Integrity in International Justice

**Morten Bergsmo and Viviane E. Dittrich
(editors)**

2020
Torkel Opsahl Academic EPublisher
Brussels

Front cover: Sir Thomas More (1478-1535) painted by the German artist Hans Holbein the Younger (1497-1543) in the late 1520s. Sir Thomas More is discussed extensively in this book as a symbol of integrity in justice.

Be grateful as your deeds become less and less associated with your name, as your feet ever more lightly tread the earth.

Dag Hammarskjöld

FOREWORD BY THE SERIES EDITOR

The *Nuremberg Academy Series* seeks to cover relevant and topical areas in the field of international criminal law, and includes work that is interdisciplinary or multidisciplinary, bringing together academics and practitioners. Grounded in the legacy of the Nuremberg Principles – the foundation of contemporary international criminal law – it addresses persistent and pressing legal issues, and explores the twenty-first century challenges encountered in pursuing accountability for core international crimes. The Series was established in April 2017 by the International Nuremberg Principles Academy, in co-operation with the Centre for International Law Research and Policy ('CILRAP'), to produce high-quality open access publications on international law published by the Torkel Opsahl Academic EPublisher ('TOAEP').

The first volume in the Series, *Two Steps Forward, One Step Back: The Deterrent Effect of International Criminal Tribunals*,[1] explored the deterrent effect in international justice, including case studies of deterrent effect in ten situations of four different international tribunals. The second volume, *Islam and International Criminal Law and Justice*,[2] focused on Islamic perspectives and criminal law, and examined the relevancy and applicability of the Nuremberg Principles to notions of justice in the Muslim world. The third volume in the Series, *The Tokyo Tribunal: Perspectives on Law, History and Memory*,[3] presented a contemporary rereading of the International Military Tribunal for the Far East ('IMTFE'), combining perspectives from law, history and social science.

This book, the fourth volume in the Series, revisits integrity in international justice through different perspectives, addressing primarily individual integrity within international justice institutions, but also including

---

[1]   Linda Carter and Jennifer Schense (eds.), *Two Steps Forward, One Step Back: The Deterrent Effect of International Criminal Tribunals*, Torkel Opsahl Academic EPublisher ('TOAEP'), Brussels, 2017 (http://www.toaep.org/nas-pdf/1-carter-schense).

[2]   Tallyn Gray (ed.), *Islam and International Criminal Law and Justice*, TOAEP, Brussels, 2018 (http://www.toaep.org/nas-pdf/2-gray).

[3]   Viviane E. Dittrich, Kerstin von Lingen, Philipp Osten and Jolana Makraiová (eds.), *The Tokyo Tribunal: Perspectives on Law, History and Memory*, TOAEP, Brussels, 2020 (http://www.toaep.org/nas-pdf/3-dittrich-lingen-osten-makraiova).

the dimension of institutional integrity. The volume advances new understandings of integrity in international justice, and includes important policy-relevant insights. The volume is of paramount relevancy in light of the environment of increased scrutiny of international justice institutions, introspection on how institutions operate, their values and purposes, and examination of a wider commitment to effective multilateralism and a rules-based international order.

The anthology draws on a number of papers that were presented at an international conference organized by CILRAP and the International Nuremberg Principles Academy in the Peace Palace in The Hague, on 1-2 December 2018. I express my gratitude to the Nuremberg Academy and CILRAP teams that made the conference possible, with the support of the Academy's Director as well as its Foundation Board and Advisory Council. I am also grateful to TOAEP and especially to my co-editor of this volume, Morten Bergsmo, for agreeing to publish the book in the *Nuremberg Academy Series*, and for his generous support and commitment to the topic of integrity.

Viviane E. Dittrich

Editor, Nuremberg Academy Series
Deputy Director, International Nuremberg Principles Academy

PREFACE BY THE CO-EDITORS

The seeds of this book were sowed in 1994-95 when one of its two co-editors, Morten Bergsmo, asked himself why the team that was forming in the Office of the Prosecutor of the International Criminal Tribunal for the Former Yugoslavia ('ICTY') was characterized by such a strong and constructive team-spirit that lasted for almost a decade. Was it caused by the mandate of the Tribunal? Or the circumstances surrounding its creation in 1993 by the United Nations Security Council acting pursuant to consensus? Was it the personality of the first Chief Prosecutor, Richard J. Goldstone, that set the tone for the team? Was it the dedication of the group of 23 United States ('US') prosecutors, investigators and other professionals who had been seconded to the Office by the US government? Or perhaps the awareness that a powerful country was supporting the work of the Tribunal? Or was it the character of specific colleagues, such as Terree A. Bowers (now Partner, Arent Fox) who in his former function as US Attorney in California led an agency of more than 300 lawyers and now accepted to sit in an open office-space as a member of one of several ICTY investigative teams without complaining? Or was it a combination of some of these and other factors?

At that time, the ICTY Office of the Prosecutor ('OTP') was doing poorly on equitable geographical distribution of staff and had a very rudimentary normative infrastructure, so diversity and strong formal ethics framework were obviously *not* the factors that created the remarkable morale, sense of common purpose, and unity within the Office in those early years. Understanding this particular period of contemporary international criminal justice more clearly – as a positive example from which lessons may be drawn – is important in order to assess how improvements can be made in other international justice agencies. We are therefore very pleased that several authors in the present anthology were involved with the work of the ICTY-OTP at that time, including Julija Bogoeva, Andrew T. Cayley, Hans Corell, Richard J. Goldstone, Hanne Sophie Greve, Karim A.A. Khan, Teresa McHenry and Christopher Staker, in addition to co-editor Bergsmo.

The next step in the process to conceive this anthology occurred in 2003. Bergsmo participated in the negotiation process to create the International Criminal Court ('ICC') between 1996 and 2002, and he had been appointed the first Senior Legal Adviser of the ICC-OTP. Working together with Klaus Rackwitz (now Director of the International Nuremberg Principles Academy), Salim A. Nakhjavani (author of Chapter 22 below), and others, Bergsmo had led the preparatory team to establish the ICC-OTP, at the request of the States Parties and the Advance Team.[1] By October 2003, Bergsmo looked back to the early days of the ICTY-OTP in 1994-95, to the monumental efforts of states between 1996 and 2002 to construct a detailed ICC normative infrastructure, the comprehensive work programme of the ICC-OTP preparatory team during 2002 and 2003, and the challenges that had already arrived in the ICC-OTP in the autumn of 2003. It was apparent that, although the process to create the ICC was led by States, more than anything, lawyers steered the process and they had crafted a very sophisticated normative framework within which the Court was being constructed. But why was the atmosphere so fundamentally different from when the ICTY-OTP was established? What, if anything, was lacking? Bergsmo concluded that there was disproportionate attention placed on legal means, and not enough on the integrity of the individuals who would fill the legal and physical structures of the Court:

> It is an intriguing case study of the sharp contrast between the elaborate legal infrastructure of the ICC and the limitations of those individuals who were elected to first run the Court. On the one hand, the legal infrastructure was developed through a massive, collective effort of the international community. On the other hand, the first Prosecutor of the Court was elected in an almost careless manner.[2]

Before the end of 2003, Bergsmo resolved to undertake a broadly-based research project on 'integrity in international justice', with a view to zooming in on the role of the individual within international justice institutions and individual integrity.

The next step towards the present book was taken in Nuremberg on 29 April 2017, when the anthology *Historical Origins of International Criminal Law: Volume 5* – co-edited by the Nuremberg Academy's Direc-

---

[1] For a detailed overview of the work of the preparatory team, see Morten Bergsmo, Klaus Rackwitz and SONG Tianying (eds.), *Historical Origins of International Criminal Law: Volume 5*, Torkel Opsahl Academic EPublisher ('TOAEP'), Brussels, 2017 (http://www.toaep.org/ps-pdf/24-bergsmo-rackwitz-song), in particular Morten Bergsmo, Chapter 1, "Institutional History, Behaviour and Development", pp. 1–31.

[2] *Ibid.*, p. 25. This strong statement does obviously not apply to all representatives of states who were involved in the process, for example the German diplomats. Bergsmo was in frequent contact with diplomats in the months leading up to the appointment of the first ICC Prosecutor, in his capacity as head of the preparatory team of the ICC-OTP.

tor Rackwitz, SONG Tianying, and Bergsmo – was launched during an event in Courtroom 600, just above the permanent premises of the Nuremberg Academy. Section 1.6. of the book ("Hammarskjöld, Integrity and the Election of Prosecutors") observes that Dag Hammarskjöld (the second United Nations Secretary-General)

> saw service as "self-oblivion", as striving towards "an unhesitant fulfilment of duty". When a team of international civil servants recognises this higher dimension of the customary requirement of "persons of high moral character", it leaves no stone unturned to make the foundations of their organisation as strong as possible. Such recognition creates a sense of unity of purpose, reducing the energy and time spent on conflict. […] If States Parties do not elect persons of adequate integrity, a young international organisation may be stillborn for many years and taxpayers' money may be wasted before it meets basic expectations of functionality.[3]

It pointed out that even if a government doubts the integrity of a candidate for prosecutor of an international criminal court,

> it may still be tempted to back him if it predicts that he will be sympathetic to its interests, perhaps out of indebtedness for being elected or established co-operation over some years. Worse, a government may possess information that the candidate does not have the requisite integrity, but nevertheless support him – or fail to raise objections when his candidacy is discussed – because it expects that he will be weak or compromised and therefore a pliant instrument should its interests become threatened during his term. Both modes of thinking are short-sighted. In effect, both make a mockery of the statutory requirements of "high moral character", "integrity" and "the highest standards of […] integrity". If States Parties do not take these standards for what they are – binding legal requirements – we cannot expect that the high officials of international organisations like the International Criminal Court will give them proper effect when they fill the organisation with staff. If we want international organisations to work according to their design, ethics cannot be an afterthought in their construction and management.[4]

The passage links the need to take integrity in international justice more seriously, to the manner in which States Parties exercise their role in

---

3 *Ibid.*, p. 30 (footnotes omitted).
4 *Ibid.*, pp. 30–31 (footnotes omitted).

the election of high officials of international courts and tribunals. It places the responsibility for failures to elect judges and prosecutors with high integrity squarely at the feet of diplomats. Three years later, in 2020, the demand that the third ICC Prosecutor possess the highest integrity became a watchword for a process that was reaching a climax around the time this book was published. While this link between concern for integrity and the election of the ICC Prosecutor is appropriate, it is only one part of the need for a broader discourse on the 'binding legal requirement' of integrity in international justice. The quoted passage amounted to a public statement of intention to pursue an 'integrity project', which the Nuremberg Academy and the Centre for International Law Research and Policy (CILRAP) gradually resolved to undertake together, with a wider focus than simply the election of high officials.

It was, however, the question of the ICC Prosecutor that attracted vigorous attention a few months later in 2017, particularly with various media revelations in October 2017 based on the hacking of an e-mail account of the first ICC Prosecutor.[5] A few weeks later, on 22 November 2017, the process was jolted by the policy brief "A Prosecutor Falls, Time for the Court to Rise" by four directors of independent organizations working on international justice issues: Wolfgang Kaleck (General Secretary, European Center for Constitutional and Human Rights), Alexander S. Muller (Chief Executive Officer, The Hague Institute for Innovation of Law), William H. Wiley (Director, Commission for International Justice and Ac-

---

[5] The media outlets included Mediapart, Der Spiegel, NRC Handelsblad, The Sunday Times, El Mundo, L'Espresso, Le Soir, ANCIR, Nacional and The Black Sea. For their articles, see, *inter alia*, *Mediapart*, "Former ICC prosecutor's lucrative links with Libyan billionaire and ex-ally of Gaddafi", 1 October 2017 (http://www.legal-tools.org/doc/895f3b); *Spiegel Online*, "Ex-Chefankläger Ocampo beschützte libyschen Milliardär", 29 September 2017 (http://www.legal-tools.org/doc/bdb5ca/); *The Sunday Times*, "Insight: Luis Moreno Ocampo, war crimes prosecutor, tipped off Gadaffi crony Hassan Tatanaki", 1 October 2017 (http://www.legal-tools.org/doc/26c605/); *NRC Handelsblad*, "Medewerker van Strafhof betaald voor lobby bij het hof", 1 October 2017 (http://www.legal-tools.org/doc/b0cc4f/); *Mediapart*, "The secret double-dealing in Kenyatta 'crimes against humanity' case", 6 October 2017 (http://www.legal-tools.org/doc/939caf/); *Mediapart*, "The devious manoeuvres behind ex-Ivorian leader Laurent Gbagbo's trial at ICC", 8 October 2017 (http://www.legal-tools.org/doc/0c5a22/); *Mediapart*, "Angelina Jolie, Omidyar et le Qatar: le cabinet cache du procureur Ocampo", 6 October 2017 (http://www.legal-tools.org/doc/ea4930/); and *Mediapart*, "How chief prosecutor at International Criminal Court owned companies in tax havens", 29 September 2017 (http://www.legal-tools.org/doc/56cfa8/).

countability), and co-editor of this volume, Morten Bergsmo (Director, Centre for International Law Research and Policy).[6] They pointed out that

> an international court will not be better than the integrity of its leaders. The Statute of the ICC requires high integrity or "moral character". International prosecutors such as Richard J. Goldstone and Louise Arbour – the first and second Chief Prosecutors of the ex-Yugoslavia and Rwanda Tribunals – show that this is a realistic qualification. In fact, integrity is a legally binding requirement to serve as Judge or Prosecutor at the ICC. States Parties are obliged to be as responsible when they elect the next chief Prosecutor as they were during the highly deliberate creation of the Statute in 1998. If the normative framework of the Court is its chassis, the OTP is the engine. It is equally important that both function well.[7]

The directors reminded us that the states that assembled in Rome's Capitol at the end of the ICC Diplomatic Conference "took an oath, not to an omniscient Jupiter, god of the sky [whose temple had stood where they met], but to an equally all-seeing humankind, pursuant to whose collective aspirations the States claimed to act, in the name of peoples, of victims".[8] They called for an "inquiry" by use of "external expert[s]" to help "turn every stone to restore trust" in the Court.

It took just over two years before the Court's Assembly of States Parties ordered an external review on 6 December 2019, with the mandate to "making concrete, achievable and actionable recommendations aimed at enhancing the performance, efficiency and effectiveness of the Court and the Rome Statute system as a whole, [...] and submit those to the Assembly and the Court for consideration".[9] This Independent Expert Review ('IER') delivered its final report on 30 September 2020.[10] The report amounts to a systemic *review*, not an *inquiry* into allegations of misconduct by high offi-

---

6   See Morten Bergsmo, Wolfgang Kaleck, Alexander S. Muller and William H. Wiley, "A Prosecutor Falls, Time for the Court to Rise", FICHL Policy Brief Series No. 86 (2017), TOAEP, Brussels, 2017 (http://www.toaep.org/pbs-pdf/86-four-directors/).

7   *Ibid.*, p. 3 (footnotes omitted).

8   *Ibid.*

9   ICC, Assembly of States Parties, Review of the International Criminal Court and the Rome Statute System, ICC-ASP/18/Res.7, 6 December 2019, para. 6 (https://www.legal-tools.org/doc/d1fyfk/).

10 See Independent Expert Review, "Review of the International Criminal Court and the Rome Status System, Final Report", 30 September 2020 ('IER Report') (https://www.legal-tools.org/doc/cv19d5/).

cials, as explained by authors in this anthology.[11] But it is an immensely useful report, with numerous insightful recommendations, and pages 83-105 deal with "Ethics and Prevention of Conflicts of Interest" and "Internal Grievance Procedures", as touched upon in the introductory chapter below.

The policy brief of the four directors was influential also in other directions. Importantly, they pointed out that formalized oversight mechanisms are

> not the ultimate overseer of the Court, nor is the Assembly of States Parties. The aspirations of individuals and communities made the Court and continue to provide its foundation. If the leaders of the Court cannot retain their trust, their aspirations will move on to other instruments for the betterment of humankind.[12]

This broadening of the perspective influenced the more detailed conceptualization of the Integrity Project of the Nuremberg Academy and CILRAP in the months following the publication of the policy brief. It was decided that the project would consider integrity in international justice from more perspectives than mere codes and compliance mechanisms – that it would also consider our understanding of integrity; historical, philosophical and religious backgrounds to the evolution of the concept of integrity in international justice frameworks; what builds awareness and cultures of integrity; the roles of States, international organizations as well as international courts in increasing respect for integrity in international justice; what (work on) specific cases can tell us about integrity in international justice; and the relationship between the principles of integrity and independence.

This wider approach was reflected in the policy brief "Revisiting Integrity in International Justice"[13] and programme[14] of the international expert conference, which the Nuremberg Academy and CILRAP held in the Peace Palace in The Hague on 1-2 December 2018. The presentations at the event were made available on the project web page as films and podcasts

---

[11] See, for example, Jan Fougner, "On Whistle-Blowing and Inquiry in Public Institutions", Chapter 16 below.

[12] See Morten Bergsmo, Wolfgang Kaleck, Alexander S. Muller and William H. Wiley, "A Prosecutor Falls, Time for the Court to Rise", *supra* note 6.

[13] See Morten Bergsmo, "Revisiting Integrity in International Justice", FICHL Policy Brief Series No. 93 (2018), TOAEP, Brussels, 2018 (http://www.toaep.org/pbs-pdf/93-bergsmo/).

[14] The project web page contains links to the programme and related resources: https://www.cilrap.org/events/181201-02-the-hague/.

shortly after the event.[15] They have been extensively referred to by authors in this book and used in the discourse leading up to the establishment of the IER and the publication of this volume.

We are pleased to publish this anthology on the heels of the submission of the IER report, shortly before the Nineteenth Session of the ICC Assembly of States Parties in December 2020. But we do not see the book against a short-term horizon. Scrutinizing and strengthening integrity in international justice is not a fleeting moment in the history of international law. It should be a constant feature of the process to build an international legal order. It is an activity and a discussion that should occur every day within international justice institutions, and also involve outside stakeholders. Our hope is that this anthology will aid such discussions – that it will become a living reference book in international courts and tribunals, and that it will inspire further analysis, research and writing.

Should there be sufficiently strong interest, we will consider whether a second, expanded edition of the anthology should be published sometime in the future. We would have liked to include even a greater variety of perspectives and experience in this first edition. We have deliberately invited different views on issues, including critical contributions. It is through such clashes of opinion that we may see the spark of truth and new ideas emerge. Needless to say, we do not necessarily agree with all views expressed by the authors, nor do they represent positions of the Nuremberg Academy or CILRAP.

Two of the premises of the Integrity Project have been that *individual* integrity in international justice institutions is the main focus, and that integrity is a *legally binding standard* in international courts and tribunals. None of the chapters disagree with the latter, but several authors have gone beyond individual integrity to also discuss institutional integrity. This is understandable: the normative and systemic context of the institutions frame the conduct of individuals serving in international courts to a considerable extent. The book therefore includes both perspectives.

Considering the scarcity of international law sources on integrity in international justice, the volume delves into a wide range of understandings of integrity, going into philosophical, religious and cultural traditions, viewing integrity as a moral authority, an ethical component, and a behavioural norm. Beyond theoretical reflections on integrity as a concept, the book addresses practical fringes for the implementation of integrity in in-

---

[15] *Ibid.*

ternational justice, while examining those actors who have a particular responsibility to uphold integrity and cultivate a culture of integrity due to their leadership roles. The ethical-legal framework on integrity in international justice and its relationship with independence is a cross-cutting topic of the anthology.

We would first of all like to thank the authors who have contributed to this volume, some of whom have spent several weeks of their time to research and draft very comprehensive chapters. We thank the Director of the Nuremberg Academy, Klaus Rackwitz, who has consistently supported the Integrity Project over the past years. We also thank those who contributed to the international expert conference in The Hague in December 2018. Furthermore, let us thank CHAN H.S. Icarus, Subham Jain and Antonio Angotti of the Torkel Opsahl Academic EPublisher and Marialejandra Moreno Mantilla and Marilena Stegbauer of the Nuremberg Academy for outstanding assistance in the making of this book.

Their dedication and enthusiasm remind us that individual integrity – or the human quality of rectitude – cannot entirely be reduced to statutory provisions, judicial codes of ethics, or grievance and oversight mechanisms. At the end of the day, integrity is about personal conduct and its motivation. That is why we quote Dag Hammarskjöld in the place of the dedication of this book: "Be grateful as your deeds become less and less associated with your name, as your feet ever more lightly tread the earth".[16] Hammarskjöld was a mere 51 years old when he wrote this on 31 December 1956. He had only served as United Nations Secretary-General for three years and eight months at this time, and his tragic, premature death was five years into the future. At the height of his power, he nevertheless expressed profound insight into what should motivate our conduct. It is not recognition, reward, election, appointment and promotion. By inviting us to tread the earth ever more lightly, Hammarskjöld speaks to what should motivate our individual service in international justice institutions (he is not suggesting that such institutions should not leave deep footprints).[17] Several authors recognize

---

[16] Dag Hammarskjöld, *Markings*, Ballantine Books, New York, 1983, p. 125. The Swedish original – *Vägmärken* – was first published by Albert Bonniers Förlag AB in 1963. Dag Hammarskjöld was Secretary-General of the United Nations Organisation from 1953 to 1961.

[17] The footprints of international justice institutions are of direct relevance for legacies and legacy building, on which there is recent literature, see, for example, Viviane E. Dittrich, "Legacies in the Making at the ICTY", in Carsten Stahn, Carmel Agius, Serge Brammertz and Colleeen Rohan (eds.), *Legacies of the International Criminal Tribunal for the Former Yugoslavia: A Multidisciplinary Approach*, Oxford University Press, 2020, p. 83; Viviane E. Dittrich, "Legacies in the Making: Assessing the Institutionalized Legacy Endeavour of the

the importance of Hammarskjöld's perspective in subsequent chapters of this book. Hans Corell – former Under-Secretary-General for Legal Affairs and the Legal Counsel of the United Nations – offers his insights in Chapter 5 dedicated to "The Dag Hammarskjöld Legacy and Integrity in International Civil Service" and in his foreword to this volume.

Individual integrity cannot be artificially disconnected from the operation of international organizations. The success of international justice institutions depends on the individual integrity of their high officials and staff members. If anything, the integrity-related challenges in the early life of the ICC offer us an opportunity to realise the significance of integrity provisions in statutory instruments of international courts and tribunals, as we strive to strengthen these institutions and the international legal order in the coming years and decades.

Morten Bergsmo and Viviane E. Dittrich

Florence and Nuremberg,
October 2020

Special Court for Sierra Leone", in Charles C. Jalloh (ed.), *The Sierra Leone Special Court and Its Legacy: The Impact for Africa and International Criminal Law*, Cambridge University Press, 2014, p. 663; and Viviane E. Dittrich, *Present at the Completion: Creating Legacies at the International Criminal Tribunals*, book manuscript, October 2020.

FOREWORD BY HANS CORELL

This book is the fruit of a remarkably interesting seminar on integrity in international justice, co-organised by the Centre for International Law Research and Policy and the International Nuremberg Principles Academy on 1-2 December 2018 in the Peace Palace in The Hague. In the seminar the participants delivered addresses that were to be developed in light of the discussions and published for the benefit of a wider audience. In the process of editing these contributions the editors received additional articles. This means that the book is now an impressive anthology that will serve as a helpful reference book for judges, prosecutors, defence counsel, registrars and other staff members of different kinds in international courts in the coming years.

The book will also be of great importance for international organisations in general. A question that often comes to my mind is: why is it so difficult to transfer wisdom from one generation to another? The book is an important source of inspiration to facilitate the spreading of knowledge from the past and from different religions and cultures. It contains valuable lessons from ancient Greece and the Roman Empire via Thomas More's focus on the need for continuous learning in integrity to contributions from individuals with personal experience from present day international courts and organisations. No doubt, the anthology will broaden the readers' perspectives.

The anthology also points to a central aspect in the process, namely the importance of leading by example. One thing that I never forget from the time when I served as a judge in my own country – see Chapter 5 on the Dag Hammarskjöld Legacy – is the seriousness with which the senior judges in the courts where I served carried out their daily duties. That taught me a lesson for life. It became a lodestar for me in all my future functions.

The book should also stimulate discussions that may lead to new or improved codes of conduct or rules on ethics and perhaps innovative mechanisms to ensure respect for the integrity standards. The analyses in Part IV will be of assistance here. And, hopefully, states will realise the great importance of giving appropriate weight to the integrity criterion when filling positions in international courts. Another indispensable criterion here, especially with respect to criminal courts, is courtroom experience.

This brings to the forefront the methods of staff recruitment in general in international courts and other international organizations. The importance of identifying individuals with the right qualifications and competences cannot be stressed enough. Ultimately, this will influence the institutional integrity of the organization.

An additional advantage, resulting from the fact that the chapters of the book will be freely available on the web in digital form, is that it should be of great assistance in raising the awareness of the importance of integrity in the courts at the national level. Therefore, national judges' associations, prosecutors' associations and bar associations should be made aware of the book. This will also put them in a position to inform their members of the same and to draw particular attention to and disseminate chapters that are of special relevance to their profession and to their country. Another obvious addressee at the national level is academia.

The articles in the book also make clear the connexion between Sustainable Development Goal 16 on equal justice for all with its targets focusing on the need for the rule of law and anti-corruption and the need for implementing this goal also at the international level. In this context the responsibility that politicians have should be highlighted. Whether they serve in the executive or the legislative branch they should find guidance in the book.

Finally, all readers of the book will no doubt ask themselves what lessons they can learn from its contents and come to the conclusion that it may influence their understanding and provide guidance in their daily activities. Against this background the book should be a must-read in wide circles both at the national and international level.

Ambassador (ret.) Hans Corell

Former Under-Secretary-General for Legal Affairs and the Legal Counsel of the United Nations

FOREWORD BY RICHARD J. GOLDSTONE

It was my privilege and pleasure to attend and participate in the conference on Integrity in International Justice that was convened at the Peace Palace in The Hague on 1-2 December 2018. This anthology is the outcome of the papers and discussions that were held on that occasion. Morten Bergsmo and Viviane E. Dittrich are to be congratulated for pursing this endeavour with their usual efficiency, insight and vigour.

The integrity of any court system lies at the very core of its mission. Without it, inevitably, there will be an absence of confidence in the judges and the outcome of cases that come before them will be questioned. Judges have no police or military force to ensure the implementation of their orders. They must perforce rely on the respect for their decisions by the other branches of government. Their allegiance must be owed solely to the application of the law and adhere to an ethical code to guide their work. This applies to all national systems of justice.

International courts are staffed by women and men from many countries around the globe. They represent different systems and traditions of legal practice. They are required to put aside those national systems and join a comparatively new endeavour. One of their most important tasks is to build confidence in their new institutions and that includes abiding by a code of ethics and a culture of integrity.

The Independent Expert Review Group appointed by the Assembly of States Parties to review the working of the International Criminal Court and the Rome Statute system recently submitted its report. It is significant, in the present context, that its many findings and recommendations include a number on "Ethics and Prevention of Conflict of Interest" and "Internal Grievance Procedures". I firmly believe that the present anthology will contribute to the momentum around the tremendous importance of integrity in international justice.

Richard J. Goldstone

Formerly, Justice of the Constitutional Court of South Africa and Chief Prosecutor, International Criminal Tribunals for the former Yugoslavia and Rwanda

TABLE OF CONTENTS

By Brigid Inder

PART V:

INTEGRITY AND THE LENS OF CASES

PART VI:
INDEPENDENCE AND INTEGRITY

Integrity as Safeguard Against
the Vicissitudes of
International Justice Institutions

By Morten Bergsmo and Viviane E. Dittrich[*]

The topical salience and urgency of recognising and revisiting integrity in international justice has come into sharper relief through countless conversations, contributions and contexts. This book is the most tangible result to date of the Integrity Project undertaken by the International Nuremberg Principles Academy and the Centre for International Law Research and Policy ('CILRAP'). It draws on papers invited for an international conference held in the Peace Palace in The Hague on 1-2 December 2018,[1] and some additional chapters. The conference brought together more than 40 leading scholars and practitioners from Africa, America, Asia and Europe engaged in high-level discussions and insightful reflections and suggestions on the upholding of integrity in international justice. During the opening session, Deputy Prosecutor of the International Criminal Court ('ICC'), James Stewart, emphasized the legal requirement of individual integrity and its relevance in the prosecution of international crimes. The importance

---

[*] **Morten Bergsmo** is Director of the Centre for International Law Research and Policy ('CILRAP'). He was the first Legal Officer hired by the Office of the Prosecutor of the International Criminal Tribunal for the Former Yugoslavia (1994-2002), and he subsequently led the preparatory team that established the International Criminal Court's Office of the Prosecutor and served as its first Senior Legal Adviser (2002-2005). He has been an academic at leading institutions in China, Europe and the United States. **Viviane E. Dittrich** is Deputy Director of the International Nuremberg Principles Academy. She is also Visiting Fellow at the Centre for International Studies, London School of Economics and Political Science ('LSE'). Previously, she has been Honorary Research Associate at Royal Holloway, University of London, and Visiting Researcher at iCourts (Centre of Excellence for International Courts), University of Copenhagen. She has published on the notion of legacy and the process of legacy building at the international criminal tribunals and has taught on international institutions, the politics of international law, global crime, and US foreign policy at the LSE, Royal Holloway, and Sciences Po Paris. Views expressed in this chapter do not necessarily reflect the views of CILRAP or the Nuremberg Academy.

[1] The Integrity Project web page contains links to the conference programme, films and podcasts of the conference presentations, and related resources, see https://www.cilrap.org/events/181201-02-the-hague/.

---

of integrity in international justice was also highlighted by Judge Marc Perrin de Brichambaut and Judge Erik Møse in their opening remarks. The book is not mere conference proceedings, but the result of deliberate conceptual development by a group of involved international lawyers and experts. Our Preface above explains the main steps that have led to the book, starting with observations made within the Office of the Prosecutor of the ex-Yugoslavia tribunal in 1994-95, until the release of the final report of the Independent Expert Review ('IER') on 30 September 2020,[2] a few weeks before the publication of the first edition of the book. The Preface provides some of the background to the development of the Integrity Project, and is thus best read in conjunction with this introductory chapter to the book.

This chapter is divided into 10 Sections. First, it considers the context of increased scrutiny of international justice institutions, against a background of more pressure on multilateralism, including from permanent members of the United Nations Security Council (*Section 1* below). *Section 2* provides an overview of the conceptual structure and direction of the book as well as the wider Integrity Project. As it turns out, there has been considerable conceptual consistency since the earlier stages of the project, through the Peace Palace conference in December 2018, to the present anthology, even if it involves 43 contributors and more than 1,100 pages of material. The main conceptual building blocks – corresponding to the six parts of this book – are described in *Sections 3 to 8* below. Each of these sections contains a summary of the chapters that fall within the part to provide a comprehensive yet succinct overview of the contributions. *Section 9* shows the growing recognition of the importance of integrity in international organizations, and discusses in some detail the final report of the Independent Expert Review of the ICC. *Section 10* distils some of the main findings and areas of convergence between the chapters in the book, focusing on issues such as individual integrity in international justice, the will or motivation to integrity, accountability for breaches of integrity, awareness of integrity, and the need to be open to multi-disciplinary perspectives in the discourse on integrity in international justice.

While this is the first book on integrity in international justice, there has been a growing corpus of writing on integrity more broadly. The con-

---

[2] See Independent Expert Review, "Review of the International Criminal Court and the Rome Status System, Final Report", 30 September 2020 ('IER report') (https://www.legal-tools.org/doc/cv19d5/).

cept of 'integrity' is used in multifarious ways in the literature.[3] This may raise methodological questions in specific contexts.[4] For example, from the perspective of institutional design, drawing on a distinction between 'the logic of consequences' and the 'logic of appropriateness', it may be useful to distinguish between formal prescription and rule-compliance, on the one hand, and norm setting and cultural approaches, on the other.[5] It goes without saying that the relevance of integrity for organizations continues to be a topic of concern, both in scholarship and in practice.[6] Overcoming any conceptual deficits in prior publications on integrity may, in some contexts, require further insightful conceptualization and operationalization of the concept of integrity. Multiple avenues for future research can be envisaged. This book will provide a source of inspiration for further conceptual work and theoretically driven yet empirically grounded research. There are risks when lawyers start defining or making distinctions with regard to the integrity standard – which is not a norm of prohibition, but a norm or standard of positive personal conduct – which is why this book includes a contextual Part I and avoids premature conceptual definitions.

As described in Section 2 below, this book emphasises individual integrity in international justice, but it does not exclude considerations of institutional integrity. It is neither 'individual-centric' nor 'institution-centric'. Rather, it invites a holistic approach, based on an accurate understanding of real integrity challenges in international justice, as well as proper command of the relevant ethics frameworks of international courts and tribunals. We have deliberately sought to avoid imposing a rigid frame on the contributors, not to stifle the discourse and to showcase the multiple understandings and perspectives when the literature on integrity in international justice is so scarce. The anthology features perceptive and incisive readings, including at times conceptually astute, while always practice-oriented reflections on integrity in international justice in a forward-looking manner.

---

[3] See multi-disciplinary literature review surveying seven disciplines (public administration, organizational science, sociology, political science, law, philosophy and international relations): Thomas Robinson, Lucinda Cadzow and Nikolas Kirby, "Investigating Integrity: A Multi-Disciplinary Literature Review", Oxford University Working Paper, May 2018.

[4] See also Andrew Stark, "Public Integrity (Book Review)", *American Political Science Review*, 2001, vol. 95, no. 1, pp. 203-4.

[5] James G. March and Johan P. Olsen, *Rediscovering Institutions: The Organizational Basis of Politics*, The Free Press, New York, 1989.

[6] See, for example, Peter Verheezen, "The (Ir)relevance of Integrity in Organizations", *Public Integrity*, 2008, vol. 10, no. 2, pp. 133-49.

The response has exceeded our expectations, with an outburst of interest in the Integrity Project, and an inspiring energy among the carefully selected authors in their drafting of the 32 chapters that follow this introductory chapter. Taken together, the chapters offer a structured multitude of perspectives on integrity in international justice, all recognizing that the integrity standard is legally binding within international courts and tribunals. Almost all the chapters draw on and are grounded in practice as they present and scrutinize proposals, venues, mechanisms, recommendations and suggestions to address integrity and its potential gaps and implementation challenges in international justice.

Their introspection of how institutions operate, their values and purposes, manifests a desire to contribute to the consolidation of the international legal order, as we face an environment of increased scrutiny of international justice organizations.

1. Multilateralism Under Pressure, Increased Scrutiny of Integrity in International Justice[7]

In a ceremony in Rome on Saturday 18 July 1998, then United Nations Secretary-General Kofi Annan proclaimed the establishment of the ICC, a "gift of hope to future generations, and a giant step forward in the march towards universal human rights and the rule of law".[8] This was a widely shared sentiment among the diplomats assembled in the Hall of the Horatii and Curiatii on Capitol and among international lawyers around the world. Twenty-two years later, there have been several changes in international relations with implications for international organizations, not excluding the United Nations ('UN') and the ICC. It has become apparent that multilateralism is under growing pressure, and that this may, among other things, increase the scrutiny of the operation of international organizations, including international courts.

---

[7] Given the conceptual continuum described above, Sections 1 through 8 below deliberately draw on elements of the Integrity Project concept paper, see Morten Bergsmo, "Revisiting Integrity in International Justice", FICHL Policy Brief Series No. 93 (2018), Torkel Opsahl Academic EPublisher ('TOAEP'), Brussels, 2018 (http://www.toaep.org/pbs-pdf/93-bergsmo/). We are pleased that more than 40 authors have agreed to contribute within this conceptual framework, the objective of which is to stimulate a discourse on integrity in international justice, eventually growing into a sub-discipline of ethics of international justice.

[8] Statement by the United Nations Secretary-General Kofi Annan at the Ceremony Held at Campidoglio Celebrating the Adoption of the Statute of the International Criminal Court, 18 July 1998 (http://www.legal-tools.org/doc/8b0ab6/).

China, India, Russia and the United States ('US') are all standing outside the ICC, watching attentively its every move, noting any weakness that could serve their perceived future interests.[9] Anne-Marie Slaughter claims that some of these leaders "support a return to an era of unfettered state sovereignty. They would dismantle international and supranational organizations of all kinds and return to multipolar 'Great Power' politics, in which alliances shift and are transactional".[10] While time may or may not verify Slaughter's fear, on 10 September 2018, just a few weeks after her article was published in the *Financial Times*, US Ambassador John Bolton delivered

> a clear and unambiguous message on behalf of the President of the United States. The United States will use any means necessary to protect our citizens and those of our allies from unjust prosecution by this illegitimate court. We will not co-operate with the ICC. We will provide no assistance to the ICC. We will not join the ICC. We will let the ICC die on its own. After all, for all intents and purposes, the ICC is already dead to us. [...] We will respond against the ICC and its personnel to the extent permitted by U.S. law. We will ban its judges and prosecutors from entering the United States. We will sanction their funds in the U.S. financial system, and, we will prosecute them in the U.S. criminal system. We will do the same for any company or state that assists an ICC investigation of Americans.[11]

Bolton continued:

> The ICC's Assembly of States Parties cannot supervise the Court any more than the United Nations General Assembly can supervise the UN bureaucracy. Recent allegations of *mismanagement and corruption among ICC personnel* make this perfectly clear. The first Prosecutor elected by the Assembly

---

[9] This risk was flagged in the policy brief published on 6 August 2018 articulating the conceptual basis of the Integrity Project, see Morten Bergsmo, "Revisiting Integrity in International Justice", *supra* note 7.

[10] See Anne-Marie Slaughter, "Donald Trump and Vladimir Putin want to create a new world order: We should take their vision of unfettered state sovereignty seriously", in *Financial Times*, 22 July 2018. She warns in the same article that it is "incumbent upon those of us who see an arc of progress bending towards peace and universal human rights to appreciate the full scope of the threat posed to our 20th-century global architecture".

[11] United States, Ambassador John Bolton, Statement, Federalist Society, 10 September 2018 (https://www.legal-tools.org/doc/84c2b4/).

of States Parties attempted to protect a high-ranking government official from prosecution, assisted a businessman with links to violations in Libya, and shared confidential court documents with Angelina Jolie.[12]

On 15 March 2019, US Secretary of State Michael R. Pompeo announced "a policy of U.S. visa restrictions on those individuals directly responsible for any ICC investigation of U.S. personnel. This includes persons who take or have taken action to request or further such an investigation".[13] On 11 June 2020, US President Donald J. Trump issued an Executive Order declaring a "national emergency to deal with the threat" of "attempt[s] by the ICC to investigate, arrest, detain, or prosecute any United States personnel without the consent of the United States, or of personnel of countries that are United States allies and who are not parties to the Rome Statute or have not otherwise consented to ICC jurisdiction".[14] In a statement shortly thereafter, US Attorney General William Barr remarked that the "U.S. Government has reason to doubt the honesty of the ICC. The Department of Justice has received substantial, credible information that raises serious concerns about a long history of *financial corruption and malfeasance* at the highest levels of the office of the prosecutor".[15] At the same press briefing, Pompeo referred to the ICC as "grossly ineffective and *corrupt*", adding that its "record of botched prosecutions and poor judgment casts grave doubt on the court's ability to function at the most basic level and demonstrates the highly politicized nature of this institution".[16] US National Security Adviser Robert O'Brien added that, "[d]espite repeated calls for reform from our allies in the United Kingdom, Japan, Germany, and other countries, the court is ineffective, unaccountable, and is a politically motivated bureaucracy", and that "we know that there is *corruption and misconduct* at the highest levels of the ICC and in the office of the

---

[12] *Ibid.* (italics added).

[13] United States, Department of State, Remarks to the Press, Michael R. Pompeo, Secretary of State, 15 March 2019 (https://www.legal-tools.org/doc/cifgr1/).

[14] United States, President Donald J. Trump, Executive Order on Blocking Property of Certain Persons Associated With The International Criminal Court, E.O. 13928 (https://www.legal-tools.org/doc/dfkvpn/).

[15] United States, Department of State, "Secretary Michael R. Pompeo at a Press Availability with Secretary of Defense Mark Esper, Attorney General William Barr, and National Security Advisor Robert O'Brien", Remarks to the Press, William Barr, US Attorney General, 11 June 2020 (italics added) (https://www.legal-tools.org/doc/h4dsqa/).

[16] *Ibid.* (italics added).

prosecutor", referring to the Court as a "corrupt international organization".[17]

On 2 September 2020, the US government imposed economic sanctions pursuant to Executive Order 13928 on the ICC Prosecutor Fatou Bensouda "for having directly engaged in an effort to investigate U.S. personnel" and Phakiso Mochochoko (Head of the Jurisdiction, Complementarity and Cooperation Division of her Office) "for having materially assisted Prosecutor Bensouda". Secretary of State Pompeo warned that "[i]ndividuals and entities that continue to support Prosecutor Bensouda and Mr. Mochochoko materially risk exposure to sanctions".[18]

It is a source of grave concern that such a relationship has evolved between the ICC and the US government, which has caused numerous strong reactions by many states, academia and civil society, in addition to the ICC itself. The President of the Bureau of the ICC Assembly of States Parties, O-Gon Kwon from Korea, issued a concise statement the very same day, saying: "I strongly reject such unprecedented and unacceptable measures against a treaty-based international organization. They only serve to weaken our common endeavor to fight impunity for mass atrocities".[19] Grave concern has been expressed regarding the "unusual and extraordinary assault on international justice" as the US President "has chosen intimidation of officials as a form of confrontation with the court".[20] On 2 November 2020, a joint statement on behalf of 72 ICC States Parties reiterated their

> commitment to uphold and defend the principles and values
> enshrined in the Rome Statute and to preserve its integrity and
> independence undeterred by any measures or threats against
> the Court, its officials and those cooperating with it. We note
> that sanctions are a tool to be used against those responsible
> for the most serious crimes, not against those seeking justice.

---

[17] *Ibid.* (italics added).

[18] United States, Department of State, "Actions to Protect U.S. Personnel from Illegitimate Investigation by the International Criminal Court", Remarks to the Press, Michael R. Pompeo, Secretary of State, 2 September 2020 (applies to all three quotations in the paragraph) (https://www.legal-tools.org/doc/2hljlk/).

[19] See also ICC, President of the Bureau of the Assembly of States Parties, "ASP President, O-Gon Kwon, rejects US measures against ICC", Press release, 2 September 2020 (https://www.legal-tools.org/doc/xaduvf/).

[20] Claus Kress, "Editorial: An Unusual and Extraordinary Assault on International Justice", *Journal of International Criminal Justice*, 2020.

Any attempt to undermine the independence of the Court should not be tolerated.[21]

Ever since US President George W. Bush signed the American Service-Members' Protection Act into law on 2 August 2002[22] – often referred to as 'The Hague Invasion Act' – it has been eminently predictable that the US government will not only be watching the ICC closely (chronicling every error that the Court makes and every allegation levelled against it), but also take action against the Court if it pursues suspects who are US citizens. This risk was being considered by those serving the preparatory team of the ICC Office of the Prosecutor in 2002-03. That is why the team invested so much work on the Draft Regulations of the Office,[23] including a carefully considered Code of Conduct,[24] to ensure that the Office and the Court would not unnecessarily feed its powerful detractors. Indeed, US Attorney General Barr confirmed on 11 June 2020 that they have "information *going back many years* about multiple matters", and that the "Department of Justice, together with partners across the United States Government, is investigating, and we are committed to uncovering and if possible holding people accountable for their wrongdoing – any wrongdoing – that we may find".[25]

International law is paramount for effective multilateralism and strong international organizations and courts and tribunals.[26] At this stage,

---

[21] United Nations General Assembly, "Adopting Draft Upholding International Criminal Court's Goal to End Impunity, Calls for Cooperation in Arresting Fugitives", Statement by Christoph Heusgen (Germany), seventy-fifth session, 2 November 2020, Meetings Coverage no. GA/12280. The full statement is available on the web site of the Permanent Mission of the Federal Republic of Germany to the United Nations.

[22] United States, The American Service-Members' Protection Act (ASPA), Title 2 of Pub.L. 107–206, H.R. 4775, 116 Stat. 820, enacted 2 August 2002 (https://www.legal-tools.org/doc/9e61d9/).

[23] See Carlos Vasconcelos, "Draft Regulations of the Office of the Prosecutor", in Morten Bergsmo, Klaus Rackwitz and SONG Tianying (eds.), *Historical Origins of International Criminal Law: Volume 5*, TOAEP, Brussels, 2017, pp. 834–93 (https://www.legal-tools.org/doc/09c8b8/).

[24] See Salim A. Nakhjavani, "The Origins and Development of the Code of Conduct", in *ibid.*, pp. 964–77. See also Suhail Mohammed and Salim A. Nakhjavani, "Does the International Criminal Court Really Need an Ethics Charter?", Chapter 22 below.

[25] *Supra* note 15.

[26] See the conference "UN at 75: Effective Multilateralism and International Law" organized by the UN Office of Legal Affairs and the Federal Foreign Office of Germany, 9 October 2020 (https://www.un75-berlin-international-law-conference.de).

---

it cannot be ruled out that the situation will get worse for the ICC and the ICC system, and that other states will articulate positions similar to those of the US government. We cannot take the achievements in multilateralism during the past century for granted. It is not so long ago that Dag Hammarskjöld cited Nikita Khrushchev's statement that "while there are neutral countries, there are no neutral men", and lamented that were this view of the international civil servant to be proven true, "we would be thrown back to 1919".[27] We have no guarantee that one or more of the great powers will not, at one stage, take a similarly dim view of international civil service, also of international justice.

2. Conceptual Structure and Direction

However uncomfortable at times, an environment of increased scrutiny also provides a welcome opportunity to revisit the role of the individual in international justice institutions, not only the institutions and their systemic context. This is what the Integrity Project and this book seek to do. They do so in a forward-looking manner with a view to contributing towards progress, while cognizant of the saying that, "[t]hough talk about ethics is cheap, silence about ethics is far too expensive".[28] When serious integrity problems within international courts become manifest, they tend to affect the external reputation of and support for the institution, and erode morale among staff. We have also seen that high-maintenance integrity problems can lead to shifts in work priorities within the agency concerned (in attempts to cover up or distract attention), thus undermining internal quality-control mechanisms.[29] Quite apart from such crisis-management after the damage is done, focusing on the standard and practice of integrity is an open-ended necessity for international justice institutions, none of which is exempted from the common challenge of professionalisation. All international justice institutions face vicissitudes from time-to-time, as the policies

---

[27] See Dag Hammarskjöld, "The International Civil Servant in Law and Fact: Lecture delivered to Congregation at Oxford University, 30 May 1961", in Wilder Foote (ed.): *The Servant of Peace: A Selection of the Speeches and Statements of Dag Hammarskjöld, Secretary-General of the United Nations, 1953-1961*, The Bodley Head, 1962, p. 329 (http://www.legal-tools.org/doc/64bcae/).

[28] See Deborah L. Rhode and David Luban, *Legal Ethics*, Fifth Edition, Foundation Press, New York, 2009, p. 1074.

[29] See the emphasis on consistency of investigation planning in Xabier Agirre Aranburu, Morten Bergsmo, Simon De Smet and Carsten Stahn (eds.), *Quality Control in Criminal Investigation*, TOAEP, Brussels, 2020.

of States Parties are dynamic and do not always evolve along rational lines. The institutions require vigilance in their defence. Erosion of the 'high moral character' standard indicates lack of progress as much as an approach of rigid moralism does. Both can undermine our mindful ability to balance moral concern with a sensitivity to complex situational differences and dilemmas.

One of the main points made by the important 1944 report "The International Secretariat of the Future: Lessons from Experience by a Group of Former Officials of the League of Nations" was that no "attribute is more essential for an international secretariat than ability to gain and hold the confidence of member Governments and of public opinion".[30] As Hans Corell has highlighted, "international judges are operating under the eyes of the whole world, and the impression they give and the way in which they perform their work will directly reflect on the standing of the institution that they serve".[31] For this reason, he argues that "the standards that international judges must uphold must be set even higher than at the national level",[32] while it should be recognized, he would agree, that "judges must first and foremost apply the law and not use it to pursue their own ethical agendas".[33]

Against this background, this book has been conceived as a contribution towards the crystallisation of a sub-discipline of ethics of international justice. This is ambitious, but it also reflects that ethics of law is taught as a subject at the domestic level in several countries, in particular in the US. The textbook by Deborah L. Rhode and David Luban[34] is an example of a broadly-based approach at the national level. Alexander Heinze and Shannon Fyfe[35] have called for a more systematic approach to ethics in international criminal justice, as do several authors in this anthology.

---

[30] See "The International Secretariat of the Future: Lessons from Experience by a Group of Former Officials of the League of Nations", Royal Institute of International Affairs, London, March 1944, p. 17 (http://www.legal-tools.org/doc/53ecbb/).

[31] Hans Corell, "Ethical Dimensions of International Jurisprudence and Adjudication", 10 June 2002, p. 6 (an excerpt from the report of the 2002 Brandeis Institute for International Judges) (http://www.legal-tools.org/doc/5eb7d4/).

[32] *Ibid.*

[33] See "The Judiciary as a New Moral Authority?", p. 3 (an excerpt from the report of the 2006 Brandeis Institute for International Judges) (http://www.legal-tools.org/doc/ad4d13/).

[34] See Deborah L. Rhode and David Luban, *Legal Ethics, supra* note 28.

[35] See Alexander Heinze and Shannon Fyfe, "Prosecutorial Ethics and Preliminary Examinations at the ICC", in Morten Bergsmo and Carsten Stahn (eds.), *Quality Control in Prelimi-*

This book, as well as the wider project, takes a comprehensive approach. It was decided not to restrict the theme to what international courts can themselves do to enhance integrity. The project was organized in six parts: Part I: Meaning of Integrity, Part II: Awareness and Culture of Integrity, Part III: Role of International Organizations and States, Part IV: Role of International Courts, Part V: Integrity and the Lens of Cases, and Part VI: Independence and Integrity.

Part I ("Meaning of Integrity") seeks to give a wider philosophical, religious, historical and comparative context to an enhanced understanding of the concept or standard of 'integrity'. For the purposes of the Integrity Project, 'integrity' is nevertheless understood as a legally binding, statutory term of international law. The project does not see integrity in international justice as a mere value judgment or moral term. The main focus is on individual integrity in international justice, less so on the institutional integrity of international courts, although one affects the other and several authors address institutional integrity in the subsequent chapters.

The intention behind Part II ("Awareness and Culture of Integrity") has been to consider some factors that may contribute towards a culture of integrity taking hold within international courts, such as frankness, decency, leadership and outstanding ability. For Part II we have invited discussions on negative and sometimes veiled dynamics such as group-thinking, collusion, and paralysis of will – also among relevant representatives of states and non-governmental organizations – as well as instrumentalisation and the stealth psychology of indebtedness. Awareness depends on understanding of the meaning of the integrity standard, and nourishing a culture of integrity depends on awareness. This is how Parts I and II relate to each other. Both exceed the traditional scope of discussions of integrity in international justice contexts. Both widen the discourse in the interest of generating fresh ideas, engaging new talent in the discussion, and facilitating broad representation and ownership in the discourse.

Parts III ("Role of International Organizations and States") and IV ("Role of International Courts") take the conventional approach, asking which measures international courts, their States Parties, and other international organizations can take to foster individual integrity and cultures of integrity in international justice. This approach may be seen as the habitual

---

nary Examination: Volume 2, TOAEP, Brussels, 2018, pp. 1-75 (http://www.toaep.org/ps-pdf/33-bergsmo-stahn).

---

element of lawyers, however it seems crucial to be properly informed of real challenges and understand clearly the wider importance of the institutions. The greatest risk to integrity in international justice may well be omissions by States Parties in treating integrity as a legally binding requirement in the election of high officials. Those who may suffer direct consequences of such failures are the successors to the high official in question, the organizational culture, the defenders of the court, and victims.

Part V ("Integrity and the Lens of Cases") considers how concrete court cases identify integrity challenges. This can be seen as the water in which lawyers swim, and it is the engine-room of subsumption of facts – real or hypothetical – under the integrity standard. However, the case-approach is at this stage of the discourse on integrity in international justice necessarily selective, and it cannot alone give the overview necessary to construct a wider typology of risks and reform options.

Finally, Part VI ("Independence and Integrity") analyses the tension between the independence of international justice and the integrity of its members and, in some of the chapters, the international justice institutions. There is often a tension between the principles of independence and integrity. This is one of the hotspots of 'integrity stress', but also where efforts to conceal threats may be most accomplished. It is an area where actors around international justice institutions may be most deserving of scrutiny and guidance.

When presenting this conceptual structure of the Integrity Project at the international conference in the Peace Palace in The Hague on 1 December 2018, Morten Bergsmo, co-editor of this volume, observed that the project seeks to be "forward-looking", but that this should not be understood "as a limitation on speech" and that we "should certainly not try to belittle problems which persist and which undermine international justice":[36]

> Indeed, there are real reasons for why we are gathered here, above and beyond theoretical interest in a normative standard of 'integrity'. We are not here to conceal or apologize. [...]
>
> We are here to develop our awareness and understanding further, to add strength and perspective to an emerging dis-

---

[36] Morten Bergsmo, "Integrity as Safeguard Against the Vicissitudes of Common Justice Institutions", CILRAP Film, The Hague, 1 December 2018 (https://www.cilrap.org/cilrap-film/181201-bergsmo/).

course on 'integrity', and to see whether we can identify measures of improvement through inclusive consultation and communitarian scholarship.

'Integrity' is a challenge in all justice – in all public administration for that matter. It should not be seen as a threatening subject. Let us de-sensitise the subject, while not relativizing its importance.[37]

He offered a visualisation of the conceptual or cognitive structure of the Integrity Project shown as Figure 1, on which this book is also based.

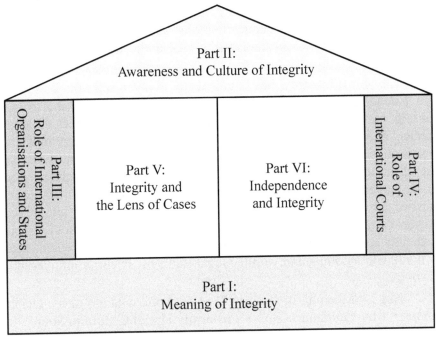

Figure 1: Visualisation of the conceptual structure of the book.

3. Meaning of 'Integrity'

In international justice, the term 'integrity' is often used in connection with the expression 'high moral character'. In the ICC Statute, for example, Article 36(3)(a) mentions both standards, whereas Article 42(3) only mentions 'high moral character'. Thus, for the purposes of the Integrity Project both are considered *legal* terms. At the same time, 'integrity' is used as

---

[37] *Ibid.*

"one of the most important and oft-cited of virtue terms", referring to "a quality of a person's character", used "virtually synonymously with 'moral'", righteous, conscientious or with rectitude.[38]

The UN International Civil Service Advisory Board observed in an influential 1954 report that 'integrity' must be judged "on the basis of the total behaviour of the person concerned. Such elementary personal or private qualities as honesty, truthfulness, fidelity, probity and freedom from corrupting influences, are clearly included".[39] Dag Hammarskjöld (the second UN Secretary-General) equated 'integrity' with "conscience" and "respect for law and respect for truth".[40] In his important monograph *The International Civil Servant*, Jacques Lemoine subsumes "the moral qualities of dedication, fairness and impartiality [...] under the concept of integrity".[41]

The word 'integrity' has linguistically evolved from the Latin adjective *'integer'*, meaning whole or complete. On one narrow and technical reading, 'integrity' could include consistent immoral conduct as long as conduct and personal principles operate in harmony. This reading is counter-intuitive to most of us and does not take fairly into account centuries of use of the term. David Luban has nevertheless made an insightful attempt to address problems associated with this narrow reading.[42] There are other narrow, conversational views that subjectivize terms such as 'integrity' and 'virtue' in manners that may not only appear rigid, but are both dissonant with how constituencies in China, India and other populous regions actually think, and incompatible with the legal status of 'integrity' in international courts.

Part I ("Meaning of Integrity") of the book contains seven chapters. *Chapter 1* by Emiliano J. Buis ("Physically Upright, Morally Sound: Recreating Ancient 'Integrity'") commences with reflections on the meaning of 'integrity' in Ancient Greece and Rome. Taking an historical and philo-

---

[38] See *Stanford Encyclopedia of Philosophy*, 9 July 2018 (https://plato.stanford.edu/entries/integrity/).

[39] See "Report on Standards of Conduct in the International Civil Service", 8 October 1954 (http://www.legal-tools.org/doc/d94c61/).

[40] See Dag Hammarskjöld, "The International Civil Servant in Law and Fact: Lecture delivered to Congregation at Oxford University, 30 May 1961", *supra* note 27, p. 348.

[41] See Jacques Lemoine, *The International Civil Servant: An Endangered Species*, Kluwer Law International, The Hague, 1995, p. 257.

[42] See Chapter 8 of his *Legal Ethics and Human Dignity*, Cambridge University Press, 2007.

sophical approach to integrity, Buis highlights the value of understanding the ethical principles underlying modern conceptions, in order to uphold them properly. Seeking the origins of 'integrity' to recreate the concept of 'integrity' in Classical Athens and Republican Rome, he illustrates, *inter alia*, the connection between an individual's physical features and moral characteristics, and its importance as an efficient rhetorical technique for integrity and justice. Integrity is thus associated with uprightness, straight bodies and honest conduct, as the antithesis to what is twisted or crooked. Although modern notions of 'integrity' do not have a physical equivalent and are often based on Christianity, the civic use of physical metaphors of rectitude and corruption remains. Buis concludes that the understanding of Classical values is therefore essential and a Classical debt.

Based on early Christian sources, *Chapter 2* by Judge Hanne Sophie Greve ("*Integer Vitae*: Christian Sources and Reflections on Integrity in Justice") presents religious and philosophical reflections on the notion of 'integrity' in justice. Hanne Sophie Greve draws on Quintus Horatius Flaccus' poem *Integer Vitae* to define *integer* as "a person not lacking in any capacity needed for moral or ethical behaviour in providing justice". From this definition, Greve addresses ethical and moral concepts such as human faculties and their controlling powers, the cardinal virtues (including prudence, justice, temperance and fortitude), and the three theological virtues (faith, hope and charity). She concludes that justice is crucial for society and, as such, the role of integrity is paramount as it materializes in relation to the Other through hope and charity.

In *Chapter 3* ("*Shari'ah* Sources and Reflections on Integrity"), Judge Adel Maged provides reflections on early *Shari'ah* sources and the notion of 'integrity' in justice. It explores the influence of Islam on the legal system and the judicial function. It examines *Shari'ah* sources and their provisions on judicial ethics, which place integrity as the core legal requirement for serving as a judge. In doing so, the chapter refers to Adab Al-Aāḍī, a compendium of early-classical Islamic jurisprudential literature. It further provides an overview of the importance of justice, judicial integrity and the judiciary in *Shari'ah*. Maged introduces *Shari'ah* concepts in relation to the Western notion of judicial 'integrity', in an effort to contribute to the consolidation of the concept in the international justice system.

In *Chapter 4* ("Sir Thomas More and Integrity in Justice"), Gunnar Ekeløve-Slydal develops a detailed analysis of Sir Thomas More and the notion of 'integrity', exploring what we can learn from his teachings in terms of principles and strategies to strengthen individual and institutional integrity. Being aware of its Classical and Biblical roots, More was among the first to use the English word 'integrity' as consistency in thought, word and action. Thus, Ekeløve-Slydal suggests that we should take More's concept of 'integrity' into account when facing current integrity challenges. He then addresses integrity failures in some inter-governmental organizations and analyses them in relation to a typology of integrity issues: politicization, instrumentalization of institutions, and professional integrity. More's integrity lessons relate to professional integrity being characterized by critical and creative reasoning to engage with conflicting demands of professional practice. He concludes that upholding professional integrity in international justice requires conforming to the promises and aims of justice.

In *Chapter 5* ("The Dag Hammarskjöld Legacy and Integrity in International Civil Service"), Ambassador Hans Corell provides a penetrating account of Dag Hammarskjöld's legacy and integrity in international civil service. Drawing on Hammarskjöld's lectures and the book *Markings* (which he prefers to call *Waymarks* in English), Corell discusses Hammarskjöld's statements on the UN and the ambiguity of the concept of 'neutrality'. He analyses how, following Hammarskjöld's guidance, integrity is ultimately an issue of conscience, and the international civil servant needs to be fully aware of human reactions, to keep them in check, so they do not interfere with decisions. He emphasizes that the standards at the international level should be higher than those at the national level, and the relevancy of accountability. Corell concludes by reminding us of the importance of forcing problems that confront us into a clearly conceived intellectual form and acting accordingly, based on a quotation by Hammarskjöld.

In *Chapter 6* ("Multicultural Understanding of Integrity in International Criminal Justice"), Juan Carlos Botero Navia seeks to develop some reflections on a multicultural understanding of 'integrity', with a focus on perspectives from the Global South. Botero examines whether the 2000 Bangalore Principles of Judicial Conduct, considered an important international standard on judicial integrity and independence, are truly universally accepted. In his understanding, international criminal justice overwhelmingly focuses on Western and elitist notions of justice, emphasizing punishment, retribution and deterrence, while excluding other forms of customary justice. He argues that this is also reflected in the Western concept of judicial integrity, which incorporates impartiality and a strict application of the law, but disregards the Global South's ideal of justice with its emphasis on restoration and community harmony (he develops an 'African Tree' consideration). He concludes that the legitimacy of international criminal tribunals, particularly the ICC, could be enhanced in the Global South by an interpretation of international criminal justice beyond what he sees as predominantly Western perspectives.

Shannon Fyfe explores theoretical approaches to the concept of 'integrity' in *Chapter 7* ("Ethics, Integrity and the *Bemba* Acquittal"). She dwells on the ICC Appeals Chamber's decision in the *Bemba* case and the Prosecutor's reaction thereto. Fyfe argues that this decision reflects that an institution must not only follow integrity standards, but it should also appear to be doing so. The chapter presents an overview of integrity as identity, as wholeness and integration, and as standing for something, concluding that the integrity of the ICC goes beyond its Prosecutor. She observes that the individual ethical obligation of prosecutors can be understood in deontological and consequentialist terms. Fyfe presents an incisive reflection on the institutional integrity of the judiciary based on an analysis of judicial ethics and individual integrity. She contributes normative tools to understand the relationship between institutions and individuals in international criminal law through the lens of integrity.

4. Awareness and Culture of Integrity

At the individual level, it is necessary to ask whether international civil servants and high officials in international courts have sufficient awareness or understanding of what 'integrity' and 'high moral character' refer to. It is problematic if these legal terms are largely seen as slogans or empty shells to which everyone is free to give equally valid content as may be convenient. The terms require interpretation according to the same methodology that applies to other binding language in the statute of the international court in question, even if there is relative scarcity of relevant international law sources.

In his biography on Dag Hammarskjöld, Brian Urquhart explains how Hammarskjöld left a personal impression on most of the people who dealt with him. He highlights Hammarskjöld's "integrity, disinterestedness and purity of intention",[43] while never questioning his practical judgment in matters of government, politics or international civil service. Hammar-

---

[43]   See Brian Urquhart, *Hammarskjold*, Harper & Row, New York, 1972, p. 33.

skjöld saw service as "self-oblivion", as striving towards "an unhesitant fulfilment of duty".[44] How is this relevant to the integrity standard? Is Hammarskjöld's legacy as a standard-bearer for civil servants and high officials in international courts relevant to how we nourish cultures of integrity in international courts?[45] For example, is there a requirement of 'intellectual integrity' for high officials and international civil servants in international courts? If prolific use of separate opinions affects the standing of an international court, could the practice bear on integrity?

These were among the more novel questions that had been formulated for the contributors to Part II of the anthology ("Awareness and Culture of Integrity"). 'Conflict of interest' is the most common arena for discussion of integrity in the preparation and adjudication of cases before international courts. This issue has received considerable attention already.[46] But while it may be decisive for the reputation of individual lawyers, it rarely has that effect on the institutions themselves. This and other 'integrity' challenges in operations – such as self-interest in recruitment, remuneration and privileges, loyalty in external activities, and propriety during missions – are also relevant here.

Part II of this anthology contains five chapters. In *Chapter 8* ("Conformity, Leadership and the Culture of Integrity at the International Criminal Court"), Brigid Inder OBE examines integrity concerns with respect to the ICC, while assessing the concepts of conformity, leadership and culture of integrity. The chapter begins with an introduction to the institutional framework of the ICC, identifying as a weakness the area of prohibited conduct, including sexual and other forms of gender-based violence committed in the workplace. She interprets it as stemming from factors such as

---

[44] Quoted in W.H. Auden, "Foreword", in Dag Hammarskjöld, *Markings*, Ballantine Books, New York, 1983, p. vii. Fair-minded readers of *Markings* can hardly perceive Hammarskjöld as naïve – he was obviously not a Brand-like character (as in the uncompromising figure in Henrik Ibsen's celebrated play *Brand* from 1866).

[45] Ever since the establishment of the Secretariat of the League of Nations and the International Labour Office in 1920, the international civil service's performance as regards "independence from any authority external to the organization, and the highest standards of efficiency, competence and integrity" has been "fragile and [...] repeatedly called into question" (Marcel A. Boisard, "Preface", in Lemoine, *supra* note 41, pp. v-vi). Boisard maintains that the preservation of these requisites "implies a continuing struggle" (*ibid.*).

[46] Brandeis University's International Center for Ethics, Justice and Public Life has produced several short reports on aspects of this problematique, see the collection at https://www.legal-tools.org?search=cajc9qcu.

---

indifference to international standards regarding oversight. The chapter addresses the ethical challenges present at the ICC, including misconduct by individual staff or high officials, failures of internal oversight mechanisms, and limited infrastructure to support and ensure the Court's institutional integrity. She presents Registry's restructuring project 'ReVision' as a factual case of leadership vacuum to illustrate the Court's ethical challenges. The author concludes that the ICC is ethically discordant with the principles that guided its foundations, and calls for States Parties to ensure that the Court fulfils its mandate and exercises proper leadership.

From a different perspective, William H. Wiley critically assesses the relationship between leadership, management and integrity in international criminal investigations in *Chapter 9* ("Effective Leadership, Management and Integrity in International Criminal Investigations"). In searching for explanations for underperformance by international judicial institutions since 1993, Wiley addresses what he describes as the insufficient institutional leadership and management of international criminal justice, drawing a distinction between the two concepts. He highlights the relevance of institutional loyalty for the success of an international criminal court or tribunal as it fosters an organizational culture that impacts staff performance. Drawing on his personal experience at the ICTR, ICTY and ICC, Wiley further chronicles examples of what he considers as successful and unsuccessful incidents of discipline and integrity in these institutions. Consequently, Wiley reflects on the intersection between leadership, professional integrity, and international criminal investigations, emphasizing the requisite harmony between investigators, analysts and counsel for the effectiveness of the case-building process. He concludes that the principles of effective leadership and management in international criminal investigations must be addressed as an essential component to guarantee the prosecutorial output of the international criminal justice system.

In *Chapter 10* ("Decency as a Prerequisite to Integrity in International Proceedings"), Andrew T. Cayley CMG QC delves into the concept of decency as a prerequisite to integrity in international criminal proceedings, embedded in standards of professional conduct that regulate the relationship between counsel and court as well as between counsel and client. He underscores how domestic regulations like those of England and Wales require a positive duty of decency, whereas the ICC expresses this duty in the negative. Cayley identifies that fundamental principles of decency are broadly the same in domestic and international jurisdictions, involving a duty of candour and honesty, in addition to independence, integrity and good faith. He provides a thoughtful reflection based on his personal experience at the ICTY, particularly in the cases of *Krstić* and *Šainović et al.*, arguing that decency often requires one to act in a way that is not self-serving, even when prosecuting in international criminal proceedings. As such, the chapter concludes with a reference to 'A Man for All Seasons' and the courage and strength required to give the Devil the benefit of the law.

Julija Bogoeva's *Chapter 11* ("Only the Best Should Prosecute and Judge in International Justice") starts by surveying some of the challenges the international community currently faces, arguing that integrity is more necessary than ever. Regarding the act of judging fellow humans for criminal conduct, Bogoeva writes that it requires the highest integrity. Based on her experience at the ICTY and a 2018 Oxford study, she proposes that integrity implies the coherence of individuals and institutions and an 'ethical climate' within the organization. Consequently, she maintains that the impunity of the most powerful must end, meaning that the influence of states should be reduced by promoting a truthful environment in international criminal justice while also protecting whistle-blowers. The chapter underscores that integrity is key to international justice.

The role of aesthetics in furthering a culture of integrity in international criminal justice is examined by Marina Aksenova in *Chapter 12* ("The Role of Aesthetics in Furthering Integrity"). Aksenova suggests that enhancing international justice through alternative means has a direct impact on the integrity of its actors, arguing that those involved in the process must embrace the values promoted. Consequently, she writes that integrity is bolstered by the connection between inner guidance and outer norms, which is fostered by aesthetics. Relying on natural law theory and theoretical frameworks such as the "visual methodology in the age of digital baroque", Aksenova notes that art allows for law to be contextualized. This relation provides for a further connection between ethics and aesthetics, which can be translated into specific ways to engage with art in the field of international justice. As such, the chapter seeks to illustrate how international criminal proceedings can be seen as ritualistic performances and how art can contribute to reparations at the ICC.

5. Role of International Organizations and States

Establishing an international court takes years of preparations and negotiations by states – if not decades, as we have seen with the ICC – to agree and adopt a statute and wider legal infrastructure. Securing near consensus on a statute negotiated by more than 150 states is a monumental undertaking, as illustrated by the Rome Diplomatic Conference on the ICC in 1998 and the two preceding years of intense discussions. When the statute finally enters into force, the process to establish and build the actual organization of the court starts. States Parties must then agree on the financing of the court, its buildings, staff, case flow, and other operational needs. This requires a further continuous investment by governments.

In contrast to the making of the law and organizational framework, the attention given to who should lead these institutions can sometimes seem surprisingly lacklustre. It is almost as if some government representatives see their job as done when the legal instruments and institutional structures are in place. This is a particular risk for positions such as prosecutor or deputy prosecutor of international criminal jurisdictions, where we have normally not seen state-driven campaigning in the same way as for international judgeships.[47]

States Parties are responsible for the election of judges and prosecutors of international courts. This is an important responsibility that requires vigilance. The high officials of international courts define the culture of integrity within their institutions. As observed by four long-standing actors in the field of international criminal justice: "we should recognize that an international court will not be better than the integrity of its leaders".[48] Do states take this responsibility seriously enough? If not, what can be done to help improve their performance? Should more be done to expose the pursuit of national interests and deal-making when that reduces the emphasis placed on 'integrity' in the election of high officials of international courts? Should there be more attention on the conduct of state officials with portfo-

---

[47] This is elaborated by Morten Bergsmo in his chapter "Institutional History, Behaviour and Development", in Morten Bergsmo, Klaus Rackwitz and SONG Tianying (eds.): *Historical Origins of International Criminal Law: Volume 5*, TOAEP, Brussels, 2017, pp. 25-27 (http://www.legal-tools.org/doc/09c8b8/).

[48] Morten Bergsmo, Wolfgang Kaleck, Alexander S. Muller and William H. Wiley, "A Prosecutor Falls, Time for the Court to Rise", FICHL Policy Brief Series No. 86 (2017), TOAEP, Brussels, 2017 (http://www.toaep.org/pbs-pdf/86-four-directors/).

lio-responsibility for an international court when they themselves have a known ambition to become one its high officials?

In addition to these questions – several of which have been touched upon by chapters throughout the anthology – Part III ("Role of Internationalal Organizations and States") explores efforts within the UN and the European Union to strengthen integrity, including in the area of sexual harassment, as well as perspectives from national inquiries into integrity violations in public agencies and the responsibilities of states as regards private international investigations.

In the first of five chapters in Part III, Dieneke de Vos in *Chapter 13* ("Institutional Ethics, Individual Integrity, and Sexual Harassment: Recent Developments in Ethics Standard-Setting and Mechanisms at the United Nations") emphasizes the role of institutional ethics, claiming that individual integrity and institutional integrity must be understood jointly since the latter will ultimately shape the former. De Vos explores the linkage between the institution and the individual by examining the UN ethics infrastructure. In setting out this regulatory framework, she notes the significance of independence, impartiality and incorruptibility in defining integrity. However, although the UN has developed mechanisms to enforce standards around individual integrity such as the UN Ethics Office, these structures are only starting to grapple with how to deal with sexual harassment as an institutional integrity concern. De Vos identifies this as a gap within the UN's ethics infrastructure, since such a framework on individual integrity should also address inter-personal conduct. She concludes that while a value-based ethics infrastructure is required to advance institutional ethics and individual integrity, accountability for all types of unethical behaviour is essential.

With a detailed focus on sexual harassment, Matthias Neuner examines the UN's efforts to address it in *Chapter 14* ("Sexual Harassment"). Analyzing the history of the definition of sexual harassment, Neuner draws on both domestic and international developments, from the US adoption of administrative regulations and judicial recognition of sexual harassment as unlawful sex discrimination in the 1970s and 1980s, to the 2008 definition provided by the UN Secretariat. Neuner considers the first UN legal definition in 1992 as the beginning of a standard-setting phase characterized by the adoption of administrative instructions and procedures in relation to sexual harassment by UN organs and sub-agencies. He then considers the evolution of the definition of sexual harassment, leading to a comprehensive analysis of the case law on sexual harassment, including more than 40 judgments issued by the UN Administrative Tribunal, the UN Dispute Tribunal, and the UN Appeals Tribunal. Neuner concludes that the UN efforts to investigate and adjudicate cases of sexual harassment are decades-long and ongoing, pursuing a 'zero tolerance' approach to the matter.

In *Chapter 15* ("Integrity and the Work of the European Ombudsman"), Marta Hirsch-Ziembinska and Vieri Biondi present the role of integrity in the work and functioning of the European Ombudsman. The chapter describes how integrity is integral to the right to good administration as enshrined in Article 41 of the European Charter of Fundamental Rights, and how it has been implemented by the European Ombudsman in practice. Hirsch-Ziembinska and Biondi elaborate on the European Ombudsman's efforts to ensure transparency and accountability. These efforts include addressing potential and actual conflicts of interest while being mindful of the so-called 'revolving doors' phenomenon, ensuring the transparency of the expert groups advising the European Commission, and the maintenance of transparent and well-regulated lobbying. The chapter concludes that the European Ombudsman places respect for integrity near the concept of good administration, ensuring the integrity of EU institutions in a reactive and safeguarding manner.

Whistleblowing and its implementation procedures in public institutions are explored by Jan Fougner in *Chapter 16* ("On Whistle-Blowing and Inquiry in Public Institutions"). He argues that whistle-blowing is conducive to eradicating misconduct, as it introduces a culture of transparency and freedom of expression. Fougner highlights that whistle-blowing procedures and private inquiries as ways to ensuring integrity and fighting misconduct and unethical behaviour also in the judiciary. Implementation of whistle-blowing procedures and appropriate mechanisms to combat corruption and violations of professional and ethical standards is, however, essential to preserve integrity. For Fougner, such implementation seeks to create conduct of openness and deterrence of wrongdoing, but it will ultimately depend on the institution's willingness. He closes by arguing that the ICC should implement such mechanisms, in order to impede absolute power, hinder corruption, and re-establish the virtue of integrity.

In *Chapter 17* ("Private International Criminal Investigations and Integrity"), Alexander Heinze offers a comprehensive analysis of private international criminal investigations and integrity. He examines their previous occurrences and advantages (such as efficiency and immediacy), and

illegal conduct of private investigators. The chapter carefully evaluates integrity as both a semantic and philosophical concept from three perspectives – object, subject and context – and analyses the application of the procedural regime, especially exclusionary rules. Moreover, Heinze considers the different contexts in which private investigations might take place: inter-investigatory, intra-investigatory, and extra-investigatory. He concludes that private investigations constitute a double-edged sword, being both necessary in the fight against impunity and dangerous when involving illegally obtained evidence. Considering this dichotomy, Heinze suggests that private conduct in international investigatory contexts must be regulated and guided by integrity, understood as fairness, due process, natural justice or judicial legitimacy.

6. Role of International Courts

The role of international courts in upholding integrity is as important as that of States Parties, if not more fundamental. The high officials of these courts set the tone of integrity for their organization as a whole. Several institutional, non-political measures are available to raise awareness and build cultures of integrity within such courts.[49] Part IV of the anthology concerns these measures.

The conceptualisation of the project raised several questions to guide the contributors to Part IV. Does, for example, our understanding of integrity-awareness, -reasoning, -intent and -behaviour within these institutions correspond to the new international environment where several permanent members of the UN Security Council show strong reservation towards the ICC and other international courts?[50] Have we overlooked or underestimated ways in which the administration of international courts can "help to create an atmosphere which is conducive to the [integrity] of international

---

[49] A statement of the Women's Initiatives for Gender Justice expressed concern that media revelations about the first ICC Prosecutor "could be considered emblematic of an underlying *culture* within the Court, rather than exceptional to the overall environment", see "A critical time for the ICC's credibility", 12 October 2017 (http://www.legal-tools.org/doc/e2fbc7/) (italics added). It observed that this "is an important moment for the ICC's evolution as a permanent court built for longevity, worthy of public trust and focused on the ethical fulfilment of its mandate".

[50] This paraphrases Deborah L. Rhode, "Where is the Leadership in Moral Leadership?", in *idem* (ed.), *Moral Leadership: The Theory and Practice of Power, Judgment, and Policy*, John Wiley & Sons, San Francisco, 2006, pp. 22-33.

officials"?[51] Are the existing statutory requirements of 'integrity' or 'high moral character' adequate or should there be stronger language to emphasise their legally binding nature, to dispel any doubts that may exist? Do the codes of conduct in international courts work or should they be developed further? Should a model code of conduct or ethics charter for international criminal justice be drawn up? Are existing mechanisms effective enough to deal with sexual misconduct within international courts and with misconduct by former high officials?[52] Part IV deals with some of these questions, including how to give maximum effect to existing integrity mechanisms, including oversight mechanisms.

In *Chapter 18* ("Codes of Judicial Ethics: An Emerging Culture of Accountability for the Judiciary?"), the first of five chapters in Part IV, Bettina Julia Spilker writes about the emergence of a culture of accountability for the judiciary of international criminal tribunals. Despite the importance of a culture of accountability for actors in judicial proceedings to guarantee integrity in international criminal proceedings, codes of judicial ethics have only been adopted recently. Spilker meticulously dissects the existing codes of judicial ethics of the ICC, ICTY, the International Residual Mechanism for Criminal Tribunals ('MICT'), Extraordinary Chamber in the Courts of Cambodia, Special Tribunal for Lebanon, and Kosovo Specialist Chambers, examining their preambles and legal bases, the applicable standards enshrined therein, and the disciplinary procedures in place. The adoption of codes and disciplinary procedures are a step towards creating a culture of accountability for judges in international criminal tribunals as effective institutional measures. Nonetheless, Spilker claims that states must improve their involvement in this regard, providing a solid legal basis for the adoption of such principles and procedures when creating these institutions.

Drawing on his personal experience at the ICTR and the European Court of Human Rights, Judge Erik Møse presents an incisive reflection on common integrity challenges in international criminal justice and regional human rights courts in *Chapter 19* ("Reflections on Integrity in Interna-

---

[51] See the influential report "The International Secretariat of the Future: Lessons from Experience by a Group of Former Officials of the League of Nations", *supra* note 30, p. 61. The bracketed word "integrity" replaces "loyalty" in the original.

[52] In a statement, the International Criminal Court Bar Association ('ICCBA') observes that the first ICC Prosecutor, "as a former elected official, falls outside the IOM's investigative mandate", see "ICCBA Statement on Allegations Against Former ICC Prosecutor", 29 November 2017 (http://www.legal-tools.org/doc/a8cdcb/).

tional Criminal Justice and Regional Human Rights Courts"). Mindful of their differences, Møse explores the similarities between international criminal justice institutions and human rights courts, including with regard to institutional legitimacy and individual integrity, an inter-related issue as institutional legitimacy requires individual integrity. Møse identifies a relationship between the reaction to criticism and legitimacy, as an institution might risk losing its legitimacy when adopting a defensive attitude or not reacting to well-founded criticisms. Consequently, he argues that these international institutions must transparently respond to such challenges, either by refuting the criticism or addressing it through measures such as investigations and reform, while creating a common culture of integrity within the institutions.

Karim A.A. Khan and Jonathan Agar further elaborate on the culture of integrity within international institutions in *Chapter 20* ("Integrity and Independence in the Delivery of Accountability: Harnessing International and Domestic Frameworks in Pursuit of Justice for ISIL Crimes"). Arguing that integrity commences at the leadership and percolates down, Khan and Agar claim that integrity in investigation and accountability mechanisms requires a self-sustaining ecosystem, in which all parties are imbued with integrity, ensuring coherence and commitment by all team members. In doing so, they offer an invaluable account of the lessons learned on integrity and independence in the delivery of accountability by the United Nations Investigative Team to promote accountability for crimes committed by Da'esh ('UNITAD') in Iraq. The authors also highlight UNITAD's deontological and consequential approaches to integrity. The chapter comprehensively presents the UN and UNITAD normative integrity frameworks and, importantly, the Investigative Team's integrity policies and their emphasis on international and domestic staffing, best practices on documentation and evidence, and engagement with survivors, witnesses and impacted communities. Khan and Agar conclude that in addition to a comprehensive integrity framework addressing individual and institutional integrity, concerted action and commitment from the institutional leadership is required.

In *Chapter 21* ("The Wider Policy Framework of Ethical Behaviour: Outspoken Observations from a True Friend of the International Criminal Court"), Cyril Laucci scrutinizes the relationship between the legal and policy frameworks of international institutions and integrity. He provides an overview of the structure of the ICC internal legal and policy frameworks, assessing the main areas of legal and policy vacuums and how they might impact the upholding of integrity at the ICC. In doing so, Laucci elaborately reflects on the administrative and labour law frameworks in place at the ICC, practically assessing their gaps and subsequent impacts on the staff and recruitment policies, particularly those concerning the selection of staff members, the conditions of field operations, disciplinary procedures, anti-fraud and whistle-blowing policies, and the protection of information. The chapter argues that whereas strong legal and policy frameworks alone are not a guarantee of integrity, gaps are pitfalls for integrity and ethical behaviour within the institution. For this reason, the institution needs to provide guidance in line with its duty of care.

The question whether the ICC really needs an ethics charter is the focus of the reflections by Salim Nakhjavani and Suhail Mohammed in *Chapter 22* ("Does the International Criminal Court Really Need an Ethics Charter?"). The chapter critically assesses the external auditor's 2018 recommendations on the need for a new ethics charter by highlighting the existence of six codes of ethical and professional conduct at the ICC. Arguing that the problem lies in that transmission does not imply reception, the authors examine whether the ICC's existing ethical framework communicates a 'moral message', considering specific incidents arising during the *Lubanga* trial, some actions by the Prosecutor in the Darfur situation, and the *Ruto and Sang* and *Gbagbo* trials. Concluding that the 'moral message' is already present in the ICC's ethical framework, the authors further reflect on its permeation at the level of culture. They conclude that the adoption of an additional ethics charter might be counter-productive or self-defeating because of double deontology, arguing that the real question is on the implementation of such ethical framework, which calls for an honest reading of the reality at the level of culture and persistent conversations on ethics among the Court's staff.

7. Integrity and the Lens of Cases

Part V contains four chapters which either look at specific cases notorious for how they engage issues of integrity, or consider how integrity relates to some central, case-related work-processes in international courts. The authors chose to focus on certain cases, which had already been the object of much scrutiny and outside commentary in the media and public arena. It is clear that more cases deserve attention and more careful analysis is needed at any given international court or tribunal and also across courts and tribunals. Certainly, a more systematic analysis of a wide scope of cases is required to comprehensively illuminate integrity in practice.

In *Chapter 23* ("Reflections on Integrity in the Prosecution of International Cases"), Teresa McHenry and Ann Marie Ursini offer a perceptive and practical reflection on integrity in the prosecution of international cases. Drawing on McHenry's experience as an international and domestic prosecutor, the chapter addresses the inside and outside perspectives, the realities of investigations and resource limitations, the issue of co-operation, and discovery and disclosure. The chapter discusses the challenges faced by prosecutors regarding witnesses, such as the dissonance between domestic and international practice concerning witness preparation, the multiplicity of witness statements, and the obligations pertaining to security and privacy. The authors argue that integrity must also be evinced from courtroom conduct, extending to the judges' behaviour and staff recruitment policies. The chapter concludes that integrity in international justice must mean integrity among its participants, as well as in the functioning of the institutions themselves.

The next three chapters provide different perspectives on particular cases. In *Chapter 24* ("Individual Integrity and Independence of Judges: The Akay Saga"), Antonio Angotti, Basil Saen and Shan Patel focus on the events following the arrest by Turkish authorities of MICT Judge Akay. The authors reflect on individual integrity and the independence of judges while examining the conduct of the involved individuals, namely, the UN Secretary-General, the UN Legal Counsel, the MICT Prosecution, the Defence Counsel for Mr. Ngirabatware, Mr. Peter Robinson, and MICT President and Pre-Review Judge Theodor Meron. The authors identify the relevant ethical codes applicable to each of the individuals and their concrete actions at relevant points of what they call the 'Akay Saga'. Nonetheless, Angotti, Saen and Patel emphasize that achieving integrity is not a one-time test and goes beyond following normative frameworks, but it is a constant struggle for international civil servants and high officials in international justice.

Mohamed Badar and Polona Florijančič analyse the disqualification of Judge Frederik Harhoff from the *Šešelj* case and its implications for the ICTY in *Chapter 25* ("The Disqualification of Judge Frederik Harhoff: Implications for Integrity"). The authors address the disqualification, the alleged bias displayed by Judge Harhoff, and the content of his much-cited letter to a group of friends. They examine whether Judge Harhoff's opinions concerning the alleged change in ICTY jurisprudence were wrong, scrutinizing concepts such as specific direction, and the *Gotovina* case and implementation of joint criminal enterprise. The chapter explores several claims regarding what is behind the disqualification of Judge Harhoff, including possible punishment for questioning the tribunal's independence and potential pressure exerted on fellow judges. Badar and Florijančič highlight the importance of valid criticism of international judicial institutions.

In *Chapter 26* ("Integrity in International Criminal Law: Post-Conviction Proceedings"), Gregory S. Gordon analyses early release proceedings at the MICT and potential integrity vacuums therein. He reviews these proceedings in the case of Ferdinand Nahimana, particularly the early release decision. Gordon provides an account of the ICTR proceedings and the involvement of Judge Theodor Meron during the merits, including his dissenting opinion. For Gordon, Judge Meron's earlier involvement in the merits and decision on early release raise ethical and due process concerns, hinting at the existence or appearance of a lack of impartiality or bias on the judicial level. Systemically, he finds that there was a lack of due process and fairness as only one judge was the decision-maker. Seeing integrity as the coherence of the entire procedural scheme, Gordon sets out several recommendations to strengthen integrity in early release proceedings, aiming to ensure fairness, transparency and due process in future post-conviction proceedings.

8. Independence and Integrity

Part VI of the anthology explores the relationship between the principles of integrity and independence. The authors in this part were asked to discuss how the integrity standard in international justice relates to the requirement of independence. This is obviously not just a conceptual question with little real-world implication. The project conceptualization asked whether recent technical developments such as WikiLeaks and proliferation of communication surveillance techniques affect the ways high officials and international civil servants of international courts should communicate with representatives of embassies or governments. Given that international civil servants meet their "most severe test in intercourse with government authorities, whether it be delegates accredited to the organization or officials of the various departments of national governments",[53] how close can they be to governments before the contact jeopardizes integrity?

Other questions asked included whether there are sufficient means to detect cases where a high official of an international court acts on feelings of *indebtedness* towards a government that ensured his or her election or appointment, especially when the government is that of a great power whose actions towards the institution are jealously guarded by other states.[54] Should there be stronger whistle-blower protection for members of staff who detect signs of such indebtedness, to deter that it be acted upon (for example in recruitment) and discourage statements in informal settings that lend themselves to the perception of bias or lack of independence on this ground? Moreover, are integrity challenges that are linked to the relations between high officials of international courts and leaders of non-governmental organizations adequately addressed (including the latter's concern for continued financial support from States Parties and the *de facto* influence of high officials of the court)? These are among the less comfortable questions that deserve careful and open analysis. The authors have answered some of them in this first edition of the anthology, leaving more work to be done in this area.

In *Chapter 27* ("Judicial Independence and Accountability at International Criminal Courts and Tribunals"), Judge Ivana Hrdličková and Adrian Plevin offer a detailed reflection on the relation between judicial independence and judicial accountability at international criminal courts and tribunals. The chapter balances the tension between independence and accountability, advocating that beyond any conflict, judicial accountability only enhances and strengthens judicial independence. Considering that judicial independence is widely deontologically recognized but lacks uniformity in its promotion and protection among judicial institutions, the authors argue that accountability mechanisms and ethics codes are required to promote it and guarantee that judges are answerable for their actions. In pursuance of uniformity, Hrdličková and Plevin conclude that the proposal of the Paris

---

[53] Lemoine, *The International Civil Servant: An Endangered Species*, *supra* note 41, p. 54.

[54] There are two sides to instrumentalisation of such feelings of indebtedness: "international civil servants are, as much as governments, guardians of their own integrity", see *ibid.*, p. 47. "[U]sing knowledge and skills acquired by virtue of official position to concoct tactical moves" in "connivance with national authorities [...] is not unknown", see *ibid.*, pp. 58-59, where he continues: "Lobbying, approaching delegations in an unofficial and unauthorized capacity, is another failing some international officials are prone to".

Declaration for the Effectiveness of International Criminal Justice for a joint accountability mechanism applicable to international courts and tribunals could lead to the development of a more detailed code of conduct applicable to all judges, improving the quality of justice and the rule of law.

Former ICTY and ICTR Chief Prosecutor Richard J. Goldstone offers his invaluable insight into the relationship between independence and integrity in *Chapter 28* ("Prosecutorial Language, Integrity and Independence"). Goldstone provides an insider's perspective on the fine line between politics and international law, and how prosecutorial language is key for international civil servants and judicial staff to navigate the diplomatic intricacies of international criminal justice. As the former Chief Prosecutor, Goldstone reflects on his experience at the *ad hoc* Tribunals, evoking his engagement with the national governments of France, Denmark and the US in relation to evidentiary matters relevant to the ICTY, his negotiations with the Rwandan government as ICTR Prosecutor, his Office's commitment to prosecuting sexual and gender-based violence at the ICTR in the face of civil society's concerns, and his efforts to uphold his independence even before the UN Secretary-General. Goldstone concludes that prosecutorial language is of paramount importance for international prosecutors to diplomatically and astutely manoeuvre international politics without compromising their independence.

In *Chapter 29* ("Integrity and the Preservation of Independence in International Criminal Justice"), David Donat-Cattin and Melissa Verpile assess the preservation of judicial independence in international criminal justice, particularly at the ICC. They shed light on the issue of integrity and judicial independence from a civil society perspective, addressing the interplay between integrity and independence at the ICC, and the perceived lack of accountability, legitimacy and integrity of international criminal tribunals. The chapter considers the early phase of the implementation of the Rome Statute, exploring the statutory requirement of integrity relating to its application. Donat-Cattin and Verpile further analyse the upholding of integrity and judicial independence in practice, looking into the role of the Assembly of States Parties, the issue of immunities in the *Al-Bashir* case, the aftermath of the *Kenyatta and Ruto* cases, and the attacks on the Court by national governments. The authors conclude that the ailments stemming from the ICC's functioning are not fatal since accountability mechanisms are already in place, highlighting the role of the Assembly in monitoring the Court's work as well as the relevance of the election of judges. Nonetheless, they caution that the Assembly must perform its tasks of proper oversight, and restate the system of nomination and elections of judges and prosecutor recommended by Parliamentarians for Global Action.

Adedeji Adekunle provides reflections on the standards and challenges on integrity and independence at the ICC in *Chapter 30* ("Integrity and Independence: Common Standards and Uneven Cost of Implementation"). Even though the concepts of integrity and impartiality are considered universal and necessary in international justice, Adekunle argues that the cultural, social or economic background or orientation of the diverse staff may play a role in their understanding and implementation. Considering this potential dissonance, he emphasizes the need for evenness and objectivity in enforcement, implying codification and a clear understanding thereof through the proper contextualization of the concepts as part of an institutional framework of beliefs and norms. Adekunle perceptively construes the different types of threats and pressures faced by prosecutors, judges and other staff at international criminal justice institutions that might require additional guidance to be dealt with, such as political, post-employment, economic, socio-cultural and even historical pressure. He concludes by suggesting an ethics compliance mechanism at the ICC beyond the Independent Oversight Mechanism that may reflect practices such as the EU Ombudsman or the UN Ethics Office.

Christopher Staker offers personal reflections addressing the anathema of political exposure of international criminal tribunals in *Chapter 31* ("Integrity and the Inevitable Political Exposure of International Criminal Justice"). While political influence in the judiciary is generally condemned, Staker argues that this exposure is necessary when the totality of criminal justice is considered. International criminal justice is probably more vulnerable to such influence given the role of states as sovereign decision-makers. ICC proceedings are often marked by political decisions made by states – from the triggering of the Court's jurisdiction, to withdrawal from the Statute. States might also seek to persuade the Court regarding prosecutorial policies. Bearing in mind the unavoidability of the Court's political exposure, Staker notes that a common understanding of the appropriate role of political decision-makers and its limitations is required for prosecutors and judges to know in light of their independence and integrity.

In concluding *Chapter 32* ("Some Reflections on Integrity in International Justice"), Judge David Re rounds off Part VI of this anthology with an appropriately sober analysis of the systemic factors that make it more difficult in practice to uphold integrity in international courts than at the national level. Through several examples of integrity dilemmas that he has observed in international(ised) criminal jurisdictions and national practice, he suggests that it is not easy to progress through mere codes of conduct and basic compliance mechanisms.

9. Growing Recognition of the Importance of Integrity

There has been a marked increase in the references to integrity in international justice since April 2017, when the steps leading to this book intensified, as detailed in our Preface above.[55] There was a palpable interest in the international conference on the topic in the Peace Palace in The Hague in December 2018, as well as in the films and podcasts of the presentations made at the conference. Integrity now appears to be in fashion. The theme of integrity in international justice even became a watchword during the months in 2020 leading up to the election of the third ICC Prosecutor and new ICC judges. This surge in interest should be welcomed wholeheartedly, although one should be weary of any attempt to instrumentalize what is a fundamentally important subject for the future of international justice (for example, pursuant to personal ambition linked to court elections or preservations of jobs). Anecdotes can obviously be valuable if they translate into proper evidence, whereas deliberate rumour mongering and prejudice must be handled with care when basic interests of international courts as well as individuals are at stake.

The Integrity Project offers a comprehensive, serious review of the integrity standard in international justice, with a view to contributing to our awareness of integrity and which measures may be best suited to strengthen respect for integrity in international justice. The book is teeming with ideas, suggestions and advice about such measures, while it at the same time offers profound theoretical perspectives and background analysis to deepen our understanding. The book does not shy away from some of the inevitably thorny issues and vigorous debates in the field, without tabloidizing serious concerns. International judges and prosecutors – and other high of-

---

[55] See, for example, Open Letter to Committee on the Election of the ICC Prosecutor: Zero Tolerance Must be Shown Towards Sexual Harassment, 17 February 2020 (https://www. legal-tools.org/doc/cx0yns/); Danya Chaikel, "ICC Prosecutor Symposium: The Next ICC Prosecutor Must Embody Integrity in #MeToo Era", in *Opinio Juris*, 16 April 2020 (available on its web site). See also UN Office on Drug and Crime, "UN Launches Global Network of Judges to Strengthen Integrity in Courts", 9 April 2018 (https://www.legal-tools.org/doc/5r526m/).

ficials of international courts – are *public figures* and their work should therefore be subjected to direct critical review. That comes with the job and this is one of the reasons why such high officials are highly remunerated. In order to execute their weighty responsibilities under the statutory instruments of international courts, the States Parties need to be assisted by clearly articulated, critical assessments that are not artificially constrained by fear of sanction or a desire to be cited in decisions or submissions. It is in the institutional interest of international courts that critical analysis not be impeded by a deference which may be appropriate *within* legal fraternities and their practice, but do not apply in the same way *outside*. As it turns out, the high officials who are mentioned by some authors in this anthology are in most cases so accomplished that their long-standing merits and achievements are well established.

Integrity is certainly lamented if it is seen as missing. It is also often referred to when discussing prescriptions for institutional reform. Interest in the integrity and ethics of governance has increased significantly in the last years, given a growing commitment of international organizations to fight corruption and safeguard integrity. More recently, the International Bar Association's '2019 International Principles on Conduct for the Legal Profession' sets out ten relevant principles for legal professionals to guide their professional duties, including independence, honesty, integrity and fairness.[56] Committees and conferences are organized and full-blown integrity programmes created.[57] Networks and institutional bodies and policies with an explicit focus on integrity are established. For example, the UNODC's Global Judicial Integrity Network was officially established in Vienna in April 2018. In March 2020, over 700 participants from 118 countries and 50 judicial associations and organizations, met for a high-level event of the Network. This shows the interest in integrity-related topics and the appeal of sharing experiences. Another example beyond the judicial arena is the High Level Panel on International Financial Accountability, Transparency and Integrity for Achieving the 2030 Agenda launched in

---

[56] See International Bar Association, IBA International Principles on Conduct for the Legal Profession, approved on 25 May 2019 by the Council of the International Bar Association (available on the IBA web site).

[57] Integrity programmes may include various measures, such as a code of conduct, an integrity office(r), integrity training, whistle-blowing procedures, policies for misconduct, and pre-employment screening. See, for example, Alain Hoekstra and Muel Kaptein, "The Integrity of Integrity Programs: Toward a Normative Framework", *Public Integrity*, 7 July 2020, pp.1-13.

April 2020 by the Presidents of the UN General Assembly and the Economic and Social Council. Furthermore, NATO's Building Integrity Programme has been in place since 2007 and a Building Integrity Policy has been endorsed since 2017. Put simply, a key challenge often observed is getting from talking the talk to walking the walk.

In his Foreword to this book, Justice Richard J. Goldstone refers to the final report of the Independent Expert Review Group ('IER') appointed by the Assembly of States Parties to review the working of the International Criminal Court and the Rome Statute system, and his hope that "the present anthology will contribute to the momentum around the tremendous importance of integrity in international justice" (see above). As described in our Preface to this book, the Assembly's 2019 establishment of the IER mandate[58] followed a recommendation at the early stages of the Integrity Project. On 30 September 2020, the IER published its final report, which runs to 348 pages and includes 384 recommendations, of which 76 are summarised as "prioritised recommendations" in Annex I.[59]

Following a description of its terms of reference,[60] the IER report first addresses Court-wide matters, such as governance, human resources, ethics and prevention of conflicts of interest, and internal grievance procedures; before addressing organ-specific matters of Chambers, the Office of the Prosecutor and Registry, delving into their working methods, the Code of Judicial Ethics, defence-related matters and victim participation, reparations, and assistance. The report also examines matters such as the Court's external governance, oversight bodies and mechanisms, and the system of nomination of judges.

The notion of integrity – its different meanings and relevancy for the legitimacy of international justice institutions – is visible throughout the report, particularly where ethical and appropriate behaviour is discussed. The report states that "ethics has been identified as an important topic for

---

[58] See, ICC, Assembly of States Parties, Review of the International Criminal Court and the Rome Statute system, ICC-ASP/18/Res.7, 6 December 2019 (https://www.legal-tools.org/doc/d1fyfk/). The task was assigned to a Group of Independent Experts comprised of nine members and chaired by Justice Richard J. Goldstone, who has also contributed Chapter 28 below ("Prosecutorial Language, Integrity and Independence").

[59] See Independent Expert Review, "Review of the International Criminal Court and the Rome Status System, Final Report", *supra* note 2, p. 331 (https://www.legal-tools.org/doc/cv19d5/).

[60] Review of the International Criminal Court and the Rome Statute system, ICC-ASP/18/Res.7, 6 December 2019, Annex I, p.4 (https://www.legal-tools.org/doc/d1fyfk/).

all stakeholders",[61] highlighting "allegations of conflicts of interest, potential ethics violations or inappropriate behaviour".[62] It further observes:

> Such events, whether truly inappropriate behaviour was involved or not, can impact the Court both externally and internally. The Court's reputation, credibility and trust is eroded, risking lower support by States Parties and civil society. Internally, it can affect staff productivity and welfare, and in some instances can represent a financial risk for the institution.[63]

The Group of Experts acknowledges the creation of the Independent Oversight Mechanism ('IOM') and the need to strengthen it,[64] as advocated by some of the contributors in Part II of this anthology in relation to the awareness and culture of integrity that should be a dominant feature of international justice. The report incisively assesses the Court's workplace culture and environment as being affected by instances of harassment and bullying,[65] and characterised by "a general reluctance, if not extreme fear, among many staff to report any alleged act of misconduct or misbehaviour" (para. 302). While the report highlights that the Court appears to suffer internally from distrust and a culture of fear at all levels (para. 62), especially concerning are those findings related to the leadership's role in fostering such a working environment.[66]

In addition to oversight and accountability mechanisms, the Group of Experts stresses "the inadequacy of existing mechanisms in the Court to deal with complaints of bullying and harassment" and emphasise the need for change regarding the environment and practices that allow inappropriate behaviour to occur (para. 210). The IER also highlights particular measures that the Court can internally adopt to foster integrity, transparency and accountability. As such, it refers to the creation of an ethics committee "to promote and ensure coherent high levels of integrity and professionalism across the organisations, advise leadership on matters related to the applicable code of conduct, offer guidance and advice on ethical issues to individuals taking part in the organisation's activities" (para. 276). Such concrete and precise mechanisms and venues are required to address the

---

[61] IER report, *supra* note 2, para. 254.

[62] *Ibid.*.

[63] *Ibid.*, para. 255.

[64] *Ibid.*, paras. 265-268, 284-289.

[65] *Ibid.*, para. 72.

[66] *Ibid.*, paras. 63, 72-74, 298.

accounts of bullying, sexual harassment and discriminatory behaviour towards women (para. 209), as it is also strongly argued in Part III of this book on the role of international organizations and states.

The IER report also lays out the ICC's ethics framework and the instruments that it is comprised of, including the Code of Judicial Ethics, the Code of Conduct of Staff, the Code of Conduct for the OTP, the Code of Professional Conduct for (external) counsel, and the Code of conduct for investigators (para. 257). This framework is extensively discussed in Part IV of this compilation, with five chapters addressing the role of international courts in upholding integrity within their organizations. While the Experts recognise the comprehensive regulatory framework of the Court's expected behaviour, they characterise the framework as fragmented, emphasising the need for "clear common principles and minimum standards applicable to all individuals affiliated with the Court, whether elected officials, staff or externals" (para. 261), to guarantee the consistent implementation across the Court. Furthermore, analysing the Court's Code of Judicial Ethics from a comparative point of view, the report finds that, "on integrity, while the Codes of IRMCT, the STL and ICTY require judges to treat other judges and staff with dignity and respect, and not to engage in any form of discrimination and harassment, including sexual harassment and abuse of office, the Court's Code is silent" (para. 456). On this matter, the Group of Experts goes as far as to suggest an improvement through a "unified, Court-wide Ethics Charter applicable to all elected officials, staff and individuals affiliated with the Court" (para. 262).

Throughout the IER report, particular attention is given to the integrity of judges as an essential component of international justice. Clear ethical standards are required for all individuals working with the Court, but special consideration must be paid to those concerning the judges. As distilled from the consultations carried out by the Group of Experts, "the growing number of requests for disqualifications of Judges that – together with the fact that Judges themselves decide on the matter – erodes public trust in the bench and the Court as a whole" (para. 256). In fact, an adjusted disciplinary arrangement and scheme for effective accountability is discussed in detail by the IER with a view to enhancing integrity in the judiciary and the credibility of the disciplinary mechanisms against judges (paras. 311-321). Cases involving the disqualification of judges and questions of integrity are also assessed in Part V of this book addressing the integrity of the judiciary through the lens of trial and post-trial proceedings.

Independence – which is a cross-cutting concern throughout this anthology, with Part VI specifically dedicated to this principle – is also underscored by the IER as being of paramount importance for integrity in international justice. The tension between the Court's independence and political exposure is noted in the IER report as it remarks that "the ICC is both a judicial entity (ICC/Court) and an international organization (ICC/IO). As a judicial entity, the Court must benefit from judicial independence. As an international organization, States Parties reasonably expect to be able to guide and shape the institution" (para. 26).

In this vein, and although it was not remitted to the Experts, the IER considered it necessary to address the need for improvement of the system of nomination of judges. Consequently, it refers to "evidence of just how significant the role that politics can play in the election of Judges" (para. 963). Nonetheless, in "the face of the indication that there is currently no appetite to abandon this practice and elect Judges solely on merit, and in the absence of confidence in the integrity of the election process, it was considered appropriate to concentrate on the nomination procedure" (para. 964).

The comprehensive final report of the IER may be seen as an important step forward in the strengthening of integrity in international justice and at the ICC. As an external review commissioned by the ICC States Parties, its recommendations are so incisive and pragmatic that it can reasonably be expected to positively impact the integrity of ICC staff members and high officials, and the performance of the Court as well as other international judicial institutions. The report should help to consolidate the recognition of integrity as fundamental to international justice. That said, one recognizes the integrity challenge faced by those who stand to lose from some of the IER recommendations, in particular members of the Secretariat of the Assembly of States Parties (some of whom are in direct contact with the same diplomats who will be making the decisions on the recommendations). Developments in the field now will depend on how the report is received and acted upon in the short and long term.

10.   The Will to Let Integrity and Uprightness Distinguish Our Acts

Looking back at the preceding sections – as elaborated in the next 32 chapters – we see that integrity is indispensable to international justice. As Justice Goldstone writes in his Foreword to this book:

> The integrity of any court system lies at the very core of its mission. Without it, inevitably, there will be an absence of confidence in the judges and the outcome of cases that come before them will be questioned. Judges have no police or military force to ensure the implementation of their orders. They must perforce rely on the respect for their decisions by the other branches of government. Their allegiance must be owed solely to the application of the law and adhere to an ethical code to guide their work. This applies to all national systems of justice.

Corruption or other forms of integrity-deficit in a justice system, whether actual or perceived, is potentially fatal. Doubts about integrity can delegitimize and paralyze organizations and individuals – even institutions whose mandate enjoys broad public support can become overwhelmed by critique. Indeed, it is discernible that the integrity performance of international justice has come to weigh directly on the will of states to further strengthen the rule of international law.[67]

Strengthening the *culture* of integrity is important to prevent integrity violations and, when they do occur, to address them effectively. Integrity, impartiality and independence are core requirements for a functioning, effective, and meaningful judiciary or justice system. Using accountability is also necessary to restore public confidence in justice institutions where there has been erosion. There is an expectation of acknowledgment of what went wrong – often referred to as truth-telling in international criminal justice – and that one or more individuals take responsibility or are held accountable. This is all the more important for international justice institutions which depend on the continued support of a diverse group of States Parties, the public, and victims of wrongdoing.

Nurturing integrity within international justice institutions requires careful and critical contemplation on the functioning of institutions, values, rules and purposes, and a wider commitment to the international legal order. Such introspection is not easy, but there would seem to be a direct interest for international lawyers and high officials within and around these courts to do so, with a view to improving the institutions from within and ena-

---

[67] Performance of international courts is being subjected to more scrutiny, see Theresa Squatrito, Oran R. Young, Andreas Føllesdal and Geir Ulfstein, *The Performance of International Courts and Tribunals*, Cambridge University Press, 2018; Stuart Ford, "How Much Money Does the ICC Need?", in Carsten Stahn (ed.), The Law and Practice of the International Criminal Court, Oxford University Press, 2015.

bling them to withstand growing scrutiny. We should do so mindful that "progress is possible on issues of professional responsibility, and that it matters".[68] This is not primarily a question of financial resources, but one of will to let integrity and uprightness distinguish our acts.

Reviewing institutional practice can be a painstaking process. But it is essential in order to build enduring institutions and to be equipped to address ethical dilemmas as addressed in this book. The IER report is an example of an external review exercise long in preparation. It thoroughly analyses the existing normative and enforcement framework and what can be done to improve it. Many chapters in this book elaborate further on these questions.

What causes integrity violations? Indications are that it is a combination of legal, social, political, organizational and individual factors, but this is an area that may require further research and analysis. Leadership is immensely important. Leaders set the tone of the organization, and model behaviour and policies through their conduct. But the high officials of international courts are not the only individuals who are important for the culture of integrity in an institution. Integrity violations are always committed by *individuals*, even when they act through institutions. This is why the main focus of this book is on individual integrity of actors within international justice institutions (although several chapters also consider institutional integrity). This is an area where the anthology adds an additional paradigm to the IER report, by exploring in detail the origins and *meaning* of the integrity standard, how *awareness* of integrity can be raised, and what contributes to reinforcing an integrity *mindset* in staff and a *culture* of integrity in the agency in question.

The interplay of formal prescription and rule-compliance, on the one hand, and norm setting and cultural approaches, on the other hand, as highlighted at the outset of this chapter, seems paramount. Discussing the already dense ethics framework of the International Criminal Court, Salim A. Nakhjavani and Suhail Mohammed make a pertinent observation in their Chapter 22 below:

> So, the ICC's "moral message" to its staff is not missing. Far from it – at least on paper. But transmission does not imply reception. *The real question is how the message is translated into action, both individually and collectively.* And the real

---

[68]   Rhode and Luban, *supra* note 28, p. 1074.

challenge is that there may be little appetite for the promulgation of yet more ethical standards in a social space already inundated by expressions of moral righteousness, and in a world weary of empty speech.[69]

They continue:

> The literature in management science makes plain that the mere existence of ethics charters and codes of conduct, does not in itself guarantee ethical conduct by staff within an organisation. This is especially true in instances when enforcement is lacking. There is no reason why this logic would not apply to the ICC, whose robust ethical framework, it would appear, has not spontaneously generated virtue in all individuals under all circumstances.[70]

The intuitive approach of lawyers – codes of conduct and compliance procedures – is simply not enough, however well-embedded in the organization. There is no way around individual will to integrity. Integrity is practiced by individuals, through their acts and omissions. Integrity is more than anything a quality or value of individuals. Individuals are the source of all the integrity breaches that have reportedly occurred within the ICC and other international courts. The harm inflicted on the reputation of these institutions originates in individual high officials and staff members, not in abstract entities, to paraphrase the Nuremberg Judgment, which added a vital reminder of the need to punish individuals who commit such breaches.[71] As pointed out by Jan Fougner – a leading expert on independent inquiries – in his chapter in this anthology, the IER is not an inquiry that prepares the ground for sanctioning of those responsible for the alleged integrity breaches at the ICC, but a systemic review.[72]

---

[69] Salim A. Nakhjavani and Suhail Mohammed, "Does the International Criminal Court Really Need an Ethics Charter?", Chapter 22 below (italics added).

[70] *Ibid.* (footnotes omitted; italics added).

[71] The sentence in the Judgment reads: "Crimes against international law are committed by men, not by abstract entities, and only by punishing individuals who commit such crimes can the provisions of international law be enforced", see International Military Tribunal, Judgment, 1 October 1946 (https://www.legal-tools.org/doc/f21343/).

[72] See Jan Fougner, "On Whistle-Blowing and Inquiry in Public Institutions", Chapter 16 below. See also the Norwegian Helsinki Committee, Letter to the President of the Bureau of the Assembly of States Parties of the International Criminal Court, 26 October 2020 (https://www.legal-tools.org/doc/jo7vkx/).

Understanding the role of the individual in ensuring integrity in international justice is therefore one of the main features of this anthology. This not only involves individual *will* to integrity – including preparedness to make personal sacrifices to uphold integrity when we come under pressure – but also *accountability* for those who violate statutory integrity requirements, including high officials who may have engaged in intimidation and retaliation against staff members merely seeking to uphold their integrity obligations. Such retaliation can in some circumstances amount to an offence against the administration of justice, also under the Statute of the ICC. Impunity for such breaches by high officials will almost unavoidably undermine the will to integrity in the organization affected, even if fear is deployed as an instrument of selective compliance. It is exceptionally difficult to achieve a culture of integrity in an international court if high officials get away with serious integrity breaches without sanction. Leaders of highly value-driven organizations may generate a charisma or atmosphere that induces the feeling that the ethical mandate justifies conduct lacking in integrity.[73] But, as was pointed out by Morten Bergsmo at the integrity conference in the Peace Palace in December 2018, we cannot operate with such a *Faustian curtain* in international justice:

> The Faustian myth – the belief that the highly talented person can deliberately compromise some standards to achieve higher knowledge or performance – is not a universally shared myth. It is actually a highly offensive proposition in Chinese culture or in Islam.[74]

This book does not only analyse these rather obvious mechanics of integrity. It also deliberately turns the coin of *motivation*, to help our understanding of what motivates conduct positively characterised by integrity – to help us not only raise ethics problems, but to do something to prevent them. This is why, for example, Part I of the book contains chapters on positive advocates of integrity such as Sir Thomas More and Dag Hammarskjöld. In case of a second edition of the book, we hope to be able to include additional role models. This is also why you find chapters on philo-

---

[73] See Dieneke T. de Vos, "Institutional Ethics, Individual Integrity, and Sexual Harassment: Recent Developments in Ethics Standard-Setting and Mechanisms at the United Nations", Chapter 13 below.

[74] See Morten Bergsmo, "Integrity as Safeguard Against the Vicissitudes of Common Justice Institutions", CILRAP Film, The Hague, 1 December 2018 (https://www.cilrap.org/cilrap-film/181201-bergsmo/).

sophical background and analysis of integrity, as well as on religious foundations of the concept of integrity.[75] We would have liked to include more such perspectives.

International organizations are there to give effect to international law in international relations. In this book it is suggested that international organizations will not succeed in fulfilling their mandate unless the integrity standard is protected within the organizations. Whether we like it or not, integrity is a prerequisite for international law to be able to serve as a 'gentle civilizer of nations'.[76] A serious discourse on integrity in international justice must be multi-disciplinary: it needs to draw on philosophy, religion, history, psychology, sociology, and law, among other perspectives. International lawyers seem to be inclined to believe in the civilizing effects of international law in international relations. But single-minded insistence on normative codes of conduct and compliance mechanisms – tools of the legal profession – is not alone solving integrity problems, as may become apparent when international justice and other multilateral organizations come under further scrutiny.

---

[75] Ethics and integrity as moral virtues and philosophical concepts have recently been revisited as the foundations of international justice. See Amartya Sen, "Ethics and the Foundation of Global Justice", in *Ethics and International Affairs*, 2017, vol. 31, no. 3, pp. 261-270; Steven Ratner, "Ethics and International Law: Integrating the Global Justice Project(s)", in *International Theory*, 2013, vol. 5, no. 1, pp. 1-34.

[76] See Martti Koskenniemi, *The Gentle Civilizer of Nations: The Rise and Fall of International Law 1870-1960*, Cambridge University Press, 2002.

PART I:
MEANING OF INTEGRITY

1

Physically Upright, Morally Sound: Recreating Ancient 'Integrity'

Emiliano J. Buis[*]

1.1. Introduction

In recent times, international justice has been the object of harsh criticism. The question concerning the ways to overcome this disapproval is a complex one. In any case, it seems quite clear that, in times of institutional crisis, a good bottom-up starting point is reassessing the role of those individuals who are personally involved in international tribunals. The standard and practice of 'integrity' become therefore an essential threshold to improve the proper functioning of courts and organizations; it is of the utmost importance to raise awareness about the high moral character that is (or should be) required when electing or appointing professionals expected to hold public office.[1] And, in this vein, a historical approach to the meaning of 'integrity' is essential. We are much better placed to discuss the sensitivities of ethical principles if the ancient values underlying our modern conception are properly understood.

The purpose of this chapter is to understand the logics behind the notion of 'integrity' in ancient Greece and Rome – including terminology and

[*] **Emiliano J. Buis** received his Ph.D. from the University of Buenos Aires, Argentina, and is Professor of Public International Law, International Humanitarian Law, the Origins of International Law in Antiquity and Ancient Greek Language and Literature at the University of Buenos Aires and the Central National University in Azul, Argentina. He is also a Researcher at the National Research Council for Science and Technology (CONICET). He is a former fellow at the Department of Classics, Brown University, the Max-Planck Institut für europäische Rechstgeschichte, the Harvard University Center for Hellenic Studies, the Alexander S. Onassis Public Benefit Foundation, the Center for Epigraphical and Paleographical Studies (Ohio State University), and the Center for Hellenic Studies at Princeton University. I wish to thank Morten Bergsmo, Viviane Dittrich and all the organizers, speakers and participants at the international expert conference on 'Integrity in International Justice' (Peace Palace, The Hague, 1-2 December 2018), for their extremely useful comments and suggestions. I am indebted to all of them. All mistakes and inexactitudes which remain in the text are obviously my own.

[1] Morten Bergsmo, "Revisiting Integrity in International Justice", FICHL Policy Brief Series No. 93 (2018), Torkel Opsahl Academic EPublisher, Brussels, p. 1 (http://www.toaep.org/pbs-pdf/93-bergsmo).

semantical scopes – taking into account its rhetorical elements. In the context of the project conference held in The Hague and this edited volume dealing with integrity in international justice, my aim here is to offer a succinct introduction to the physical and moral, and thus, political, dimensions of integrity in some Greek and Latin texts that can be relevant to appreciating its implications. In that sense, although there does not seem to be in antiquity a single notion that can deliver the complex meaning of integrity, my intention is to explain how ancient sources dealing with physical and ethical values may contribute to a better understanding of the multifaceted relationship between integrity and the administration of justice today.

The first part of my chapter will deal with the pre-classical image of justice and rightness as related to truth, which becomes relevant when exploring the nature of ethical integrity. Ancient texts show a close association between telling lies and corruption, which would be later developed in the politics of integrity laid in classical Greek and Roman testimonies, as examined in the second and third part of the chapter. In my conclusions, I will reveal why I believe that revisiting these pre-Christian sources becomes a useful exercise in the quest for a comprehensive view of integrity as a key concept in modern international law.

1.2. Origins of 'Integrity'?

In a ground-breaking book published in Paris in 1967, Marcel Detienne focused his attention on what he called the 'masters of truth' (*les maîtres de vérité*) in archaic Greece. He stated that figures of authority such as the prophet, the poet, and the king-judge, always spoke the truth because they represented the voice of the gods; an inspired ruler could never act in a wrongful manner. According to this reading, in pre-classical times, these three leading figures – the diviner, the bard, and the king of justice – shared the privilege of dispensing truth purely by virtue of their qualities: they could tell 'what was', 'what is' and 'what will be' because of their possession of a similar type of speech. By means of the religious power of memory, *Mnemosýne*, they had direct access to the divine authority.[2]

In ancient Greece, the notion of truth (ἀλήθεια, *alétheia*) was directly related to justice (δίκη, *díke*), since it asserted a *parole efficace* which con-

---

[2] Marcel Detienne, *Les maîtres de la vérité dans la Grèce archaïque*, Maspero, Paris, 1967, pp. 15–16.

tributed to the creation of the world.[3] In the archaic world, the judicial sentences, or θέμιστες (*thémistes*), were possessed by the king, who acted as judge and had been granted authority directly through a divine agent.[4] The judicial word, in this context, constituted an authorized statement about good and evil: the judge, inspired or plunged into *enthousiasmós*, simply dictated a verdict that was enunciated to his mind by a higher power. Sentences, far from constituting a human manifestation, derived from the exclusive will of the gods – they were a means of reproducing Olympic decisions among mortals.[5]

This close contact between judicial activity and religious support led Louis Gernet, one of the most recognized experts in Greek legal anthropology, to postulate a strong bond between legal institutions and ritualism, based on what he denominated pre-law (*pré-droit*). In that context, decisions pronounced by a king-judge – through whom the gods expressed themselves – had the character of obscure revelations or self-imposing oracles.[6] It was because of the association with the goddess *Thémis* (a divinity usually related to oracular discourse) that the discussion of law (θέμις,

---

[3] Jean-Pierre Levet, *Le vrai et le faux dans la pensée grecque archaique*, Étude de vocabulaire, Les Belles Lettres, Paris, 1976, pp. 1–3, points out that in Greek the notion of truth is expressed through terms presented as negative: the most frequent words – the adjective ἀληθής and the noun ἀλήθεια (lit. 'lack of remembrance') – show that obtaining the truth implied etymologically a concrete activity destined to unveil, to get out of oblivion, to bring something to memory as an act of justice. From that place, then, ἀ-λήθεια conceptually implies an active movement and expresses a step of discovery: the truth does not seem to be given in the abstract for its knowledge or apprehension. From the pre-philosophical thinking of the archaic world onwards, the notion of truth has been associated with discourse, stories, and verbal expression of thought. I have explored the notiong of legal truth in ancient Greece elsewhere; see Emiliano J. Buis, "Ficciones y p(ersu)asiones de la verdad: la retórica judicial de la *alétheia* en el derecho griego arcaico y clásico", in Germán Sucar and Jorge Cerdio Herrán (eds.), *Derecho y verdad II "Genealogía(s)"*, Tirant lo Blanch, Madrid, 2015, pp. 247–320.

[4] Henry Sumner Maine, *Ancient Law. Its Connection with the Early History of Society and its Relation to Modern Ideas*, John Murray, London, 1861, considered with certain exaggeration that every single aspect of ancient law was dependent, in its first manifestations, on divine authority.

[5] Karl-Joachim Hölkeskamp, *Schiedsrichter, Gesetzgeber und Gesetzgebung im archaischen Griechenland*, Franz Steiner, Stuttgart, 1999.

[6] Louis Gernet, "Droit et pré-droit en Grèce ancienne", in *L'année sociologique*, 1951, no. 3, pp. 21–119.

---

thémis) was transferred to the field of mantic.[7] Therefore, in pre-classical times, judgments and oracles had a common origin based on an authority located beyond the world of mortals.[8] The judge was a divine spokesperson, and the ordeal implied a test whose religious virtue, according to Gernet, immediately decided a controversy by translating, without active intermediaries, the undisputed will of the gods: the symbols of pre-law acquired full significance through the unbeatable force of religion. Knowing the principles of divine justice meant participating in an unquestionable truth, as Hesiod conveys in describing the birth of Nereus and his wisdom (*Theogony*, 234-237):

> Νηρέα δ᾽ ἀψευδέα καὶ ἀληθέα γείνατο Πόντος,
> πρεσβύτατον παίδων· αὐτὰρ καλέουσι γέροντα,
> οὕνεκα νημερτής τε καὶ ἤπιος, οὐδὲ θεμιστέων
> λήθεται, ἀλλὰ δίκαια καὶ ἤπια δήνεα οἶδεν·

> And Sea begat Nereus, the eldest of his children, who is true (*alethéa*) and lies not (*apseudéa*): and men call him the Old Man because he is trusty and gentle and does not forget the laws of righteousness, but thinks just (*díkaia*) and kindly thoughts.[9]

The quotation clearly shows a set of terms through which the adjectives (morphologically negative) that refer to truthfulness and lack of lies (ἀ-ψευδέα, *a-pseudéa*; ἀ-ληθέα, *a-lethéa*) are connected to the value of memory as a rejection of forgetfulness (οὐδὲ [...] λήθεται, *oudè [...] léthetai*), as a way of imposing the laws of Zeus: θεμιστέων (*themistéon*).

Justice seemed to respond to the purposes of the gods, and therefore 'straight' rulers were required to translate divine inspiration when deciding a case.

Nevertheless, this strict relationship between justice, truth and correctness could be shattered when kings chose to oppose the will of the gods,

---

[7] On *thémis* and its relationship to its particular statutes (*thémistes*), see Jean Rudhardt, *Thémis et les Hôrai. Recherches sur les divinités grecques de la justice et de la paix*, Droz, Genève, 1999.

[8] Arnaldo Biscardi, *Diritto Greco Antico*, Giuffrè, Milano, 1982, pp. 352–354, argues that *thémistes* were public expressions of the ineluctable will of the gods.

[9] Here and elsewhere, the Greek text of Hesiod and its translation are taken from Hugh G. Evelyn-White, *Hesiod. The Homeric Hymns and Homerica*, Harvard University Press and William Heinemann, Cambridge (MA) and London, 1914.

as presented in epic poetry.[10] In Book XVI of the *Iliad*, for instance, Patroclus fails to comply with Achilles' request to return to the ships. Instead, he attacks the Trojans, forcing them to escape. The snorts of the horses of the enemies fleeing from Patroclus are compared, with a typically Homeric simile, with the excess of those who sentenced incorrectly and deserved divine punishment (*Iliad* XVI.384-393):

> ὡς δ' ὑπὸ λαίλαπι πᾶσα κελαινὴ βέβριθε χθὼν
> ἤματ' ὀπωρινῷ, ὅτε λαβρότατον χέει ὕδωρ
> Ζεύς, ὅτε δή ῥ' ἄνδρεσσι κοτεσσάμενος χαλεπήνῃ,
> οἳ βίῃ εἰν ἀγορῇ σκολιὰς κρίνωσι θέμιστας,
> ἐκ δὲ δίκην ἐλάσωσι θεῶν ὄπιν οὐκ ἀλέγοντες·
> τῶν δέ τε πάντες μὲν ποταμοὶ πλήθουσι ῥέοντες,
> πολλὰς δὲ κλιτῦς τότ' ἀποτμήγουσι χαράδραι,
> ἐς δ' ἅλα πορφυρέην μεγάλα στενάχουσι ῥέουσαι
> ἐξ ὀρέων ἐπικάρ, μινύθει δέ τε ἔργ' ἀνθρώπων·
> ὡς ἵπποι Τρῳαὶ μεγάλα στενάχοντο θέουσαι.

> As the whole dark earth bows before some tempest on an autumn day, when Zeus rains his hardest to punish men for judging crookedly in their courts, and arriving justice there from without heed to the decrees of heaven – all the rivers run full and the torrents tear many a new channel as they roar headlong from the mountains to the dark sea, and it fares ill with the works of men – even such was the stress and strain of the Trojan horses in their flight.[11]

---

[10] On the debates surrounding justice in archaic Greece, see Michael Gagarin, "*Dikē* in Archaic Greek Thought", in *Classical Philology*, 1974, no. 69, pp. 186–197; Matthew W. Dickie, "*Dike* as a moral term in Homer and Hesiod", in *Classical Philology*, 1978, no. 73, pp. 91–101; Joanna Janik, "*Dike* and *themis* in the works of Homer", in *Eos*, 2000, no. 87, pp. 5–31, and more recently Christos Antypas, "*Dike* in a pre-polis society: the evidence from Homeric epic", in Menelaos Christopoulos and Machi Païzi-Apostolopoulou (eds.), *Crime and Punishment in Homer and Archaic Epic* (Proceedings of the 12th international Symposium on the *Odyssey*, Ithaca, September 3-7, 2013), Center for Odyssean Studies, Ithaca, 2014, pp. 39–46. A study on the vocabulary of justice in archaic Greek literature can be found in Joanna Janik, *Terms of the Semantic Sphere of δίκη and θέμις in the Early Greek Epic* (Studies of the Commission on Classical Philology, vol. 30), PAU, Krakow, 2003.

[11] The Greek text has been taken from A.T. Murray, *Homer. The Iliad*, Cambridge (MA)/London, Harvard University Press/William Heinemann, 1924. The translation corresponds to Samuel Butler, *The* Iliad *of Homer*, Longmans, Green & Co., London, 1898.

Set in the *agora* – the public square understood as a space for verbal exchange[12] – the image contained in these verses describes those who solve cases against the guidelines established by the gods. These men alluded in the passage are the Homeric kings (βασιλῆες, *basilées*) who were in charge of the task of imparting justice. Achilles himself had mentioned them before (*Iliad* I.237-239), asserting that the sons of the Achaeans behaved as administrators of justice (δικασπόλοι, *dikaspóloi*) and were guardians of the decrees of Zeus (θέμιστας πρὸς Διός, *thémistas pròs Diòs*). Since the *agora* was the open area in which men proclaimed their statements (as can be seen in the verb ἀγορεύειν, *agoreúein*, 'to give a speech'), and this ability to judge may imply telling the truth or lying, those kings who behaved in an excessive manner, who issued unjust sentences, were frowned upon by the angered gods. To pronounce crooked decisions meant, in short, to advocate for a lack of truth and thus represented a disruption of the magical-religious continuity that pervaded the archaic vision of truth-telling as a result of endorsing the will of the gods. Human rulers, through their speech, were therefore able to alter the will of Zeus. They could behave incorrectly, breaking the inherent link between justice and truth, hence endorsing corrupted decisions. When judging according to their own interests or lying to the people, they could walk away from the path of divine justice.

Another passage in the *Iliad* is relevant to complement these reflections. When Achilles' shield is depicted in Book XVIII, the poem mentions the representation of two cities in the centre, one in peace and the other besieged by enemies. In the first of the two *póleis*, the daily scenes that were crafted by Hephaestus are described in detail: on the one hand, weddings and parties; on the other hand, a judicial process mentioned in the following terms (*Iliad* XVIII.497-508):

> λαοὶ δ' εἰν ἀγορῇ ἔσαν ἀθρόοι· ἔνθα δὲ νεῖκος
> ὠρώρει, δύο δ' ἄνδρες ἐνείκεον εἵνεκα ποινῆς
> ἀνδρὸς ἀποφθιμένου· ὃ μὲν εὔχετο πάντ' ἀποδοῦναι

---

[12] Already in epic poetry, the *agora* constituted the place in which justice was administered and quarrels among litigants were dealt with: ἦμος δ ἐπὶ δόρπον ἀνὴρ ἀγορῆθεν ἀνέστη / κρίνων νείκεα πολλὰ δικαζομένων αἰζηῶν, / τῆμος δὴ τά γε δοῦρα Χαρύβδιος ἐξεφαάνθη (*Odyssey*, XII.439-441). This explains, for example, the opposition between the civilized world of the Greeks and the land of the Cyclops, which lacked an *agora* to hold councils and implement rules from the gods (τοῖσιν δ' οὔτ' ἀγοραὶ βουληφόροι οὔτε θέμιστες, *Odyssey* IX.112). Few verses later, in the same book, Polyphemus himself was presented by similar expressions as a savage, ignorant of judicial processes and norms: ἄγριον, οὔτε δίκας εὖ εἰδότα οὔτε θέμιστας (*Odyssey* IX.215).

δήμῳ πιφαύσκων, ὃ δ' ἀναίνετο μηδὲν ἑλέσθαι·
ἄμφω δ' ἱέσθην ἐπὶ ἴστορι πεῖραρ ἑλέσθαι.
λαοὶ δ' ἀμφοτέροισιν ἐπήπυον ἀμφὶς ἀρωγοί·
κήρυκες δ' ἄρα λαὸν ἐρήτυον· οἳ δὲ γέροντες
εἵατ' ἐπὶ ξεστοῖσι λίθοις ἱερῷ ἐνὶ κύκλῳ,
σκῆπτρα δὲ κηρύκων ἐν χέρσ' ἔχον ἠεροφώνων·
τοῖσιν ἔπειτ' ἤϊσσον, ἀμοιβηδὶς δ' ἐδίκαζον.
κεῖτο δ' ἄρ' ἐν μέσσοισι δύω χρυσοῖο τάλαντα,
τῷ δόμεν ὃς μετὰ τοῖσι δίκην ἰθύντατα εἴποι.

Meanwhile the people were gathered in assembly, for there was a quarrel, and two men were wrangling about the blood-price for a man who had died, the one claiming to the *dêmos* that he had the right to pay off the damages in full, and the other refusing to accept anything. Each was seeking a limit, in the presence of an arbitrator (*hístor*), and the people took sides, each man backing the side that he had taken; but the heralds kept them back, and the elders sat on their seats of stone in a solemn circle, holding the staves which the heralds had put in-to their hands. Then they rose and each in his turn gave judg-ment, and there were two measures of gold laid down, to be given to him whose judgment should be deemed the fairest.

In the context of an epic which is seldom concerned with the practice of institutional justice,[13] this scene depicted corresponds to a murder trial, in which two litigants plead over different modes of reparation. Interesting-ly enough, the judgment in this case did not rely on a powerful king but rather on a number of elders who voted individually.[14] The interpretations of the judicial episode have been varied.[15] For the purposes of our reading,

---

[13] The legal references are in general more related to the values of private justice, based on retribution and redress. See Robert J. Bonner, "Administration of justice in the age of Homer" in *Classical Philology*, 1911, no. 6, pp. 12–36; Eva Cantarella, "Private revenge and public justice: the settlement of disputes in Homer's *Iliad*", in *Punishment and Society*, 2001, no. 3, pp. 473–483. The moral aspects of these legal allusions have been studied in two monographs by Arthur W. H. Adkins: *Merit and responsibility: A study in Greek values*, Ox-ford University Press, Oxford, 1960, and *Moral values and political behaviour in ancient Greece: from Homer to the end of the fifth century*, Chatto & Windus, New York, 1972.

[14] On these two models of justice, see Eva Cantarella, "Modelli giurisdizionali omerici: il giudice unico, la giustizia dei vecchi", in Gerhard Thür and Eva Cantarella (eds.) *Symposion 1997* (Akten der Gesellschaft für griechische und hellenistische Rechtsgeschichte, vol. 13), Böhlau Verlag, Köln, Weimar and Wien, 2001, pp. 3–19.

[15] The judicial image included in the shield has been the object of different interpretations across the decades. See Hans J. Wolff, "The Origin of Judicial Litigation among the Greeks", in *Traditio*, 1946, no. 4, pp. 31–87; H. Hommel, "Die Gerichtsszene auf dem Schild des

however, it is simply worth noting the similarities between the description of the passage and the simile described above. Also located in the *agora* (εἰν ἀγορῇ), the image presupposes a group of elders (γέροντες, *gérontes*) who resolve the dispute in a typically sacred environment (ἱερῷ ἐνὶ κύκλῳ, *hierôi ení kýkloi*).[16] In that sense, it is possible to uphold that the decision regarding the legal solution of the matter could be explained within a system marked by the legal authority of the divinities and by a judicial role in which ritual formulae became important to validate law. Nevertheless, an award was granted to that old man who gave the fairest judgment. This is significant, since it shows that, in pre-classical Greece, human judgments could be valued differently. As explained when discussing the crooked verdicts sanctioned by Zeus' wrath in Book XVI, judges here are said to be able either to take fair decisions or to uphold unfair verdicts. The opposition between 'straight' and 'crooked' decisions, between correct and incorrect judgments, seems to suggest that, already in early Greek times, absolute values collided with a more relative approach: human behaviour could either follow the right path of superior orders or respond to personal interests instead.

In *Works and Days*, Hesiod reproduces a similar line of thought.[17] In vv. 37-39, he claims to have invited his brother to settle his controversies

---

Achilleus. Zur Pflege des Rechts in homerischer Zeit", in Peter Steinmetz (ed.), *Politeia und Res Publica. Beiträge zum Verständnis von Politik, Recht und Staat in der Antike, dem Andenken Rudolf Starks gewidmet*, Franz Steiner, Wiesbaden, 1969, pp. 11–38; Gerhard Thür, "Zum *dikazein* bei Homer", in *Zeitschrift der Savigny-Stiftung für Rechtsgeschichte*, 1979, no. 87, pp. 426–44; Øivind Andersen, "Some thoughts on the shield of Achilleus", in *Symbolae Osloenses*, 1976, no. 51, pp. 5–18; Raymond Westbrook, "The Trial Scene in the *Iliad*", in *Harvard Studies in Classical Philology*, 1992, no. 94, pp. 53–76; Eva Cantarella, "Dispute Settlement in Homer: Once Again on the Shield of Achilles", in *Droits antiques et société. Mélanges en l'honneur de Panayotis D. Dimakis*, Sakkoulas, Athènes, 2002, pp. 147–164; Henri van Effenterre, "Un mort parle toujours", in Gerhard Thür and Francisco Javier Fernández Nieto (eds.), *Symposion 1999* (Akten der Gesellschaft für griechische und hellenistische Rechtsgeschichte, vol. 14), Böhlau Verlag, Köln, Weimar and Wien, 2003, pp. 21–26; Giuseppe Lentini, "La scena giudiziaria dello Scudo di Achille e l'immaginario della giustizia nella Grecia arcaica", in *Materiali e Discussioni per l'analisi dei testi classici*, 2016, no. 76, pp. 15–31; Sima Avramovic, "Blood money in Homer – Role of *istor* in the trial scene on the shield of Achilles (*Il.* 18.497-508)", in *Zbornik PFZ 67/5*, 2017, pp. 723–756.

[16] On the figure of these old kings, see Pierre Carlier, "Les *basileis* homériques sont-ils des rois?", in *Ktèma*, 1996, no. 21, pp. 5–22.

[17] Michael Gagarin, "The Poetry of Justice: Hesiod and the Origins of Greek Law", in *Ramus*, 1992, no. 21, pp. 61–78. See also Michael Gagarin, "*Dikē* in the *Works and Days*", in *Clas-*

with straight sentences (ἰθείῃσι δίκης) which, coming from Zeus, were the best (αἵ τ' ἐκ Διός εἰσιν ἄρισται). Among men there were corrupt judges – considered as "devourers of gifts" (δωροφάγους) – who were willing to make a decision (οἳ τήνδε δίκην ἐθέλουσι δίκασσαι) after being flattered. These outraged Dike when they sentenced in a crooked way (τῆς δὲ Δίκης ῥόθος ἑλκομένης, ᾗ κ ἄνδρες ἄγωσι / δωροφάγοι, σκολιῆς δὲ δίκης κρίνωσι θέμιστας, vv. 220-221), whereas good rulers gave fair sentences to foreigners and allowed the city to prosper and the people to flourish (Οἳ δὲ δίκας ξείνοισι καὶ ἐνδήμοισι διδοῦσιν / ἰθείας καὶ μή τι παρεκβαίνουσι δικαίου, / τοῖσι τέθηλε πόλις, λαοὶ δ ἀνθεῦσιν ἐν αὐτῇ, vv. 225-227). This distortion, as Hesiod seems to confirm, had clear political effects.[18] Contrary to what happened in the past, during the new iron age, evil people would forget about truth and pronounce false oaths in a crooked manner (vv. 190-194):

οὐδέ τις εὐόρκου χάρις ἔσσεται οὔτε δικαίου
οὔτ' ἀγαθοῦ, μᾶλλον δὲ κακῶν ῥεκτῆρα καὶ ὕβριν
ἀνέρες αἰνήσουσι· δίκη δ' ἐν χερσί· καὶ αἰδὼς
οὐκ ἔσται, βλάψει δ' ὁ κακὸς τὸν ἀρείονα φῶτα
μύθοισιν σκολιοῖς ἐνέπων, ἐπὶ δ' ὅρκον ὀμεῖται.

There will be no favour for the man who keeps his oath or for the just or for the good; but rather men will praise the evil-doer and his violent dealing. Strength will be right, and reverence will cease to be; and the wicked will hurt the worthy man, speaking crooked words against him, and will swear an oath upon them.

The corrosive effects of wrongful acts were a symbol of political deterioration. Overcoming the idea that archaic values were endorsed by absolute principles derived from the authority of gods – as suggested by Marcel Detienne – a relativistic opposition rather implied the acknowledgment of moral limits in human behaviour. The corrupt intervention of judges and

---

sical Philology, 1973, no. 68, pp. 81–94; Robert J. Bonner, "Administration of justice in the age of Hesiod", in Classical Philology, 1912, no. 7, pp. 17–23.

[18] Daniel Malamis, "Crimes of the Agora: Corruption in Homer and Hesiod", in Philip Bosman (ed.), Corruption and Integrity in Ancient Greece and Rome, Classical Association of South Africa, Pretoria, 2012, pp. 17–29, identifies in this Homeric and Hesiodic passages a reference to political degradation, what he calls "institutional corruption": "Institutional corruption may then take the form of advice within a deliberative council that should operate in the community's interest, but advice that actually promotes the interest of the adviser, either because it is personally beneficial or because the council member in question has been bribed" (p. 22).

rulers did not only generate the fury of the Olympians, but also the rejection of those poets who supported communal solidarity and fairness. This axiomatic system set the ground for the endorsement of a politics of integrity, which held physical rectitude and moral righteousness as positive social values both in classical Greek and ancient Rome.

1.3. Recreating Integrity in Classical Athens

Rude, lewd and bad-mannered, Thersites is said to have disturbed the assembly of the Achaean army in Book II of the *Iliad* (II.211-218):

> ἄλλοι μέν ῥ᾽ ἕζοντο, ἐρήτυθεν δὲ καθ᾽ ἕδρας·
> Θερσίτης δ᾽ ἔτι μοῦνος ἀμετροεπὴς ἐκολῴα,
> ὃς ἔπεα φρεσὶν ᾗσιν ἄκοσμά τε πολλά τε ᾔδη
> μάψ, ἀτὰρ οὐ κατὰ κόσμον, ἐριζέμεναι βασιλεῦσιν,
> ἀλλ᾽ ὅ τι οἱ εἴσαιτο γελοίϊον Ἀργείοισιν
> ἔμμεναι· αἴσχιστος δὲ ἀνὴρ ὑπὸ Ἴλιον ἦλθε·
> φολκὸς ἔην, χωλὸς δ᾽ ἕτερον πόδα· τὼ δέ οἱ ὤμω
> κυρτὼ ἐπὶ στῆθος συνοχωκότε· αὐτὰρ ὕπερθε
> φοξὸς ἔην κεφαλήν, ψεδνὴ δ᾽ ἐπενήνοθε λάχνη.

> The rest now took their seats and kept to their own several places, but Thersites still went on wagging his unbridled tongue – a man of many words, and those unseemly; a monger of sedition, a railer against all who were in authority, who cared not what he said, so that he might set the Achaeans in a laugh. He was the ugliest man of all those that came before Troy – bandy-legged, lame of one foot, with his two shoulders rounded and hunched over his chest. His head ran up to a point, but there was little hair on the top of it.

Unlike the rest of the Greek warriors, Thersites is described as bow-legged and lame, a grotesque figure of wickedness. His shoulders are caved inward, and his head is covered with few hairs.[19] When he launches an abusive attack against Agamemnon in the assembly (II.225-242), he is called greedy and coward. His physical representation was therefore coupled with moral depravation. Not surprisingly, he is the only one in the passage to lack a patronymic.[20]

---

[19] On his poor bodily condition and the possible puns intended in the *Iliad*, see R. Clinton Simms, "The Missing Bones of Thersites: A Note on *Iliad* 2.212-19", in *American Journal of Philology*, 2005, no. 126, pp. 33–40

[20] Andrea Kouklanakis, "Thersites, Odysseus, and the Social Order", in Miriam Carlisle and Olga Levaniouk (eds.), *Nine Essays on Homer*, Rowman & Littlefield, Lanham, 1999, p. 40.

Some centuries later, Greek sources would rely again on this physical and moral construction of characters as an efficient rhetorical technique. Through the technique of *ethopoiía*, for example, forensic speechwriters such as Lysias delineated personalities, opposing their own clients, portrayed as pure and undamaged, to their rivals, constantly presented as ethically corrupted. If speakers endorsed moral qualities, such as altruism and integrity, the disposition of their bodies corresponded to required uprightness, as opposed to crookedness presented in their corrupt and perverse enemies in court.

The symbolic value of body language in communication deserves special attention.[21] Gestures such as the position of hands, the inclination of the head, and the movement of the eyes are significant ways of expressing intention, and can therefore transmit relevant evidence on attitudes.[22] A number of recent contributions have attempted to offer some insights into the role of gestures and their meaning in classical civilizations.[23] However, in spite of the obvious political character of gestures as a means of expressing personal relationships within a society, the relevance of gestures has also been neglected in the study of judicial administration, due again to the

---

See Norman Postlethwaite, "Tersites in the *Iliad*", in *Greece and Rome*, 1992, no. 35, pp. 123–136.

[21] See Pierre Guiraud, *Le langage du corps*, Presses Universitaires de France, Paris, 1980.

[22] According to Keith Thomas, "Introduction", in Jan Bremmer and Herman Roodenburg (eds.), *A Cultural History of Gesture. From Antiquity to the Present Day*, Polity Press, Cambridge, 1991, p. 1, gestures include any kind of bodily movement or posture (including facial expression), which transmits a message to the observer. This definition seems to presuppose the existence of at least two bodies interacting with each other: one of them performing the gesture, and the second one decoding its explicit or implicit significance. On the cultural importance of gesture and its relationship to speech, see Adam Kendon, "Gesture", in *Annual Review of Anthropology*, 1997, no. 26, pp. 109–128. Gerhard Neumann, *Gesten und Gebärden in der griechischen Kunst*, Walter de Gruyter, Berlin and Boston, 1965, pp. 10–12, uses the expression "rhetorische Geste" to indicate the "geformte und schalgkräftig pointierte Geste". According to Carolin Hahnemann, "A Gesture in Archilochus 118 (West)?", in Geoffrey W. Bakewell and James P. Sickinger (eds.), *Gestures. Essays in Ancient History, Literature and Philosophy presented to Alan L. Boegehold on the occasion of his retirement and his 75th birthday*, Oxbow, Oxford, 2003, p. 55, rhetorical gestures include any motion of head and hand that accompany a speech-act. These gestures will be relevant in the context of legal proceedings.

[23] Anthony Corbeill, *Nature Embodied. Gestures in Ancient Rome*, Princeton University Press, Princeton and Oxford, 2004, and Douglas L. Cairns, "Introduction", in Douglas L. Cairns (ed.) *Body Language in the Greek and Roman Worlds*, Classical Press of Wales, Swansea, 2015, pp. ix–xxii.

---

biased nature of our sources.[24] I argue that, both in Greek and Roman sources, the information that can be obtained from the identification and observation of different gestures and corporal postures can greatly contribute to the ancient perception of integrity in public fora.

Aristotle discussed the symbolic value arising from the difference between straight and crooked bodies. In his *Politics*, the unbent body represents the ideal physical support of the male citizen, whereas crooked or curve figures are deemed useless for civic activities, and become therefore associated to slaves (1254b 27-31):

> βούλεται μὲν οὖν ἡ φύσις καὶ τὰ σώματα διαφέροντα ποιεῖν
> τὰ τῶν ἐλευθέρων καὶ τῶν δούλων, τὰ μὲν ἰσχυρὰ πρὸς τὴν
> ἀναγκαίαν χρῆσιν, τὰ δ' ὀρθὰ καὶ ἄχρηστα πρὸς τὰς τοιαύτας
> ἐργασίας, ἀλλὰ χρήσιμα πρὸς πολιτικὸν βίον.

> The intention of nature therefore is to make the bodies also of freemen and of slaves different – the latter strong for necessary service, the former erect and unserviceable for such occupations, but serviceable for a life of citizenship.[25]

Bodies which were erect (ὀρθὰ, *orthá*) seemed prepared for a life devoted to the *pólis*. Body language helps to understand the relationship between social status and physical disposition, since curved anatomies meant submission as opposed to self-sufficiency and autonomy.[26]

---

[24] An interesting contribution by Anthony Corbeill, "Gesture in Early Roman Law: Empty Forms or Essential Formalities?", in Cairns, 2015, pp. 157–171, see above note 23, has discussed the importance of gesture and body contact in early Roman law considering that, far from being symbolic adjuncts, they were truly constitutive elements of some legal processes. Another exception is the recent book by Peter A. O'Connell, *The Rhetoric of Seeing in Attic Forensic Oratory*, The University of Texas Press, Austin, 2017, which, although focused on the importance of sight, refers to the relevance of non-verbal expressions and physical movements in classical Greek forensic oratory.

[25] The Greek text corresponds to W.D. Ross (ed.), *Aristotle. Politica*, Clarendon Press, Oxford, 1957. The translation has been taken from H. Rackham (ed.), *Aristotle*, vol. 21, Harvard University Press and William Heinemann, Cambridge (MA) and London, 1944.

[26] On the difference between "normal" and "deviant" bodies in antiquity and its relationship to social values, see also Christopher Goody and Martha Lynn Rose, "Mental states, bodily dispositions and table manners: a guide to reading 'intellectual' disability from Homer to late antiquity", in Christian Laes, Christopher Goodey and Martha Lynn Rose (eds.), *Disabilities in Roman Antiquity: Disparate Bodies; a Capite ad Calcem*, Brill, Leiden and Boston, 2013, pp. 17–44. On the deformed and disabled body and its figured "otherness", see more recently Lisa Trentin, *The Hunchback in Hellenistic and Roman Art*, Bloomsbury, London, 2015.

According to Aristotle's *On the Parts of Animals*, human beings were the only creatures with straight bodies: μόνον γὰρ ὀρθόν ἐστι τῶν ζῴων ἄνθρωπος (656a 12-13). In his *Timaeus*, Plato had considered already that an "upright" attitude is a consequence of the human attempt to reach the gods (τὸ θεῖον τὴν κεφαλὴν καὶ ῥίζαν ἡμῶν ἀνακρεμαννὺν ὀρθοῖ πᾶν τὸ σῶμα, 90b1), whereas wild animals had curved bodies because they dragged their front limbs and their head down to the earth (ἐκ τούτων οὖν τῶν ἐπιτηδευμάτων τά τ' ἐμπρόσθια κῶλα καὶ τὰς κεφαλὰς εἰς γῆν ἑλκόμενα ὑπὸ συγγενείας ἤρεισαν, 91e 6-8).

The opposition between straight and curved bodies is not only relevant in biological and political terms, but also with regard to judicial activities. It materially reproduces the difference between rightness and corruption, which archaic sources attributed to judicial decision-making, helping to understand the physical and moral logics behind ancient 'integrity'. We should bear in mind that, in Aristotle's *Republic*, office-holders had a duty to govern with a view to the public interest. Political regimes aimed at protecting private interests were considered to be "deviations" (παρεκβάσεις, *parekbáseis*, 1279b 5) instead.[27] In Aristotle and elsewhere, the vocabulary of rectitude and crookedness was employed to address the problems arising from political 'integrity'.

An example from Athenian comedy can shed light on how bodily attitudes represent ethical qualities. In Aristophanes' *Wasps* – a comedy focused on the administration of justice in popular tribunals – the main character, Philocleon, was depicted as hard and stiff when dreaming of becoming a judge every day, in opposition to the softness of those defendants who would try to convince him of acquitting them through mercy and compassion. In the protagonist's own words, his corporal attitude of walking straight into the courtroom had to be contrasted to the womanly gestures of the litigants: "As I walk past, one of them places his soft hand in mine" (κἄπειτ' εὐθὺς προσιόντι / ἐμβάλλει μοι τὴν χεῖρ' ἀπαλήν, vv. 552-553).[28]

---

[27] The overlapping of personal economic motives and public interests was frequently seen as a symbol of corrupt behavior. See Barry Strauss, "The Cultural Significance of Bribery and Embezzlement in Athenian Politics: The Evidence of the Period 403–386 B.C.", in *The Ancient World*, 1985, no. 11, p. 73.

[28] The Greek text of the play corresponds to the edition of Zachary P. Biles and S. Douglas Olson (eds.), *Aristophanes. Wasps*, Oxford University Press, Oxford, 2015. Translations are taken from Alan H. Sommerstein (ed.), *The Comedies of Aristophanes*, vol. 4. Wasps, Aris & Phillips, Warminster, 1983.

Such a representation of legal relationships on the dramatic stage can illustrate the direct correspondence between straight bodies and a claim for honest conduct.[29] It is well known that reciprocal positions and distance between bodies are indicative of the intentions of those who interact.[30] In a proxemic analysis, what Philocleon acknowledged is that his body got in contact with the bodies of the defendants, but this touching experience was not described as an interaction between equals, as it could be expected in physical contact between citizens. Whereas he stood up, the defendants bent in front of him and begged after fawning and crawling: "they bow down and supplicate me" (ἱκετεύουσίν θ᾽ ὑποκύπτοντες, v. 559). The participle ὑποκύπτοντες (hypokýptontes, v. 555), 'bowing down', shows the distance between the superiority of the juror and the humility of the beggars.[31]

A physiognomic interpretation of this antithesis pays attention to the corporal representation of jurors and offenders at court.[32] The opposition between a body that stands, keeps firm and looks down, on the one hand, and a soft body that twists and curves, on the other, reproduces the legal inequality that Aristophanes is fond of criticizing in judicial interactions. Far away from *isonomía*, an equality of looks, in Philocleon's perception his straight attitude of superiority was clearly different from the crooked bodies of the pleaders. While he was "like a Zeus", flashing verdicts as a lightning from above, the accused bent and shook in fear (vv. 619-627):

ἆρ᾽ οὐ μεγάλην ἀρχὴν ἄρχω καὶ τοῦ Διὸς οὐδὲν ἐλάττω, ὅστις
ἀκούω ταῦθ᾽ ἅπερ ὁ Ζεύς;
ἢν γοῦν ἡμεῖς θορυβήσωμεν,

---

[29] Mariel Vázquez, "'Cuerpos curvados' en *Asambleístas* de Aristófanes: la postura corporal y sus implicancias biológico-políticas", in Alicia Atienza, Emiliano J. Buis and Elsa Rodríguez Cidre (eds.), *Anatomías poéticas. Pliegues y despliegues del cuerpo en el mundo griego antiguo* (Colección Saberes), Editorial de la Facultad de Filosofía y Letras de la UBA, Buenos Aires, 2020, pp. 205–232, has recently worked on the political implications of the female image of crooked bodies in Aristophanes' *Ecclesiazusae*.

[30] Guiraud, 1980, see above note 21, considers that the interpretation of this connection of bodies is part of proxemics, since it is related to the physical communication between people in a specific spatial environment.

[31] Biles and Olson, 2015, p. 259, see above note 28. On this verb, see Diphilus fr. 42, 23-24 and Herodotus 1.130.1, 6.25.2 and 109.3.

[32] Jon Hesk, "The Rhetoric of Anti-rhetoric in Athenian oratory", in Simon Goldhill and Robin Osborne (eds.), *Performance Culture and Athenian Democracy*, Cambridge University Press, Cambridge, 1999, pp. 220–226, has coined the expression 'physiognomic interpretation' in order to describe the ways in which orators matched some physical traits to specific character types in their speeches.

πᾶς τίς φησιν τῶν παριόντων·
"οἷον βροντᾷ τὸ δικαστήριον,
ὦ Ζεῦ βασιλεῦ." κἂν ἀστράψω,
ποππύζουσιν κἀγκεχόδασίν μ᾽
οἱ πλουτοῦντες καὶ πάνυ σεμνοί.

Do I not wield great power, in no way inferior to that of
Zeus – seeing that the same things are said of Zeus and of me?
For example, if we get noisy, every passer-by says: "What a
thunder's coming from the court! Lord Zeus!" and if I make
lightning, the rich and the very grand all cluck and defecate in
their clouds from fear of me.

However, Philocleon's son Bdelycleon would soon try to prove his
father wrong. When explaining to him that he was in fact a δοῦλος (*doûlos*,
'slave'), and not a king, Bdelycleon criticized the relationship between jurors and demagogues and compared it to the treatment of masters and
slaves (vv. 515-517):

καταγελώμενος μὲν οὖν
οὐκ ἐπαΐεις ὑπ᾽ ἀνδρῶν, οὓς σὺ μόνον οὐ προσκυνεῖς.
ἀλλὰ δουλεύων λέληθας.

More than that, you don't understand that you're being made a
fool of by men whom you all but worship. You're a slave, and
you're not aware of it.

The verb used here to indicate the superiority of politicians,
προσκυνεῖς (*proskyneîs*), referred to *proskýnesis*, a form of veneration involving abasement by prostration and hand gestures which was frequent in
prayers to the gods. It was a gesture which, when applied to human beings
who bent their knees in front of other individuals, resulted in an inadequate
submission which would not be considered appropriate among decent citizens. Curving the body in front of another *polítes* would imply affecting
one's own τιμή (*timé*, 'honour').

The antithesis between upright and twisted positions of the body
served as an efficient way of denouncing the inequality of litigants and jurors. This breakup repudiated what should be considered an ideal democratic balance of those who were involved in civic activities. The ways in
which bodies were presented provide us with interesting information on the
relationship between accusers and defendants and between litigants and
jurors. A study of their corporal language allows us to discover their perceptions of the other and their subjective modes of dealing with adversaries.

Taking advantage of the importance of visual representation in the comic scene, the physicality of the movements of the actors on stage, and their body-to-body contact, reveal a lot about the material dynamics of judicial procedure in classical Athens and about the complex nature of integrity, as opposed to ruin and corruption.

In forensic oratory, a frequent rhetorical technique consisted of denoting the construction (or simulation) of character in discourse, delineating personality on the basis of reputation and the importance of public image. In Athenian forensic discourse, accusing the enemy of being a traitor, a turncoat and a liar, meant placing him out of the limits of socially accepted behaviour. Showing the defendants as untrustworthy, impious, and greedy, was a way of presenting them "in the worst light possible".[33] In that sense, the self-construction of the speaker as upholding the common values of the *pólis* depended on the presentation of positive virtues that could relate to our modern concept of integrity.

Whereas the speaker was always portrayed as undamaged by decay, embodying a standard of high moral character, his rival was portrayed as ruined, characterized by a damaged reputation and a lack of ethical values. This was the case of Aeschines' depiction of Timarchus, who was presented not just as morally dissolute – that is, as a male prostitute – but as physically dissipated too (1.26):

> ἐκεῖνοι μέν γε ᾐσχύνοντο ἔξω τὴν χεῖρα ἔχοντες λέγειν, οὑτοσὶ
> δὲ οὐ πάλαι, ἀλλὰ πρώην ποτὲ ῥίψας θοἰμάτιον γυμνὸς
> ἐπαγκρατίαζεν ἐν τῇ ἐκκλησίᾳ, οὕτω κακῶς καὶ αἰσχρῶς
> διακείμενος τὸ σῶμα ὑπὸ μέθης καὶ βδελυρίας, ὥστε τούς γε
> εὖ φρονοῦντας ἐγκαλύψασθαι, αἰσχυνθέντας ὑπὲρ τῆς πόλεως,
> εἰ τοιούτοις συμβούλοις χρώμεθα.

> They [the citizens] were too modest to speak with the arm outside the cloak, but this man not long ago, yes, only the other day, in an assembly of the people threw off his cloak and leaped about like a gymnast, half naked, his body so reduced and befouled through drunkenness and lewdness that right-

---

33   Claire Taylor, "Corruption and Anticorruption in Democratic Athens", in Ronald Kroeze, André Vitória and Guy Geltner (eds.), *Anti-corruption in History: From Antiquity to the Modern Era*, Oxford University Press, Oxford, 2017, pp. 21–33, at p. 29.

minded men, at least, covered their eyes, being ashamed for the city, that we should let such men as he be our advisers.[34]

Showing the rightness and closeness of a standing body, as opposed to those bodies which are seen naked or dancing, meant praising the moral quality of a person who appeared to take decisions or actions with the purpose of defending the values of the city against self-interest. [35]

At the crossroad between bodily posture and moral reliability, the words in ancient Greek terms indicating aspects which could be related to our concept of integrity included χρηστότης (*khrestótes*), "uprightness, honesty"; σωφροσύνη (*sophrosýne*), "self-mastery"; ἀφελεία (*apheleía*), "simplicity", and especially ἀκεραιότης (*akeraiótes*), "intactness, purity". In a (typically Greek) system of lexical oppositions, terms related to corruption embraced nouns such as μοχθηρία (*mokhtería*), "depravity"; δωροδοκία (*dorodokía*): "corruption"; and verbs such as διαφθείρειν (*diaphteírein*), "to utterly destroy", and λωβᾶσθαι (*lobâsthai*), "to harm/seduce".[36]

In short, this antithetical political perspective, based on the distance between corruption and uprightness, was rhetorically built upon both physical and moral considerations (see Graph 1 below). Whereas purity and wholeness were validated as positive notions, putrefaction and degeneration identified decadent and unscrupulous men. In moral terms, this was perceived as the antagonism between guilt and innocence, depravity and honesty, lies and truth.

---

[34] The Greek text and its translation are taken from Charles Darwin Adams (ed.), *Aeschines,* Harvard University Press and William Heinemann, Cambridge (MA) and London, 1919.

[35] Philip Bosman, "Corruption and Integrity: A Survey of the Ancient Terms", in Bosman, 2012, p. 2, see above note 18.

[36] Bosman, 2012, pp. 5–6 and 10-14, see above note 18. On the legal and political implications of these terms, see Mark Philp, "Defining Political Corruption", in *Political Studies*, 1997, no. 45, pp. 436–62, at p. 442; F. David Harvey, "*Dona Ferentes*: Some Aspects of Bribery in Greek Politics", in *History of Political Thought*, 1985, no. 6, pp. 76–117, at p. 105, and Lisa Hill, "Conceptions of Political Corruption in Antiquity", in *History of Political Thought*, 2013, no. 34, at pp. 567–568.

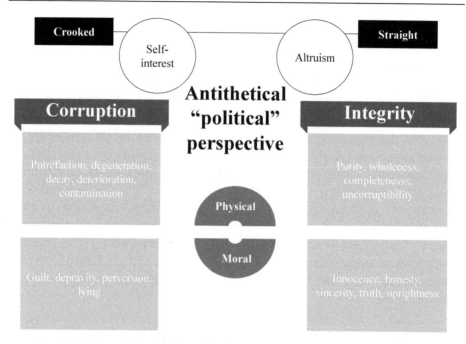

Graph 1: The antithetical 'political' perspective of 'integrity' in antiquity.

Defective individuals and degenerated political regimes went together.[37] This is the reason why the appeal to democratic values was so important in political and forensic oratory – it aimed to create a closer connection between the speaker and the δῆμος (*dêmos*, 'the people'). The orator Aeschines, for instance, described the perfect virtues of the democratic citizen in a passage of his speech *Against Ctesiphon*. By contrast to an oligarch, the admirable *polítes* ought to be a man of good judgment, who would be able to serve the Athenian people wholeheartedly, without any personal bias or interest (3.169-170):

> οἶμαι τοίνυν ἅπαντας ἂν ὑμᾶς ὁμολογῆσαι τάδε δεῖν ὑπάρξαι
> τῷ δημοτικῷ, πρῶτον μὲν ἐλεύθερον εἶναι καὶ πρὸς πατρὸς
> καὶ πρὸς μητρός, ἵνα μὴ διὰ τὴν περὶ τὸ γένος ἀτυχίαν
> δυσμενὴς ᾖ τοῖς νόμοις, οἳ σῴζουσι τὴν δημοκρατίαν,
> δεύτερον δ᾽ ἀπὸ τῶν προγόνων εὐεργεσίαν τινὰ αὐτῷ πρὸς
> τὸν δῆμον ὑπάρχειν, ἢ τό γ᾽ ἀναγκαιότατον μηδεμίαν ἔχθραν,
> ἵνα μὴ βοηθῶν τοῖς τῶν προγόνων ἀτυχήμασι κακῶς ἐπιχειρῇ

---

[37] William J. Prior, *Virtue and Knowledge: An Introduction to Ancient Greek Ethics*, Routledge, New York and London, 2016 [1991], pp. 261–275.

ποιεῖν τὴν πόλιν. τρίτον σώφρονα καὶ μέτριον χρὴ πεφυκέναι
αὐτὸν πρὸς τὴν καθ᾽ ἡμέραν δίαιταν, ὅπως μὴ διὰ τὴν
ἀσέλγειαν τῆς δαπάνης δωροδοκῇ κατὰ τοῦ δήμου. τέταρτον
εὐγνώμονα καὶ δυνατὸν εἰπεῖν· καλὸν γὰρ τὴν μὲν διάνοιαν
προαιρεῖσθαι τὰ βέλτιστα, τὴν δὲ παιδείαν τὴν τοῦ ῥήτορος
καὶ τὸν λόγον πείθειν τοὺς ἀκούοντας· εἰ δὲ μή, τήν γ᾽
εὐγνωμοσύνην ἀεὶ προτακτέον τοῦ λόγου. πέμπτον ἀνδρεῖον
εἶναι τὴν ψυχήν, ἵνα μὴ παρὰ τὰ δεινὰ καὶ τοὺς κινδύνους
ἐγκαταλίπῃ τὸν δῆμον.

I think you would all acknowledge that the following qualities ought to be found in the "friend of the people": in the first place, he should be free-born, on both his father's and his mother's side, lest because of misfortune of birth he be disloyal to the laws that preserve the democracy. In the second place, he should have as a legacy from his ancestors some service which they have done to the democracy, or at the very least there must be no inherited enmity against it, lest in the attempt to avenge the misfortunes of his family he undertake to injure the city. Thirdly, he ought to be temperate and self-restrained in his daily life, lest to support his wanton extravagance he take bribes against the people. Fourthly, he ought to be a man of good judgment and an able speaker; for it is well that his discernment choose the wisest course, and his training in rhetoric and his eloquence persuade the hearers; but if he cannot have both, good judgment is always to be preferred to eloquence of speech. Fifthly, he ought to be a man of brave heart, that in danger and peril he may not desert the people.[38]

A noble character constituted a proof of patriotism; it was a symbol of self-conscious dedication to the political community.[39] Thus, when responding to Aeschines' criticism, Demosthenes centred his speech *On the Crown* around the description of his own private and public integrity: as expected, he claimed to have lived up to the highest standards of self-sacrifice and courage. In front of his fellow Athenians, he explained that he

---

[38] The Greek text and the English translation correspond to the edition prepared by Charles Darwin Adams, *Aeschines*, Harvard University Press and William Heinemann, Cambridge (MA) and London, 1919.

[39] Ryan K. Balot, "The Virtue Politics of Democratic Athens", in Stephen Salkever (ed.) *The Cambridge Companion to Ancient Greek Political Thought*, Cambridge University Press, Cambridge, 2009, at pp. 284–285.

had always acted with zeal, loyalty, eagerness, generosity, and well-informed rationality, in order to pursue the city's welfare (18.62-71).

Together with the Assembly, the judicial arena was a crucial setting in classical Athens, where citizens could display their virtuous characters and show their normatively appropriate feelings in front of others. This was the case of Socrates' famous prosecution under the charges of impiety (ἀσέβεια, *asébeia*) and corruption of the youth, maybe the best-known example of the need for a philosopher to inform of his ethical integrity. According to Plato's *Apology*, Socrates claimed to have acted in a proper way, respecting both law and religion: μηδὲν ἄδικον μηδ᾽ ἀνόσιον ἐργάζεσθαι ("I should do nothing wrong or contrary to the sacred") (*Apology* 33c-d). Interestingly, in Socrates' words there was an insistence in the maintenance of unity and harmony within the soul, a correspondence between word and action which, again, implied that integrity could not only be achieved by a mental disposition, but also involved tangible behaviour.[40] In the case of Socrates, it has been stated that his integrity derived mainly from negativity, since he departed from ignorance (instead of knowledge), and he knew what injustice was (rather than what virtuous excellence was).[41] His integrity only turned out to be positive when caring for others.[42] In this sense, moral integrity was seen as an individual virtue related to a social environment because of the effects it could produce on the rest of the citizens. Socrates' integrity also entailed the civic courage of opposing the Athenians when the *dêmos* decided to infringe the law.[43]

Similar to comedy and forensic oratory, Athenian tragedy made frequent allusions to this set of opposing core values as well. In ancient Greece, in spite of the close nexus between corporal deportment and ethical

---

[40]   Bosman, 2012, pp. 9-10, see above note 18.

[41]   George Kateb, *Patriotism and Other Mistakes*, Yale University Press, New Haven, 2006, p. 216.

[42]   Kateb, 2006, p. 241, see above note 41: "The whole image of Socrates as a model of intellectual and moral integrity, as a supreme hero of self-denial and self-sacrifice, as a master of negativity, needs one, if only one, positivity, and that must be a positive commitment to others. He cared for them more than he cared for himself. He lived and died for them. He made them his superiors by deeming them worthy of his self-sacrifice. But he did not think that they were his equals, and this is precisely why he had to care for them and in the way that he did".

[43]   Claude Mossé, *Le procès de Socrate. Un philosophe victim de la démocratie?*, André Versaille, Bruxelles, 2012, p. 69 argues that "Socrate demeurait fidèle à lui-même et à ses convictions, et n'hésitait pas à braver ceux dont les ordres lui paraissent injustes et contraires aux lois".

manners, tragedy presented examples in which the proximity of physical beauty and moral carriage was compromised. In these exceptional cases, a specific reference was made to the lack of balance between body and personality, as it happened in Euripides' *Orestes* when a messenger on stage described a good citizen, although bad-looking, as "manly uncorrupted" (ἀκέραιος, *akéraios*) and well-behaved, far from censure or blame (vv. 919-923):

> μορφῇ μὲν οὐκ εὐωπός, ἀνδρεῖος δ᾿ ἀνήρ,
> ὀλιγάκις ἄστυ κἀγορᾶς χραίνων κύκλον,
> αὐτουργός – οἵπερ καὶ μόνοι σῴζουσι γῆν –
> ξυνετὸς δέ, χωρεῖν ὁμόσε τοῖς λόγοις θέλων,
> ἀκέραιος, ἀνεπίπληκτον ἠσκηκὼς βίον·

> He was not physically good-looking but a manly man (*andreîos*), one who rarely impinges on the town or the market circle; a working farmer (it is these alone that ensure the land's survival), but intelligent, willing to come to grips with the argument, uncorrupted (*akéraios*), self-disciplined to a life above reproach (*anepíplekton eskekòs bíon*).[44]

In the strict field of jurisdiction, for instance, straightness and correction also played a relevant role according to tragedy. In Aeschylus' *Eumenides*, for instance, the goddess Athena created the prestigious criminal tribunal of the Areopagus for the Athenians, an unbiased court described as "untouched by greed" (vv. 681-705):

> κλύοιτ᾿ ἂν ἤδη θεσμόν, Ἀττικὸς λεώς,
> πρώτας δίκας κρίνοντες αἵματος χυτοῦ.
> ἔσται δὲ καὶ τὸ λοιπὸν Αἰγέως στρατῷ
> αἰεὶ δικαστῶν τοῦτο βουλευτήριον.
> πάγον δ᾿ Ἄρειον τόνδ᾿, Ἀμαζόνων ἕδραν
> σκηνάς θ᾿, ὅτ᾿ ἦλθον Θησέως κατὰ φθόνον
> στρατηλατοῦσαι, καὶ πόλιν νεόπτολιν
> τήνδ᾿ ὑψίπυργον ἀντεπύργωσαν τότε,
> Ἄρει δ᾿ ἔθυον, ἔνθεν ἔστ᾿ ἐπώνυμος
> πέτρα, πάγος τ᾿ Ἄρειος· ἐν δὲ τῷ σέβας
> ἀστῶν φόβος τε ξυγγενὴς τὸ μὴ ἀδικεῖν
> σχήσει τό τ᾿ ἦμαρ καὶ κατ᾿ εὐφρόνην ὁμῶς,
> αὐτῶν πολιτῶν μὴ 'πιχραινόντων νόμους

---

[44] The Greek text is taken from Gilbert Murray, *Euripidis Fabulae, vol. 3*, Clarendon Press, Oxford, 1913. The translation is taken from Martin L. West, *Euripides. Orestes*, Aris & Phillips, Warminster, 1987.

κακαῖς ἐπιρροαῖσι· βορβόρῳ δ᾽ ὕδωρ
λαμπρὸν μιαίνων οὔποθ᾽ εὑρήσεις ποτόν.
τὸ μήτ᾽ ἄναρχον μήτε δεσποτούμενον
ἀστοῖς περιστέλλουσι βουλεύω σέβειν,
καὶ μὴ τὸ δεινὸν πᾶν πόλεως ἔξω βαλεῖν.
τίς γὰρ δεδοικὼς μηδὲν ἔνδικος βροτῶν;
τοιόνδε τοι ταρβοῦντες ἐνδίκως σέβας
ἔρυμά τε χώρας καὶ πόλεως σωτήριον
ἔχοιτ᾽ ἄν, οἷον οὔτις ἀνθρώπων ἔχει,
οὔτ᾽ ἐν Σκύθῃσιν οὔτε Πέλοπος ἐν τόποις.
κερδῶν ἄθικτον τοῦτο βουλευτήριον,
αἰδοῖον, ὀξύθυμον, εὐδόντων ὕπερ
ἐγρηγορὸς φρούρημα γῆς καθίσταμαι.

Hear now my ordinance, people of Attica, as you judge the first trial for bloodshed. In the future, even as now, this court of judges will always exist for the people of Aegeus. And this Hill of Ares, the seat and camp of the Amazons, when they came with an army in resentment against Theseus, and in those days built up this new citadel with lofty towers to rival his, and sacrificed to Ares, from which this rock takes its name, the Hill of Ares: on this hill, the reverence of the citizens, and fear, its kinsman, will hold them back from doing wrong by day and night alike, so long as they themselves do not pollute the laws with evil streams; if you stain clear water with filth, you will never find a drink. Neither anarchy nor tyranny – this I counsel my citizens to support and respect, and not to drive fear wholly out of the city. For who among mortals, if he fears nothing, is righteous? Stand in just awe of such majesty, and you will have a defence for your land and salvation of your city, such as no man has, either among the Scythians or in Pelops' realm. I establish this tribunal, untouched by greed (*kerdôn áthikton* [...] *bouleutérion*), worthy of reverence, quick to anger, awake on behalf of those who sleep, a guardian of the land.[45]

This founding myth of the Areopagus, which was presented as a creation of Athena during the trial of Orestes for the crime of his mother, exhibited the image of the tribunal as a place for veracity and honour. Its judicial integrity pointed to moral uprightness and material inviolability,

---

[45] The Greek text and its translation are taken from Herbert Weir Smyth (ed.), *Aeschylus, vol. 2, Eumenides*, Harvard University Press, Cambrige (MA), 1926.

which seemed to complement the ethical rectitude of those who administered justice. In the so-called "dikastic oath", which was pronounced by Athenian citizens before acting as jurors (δικασταί, *dikastaí*), relying on favour or enmity was explicitly excluded when taking decisions, and it was provided that both parties had to be listened on an equal footing during the proceedings to guarantee a fair trial. A vote in accordance with "the most equitable opinion" (γνώμη δικαιοτάτη, *gnóme dikaiotáte*) was also required.[46]

The importance of upholding ethical standards was not only presented in the judicial business of classical Greek cities. This is not surprising. Medical integrity constituted an example, since the practice of medicine, which also heavily influenced political thought,[47] was also subject to clear patterns of rectitude and soundness, as suggested by the famous Hippocratic oath. Under this oath, new doctors were expected to recite the pledge to promise to abstain from whatever was deleterious and mischievous, to re-

---

[46] We do not have any ancient source transmitting the text of the oath. Nevertheless, following possible reconstructions, it may well have included these provisions according to Alan H. Sommerstein, "The Judicial Sphere", in Alan H. Sommerstein and Andrew J. Bayliss, *Oath and State in Ancient Greece*, Walter de Gruyter, Berlin and Boston, 2013, p. 79: "I will vote according to the laws and decrees of the Athenian people and of the Council of Five Hundred; and on matters about which there are no laws, I will vote according to the justest opinion. And I will give an equal hearing both to the accuser and to the defendant, and I will cast my vote upon the actual matter which is the subject of the charge. And I will not accept any gift on account of my service as a juror, neither I nor any other man or woman with my knowledge, by any means or device whatsoever. And I am not less than thirty years old. I swear this by Apollo Patroios, Demeter, and Zeus the King; if I transgress any of these provisions, then may I be utterly destroyed, myself and my house, but if I keep my oath may I have many blessings". The most famous reconstruction is owed to Max Fränkel, "Der attische Heliasteneid", in *Hermes*, 1878, no. 13, pp. 452–466, and has been extensively studied by David C. Mirhady, "The Dikast's Oath and the Question of Fact", in Alan H. Sommerstein and Judith Fletcher (eds.), *Horkos. The Oath in Greek Society*, Liverpool University Press, Liverpool, 2008, pp. 49–51. On the nature of the dikastic oath under the light of Aristotle's *Politics*, see the recent contribution by Anders Dahl Sørensen, "Hippodamus of Miletus and the Character of the Athenian Dikastic Oath (Arist. *Pol.* 2.8)", in *Greek, Roman, and Byzantine Studies*, 2018, no. 58, pp. 324–348.

[47] See Giuseppe Cambiano, "Pathologie et analogie politique", in François Lasserre and Philippe Mudry (eds.), *Formes de pensée dans la Collection Hippocratique* (Actes du IVe Colloque international hippocratique, Lausanne, 21-26 septembre 1981), Droz, Genève, 1983, pp. 441–458. On the overlapping between medicine and politics, see also Roger Brock, "Sickness in the body politic: medical imagery in the Greek polis", in Valerie M. Hope and Eireann Marshall (eds.), *Death and Disease in the Ancient City*, Routledge, London and New York, 2000, pp. 24–34.

frain from giving deadly medicine to anyone if asked, and to abstain from every voluntary act of mischief and corruption.[48]

In sum, integrity was part of what a city would endorse as general patterns of social behaviour in different professions and activities. This correctness also included intellectual pursuit, which was an activity related to political performance as well. For example, moral considerations would be attributed to virtuous historians many centuries later by Lucian, with a similar vocabulary placing emphasis on integrity and rightness (*How to write History*, 41):

> τοιοῦτος οὖν μοι ὁ συγγραφεὺς ἔστω, ἄφοβος, ἀδέκαστος, ἐλεύθερος, παρρησίας καὶ ἀληθείας φίλος [...] οὐ μίσει οὐδὲ φιλίᾳ τι νέμων οὐδὲ φειδόμενος ἢ ἐλεῶν ἢ αἰσχυνόμενος ἢ δυσωπούμενος, ἴσος δικαστής, εὔνους ἅπασιν ἄχρι τοῦ μὴ θατέρῳ ἀπονεῖμαι πλεῖον τοῦ δέοντος, ξένος ἐν τοῖς βιβλίοις καὶ ἄπολις, αὐτόνομος, ἀβασίλευτος, οὐ τί τῷδε ἢ τῷδε δόξει λογιζόμενος, ἀλλὰ τί πέπρακται λέγων.

> This, then, is the sort of man the historian should be: fearless, incorruptible (*adékastos*), free (*eleútheros*), a friend of free expression and the truth (*parrhesías kaì aletheías phílos*), [...] giving nothing to hatred or to friendship, sparing no one, showing neither pity nor shame nor obsequiousness, an impartial judge (*ísos dikastés*), well disposed to all men up to the point of not giving one side more than its due, in his books a stranger and a man without a country, independent, subject to no sovereign, not reckoning what this or that man will think, but stating the facts.[49]

1.4. Recreating Integrity in Republican Rome

Concerning Republican Rome, the sources available to us seem to follow a similar path – physical uprightness and moral honesty were closely linked.

---

[48] The Greek text can be found in W.H.S. Jones (ed.), *Hippocrates Collected Works*, vol. I, Cambridge (MA), Harvard University Press, 1868. On its importance for the history of medical thought, see Robert M. Veatch, *Hippocratic, Religious, and Secular Medical Ethics: The Points of Conflict*, Georgetown University Press, Washington, DC, 2012. On the 'legal' character of this oath and the obligations which arise from its text, see Lisa R. Hasday, "The Hippocratic Oath as Literary Text: A Dialogue Between Law and Medicine", in *Yale Journal of Health Policy, Law, and Ethics*, 2002, no. 2, pp. 299–324.

[49] The Greek text is taken from Karl Jacobitz (ed.), *Luciani Samosatensis Opera*, vol. II, B.G. Teubner, Leipzig, 1913. The translation corresponds to K. Kilburn, *Lucian*, vol. VI, Harvard University Press, Cambridge (MA), 1959.

The ethical and political centre was the *vir*, the adult male citizen. In the social hierarchy of *status*, the role of Roman men was heavily dependent on the nature of their body: a Roman citizen was seen in sexual terms as an agent of penetration, whereas in the political and legal dimensions he was expected to enforce domestic authority as a *pater familias*. Since defending the body from external assault was the cornerstone of masculinity, the idealized image of Roman men involved a sexual protocol based on the clear establishment of physical boundaries, which turned their bodies into impenetrable constructions.[50] Manhood therefore meant, at the same time, immunity from physical invasion, and civic autonomy. Once again, at the crossroad between physicality and ethics, integrity was definitely a significant feature of these two complementary dimensions.

Following the Greek tradition, external and internal connotations also conflated in the Latin vocabulary involving integrity and corruption. Thus, the word *corruptio* meant "dishonest conduct, seduction, harm, bribery" and the related verb *corrumpere* similarly translatable as "to utterly destroy, ruin, spoil, damage, adulterate". Integrity, on the other side, was expressed through nouns such as *temperantia*, "self-control"; *innocentia*, "blamelessness" and *integritas*, "intactness, completeness, wholeness", which originated our correspondent words.[51] Significantly, *integritas* came from *intangere* ("not to touch") and therefore remained close to the Greek ἀκεραιότης *(akeraiótes)*, which, according to Bosman, also derived from *a-keránnymi* ("not to mix").

Unlike our modern perception, in which integrity seems to relate to innocence and honesty – and more recently became associated with interiority, autonomy, and reflection – in Republican Rome the idea of *integritas* involved strong physical traits.[52] This can be noted when examining the relevant passages, where the concept is placed next to adjectives indicating purity and intangibility. Expressions such as *integer intactusque*, which is ubiquitous in Livy,[53] *integer et incorruptus*,[54] *integer et inlibatus*,[55] or *integer et inviolatus*[56] easily demonstrate the nature of this semantic scope.

---

[50] Jonathan Walters, "Invading the Roman Body: Manliness and Impenetrability in Roman Thought", in Judith P. Hallett and Marilyn B. Skinner (eds.), *Roman Sexualities*, Princeton University Press, Princeton, 1997, pp. 29–46.

[51] Bosman, 2012, pp. 3–5, see above note 18.

[52] Robert A. Kaster, *Emotion, Restraint and Community in Ancient Rome*, Oxford University Press, Oxford, 2005, pp. 135–137.

[53] Livy 5. 38. 7, 10.14. 20, 10. 27. 9, 10. 36. 3, *inter alia multa*.

In fact, the adjective *integer* was mostly used with physical entities in order to refer to those characteristics which made it entirely what they were: this implied that something which was described as *integer* remained unaltered since it had not suffered from any addition (which might eventually spoil its purity) or subtraction (which would undermine its wholeness).[57] The idea behind this material sense of integrity is clearly seen in the way the Romans referred to the movement of rivers in which waters were deemed to be neither contaminated nor compromised. In Tacitus' *Histories*, for instance, the river Jordan "is not received by the open ocean but flows *integer* through one lake, then another, and is captured by a third" (*nec Iordanes pelago accipitur, sed unum atque alterum lacum integer perfluit, tertio retinetur*, 5.6).[58] When defined as *integer*, a river was conceived as both pure and complete, in accordance with its original essence.

The transferal of the material implications of *integritas* to the moral realm keeps this idea of purity and completeness. Not surprisingly, Cicero explicitly mentioned the close relationship between physical qualities and spiritual virtues. Bodies and minds could become impure and crooked when altered. Corruption was in fact a sort of disease affecting both the body and the soul, but the mind could be as beautiful as the body if characterized by equality, constancy of opinions and judgments, firmness and stability, as suggested in *Tusculan Disputations* 4.28-31:

> *morbum appellant totius corporis corruptionem, aegrotationem morbum cum imbecillitate, vitium, cum partes corporis inter se dissident, ex quo pravitas membrorum, distortio, deformitas (...) Atque ut in malis attingit animi naturam corporis similitudo, sic in bonis. sunt enim in corpore praecipua, pulchritudo, vires, valetudo, firmitas,*

---

[54] Cicero, *For Marcus Fonteius* 3, *De Natura Deorum* 2. 71, etc.

[55] Seneca, *Dialogue* 2. 6. 7; Pliny, *Panegyricus* 25. 1.

[56] Cicero, *Against Verres* 2. 4. 130, Livy 6. 3. 10.

[57] Bosman, 2012, pp. 4–5, see above note 18.

[58] Similarly, Pomponius Mela – the first Roman geographer – explained that the Rhône "maintains its course, passing unaltered (*integer*) through the middle of the lake and emerging with its volume undiminished" (*tenet impetum, seque per medium integer agens quantus venit egreditur*, 2.79). Speaking of the Tigris, Seneca stated that its course was restored with its full size (*integrae magnitudinis redditur, Ad Lucilium Epistulae Morales* 104. 15). Also, in his *Dialogues,* the spring Arethusa was said to remain unchanged (*integrum*) beneath many seas, saved from mingling with water of lesser quality (*inlapsum terris flumen integrum subter tot maria et a confusione peioris undae servatum*, 6.17.3).

velocitas, sunt item in animo (...) sic in animo opinionum iudiciorumque aequabilitas et constantia cum firmitate quadam et stabilitate virtutem subsequens aut virtutis vim ipsam continens pulchritudo vocatur.[59]

They call that a disease where the whole body is corrupted; they call that sickness where a disease is attended with a weakness, and that a defect where the parts of the body are not well compacted together; from whence it follows that the members are misshapen, crooked, and deformed (...) As there is some analogy between the nature of the body and mind in evil, so is there in good; for the distinctions of the body are beauty, strength, health, firmness, quickness of motion: the same may be said of the mind. (...) The beauty of the mind consists in an equality and constancy of opinions and judgments, joined to a certain firmness and stability, pursuing virtue, or containing within itself the very essence of virtue.[60]

Straight or firm bodies were described as "whole", in the sense that their parts were not separated but rather formed a single unity. As already indicated for the Greek texts, deformations and crookedness became here indicative of physical corruption (which was presented in turn as a disease, *morbus*). The link between bodily weakness and mental deterioration showed the extent to which the physical elements could underline intellectual virtues.

The political implications of this image of corporal and spiritual vices cannot be underestimated, especially since the Roman community was perceived as a body politic which needed to stay as healthy, pure and intact (and therefore exempt from corruption) as its citizens. In his treatise *De officiis* – which has been accurately described as "a contemporary handbook of the elite's behaviour"[61] – Cicero described that, when performing civic activities, the duties of public officials should encompass appropriate behaviour and uprightness. In particular, this entailed the rejection of individual benefits for the sake of collective interests (1.85):

---

[59] The Latin text is taken from the edition prepared by Max Pohlenz (ed.), *M. Tullius Cicero. Tusculanae Disputationes*, Teubner, Leipzig, 1918.

[60] The translation belongs to C.D. Yonge (ed.), *Cicero's* Tusculan Disputations, Harper & Brothers, New York, 1877.

[61] Valentina Arena, "Fighting Corruption. Political Thought and Practice in the Late Roman Republic", in Kroeze, Vitória and Geltner, 2017, pp. 35–47, at p. 40, see above note 33.

Omnino qui rei publicae praefuturi sunt, duo Platonis praecepta teneant, unum, ut utilitatem civium sic tueantur, ut, quaecumque agunt, ad eam referant obliti commodorum suorum, alterum, ut totum corpus rei publicae curent, ne, dum partem aliquam tuentur, reliquas deserant. Ut enim tutela, sic procuratio rei publicae ad eorum utilitatem, qui commissi sunt, non ad eorum, quibus commissa est, gerenda est. Qui autem parti civium consulunt, partem neglegunt, rem perniciosissimam in civitatem inducunt, seditionem atque discordiam.

Those who propose to take charge of the affairs of government should not fail to remember two of Plato's rules: first, to keep the good of the people so clearly in view that regardless of their own interests they will make their every action conform to that; second, to care for the welfare of the whole body politic and not in serving the interests of some one party to betray the rest. For the administration of the government, like the office of a trustee, must be conducted for the benefit of those entrusted to one's care, not of those to whom it is entrusted. Now, those who care for the interests of a part of the citizens and neglect another part, introduce into the civil service a dangerous element – dissension and party strife.[62]

As far as vocabulary is concerned, the expected political conduct of public officers remained close to the descriptions provided by Cicero in his forensic speeches, when praising his clients to the courts. Taking into account the importance of endorsing shared values in Roman tribunals in order to ensure a favourable verdict, Cicero focused on a particular set of recurrent key moral characteristics which shaped the ethical assessment of a person.[63] When describing Balbus' military service, for example (*For Cornelius Balbus* 6), he noted his "industry, determination, fighting spirit, and valour worthy of a general" (*labor, adsiduitas, dimicatio, virtus digna*

---

[62] Both the Latin text and the English translation have been taken from Walter Miller (ed.), *M. Tullius Cicero. De Officiis*, Harvard University Press, Cambridge (MA) and London, 1913. Later in the text, Cicero affirmed again that exploiting the state for selfish profit was not only immoral, but also criminal and infamous (*habere enim quaestui rem publicam non modo turpe est, sed sceleratum etiam et nefarium*, 2.77). Cicero laid the foundations for the moral obligations that need to be met in modern times by those holding a public office; see Steve Sheppard, *I Do Solemnly Swear: The Moral Obligations of Legal Officials*, Cambridge University Press, Cambridge, 2009, p. 49.

[63] Claudia I. Arno, *How Romans Became "Roman": Creating Identity in an Expanding World*, Ph.D. Dissertation, University of Michigan, Ann Arbor, 2012, pp. 25–27.

summo imperatore), referring later to his *pudor, integritas, religio*, and *diligentia* and his well-known *castitas, sanctitas* and *moderatio*. In political terms, integrity comprised a wide range of private and public virtues related to the essential qualities of "wholeness" and "purity". As with rivers, these positive values were described as essential in the characterization of an individual, who possessed them in spite of the many changing circumstances surrounding his life.[64]

Civic virtues were extremely useful to distinguish good and bad citizens. In *Against Verres*, Cicero stated that – unlike his rival – he cherished *fides, pudor, pudicitia, religio* and *ius aequum* (2.3.6). He then described Verres' corrupt way of acting by accusing his listeners of not being able to appreciate values which were inherent to Roman citizens, such as virtue, trustworthiness (*integritas*), hard work, frugality, and modesty (2.3.7-8):

> *illa quae leviora videntur esse non cuiusvis animum possunt movere, quod ad tuam ipsius amicitiam ceterorumque hominum magnorum atque nobilium faciliorem aditum istius habet nequitia et audacia quam cuiusquam nostrum virtus et integritas? odistis hominum novorum industriam, despicitis eorum frugalitatem, pudorem contemnitis, ingenium vero et virtutem depressam exstinctamque cupitis: Verrem amatis! Ita credo; si non virtute, non industria, non innocentia, non pudore, non pudicitia, at sermone, at litteris, at humanitate eius delectamini. Nihil eorum est, contraque sunt omnia cum summo dedecore ac turpitudine tum singulari stultitia atque inhumanitate oblita.*[65]

What? cannot even those matters, which seem more trifling, move any one's mind, – that the worthlessness and audacity of that man should have a more easy access to your own friendship and to that of other great and noble men, than the virtue and integrity of any one of us? You hate the industry of new men; you despise their economy; you scorn their modesty; you wish their talents and virtues to be depressed and extinguished. You are fond of Verres: I suppose so. If you are not gratified with his virtue, and his innocence, and his industry, and his modesty, and his chastity, at least you are transported at his conversation, his accomplishments, and his high breed-

---

[64] Kaster, 2005, pp. 137, 142, see above note 52.

[65] The Latin text is taken from William Peterson (ed.), *M. Tvlli Ciceronis Orationes*, Clarendon Press, Oxford, 1917.

ing. He has no such gifts; but, on the contrary, all his qualities are stained with the most extreme disgrace and infamy, with most extraordinary stupidity and boorishness.[66]

Other relevant passages in the *Verrine Orations* complemented this axiological model by providing us with a larger picture of 'integrity': on some occasions we see that several references were made to identify the public display of virtues by jury members and even by women. As far as the first group is concerned, unlike other magistrates, both Quintus Manlius and Quintus Cornificius were presented by Cicero under a positive light that pointed directly to their ethically "upright" comportment (1.1.30):

> *Q. Manlium et Q. Cornificium, duos severissimos atque integerrimos iudices, quod tribuni plebis tum erunt, iudices non habebimus; P. Sulpicius, iudex tristis et integer, magistratum ineat oportet Nonis Decembribus.*

> We shall not have Quintus Manlius and Quintus Cornificius, two most severe and upright judges, for judges, because they will then be tribunes of the people. Publius Sulpicius, a solemn and upright judge, must enter on his magistracy on the fifth of December.

With regards to women, when presenting Philodamus' unmarried daughter, she was described by Cicero as "a woman of extraordinary beauty, who was judged to be exceedingly modest and virtuous" (*mulierem eximia pulchritudine; sed eam summa integritate pudicitiaque existimari*, 2.1.64). In this case, *integritas* corresponded to a female value, since it was connected to *pudicitia* with the purpose of showing her virginal purity and respectability.[67]

These examples show that *integritas*, as an abstract notion which could adapt to different contexts, mainly conveyed the idea of physical and moral "wholeness", implying not only strictness in public performances but also chastity and honesty.[68] It encompassed then a large set of personal dis-

---

[66] With slight modifications, the translation belongs to C.D. Yonge (ed.), *The Orations of Marcus Tullius Cicero*, George Bell & Sons, London, 1903.

[67] In Cicero – and elsewhere in Roman oratory – it was a common strategy to present the morality of individuals in relation to their families. Nobility and excellence (*virtus, dignitas*) were intertwined to shape one's reputation, as examined by Susan Treggiari, "Ancestral Virtues and Vices: Cicero on Nature, Nurture, and Presentation", in Emma Gee (ed.), *Myth, History and Culture in Republican Rome: Studies in Honour of T.P. Wiseman*, University of Exeter Press, Exeter, 2003, pp. 139–164.

[68] Kaster, 2005, p. 138, see above note 52.

positions, which had made their way into the public sphere when a conscientious behaviour had to be shown in front of others, but in reality responded to an individual nature which was generally seen as all-embracing
and unadulterated.[69] Also in a highly political context, a passage of Sallust's *Conspiracy of Catiline*, where Caesar and Cato are compared and
judged, complements our reading of the private and public dimensions of
integritas by alluding to self-containment and firmness (54.2-6):

> *Caesar beneficiis ac munificentia magnus habebatur, integri-*
> *tate vitae Cato. Ille mansuetudine et misericordia clarus fac-*
> *tus, huic severitas dignitatem addiderat. Caesar dando suble-*
> *vando ignoscundo, Cato nihil largiundo gloriam adeptus est.*
> *In altero miseris perfugium erat, in altero malis pernicies.*
> *Illius facilitas, huius constantia laudabatur. Postremo Caesar*
> *in animum induxerat laborare, vigilare; negotiis amicorum*
> *intentus sua neglegere, nihil denegare quod dono dignum*
> *esset; sibi magnum imperium, exercitum, bellum novom*
> *exoptabat, ubi virtus enitescere posset. At Catoni studium*
> *modestiae, decoris, sed maxume severitatis erat; non divitiis*
> *cum divite neque factione cum factioso, sed cum strenuo*
> *virtute, cum modesto pudore, cum innocente abstinentia*
> *certabat; esse quam videri bonus malebat: ita, quo minus*
> *petebat gloriam, eo magis illum [ad]sequebatur.*[70]

Caesar grew eminent by generosity and munificence; Cato by
the integrity of his life. Caesar was esteemed for his humanity
and benevolence; austereness had given dignity to Cato. Caesar acquired renown by giving, relieving, and pardoning; Cato
by bestowing nothing. In Caesar, there was a refuge for the
unfortunate; in Cato, destruction for the bad. In Caesar, his
easiness of temper was admired; in Cato, his firmness. Caesar,
in fine, had applied himself to a life of energy and activity; intent upon the interest of his friends, he was neglectful of his
own; he refused nothing to others that was worthy of acceptance, while for himself he desired great power, the command of an army, and a new war in which his talents might be
displayed. But Cato's ambition was that of temperance, discre-

---

[69] According to Kaster, 2005, p. 140, see above note 52, "taken together, these personal and
social behaviors and dispositions are constitutive of *integritas*: being ethically *integer* just
means that you possess these dispositions and display these behaviors".

[70] The Latin text has been taken from Axel W. Ahlberg (ed.), *C. Sallusti Crispi. Catilina,
Iugurtha, Orationes et epistulae excerptae de historiis*, Teubner, Leipzig, 1919.

tion, and, above all, of austerity; he did not contend in splendour with the rich, or in faction with the seditious, but with the brave in fortitude, with the modest in simplicity, with the temperate in abstinence; he was more desirous to be, than to appear, virtuous; and thus, the less he courted popularity, the more it pursued him.[71]

The opposition between the two characters is built on the basis of contradictory virtues. Whereas Caesar was considered great as a consequence of his benevolence and generosity, Cato's personality was defined by the *integritas* of his life. The former was famous for his gentle and compassionate character, while the latter derived standing from his sternness. Affability, on the one side; resolution, on the other one. It seems evident that the attributes ascribed to Caesar were mainly external, insofar as they were directed towards others. On the contrary, Cato's traits were basically internal: they referred to self-centeredness, personal harshness and austerity. His honesty was revealed by means of strictness and gravity (*severitas*). His virtues undermined Caesar's merits because they referred to absolute ethics. It follows that perhaps the core of integrity, for the Roman mind, concerned a set of normative principles that were born in the inner self.[72]

Cicero's speech *For Lucius Murena* also mentioned Cato's *gravitas*. When responding to the prosecution, he launched his arguments for the defense by firstly endorsing Cato's conscientiousness, identifying him as "a man of the utmost seriousness and integrity" (*gravissimo atque integrissimo viro, Mur.* 3).[73] As it happened with the description of Cato's ethics in *For Sestius* 60, his *virtus* was related here to *gravitas* ("earnestness") and *integritas* ("probity").

Sallust provided us elsewhere in his text with antithetical characters. By heavily criticizing the corrosive political environment of his time – as

---

71 The translation is taken from John Selby Watson (ed.), *Sallust. Conspiracy of Catiline*, Harper & Brothers, New York and London, 1899.

72 Even the expression of the antithesis is relevant when the Catonian subordination of self to ethics is presented. This subordination is paralleled with a chiasmus, which allows *integritas vitae* to be placed in a privileged position. See William W. Batstone, "The Antithesis of Virtue: Sallust's 'Synkrisis' and the Crisis of the Late Republic", in *Classical Antiquity*, 1989, no. 7, pp. 1–29. On this passage, see also Myles Anthony McDonnell, *Roman Manliness. Virtus and the Roman Republic*, Cambridge University Press, Cambridge, 2006, p. 341.

73 Malcolm Schofield, "Republican Virtues", in Ryan K. Balot (ed.), *A Companion to Greek and Roman Political Thought*, Blackwell, London, 2009, pp. 199–213, at p. 204.

opposed to the greatness of the ancestors – Sallust described Lucius Cati-line's moral degradation at the beginning of his speech. Apart from his per-sonal inclinations, Catiline's violent spirit responded to the circumstances which prompted his lack of integrity: "The corrupt morals of the state, too, which extravagance and selfishness, pernicious and contending vices, ren-dered thoroughly depraved, furnished him with additional incentives to ac-tion" (*incitabant praeterea corrupti civitatis mores, quos pessuma ac di-vorsa inter se mala, luxuria atque avaritia, vexabant, Cat.* 5).

Like in classical Athenian oratory, here Sallust's prose confirmed that corrupted characters echoed the political ruin of the community. However, the text itself leaves room for change since an example involving the au-thor himself suggests that, in very specific circumstances, a negative social background could be overcome by the personal qualities of a subject. By endorsing the possibility of moral recovery, Sallust presented a *mea culpa* when describing his own youth, marked by shamelessness, bribery, rapacity, and ambition. To explain his moral evolution, he compared his early depra-vation with the modesty, chastity and honesty he developed later in life when becoming a historian for the Roman people. It becomes an interesting account of the birth of his own intellectual integrity (3.3-5):

> *Sed ego adulescentulus initio, sicuti plerique, studio ad rem publicam latus sum ibique mihi multa advorsa fuere. Nam pro pudore, pro abstinentia, pro virtute audacia, largitio, avaritia vigebant. Quae tametsi animus aspernabatur insolens mala-rum artium, tamen inter tanta vitia imbecilla aetas ambitione corrupta tenebatur.*

> When I myself was a young man, my inclinations at first led me, like many others, into public life, and there I encountered many obstacles; for, instead of modesty, chastity and honesty, shamelessness, bribery and rapacity held sway. And, although my soul, a stranger to evil ways, recoiled from such faults, yet amid so many vices my youthful weakness was corrupted and held captive by ambition.[74]

If political action required moral standards of suitable behaviour, it is not surprising that the same Republican virtues had to be displayed by those in charge of explaining facts and analyzing the past: "On the contrary, I resolved to return to a cherished purpose from which ill-starred ambition

---

[74] The English translation is taken from J.T. Ramsey (ed.), *Sallust's* Bellum Catilinae, Oxford University Press, Oxford, 1984.

had diverted me, and write a history of the Roman people" (*sed, a quo incepto studioque me ambitio mala detinuerat, eodem regressus statui res gestas populi Romani carptim*, 4.2).

In Sallust's wording, therefore, *pudor, abstinentia* and *virtus* should not be overcome by *audacia, largitio and avaritia*. A good citizen needed to uphold the pure values of *virtus, pietas, iustitia, modestia* and *integritas*, thus rejecting being contaminated or altered by *corruptio* and *ambitio*.[75] A final comment should be made on this effort to circumvent the pollution of venality.

The idea of corruption pervaded ancient Rome since early times,[76] so the moral qualities of Roman men were expected to protect the public interests from the selfish desires of worthless politicians. So far, little difference can be seen when comparing this experience with the ethical condemnation of corruption that we portrayed for classical Athens. However, unlike the Athenian practice, in ancient Roman law, one of the best-recorded crimes of political corruption was *ambitus*, which consisted mainly of a candidate's effort to influence the result of an election through bribes or other subtler methods of soft power. Since "going around" in order to appeal to the people could easily lead to unethical excesses, the moral risks involved in *ambitus* soon led to the emergence of legislation aimed at criminalizing electoral bribery.[77] Once again, the need to endorse the high standard and practice of integrity fostered an institutional reaction to fight bribery. The moral idea behind these legal-political measures was to curb

---

[75] These Republican virtues can be explored in contemporary Roman theater as well. Not unlike its Athenian precedent, drama engaged with a variety of these expected qualities; see Gesine Manuwald, *Roman Republican Theater*, Cambridge University Press, Cambridge, pp. 294–295.

[76] Carlo Alberto Brioschi, *Corruption: A Short Story*, Brookings Institution, Washington, DC, 2017, pp. 39–50.

[77] The so-called *Lex Baebia* was the first law against *ambitus*, instituted by M. Baebius Tamphilus during his consulship in 181 BCE. On the reactions to *ambitus* and electoral corruption in Republican Rome, see for instance Georges Chaigne, *L'ambitus et les moeurs électorales des Romains*, E. Larose, Paris, 1911; Élisabeth Deniaux, "De l'*ambitio* à l'*ambitus* : les lieux de la propagande et de la corruption électorale à la fin de la République", in *L'Urbs, espace urbain et histoire (Ier siècle av. J.-C. – IIIe siècle ap. J.-C.)* (Actes du colloque de Rome, 8-12 mai 1985), École française de Rome, Rome, 1987, pp. 279–304; Tammo Wallinga, "*Ambitus* in the Roman Republic", in *Revue Internationale des Droits de l'Antiquité* 41, 1994, pp. 411–442; Peter Nadig, *Ardet Ambitus. Untersuchungen zum Phänomen der Wahlbestechungen in der römischen Republik*, Peter Lang, Frankfurt am Main and New York, 1997, and Brahm H. Kleinman, *Ambitus in the Late Roman Republic (80-50 B.C.)*, MA Thesis, Department of History and Classical Studies, McGill University, Montreal, 2012.

corruption and improve government by strengthening the basis of the Republic under the traditional values of *libertas, concordia, virtus* and *fides*.[78]

As conveyed by the examples of Cicero or Sallust, the fall of Republican Rome has been frequently ascribed by Latin authors to ethical failure.[79] The image of a corrupted political system, immersed in vice, was facilitated by the fact that the whole community was regarded as a single body politic,[80] and therefore the physical and moral deterioration of a person – which has been addressed in the sources – could be easily applied to the society as a whole.[81] In sum, the interpretation of political decline being the result of the moral neglect of traditional principles shows the importance attached by the Romans to integrity and its associated values, considered to be high-level standards that enabled a community to live together under common criteria of unity, mutual respect and concord.

1.5. Ancient Integrity Today: A Reappraisal of Classical Values in Times of Moral Crisis?

Some final remarks can be drawn from the ancient sources, which have been discussed along this chapter. Firstly, it should be noticed that, through the repetition of a similar vocabulary, the ancient Greek and Roman texts make reference to the (necessary) opposition between corruption and integrity in order to identify contradictory opinions regarding vice and virtue in society. When referring to virtues that can be related to our modern sense of integrity, the terms used in Greek and Latin indicate an overlapping of concrete and abstract senses (straight/crooked; altered/unaltered; deteriorated/pure) that deal both with a physical and a moral dimension at the same time. Integrity thus is firmly constructed over a metaphorical use of body imagery which tends to appeal to the merits of purity and untouchability.

---

[78] Arena, 2017, pp. 35–47, at p. 47, see above note 61.

[79] On Cicero's texts, see Thomas N. Mitchell, "Cicero on the moral crisis of the late Republic", in *Hermathena*, 1984, no. 136, pp. 21–41.

[80] Barbara Levick, "Morals, Politics, and the Fall of the Roman Republic", in *Greece and Rome*, 1982, no. 29, pp. 53–62.

[81] Ramsay MacMullen, *Corruption and the Decline of Rome*, Yale University Press, New Haven, 1990, has argued that a key factor in Rome's fall was the steady loss of focus and control over government as its aims were thwarted for private gain by high-ranking bureaucrats and military leaders.

Since uprightness and rectitude were considered appropriate values for citizenship, the original features of 'integrity' were soon enlarged to adopt a strong political background. This new civic setting explains its use as a regular motif in assembly performances, dramatic representations, and judicial activities. In different literary genres – such as oratory, tragedy, comedy or philosophical treatises – Athenian and Roman sources frequently resorted to a rhetorical construction of 'integrity' which relied on the pre-existing positive consideration of moral soundness, truthfulness and honesty, and the need to attribute the opposing standards of spiritual decay to those 'others' who did not share the private and public values endorsed by the community.

It may be true that the original bodily dimension of integrity, which was present in classical Greece and Rome, has been lost today, but the civic use of physical metaphors to describe rectitude or corruption remains in our time. Since the earliest sources, there has been a clear idea in antiquity about the need to eradicate corruption and to challenge litigants, judges or politicians who did not behave according to the principles of justice, righteousness and decency. Authors such as Hesiod, Aristotle or Cicero – to take only some samples – understood the distinction between the private good and the public interest, and were very well aware of the duty to comply with the dictates of high morality when acting publicly.[82]

A final question remains to be addressed: why should we come back to classical sources when dealing with integrity today? First of all, we have to acknowledge that our modern idea of 'integrity' in the Western world depends heavily on its Christian background. The meaning of *integritas* in early Christianity and medieval times still relied on its ancient roots but, contrary to the examples from classical Greece or Republican Rome, soon expanded for religious concerns to cover a mental state of divine grace,

---

[82] Hill, 2013, p. 587, see above note 36. Further reading on ancient corruption should include Wolfgang Schuller (ed.), in *Korruption im Altertum*, R. Oldenbourg Verlag, München/ Wien, 1982; Carine K. Doganis, *Aux origines de la corruption : démocratie et délation en Grèce ancienne*, Presses Universitaires de France, Paris, 2007; Arlene W. Saxonhouse, "Corruption and Justice: The View from Ancient Athens", in William C. Heffernan and John Kleinig (eds.), *Private and Public Corruption*, Rowman & Littlefield, Lanham, 2004, pp. 25–51; and Cristina Rosillo López, *La corruption à la fin de la république romaine (IIᵉ-Iᵉʳ s. av. J.-C.): aspects politiques et financiers*, Franz Steiner, Stuttgart, 2010.

original or restored.[83] In this moral theology based on the Bible – which is the main source allowing to teach and train in righteousness – virtuous and wrong behaviour have been examined through the lens of the compliance with cardinal and theological virtues, and specifically with the commandments.[84]

As presented here, the complex politics of ancient 'integrity' can contribute to overcoming the cultural bias of Christianity and giving a different (more global and less inclined) viewpoint on moral responsibility and elevated standards of ethical behaviour when examining the administration of international justice.[85]

A second argument involves classical debt. In an interesting book recently published, Johanna Hanink argues that contemporary discussions on the Greek crisis have included interesting references to the debt we owe to antiquity, imagined as a symbolic return to the fantasy of a past characterized by exceptional achievements which are very different from our current state of despair.[86] In a hectic twenty-first century, where values seem eroded and morality is said to have been replaced by self-interest and venality, antiquity can still offer a well-founded set of criteria that can serve to identify an alternative discourse to the moral shortfall of contemporary societies.

When the first universal permanent international criminal court was created, the designated location for discussions and negotiation was eternal Rome. Perhaps the international community decided to reappraise the legacy of ancient values and follow their traces. Under the close scrutiny of Zeus or Jupiter, history can provide contemporary judges or politicians

---

[83] On the notion of *integritas* in Ambrose, Augustine and Thomas, see Margaret E. Mohrmann, "Integrity; *Integritas, Innocentia, Simplicitas*", in *Journal of the Society of Christian Ethics*, 2004, vol. 24, no. 2, pp. 25–32.

[84] D. Stephen Long, *Christian Ethics: A Very Short Introduction*, Oxford University Press, Oxford, 2010. On the main concepts involved in Christian moral theology, see James F. Childress and John Macquarrie (eds.), *The Westminster Dictionary of Christian Ethics*, Westminster Press, Philadelphia, 1986.

[85] Bergsmo, 2018, p. 4, see above note 1.

[86] Johanna Hanink, *The Classical Debt. Greek Antiquity in an Era of Austerity*, Belknap Press, Cambridge (MA) and London, 2017. Similarly, Dean Hammer, *Roman Political Thought and the Modern Theoretical Imagination*, University of Oklahoma Press, Norman, 2008, p. 14, deals with ancient Rome and considers that the idealist conception of a Western tradition "saw the world as organized by eternal essences, linked the past with the present, envisioned a progressive conception of historical development, and provided a moral foundation to contemporary conceptions of the state".

with the uppermost standards of moral behaviour. If we feel proud to stand on the shoulders of giants, then we have no option but to live up to their higher ethical aspirations.[87]

---

[87] See Morten Bergsmo, Wolfgang Kaleck, Sam Muller and William H. Wiley, "A Prosecutor Falls, Time for the Court to Rise", FICHL Policy Brief Series No. 86 (2017), Brussels, 2017 (http://www.toaep.org/pbs-pdf/86-four-directors/), pp. 1, 4.

2

Integer Vitae:
Christian Sources and Reflections on
Integrity in Justice

Hanne Sophie Greve[*]

2.1. Introduction

2.1.1. Definition

In his poem "Integer Vitae", Quintus Horatius Flaccus describes his hero as *"Integer vitae scelerisque purus"* – a man of uprightness and stainless integrity".[1] In antiquity, *integer* was not used with the meaning as later given to it. *Integer* means 'whole', 'unimpaired' and 'untouched'. Its specific meaning is evinced by its context. In relation to political activity, it may be read as 'incorruptible', in friendship as 'loyal', and in love as 'faithful'.

I shall here define *integer* to denote a person not lacking in any capacity needed for moral or ethical behaviour in providing justice.

Intellectual virtues – the five ways the soul arrives at truth by affirmation or denial – make the human mind a more efficient instrument of knowledge and promote intellectual flourishing, critical thinking and the pursuit of truth. The three speculative intellectual virtues are understanding, scientific knowledge and wisdom. The two practical ones are art and practical wisdom.

A measure of intellectual virtues is an 'obvious' requirement for legal office. I will pay no further attention to them, as my focus is moral or ethical behaviour in providing justice.

---

[*]   **Hanne Sophie Greve** is Vice President of the Gulating High Court, Norway, and member of the International Commission against the Death Penalty. She has previously served, *inter alia*, as an Expert in the UN Commission of Experts for the Former Yugoslavia established pursuant to UN Security Council resolution 780 (1992) (1993–94); and Judge at the European Court of Human Rights (1998–2004). She has served as UNHCR Assistant Protection Officer (1979–1981, Bangkok), and as a mediator for the UN Transitional Authority in Cambodia (1992–beginning of 1993, Phnom Penh). She has had several consultancies in and lectured extensively on international law (human rights, refugee law, law of war and criminal justice).

[1]   Quintus Horatius Flaccus (Horace), "Integer Vitae", in *Odes*, Book 1, 23 BC.

2.1.2. Ethics

> So God created man in his own image, in the image of God
> created he him; male and female created he them.[2]

Thus, the extraordinary simplicity and absolute complexity of our shared human existence. The human person partakes of the divine nature of God by the act of creation. In this, all human beings are equals and the human worth is inherent. Human plurality has the dual character of equality and distinction.

Human life is a conditioned reality. The individual is a party to conditioning her or his own circumstances, and a party to conditioning the circumstances of fellow human beings.

Each person is both 'self' and 'the other'. I am both I and – in relation to everyone else – I am the Other, You. For a human being to be mindful of the human condition and to understand the reality of life is to recognise her or his dual character as living as a human being among humans – all subjects.

The Golden Rule – "Do unto others as if you were the others" – is the epitome of ethical action articulated in almost every religion and culture.[3]

Normative ethics is concerned with developing moral standards that regulate right and wrong conduct. Virtue ethics are one of the oldest normative traditions in Western civilization.

2.2. Basic Concepts

2.2.1. Human Faculties

Human faculties are abilities. The four human faculties contributing to our moral acts are:

- the intellect;
- the will;
- the appetite of desire; and
- the appetite of aversion.

---

[2] Genesis 1:27, King James Version (the publisher's preferred version). An alternative translation from the English Standard Version and the Revised Standard version reads as follows: "So God created man in his own image, in the image of God he created him; male and female he created them".

[3] In the Bible referred to in Leviticus 19:18, Matthew 7:12 and Luke 6:31.

2.2.2. Controlling Powers

Each of these four faculties is in need of corresponding controlling powers to keep them straight:

- prudence for the mind;
- justice for the will;
- temperance for the urge to what is pleasant; and
- fortitude for the instinct away from what is painful.

Their functions can be summarised as: look around, act, keep away from, and bear up with. For the controlling powers, Thomas Aquinas invented the word 'virtue' from '*vir*' – man – and '*vis*' – power.[4]

The Scriptures have several words for virtue signifying strength or power, might, moral excellence or perfection. Moral virtue is true, honourable, upright and pure.

Virtue ethics emphasise education to develop good habits of character. Human virtues are firm attitudes, habitual perfections of intellect and will that govern our actions, order our passions and guide our conduct according to reason inclining it towards the Good. Habits reside in the faculties as stable dispositions that prompt the faculties to act with ease and dexterity in a certain way.

Aristotle was the basic source on which Aquinas built the structure of the core virtues – four due to the objective order of morality. The mind must first discover this order and propose its commands to the will; prudence, or the habit of doing the right thing at the right time, is reason's helper. The will, in turn, must execute the commands that are justice, or the habit of giving every person her or his due. Temperance helps the will to control the appetite's desires, and fortitude aids to manage the same appetite's aversions.

A person is virtuous because her or his actions correspond to an objective norm that for Aristotle was knowable by reason and for Aquinas by reason and faith. Aquinas represents the backbone of an ethical system that believes that God and religious values are primary, and that true goodness is to be measured in terms of an ultimate finality, reasoned by the human being's natural intellect and fully possessed on the basis of Christianity.

---

[4] Thomas Aquinas, *Summa Theologica*, Fathers of the English Dominican Province (trans.), Notre Dame, IN, 1981 [1265-1274].

2.3. The Cardinal Virtues

The root of 'cardinal' is the Latin word *cardo*, meaning 'hinge' – the device on which a door turns. To be 'cardinal' means to belong to the very nature of a thing so that it cannot be removed without destroying the thing or its character.

There are four cardinal virtues – prudence, justice, temperance and fortitude. All other moral virtues can be subsumed under them as being their potential parts.

A moral virtue is a certain habit of the faculty of choice, consisting of a mean suitable to our nature and fixed by reason in the manner in which a prudent person would fix it. A moral virtue does not offend against right reason by excess or by defect. What is needed is a reasonable balance between behaviouristic extremes. Virtue ethics advocate that a person should avoid acquiring bad character traits or vices. To find the mean between extremes, the human being needs reason's assistance.

For Aristotle, a human being is virtuous when displaying a beautiful balance in the person's moral actions, not unlike the harmony in a work of art. Christianity added new dimensions of morality. Internal dispositions and their consequent actions are virtuous because they advance their possessor in the direction of her or his final destiny to eternal life. Virtue, moreover, postulates a primal obligation to a divine Lawgiver, whose will is manifest in conscience and faith, and to whom obedience is due as the human being's Creator and God.

2.3.1. Prudence

Prudence treads a careful path. The human existence is conditioned. Moral reflections have to take into consideration whatever such confines. One needs to seek harmony of agent, conduct and environment.

Prudence is "right reason in action", writes Aquinas.[5] Prudence is the virtue that disposes practical reason to discern our true Good in every circumstance and to choose the right means of achieving it.

The functions of prudence have been summarised in the word *circumspice* – to look around and to look for, to survey, to inspect, to search for, to examine and to ponder. That is, to seek the necessary insight to make the appropriate choices. 'Appropriate' means taking into consideration the

---

[5]   *Ibid.*, II-II, q. 47, a. 2

reality of the human existence, every human being created in the image of God, ordained for a divine order. Prudence guides the judgment of conscience.

Prudence is called 'the charioteer of the virtues' because it steers the other virtues by setting rule and measure.[6]

The principal act of prudence is the practical executive command of right reason. Within its orbit come good counsel and sound judgment, *and* the ability to deal with exceptional cases.

Prudence as such is not in search of a mean between behaviouristic extremes. The core is that prudence has to be utilised within a reasonable time considering the circumstances. Developing the habit of applying right reason – reaching the understanding needed for the correct choices – is what is sought for. Prudence may, nevertheless, be construed as a mean between being insensible and overly thorough.

2.3.2.   Justice

My focus here is the cardinal virtue known as 'justice'. 'Justice' and 'integrity in international justice' are not interchangeable.

The functions of the cardinal virtue 'justice' is summarised in the word *age* – to act, to live, to work, to deal with and to defend a cause. It is, moreover, deliberate inactivity such as to wait and to restrain. Justice is premeditated human behaviour.

First, there is prudence – light for the mind, both of principles and practical knowledge – and then there must be rectitude for the will to have it tend naturally to the Good as defined by reason. Justice is the moral virtue that consists in the constant and firm will to give everyone their due, and to establish in human relationships the harmony that promotes equity with regard to persons and to the common Good.

The Scriptures frequently refer to 'the just person' as being distinguished by habitual right thinking and the uprightness of her or his conduct toward fellow human beings.

The one innate right of every human being is freedom, the freedom that is compatible with the freedom of everyone else. The virtue of justice must imply that one acts to promote the freedom of every human being by working for the three main – and intertwined – common Goods as known

---

[6]   *Ibid.*

to human societies: security, human flourishing and social cohesion. To secure these common Goods, there has to be vindication when an injury has been done.

Attributes to justice such as decency and fidelity have a role to play as well. For the virtue of justice, there is a mean – too much or too little is injustice.

2.3.3. Temperance

"Go not after thy lusts, but refrain thyself from thine appetites."[7] The New Testament refers to temperance as 'moderation' or 'sobriety'.

The functions of temperance are summarised in the word *abstine* – to keep away from, to hold or retain, to abstain or renounce and to moderate oneself.

For temperance in particular, Aristotle's view of the aesthetic harmony of agent, conduct and environment, is evident. However, in the Christian understanding, temperance more importantly responds to a primal obligation to the divine Lawgiver and the natural order for His creation – humankind.

Temperance is the moral virtue that moderates the attraction of pleasures – hereunder personal gains and advantages – and provides balance in the use of created goods. It ensures the will's mastery over instincts and keeps desires within the limits of what is honourable.

2.3.4. Fortitude

Per ardua – through adversity.

A key characteristic of the human condition is its frailty. The human being is vulnerable in every respect. It is deeply human to fear adversity and danger. As for international justice, many are the applicants and witnesses who have made immense sacrifices and taken huge risks to contribute to the reign of justice. Humankind has a right to demand the needed fortitude or courage from every person involved in administering international justice. Courage keeps the balance between cowardice and reckless daring.

Fortitude ensures firmness in difficulties and constancy in the pursuit of the Good. Fortitude strengthens the resolve to surmount obstacles and

---

[7] Sirach 18:30. An alternative translation from the *New Jerusalem Bible: Standard Edition* reads as follows: "Do not be governed by your passions, restrain your desires".

enables the person to defeat fear. The functions of fortitude may be summarised in the word *sustine* – to bear up with and endure, to hold in check and to sustain. Confidence is part of fortitude as is the patience that keeps an unconquered spirit.

2.4. The Theological Virtues

The Greek list of virtues has been supplemented with three Christian ones: faith, hope and charity. These theological virtues have God for their origin, their motive and their object. God known by faith, God hoped in, and loved for His own sake. They inform the moral virtues and give them life. That is, the grace of God animates and enhances the moral virtues as well – the virtues cardinal in human conduct, but penultimate and subordinate to the final end of human beings as created in the image of God. The theological virtues bring the ethics of the Genesis into full understanding. Aquinas believes that a person in the state of grace, or divine friendship, possesses certain enduring powers, the infused virtues and gifts, that raise her or him to an orbit of a superior existence and that give abilities of thought and operation that are of God. An approach distinctively theological but strongly conversant with philosophy. The theological virtues have a centre of gravity – a mean in the sense that a human being should exercise these virtues according to the measure of her or his condition. Aquinas teaches that the theological virtues faith, hope and charity correspond in the supernatural order to natural knowledge, hope and love.

2.4.1. Faith

Faith is the theological virtue by which we believe in God. By faith, the human being freely commits itself to God and seeks to know and do God's will. Natural law as dictated by human nature – the eternal law – is instilled in the human being as endowed with reason, and is inclining the person towards its right action and end. Aquinas argues that divine wisdom's conception has the character of 'law' insofar as it moves all things to their appropriate ends. The gift of faith should not be deprived of hope and charity. The gift of faith is intertwined with, or rather it is, *meaning* – the meaning of the human existence and the natural order.

2.4.2. Hope

Life is change, constant change – it is unpredictable. The first Christians depicted hope as an anchor fixed to the shores beyond, to God. Hope is a source of life, but different from optimism, or merely a positive attitude. Hope is the humblest of the three theological virtues. It frequently remains rather invisible. In hope, we place trust in Christ's promises and rely not merely on our own strength, but on the help of the grace of the Holy Spirit. Hope changes us from within. It changes our attitudes. The virtue of hope teaches us that no human being is ever beyond hope. The virtue of hope responds to the human aspiration to happiness and inspires human activities. It keeps the human being from despair and upholds the person during times of abandonment.

2.4.3. Charity

Charity is the theological virtue by which we love God above all things for His own sake, and our neighbour – every other human being – as ourselves for the love of God. All other virtues are animated and inspired by charity that binds everything together in perfect harmony. Charity is superior to all other virtues. "And now abideth faith, hope, charity, these three; but the greatest of these is charity."[8]

2.5. Some Concluding Remarks

Justice is crucial for society to be able to provide security, human flourishing and social cohesion. Justice cannot be dissociated from these overarching purposes. Integrity cannot be about me only – it materialises in a context where I have to see the Other in the light of hope and charity as well. Integrity – as justice – is embedded in the human condition and our shared human reality. One may not be fully able to describe the plurality of virtues that come together in integrity – but we recognize them when we see them. It is immediately recognisable when these virtues are lacking as well. It is not the oath that makes us believe the person, but the person who makes us believe the oath. When Solomon inherited his father David's great kingdom, God asked him what gift he would want. It was neither more power nor greater wealth. Solomon asked for a listening heart, so that he could be able to make good decisions.[9]

---

[8] 1 Corinthians 13:13. Another translation would be: "As it is, these three remain: faith, hope and love, the three of them; and the greatest of them is love".

[9] 1 Kings 3:9.

3

Shari'ah Sources and Reflections on Integrity

Adel Maged[*]

> He who is entrusted with the function of a judge, is slaughtered without a knife.[1]

3.1. Introduction

In most nations, judges, and other judicial officials, such as prosecutors, play a vital role in dispensing justice and upholding the rule of law. As illustrated in the Bangalore Principles of Judicial Conduct:

> A judiciary of undisputed integrity is the bedrock institution essential for ensuring compliance with democracy and the rule of law. Even when all other protections fail, it provides a bul-

---

[*]   **Adel Maged** is the Judge and Vice President of the Egyptian Court of Cassation (Criminal Chambers). He was appointed Public Prosecutor in April 1987, and served as a Judge at the Courts of First Instance, Chief Prosecutor at the Criminal Division of the Court of Cassation, Judge at the Egyptian Court of Appeals, and for several years on secondment to the Ministry of Justice of the United Arab Emirates as a Legal Advisor on International Law and Treatise. Justice Maged is also a lecturer in criminal law and criminal procedural law at the Faculty of _Shari'ah_ and Law, al-Azhar University in Cairo, and founding member of the research group 'Islám, Law and Modernity' at Durham Law School. He has advised the ICC Office of the Prosecutor and the Arab League of States on international criminal law issues. His publications include books and articles, in Arabic and English, on international criminal law, Islámic law, justice reform, transitional justice, combating extremism, terrorism and combating human trafficking. He holds a Bachelor of Law from Alexandria University; LL.M. on Internationalization of Crime and Criminal Justice from Utrecht University; and a Diploma on International Law and Organisation for Development from the Institute of Social Studies, The Hague. The author thanks co-editor Morten Bergsmo for his conceptual input. The author also thanks Fathi M. Abdelraouf Ahmed, Arabic translator and reviser, for his advice on the translation of the Caliphs' Letters on the Judiciary referred to in this chapter, and Ms. Rawan Maged, Bachelor of Political Science, the American University in Cairo and LL.B. Cairo University, for her research assistance. TOAEP has adopted the Transliteration System approved at the 10th International Congress of Orientalists held in Geneva in 1894, and that has been implemented here for Arabic terms to the extent feasible.

[1]   Al-Tirmidhi, _Sunan al-Tirmidhi_, Sheikh Saleh Al-Sheikh (ed.), Saudi Ministry of Islamic Affairs, Dawah and Guidance, _hadith_ no. 1325, p. 321.

---

wark to the public against any encroachments on rights and freedoms under the law.[2]

From the earliest times, in all cultural and religious traditions, the judge has been perceived as an individual of high moral stature, possessing qualities distinct from those of ordinary individuals and is subject to more rigorous constraints than others. Thus, judges are required to observe a form of life different from that of the rest of the community, in order to preserve their integrity.[3] Accordingly, in discharging their judicial duties, judges should adhere to a combination of values and characteristics that are essential for the very legitimacy of the judicial function. Judges should perform their functions with integrity, impartiality and independence as well as diligence.[4] This approach has been asserted in various documents of the United Nations ('UN') and other respected organisations. For the purposes of this chapter, and without prejudice, two documents have singled out for particular consideration, namely the Bangalore Principles of Judicial Conduct[5] and the Bangalore Draft Code of Judicial Conduct of 2002.[6] These principles are articulated around six basic values and qualities: 'independence', 'impartiality', 'integrity', 'propriety', 'equality', and 'competence and diligence'.

It is recognised at both the international and domestic levels that integrity is essential for the proper discharge of the judicial office.[7] A judicial system which operates without regard to professional ethics standards is unable to build and retain public trust in the fairness and objectivity of its decisions and outcomes.

---

[2]   United Nations Office on Drugs and Crime ('UNODC'), *Commentary on the Bangalore Principles of Judicial Conduct*, Vienna, 2011, p. 5.

[3]   *Ibid.*, p. 117.

[4]   UNODC, *Resource Guide on Strengthening Judicial Integrity and Capacity*, Vienna, 2007, p. 127.

[5]   Basic Principles on the Independence of the Judiciary, adopted by the Seventh United Nations Congress on the Prevention of Crime and the Treatment of Offenders held at Milan from 26 August to 6 September 1985 and endorsed by General Assembly resolutions 40/32 of 29 November 1985 and 40/146 of 13 December 1985 (https://www.legal-tools.org/doc/rnabsy/).

[6]   The Bangalore Draft Code of Judicial Conduct of 2001, adopted by the Judicial Group on Strengthening Judicial Integrity, as revised at the Round Table Meeting of Chief Justices held at the Peace Palace, The Hague, November 25–26, 2002 ('Bangalore Principles of Judicial Conduct') (https://www.legal-tools.org/doc/xwake8/).

[7]   *Ibid.*, Value 3.

From a practitioner's point of view, judicial integrity is a key judicial value and comes at the heart of the judicial profession. However, it should be noted that the responsibilities and the public's perception of the standards of integrity to which judges should adhere to are continuously evolving.[8] Therefore, it is important to understand the sources and pillars of integrity from different perspectives.

In the Muslim world, religion has great influence, not only on the societal attitudes, but also on the legal system governing their relations with each other.[9] In the early Islamic era, and recently in some Arab and Islamic countries, Muslim judges have rendered decisions according to the provisions of *Sharí'ah*.

As one of the main legal traditions of humanity, *Sharí'ah* emphasises the notion of justice, highly regards the judicial function, and supports judicial integrity. In general, *Sharí'ah* allocates special attention to justice and addresses the judicial traditions and ethics required to uphold the rule of law. Captivatingly, *Sharí'ah* provides detailed provisions on judicial ethics that regulate the conduct of judges in a precise manner that could be considered as an 'Islamic Code of Judicial Ethics'.[10] The provisions of such code are strewn in different (primary) sources of *Sharí'ah*: Qur'án,[11] Sunnah,[12] Ijmā[13] and Qiyās.[14]

---

[8] Courts and Tribunals Judiciary, "Guide to Judicial Conduct – Revised March 2018 (Updated March 2020)", *Judiciary UK* (available on its web site).

[9] *Sharí'ah*, in general terms, also contains the rules by which the Muslim nation, in the broadest sense of the word, is organised, and it provides all the means necessary for resolving conflicts among individuals, between individuals and the state, as well as between the states themselves.

[10] Various justice systems have drafted Codes of Judicial Conduct. In some Member States, violations of the code may result in sanctions, including in Italy and in the United States (both at the federal and state levels). In other Member States, the codes of judicial conduct are not conceived as a set of enforceable rules, but rather as an ideal guide of judicial behaviour.

[11] The *Qur'án* is the words of God conveyed to the people by his Messenger (Prophet Muhammad (ﷺ), the earliest and the central religious text of Islám. Many Western scholars consider the *Qur'án* – in addition to containing timeless moral and spiritual injections – as a rich repository of guidance on real-life situations, with injunctions regulating a vast field, that also covers rules on adjudication and the responsibility of the judiciary. See, for example, Onder Bakircioglu, "The Principal Sources of Islamic Law", in Tallyn Gray (ed.), *Islam and International Criminal Law and Justice*, Torkel Opsahl Academic EPublisher, Brussels, 2018, p. 20.

[12] The *Sunnah* is Prophetic *hadíth* (sayings) as well as practices and deeds attributed to the Prophet Mohammad, that were narrated to us via the Prophet's companions and their succes-

Both the *Qur'án* and the *Sunnah* are the principal primary sources of *Sharí'ah*.[15] Noticeably, *Sharí'ah*'s jurisprudence (*fiqh*)[16] has vividly assembled and interpreted those provisions to formulate such code. As we will see below, early-classical Muslim jurists require 'extra judicial qualities' more than the 'standard criteria' embedded in national and international instruments for the appointment in judicial positions, and integrity comes at the top of this list of qualities. In fact, integrity in *Sharí'ah* is a legally binding requirement to be able to serve as a judge.

An international high-ranking civil servant has noted that "while there are neutral countries, there are no neutral men".[17] In this chapter, I argue that in Islamic traditions such men do exist. We will see examples of judges who disobeyed great rulers to protect their integrity and independence, without any regard of indebtedness towards anyone.

---

sors. The *Sunnah* constitutes the normative pattern of life established by the Prophet Muhammad (ﷺ). The *Sunnah* in the form of *hadíth* is supplementary to the *Qur'án* itself. It helps to explain and clarify the *Qur'án* and provides practical applications of its teachings.

13   *Ijmá'* is the consensus of the Companion of the Prophet and later on the Muslim jurists on a certain issue.

14   *Qiyás* (analogy) is a recognised source of *Sharí'ah* that can be utilised by Muslim jurists and scholars to reach legal norms.

15   For more information, see Adel Maged, "The Impact of Religion on Military Self-Interest in Accountability: A *Sharí'ah* Perspective", in Morten Bergsmo and SONG Tianying (eds.), *Military Self-Interest in Accountability for Core International Crimes*, Torkel Opsahl Academic Publisher, Brussels, 2015, pp. 141–166 (http://www.toaep.org/ps-pdf/25-bergsmo-song-second).

16   *Fiqh* is a process by means of which jurists derive sets of guidelines, rules and regulations from the rulings laid down in the *Qur'án* and the teachings and living example of the Prophet Muhammad (ﷺ), the *Sunnah*. The science of *fiqh* is a discipline, intellectual-methodological application, and a set of tools for other sciences that is used to reach rulings in *Sharí'ah* questions, mostly through *ijtihád*. Over the centuries, *fiqh* has been formulated and elaborated upon by successive generations of learned jurists, through interpretation, analogy, consensus and disciplined research. While the principles of the *Qur'án* and the *Sunnah* are permanent, it is the nature of Islámic jurisprudence to facilitate for human beings the application of those principles to their daily-life activities and dealings. In other words, *Sharí'ah fiqh* is the human understanding and implementation of *Sharí'ah* and the process by which Muslim jurists (*fuqaha*) extract legal rulings (*ahkam*) from the primary sources of Islám (*Qur'án, Sunnah, Ijmá and Qiyás*). It encompasses the vast corpus of juristic scholarship and jurisprudential texts produced by early and modern Muslim jurists.

17   See Morten Bergsmo, Wolfgang Kaleck, Alexander Muller and William H. Wiley, "A Prosecutor Falls, Time for the Court to Rise", FICHL Policy Brief Series no. 86 (2017), Torkel Opsahl Academic Publisher, Brussels, 2017, p. 4 (https://www.toaep.org/pbs-pdf/86-four-directors/).

Moreover, one will be surprised to know the strict conditions *Sha-ri'ah* requires of a person to be appointed in the judiciary. The wealth of information that Islamic jurisprudence provides on different aspects of judges' qualities and the abundance of books and chapters that were written by early-classical Muslim jurists are also remarkable. These sources should have a significant impact on the emerging body of judicial ethics that govern the administration of justice at the international level.

Some contemporary Western scholars consider integrity as 'moral character', and they refer to Articles 36(3)(a) and 42(3) of the Rome Statute of the International Criminal Court ('ICC Statute') to support this view.[18] Indeed, such characterisation converges with *Shari'ah* sources, which also recognise it as 'moral character', reflecting an 'ethical value' required for those who occupy judicial office. Accordingly, a judge or prosecutor who has such 'saintly character' lifts the entire institution, and underpins public confidence in the judiciary. This is where spirituality and justice meet, and this, I fear, has not been a priority in international criminal justice since the 1990s.

Some Western scholars have raised concerns about alleged integrity problems within the current international justice system,[19] especially after the announcement made by the International Criminal Court Bar Association ('ICCBA') of "serious allegations of improper and potentially illegal activity by former ICC Prosecutor Luis Moreno-Ocampo".[20] This chapter is designed to introduce the basic *Shari'ah* concepts that govern judicial integrity to Western readers, and support the ongoing efforts that aim to consolidate the concept in the international justice system, in accordance with the highest applicable standards of integrity in different legal traditions. These efforts are important for more reasons than what may first meet the eye. It would be unwise to underestimate the significance of integrity in the ranks of high officials of international criminal justice among the populations in mainly-Muslim countries, as well as other societies that may seem more 'traditional' (combined, these countries may well represent more than half the world's population).

---

[18] *Ibid.*, p. 3.

[19] *Ibid.*, p. 2.

[20] ICCBA Statement on Allegations Against Former ICC Prosecutor, 29 November 2017.

3.2. Methodology

It is admitted among the majority of Western legal scholars that there is no consensus on the meaning of judicial integrity, nor on its functioning in practice. Conspicuously, some contend that integrity discourses differ from one jurisdiction to another, and that the meaning of the term itself, differs significantly per profession and, in the case of judges, per jurisdiction.[21] This has had a great impact on the comprehension and the adoption of the term at the international level. The term has not yet been comprehensively addressed in a single document issued by existing international courts.

To address this loophole, I will revisit *Shari'ah* sources to see how they approach the judiciary in general, and, specifically, how they address the concept of judicial integrity. Hence, I will carefully inquire into those sources to explore whether *Shari'ah* is a norm of its own or a holistic concept that encompasses other norms and/or values; and examine whether integrity is a legally binding requirement and a prerequisite quality for a person to assume the judicial position. This requires delving into early-classical and original literature by eminent *Shari'ah* jurists (hereafter, 'classical *Shari'ah* literature'), as experience has proven that intermediary references on *Shari'ah*, especially those written in non-Arabic languages, may not have authenticity and confidence, and could disrupt the real meaning of the original sources, or at least "evaporate their authentic aroma".[22] Unfortunately, the intermediary non-Arabic literature on *Shari'ah* very often cannot fully convey the letter and spirit of the text to the reader. Accordingly, it is preferable for those who research *Shari'ah*'s sources and jurisprudence (*fiqh*) to have an excellent command of the Arabic language and to be well acquainted with *Shari'ah* sciences in order to be able to search and interpret provisions in accordance with required scholarly standards. As we will see below, there is *ijmā'* among Muslim jurists that one who practices *ijtihād*[23] should be skilful in the Arabic language, as the original sources of *Shari'ah* are in Arabic. Unfortunately, a very small portion of the tools of knowledge required for *ijtihād* is available in other languages.

---

[21] See Jonathan Soeharno, "Is judicial integrity a norm? An inquiry into the concept of judicial integrity in England and the Netherlands", in *Utrecht Law Review*, vol. 3, no. 1, 2007, p. 8.

[22] Jeffrey Einboden, *Nineteenth-Century U.S. Literature in Middle Eastern Languages*, Edinburgh University Press, 2013, p. 55.

[23] *Ijtihād* is an individual and independent juristic reasoning exercised to provide answers to legal or other religious questions that there is no basis in the *Qur'ān* and *Sunnah*.

Despite my excellent command of the Arabic language, one challenge that I encountered when I decided to write on this topic was to identify the best methodology, through which I can convey to the Western readers the correct *Sharī'ah* jurisprudential terminology, norms and rules that address the topic of judicial integrity.

To ensure credibility of my work, this chapter mainly relies on classical *Sharī'ah* literature, including learned treatises written by eminent *Sharī'ah* jurists in Arabic. However, I would like to mention that the religious texts addressing the topic in *Sharī'ah* sources are written in classical, eloquent Arabic, enriched with metaphors, orthodox terms, and complex expressions that are, sometimes, difficult to comprehend, even for a proficient Arabic speaker. Moreover, Arabic words can have a variety of different meanings depending on the context, and didactical symbols used in the Arabic language can change the meaning of a word significantly. Therefore, to ensure that I transfer the correct meaning of the religious texts from Arabic into English, I have consulted on the meaning and translation of those texts with translation experts and Islamic scholars to ensure accuracy and that the translation is reliable and close to the original.

My focus in this chapter will be on the following classical *Sharī'ah* sources that are considered to be the principal references for those interested in studying the central rules of adjudication and judicial ethics in *Sharī'ah*:

1. The Message of Caliph Umar Ibn Al-Khaṭṭáb on the Judiciary,[24] which is considered a judges' charter and an Islamic code of judicial conduct.[25] Early-classical *Sharī'ah* jurists called it "the judges' policy" and "the judicial constitution".[26]

2. The Message of Alī Ibn Abī Ṭālib, the fourth of the rightly-guided Caliphs, to Mālik Al-Ashtar on the Judiciary, in which he instructed

---

[24] See Appendix I for further details. To review the original texts of the Message in Arabic, see Imam Al-Mawardi, *Al-Ahkam as-Sultaniyyah*, Ahmad Mubarak Al-Baghdadi (ed.), Dar Ibn Qutaibah, Kuwait, 1989, pp. 95–96; Ibn Khaldun, *Muqaddimah Ibn Khaldun*, Abdallah Muhammad al-Darwish (ed.), first edition, Dar Yareb, Damascus, 2004, vol. 1, pp. 402–403.

[25] The message of Umar Ibn al-Khattab on the Judiciary is known among Muslim scholars as the first comprehensive Islámic directive on the judiciary. Many consider it as the basis of a functional Islámic judicial system and at the same time the code of conduct of judges, as it gave comprehensive instructions in regard of conduct of al-*qāḍī*.

[26] Al-Shahīd Al-Sadr, *sharh Adab Al-Qāḍī Al-Khaṣṣāf* (Commentary on *Adab Al-Qāḍī* by Al-Khaṣṣāf), Mohie Eldien Sarhan (ed.), first edition, Iraqi Ministry of Endowments and Religious Affairs, Baghdād, 1977, vol. 1, pp. 213–214.

him of the qualities that he should observe when selecting a person to act as a judge.[27]

3. Reliable *hadíth* reports, which were narrated by the Prophet's companions and underwent a rigorous process of authentication, for example, the commentaries on the *Sunnah*, written by eminent classical *Sharí'ah* jurists such as Sahih Muslim and Sunnan Abī Dāwūd.

4. The renowned Islamic jurisprudential exegesis on *Adab Al-Qāḍī*, referred to in some contemporary Western literature, in the English language, as 'etiquette of the judge', written by early eminent Muslim jurists, for example, Imam Al-Khaṣṣāf,[28] Imam Al-Ṭabarī[29] and Imam Ibn Abī' Al-Dam.[30]

Obviously, reference will also be made to relevant verses of the *Qur'án*. Yet, we have to bear in mind that the *Qur'án* is written in a highly symbolic and classical, eloquent form of the Arabic language. Accordingly, translating verses of the *Qur'án* requires a profound understanding of its meaning and an ability to reflect those meanings into English. As a matter of fact, due to the sacred nature of the *Qur'án*, all translation attempts are considered interpretations of the meanings, rather than an actual translation

---

[27] See Appendix II for further details. To review the original texts of the Message in Arabic, see Alī Al-Salaby, *Alī Ibn Abī Ṭālib: shaghsyaton wa asroh* (Alī Ibn Abī Ṭālib: His Personality and Era), in *History of Rashid Caliph Series*, Maktabat Al-Sahaba, UAE, 2004, vol. 2, p. 369. This Letter is to be considered as an original reference for those who study *Sharí'ah* jurisprudence, and is found under 'Letter 53' of the famous *Nahj al-Balāgha* collection (The way of Eloquence), which contains 240 sermons given by Caliph Alī Ibn Abī Ṭālib dealing with a wide variety of topics including human existence, relationship with God, building a God-fearing personality, and other reflections upon historical incidents.

[28] Imam Abú Bakr Aḥmad Ibn Umar Ibn Mahir al-Shaybānī, known as Al-Khaṣṣāf, an early-classical Muslim scholar, belongs to the *Hanafite* School of *fiqh*, and author of voluminous compendiums of early Islámic history.

[29] Imam Ahmmad Ibn Abi Ahmmad Abú Abbas Al-Ṭabarī, known as Ibn Al-Kāss, an early-classical Muslim scholar, belongs to the *Shāfi* School of *fiqh*, and author of large compendiums of early Islámic history and *Qur'ānic* exegesis.

[30] Imam Abū Ishāq Shihāb Al-Dīn Ibrāhīm Ibn 'Abd Allāh al-Ḥamawī, better known as Ibn Abī' Al-Dam , an early-classical Muslim scholar, belongs to *Shāfi'ī* School of Islámic *fiqh*, and was the chief Islámic judge in his native Ḥamāt, Syria. F. Rosenthal, "Ibn Abī' Al-Dam", in P. Bearman, Th. Bianquis, C.E. Bosworth, E. van Donzel and W.P. Heinrichs (eds.), *Encyclopedia of Islám*, second edition, Brill Academic, 1986.

of the holy text. Hence, I will try my best to simplify the meaning of its verses to the reader, without disrupting its original connotations.[31]

3.3. *Adab Al-Qāḍī*: A Comprehensive Resource in <u>Shar</u>íʻah on the Judiciary

Adab Al-Qāḍī refers to a compendium of early-classical Islamic jurisprudential literature written by renowned Muslim jurists belonging to all Islamic schools of thought. The authors of *Adab Al-Qāḍī* gathered and commented on various legal and judicial issues in light of the primary sources of <u>Shar</u>íʻah, with detailed explanation, in accordance with established rules of research in Islamic *fiqh*.

Adab Al-Qāḍī is an important original jurisprudential source of <u>Sha</u>ríʻah that studies in depth the institution and discipline of judgeship in Muslim societies. It expounds the basic principles of the Islamic judicial system and the function of the judiciary, for instance, court proceedings, litigations, and the taking of testimony. It also addresses issues related to the qualifications and qualities of the judges,[32] their appointment, and removal from office. It goes further to explore the relationship between *al-qāḍī* and a ruler, and sheds some light on judicial integrity questions, such as the nature of judgeship, the manners and propriety of judges, in particular, what they must do, what they may do, what is forbidden to them, and what is abhorred. Noticeably, it covers the ethics and conduct of judges and is designed to enable judges to administer justice on the foundations of <u>Shar</u>íʻah sources.[33]

Indeed, early-classical Muslim jurists have left great treasures of legal knowledge, awaiting to be explored. The wealth of knowledge on *al-qāḍī* behaviour in his daily life and conduct while undertaking his judicial function that *Adab Al-Qāḍī* presents is broad, comprehensive and needs more in-depth research. Each treatise is interspersed with actual cases and models that cover these topics. As stated in one contemporary English

---

[31]   The author used several translations of the *Qurʼán* on a case-by-case basis depending on his agreement on the strategy used in transferring the meaning of each verse.

[32]   Ibn Abī Al-Dam, *Adab Al-Qāḍī*, 1984, first edition, Iraqi Ministry of Endowments and Religious Affairs, Baghdād, vol. 1, p. 6.

[33]   *Ibid.*, pp. 136–137.

source commending *Adab Al-Qāḍī*: "It is important for the wealth of materials it offers the practitioner in terms of both procedures and substance".[34]

3.4. Methodological Consideration Regarding the Meaning of *Adab Al-Qāḍī*

Some authors have endeavoured to write commentaries on *Adab Al-Qāḍī* in contemporary Western scholarship. However, some have committed a methodological mistake by referring to *Adab Al-Qāḍī* as "etiquette of the judge". Unfortunately, this translation does not reflect the true meaning or the content and subject-matter of *Adab Al-Qāḍī*.

In classical Arabic dictionaries, the word '*adab*' has two connotations. First, in literature which mainly refers to the products of the human-thinking in different fields of knowledge. In other words, it refers to sophisticated collections of spoken and written works on certain or particular subjects, that may be classified according to a variety of systems and fields of knowledge, which are deemed to have artistic or intellectual value.[35] It may also refer to articulated works of poetry and prose of lasting artistic merits, which require the knowledge of Arabic and *Sharī'ah* sciences.[36] Second, literally, it means politeness and propriety.[37] In his renowned Arabic dictionary *al- Qamous al-Muheet*, al-Fairūzābādī refers to the word '*adab*' as "good manners".[38]

Adab Al-Qāḍī refers to sophisticated collections and literature written on the art of adjudication that focus on the conduct of *Al-Qāḍī*. As one authority explained, *Adab Al-Qāḍī* refers to a "compendium of the principles of adjudications". Therefore, the title *Adab Al-Qāḍī* does not reflect only the etiquette or manners of *al-qāḍī*, but it covers different branches of sciences related to the judiciary and legal proceedings before the courts.

Linguistically, the word 'etiquette' in English literature refers to a set of rules or customs for polite behaviour in particular in social groups or

---

[34] Chibli Mallat, "Comparative Law and the Islámic (Middle Eastern) Legal Culture", in Mathias Reimann and Reinhard Zimmermann (eds.), *The Oxford Handbook of Comparative Law*, second edition, Oxford University Press, 2019, p. 630.

[35] See Al-Waseet Dictionary, second edition, Arabic Language Academy, vol. 2, 1985, pp. 9–10.

[36] See Ibn Khaldun, 2004, vol. 2, p. 376, see above note 24.

[37] *Ibid.*, pp. 9–10.

[38] Al-Fairūzābādī, *Al- Qamous al-Muheet*, third edition, The General Egyptian Book Organisation, vol. 1, 1977, p. 36.

social situations, or, in other words, as stipulated in *Encyclopaedia Britannica*, a system of rules and conventions that regulate social and professional behaviour.[39] Such a system is usually built and formulated on social rubrics, which are changing and subject to alteration, while *Adab Al-Qāḍī* represents permanent values that find their roots in established *Sharí'ah* sources, which have a divine nature.[40] As has been shown, "etiquette of the judge" is an incorrect translation of *Adab Al-Qāḍī* both in literal meaning and in scope.

3.5. The Concept of Judicial Integrity?

As mentioned above, behind the single word 'integrity' lurks several distinct issues and values that could be disentangled. As will be shown later, according to its meaning in the classical Arabic language and in *Sharí'ah*, the concept of judicial integrity is a holistic notion that covers various judicial qualities. Hence, after explaining the meaning of the concept in the Arabic language and in *Sharí'ah*, I will distinguish its various components, which reflect respected values and qualities. Then I will address each of them from a *Sharí'ah* perspective. To show the extent to which *Sharí'ah* rules on judicial integrity conform to, and mostly exceed, contemporary standards of judicial integrity, I will compare these rules to those included in the above-identified international documents that deal with the concept of judicial integrity, primarily the Bangalore Principles of Judicial Conduct.

To facilitate the presentation of the *Sharí'ah* rulings addressing the concept of judicial integrity, I will make a distinction between personal and professional judicial integrity. For conformity with the recent international standards addressing the topic, it is understood that for the purpose of this chapter, the principle of integrity does not only apply to judges, but also to those holding prosecutorial positions in the international justice system.

However, before exploring the components of the concept in different sources of *Sharí'ah*, I will shed some light on the status of *Sharí'ah* among other legal traditions, as well as the status of the judiciary as such in Islam.

---

[39] "Etiquette", *Encyclopaedia Britannica* (available on its web site).
[40] See, for example, Mohamed Emam, *Ausoul Al-Hesba in Islám*, Dar Al-Hedayah, 1986, p. 71.

3.6. The Status of _Sharí'ah_: An Overview

It is nowadays admitted that Islamic law has a significant impact not only on the Muslim world, but also on the international community as a whole, as it remains one of the recognised legal systems of the world today.[41] Moreover, _Sharí'ah_ is the primary or one of the main sources of legislation in the majority of Arab States, and contains the rules by which the Muslim nation, in the broadest sense of the word, is organised. It provides the means necessary for resolving conflicts among individuals, between individuals and the State, as well as between States themselves.[42] Obviously, it is recommended that we look at the influence of _Sharí'ah_ when examining issues related to justice and the judicial function.

We have to bear in mind that the term '_Sharí'ah_' is different in meaning from the term 'Islamic law'. '_Sharí'ah_' has a broader meaning than 'Islamic law'. '_Sharí'ah_' entails divine-made rules by God and His Messenger, while 'Islamic law' refers to a heterogeneous body of human-made interpretations of Islam's sacred texts by early and contemporary Islamic jurists. These include legal principles and doctrines, derived from the _Qur'án_, _Sunnah_ and by using jurisprudential reasoning (_fiqh_), formulated by early-classical Muslim jurists, as well as diverse rulings implemented by pre-modern _Sharí'ah_ courts and scholars, based on '_Sharí'ah_' primary sources. Accordingly, in our modern era, there is an accumulation of all these human efforts that constitute a rich Muslim legal tradition yet to be investigated by Western academia. Conspicuously, general principles of law derived from the _Sharí'ah_ legal system could provide a major source of jurisprudence in the international field.

Although Islamic law remains one of the main legal systems of the world today – one that governs the lives of a substantial portion of the world's population – it has so far been poorly represented. The experience of recent years has shown that examples of meaningful research in the areas of Islamic law are few, even though it can provide answers to countless legal questions currently confronted by Western academia, including ques-

---

[41] See, René David and John E.C. Brierley (eds.), _Major Legal Systems in the World Today: An Introduction to the Comparative Study of Law_, second edition, Stevens and Sons, London, 1978, p. 421; Mashood A. Baderin, "Effective Legal Representation in '_Shari'ah_' Courts as a Means of Addressing Human Rights Concerns in the Islámic Criminal Justice System of Muslim States", in Eugene Cotran, Martin Lau and Victor Kattan (eds.), _Yearbook of Islámic and Middle Eastern Law_, vol. 11, no. 1, Brill, Leiden, 2004, pp. 135–67.

[42] Maged, 2015, p. 142, see above note 15.

tions on the concept of judicial integrity and their implications for the international justice system.

Succinctly, classical Muslim jurists have formulated a coherent system of Islamic legal jurisprudence that covers issues related to justice and the qualifications of judges, and, interestingly, addressing the core issues of integrity in justice. Accordingly, it is imperative to look at the sources of *Sharí'ah* when examining this central concept. Before doing so, as a logical development of the topic under research, I will first shed some light on the status of the judiciary as such in *Sharí'ah*.

3.7. The Importance of Justice in *Sharí'ah*

Justice in Islam means giving equal rights and treatment to others. The meaning of justice in Arabic is close to 'equality' in the sense that it creates a state of equilibrium in the distribution of rights and duties. Justice in Islam is a religious duty, and it is a cornerstone of the tenets of Islam. It is also a basic objective and a supreme virtue, as stipulated in the *Qur'án* and *Sunnah*. No wonder that *al-'Adl* (The utterly just) is one of the 99 divine Names of God, stipulated in the *Qur'án* and the *Sunnah*, called in Arabic *asmāullah al-ḥusnā*.

It is forbidden in Islam to punish unjustly or to do injustice to others. It is narrated by the Prophet Muḥammad (ﷺ) that God said:

> O My worshipers, I have forbidden injustice for Myself and forbade it also for you. So, avoid being unjust to one another.[43]

Upholding this concept, Imam Ibn Taymiyyah[44] said: "God upholds the just State even if it is disbelieving, and does not uphold the unjust one even if it is a Muslim believing State".[45]

As we will see below, God commanded the Prophet Muḥammad (ﷺ) to promote and observe justice, as a divine duty and an attribute of human personality, which carries a great burden. In this context, the Prophet

---

[43] Sahih Muslim, *Sharh al-Nawāwy*, Kortoba Foundation Publisher, Cairo, first edition, 1999, vol. 16, *ḥadíth* no. 2577, p. 199.

[44] Taqī Ad-Dīn Aḥmad Ibn Taymiyyah, early-classical Sunni Muslim scholar.

[45] Imam Ibn Taymiyyah, *majmou fatawa Ibn Taymiyyah* (The Compendium of Juristic Opinions of Emam Ibn Taymiyyah), Abdelrahman Kassem (ed.), King Fahd Complex for Printing The Holy Quran, Saudi Ministry of Islámic Affairs Dawah and Guidance, KSA, 2004, vol. 28, p. 63.

Muḥammad (ﷺ) warned his followers of the burden of delivering justice. He said:

> You submit your disputes to me, and I am only human. Perhaps some of you may be more eloquent in presenting your case than others, so I rule in your favour because of what I hear from you. If I pass a judgement in favour of one of you that detracts from his brother's rights, then he should not take it, because it is a piece of fire that is given to him which he will bring forth on the Day Resurrection.[46]

The *Qur'án* goes further to instruct the believers to disregard their emotional predisposition towards their enemies and be just with them. In *surat* Al-Ma'idah, God said:

> O you who have believed, be persistently standing firm for God, witnesses in justice, and let not the hatred of a people swerve you away from justice. Be just, for this is closest to piety. And fear God; indeed, God is Acquainted with what you do.[47]

3.8.   The Status of the Judiciary in *Sharí'ah*

Early-classical Muslim jurists underscored that the basis of the necessity of the judiciary in the Islamic nation is stipulated in the *Qur'án*, *Sunnah* and *Ijmā'*. In addition, they considered it as a religious duty. They referred to many verses in the *Qur'án*, in which God advocates justice and requires His messengers to observe it as a religious duty. And thus, they stressed that the administration of justice is an attribute of God and is considered as a moral virtue.[48]

Imam Al-Mawardi asserts in his famous book *Al-Ahkam as-Sultaniyyah* that the existence of a (judicial) power to uphold justice is essential to the Muslim community.[49] Imam Ibn Qudāmah[50] refers to the fol-

---

[46] Sahih Muslim, *Sharh Al-Nawāwy*, Egyptian Press Al-Azhar, Cairo, first edition, 1930, vol. 12, p. 4–6; Imam Mālik Ibn Anas, *Al-Muwatta*, Dar Al-Taeseel, first edition, 2016, vol. 2, p. 183.

[47] *Qur'án, surat* Al-Ma'idah, 5:8.

[48] Al-Mawardi, 1989, p. 100, see above note 24.

[49] *Ibid.*, p. h.

[50] Imam Ibn Qudāmah Al-Maqdīsī Muwaffaq Al-Dīn Abū Muḥammad ʿAbd Allāh Ibn Aḥmad Ibn Muḥammad is an early renowned Sunni Muslim jurist who contributed many important treatises on jurisprudence and religious doctrine, including one of the classical works of Hanbali school of jurisprudence, Al-Mughnī.

lowing *hadíth* of the Prophet Muḥammad (ﷺ) as another base for the necessity of the judiciary in the Muslim community:

> When a judge delivers a judgement, having striven to decide correctly and is right, then he will receive double the reward, and if he delivers a judgement, having striven to decide correctly but erred, then he receives a single reward.[51]

This means that a fair and righteous judge is rewarded in all cases; yet, he has to exert his best efforts to reach a judgement.

Captivatingly, the Prophet (ﷺ) described the judicial function as one of the blessings for which envy is permitted, as he said:

> There should be no envy except in two cases: a man to whom God has given wealth and granted him the authority to spend it in a rightful manner and a man to whom God has given wisdom and he judges and acts on the basis of it.[52]

Acknowledging the importance of the judiciary and its supreme status and solemn message, Umar Ibn Al-Khaṭṭáb used to send messages to the judges he had appointed all over the Muslim nation,[53] which included advice to them.[54] He addressed the function of the judiciary and the conduct of judges in his famous message to Abú Moussa Al-Ash'ari. The majority of Islamic scholars consider it as the judges' charter, and some call it 'the Book of Judicial Policy'. In the first paragraph of this message, Caliph Umar Ibn Al-Khaṭṭáb stated that: "The right to adjudication is an absolute (religious) duty and a followed Prophetic Tradition". In his renowned "Message to the Judiciary", Ibn Khaldun asserts the divine nature of judging between people, which requires a complete devotion to God and His support.[55]

---

[51] Sahih Muslim, *Sharh al-Nawāwy*, Dar al-Shāb, vol. 4, *hadíth* no. 13, p. 310; Imam ibn Qudāmah, *Al-Mughnī*, commentary by Sheikh Mahmoud Fayed, Cairo Library, Cairo, vol. 10, p. 32.

[52] Al-Shahīd al-Sadr, 1977, p. 72, see above note 26.

[53] For more information, see, Mahe Abd Elmajid Aboud, "The Juridical Bases in the Letter of Umar Ibn al-Khattab", vol. 1, Dar Al-Kotob Al-Ilmiyah, Beirut, 2009, p. 11.

[54] Sliman Mohamed El-Tamawy, *Judicial Policy in the Umar Ibn Al-Khaṭṭáb Epoch and its Impact on our Modern Era*, Dar Elfekr El-Araby, Cairo, 1969, p. 329.

[55] See Ibn Khaldun, *mozil al-malam an hukam al-anam*, Foad Abdelmonem Ahmed (ed.), first edition, Dar al-Watan, Riyadh, 1996, p. 105.

Imam Ibn Qudāmah asserted the importance of the existence of a judicial system in a nation by saying: "The Muslims unanimously agreed that a judicial system must be established to adjudicate between people".[56]

In *Sharí'ah*, the judiciary is considered an important pillar in the Islamic nation and accordingly has supreme religious status. It is not only a moral virtue but also an obligation to be fulfilled under all circumstances. It is stated in the *Qur'án*: "Indeed, God commands you to render trust to whom they are due and when you judge between people, judge with justice. Excellent is that which God instructs you. Indeed, God is ever Hearing and Seeing".[57]

As a result of their divine mission, judges should discharge their duties with the utmost form of justice. In various verses of the *Qur'án*, God advised His Messengers to judge between people fairly: "And if you judge (O Muhammad), judge between them with justice. Verily, God loves those who act justly".[58]

However, justice needs a functional judicial system to be achieved. Early Muslim jurists consider the following verses of the *Qur'án* to be the bases of such a system: "O David, verily we have placed you as a successor on Earth, so judge between people in truth".[59]

Elaborating on the previous concept, Imam Ahmad, one of the most prominent classical jurists of Islam, once said: "People have to have a judicial authority or their rights will disappear".[60] As stipulated in early Islamic jurisprudence, the main goal of such a system is to "explore *Sharí'ah* rulings, reinforce these rulings and adjudicate disputes".[61] Accordingly, the science of judgeship has a supreme status in Islamic jurisprudence.[62]

3.8.1. *Sharí'ah* on the Appointment of Judges

In the early era of the Rightly Guided Caliphs (the successors of Prophet Muḥammad), the position of *al-qāḍī* was instituted by the Caliph himself,

---

[56] Ibn Qudāmah, p. 32, see above note 51.

[57] *Qur'án, surat* An-Nisaa', 4:58.

[58] *Qur'án, surat* Al-Ma'idah, 5:42.

[59] *Qur'án, Surat* Sad, 38:26.

[60] Al-Syuti al-Raihabany, *mataleb oly al-nahy fe sharh ghayet al-montha*, Sheihk Hassan al-Shaty (ed.), first edition, the Islámic Bureau, Damascus, 1961, vol. 6, p. 454.

[61] *Ibid.*

[62] Abī'Al-Dam, 1984, p. 126, see above note 32.

who was responsible for selecting and appointing judges, governing their affairs, supervising their work, as well as protect their independence. Subsequently, the appointment and removal of judges was the responsibility of the Muslim nation's ruler. He was responsible for supervising their behaviour and monitoring their performance. In all cases, it was considered a religious duty for the ruler to provide for the administration of justice through the appointment of judges.[63]

At that time, the *al-qāḍī* court was a single-judge court with general jurisdiction, hence *al-qāḍī* was competent to adjudicate all kinds of litigations brought before him. His basic function was to settle disputes and allocate rights to litigants, in accordance with the injunctions (both commandments and prohibitions) of the divine rules of Islamic law. In other words, *al-qāḍī* must apply the rules stipulated mainly in the *Qur'án* and *Sunnah*, or resort to *ijtihád* when the *Qur'án* and Sunnah are silent.

As mentioned before, one of the most comprehensive, while succinct, instruments in *Sharí'ah* that contains the required criteria for the appointment of judges is the Message of Caliph Alī Ibn Abī Ṭālib to his commissioner in Egypt, Malik al-Ashtar on the Judiciary, in which he instructed him of the qualities that he should observe when selecting a person to act as *qāḍī*.[64]

3.8.2. The Status of Judges in *Sharí'ah*

The foregoing has established that the existence of a functional judicial system is imperative for the Muslim nation. However, such judicial system requires highly qualified judges. The existence of judges is considered by Islamic law to be both a religious duty and a necessity for the functioning of society. Reflecting this fact, God says: "We have sent Messengers with clear proofs, and sent down with them the Scripture and the balance that mankind can establish justice".[65]

Upholding justice is considered in Islam as a divine mission compensated by God. In this context, the Prophet (ﷺ) said: "A day of just leadership is better than sixty years of worship".[66]

---

[63] Rulers of the Muslim nation who were appointed after the Prophet Muhammad and subsequently in medieval Islám.

[64] Alī Al-Salaby, 2004, p. 369, see above note 27.

[65] Qur'án *surat* Al-Hadid, 57:25.

[66] Al-Shahīd Al-Sadr, 1977, vol. 1, p. 127, see above note 26.

To assert the divine mission of *al-qāḍī*, the Prophet (ﷺ) said: "When *al-qāḍī* sits two angles descend to guide, direct and support him, as long as he is not unjust. If he delivers injustice, they will abandon him and ascend".[67]

If *al-qāḍī* performs his function correctly and fairly, he will receive the divine blessings. This approach was emphasised by the companion of the Prophet Muḥammad (ﷺ), Ibn Masud, who once said: "To spend one-day judging between people is more pleasing to me than engaging in worship for seventy years".[68]

Islamic *fiqh* views the act of judging between people as an esteemed religious function that is to be considered a supreme act of worship. Consequently, Islamic *fiqh* allocates high status to judges.[69] The names of many just and qualified judges have been preserved in Islamic history and the concepts of fairness and integrity were attached to their names. Many pages in history books are devoted to the lives and careers of early eminent Muslim judges like Mu'adh Ibn Jabal in Yemen, Iyâs Ibn Muawiyah in Basra, Shuraih Ibn al-Hârith in Kufah, Abú Moussa Al-Ash'ari in Kufa, Yaqub Ibn Ibrahim al-Ansari better known as Abú Yusuf (the student of the great jurist Abú Ḥanífa) in Baghdad, and others who applied the teachings of Islam in their judgements in the best possible manner and gave us living examples of morality and integrity.

3.8.3. The Gravity of the Function of *Al-Qāḍī* in *Sharí'ah*

Taking up the position of *qāḍī* has grave consequences. The Prophet Muḥammad (ﷺ) warned of the gravity of this position. In one of his *ḥadíth*, he is reported to have said:

> Out of three Judges, two are destined to Hell and one is destined to heaven: A man who, knowingly, judges by other than truth is destined to Hell; a man who, unknowingly judges is destined to Hell; and a man who recognises the truth and judges accordingly, is destined to Heaven.[70]

---

[67] Imam Al-Baihaqi, "Al-Sunan Al-Kobrá", Abdallh Al-Turkey (ed.), first edition, Hagar Centre for Research, Arabic and Islámic Studies, Cairo, 2011, vol. 20, p. 245.

[68] Imam Ibn Qudāmah, *Al-Mughnī yalih al-sharh al-kabeer*, Dar al-Kitab al-Araby, Cairo, vol. 11, p. 374.

[69] Ibn Abī Al-Dam, 1984, p. 6, see above note 32.

[70] Al-Tirmidhi, *ḥadíth* no. 1322, p. 321, see above note 1.

In another *ḥadíth*, asserting the sacredness of the responsibility of judges in *Sharí'ah*, the Prophet (ﷺ) said: "There are seven categories of people whom God will shelter under His shade on the Day when there will be no shade except His. (One is) the just leader".[71]

Further, it was narrated that the Messenger of God (ﷺ) said: "God is with the judge so long as he is not unjust, but if he rules unjustly, He entrusts him to himself".[72]

These religious texts illustrate a burdensome responsibility that *Sharí'ah* laid down on the part of the judges. In this case, the judge is rewarded for his *ijtihád* and efforts, not for his mistakes. This illustrates that Islam stresses and places a responsibility on a judge to the extent to which he exerts efforts in his judgments.

According to *Sharí'ah*, a judge should strive to establish justice, based on primary rules set in the *Qur'án* and *Sunnah*. Otherwise, he has to practice *ijtihád* to establish the applicable rules. Reportedly, the permissibility of deducing secondary rulings through critical thinking had been encouraged by the Prophet (ﷺ) himself in the form of *ijtihád*.[73] *Ijtihád* is often dubbed as independent or critical reasoning, and is considered a fundamental requirement for acquiring the position of *al-qáḍí*, according to early Muslim jurists.[74] However, one who is qualified for *ijtihád*, should possess certain qualifications: piety (*taqwa*), knowledge of the objectives (*maqáṣid*) of *Sharí'ah*, knowledge of the *Qur'án* and the *Sunnah*, and skill in the Arabic language.[75]

Surprisingly, many early Muslim jurists actively avoided being appointed as judges, even though they are qualified for this position. In his treatise *Guide for the Rulers on the Rules of Litigations*, renowned classical jurists Sheikh 'Ala Al-Deen Al-Taraabulsi explained the dilemma, which early-Muslims jurists and Imams faced when they were requested to act as judges. He clarified that a number of exemplary Imams endured hardship

---

[71] Sahih Muslim, *Darussalam,* 2007, vol. 7, *ḥadíth* no. 1031, p. 76.

[72] Ibn Majah, *Sunan Ibn Majah*, Centre of Research and Information Technology, Dar al-Taseel, 2014, first edition, vol. 2, no. 2312, p. 455.

[73] Ibn Qudāmah, *Al-Mughní*, vol. 10 p. 35, see above note 51.

[74] Onder Bakircioglu, "The Principal Sources of Islamic Law", in Tallyn Gray (ed.), *Islam and International Criminal Law and Justice*, Torkel Opsahl Academic EPublisher, Brussels, 2018 (https://www.legal-tools.org/doc/0528c5/).

[75] Imam Abú Isaaq Al-Shatby, *Al-Muwafaqat*, Dar Ibn Afan for Publication and Disruption, KSA, 1997, vol. 3, p. 213.

in order to avoid assuming this position and they bore it with patience. Some of them even accepted being beaten and imprisoned instead of being appointed, and others fled from their homelands in order to avoid being appointed as judges. He explained that "[t]hey feared the serious responsibility of judging between people, in the assumption that they did not fulfil the required conditions".[76] Some others feared the grave danger of passing incorrect judgements, as indicated in many of the *ḥadīth* of the Prophet (ﷺ), in which a stern warning is issued to the one who is appointed as a judge and does not fulfil the obligations and requirements needed to be a judge.

The gravity of the responsibility of *al-qāḍī* is illustrated in a famous *ḥadīth* by the Prophet Muḥammad (ﷺ), in which he mentioned how God would hold *al-qāḍī* accountable for all his deeds. He said: "*Al-qāḍī*, though the just one, will be brought (before God) in the day of Resurrection, due to the severe accountability he will face, he would have wished that he did not decide between two (even in half a date)".[77]

In his commentary on *Adab Al-Qāḍī*, Al-Shahīd Al-Sadr interprets the meaning of this *ḥadīth* by stating that: "Islamic jurists warn of the gravity of judgeship even for a just *qāḍī*, accordingly, unjust *qāḍī* will be faced by severe measures of accountability". Al-Shahīd al-Sadr stresses that all judges will be held accountable in the day of judgement, but a just *qāḍī* will be spared by God.[78]

Additionally, in his book, *Al-Mughnī*, Imam Ibn Qudāmah points out: "In acting as a judge there is a grave danger and a huge burden for the one who does not undertake this function properly. Hence the *salaf* (prominent predecessors) would refuse it emphatically, fearing its dangers".[79]

Nonetheless, the Prophet (ﷺ) encouraged his companions to accept the position of *al-qāḍī*. Conveying the *Sunnah* of the Prophet (ﷺ) Alī Ibn Abī Ṭālib once said:

> The Messenger of God (ﷺ) sent me to Yemen. I said: O Messenger of God, you are sending me to judge between them while I am a young man, and I do not know how to judge? He patted me on the chest with his hand and said: 'O God, guide

---

[76] Sheikh 'Ala Al-Deen Al-Taraabulsi, *Mu'een al-Hukkaam fima yataraddadu bayna al-Khasmayni min al-Ahkaam*, p. 9.

[77] Al-Baihaqi, 2011, p. 275, see above note 67.

[78] Al-Shahīd al-Sadr, 1977, vol. 1, p. 127, see above note 26.

[79] Ibn Qudāmah, *Al-Mughnī*, vol. 10, p. 33, see above note 51.

his heart and make his tongue steadfast. When two litigants sit in front of you, do not decide until you hear what the other has to say as you heard what the first had to say; for it is best that you should have a clear idea of the best decision. Alī said: I had never doubted about a decision that I made between two (people) ever after.[80]

The foregoing reflects the meaning of the Prophet's *hadíth* that was situated at the beginning of this chapter: "He who is appointed as a judge is slaughtered without a knife". In his treatise on *Adab Al-Qāḍī*, Imam Ibn Abī'Al-Dam recounted two meanings reported by an early-Muslim jurist. He who has appointed as *qāḍī* is like a man who is slaughtered because (1) he has to suppress his desires, defeat his inclinations and prevent himself from social life; and (2) he is exposed to great danger, as he cannot fulfil the necessities of this job.[81]

Imam Ibn Abī'Al-Dam goes further in explaining that the word 'slaughter' should be understood metaphorically to mean that *al-qāḍī* should exert his utmost efforts to ensure that he justly adjudicate cases brought before him according to the highest standards of *Shari'ah*.[82]

As explained by Imam Al-Syuti, this *hadíth* of the Prophet (ﷺ) warns of the gravity of *al-qāḍī*'s duties, and the word slaughter is used as a metaphor which refers to the grave consequences that a judge could suffer if he erred in his judgement.[83]

3.9. Qualifications of Judges in *Shari'ah*

The *Al-qāḍī* is comparable to a magistrate or a judge in contemporary Western judicial systems. He holds a distinct position with great respect in the Muslim nation. Given his prestigious social status, and his knowledge of the *Shari'ah* jurisprudence, the *al-qāḍī* is perceived as the key institution for the application and preservation of Islamic law. Because the *al-qāḍī* performed an essential function in early Muslim society, requirements for

---

[80] Al-Baihaqi, Ahmed Ibn El-Hussein, *Al-sunan we al-athar* (*The Sunah and Traces*), Sayed Kasrawy Hassan (ed.), Dar Al-Kotob Al-Ilmiyah, Beirut, first edition, 1991, vol. 7, Book of *Adab Al-Qadi*, *hadíth* no. 5874, p. 368; Sunan Abī Dāwūd, Abī Trab Adel Ibn Muhammad and Abi Amr Ibn Abbas (eds.), Dar al-Taseel, first edition, 2015, vol. 5, no. 3537, pp. 578–588; Alī Al-Salaby, 2004, p. 153, see above note 27.

[81] Ibn Abī'Al-Dam, 1984, p. 259, see above note 32.

[82] *Ibid.*, pp. 260–261.

[83] Al-Syuti al-Raihabany, 1961 p. 454, see above note 60; See also Ibn Qudāmah, *Al-Mughnī yalih al-sharh al-kabeer*, vol. 11, p. 374, see above note 68.

---

the post were strict. A person selected to act as *al-qāḍī* should be suitably qualified to fulfil such a position and fulfil the prerequisite qualifications required by *Sharí'ah* law.

3.9.1.   Prerequisite Qualifications of the *Al-Qāḍī*

Sharí'ah rules on the judicial function are stringent when it comes to the qualifications that a *qāḍī* should possess. In order to be appointed as *qāḍī*, early-classical Muslim jurists identified basic requirements that a person should enjoy: he must be a free Muslim of legal capacity, be of sound mind, with full sensory perception, and possess high moral probity or rectitude. This means that *al-qāḍī* should be one of upright character, of a mature and balanced personality, with no ulterior motives, physically and psychologically healthy, of sound hearing and sight, and is able to communicate verbally in the language used in court.

Besides the above-mentioned requirements, the majority of Muslim jurists agree that it is a prerequisite in *Sharí'ah* that any individual seeking to act as a *qāḍī* should possesses sound knowledge of *Qur'án*, *Sunnah* and *fiqh*, as his work must be totally congruent with Islamic law. Therefore, he should have the capacity to exercise *ijtihád*. This requires that the *al-qāḍī* must be sufficiently educated and knowledgeable about the law that he applies, and able to perform *ijtihád* to extract legal rulings from original sources.[84]

This approach was illustrated in the tradition of the Prophet Muhammad (ﷺ) narrated by his companions. It was narrated by Mu'adh Ibn Jabal when the Prophet appointed him as *al-qāḍī* in Yemen. Some companions of Mu'adh Ibn Jabal said: "When the Messenger of God (ﷺ) intended to send Mu'adh Ibn Jabal to Yemen", he asked: "What will you do if a matter is referred to you for judgement?". Mu'adh said: "I will judge according to the Book of God". The Prophet asked: "What if you find no solution in the Book of God?". Mu'adh said: "Then I will judge by the *Sunnah* of the Prophet". The Prophet asked: "And what if you do not find it in the Sunnah of the Prophet?". Mu'adh said: "Then I will delicately exert *ijtihád* to reach a resolution". The Prophet patted Mu'adh's chest and said: "Praise be to

---

[84]   Ibn Abī Al-Dam, 1984, pp. 134–135, see above note 32.

God who has guided the messenger of His Prophet to that which pleases His Prophet".[85]

Asserting the responsibilities of *al-qāḍī* attached to this religious duty, in his message to Abú Moussa Al-Ash'ari, Caliph Umar Ibn Al-Khaṭṭáb instructed him as follows:

> If a case is brought before you and you cannot find applicable rule(s) neither in the Qu'ran nor in the *Sunnah*, then you must resort to logical reasoning, and use analogy, comparison and parallelism (to reach a judgement). Consequently, apply the ruling that you consider closest to what is right and fair and that would please God Almighty.

Numerous early-classical literature is written on *ijtihád* as a prerequisite to occupy the judicial office. According to a contemporary Muslim scholar, as stated in his article on "The Requirement of Ijtihád to Occupy the Judicial Office": "The majority of early Muslim jurists regard *ijtihád* as inevitable quality".[86] Thus, according to *Sharí'ah* provisions, judges are chosen from among people who already have a consolidated experience in the interpretation and application of *Sharí'ah*. However, Muslim jurists belonging to modern jurisprudential schools argue that in the modern eras, it is difficult to find judges who have the skills to exercise *ijtihád*, as recognised in *Sharí'ah*.[87] Thus, in many Arab countries nowadays, the requirement of *ijtihád* is no longer a prerequisite for the appointment in the judiciary, it suffices that the judge has commendable legal knowledge, and judicial skills necessary for the proper performance of his judicial duties.

Further, to assume the judicial function, *al-qāḍī* should possess the highest standards of integrity. Ibn Qayyim al-Jawziyyah[88] asserted that the person appointed for this task should be the best of the nominees. He should also be religious and pious.[89] Alī Ibn Abī Ṭālib said: "A person

---

[85]   Sunan Abī Dāwūd, vol. 5, no. 3547, pp. 584–585, see above note 80; Al-Shaid al-Sadr, Al-Khaṣṣāf, 1977, vol. 1, p. 127; Al-Mawardi, 1989, p. 90, see above note 24.

[86]   Abd Al-Aziz Al-Meshal, *Shart al-ijtihád fiman yaly al-qada*, Megalat Al-Adel (Justice Journal), 2009, vol. 43, p. 127.

[87]   Al-Shahīd Al-Sadr, 1977, vol. 1, p. 206, see above note 26.

[88]   Ibn Qayyim al-Jawziyyah (691/1292-751/1350) was born in a village near Damascus, Syria. His contributions to Islámic writings are extensive, dealing most with Qur'ánic commentaries and prophetic traditions. He was a student of Ibn Taymiyyah, but did not restrict himself to the Hanbali madhab and sometimes took view from other madhabs or no madhab.

[89]   Ibn Qayyim al-Jawziyyah, I'lam al-Muwaqqi'in 'an Rabb al'Alamin, Narrated by Abd El-Rahman El-Wakeel, vol. I, Dar Ehya al Turath al Araby, Beirut, p. 114.

could not be appointed as a judge unless he has five characteristics: virtuousness, modesty, knowledge of precedents, be willing to deliberate with prudent scholars, and does not fear but only God and no one else".[90]

The strongest proof that judges are carefully selected in the Islamic tradition is stipulated in Caliph Alī Ibn Abī Ṭālib's Message to his commissioner in Egypt, Malik al-Ashtar, in which he entrusted him with selecting judges according to the highest integrity standards. I will address those integrity standards stipulated in this message later.

Other jurists required more qualities to guarantee that the person holding the position of *al-qāḍī* possess required conditions, such as being authoritative, having extensive knowledge, and being trustworthy. Such qualities also include uprightness, truthfulness, fidelity, probity and freedom from corrupting influences.

Addressing the same issue, Caliph Umar Ibn Abd Al-Aziz is reported to have said: "*Al-qāḍī* should possess seven qualities: Sanity, jurisprudence, pious, integrity, firmness, knowledge of precedents, and wisdom". He added: "if he misses one of these qualities, then he is unqualified".[91]

Imam Ibn Qudāmah has summarised the required qualities of judgeship in the following three conditions:

1. Integrity: As a basic condition that guarantees that a judge is selected according to *Sharí'ah* rules and is complete in his personal qualities;

2. Uprightness: Uprightness has been reflected by an early Muslim authority in three virtues: truthfulness, evade heresy, and avoid major sins.[92] Hence, a sinner or corrupt person cannot be selected as a judge;

3. Ijtihád: Al-qāḍī should be capable of conducting individual independent legal reasoning based on *Sharí'ah* disciplines.[93]

The foregoing demonstrates that the application of *Sharí'ah* requires righteous, reliable, and learned judges who enjoy both personal and professional judicial integrity.

---

[90] Ibn Qudāmah, *Al-Mughnī*, vol. 10, p. 40, see above note 51.

[91] *Ibid.*; Ibn Qudāmah, vol. 11, p. 386, see above note 68.

[92] Muhammad Taher, *al-garh we al-taeddl, al-Dar al-Arabia Llketab*, 1997, p. 249.

[93] Ibn Qudāmah, vol. 22, pp. 380–384, see above note 68.

3.10. Meaning of Integrity in the Arabic Language

The term 'integrity' in Arabic is close to the meaning of the Latin adjective '*integer*', which refers to the state of being whole or complete and would also reflect the term 'coherent', as explained in Chapters 1 and 2 above. Similar to what has been stipulated in an important international document, the term in Arabic also reflects the attribute of honesty, rectitude and righteousness;[94] in other words, a 'principled behaviour' or a 'clear intrinsic moral value'. For ordinary Arab citizens, the first meaning that will come to mind when hearing the term 'integrity' in the abstract, is morals or virtues, and sometimes the terms are used interchangeably. In general, it is understood as a high moral character that distinguishes a person, and as a central value impeded in his conduct such as honesty, purity and fairness. Those who have such a characteristic should be considered as 'virtuous persons'.

In classical Arabic dictionaries, the classical source of the word means 'distance', or keeping distant from something, especially dirt. The term is pronounced in Arabic as '*nazamā*', which literally means 'to distance oneself from malice and avoid suspicions'. Thus, the term is also attached to a person's conduct and manners.[95] From a legal perspective, the term means 'to distance oneself from corruption in all its forms'. And in a judicial context, the term is considered as a core quality of a judge. It refers to purity of intention, and may also cover the value of incorruptibility, while carrying out a judicial function.

In Arabic culture, a person with 'integrity' should have a high degree of conscientiousness. This special characteristic controls a person's attitude in both the personal and professional life and encourages a judge to perform his duties thoroughly and diligently. In the Arab tradition, a judge with 'integrity' should possess the following characteristics: conscientiousness, uprightness and fairness. This illustrates that 'integrity' is a set of values that reflect the core characteristic of a judge.

3.11. Meaning of Judicial Integrity in *Shari'ah*

As stated above, judges in the Islamic tradition occupy a supreme status and are regarded as implementing a divine function on Earth. Accordingly, those who are selected to serve as judges should possess the highest stand-

---

[94]   UNODC, 2011, p. 79, see above note 2.

[95]   Al-Waseet Dictionary, p. 952, see above note 35.

ards of integrity. Integrity in this regard should be considered as an ethical quality of those who occupy the judicial office.

As we will see, in *Sharí'ah* sources, integrity and morality are interrelated. 'Morality' in Islam is a comprehensive term that serves to include the concept of righteousness, uprightness and good character. In addition, it is the body of moral qualities and virtues prescribed in the *Qur'án* and the *Sunnah*, which often speak in emphatic manners to instruct Muslims to adopt morally good characteristics.

Obviously, the term integrity, as such, in a judicial context, is not frequently used in the primary sources of *Sharí'ah* (*Qur'án* and *Sunnah*). Instead, other terms such as fairness, righteousness and impartiality or impartial justice are used to reflect it, especially during trial proceedings, while other terms like virtuousness, uprightness and piety are used to describe a judge's integral qualities. These abstract characteristics are required to be realised in the form of a concrete principle, the attitudes of a judge, either in the workplace or in private life. Notwithstanding these facts, the term is used explicitly in some major early jurisprudential treatises and exegeses like *Al-Mughní* and *Adab Al-Qáḍí*. Obviously, it is frequently used in scholarly and judicial works that tackle *Sharí'ah* in our modern era as a key judicial value.

In fact, upon reading the provisions of *Sharí'ah* that exclusively address the qualities required to occupy judicial office, it is easily inferred that integrity is a core judicial value that encompasses other well-established virtues in Islam. Those occupying a judicial office are required to maintain the highest standards of decorum and decency in his frequent dealings with other people, and behave beyond reproach.

Subsequently, this central characteristic encompasses other values essential to exercise the sacred judicial function. In my view, integrity represents a moral value that encompasses a long list of factors that are continuously adapted in a fast-changing world. According to the message of Caliph Umar Ibn Al-Khaṭṭáb, conscientiousness, patience, dedication, righteousness, fairness and dignity are all components of a judge's integrity. Each of these characteristics is not equivalent to the concept of integrity, but they all come under it.

Conclusively, after looking at the rulings of *Sharí'ah*, integrity should be considered as the bond that unites many judicial qualities together and acts as an umbrella for many other virtues required to hold a judicial position.

It seems that occasional contemporary scholars and practitioners started to support the same approach of *Shari'ah* towards judicial integrity as a 'virtue' and a 'moral' character required for appointment in a judicial position. For example, Andrzej Rzeplinski, the President of the Constitutional Tribunal of Poland, admits that a judge without morals or integrity is no judge at all. He stated that:

> The profession of being a judge is not a good career for persons who do not possess a sufficiently well-established sense of personal and professional dignity, the virtue of personal integrity, impeccable past, professional and practical knowledge, social and family maturity, and personal maturity to be able to assume full responsibility for each ruling passed in accordance with the law and with their own conscience.[96]

3.12. Why Judicial Integrity Is Significant in *Shari'ah*

So far, the study of *Shari'ah* signifies that judicial integrity is a virtue required to carry out the judicial function. In this sense, we cannot separate a judge's character from his actions. Only a judge with integrity is a good judge, while a judge without integrity is a bad judge. This moral approach is embedded in the normative underpinnings of the concept of judicial integrity in Islam. This is why *Shari'ah* concentrates on the moral character of the judge reflected in his integrity.

It is asserted that the faith and confidence of the common people in the judiciary will be maintained only if the highest possible standards are adhered to by judges.[97] There is no doubt that judicial integrity fortifies the faith of the public in judges and judicial institutions. It is, therefore, imperative that judges must endeavour to realise the utmost standards of integrity both in their professional and personal lives.[98] As we will see, this essential quality was explicitly mentioned in the *Shari'ah*'s *fiqh*.

---

[96] UNODC, *Judicial Conduct and Ethics*, Self-Directed Course, Vienna, 2019, p. vii.

[97] R.N. Prasad and P. Chakraborty, *Administration of Justice and the Judicial Administration in Mizoram*, Mittal Publications, New Delhi, 2006, p. 4.

[98] Md. Manjur Hossain Patoari *et al.*, "The Desired Qualities of a Good Judge", in *Academic Journal of Interdisciplinary Studies*, MCSER Publishing, Rome-Italy, vol. 3, no. 1, March 2014, p. 97.

3.13. Reflections in _Sharí'ah_ Sources on Judicial Integrity

According to international standards, a judge shall exhibit and promote high standards of judicial conduct in order to reinforce public confidence in the judiciary which is fundamental to the maintenance of judicial independence.[99] Accordingly, as a reflection of the concept of 'high standards of judicial conduct', integrity is vital to the independence of the judiciary. Judges should, therefore, demonstrate and promote a high standard of judicial integrity as one element of assuring the independence of the judiciary. They should also ensure that their conduct is above reproach in the view of a reasonable observer.[100] In other words, their behaviour must reaffirm the people's faith in the integrity of the judiciary,[101] as justice must not merely be done but must also be seen to be done.[102]

While the basics of judicial integrity have been agreed and enumerated, _inter alia_, in the Bangalore Principles of Judicial Conduct, the guidelines on some topical matters may not be up to the required standards and might need more research. In addition, some required criteria have not been addressed in those principles. For example, subjects like the personal qualities of the judge in his daily life, and the standards governing the relationships between the prosecutor and his subordinates and the judges and their governments, have recently become more relevant to judicial work and are in need of closer scrutiny.

The importance of judicial integrity rests on the fact that judges are a pillar of the justice system they serve and the public expects the highest and irreproachable conduct from anyone performing a judicial function. In the following, I will delve into _Sharí'ah_'s sources to see how they address the concept of judicial integrity.

Reflections in _Sharí'ah_ on the concept of judicial integrity can be traced in several verses of the _Qur'án_, where God demands from the believers in general and His messengers in particular, to deliver justice firmly in accordance to the highest standards of integrity.

---

[99] Bangalore Principles of Judicial Conduct, Article 1.6, see above note 6.
[100] _Ibid._, Value 3.1.
[101] _Ibid._, Value 3.2.
[102] _Ibid._, Value 3.2.

In *surat Al-Nisaa'*, God commands His believers to stand up for justice and fairness and be cautious of deviating from it. He said: "O you who believe! Stand out firmly for justice".[103]

The same applies to the Prophet of God, Muḥammad (ﷺ). God advised him to deliver judgements according to the rules stipulated in the *Qur'án* with justice and to avoid people's interferences and whims: "So judge (O Muḥammad) between them by what God has revealed and do not follow their vain desires, but beware of them lest they turn you away from some of what God has sent down to you".[104]

Those who had the opportunity to read the most renowned literature on *Adab Al-Qāḍī*, would recognise that *Sharí'ah* requires extra judicial qualities that the *al-qāḍī* should possess. In his treatise on *Adab Al-Qāḍī*, Ibn Abī'Al-Dam addressed the qualities that the *al-qāḍī* should possess, and the environment that should surround him in court, classifying them under the title *Adab Al-Qāḍī*. He divided such qualities and conditions into three categories: the first category includes forms of conduct attached to the personality of the *al-qāḍī* (personal qualities); the second category covers traditions and formalities that surround the judicial function, mostly attached to the judicial institution itself (judicial institutional formalities); and the third category covers specific professional qualities required for the proper execution of *al-qāḍī* judicial duties (professional qualities).[105]

As I have already mentioned, judicial integrity is a holistic term that encompasses various qualities that *al-qāḍī* should possess. Those qualities reflect intrinsic values that are manifested in the *al-qāḍī*'s personal characteristics, such as 'piousness', 'conscientiousness', 'righteousness', 'uprightness', 'propriety', 'dignity', 'esteem', 'firmness', 'patience' and 'courtesy'. Some of these qualities are purely personal qualities that every Muslim should practice, while some other qualities are attached to the conduct of judges. Other qualities are associated to the *al-qāḍī*'s professional conduct during the performance of his judicial duties, such as 'independence', 'impartiality', 'equality', and 'competence and diligence', as affirmed in the Bangalore Principles of Judicial Conduct.

Bearing in mind the purpose of this chapter, and for the sake of simplicity, I will examine how *Sharí'ah* sources address judicial integrity ac-

---

[103] *Qur'án, surat* An-Nisaa', 4:135.

[104] *Qur'án, surat* Al-Ma'ida, 5:49.

[105] Ibn Abī'Al-Dam, 1984, vol. 1, p. 136, see above note 32.

cording to the above-mentioned distinction between personal and professional judicial integrity, while leaving the topic of judicial institutional integrity out of the analysis here.

3.14. Personal Judicial Integrity of the *Al-Qāḍī* in *Sharī'ah*

According to applicable international standards, judges are expected to behave with honesty and propriety both on the bench and in their private lives so as to inspire trust and confidence in the community.[106] Notably, *Sharī'ah*'s approach to the qualities of *al-qāḍī* is different from that of contemporary judicial systems, in particular with respect to good manners reflected in modern systems in the term 'propriety'. Ethics and good manners are deemed to be inherent characteristics of every Muslim within his community and in his relation to God, as exemplified in the Prophet's manners.

According to the *Sharī'ah* provisions, one can infer that an intrinsic quality of the concept of personal integrity of the *al-qāḍī* is presented in his conscientiousness. In that sense, the *al-qāḍī*'s personal integrity means that he enjoys a conscious and consistent system of values, based on his faith, which guides him in his demeanour and actions.

Imam Ibn Abī' Al-Dam addressed certain central personal qualities that the *al-qāḍī* should possess and the conduct that he should follow, both in his daily life and in court. The *al-qāḍī* should be God-fearing and at the same time have a dignified demeanour distinguished by sobriety and piety. Further, he should bear an absolutely irreproachable character. For example, according to *Adab Al-Qāḍī* literature, the *al-qāḍī* should be acquainted with piety, and distance himself from morally questionable companions.[107] To preserve his integrity, he should avoid requesting favours or borrowing from people, except close relatives.[108]

In *Sharī'ah* literature, there is always a reference to righteousness as an inherent quality of the *al-qāḍī*. For the purposes of this chapter, 'righteousness' is used to mean the individual quality of being morally right or justifiable. This is a key notion for the common sense of the concept of 'integrity'. Regrettably, the negative term 'self-righteousness' has become so

---

[106] UNODC, *Resource Guide on Strengthening Judicial Integrity and Capacity*, Vienna, 2011, p. 127.

[107] Imam Ibn Farhoun, *Tabsrat Al-Hukam fe Osool Al-Akdiah we Manaheg Al-Ahkam* (Insight the Rulers of Fundamentals of Cases and Methodology of Judgements), Gamal Marashly (ed.), Dar Alam Al-Kotob, Riyadh, 2003, vol. 1, p. 28.

[108] *Ibid.*, p. 28.

commonplace – often as an appropriate reaction to hypocrisy or moralising – that utility of the compass virtue of 'righteousness' may have become undermined. According to this quality, *Sharí'ah* requires that the *al-qāḍī* should strive to find the truth and uphold justice, especially in *Qisás* crimes as it is based on the principle 'no blood goes in vain in Islam'.

In the ninth paragraph of his message, Caliph Umar Ibn Al-Khaṭṭáb instructed Abú Moussa Al-Ashari, as follows:

> Judging fairly is rewarded by God Almighty and praised by people. He whose heart's intention is to establish justice and rule fairly, even if his rulings would be against his own interest, will be protected and supported by God Almighty, whereas he who, out of hypocrisy, acts contrary to his heart's conviction, will be disgraced by Him. God accepts only pure and honest deeds and intentions.

According to applicable international standards, judges are expected to treat the litigants, witnesses and attorneys with courtesy and respect,[109] as disrespectful behaviour towards a litigant infringes on the litigant's right to be heard, and compromises the dignity and decorum of the courtroom. Lack of courtesy also affects a litigant's satisfaction with the handling of the case, thus creating a negative impression of courts in general.

Sharí'ah had contemplated those qualities centuries ago. The *al-qāḍī* must not show any sense of disrespect towards the litigants. For example, he should not laugh at litigants, nor should he make fun of them; according to established rules of Islam, as stated in the *Qur'án*: "O you who have believed, let not a people ridicule another people; perhaps they may be better than them".[110] According to Imam Ibn Abī' Al-Dam, the *al-qāḍī* should receive the witnesses well and treat them with courtesy and respect.[111] It is narrated that Caliph Alī Ibn Abī Ṭālib has removed the *al-qāḍī* Aba Al-Asoud Al-Dialy one hour after he appointed him. Then, Aba Al-Asoud asked Caliph Alī Ibn Abī Ṭālib: "Why did you remove me from office?". Caliph Alī responded: "Because it was reported to me that you raised your voice over the voice of the litigants".[112]

---

[109] UNODC, 2011, p. 127, see above note 106.

[110] *Qur'án, surat Al-Hujurat*, 49:11.

[111] Ibn Abī' Al-Dam, 1984, vol. 1, pp. 367–370, see above note 32.

[112] Imam Ibn Al-Kāss, *Adab Al-Qāḍī*, Hussein Khalaf Al-Jobory (ed.), Maktabat Al-Sedeek, KSA, 1989, vol. 1, p. 99.

In general, the *al-qāḍī* should adopt respectful behaviour towards everyone who stands before him. He may return the greetings of the litigants and witnesses when they enter the courtroom. However, he should greet all parties equally, and it is also recommended not to greet them after beginning the judicial proceedings to avoid creating any doubt of his attitude towards the parties.[113]

In his famous treatise on *Adab Al-Qāḍī*, Imam Ibn Abī' Al-Dam indicated some qualities that the *al-qāḍī* should observe during the performance of his judicial duties. The *al-qāḍī* should observe the highest standards of propriety during court proceedings, and ensure that his conduct is above reproach.[114] In this context, he retrieved the essence of the Message by Caliph Umar Ibn Al-Khaṭṭáb on the Judiciary.

The *al-qāḍī* should not accept gifts or social hospitability from litigants or people of interests,[115] unless from his relative who could not appear as litigants before him.[116] According to Imam Al-Khaṣṣāf, the *al-qāḍī* may continue to accept gifts from those who used to send him gifts before he is appointed as *qāḍī*.[117]

In general, gifts are praised in *Sharí'ah*. However, great precautions are taken when it comes to *al-qāḍī*.[118] Acceptance of gifts or benefits from the public is prohibited by Islam as it raises doubts about the *al-qāḍī*'s integrity,[119] and may pave the way for corruption.[120] Moreover, he should avoid private communications with any of the parties to the legal dispute presented before him, and should never see any party in private, nor should he ask any party to do him any favours. He also should not engage in trade or private business, or other activities that may compromise his position or

---

[113] Al-Shahīd al-Sadr, 1977, vol. 2, p. 66–69, see above note 26.

[114] Ibn Abī' Al-Dam, 1984, p. 137, see above note 32.

[115] Al-Mawardi, 1989, p. 100, see above note 24.

[116] Ibn Farhoun, 2003, vol. 1, p. 26, see above note 107.

[117] Al-Shahīd al-Sadr, 1977, vol. 2, p. 65, see above note 26.

[118] *Ibid.*, p. 34–37.

[119] Ibn Farhoun, 2003, vol. 1, p. 100, see above note 107; see also Al-Shahīd Al-Sadr, 1977, vol. 1, pp. 353–354, see above note 26.

[120] Ibn Farhoun, 2003, vol. 1, p. 26, see above note 107.

cast doubts upon his demeanour and open the door for bribes or show favouritism to any party to a dispute before him.[121]

The prohibition of accepting gifts and other privileges offered to *al-qāḍī* is affirmed in various classical Islamic sources, as it raises suspensions and subjects him to covet".[122] Moreover, this type of conduct may open the doors for the public to question his integrity and may consider such gifts as bribes or favours.[123] In his treatise on *Adab Al-Qāḍī*, Imam Al-Khaṣṣāf classifies such acts as pure bribes.[124] In all cases, the *al-qāḍī* should never accept money from litigants to adjudicate between them, as this is considered in Islam as a form of bribe.[125] It goes without saying that he must not accept bribes in any forms. In this context, it is reported that the Prophet Muḥammad (ﷺ) said: "May the curse of God be upon the one who pays a bribe and the one who takes it".[126] Bribery is a major sin in *Shari'ah*, and falls under *fisq* (a term that will be explained later).

However, there is a consensus among *Shari'ah* jurists that the *al-qāḍī* may accept gifts from his relatives, except for those having cases pending before him. As stated above, he may also continue to accept gifts from those who gave him gifts before his appointment as *qāḍī*, but if they increase the value of the gift after his appointment, then he should cease accepting such gifts. As such, the *al-qāḍī* should never compromise his value for any reason. Thus, he must not appear to use his judicial position to personal advantage, nor must he act in a manner that raises suspicions about his conduct.

On the basis of the foregoing, it is clear that, in Islam, the personality of the *al-qāḍī* and his uprightness are traditionally viewed as being subordinate to his judicial function. Bearing in mind the social discrepancies in the early Islamic era, and for the proper administration of justice as exists in our modern era, I can infer from *Shari'ah* sources that the following personal integrity values are required in order to assume a judicial position as

---

[121] Ahmed Sharkawy, *Haibat al-qāḍī fe al-fiqh al-Islámy wa al-kanoon al-wadey* (Judge's Prestige in Islámic Jurisprudence and Positive Law), al-Wafaa Library, first edition, 2018, pp. 70–72.

[122] Ibn Qudāmah, *Al-Mughnī*, vol. 10, p. 68, see above note 51.

[123] Al-Mawardi, 1989, p. 100, see above note 24.

[124] Al-Shahīd al-Sadr, 1977, vol. 2, p. 37, see above note 26.

[125] *Ibid.*, p. 100.

[126] Ibn Majah, 2014, vol. 2, no. 2316, p. 456, see above note 72.

alluded to above: 'conscientiousness', 'uprightness', 'propriety', 'patience', 'dignity', 'esteem', 'firmness' and 'courtesy'.

3.15. Professional Judicial Integrity of *Al-Qāḍī* in <u>Sharī'ah</u>

We have seen that the qualities attached to the personality of the *al-qāḍī* have a great impact on the public respect for and confidence in him. Other professional qualities that have an impact on the performance of the *al-qāḍī* during the court proceedings are also of great importance. In <u>Sharī'ah</u>, integrity is not only a quality of the judge related to his judicial office, it extends to encompass his behaviour during the trial. We will note that personal and professional integrity requirements overlap and complement each other during the judicial process.

According to <u>Sharī'ah</u>, the *al-qāḍī* should observe the highest standards of professional integrity during the trial, as we have seen above. In his Message to the Judiciary, Ibn Khaldun identified certain commands that the *al-qāḍī* should observe and follow before adjudication. Some of those commands address the *al-qāḍī*'s divine duties, while others concern the *al-qāḍī*'s attitude when he is on the bench and assumes the judicial process. The first command requires the *al-qāḍī* to resort to God asking His support and insight. He commanded the *al-qāḍī* to recite certain verses of the *Qur'án*, in particular verse 255 of *surat al-Baqarah*, which reads:

> God! There is no deity save Him, the Alive, the Eternal. Neither slumber nor sleep overtaketh Him. Unto Him belongeth whatsoever is in the heavens and whatsoever is in the earth. Who is he that intercedeth with Him save by His leave? He knoweth that which is in front of them and that which is behind them, while they encompass nothing of His knowledge save what He will. His throne includeth the heavens and the earth, and He is never weary of preserving them. He is the Sublime, the Tremendous.

After this, according to Ibn Khaldun, the *al-qāḍī* should recite a famous *ḥadīth* of the Prophet Muḥammad, narrated by Umm Salamah, Ummul Mu'minin, in which she said:

> The Messenger of God (ﷺ) never went out of my house without raising his eye to the sky and saying: "O God! I seek refuge in Thee lest I stray or be led astray, or slip or made to slip,

or cause injustice, or suffer injustice, or do wrong, or have wrong done to me".[127]

The second command instructs the *al-qāḍī* to observe the qualities included in the Prophet's *ḥadíth* on good manners, which states: "Forbearance, sobriety, and propriety make up one of the twenty-five constituents of prophethood".[128]

Firmness is a personal quality, which has a great impact on the judge's professional performance and is necessary during court proceedings. It was reported that Caliph Umar Ibn Al-Khaṭṭāb preferred to appoint to the judicial office a person who is firm enough that a suspect would fear him.[129] An appropriate measure of firmness is necessary to achieve this end. However, a fine balance has to be drawn by the *al-qāḍī*, who is expected to conduct the process effectively as well as to avoid creating in the mind of a reasonable observer any impression of a lack of impartiality. According to *Adab Al-Qāḍī* literature, the *al-qāḍī* should possess a commanding personality that enables him to control the courtroom. He should not leave a room for the litigants to disturb the proceedings.[130] However, he should behave tolerantly with all parties who appear before him. The *al-qāḍī* should display patience in court. Recognising the interrelation between these two qualities, Caliph Alī ibn Abī Ṭālib instructed Malik al-Ashtar to select for the position of *al-qāḍī*: "[o]ne who is most patient at probing into matters, and is most decisive once the truth is revealed and the verdict becomes clear in his mind".[131]

Adherence to the above-mentioned qualities will ultimately strengthen judicial prestige. Contemporary judicial scholars admit that juridical prestige is an important topic that needs to be explored to identify its implications on the judicial process.[132] *Sharí'ah* has long ago addressed that topic and early Muslim scholars allocated an imperative role to prestige in securing the efficiency of the judicial process. Meanwhile, they emphasise

---

[127] Al-Tirmidhi, *ḥadíth* no. 3472, p. 782, see above note 1.

[128] Imam Mālik, 2016, vol. 2, no. 1492, p. 392, see above note 46; Sunan Abī Dāwūd, 2015, vol. 7, no. 4695, p. 291, see above note 80.

[129] Al-Baihaqi, 2011, p. 315, see above note 67.

[130] Ibn Qudāmah, vol. 11, p. 386, see above note 68.

[131] Alī Al-Salaby, 2004, p. 369, see above note 27.

[132] See, for example, David Klein and Darby Morrisroe, "The Prestige and Influence of Individual Judges on the U.S. Courts of Appeals", in *Journal of Legal Studies*, 1999, vol. 28, no. 2, p. 371.

that prestige only exists where justice and equality prevail.[133] Thus, judges should aspire to preserve their judicial prestige, in order to increase the amount of respect, regard and esteem to their courts. This requires that they maintain order and decorum in all proceedings before the court and be patient, dignified and courteous in relation to litigants, jurors, witnesses, lawyers and others with whom the judge deals in an official capacity.[134]

To preserve his prestige, the *al-qāḍī* should present himself in a dignified manner that commands the respect of others, even in his way of sitting, dressing and grooming.[135] Dignity and esteem should be manifested in *al-qāḍī* conduct in his private life and at court, as these qualities boost respect of the public toward those who hold the judicial office and strengthen the judicial function.

According to *Sharíʿah* sources, it is important that the *al-qāḍī* should be paid handsomely to preserve his dignity and prestige, Caliph Alī Ibn Abī Ṭālib instructed Malik al-Ashtar accordingly:

> Pay *al-qāḍī* handsomely enough, this removes his necessity and there remain no occasion for him to go to others for his need. Confer on him such a high stature so that persons who are most close to you could not covet. Consequently, he would be protected from their malign and back-biting.

From his side, the *al-qāḍī* should avoid with care any behaviour that demeans his prestige and high office or diminish his chivalry. Accordingly, the *al-qāḍī* in Islam should avoid laughing in the courtroom,[136] or being humorous with the parties as this could diminish his esteem.[137] The *al-qāḍī*'s esteem also requires that he should observe his demeanour inside and outside the courtroom. The *al-qāḍī* should neither lend the prestige of the judicial office to advance his private interests, to show off; nor should he allow others to convey the impression that they are in a special position to influence the judge.[138] In any case, according to the majority of early-classical Muslim jurists, the *al-qāḍī* should never aspire to judicial prestige as a modality to brag.[139]

---

[133] Ahmed Sharkawy, 2018, p. 3 see above note 121.

[134] Ibn Farhoun, 2003, vol. 1, pp. 30–32, see above note 107.

[135] *Ibid.*, p. 26.

[136] *Ibid.*, p. 33.

[137] Al-Shahīd al-Sadr, 1977, vol. 1, p. 343, see above note 26.

[138] *Ibid.*, pp. 16–17.

[139] Al-Mawardi, 1989, p. 99, see above note 24.

This illustrates that dignity, esteem and firmness are important safe-guards against improper influences, inducements, pressures, threats or interferences, direct or indirect, in the judicial affairs, from any quarter or for any reason.

As seen before, 'independence', 'impartiality', 'equality' and 'competence and diligence' are recognised qualities, both in *Sharī'ah* and contemporary international standards. Below I will explore how *Sharī'ah* addresses these qualities.

3.15.1. Integrity and Recognised Professional Qualities

3.15.1.1. Equality

As recognised in current international standards, a judge in the performance of his duties shall ensure the principle of equality before the courts and the law, and pay the same attention to all participants in the process regardless of their gender, race, nationality, property and social status, religion, or membership in public associations.[140]

The virtue of equality requires the *al-qāḍī* to treat both parties to litigation equally from the beginning to the end of the proceedings. According to *Sharī'ah* principles, the *al-qāḍī* has to treat litigants at his court equally, so that people could never doubt his impartiality.[141] He should invite them to his court at the same time, allow them to enter together, and let them sit before him at similar places and listen to them equally without any distinction.[142] Imam Al-Khaṣṣāf, had addressed in details the manner in which the litigants should sit before the *al-qāḍī*.[143]

Equal treatment should apply to both the strong and the weak, the ruler and the subjects, and so on.[144] Acknowledging that equality is an essential principle for due performance of the judicial office, in his message, Caliph Umar Ibn Al-Khaṭṭāb advises the *al-qāḍī* to be aware of that principle in the way he treats all litigants who appear before him. In the third paragraph of his message, Caliph Umar Ibn Al-Khaṭṭāb (may God be pleased with him) instructed Abú Moussa Al-Ash'ari on the qualities that he

---

[140] Draft Codes of Ethics of Judges in the Republic of Kazakhstan, Venice Commission, Strasbourg, 2 April 2016, CDL-REF(2016)023, p. 4 (https://www.legal-tools.org/doc/klnjt7/).

[141] Ibn Abī Al-Dam, 1984, p. 137, see above note 32.

[142] *Ibid.*, p. 353.

[143] Al-Shahīd al-Sadr, 1977, vol. 2, pp. 84–87, see above note 26.

[144] Al-Mawardi, 1989, p. 95, see above note 24.

should administer concerning the litigants who will appear before him. He wrote to him:

> Be equal to the parties appearing before you, and let your fairness be manifested in the way they seat in your divan (courtroom), in your face (facial expressions) and in your judgement, so that no noble person can ever hope that you will favour him/her unfairly, nor can a layman ever doubt your fairness;

Caliph Umar Ibn Al-Khaṭṭáb went beyond the required standard of equality to ask the *al-qāḍī* to observe his demeanours as a crucial element to maintain his impartiality during the proceedings, because it is what others see. In this respect, Caliph Umar Ibn Al-Khaṭṭáb advises the *al-qāḍī* to observe his conduct, which appears in his facial expressions or even in the way the litigants are seated before him. This approach of Caliph Umar Ibn Al-Khaṭṭáb demonstrates his aim to preserve public confidence in the integrity of the judiciary.

The highest standards of equality and impartiality are manifested in the following statement of Caliph Umar Ibn Al-Khaṭṭáb on the Judiciary: "let your fairness be manifest in your face".

Imam Al-Khaṣṣāf emphasises that the *al-qāḍī* should be equal to the parties who appear before him, even in the way he looks at them.[145] According to Ibn Qayyim al-Jawziyyah, this clause elaborates how the *al-qāḍī* should treat all parties who appear before him on equal terms, without any distinction. The *al-qāḍī* should not smile at one of the litigants or give him/her special attention, as this may manifest a sense of impartiality.[146] According to Imam Al-Khaṣṣāf, *al-qāḍī* should speak to all litigants in the same tone of voice.[147]

A famous case in the Islamic tradition that illustrates how equality is well-observed among early Muslim judges is the case of *Caliph Alī Ibn Abī Ṭālib v. the Jew*. Caliph Alī lost his armour during the war. When the war was over and he returned to Kufah-Iraq, he came across the armour in the hands of a Jew. The Jew said to Caliph Alī: "It is my armour and it is in my hand". Caliph Alī brought a claim before the appointed *qāḍī* (the famous judge Shuraih) alleging that the Jew had stolen his shield. The *al-qāḍī*

---

[145] Al-Shaid al-Sadr, 1977, vol. 1, p. 218, see above note 85.

[146] Ibn Qayyim al-Jawziyyah, I'lam al-Muwaqqi'in 'an Rabb al 'Alamin, Narrated by Abd El-Rahman El-Wakeel, vol. I, Dar Ehya al Turath al Araby, Beirut, p. 96.

[147] Al-Shaid al-Sadr, 1977, vol. 2, p. 92, see above note 85.

asked Caliph Alī to produce his witnesses to prove his claim. Caliph Alī presented his son and then his emancipated slave. According to *al-qāḍī* Shuraih, the testimony of a son in favour of his father or of the emancipated slave was not admissible, before him; hence he ordered Alī to present another witness. When Caliph Alī was unable to do so, *al-qāḍī* Shuraih dismissed his original claim to the armour. Caliph Alī, the caliph of the time, emerged from the court cheerfully, even though the judgment went against him. Then, the Jew said: "The Amir al-Muminin (Caliph Alī) brought me before his *qāḍī*, and his *qāḍī* gave a judgement against him. I witness that this is the truth, and I witness that there is no god but God and I witness that Muḥammad is the messenger of God, and that the armour is your armour". Caliph Alī responded: "I have made it a gift for you".[148]

3.15.1.2. Impartiality

It is admitted nowadays that improper demeanour by members of the judiciary can undermine the judicial process by conveying an impression of bias or indifference to the litigants or other persons attending the trials.[149] As such, impartiality is essential to the proper discharge of the judicial office. It applies not only to the decision itself but also to the process by which the decision is made.[150] Article 2 of the Basic Principles on the Independence of the Judiciary specifies some of the qualities of the judge, which reflects some elements of judicial integrity, related to the principle of impartiality. Accordingly, the judiciary shall decide matters before them impartially, on the basis of facts and in accordance with the law.

Acknowledging that impartiality is the cornerstone of any judicial system, Lord Denning once said:

> Justice is rooted in confidence, and confidence is destroyed when the right-minded go away thinking that the judge is biased. The judge shouldn't be diverted from their duties by any extraneous influences, nor by any hope of reward, nor by the fear of penalties, nor by flattering, nor by indignant reproach. It is the sure knowledge of this that gives the people confidence in judges.

Accordingly, all partisan political activities should cease upon the holding of the judicial office, as this may undermine the judge's impartiali-

---

[148] Ibn Abī'l-Dam, 1984, p. 258, see above note 32.

[149] UNODC, p. 112, see above note 2.

[150] See Bangalore Principles of Judicial Conduct, Value 2, p. 3, see above note 6.

ty and lead to public confusion about the nature of his relationship with other authorities. This approach was recognised in *Sharí'ah* more than 14 centuries ago. According to *Sharí'ah*'s different sources, judges are required to exercise maximum discretion in the courts' proceedings, in order to preserve their image of impartiality. While in judicial office, a judge should not choose, in public, one side of a debate over another. In addition, to preserve integrity, a judge must be careful to avoid, as far as possible, entanglements in controversies that may reasonably be seen as politically partisan.

In *surat Sad*, God advises his messenger David to avoid his own whims when judging between people:

> O David, verily we have placed you as a successor on Earth, so judge between people in truth, and do not follow your desires – for it will mislead you from the path of God. Verily, those who wander stray from the path of God (shall) have a severe punishment, because they forgot the day of reckoning.[151]

According to these verses, those who are in positions of authority should judge according to truth and justice impartially, without any distinction between litigants.

Certain personal qualities like piety, sobriety and propriety are interacting with the professional quality 'impartiality' to keep the *al-qāḍī* unbiased. A judge will have to excuse himself, if he feels that his judgement might benefit one of his acquaintances, such as a member of his family, close relatives or friends.

In addition, the *al-qāḍī* must not favour one party, for example, by showing any sign or gesture towards any party to a dispute before him, which might give suspicion that he is in favour of that party. The foregoing shows that established rules by *Sharí'ah*, assert that the *al-qāḍī* should perform his judicial duties without favour, bias or prejudice.

3.15.1.3. Independence

It is understood that judicial independence is not an exclusive privilege accorded to judges in the performance of their duty, but it is also a right enjoyed by citizens when they seek justice in courts. There is no doubt that the concept of 'integrity' and the principle of 'independence' are comple-

---

[151] *Qur'án, surat Sad*, 38:26.

mentary and intermingled. Maintaining judicial independence will increase confidence in the judiciary. If the general public loses faith in the integrity of judges, this would pose the greatest threat to the independence of the judiciary.

Influences, inducements, pressures, threats or interferences on a judge or in his judicial function, direct or indirect, from any quarter or for any reason, could be described as a threat to judicial impartiality and independence and thereby, judicial integrity. The *al-qāḍī* must not deviate from the truth for fear of someone's anger. The *al-qāḍī*'s esteem should be maintained and he should not be exposed to undue approaches of interested parties. Accordingly, the *al-qāḍī* should not be diverted from his duties by any extraneous factor, nor by any hope of reward as this could be characterised as a threat to their independence and therefore integrity.

It is widely believed among Islamic scholars that during the historical period of the guided Caliphs, the judiciary enshrined both institutional and personal independence to a level comparable to advanced legal systems today. Many examples exist within Islamic history to illustrate the extent of independence early Muslim judges had. An illustrative example is that when Caliph Umar Ibn Al-Khaṭṭáb diminished any authority of Muawya Ibn Abi Sufian, the ruler of Palestine at the time, on *Al-Qāḍī* Ebadah Ibn Elsamet, to consolidate his independence.[152]

3.15.1.4. Competence and Diligence

As previously mentioned, competence and due diligence are essential requirements for assuming the judicial office. These required criteria are manifested in both the Messages of Caliph Umar Ibn Al-Khaṭṭáb and Caliph Alī Ibn Abī Ṭālib on the Judiciary. Both messages affirm that *Sharí'ah* criteria in that respect surpass the conditions of appointment at the judicial office in contemporary judicial systems, whether at the national or international levels. Competence in the performance of judicial duties requires legal knowledge and skills of *Sharí'ah* sciences. To achieve this level, according to *Adab Al-Qāḍī* literature, the *al-qāḍī* should be acquainted with the jurists. The *al-qāḍī*'s professional competence should be evident in the discharge of his duties. This will never be achieved unless he has the ca-

---

[152] For more details, see Ibn Al-Atheer, *Asad al-ghaba fe merefat al-sahaba*, Dar ibn Hazm, 2012, no. 2792, p. 630.

pacity to exercise independent juristic reasoning; in other words, is capable of practicing *ijtihád*.[153]

3.15.2. <u>Sharí'ah</u> Perspectives on the Emotional Integrity of *Al-Qādī*

As we have seen before, *Sharí'ah* considers the concept of judicial integrity as a moral value, which incorporates a multiplicity of virtues. Unlike man-made laws and regulations, in Islam, as a divine religion, internal sentiment and behavioural responses of the *al-qādī* do count. *Sharí'ah* puts emphasis on the *al-qādī*'s emotions to guarantee that such emotions do not affect his ability to judge fairly.

Before addressing the impact of the *al-qādī*'s emotions on his judgements, one should explore the meaning of the word 'emotion', as required by this chapter and to understand to which extent it affects the *al-qādī* actions and reactions. As illustrated by a renowned physiologist: "There is no consensus in the literature on the definition of emotions. The term is taken for granted in itself and, most often, emotion is defined with reference to a list: anger, disgust, fear, joy, sadness, and surprise".[154] Some think that emotions are always associated with thoughts, feelings, behavioural responses, and a degree of pleasure or displeasure.[155] Hence, it is admitted by some contemporary legal scholars that emotions almost certainly have a substantial impact on peoples' behaviour, as well as on judges' conduct, while carrying on their judicial responsibilities.[156] Therefore, wisdom requires that 'emotional integrity' should be regarded as an essential aspect of good character, something that also applies to judges.

However, we have to bear in mind that emotions, as opposed to values, are subjective, and may come into conflict with established judicial values. Accordingly, they view some emotions as signs of either a lack or plenitude of integrity.[157] Hate and anger are examples of the latter. Inadequate emotional integrity may lead to inappropriate behavioural responses,

---

[153] For more details, see Al-Mawardi, 1989, pp. 89–91, see above note 24.

[154] Michel Cabanac, "What Is Emotion?", in *Behavioural Processes*, 2002, vol. 60, no. 2, p. 2.

[155] See Paul Ekman and Richard Davidson (eds.), *The Nature of Emotion: Fundamental Questions*, in Series in affective Science, Oxford University Press, 1994.

[156] Terry A. Maroney, "The Emotional Intelligent Judge: A New (and Realistic) Ideal", in *Court Review: The Journal of the American Judges Association*, November 2013, vol. 49, no. 2, p. 100.

[157] See Damian Cox, Marguerite La Caze and Michael P. Levine, *Integrity and the Fragile Self*, Routledge, 2018.

which will negatively affect the judicial performance of the *al-qāḍī* and compromise his judgements.

As a Western scholar recently observed, like any other persons, judges have emotions, and their emotions may influence the decision-making process.[158] Therefore, a judge with emotional integrity, has strong core values, such as serenity and honesty, that subsequently influence his judicial 'outer' conduct.

As stated several decades ago by a renowned judicial authority:

> Deep below consciousness are other forces, the likes and the dislikes, the predilections and the prejudices, the complex of instincts and emotions and habits and convictions, which make the man, whether he be litigant or judge.[159]

While existing codes of judicial conduct, both at the international and national levels, do not address certain emotional characteristics of judges, such as hatred, anger, empathy and patience, *Shari'ah* addressed such emotions, in details, in its different sources. Moreover, as we will see below, when addressing the *al-qāḍī*'s emotions, *Shari'ah* does not only deal with his expressions, anger and what he likes, but it does also address his deep inner state of mind, to guarantee his emotional balance and harmony.

As we have seen before, the *Qur'án* encourages the believers to do justice in all circumstances, without regard to their emotional inclinations for others or *vice versa*. It is inspiring to see how the *Qur'án* addressed this issue 1,400 years ago in *surat Al-Ma'idah*, in which God commanded the believers to conquer their emotional inclinations and do justice, even towards their enemies.[160]

In his letter to Mālik Al-Ashtar, Caliph Alī Ibn Abī Ṭālib addressed the *al-qāḍī*'s emotions and inner-feelings in the context of the judicial process. He advised him to select for the position of the *al-qāḍī* "one who does not have any tendency to covetousness". And to guarantee ample emotional balance and serenity of the *al-qāḍī* during his work Caliph Alī Ibn Abī Ṭālib asked Mālik Al-Ashtar to appoint "one who does not vain to flattery

---

[158] Maroney, 2013, p. 100, see above note 156.

[159] Benjamin N. Cardozo, *The Nature of the Judicial Process*, Yale University Press, 1921, p. 167.

[160] See Tafsir Ibn Kathir (interpretation of Noble *Qur'án* in English), Darussalam, Riyadh, January 2000, vol. 3, p. 122.

and who is not easily tempted".[161] This shows how *Sharí'ah* is not only concerned with the outer expressions of the judge during adjudication, but also with his inner emotions. In this context, early Muslim jurists required the *al-qāḍī* to have a balanced attitude with peace of mind and serenity.[162]

Acknowledging the fact that the *al-qāḍī's* emotions could affect his conduct towards the litigants, and therefore could be very detrimental to the cause of justice, *Sharí'ah* instructs the *al-qāḍī* to avoid anger, anxiety and weariness during the performance of his judicial duties.[163] He should also avoid to be annoyed by litigants. The Prophet Muḥammad (ﷺ) underscored this in one of his famous *hadíth*: "Let *al-qāḍī* not pass a judgment when he is angry".[164]

In the ninth paragraph of his Message on the Judiciary, Caliph Umar Ibn Al-Khaṭṭáb instructed Abú Moussa Al-Ash'ari to "[b]e cautious of anger, anxiety, weariness, and impatience when adjudicating on people's disputes".

Adab Al-Qāḍī literature provide more example of certain emotions that could prevent the *al-qāḍī* from judging adequately. For example, he must not give judgement when under emotional strain. The reason for this is very simple; when the *al-qāḍī* is emotionally disturbed, his reasoning power and judgement may be impaired.

This leads to the fact that that the *al-qāḍī* should retain peace of mind while hearing cases brought before him, as this will enable him to focus on the hearing with full attention so that he will be able to decide fairly and correctly. Subsequently, the *al-qāḍī* should not decide cases when he is angry, hungry, worried or suffering weariness.[165]

Contemporary judicial systems in some Arab States acknowledge the fact that some emotions could affect the judge's eligibility to decide a case before him; although they consider them as internal feelings that are difficult to assess in most cases, however, they relate to the judge's conscience. In this sense, the Egyptian Court of Cassation has established that: "The state of anger, the desire to condemn and the feeling of embarrassment are

---

[161] Alī Al-Salaby, 2004, p. 369, see above note 27.

[162] Ibn Farhoun, 2003, vol. 1, p. 32, see above note 107.

[163] Al-Baihaqi, 2011, p. 307, see above note 67.

[164] Sunan Abī Dāwūd, the Book of Judgements, vol. 5, no. 3544, p. 582.

[165] Al-Shahīd al-Sadr, 1977, vol. 1, p. 340–341, see above note 26.

all internal issues within the judge's mind-set, which relate to his disposition and conscience".[166]

However, if such emotions are established, any party to the dispute can challenge the judge's eligibility to perform his judicial function, with respect to the case over which he is presiding, because of a possible lack of impartiality. In such instance, the judge can recuse himself from the case. Integrity requirements oblige the judge to disqualify himself in any proceeding in which his impartiality might reasonably be questioned. However, in some jurisdictions, unless the legislator has left the matter of determining the existence of such emotions to the judge's discretion, to what reassures him and to what rests his sentiment.[167]

Interestingly, *Shari'ah* does not limit the conditions that prevent the *al-qāḍī* from deciding a case to emotional disturbance or strain only. It goes further to prevent the *al-qāḍī* from deciding cases when his physical conditions could affect his well-being, feelings or reactions. In this regard the Prophet Muḥammad (ﷺ) said: "Let the judge not pass a judgment unless he is comfortable (should not be in state of hunger or thirst)".[168]

Notably, *Shari'ah* places noticeable considerations on the well-being of the *al-qāḍī* during the performance of his judicial function, as this will guarantee that he will be able to provide full attention to his work. For example, he should avoid fatigue and must not weaken himself with non-obligatory fasting when he is deciding cases.

Many examples of certain emotions that could prevent the *al-qāḍī* from judging fairly are found in *Adab Al-Qāḍī* literature. According to *Adab Al-Qāḍī*, the *al-qāḍī* should not sit on the bench or decide on a case when he is unduly tired or overjoyed. He goes further to stipulate that he must not decide a case when sleep overcomes him, nor when he is hungry or has overeaten.[169] Moreover, the *al-qāḍī*'s emotions should not influence him to show compassion to one of the parties in a dispute before him.

It is argued that the psychology of emotional regulation can help judges learn how to prepare realistically for, and respond thoughtfully to

---

[166] Appeal No. 25649 before the Egyptian Court of Cassation, Judicial Year 64, Technical Bureau 47, p. 1362.

[167] *Ibid.*

[168] Al-Baihaqi, 2011, pp. 306–307, see above note 67.

[169] Imam Ibn Al- Kāss, 1989, pp. 157–159, see above note 112.

the emotions they are bound to feel.[170] Of course, this requires skilful emotional management and strong emotional integrity. Apparently, a judge with emotional integrity is a judge who can control his demeanours.

Evidently, *Sharíʿah* is well equipped to tackle judges' emotions during the performance of their duties. Recalling the divine nature of Islam, its affiliation with inner peace (*iṭmīnān*), and its call for contentment (*riḍā*) and serenity (*sakīna*), a faithful Muslim judge would rely on his religious convention and Prophetical teachings to manage his anger, anxiety, weariness and impatience.

We can infer from the foregoing that *Sharíʿah* does not only inspire certain emotions in the *al-qāḍī*, such as serenity and peace of mind, which lead to emotional balance and harmony. It also asks the *al-qāḍī* to detach himself from any type of personal emotions that may influence his judgment. It even gives regard to the *al-qāḍī*'s inside inclinations, such as a tendency towards avariciousness and temptations.

To summarise, according to *Sharíʿah*, a 'good judge', is one who is not influenced in his decisions by personal desires, or by fear or hope, one who has no inclination towards favouritism, but takes a neutral attitude towards all that comes before him, and finally, one who could manage his anger, anxiety, weariness, and impatience.

3.15.3. A Proposed Definition of Judicial Integrity Derived from *Sharíʿah* Sources

As shown in this chapter, in *Sharíʿah*, the basis of judicial integrity, as an ethical value, is found in the conscientiousness of the person concerned, as a virtue derived from the religion itself.

The approach of *Sharíʿah* towards integrity as a moral value is reflected in the approach of the second United Nations Secretary-General Dag Hammarskjöld's understanding of integrity, in which he associates it with purity of intention and equates it with conscience.[171]

One important character of judicial integrity as established in this chapter is that it motivates the person in question to adhere to certain quali-

---

[170] Maroney, 2013, p. 113, see above note 156.

[171] See Dag Hammarskjöld, "The International Civil Servant in Law and Fact: Lecture delivered to Congregation at Oxford University, 30 May 1961", in Wilder Foote (ed.), *The Servant of Peace: A Selection of the Speeches and Statements of Dag Hammarskjöld, Secretary-General of the United Nations*, 1953-1961, The Bodley Head, 1962, p. 348 (https://www.legal-tools.org/doc/64bcae/).

ties, mainly uprightness and propriety, thus it distances the person concerned from malice and suspicion.

On the basis of the provisions of *Shari'ah* sources stipulated in this chapter, judicial integrity can be defined as: a core judicial value, which reflects a holistic concept incorporating intrinsic core personal virtues that those who hold a judicial office should possess, such as 'conscientiousness', 'uprightness', 'propriety', 'dignity', 'esteem', 'firmness' and 'courtesy', requiring them to distance themselves from malice and avoid suspicion, by refraining from any conduct that could cast any doubt on their behaviour, while fully respecting other professional qualities such as 'independence', 'impartiality', 'equality', and 'competence and diligence'.

An in-depth comprehension of the concept, from an Arab *Shari'ah* perspective, reveals that judicial integrity is based on and revolves around the core value of distancing oneself from malice and avoiding attracting suspicion, thus freeing oneself from any corrupting influences. A person who possesses such quality is, ultimately, expected to discharge his judicial duties according to the highest standards of integrity. Furthermore, adherence to the 'elements of integrity' stipulated in this definition, would allow those who are appointed in any judicial position to preserve their sacred judicial function.

As we have seen, emotions might have a great impact on the *al-qāḍī*'s judicial performance. This raises the question whether there is a requirement of 'emotional integrity' for those who occupy judicial positions whether at the national or international levels.

3.15.4. Some Indications of Judicial Integrity from a *Shari'ah* Perspective

The existence of a judicial performance-indicator mechanism may be important to assess judges' conduct, and ensure the independence, impartiality and fairness of the judiciary.

From my analysis and interpretation of *Shari'ah* sources specified in this chapter, I can infer the following indications of the existence of judicial integrity:

- abide by Islamic judicial traditions and courts' practice;
- acquaintance with the jurists, as well as with the pious;
- avoid malicious and corrupt behaviour;

- uphold the highest standards of judicial characteristics, such as impartiality, righteousness, dignity, esteem and propriety; and
- consistency, coherence and equality in judicial decision-making.

3.15.5. Loss of Integrity

It has been established in this chapter that, according to _Sharíʿah_, the _al-qāḍī_ should distance himself from malice and avoid suspicion; otherwise he would lose his integrity. Consequently, he should behave in a manner that does not cast doubt upon his independence, integrity and impartiality. As integrity is a core value that is an ornament of the judicial function, being without it, the judiciary loses its credentials.

As we have seen before, through different sources of _Sharíʿah_, the concept of judicial integrity, as understood in the Islamic tradition, is a central value that contains a variety of virtues attached to the judicial office. It is, therefore, very important that the _al-qāḍī_'s conducts is within the parameters set by _Sharíʿah_. The _al-qāḍī_ should observe the standards of integrity set by _Sharíʿah_, in all its components, and should be held accountable in case if he infringes these standards. This is totally understood, as _al-qāḍī_ misbehaviour could erode the credibility of the judicial institution in the public mind, which is so destructive to the independence of the judiciary.

However, it is unfortunate that in current judicial systems, not every violation of the judicial integrity qualities, as illustrated in this chapter, leads to disciplinary action. Notwithstanding this fact, in some judicial systems, if a certain violation is not grave, a judge could be held accountable on the basis of his overall conduct. For instance, in the Egyptian judicial system, it is established that judicial integrity is judged on the basis of the totality of the behaviour of the person concerned. This means that the accumulation of infringements of judicial integrity qualities might lead to removal from office, even though each of those infringements alone is not alone punishable. According to relevant decisions by the respected Chamber of the Egyptian Court of Cassation, integrity must be judged "on the basis of the aggregate behaviour of the judge concerned".[172]

Accordingly, when assessing certain conduct of a judge under scrutiny, to decide on his eligibility, during disciplinary measures, focus should

---

[172] Court of Cassation, Civil Chamber, Appeal no. 5, Judicial Year 52, Session 18/1/1983, Technical Bureau Year 34, p. 5.

be on the 'wholeness' of the person concerned and on all his past and present acts, by examining both his personal and judicial integrity. In the final analysis, the question that must always be asked is whether in the particular social context and in the eyes of a reasonable observer, the judge has engaged in an activity that could objectively compromise his or her independence or impartiality or that might appear to do so. As stipulated in Caliph Alī Ibn Abī Ṭālib Letter on the Judiciary, Islamic rulers used to periodically evaluate the professional performance and behaviour of the judges they had previously appointed.[173] In case of biased judgements,[174] or established corruption or misconduct, the judge could be removed from office.

3.15.5.1. *Fisq* (Corruption): A Flagrant Threat to Integrity

Corruption of members of the judiciary undermines the rule of law and affects public confidence in the judicial system.[175] Therefore, the United Nations Convention against Corruption, in its Article 11, obliges States Parties, in accordance with the fundamental principles of their legal systems and without prejudice to judicial independence, to take measures to strengthen integrity and to prevent opportunities for corruption among members of the judiciary, including rules with respect to the conduct of members of the judiciary.[176] Since the mid-1990s, the interplay between corruption, good governance, and integrity has become a crucial issue in the global setting. Situations and abuses can challenge one's personal integrity and create a conflict between the person and the judicial institution. Therefore, a judge acting in a way that is corrupt (for example, through accepting bribes or other favours to make favourable judicial decisions), acts without integrity.[177]

Sharí'ah despises corruption and the corrupted, and has attributed prodigious emphasis on issues related to the incorruptibility of the *al-qāḍī*. To ensure that a judge's behaviour and conduct is acceptable to the public, and does not provide an opportunity for people to doubt his integrity or im-

---

[173] Alī Al-Salaby, 2004, p. 369, see above note 27.

[174] Ibn Farhoun, 2003, vol. 1, p. 15, see above note 107.

[175] See the Economic and Social Council, Strengthening basic principles of judicial conduct, 27 July 2006, ECOSOC 2006/23 (https://www.legal-tools.org/doc/yiyqyy/).

[176] UN General Assembly, United Nations Convention against Corruption, 21 November 2003, A/RES/58/4 (https://www.legal-tools.org/doc/hwuihi/).

[177] Agata Gurzawska, Institutional Integrity, SATORI, European Commission's Seventh Framework Programme, June 2015, p. 5.

partiality, Muslim jurists require that a judge should refrain from any conduct that could cast doubt in his behaviour. Therefore, a judge should avoid any activities that may attract criticism or rebuttal from the public.

In his famous letter to Mālik Al-Ashtar on the Judiciary, Caliph Alī Ibn Abī Ṭālib had eloquently used a short paragraph reflecting a specific character that should not exist in *al-qāḍī* that might lead him to corruption. As mentioned before, he advised Mālik Al-Ashtar to select: "One who does not have any tendency to covetousness".[178] Moreover, he advised him to: "pay him handsomely enough, that removes his necessity and there remain no occasion for him to go to others for his need", a theme touched on above. The aforementioned approach of Caliph Alī Ibn Abī Ṭālib could be considered as a preventive measure of graft and corruption of judges.

3.15.5.2. Disciplinary Measures in <u>Sharí'ah</u>

<u>Sharí'ah</u> has recognized forms of disciplinary measures for judges, such as disqualification and removal from office, in case they lose their judicial integrity.

3.15.5.2.1. Disqualification

The meaning of the term 'disqualification' might vary in the Arab and Islamic States and differ from the meaning prevalent in Western States. The term 'disqualification' in the Arabic language is not only restricted to losing impartiality, competency of other professional qualifications, as it extends to cover some personal qualities. In general, a judge could be disqualified only for any conduct that could undermine the judiciary or the judicial institution.

In a book titled 'Fair Trial, and Values and Traditions of the Judiciary', a renowned Egyptian judicial authority stated:

> The value of the eligibility/qualification, in the judicial domain, means that the judge or the prosecutor possesses good manners and reputation, absolute objectivity, in his judicial convection and the application of the law, impartiality manifested in avoiding inclination towards personal desires and

---

[178] Alī Al-Salaby, 2004, p. 369, see above note 27.

whims. Infringement of these values may result in disciplinary measures that could lead to his disqualification.[179]

3.15.5.2.2. Removal from Office

In the majority of legal systems, removal from office might only occur in cases of infirmity of body or mind or serious misbehaviour according to established principles of *Sharí'ah*. In cases of clear proof of corruption (*fisq*) on the part of a judge, he could be disqualified and removed from office, not only the case.[180] According to the foregoing, the *al-qāḍī* could be subjected to disciplinary measures, not merely for professional reasons, but also because of allegations about his personal misbehaviour. It is worth noting that this approach has already been adopted by the European Court of Human Rights. It has previously acknowledged that a judge's duty to observe professional ethics may impinge to a certain extent upon his or her private life.[181]

The question of when *al-qāḍī* may be removed from office is of vital importance in *Sharí'ah*. The literature on *al-qāḍī* has clearly determined three mechanisms for the removal of *al-qāḍī* from office:

1. The *al-qāḍī* may remove himself, with the knowledge of the Muslim ruler;

2. The *al-qāḍī* should remove himself or be removed by the ruler In case of fisq;

3. The Islamic ruler may remove the *al-qāḍī* from his office.

Al-fisq is a shameful quality both in the Arab traditions and *Sharí'ah*. In Arabic language it means departing from the right path and disobedience.[182] The term *fisq* may also be understood as 'impious' or 'corrupt' that may constitute an act of debauchery; thus, the term refers to a person of loose character who is guilty of committing major sins. It reflects severe disobedience of the Commands of God and violations of *Sharí'ah* norms as well as deviating from the path of truth, as such it diminish and important Islamic judicial quality, which is 'uprightness'.

---

[179] Serry Siam, *Al-muhakamah al-monsifa wa keiam wa takaleed al-qadaa*, Dar al-Shorouk, first edition, 2017, p. 67.

[180] Ibn Farhoun, 2003, vol. 1, p. 15, see above note 107.

[181] See *Özpınar v. Turkey*, no. 20999/04, 19 October 2010.

[182] Muhammad Taher, *al-garh we al-taedeel bayen al-mutashadedin we al-mutasahlin*, Al-Dar Al-Arabia Llketab, Tunis, 1997, p. 366.

Imam Al-Shawkany cited the opinion of Imam al-Qurtubi which indicated that the term *fisq* meant by *Sharí'ah* is: actions that lead to a deviation from the obedience of God and may be categorised as *ma'siah* (sin).[183] Obviously, the term *fisq* covers cases of violation of personal and professional integrity. Personal and professional misconduct fall under this term. Accordingly, the *al-qāḍī* may be removed from office if he is found in a state of *fisq*,[184] in case he is engaged in serious corruptive conduct or misbehaviour that clearly renders him unfit to discharge his duties.

Commonly, in most legal systems, judges are removed from office in cases of serious ethical or criminal misconduct, such as accepting bribes, sexual misbehaviour, obstructing an official proceeding, and making false statements. If it is proven that the judge has violated terms of judicial integrity that affects his personal judicial credibility, which poses a threat to the administration of justice, then he could be dismissed from the judiciary according to applicable disciplinary mechanisms.

It has to be mentioned that the rigorous requirements for the appointment in the judicial office and the high standards of ethical conduct help to minimize the resort to the removal mechanism.

To maintain the appearance of judicial independence, Islamic law does not permit the ruler to remove the *al-qāḍī* from office unless in cases of *fisq* or serious acts of misconduct that undermine the public confidence in the judiciary. In this case, the ruler shall appoint another person who is much better qualified for the post.[185] If a judge is removed without a valid reason, his appointment remains intact.

3.16. Conclusion

We have seen in this chapter that Islam emphasises the function of the judiciary as it is, according to *Sharí'ah* principles, close to piety. Therefore, a review of *Sharí'ah* sources shows that judges are selected after a credible inquiry by the Caliphs and other Muslim rulers to ensure that the judge being appointed is reliable and fulfils the prerequisite qualities required by *Sharí'ah*.

---

[183] Imam Al-Shawkani, *Fath Al-Qadir Al-Jame*, Youssef Al-Ghoush (ed.), Dar Al-Marefah, Beirut, vol. 1, pp. 40–41.

[184] Al-Shaid al-Sadr, 1977, p. 129, see above note 85.

[185] Ibn Farhoun, 2003, p. 15, see above note 107.

In-depth research in *Shari'ah* sources has revealed that the term 'integrity' refers to a combination of values intrinsic in a person's character and is an established norm in *Shari'ah*. In the context of the judicial function, it refers to certain qualities manifested in the *al-qāḍī's* personal and professional characteristics during the performance of his judicial duties. One important core value that reflects the concept of judicial integrity in *Shari'ah* is to distance oneself from malice and avoid attracting suspicion, thus freeing oneself from any corrupting influences.

This chapter has also affirmed that integrity is essential to the proper administration of justice, and that *Shari'ah* provisions adopt a high standard approach to judicial integrity and considers it as a moral value and a legal requirement for the discharge of the judicial function. Further, it has asserted that integrity is a condition of general ethical conduct and virtue both before and after appointment, in *Shari'ah*, which is honoured in national legal systems of Islamic countries.

Interestingly, the research in this chapter has revealed that the rules of *Shari'ah* on integrity converge with the ancient Roman/Greek 'virtue ethical theory'. Further research may show the interactions between these traditions. Apparently, the meaning of judicial integrity does not differ significantly between various traditions, and should be recognised as a common, universal legal quality-requirement to hold judicial office.

However, notwithstanding this, *Shari'ah* would seem to be more encompassing than contemporary approaches to judicial integrity, stipulated in modern international documents, and granted special attention to the management of judges' emotions during the performance of their judicial function, acknowledging that inadequate emotional integrity may undesirably influence the judicial decision-making process.

In my view, the qualities of judges required in the Messages on the Judiciary of the two guided Caliphs Umar Ibn Al-Khaṭṭáb and Alī Ibn Abī Ṭāleb, exceed those that exist in contemporary international documents. As stipulated in those messages, we should ask ourselves whether we nowadays find judges whose fairness is manifested in their face? One who is cautious of anger, anxiety, weariness, and impatience when adjudicating people's disputes? One who does not have any tendency to covetousness? One who is immune to flattery and elation? I think there are very few who have such characteristics and are thus qualified for the appointment to such a *sacred* position as judge.

According to my reading of the _Sharí'ah_ provisions stipulated in this chapter, and beyond, based on logical reasoning, derived from _fiqh_, I concluded that the judicial integrity concept entails two meanings: personal integrity and professional integrity. A person who holds judicial office should have and demonstrate both qualities. The stringent requirements of both personal and professional judicial integrity in _Sharí'ah_ explain why one who is appointed as a judge is slaughtered without a knife, according to the Prophet Muḥammad's (ﷺ) _hadíth_.

On the basis of provisions of _Sharí'ah_ sources stipulated in this chapter, I propose the following definition of judicial integrity:

> A holistic concept that incorporates the intrinsic core personal and professional qualities that those who hold a judicial office should possess, which requires them to distance themselves from malice and avoid suspicion, by refraining from any conduct that could cast any doubt on their behaviour, while fully respecting equality, fairness, impartiality, and independence of the judiciary.

I believe that _Sharí'ah_ standards on integrity, which are spread out in its sources, could assist in developing a model code of conduct that can help to reinforce judicial ethical standards and to create a _culture_ of integrity in relevant judicial systems. It may also assist various judicial institutions not only to render their judges ethically stronger, but also to consolidate their integrity. Developing such a code in international justice institutions may contribute to holding those who violate judicial ethics accountable. The existence of personal and professional judicial integrity will create the realisation and the public perception regarding the efficiency and transparency of the judicial system and will ultimately raise the public's trust in that system.

I hope to have conveyed to the Western reader, the normative structure of the concept of judicial integrity that exists in _Sharí'ah_, in a manner that inspires more terminological clarity. The hope is that the values on judicial integrity included in this chapter could assist in realising the highest standards of judicial integrity, in a way that could provide concrete ideas for the strengthening of judicial integrity in national and international institutions. For the purposes of this book, it bears repeating that the standards that international judges must uphold must be set even higher than at the national level.

An in-depth examination of available jurisprudential *Sharí'ah* sources on the subject-matter goes beyond the scope of this chapter. Other colleagues or institutions may have curiosity to continue researching this topic, in more depth. Indeed, the Centre for International Law Research and Policy (CILRAP) deserves tribute for supporting projects that cover classical jurisprudential sources of *Sharí'ah*. We have seen that early-classical Muslim jurists left the comprehensive *fiqh* treatise *Adab Al-Qāḍī*. This wealth of knowledge should be translated from Arabic into other languages, with commentaries, to assist non-Arabic speaking readers to have access to that original *Sharí'ah* literature, to see how *Sharí'ah* has adopted the highest standards of integrity for the discharge of judicial responsibilities. I believe that this could help to revive Dag Hammarskjöld's legacy of 'integrity' as a standard-bearer for civil servants and high officials in international courts.

Appendix I: The Message of Caliph Umar Ibn Al-Khaṭṭáb on the Judiciary

The Message of Caliph Umar Ibn Al-Khaṭṭáb on the Judiciary (may God be pleased with him) to *Abú Moussa Al-Ash'ari* upon entrusting him with the mandate of adjudicating on people's disputes; which should be considered a judge's charter.

In the Name of God the Merciful and the Gracious

- Adjudication in (Islam) is based on a precise obligation (*Qur'án*) and a followed *Prophetic Tradition* (sayings and practices of Prophet Muhammad, peace be upon him);

- Comprehend any dispute brought before you, and note that it is futile to reach a right judgement without executing it;

- Be equal to the parties appearing before you, and let your fairness be manifested in the way they seat in your *divan* (courtroom), in your face (facial expressions) and in your judgement, so that no noble person can ever hope that you will favour him/her unfairly, nor can a layman ever doubt your fairness;

- The burden of proof is on the plaintiff, and if the defendant denies, he/she must take the oath;

- He who claims an infringed entitlement or missing evidence should be allowed to provide the evidence within a deadline. If he/she supplies the evidence, grant him/her the right he/she claims, otherwise rule against him/her. In that way, you give the plaintiff a fair chance to prove his/her right/entitlement and place the case under proper scrutiny;

- If you render a judgment and then later find out, after re-visiting it, that you were not right, do not hesitate to renounce that judgment in order to establish justice, as justice is primordial and should not be deviated from. A revision of unfair judgement is better than establishing injustice;

- Muslims are credible witnesses whose testimony should be admitted, except those proven to have committed punishable sins, those known to have given false testimony, or those suspected of bias due to loyalty or kinship. Only God Almighty knows what is in the minds of people.

Therefore, no one should be condemned without reliable evidence or proper oath;

- If a case is brought before you and you cannot find applicable rule(s) neither in the *Qur'án* nor in the *Sunnah*, then you must resort to logical reasoning, and use analogy, comparison and parallelism (to reach a judgement). Consequently, apply the ruling that you consider closest to what is right and fair and that would please God Almighty;

- Be cautious of anger, anxiety, weariness, and impatience when adjudicating on people's disputes, and never be annoyed with litigants or deny a litigation. Judging fairly is rewarded by God Almighty and praised by people. He whose heart's intention is to establish justice and rule fairly, even if his/her rulings would be against his/her own interest, will be protected and supported by God Almighty, whereas he/she who, out of hypocrisy, acts contrary to his/her heart's conviction, will be disgraced by Him. God accepts only pure and honest deeds and intentions;

- Contemplate and never forget God's rewards as manifested in both His worldly blessings and plentiful mercy in the Hereafter.

Appendix II: The Message of Alī Ibn Abī Ṭālib to Mālik Al-Ashtar on the Judiciary

The Message of Alī Ibn Abī Ṭālib to his commissioner in Egypt, Mālik Al-Ashtar on the Judiciary is to be considered as one of the most comprehensive *Sharí'ah* instruments on the concept of judicial integrity:

> For adjudicating on people's disputes, select one whom you trust, is by far the best among your subjects in your view; one who is patient and imperturbable; one who is not influenced by the importunity of the litigants; one who does not persist if he commits an error, and hold back the truth once he knew it; one who does not have any tendency to covetousness, nor is satisfied with cursory understanding (of a matter brought before him) without going thoroughly into it (scrupulously goes beyond that to contemplate the case before him to the maximum extent); one who stops whenever he is faced with doubts and only approves reliable evidence; one who is least repined at the quarrel of litigants; one who is most patient at probing into matters, and is most decisive once the truth is revealed and the verdict becomes clear in his mind; and one who does not vain to flattery and is not easily tempted. Few are those who meet all of these criteria. Thereafter, check regularly his judgements, and pay him handsomely enough, that removes his necessity and there remain no occasion for him to go to others for his need. Confer on him such a high stature so that persons who are most close to you could not covet. Consequently, he would be protected from their malign and backbiting.

This letter is to be considered as a model of the qualities that a person should have to be selected as *al-qāḍī* – all components of 'integrity'. While it speaks of both personal and professional judicial qualities, it places more emphasis on the intrinsic values of the person in question. According to Caliph Ali's letter, the *al-qāḍī* should be the most qualified, yet virtuous, patient, honest, truthful and pious person in order to be selected for this position. Indeed, the *al-qāḍī*'s criteria enumerated in Alī Ibn Abī Ṭālib's Letter to Mālik Al-Ashtar fulfil the judicial integrity requirements.

The Letter covers certain safeguards that protect the *al-qāḍī* from malice, corruption and temptations. Specifically, it requires the governor to observe certain virtues for judicial office, including pure intention, having an upright character, and immunity from greed.

4

Sir Thomas More and Integrity in Justice

Gunnar M. Ekeløve-Slydal[*]

Beati quorum via integra est: qui ambulant in lege Domini[1]

Integrity issues in international organizations have gained wide attention in recent years due to extensive media coverage of problematic practices and non-compliance with codes of ethics by actors within such organizations. Particularly shocking were revelations by eight international media organizations of the European Investigative Collaborations in 2017 that undermined the credibility of the International Criminal Court ('ICC').

The revelations included serious allegations that members of the ICC Office of the Prosecutor had helped the first Prosecutor of the ICC, Luis Moreno-Ocampo, to make money by assisting persons suspected of having aided ICC crimes in Libya. There were also issues connected with situations under ICC investigations in Côte d'Ivoire and Kenya as well as some broader issues linked to the heritage of the first Prosecutor.[2]

---

[*] **Gunnar M. Ekeløve-Slydal** is Acting Secretary General, Norwegian Helsinki Committee, and Adjunct Lecturer at the University of South East Norway. He studied philosophy at the University of Oslo and worked for many years for the Norwegian Centre for Human Rights at the University of Oslo and as Editor of the *Nordic Journal on Human Rights*. He has written extensively on human rights, international institutions, and philosophical themes, including textbooks, reports, and articles. The author wants to extend his gratitude to Berit Lindeman for input to Section 4.1.1. on election observation and Section 4.1.2. on corruption in the Parliamentary Assembly of the Council of Europe.

[1] "Blessed are the undefiled in the way, who walk in the law of the Lord." Book of Psalms 119:1, King James Version. An alternative translation from the New International Version reads as follows: "Blessed are those whose ways are blameless, who walk according to the law of the Lord".

[2] For a short account of the issues, see Pierre Hassan, "Scandals rocks international criminal court", *Justiceinfo*, 8 October 2017 (available on its web site). For the broader issues, see Morten Bergsmo, Wolfgang Kaleck, Sam Muller and William H. Wiley, "A Prosecutor Falls, Time for the Court to Rise", FICHL Policy Brief Series No. 86 (2017), Torkel Opsahl Academic EPublisher, Brussels, 2017 (http://www.legal-tools.org/doc/41b41a/). At the heart of many of the issues related to the ICC Office of the Prosecutor may be Mr. Moreno-Ocampo's unwillingness to follow-up on the ground-breaking work of the ICC preparatory team, see Morten Bergsmo, Klaus Rackwitz and SONG Tianying (eds.), *Historical Origins*

In the following, I engage in finding out what Sir Thomas More (1478–1535) may offer in terms of principles and strategies on how to strengthen personal and institutional integrity within international justice institutions. His image is on the cover of this book, and I have had the honour of writing the chapter on him. What can an outstanding representative of so-called 'Northern Humanism', a friend and ally of Erasmus of Rotterdam (1466–1536), and a statesman serving in the highest positions during large parts of King Henry VIII's reign (1509–47) offer to contemporary debates about integrity issues, in particular in international justice institutions?

It is well known that More, despite his long and outstanding service, was unjustly executed by the King. What is less well known is the reason More offered so as not to give in to the immense pressure to condone the King and Parliament abolishing the independence of the Church of England and making the King its head. More dealt with the issue of integrity in many of his works, including his famous *Utopia* (1516)[3] and *The History of King Richard the Third* (1557).[4] An underlying question for much of his political writings was how a wise man with integrity ("a first citizen")[5] could serve a King or prince with tyrannical inclinations. (The references to the "King" and "Kings" throughout this chapter should be understood as a legacy of More's times and for consistency, not a deliberate exclusion.)

Central to More's thinking on how to develop and preserve integrity was to train yourself to be faithful to your conscience. He also frequently referred to respect for the law, which in his view justly limited the power of the King and protected the right to dissent. Leaders should serve the people, not their own narrow interests.

Among the reasons to include More in contemporary discussions on integrity is also that he was the first English writer to use the word 'integri-

---

   of International Criminal Law: Volume 5, Torkel Opsahl Academic EPublisher, Brussels, 2017 (http://www.legal-tools.org/doc/09c8b8/).

3   *Utopia* is available in several editions. I consulted the following: Thomas More, *Utopia*, Cambridge University Press, 2016 [1516].

4   Thomas More, *The History of King Richard the Third*, in Richard S. Sylvester (ed.), *The Complete Works of St. Thomas More*, vol. 2, Yale University Press, New Haven, 1963.

5   Thomas More, epigram 111.

ty', being well aware of the concept's both classical and biblical roots.[6] For him, integrity signifies consistency in thought, word and action, based on conscience and comprehensive understanding. It is the fruit of a successful struggle to be just *one* person, rather than to be several. It is "what makes a person a unity rather than a duplicity. Integrity makes a particular life resemble a good poem rather than a dubious collection of fragments, with doubtful authorship".[7]

This chapter deals with the arguments and stance of Thomas More, situating them in a context of modern integrity. The first section deals with integrity issues recently faced by international organizations, such as biased election observation, lack of quality control and transparent procedures in both the Council of Europe and the International Criminal Police Organization ('INTERPOL'), acquittals in the international tribunals, as well as misconduct by members of the ICC Office of the Prosecutor (Section 4.1.). To ground the discussion of More's relevancy for current integrity discussions, I provide a typography of these problems, focusing on individual versus institutional integrity, politicization or instrumentalization of institutions, and the specificities of *professional* integrity (Section 4.2.). These challenges to integrity form the basis upon which we turn to More for guidance, which is the subject of the following sections. The chapter progresses with a discussion on More's thoughts on tyranny and how to confront it (Section 4.3), before turning to More as a statesman and his views on heresy (Section 4.4.). Finally, the chapter turns briefly to More's conflict with Henry VIII (Section 4.5.), before concluding with More's lessons as well as returning to the topic of integrity in justice (Sections 4.6. and 4.7.).

4.1. Integrity Failures in International Political Institutions

My organization, the Norwegian Helsinki Committee, has a history of addressing integrity issues publicly, rather than only raising them discretely behind the scenes. Maybe it is part of a wider Nordic tradition that to demonstrate your support for an institution, you do not shy away from publicly criticizing it and appeal for effective measures to address failings.

---

[6] "Conscience and Integrity", in Gerard B. Wegemer and Stephen W. Smith (eds.), *A Thomas More Sourcebook*, Catholic University of America Press, Washington, DC, 2004, pp. 212–214.

[7] Stephen W. Smith, "Thomas More: Patron Saint of Leading Citizens", in Travis Curtright (ed.), *Thomas More: Why Patron of Statesmen?* Lexington books, New York, 2015, p. 145.

Part of this tradition is a perception that for criticism to be effective, it must be *constructive*. Only denouncing practices, without pointing to remedies and good examples that could help improve them, is not enough. External inquiries into institutional misbehaviour, which is widely used in the Nordic countries, is expected to produce recommendations on remedies as well as to clarify and evaluate the facts.

I will point to a few examples of recent integrity issues in international organizations. These examples are telling in themselves but also help to characterize *main types* of contemporary integrity issues. Such a typology, as further developed in Section 4.2., may make it easier to answer questions about the relevance of More's approach to developing and preserving integrity.

4.1.1. Biased Election Observation

During the 1990s, election observation as a distinct form of human rights monitoring developed rapidly. In post-conflict situations and in societies in transition from communist dictatorship to democratic rule, Western States, the United Nations ('UN'), the Council of Europe, the Conference on Security and Co-operation in Europe ('CSCE', renamed the 'OSCE' on 1 January 1995)[8] and some other international organizations put great emphasis on promoting free and fair elections as necessary steps towards democratic rule.

A telling expression of this view is to be found in the landmark 1990 CSCE Copenhagen Document, where all 35 Participating States at the time declared that "the will of the people, freely and fairly expressed through periodic and genuine elections, is the basis of the authority and legitimacy of all government".[9]

The CSCE/OSCE Office of Democratic Institutions and Human Rights ('ODIHR') played an important role – as did several academic institutions and non-governmental organizations – in developing a methodology

---

[8] Budapest Summit Declaration, Towards a genuine partnership in a new era, 21 December 2004, paragraph 3.

[9] Conference on the Security and Co-operation in Europe, Document of the Copenhagen Meeting of the Conference on the Human Dimension of the CSCE, 29 June 1990, para. 6 (https://www.legal-tools.org/doc/f85146).

to ensure that findings reflected both election day performance of elections as well as contextual factors.[10]

In some of the transitional countries, hopes for democratic developments were soon to be replaced by the reality of 'managed' democracy. States like the Russian Federation, Belarus, Azerbaijan and the Central Asian States do perform elections, but they adhere to systems where the 'elected' government weakens and/or controls the judiciary, the media, the parliament, and other State institutions to such an extent that there are little, if any, checks and balances. Furthermore, no effective opposition in the parliament exists.

In some of the countries, widespread cheating on election day does take place. However, the States increasingly adhere to more sophisticated ways of controlling the election results.[11]

Even if these States centralize power and are intolerant of criticism, they make efforts to retain an institutional set-up that mimics democratic governance. Among former communist countries, the Russian Federation has often played the role of pioneering the development of methods of 'controlling' and 'faking' democracy.

It is precisely because these States do not adhere to principles of separation of power and rule of law, and do not tolerate free media and independent civil society, that arranging elections is of crucial importance to strengthen legitimacy and present themselves as adhering to democratic principles.

Sometimes leaders of the States recognize that the governance model is not democratic in the full sense. President Vladimir Putin refers to 'managed' or 'controlled' democracy,[12] while Prime Minister Viktor Orbán be-

---

[10] ODIHR, *Election Observation Handbook*, sixth edition, OSCE/ODIHR, Warsaw, 2010. An extensive library of election related guidelines and tools are available at the OSCE web page.

[11] For a compelling account of the main methods used to 'control' democracy, see Andrew Wilson, *Virtual Politics: Faking democracy in the Post-Soviet World*, Yale University Press, 2005. He argues that the post-Bolshevik culture of 'political technology' is the main obstacle to better governance in the region. There is no real popular participation in public affairs, and no systematic modernization of the political economy.

[12] This term may be inspired by the concept of 'guided democracy', coined by the American journalist Walter Lippmann in his influential book *Public Opinion* from 1922. In such a system, a formal democratic government function as a de facto autocracy. For an early criticism of Putin's managed democracy, see Masha Lipman and Michael McFaul, "Managed democracy in Russia", in *Harvard International Journal of Press/Politics*, 2001, vol. 6, no. 3, pp. 116–127.

came infamous for characterizing the European Union ('EU') Member State Hungary as an 'illiberal State'.[13] Other leaders resorted to terms like 'transitional democracy', indicating that the State might not be fully democratic yet, but is *en route* towards that end goal.[14]

Faced with increasingly professional independent election observation, which is able to detect election fraud not only on election day, but also pre- and post-election day measures that were initiated to produce the desired election results, the regimes set out to tackle this challenge as well. They organized, *inter alia, alternative* election observation missions, which stated that elections were free and fair even if they were not.

A group of parliamentarians from Western countries constituted a special problem. Being members of respected international election observation missions, they breached codes of conduct, made positive statements on Election Day, and tried to influence mission statements to become more positive than justified. These problems were in particular linked to elections in Azerbaijan, and the Parliamentary Assembly of the Council of Europe ('PACE') eventually initiated an investigation into alleged corruption among its members.[15]

To respond to biased election observation, a coalition of non-governmental organizations, the European Platform for Democratic Elections ('EPDE'),[16] initiated several studies of threats to the integrity of election observation in 2016.[17]

---

[13] Prime Minister Orbán proclaimed Hungary as an illiberal democratic State in a speech at the Tusványos Summer University and Student Camp on 26 July 2014. "Proclamation of the Illiberal Hungarian State", *The Orange Files*, 1 August 2014 (available on its web site).

[14] Freedom House has since 1995 run a project called "Nations in transit", which according to a certain methodology survey democratic reforms in 29 former communist countries. The report covering developments in 2018 registered the most score declines in the project's 23-year history: 19 of the 29 countries had declines in their overall Democracy Scores. For the second year in a row, there were more Consolidated Authoritarian Regimes than Consolidated Democracies (Freedom House, "Nations in Transit 2018" (available on Freedom House's web site)).

[15] Council of Europe, *Report of the Independent Investigation Body of the allegations of corruption within the Parliamentary Assembly*, 15 April 2018 (available on the Parliamentary Assembly's web site). For extensive coverage of the so-called 'caviar diplomacy' in PACE, see European Stability Initiative thematic web site on corruption problems in the PACE.

[16] Members of the coalition include Helsinki Citizens' Assembly Vanadzor, Election Monitoring and Democracy Studies Centre (EMDS), Belarusian Helsinki Committee, International Society for Fair Elections and Democracy, European Exchange, International Elections Study Centre, Promo-LEX Association, The Norwegian Helsinki Committee, Stefan Batory

According to the EPDE, the main integrity issues were:

- "a growing tendency among authoritarian regimes in the OSCE region to orchestrate benevolent election observation in order to give legitimacy to fraudulent elections";[18]

- "a series of cases where European parliamentarians *individually* make public assessments of elections abroad, giving an impression to represent the position of their parliament also while their activity is not endorsed by their parliament or their faction, and when they are not member of any official Election Observation Mission. By that, they discredit not only the parliament and the faction they represent but election observation as such";[19]

- "there are European parliaments which did not sufficiently elaborate effective internal control mechanisms (i.e. Codes of Conduct) to discourage their members from participating in biased international election observation missions";[20]

- "an increasing number of GONGOs (governmental organized NGOs) publish assessments on election processes which are not based on any methodological election observation, while often being purely politically motivated";[21]

- "election administrations in some countries of the OSCE region deliberately deny accreditation to independent international Election Observation Missions adhering to international standards as the ODIHR methodology";[22]

- several parliamentary assemblies send election observation missions that "do not operate on the basis of a transparent and clearly defined

---

Foundation, Golos, Swedish International Liberal Centre, and Committee of Voters of Ukraine.

[17] EPDE, *Politically biased election observation – A threat to the integrity of international institutions*, July 13, 2018 (available on EDPE's web site).

[18] *Ibid.*, p. 8.

[19] *Ibid.*

[20] *Ibid.*

[21] *Ibid.*, p. 9.

[22] *Ibid.*

election observation methodology for the assessment of the election process".[23]

4.1.2. Corruption in the Parliamentary Assembly of the Council of Europe

An enabling factor for these unfortunate developments was a lack of quality control mechanisms. There were, *inter alia*, no established mechanisms to monitor the conduct of parliamentarians participating in observation missions of PACE, the OSCE Parliamentary Assembly, or the European Parliament. Nor were there procedures to establish the basis for reaching conclusions that significantly differed from those of the long-term professional missions of the OSCE's specialized agency for conducting election observation, ODIHR.

Lack of quality control and transparent procedures may also have been at the core of the integrity issues connected with the so-called 'caviar diplomacy' in PACE. In short, this diplomacy may have started as early as in 2001 and consisted in bribing members of PACE with money and gifts to influence their voting in favour of Azerbaijan and possibly some other Council of Europe Member States.[24]

The conclusion of the external review of the allegations was as follows:

> The key deficiency in the organisation of work and political processes in PACE was found to relate to the manner in which the decisions on appointments to different functions were made. This in particular concerned the lack of transparency and sufficient regulation of the procedures for such appointments, especially the appointments of members of the Monitoring Committee and the Rules Committee, as well as the appointments of rapporteurs in general. An issue of lack of transparency and an absence of safeguards against abuse was also found to arise with regard to the voting processes in the committees, which might affect the voting results and open the door to the possibility of exertion of improper influence, including that of a financial nature.

---

[23] *Ibid.*

[24] For a short description of the problems, see Organized Crime and Corruption Reporting Project ('OCCRP'), "Council of Europe Expels 13 in Azerbaijan Bribe Case", 3 July 2018 (available on OCCRP's web site).

As to the functioning of PACE in matters concerning Azerbaijan, the Investigation Body established that there was a group of persons working in PACE in favour of Azerbaijan. A certain level of cohesion in their various activities existed, although the Investigation Body found it difficult to establish with a sufficient degree of certainty that they all formed part of a single orchestrated structure. In this context, the Investigation Body found that, in their activities concerning Azerbaijan, several members and former members of PACE had acted contrary to the PACE ethical standards.[25]

The review also found that

the Guidelines on the observation of elections by the Parliamentary Assembly required to be further strengthened and clarified and that PACE should consider including in the ethical framework a specific part dedicated to election observation, in order to ensure that members of PACE participating in that type of missions complied with those guidelines.[26]

The conclusions on corrupt behaviour of former and present members of PACE was also fairly clear, namely

that a number of former PACE MPs who had performed ... [lobbying activities on behalf of Azerbaijan] had acted contrary to the PACE Code of Conduct. As to the corruptive activities in favour of Azerbaijan, the Investigation Body established that there was a strong suspicion that certain current and former members of PACE had engaged in activity of a corruptive nature.[27]

The review was, however, limited in time and resources, and therefore also concluded that there was a need for further investigations, *inter alia*, to elucidate whether countries other than Azerbaijan had been involved in corruption as well as more detailed questions about the extent and planned nature of the corruption schemes.

A trial in Milan, which started 10 December 2018, has so far been the only follow-up to hold anyone criminally responsible for the biggest scandal in the history of the Council of Europe. In this case, three former members of PACE were charged with corruption, namely Luca Volonte (Italian

---

[25] Council of Europe, *Report of the Independent Investigation Body of the allegations of corruption within the Parliamentary Assembly*, p. x, see above note 15.

[26] *Ibid.*, pp. x-xi.

[27] *Ibid.*, p. xi.

member, 2008–2013), Elkhan Suleymanov (Azerbaijani member, 2011–2018), and Muslum Mammadov (Azerbajani member, 2016–2018).[28]

The facts of the case were not disputed: in the period 2012–2014 the two Azerbaijanis transferred large sums of money to the Italian, who as a leader of the biggest political group in PACE, the European People's Party, had considerable influence on voting results in the Assembly.

Among the evidence in the case were e-mail communications between the three PACE members. One of them, from 1 February 2013, is especially telling of their relationship. It was written after a vote on a resolution on political prisoners that Azerbaijan's government wanted to see defeated and which to the surprise of both members of PACE and external observers was rejected by a large majority. In the e-mail, Volonte addressed Mammadov with the following words: "Your wish is my command, so I think that we should discuss the new version [of a motion] during the next meeting in Baku with Elkhan [Suleymanov] and Pushkov", the then powerful leader of the Russian delegation to PACE.[29]

4.1.3. Integrity Issues in International Police and Judicial Institutions

In recent years, documentation has been presented on abuse by a range of authoritarian States of the INTERPOL's 'wanted person' alerts in politicized criminal cases. The background is an extensive increase in the use of INTERPOL Red Notices and Diffusions, which has heightened the risk of misuse. For example, the number of Red Notices issued each year increased from 1,418 in 2001 to 13,048 in 2017 and to 13,516 in 2018. There are currently approximately 58,000 valid Red Notices, of which some 7,000 are public.[30]

The high numbers of alerts increase demands on resources for control. According to its Constitution, INTERPOL's main goal is "to ensure and promote the widest possible mutual assistance between all criminal police authorities within the limits of the laws existing in the different

---

[28] European Stability Initiative ('ESI'), "Human Rights with Teeth (I) – Battle of Europe", *ESI Newsletter*, 2018, no. 9, p. 2.

[29] *Ibid.*

[30] Amy Mackinnon, "The Scourge of the Red Notice: How some countries go after dissidents and debtors", *Foreign Affairs*, 3 December 2018 (available on its web site). See also, David Satter, "Russia's abuse of Interpol", *Russia Studies Centre Policy Paper No. 6 (2015)*, The Henry Jackson Society, July 2015. The figures were taken from Interpol's web site.

countries and in the spirit of the 'Universal Declaration of Human Rights'".[31]

In other words, a constitutional requirement exists that the mutual assistance provided by INTERPOL and the cases presented by national police authorities to its platforms should be based on investigative or other activities that respect international human rights. This is further underlined by Article 3 of the Constitution, which states that "it is strictly forbidden for the Organization to undertake any intervention or activities of a political, military, religious or racial character".[32]

Fair Trials, a UK-based non-governmental organization that works for fair trials according to international standards of justice, has documented such abuse since 2013.[33] According to the organization, INTERPOL has started to make reforms to strengthen control, but there are still major problems with "transparency, missing statistics and a simple lack of resources".[34] The solution, according to Fair Trials, is not to exclude any of the 194 Member States of INTERPOL: "We need strong international organisations to tackle international crime and keep the world safe. We don't want countries like Russia and Turkey to become safe havens for criminals by excluding them from Interpol altogether".[35]

To strengthen the integrity of the organization, there is rather a need to speed up implementation of its reform programme. The programme is designed to make it harder to abuse its systems as a vehicle of political repression. The Council of Europe and other international organizations may

---

[31] Constitution of the International Criminal Police Organization-INTERPOL, 1956 (2017), Article 1 (https://www.legal-tools.org/doc/07a066).

[32] *Ibid.*, Article 3

[33] Fair Trials International, *Strengthening respect for human rights: Strengthening Interpol*, 2013 (available on Fair Trials' web site). The report documented abuse in specific cases and recommended measures to detect and prevent such abuse. It also referred to resolutions and statements by international organizations since 2010 about the need to strengthen control mechanisms within the organization.

[34] Fair Trials, "How to end the abuse of INTERPOL: insights from America and Europe", 18 December 2018 (available on Fair Trials' web site). On measures to strengthening safeguards against abuse, see INTERPOL: "New measures approved to strengthen INTERPOL information sharing system", 9 November 2016 (available on its web site).

[35] Fair Trials, "How to end the abuse of INTERPOL: insights from America and Europe", see above note 34.

play important roles in monitoring how well INTERPOL implements the programme.[36]

Part of the programme is to 'clean up' its databases to identify and delete alerts that were circulated without proper review. INTERPOL may also restrict certain countries' access to databases if they believe that they are repeatedly and systemically violating its rules.

Similar to the 'caviar diplomacy' scandal in PACE, at the core of IN-TERPOL's problems are actions of Member States that undermine the integrity of the institution. The problem is then aggravated by the institution's lack of proper safeguards and capacity to detect and prevent the misuse of its systems.[37]

In PACE, an additional problem was that several members from democratic countries by corruptive influence were willing to compromise the integrity of the organization. There were both an institutional integrity problem – among others, lack of safeguards which enabled corrupt members to change the course of the institution – as well as individual integrity issues.

As a result, well-intended Member States may not rely on INTER-POL alerts without conducting thorough investigations into the background of persons that have been put into the system. Several persons have been repeatedly arrested or questioned by police based on politicized INTER-

---

[36] PACE, *Abusive use of the INTERPOL system: the need for more stringent legal safeguards*, Doc. 14277, 29 March 2017. It should be noted that even if PACE has had serious integrity issues of its own to deal with, it often played strong and beneficial external roles in promoting and securing adherence to human rights, democracy, and integrity norms.

[37] Commission of Security and Co-operation in Europe, "Helsinki Commission leaders introduce translational repression accountability and prevention (TRAP) act", 12 September 2019 (available on its web site). Recognizing the extent of the problem, the leaders of the US Helsinki Commission on 12 September 2019 introduced the Transnational Repression Accountability and Prevention (TRAP) Act in the House of Representatives. The Act declares that it is the policy of the United States to pursue specific reforms within INTERPOL and use its diplomatic clout internationally to protect the rights of victims and denounce abusers. The bill requires the Departments of Justice, Homeland Security, and State, in consultation with other relevant agencies, to provide Congress with an assessment of autocratic abuse of INTERPOL, what the United States is doing to counteract it, and how to adapt United States policy to this evolving autocratic practice. The State Department would also be required to publicly report on the abuse of INTERPOL in its annual Country Reports on Human Rights to create a transparent, public record of these violations of the rule of law.

POL alerts. The result is often that their freedom of movement becomes severely restricted.[38]

In an exposé of recent international integrity failures, acquittals in 2012–2013 by the Appeals Chamber of the International Criminal Tribunal for the former Yugoslavia ('ICTY'), and media revelations about a deep split among its judges should also be mentioned. The acquitted included high-ranking Croat and Serb officials, such as Ante Gotovina, Mladen Markač, Momčilo Perišić, Jovica Stanišić and Franko Simatović, and generated concerns about the quality of the legacy of the ICTY. Much of the criticism focused on the role of the then ICTY President Theodor Meron, thus challenging his impartiality and alleging that he sought to unduly influence other Tribunal judges. According to diplomatic cables released by WikiLeaks, he was close to the US government, being characterized by US diplomatic personnel as a pre-eminent supporter of specific government interests. The criticism extended to the International Criminal Tribunal for Rwanda ('ICTR') which shared its Appeals Chamber with the ICTY.[39] The acquittals did not come as a result of new evidence, but rather as a consequence of changes in judicial interpretation at a late stage in the life of the ICTY affecting the ability of the Tribunal to hold leaders accountable. Combined with revelations of an apparent power struggle between the then American Tribunal President and the Danish judge Frederik Harhoff, leading to the exclusion of the latter, this not only revealed serious disunity among the judges, but at the time reduced trust in the Tribunal in ways that disoriented victims, their families, and the wider struggle against impunity. According to Judge Harhoff, his main concern was undue influence by "the

---

[38] A telling example is former hedge fund investor in Russia, William Browder, who since 2009 has led an international human rights campaign, 'Justice for Sergei Magnitsky'. He has been placed on Interpol's red alert list seven times by Russia, which wants him extradited for alleged tax evasion. See Reuters, "Russia asks Interpol to arrest Kremlin critic Bill Browder: letter", 9 April 2018 (available on Reuters' web site). For Browder's best-selling auto-biographical book see William Browder, *Red Notice: How I became Putin's No. 1 Enemy*, Transworld Publishers Ltd., London, 2015.

[39] Gunnar M. Ekeløve-Slydal, "ICTY Shifts Have Made Its Credibility Quake", FICHL Policy Brief Series 49 (2016), Torkel Opsahl Academic EPublisher, Brussels, 2016 (http://www.legal-tools.org/doc/18ba48/) See also Julija Bogoeva, "International Judges and Government Interests: The Case of President Meron", FICHL Policy Brief Series 48 (2016), Torkel Opsahl Academic EPublisher, Brussels, 2016 (http://www.legal-tools.org/doc/56a576/); and Frederik Harhoff, "Mystery Lane: A Note on Independence and Impartiality in International Criminal Trials", FICHL Policy Brief Series 47 (2016), Torkel Opsahl Academic EPublisher, Brussels, 2016 (http://www.legal-tools.org/doc/c2e5ad/).

military establishments in countries involved in armed conflicts in other parts of the world, such as the United States and Israel – and [...] Russia, France, the UK and others".[40]

My own conclusion at the time was that there existed a

> persistent reason to doubt the impartiality of President Meron. Regrettably, this doubt has a cancerous staying power. We are so-called 'informed observers', a part of the community of actors that has helped make and protect the ICTY for more than 20 years. If such 'informed observers' perceive bias on the part of an ICTY Judge and MICT President, and have the courage to say so publicly, that has immediate relevancy under the ICTY's law. Losing trust among the informed part of the public is detrimental for a judge of an institution whose authority depends on being – and being perceived as – impartial.[41]

My final example is the media revelations in 2017 about possible misconduct by members of the ICC Office of the Prosecutor and the first ICC Prosecutor, Luis Moreno-Ocampo. Even if there have been serious integrity issues in other international institutions – as shown by the far from exhaustive exposé presented above – there was something particularly disturbing about these revelations. A former high official of the ICC, its first Prosecutor, who had been elected based on legal requirements of "high moral character" in addition to professional skills (being "highly competent in and [...] [having] extensive practical experience in the prosecution or trial of criminal cases"),[42] had allegedly been making money by assisting a potential suspect in the Libya situation under ICC investigation.

It is not infrequent that prosecutors become private lawyers or legal advisors after their tenure (and after a regulated quarantine period ends), but one part of the revelations was far from acceptable: the first prosecutor relied on ICC staff members sharing information with him.

In addition, there were a range of broader issues resulting from a culture institutionalized by the first Prosecutor which weakened quality control, removed open internal discussions, and resulted in a "sense of fear"

---

[40] Harhoff, 2016, p. 2, see above note 39.

[41] Ekeløve-Slydal, "ICTY Shifts Have Made Its Credibility Quake", p. 4, see above note 39.

[42] Rome Statute of the International Criminal Court, 17 July 1997, Article 42(3) ('ICC statute'] (https://www.legal-tools.org/doc/7b9af9/).

and "intimidation" among staff members.[43] Within a few years, 22 top staff members had left his office. These internal problems were known by several government officials and leaders of non-governmental organizations since late 2003.[44]

A further aggravating fact was that the ICC's achievements in terms of convictions of major war criminals have been very disappointing. There have been only three convictions so far. Cases against 12 persons have collapsed.[45]

Two other factors were also at play. When created, the ICC received widespread support from large parts of the international community, even though some influential States showed reservation and sometimes acted in a hostile manner to the institution.[46] For the human rights community, the adoption of the Rome Statute and its rapid ratification by the required number of States created widespread optimism that the ICC would help create an effective system to fight impunity for core international crimes. In general, institutions do create expectations and provide implicit promises. The establishment of the ICC had created high expectations, some of them perhaps unrealistic.

The second factor is linked to the concept of 'professional integrity'. As a physician is not evaluated only based on his or her personal integrity – being a morally solid and consistent person – but as a person who honours profession-specific requirements, the same goes for prosecutors in international justice. During his time as ICC Prosecutor, Moreno-Ocampo was often hailed in popular culture as a hero in the fight against unspeakable crimes and criminal leaders. His fall due to his failure to uphold profes-

---

[43] Morten Bergsmo, "Institutional History, Behaviour and Development", in Bergsmo, Rackwitz and SONG (eds.), 2017, p. 24, see above note 2.

[44] Morten Bergsmo, Wolfgang Kaleck, Sam Muller and William H. Wiley, "A Prosecutor Falls, Time for the Court to Rise", FICHL Policy Brief Series No. 86 (2017), Torkel Opsahl Academic EPublisher, Brussels, 2017, page 2 (http://www.legal-tools.org/doc/41b41a/)

[45] Morten Bergsmo, «La CPI, l'affaire Gbagbo et le rôle de la France», *Le Monde*, 18 January 2019 (http://www.legal-tools.org/doc/d499f6 and https://www.legal-tools.org/en/doc/693bee (English version)).

[46] For an overview and evaluation of US relations with the ICC since 2002, see William Pace: "The Hague Invasion Act remains dangerous", *Diplomat Magazine*, February 9, 2019 (available on Diplomat Magazine's web site).

sional and integrity requirements consequently created great disappointment, along with the collapse of the cases he had initiated.[47]

In a letter to Fatou Bensouda, the ICC Prosecutor since 2012, the Norwegian Helsinki Committee raised these issues and asked her to use her "full authority over the management and administration of the Office" to conduct credible and transparent reviews of the legacy of the first Prosecutor in order to establish relevant facts of professional and ethical misconduct".[48]

In her 22 May 2018 reply, Bensouda concluded that

> my staff and I have made every effort to learn from past experience, improve the culture of the Office of the Prosecutor to encourage openness and critical thinking, and transform our working methods to achieve success. We have endeavoured to be transparent. We uphold ethical standards of the highest order. Should credible allegations of misconduct arise, they are dealt with appropriately and according to a fair process. As such, I am of the respectful view that the sort of broad inquiry you call for is unnecessary considering the steps the Office itself has taken, what we are already accomplishing and have put in place.[49]

In her letter, Bensouda failed to address the most serious allegations referred to in our letter, which implicated the first Prosecutor as well as his *Chef de cabinet* at the time. There were, however, indications in her letter that could be interpreted in the direction that "further measures" could be taken that included "fact-finding concerning the first Prosecutor and former staff members".[50]

---

[47] For portraits of Mr. Ocampo that build the hero-narrative, see for instance the films: Edet Belzberg, Kerry Propper, Amelia Green-Dove and Taylor Krauss (Producers) and Edet Belzberg (Director), "Watchers of the sky", motion picture, 2014, United States, Propeller Films; and Paco de Onis (Producer) and Pamela Yates (Director), "The reckoning: the battle for the International Criminal Court", motion picture, 2009, United States, Skylight Pictures.

[48] Norwegian Helsinki Committee, "Letter to Mrs. Fatou Bensouda, Prosecutor of the ICC", 12 March 2018 (http://www.legal-tools.org/doc/b745e4/).

[49] Fatou Bensouda, "Letter to Messr Engesland and Ekelove-Slydal", 22 May 2018 (available on the Norwegian Helsinki Committee's web site).

[50] Norwegian Helsinki Committee, "Letter to Mrs. Fatou Bensouda, Prosecutor of the ICC", 8 June 2018 (available on the Norwegian Helsinki Committee's web site). Also Women's Initiatives for Gender Justice argued for "external review of the practices relevant to the allegations", see Women's Initiatives for Gender Justice, "A critical time for the ICC's credibility", 18 November 2017 (http://www.legal-tools.org/doc/e2fbc7). The ICC Bar Association ('IC-

4.2. Typology of Integrity Issues

There may exist several motives for criticizing integrity failures of institutions and high officials. Most of them fall into two categories: either one wants to *undermine the credibility of the institutions or the officials*, or one wants to *improve, modify and eventually strengthen them*. While critics falling into the first category may wish for the institution to become irrelevant or closed down, those falling into the second category may wish for the opposite. Their vision is a renewed and strengthened institution that plays a stronger beneficial role in its mandated field.

A third category may include critics with motives that are less definite, simply wanting to place failures and problems into the open to initiate debates that may lead in different directions.

To act on any of these motives may, due to circumstances, be quite risky. Consequences of public criticism and debates are difficult to predict. It might be next to impossible to carry out the *utilitarian test* with any degree of certainty, that is, to answer the question whether consequences of a critical engagement will be more beneficial than harmful for the overall goal of advancing the mandate of the institution in question. Is the criticism doing more good than harm?

Such questions were not alien to Thomas More. Regardless of views on whether he was right in his conflict with the King and the legal establishment of his time, it cannot be denied that he was exceptionally skilful in the way he navigated impossible waters. He was in no way seeking martyrdom, but he held steadfastly to viewpoints and strategies he though would lead to the best results.

In his writings, he publicly criticized the Kings that ruled in England and other European States. Sometimes he did so in very direct ways, using strong language to depict the wretchedness of the character of the person he denounced.

At the same time, he eventually decided to serve at high positions in the developing State bureaucracy of England under King Henry VIII (1491–1547). His intention was never to undermine the authority of the King and to instigate a revolt against him. On the contrary, he wanted to

---

CBA'), urged in a statement, "States Parties and the ASP to initiate a thorough, effective and independent investigation into the serious allegations raised in these recent public reports", see ICCBA, "ICCBA Statement on Allegations Against Former ICC Prosecutor", 29 November 2017 (http://www.legal-tools.org/doc/a8cdcb).

---

improve and thereby strengthen the legitimacy of his rule. Overall, it seems that his main goal was to promote peace and improve the lot of ordinary people.

One of his best-known books, *The History of King Richard the Third*, is a sharply formulated Christian humanist attack on tyrannical rule and a King that personalized excesses connected with ruthless power-struggle and disregard for the well-being of his people.[51]

More's world-famous *Utopia* (1516) criticizes the state of European politics and exemplifies how politics governed by reason may function by way of describing the state of affairs at a fictive island State.[52] Interestingly, it also includes discussions on whether a wise person should separate himself from politics, or rather serve leaders who are less than ideal and at least contribute to moderating their evils and mistakes.

According to More, a good leader has a duty to "take more care of his people's welfare than of his own, just as it is the duty of a shepherd who cares about his job to feed the sheep rather than himself".[53] If a King departs from his duty, his servant should do what he or she could to minimize the negative consequences of such departure.

More presented strong arguments against the execution of or other harsh penalties imposed on thieves. He was behind legal reforms that would ease access of the poor to justice. Stealing was the only way of surviving for many poor people. Executing them would not contribute to solving any problems, More argued. Part of his progressive agenda was also arguments that leaders should accept free speech, and that Parliament should have a decisive say on legislation.

Even if realities were far from these ideals, More decided eventually to serve for many years under one of the Kings he had both hailed and criticized, Henry VIII. First serving in high legal positions in the city of Lon-

---

[51] More probably started to write the book in 1513 and did never finish it. He wrote two versions simultaneously, one in English and one in Latin for a wider European audience. It was published only after More's death, in 1557. A modernised and easy to read version of the book has been made available online by The Centre for Thomas More studies: Thomas More, *The History of King Richard the Third*, Mary Gottschalk (ed.), 2012 [c. 1513]. This version is based on the 1557-edition that inspired William Shakespeare (1564-1616) to write his play 'Richard III'. Whether More's negative account of King Richard was wholly justified, is another question, which I do not intend to discuss here.

[52] More, *Utopia*, see above note 3

[53] *Ibid.*, p. 33

don, he had accepted prominent positions offered by the King from 1518. He was Chancellor of England from 1529 to 1532.

When entering the King's Council in 1518, More was well aware of the conflicting demands such service would entail. What he did not know, of course, was that Henry VIII would develop into a tyrant, killing wives, high officials that had served him, among many others. He could not foresee that he himself would eventually be killed by the King because of a conflict about fundamental principles concerning the relationship between State and church. In 1535, More was beheaded after a show trial, on the order of the King, for refusing to accept Henry VIII as head of the Church of England. His vision was an internationally unified and independent church.

More has been recognized as a saint by the Roman Catholic Church (1935). Even more important in the context of integrity discussions, he has been proclaimed as a Patron Saint of Statesmen (2000).[54] His example of integrity is not only recognized by the Catholic Church, but by people belonging to different religions and beliefs.

His example remains to a certain degree controversial. The critics claim that he was a fanatic responsible for the execution of heretics during his tenure. It is undisputed that he was responsible for such executions, and it is therefore mandatory in discussions about his enduring legacy to identify exactly what to keep and what to disregard from his thought and practice. Before discussing further More's relevancy for current integrity discussions, though, I will return to the above examples of such issues within international institutions, providing a categorization of the problems.

4.2.1. Politicization or Instrumentalization of Institutions

The examples include issues related to integrity both on institutional as well as individual levels. There were issues related to both current and former officials within the institutions, which enjoyed certain 'privileges' which they reportedly abused (that is, former members of PACE lobbying for Azerbaijan and the first Prosecutor of the ICC).

By institutional integrity, I mean upholding institutional activities and views in line with reasonable interpretations of the institution's man-

---

[54] Pope John Paul II, Apostolic Letter Issued Moto Proprio, *Proclaiming Saint Thomas More Patron of Statesmen and Politicians*, 31 October 2000 (available on The Holy See's web site).

date. The mandate of the Council of Europe, for instance, is to promote and protect human rights, democracy and the rule of law in its Member States.[55] Mandates of institutions of international justice are typically to "exercise [...] jurisdiction over persons for the most serious crimes of international concern".[56] The institutions may have different rules concerning that jurisdiction, but the core purpose remains the same: to hold persons (at high places) accountable for international crimes they conducted, were responsible for, or failed to prevent.

If institutions fail to fulfil their mandates in specific cases or situations because of *corruption, giving in to political pressure*, or *neglect*, these may amount to instances of institutional integrity failures. In international justice institutions, the ICTY's 2012–2013 acquittals may be a case at hand. The point here is that failures to uphold integrity at a personal level may translate into *institutional failure*.

Justice institutions are particularly vulnerable to such failure, since the number of people taking binding decisions is limited. The example of PACE's failure to adopt a resolution on political prisoners in Azerbaijan mentioned above indicate that also in bodies where decision-making includes hundreds of persons (PACE has 324 members), this risk is still present.

4.2.1.1. Establishing Fake Institutions

As we have seen, one way of undermining genuine international institutions is to establish *alternative* institutions with a similar mandate, but which applies the mandate in a politicized or biased way.

The purpose may be to undermine the views of genuine institutions in front of the international community or at domestic levels. By presenting alternative views as if they were based on systematic and methodologically sound research, the institutions serve to disorient public opinion and undermine trust in genuine institutions.

The primary example given above was biased election observation. There might, however, also be discussions about whether specific justice institutions should be placed in this category. It is hardly controversial to place highly politicized courts and prosecutorial services in authoritarian

---

[55] Statute of the Council of Europe, 5 May 1949. For an updated presentation of the organization's aim and prioritized areas of activity, see the Council of Europe's official web site.

[56] ICC Statute, Article 1, see above note 42.

States in this category. Such institutions 'mimic' independent courts and prosecutorial services, but in reality, they often function as tools of the highest political authorities or other powerful circles to further their interests.[57]

More controversial – and in my view misleading – would be to place internationalized or international jurisdictions in this category, due to claims that they were one-sided, applied double standards, or professed other mandate restrictions preventing them from applying a strict criteria-based approach to case selection.

The main challenges to their legitimacy centred around the way they were created or their assertion of jurisdiction over heads of States.[58] Another important issue is related to the application of double standards. Double standards in international criminal law raises important and difficult questions about the legitimacy and credibility of the project of ensuring accountability for core international crimes since there is not yet equality before the law. However, this is a different problem from justice institutions that are created to 'mimic' justice, while serving only or mainly political purposes, and which are continuously unduly influenced.[59]

As the ICTY example shows, there reportedly were instances of undue political influence on high officials of international justice institutions, but not of such a systematic and massive scale as to question the genuine character of the institutions as such.

In my view, the main remedy against the fake institution threat to integrity is principled and fact-based criticism exposing the failure of the institutions to uphold agreed standards and professional implementation of their mandate.

---

[57] See among others, Maria Popova, *Politicized Justice in Emerging Democracies: A Study of Courts in Russia and Ukraine*, Cambridge University Press, 2012. In particular, chapter 6 gives an instructive overview of how the integrity of the courts are jeopardized by so-called informal practices of influence, such as 'ex parte communication' between judges and litigants and 'telephone justice' between politicians (or other important players) and judges.

[58] For examples of how high-profile defendants have challenged the legitimacy of the international(ized) courts they were brought for, see Michael A. Newton, "The Iraqi High Criminal Court: controversy and contributions", in *International Review of the Red Cross*, 2006, vol. 88, no. 862, p. 405.

[59] For a description and discussion of the problem of double standards in international justice, see Wolfgang Kaleck, *Double Standards: International Criminal Law and the West*, Torkel Opsahl Academic EPublisher, Brussels, 2015.

4.2.1.2.   Undermining Integrity of Genuine Institutions

Concepts of personal integrity mainly fall into two categories: those that underline "formal relations one has to oneself, or between parts or aspects of one's self" and those that see integrity as an "important way to acting morally, in other words, [that] there are some substantive or normative constraints on what it is to act with integrity".[60]

In the first category fall conceptions of persons with "a harmonious, intact whole";[61] persons that are able to keep "the self intact and uncorrupted".[62] Other important characteristics are wholeheartedness and being steadfastly true to one's commitments, especially commitments that are most important for the person's self-respect.

A step further, inspired by existentialist and Kantian thoughts on categorical imperatives, is a view that underlines integrity as 'self-constitution'. The point here is that in addition to coherence, there is an act of rational endorsement of the principles by which a person decides his or her projects. The way to make yourself into a particular person, who can interact well with yourself and others, "is to be consistent and unified and whole – to have integrity".[63]

The second category includes views that point to integrity as a social virtue, which is defined by a person's relations with others. Persons with integrity stand for something, but not in the same way as fanatics do because they respect the deliberations of others. This might be one of the more difficult questions related to integrity: what does it mean to respect other's views, when you in the end are willing to sacrifice even your life, as was the case with More, to stand by your own view?

More, like Socrates (c. 470–399 BC) and several other exemplary figures of integrity, stood by their judgment in the face of enormous pressure to recant. There is a strong argument that it is exactly from such examples we may detect the essence of integrity. These are persons who hold to their views despite pressure, efforts to help them escape, efforts to bribe them, or blaming them for letting down their family, friends and social obligations because of their perceived stubbornness.

---

[60]   Stanford Encyclopedia of Philosophy, "Integrity", 9 April 2001 (available on its web site).
[61]   *Ibid.*
[62]   *Ibid.*
[63]   *Ibid.*

In the case of More, it is clear that he thought the judges in the trial against him to be both morally and legally wrong in convicting him to death for treason. He had remained silent about his views, and the law protected silence in a case like his. At the same time, he did not denounce his judges, some of whom were his long-term friends. One way of interpreting this seemingly paradoxical situation might be to conclude that as he thought the judges to be wrong, he still respected their right to be wrong in the way they were. He knew, and the judges knew, that to oppose the will of the King equalled endangering your life.[64]

More fought for the unity and integrity of the Catholic Church. While England's bishops (except Bishop John Fisher (1469–1535)), universities and other institutions had given in to the demands of the King to be the head of the Church of England, he would not. He fought for something he believed in very deeply. To give in would be to betray his own convictions, but also to fail in upholding the integrity of a unified church and the future of Christendom.

He fought both to uphold his own integrity and the integrity of an institution he deemed to be of unique importance to upholding the material and spiritual existence of human beings. Dividing the church and placing it under the leadership of Kings would weaken it, lead to violent conflict, and eventually undermining the standing of the Christian States, which at his time was under considerable pressure from the Ottoman Empire as well as from internal conflicts in the Christian world.[65]

The examples presented above primarily illustrated weakening of the integrity of genuine institutions. While INTERPOL's problem was the lack of sufficient institutional safeguards to detect and prevent politicized alerts from its Member States, the other examples showed how institutional integrity was undermined by individual actors within the institutions or by external actors with a privileged access to the institutions. The methods were among others *bribing, exertion of pressure*, and *abuse of personal relationships*.

---

[64] See Gerard B. Wegemer, "The Trial of Thomas More: July 1, 1535", in *Portrait of Courage*, Scepter, Cleveland, 1995, pp. 210–217.

[65] For a vivid description of the challenging times of More for Britain and, in particular, for Europe, see Robert Tombs, *The English and Their History*, Penguin Books, London, 2015, pp. 157–160.

Corruption of high officials may be both internally and externally directed. It may be facilitated by clearly illegitimate methods, but there is also a vast area of less clear but still *integrity-sensitive* ways of changing institutional policies or even outcomes of trials in justice institutions. Such methods may include *forceful argumentation* towards persons in lower positions, reference to *perceived interests of important allies of the institution*, or *gradual undermining of a culture of quality control*.

The examples illustrate the close nexus between professionalism and integrity: if you are weak on the practice of your profession, you may be easy prey for someone who wants to instrumentalize your professional role in ways that weakens institutional integrity.

To counter the threats to institutional integrity, the main methods are institutional safeguards, transparency in appointments and elections of high officials, adherence to codes of conduct, and proper oversight mechanisms. But even an institution that is well set up and protected against corrupt practices may fail.

A culture of individual adherence to norms of professional integrity is vital. In particular, leaders of institutions play an important role in this regard. They may set examples and nourish cultures of integrity. Or they may fail to do so with detrimental consequences for the institution.[66]

In my view, More is especially relevant in this regard. His foremost contribution may be his insight into the importance of leaders exemplifying and talking convincingly about integrity.

4.2.2. Professional Integrity

Each profession creates its own framework of integrity. The reason we trust our health to physicians we do not personally know, is that they represent competence and a wider practice that we confide with. The same goes for justice professionals. We respect and adhere to court decisions because we confide with the wider practice of courts and the professional competence and integrity of the key actors taking decisions.

---

[66] For a powerful account of the important role of leaders adhering to democratic norms and functioning as gatekeepers to uphold democratic rule, see Steven Levitsky and Daniel Ziblatt, *How Democracies Die*, Broadway Books, New York, 2018. While their analysis mainly deals with the question of how to uphold democratic *political* institutions, their insistence on the important role of leaders or gatekeepers is also highly relevant for discussions on how to uphold and strengthen integrity of justice institutions.

There are several reasons to conceptualize *professional* integrity as a distinct virtue, and not as 'ordinary' integrity placed in a specialized context. Firstly, any profession has specific ends, such as health for medical personnel and justice for prosecutors, defence lawyers, and judges. Loyalty to such profession-specific ends may be perceived as an integrity factor *sui generis*. It is precisely because we expect this form of integrity that we entrust important aspects of our lives to professionals.[67]

Secondly, we expect role holders within specialized institutions to put professional standards above self-interest. When issues of corruption or conflict of interests are brought up, professional integrity is seen as the virtue of honouring norms of the profession more than any personal interest. A judge that gives in to political pressure or accepts bribes to decide in favour of one of the parties is not living up to the assurances or promises of her or his profession.

Professionals should not be like people who constantly question their own decisions or backslide in the face of social pressure. Professionals trust their own convictions. They may change their views, but only in light of compelling reasons.

Upholding professional standards may at times be hard, not because of pressures or temptations, but because issues are hard to solve. Such hard cases demand a certain degree of interpretive skills, deliberative capacity and competence and ability to balance different views and concerns. In these situations, professional competence is not only about finding a solution but to be able to *demonstrate* why this is the preferred solution in terms of professional standards and practice.

In this view, professional integrity is characterized by a mode of reasoning that calls for the role holder to engage critically and creatively with the varied and sometimes conflicting demands of practice. The 'fundamental normative relation' that governs the situation is a promissory relation: the profession has given its word to the public, and role holders are given the task of keeping the promises. In keeping the promises, they must both honour professional standards and have a wider understanding of the practice they fulfil.[68]

---

[67] Andreas Eriksen, "What is Professional Integrity?", in *Nordic Journal of Applied Ethics*, 2015, vol. 9, no. 2, pp. 3–17.

[68] *Ibid.*, p. 10. Eriksen uses Ronald Dworkin's figure of a "chain novelist" to illustrate this interpretive view of professional integrity. The task of judges is like the task of authors en-

In important aspects, this view balances the responsibility of the role holder with the practice of the profession. The judge remains responsible because he or she has to interpret with a view to deciding the case according to his or her best reading of practice. The responsibility is nevertheless shared with the practice of the profession, which is regarded as a justifiable social institution.

Ordinary or personal integrity is about consistency in upholding moral values one has chosen to be guided by – in words and deeds. Professionals, in addition, have to honour the standards and practice of their profession. But not in a careless and automatic way. They have to give their own contribution by interpreting previous practice and decide on new cases based on the best reading of that practice. Sometimes they have to depart from previous judgments, but only if they can base that departure on a justifiable reading of previous practice.

4.2.2.1. Disregard of Professional Norms and Interpretive Requirements

Seen from this view on integrity it appears that many current integrity issues stem from the failure of leaders of the institutions to uphold their own professional integrity, to uphold a culture of integrity within the institution, as well as weak oversight mechanisms. They fail to honour the inherent promises, the standards and practices of their profession.

Pedro Agramunt, a Spanish conservative politician, resigned as President of PACE after conducting a visit to Syria's president Bashar al-Assad in March 2017, together with Russian Duma members. Although he underlined that he undertook the visit only in his capacity as Spanish Senator, the Bureau of PACE stated that he was no longer "authorized to undertake any official visits, attend meetings, or make public statements on behalf of the Assembly in his capacity as president".[69] His resignation, however, had a

---

gaged in a "chain novel". This novel is written one chapter at a time. Each finished chapter is passed along to a new author, who writes the next one. The task of each author is to make this the best novel it can be. According to Dworkin, the good judge views earlier decisions "as part of a long story he must interpret and then continue, according to his own judgment of how to make the developing story as good as it can be".

69 Rikard Jozwiak, "PACE President Stripped of Powers After Meeting Syria's Assad", on *Radio Free Europe*, 28 April 2017 (available on Radio Free Europe's web site). A Motion for dismissal was tabled by Ingjerd Schou, a Norwegian member of the PACE, on 30 June 2017, see PACE, *Dismissal of Mr Pedro Agramunt, President of the Parliamentary Assembly*, Doc. 4383, 30 June 2017. The Motion reads: "We, the undersigned, consider that the

wider context. Already as PACE Rapporteur on political prisoners in Azerbaijan, he became controversial by human rights groups for not reporting accurately on the problems in the country. This criticism continued and was strengthened during his tenure as PACE President, 2016–2017. Several others of the members that were involved in the so-called 'caviar diplomacy', also had leading roles. Luka Volonté was heading the European People's Party in PACE.

Members of the ICC Office of the Prosecutor continued to stay in close contact with the first Prosecutor, reportedly based on personal relationships. In the example of ICTY given above, the situation was complex: the ICTY President may have felt pressure from military establishments to change judicial interpretation. He then himself may have exerted undue pressure on some of his colleagues.

From these examples, four main categories of breaches with professional integrity may be detected:

1. Integrity failures may result from giving in to *external political* or *undue internal collegial pressure*. The colleague exerting undue pressure often has a superior role, but this may not necessarily be the case.

   a. A subcategory, not exemplified above, is the famous Soviet and Russian use of '*Kompromat*' or 'compromising material' to blackmail for instance judges to receive certain outcomes of criminal or other cases before a court. In these cases, the pressure was based on exerting fear of a ruined career or reputation.

   b. The position of power necessary for exerting effective pressure to undermine the integrity of professionals may vary, from being able to obstruct promotions, making sure the person loses her or his job, or more serious consequences, as the one faced by Thomas More: risking losing his life.

   c. The position of power may also be of such a nature that not only the fate of the professional but the survival of the institution she or he serves is at stake. In such situations, professionals may feel

---

President of the Parliamentary Assembly no longer enjoys the confidence of the Assembly, on the grounds that his behaviour seriously harms the reputation of the Parliamentary Assembly and tarnishes its image". Agramunt, however, resigned on 6 October 2017 before the Motion was scheduled to be decided on, see PACE, "Pedro Agramunt resigns as PACE President", 6 October 2017 (available on PACE's web site).

obliged to give in to undue pressure to save the institution while losing out on integrity.

2. Giving up integrity may result from giving in to *material temptations*, such as bribes, luxury travels, or other forms of material gains, such as reportedly was the case in the PACE 'caviar diplomacy' scandal. Bribery can come from both colleagues and from external actors. The effect of the bribes may be augmented by the development of a personal relationship, which places the person who bribes and the person who receives bribes in a relationship of mutual loyalty.

3. A third category comprises *personal relationships as such*. This factor may often remain neglected in dealing with integrity issues. However, in any institution personal bounds may play an important role in weakening scrutiny of decisions and decision-making processes. An important part of creating a culture of integrity is to uphold norms of quality control, professionalism and internal oversight not only in situations of *difficult* personal relations between staff members but also in situations of *strong reciprocal sympathies*. Such sympathies may weaken the willingness to challenge decisions that violate professional integrity.

4. A fourth category comprises of *lack of professional and moral convictions*. Stories of professionals who give in to pressure or material temptations may not only be diagnosed as lack of will-power, but also as lack of basic identification with the profession's ends and means. Such identification may develop over time from education and experiences in the profession, but it may also be weakened by cynicism and pessimism about the achievements of the profession and institutions. The idealism of the newly educated staff member may over time be taken over by cynicism and lack of identification with the practice of the profession.

4.2.2.2. Failure by External Actors to Hold Institutions to Account

Finally, the role of external actors should be mentioned. There are several differences in the accounts of integrity issues in PACE and in the ICC given above. One of the most striking is that the call for external review was successful in the case of PACE, while the Prosecutor of the ICC did not initiate such review. One of the likely explanations for this may be the lack of consistent public pressure on the ICC from 'informed observers' and watchdogs to do so.

In the case of PACE, a large number of non-governmental organizations, think-tanks as well as members of PACE were alerted of the situation and strongly requested such review.

Justice institutions are obviously different from political bodies in several aspects. There are fewer persons involved in decision-making and for external supportive actors, the concern of upholding and respecting the independence of prosecutors and judges may lead to more muted criticism than warranted by the seriousness of their failures.

The important role of external guardians of integrity for justice institution should not be understated. Independent media, professionalized civil society organizations, academics and other informed observers are vital parts of a necessary structure to uphold institutional integrity. Without such a structure, consistently challenging the institution on professional and integrity issues, it becomes increasingly vulnerable to under-performing.

4.2.3. The Role of Exemplary Stories and Personalities

As described above, international institutions face a range of integrity challenges. These are the basis for the questions we ask More for guidance on in the following.

There are questions related to 'professionalism', in particular for legal personnel, who are tasked to take decisions based on legal rather than on purely political grounds. There is an inherent requirement not to adhere to 'horse-trading' to get support from important States or other powerful actors.

There are questions related to upholding institutional consistency and being in line with the mandate and aim of the institution. 'Independence', 'incorruptness' and 'not giving in to political pressure' are among the key words in this context, as well as 'professional competence'.

Given the difficult political environment of international justice, 'integrity' may play a crucial role in upholding the authority of an institution. Arguably, a culture of professional integrity is decisive to ensure that international justice institutions live up to expectations, create public trust, and withstand unfounded criticism.

There are large integrity deficits in justice institutions at the national level in many States, and international jurisdictions are therefore needed as integrity models.[70] The complementarity principle of the ICC Statute implies that the ICC may prosecute only when national jurisdictions fail to uphold justice, including because of integrity deficits. That puts an additional pressure on the ICC to be exemplary on integrity.

Studying personalities and stories of the past to get guidance on current integrity issues obviously carries a risk of misrepresenting them to extract relevant messages. Nevertheless, integrity issues being inherent in personal and professional relationships of all times, there are remarkable similarities between the contemporary issues and the issues inherent in the writings and life of More and other heroes of integrity of the past.

In the story about More's conflict with King Henry VIII, and central to his thinking on political issues, all four challenges to upholding integrity as described above are to be found. He reflected on and exemplified how to withstand strong *pressure* from both the political leadership of his time, headed by King Henry VIII and his chief minister, Thomas Cromwell (1480–1540), his colleagues, many of whom had been his personal friends for a long time, and even his own family.

During his service both for the city of London and for King Henry VIII he was well known for his uncorrupted and efficient dealing with public affairs under his responsibility. Based on Christian beliefs, he seemed to endorse a simple lifestyle, although he ran a big family estate with frequent guests, and sometimes provided meals for the poor.[71]

When it comes to integrity being weakened by personal relationships and lack of personal or professional convictions, More stands out as particularly serious about his role as a lawyer, high official and a leading citizen.

---

[70] As an indicator of possible lack of integrity in national jurisdictions, I take low scores on civil and criminal justice in the World Justice Project Rule of Law Index (available on the World Justice Project's web site). A further indication of issues of integrity being widespread at the national level, is the renewed focus by the United Nations Office on Drugs and Crime (UNODC) on integrity issues in the Criminal Justice System. See also above note 57.

[71] The literature on Thomas More's life and thinking is vast. For general introductions, I consulted John Guy, *Thomas More: A Very Brief History*, Society for Promotion of Christian Knowledge, London, 2017; Richard Marius, *Thomas More: A Biography*, Alfred A. Knopf, New York, 1984; Raymond Wilson Chambers, *Thomas More*, Endeavor Press, London, 2017 (first published 1935); George M. Logan (ed.), *The Cambridge Companion to Thomas More*, Cambridge University Press, 2011; and Peter Berglar, *Thomas More: A Lonely Voice Against the Power of the State*, Scepter Publishers, Cleveland, 2009 (first published in German, 1999).

In his twenties, he may seriously have doubted whether to become part of public affairs. He was attracted to a life secluded from the temporal world, living in or next to the London Charterhouse from around 1500–1503, a Carthusian Monastery at the time.[72] There he tested his vocation for the priesthood, although without withdrawing completely from the world. He continued to teach his students and gave public lectures on St. Augustine's *City of God* during this period.

In the end, he decided to seek political engagement. This was not based on naïve or utterly idealistic ideas that he could drastically change things for the better. But he had ideas of legal and political reform, the need to balance executive power with adherence to reasonable laws, and about developing amicable relations with foreign States. He realized that the best way to improve society was not to stay in a cloister, but to become an active citizen of a Christian commonwealth in line with the humanist thinking of his day.[73]

In seeking political engagement, he knew that abuse of power was frequent. Among his lasting contributions as a political thinker is his discussions on how to confront tyranny.

4.3. Civilizing Politics

Abuse of power may be as old as power itself. Since power-relations are part of any human society – and human beings per definition are political creatures, living in more or less stable societies – such abuse and how to stem it constitutes fundamental issues of political and moral philosophy.

In his thinking on such issues, More applied concepts and doctrines framed by Greek philosophers such as Plato (427–347 BC) and Aristoteles (384–322 BC). He belonged to a small group of English intellectuals who were influenced by Italian Renaissance philosophers' re-reading and trans-

---

[72] The London Charterhouse was a Carthusian Priory 1371-1537, when it was dissolved by Henry VIII. The Carthusian order, also called the Order of Saint Bruno, is a Catholic religious order of enclosed monastics. It was founded by Bruno of Cologne in 1084 and includes both monks and nuns. The order has its own Rule, called the *Statutes*, rather than the Rule of Saint Benedict, and combines eremitical and coenobitic monasticism. The motto of the Carthusians is *Stat crux dum volvitur orbis*, Latin for "The Cross is steady while the world is turning"; Wikiwand, "London Charterhouse" (available on its web site).

[73] For a short discussion of More's motivations to seek political engagement, see John Guy, "Shaping a mind", in *Thomas More: A Very Brief History*, Society for Promotion of Christian Knowledge, London, 2017, pp. 1–8.

lations of original Greek philosophical texts, in particular Plato's and Aristoteles' texts on governance and the best ways to organize society.

Renaissance humanism did not form a coherent ideology or school of philosophy. Rather, it provided new readings of some of the same antique texts that Medieval philosophy was based on. In its Northern version, humanism also relied heavily on the foundational texts of Christian antiquity, notably those of the New Testament and the Church Fathers.[74] It represented a break with Medieval metaphysical system-building and speculation, scholastic culture, arts of disputation and dialectic and a renewed focus on reforms of church and society to improve the situation of its members. Its educational programmes, designed to enable active citizens to cope with the needs of the day, "carried an inherent moral purpose in the furtherance of the common good, so that another component was moral philosophy, especially directed to the obligations of the ruler and the citizen".[75]

In More's thinking, a shift took place with ancient Greek values of *equality* and *justice*, breaking with the Roman influenced values prevailing in his society of *glory, honour, ambition* and *private property*.[76] The humanist emphasis on moral and political philosophy may also have made it easier for More to combine his extensive humanist studies with his study of law, which his father John More (1450/53–1530), a highly respected lawyer and judge, favoured. The proper role of law in society, being binding on both rulers and citizens, was at the core of the humanist reform agenda. The impulses from Italy seem first to have made its way to court circles and to the legal world of the Inns court, where More learnt law from 1494.[77]

It may seem paradoxical that Plato was among the foundational thinkers of this paradigm shift in Western philosophy. He is primarily known for his belief in a world of invisible *forms* or *ideas*, which he held to be the *real* world, and for abstract speculation. However, the larger parts of

---

[74] James McComica, "Thomas More as Humanist", in George M. Lugan (ed.), *The Cambridge Companion to Thomas More* (Cambridge Companions to Religion), Cambridge University Press, 2011, p. 22.

[75] *Ibid.*, p. 23.

[76] *Ibid.* Several of More's friends and teachers were prominent scholars and linguists who had travelled to Florence and Rome to study Greek language and philosophy, such as William Grocyn (1446–1519), Thomas Linacre (1460–1524), John Colet (1467–1519), and William Lily (1468–1522).

[77] *Ibid.*, p. 26.

his works – such as *The Republic* and *The Laws*, but also many of the Socratic dialogues – focus on how to improve the less than perfect material and political world.[78]

A central point for Plato, resonated in the writings of Cicero (106–43 BC), one of the few Roman thinkers that More held in high esteem, was that humans are not born for themselves alone, "but our country claims a share of our being, and our friends a share".[79] In developing this perception of humans as socially inter-connected, More warned against misconstrued views on *human liberty*.

False expectations of life arise from such views, namely that *a free person is the one that can do whatever he wants*. Rather, inherent in liberty are to be guided by constraints such as the high commandments of God, the laws made by humans to rule society, and the commands of those with legitimate power. Given human nature, persons may easily fall prey to enslavement by obsessions, sins, or by society and rulers. One part of society often enslaves another.

An antidote to such enslavement is to connect liberty with law, as advocated by Cicero and further developed by More.[80] In his early works, More underlined that liberty without law, even if you are a rich person, is tantamount to bondage. In particular, he points to the importance of 'skilled princeps', 'leading citizens' respecting the law. These are leaders that have the virtues, training and ingenuity needed to secure the safety of the people and provide justice. Their integrity is of utmost importance for society.

Leaders who do not respect law and liberty, develop into tyrants. The quality of a ruler is made clear only by the actual liberty, prosperity, peace, and joy of his people.[81]

4.3.1. The Ever-Present Danger of Tyranny

There is a strong continuity in More's thinking about the duties of leaders, from his first literary works until his last works written during his 14 and a half months of imprisonment before he was beheaded. A main theme is that

---

[78] See *Stanford Encyclopedia of Philosophy*, "Plato", 20 March 2004 (available on its web site).

[79] Marcus Tullius Cicero, *De Officiis*, Walter Miller (trans.), Harvard University Press, Cambridge, 1913 [44 BC].

[80] More was shortly after his death called "the Christian English Cicero", see Nicholas Harpfield, *Life and Death of Sir Thomas More*, Early English Text Society, London, 1932, p. 217.

[81] Gerard Wegemer, "Thomas More on Liberty, Law, and Good Rule", in Curtright (ed.), 2015, pp. 5–13, see above note 7.

true leading citizens have a duty to ensure that justice is done. To neglect to do what the duty of his office requires is "like a cowardly ship's captain who [...] deserts the helm, hides away covering in some cranny, and abandons the ship to the waves".[82]

Even though More was a Christian thinker and statesman, many of his ideas have resonated well beyond Christian circles. This is no surprise since More's humanist writings conveyed arguments and views which were based on philosophical ideas. He held the view that reason and practical wisdom led to conclusions that would not be contradicted but rather further enlightened by Christian revelation.

More's example has appealed to Christians, persons with other faiths, as well as to non-believers. This is an important part of the reasoning behind pope John Paul II's proclamation of More as "Patron of Statesmen and Politicians". In the apostolic letter making the proclamation, the pope referred to support from "different political, cultural, and religious allegiances", indicating a "deep and widespread interest in the thought and activity of this outstanding statesman".[83]

A fundamental issue for More and the tradition of thought he belonged to, was how a leading citizen, a statesman, or a philosopher should respond to tyranny. Rulers developing into tyrants was seen as an ever-present danger, given the temptations of power and the lack of strong institutional set-ups that could temper the ruler's tyrannical inclinations. More certainly realized that serving King Henry VIII could become precariously difficult, given the Kings propensity to pass from mild rule into repressive and arbitrary rule. In general, More favoured republican and consultative government over that of a single ruler to avoid abuse of power.[84]

More also favoured that members of Parliament should be given freedom of expression, so that the King would know what they really felt about his propositions. In April 1523 he was chosen as speaker of the House of Commons, and in a speech there he made the first recorded petition for the exercise of freedom of speech in parliament. Effective governance depended on parliamentarians' freedom to speak their mind without

---

[82] Thomas More, *De Tristita Cristi*, in *The Complete Works of St. Thomas More (CW)*, 15 vols., Yale University Press, New Haven, 1963–97, vol. 14, p. 265.

[83] John Paul II, *Apostolic Letter Issued Motu Proprio: Proclaiming Saint Thomas More Patron of Statesmen and Politicians*, section 1, see above note 54.

[84] Cathy Curtis, "More's public life", in Logan (ed.), 2011, p. 74, see above note 71.

fear of reprisals, he argued.[85] He also practised free speech in Parliament himself, by speaking against Henry VII's and later against Henry VIII's proposals for funding of wars or other purposes by increasing taxation. He was influential in convincing Parliament to reduce the demanded amounts, much to the Kings' displeasure.

These views and practices were part of a well-thought-out strategy that More in his humanist works advised to confront and minimize the consequences of tyranny or abusive rule. They were based on a realistic view that to influence rule by a tyrant so it at least to some extent benefitted the people, and not only the ruler, killing the tyrant or rebelling against him would not lead to the desired results. More's theorizing on tyranny and how to confront it, is an important key to understanding him as a statesman and his motivation for serving King Henry VIII at the highest levels, despite his knowledge of the Kings tyrannical inclinations.

More elaborated his view in *Declamation* in response to Lucian's *The Tyrannicide*, a text More translated from Greek into Latin in 1506.[86] Lucian of Samosata (120-after 180 AD) was a Greek rhetorician, pamphleteer, and satirist who wielded considerable influence on both More and Erasmus. His writings embody a sophisticated and often embittered critique of the shams and follies of the literature, philosophy, and intellectual life of his day.

The Tyrannicide presents a fictional court speech in which a citizen claims to deserve the city's reward, provided for by law, for having killed the tyrant, although indirectly. He had actually only managed to kill the tyrant's son, but when the tyrant found his son killed, he committed suicide. The speaker nonetheless presents himself as a tyrannicide and the city's saviour.

More's *Declamation* presents a court speech of a fellow citizen who challenges the tyrannicide's right to the legal reward. In effect, the *Decla-*

---

[85] *Ibid.*, p. 77.

[86] More's *Declamation* is available in: *The Complete Works of St. Thomas More*, 15 vols., Yale University Press, New Haven, 1963–97, vol. 3, part 1. In 1505–1506, More and Erasmus translated some of Lucian's writing into Latin. More translated the *Cynicus, Minippus, Philopseudes* and *Tyrannicide*, and both he and Erasmus wrote declamations replying to the latter work.

mation provides a diagnosis of tyranny and an account of how best to confront it.[87]

There are several noteworthy points in More's account. Firstly, he shows how tyranny represents an ever-present danger. Even benevolent rulers may decay into tyrants. True, the tyrant is a disturbed individual, caring for his own interests only despite being a leader with a duty to care for the interests of his people. He is, however, not so different from other people as we like to think. As More showed in his history of *Richard III*[88] and in the first book of *Utopia*,[89] European rulers of his own time were prepared to use several measures associated with tyranny, such as aggressive wars, killing their opponents, and manipulating currency and law to serve their interests.[90]

Secondly, since tyranny is an ever-present danger, those with influence and political authority must make efforts to learn how to respond to it intelligently and efficiently. Killing the tyrant (or his son) is not to produce sustainable results. We need to think as a physician, who knows that to cure a disease you must know its cause as well as which treatment are best suited to cure it.

In understanding tyranny, More refers to Plato (*The Republic*) and Aristotle (*Politics*), who define a tyrant as a solitary ruler.[91] However, not all solitary rulers are tyrants. For Aristotle, the difference is that a King rules for the good of his subjects, while a tyrant rules only with a view to his own advantage. For More, the solitary status of the tyrant is a consequence of the disorder of his soul. He has an unrestrained desire that respects no limitations. He cannot have a partner; not even his son.

In analysing the tyrant's desire, More follows Plato and Cicero in perceiving the human soul as composed of three parts, each with its own object of desire. *Reason* desires truth and the good of the whole individual, the *spirit* is preoccupied with honour and competitive values, while *appetite* has the traditional low tastes for food, drink, and sex.

---

[87] For a detailed account of the *Declamation*, see Carson Holloway, "Statesmanship, Tyranny, and Piety", in Curtright (ed.), , 2015, pp. 17–36, see above note 7.

[88] More, 1513, see above note 4.

[89] More, 1516, see above note 3.

[90] Holloway, 2015, p. 19, see above note 87.

[91] Plato, *The Republic*, Allan Bloom (trans.), Basic Books, New York, 1991 [376 BC], book 9; and Aristotle, *Politics*, Carnes Lord (trans.), University of Chicago Press, 1984, book 3, chapter 7.

Because the soul is complex, an erroneous calculation is not the only way it can go wrong. The three parts pull in different directions, and the low element in a soul in which it is overdeveloped, can win out. It follows that a good condition of the soul requires more than just cognitive excellence. The healthy or just soul has harmony in which its three parts all functions properly. Reason understands the Good, while spirit and appetite desire what is good for them to desire, being guided by reason.

The soul of the tyrant has departed from this order. He is, according to Plato, ruled not by his reason but by his appetite, which craves for satisfaction without boundaries. He is driven by lust for money, food and sex.[92] More agrees with Plato on the distorted order of the tyrant's soul. Tyranny involves the rule in the soul of the lower parts. But he lays the emphasis on the role of *spiritedness*, the desire for honour and a unique position in society, rather than on the bodily desires. A tyrant is dominated by ambition, lust of power, greed, and thirst for fame. He wants to elevate himself above other human beings by becoming the supreme power in the city or the realm.[93]

In arguing for this position, More points that beasts that are driven by bodily desires such as hunger, can only show certain elements of a tyrannical nature. Human beings go further in succumbing more completely to tyranny. Appetite or bodily desires are not in themselves enough to bring tyranny into being.[94]

If satisfying bodily desires was the main desires of tyranny, becoming a wealthy businessman would probably give better results. A tyrant, in contrast, lives under threat of violent death at the hands of oppressed and desperate subjects. His ability to enjoy bodily pleasures would be limited.

Because the tyrant is driven by spirited desires, he cannot share power with anyone. If the beast does not tolerate partners in the hunt due to their hunger (appetite), how can we "imagine that a human tyrant, puffed up by pride, driven by the lust of power, impelled by greed, provoked by the thirst for fame, can share his tyranny with anyone?".[95]

Thirdly, even if the tyrant is driven by spirited desires, he also lacks restraint in relation to bodily desires, resulting in him resorting to murder,

---

[92] Plato, 1991, 572d–575d, see above note 91.

[93] Holloway, 2015, pp. 22–23, see above note 87.

[94] *Ibid.*

[95] More, *Declamation*, p. 101, see above note 86.

rape, and robbery. This is so because he may use objects of bodily desires to ascertain his total dominance over his realm. To keep public order and rule moderately, would not satisfy his lust for complete dominance. He cannot accept any kind of equality between his subjects and himself. He murders, robs, and rapes to manifest his supremacy and humiliate those he rules over.

There is also an important impunity factor, explaining the tyrant's excessive abuses. Since he is placed totally above the law, he is free to fulfil any bodily desire. In his soul, the worst parts dominate the best (reason), and this results in him being unhappy and "full of confusion and regret".[96] He is therefore constantly seeking distractions by fulfilling his bodily desires.

Fourthly, the resulting characteristics of tyrannical rule may be summarized as a lawless form of rule in contrast to legitimate authority, that governs by laws and obeys laws. The tyrant may call his directives 'laws', but they hardly deserve the name since he can change them at any time. A law is a settled rule superior to any single man's will, and the tyrant therefore cannot accept it. His rule becomes unpredictable, spreading fear and distress among his subjects.[97]

Tyranny is also a regime devoid of any freedom. All of the tyrant's subjects evidently lack freedom, living at the mercy of the tyrant. However, the tyrant himself also lacks genuine freedom. He cannot choose what is good for human beings, namely to be governed by reason and laws. He does not know real friendship; he reduces other human beings to become tools of his own desires. His freedom is therefore empty and illusory. He is enslaved by his own desires, dominated by forces within his own distorted soul.

More's teaching on tyranny is a dark tale. Not the least because of his insistence that it is rooted in human nature and its strong desires. It is extreme and evil, but it is not as rare as we would like to think. It tends to develop from the normal functioning of the human soul, which is often not properly regulated. When the man who killed the tyrant's son claims to have eradicated tyranny and demand to be rewarded, it is another example of the spirited desire for public recognition beyond what is truly reasonable.

---

[96] Plato, 1991, 577e, see above note 91.
[97] More, *Declamation*, p. 101, see above note 86; Holloway, 2015, p. 24, see above note 87.

That means that the impulses – the inflated desire for honour and public praise – that led to tyranny is also present in the attempted destruction of tyranny. In addition, there is a question about the motives: was the attack on the tyrant based on a genuine will to eradicate tyranny or was it done "in revenge or retaliation for some private injury done to you"?.[98] Those acting against the tyrant may include decent men who suffered under brutal oppression, but it could also include selfish men who resented the fact that the tyranny operated against their own benefit. There might even be men included who want to replace the tyrant, while upholding tyranny.

According to More, in any society there is a part of the population that must be categorized as wicked. Even if they form just a small part, their views might influence the deliberations of the society if they are not refuted. The recognition that wickedness is always part of politics, also in non-tyrannical regimes, must make us realize that any regime carries the seeds of tyranny.[99]

In More's own words, even "legitimate authorities, not only governing by laws but also obeying laws, and so very much milder than a tyranny, are nevertheless so dominated by the desire for power that they spare not the lives of intimate friends rather than allow them to share their rule".[100]

More's conclusion is that it is naïve to think about the tyrant as an exceptional person, a monster or a psychopath, and that lawful rulers could not become tyrants. The same spirited motives that result in tyranny – love of power and fame – are present even in legitimate rulers. The difference is that they are present in more restrained forms.

Finally, it must not be forgotten that even if the tyrant does not tolerate co-rulers, there are plenty of enablers, supporters and henchmen. You may succeed in killing the tyrant, but utterly fail in eradicating tyranny which is brought forward by those who willingly benefited from his rule, were protected by it and themselves committed outrageous crimes.

4.3.2. The Fundamental Question of Integrity

We have now reached the point in discussing tyranny where what could be called the fundamental question of integrity should be asked: *How to con-*

---

[98] More, *Declamation*, p. 107, see above note 86.
[99] Holloway, 2015, p. 27, see above note 87.
[100] More, *Declamation*, p. 101, see above note 86.

front tyranny in such a way that you don't sow the seeds of further tyranny, neither in your own soul nor in society?

According to More, the answer is that you should rebalance your soul and leave the level of spiritedness. Reason should become the guide of your actions, not motives of being recognized for courage, becoming famous and publicly praised. Since the cause of tyranny is the domination of spirited desires, actions based on these desires cannot be the solution.

It does not mean, however, that there is no need for courage and other spirited desires in confronting tyranny. The problem arises, however, when desires of fame, honour, and power remain uncontrolled. What is needed is courageous actions under the direction of reason.

The fundamental question could thus be rephrased as *how to ensure that reason remain in control of spirit and appetite in confronting tyranny*?

More makes this point clear by comparing the tyrannicide with a doctor. The criteria by which to judge the professional quality of a doctor is whether he heals or improves the condition of a patient, not how strongly he *wants* or *tries* to do so. If he pretends to know how to heal me, without being competent, he deserves only "condemnation for rashly meddling, to my danger, in this matter in which he was unskilled".[101]

In a similar way, what the law seeks in rewarding killing of the tyrant and eradicating tyranny, is a "resourceful man, one not only stronghanded but (much more) strong-hearted; able in stratagem rather than in force; one who knows how to lay plots, hide his traps, make the most of his opportunities".[102]

Confronting tyranny effectively requires intelligence and skill. An incompetent doctor may leave the patient in a worse condition than before his intervention. Likewise, confronting tyranny without proper strategies and skills may strengthen it and increase the suffering of ordinary people who now may be targeted innocently by an enraged tyrant.

Even if Lucian's character, claiming that he should be rewarded for tyrannicide, had succeeded in killing the tyrant himself, the forces that had enabled tyranny would still be operational. There would be men who had been privileged by his rule, stealing from and suppressing their fellow citizens, and who would be eager to find a successor to the tyrant. Even if they

---

[101] *Ibid.*, p. 109.
[102] *Ibid.*

failed, there would be civil war or uprisings, people would die and the goal of establishing a legitimate free public order would be hard to attain.

More returns to the question of how a leading citizen or a statesman could confront tyranny or milder forms of corrupted politics in the first book of *Utopia*, which was written about 10 years later than the *Declamation* (in 1515-6).[103] Here the focus is on the problem of ensuring that rulers receive – and take – appropriate advice. Given the corrupted nature of politics, from the point of view of a prospective councillor, the question is if he should commit himself to public affairs at all. The discussion between the philosopher-traveller, Raphael Hythloday (who in the second part recounts his experiences from Utopia, an island State based on socialist, tolerant, and equality principles), Peter Giles (a humanist official, based on a real person), and Thomas More (the author, but not necessarily always presenting the author's views) on this issue is revealing:

> 'My dear Raphael', he said, 'I'm surprised that you don't enter some King's service; for I don't know of a single prince who wouldn't be very glad to have you. Your learning and your knowledge of various countries and peoples would entertain him while your advice and supply of examples would be helpful at the counsel board. Thus you might admirably advance your own interests and be of great use at the same time to all your relatives and friends.'
>
> 'About my relatives and friends', he replied, 'I'm not much concerned, because I consider I've already done my duty by them tolerably well. While still young and healthy, I distributed among my relatives and friends the possessions that most men do not part with till they're old and sick (and then only reluctantly, when they can no longer keep them). I think they should be content with this gift of mine, and not insist, or even expect, that for their sake I should enslave myself to any King whatever.'
>
> 'Well said', Peter replied; 'but I do not mean that you should be in servitude to any King, only in his service.'
>
> 'The difference is only a matter of one syllable', said Raphael.
>
> 'All right', said Peter, 'but whatever you call it, I do not see any other way in which you can be so useful to your

---

[103] More, 1516, see above note 3.

friends or to the general public, in addition to making yourself happier.'

'Happier indeed!' said Raphael. 'Would a way of life so absolutely repellent to my spirit make my life happier? As it is now, I live as I please, and I fancy very few courtiers, however splendid, can say that. As a matter of fact, there are so many men soliciting favours from the powerful that you need not think it will be a great loss if they have to do without me and a couple of others like me.'

Then I [More] said, 'It is clear, my dear Raphael, that you seek neither wealth nor power, and indeed I prize and revere a man of your disposition no less than I do the mightiest persons in the world. Yet I think if you could bring yourself to devote your intelligence and energy to public affairs, you would be doing something worthy of your noble and truly philosophical nature, even if you did not much like it. You could best perform such a service by joining the council of some great prince and inciting him to just and noble actions (as I'm sure you would): for a people's welfare or misery flows in a stream from their prince as from a never-failing spring. Your learning is so full, even if it weren't combined with experience, and your experience is so great, even apart from your learning, that you would be an extraordinary counsellor to any King in the world.'

'You are twice mistaken, my dear More', he said, 'first in me and then in the situation itself. I don't have the capacity you ascribe to me, and if I had it in the highest degree, the public would still not be any better off if I exchanged my contemplative leisure for active endeavour. In the first place, most princes apply themselves to the arts of war, in which I have neither ability nor interest, instead of to the good arts of peace. They are generally more set on acquiring new Kingdoms by hook or crook than on governing well those they already have. Moreover, the counsellors of Kings are so wise already that they don't need to accept or approve advice from anyone else – or at least they have that opinion of themselves. At the same time, they endorse and flatter the most absurd statements of the prince's special favourites, through whose influence they hope to stand well with the prince. It's only natural, of course, that each man should think his own inventions best: the crow loves his fledgling and the ape his cub.

'Now in a court composed of people who envy everyone else and admire only themselves, if a man should suggest something he has read of in other ages or seen in practice elsewhere, those who hear it act as if their whole reputation for wisdom would be endangered, [...].'[104]

In the further discussion, More holds on to his conviction that if Raphael could overcome his aversion to court life, his

advice to a prince would be of the greatest advantage to the public welfare. No part of a good man's duty [...] is more important than this. Your friend Plato thinks that commonwealths will be happy only when philosophers become Kings or Kings become philosophers. No wonder we are so far from happiness when philosophers do not condescend even to assist Kings with their counsels.[105]

Raphael reacts by asking More if he thinks his advice to the King of France to give up all ideas of conquering Italy or other realms would be well received when all other advisors were presenting ingenious plans for successful military campaigns to expand his Kingdom. He would argue that one King can only manage to rule a limited Kingdom ("the Kingdom of France by itself is almost too much for one man to govern well"), and that war always makes life worse for the people.[106]

More concedes that in such a setting, advices for peace and better domestic rule would not be enthusiastically received.[107]

Then Raphael continues by referring to advice to the King on various schemes on how to fill the treasury; one more manipulative of the people than the other. His councillors maintain that it will only benefit the King that his people remain destitute due to heavy taxation, since "his own safety depends on keeping them from getting too frisky with wealth and freedom. For riches and liberty make people less patient to endure harsh and unjust commands, whereas poverty and want blunt their spirits, make them docile, and grind out of the oppressed the lofty spirit of rebellion".[108]

When Raphael again argues that his views, refuting the premises of such advice, and maintaining that a King can only succeed when genuinely

---

[104] More, 1516, pp. 14–15, see above note 3.

[105] *Ibid.*, pp. 28–29.

[106] *Ibid.*, p. 31

[107] *Ibid.*, p. 32.

[108] *Ibid.*, p. 33.

caring for the people, More again concedes that such views will indeed be met by deaf ears. Raphael should therefore refrain from giving advice that he "knows for certain will not be listened to".[109]

In the councils of Kings, there is no room for lofty academic philosophy, ill adapted to the situation, continues More.

> But there is another philosophy, better suited for the role of a citizen, that takes its cue, adapts itself to the drama in hand and acts its part neatly and appropriately. This is the philosophy for you to use. […] If you cannot pluck up bad ideas by the root, or cure longstanding evils to your heart's content, you must not therefore abandon the commonwealth. Don't give up the ship in a storm because you cannot hold back the winds. […] Instead, by an indirect approach, you must strive and struggle as best you can to handle everything tactfully – and thus what you cannot turn to good, you may at least make as little bad as possible. For it is impossible to make everything good unless all men are good, and that I don't expect to see for quite a few years yet.[110]

In reply, Raphael explains that he cannot give up his convictions and lie. He is not sure what More means by 'indirect approach' either. Besides, in a council,

> there is no way to dissemble or look the other way. You must openly approve the worst proposals and endorse the most vicious policies. A man who praised wicked counsels only half-heartedly would be suspected as a spy, perhaps a traitor. And there is no way for you to do any good when you are thrown among colleagues who would more readily corrupt the best of men than be reformed themselves. Either they will seduce you by their evil ways, or, if you remain honest and innocent, you will be made a screen for the knavery and folly of others. You wouldn't stand a chance of changing anything for the better by that "indirect approach".
>
> This is why Plato in a very fine comparison declares that wise men are right in keeping away from public business. They see the people swarming through the streets and getting soaked with rain; they cannot persuade them to go indoors and get out of the wet. If they go out themselves, they know they

---

[109] *Ibid.*, p. 36

[110] *Ibid.*, pp. 36–37.

will do no good, but only get drenched with the others. So they stay indoors and are content to keep at least themselves dry, since they cannot remedy the folly of others.[111]

Where does this intriguing discussion leave us? Undoubtedly, More was receptive to see the strong points of both views. His preference of using dialogues in his writings was not only a tool he used to create interesting texts but reflected a fundamental feature of his mind. He strove to understand and measure the strength of opposing views and arguments. Settling the issue of whether to enter the King's service was not easy for him.

There was a fundamental integrity issue at stake: would he be able to sustain his principles as a leading citizen, putting the well-being of the people first, contribute to just outcomes of trials, and turn ruthless decisions to be "as little bad as possible"?[112] Or would he be corrupted himself, unable to withstand the pressure inherent in a position where lack of explicit consent could be seen as proof of betrayal?

Such reflections pave the way for a third formulation of the fundamental question of integrity: *How can a person enter service of a ruler guided by spirited desires being convinced that he or she will be able to remain guided by reason?*

4.4. More as Statesman

This was a fundamental question for More when considering entering the King's service. He realized early one that Henry VIII was at least a potential tyrant. When he on 25 October 1529 succeeded Thomas Wolsey (1473–1530) as lord chancellor, the King was already at war against the Catholic Church and against ancient principles of English and European civilization.

At the beginning of his public life, More could not have predicted that Martin Luther (1483–1546) and other religious reformers would split the Church and reshape Europe, that Ottoman military forces would advance as far as Vienna, and that Henry VIII would desire both an annulment of his marriage to Catherine of Aragon (1485–1536) and to establish England as an independent realm of Rome.[113]

He had however, as I have shown above, long before he left his post as under-sheriff of London and became a member of the King's Council in

---

[111] *Ibid.*, p. 39.

[112] *Ibid.*, p. 35

[113] Curtis, 2011, p. 70, see above note 84.

1518, reflected extensively on the costs and dangers for a wise and just man in serving the King.[114] In accepting to do so, he kept to the main principles he had formulated in his writings on how to civilize politics; by applying an 'indirect approach' and practical wisdom, always adapt to the situation at hand, refraining from radical and sweeping actions. During his conflict with the King he never conspired against him, plotted against him or even denounced him publicly. Nevertheless, both while in office and after stepping down, he continued to work for what he thought was the best for the commonwealth and its people.

More's background as both lawyer, humanist scholar and a devout Christian with inclinations for a life of contemplation and religious studies seems to have prepared him well for the kind of uncorrupted office he became known for. There are, however, considerable debate among scholars about the reasons for him to enter the King's council in 1518, and later climb to ever higher positions. Initially, he expressed reservations about the inconveniences and threats to reputation entailed in such service.[115]

The simplest explanation may be that he felt obliged to contribute to making things as little bad as possible, along the lines of the discussion in *Utopia* rendered above.[116] Entering the King's service would increase his influence in reforming the English legal and political order in a way that benefitted the people.

There might, however, also have been more specific reasons. Pope Leo X hade proposed in a bull of 6 March 1518 a truce among European powers, which would enable a united front against the Turks in response to Ottoman successes in Egypt and Syria. More may have thought that by entering royal service at this point, he could ensure that England supported such a collective security initiative to European peace-making. England's role in entering the October 1518 Universal Peace Treaty (proclaimed in London), created needs for additional skilled public servants to bring it to fruition. The treaty represented an early and important attempt to address

---

[114] More was appointed under-sheriff in 1510. As such, he was a permanent official who advised the sheriffs and sat as judge in the sheriff's court. He received a generous stipend and had a lucrative right to represent the City in the royal courts at Westminster.

[115] Curtis, 2011, p. 73, see above note 84.

[116] More, 1516, p. 35, see above note 3.

European international relations by peaceful agreements, and it must have been attractive for More to assist in its adoption and implementation.[117]

A further explanation could be that More already successfully had taken part in extensive trade negotiations on behalf of the King before he decided to enter the King's council. When he was offered a permanent position by the King, he may have seen the advancement as a natural development in serving the country.

He had also recently shown his ability to intervene to restore public order, acting in his undersheriff capacity to quell riots in London by a group of young English apprentices. They had looted the houses, shops and warehouses of immigrant communities on a May day in 1517. More had called the rioters to order. His eloquence alone, according to the chroniclers, stemmed the worst of the violence.[118]

When More took his oath as a councillor, Henry VIII gave him some advice, urging him to "first look unto God and after God unto him".[119] This could be interpreted as an assurance by the King that More could stay true to his principles; an assurance the King later would depart from.[120]

4.4.1. Uncorrupted Fairness

During his career as a lawyer, judge, speaker in Parliament, ambassador, and in the King's service, More was highly respected for being uncorrupted and fair. In summing up his achievements, he underlined though that he had been "a source of trouble to thieves, murderers, and heretics".[121] As a judge, he would avoid any conflict of interests, for example by not hearing cases concerning related persons.

As lord chancellor he would continue reforms of his predecessor, Thomas Wolsey, simplifying procedures and increasing access to equity courts. More regarded law as applying equally to all, and its proper application was fundamental to a healthy secular and ecclesiastical society. The

---

[117] For further explanation, see Curtis, 2011, pp. 75–76, see above note 84. The treaty did not succeed in securing long-term peace in Europe.

[118] Guy, 2017, chap. 3, "The King's servant", see above note 71.

[119] *Ibid.*

[120] *Ibid.*

[121] From More's epitaph for the Tomb in Chelsea Old Church, which he wrote himself in 1532. T.E. Bridgett, "Sir Thomas More's Epitaph", in *Life and Writings of Sir Thomas More*, Burns & Oates, London, 1892, pp. 250–252.

administration of the laws required the greatest prudence, courage and moderation.

More's training as a lawyer was by intense oral instruction and exercises of solving cases. From 1496, he had studied at Lincoln's Inn, being constantly challenged together with his fellow students by senior barristers to solve difficult legal questions. The instruction was also organized as trials, where the students had to act as opposing counsel. In addition, there were periods of lectures given by skilled lawyers on a statute or branch of law. Legal education at the time has been characterized as "rigorous and detailed, and fostered exceptional skills in memory, forensic analysis and argumentation that would serve More well throughout his legal and political life".[122]

He was portrayed by his first biographer and son-in-law, William Roper (1496-1578), as "patient, moderate, affable and as a master of his passions through the exercise of reason, years of study and religious reflection", in contrast to the King who could move swiftly from "personal intimacy to mortal threat if policy or passion required, indicating his [...] lack of capacity for constant friendship".[123]

More underlined that his pre-occupation with humanist studies, poetry, literature and rhetoric had served him immensely in his public role. The study of poets, orators, and histories is of unrivalled value in the acquisition of the "practical skill" of "prudence in human affairs".[124]

4.4.2. Why Did More Hunt Heretics?

I have portrayed More as an eminent lawyer, highly respected by his fellow citizens in London, a statesman holding the highest positions in the emerging English State and a renowned humanist throughout Europe. He was a man of faith and reason, a man for all seasons, one who solved conflicts rather than exaggerating them.[125]

---

[122] Curtis, 2011, p. 71, see above note 84.

[123] *Ibid.*, p. 79.

[124] *Ibid.*, p. 72.

[125] More was called a "man for all seasons" during his lifetime. Robert Bolt's play "A Man for All Seasons" (1954) about More's life and conflict with Henry VIII, made the phrase famous. The play was subsequently made into a multi-Academy Award-winning 1966 feature film and a 1988 television movie, see Fred Zinnemann (Producer and Director), "A Man for All Seasons", motion picture, 1966, United Kingdom, Highland Films; and Robert Bolt (Pro-

Some would argue, however, that this is to give him too much praise. He should rather be portrayed as a fanatic, responsible for the burning of heretics, lacking in pragmatism and willingness to compromise. Such criticism was mounted already during his lifetime and in the aftermath of his conflict with Henry VIII. It has also found expression in contemporary popular culture and scholarship.[126]

To reconcile the dissonance between the tolerance demonstrated in his humanist writings and his intolerance of Protestantism may not be easy in our time, where freedom of religion is solidly anchored in international law as well as in most national jurisdictions.[127] In *Utopia*, there is freedom of religion (except for atheism), but More was strongly against such freedom in his native England.

He treated Luther and Protestantism very harshly. During his last 10 years of service for the King, he devoted considerable energy and time to enforce England's heresy laws. This was not an incidental part of his life and work. It was central to his understanding of his professional duties.[128]

He, however, denied any involvement in torture, although he was not against the death penalty for heresy, which was part of the legislation and culture of the time he lived in. Historians believe that six heretics were condemned to be burned during More's tenure as lord chancellor.[129]

Heretic dissent from the dominant catholic Christianity was known in England from the late fourteenth century, when John Wycliff (1330–1384) preached a theology anticipating Protestantism. The movement became

---

ducer) and Charlton Heston (Director), "A Man for All Seasons", motion picture, 1988, United States, Turner Network Television.

[126] The most important early example is John Foxe's (1516–1587) famous *Book of Martyrs* (1563), a graphic and polemic account of those who suffered for the cause of Protestantism, including in the hands of Thomas More: John Fox, *Book of Martyrs*, John Day, London, 1563. In 2009 a novelist won the Man Booker Prize for Fiction with a story in which she has More admit in conversation the allegations of torture he denied in print: Hilary Mantel, *Wolf Hall*, Fourth Estate, London, 2009, pp. 628–9. *Wolf Hall* is also the title of a widely seen TV series by the BBC2, based on the book.

[127] Although far from being practiced everywhere, as documented by among others, Pew Research Centre.

[128] Richard Rex, "Thomas More and the heretics: statesman or fanatic?", in Logan (ed.), 2011, p. 94, see above note 71. The modern tradition of portraying More as an unbalanced inquisitor derives chiefly from Marius, 1984, see above note 71; and from Geoffrey Elton, *Studies in Tudor and Stuart Politics and Government*, 4 vols., Cambridge University Press, 1974–92.

[129] *Ibid.*

known as *Lollardy*, and ecclesiastical and royal authorities co-operated in repressing it. A statute was adopted in 1401 that provided for the burning of heretics. Another result was a profound suspicion of English translations of the Bible, which were produced by members of the Lollardy movements.[130] Finally, a concern grew among authorities that heresy led to sedition, due to the outbreak of the Peasants' Revolt (1381) at the same time when Wycliffe's teachings were attracting popular support.[131]

Under Henry VII and Henry VIII, persecution of perceived heretics intensified. More became actively involved in proceedings against followers of Luther in 1521. Henry VIII decided to write against Luther's attack on the Catholic church in his pamphlet, *Babylonian Captivity of the Church* (1520). More was called in to help with Henry's *Assertion of the Seven Sacraments* (1521).[132]

The impact of the new ideas was found by English authorities to be a threat that had to be defeated from around the mid-1520s. This was at the same time as the bloody Peasants War took place in Germany. In particular, measures to hinder the spread of a new translation of the New Testament by William Tyndale (1494–1536) was seen as important. The book was smuggled into England from 1526 on, despite efforts by the English bishops to stop it. By the end of the 1520s, networks of Lutherans and Lollards were exposed, further alarming the authorities.

In the 1530s, the religious situation became more complicated, due to Henry VIII's 'Great Matter'. He needed to divorce from his first wife in order to re-marry (see Section 4.5.). Evangelicals tended to support divorce, while conservative Catholics were against it. When separating the English church from the papacy, Henry started a process that eventually (after his death) led to a Protestant settlement.

More ended up being the most well-known victim of Henry's Reformation despite having acted together with the King against Luther and other reformers during the 1520s.

---

[130] More was, nevertheless, in favour of the church producing an English translation of the Bible. It should, however, be without all the mistakes that the reformers' translations contained. A true English translation should be undertaken as soon as possible. Guy, 2017, chapter three: "The King's servant", see above note 71.

[131] *Ibid.*

[132] Rex, 2011, p. 95, see above note 128.

More defined heretics as persons who held "self-defined opinions contrary to the doctrine that the commonly known Catholic church teach and hold necessary for salvation".[133] The main problem was that heretics placed their own personal opinion above the consensus of the church, which was guaranteed by the Holy Spirit. He was not willing to accept the arguments by Protestants that they based their theological views on their own reading of the Bible, as in his view it was only the Church that could determine the true meaning of Biblical texts.

For More religion was crucial not only for salvation, but for the order of society. Heresy resulted in conflict, wars and misery. But there were more at stake: heretics also destroyed people's prospects of eternal salvation and their immortal soul. It represented treason against God and was the worst of all crimes. He thought Christian Kings to be "sacral figures", who were responsible even for their subjects' spiritual affairs. But only within the boundaries of a united church.[134]

In 1529, More was commissioned by the bishop of London, Cuthbert Tunstall (1474-1559), to possess and read forbidden books for the purpose of refuting them in English. The result was, among others, *Dialogue Concerning Heresies* (1529) [135] and *Confutation of Tyndale's Answer* (1532/33).[136] In 1533 he published *Apology*, a pamphlet where he defended and clarified his actions as lord chancellor concerning heretics.[137]

More has been criticized for being unpolite and rude in his polemic against the Protestants. However, the reformers used very harsh language themselves, for example by coining the pope as Antichrist and featuring Catholic clergy as obscene. More reasoned that he had to fight in a similar language, applying his considerable rhetoric skills.

On the argument that by burning heretics there was a risk of convicting innocent persons, he replied that there was the same risk in other criminal cases. Besides, a first offence could be atoned for by abjuration and penance. The obstinate or relapsed, on the other hand, were "well and worthily burned".[138]

---

133 CW, vol. 10, p. 30, see above note 82.
134 Rex, 2011, p. 98, see above note 128.
135 Thomas More, *Dialogue Concerning Heresies*, in CW, vol. 6, see above note 82.
136 Thomas More, *Confutation of Tyndale's Answer*, in CW, vol. 8, see above note 82.
137 Thomas More, *Apology*, in CW, vol. 9, see above note 82.
138 Rex, 2011, p. 105, see above note 128.

During his last 10 years of service, both before and during his period as lord chancellor, "heresy was the single most time-consuming issue Thomas More dealt with".[139] He was very concerned, however, that actions against heretics should be in compliance with the laws. When accused of transgressing legal bonds in heresy cases, he refuted that strongly.

The policies More implemented were also in line with what the bishops of the Catholic church wanted of him. At the time, it was highly unusual that a layman played such an important role as theological polemist, demonstrating the church leaders' unusual confidence in him.

His role in confronting heresy in the service of the King was more conventional. It was first and foremost a function of his public position. "Since the time of Henry V, the oath sworn by every man who took office under the crown had included an undertaking to assist the Church in the struggle against heresy." As lord chancellor, being the head of the judiciary, he was under an obligation to repress heresy.[140]

However, More's motivation to write extensively against Protestantism was also based on personal conviction. He perceived that Protestantism represented a serious threat to the existing order in England and Europe. It rapidly attracted support from learned men such as himself. The Reformation introduced a new version of Christianity, which would lead to violent social and political revolutions in Europe.

Regardless of how convincing such justifications may appear, difficult questions remain. Could such beliefs justify that he acted against heretics in the way he did? Should he rather have made efforts to temper the bishops' and the King's wishes for repressive measures? Did More stay governed by reason in his actions against heretics or did he let spirited desires rule?

In answering such questions, one must take into account the context of More's thinking and actions. One's judgment should not be based on solely modern prepositions. By taking a contextual stand, I believe the conclusion must be that More remained governed by reason. He acted like a first citizen and not as a fanatic.

This conclusion does not imply that his reasons should not be criticized. We should not endorse his intolerance, even if we can understand his

---

[139] *Ibid.*, p. 107.
[140] *Ibid.*, p. 108.

reasoning. It does, however, mean that we can still learn about integrity from More. He stayed a man of reason, even if his reasons were wrong.

His mistake entails important lessons. Even if you preserve integrity in the More-sense by letting your reason and faith rule, following your conscience, you may be wrong. Infallible religious or philosophical truths are unattainable, even though, at a personal level, you may choose to base your life on them. At the State level, however, you should not operate according to such convictions. You should refrain from appealing to the consensus of any institution, such as the church, as something that cannot be criticized. States that present themselves as built on infallible truths lead to tyranny and oppression, even if they treat all but the heretics nice.

The full meaning of religious tolerance in the affairs of the State may not have been explicitly taught by More at any time, although his humanist writings pointed in that direction. In *Utopia*, at least, he showed that a society could function well even if it practised a lot more tolerance than England and himself as a State official.

4.5. More's Conflict with Henry VIII

The main controversy with Henry VIII was about the independence of the English Church. The King wanted The English Church to depart from the Catholic Church because of the Pope's unwillingness to accept his divorce from his first wife, Catherine of Aragon, who did not give him a son. The King wanted to marry Anne Boleyn and did so secretly on 25 January 1532, when she was already pregnant with his child. Because of the pregnancy, divorce with Catherine to avoid bigamy and his child to be born outside wedlock became urgent. An independent English Church, under the King's own leadership, would help formalize divorce and re-marriage.

To accomplish the break with Rome and destroy the power of the medieval church, the so-called Reformation Parliament played a vital role. It first met in November 1529 and lasted seven years, enacting 137 statues of which 32 were of vital importance. In addition, the King also pressured the church Convocation to accept his demands.

Some of the most important acts and submissions that ensured that Henry VIII became head of the English Church and separated England from the Pope's influence was:

- The Annates Statute of 1532, which empowered the King to abolish payment to Rome of the first year's income of all newly installed bishops;[141]

- The Submission of the Clergy of 15 May 1532, in which the clergy promised not to legislate without royal consent;[142]

- The Act of Restraint of Appeals of April 1533,[143] which decreed that "this realm of England is an empire", cutting the constitutional cords holding England to the papacy. A month later an archbishop annulled the King's first marriage, and on 1 June Anne was crowned rightful queen of England;

- The Act of Succession of March 1534 ordered subjects to accept the King's marriage to Anne as "undoubted, true, sincere and perfect";[144]

- A second Statute "in Restraint of Annates" severed most of the financial ties with Rome while in November 1534, the Act of Supremacy announced that Henry was and always had been "Supreme Head of the Church of England;[145]

- The Act of Treason of December 1534, which made it punishable by death, to disavow the Act of Supremacy.[146] It was designed to root

---

[141] Parliament of England, Act in Conditional Restraint of Annates (23 Hen. VIII c. 20), 1532 (Annates Statute).

[142] The document was adopted in Convocation on 15 May 1532 under intense pressure from Henry VIII and handed to the King on the following day. It contained a submission to the King's demands, promising,

> in verbo sacerdotii, here unto your highness, submitting ourselves most humbly to the same, that we will never from henceforth [enact], put in use, promulge, or execute, any [new canons or constitutions provincial, or any other new ordinance, provincial or synodal], in our Convocation [or synod] in time coming, which Convocation is, always has been, and must be, assembled only by your highness' commandment of writ, unless your highness by your royal assent shall license us to [assemble our Convocation, and] to make, promulge, and execute [such constitutions and ordinances as shall be made in] the same; and thereto give your royal assent and authority.

Henry VIII, The Reign, "Submission of the Clergy 1532" (available on its web site).

[143] Parliament of England, An Acte that the Appeles in suche Cases as have ben used to be pursued to the See of Rome shall not be from hensforth had ne used but within this Realme (24 Hen. VIII c. 12), April 1533 (Act of Restraint of Appeals).

[144] Parliament of England, Act of Succession (25 Hen. VIII c. 22), March 1534.

[145] Parliament of England, Act in Absolute Restraint of Annates (25 Hen. VIII c. 20), November 1534.

[146] Parliament of England, Act of Treason (26 Hen. VIII c. 13), December 1534.

---

out and liquidate dissent, extending the meaning of treason to include all those who did "maliciously wish, will or desire by words or writing or by craft imagine" the King's death or slandered this marriage. It was eventually used against More.[147]

By these acts, the medieval order that church and State were separate entities with divine law standing higher than human law had been legislated out of existence. The English church had become a department of the Tudor State, monasteries were dissolved, and at least 13 percent of the land of England and Wales were nationalized, making the King much wealthier and able to finance wars.[148]

Although More referred to health issues and his need for devoting more time to spiritual matters when stepping down as lord chancellor on 16 May 1532, the real reason was his unwillingness to accept that the King now possessed veto power over ecclesiastical legislation as put in place by the Submission of the Clergy. In effect, the submission meant that the leaders of the church had given up defending its institutional integrity. In his explanation to the King, he said that he would "bestow the residue of my life in mine age now to come, about the provision for my soul in the service of God, and to be your Grace's beadsman and pray for you".[149]

The remaining three years of his life would rather be characterized by both intensive activity and dramatic incidents. He would not give up his fight against the King's efforts to subdue the church, while at the same time presenting himself as the Kings good servant.[150]

More refused to attend the coronation of Anne Boleyn in June 1533, despite being officially invited and approached by bishops who wanted him to attend together with them. The refusal surely contributed to determining the fatal outcome of his struggle, putting a "sword in his enemies' hands", as one scholar put it.[151] Charges were brought against him, including for complicity with Elizabeth Barton (1506–1534), a nun who had uttered

---

[147] The overview is based on: Patrick Joyce, Ralph Charles Atkins and Others, "United Kingdom: The Break with Rome", *Encyclopædia Britannica* (available on its web site).

[148] *Ibid.*

[149] Peter Marshall, "The last years", in Logan (ed.), 2011, p. 116, see above note 71; Curtis, 2011, p. 69, see above note 84.

[150] Travis Curtright, "Sir Thomas More and his Opposition to Henry VIII in 1533", in Curtright (ed.), 2015, pp. 111, see above note 7.

[151] *Ibid.*, p. 112.

prophecies against Henry's divorce. More was, however, able to prove his innocence.

In April 1533, More refused the Oath of Succession because it transgressed on the freedom of the English Church. He was imprisoned on 17 April 1534 and tried on 1 July 1535, for denying the King's title as supreme head of the Church of England. In the trial, he was found guilty of treason despite his denial of what he considered perjured evidence. He was beheaded five days later.

4.5.1. The Ultimate Test of Integrity

What More endured after his arrest may be termed as his ultimate test of integrity. Pressure mounted against him because of his unwillingness to state his acceptance of the King's new power over the Church – from representatives of the King in the forms of threats, interrogations, and traps; from friends and former colleagues in the form of appeals of giving in; and from family members who suffered because of his imprisonment and his loss of income and estate.

The indictment comprised of four counts:[152]

1. More had maliciously refused on 7 May 1535, to accept the King's supremacy over the Church of England;

2. He had conspired against the King by writing treasonous letters to bishop John Fisher;

3. He had stirred up sedition by describing the Act of Supremacy as a two-edged sword, that is, a law that if disobeyed would mean bodily death, and if obeyed would mean spiritual death;

4. He had "maliciously, traitorously, and diabolically" denied Parliament's power to declare the King to be head of the Church.[153]

In his defence, which he had to present himself without written notes, More underlined that he had remained silent on whether the King could be the head of the English Church. His argument was based on a legal norm established by English precedent, that "silence is not a crime; in fact, silence means consent".[154]

---

[152] This section is based on Wegemer, 1995, see above note 64.

[153] *Ibid.*, p. 210.

[154] *Ibid.*, p. 211.

Furthermore, none of his letters to bishop Fisher had touched upon matters of State, and they did not exist any longer. He had only expressed himself hypothetically about the Act of Supremacy (Oath of Succession): "if it was like a two-edged sword forcing a person to make a choice between physical and spiritual life, then the statute might at a later time be considered illegitimate".[155]

Refuting the fourth count, he underlined that he had never denied Parliament's power to make the King Head of the Church.

At the trial, More faced 15 judges and 12 jurors. The judges included Chancellor Thomas Audley (1488–1544), Royal Secretary Thomas Cromwell (1485–1540), and Thomas Howard 3rd Duke of Norfolk (1473–1554), as well as an uncle, a brother, and the father of Anne Boleyn, the King's new wife. They all had strong interests in convicting More.

The jury of twelve was also partial, being put together to ensure the result wanted by the King. More did not have counsel or was not permitted a written account of his defence or the indictment.

The court seems to have accepted More's first three arguments, but not the fourth; that he had not denied Parliament's right to make the King head of the Church. The rest of the trial focused on this count.

The prosecution witness, Solicitor General Richard Rich (1496/97–1567), stated that More had told him on 12 June 1535 in his cell that Parliament did not have authority to make the King head of the Church. More denied having said anything of the kind, stating that Rich was committing perjury. He then demonstrated Rich's lack of credibility as a witness. He would never have trusted him with secrets "of my conscience touching the King's Supremacy".[156]

The jury of the court still found him guilty.

More's defence was of high legal quality. He was able to demonstrate that he had done none of the illegal acts he was charged for. He referred to over 20 years of trusted positions in the State and an untainted reputation showed the credibility of his character. He demonstrated that the Act of Parliament, which the indictment against him was grounded on, was in conflict both with the laws of God and with many other "laws and statutes of our own land", including the Magna Carta (1215), which states that "the

---

[155] *Ibid.*

[156] *Ibid.*, p. 213.

English Church shall be free, and shall have its rights undiminished and its liberties unimpaired".[157]

He knew, however, that even if there were no evidence against him, this would not be enough to save him. His real opponent was the King, and the King could not accept anything but surrender.

He did not surrender. Nor did he try to escape. He referred to his conscience, which was bound by faith and reason to defend the unity of the church. He stood the test of integrity as a lawyer, providing a solid defence for himself in line with ethical and professional standards.

He also stood the test of integrity as a person, not making concessions conflicting his personal views, while caring for his family and friends, expressing gratitude to those who supported him, and forbearance to those who facilitated the injustice that caused his death.

Few persons could have done so well in terms of upholding his integrity – being ruled by reason and faithful to his professional and personal convictions – under such pressure, knowing that death was a certain outcome. It is a remarkable story about skill and courage.

However, in my view, the main lesson to take from More is not that we shall never give in to pressure when confronted with lethal threats. We should rather follow More's own reasoning in his humanistic writings and learn how courage and other spirited desires should always be governed by reason. A well-trained and educated reason.

What we should learn from him is how he did what he thought reasonable to avert the King's measures that would undermine justice and peace in England and in Christian States in Europe.

According to his view of the world, this could be summarized as being more faithful to God than to the King. He ended his life by stating that "I die the King's faithful servant, but God's first".[158]

---

[157] England, Magna Carta Libertatum, 15 June 1215, clause 1.

[158] Quoted from Peter Marshall, "The last years", in Logan (ed.), 2011, p. 133, see above note 71. Some scholars doubt the authenticity of the quote, which was reported first by the Paris News Letter, 4 August, 1535. It is, however, little doubt that it reflects More's understanding of his relation to the King; an understanding he had believed the King shared. Cf. the Center for Thomas More Studies, "About Famous Quotes" (available on its web site).

4.6. More's Integrity Lessons

When confronted with the fact that almost all bishops and universities had agreed to the new legislation, More responded that even if that was so, throughout Christendom many more would support his view. His conscience was bound to conform to a General Council of Christendom, rather than to the council of one realm only. In this way he was denying the legal justification by Parliament of placing the King above the law, epitomized in Cromwell's statement: "You're absolutely right. It must be done by law. It's just a matter of finding the right law. Or making one".[159]

More was referring to the conscience as the bedrock of personhood, and moral and professional integrity. A conscience bound by Christian principles and by law; not by personal opinion.

In defending the church against interference from the State, he also defended individual freedom *vis-à-vis* political power, as Pope John Paul II has put it. The State should not interfere with the freedom of conscience.[160]

In his so-called 'tower works', More elaborated on the concepts of conscience, courage, and grace.[161] It is necessary to gather comfort and courage, and let it sink into the heart, even though belief in God and grace also plays a strong role. By right imagining, the abstract argument is transformed into a habitual, fast, and deep-rooted purpose. There is a form of internalized rhetoric involved, based on study and training.

---

[159] Wegemer, 1995, see above note 64.

[160] This is a prevailing view in Peter Berglar, *Thomas More: A Lonely Voice Against the Power of the State*, Scepter Publishers, Cleveland, 2009 (First Published in German, 1999), summarized in the foreword as follows: "More generally, what was involved was the breaking away of society and the state from the medieval political order and the birth of the modern concept of independent nationhood. But something else also was implicated in these events, namely, the state's ambition to impose not just de facto obedience but also active assent. Now, for the first time in history, simply tolerating the unilateral decisions of an establishment was not enough; explicit approval was demanded, and not only defiance but personal opinion was subject to persecution, with nonconformity treated as the equivalent of rebellion. In the cradle of modern Europe, then, we witness a power struggle to preserve the freedom of the individual in the face of organized power, something not always or necessarily identified with the state".

[161] The tower works include: Thomas More, *A Dialogue of Comfort Against Tribulation*, in CW, vol. 12, 1534, see above note 82; Thomas More, *Treatise Upon the Passion*, in CW vol. 13, 1534, see above note 82; Thomas More, *Treatise on the Blessed Body*, in CW, vol. 13, 1535, see above note 82; Thomas More, *De Tristitia Christi*, in CW, vol. 14, 1535, see above note 82.

More stood almost alone against immense political pressure, including from colleagues, friends and family. He frequently referred to his conscience in scrutinizing the soundness of his own motives, which were criticized of being over-scrupulous. He navigated a course between the scrupulous conscience and the over-large or elastic conscience.

He also referred to an 'informed conscience'; shaped by years of study and reflection. From early one, in his humanist writings More had raised the fundamental integrity question: *How to serve with integrity in a brutal political environment, full of intrigues, flattering, and dishonesty.* The notion of an 'informed' conscience may be interpreted to summarize that this inner voice of truth is not based on spirited desires for honour or fame, but rather on faith and reason's efforts to do as good as possible in every difficult circumstance.

He was loyal to the Catholic Church and to a settled consensus within that church. He appealed to the views throughout Christendom, that would support his view on the unity of the church. At the same time, he acted on his own conscience: "I never intend […] to pin my soul to another man's back, not even the best man that I know this day living: for I know not where he may lead it".[162] The responsibility must be his alone.

He is very clear that he will not criticize others or condemn their conscience, but for his own part, he is content "to lose goods, land, and life too, rather than swear against my conscience".[163] Many of those who took the decisions that would end his life were former friends and colleagues. To them he stated that he looked forward to seeing them again, in another world.

In conclusion, More exemplified great personal integrity. When he was pressed for why he would not give up his convictions, when his friends and colleagues did, he referred to his conscience. But he also defended his views and rights with legal, theological and philosophical reasoning. He linked his conscience to religious beliefs and values, and underlined that conscience has to be trained and developed through study and reflection.

---

[162] Thomas More to his daughter, in prison, August 1534. Quoted from Curtright (ed.), 2015, beginning of book, before pagination, see above note 7.

[163] Gerard B. Wegemer and Stephen W. Smith, *A Thomas More Source Book*, The Catholic University of America Press, Washington, DC, 2004, p. 334.

He did not perceive his courage as entirely a gift of grace. It also had to be nurtured through imagination, internalization of words and preparations, and to be controlled by reason.

More exemplified integrity as self-integration and consistency throughout his career. He stood for something, not giving in to pressure, at the same time always willing to reason and provide his arguments.

More is not an example of 'civil disobedience' based on personal convictions, I would argue. His reasoning and practice during the ultimate integrity test are instead closer to modern conceptions of professional integrity. As outlined above, professional integrity is characterized by a mode of reasoning that calls for the role holder to engage critically and creatively with the varied and sometimes conflicting demands of professional practice. More as a 'first citizen' was a professional, applying legal and theological arguments in line with professional standards and practice of his time.

His defence of the unity of the church and church doctrine may be seen as a reference to authoritative theological practice. In his conflict with Henry VIII, he makes efforts to give his best reading of that practice.

The same goes for his acting as a lawyer, throughout his career, and certainly in his own final case. In his defence, he provides what he believes is the best reading of English jurisprudence in a treason case like his.

It may seem paradoxical, but because More is not a modern in the sense that he linked his conscience to private opinion, he becomes interesting in terms of professional integrity, which primarily refers to institutional practice and not to personal opinion.

More favoured reforms, that is, improving the standards and practice of church, law and politics gradually. Concerning church doctrine and practice, he referred to the General Council of Christendom as the final arbiter.

He argued that new legislation should be adopted by Parliament, while judges should have discretion to apply written and unwritten law according to circumstances and their own interpretation.

4.7. Integrity in Justice

There are thus several ways in which More is relevant for discussions on how to strengthen integrity in justice.

For individuals considering the fundamental integrity question – whether to enter the world of justice professionals – there is great inspiration to take from him. He would tell them that there is a fundamental question anyone who considers working for justice institutions have to ask themselves: *Will I be able to honour the promises of my profession, despite all the pressure, cynicism and temptations I will be exposed to? Will I be able to hold my spirited desires and appetite (for money, sex, luxury) governed by reason?*

From More's writings, we know that he believed that an initial determination to live up to integrity standards is not enough. His method was to continuously train himself in integrity by binding his conscience to the standards and promises of his profession, and by reflecting on how to moderate the effects of wickedness and evil.

Safeguarding the integrity of the church, justice institutions, and Parliament was a central part of More's efforts as a statesman and lawyer. He knew well that institutions could be corrupted and manipulated, and how important leadership were in setting and practising high standards. Well-functioning institutions could improve societies and human affairs vastly. They should be protected.

The catalogue of integrity failures listed in Section 4.2.2.1. above would not be unknown to More. I suspect he would respond that to let undue pressure, material temptations, personal relationships, or lack of professional and moral convictions lead you away from professional duties would be the result of the lower parts of your soul being too dominant. The antidote would be to rebalance your soul and let reason rule. He would know well that this is easier said than done. To succeed may require hard work over a long time.

However, if you are going to make advances in confronting tyranny and injustices that is what is necessary. This is also what an institution such as a court promises. Maintaining professional integrity as a leader or staff member of such institutions requires conforming your conscience to the promises and aims of justice – and follow it.

That seems to me to be the essence of Thomas More's thoughts and practice of integrity.

5

The Dag Hammarskjöld Legacy and Integrity in International Civil Service

Hans Corell[*]

5.1. Dag Hammarskjöld on the International Civil Servant in Law and in Fact

On 30 May 1961, Dag Hammarskjöld delivered his famous lecture to Congregation at Oxford University entitled 'The International Civil Servant in Law and in Fact".[1]

The point of departure in this lecture is Dag Hammarskjöld's reference to the fact that the international civil service had its genesis in the League of Nations.[2] He then makes an intriguing analysis of the provisions that governed the permanent Secretariat of the League of Nations and the corresponding provisions in the Charter of the United Nations.[3] In his view, the legacy of the international Secretariat of the League of Nations is marked in the first paragraph of Article 100 of the Charter of the United Nations ('UN'),[4] which reads:

> In the performance of their duties the Secretary-General and the staff shall not seek or receive instructions from any government or from any other authority external to the Organization. They shall refrain from any action which might reflect on

---

[*] **Hans Corell** is the former Under-Secretary-General for Legal Affairs and the Legal Counsel of the United Nations, Ambassador and Under-Secretary for Legal and Consular Affairs in the Swedish Ministry for Foreign Affairs, Chief Legal Officer of the Swedish Ministry of Justice, and a judge in Sweden. The present chapter is based on an oral presentation that the author gave at the Peace Palace in The Hague on 1 December 2018. There were a few footnotes in that presentation. All additional footnotes have been added by the editors.

[1] Dag Hammarskjöld, "The International Civil Servant in Law and in Fact", Oxford, 30 May 1961 (http://www.legal-tools.org/doc/64bcae/).

[2] *Ibid.*, sect. II, p. 329.

[3] *Ibid.*, pp. 330 ff.

[4] *Ibid.*, sect. III, pp. 332–33.

their position as international officials responsible only to the Organization.[5]

However, with respect to the functions and authority of the Secretary-General, the UN Charter "broke new ground".[6] Here, Dag Hammarskjöld refers to Articles 97, 98 and 99:[7]

Article 97

The Secretariat shall comprise a Secretary-General and such staff as the Organization may require. The Secretary-General shall be appointed by the General Assembly upon the recommendation of the Security Council. He shall be the chief administrative officer of the Organization.

Article 98

The Secretary-General shall act in that capacity in all meetings of the General Assembly, of the Security Council, of the Economic and Social Council, and of the Trusteeship Council, and shall perform such other functions as are entrusted to him by these organs. The Secretary-General shall make an annual report to the General Assembly on the work of the Organization.

Article 99

The Secretary-General may bring to the attention of the Security Council any matter which in his opinion may threaten the maintenance of international peace and security.

It is also important to note that, according to Article 101 of the UN Charter, the staff shall be appointed by the Secretary-General under regulations established by the General Assembly. "The paramount consideration in the employment of the staff and in the determination of the conditions of service shall be the necessity of securing the highest standards of efficiency, competence, and integrity."[8] Due regard should be paid to the importance of recruiting the staff on as wide a geographical basis as possible.[9]

---

[5] See Charter of the United Nations, 26 June 1945 (http://www.legal-tools.org/doc/6b3cd5/) ('UN Charter').

[6] Hammarskjöld, 1961, p. 334, above note 1.

[7] See *ibid.*, pp. 334–38.

[8] UN Charter, Article 101, see above note 5. See also Hammarskjöld, 1961, p. 337, above note 1.

[9] *Ibid.*

Dag Hammarskjöld's conclusions are "that the administration of the Organization shall be left to the Secretary-General" and that the Secretariat has "a position, administratively, of full political independence", which also reflects on international civil servants employed by the Organization.[10]

However, Articles 98 and 99 "together open the door to the problem of neutrality in a sense unknown in the history of the League of Nations".[11] Dag Hammarskjöld focuses on the fact that the Charter "entitles the General Assembly and the Security Council to entrust the Secretary-General with tasks involving the execution of political decisions, even when this would bring him – and with him the Secretariat and its members – into the arena of possible political conflict".[12]

Of particular importance is that the Secretary-General has "a right to bring matters to the attention of the Security Council".[13] This would bring with it "a broad discretion to conduct inquiries and to engage in informal diplomatic activity in regard to matters which 'may threaten the maintenance of international peace and security.'"[14] Dag Hammarskjöld also makes special reference to the use of the word "integrity" in Article 101.[15]

According to Dag Hammarskjöld,

> [t]he independence and international character of the Secretariat required not only resistance to national pressures in matters of personnel, but also—and this was more complex—the independent implementation of controversial political decisions in a manner fully consistent with the exclusively international responsibility of the Secretary-General.[16]

In particular, in controversial situations,

> the Secretary-General was confronted with mandates of a highly general character, expressing the bare minimum of agreement attainable in the organs. That the execution of these tasks involved the exercise of political judgment by the Secre-

---

[10] *Ibid.*, p. 334.
[11] *Ibid.*, p. 335.
[12] *Ibid.*
[13] *Ibid.*
[14] *Ibid.*
[15] *Ibid.*, p. 337.
[16] *Ibid.*, sect. V, p. 342.

tary-General was, of course, evident to the Member States themselves.[17]

As examples, Dag Hammarskjöld mentions the situations in Palestine, Egypt, Lebanon, Jordan and the Congo during his tenure.[18] He concludes by stating that these examples "demonstrate the extent to which the Member States have entrusted the Secretary-General with tasks that have required him to take action which unavoidably may have to run counter to the views of at least some of these Member States".[19]

5.2. The Conclusions in Dag Hammarskjöld's Lecture

Focusing on the conclusions in Dag Hammarskjöld's lecture is of great importance. The best way of conveying his legacy here is through references to his lecture, in particular to three direct quotes.

First, Dag Hammarskjöld points to "the serious problems" that

> arise precisely because it is so often not possible for the organs themselves to resolve the controversial issue faced by the Secretary-General. When brought down to specific cases involving a clash of interests and positions, the required majority in the Security Council or General Assembly may not be available for any particular solution.[20]

He then continues:

> It might be said that in this situation the Secretary-General should refuse to implement the resolution, since implementation would offend one or another group of Member States and open him to the charge that he has abandoned the political neutrality and impartiality essential to his office. The only way to avoid such criticism, it is said, is for the Secretary-General to refrain from execution of the original resolution until the organs have decided the issue by the required majority (and, in the case of the Security Council, with the unanimous concurrence of the permanent members) or he, maybe, has found another way to pass responsibility over on to governments.[21]

---

[17]   *Ibid.*

[18]   See *ibid.*, pp. 343 ff.

[19]   *Ibid.*, p. 344.

[20]   *Ibid.*, p. 345.

[21]   *Ibid.*

However, in his lecture, Dag Hammarskjöld takes a different position, stating that "[t]he answers seemed clear enough in law".[22] He concludes that "the responsibilities of the Secretary-General under the Charter cannot be laid aside merely because the execution of decisions by him is likely to be politically controversial. The Secretary-General remains under the obligation to carry out the policies as adopted by the organs".[23] The "essential requirement", according to Dag Hammarskjöld, is that the Secretary-General "does this on the basis of this exclusively international responsibility and not in the interest of any particular State or group of States".[24]

Second, he draws attention to the ambiguity of the word "neutrality" in such a context:

> It is obvious from what I have said that the international civil servant cannot be accused of lack of neutrality simply for taking a stand on a controversial issue when this is his duty and cannot be avoided. But there remains a serious intellectual and moral problem as we move within an area inside which personal judgement must come into play. Finally, we have to deal with the question of integrity or with, if you please, a question of conscience.[25]

Against this background, Dag Hammarskjöld maintains that

> [t]he international civil servants must keep himself under the strictest observation. He is not requested to be a neuter in the sense that he has to have no sympathies or antipathies, that there are to be no interests which are close to him in his personal capacity or that he is to have no ideas or ideals that matter for him.[26]

"However", says Dag Hammarskjöld, "he is requested to be fully aware of those human reactions and meticulously check himself so that they are not permitted to influence his actions".[27] "This is nothing unique", he says, and ends with the following question: "Is not every judge professionally under the same obligation?".[28]

---

[22] *Ibid.*, p. 346.
[23] *Ibid.*
[24] *Ibid.*
[25] *Ibid.*, p. 348.
[26] *Ibid.*
[27] *Ibid.*
[28] *Ibid.*

In the final analysis, Dag Hammarskjöld concludes:

> If the international civil servant knows himself to be free from such personal influences in his actions and guided solely by the common aims and rules laid down for, and by the Organization he serves and by recognized legal principles, then he has done his duty, and then he can face the criticism which, even so, will be unavoidable. As I said, at the final last, this is a question of integrity, and if integrity in the sense of respect for law and respect for truth were to drive him into positions of conflict with this or that interest, then that conflict is a sign of his neutrality and not of his failure to observe neutrality— then it is in line, not in conflict, with his duties as an international civil servant.[29]

This is a powerful message both to the Member States and to the international civil service. On another occasion where the same was discussed, I drew the following conclusions with respect to the United Nations: The lecture should serve as a reminder both to those who are already employed and to those who are involved with recruitment. What the United Nations needs are individuals who can be deemed to observe the standards required and who do not give in to pressure. If they do not demonstrate the kind of integrity that Dag Hammarskjöld refers to, they will sooner or later put the functioning of the Organization at risk.[30]

I then went on to say:

> What the Organisation needs are persons who can make assessments and decisions in accordance with the clear guidelines that follow from Dag Hammarskjöld's address. This also means that it is inevitable that the Secretary-General of the United Nations from time to time is likely to have an argument with one or more member states, notably the major powers. This is certainly not something that he or she should be looking for, but it is the unavoidable result of the Secretary-General performing the duty that follows with the position.
>
> If this situation should occur, the member states should not simply jump to conclusions that produce confrontation but

---

[29] *Ibid.*

[30] Hans Corell, "The Need for the Rule of Law in International Affairs – Reflections on Dag Hammarskjöld's address at Oxford University on 30 May 1961, 'The International Civil Service in Law and in Fact'", in Henning Melber (ed.), *The Ethics of Dag Hammarskjöld*, Dag Hammarskjöld Foundation, Uppsala, 2010, p. 15.

rather step back for a moment and reflect. Is this situation not, rather, a sign of health – that the Secretary-General is doing his or her job? On second thoughts, maybe the firm stand of the Secretary-General is in both the short and long term interest of the member states, including those that may have been displeased in the particular situation.[31]

5.3. Integrity in International Justice

When reading Dag Hammarskjöld's lecture from the perspective of integrity in international justice, I find the reference to the obligations of every judge of particular interest. Having served in the judiciary of my own country Sweden from 1962 to 1973, I recognize this duty immediately. As a matter of fact, in Sweden there is a tradition that might have inspired Dag Hammarskjöld in his role as UN Secretary-General, namely the so-called 'public service tradition',[32] guided by principles of uprightness, integrity, impartiality and incorruptibility.

Under all circumstances, the manner in which Dag Hammarskjöld analyses the concept of integrity in his lecture is a crucial legacy for international civil servants, and in particular for international judges. This is for the simple reason that they have to observe an even greater level of independence than international civil servants in general. I would therefore suggest that all persons elected to such functions in international courts be made aware of the lecture, since Dag Hammarskjöld's analysis is of direct relevance in the field of international justice. The dilemma that he analyses is omnipresent in this field. This is also why he uses the expression "professionally" when he refers to the obligation of every judge – it comes with the profession.

Let us now look at the manner in which the obligations of judges are described in two court statutes. I have chosen the Statute of the International Court of Justice and the Rome Statute of the International Criminal Court as examples.

According to Article 2 of the Statute of the International Court of Justice,[33] "[t]he Court shall be composed of a body of independent judges, elected regardless of their nationality from among persons of high moral

---

[31] *Ibid.*, p. 16.

[32] In Swedish: *ämbetsmannatraditionen.*

[33] Statute of the International Court of Justice, 26 June 1945 (http://www.legal-tools.org/doc/fdd2d2/).

character, who possess the qualifications required in their respective countries for appointment to the highest judicial offices, or are jurisconsults of recognized competence in international law". Article 16(1) prescribes that "[n]o member of the Court may exercise any political or administrative function, or engage in any other occupation of a professional nature". Furthermore, according to Article 17, "[n]o member of the Court may act as agent, counsel, or advocate in any case", or "participate in the decision of any case in which he has previously taken part as agent, counsel, or advocate for one of the parties, or as a member of a national or international court, or of a commission of enquiry, or in any other capacity". Article 20 prescribes that "[e]very member of the Court shall, before taking up his duties, make a solemn declaration in open court that he will exercise his powers impartially and conscientiously".

In the Rome Statute of the International Criminal Court,[34] Article 36(3)(a) prescribes that "[t]he judges shall be chosen from among persons of high moral character, impartiality and integrity who possess the qualifications required in their respective States for appointment to the highest judicial offices".

In a criminal court, one must also look at the prosecutor in this context. According to Article 42(3) of the Rome Statute, "[t]he Prosecutor and the Deputy Prosecutors shall be persons of high moral character, be highly competent in and have extensive practical experience in the prosecution or trial of criminal cases". With respect to the employment of staff, Article 44(2) prescribes that "the Prosecutor and the Registrar shall ensure the highest standards of efficiency, competency and integrity".

As it appears, there are references to "high moral character" in the Statute of the International Court of Justice and to "integrity" in the Rome Statute. It is obvious that the standards that Dag Hammarskjöld recognizes in his lecture must also apply in the field of international justice.

The analysis that Dag Hammarskjöld makes in his lecture, and the manner in which he applies the standards that he explains, set an extraordinary example as guidance for us in later generations. I often thought of this when I served as the United Nations Legal Counsel from 1994 to 2004, three years with Boutros Boutros-Ghali, and seven years with Kofi Annan. I have also had the privilege of interacting with international judges in dif-

---

[34] Rome Statute of the International Criminal Court, 17 July 1998 (http://www.legal-tools.org/doc/7b9af9/).

ferent settings over the years since I was involved in the establishment of the International Criminal Tribunal for the former Yugoslavia, the International Criminal Tribunal for Rwanda, the International Tribunal for the Law of the Sea, the Special Court for Sierra Leone, and the Extraordinary Chambers in the Courts of Cambodia. I was also the Secretary-General's Representative at the Rome Conference in 1998, and was involved in the initial stages of the establishment of the International Criminal Court. And, of course, the International Court of Justice is one of the six main organs of the United Nations. This means that I have interacted with international judges in many contexts.

Of particular interest were the discussions with the judges who attended the Brandeis Institutes for International Judges, to which I was invited[35] and asked to deliver a keynote address in June 2002 as the United Nations Legal Counsel.[36]

On that occasion, I made two specific points that can be seen as reflecting the legacy of Dag Hammarskjöld. I first pointed out that international judges must uphold standards which are set even *higher* than at the national level. The reason is that international judges are operating under the eyes of the whole world. The impression they give and the way in which they perform their work will directly reflect on the standing of the institution that they serve.

I then pointed to a classic dilemma at the international level: *Quis custodiet custodes?* Who supervises the supervisors? This must always be present in the minds of judges who serve at the international level. I said that I could think of no higher calling for a lawyer than to serve as an international judge. But precisely because it is a high judicial office with limited ways of establishing accountability, it must be assumed with a humble mind. What is required is a deep insight that a competent, independent, and impartial international judiciary is an indispensable element when we are making our best efforts to establish the rule of law in international relations.

Against this background, it is clear that Dag Hammarskjöld's analysis of neutrality and integrity in his 1961 lecture is an important part of his legacy with respect to international justice.

---

[35] See Brandeis University's web site.
[36] Hans Corell, "Ethical Dimensions of International Jurisprudence and Adjudication", Waltham, Massachusetts, 10 June 2002 (http://www.legal-tools.org/doc/5eb7d4/).

5.4. Dag Hammarskjöld's *Waymarks* – Also Named *Markings*

After Dag Hammarskjöld's death in September 1961, a manuscript was found in his New York apartment entitled *Vägmärken*, in English best translated as *Waymarks*. Attached to the manuscript was an undated letter, addressed to an official in the Swedish Ministry for Foreign Affairs, authorizing him to publish it "as a sort of 'White Book' concerning my negotiations with myself — and with God".[37] (The manuscript was published in Sweden in 1963. In 1964, an English translation by W.H. Auden in collaboration with Leif Sjöberg, entitled *Markings*, was published by Alfred A. Knopf, New York, and Faber & Faber, London. This translation has been criticized by some, and I myself have found language and expressions in the book that I prefer to translate myself. In fact, an interesting guide to the *Waymarks* is now available, in which these problems are discussed.[38] With respect to the quote from the undated letter, reference is made to W.H. Auden's Foreword to *Markings*.[39])

When my father presented me with *Vägmärken* in 1963, I understood that reading and writing poetry was an important source of strength and inspiration to Dag Hammarskjöld. I came to realize that a few lines of a poem often make a greater impression on the human mind than the ordinary prose of an essay or a novel.

In this context, I will reflect on Dag Hammarskjöld's *Waymarks* from a lawyer's perspective. Lawyers have a role of great importance to fulfil both at the national and international levels. Irrespective of where we discharge our professional duties – be it at the bar; the judiciary; national, regional or local government; business; inter-governmental organizations; or non-governmental organizations – we have an obligation to engage in establishing the rule of law and in explaining that the rule of law is an indispensable element in creating a world society where humans can live in peace and dignity with their human rights protected. It goes without saying

---

[37] Dag Hammarskjöld, *Markings*, Leif Sjöberg and W.H. Auden (trans.), Faber & Faber, London, 1964, p. 7.

[38] Bernhard Erling, *A Reader's Guide to Dag Hammarskjöld's* Waymarks, St. Peter, Minnesota, 1999 (updated Introduction in 2009).

[39] Reference can also be made to Inge Lønning, "Politics, Morality and Religion – The Legacy of Dag Hammarskjöld", and Henning Melber, "Dag Hammarskjöld's *zeitgemäße Betrachtungen* – Reflections on Inge Lønning's Dag Hammarskjöld Lecture", both in Henning Melber (ed.), *The Ethics of Dag Hammarskjöld*, Dag Hammarskjöld Foundation, Uppsala, 2010.

that those who serve in the field of international justice have unique obligations here.

When I first read the *Waymarks*, one of them caught my attention in particular. In fact, it became a lodestar to me. (Among other things, I would quote it when greeting new staff members welcome to the United Nations Office of Legal Affairs.) This 'waymark' reads, in my own translation:

> Openness to life grants a swift insight – like a flash of lightning – into the life situation of others. A must: to force the problem from its emotional sting into a clearly conceived intellectual form – and act accordingly.[40]

This waymark reflects the fact that we are constantly exposed to various impressions depending on what we do, where we are, and the circumstances of the time. A common experience is hearing in the news and reading in the papers about atrocities that human beings are exposed to, in particular in connection with armed conflicts. Most people react very strongly against this, getting upset and condemning the actions by the perpetrators. Lawyers are no different in this respect. We react in the same manner here as other people do.

However, there is a tremendous difference if the lawyer all of a sudden finds him- or herself involved in a law enforcement process, dealing with the criminal acts that caused the human suffering. Whether we act in this context as an investigator, a prosecutor, a defence counsel or a judge, we must be absolutely certain that we act in a professional manner as described in the waymark. We have to force the problem we are confronted with from its emotional sting into a clearly conceived intellectual form – and act accordingly.

For me, this became clear already when I served as a law clerk and as a young judge. A common experience is that one reads in the local press about crimes committed and gets upset. However, in a matter of time, the case will appear before the court where one serves, and then one has to act in a professional manner. I would suggest that this is the typical situation at the international level, in particular in international criminal courts. The waymark should therefore serve as an important lodestar here.

Another waymark that caught my attention at an early stage was the following in Sjöberg and Auden's translation:

---

[40] Dag Hammarskjöld, *Vägmärken*, Albert Bonniers Förlag, Stockholm, 1963, p. 16 (the present author's translation).

> Never look down to test the ground before taking your next
> step: only he who keeps his eye fixed on the far horizon will
> find his right road.[41]

This waymark came back to me when I observed the work of the United Nations during my tenure as UN Legal Counsel. Of particular concern to me was the fact that the Security Council often fails to fulfil its foremost obligation laid down in Article 24 of the UN Charter: the primary responsibility for the maintenance of international peace and security. The waymark also tallies with my experiences serving as a sailor in the Swedish merchant marine during 12 months across four summer holidays when I was a student: the importance of looking to the horizon.

What all this boils down to is the need for statesmanship. What the world needs is statesmanship – statesmen and -women who realize that we need an international order based on the rule of law, and who can look to the future with determination based on this conviction. They must look to the horizon to understand that they must define the interests of their countries in a manner that protects the world population, and that international co-operation must be based on international law.

A third waymark that caught my attention in later years is the following, in my own translation:

> You will never return.
> Another man
> will find another city.[42]

The message here is true, in particular if one serves in an international organization. One is constantly confronted with new experiences and impressions. This is of tremendous importance. In a sense, it is a learning process that is of great value since it teaches one to view questions with which one is confronted from different perspectives. It also broadens one's knowledge and may cause one to view one's impressions from back home in a new light.

Furthermore, the privilege of working with colleagues from other countries is great. It also means that one should listen carefully to what these colleagues say, not least if they express opinions that are different from one's own. In the final analysis, one must of course make one's own decision with independence and integrity.

---

[41] Hammarskjöld, 1964, p. 32, see above note 37.
[42] Hammarskjöld, 1963, p. 147, see above note 40 (the present author's translation).

Upon re-reading the book to see whether there were other components that could be of interest to lawyers serving in the field of international justice, I came across the following short components, all in Sjöberg and Auden's translation:

> Our secret creative will divines its counterpart in others, experiencing its own universality, and this intuition builds a road towards knowledge of the power which is itself a spark within us.[43]

*

> Never, 'for the sake of peace and quiet', deny your own experience or convictions.[44]

*

> Your position never gives you the right to command. It only imposes on you the duty of so living your life that others can receive your orders without being humiliated.[45]

*

> The only kind of dignity which is genuine is that which is not diminished by the indifference of others.[46]

*

> A task becomes a duty from the moment you suspect it to be an essential part of that integrity which alone entitles a man to assume responsibility.[47]

*

> Do what you can — and the task will rest lightly in your hand, so lightly that you will be able to look forward to the more difficult tests which may be awaiting you.[48]

*

> Twice now you have done him an injustice. In spite of the fact that you were 'right' or, more correctly, *because* you were, in

---

[43] Hammarskjöld, 1964, p. 37, see above note 37.

[44] *Ibid.*, p. 85.

[45] *Ibid.*, p. 96.

[46] *Ibid.*, p. 97.

[47] *Ibid.*, p. 100.

[48] *Ibid.*, p. 109.

your conceit and your stupid pride in your powers you went stumping on over ground where each step gave him pain.[49]

*

Be grateful as your deeds become less and less associated with your name, as your feet ever more lightly tread the earth.[50]

*

You have not done enough, you have never done enough, so long as it is still possible that you have something of value to contribute.

This is the answer when you are groaning under what you consider a burden and an uncertainty prolonged ad infinitum.[51]

*

Did'st Thou give me this inescapable loneliness so that it would be easier for me to give Thee all?[52]

I leave it to the reader to reflect on these quotes from Dag Hammarskjöld's *Waymarks*. They should speak for themselves. The main thing is that we realize that they were produced by an extraordinary personality with great moral integrity who lost his life in the service of the United Nations. The best way in which we can honour his memory – and also the memories of others who have paid the ultimate sacrifice in the service of the Organization – is to contribute to establishing the rule of law at the national and international levels.

5.5. Conclusion

From the foregoing, it should be clear that the Dag Hammarskjöld legacy is of great importance when the integrity in international justice is defined. Both his legal analysis and his *Waymarks* should serve as lodestars here. Integrity in international justice is an important component in world governance which is facing major challenges in today's world. Much could be said about these challenges: genocide, war crimes and crimes against humanity; terrorism and transnational crimes; the need for strengthening human rights and gender equality; the need to address poverty and disease;

---

[49]   *Ibid.*, p. 119.
[50]   *Ibid.*, p. 126.
[51]   *Ibid.*, p. 135.
[52]   *Ibid.*, p. 139.

and the need for environmental protection. As lawyers, we must focus on the legal prerequisites for achieving this.

Nowadays, I never miss an opportunity to refer to one of the 17 Sustainable Development Goals adopted by the United Nations General Assembly in September 2015.[53] In my view, one of these goals is necessary to attain all the other goals. I refer to Goal 16: "Promote peaceful and inclusive societies for sustainable development, provide access to justice for all and build effective, accountable and inclusive institutions at all levels".[54]

Among the targets of this goal are "promote the rule of law at the national and international levels", and "substantially reduce corruption and bribery in all its forms". These are absolutely crucial elements for creating the legal order that is a prerequisite for achieving all the other goals.

This is where I see a vital role for lawyers irrespective of where we discharge our professional duties. When we force the problems that we face here into a clearly conceived intellectual form, the obvious legacy of Dag Hammarskjöld is: we must act accordingly.

---

[53] Transforming our world: the 2030 Agenda for Sustainable Development, 25 September 2015, UN Doc. A/RES/70/1 (http://www.legal-tools.org/doc/d52143/).

[54] *Ibid.*, p. 25.

6

Multicultural Understanding of Integrity in International Criminal Justice

Juan Carlos Botero[*]

6.1. Introduction

The International Criminal Court ('ICC') has been facing a legitimacy crisis for a long time.[1] Serious allegations of integrity lapses by the ICC's first prosecutor, Luis Moreno-Ocampo,[2] have been compounded by a growing perception among the international criminal justice community, that the court is missing in action – with judges more concerned about raising their already plentiful, tax-free salaries in The Hague, than in fulfilling the

---

[*] **Juan Carlos Botero** (LL.M., S.J.D.) is Associate Professor, Department of Philosophy and History of Law, Pontificia Universidad Javeriana Law School.

[1] The ICC's legitimacy crisis has multiple dimensions. See, for example, Jessica Hatcher-Moore, "Is the world's highest court fit for purpose?", *The Guardian*, 5 April 2017 (available on its web site). See also James A. Goldston, "Don't Give Up on the ICC", in *Foreign Policy*, 8 August 2019; Yvonne Dutton, "Bridging the Legitimacy Divide: The International Criminal Court's Domestic Perception Challenge", in *Columbia Journal of Transnational Law*, 2017, vol. 56, no. 70; Mandiaye Niang, "Africa and the Legitimacy of the ICC in Question", in International Criminal Law Review, 2017, vol. *17, no.* 4, pp. 615–624; Catherine Gegout, "The International Criminal Court: limits, potential and conditions for the promotion of justice and peace", in *Third World Quarterly*, 2013, vol. 34, no. 5, pp. 800–818; Margaret M. deGuzman, "The Global–Local Dilemma and the ICC's Legitimacy", in Nienke Grossman, Harlan Cohen, Andreas Follesdal and Geir Ulfstein (eds.), *Legitimacy and International Courts*, Cambridge University Press, 2018, pp. 62–82; Jeff Handmaker, "The Legitimacy Crisis Within International Criminal Justice and the Importance of Critical, Reflexive Learning", in Bob Jessop and Karim Knio (eds.), *The Pedagogy of Economic, Political and Social Crises: Dynamics, Construals and Lessons*, Routledge, London, 2018, pp. 189–206; Mihret Getabicha, "Decolonizing the International Criminal Court: Considering Questions of Bias in the Prosecution of African Leaders", in *Rapoport Center Working Paper Series*, 2018, no. 1; Mathew Lee, "Bolton: International Criminal Court 'already dead to us'", *AP News*, 11 September 2018; Ramesh Thakur, "The end of the International Criminal Court?", *The Japan Times*, 17 May 2019; Michèle Laborde-Barbanègre and Roxane Cassehgari, "Reflections on ICC Jurisprudence Regarding the Democratic Republic of the Congo", in *International Center for Transitional Justice Briefing*, 1 September 2014.

[2] See, for example, Morten Bergsmo, Wolfgang Kaleck, Sam Muller and William H. Wiley, "A Prosecutor Falls, Time for the Court to Rise", FICHL Policy Brief Series No. 86 (2017), Torkel Opsahl Academic EPublisher, Brussels, 2017 (https://www.toaep.org/pbs-pdf/86-four-directors/).

---

court's high mission.[3] Other chapters in this volume[4] deal with the causes, operational and legal mechanisms, and potential solutions to the integrity issues currently facing the ICC. This chapter does not primarily concern itself with these questions. Instead, it takes a broader perspective on *integrity* in international criminal justice and considers it from the perspective of large segments of the world's population – particularly in the Global South – whose perception of judicial integrity may diverge from the standard consensus among the world's legal elites.

This chapter explores how the principles of integrity and independence relate to each other in international criminal justice, in the multicultural world of the twenty-first century. In particular, it explores if 'Western' notions of integrity and independence that have characterized international criminal justice since the Nuremberg trials – which emphasize punishment, *retributive* justice, and deterrence,[5] as opposed to customary justice's long-

---

[3] See, for example, Goldston, 2019, see above note 1 ("it is disconcerting that one-third of the court's judges are suing for a pay raise plus pension increases and damages that could run into the millions. Why, when the court has been underperforming and the budget is strained, are its judges dedicating precious time and energy to increase their already generous compensation—which at around $200,000 tax-free exceeds that of judges on many national courts?"); Hatcher-Moore, 2017, see above note 1; Thakur, 2019, see above note 1. But see Elian Peltier and Fatima Faizi, "I.C.C. Allows Afghanistan War Crimes Inquiry to Proceed, Angering U.S.", *The New York Times*, 5 March 2020 (available on its web site); Declan Walsh and Abid Latif Dahir, "Sudan's Ex-Ruler May Face War Crimes Trial, Official Says", *The New York Times*, 11 February 2020; and Marlise Simons, "Myanmar Genocide Lawsuit Is Filed at United Nations Court", *The New York Times*, 11 November 2019 (available on its web site).

[4] The conceptual framework for this project on integrity in international criminal justice, is developed in Morten Bergsmo, "Revisiting Integrity in International Justice", FICHL Policy Brief Series No. 93 (2018), Torkel Opsahl Academic EPublisher, Brussels, 2018 (https://www.toaep.org/pbs-pdf/93-bergsmo/).

[5] See, for example, David Wippman, "Atrocities, Deterrence, and the Limits of International Justice", in *Fordham International Law Journal*, vol. 23, no. 2, 1999, p. 474 ("the connection between international prosecutions and the actual deterrence of future atrocities is at best a plausible but largely untested assumption. Actual experience with efforts at deterrence is not encouraging"); Juan Carlos Botero and Mateo Merchán, "Rethinking Peace and Justice: Lessons from the Colombian Transitional Justice Experience", *Justice in Conflict*, 27 April 2020 (https://justiceinconflict.org/2020/04/27/rethinking-peace-and-justice-lessons-from-the-colombian-transitional-justice-experience/). But see Jennifer Schense and Linda Carter (eds.), *Two Steps Forward, One Step Back: The Deterrent Effect of International Criminal Tribunals*, Torkel Opsahl Academic EPublisher, Brussels, 2017 (https://www.toaep.org/nas-pdf/1-carter-schense). On empirical evidence of the effectiveness of punishment and deterrence of criminal sanctions in domestic jurisdictions, see Anthony Bottoms and Andrew von Hirsch, "The Crime-preventive impact of penal sanctions", in Peter Cane

established emphasis on *restorative* justice and community harmony[6] – may influence the legitimacy and perception of fairness of international criminal tribunals among the broader population (not just lawyers and judges) in developing countries around the world today.

Under the auspices of the United Nations ('UN'), great efforts have been made during the past few decades to develop universal standards of judicial conduct that are applicable to all cultures and legal traditions of the world. Two milestones in this process of global convergence, are the Basic Principles on the Independence of the Judiciary, endorsed by the UN General Assembly ('UNGA') in its Resolutions 40/32 and 40/146 of 1985,[7] and the Bangalore Principles of Judicial Conduct, developed by the Judicial Integrity Group convened by the UN in Vienna in 2000.[8] The Bangalore Principles were initially adopted in 2001 and revised to their current form

---

and Herbert Kritzner (eds.), *The Oxford Handbook of Empirical Legal Research*, Oxford University Press, Oxford, 2010.

[6] The notion of 'community-harmonizing justice' is described in Juan Carlos Botero, *The Three Faces of Justice: Legal Traditions, Legal Transplants and Customary Justice in a Multicultural World*, in *SSRN Electronic Journal*, 2013, on which this chapter draws. According to Zehr and Gohar,

> [b]oth retributive and restorative theories of justice acknowledge a basic moral intuition that a balance has been thrown off by the wrongdoing. Consequently, the victim deserves something and the offender owes something. Both approaches argue that there must be a proportional relationship between the act and the response. They differ, however, on the currency that will fulfill the obligations and right the balance. Retributive theory believes that pain will vindicate, but in practice that is often counterproductive for both victim and offender. Restorative justice theory, on the other hand, argues that what truly vindicates is acknowledgment of victims' harms and needs combined with an active effort to encourage offenders to take responsibility, make right the wrongs and address the causes of their behavior. By addressing this need for vindication in a positive way, restorative justice has the potential to affirm both victim and offender and help them transform their lives.

Howard Zehr and Ali Gohar, *The Little Book of Restorative Justice*, Good Books, Intercourse, PA, p. 59.

[7] United Nations General Assembly ('UNGA'), Basic Principles on the Independence of the Judiciary, UN Doc. A/RES/40/146, 13 December 1985 ('Basic Principles on the Independence of the Judiciary') (https://www.legal-tools.org/doc/rnabsy/).

[8] United Nations Office on Drugs and Crime ('UNODC'), The Bangalore Principles of Judicial Conduct, 26 November 2012 ('Bangalore Principles') (https://www.legal-tools.org/doc/xwake8/).

in 2002. These documents represent two of the most authoritative international standards on judicial integrity and independence available today.[9]

In the Preface to United Nations Office on Drugs and Crime's ('UNODC') influential *Commentary on the Bangalore Principles of Judicial Conduct*,[10] late Judge C.G. Weeramantry, former Vice President of the International Court of Justice and Chairperson of the Judicial Integrity Group, declared as follows:

> A judiciary of undisputed integrity is the bedrock of democracy and the rule of law. Even when all other protections fail, the judiciary provides a bulwark to the public against any encroachments on rights and freedoms under the law.
>
> These observations apply both domestically—in the context of each nation State—and globally, for the global judiciary is seen as one great bastion of the rule of law throughout the world. Ensuring the integrity of the global judiciary is thus a task to which much energy, skill and experience must be devoted.
>
> This is precisely what the Judicial Group on Strengthening Judicial Integrity (the Judicial Integrity Group) has sought to do since 2000. The Group commenced as an informal gathering of chief justices and superior court judges from around the world who combined their experience and skill with a sense of dedication to this noble task. Since then, the Group's work and achievements have grown to a point where they have made a significant impact on the global judicial scene.
>
> The principles were first worked out only tentatively, but have increasingly been accepted over the past few years by the different sectors of the global judiciary and by international agencies interested in the integrity of the judicial process. As a result, the Bangalore Principles of Judicial Conduct are seen more and more as a document which all judiciaries and legal systems can accept unreservedly. *In short, these principles give expression to the highest traditions relating to the judicial function as visualized in all cultures and legal systems.*

---

[9] Another authoritative standard is the notion of 'high moral character' in international criminal justice, which is explained in Morten Bergsmo's concept paper for this research project, see note 4 above. See also Chapter 18 by Bettina Spilker.

[10] UNODC, *Commentary on the Bangalore Principles of Judicial Conduct*, 2007, pp. 1–6.

Reaching agreement on these core principles has been difficult but the Judicial Integrity Group's unwavering commitment to achieving a *result which would command universal acceptance* has allowed it to surmount the barriers in its path.

Not only have some States adopted the Bangalore Principles, but others have even modelled their own principles of judicial conduct on them. International organizations have also looked on them with favour and endorsed them. The United Nations Economic and Social Council, in its resolution 2006/23 of 27 July 2006, invited States Members of the United Nations to encourage their judiciaries, in line with their domestic legal systems, to take into consideration the Bangalore Principles when reviewing or developing rules on the professional and ethical conduct of the members of the judiciary [...].

It should be noted that just as *all traditional systems of law* insist unanimously on abiding by the highest standards of judicial rectitude, so do *all the great religious systems of the world*. In recognition of this, this Commentary contains, in an annex, a brief outline of how religious teachings approach the subject of judicial integrity.

We have, in the Bangalore Principles, an instrument that is of great potential value, not only for the judiciaries of all nations, but also for the general public and for all those concerned with laying down a firm foundation for a global judiciary of unimpeachable integrity.[11]

This chapter has three concrete aims. First, it seeks to address the question on whether the Bangalore Principles command – as Judge Weeramantry claims – truly "universal acceptance", and whether they indeed "give expression to the highest traditions relating to the judicial function as visualized in all cultures and legal systems" and "all the great religious systems of the world". Second, this chapter explores whether a multicultural understanding of integrity and independence in international criminal justice (not the specific standards of the ICC – or any other tribunal), implies a move towards 'relativizing' these standards. Third, the paper explores whether there are notions of judicial integrity and independence that underlie the world's broader understanding of Justice (with capital 'J'), regard-

---

[11] *Ibid.*, pp. 5–6 (emphasis added).

less of legal tradition, and how this global perspective may influence the way we see international criminal justice in the multicultural world of the twenty-first century. Some tentative implications for the ICC and other international courts and tribunals, of adopting a broader perspective of judicial integrity and independence in international criminal justice, are suggested at the end.

At a time when the ICC and the principles for which this institution stands are under attack from so many fronts,[12] supporters of the principles of international criminal justice should explore whether the legal profession's narrow conceptions of judicial integrity and independence may be undermining the Court's legitimacy among the broader public in developing countries. But please do not misinterpret my words: I do not suggest that the Rome Statute[13] needs to be amended, which would be impossible in today's highly polarized geo-political environment. I am only wondering whether various ICC constituencies, particularly the Prosecutor, Judges, and the Assembly of States Parties, might need to read the Statute in a different light – lessening the emphasis on legal process, punishment, retributive justice, and deterrence, while giving proper attention to customary justice's long-established emphasis on restorative justice and community harmony or unity.[14] Three key findings of the International Nuremberg Princi-

---

[12] For example, Lee, 2018, see above note 1; Hatcher-Moore, 2017, see above note 1; Thakur, 2019, see above note 1. Cf., Goldston, 2019, see above note 1.

[13] Rome Statute of the International Criminal Court, 17 July 1998 (http://www.legal-tools.org/doc/e5faa8/).

[14] One of the main lessons from international criminal justice experiences over the past 75 years since the Nuremberg trials, is that its understanding of 'justice' mainly as retributive justice, is not shared by large segments of the world's population. For a comprehensive review of the limits of retributive justice and its negative impact on global acceptance of international criminal justice principles in developing countries, see Friederike Mieth, "Acceptance of International Criminal Justice A Review", in Susanne Buckley-Zistel, Friederike Mieth and Marjana Papa (eds.), *After Nuremberg: Exploring Multiple Dimensions of the Acceptance of International Criminal Justice*, International Nuremberg Principles Academy, Nuremberg, 2016. Throughout this chapter, I refer mostly to 'formal courts' and 'customary justice' as the two main mechanisms of justice in low and middle-income countries. The difference between them is sometimes blurred, as in some countries both systems are integrated (see Botero, 2013, pt. 4, chap. 6, above note 6). I use the term 'formal court' to include the civil and criminal court system inherited from Europe throughout the world, as well as any other formal, State-governed dispute resolution institution. The term 'customary justice' is employed here to include traditional justice, indigenous and ethnic dispute resolution, community-based dispute resolution, and in some cases also religious courts. The dividing line is often blurred, as it is explained in pts. 3 and 4 of Botero, 2013, see above note 6. A major limitation of this chapter is that Islamic law and courts are mostly outside of its scope. I

ples Academy's ground-breaking project on *Acceptance of International Criminal Justice in Situation Countries*,[15] are:

1. that acceptance of international criminal justice "is a dynamic process" and actors' "activities may elicit different responses from different groups of society";
2. that "[s]ocieties marked by violence, like all societies, are composed of many often highly diverse identity groups, amongst which acceptance of [international criminal justice] can vary", so "[t]here is thus not one society which accepts [international criminal justice], but many groups with very diverse views regarding acceptance"; and
3. that there is a large degree of "[i]nterdependence of different justice mechanisms".

Indeed, international criminal justice's overwhelmingly narrow focus on retributive justice, to the exclusion of other forms of justice, is one of the key factors limiting its global acceptance. According to Susanne Buckley-Zistel, Friederike Mieth and Marjana Papa:

> ICJ [international criminal justice] is based on the principle of *retributive justice*. In some contexts, alternative forms of providing justice such as *restorative mechanisms* are equally important so that the acceptance of ICJ also depends on the availability and/or success of other justice mechanisms.[16]

What does judicial integrity and independence in international criminal justice mean for vast segments of the world's population in the Global South today? Until recently, there were less than 200 registered lawyers in the entire country of Liberia; and there are just a few dozen judges in the entire country of Malawi.[17] In both countries, justice is delivered by thou-

---

acknowledge that many of the same questions that arise out of the interplay among legal traditions, legal transplants and customary justice institutions in Africa, Asia and Latin America, also apply to the interaction between Western and Islamic laws, procedures and courts, in both Muslim majority and Muslim minority countries. Nonetheless, Sharia's complexity and sophistication – as explained in the chapter above by Judge Adel Maged – sets it apart from other dispute resolution systems existing in the world today. Addressing these questions properly would require an effort which is currently beyond my limited knowledge of various Islamic legal traditions.

[15] Susanne Buckley-Zistel, Friederike Mieth and Marjana Papa, "Acceptance of International Criminal Justice in Situation Countries. 10 Key Findings", International Nuremberg Principles Academy, Nuremberg, 2017 (available on its web site).

[16] *Ibid* (emphasis added).

[17] Botero, 2013, at pt. 4, chap. 7, see above note 6.

sands of 'chiefs', or customary justice authorities in accordance with im-memorial notions of restorative justice, as opposed to the 'Western' law of the colonizers. For the overwhelming majority of people in both coun-tries – and for several billion people around the world today – the 'Western' legal traditions of the *civil law* and the *common law* (embraced by the legal profession in virtually all countries), have very little resemblance to the people's understanding of Justice. For most people in the Global South to-day, Justice is not represented by the European colonizer's impartial and independent 'Lady Justice' (blindfolded and holding the scales and the sword), but rather by the 'African Tree', the friendly meeting place where the community comes together to restore the broken bonds.[18] This broader notion of Justice, I argue, is the light under which the Rome Statute must be read today, if it is ever to achieve universal legitimacy. Indeed, "[v]ery often people in affected regions want restorative and distributive justice, as well as punitive justice".[19]

Legal elites in the Global North and the Global South alike – for ex-ample, Judge Weeramantry, quoted above[20] – claim that the UN Basic Prin-ciples on the Independence of the Judiciary,[21] the Bangalore Principles of Judicial Conduct,[22] and the Rome Statute,\ command universal legitimacy precisely because they were adopted by representatives from a large num-ber of countries, from a variety of legal traditions. This claim is only par-

---

[18] Botero, 2013, p. 3, see above note 6. The 'African Tree' justice is essentially a conversation, which may last for a few minutes or several months. It is a dialogue between the contending parties and the chief or mediator, whose overall objective is not only (or even mainly) to re-solve a specific dispute among two parties – as it is among the 'conflict-solving' understand-ing of justice – but more broadly to harmonize the broken bonds within the community. In some instances, the whole village gets involved in the healing process. The African Tree no-tion of justice is not exclusive of the African continent. Dispute resolution among indige-nous communities in other latitudes show similar characteristics. The community-harmonizing justice of the African Tree is explained in detail in pts. 4 and 5 of Botero, 2013, see above note 6. I am grateful to Hassan Bubacar Jallow and Murtaza Jaffar, from the In-ternational Criminal Tribunal for Rwanda, for insightful comments about the nature of dis-pute resolution in Sub-Saharan Africa.

[19] Mieth, 2016, p. 7, see above note 14.

[20] UNODC, 2007, pp. 1–6, see above note 10.

[21] Basic Principles on the Independence of the Judiciary, see above note 7.

[22] Bangalore Principles, see above note 8.

tially true,[23] and it undermines the ICC's legitimacy among the broader public in the Global South.[24]

From the perspective of large segments of the population in developing countries today, the ICC's vision of justice – with its 'Western' emphasis on legal procedure, punishment, retribution, and deterrence – represent the law of the European colonizers.[25] In contrast, restorative justice principles embedded in ancestral customary justice mechanisms in the four corners of the world, represent a more legitimate way to deal with conflict, including grave crimes.[26] The ICC's survival depends on its legitimacy, and its legitimacy partly depends on its broader appeal to the public in develop-

---

[23] Participation of legal elites from a large number of countries in the drafting of these international instruments, confer global legitimacy to these documents among the legal elites of virtually all countries in the world, whose laws are based on the European *civil law* and *common law* traditions. However, this fact does not automatically confer legitimacy of the same documents across the wider population in the Global South. The low legitimacy of 'Western' institutions of justice among broad segments of the population in developing countries has been extensively documented in the literature throughout Latin America, Sub-Saharan Africa, and Asia. See, for example, Julio Faundez, "Access to Justice and Indigenous Communities in Latin America", in Yash Ghai and Jill Cottrell (eds.), *Marginalized Communities and Access to Justice*, Routledge, New York, 2010, p. 83, ("the indigenous communities' views about legal institutions bear little resemblance to liberal views about law. Instead of seeing them as friendly institutions that empower and liberate individuals, they regard them as the cause and symbol of their longstanding economic and political oppression"); also pp. 93–94. Hannah Irfan, *Honor Related Violence Against Women in Pakistan*, American Bar Association, 2008, p. 19 (in Pakistan "one of the major reasons that women victims are reluctant to take action against violence through the courts is that *they fear the system of which they have no knowledge*. The inadequacy of knowledge and information about the legal processes made the thought of even going to court frightening"); Deborah H. Isser, Stephen C. Lubkemann, and Saah N'Tow, *Looking for Justice, Liberian experiences with and perceptions of local justice options*, United States Institute of Peace, Washington, DC, 2009, p. 3 ("Most Liberians would still be unsatisfied with the justice meted out by the formal system, even if it were able to deliver on the basics").

[24] The legitimacy crisis of the ICC among the broad public in developing countries is compounded by a variety of factors, including the court's many structural and operational limitations, see above note 1.

[25] Faundez, 2010, see above note 23; Irfan, 2008, see above note 23; Stuart Banner, *How the Indians Lost Their Lands*, Harvard University Press, 2007; Lidsay Robertson, *Conquest by Law*, at Preface, Oxford University Press, 2005; N. Bruce Duthu, *American Indians and the Law*, Penguin, New York, 2008; Stephen Breyer, "'For Their Own Good": The Cherokees, the Supreme Court, and the Early History of American Conscience", *The New Republic*, 4 December 2008.

[26] A comprehensive review of alternative mechanisms available to deal with mass atrocities, is available at Open Society Justice Initiative, *Options for Justice: A Handbook for Designing Accountability Mechanisms for Grave Crimes*, Open Society Foundations, 2018.

ing countries. This legitimacy, in turn, could be greatly enhanced by rein-terpreting the Rome Statute (and the international criminal justice system more broadly), in light of ancestral restorative justice principles. This chapter suggests a few ways in which this may be advanced.

6.2. Judicial Integrity and Independence in the 'Western' Legal Tradition – Historical Divergence

The shape and character of the laws and institutions of all countries are closely tied to their history. To some extent, they respond to the cultural, philosophical and religious foundation of society.[27] However, in many countries, a number of laws and institutions do not stem from local culture; they are simply legal 'transplants' copied or received from 'mother' countries.[28]

Comparativists have long proposed the idea that the laws of all countries may be aggregated into a handful of legal families.[29] Similar institutional designs within these families have been said to stem from shared legal traditions. As late Merryman defined it:

> A legal tradition, as the term implies, is not a set of rules of law about contracts, corporations, and crimes, although such rules will almost always be in some sense a reflection of that tradition. Rather it is a set of deeply rooted, historically conditioned attitudes about the nature of the law, about the role of law in the society and the polity, about the proper organization and operation of a legal system, and about the way law is or should be made, applied, studied, perfected, and taught. *The legal tradition relates the legal system to the culture of which*

---

[27] See generally, for example, Hans Kelsen, *What is Justice?*, University of California Press, Berkeley, 1957.

[28] See generally, for example, Alan Watson, *Legal Transplants: An Approach to Comparative Law*, University of Virginia Press, Charlottesville, 1974; Michele Graziadei, "Comparative Law as the Study of Transplants and Receptions", in Mathias Reimann and Reinhard Zimmermann (eds.), *The Oxford Handbook of Comparative Law*, Oxford University Press, 2006.

[29] See, for example, Rene David and John Brierley, *Major Legal Systems in the World Today: An introduction to the Comparative study of Law*, The Free Press, New York, 1978; John Dawson, *The Oracles of the Law*, William S. Hein, New York; Rudolph Schlesinger, Ugo Mattei, Teemu Ruskola and Antonio Gidi, *Comparative Law, Case- Text- Materials*, The Foundation Press, New York, 1988; Konrad Zweigert and Hein Kotz, *Introduction to Comparative Law* (vol. I – The Framework/vol. II – The Institutions of Private Law), Clarendon Press, Oxford, 1987; John Henry Merryman, *The Civil Law Tradition. An Introduction to the Legal Systems of Western Europe and Latin America*, Stanford University Press, California, 1985.

> *it is a partial expression. It puts the legal system into cultural perspective.*[30]

This chapter briefly traces the historical context of the notions of judicial integrity and independence – particularly in the two most prevalent of these traditions, the *civil law* and the *common law*[31] – we open up a conceptual background to the analysis of integrity which may be useful.

Most of the judicial institutions that we know today can trace back their origins in one way or another to Rome.[32] The Roman Empire enjoyed a highly developed legal system where written law evolved over centuries and was codified into systematic and comprehensive bodies of law. There was a centralized and hierarchical apparatus of courts that contributed to unifying the system. The application of the law was guided by sophisticated legal principles and procedures, developed by professional judges.

With the fall of the Roman Empire, the early Middle Ages were characterized by the fractionalization of the Roman legal system into multiple local jurisdictions. Justice was largely a matter of basic rules mixed with superstition and religion, which were erratically created and enforced by local lords.[33] During the late Middle Ages, the old customs of the Germanic tribes clashed with the rediscovered Roman law, and this uneasy mix evolved over the centuries into the various modern legal families. Italy remained closely attached to the Roman law. The French legal system resulted from the Napoleonic combination of Roman and Germanic customary law, where the later element predominated. Germany rediscovered and adopted the Roman law in the process called 'The Reception'. In England, the Roman influence was largely diluted over time, and the law developed mainly from Germanic and feudal customs; from the twelfth century, the

---

[30] Merryman, 1985, p. 2, see above note 29 (emphasis added).

[31] *Ibid.*, p. 1: "There are three highly influential legal traditions in the contemporary world: civil law, common-law, and socialist law". With the fall of the Soviet Union, the third one lost significance. On Islamic law, see above note 24.

[32] "It is no exaggeration to say that, next to the Bible, no book has left a deeper mark upon the history of mankind than the Corpus Iuris Civilis", Justinian, "General Introduction", in *The Digest of Roman Law*, Penguin Classics, reprint edition, 1979, p. 8.

[33] See generally, for example, William Sidney Gibson, *On some Ancient Modes of Trial, especially the Ordeals of Water, Fire and other Judicia Dei: Communicated to the Society of Antiquaries.*, Nichols & Son, London, 1848.

common law was created by English royal courts and evolved gradually until present times.[34]

Through the process of European conquest and colonization, these 'Western' legal traditions were imposed by might of the sword on virtually all peoples of the world. When European colonization ended in the nineteenth and twentieth centuries, 'Western' legal traditions were maintained in all countries by local legal elites. Yet, vast segments of the population in developing countries continued to perceive these 'Western' laws and procedures with contempt. The 'original sin' of violent conquest and colonization, which underlies the 'Western' institutions of Justice, continues to undermine the ICC's legitimacy in the Global South today.[35]

6.3. Judicial Integrity and Independence in the 'Western' Legal Tradition in Historical Perspective

What are the implications of the historical evolution of justice in England and continental Europe for current notions of judicial integrity and impartiality? Renowned comparativists – Caenegem, Damaška, David, Dawson, Glendon, Merryman, Schlesinger, Zweigert and Kotz – differ on a number of issues related to the divide between *civil law* and *common law*, but they all tend to agree on the fact that specific historical developments led to a rather distinct view of the role of the judge in society.[36]

---

[34] Although some Roman elements continued to influence procedure well into the nineteenth century. For example, R.C. van Caenegem, "History of European Civil Procedure", in Mauro Cappelletti (ed.), *International Encyclopedia of Comparative Law: Volume XVI, Civil Procedure*, 1982, p. 15. See also, Mary Ann Glendon, Michael Gordon and Christopher Osakwe, *Comparative Legal Traditions*, West Publishing, St. Paul, 1994; R.C. van Caenegem, *European Law in the Past and the Future: Unity and Diversity over Two Millennia*, Cambridge University Press, 2002.

[35] The legitimacy gap of 'Western' justice institutions between legal elites and the broad public in developing countries, is not only documented in the literature (see, for example, above note 23), but it is also supported by the author's personal experience measuring people's experiences and perceptions of justice in over one hundred countries over the past two decades, including hundreds of thousands of household surveys in over 300 cities around the world, and hundreds of conversations and interviews with formal and customary justice authorities from dozens of countries throughout Latin America, Sub-Saharan Africa and Asia. Botero, 2013, see above note 6. On the legitimacy crisis of the International Criminal Court, see above note 1.

[36] Juan Carlos Botero, "The delivery of justice in middle-income countries", in Randall Peerenboom and Tom Ginsburg (eds.), *Law and Development of Middle-Income Countries*, Cambridge University Press, 2014, p. 196.

As Carl Goodman reminds us, "because the King of England utilized the legal system and his Royal Courts and traveling judges to extend his rule throughout England it was important that the populous view the Royal Courts as fair and honest".[37] In the United States 'justice' means 'fair play', the judicial process is a contest, and the judge is an umpire. The function of the American judge is to guarantee an *efficient and fair process*. In this context, *judicial integrity means impartiality*.

In contrast, in *civil law* countries, the judge is the good old Roman *pater familias*, who has a say and becomes involved in every dispute within the family. The function of the civil law judge is to ensure a *fair outcome*.[38] Moreover, in other civil law countries that have millenary autochthonous traditions, justice is represented by the Buddha of Compassion. In Japan, for example, the "criminal law system has harmony as its goal".[39] In this *civil law* variant, the function of the judge is to restore social harmony. More broadly, the historical function of the civil law judge is to implement State policy.[40]

These diverging attitudes, which may be traced back to the twelfth century,[41] partly stem from the revolutionary France's deeply rooted concern with the 'tyranny of justice'. For the revolutionary France, 'justice' is the tool of the tyrant, a mechanism of oppression. In eighteenth-century France, the judge shall be "no more than the mouth that pronounces the words of the law".[42] Real justice can only be achieved through strict adherence to the people's law – not by the aristocratic judges' free interpretation

---

[37] Carl Goodman, *The Rule of Law in Japan*, Kluwer Law International, the Netherlands, 2008, p. 9.

[38] See, for example, Benjamin Kaplan, "Civil Procedure—Reflections on the Comparison of Systems", in *Buffalo Law Review*, 1960, p. 431 (US system "exploits the free-wheeling energies of counsel and places them in adversary confrontation before a detached judge"; "German system puts its trust in a judge of paternalistic bent acting in cooperation with counsel of somewhat muted adversary zeal").

[39] Goodman, 2008, p. 504, see above note 37.

[40] Mirjan Damaška, *The Faces of Justice and State Authority. A Comparative Approach to the Legal Process*, Yale University Press, New Haven, 1986.

[41] See generally, Caenegem, 2002, see above note 34; Caenegem, 1982, see above note 34; Damaška, 1986, see above note 40.

[42] Montesquieu, *The Spirit of Laws*, 1748 ("But as we have already observed, the national judges are no more than the mouth that pronounces the words of the law, mere passive beings, incapable of moderating either its force or rigor").

thereof. Thus, a judge with integrity is a judge that follows the law. In this context, judicial integrity means the strict application of the law.

Do these notions of judicial integrity correspond to the currently prevailing notion of justice outside of the metropolis (Europe and North America)? For historical reasons, 'Western' adjudication has placed particular emphasis on two relations: a dispute between two individuals (as in thirteenth century England), and the relationship between one individual and the State (as in Imperial Rome or the Kingdom of France). In contrast, customary justice throughout the Global South focuses on the multiple relations that are co-existing and evolving over time within a specific community over time.

6.4. The Bangalore Principles of Judicial Conduct: A 'Universal' Understanding of Integrity and Independence in Justice

In July 2006, the UN Economic and Social Council adopted a resolution that "[e]mphasizes that the Bangalore Principles of Judicial Conduct represent a further development and are complementary to the Basic Principles on the Independence of the Judiciary, endorsed by UNGA in its resolutions 40/32 and 40/146".[43] Taken together, these two documents – the UNGA's Basic Principles[44] and the Bangalore Principles of 2001, as revised in 2002[45] – represent two of the most authoritative international standards on the notions of integrity and independence of justice available today.

The Bangalore Principles recognize integrity and independence of justice as follows:

> Value 1. Independence.
>
> Principle: Judicial independence is a prerequisite to the rule of law and a fundamental guarantee of a fair trial. A judge shall therefore uphold and exemplify judicial independence in both its individual and institutional aspects.
>
> Application:
>
> 1.1. A judge shall exercise the judicial function independently on the basis of the judge's assessment of the facts and in accordance with a conscientious understanding of the law,

---

[43] United Nations Economic and Social Council, Strengthening basic principles of judicial conduct, 27 July 2006, ECOSOC 2006/23 (https://www.legal-tools.org/doc/yiyqyy/).

[44] Basic Principles on the Independence of the Judiciary, see above note 7.

[45] The Bangalore Principles, see above note 8.

free of any extraneous influences, inducements, pressures, threats or interference, direct or indirect, from any quarter or for any reason.

1.2. A judge shall be independent in relation to society in general and in relation to the particular parties to a dispute that the judge has to adjudicate.

1.3. A judge shall not only be free from inappropriate connections with, and influence by, the executive and legislative branches of government, but must also appear to a reasonable observer to be free therefrom.

1.4. In performing judicial duties, a judge shall be independent of judicial colleagues in respect of decisions that the judge is obliged to make independently.

1.5. A judge shall encourage and uphold safeguards for the discharge of judicial duties in order to maintain and enhance the institutional and operational independence of the judiciary.

1.6. A judge shall exhibit and promote high standards of judicial conduct in order to reinforce public confidence in the judiciary, which is fundamental to the maintenance of judicial independence.

Value 3. Integrity.

Principle: Integrity is essential to the proper discharge of the judicial office.

Application:

3.1. A judge shall ensure that his or her conduct is above reproach in the view of a reasonable observer.

3.2. The behaviour and conduct of a judge must reaffirm the people's faith in the integrity of the judiciary. Justice must not merely be done but must also be seen to be done.

The Bangalore Principles also recognize three closely related concepts, impartiality, propriety and equality, as essential values that define the conduct of judicial officers under international standards. These principles are as follows:

Value 2: IMPARTIALITY.

Principle: Impartiality is essential to the proper discharge of the judicial office. It applies not only to the decision itself but also to the process by which the decision is made.

Value 4: PROPRIETY.

Principle: Propriety, and the appearance of propriety, are essential to the performance of all of the activities of a judge.

Value 5: EQUALITY.

Principle: Ensuring equality of treatment to all before the courts is essential to the due performance of the judicial office.

Finally, the Bangalore Principles of Judicial Conduct recognize a sixth value, competence and diligence, as follows:

Value 6: COMPETENCE AND DILIGENCE.

Principle: Competence and diligence are prerequisites to the due performance of judicial office.

A central question of this chapter, as stated in the introduction, is whether the Bangalore Principles command truly "universal acceptance", and whether they indeed "give expression to the highest traditions relating to the judicial function as visualized in all cultures and legal systems" and "all the great religious systems of the world".

The detailed account of the process of creation of these principles,[46] suggests a bias in favour of the principles of judicial integrity and independence of the *common law* tradition, by virtue of the overwhelmingly majoritarian membership of judges from this tradition in the drafting group, and the predominantly *common law* nature of the national codes used as reference material in the drafting process.[47] As stated above, this *common law* emphasis implies an understanding of *judicial integrity primarily as a function of judicial impartiality*.

It is also clear that the drafting group made great efforts in 2002 to socialize and integrate principles pertaining to the *civil law* tradition into these 'universal' standards.[48] Thus, the *civil law's* flavour of *judicial integ-*

---

[46] UNODC, 2007, pp. 1–6, see above note 10.

[47] *Ibid.*, A detailed list of National Codes that were consulted is included in the Commentary.

[48] There was significant agreement among the common and civil law judges who participated in the meeting concerning core values, and some disagreement on the scheme and order in which these values ought to be placed. For instance: "[...] *(c)* The statement in the preamble of the Bangalore Draft that the "real source of judicial power is public acceptance of the moral authority and integrity of the judiciary" was questioned. It was argued that the "real

rity as a function of strict adherence to the law, may also be observed in the same principles.

In sum, it seems fair to argue that the Bangalore Principles "give expression to the highest traditions relating to the judicial function as visualized [by judges and lawyers] in all ['Western'] legal systems". Whether these principles developed by high court justices from a variety of countries actually reflect the 'cultures' and 'religions' of all peoples of the world, remains to be seen.

6.5. A Multicultural Understanding of Integrity and Independence as Viewed by Citizens

Ordinary people in low and middle-income countries generally know two faces of justice, the so-called 'Wig and Gown' justice of the colonizers, and the customary justice system that predates the arrival of the Europeans. These two faces of justice are increasingly misaligned with the changing reality of a globalized yet multicultural world.

There are profound differences among societies on fundamental social values, which have impacted the role assigned to law and justice in them.[49] Yet, regardless of these cultural differences about the notion of justice1, the underlying truth is that all peoples need accessible and effective dispute settlement systems:

---

source" was the Constitution and that placing too great an emphasis on the ultimate dependence of the judicial power upon general acceptance could, in some circumstances, be dangerous". UNODC, 2007, pp. 6–10, see above note 10.

[49] Huntington – whose work has spurred controversy – describes these differences between two cultures (China and the USA), as follows:

At the broadest level the Confucian ethos pervading many Asian societies stressed the values of authority, hierarchy, the subordination of individual rights and interests, the importance of consensus, the avoidance of confrontation, 'saving face,' and, in general, the supremacy of the state over society and of society over the individual. In addition, Asians tended to think of the evolution of their societies in terms of centuries and millennia and to give priority to maximizing long-term gains. These attitudes contrasted with the primacy in American beliefs of liberty, equality, democracy, and individualism, and the American propensity to distrust government, oppose authority, promote checks and balances, encourage competition, sanctify human rights, and to forget the past, ignore the future, and focus on maximizing immediate gains. The sources of conflict are in fundamental differences in society and culture.

Samuel P. Huntington, The Clash of Civilizations and the Remaking of the World Order, Simon & Schuster, 1996, p. 225.

In old ages, people used customary justice systems to resolve their disputes, ranging from the Cheyenne "conference of tribal chiefs", to the Afghan *Jirgas*, to the Liberian chiefdoms, to the Amazonian shamans. While many of these systems continue to operate today, the European colonization process of the past few centuries brought with it a new dispute-resolution system to all corners of the planet. In some places, the old forms were completely abandoned while, in others, a dual arrangement emerged. Parallel systems of dispute resolution co-existed and interacted in most countries. In some places customary justice was formally and hierarchically integrated into the formal (European) judicial machinery, while in others they remained in operation de facto, mostly ignored or tolerated by the formal courts. For decades (in Africa and parts of Asia) or centuries (in Latin America and other parts of Asia), the formal courts were perceived mostly as instruments for resolving disputes among the descendants of European colonizers, the global and local business community, and the local elites. By design, in most colonies and pseudocolonies around the world formal courts were not intended to be widely accessible to ordinary folk.[50]

Formal courts were not seen and embraced by the masses as their cherished property, as "a progressive force on the side of the individual against the abuse of power by the ruler".[51] However, this was not necessarily a problem, because people still had access to their customary justice systems.

Several new factors have emerged in the last few decades, starting with the end of the Cold War, which pose a serious challenge to the existing arrangements. These factors include, among others, increasing globalization and integration of markets; growing migration and urbanization; exponential expansion of access to communication technologies; unprece-

---

[50] Botero, 2014, p. 196, see above note 36.

[51] "In the United States and England [...] there was a different kind of judicial tradition, one in which judges had often been a progressive force on the side of the individual against the abuse of power by the ruler", see Merryman, 1985, p. 16, see above note 29. In contrast, in colonies throughout the world "the indigenous communities' views about legal institutions bear little resemblance to liberal views about law. Instead of seeing them as friendly institutions that empower and liberate individuals, they regard them as the cause and symbol of their longstanding economic and political oppression", see Faundez, 2010, pp. 83, 93-94, see above note 23.

dented universal access to information for all segments of the population; growing cultural self-assertiveness; and growing awareness among marginalized populations about their own rights (and decreasing tolerance to abuses and exclusion).[52]

For several decades, we have been witnessing a revival of deeply-rooted cultural traditions in various parts of the world. For instance, "Shamanism is becoming more popular in South Korea in recent years, after being dismissed as 'superstition' and 'delusion' by past military governments",[53] which often go hand-in-hand with increasingly anti-elitist sentiments.[54]

The impact of these changes for the machinery of justice is clear: the "Wig and Gown" justice of the colonizers and their heirs is no longer acceptable to an increasingly cultural assertive and well informed population, at the same time that the [customary] justice of the local chiefs is no longer effective in a globalized world.[55]

Ghana's formal courts are as nicely adapted to the needs of ordinary citizens, as the wig and gown of Madam Chief Justice are adapted to the weather conditions of this beautiful tropical country. There is a fundamental disconnect between the elegant wig and gown of Madam Chief Justice and the hot, humid, tropical weather of Ghana. The laws that go with the wig are no different. The system is broken.

For most native-Americans in the United States – the original indigenous communities – the European institutions of law and justice have generally been perceived for centuries as a foreign imposition.[56] The atti-

---

[52] Botero, 2014, p. 196, see above note 36.

[53] "Shamans' newfound popularity in South Korea", *BBC News*, 29 July 2012 (available on its web site).

[54] See, for example, Simon Kuper, "The revenge of the middle-class anti-elitist: Why the comfortably well-off voted for Trump, Brexit and Italy's Lega", *Financial Times Magazine*, 13 February 2020 (available on its web site).

[55] Botero, 2014, p. 196, see above note 36.

[56] See, for example, Banner, 2007, p. 1, see above note 25 ("The Indians were really conquered by force [...], but Americans and their British colonial predecessors papered over their conquest with these documents [treaties] to make the process look proper and legal"); Robertson, 2005, at Preface, p. IX, see above note 25 ("Over a succession of generations, Europeans devised rules intended to justify the dispossession and subjugation of the native peoples of the Western Hemisphere"); Duthu, 2008, p. xxii, see above note 25 ("on June 9, 1855, Kamiakin rose last among his fellow tribal leaders, made his mark on the treaty and returned to his seat with his lips 'covered with blood, having bitten them with suppressed rage'");

tudes of native-Americans about European law in the United States are similar to those of vast segments of the population in most countries in Africa, Asia and Latin America, where European laws and institutions were transplanted by the colonizers.[57] As Hannah Irfan tells us, in Pakistan, "one of the major reasons that women victims are reluctant to take action against violence through the courts is that *they fear the system of which they have no knowledge*. The inadequacy of knowledge and information about the legal processes made the thought of even going to court frightening".[58]

More often than not, from the point of view of the common citizen, legal institutions in low- and middle-income countries throughout the world feel like a foreign intrusion. Transplant institutions, laws and procedures were often kept for decades or centuries after independence because they helped to maintain stability during tumultuous times. Elites in those countries tended to support the foreign transplants as they contributed to sustain the status quo, which favoured the interests of the heirs of the original colonizers once formal colonization ended – for instance, those of white *creoles*[59] in Latin America, *Afrikaans* in South Africa, and Americo-Liberians in Liberia. But it shall not escape the reader that for the vast majority of the population in most low and middle-income countries, transplant institutions may not reflect the idiosyncratic aspirations and needs of the people.

Merryman was wrong; the legal tradition does not "relate the legal system [of a particular country] to the culture of which it is a partial expression". [60] Outside of the 'metropolis', it relates the legal system only to the culture and needs of the colonizers. For vast segments of the population in developing countries, the legal system often remains a distant and even frightening 'transplant',[61] not an integral part of their culture. Legal and

---

Breyer, 2000, p. 30, see above note 25 ("In 1836, the United States and the State of Georgia forced the Cherokee Indian tribe to leave its home in Georgia and to move to the West. The Tribe did not want to move. It believed it had a legal right to stay [...] [The outcome of this engagement is a] tragic story in the history of the Cherokee Tribe").

[57] Faundez, 2010, see above note 23.

[58] Irfan, 2008, p. 19, see above note 23 (emphasis added).

[59] French, Spanish and Portuguese descendants, Encyclopaedia Britannica on-line. "**Creole**, Spanish *Criollo*, French *Créole*, originally, any person of European (mostly French or Spanish) or African descent born in the West Indies or parts of French or Spanish America (and thus naturalized in those regions rather than in the parents' home country)".

[60] Merryman, 1985, p. 2, see above note 29 (emphasis added).

[61] Botero, 2014, see above note 36.

procedural restrictions in developing countries are as much safeguards of Justice as they are instruments of monopoly power and exclusion.[62]

In most developing countries, the cost of litigation (court and attorney fees) for even the most basic disputes is significantly higher than the monthly minimum wage. Local elites justify this on the 'sanctity of procedure;' as Gandasubrata declared, "in connection with the nature of the judicial process itself and considering the formal, punctual and rather complicated manners and usages upheld by the courts according to the Law on Procedure, it could be said that *correct judgment cannot be performed in a short time*".[63] Of course, lengthier and more complex proceedings often mean more lucrative attorney fees. Moreover, they produce a very steep barrier to access the market for potential competitors (including the litigants themselves, if they consider handling their own disputes without the assistance of a lawyer), which may guarantee a stream of revenue in the long run. From the users' perspective, lengthy and cumbersome proceedings translate into judicial inefficiency, which is generally perceived as a form of corruption or lack of integrity.

6.6. Judicial Integrity from the People's Perspective: Implications for the ICC

The negative effect of 'foreign impositions' on the legitimacy of justice among the people, is often compounded in the application of international criminal justice within the context of societies that have undergone severe conflict and mass atrocities:

> The feelings of 'imposition' seem particularly critical in contexts where international justice mechanisms threaten to jeopardise peace in a certain region. Two much-debated situations in this regard are Northern Uganda and the Darfur region, both investigated by the ICC. In these instances, the ICC investigations were instigated by perceived outside actors. From the perspective of Ugandans living in the north of the country, the referral by President Museveni of the situation to the ICC can be seen very much as an 'outside' intervention, as was the UN Security Council decision to open investigations for the Darfur region. It has been claimed that when victims of war

---

[62] As explained in pt. 3 of chap. 4 of Botero, 2013, see above note 6.

[63] Purwoto Gandasubrata, "Indonesia, Administration of Justice: Procedural Reforms on Court Congestion", in Purificación Valera-Quisumbing (ed.), *Asian Comparative Law Series*, 1980, vol. 2, p. 7 (emphasis added).

crimes and other affected groups feel that their immediate need for peace is not mirrored by actions of an international body such as the ICC, the latter will not be appreciated.

When international justice feels imposed, a typical reaction is to question whether the crimes should be dealt with at an international level rather than domestically, which can ultimately affect acceptance of the respective institution which becomes involved.

Such debates can be seen in some of the recent cases that have experienced ICC engagement, such as Côte d'Ivoire, Kenya, and Mali.[64]

Popular dissatisfaction with domestic formal ('Western') institutions of justice in virtually all countries across the Global South,[65] has grave implications for the local buy-in (legitimacy) of international courts and tribunals, including the ICC:

People's previous experiences with domestic judicial systems influence the acceptance of international justice. In many regions where international justice operates, people are faced with inadequate and often corrupt domestic justice systems. In Sierra Leone, for example, the author found that citizens' low interest in the Special Court for Sierra Leone was partly rooted in the low expectations in judiciary procedures in general, which stemmed from their negative experiences with both the formal and customary justice systems in the country. These two justice systems coexist, but are perceived equally corrupt and unfair. Similarly, a 2010 study in Kenya on attitudes to-

---

[64] Mieth, 2017, p. 4, see above note 14 (citations omitted). Similarly, according to Laborde-Barbanègre and Cassehgari, 2014, see above note 1, the ICC's

results could be interpreted as disappointing when compared with the amount of resources invested in the process. In particular, the proceedings were slow, complicated, and expensive, and the court's operations attracted serious criticism. For Congolese civil society, the picture is more mixed or even negative. The main criticism of the court pertains to the prosecutorial and investigative strategy of the Office of the Prosecutor. One of the primary criticisms of the ICC's investigations in the DRC cases is that they lack representativeness, reflecting only part of the conflict, in terms of both affected victims and temporal scope.

[65] The level of people's satisfaction/legitimacy of civil and criminal justice institutions has been measured by the World Justice Project through surveys conducted among a random sample of 1,000 households per country, in over 100 countries. See, for example, "WJP Rule of Law Index 2017-2018", *World Justice Project* (available on its web site). The author led the team that developed and deployed these surveys around the world for ten years.

wards transitional justice found that the majority of the respondents sampled in regions most affected by the 2007-2008
post-electoral violence, did not trust their justice system as it
was perceived to be extremely corrupt. A study of people's
perception of justice and peace in the eastern DRC [Demo-
cratic Republic of the Congo] revealed overall negative perceptions of the national justice system, citing that people
found it corrupt, non-existent, favouring the rich, or requiring
payment. Finally, in Mali, respondents to a small assessment
on transitional justice in the country explained that "justice
isn't really respected here. We resolve many of our problems
among ourselves, rather than going to the formal justice system", as one artist was quoted as saying.[66]

6.7. Judicial Integrity and Independence under the 'African Tree': Customary Justice as Perceived by Users

Customary justice is widely used by vast segments of the population in developing countries, for a variety of reasons:

> Many observers point to the practical needs of rural popula-
> tions when explaining the popularity and functionality of in-
> formal justice institutions. Rural populations often have better
> access to informal justice systems than to the state judiciary
> and they prefer them for a number of significant reasons: typi-
> cally, the procedure takes place *on site*, it is more or less *free
> of cost* and *less prone to corruption,* it is exercised by *trusted
> people* in the *language everybody speaks*, and decisions are
> taken according to *rules known to all community members*. In-
> formal *procedures typically aim at restoring social peace in-
> stead of enforcing abstract legislation.* They are consent and
> justice oriented. In this sense, informal justice systems allow
> for better 'access to justice'.

> Apart from these common features, informal justice insti-
> tutions are, in large geographical areas, the only choice due to
> the absence of the state. This is often the case in regions
> where colonial powers did not attempt to establish formal
> court systems, such as North Yemen or Afghanistan. In the
> situation of armed conflict, informal justice institutions often
> gain more importance due to the breakdown of the formal

---

[66] Mieth, 2017, p. 8, see above note 14 (citations omitted).

court systems. In post-conflict societies they can play a crucial role in the stabilisation and reconciliation process.[67]

In Pakistan,

the formal legal system proves less efficient and less accessible in terms of infrastructure, language and facilities as well as actual delivery of justice to the citizens, and hence there has been an increased reliance on this alternative and traditional form of dispute resolution in Pakistan. It is argued that local tribunals because of their proximity substantially reduce the cost of dispute settlement for the poor, and are decided on the basis of customary law, which the villagers can comprehend. Most importantly, however, the contrast drawn between the formal system and the informal tribal system is that the decisions of the tribal system enjoy the 'sanction of tradition and are more readily and willingly acceptable' by the parties. State laws are rarely understood by the uneducated masses and 'court decisions do not inspire confidence either in merit or impartiality'.[68]

Similarly, in Afghanistan,

the main reasons that Afghan people have preferred *jirga/shura* to formal justice is because the former is conducted by respected elders with established social status and the reputation for piety and fairness. In many cases, the disputants personally know the local elders and trust them. In addition, in the context of *jirga/shura*, elders reach decisions in accordance with accepted local traditions/values (customary law) that are deeply ingrained in the collective conscience of the village/tribe – they have a profound existence in the collective mind of the village and in the minds of its individual members. Also unlike state courts, *jirga/shura* settle disputes without long delays and without financial costs. Illiteracy plays an important role in discouraging people from using the formal courts – the overwhelming majority of Afghans are unable to

---

[67] Tilmann J. Röder, "Informal Justice Systems: Challenges and Perspectives", in Juan Carlos Botero, Ronald Janse, Sam Muller and Christine Pratt (eds.), *Innovations in Rule of Law*, HiiL and The World Justice Project, Washington, DC, 2012, pp. 58–61 (emphasis added).

[68] Rehman, I.A. Dark Justice, News Line, August 2002. Irfan, 2008, p. 24, see above note 23.

make applications, read/understand the laws or complete the paper work.[69]

Furthermore, for many Liberians, the punishing system of formal justice is widely regarded in disbelief as it is not concerned about getting to the root of the problem, but in placing blame and punishing, eventually further dividing society. To many people, this system is not constructive and not worth it; they are rather interested in making amends, forgiving, and strengthening the community through the dispute resolution process. More than tradition, restorative justice, which favours social reconciliation – the African Tree – is linked to the socio-economic context in which the majority of Liberians live; bearing in mind the means of subsistence and economic interdependence of rural societies, confrontational relations amid neighbours can have serious costs.[70]

Survey after survey around the world[71] tends to confirm the users' preference for customary justice, for the reasons explained in the previous paragraphs. According to a study published by several agencies of the UN,

> [t]he data collected [in Malawi] confirmed previous conclusions that a major proportion of the population primarily use IJS [informal justice systems]. In the qualitative data collected, approximately one third of the respondents said they preferred to take a case to the traditional leaders first (see below), while another third would first go to church leaders. While the nature of the services provided by church leaders tends to differ from IJS, and a religious official or paralegal might provide advice rather than dispute resolution as such, it can be said that the main sources of help for people facing disputes are the family counselors, religious leaders, NGOs/CBOs, and traditional authorities (TAs).[72]

---

[69] Ali Wardak, "Building a post-war justice system in Afghanistan", in *Crime, Law and Social Change*, Kluwer Academic Publishers, Netherlands, 2004, vol. 41, p. 319–341.

[70] See, for example, Isser *et al.*, 2009, see above note 23.

[71] For example, *Law and Justice in Timor-Leste: A Survey of Citizen Awareness and Attitudes Regarding Law and Justice*, USAID and Asia Foundation, 2008, p. 33; *Informal Justice Systems, Charting a Course for Human Rights-Based Engagement*, UN Women, the United Nations Children's Fund ('UNICEF') and United Nations Development Programme ('UNDP'), United Nations, New York, 2012, p. 321; Isser *et al.*, 2009, see above note 23; World Justice Project's surveys in over 100 countries, described in Juan Botero and Alejandro Ponce, *Measuring the Rule of Law*, The World Justice Project, 2011.

[72] UN Women, UNICEF and UNDP, 2012, p. 321, see above note 71.

For most people around the world, the notion of 'customary justice' is more readily identified with the notion of the 'African Tree' – the friendly meeting place where the community comes together to amend the broken bonds.[73] Skelton presents the South African variant of this notion as follows:

> The 'African philosophy' [...] is known as *ubuntu*. It has been described as an African worldview, which is both a guide for social conduct as well as a philosophy of life. Archbishop Desmond Tutu explains in his book about the TRC [Truth and Reconciliation Commission] that during the negotiation process, a decision had to be made about what form the commission to deal with South Africa's past should take. The two possibilities of the Nuremberg-type trials or an unconditional amnesty process were overtaken by a third approach of conditional amnesty, and that this approach was consistent with Ubuntu. He explains further:
>
> > Ubuntu is very difficult to render into a Western language. It speaks of the very essence of being human. When we want to give high praise to someone we say 'yu, u nobuntu' (hey, he or she has ubuntu). This means they are generous, hospitable, friendly, caring and compassionate. They share what they have. It also means my humanity is caught up, is inextricably bound up, in theirs. We belong to a bundle of life. We say, 'a person is a person thought other people'.
>
> He goes on to clarify how ubuntu is linked to the idea of forgiveness. He asserts that to forgive is not just to be altruistic, it is the best form of self-interest because forgiveness gives people resilience, enabling them to survive and emerge still human despite all efforts to dehumanize them. He concludes that even the supporters of apartheid were victims of the vicious system which they implemented, because within the context of ubuntu, our humanity is intertwined.
>
> The concept of ubuntu has underpinned societal harmony in Africa for many years, and guided traditional conflict resolution. Traditional mechanisms to deal with problems arising in communities have been effective structures for upholding African customary law. It has been said that 'reconciliation,

---

[73] The notion of justice as the 'African Tree' is introduced at above note 18.

restoration and harmony lie at the heart of African adjudication', and that the central purpose of a customary law court was to acknowledge that a wrong had been done and to determine what amends should be made. Some of these customary courts, known as Izinkundla, Izigcawu or Makgotla are still in operation throughout South Africa today, mostly in rural areas.

The traditional model currently practiced in rural areas in South Africa is similar to indigenous traditions in other countries such as New Zealand and Canada. It involves elders (almost exclusively men) who preside over the resolution of problems experienced by members of the community, which have not been resolved at the family or community level. *With the emphasis on 'problems' rather than offences, these structures hear the stories of the parties involved and then make decisions regarding outcomes. These outcomes aim to heal relationships, and they ensure restitution or compensation to victims. Symbolic gestures such as sacrifice of animals and the sharing of a meal indicate that the crime has been expiated and the offender can now be reintegrated.*[74]

The 'African Tree' notion of justice includes many variants and is not exclusive to the African continent; manifestations of the same concept of justice in other latitudes, including the Middle East, South Asia, East Asia, and North and South America, are presented in detail elsewhere.[75]

This contrasting views on the role of justice in society have been debated in the context of international criminal justice:

A limit to the Western-based models of international justice is their primary focus on prosecuting individuals. In many African societies there is often an additional communal dimension of culpability which points more to the necessity of reconciliation rather than punishment. This is an argument that can well be extended beyond Africa.[76]

But before we proceed any further with the idea that the solution to the ailing field of international criminal justice may include a move in the

---

[74] Ann Skelton, "Restorative Justice as a Framework for Juvenile Justice Reform: A South African Perspective", in *British Journal of Criminology*, 2002, vol. 42, no. 3, pp. 496, 498-499 (emphasis added) (citations omitted).

[75] Botero, 2013, see above note 6.

[76] Mieth, 2017, p. 7, see above note 14 (citations omitted).

direction of customary justice, it is important to state the following caveat: Customary justice is not deprived of shortcomings, including severely biased treatment of segments of the population (often amounting to violations of international human rights, including discrimination). There are egregious violations of universal human rights committed by customary justice authorities in various continents, in the name of 'community harmonizing justice'.[77] Some examples include the 'tar and feather' justice of Cameroon, the stoning of child witches in Nigeria, the gang-raping of Mukhtar Mai in Pakistan, and pervasive gender discrimination among customary justice authorities in Colombia. Moreover, restorative justice approaches in the face of mass atrocities, such as the *gacaca* courts in Rwanda, are not without severe limitations and critics.[78]

6.8. The Bangalore Principles of Judicial Conduct and Articles 36(3)(a) and 42(3) of the Rome Statute, under the 'African Tree'

As stated in Section 6.1. above, this chapter's first goal was to address whether the Bangalore Principles of Judicial Conduct command truly universal acceptance, and whether they indeed "give expression to the highest traditions relating to the judicial function as visualized in all cultures and legal systems" and "all the great religious systems of the world", as Judge Weeramantry claims.

What has been explained so far should suffice to conclude that, while the Bangalore Principles vividly reflect core values of adjudication across *civil* and *common law* traditions (embraced by legal elites in all countries), the same principles do not reflect a truly 'universal' understanding of judicial integrity and independence.

For instance, the Bangalore Principles are grounded on the *Virtues of Tunnel Vision*[79] and the *Ideal of Tabula Rasa*,[80] which became 'black-

---

[77] Botero, 2013, at Part IV, see above note 6.

[78] Lars Waldorf, "Rwanda's Failing Experiment in Restorative Justice", in Carolyn Hoyle, *Restorative Justice: Critical Concepts in Criminology*, Routledge, 2008, vol. 2, pp. 364–381.

[79] "The Virtues of Tunnel Vision. The pure conflict-solving process demands more from the decision maker than neutrality as between the parties; he must also be blind to any considerations that transcend the resolution of the dispute before him", see Damaška, 1986, p. 140, see above note 40.

[80] "The Ideal of Tabula Rasa. If in the conflict-solving process the decision is to emerge from the dialectic of party debate, ideally the decision maker must enter the case unprepared, unaware of all matters specifically related to the issue. He should have a 'virgin mind,' to be

boxed' within the legal process of the common law about seven hundred years ago.[81] As it was explained above, these principles are by essence incompatible with the 'African Tree', which is the prevailing notion of Justice among vast segments of the population today, not only in Africa but also in Asia and Latin America.

The Rome Statute is, by essence, incompatible with basic customary justice tenets around the world. For instance, the personal, intimate relation existing between the *Mamo* and each member of the community among the Kogi people of Colombia – which constitutes the essence of the Kogi system of fact-finding and adjudication – would not only be inappropriate, but also highly indicative of bias under the lens of UNODC's *Commentary on the Bangalore Principles of Judicial Conduct*.[82] According to these principles:

> 90. Depending on the circumstances, a reasonable apprehension of bias might be thought to arise in the following cases: [...] (b) *If the judge is closely acquainted with any member of the public involved in the case*, particularly if that person's credibility may be significant in the outcome of the case;

> 111. Propriety and the appearance of propriety, both professional and personal, are essential elements of a judge's life. What matters is more not what a judge does or does not do, but what others think the judge has done or might do. *For example, a judge who speaks privately and at length with a litigant in a pending case will appear to be giving that party an advantage, even if in fact the conversation is completely unrelated to the case.* Since the public expects a high standard of conduct from a judge, he or she must, when in doubt about attending an event or receiving a gift, however small, ask the question, "How might this look in the eyes of the public?"[83]

In other words, when 'Western' notions of judicial integrity and independence – which emphasize legal process, punishment, retributive justice, and deterrence – demand a distant (blindfolded) judge, customary justice's long-established emphasis on restorative justice and community har-

---

tutored only through the bilateral process of evidentiary presentation and argument." *Ibid.*, p. 138.

[81] A detailed explanation of the notion of 'black boxing' of legal principles in the civil law and common law traditions, is provided in Botero, 2013, pt. 5, chap. 3, see above note 6.

[82] UNODC, 2007, see above note 10.

[83] UNODC, 2007, pp. 57 and 69, see above note 10 (emphasis added).

mony require the exact opposite – a deeply-rooted elder, a wise member of the community, who must have intimate knowledge of the parties involved in the dispute.

Around the thirteenth century, Europe experienced a fundamental transformation about the understanding of the world, and this philosophical revolution left a profound impact on the European notions of law and justice. Roman law was rediscovered and embraced wholeheartedly. Lady Justice – the Roman Goddess of Justice represented as an austere and impartial (blindfolded) woman, holding a sword in one hand and the scales in the other – slowly came to replace the Christian cross as the prevailing image of justice in the community. Most saliently, the law of procedure became the scales of justice, the tool through which Justice with capital J materializes in the world. And the instrument of this transformation was the rediscovered Roman law.[84] This process had its climax at the Enlightenment, when reason finally triumphed, as the last remnants of the trial by ordeal were abolished,[85] and the law of the 'civilized world' achieved its final shape. Through parallel processes evolving over a thousand years in England and in Continental Europe, *judicial integrity came to signify impartiality* (the scales of Lady Justice of the *common law*) *and strict application of the law* (the sword of Lady Justice of the *civil law*).

While these transformations were enormously significant, something else was lost in translation. This 'something' is precisely the 'African Tree'.[86] The idea that justice is not a sword used by a powerful judge to cut and remove the transgressors of the law, or a scale that requires all situations to be treated equally regardless of context, but rather a friendly meeting place around which the community may unite once again, to heal and re-establish the bonds that were broken. This accident of history has had profound implications on the way lawyers and judges see judicial integrity today, and it may contribute to explain the fading support for the ICC, particularly in the Global South. But is this distant and blindfolded Lady Jus-

---

[84] "The law of Rome stood for reason, organization, and administrative efficiency under central control. Embodied in the superb bodies of the Corpus Juris Civilis, it was rediscovered and studied as a revelation, the lawyer's ultima ratio", see Caenegem, 1982, p. 11, see above note 34.

[85] "The last-mentioned method of ordeal, viz. that by cold water, was resorted to in England for the detection of witches, until the beginning of the last [eighteenth] century", see Gibson, 1848, p. 15, see above note 29.

[86] See above note 18.

tice of the 'Western' legal tradition (which was embraced by legal elites in the Global South), a mandatory requirement under the Rome Statute?

According to Article 36(3)(a) of the ICC Statute,

> 3. (a) The judges shall be chosen from among persons of high moral character, impartiality and integrity who possess the qualifications required in their respective States for appointment to the highest judicial offices.

And pursuant to Article 42(3) of the same statute:

> The Prosecutor and the Deputy Prosecutors shall be persons of high moral character, be highly competent in and have extensive practical experience in the prosecution or trial of criminal cases. They shall have an excellent knowledge of and be fluent in at least one of the working languages of the Court.

Again, when 'Western' notions of judicial integrity and independence demand a distant (blindfolded) judge, customary justice's long-established emphasis on restorative justice and community harmony require the exact opposite – a deeply-rooted elder, a wise member of the community, who must have intimate knowledge of the parties involved in the dispute. Unless ICC constituencies are able to reinterpret these standards under a community-harmonizing Justice perspective, the ICC legitimacy crisis in the Global South will not be remedied.

Nothing in the Rome Statute prevents the Office of the Prosecutor ('OTP') to approach cases from the ground-up, in close contact with the community, and from the perspective of the community. Nothing in the Rome Statute prevents ICC judges to pay a bit less attention to the global human rights movement (which played an invaluable role in the creation of the ICC and have sustained it for two decades) and sharpen their ears to the justice needs and aspirations of the community. Do Rohingyas, the Kenyans and the rural Colombians who face violations have the same justice needs and aspirations? If the ICC only acts from The Hague, from the perspective of The Hague, and is ultimately unaccountable to the particular community that was affected by grave crimes, the ICC will never achieve truly universal acceptance. While this distance is in part a problem caused by lack of resources, it is also a problem of perspective.[87]

---

[87] "[D]elays are a product of scarce investigative resources, a lack of state cooperation, and other factors. But with limited communication and outreach, victims and members of affected communities have been left wondering what, if anything, the court is doing", see Goldston, 2019, see above note 1.

While the global criminal court has an important role to play as court of last resort for mass atrocities, it cannot behave as the continuation of the old judicial institutions of the European colonizers, as it is currently perceived by vast segments of the population in the Global South.

6.9. Is There a Truly Universal Understanding of Judicial Integrity and Independence?

This chapter's second research question was whether a truly multicultural understanding of integrity and independence in international criminal justice (not the specific standards of the ICC or other tribunals), implies a move towards 'relativizing' these standards.

At a basic level, this research shows that adopting a broader cultural perspective that goes beyond the narrow standpoint of the world's legal elites, necessarily implies a move towards relativizing the aforementioned global standards of judicial integrity and independence. Indeed, if the notions of judicial integrity and independence underlying the views on justice and due process prevailing among the Navajo Nation in North America,[88] the Kogi community in Colombia,[89] or the Liberian chiefs,[90] are examined under the light of the UN-sponsored standards of judicial integrity and independence, it becomes apparent that the meaning of 'justice' and 'due process' among these communities does not match that of the *civil law* and the *common law* traditions (that is, the 'Western' legal tradition), which underlie the Bangalore Principles of Judicial Conduct.[91]

Yet, at a higher level of abstraction, it is also argued that the core components of integrity and independence transcend all legal traditions. From time immemorial, dispute resolution systems were (at least in theory) created to provide equal justice among unequal parties, that is, to protect the weak – the strong did not need protection. This ideal is present in all legal traditions of the world:

> [I was called] to bring about the rule of righteousness in the land [...] so that the strong should not harm the weak.
>
> Prologue, Hammurabi's Code, 1772 BCE

---

[88] See, for example, Paul Spruhan, "The Meaning of Due Process in the Navajo Nation", in *The Indian Civil Rights Act at Forty*, UCLA American Indian Studies Center Publications, 2012.

[89] Botero, 2013, at pt. 4, chap. 5, see above note 6.

[90] *Ibid.*, at pt. 4, chap. 4.

[91] The Bangalore Principles, see above note 8.

> If someone disobeys the law, even if he is worthy, he must be punished. If someone meets the standard, even if he is unworthy, he must be found innocent. Thus the Way of the public good will be opened up, and that of private interest will be blocked.
>
> The Huainanzi, 139 BCE, Han Dynasty, China

> Treat the people equally in your court and give them equal attention, so that the noble shall not aspire to your partiality, nor the humble despair of your justice.
>
> Judicial Guidelines from 'Umar Bin Al-Khattab,
the Second Khalif of Islam, 634-644 CE

From time immemorial, the litmus test of a judge's *integrity* is whether he or she actually protected the weak, when he or she was called upon to do so. Of course, holding the 'strong' accountable for violations, is one way to protect the 'weak'. A more culturally competent and inclusive (less Euro-centric, legalistic and patronizing) reading of the Rome Statue, could potentially tap into this common well of wisdom of all humanity.

Sine the Nuremberg trials, international criminal justice appears to have converged around the notion that a court's true measure is given by its ability to bring about universal accountability for grave crimes. In the words of Teitel:

> Nuremberg established the principle of individual criminal accountability for human rights violations perpetrated against civilians in wartime: that certain crimes are so heinous that they violate the "law of nations" and may be prosecuted anywhere. [92]

The courts and tribunals established since Nuremberg, including the International Criminal Tribunal for the former Yugoslavia, the International Criminal Tribunal for Rwanda, the Special Court for Sierra Leone, and, ultimately, the ICC, all function under the same basic understanding. In other words, the true measure of their *integrity*, from a 'universal' perspective, seems to be their ability to bring about accountability. Yet, accountability has many flavours. It can take the form of purely retributive punishment, or more community-harmonizing, culturally competent restorative justice.

---

[92] Ruti Teitel, "Transitional Justice: Postwar Legacies", in *Cardozo Law Review*, 2006, vol. 27, no. 4, p. 1615.

Arguably, one of ICC's greatest successes – its relentless push for accountability in Colombia, gently implemented through positive complementarity[93] – is a manifestation of the OTP and the whole court's community-harmonizing and culturally-competent understanding of the justice needs and aspirations of Colombian people, beyond black and white accountability under immutable international standards. According to Goldston:

> Despite its problems, the ICC has had important impacts outside the courtroom. Even as it has refrained from pursuing its own investigation of possible war crimes and crimes against humanity in Colombia, the court's quiet monitoring and oversight of postwar developments in the country have helped ensure that accountability is a critical part of a national peace process following a decadeslong civil war.[94]

Similarly, according to International Centre for Transitional Justice, "Colombia's obligations as a State Party to the Rome Statute appear to have weakened domestic tolerance of impunity".[95] Most informed observers in Colombia perceive the ICC's role during the peace process with the Revolutionary Armed Forces of Colombia (FARC) as a more culturally-competent and inclusive (less Euro-centric, legalistic and patronizing) reading of the Rome Statue. Perhaps this success is owed, at least in part, to the Prosecutor's ability to understand Colombia's language and culture – in contrast to his apparent inability to read Kenyan culture, and the justice needs and aspirations of the Kenyan people during the same period. "The Kenyan case shows how a government has consistently and effectively employed the rhetoric of 'imposed international justice' throughout its ICC proceedings."[96]

The contrasting outcome of the Colombian and Kenyan cases respond to a plurality of causes that would be impossible to explore within the limited scope of this chapter. Nonetheless, at least in principle, these two cases seem to suggest that unless international criminal justice moves

---

[93] William W. Burke-White, "Proactive Complementarity: The International Criminal Court and National Courts in the Rome System of International Justice", in *Harvard International Law Journal*, 2008, vol. 49, no. 53.

[94] Goldston, 2019, see above note 1.

[95] Amanda Lyons and Michael Reed-Hurtado, "Colombia: Impact of the Rome Statute and the International Criminal Court", in *International Center for Transitional Justice*, 2010, p. 1.

[96] Mieth, 2017, p. 5, see above note 14.

further in the direction of recognizing and accommodating to some extent regional standards regarding the trade-off between peace and justice in transitional situations, it will not be perceived as truly universal and legitimate by large segments of the population in the Global South.

The OTP's reading of the Colombian situation is an example of the ICC taking unprecedented steps (despite strong pressure to the contrary) to interpret the Rome Statute under the light of a country's particular situation and in harmony with its people's unique justice needs and aspirations, without sacrificing universal principles of accountability for grave crimes.[97]

---

[97] For information on recent experiences with transitional justice in Colombia, particularly in the context of the *Special Jurisdiction of Peace* created by the 2016 Peace Agreement with FARC, and the *Justice and Peace* process created by Law 975 of 2005, regarding paramilitary groups, see, for example, Nelson Camilo Sánchez León, *Acceptance of International Criminal Justice - Country Study on Colombia*, in International Nuremberg Principles Academy, 2017; Paul Seils, *Squaring Colombia's Circle: The Objectives of Punishment and the Pursuit of Peace*, International Center for Transitional Justice ('ICTJ'), New York, 2015; Botero and Merchán, 2020, see above note 5; *El enfoque de macro criminalidad en el proceso penal de Justicia y Paz. Lecciones para la Jurisdicción Especial para la Paz*, ICTJ, New York, 2019; Institute for Integrated Transitions ('IFIT'), *Rethinking Peace and Justice* (available on its web site); Julieta Lemaitre and Lina Rondón, "La justicia restaurativa y la escucha: un análisis del componente oral de los informes mixtos y de las versiones voluntarias en el Caso 01", in Danilo Rojas Betancourth (ed.), *La JEP vista por sus jueces (2018-2019)*, Jurisdicción Especial para la Paz, Bogotá; Rafael A Prieto Sanjuán, "La jurisdicción especial para la paz: internacional, a pesar de todo", in Ruiz-Rico, Szegedy, Prieto and Garzon (eds.), *Retos en la implementación de los acuerdos de paz en Colombia*, Tirant lo Blanch, 2018; Orlando Humberto de la Vega Martins, "Juicio al mal radical? Dos reflexiones acerca de la justicia transicional en Colombia", in Ruiz-Rico, Szegedy, Prieto and Garzon (eds.), *Retos en la implementación de los acuerdos de paz en Colombia*, Tirant lo Blanch, 2018; Carlos Ignacio Jaramillo, "El 'derecho a no ser victima', y su incidencia en el 'posconflicto' colombiano", in Ruiz-Rico, Szegedy, Prieto and Garzon (eds.), *Retos en la implementación de los acuerdos de paz en Colombia*, Tirant lo Blanch, 2018; Lorena Cecilia Vega Dueñas, "Modelo de justicia transicional: el caso colombiano", in Ruiz-Rico, Szegedy, Prieto and Garzon (eds.), *Retos en la implementación de los acuerdos de paz en Colombia*, Tirant lo Blanch, 2018; Open Society Justice Initiative, 2018, p. 362, see above note 26; Lorena Cecilia Vega Dueñas and Alberto José Olalde Altarejos, "La justicia restaurativa como paradigma orientador de paz: los encuentros restaurativos", in *Revista Icade: Revista de las Facultades de Derecho y Ciencias Económicas y Empresariales*, 2018; Gustavo Emilio Cote Barco, "Responsibility for leadership in the Peace Agreement signed by the Colombian Government and the FARC-EP: An analysis based on the Bemba case of the International Criminal Court", in *Nuevo Foro Penal*, 2019, vol. 15, no. 92; Laura Bernal-Bermudez and Daniel Marin Lopez, "Los empresarios en la guerra: verdad judicial sobre la complicidad empresarial en Colombia", in *Cuentas Claras: El Papel de la Comisión de la Verdad en la develación de la responsabilidad de empresas en el conflicto armado colombiano*, 2018, pp. 39–66, Centro de Estudios de Derecho, Justicia y Sociedad, Colombia; Comisión Internacional de Juristas,

In sum, a truly universal understanding of *integrity* in international criminal justice does not emerge from a purist and unyielding reading of the Rome Statute. At least from the perspective of large segments of the population in the Global South, the ICC's *integrity* as an institution, significantly depends upon its ability to read the cultural nuances of the situations under review. In the timeless words of Jean-Étienne-Marie Portalis:

> Les lois ne sont pas de purs actes de puissance; ce sont des actes de sagesse, de justice et de raison. Le législateur exerce moins une autorité qu'un sacerdoce. Il ne doit point perdre de vue que les lois sont faites pour les hommes, et non les hommes pour les lois; qu'elles doivent être adaptées au caractère, aux habitudes, à la situation du peuple pour lequel elles sont faites.[98]

Colombia: Jurisdicción Especial para la Paz, análisis a un año y medio de su entrada en funcionamento, Junio 2019; Heidi Abuchaibe, Andrei Gómez-Suárez, and Camilo Eduardo Umaña Hernández, *Justicia Restaurativa: oportunidades y retos para construir una paz estable y duradera*, Defensoría del Pueblo, Republica de Colombia, 2018; Lilia Inés, Ávila Alférez and Juanita Cardona Pachón, *Jurisdicción Especial para la Paz*, Defensoría del Pueblo, Republica de Colombia, 2018; Juan Felipe García and Norberto Hernández, "Amnistías, indultos y tratamientos especiales diferenciados como mecanismos de justicia transicional en Colombia: El modelo del acuerdo de paz de 2016", Pontifica Universidad Javeriana (forthcoming 2020); Juan Felipe García, "Los debates de la justicia transicional en Colombia", in Sebastián Peñuela Camacho, Eduardo F. Gutiérrez González, and María Lucía Zapata Cancelado (eds.), *Retos de la implementación de la justicia transicional en Colombia*, Editorial Pontificia Universidad Javeriana, Bogotá, 2020; Norberto Hernández, "El 'nuevo' acuerdo final para la paz a través del lente del derecho penal", *Revista Nuevo Foro Penal*, vol. 13, no. 88, 2017, Universidad EAFIT; Alejandro Aponte Cardona, *El proceso penal especial de justicia y paz alcances y límites de un proceso penal concebido en clave transicional*, Citpax, 2011; Gustavo Emilio Cote-Barco, "Responsabilidad del superior jerárquico y responsabilidad penal por omisión de miembros de la fuerza pública en Colombia: ¿convergencia entre el derecho penal nacional e internacional?", *International Law, Revista Colombiana de Derecho Internacional*, 2016, vol. 14, no. 28, pp. 49–112; Gustavo Cote-Barco, "El proceso penal especial de justicia y paz: ¿verdadera alternativa para la transición a la paz u otro intento fallido de consolidación del estado en medio de la guerra?", *International Law: Revista Colombiana De Derecho Internacional*, 2010, vol. 8, no. 17; Gustavo Cote Barco, "Complicidad, responsabilidad penal de directivos empresariales y violaciones de Derechos Humanos cometidas por grupos armados ilegales: lecciones del Derecho Penal Internacional para Colombia", *Vniversitas*, 2019, vol. 68, no. 138; Leigh Payne, Gabriel Pereira and Laura Bernal-Bermúdez, *Transitional Justice and Corporate Accountability from Below: Deploying Archimedes' Lever*, Cambridge University Press, 2020; Astrid Liliana Sánchez, *Victims' Rights in Flux: Criminal Justice Reform in Colombia*, Springer, 2017.

[98]   Jean-Étienne-Marie Portalis, *Discours préliminaire du premier projet de Code civil*, 1801.

6.10. People Need Justice: Integrity Also Means Timeliness

For ordinary citizens around the world, expectations about justice are the same as those of someone waiting for a tram in a lonely city in the middle of the night: they want it 'reasonably fast', 'reasonably affordable', and 'reliable'. Based on my experience measuring people's perceptions of justice in over one hundred countries over the past two decades, for ordinary citizens, Justice is perceived as 'corrupt' if it is: 'too slow', 'too expensive', 'unreliable', or it 'only persecutes the weak'.

In this light, the sixth principle recognized by the Bangalore Principles of Judicial Conduct, the value of 'Competence and Diligence', is perhaps the one that most directly influences current global perceptions of judicial integrity in international criminal law. Some civil society observers of the ICC acknowledge "a string of disappointments that have shaken confidence in the institution".[99]

The disappointment largely stems from the perceived inaction of the ICC while continuing to incur costs.[100] Even the staunchest ICC supporters might wonder whether the ICC is fit to carry out its purpose.[101] The ICC's inability to hold the powerful accountable for so long, has seriously undermined the court's legitimacy and the perception of integrity of the court across the Global South. The court's inclination to allow the investigation of the situation in Afghanistan, may constitute a first step to re-establish its credibility as an impartial arbiter in the eyes of ordinary folk in developing countries.[102]

6.11. Implications for International Criminal Justice and the ICC

This chapter's final goal was to explore whether there are notions of judicial integrity and independence that underlie the world's broader understanding of Justice (with capital 'J'), regardless of legal tradition, and how

---

[99] Goldston, 2019, see above note 1.

[100] Goldston, 2019, see above note 1 (and the familiar passage: "it is disconcerting that one-third of the court's judges are suing for a pay raise plus pension increases and damages that could run into the millions. Why, when the court has been underperforming and the budget is strained, are its judges dedicating precious time and energy to increase their already generous compensation—which at around $200,000 tax-free exceeds that of judges on many national courts?").

[101] Hatcher-Moore, 2017, see above note 1.

[102] Peltier and Faizi, 2020, see above note 3.

these global perspectives may influence the way we see international criminal justice in the multi-cultural world of the twenty-first century.

The growing disconnection between legal elites and the rest of the people throughout the world, may also affect the ICC – an institution that has been perceived as 'foreign' or 'alien' by large segments of the world's population. The time has come for friends of international criminal law principles to give serious consideration to the 'African Tree'. This does not mean to question the validity of the Rome Statute in any way. It is rather a gentle suggestion to try to read the same statute under the light of ancestral notions of community-harmonizing justice.

Some criticize South Africa for depicting the ICC "as a so-called Western institution imposing double standards".[103] With all due respect for these opinions – even though the Rome Statute was negotiated by judges and lawyers from around the world, and the ICC's staff comes "from more than 90 countries, each with their own legal cultures and traditions"[104] – the court is an expression of the European ideal of Justice, not a manifestation of a truly global understanding of Justice; "if ideas and institutions about as fundamental and personal a value as justice are imposed from outside without an internal resonance, they may flounder, notwithstanding their assertion of universality".[105]

At the very minimum, international criminal law experts should bear in mind that the fact that the Bangalore Principles and the Rome Statute were negotiated by High Court Justices and lawyers from over one hundred countries does not mean that these global standards and rules represent the cultural traditions of an increasingly interconnected, anti-elitist, and culturally self-assertive global population. Legal elites throughout the world find it hard to acknowledge that the 'Western' legal tradition, in which they were educated, does not necessarily reflect the Justice needs and aspirations of people in the Global South of the twenty-first century.

In the context of the common law tradition, *judicial integrity means impartiality.* In the civil law tradition, it means *strict application of the law.* None of them reflects the ideal of justice of ordinary people in the Global South. As it was explained above, customary justice is widely used by vast

---

[103] Goldston, 2019, see above note 1.

[104] *Ibid.*

[105] Rama Mani, *Beyond Retribution: Seeking Justice in the Shadows of War*, Polity Press, Cambridge, 2002, p. 49.

segments of the population in developing countries, for a variety of reasons. The same reasons may apply to public perceptions of international criminal justice in the Global South.[106]

A twentieth century institution that is perceived as 'patronizing' and 'neo-colonial' by significant segments of the world's population, can hardly be perceived to have *integrity* in the globalized, hyper-connected, anti-elitist, and culturally self-assertive world of the twenty-first century. While the Rome Statute cannot be renegotiated in today's polarized geopolitical environment, incremental change may be made to bring the international criminal justice system closer to the people, to increase the system's legitimacy at the regional level, and to ultimately advance its high goals. At an age characterized by profound mistrust for elites, Humpty Dumpty has fallen[107] and it cannot be made whole again by simply keep hailing the Court's elevated goals.

The Colombian experience dealing with pervasive and long-lasting violations through the Special Jurisdiction of Peace (JEP), may shed some light on alternative ways to consider international criminal law principles in the context of peace and reconciliation needs of the community.[108]

Perhaps in a not so distant future, the international criminal justice system will encompass, in addition to a down-scaled and more efficient ICC, a network of smaller and more agile, loosely affiliated regional mechanisms, which give proper consideration to local customs, languages and traditions, in the conceptualization and application of judicial process, forms of punishment, and community outreach – perhaps a bit more in line with the 'African Tree'.

This chapter's conclusion is also a gentle suggestion for international criminal law experts to revisit the sixth principle of the Bangalore Princi-

---

[106] Röder, 2012, pp. 58–61, see above note 67 (emphasis added):

Rural populations often have better access to informal justice systems than to the state judiciary and they prefer them for a number of significant reasons: typically, the procedure takes place *on site*, it is more or less *free of cost* and *less prone to corruption*, it is exercised by *trusted people* in the *language everybody speaks,* and decisions are taken according to *rules known to all community members.* Informal *procedures typically aim at restoring social peace instead of enforcing abstract legislation.* They are consent and justice oriented. In this sense, informal justice systems allow for better 'access to justice'.

[107] As the popular rime reads: "Humpty Dumpty sat on a wall. Humpty Dumpty had a great fall. All the king's horses and all the king's men. Couldn't put Humpty together again".

[108] For a description of the Colombian Peace Jurisdiction and its departures from standard canons of international criminal justice, see above note 97.

ples of Judicial Conduct – the principle of 'Competence and Diligence' – as the main driver of perceptions about *integrity* of justice. For ordinary citizens throughout the world, Justice is perceived as 'corrupt' if it is too slow, too expensive, unreliable or it only persecutes the weak. At the very minimum, the threat of increased competition at the regional level may motivate Humpty to bring its act together again.

7

Ethics, Integrity and the *Bemba* Acquittal

Shannon Fyfe[*]

7.1. Introduction

On 8 June 2018, the Appeals Chamber of the International Criminal Court ('ICC') acquitted Jean-Pierre Bemba Gombo ('Bemba') of the charges of war crimes and crimes against humanity, overturning the decision of Trial Chamber III to convict the defendant.[1] Three judges joined in the Judgment issued by the majority, while two judges dissented.[2] The conviction had been appealed on six separate grounds, but the Judgment overturning the conviction focused on two grounds: first, that the conviction exceeded the charges, and second, that Bemba was not liable as a superior.[3]

On 13 June 2018, Prosecutor Bensouda released a statement[4] expressing concern with the Appeals Chamber's decision. Notably, she stated that she "must uphold the integrity of the Court's processes and accept the outcome".[5] Yet, she went on to indicate her worries that the Appeals Chamber's judgment reflected radical interpretations of jurisprudence and

---

[*] **Shannon Fyfe** is an Assistant Professor of Philosophy at George Mason University, where she is also a Fellow at the Institute for Philosophy and Public Policy and an Adjunct Professor at the Antonin Scalia Law School. She holds both a Ph.D. in philosophy and a J.D. from Vanderbilt University. Her prior work includes an internship with the International Criminal Tribunal for Rwanda's Office of the Prosecutor, the American Society of International Law's Arthur C. Helton Fellowship for international human rights law in Tanzania, and a fellowship with the Syria Justice and Accountability Centre. She has published *International Criminal Tribunals: A Normative Defense*, Cambridge University Press, Cambridge, 2017 (co-author with Larry May).

[1] International Criminal Court ('ICC'), Situation in the Central African Republic, *Prosecutor v. Jean-Pierre Bemba Gombo*, Appeals Chamber, Judgment on the appeal of Mr Jean-Pierre Bemba Gombo against Trial Chamber III's "Judgment pursuant to Article 74 of the Statute", 8 June 2018, ICC-01/05-01/08A ('Judgment') (https://www.legal-tools.org/doc/40d35b).

[2] *Ibid.*

[3] *Ibid.*, para. 32.

[4] ICC Office of the Prosecutor ('OTP'), "Statement of ICC Prosecutor, Fatou Bensouda, on the recent judgment of the ICC Appeals Chamber acquitting Mr Jean-Pierre Bemba Gombo", 13 June 2018.

[5] *Ibid.*

---

precedent.[6] Prosecutor Bensouda closed her statement by acknowledging the victims of violence in the Central African Republic ('CAR') and proclaiming the solidarity of the Office of the Prosecutor ('OTP') with these victims.[7]

The Appeals Chamber judgment and the corresponding statement from the Prosecutor reveal the challenge faced by the OTP in balancing ethical obligations demanded by particular legal and moral standards, and maintaining the integrity of both the Office and the institution as a whole. Prosecutor Bensouda faced the seemingly impossible task of defending the processes of and prospects for the Court as an international criminal justice institution, while acknowledging her view that the Court had failed with respect to the substantive outcome of a particular trial, and the corresponding failure to achieve justice for particular victims of violence. The Prosecutor's public statement illustrates the tension the OTP often faces in seeking short-term international criminal justice and investing in the long-term sustainability of international criminal justice institutions. It also reflects the fact that an institution must be dedicated to both actual integrity and the appearance of integrity, as the lack of one threatens the other.

In this chapter, I consider the role of integrity in decisions made by individuals, both as individuals and as part of institutional structures, at the ICC. I begin by arguing that we should take a more systematic approach to understanding the role of integrity in individual and institutional obligations, and I attempt to construct such a normative framework. I argue that in order to answer the primary ethical question for actors in a legal system, that is, how we should act, we must understand our obligations in terms of integrity, normative ethical considerations, and specific legal obligations.

I then use the case of the *Bemba* acquittal and its aftermath to draw out the various obligations and tensions that exist for prosecutors, judges, and other actors attempting to defend the cause of international criminal justice. I argue that in this case, Prosecutor Bensouda may have failed to achieve her aim of not undermining the institution, and that this failure may in fact undermine institutional integrity mechanisms of the Court. At the same time, the Appeals Chamber appears to have failed to meet its own integrity requirements, and if so, this speaks again to Prosecutor Bensouda's urge to defend the institution. Unfortunately, I conclude, she cannot be

---

[6]   *Ibid.*

[7]   *Ibid.*

responsible for maintaining the integrity of the entire institution if a separate branch fails in meeting its own integrity requirements.

7.2. Individual Integrity

The first distinction I draw is between individual integrity and institutional integrity. Before we can answer questions about what it means for a group or an organization to 'act with integrity', we must understand the more straightforward question of what this means for an individual. I begin with the broad concept of individual integrity before examining the demands of integrity within the other legal and ethical obligations of prosecutors and judges.

7.2.1. Integrity for Individual Actors

In this Section 7.2.1., I construct an account of necessary features for individual integrity. There are many ways of understanding the philosophical concept of individual integrity, and I will not attempt to provide a comprehensive overview of these views. Rather, I understand integrity to involve two necessary features: a structural sense of integrity and a substantive sense of integrity. Within these two camps, I will explore several prominent possibilities for understanding integrity. Each of these ways of understanding integrity, I argue, can introduce important considerations to an individual actor's decision-making process.

7.2.1.1. Structural Conceptions of Integrity

Integrity can be understood as a formal relation an entity has to itself, between parts of itself, or with other entities. These types of views consider integrity to be a formal, structural concept. Each conception provides a helpful way to think about what it means for an individual to make decisions 'with integrity', thus I do not find it necessary to adopt one structural view of integrity to the exclusion of the others.

7.2.1.1.1. Identity and Commitments

Bernard Williams defends a view of integrity based on 'identity-conferring commitments'.[8] An identity-conferring commitment is "the condition of

---

[8] See Bernard Williams, "Integrity", in J.J.C. Smart and Bernard Williams (eds.), *Utilitarianism: For and Against*, Cambridge University Press, New York, 1973, pp. 108–117; see also Bernard Williams, *Moral Luck: Philosophical Papers 1973-1980*, Cambridge University Press, Cambridge, 1981.

my existence, in the sense that unless I am propelled forward by the conatus of desire, project and interest, it is unclear why I should go on at all".[9]
If an individual abandons such a commitment, according to Williams, then
the individual begins to lose what gives his or her life its moral identity.
For Williams, an individual is "identified with his actions as flowing from
projects and attitudes which in some cases he takes seriously at the deepest
level, as what his life is about"[10] – and when he makes a choice that alien-
ates him from these projects and attitudes, he fails to act with integrity.[11]
While many consider integrity to be a virtue,[12] as we will explore shortly,
Williams argues that this is not the case. Integrity is neither motivating nor
enabling; rather "one who displays integrity acts from those dispositions
and motives which are most deeply his, and has also the virtues that enable
him to do that. Integrity does not enable him to do it, nor is it what he acts
from when he does so".[13]

Despite his claim that integrity is not a virtue (but perhaps depends
on virtues?), Williams' view of integrity in terms of relationship to one's
identity is intuitive. A reference to integrity can easily conjure a sense of
one's deep commitments and values. The question remains as to whether
on a defensible view of integrity, there must also be substantive constraints
on what these deep commitments might be.

7.2.1.1.2. Wholeness and Integration

Another related way to think about integrity is in terms of wholeness and
integration. Gabriele Taylor defines a person who possesses integrity as
"the person who 'keeps his inmost self intact', whose life is 'of a piece',
whose self is whole and integrated".[14] For Taylor, a person of integrity
"lacks corrupt in the sense that his self is disintegrated".[15] Taylor argues
that a person of integrity will usually possess moral qualities like honesty

---

[9] Bernard Williams, "Persons, Character and Morality", in Williams, 1981, pp. 1–19, 12, see
     above note 8.
[10] Williams, 1973, p. 116, see above note 8.
[11] *Ibid.*
[12] A trait is a virtue if there is something about the trait itself that is intrinsically valuable.
[13] Bernard Williams, "Utilitarianism and Self-Indulgence", in Williams, 1981, pp. 40–53, 49,
     see above note 8.
[14] Gabriele Taylor, "Integrity", in *Proceedings of the Aristotelian Society, Supplementary Vol-
     ume*, 1981, vol. 55, pp. 143–159, 143.
[15] *Ibid.*, p. 144.

and loyalty, but that "we ascribe integrity to him who behaves in socially acceptable ways, or to him who sticks to his principles however adverse the circumstances".[16] We must assume, however, that someone who behaves in these ways is someone who "keeps his self intact", given our epistemic position with respect to an individual's self.[17]

But what does it mean for a self to be integrated or intact? Taylor's view of integrity requires that a person be rational: he "will not ignore relevant evidence, he will be consistent in his behaviour, he will not act on reasons which, given the circumstances, are insufficient reasons for action".[18] Further, an individual with integrity is "not inconsistent in ways that somehow matter", and for Taylor this refers to inconsistencies that are connected to a person's identity (similar to Williams' view above).[19] But Taylor generates further requirements related to identity, such as the condition that "a person who keeps his self intact will be under 'due' influence of his past".[20] In other words, a person must have a memory of his past and an understanding of how it relates to his identity in the present.[21]

Like Williams, Taylor does not identify integrity as a virtue, but rather as something "we hope to get hold of through the virtues".[22] She explicitly acknowledges that her view "seems to have the defect that it fails to account for our thinking of it as some sort of moral quality", since we are "reluctant at least to think of the wholly wicked as candidates for integrity".[23] She contends that we want "to think that the whole or integrated person is also the wholly good person", but she admits that this is only an assumption under her definition.[24]

David Luban offers an alternative view of integrity based on the concept of wholeness in the form of avoiding cognitive dissonance. He defines integrity as "wholeness or unity of a person, an inner consistency between

---

[16] *Ibid.*

[17] *Ibid.*

[18] *Ibid.*, p. 148.

[19] *Ibid.*

[20] *Ibid.*, p. 149.

[21] *Ibid.*

[22] *Ibid.*, p. 152.

[23] *Ibid.*

[24] *Ibid.*

deed and principle".[25] A person of integrity, according to Luban, is "the person whose conduct and principles operate in happy harmony".[26] On this view, then, cognitive dissonance, or the clashing of our conduct and our principles, threatens our intuitions about integrity.[27] Luban identifies examples like the Stanford Prison Experiment[28] and the Milgram Experiment[29] as instances where individuals follow along with the prevailing social norms and then try to justify their otherwise incomprehensible behaviour.[30] Because we are "highly resistant to the thought of our own wrongdoing",[31] research suggests that "we will bend our moral beliefs and even our perceptions to fight off the harsh judgment of our own behavior".[32] Thus, it results in a "kind of integrity in which [one's] beliefs always rationalize [one's] actions after the fact",[33] instead of acknowledging that we might have done something wrong.

But Luban goes on to distinguish this so-called integrity from genuine integrity, and instead classifies this behaviour as 'dissonance reduc-

---

[25]   David Luban, "Integrity: Its Causes and Cures", in *Fordham Law Review*, 2003, vol. 72, p. 279.

[26]   *Ibid.*

[27]   *Ibid.*

[28]   This refers to an experiment in which volunteer undergraduate subjects were divided randomly into 'guards' and 'inmates' in a mock prison. In less than a day, those labeled 'guards' began bullying and brutalizing the 'inmates', while the inmates began to exhibit the pathologies of real-life prisoners. Five of the inmates had to be released quickly due to "extreme emotional depression, crying, rage and acute anxiety". See Craig Haney *et al.*, "Interpersonal Dynamics of a Simulated Prison", in *International Journal of Criminology and Penology*, 1973, vol. 1, p. 81. On the second day, the prisoners revolted and the guards put down the rebellion by blasting them with fire extinguishers. See Philip Zimbardo *et al.*, "The Mind Is a Formidable Jailer: A Pirandellian Prison", in *New York Times*, 8 April 1973, §6 (Magazine), p. 41.

[29]   In the Milgram experiments, subjects were ordered to administer escalating electrical shocks to another subject in an experiment on the effects of pain on learning. The victim was a confederate of the experimenter, and the shocks were fake, but almost two-thirds of the subjects prove willing to go all the way to the end of the sequence of shocks, despite the fact that the victim spends much of the time screaming for the experiment to stop, and eventually falls ominously silent, while the label on the shock-generator reads 'Danger: Severe Shock'. See Stanley Milgram, *Obedience to Authority: An Experimental View*, Harper & Row, New York, 1974.

[30]   See Luban, 2003, see above note 25.

[31]   *Ibid.*, p. 281.

[32]   *Ibid.*

[33]   *Ibid.*

---

tion'.[34] Integrity, according to Luban, "does not consist of molding and adapting one's principles to whatever behaviors we and those around us find convenient".[35] Instead, integrity operates in the opposite direction. It "consists of taking the high road, the road of conforming our behavior to our principles".[36] An individual (or as we will see, an institution) is "whole if it is untouched, unsullied", and this excludes those who engage in mere dissonance reduction from meeting the standard for integrity.[37] For Luban, "the person of integrity is not merely the person whose principles and behavior harmonize, regardless of how that harmony gets achieved, but rather the person who has kept her principles intact ('intact' is another word whose Latin root means 'untouched')".[38]

Like Williams and Taylor, Luban acknowledges that his view lacks a substantive requirement for what those principles must be.[39] He considers that genuine integrity might consist "not simply of adherence to principles, but adherence to the right principles, or at any rate to reasonable principles".[40] But the problem, according to Luban, is that it is not always possible for someone to identify the right principles from the inside.[41] He notes that "the ethical value of integrity is experienced from the inside as a kind of harmony or equilibrium between values and actions, whereby one does what one does without departing a nail's breadth from oneself".[42] Yet we are psychologically predisposed to want to "see ourselves as ethically righteous people regardless of the knavery of our calling", and thus we can easily pursue dissonance reduction when we seek genuine integrity.[43] This presents us with, by my lights, another call for substantive integrity requirements.

---

[34] *Ibid.*

[35] *Ibid.*, p. 298

[36] *Ibid.*

[37] *Ibid.*

[38] *Ibid.*

[39] *Ibid.*, p. 299

[40] *Ibid.*; see also Deborah L. Rhode, "If Integrity Is the Answer, What Is the Question?", in *Fordham Law Review*, 2003, vol. 72, pp. 335–36.

[41] Luban, 2003, p. 299, see above note 25.

[42] *Ibid.*, p. 304.

[43] *Ibid.*

7.2.1.1.3. Standing for Something

Cheshire Calhoun understands integrity to refer to relationships with others, as a 'social virtue', rather than oneself. She argues that "the notion of 'standing for something' is central to the meaning of integrity".[44] Calhoun distinguishes 'standing by' one's principles, which one can do alone, from 'standing for' one's principles, which implies membership in a community where there may be conflicting views.[45] The former is "intimately, tied to protecting the boundaries of the self – to protecting it against disintegration, against loss of self-identity, and against pollution by evil".[46] Conversely, Calhoun argues, integrity should be "tightly connected to viewing oneself as a member of an evaluating community and to caring about what that community endorses. That is, it seems to be a social virtue".[47]

Considering integrity to be a social virtue follows, according to Calhoun, from the idea that "acting on one's own best judgment is integral to some common project" or "to a way of comporting ourselves among others".[48] This means we must see integrity as something more than just "a matter of the individual's proper relation to herself", and instead as "a matter of her proper relation to common projects and to the fellows with whom one engages in those common projects".[49] Calhoun argues that seeing "integrity as a social virtue enables us to see persons of integrity as insisting that it is in some important sense for us, for the sake of what ought to be our project or character as a people, to preserve what ought to be the purity of our agency that they stick by their best judgment".[50]

Calhoun claims that individuals with integrity

> treat their own endorsements as ones that matter, or ought to matter, to fellow deliberators. Absent a special sort of story, lying about one's views, concealing them, recanting them under pressure, selling them out for rewards or to avoid penalties, and pandering to what one regards as the bad views of others,

---

[44] Cheshire Calhoun, "Standing for Something", in *The Journal of Philosophy*, 1995, vol. 92, no. 5, p. 253.

[45] *Ibid.*, pp. 253–54.

[46] *Ibid.*, p. 254.

[47] *Ibid.*

[48] *Ibid.*, p. 256.

[49] *Ibid.*, pp. 256–57.

[50] *Ibid.*, p. 257.

---

all indicate a failure to regard one's own judgment as one that should matter to others.[51]

Calhoun's account of integrity speaks to "why we care that persons have the courage of their convictions" when engaged in deliberation with other members of a community.[52] Her view will be particularly appealing when we begin to consider institutional integrity because it speaks to the value of individual integrity for collective decision-making, so we return to Calhoun in Section 7.3.

As I have already noted, there is much to be drawn from each of these accounts that accords with our intuitions about integrity. Yet, these structural conceptions of integrity are insufficient because they would permit immoral individuals, either alone or in immoral communities, to meet the formal requirements for integrity while acting in a morally reprehensible manner. In the sub-section that follows, I offer a complement to the structural views of integrity.

7.2.1.2. Substantive Conceptions of Integrity

The other main intuition we often have about the concept of integrity relates to its substance. It is, however, possible to act with complete structural integrity and yet still act in ways that most would find to be intuitively immoral. Thus, it is necessary, on my view,[53] for there to be substantive constraints on what it means to act with integrity. I now consider two ways of understanding these substantive constraints.

7.2.1.2.1. Virtue

The thought that integrity is a virtue, in the most general sense of the term, is highly intuitive. We commonly think of integrity as "an admirable trait of character and genuine excellence of persons in its own right".[54] Williams challenges this intuition based on his claim that while integrity "is an admirable human property, it is not related to motivation as the virtues are. It is not a disposition which itself yields motivations, as generosity and benevo-

---

[51] *Ibid.*, p. 258.

[52] *Ibid.*, p. 259.

[53] While they do not use the same terminology I use, other views that require two discrete aspects of integrity include those espoused by Lynne McFall, "Integrity", in *Ethics*, 1987, vol. 98, pp. 5–20; and Rhode, 2003, see above note 40.

[54] Greg Scherkoske, "Could Integrity Be an Epistemic Virtue?", in *International Journal of Philosophical Studies*, 2012, vol. 20, no. 2, p. 185.

lence do", nor is it a virtue that is "necessary for that relation to oneself and the world which enables one to act from desirable motives in desirable ways", as courage and self-control do.[55] Because Williams sees acting with integrity as maintaining one's identity-conferring commitments, integrity is not tied to particular sorts of thoughts, as one might think would be required of a virtue.

One compelling way to respond to Williams is to claim that integrity is a virtue, but that it is a 'cluster concept', representing "a cluster of morally praiseworthy attributes including such things as the sincerity and steadfastness with which [an individual's] moral beliefs are held, the struggle [an individual] ha[s] undergone to achieve them, [an individual's] willingness and capacity to question them".[56] Damian Cox, Marguerite LaCaze, and Michael Levine defend such a view, and challenge Williams' view as incomplete without any requirement that an individual maintain second-order moral commitments.[57] They argue that an individual who exemplifies the virtue of integrity finds an Aristotelian mean between excesses of virtues (such as steadfastness where integrity demands change) and vices (such as hypocrisy) that stand to undermine integrity.[58]

Conceiving of integrity as a virtue, as either an intrinsically valuable feature or as a cluster of praiseworthy attributes, is compatible with the structural constraints identified in the previous sub-section, and provides an option for defeating claims of integrity where clearly immoral principles have been upheld.

7.2.1.2.2. Moral Purpose

A more concrete way to undergird the moral substance of integrity is to adopt a view about what sorts of commitments are acceptably defended on a structural account of integrity. Mark Halfon describes an individual of integrity as one who embraces "a moral point of view that urges them to be conceptually clear, logically consistent, apprised of relevant empirical evidence, and careful about acknowledging as well as weighing relevant moral

---

[55] Williams, 1981, "Utilitarianism", p. 49, see above note 13.

[56] Damian Cox, Marguerite LaCaze, and Michael P. Levine, "Should We Strive for Integrity?", in *Journal of Value Inquiry*, 1999, vol. 33, no. 4, p. 521.

[57] *Ibid.*, pp. 521, 523.

[58] Damian Cox, Marguerite LaCaze, and Michael P. Levine, *Integrity and the Fragile Self*, Ashgate Publishing, Aldershot, 2003, p. 49.

considerations".[59] He identifies these constraints as those which ensure that an individual attempts to do 'what is best' rather than just what can be plausibly defended.[60] Persons of integrity impose these restrictions on themselves since they are concerned, not simply with taking any moral position, but with pursuing a commitment to do what is best. Elizabeth Ashford takes this view a step further and defends an account of 'objective integrity'. For Ashford, an attribution of integrity requires that an individual's

> self-conception must be grounded in reality: it must not be based on her being seriously deceived either about empirical facts or about the moral obligations she actually has. In particular, her self-conception as being morally decent must be grounded in her leading a genuinely morally decent life.[61]

This account of integrity tracks what we think is valuable about integrity: the genuine attributes an individual actually possesses. Without the objectivity requirement, according to Ashford, an individual could claim integrity based on her belief that she is leading a worthwhile life, despite her failure to genuinely accomplish this feat.[62]

Given our epistemic position with respect to objective morality, Halfon's emphasis on moral reasoning might be more appealing than Ashford's demand for objective integrity. But his view, as he admits, leaves significant room for justifying 'moral views' that are intuitively immoral. He admits that his account allows for the possibility that a Nazi plotting the genocide of the Jewish people could meet the qualifications for being a person of integrity.[63] Thus Ashford's objective view, despite its practical challenges, is a better option for grounding the substance of a structural account of integrity.

We can now see why the concept of integrity needs both structural and substantive elements. As Morten Bergsmo noted in the concept note for this project,

> at the individual level, it is necessary to ask whether international civil servants and high officials in international courts

---

[59] Mark Halfon, *Integrity: A Philosophical Inquiry*, Temple University Press, Philadelphia, 1989, p. 37.

[60] *Ibid.*

[61] Elizabeth Ashford, "Utilitarianism, Integrity and Partiality", in *Journal of Philosophy*, 2000, vol. 97, p. 4.

[62] *Ibid.*, pp. 424–45.

[63] Halfon 1989, pp. 134–36, see above note 59.

> have a sufficient understanding of what 'integrity' and 'high moral character' refer to. It is problematic if these legal terms are largely seen as slogans or empty shells to which everyone is free to give equally valid content as may be convenient.[64]

If integrity is thought of purely in substantive terms, then the existence of the term is likely superfluous. And if acting with integrity is just acting while possessing 'high moral character', then the quality does little to inform how we should act.

As we will see in the next two sub-sections, prosecutors and judges are expected to possess both 'integrity' and 'high moral character', and therefore it makes sense that the terms should have distinct definitions. Demanding that one act 'virtuously' or 'with objectively good reasons' does not give us *deontic verdicts* – verdicts about which actions are required, optional, or forbidden. Thus, we need the aforementioned structural conception to help shape what an individual should do in order to act with integrity. Further, we will need a normative ethical framework to help us know how to balance competing claims and how to make ethical decisions within the context of a criminal justice system, which we consider in the next two sub-sections.

7.2.2. Prosecutorial Ethics and Individual Integrity

I turn now to the individual ethical constraints on a prosecutor at the ICC and briefly consider the relationship between individual integrity and prosecutorial ethics.[65] In the previous sub-section, I argued that integrity requires moral commitments of a particular substance, and that virtue ethics is insufficient to flesh out that substance. Here, I frame substantive prosecutorial obligations at the ICC in terms of deontological and consequentialist norms. I then identify specific legal rules for ethical conduct that apply to individuals in the OTP.

---

[64] Morten Bergsmo, "Revisiting Integrity in International Justice", FICHL Policy Brief Series No. 93, Torkel Opsahl Academic EPublisher, 2018, p. 3 (https://www.legal-tools.org/doc/e550f7).

[65] For a comprehensive analysis of prosecutorial ethics at the ICC, see Alexander Heinze and Shannon Fyfe, "Prosecutorial Ethics and Preliminary Examinations at the ICC", in Morten Bergsmo and Carsten Stahn (eds.), *Quality Control in Preliminary Examination: Volume 2*, Torkel Opsahl Academic EPublisher, Brussels, 2018 (https://www.legal-tools.org/doc/dff594), in which we call for a more systematic approach to ethics in international criminal justice.

7.2.2.1. Normative Ethics

A prosecutor's individual ethical obligations toward her role in the criminal justice system can be thought of in terms of deontological norms and consequentialist norms. Deontological norms identify actions as obligatory, prohibited, or permitted (deontic verdicts) based on the intrinsic nature of the actions and regardless of the outcomes they produce. Kant argues that one should: "[a]ct so that you use humanity, as much in your own person as in the person of every other, always at the same time as end and never merely as means".[66] A prosecutor "who is focused on deontological norms will be concerned with the way choices are made, defendants' rights are respected, and trials are conducted, independent of the end-states the trials produce".[67]

Luban argues for a view of integrity for lawyers that appears to align individual integrity with deontological norms. He claims that a lawyer's objective should always be to protect the human dignity of the client. Thus, prosecutors must make choices with the aim of treating individuals as subjects of their experience and their testimony, and as individuals, rather than as entities that can be "entirely subsumed into larger communities" if doing so serves some desirable end-state.[68] Human dignity, according to Luban, requires that individuals not be treated "as an instrument of [their] own condemnation".[69] In order to uphold this standard of human dignity, prosecutors must never humiliate victims or defendants, or treat them as mere resources to be used in furtherance of a particular outcome.[70]

Yet, a prosecutor who is solely focused on the intrinsic nature of her actions may not consider necessary strategic aspects of a trial, and this could lead to consistent failures to achieve substantive results, and ultimately the downfall of the criminal justice institution altogether. Enter consequentialist norms, which identify right actions (deontic verdicts) based solely on the outcomes they produce. So, a prosecutor who aims to reach the "the correct substantive outcome in every case, and considers this to be

---

[66] Immanuel Kant, Allen W. Wood (ed. and trans.), *Groundwork for the Metaphysics of Morals*, Yale University Press, New Haven, CT, 2002, G4:429.

[67] Heinze and Fyfe, 2018, p. 10, see above note 65.

[68] David Luban, *Legal Ethics and Human Dignity*, Cambridge University Press, New York, 2007, p. 88.

[69] *Ibid.*

[70] *Ibid.*

the standard of what constitutes a fair trial, adopts a purely consequentialist view of her ethical obligations".[71]

However, a prosecutor could also justify dishonest behaviour or offensive treatment of defendants, in pursuit of a desired conviction, if she adopts purely consequentialist norms as her normative ethical framework. We could imagine an OTP in which the individual lawyers engage in insidious group-think, justifying actions that violate deontological norms. If the individuals know that horrific events like genocide or crimes against humanity have occurred, and that there is a lot of evidence for them, this could lead to the adversarial commitment to making *someone* pay for the crimes against the victims, regardless of an individual defendant's actual guilt. The individual members of the OTP must keep the power of the situation in mind, and not allow it to result in a deterministic or fully consequentialist view of prosecution.

Thus, I argue that prosecutors are obligated to take into account both deontological and consequentialist norms when making decisions. Individual integrity for prosecutors requires reflection on substantive moral values, and deontological and consequentialist norms, but also an awareness of the human tendency to justify behaviour that should not be justified in order to avoid cognitive dissonance. Individual integrity requires one to keep one's guiding principles intact, but not by justifying immoral decisions. Deontological constraints (and the corresponding demands of individual integrity) will therefore always apply, as a prosecutor is never permitted to engage in deception in order to obtain a conviction. Yet sometimes a prosecutor, and the ICC Prosecutor in particular, may also be obligated to take into account the end-states that are reasonably expected to be produced by her decisions.

We now have two sources informing the decision-making of individuals who work at the OTP, which are the structural and substantive requirements of integrity, and consequentialist and deontological considerations. One might think that the wealth of 'obligations' will paralyse actors in a legal justice system, as it might be argued that there are too many considerations informing any given decision. I would counter that if the aim of ethics is to issue deontic verdicts, we must have specific considerations in order to obtain those verdicts. Again, a broad appeal to morality or integrity in general terms will not suffice. While there will still be conflicts and epistemic challenges in obtaining deontic verdicts at times, we should seek to

---

[71] Heinze and Fyfe, 2018, p. 9, see above note 65.

include as much guidance as possible for individuals working in a legal justice system.

7.2.2.2. Legal Ethics Rules

I now add the legal ethics rules as the final piece of our normative framework. There are two main texts from which we can draw these requirements as they pertain to individuals: the ICC Statute and the OTP Code of Conduct.[72]

7.2.2.2.1. ICC Statute

The ICC Statute contains specific ethical requirements for individuals working in the OTP in several sections of the Statute. Article 42(3) notes that the "Prosecutor and the Deputy Prosecutors shall be persons of high moral character".[73] Article 45 requires that the Prosecutor and the Deputy Prosecutors must "make a solemn undertaking in open court to exercise his or her respective functions impartially and conscientiously" before beginning their duties.[74] The Court maintains a high level of internal independence, and thus there is also a rule that no OTP member[75] shall "seek or act on instructions from any *external* source".[76] This reaffirms that the OTP shall exercise its authority on its own behalf, and should not succumb to external pressure from governments, international organizations, NGOs or individuals.[77]

---

[72] Again, this is a brief overview of these sources of legal ethical rules. For a more comprehensive treatment, please refer to Heinze and Fyfe, 2018, see above note 65.

[73] Rome Statute of the International Criminal Court, adopted 17 July 1998, entry into force 1 July 2002, Article 42(3) ('ICC Statute') (http://www.legal-tools.org/doc/7b9af9/).

[74] *Ibid.*, Article 45.

[75] This provision applies to the Prosecutor, the Deputy Prosecutors, staff and gratis personal; see William A. Schabas, *The International Criminal Court: A Commentary on the Rome Statute*, second edition, Oxford University Press, 2016, p. 740.

[76] ICC Statute, Article 42(1) clause 3, see above note 73. Cf. also Yvonne McDermott, "Article 42", in Mark Klamberg, *Commentary on the Law of the International Criminal Court*, Torkel Opsahl Academic EPublisher, Brussels, 2017, para. 1 (https://www.legal-tools.org/doc/aa0e2b/).

[77] ICC, Situation in the Democratic Republic of the Congo, Pre-Trial Chamber, Prosecution's Reply on the Applications for Participation 01/04-1/dp to 01/04-6/dp, 15 August 2005, ICC-01/04-84, para. 32 (http://www.legal-tools.org/doc/4aa811/); see also ICC, Staff Rules of the International Criminal Court, adopted 21 April 2005, entry into force 3 December 2005, Rule 101.3(a) (http://www.legal-tools.org/doc/10f5c7/) ("Staff members shall ensure their independence from any person, entity or authority outside the Court.").

As for the OTP's external independence, the Prosecutor and Deputy Prosecutors must not engage in any activity that is likely to interfere with their prosecutorial functions or affect confidence in their independence.[78] This requirement is deontological, in that it requires that members of the OTP hold themselves to a high standard and refuse to permit others to bias their decisions. Yet, it also reflects a consequentialist concern about the likely result – unfairness – of permitting such biases to influence the individuals who work at the OTP.

7.2.2.2.2. OTP Code of Conduct

The ICC also has Codes of Conduct that ensure the compliance of lawyers with ethical rules and values. Rule 9 of the ICC Rules of Procedure and Evidence provides that the Prosecutor is responsible for governing "the operation of the office", including whether or not the OTP would have a code of conduct and regulations.[79] The OTP finally published regulations on 23 April 2009, and on 5 September 2013, the OTP Code was adopted to regulate the ethical conduct of the individuals working at the OTP.[80] Prior to 2013, there was no set of ethical standards "specifically regulat[ing] the conduct of members of the OTP".[81] Many of the rules and regulations listed in the following sub-sections, which were in place prior to the adoption of the OTP Code, were "general in scope and not tailored to apply to the specific role that the OTP plays at the ICC and the specific obligations and duties which that role entails".[82]

The OTP Code includes many general deontological constraints on the conduct of the OTP, and virtues that relate to individual integrity, which are also applied to other counsel acting before the ICC, such as those relat-

---

[78] ICC Statute, Article 42(5), see above note 73.

[79] See Theresa Roosevelt, "Ethics for the Ethical: A Code of Conduct for the International Criminal Court Office of the Prosecutor", in *Georgetown Journal of Legal Ethics*, 2011, vol. 24, no. 1, p. 840.

[80] See Alexander Heinze, *International Criminal Procedure and Disclosure*, Duncker & Humblot, Berlin, 2014, pp. 454 ff.

[81] Lawrence Pacewicz, "Introductory Note to International Criminal Court Code of Conduct for the Office of the Prosecutor", in *International Legal Materials*, 2014, vol. 53, no. 2, p. 397. For a thorough overview by a former insider, see Salim A. Nakhjavani, "The Origins and Development of the Code of Conduct", in Morten Bergsmo, Klaus Rackwitz and SONG Tianying (eds.), *Historical Origins of International Criminal Law: Volume 5*, Torkel Opsahl Academic EPublisher, Brussels, 2017, pp. 951–1006 (https://www.toaep.org/ps-pdf/24-bergsmo-rackwitz-song).

[82] *Ibid.*

ed to faithfulness, conscientiousness, impartiality, independence, confidentiality, and conflicts of interest.[83] The OTP Code contains other deontological constraints on or demands for individual integrity in the effective investigation and prosecution practices of the OTP, including the requirements to "act with competence and diligence, make impartial judgments based on the evidence and consider foremost the interests of justice in determining whether or not to proceed" and to "fully respect the rights of persons under investigation and the accused and ensure that proceedings are conducted in a fair manner".[84]

Arguably, these rules do not add anything substantive to our normative framework, but they do provide concrete legal obligations for prosecutors that align with the framework. Now that we have filled in the relevant aspects of the framework for individual integrity at the OTP, we can turn to individual integrity for judges.

7.2.3. Judicial Ethics and Individual Integrity

In this section, I refrain from reiterating the entire normative framework from the previous sub-section. Instead, I identify notable differences between prosecutorial ethical obligations and judicial ethical obligations in terms of the different sorts of decisions that must be made by prosecutors and judges. I then identify the specific legal rules for ethical conduct that apply to individual judges.

7.2.3.1. Normative Ethics

A judge's individual ethical obligations toward her role in the criminal justice system can also be thought of in terms of deontological norms and consequentialist norms. A judge focused on deontological norms will, like her prosecutor counterpart, be concerned with the way decisions are made, defendants' rights are respected, and trials are conducted, independent of the end-states produced by the trials. A judge who is focused on consequentialist norms may utilize her discretion or read the evidence in a particular way that veers a case toward a particular outcome, which may or may not be warranted (or permissible) depending on the circumstances. Although Luban's account of integrity is aimed at lawyers who represent clients ra-

---

[83] ICC, "OTP Code", in *Code of Conduct for the Office of the Prosecutor*, 5 September 2013, chap. 2 (http://www.legal-tools.org/doc/3e11eb/).

[84] *Ibid.*, chap. 3, sect. 2.

ther than at judges,[85] a judge who acts with integrity should also treat everyone who comes before her with dignity, and avoid acting in ways that humiliate victims, defendants, or their representation.

Like prosecutors, judges are obligated to take into account both deontological and consequentialist norms when making decisions. Individual integrity for judges requires reflection on substantive moral values, and deontological and consequentialist norms. Deontological constraints (and the corresponding demands of individual integrity) will therefore always apply, but sometimes a judge may also be obligated to take into account the end-states that are reasonably expected to be produced by her decisions, both in judgments and in the courtroom.

We now have established the two sources informing the decision-making of judges, which are the same as those informing prosecutors: the structural and substantive requirements of integrity, and consequentialist and deontological considerations.

7.2.3.2. Legal Ethical Rules

Here, I add the legal ethics rules as the final piece of our normative framework for judges. There are two main texts from which we can draw these requirements as they pertain to individual judges: the ICC Statute and the Judicial Code of Conduct.[86]

7.2.3.2.1. ICC Statute

The ICC Statute contains specific ethical requirements for individual judges at the ICC in several sections of the Statute. Article 36(3)(a) notes that "judges shall be chosen from among persons of high moral character, impartiality and integrity who possess the qualifications required in their respective States for appointment to the highest judicial offices".[87]

Judges are required to be independent in the performance of their judicial functions, as outlined in Article 40, which further explains that judges "shall not engage in any activity which is likely to interfere with their judicial functions or to affect confidence in their independence", and that they are not permitted to have any other professional occupation during

---

[85]   See Luban, 2007, see above note 68.

[86]   This is also a brief overview of the sources of legal ethical rules for judges.

[87]   ICC Statute, Article 36(3)(a), see above note 73.

their tenure on the Court.[88] If there are concerns about a judge's impartiality with respect to a given case, he or she will be disqualified from the case pursuant to the procedure outlined under Article 41.[89] Article 45 requires that judges must "make a solemn undertaking in open court to exercise his or her respective functions impartially and conscientiously" before beginning their duties.[90]

7.2.3.2.2. Judicial Code of Conduct

The Code of Judicial Ethics ('Judicial Code') has been adopted to further regulate the ethical obligations of judges at the ICC. The Judicial Code, like the OTP Code, includes many general deontological constraints on the conduct of judges, and virtues that relate to individual integrity, such as those related to impartiality, independence, diligence, proper conduct, and confidentiality.[91] The Judicial Code contains other deontological constraints on or demands for individual integrity to ensure the "legitimacy and effectiveness of the international judicial process", including requirements to "avoid any conflict of interest, or being placed in a situation which might reasonably be perceived as giving rise to a conflict of interest",[92] and to "conduct themselves with probity and integrity in accordance with their office, thereby enhancing public confidence in the judiciary".[93]

In this section, I constructed a multi-level normative framework for understanding the ethical obligations for individual prosecutors and judges at the ICC. I generated the normative framework by working through the meaning of individual integrity as a substantive and structural concept, identifying both deontological and consequentialist constraints that inform prosecutorial and judicial decision-making, and laying out the legal rules that govern the ethical obligations of prosecutors and judges. When tasked with making decisions as individuals, each level of the framework should feature in ensuring that individuals at the ICC act with integrity. We will turn now to understanding institutional integrity at the ICC.

---

[88] *Ibid.*, Article 40.

[89] *Ibid.*, Article 41.

[90] *Ibid.*, Article 45.

[91] See ICC, *Code of Judicial Ethics*, 9 March 2005, ICC-BD/02-01-05 (https://www.legal-tools.org/doc/383f8f).

[92] *Ibid.*, Article 4.

[93] *Ibid.*, Article 5.

7.3. Institutional Integrity

7.3.1. Integrity for Institutional Actors

One way to think about the integrity (or any other characteristic) of institutional actors is to think of institutions as possessing an aggregation of the individuals which make up the organization. If there is nothing (or little) more to, say, a corporate board of directors than the individuals who sit on the board, then we can reduce the concept of the board of directors to these individuals, with no remainder. On an individualist account of an organization, individuals "are not, when brought together, converted into another kind of substance",[94] but they remain individuals. So in a sense, a reference to the integrity of the board of directors would merely refer to the aggregation of the individual integrity of each director.

However, it is incoherent to think of most organizations in this limited manner. An organization of persons that constitutes a group or institution must engage in collective decision-making, and the outputs of that organization are *collective* decisions, to some extent. It may be that one individual represents an organization and has the final decision-making power, or it may be that there is a collective decision-making procedure that results in a 'judgment' or decision on behalf of an organization. Regardless, while the individual integrity of the members of an organization may be necessary for institutional integrity, it is not sufficient.

Another feature of institutional integrity that arguably distinguishes institutional integrity from individual integrity is the impact on the legitimacy of the entity. Although there are some views of individual integrity that claim individuals who do not act with integrity do not act as agents at all,[95] this view is much too radical, by my lights. Individuals who fail to act with integrity may not be trusted or taken seriously by their friends and colleagues, but they will go on existing despite their lack of integrity. Institutions, on the other hand, may collapse without integrity. It may be that the institution becomes illegitimate because it lacks integrity, if integrity is a crucial feature of the institution's identity or mandate, and it may cease to function. Or it may be that the perception of the institution as illegitimate causes the institution to collapse due to lack of support from external actors. In either case, the loss of integrity may prove fatal to an institution.

---

[94] John Stuart Mill, *A System of Logic*, book VI, chap. 7, §1.

[95] See Christine M. Korsgaard, *Self-Constitution: Agency, Identity, and Integrity*, Oxford University Press, Oxford, 2009.

7.3.1.1. Substantive Integrity of Institutional Actors

I begin in this section with the intuition we often have that the concept of integrity relates to its substance, because it involves a fairly straightforward set of moves from individual integrity to institutional integrity. It is, however, possible to act with complete structural integrity and yet still act in ways that most would find to be intuitively immoral. On my view, it cannot be the case that an institution aimed at something intuitively immoral can act with substantive integrity, and thus there must be substantive constraints on what it means to act with institutional integrity.

As noted above, the individual integrity of the members of an organization is likely a necessary feature of an organization with institutional integrity. Certainly, an institutional actor must operate with a commitment to some moral principles, whether those moral principles are explicitly outlined in the governing documentation of the organization, or they are accidentally maintained by the individuals who make up the body of the organization. While an organization likely cannot maintain structural institutional integrity by accident, it seems possible that the moral content underpinning the structural integrity could come about by accident. This is because not all organizations will have explicit statements about their moral principles and values, but they will nearly always have explicit statements regarding the aims, purposes, and general structure of the organization. An institution will fail to meet a test for institutional integrity, regardless of structural integrity in terms of cohesion or integration, if it operates pursuant to a clearly repugnant moral commitment (such as the promotion of genocide). Conversely, the substantive integrity requirement for an institutional actor may be met by encouraging individuals who make up the organization to act virtuously (in a broad sense), or it may be met by explicitly outlining the virtues that are crucial to the aims of the institution, or it may be met by constructing a set of procedures to ensure that institutional decision-making is based on 'objectively good reasons' or an 'objective moral purpose'.

7.3.1.2. Structural Integrity of Institutional Actors

The structural integrity of institutional actors, like individual actors, can be understood as a formal relation an institution has to itself, between parts of itself (sub-institutions or individuals), or with other institutions. As with individual structural integrity, I do not find it necessary to adopt one view to the exclusion of others. Each of the following conceptions can contribute to an understanding of institutional decision-making with integrity.

7.3.1.2.1. Identity and Commitments

Recall that Williams' view of integrity is based on 'identity-conferring commitments', which are "the condition[s] of my existence, in the sense that unless I am propelled forward by the conatus of desire, project and interest, it is unclear why I should go on at all".[96] If an individual abandons such a commitment, according to Williams, then the individual begins to lose what gives their life its moral identity. From an institutional perspective, it is coherent to think of organizations coming into existence for reasons, in order to achieve a discrete purpose or further a particular project. Even more so than with individuals, an institution that abandons an identity-conferring commitment may lose what gives the institution its identity. This may, in turn, cause the institution to lose legitimacy or collapse altogether. Depending on the type of organization or institution, it may be able to reorganize itself under different 'conditions of existence'. But for purposes of this chapter, the institutions in question are unlikely to survive a significant change to their identity-conferring commitments.

7.3.1.2.2. Wholeness and Integration

On a related view, integrity is understood in terms of wholeness and integration. Taylor's account of integrity ascribes the trait to one who 'keeps his self intact', which means an individual "will not ignore relevant evidence, he will be consistent in his behaviour, he will not act on reasons which, given the circumstances, are insufficient reasons for action".[97] Her view also requires that an individual have the right relationship with the past.[98] An institution can be understood through this lens as well. Assuming that the institution was created with a sense of what it is meant to do, or it grows to develop such a sense, an institution can act rationally to maintain this sense of institutional self, and can discourage conflict or disintegration between sub-institutions and/or individuals who make up the institution. Luban's view of genuine integrity maps onto institutions as well. Like an individual, an institution can be thought of as having structural integrity if

---

[96] Williams, 1981, "Persons", p. 12, see above note 9.
[97] Taylor, 1981, p. 148, see above note 14.
[98] *Ibid.*, p. 149.

it is "untouched, unsullied".[99] An institution with integrity keeps its principles intact.[100]

7.3.1.2.3.   Standing for Something

Calhoun's understanding of integrity as 'standing for something' is useful on two levels. On the institutional level, the social virtue of integrity can refer to an institution's decision to stand up for itself and its principles in the face of conflicting views from external institutions or individuals. But Calhoun's view can also be used to understand how individual components of the institution engage in collective decision-making. If the institution has a common project, individuals are tasked with "acting on one's own best judgment" while engaging in debate with other individuals within the institution.[101] As noted earlier, Calhoun's account of integrity speaks to "why we care that persons have the courage of their convictions" when engaged in deliberation with other members of a community.[102]

7.3.1.3. Structural Integrity of Institutional Judicial Actors

It is worth adding an additional normative sub-section addressing the structural integrity of institutional judicial actors in particular, due to their individual or collective power within a criminal justice system. It has been argued that the output of a judicial body ought to reflect a particular kind of integrity in the structural sense of the term. I will look at two sources of this argument: Dworkin's philosophical argument that we should understand law as integrity, and the Australian legal principle of 'institutional integrity'.

7.3.1.3.1.   Law as Integrity (Dworkin)

In *Law's Empire*, Ronald Dworkin gives us a model of adjudication known as 'law as integrity'.[103] This view secures a "kind of equality among citizens that makes their community more genuine and improves its moral justification for exercising the political power it does".[104] It does this because it sees that rights and responsibilities of individuals "flow from past deci-

---

[99]   See Luban, 2003, p. 298, see above note 25.

[100] *Ibid.*

[101] Calhoun, 1995, p. 256, see above note 44.

[102] *Ibid.*, p. 259.

[103] See Ronald Dworkin, *Law's Empire*, Harvard University Press, Cambridge, 1986.

[104] *Ibid.*, p. 96.

sions" and thus "count as legal, not just when they are explicit in these decisions but also when they follow from the principles of personal and political morality the explicit decisions presuppose by way of justification".[105] Individuals are entitled to this extension of past decisions, "even when judges profoundly disagree about what this means".[106]

Judges, then, are required to "identify legal rights and duties, so far as possible, on the assumption that they were all created by a single author – the community personified – expressing a coherent conception of justice and fairness".[107] Dworkin uses the analogy of a chain novel to describe this process of adjudication, and he sets up a scenario in which a group of novelists seeks to write a novel together.[108] Each novelist is tasked with interpreting the chapters that have been written previously before writing a new chapter.[109] Dworkin depicts how each novelist "has the job of writing his chapter so as to make the novel being constructed the best it can be, and the complexity of this task models the complexity of deciding a hard case under law as integrity".[110] The novelists, according to Dworkin, "aim jointly to create, so far as they can, a single unified novel that is the best it can be".[111] A judge, similarly, must try to create a single, unified story about the law, and this means that

> the actual political history of his community will sometimes check his other political convictions in his overall interpretive judgment. If he does not – if his threshold of fit is wholly derivative from and adjustable to his convictions of justice, so that the latter automatically provide an eligible interpretation – then he cannot claim in good faith to be interpreting his legal practice at all.[112]

---

[105] *Ibid.*

[106] *Ibid.*, p. 134.

[107] *Ibid.*, p. 225.

[108] *Ibid.*, p. 229.

[109] *Ibid.*

[110] *Ibid.*

[111] *Ibid.*

[112] *Ibid.*, p. 255.

7.3.1.3.2. Institutional Integrity (Australia)

In Australia, there is a constitutional principle known as the *institutional integrity principle* or the *Kable doctrine*.[113] This principle developed out of a 1996 case in which a majority of the High Court found that a function furnished by the Community Protection Act 1994 to the Supreme Court of New South Wales was invalid because it was incompatible with the institutional integrity of the Australian judiciary.[114] In *Kable*, the High Court's assessment was based upon "the effect of the impugned legislation on the capacity of the institution to be a fit repository for Commonwealth jurisdiction".[115] The High Court's majority opinion notes that "the underlying concern was to maintain public confidence in the independence of State courts".[116] While the details of this doctrine are not particularly relevant for the purposes of this chapter, it is worth briefly noting that Australia maintains a constitutional principle that allows courts to overturn legislation in order to maintain the integrity (in the sense of integration or wholeness) of a judicial institution.

As with individual integrity, institutional integrity requires both structural and substantive components in order to obtain. There are arguably several ways of meeting the substantive requirements, through individual moral commitments or through explicit institutional moral commitments, but structural integrity may be harder to obtain due to the multilevel demands for integration, commitment to identity, and/or taking a principled stand. In the next sub-section, we will consider what the normative framework for institutional integrity looks like for the OTP, judges, and the ICC as a whole.

7.3.2. Integrity of the OTP

The next step is to think about institutional integrity of the OTP, which involves the integrity of the individuals who make up the OTP, in light of the

---

[113] See Chris Steytler and Iain Field, "The Institutional Integrity Principle: Where are We Now, and Where are We Headed", in *University of Western Australia Law Review*, 2011, vol. 35, pp. 227–264.

[114] *Ibid.*, p. 229; see also High Court of Australia, *Kable v. Director of Public Prosecutions (NSW)*, 12 September 1996, 189 CLR 51.

[115] Steytler and Field, 2011, p. 229, see above note 113; see also High Court of Australia, *Gypsy Jokers Motorcycle Club Inc v. Commissioner of Police*, 2007, 33 WAR 245, p. 268.

[116] Peter Johnston and Rohan Hardcastle, "State Courts: The Limits of Kable", in *Sydney Law Review*, 1998, vol. 20, p. 220; see also *Kable*, 1996, p. 98, see above note 114.

culture of integrity that is promoted by the leadership. While this goes beyond individual integrity, especially with respect to collective decision-making, it is still cashed out, in some ways, in terms of the virtues and ethical considerations that are adopted by and reflected in the individual actions of the OTP. Additionally, the OTP is structured with the Prosecutor at the top, thus she is in a position to individually overrule any decisions that are made 'collectively'.

The deontological and consequentialist considerations are the same whether we think about the OTP as the Prosecutor or as an institution presided over by the Prosecutor and made up of deputy prosecutors and staff. Thus, I do not rehash the normative ethical framework presented in Section 7.2.2.1. I also will not reiterate the specific rules outlining individual ethical obligations in Section 7.2.2.2., but I briefly identify some ethical rules that could be seen as applying to the OTP as an institution rather than as represented by an individual. This will also include a short discussion of the OTP strategy and policy papers.

7.3.2.1. ICC Statute

The ICC Statute contains specific ethical requirements for the OTP as an institution in several sections of the Statute. Article 44 provides for the appointment of staff, including the requirement that the OTP "shall ensure the highest standards of efficiency, competency and integrity" in its employment of staff.[117] Article 54(1) relates to the investigations phase and requires that the Prosecutor "investigate incriminating and exonerating circumstances equally",[118] take measures to "respect the interests and personal circumstances of victims and witnesses, including age, gender as defined in Article 7, paragraph 3, and health, and take into account the nature of the crime, in particular where it involves sexual violence, gender violence or violence against children" in the investigations,[119] and "[f]ully respect the rights of persons arising under this Statute".[120] The obligations under Article 54(1) are deontological, where they correspond to specific procedural requirements or the rights of individuals, and they also reflect the demands of individual integrity regarding respect for the dignity of all persons. Yet the OTP is also obligated to consider the results of the Prosecutor's discre-

---

[117] ICC Statute, Article 44(2), see above note 73.
[118] *Ibid.*, Article 54(1)(a).
[119] *Ibid.*, Article 54(1)(b).
[120] *Ibid.*, Article 54(1)(c).

tionary choices when balancing deontological obligations to defendants with deontological obligations to victims and witnesses.

There are other ethical obligations that the OTP incurs indirectly, such as those from sections of the ICC Statute that grant rights on other parties. Article 55, for instance, provides for specific rights on the part of persons during an investigation. These rights create corresponding deontological obligations on the part of the OTP, such as the obligation that the OTP not subject an individual "to arbitrary arrest or detention", nor deprive an individual "of his or her liberty except on such grounds and in accordance with such procedures as are established in this Statute".[121]

7.3.2.2. OTP Code of Conduct

The OTP Code is largely directed at the conduct of individuals, but it includes several features that are applicable to the OTP as an institution. Chapter 3 outlines the duties of the OTP as they pertain to the OTP's duty to objectively seek the truth under Article 54(1)(a) of the ICC Statute, the OTP's obligation to ensure effective investigation and prosecution under Article 54(1)(b) of the ICC Statute, rules for disclosing and handling information and evidence, and the obligation to ensure security for anyone who interacts with the OTP.[122] Chapter 4, which addresses working relations within the OTP, with other sub-institutions within the Court, and with other individuals, includes both individual and institutional requirements for integrity. While these constraints are largely deontological, they can also be seen as consequentialist in that they attempt to protect individuals and the OTP from negative outcomes and ensure ongoing co-operation between sub-institutions and between individuals.

7.3.2.3. Strategy and Policy Papers

The OTP has also adopted strategy papers, which clarify the OTP's strategic objectives for a time period of three to four years, as well as policy papers, which address particular fundamental issues on which the OTP seeks to provide more clarity and transparency. Regulation 14 of the Regulations of the OTP requires that the OTP make public its strategy and make use of policy papers that reflect the key principles and criteria of this strategy.[123]

---

[121] *Ibid.*, Article 55(1)(d).

[122] OTP Code, chap. 3., see above note 83.

[123] This corresponds to No. 17 of the UN Guidelines on the Role of Prosecutors ("In countries where prosecutors are vested with discretionary functions, the law or published rules or reg-

The practice involves a broad ethical obligation on the part of the OTP, which could be considered deontological, in that the duty might be seen as reflective of an obligation to be transparent with the international community, the general public, and all possible defendants that could come before the ICC. Such a commitment to transparency can also be seen as consequentialist, as one of its aims might be to support the appearance of the legitimacy of the OTP and the Court as a whole.[124]

7.3.3. Integrity of the Judiciary

Turning to the judiciary at the ICC, we can begin by thinking about its institutional integrity in terms of the integrity of the individuals who serve as judges, in light of the culture of integrity that exists in Chambers. The institutional integrity will be, again, cashed out in some ways in terms of the virtues and ethical considerations that are adopted by and reflected in the individual actions of judges. Yet, collective decision-making will play a much greater role in judicial settings than it does in the OTP. The institutional integrity of the judiciary will involve more than just the aggregation of the integrity of individual judges. Namely, it will require something akin to Dworkin's adjudicative theory of law as integrity. It is also worth noting that there is a difference between the judges who sign on to a majority opinion, which represents the decision of the judiciary as an institution, and those who sign on to a dissenting opinion, who arguably maintain their status as individual judges since they do not represent the institution.

The deontological and consequentialist considerations considered in Sections 7.2.1. and 7.2.3.1. are largely the same whether we think about judges as individuals or as institutions engaged in collective decision-making, and the individual ethical rules are contained in Section 7.2.3.2. So, I turn directly to identifying ethical rules that could be seen as applying to the judiciary as an institution rather than as individual judges.

---

ulations shall provide guidelines to enhance fairness and consistency of approach in taking decisions in the prosecution process, including institution or waiver of prosecution."). An example is ICC-OTP, *OTP Report on Preliminary Examination Activities 2013*, 25 November 2013 (http://www.legal-tools.org/doc/dbf75e/), which sets out the principles and criteria of preliminary examinations (paras. 1 *et seq.*) and aims to promote transparency (para. 15).

[124] Stahn appears to view transparency (including publicity) as involving consequentialist considerations, when he points out: "Publicity is in line with the public nature of criminal proceedings. It may facilitate the alert effect and strengthen prevention". Carsten Stahn, "Damned If You Do, Damned If You Don't: Challenges and Critiques of Preliminary Examinations at the ICC", in *Journal of International Criminal Justice*, 2017, vol. 15, no. 3, p. 18.

7.3.3.1. ICC Statute

The ICC Statute contains specific ethical requirements for the judiciary as an institution in several sections of the Statute. Articles 60 and 61 require that the Pre-Trial Chamber ensure procedural protections for defendants.[125] In Article 64, the Trial Chamber is called to "ensure that a trial is fair and expeditious and is conducted with full respect for the rights of the accused and due regard for the protection of victims and witnesses".[126] Article 68 provides for the protection of victims and witnesses who participate in the court proceedings, and some of the protections are to be ensured by the judiciary.[127] The discretionary aspects of evidence admissibility are outlined in Article 69, which establishes several specific obligations on the part of the judiciary.[128] Article 74 outlines the requirements for judges in making a decision on a case,[129] while Articles 76 and 78 outline the requirements for judges in handing down a sentence following a conviction.[130] In the event of an appeal, Articles 83 and 84 outline the obligations of judges who make up the Appeals Chamber.[131]

7.3.4. Integrity of the Court and International Criminal Law

A further move we can make at this point is from the integrity of sub-institutions like the OTP and the judiciary to the institutional integrity of the ICC as a whole. This cannot be separated from the individual integrity of those who work at the institution, nor can it be separated from the integrity of institutions like the OTP and the judiciary. The institutional integrity of the ICC is fragile, as the failure of any individual or sub-institution could threaten the integrity of the ICC as a whole. One of the consequentialist considerations that individuals and sub-institutions must take into account, therefore, is whether or not a given individual or collective decision is likely to threaten the continued existence of the institution of the ICC – which would also threaten the greater institution of international criminal law.

---

[125] ICC Statute, Articles 60, 61, see above note 73.
[126] *Ibid.*, Article 64.
[127] *Ibid.*, Article 68.
[128] *Ibid.*, Article 69.
[129] *Ibid.*, Article 74.
[130] *Ibid.*, Articles 76, 78.
[131] *Ibid.*, Articles 83, 84.

It is here that we can see the need for a robust normative ethical framework to guide individuals and institutions and offer assistance in reaching deontic verdicts. For these decisions require more than broad statements about virtue. How could a commitment to 'act courageously' help an individual decide whether or not to take a particular action? This actually requires an individual or collective to make a prediction about the future, which in turn requires courage, both structural and substantive integrity, balancing ethical considerations, and also an understanding of the institution as a whole. The accounts that we have from Taylor and Luban of integrity as wholeness are particularly salient here, applied to both the individual and the institution, in terms of demanding decisions that are unlikely to threaten the continued existence of the institution. If the institution is to remain, it must also remain focused on identity-conferring commitments (in the vein of Williams), such as those listed in the Preamble to the ICC Statute, including the idea that "the most serious crimes of concern to the international community as a whole must not go unpunished and that their effective prosecution must be ensured by taking measures at the national level and by enhancing international cooperation",[132] the determination to "put an end to impunity for the perpetrators of these crimes and thus to contribute to the prevention of such crimes",[133] and the resolution to "guarantee lasting respect for and the enforcement of international justice".[134]

Now that I have examined the complete normative ethical framework for both individual and institutional integrity at the ICC, I consider what the framework implies about the *Bemba* case introduced at the beginning of the chapter.

7.4. Case Study: The *Bemba* Acquittal

My aim in this final section is to reveal the challenges inherent in a more complex assessment of individual or institutional integrity, despite the existence of a comprehensive normative ethical framework. I do not intend to offer a meticulous analysis of the *Bemba* judgement at the trial level or either opinion issued by the Appeals Chamber. Rather, I sketch out the fea-

---

[132] *Ibid.*, Preamble.
[133] *Ibid.*
[134] *Ibid.*

tures of the appeal that bear directly on issues of individual and institutional integrity at the ICC.

7.4.1. *Bemba* Judgment and Appeal

As noted at the beginning of this chapter, the Appeals Chamber of the ICC acquitted Bemba of the charges of war crimes and crimes against humanity in June 2018, overturning the decision of Trial Chamber III to convict the defendant. The majority adopted the standard of review on appeal that the Appeals Chamber must overturn factual findings of the Trial Chamber if they can reasonably be called into doubt.[135] The opinion of the majority of the Appeals Chamber focused on two grounds of Bemba's appeal: first, that the conviction exceeded the charges, and second, that Bemba was not liable as a superior.[136]

7.4.1.1. Standard of Review – Dissenting Opinion

In the dissenting opinion, the judges challenged the majority's view that that Appeals Chamber must overturn factual findings of the Trial Chamber if they can reasonably be called into doubt.[137] They viewed the adoption of this standard as a significant and unexplained departure from the conventional standard of review for factual errors applied to date by the Appeals Chamber, as well as of all other international and internationalised courts and tribunals.[138] The dissenting opinion states that it is not sufficient that there are "serious doubts" about a factual finding entered by the Trial Chamber.[139] In case of doubt, they argued that the Appeals Chamber should review the evidence supporting the factual findings in question to itself determine the issue or to remand the matter to a trial chamber for that purpose.[140] The dissenting judges would have applied the conventional standard of appeal in assessing Bemba's grounds of appeal, which accords some deference to the Trial Chamber's findings of fact, and they considered that

---

[135] Judgment, para. 35 *et seq.*, see above note 1.

[136] See *ibid.*

[137] ICC, Situation in the Central African Republic, *Prosecutor v. Jean-Pierre Bemba Gombo*, Appeals Chamber, Dissenting Opinion of Judge Sanji Mmasenono Monageng and Judge Piotr Hofmański to the Judgment on the appeal of Mr Jean-Pierre Bemba Gombo against Trial Chamber III's "Judgment pursuant to Article 74 of the Statute", 8 June 2018, ICC-01/05-01/08-3636 ('Dissenting Opinion') (https://www.legal-tools.org/doc/dc2518).

[138] *Ibid.*, paras. 2–18.

[139] *Ibid.*, para. 10.

[140] *Ibid.*, para. 92.

this modified standard of review has led the majority of the Appeals Chamber to an erroneous conclusion.[141]

7.4.1.2. Second Ground of Appeal – Majority Opinion

On the second ground of appeal, the majority of the Appeals Chamber noted that the Prosecutor provided a "non-exhaustive" list of alleged criminal acts, including murder, rape, and pillaging, which was then confirmed by the Pre-Trial Chamber in broad terms.[142] The Prosecutor went on to provide information on individual criminal acts which had not been expressly stated in the initial charging document.[143] The Trial Chamber convicted Bemba of a number of these criminal acts.[144] On appeal, Bemba alleged that "[n]early two thirds of the underlying acts for which [he] was convicted were not included or improperly included in the Amended Document Containing the Charges and fall outside the scope of the charges",[145] and he asserted that the Trial Chamber erred in relying on these acts for the conviction.[146]

The majority of the Appeals Chamber found that Bemba's convictions were for specific acts not substantiated in the Trial Chamber's conviction document, and that the charging document was too broad to amount to a meaningful description of the charges against Bemba.[147] Despite the Appeals Chamber's acknowledgement of amended documents containing more specific factual allegations against Bemba, the majority of the Appeals Chamber concluded that both the formulation in the operative part of the Confirmation Decision as well as that in the relevant parts of the Document Containing the Charges are too broad to amount to a meaningful "description" of the charges against Bemba.[148] An amendment to the charges would have been required to effectuate the more specific factual allegations.[149] The Appeals Chamber therefore granted this ground of appeal and found, by majority, that the Trial Chamber erred when it convicted Bemba

---

[141] *Ibid.*, para. 1.

[142] Judgment, para. 75, see above note 1.

[143] *Ibid.*, para. 76.

[144] *Ibid.*, para. 83.

[145] *Ibid.*, paras. 77–78.

[146] *Ibid.*, para. 74.

[147] *Ibid.*, paras. 116–118.

[148] *Ibid.*

[149] *Ibid.*, para. 115.

of acts which did not fall within the "facts and circumstances described in the charges".[150]

7.4.1.3. Second Ground of Appeal – Dissenting Opinion

The dissenting judges argued that the Prosecutor's case against Bemba was brought by geographical, temporal and other substantive parameters, and the Pre-Trial Chamber confirmed the charges as such.[151] The Trial Chamber therefore could consider any criminal acts that fell within these parameters, subject to the requirement of proper notice to the accused.[152] The dissenting judges considered that the Prosecutor may set broad parameters for the charges depending on the circumstances of the case she intends to bring.[153] Therefore, if the Prosecutor formulates the charges broadly, this means that additional individual criminal acts may be alleged for the purpose of the trial, provided that they fall within the scope of the crimes confirmed and provided that the rights of the accused to notice and time for the preparation of his or her defence are respected.[154] The dissenting judges considered this description of the facts and circumstances described in the charges to be adequate, and they would have found that Bemba's conviction did not exceed the facts and circumstances described in the charges that were brought against him.[155]

7.4.1.4. Third Ground of Appeal – Majority Opinion

With respect to the third ground of appeal, Bemba argued that the Trial Chamber erred in finding that he failed to take all measures that were necessary and reasonable to prevent or repress the crimes committed by MLC (the Movement for the Liberation of the Congo) forces, or to submit the matter to the competent authorities.[156] He made five separate claims regarding this error on the part of the Trial Chamber.[157] The majority of the Appeals Chamber concluded that the Trial Chamber did err in concluding that Bemba failed to take all necessary and reasonable measures in re-

---

[150] *Ibid.*, paras. 116–118.

[151] Dissenting Opinion, para. 32, see above note 137.

[152] *Ibid.*, para. 36.

[153] *Ibid.*

[154] *Ibid.*

[155] *Ibid.*, para. 32.

[156] Judgment, para. 137, see above note 1.

[157] *Ibid.*, para. 30.

sponse to MLC crimes in the CAR, was materially affected by these errors, and that Bemba cannot be held criminally liable for crimes committed by MLC troops during the CAR operation.[158] The majority of the Appeals Chamber found, in several different instances, that the Trial Chamber ignored significant evidence relevant to Bemba's liability for the crimes committed by MLC forces.[159]

7.4.1.5. Third Ground of Appeal – Dissenting Opinion

The dissenting judges argued that the Trial Chamber's conclusion that "Bemba failed to take all necessary and reasonable measures within his power to prevent or repress the commission of crimes or to refer the matter to the competent authorities" was in fact supported by the evidence.[160] With respect to this ground of appeal, the dissenting judges could not identify any errors in the Trial Chamber's findings or unreasonableness in the overall conclusions, and thus they would have confirmed the Trial Chamber's finding that Bemba had failed to take all necessary and reasonable measures.[161]

7.4.2. Integrity of the Prosecutor and the OTP

Prosecutor Bensouda released a statement several days after the judgment was handed down, in which she expressed concern with the Appeals Chamber's decision.[162] She stated that she "must uphold the integrity of the Court's processes and accept the outcome",[163] yet she went on to indicate her worries that the Appeals Chamber adopted a radical model of appellate review of factual errors, and a radical view of the manner in which the Prosecution ought to charge cases involving mass criminality.[164] Prosecutor Bensouda closed her statement by acknowledging the victims of violence in the CAR and proclaiming the solidarity of the OTP with these victims.[165]

Based on what I have argued thus far, an assessment of Prosecutor Bensouda's integrity requires us to consider her structural and substantive

---

[158] *Ibid.*, para. 194.

[159] *Ibid.*, paras. 166–194.

[160] Dissenting Opinion, paras. 185–191, see above note 137.

[161] *Ibid.*, para. 191.

[162] See Statement of ICC Prosecutor, 2018, above note 4.

[163] *Ibid.*

[164] *Ibid.*

[165] *Ibid.*

integrity in light of the relevant ethical norms and rules. It appears that the Prosecutor sought to reassure the specific victims of violence in the CAR, and the global community as a whole, that this outcome was undesirable and that she (as both an individual and the face of the institution of the OTP) would do everything she could to avoid such an unsatisfying outcome in the future. At the same time, she attempted to avoid undermining the institution of the Court by accepting the Appeals Chamber's decision and the validity of the processes that lead to the decision.

There is no indication that Prosecutor Bensouda acted based on immoral commitments; rather, it appears that she sought to ground the substance of her actions in the commitments of the ICC as an institution, such as ending impunity, which is (by my lights) an objectively moral purpose. She sought to align herself, the OTP, and the Court with arguably identity-conferring commitments. Presumably, Prosecutor Bensouda made the statement in light of these aspects of integrity, while considering the demands of deontological and consequentialist norms, and as an intact reflection of her principles that require her to 'stand up for' and support victims. She certainly aimed to treat victims of violence in the CAR with dignity, thereby meeting one aspect of Luban's requirements. In this light, she made her statement with individual integrity.

Yet, it is not clear that she acted with institutional integrity from the standpoint of wholeness or integration. But this does not speak to what her individual integrity should be as the head of the OTP rather than an individual, nor does it speak to keeping the principles or harmony of the institution intact. The OTP's decisions must reflect reasoned deliberation, not just loyalty or a commitment to consequentialist considerations. Accordingly, I ultimately conclude that, while the OTP should use its outreach capacity to assure victims of violence that the Court is not a futile source of international criminal justice, the Prosecutor should not use the OTP's official platform to suggest the opposite, with respect to individual cases or the Court's practices as a whole, thereby undermining the integrity of the Court and the OTP.

7.4.3. Integrity of the Judges and the Appeals Chamber

Without engaging in an extensive analysis of either the majority opinion or the dissenting opinion, based on the above summary, it may be the case that some of the judges in the Appeals Chamber also failed to meet the requirements for institutional integrity. We have no evidence that any of the judges failed to meet the demands of individual integrity, so I will proceed directly to an analysis of the institutional integrity of the judges who constitute the majority.

On the Dworkinian view of law as integrity, judges must interpret the law and make decisions as part of the long story of their institutions. The dissenting judges argue that the standard of review of the Trial Chamber decision, requirements for charging individuals with crimes, and requirements for establishing liability under a theory of command responsibility each depart significantly from previous jurisprudence, such that the ICC is no longer telling a consistent, unified story. The majority of the Appeals Chamber may have failed to express a "coherent conception of justice and fairness"[166] and failed to take into account the actual political history of its community and institution.[167] Importantly, the ICC was set up to prosecute 'big fish', accused of co-ordinating heinous crimes. There is a good argument to be made that the majority of the Appeals Chamber may not be acting in good faith in their interpretation due to their failure to consider the previous decisions and the political history of the Court, and this would reflect a breach of the requirements for institutional integrity.

7.4.4. Integrity of the Court

If the majority of the Appeals Chamber has, in fact, failed to act with institutional integrity, this is concerning for the Appeals Chamber, for the future of appellate jurisprudence at the ICC, and for the Court itself. The potential casualties of the majority's decision speak again to Prosecutor Bensouda's likely urge to defend the institution of the ICC. Unfortunately, she cannot be responsible for maintaining the integrity of the entire institution if a separate branch fails in its own sub-institutional integrity requirements. She cannot and should not save the institution, even through her commitments to individual and institutional integrity, if the institution folds from within.

7.5. Conclusion

While Bemba's recent acquittal by the Appeals Chamber has been a lightning rod for those concerned with defending and challenging the legitimacy of the ICC and the enterprise of international criminal law, it is important to remember that it is not our only site for analysing the integrity of

---

[166] Dworkin, 1986, p. 225, see above note 103.
[167] *Ibid.*, p. 255.

the institution of the ICC, its sub-institutions, and the individuals who engage in decision-making, with or without integrity, every day. Here, I have considered two decisions related to this acquittal, disseminated by individuals but purportedly, definitively, or in the face of strong dissent, representing their respective institutions. My aim has been to provide normative tools for assessing the integrity of these decisions, and perhaps to better understand the relationship between institutions and individuals in international criminal law.

PART II:
AWARENESS AND CULTURE OF INTEGRITY

8

Conformity, Leadership and the Culture of Integrity at the International Criminal Court

Brigid Inder[*]

8.1. Introduction

For public institutions to succeed and to have long-term viability, they must be motivated by mandate and driven by values. Above all, they must not betray or compromise the trust and confidence of the public, whose interest these institutions serve.

In the Policy Brief "Revisiting Integrity in International Justice", Morten Bergsmo describes a number of integrity-related challenges before the International Criminal Court ('ICC').[1] Whilst acknowledging the powerful external politics surrounding the ICC, the brief considers the concept of integrity to be primarily an issue of leadership and recognizes the complex interplay between the exercise of individual integrity and the culture of an institution.

This chapter examines these issues from a practitioner's perspective, with a focus on the respective leadership roles of the ICC and States Parties in addressing integrity issues within the challenging political, operational and judicial contexts, which both affect and inform the Court's work.

The chapter draws upon 16 years of institutional monitoring of the ICC since its beginning, as well as advocacy efforts urging its development as an institutionally sound and transparent Court. These initiatives were based upon the premise that, without an ethical and robust foundation, the

---

[*] **Brigid Inder**, OBE, a global pioneer of women's human rights, has served as the co-founder and Executive Director of the Women's Initiatives for Gender Justice. She is a former Special Advisor on Gender to the Prosecutor of the International Criminal Court. She has been awarded an Order of the British Empire (OBE) in 2014 by Her Majesty, The Queen, for services to women's rights and international justice. She is also the recipient of the inaugural Bertha von Suttner Peace Prize.

[1] Morten Bergsmo, "Revisiting Integrity in International Justice", FICHL Policy Brief Series No. 93 (2018), Torkel Opsahl Academic EPublisher, Brussels, 2018. (http://www.toaep.org/pbs-pdf/93-bergsmo/).

ICC would not have the structural integrity needed to implement its challenging mandate, to withstand the inevitable attacks on its legitimacy, and to ensure its long-term credibility in the eyes of the public, including the victims of crimes within its jurisdiction.

The genesis of the ICC's approach to integrating ethical considerations within the core of its identity is revealed in a review of some of the factors influencing the development of the Court's regulatory framework. This includes an analysis of the staggered and incomplete emergence of its internal and external control systems, the complicated dynamics between ICC officials and States Parties that shape the ethical terrain of the Court, and the challenges associated with institution-building. The chapter relies primarily on reports, documents and data in the public domain. This material is supplemented by first-hand insights and accounts of debates and decisions related to the Court's organizational development; the chapter recalls interactions with former and current Court staff, officials and diplomats over the past decade and a half, including decision-makers responsible for transforming the Rome Statute into a viable court. It also considers some of the major institutional integrity-related crises to have affected the Court in its first two decades.

We rarely examine or consider the ICC through an ethics, or conversely, a corruption lens. Its mandate is assumed to elevate the Court beyond prosaic questions of compliance, conduct and oversight. Such managerial aspects are assumed to be either inherent within or secondary to the pursuit of the Court's unimpeachable mandate. This chapter suggests that long-term neglect of the ICC's institutional integrity has led to practices that have inevitably called into question the Court's trustworthiness as a public institution. Left unaddressed, this neglect may ultimately compromise the ICC's credibility to exercise its moral and legal authority and implement its mandate.

Authored by a devotee of the Rome Statute and a supporter of the Court, this chapter is offered in the hope that it may draw attention to the urgency of the integrity crisis at the ICC and contribute, in some way, towards its organizational transformation.

8.2. Mandate and Significance of the ICC

The adoption of the Rome Statute on 17 July 1998,[2] and its entry into force
on 1 July 2002, ushered in a potential new era of international justice and
further globalization of the rule of law as a shared collective standard. No
longer in the realm of aspiration, this ground-breaking treaty established
the first permanent international criminal court with jurisdiction over war
crimes, crimes against humanity, genocide and, more recently, the crime of
aggression.[3] The treaty balances national sovereignty with the responsibility for the investigation and prosecution of such crimes, while also ensuring that, should States prove unwilling or unable to do so, the ICC would
fill the accountability gap previously occupied by impunity. The Statute's
promise of a court which would prosecute these most serious crimes was
further elevated by its Article 27, ensuring that Heads of State would not be
immune to such prosecutions, thus opening the way for those historically
beyond the reach of domestic courts to be held accountable through this
new justice mechanism.

The impetus for the negotiations towards an international criminal
court arose from the conflicts and genocides committed in Rwanda in 1994
and the former Yugoslavia between 1991 and 1999. The brutality, scale and
rapid escalation of these conflicts and the commission of genocide on two
continents in quick succession, galvanized the global community to begin
discussions towards the establishment of a permanent court that could
prosecute, and in time, possibly deter perpetrators of mass crimes.

In the intervening years, the impact of armed conflicts around the
world has escalated. According to the United Nations ('UN') Secretary-
General, the number of countries currently involved in "violent conflicts"

---

[2]   Rome Statute of the International Criminal Court ('ICC'), 17 July 1998, in force 1 July 2002
    ('ICC Statute') (https://www.legal-tools.org/doc/7b9af9).

[3]   *Ibid.*, Articles 5–8. The definitions and the conditions for the exercise of jurisdiction over
    crimes of aggression were adopted by consensus at the 2010 Kampala Review Conference
    by the States Parties to the Court. The adopted amendments to the Rome Statute included,
    inter alia, deletion of Article 5(2) of the Rome Statute that formerly stated: "The Court shall
    exercise jurisdiction over the crime of aggression once a provision is adopted in accordance
    with articles 121 and 123 defining the crime and setting out the conditions under which the
    Court shall exercise jurisdiction with respect to this crime. Such a provision shall be con-
    sistent with the relevant provisions of the Charter of the United Nations.", and additions of
    Article 8*bis* and Article 15*bis/ter* that defined the "crime of aggression" and conditions on
    the exercise of jurisdiction over the "crime of aggression", respectively. The Court's juris-
    diction over the crime of aggression was activated on 17 July 2018.

is the highest in 30 years, while the number of people killed in conflicts has risen tenfold since 2005.[4] The volume of "violent situations" classifiable as wars, based on the number of casualties, has tripled since 2007.[5] In addition, "low-intensity conflicts" have risen by 60 per cent in the last decade.[6]

A recent edition of the Global Peace Index, produced annually by the Institute for Economics and Peace, found, based on an assessment of 163 States and territories,[7] that conflict levels in the last decade are in contrast to the trends over the past century, which have moved towards an increase in peacefulness world-wide.[8] Using 23 qualitative and quantitative indicators, it measures three thematic domains: "Safety and Security"; "Ongoing Domestic and International Conflict"; and "Militarisation".[9] According to the report, all three domains have worsened in recent years,[10] and the key indicators of peace have deteriorated globally over the past decade, in steady increments.[11] The current situation appears to be mostly due to long-term and entrenched conflicts remaining unresolved, and conflicts that have emerged in the last decade continuing unabated.[12]

According to the UN Refugee Agency, 68.5 million people fleeing conflict, violence and persecution were forcibly displaced in 2017, a record number.[13] For the first time in history, 1 per cent of the world's population is displaced.[14]

In light of the current levels of conflict, with a heightened need for multilateral responses and recognizing the important role of justice within

---

[4] UN News, "Rise in violent conflict shows prevention 'more necessary than ever': UN chief", Statement made to journalists at the Annual Retreat for International Conflict Mediators and other high-level decision makers, Norway, 19 June 2018.

[5] *Ibid.*

[6] UN News, "Preventing and resolving conflicts must form 'backbone' of collective efforts – UN chief", Statement made to the United Nations Security Council on the issue of regional conflicts, New York, 6 December 2018.

[7] Institute for Economics and Peace, *Global Peace Index 2018: Measuring Peace in a Complex World*, Sydney, June 2018, p. 2 ('Global Peace Index 2018').

[8] *Ibid.*

[9] *Ibid.*

[10] *Ibid.*, p. 10.

[11] *Ibid.*, p. 26.

[12] *Ibid.*, p. 7.

[13] United Nations High Commissioner for Refugees ('UNHCR'), *Global Trends Report: Forced Displacement in 2017*, Geneva, 2018, p. 2.

[14] Global Peace Index 2018, p. 33, see above note 7.

the global peace and security framework, the ICC's mandate is more relevant than ever. Its significance as an impartial arbiter of criminal justice for
the most serious crimes is without parallel in the international multi-lateral
system. There is no other entity in the world entrusted with the mandate to
stand uniquely and exclusively on the side of justice at the complicated intersection of global politics, international humanitarian and criminal law,
and security challenges.

8.3. Credibility in Question

While the ICC's moral and legal authority is derived from the Rome Statute,
its credibility comes from its perceived impartiality and the manner in
which it undertakes its statutory responsibilities. This is demonstrated primarily in its judicial work – the selection of cases, the fairness of its proceedings, the demonstrable capacity of the Court to implement its mandate – as well as in its organizational integrity as a global public institution
for justice. This chapter will focus on the latter aspect of the ICC's credibility.

Although the relevance and necessity of the Court's mandate are beyond dispute, its credibility, with respect to both its judicial achievements
and its institutional ethics, has been called into question. For the former,
this is due to its relatively modest impact, to date, concerning its prosecutorial record within which the performance of the Office of the Prosecutor
('OTP'), as well as genuine complexities, demanding disclosure requirements and at times innovative jurisprudence have all played a part.[15]

The ICC has also made an unsteady contribution to furthering the jurisprudence associated with international crimes with some notable exceptions, including the Judgement in the *Prosecutor v. Bosco Ntaganda* case,[16]
and the earlier decisions in the same case by the Trial and Appeals Cham-

---

[15] See, for example, Coalition of NGOs for the ICC, "Jean-Pierre Bemba Gombo acquitted by
ICC Appeals Chamber", 13 June 2018; Women's Initiatives for Gender Justice, "Appeals
withdrawn by Prosecution and Defence, Prosecutor v Germain Katanga", 26 June 2014;
Women's Initiatives for Gender Justice, "The Compendium: An Overview of Situations and
Cases Before the International Criminal Court", 2017; Douglas Guilfoyle, "Part III - This is
Not Fine: The International Criminal Court in Trouble", in *European Journal of Interna-
tional Law*, 25 March 2019; and Women's Initiatives for Gender Justice, "Gender Report
Card on the International Criminal Court", 2007–2014 and 2018.

[16] ICC, Situation in the Democratic Republic of the Congo, *Prosecutor v. Bosco Ntaganda*
('*Ntaganda*'), Trial Chamber, Judgment, 8 July 2019, ICC-01/04-02/ 06-2359 (https://
www.legal-tools.org/doc/80578a/).

bers with respect to the charges of rape and sexual slavery committed against children within Ntaganda's own militia group.[17]

For the latter credibility issue, its institutional integrity has been called into question due to what appears to be improper, unethical or unlawful conduct by ICC staff, specifically senior leaders and Court officials. Some of these incidents are in the public domain, several have been exposed by the media.[18]

Arguably, its institutional credibility has also been compromised, perhaps most damagingly, by the more mundane but less widely known repetitive breaches of ICC staff regulations, rules, policies and resolutions. These violations, small and large, have been committed by those who have both shaped and taken advantage of a culture of non-compliance and unaccountability. This environment has been enabled and facilitated by the manner in which the Assembly of States Parties ('ASP', or the 'Assembly') has exercised its governance responsibilities.

Based on longitudinal monitoring of the Court,[19] there is now compelling evidence to suggest that the ICC is in a precarious position with

---

[17] *Ntaganda*, Trial Chamber, Second Decision on the Defence's challenge to the jurisdiction of the Court in respect of Counts 6 and 9, 4 January 2017, ICC-01/04-02/06-1707, para. 54 (https://www.legal-tools.org/doc/2de239/); *Ntaganda*, Appeals Chamber, Judgment on the appeal of Mr Ntaganda against the "Second decision on the Defence's challenge to the jurisdiction of the Court in respect of Counts 6 and 9", 15 June 2017, ICC-01/04-02/06-1962 (https://www.legal-tools.org/doc/a3ec20).

[18] Sven Becker, Marian Blasberg and Dietmar Pieper, "The Ocampo Affair: A Former ICC Chief's Dubious Links", in *Spiegel International*, 5 October 2017; EIC Network, "Secrets of the International Criminal Court Revealed", in *The Black Sea*, 29 September 2017; EIC Network, Stephanie Maupas, "Secrets of the International Criminal Court: The Kenya U-Turn", in *The Black Sea*, 6 October 2017; Barney Thompson, "Former ICC Prosecutor in row over lucrative consultancy work", in *Financial Times*, 6 October 2017; Stephanie Maupas, "ICC Under Fire for Internal Mismanagement", *JusticeInfo.net*, 26 February 2018; and Morten Bergsmo, "Integrity as Safeguard Against the Vicissitudes of Common Justice Institutions", Centre for International Law Research and Policy ('CILRAP'), 1 December 2018, at 8.53-11.44 mins (https://www.cilrap.org/cilrap-film/181201-bergsmo).

[19] Between 2004 and 2017, the author was the Executive Director of the Women's Initiatives for Gender Justice. During this time, the organization monitored the institutional development of the ICC regarding recruitment and the gender and geographical profile of the staff of the Court, and its elected officials. It also conducted reviews of selected ICC policies and training activities, analysed and advocated for the elaboration of the Court's institutional framework, including the development of the Independent Oversight Mechanism, and scrutinized the annual budget submissions of each of the organs of the ICC. The organization provided briefings to States Parties, to the Committee on Budget and Finance ('CBF'), and the Assembly of States Parties ('ASP'), specifically addressing issues associated with the in-

respect to its institutional integrity. This appears to be the result of a long, slow, burn of ethical compromises, violations and questionable conduct cumulating in a credibility crisis for the Court. Alarmingly, these violations, both subtle and blatant, have occurred on a significant scale, over a long period of time, largely without consequence or accountability. Breaches left unchecked have inevitably contributed to an ever-increasing tolerance for impropriety, and predictably, ever-more serious violations.

Given the ICC is a relatively new international mechanism, the volume and range of institutional challenges appear to be excessive for its mere 17 years of operations. This is all the more discombobulating given the sophistication of management practices employed in contemporary public and private institutions; and that this is a Court created in and for a new millennium when there is heightened public access to information and consequently, greater scrutiny of institutions and public officials.[20]

How did the ICC arrive at this point where its institutional integrity has been compromised and is justifiably questioned?

8.4. Relationship between the ICC and the United Nations

8.4.1. Independence of the ICC

In creating the ICC, the governments participating in the Rome negotiation process agreed upon a model obligating the Court to work in close association with, but remain independent from, the UN, including the UN Security Council.

Unlike the International Court of Justice, where all UN Member States are automatically its members, the ICC is a court of choice. Membership to the ICC is by voluntary accession to the Rome Statute. States are also able to accept the Court's authority, without being a member, under an Article 12(3) declaration.[21] At the time of writing, 123 States have ratified

---

stitutional development of the Court. The Women's Initiatives for Gender Justice produced annual Gender Reports Cards on the ICC ('Gender Report Cards') that summarized important developments in the ICC's substantive work, as well as providing assessments and detailed recommendations on aspects of its internal control system, governance issues, the budget, staff profile, and the election of Court officials. The Gender Report Cards also assessed the implementation of the gender mandates of the Rome Statute with respect to the institutional development of the Court. Since 2018, the author has, on an independent basis, continued to monitor a select number of institutional development issues before the ICC.

[20] Bergsmo, 2018, p. 1, see above note 1.

[21] Rome Statute of the International Criminal Court, 17 July 1998, Article 12(3) (http://www.legal-tools.org/doc/7b9af9/):

the Rome Statute and are members of the ICC.[22] This membership provides a legal remedy for nationals of States Parties who are victims of crimes within the ICC's jurisdiction. It also subjects their citizens, including military leaders and elected public officials, to potential prosecutions and the judgments of the Court.

The ICC was created to be an independent institution driven by its jurisdictional imperatives but operating in a clearly defined relationship with the UN system.[23] The intention behind its unique status was to remove, or perhaps more realistically reduce, the potential political influence of the Security Council on this new global justice mechanism. The goal was to establish a Court accessible to all States, beyond the power centres created after the Second World War and subsequently instituted in the permanent membership of five States on the Security Council, each with veto powers. Whilst keenly aware that it would likely operate in highly politicized environments, the Court was established on the basis that it would be driven by the jurisdiction with which it was entrusted and in so doing act as an equalizer in the world of the powerful and powerless.

However, the notion that the Court is a politically neutral zone is an ideal rather than a reality. All of the States Parties to the ICC are also all UN members and therefore well versed in the economic relationships, consensus-building activities, transactional co-operation and the geopolitical and historic alliances that constitute international diplomacy. Two of the five permanent members of the Security Council are States Parties of the ICC – France and the United Kingdom. Although the three permanent members of the Security Council that are not States Parties to the Court, namely the United States of America ('US'), Russia and China, do not have

---

If the acceptance of a State which is not a Party to this Statute is required under Paragraph 2, that State may, by declaration lodged with the Registrar, accept the exercise of jurisdiction by the Court with respect to the crime in question. The accepting State shall cooperate with the Court without any delay or exception in accordance with Part 9.

[22] States Parties to the Rome Statute (available on the ICC's web site); ICC, "President of the Assembly welcomes Malaysia's accession to the Rome Statute", 5 March 2019 (https://www.legal-tools.org/doc/5f783c).

[23] ICC, "Negotiated draft Relationship Agreement between the International Criminal Court and the United Nations", adopted at the third plenary of the Assembly of States Parties on 7 September 2004, entered into force on 4 October 2004, ICC-ASP/3/Res.1 ('Relationship Agreement') (https://www.legal-tools.org/doc/9432c6). There, Member States reminded themselves that "in accordance with the Rome Statute, the International Criminal Court is established as an independent permanent institution in relationship with the United Nations system".

any formal influence with the ICC, it would be fanciful to assume that at least some of their interests are not readily communicated to the Court via surrogate States or through direct communication between their diplomats and Court officials.

As a permanent and independent entity within the multi-lateral community associated with the UN, the ICC is an important and irreplaceable component of the international peace and security architecture.

8.4.2. Relationship Agreement

With its independence in mind and highly cognizant of its interface with the Security Council, the negotiators of the Rome Statute designated two specific statutory roles for the Security Council with respect to the potential opening of investigations into crimes falling within the ICC's temporal and subject matter jurisdiction. These are outlined in Articles 13 and 16 of the Rome Statute, respectively, and address the ability of the Security Council, acting under Chapter VII of the UN Charter to: refer a situation to the ICC Prosecutor in which one or more crimes within the ICC's jurisdiction appear to have been committed;[24] or alternatively, to defer an ICC investigation or prosecution for up to 12 months, with the possibility of renewing such a deferral.[25]

With the specific roles for the Security Council defined and the jurisdictional independence of the Court enshrined within the Statute, the ICC and the UN entered into a relationship agreement (the 'Agreement'), as required under Article 2 of the Rome Statute.[26] Within two years of the Statute coming into force, an agreement specifying and clarifying the relationship between the new Court and the UN was adopted by both parties.[27]

The Agreement recognizes the ICC as an independent permanent judicial institution and, reciprocally, the ICC recognizes the responsibilities of the UN under the UN Charter.[28] It also addresses a range of pragmatic issues and provides procedures, outlined in Article 17 of the Agreement, regarding the use of powers designated to the Security Council to refer situations and defer investigations or prosecutions. The Agreement also de-

---

[24] ICC Statute, Article 13(b), see above note 2.

[25] *Ibid.*, Article 16.

[26] *Ibid.*, Article 2.

[27] Relationship Agreement, see above note 23.

[28] ICC Statute, Article 2, see above note 2.

scribes the conditions under which the UN may provide documents or information to the Prosecutor on condition of confidentiality and solely for the purpose of generating new evidence.[29]

Overall, the Agreement defines the terms of "a mutually beneficial relationship whereby the discharge of respective responsibilities of the United Nations and the International Criminal Court may be facilitated".[30]

In practice, the Agreement has been readily and regularly utilized. The UN has played important roles with the ICC in a number of ways and has contributed to the Court's work both in its prosecutorial activities as well as operationally, including, but not limited to:

1. The voluntary participation of UN personnel as expert witnesses in ICC cases;

2. Acting as a confidential source of information for the OTP from which it could generate evidence during its investigations;

3. Providing assistance for the arrest of ICC indictees and their transfers to the Court; and

4. The provision of logistic, operational and security support to ICC missions and field offices.

In addition to the statutory independence of the ICC's investigations and cases, there is also an important institutional separation between the Security Council and the Court, specifically in the area of governance. Unlike, for instance, the International Criminal Tribunal for the former Yugoslavia ('ICTY') and the International Criminal Tribunal for Rwanda ('ICTR'), which reported solely to the Security Council,[31] the ICC uniquely reports only to its membership of States Parties (except the Prosecutor's report to the Security Council on the cases the latter referred) and elects its own officials. In this respect, the UN does not have a governance role or decision-making responsibilities regarding the institutional development and oversight of the ICC.

---

[29] *Ibid.*, Article 18.

[30] *Ibid.*, Preamble.

[31] With the closure of both the ICTR in 2015 and the ICTY in 2017, all remaining cases and appeals associated with these courts are dealt with by the International Residual Mechanism for Criminal Tribunals (the 'Mechanism'). The President of the Mechanism reports on a six-monthly basis to the UN Security Council, and annual reports on the work of the Mechanism are submitted to the General Assembly and the Security Council.

It was hoped that this structure would further protect the Court's independence and that a nimble court unencumbered by UN bureaucracy could design systems to suit its specific requirements and operational needs. In practice, this means that the ICC is not obligated to comply with the UN's ethics-related policies and frameworks; it is not subject to its internal control system, nor the UN's conduct and accountability requirements.

This independence could have propelled the Court to become the preeminent global institution demonstrating institutional authenticity in harmony with the nobility of its mandate. Instead, the ICC stumbled into an institutional void in which its ethical practices and internal control systems lag behind international standards.

8.5. Building the Institution

8.5.1. ICC Staff Regulations and Rules

Since its beginning, the ICC appears to have been more mission-driven than values-oriented. During the early years of its establishment, the ICC and the ASP passed a number of policies and resolutions to transform the Rome Statute into a working, viable Court. However, the strong focus on its jurisdictional mandate largely overpowered attention to the regulatory, organizational and ethics-related considerations necessary in building an institution.

The starting point of an organization's integrity always lies in its foundations and internal architecture.

In developing its Staff Regulations in 2003,[32] and Staff Rules in 2005,[33] the ICC closely followed the relevant regulations and rules of the UN at that time.[34] For ease, to hasten 'construction' of the Court and perhaps to take advantage of the experience of staff who were serving in the UN-related tribunals, the ICC adopted the same professional categories,

---

[32] ICC, Staff Regulations for the International Criminal Court, adopted at the second session of the Assembly of States Parties, 8-12 September 2003, ICC-ASP/2/10 ('ICC Staff Regulations') (http://www.legal-tools.org/doc/3542d3/).

[33] ICC, Staff Rules of the International Criminal Court, adopted by the Assembly of States Parties on 3 December 2005, entered into force on 25 August 2005, ICC-ASP/4/3 ('ICC Staff Rules') (https://www.legal-tools.org/doc/10f5c7/).

[34] The UN Staff Regulations and Rules relevant to this chapter and utilized in the comparison with the ICC are contained within the United Nations Regulations Governing the Status, Basic Rights and Duties of Officials other than Secretariat Officials, and Experts on Mission, 1 January 2002, ST/SGB/2002/1 ('UN Staff Rules') (https://www.legal-tools.org/doc/wv8h0w/).

staff salary specifications, and related allowances, as the UN and sought and was granted admittance to the UN Joint Staff Pension Fund for ICC staff,[35] as compelled by ICC Staff Regulations.[36]

A comparative read of the ICC texts and the UN Staff Regulations and Rules as they existed at the time of the Court's development, reveal a striking similarity in both the structure and content between the respective documents. This is to be expected given the ICC chose to follow the UN common system with respect to employee-related entitlements and conditions.

Whilst most of the ICC's provisions strongly reflect those of the UN's Staff Regulations and Rules, there are differences with respect to: a greater emphasis placed on confidentiality by the ICC; a more explicit annunciation of due process for staff regarding the disciplinary procedures; and subtle but specific reductions in the ethical requirements, conduct, and accountability by the ICC, compared to the provisions established by the UN. In these latter areas, the ICC departed from the pre-existing UN texts and established standards.

For example, the ICC's Staff Rules adopted by the ASP in 2005, subtly downgraded references to 'misconduct', as referenced in the UN Staff Rules, to 'unsatisfactory conduct' within the ICC context.[37] References to 'serious misconduct' are included in both sets of rules, but the ICC reduced one of the levels of improper behaviour from the usual standard of 'misconduct' to the lesser standard of 'unsatisfactory conduct.'

This diminished level of impropriety was advocated for and insisted upon by the OTP, specifically the Prosecutor,[38] on the basis of the statutory independence of the OTP and his authority over all areas associated with the management of the Office and its staff.[39] The Prosecutor's approach appeared to either inadvertently or deliberately diminish the manner in which improper behaviour would be viewed generally, by reducing the seriousness of specific conduct that would ordinarily be regarded as misconduct, but at the ICC would only be considered unsatisfactory. This recali-

---

[35] United Nations General Assembly, by its resolution 58/262 of 23 December 2003, effective 1 January 2004.

[36] ICC Staff Regulations, Regulation 2.1 and 3.1-3.4, see above note 32.

[37] ICC Staff Rules, Rule 110.1, p. 64, see above note 33.

[38] Conversations with former OTP staff members on file with the author.

[39] ICC Statute, Article 42(2), see above note 2.

bration of conduct and by implication the consequences associated with it should be considered in light of a pattern of similar positions advocated by the Prosecutor and the OTP in the first ten years of its operations,[40] as well as the specific issues reported by the media in 2017 with respect to the Prosecutor's professional conduct both during and after his time in office.[41]

Also absent from the ICC Staff Rules and Regulations are provisions relating to the conduct and accountability requirements of Court officials, including elected leaders and heads of organs. Specifically omitted are the requirements for Assistant Secretary-General staff and above to file financial disclosure statements, which at the ICC relate to the level of elected officials. This provision, included within the UN Staff Rules and Regulations,[42] was omitted from the equivalent ICC documents.

By comparison with the UN's Staff Rules, the section on Disciplinary Measures within the ICC Staff Rules also differed from the comparable UN regulatory requirement. The UN requirement states that:

> Any staff member may be required to reimburse the United Nations either partially or in full for any financial loss suffered by the United Nations as a result of the staff member's negligence or of his or her having violated any regulation, rule or administrative instruction.[43]

The ICC Staff Rules state that:

> Staff members may be required to reimburse or compensate the Court, either partially or in full, for any financial loss suffered by the Court as a result of gross negligence, malice, fraud or failure to observe any obligation under the instruments of the Court, such as the Staff Regulations and Rules, the Financial Regulations and Rules, and administrative issuances.[44]

Some may reasonably argue that the ICC rule is more robust than the UN equivalent because it explicitly identifies serious breaches such as gross negligence, malice, and fraud, for which ICC staff could be held accountable. The intention behind listing these specific forms of misconduct may have been genuinely motivated. However, in practice, the ICC provi-

---

[40] See Sections 8.5.4., 8.6.2.1., and 8.6.2.2. of this chapter.

[41] See above note 18.

[42] ICC Staff Regulations, Regulation, 1.2(n), see above note 32.

[43] UN Staff Rules, Rule 112.3, see above note 34.

[44] ICC Staff Rules, para. 101.3(d), see above note 33.

sion of gross negligence is a higher threshold to prove than ordinary negligence. Similarly, malice and fraud are more difficult breaches to substantiate than the straightforward provision and language adopted by the UN with respect to a violation of any regulation, rule or administrative instruction. Most of the ICC standards in this regulatory provision require additional proof of deliberateness, intention, or deception for unfair gain, regarding the decisions taken by an ICC staff member, compared to the UN rule applicable to standards of negligence or violations.

It is possible that by raising the threshold of conduct that would be considered a breach of this regulation, the ICC may have inadvertently reduced the likelihood of accountability. The Court's approach potentially expands the scope of conduct that could negatively impact on the Court, including reckless and wilful conduct and decision-making, not automatically considered gross negligence, fraud or malice, for which there could be no consequences for those responsible. To date, despite evidence suggesting such violations may have occurred, no ICC staff member or elected official has been held accountable for breaches outlined in this regulation, even under the ordinary threshold of "failure to observe any obligation".[45]

Missing from the ICC Staff Regulations and Rules and the same UN documents at the time, were provisions relating to the duty of staff to report violations of the legal and policy frameworks; ensuring the protection from retaliation for those who report breaches and the associated procedures in place for this process; and a definition of conflict of interest. Both sets of regulations and rules address conflicts of interest but limit this to financial interests and are silent on the range of issues and influences that may give rise to a potential conflict of interest in the commission of one's duty.

8.5.2. International Civil Servants

The UN and ICC Staff Regulations and Rules both identify the status of their respective staff as 'international civil servants'.[46] This status has a long history within the UN and has been a pivotal component of its institutional identity. The *Standards of Conduct for the International Civil Service* (the 'Standards'), first produced in 1954 and subsequently updated in 2001 and 2013, were adopted early on in the tenure of the second Secretary-

---

[45] See, for example, below Section 8.7. ("Case Study: ReVision").

[46] UN Staff Rules, Rule 101.1, see above note 34; ICC Staff Regulations, Regulation 1.1(a), see above note 32.

General of the United Nations, Dag Hammarskjöld. Perhaps more than any
other Secretary-General, Dag Hammarskjöld actively promoted and embodied the identity and practice of the international civil service and equated the concept of integrity with "conscience" and "respect for law and respect for truth".[47]

According to the Standards,

> international civil servants have a special calling: to serve the
> ideals of peace, of respect for fundamental rights, of economic
> and social progress, and of international cooperation. It is
> therefore incumbent on international civil servants to adhere
> to the highest standards of conduct; for, ultimately, it is the in-
> ternational civil service that will enable the United Nations
> system to bring about a just and peaceful world.[48]

The Standards of 2001, available to the ICC at the time of its establishment, had been recently updated by the UN in response to new ethical
challenges not fully addressed by the earlier Standards and in order to reflect a more modern era with the evolution of new concepts and global advances.[49]

The Standards issued at that time addressed a number of practical issues, including ethical aspects of the role and the working relationships of
civil servants;[50] the obligation to report the commission of violations;[51]
personal conduct and protection of information;[52] loyalty to the organization and its vision;[53] and the requirement to place the interests of the institution above their own and ensure responsible use its resources.[54]

---

[47] Bergsmo, 2018, p. 2, see above note 1.

[48] International Civil Service Commission, Standards of Conduct for the International Civil
Service, January 2002, para. 2, adopted by the United Nations General Assembly, A/RES/
56/244, December 2001, distributed 5 February 2002 ('Standards of Conduct') (https://www.
legal-tools.org/doc/y77yzh/).

[49] *Ibid.*

[50] *Ibid.*, paras. 15–19, 31-33, 38-45.

[51] *Ibid.*, para. 19.

[52] *Ibid.*, paras. 35, 38–40.

[53] *Ibid.*, paras. 4 and 7.

[54] *Ibid.*, para. 4.

The Standards also included a specific reference to the conduct of those in management and leadership positions emphasizing their enhanced responsibility to be models of exemplary conduct.[55]

The Standards repeatedly stressed the qualities of integrity, honesty and impartiality;[56] and urged harmonization between the mission of the international civil service and the conduct of international civil servants.

The Standards were understood to complement and to some extent supplement the UN's Staff Regulations and Rules. Thus, gaps as noted earlier in the employee documents with respect to the duty to report breaches and protection from reprisals,[57] and conflicts of interest beyond the limited focus of financial interests were addressed within the Standards[58] The UN at the time recognized that although, "[t]he standards of conduct do not have the force of law" unlike the staff regulations and rules, importantly they "provide a discussion of expected standards to help staff understand their role as international civil servants".[59]

Similarly, the ICC also claims the bold and apt identity of international civil servants for its staff as reflected in the ICC Staff Regulations and Rules,[60] and even refers to the UN Standards within the ICC's *Code of Conduct for Staff Members* (the 'Code of Conduct').[61]

However, unlike the UN, the ICC does not appear to consider the Standards to be complementary to the Staff Regulations and Rules. As such, the regulatory gaps in the ICC's internal policy regime either remain unaddressed or have been gradually and partially filled over time, but several

---

[55] *Ibid.*, para. 16: "It is natural for managers to be seen as role models and they have therefore a special obligation to uphold the highest standards of conduct".

[56] *Ibid.*, paras. 2, 4- 5, 8-9, 27, 30, and 48.

[57] *Ibid.*, para. 19.

[58] *Ibid.*, paras. 21, 22, and 41.

[59] United Nations, Status, Basic Rights and Duties of UN Staff Members, 1 November 2002, ST/SGB/2002/13, Section I, para. 7, p. 5 (https://www.legal-tools.org/doc/f9e724/).

[60] ICC Staff Regulations, see above note 32 and ICC Staff Rules, see above note 33. The term 'international civil servant' appears eleven times in the ICC Staff Regulations and Rules, including in their pre-eminent provisions where both declare that "ICC staff are international civil servants", see ICC Staff Regulations, 30 September 2016, Ref. ICC/PRESD/G/2016/002, Regulation 1.1(a) (https://www.legal-tools.org/doc/bc0ddb) and ICC, Staff Rules of the International Criminal Court, 2015, Rule 101.1 (https://www.legal-tools.org/doc/b14f3a).

[61] ICC, Code of Conduct for Staff Members, 4 April 2011, ICC/AI/2011/002, Introduction and Section 1 (https://www.legal-tools.org/doc/75f9db).

years after the ICC began its judicial work and field operations. For example, a broad range of conflicts of interest were eventually included in the Court's 2011 Code of Conduct.[62] A financial disclosure programme was introduced at the Court in 2016 applicable to principals and staff involved with specific finance and procurement activities, as well as staff associated with the system of internal control and oversight.[63] The ICC's Whistleblower Policy, adopted in 2014, addresses the duty to report violations and provides protection from retaliation.[64] The creation of the Independent Oversight Mechanism ('IOM'), deemed fully functional in 2017, finally addresses misconduct, encompassing both unsatisfactory and serious misconduct.[65] Unfortunately, this staggered and piecemeal approach to the ICC's institutional development created an internal environment without sufficient guidance and regulatory clarity, and delayed the conscious evolution of an ethics-based culture.

Despite references to its staff as international civil servants, the Court does not appear to have fully accepted the responsibilities of this status within its organizational culture or policy and legal frameworks. At the same time, States Parties have not exercised oversight of the Court through

---

[62] *Ibid.*, Section 4, paras. 4.1-4.5.

[63] ICC, Disclosure Requirements - Financial Disclosure Programme of the Court (ICC-FDP) and IPSAS Related Party Disclosures, 6 October, 2015, ICC/AI/2015/05 (https://www.legal-tools.org/doc/bbdb4c/). See also ICC, Report of the Court on Policy Issues (Anti-fraud, Whistle-blower Policies, Financial Disclosure Programme, Longer-term Investment Options and Employee Benefit Liabilities), 4 May 2015, ICC-ASP/14/17 (https://www.legal-tools.org/doc/lpfxdi/). In para. 8:

> The Court has identified the following classification of personnel required to file: (a) The Prosecutor, Deputy Prosecutor, Registrar and Deputy Registrar; (b) All staff members and officials at D-1 level or above; (c) All Certifying Officers; (d) All Procurement staff members, or those whose principal occupational duties are the procurement of goods and services for the Court; (e) All staff members whose principal occupational duties are related to the investment of the assets of the Court; (f) Other staff members and officials whose direct access to confidential procurement or investment information warrants the filing of disclosure statements; and (g) All staff members serving in the Independent Oversight Mechanism and the Internal Audit Office.

[64] ICC, Whistleblowing and Whistleblower Protection Policy, 8 October 2014, ICC/PRESD/G/2014/003, Article 1.1–1.3 (https://www.legal-tools.org/doc/0c36ff/).

[65] The Independent Oversight Mechanism (IOM) was established by the Assembly at its eighth session in accordance with Article 112, para. 4, of the 'ICC Statute'. The IOM became fully operational in 2017. It is an operationally independent office with the head of the IOM reporting to the President of the Assembly of States Parties. See also ICC, Establishment of an Independent Oversight Mechanism, 26 November 2009, ICC-ASP/8/Res.1 ('ICC-ASP/8/Res.1') (https://www.legal-tools.org/doc/bf0e8c/).

the prism of the Standards, and the prestige of being an international civil servant has perhaps been under-utilized by the ICC as a source of motivation for its employees. Nevertheless, the Court's assertion of this status for its staff carries with it the responsibility to adhere to the standards of ethical conduct expected of those in the international civil service.

Not relying on the Standards alone to fill some of the policy gaps, the UN has continuously amended and updated its staff regulations and rules as well as other workplace and ethics-related policies. By contrast, the ICC has not.

Since the UN Regulations were first published in 1952, there have been more than 60 amendments to the staff-related legal framework.[66] This reflects an ongoing process of review, adaption, and possibly learning by the UN, often preceded by crisis and scandals, as well as the adoption of management practices normative in many parts of the world. For comparison with the ICC, in the first 17 years of UN operations (1952-1969), it amended its staff regulations and rules on 17 occasions.[67] During the institutional lifespan of the Court, since the adoption of its Rules to the time of writing (2003-2020), the UN has revised its Staff Regulations and Rules more than 20 times. According to the ICC web site, in the same 17-year period, it appears that the ICC has amended its Staff Regulations twice,[68] and its Staff Rules appear to have been amended three times.[69]

Evidently, the ICC has not demonstrated the same attention and necessary commitment to the ongoing evolution of its institutional framework. Whereas one might have expected the ICC, as a modern and unprecedented institution, to have adopted the highest standards possible in its founding institutional documents, it opted instead for diminished versions of some

---

[66] United Nations, "Staff Regulations and Rules of the United Nations", 1 January 2018, ST/SGB/2018/1 (https://www.legal-tools.org/doc/6d5d9j/).

[67] *Ibid.*, p. 7.

[68] ICC, Amendment to the ICC Staff Regulations, 22 January 2014, ICC/PRESD/G/2014/001 (https://www.legal-tools.org/doc/d562a8/); ICC Staff Regulations, ICC-PRESD/G/2016/002, 30 September 2016 (https://www.legal-tools.org/doc/bc0ddb/).

[69] ICC, Promulgation of the Amendments to the ICC Staff Rules, ICC/AI/2015/004, 24 July 2015 and related corrigendum, ICC Promulgation of the Staff Rules of the International Criminal Court, 27 July 2015, ICC/AI/2015/004/Cor.1 (https://www.legal-tools.org/doc/2a5274/); Promulgation of the Amended Provisional Staff Rules of the International Criminal Court, ICC/AI/2016/003, 30 December 2016 (https://www.legal-tools.org/doc/65ab39/); Promulgation of the Amended Provisional Staff Rules of the International Criminal Court, 3 May 2017, ICC/AI/2016/003 Rev.1 (https://www.legal-tools.org/doc/f5e9c7/).

key international standards, specifically in the areas of conduct and accountability. Over time, these subtle but consistent reductions had a numbing effect on the Court and weakened the ethical orientation of the ICC as an employer and as a public institution. In hindsight, these were tell-tale signs of what lay ahead.

8.5.3. Prohibited Behaviour: Sexual and Other Forms of Harassment

A specific area of weakness in the ICC regulatory framework is a comprehensive and robust articulation of prohibited behaviour inclusive of sexual and other forms of gender-based violence committed within the workplace as well as by ICC staff, or others acting on behalf of the Court, in the course of their work and official duties.

In 2005, the ICC issued an Administrative Instruction on *Sexual and Other Forms of Harassment* (the 'Sexual Harassment Administrative Instruction' or the 'Policy').[70] At the time of its issuance, the Policy was not considered to reflect best practice standards with several areas of substantive and procedural weakness.[71] Specific and ongoing concerns include the general orientation of the Policy regarding its emphasis on courtesy, dignity and congeniality in the introductory paragraphs.[72] This language is suggestive of an era when harassment was trivialized and considered impolite or overly friendly. Whilst qualities such as courtesy and congeniality, as suggested by the Court, are valid as components of an overall workplace culture, they are perhaps less pertinent in the context of a sexual harassment policy compared with concepts such as equality, respect and workplace safety.

---

[70] ICC, Sexual and Other Forms of Harassment, Administrative Instruction, 14 July 2005, ICC/AI/2005/005 ('Sexual Harassment Administrative Instruction') (https://www.legal-tools.org/doc/hyvqzp/).

[71] Specifically, the ICC Policy does not sufficiently address the following issues: the identification of focal points with expertise in this area; the intended dissemination of the Policy and support for staff; the lack of preventive measures; the importance of prompt and concrete responses by managers to complaints under this Policy, with failure to do so possibly considered a breach of duty and/or a performance-related issue for the manager/supervisor; an expansive list of options available for reporting incidents; monitoring implementation and use of the Policy; and the absence of any references to or definition of discrimination, one of the potential precursors to the commission of conduct which is either intended to harass or could be experienced as harassment.

[72] Sexual Harassment Administrative Instruction, paras. 1.1 and 1.2, see above note 70.

Additional provisions indicating that proven cases of harassment *may* result in disciplinary measures, suggest that proven cases may also result in no disciplinary action being taken.[73]

This is further exacerbated by provisions that could be seen to disincentivize staff from reporting incidents. For example, paragraph 3.7 of the Policy indicates that individuals have a responsibility to communicate clearly to their colleagues about behaviour they find offensive and when doing so, they must also listen and respond to comments about their own behaviour. In the context of a sexual harassment policy, such a provision contains a subtle but clear suggestion that the alleged harassment or offensive conduct may be considered to have been provoked by the behaviour of the persons harassed, further implying that they could be blamed or held mutually responsible for the harassing behaviour they experienced. The apparent victim-blaming orientation of this provision and the weakness of the Policy in general, are in contrast with the explicit and unambiguous gender-responsive provisions contained within the Rome Statute. Unfortunately, the current Policy does not appear to effectively locate sexual harassment on the continuum of gender-based crimes embedded in the Statute, all of which are premised, amongst other factors, upon the recognition and experience of inequality. This contrast exposes a perhaps revealing disconnect between the Rome Statute and the high intentions of the drafters integrating gender issues, and the institutional foundations and the mindset of the implementers enacting a policy on sexual and other harassment.

With reference to the development of the OTP generally, Morten Bergsmo has described a similar quandary between the careful negotiations determining the ICC's legal infrastructure and the reality of its implementation as "a fundamental contrast between the making of the law and the making of an institution".[74]

The importance of aligning an institution with its mandate has also been underscored by Justice Richard Goldstone, specifically regarding gender-related issues. As the first Prosecutor of the ICTY and the ICTR, one of the immediate actions undertaken by his office was to consider how it would respond to gender-based crimes, given the limitations in the Tri-

---

[73] *Ibid.*, para. 7.4.

[74] Morten Bergsmo, "Institutional History, Behaviour and Development", in Morten Bergsmo, Klaus Rackwitz and SONG Tianying (eds.), *Historical Origins of International Criminal Law: Volume 5*, Torkel Opsahl Academic EPublisher, 2017, p. 25 (https://www.toaep.org/ps-pdf/24-bergsmo-rackwitz-song).

bunals' Statutes and the Geneva Conventions in this area.[75] Justice Gold-stone's view was that they would need to be inventive to address the lacuna that existed around these specific crimes in the early 1990s.[76] Mindful of his jurisdictional responsibilities and understanding the importance of organizational coherence between its prosecutorial approach and the culture within the OTP itself, Justice Goldstone urged staff to be attentive to gender issues in all spheres, believing that, "if we don't get gender issues right in the office, we're not going to get it right out of the office".[77]

Unlike the UN's comparable sexual harassment and discrimination policies (in place at the time the ICC was drafting its Sexual Harassment Administrative Instruction),[78] the Court's policy differs in three key aspects:

1. The ICC's policy does not include an explicit reference to sexual harassment being particularly serious when behaviour of this kind is engaged in by Court officials. Paragraph 2.2 of the ICC's policy closely reflects paragraph 2 of the relevant UN Administrative Instruction, with the specific exception of the language expressing that harassment is "particularly serious when behaviour of this kind is engaged in by any official". This phrase was omitted from the ICC's policy.

2. It does not acknowledge the barriers to reporting harassment created by power differentials between the harassed person and the alleged harasser. Recognizing and explicitly naming the issue of power embedded in the acts of harassment and concomitantly inherent within the challenges to report such violations, is an appropriate lens through which to develop effective policies and practices in this area. The power imbalance is magnified if the person allegedly responsible for the harassment is more senior to the harassed person, which is often the reality. Reporting is exponentially more difficult if the alleged harasser is the head of an organ or elected official of the Court or the ASP or affiliated with one of these officials.

---

[75] Richard J. Goldstone, "Prosecutorial Language, Integrity and Independence", CILRAP, 2 December 2018, at 6.50-7.25 minutes (www.cilrap.org/cilrap-film/181202-goldstone/)

[76] *Ibid.*

[77] *Ibid.*, at 8.50-9.12 minutes.

[78] United Nations, Administrative Instruction, 29 October 1992, ST/AI/379 (https://www.legal-tools.org/doc/juboyq/).

3. Paragraph 6.1 of the ICC policy states that staff members "shall have reasonable grounds before making a complaint of harassment", and paragraph 7.6 indicates that if such a complaint is found to be baseless or malicious, "the complainant may be subject to disciplinary procedures". These provisions, not within the UN's Administrative Instruction, could be considered intimidating for those contemplating reporting harassment and may be indicative of an environment hostile to, and inclined towards disbelief of, those reporting such conduct.

These policy gaps were subsequently reflected in the systemic indifference demonstrated by the Court's leadership regarding the lack of meaningful implementation of the Policy and monitoring of its use and accessibility. This inaction prevailed despite information that began to surface as early as 2005 with respect to the alleged conduct of staff and some Court officials in relation to possible harassment, especially of female staff and interns.[79]

In 2018, the ICC Disciplinary Advisory Board[80] determined that the Sexual Harassment Administrative Instruction did not apply to support staff members of either Defence Counsel or Victims Representatives, leaving these ICC-related contractors without redress or policy protection.[81] Support staff are particularly vulnerable because their contracts are negotiated directly with the Defence Counsel or Victims Legal Representatives who are not obliged to ensure that these employment arrangements comply with the standards or conditions within contracts issued directly by the ICC. The Court does not require any minimum employment protections and standards within such contracts, thus leaving support staff at the whims of the Counsel/Legal Representatives with little bargaining power and no contrac-

---

[79] Conversations with former Court staff on file with the author.

[80] ICC, "Disciplinary Procedure" (available on the ICC's web site).

[81] ICC, *The Prosecutor v.* Jean-Pierre Bemba Gombo, Aimé Kilolo Musamba, Jean-Jacques Mangenda Kabongo, Fidèle Babala Wandu and Narcisse Arido, *Trial Chamber,* Request to Review the Registry's Decision to Neither Apply or Comply With Legal Service Agreements with Defence Support Staff, *20 June 2018,* ICC-01/05-01/13-2292, paras. 21–23 ('Jean-Pierre Bemba Gombo case') (https://www.legal-tools.org/doc/dd9acd); ICC, Jean-Pierre Bemba Gombo case, Registry's Observations on the "Request to Review the Registry's Decision to Neither Apply or Comply With Legal Service Agreements with Defence Support Staff", Trial Chamber, *20 June 2018,* ICC-01/05-01/13-2292, paras. 21–27 (https://www.legal-tools.org/doc/d48f7e).

tual rights to sick leave, paid leave, and other standard conditions.[82] Although they are acting on behalf of the ICC, the Court does not extend any services to the Defence/Victims support staff and, as such, they may be unable to access the Court's medical practitioners, staff welfare services or the focal points indicated within the Policy to whom incidents of harassment can be reported. These conditions magnify the vulnerability of support staff, predominantly female, in relation to their direct service on behalf of the Court.

In 2018, 46 defence and victim's support staff members raised specific concerns with the Registry regarding the lack of institutional protection against harassment and exploitation in the workplace.[83] In March 2018, the International Criminal Court Bar Association issued a declaration reminding Defence Counsel of their obligations under the Code of Conduct for Counsel.[84] Despite the Registry's awareness of the policy gaps, the specific issues raised by support staff, and the associated vulnerability of these actors, it has not initiated any remedies or interim arrangements establishing minimum employment standards for these positions. In 2019, the Registry finally undertook a review of the Policy. However, as noted in the Final Report of the Independent Expert Review on the International Criminal Court and the Rome Statute System (the 'Independent Expert Review'), the new Administrative Instruction updating this policy area has been "stuck at inter-organ consultations for too long and remains unissued".[85]

This is an alarming oversight in the era of the #MeToo movement and unfathomably reckless with respect to the protection and well-being of individuals as well as the institution.

It is perhaps all the more startling in light of advocacy by civil society representatives between 2005 and 2014 noting the gaps in the training and procedures associated with the Policy, and the lack of progress in creat-

---

[82] *Ibid.*, paras. 3, 4, 10, 17, 18a-c.

[83] *Ibid.*, para. 21.

[84] International Criminal Court Bar Association, ICCBA Declaration on Obligations under the Code of Conduct for Counsel and Proposed Amendments thereto, 2 March 2018 (https://www.legal-tools.org/doc/tie947/).

[85] ICC, Independent Expert Review of the International Criminal Court and Rome Statute System, Final Report, 30 September 2020, para. 214, p. 68 ('Independent Expert Review') (https://www.legal-tools.org/doc/cv19d5/).

ing focal points.[86] Since 2008, these representatives have called on the ICC Presidency to oversee an audit of the Policy and its implementation, including: a review of the issues covered by the Policy; the adequacy of training; the creation of focal points; and the inclusion of the Policy within the induction process for new staff.[87] The civil society organization further suggested that the results of the audit should be shared with the Bureau and the ASP and called on the Court to develop recommendations to address any incidents or patterns of harassment and to ensure that the ICC provided a "non-discriminatory, equality-based, human-rights respecting work environment".[88]

8.5.4. Office of the Prosecutor

Beyond individual gaps in the institutional platform, deficiencies across multiple areas of employment suggest a systemic indifference within the Court to developing robust, ethical standards and an aversion, perhaps intentional, to complying with its regulatory framework, exercising oversight and responding to deviations from these obligations.

During the Court's first decade, this antipathy was perhaps most exemplified by the Prosecutor and the positions assumed by his Office on key policy issues including with respect to the creation and implementation of internal control systems across the Court as well as within the OTP.

In hindsight, possibly one of the first signs of this penchant for non-compliance within the OTP was the decision by the Prosecutor against adopting the draft Code of Conduct (the 'draft Code' or simply the 'Code'), included within the OTP's draft Regulations prepared by members of the Advance Team.[89] This preparatory team was established by States Parties

---

[86] Women's Initiatives for Gender Justice, *Gender Report Card on the International Criminal Court 2005*, Policy Section; *Gender Report Card on the International Criminal Court 2006*, p. 9; and *Gender Report Card on the International Criminal Court 2007*, p.14.

[87] Women's Initiatives for Gender Justice, *Gender Report Card on the International Criminal Court 2008*, para. 19, p. 107; *Gender Report Card on the International Criminal Court 2009*, p. 161; *Gender Report Card on the International Criminal Court 2010*, p. 65; *Gender Report Card on the International Criminal Court 2011*, p. 85; *Gender Report Card on the International Criminal Court 2012*, p. 60; *Gender Report Card on the International Criminal Court 2013*, pp. 243, 254; *Gender Report Card on the International Criminal Court 2014*, p. 277.

[88] *Ibid.*

[89] Salim A. Nakhjavani, "The Origins and Development of the Code of Conduct", in Bergsmo, Rackwitz and SONG (eds.), 2017, pp. 951–952, see above note 74.

to assist in setting up the OTP and the ICC as a whole in advance of Court officials assuming office.[90] According to Salim Nakhjavani in his analysis of the origins and development of the draft Code, the decision by the Advance Team to include a Code of Conduct within the draft Regulations of the OTP and therefore at the outset of the work of the Office, was an effort to "establish a universalised, virtues-based framework to guide behaviour and to contribute to establishing a genuinely international, professional legal culture within a nascent Office".[91] Amongst other features, the original draft of the Code included the provision for an in-house adviser for standards of conduct.[92] Far from envisaged as a set of rules, the draft Code of Conduct was intended to "unify the vision and harmonise the activities"[93] of a diverse body of staff members and ultimately to cultivate "coherence between the *being* of prosecutors and the *doing* of prosecutions".[94] Regrettably, although the Regulations were adopted by the first Prosecutor in September 2003, the OTP Code of Conduct was ignored for a decade until it was promulgated by Prosecutor Bensouda in 2013 within her first 18 months in office,[95] although without the position of an in-house adviser.[96]

Had it been adopted in a timely manner, the foresight of integrating a Code of Conduct within the Regulations and at the outset of the OTP's work may have gone some way towards inoculating the Office from the series of ethical issues that have confronted the OTP over the past 17 years, or perhaps at least provided a framework for corrective action.[97] As noted by Nakhjavani, with respect to the OTP, "effective, binding ethical and professional standards of conduct would have been *indispensable* from an early stage".[98]

---

[90] Bergsmo, 2017, p. 2, see above note 74.

[91] Nakhjavani, 2017, p. 962, see above note 89.

[92] *Ibid.*, p. 957.

[93] *Ibid.*, p. 955.

[94] *Ibid.*, p. 954.

[95] *Ibid.*, p. 952.

[96] *Ibid.*, p. 958.

[97] See, for example, *ibid.*, p. 952, fns. 5 and 6; Morten Bergsmo, Wolfgang Kaleck, Sam Muller and William H. Wiley, "A Prosecutor Falls: Time of the Court to Rise", FICHL Policy Brief Series No. 86 (2017), Torkel Opsahl Academic EPublisher, Brussels, 2017 (https://www.toaep.org/pbs-pdf/86-four-directors/); Women's Initiatives for Gender Justice, *Gender Report Cards on the International Criminal 2005-2014*, 2018; Women's Initiatives for Gender Justice, "A critical time for the ICC's credibility", 2 October 2017.

[98] Nakhjavani, 2017, p. 953, see above note 89.

In its absence, there appeared to be a consistent tendency in the leadership of the OTP towards ignoring institutional and individual accountability. This was primarily justified by the Prosecutor's assertion of the OTP's prosecutorial independence, as provided for in Article 42(1) of the Rome Statute,[99] as well as Article 42(2) of the Statute which states: "The Prosecutor shall have full authority over the management and administration of the Office, including the staff, facilities, and other resources thereof".

The Prosecutor's authority over the Office is indisputable. However, these statutory provisions were not intended to imply that OTP staff and officials, including the Prosecutor, operated outside of the ICC's rules, regulations, policies, and the requirements of the Rome Statute. During the first decade of the Court, it sometimes appeared as if the Prosecutor believed that OTP staff members were accountable to the standards set within the Office rather than to those established by the institution. This is not intended as a commentary on the integrity of the staff members of the OTP who should be assumed to be serious professionals largely mindful of their ethical responsibilities, duties, and regulatory obligations. It is simply a reflection that the ethical tone is always set from the top and that the "high officials of international courts define the culture of integrity within their institutions".[100]

It appears that at no time during the Prosecutor's tenure was the statutory imperative of independence sufficiently balanced with the equally important principles of accountability and compliance, as well as individual and institutional integrity. As exposed in the media revelations in 2017 regarding the former Prosecutor and his interactions with staff within the OTP at that time, this underlying culture appears to have had a lasting effect on at least some members of the Office. Reflecting on the workplace culture within the Court, the Independent Expert Review observed a general sense of stagnation within the overall ICC workforce that they found was "not being sufficiently rejuvenated through a process of staff turnover (particularly at the senior management level)".[101] This was particularly concerning, in their view, given that "senior management staff have sub-

---

[99] ICC Statute, Article 42(1), see above note 2.

[100] Bergsmo, 2018, p. 2, see above note 1.

[101] Independent Expert Review, 2020, para. 202, see above note 85.

stantial influence on maintaining organisational culture, thus making change more difficult".[102]

The Prosecutor's apparent aversion to checks and balances also directly contributed to weakening the internal oversight system within the Court as a whole, both during his tenure and beyond. Specifically, this contributed to: delaying the establishment of the IOM and constraining the conditions under which it operates (see Section 8.6.2.2.); curbing, along with other Heads of Organs, the independence of the Office of Internal Audit ('OIA') in its work and the submission of its findings (see Section 8.6.2.1.); and diminishing the oversight of the States Parties Committee on Budget and Finance ('CBF') and the External Auditor by ignoring their recommendations and concerns.[103]

Perhaps it is unfair to single out the ICC Prosecutor after all, as suggested by at least one commentator, the tendency towards unaccountability and "a sense that misconduct is beyond them" is not uncommon within judicial institutions or amongst international prosecutors.[104] However, if true, it is difficult to readily identify a peer who has matched this tendency to the same degree as the first chief Prosecutor of the ICC.

The underlying approach of downplaying and minimizing wrongdoing and subverting accountability during this period of the Court's establishment, laid the groundwork for the development of a high level of tolerance for impropriety and for underestimating the impact of wrong-doing on the reputation and culture of the institution. As a result, it provided fertile ground for invincibility to grow, especially amongst Court officials, ultimately compromising the integrity of the ICC. Regrettably, it also devoured the space for genuine dialogue amongst ICC staff members regarding the ethical challenges they encountered within the context of their work.

8.5.5. An Enabling Political Environment

The ICC's eagerness to exercise its jurisdiction whilst still in its infancy as an institution was widely supported, but may also have been its initial undoing. Significant expectations on the Court and assumptions about how its legitimacy would be secured, defined the pace of its work and the issues to

---

[102] *Ibid.*, para. 203.

[103] See, for example, ICC, Report of the Committee on Budget and Finance, 13 August 2004, ICC-ASP/3/18, paras. 60–62 ('ICC-ASP/3/18') (https://www.legal-tools.org/doc/63ilat/).

[104] Frédéric Mégret, "Accountability and Ethics", in Luc Reydams, Jan Wouters and Cedric Ryngaert (eds.), *International Prosecutors*, Oxford University Press, 2012, p. 417.

which it was attentive. There was an almost universal belief within the ICC, amongst States Parties and other stakeholders, that the ICC's legitimacy would be achieved through the exercise of its jurisdiction alone, and not also through its institutional integrity as a global publicly accountable institution. Its jurisdictional firepower was potentially formidable and perhaps a little intoxicating, and the establishment of the Court was justifiably a source of pride, excitement and anticipation.

Staff and external supporters wanted to close the 'impunity gap'[105] for the commission of international crimes as quickly as possible and expand the rule of law. Many were motivated by concern for the harm experienced by victims of these crimes and the urgency to halt the ongoing commission of mass violence. Some wanted to see how this new institution would interface with the global peace and security agenda, its potential to advance human rights more broadly and its effect, if any, on the pursuit of accountability within the existing world order. A wide array of legitimate and genuine motivations fuelled the significant expectations on the Court when it was first established and may have added to the pressure to produce unrealistic results.

As early as August 2004, the CBF declared that the ICC was now moving from the "start-up phase", which they described as "designing systems and recruiting personnel", into "an operational phase".[106] The following year, the staff strategy unit within the OTP was abolished because "the initial stage of creating staff policies and guidelines was nearing its end".[107] These decisions appeared to be somewhat premature given both the OTP and the Court as a whole were in the throes of a voluminous hiring process. For example, between March 2004 and August 2006, the number of ICC staff members grew from 177 to 441 positions with a total of 624 posts approved for recruitment by the end of the 2006 financial year.[108] With insuf-

---

[105] A term coined by Morten Bergsmo in 2002 which has become widely used in the international justice field. Bergsmo, 2017, pp. 14–15, see above note 74.

[106] ICC-ASP/3/18, para. 34, see above note 103.

[107] ICC, Report of the Committee on Budget and Finance on the work of its fifth session, 21 October 2005, ICC-ASP/4/27, para. 37 ('ICC-ASP/4/27') (https://www.legal-tools.org/doc/gz9soy/).

[108] ICC, Reports of the Committee on Budget and Finance, 19 August 2004, ICC-ASP/3/22, para. 20 (https://www.legal-tools.org/doc/l66zci/); ICC-ASP/4/3, 15 April 2005, para. 45; ICC, Report of the Committee on Budget and Finance on the work of its seventh session, 1 November 2006, ICC-ASP/5/23, para. 39 ('ICC-ASP/5/23') (https://www.legal-tools.org/doc/l66zci/). These figures are based on staff employed by the ICC on fixed term contracts

ficient staff policies, training and workplace procedures in place and with little time to establish the internal environment, operating methods, and ethical culture, the ICC was propelled towards exercising its mandate.

A reconstruction of the timeline demonstrates how quickly the ICC's jurisdiction was activated. The Rome Statute came into force on 1 July 2002. The first set of judges to the ICC was elected in February 2003 and quickly sworn in at the seat of the Court, in The Hague on 11 March of the same year. A short time later, the Prosecutor was sworn in on 16 June 2003, and the Registrar was appointed and sworn in by the judges on 3 July 2003. Within six months of these appointments, the ICC received its first referral,[109] and by March 2005, the OTP had received four referrals from States and non-States Parties within a 14-month period.[110]

The Court faced mounting and unrealistic expectations, many of which the OTP itself fostered and encouraged, including through its budget projections to the CBF. At times, these submissions appeared to greatly exaggerate the speed of its investigations, its readiness for trials and its prediction about the length of the legal proceedings.[111] Inaccurate early projections would not ordinarily be worthy of attention. An error in assessment does not demonstrate unreliability and mistakes are inevitable in undertakings as audacious as the mandate of the ICC. But bold pronouncements by the Prosecutor throughout the first decade often over-estimated the preparedness of the OTP. They also seemed to be regularly at odds with effective prosecutorial strategy and good management, as suggested by the results of the cases launched during this period. In hindsight, these projections also suggest four noteworthy aspects associated with the Prosecutor's assertions.

First, there was a ready audience amongst stakeholders for ambitious pronouncements by the Prosecutor, and in this area, he would not disap-

---

and exclude those hired on general temporary assistance, consultants, as well as interns and visiting fellows.

[109] ICC, *The Prosecutor v. Dominic Ongwen*, Case information Sheet, 16 December 2003, ICC-PIDS-CIS-UGA-02-018/20 (https://www.legal-tools.org/doc/sn4msm/).

[110] Referral by the Government of Uganda, 16 December 2003; referral by the Democratic Republic of the Congo, 3 March 2004; referral by the Government of the Central African Republic, 21 December 2004; referral by the United Nations Security Council of the situation in Darfur, Sudan, 31 March 2005, UNSC Resolution 1593.

[111] ICC-ASP/3/18, para. 35, see above note 103. "Situation 1, with a single case, would be ready for trial in January 2005 and would last eight months. Investigations for two cases in situation 2 would continue until May 2005, at which time they would be ready for trial. Trials in situation 2 would continue for the rest of 2005".

point. Although there is evidence that some people urged caution and encouraged the Prosecutor to take the time to build the institution,[112] the Prosecutor, himself, believed that "the institution would be built through *activity*, by doing cases and demonstrating that the Court could function".[113] He felt he needed to show results as quickly as possible,[114] and this was fuelled by the genuine intentions of supporters of the Court and the indisputable needs of victims of mass crimes.

Second, the impulse to make extravagant statements appeared to signal a pattern of bravado that came to be associated with the Prosecutor and many of the decisions of his office, some of which are considered to have compromised the reputation of the Court with respect to the OTP's prosecutorial performance.[115]

Third, the decision-making by the Prosecutor and the Executive Committee set an investigative and prosecutorial pace that the OTP (and the Court) was ill-prepared for substantively, as well as in relation to its staff levels and working methods. This extended to and impacted the organizational development of the Office.

Finally, in responding to these assertions, States Parties demonstrated an appetite for public aggrandizement and an inclination to forego critical evaluation. Concurrently, States also displayed a willingness to overlook the Prosecutor's professional conduct as an international civil servant, either because they were not personally disturbed by it or because any individual failings paled in comparison to the importance of the Court.[116]

---

[112] Alex Whiting, "Investigations and Institutional Imperatives at the International Criminal Court", in Martha Minow, C. Cora True-Frost and Alex Whiting (eds.), *The First Global Prosecutor: Promise and Constraints*, University of Michigan Press, Ann Arbor, 2015, p. 103. "Six months after my beginning I received a referral from Uganda. And some people were advising me, be careful, you have to build an institution for the next two centuries. I knew I had to run. I had to show very quickly, some outcome, some results".

[113] *Ibid.*

[114] *Ibid.*

[115] See, for example, Bergsmo, Kaleck, Muller and Wiley, 2017, see above note 97; Bergsmo, 2017, pp. 21–31, see above note 74; Scott Horton, "Unimaginable Atrocities: Six Questions for William Schabas", in *Harpers Blog*, 18 May 2012; Brigid Inder, "Launch of the Gender Report Card for 2010", Women's Initiatives for Gender Justice, 6 December 2010; Women's Initiatives for Gender Justice, *Gender Report Card on the International Criminal Court 2012*, pp. 132–163; Women's Initiatives for Gender Justice, *Gender Report Card on the International Criminal Court 2014*, pp. 157–193.

[116] Conversations with diplomats and civil society organizations on file with the author.

The first Prosecutor has been the subject of significant critique and criticism, much of it arguably warranted and justified. But his decisions, actions and conduct, while part of his professional responsibility as the Prosecutor, existed within a system that allowed and enabled these factors to occur. A balanced view of the Prosecutor immediately recognizes that he brought significant energy and dynamism to the role and displayed an indefatigable ability to generate ideas, interest and prosecutorial activity. His personal communication and rapport-building skills were an undeniable asset in his interactions with States Parties, NGOs and the media; his willingness to be the public face of the ICC provided a ready focal point for a court that may otherwise have seemed even more remote and unknowable. The Prosecutor's ability to inspire young people and their interest in international justice as well as his intuitive understanding of the allure of his office and the associated ability to engage influencers and celebrities added to the sense of momentum, purpose and global visibility of the Court. As asserted in the *Reckoning*, one of the films made about the ICC and the Prosecutor, he perhaps did more than anyone to put the Court on the map.[117] However, if true, having galvanized attention, the Prosecutor was unable to deliver on his promises to an expectant global audience.

Less ambition would not have been better. Timidity was not the way forward for a new Court. But the provision of a counter-balance by States Parties – insisting upon institution-building; being less focused on numbers (of cases and arrest warrants) in favour of quality; requiring conduct befitting international civil servants; using their oversight responsibilities to ensure a solid framework of ethical standards and compliance benchmarks; and being prepared to use their statutory obligations to address misconduct – could have brought some equilibrium to the Court and reduced the gap between the expectations generated and the outcomes that materialized. It would also have safeguarded the Court's institutional integrity.

It is understandable that the ICC would assume a high level of focus on its mandate. However, it is difficult for the Court to justify its almost exclusive focus on the exercise of its jurisdiction with insufficient attention also devoted to creating a solid and ethical foundation, ensuring the integrity and sustainability of the institution and a reliable base from which it could fulfil its jurisdictional responsibilities.

---

[117] Pamela Yates and Paco de Onis, *The Reckoning: The Battle for the International Criminal Court*, Skylight 2009; Whiting, 2015, see above note 112.

It is eminently conceivable that complacency about the ICC's institutional integrity may have been rationalized by a belief that the absolute moral imperative of the Court's mandate, somehow organically imbibed the Court's day-to-day decisions with the same moral superiority, even if the actions and decisions at hand were objectively unethical, a violation of the rules or akin to misconduct.

ICC officials and States Parties may have instinctively equated their actions and decisions as having the same high standing as the mandate of the Statute. In reality, there is no guarantee that working for or governing an institution with noble intentions and high aspirations will automatically infuse every decision with the same fragrance of authenticity. The integrity of an institution is the sum of its choices, on issues small and large, which decision-by-decision defines its character. Every individual choice has a consequence for the whole. Each time a decision was made at the ICC to ignore the policies, bend the rules, or excuse conflicts of interest, it reinforced impropriety, and what started out as just making an exception, soon became a habit that turned into a practice and evolved into a culture.

The urgency with which Court officials, member States and other stakeholders wanted the ICC to exercise its jurisdiction may have inadvertently compromised the integrity of the Court as a public institution. Its organizational foundations were not sufficiently established before it became operationally active. The Court's internal control systems and the policies regulating conduct and conflicts of interest, amongst other areas, were incomplete, untested or non-existent. Just as importantly, the ICC had not established an environment in which genuine ethical dilemmas could be identified and safely discussed as they arose. Once cases began, most institutional development issues were put on hold, and several aspects of the organizational bedrock that would ordinarily underpin an international institution were never completed.

8.6. Ethical Challenges at the ICC

Whilst the ethical challenges before the ICC are substantial, it is important to make a clear distinction between honest mistakes and impropriety.[118] Many new endeavours will experience errors and set-backs before they experience success. Mistakes in direction and decision-making can be a rich

---

[118] See M.E. Newhouse, "Institutional Corruption: A Fiduciary Theory", in *Cornell Journal of Law and Public Policy*, 2014, vol. 23, no. 3, Article 2, p. 560.

source of learning for an institution as it refines its practices, further clarifies its values, and evolves its organizational culture.[119] There needs to be room for errors to occur in order for innovation to exist. In this context, the ICC has made honest mistakes. This was inevitable given its challenging jurisdictional mandate, the complexity of the contexts within which it is working, the newness of the institution, and as the Statute was translated into practice.

In addition to genuine good-faith mistakes, the ICC has also faced avoidable ethical transgressions. Patterns of impropriety and the exercise of questionable individual and institutional integrity have had a corrosive effect on the culture of the ICC.

Importantly, all stakeholders – ICC officials and staff, States Parties and civil society – share some responsibility, to varying degrees, for the fragility of the Court's institutional integrity because each one, with few exceptions, has been willing to overlook impropriety at the ICC when it occurred and to remain silent. The high level of conformity to this practice by genuine supporters of the Court may have unintentionally contributed to a collective deception about the Court's institutional well-being and its ethical resilience. It may also have led to under-estimating the important link between the ICC's institutional integrity and its legitimacy as a trusted purveyor of global justice in an increasingly polarized world. Not only is it critical for the Court to maintain or regain its credibility but, as Karim Khan urges, we must also be aware of what is at stake in the politically fractured environment around international justice, warning that, "an understanding of what we could lose must be born very close to one's heart and upper most in one's mind".[120]

The ethical challenges confronting the ICC can be characterized into three major categories of vulnerability, which will be listed in turn:

1. public crises arising from serious misconduct by individual staff or Court officials, some of which have been exposed by the media;

2. checks and balances at the ICC that have at times lacked rigour, and internal oversight mechanisms that have at critical moments wanted independence or ability to fulfil their mandates; and

---

[119] See, for example, Amy Rees Anderson, "Good Employees Make Mistakes, Great Leaders Allow Them To", *Forbes*, 17 April 2013; Brené Brown, *Dare to Lead*, Random House, 2018.

[120] Karim A.A. Khan, "Integrity and the Limits of Internal Oversight Mechanisms", CILRAP, 2 December 2018, at 14-14.18 minutes (www.cilrap.org/cilrap-film/181202-khan/).

3. insufficient infrastructure to support and ensure the Court's institutional integrity.

8.6.1. Public Crises Exposed by the Media

The revelations in the public domain include:

- allegations regarding conflicts of interest of the former Prosecutor since leaving office and possible attempts to interfere in an ongoing ICC case;[121]

- allegations regarding the leaking and/or sharing of confidential material by the staff of the OTP to the former Prosecutor relevant to an individual client for whom the former Prosecutor was providing consultancy services;[122]

- the OTP sharing confidential information related to its investigations and cases with selected States Parties;[123]

- OTP staff moonlighting in roles which are in conflict with their status as employees of the ICC along with alleged attempts to conceal these activities;[124]

- abuse of power, and retaliatory and bad faith behaviour by the Registrar;[125]

- the illegality of the restructuring project of the Registry;[126]

---

[121] Becker, Blasberg and Pieper, 2017; EIC Network, 2017; Maupas, 2017; Thompson, 2017, see above note 18. In 2017, a series of media reports revealed allegations regarding improper and potentially unlawful activity by the former Prosecutor, Moreno-Ocampo, and staff employed by the OTP. The allegations involved the provision of confidential information about the OTP's ongoing investigation in Libya, by staff of the OTP, to Moreno-Ocampo based on its relevance to one of his clients, a Libyan national. Amongst several issues, the media reports also allege that OTP staff members provided communication and other assistance to the former Prosecutor in relation to this same client. It is also alleged that the former Prosecutor may have attempted to intervene in the OTP's cases in the Kenya Situation.

[122] *Ibid.*

[123] *Ibid.*

[124] *Ibid.*

[125] Administrative Tribunal of the International Labour Organization ('ILOAT'), *A. v. ICC*, Judgment No. 4003, paras. 15 and 17 ('Judgment No. 4003') (https://www.legal-tools.org/doc/iu7r5q/).

[126] ILOAT, *F. v. ICC*, Judgment No. 3907, para. 26 ('Judgment No. 3907') (https://www.legal-tools.org/doc/w87k12/).

- the alleged rape of ICC witnesses by Registry staff in safe houses in the Democratic Republic of the Congo over an extended period of time;[127]

- the International Labour Organisation and Tribunal ('ILOAT') judgment regarding the unlawful dismissal of an OTP staff member by the Prosecutor in retaliation for the employee reporting allegations of serious misconduct by the Prosecutor in the course of his official duties;[128] and

- the failure by the ICC to meet its duty of care to its staff, including its failure to ensure the necessary security protocols were implemented to guarantee the safety of staff members on a mission in Libya.[129] This resulted in the staff members being held by a Libyan militia group for over three weeks and an international incident in which the reputations of the staff were impugned in the media as a result of the ICC failing to take responsibility for sending staff on the mission without the required Memorandum of Understanding with the Libyan authorities.[130]

For most of these serious incidents, there has not been any demonstrable accountability by the Court, internally, to States Parties or to the public, regarding its actions, if any, to address those responsible, tackle the underlying institutional culture or examine the weaknesses in the oversight system. For their part, States Parties have been consistently willing to look the other way, especially when the misconduct involved Court officials.

There are two exceptions to this pattern that demonstrate a level of willingness by the Court to apply limited accountability measures when under significant external pressure to do so.

The first was in relation to the independent inquiry initiated by the Registry in 2013 into the sexual assault of ICC witnesses followed by a public report summarizing the key findings and recommendations to address practices within the Victims and Witness Unit.[131] Prior to the active

---

[127] Women's Initiatives for Gender Justice, *Gender Report Card on the International Criminal Court 2013*, pp. 235–241 ('Gender Report Card 2013').

[128] ILOAT, Judgment No. 2757, paras. 2–20 (https://www.legal-tools.org/doc/73bd48/).

[129] Judgment No. 4003, para. 16, see above note 125.

[130] *Ibid.*

[131] The Court's report is no longer on the ICC web site; Gender Report Card 2013, pp. 238–241, see above note 127.

involvement of the President of the ASP, and a few States Parties that strongly urged the Court to address these issues and whose interventions were triggered by civil society, the Court did not appear to have taken any serious action to investigate and determine the systemic issues enabling the rape of witnesses by ICC staff members.[132] States were alerted to this crisis in a letter by civil society submitted to the Presidents of the ASP and the Court along with a small number of selected States Parties, drawing their attention to the serious incident and calling for an independent inquiry.[133] The prompt action of the ASP President and States successfully invoked a response from the Court.

The second exception was the OTP's response to the numerous allegations made in the media between September and October 2017 involving the former Prosecutor and two OTP staff members.[134] The current Prosecutor referred these issues to the IOM for investigation as well as to the Disciplinary Advisory Board whose review and recommendations ultimately resulted in the dismissal of the staff members involved for serious misconduct.[135] A summary of the OTP's response to the specific allegations as well as steps taken by the office to strengthen standards of integrity and personal conduct was presented to States Parties in The Hague Working Group in November 2018 and subsequently made available to States Parties in the context of the ASP later that same year.[136]

However, for the most part, the Court, with the complicit agreement of other stakeholders, has generally taken the position that acknowledging and addressing wrongdoing would undermine the ICC's reputation; and, as a result, its pattern over many years has been to ignore, deny, conceal or deflect. The challenge with this approach is that it further embeds impropriety into the organizational culture and prolongs the vulnerability of these episodes for the Court because inevitably, as has been demonstrated by the series of media revelations, these issues will eventually be exposed. While

---

[132] *Ibid.*, pp. 235–241.

[133] *Ibid.*, pp. 235–237. Letter from the Women's Initiatives for Gender Justice.

[134] Becker, Blasberg and Pieper, 2017; EIC Network, 2017; Maupas, 2017; Thompson, 2017, see above note 18.

[135] ICC, Briefing by the Prosecutor, 14 November 2018, ICC-ASP/17/INF.5, paras. 18, 24(a), 24(c) ('Prosecutor's Briefing').

[136] *Ibid.*; see also comments by Deputy Prosecutor, James Stewart, "The Legal Requirement of Individual Integrity and the Prosecution of International Crimes", CILRAP Film, The Hague, 1 December 2018 (https://www.cilrap.org/cilrap-film/181201-stewart/).

they exist, they are ripe for exploitation by those who may want to discredit the Court. As many institutions, governments and private sector leaders have learned the hard way, cover-ups, obfuscation and dishonesty are often more damaging to public trust than the original error.

In addition to affecting its external reputation, integrity issues are also demoralizing for ICC staff,[137] who are predominantly rule compliant and exercise their personal ethics within the workplace. But they also take their cues from those higher up. The ethical culture of an institution affects the ability of good people to do the right thing.[138] This becomes increasingly challenging when there are no consequences or inadequate consequences for violations, or when the violations involve senior leaders and Court officials. A lack of healthy accountability both for individuals and the institution is one of the hallmarks of an ethically fragile system.

8.6.2. Checks and Balances

Leadership and oversight of the ICC are responsibilities shared between the Court and States Parties. Put simply, the ICC, specifically through the heads of organs, is responsible for the day-to-day leadership, decisions and operations of the Court, whereas States, through the ASP, are responsible for the overall governance of the ICC.

With respect to the Court's functions, it has been slow and unresponsive to the usual checks and balances essential to the effective internal oversight of a complex organization. At times, these mechanisms have lacked rigour and during critical periods for the Court, the independence of the internal oversight mechanisms has been compromised or they have been unable to fulfil their mandates. Similarly, the ASP and its key subsidiary bodies have been narrowly focused with respect to their governance responsibilities with the exception of the annual forensic budget review process. Although the ASP adopted resolutions regulating the Court, it has done little to monitor the Court's compliance with the legal framework. It has also consistently ignored and underfunded the oversight system.

---

[137] Bergsmo, 2018, p. 1, see above note 1.

[138] See, for example, Caterina Bulgarella, "Why good words can produce bad acts", in *FCPA Blog*, 26 June 2018.

8.6.2.1.   Internal Oversight

The history of the OIA is one piece of the puzzle about where and how the institutional ethics and integrity of the Court went off track so quickly.

The OIA was established under Rule 110.1 of the ICC's Financial Regulations and Rules adopted at the first plenary of the Assembly of States Parties, held 3-10 September 2002.[139] Its mandate was set out in the Financial Regulations and in the 2003 Report of the CBF adopted by the ASP wherein

> the internal auditor should be able to decide his or her annual work programme independently, including any issues raised by the Committee, and that the internal auditor should submit an annual report about the activities of the Office to the Assembly, through the Committee.[140]

The OIA commenced operations in July 2004 and for the first three years, 2005-2007, it provided reports directly to the ASP.[141] These are the only internal audit reports submitted directly to the Assembly and the only reports produced by the OIA that are publicly available. The reports summarized its activities in some detail, including work it had undertaken on its own initiative as well as audits conducted at the request of the heads of organs and other managers, as they were confronted with a range of institution-building issues. The OIA reported on these audits with a summary of its main findings and recommendations, as well as management's responses to its recommendations in general terms. It identified issues and areas for attention, supported the progress being made by the Court, and provided a number of constructive suggestions, appropriate for an office of internal audit and consistent with its oversight responsibilities.

Despite the mandate, role, and reporting lines of the OIA being addressed by the financial regulations and the 2003 CBF report, respectively, a sense of "ambiguity existed within the Court concerning how the office

---

[139] ICC, Financial Regulations and Rules, 3-10 September 2002, ICC-ASP/1/3, Part II-D (https://www.legal-tools.org/doc/6158e2-1).

[140] Official Records of the Assembly of States Parties to the Rome Statute of the International Criminal Court, 8-12 September 2003, ICC-ASP/2/10, Section II, para. 29 (https://www.legal-tools.org/doc/446e04).

[141] ICC, Report of the Office of Internal Audit, 3 August 2005, ICC-ASP/4/4 ('ICC-ASP/4/4') (https://www.legal-tools.org/doc/3zz1ki/); ICC, Report of the Office of Internal Audit, 4 August 2006, ICC-ASP/5/5 ('ICC-ASP/5/5') (https://www.legal-tools.org/doc/k4ukb6/); ICC, Report of the Office of Internal Audit, 17 July 2007, ICC-ASP/6/7 ('ICC-ASP/6/7') (https://www.legal-tools.org/doc/marcyi/).

would operate and report in practice".[142] In response to this "ambiguity" and in an act of good faith, the Director of OIA commenced a process of working with the heads of organs to develop the *Charter for Internal Audit for the Court*, which was adopted by the Coordination Council (comprised of the three heads of organs – the President, the Prosecutor and the Registrar) in June 2005.[143]

According to the first report of the OIA to the ASP, the Charter clarified and elaborated the legal mandate of the office, including its operating and reporting mechanisms, and described the interface between the External Auditor and the OIA. One of the key features of the Charter was the establishment of an Oversight Committee whose main function was to "act as an advisory panel to the Office of Internal Audit in the exercise of its audit functions and to monitor the implementation of relevant recommendations".[144]

The composition of the Oversight Committee was designated to the heads of organs, with the OIA providing secretarial support.[145] Although external experts could be added to the Oversight Committee, the primary roles were dedicated to the heads of organs.[146]

The Charter left it to the Oversight Committee to determine the terms of its working relationship with the CBF, [147] and gave authority to the Oversight Committee to decide on the dissemination of audit reports, except for those audits requested by the CBF or the ASP.[148] In other words, the findings of audits into certain areas of work, if requested by a head of organ, could be concealed from the oversight of the CBF, the External Auditor and the ICC's governance body, the ASP. Such audit reports do not always need to be made public, but they should be made available to the governing structures, including the External Auditor for review. Creating the ability to withhold the audit reports from the governing authorities cre-

---

[142] ICC-ASP/4/4, para. 10, see above note 141.

[143] *Ibid.*, Annex 1, para. 7(i).

[144] *Ibid.*, Annex 1, para. 4(ii).

[145] *Ibid.*, Annex 1, para. 4(iv).

[146] *Ibid.*, Annex 1, para. 4(iii).

[147] *Ibid.*

[148] *Ibid.*, Annex 1, para. 4(ii): "The Oversight Committee authorizes the dissemination of audit reports, except for those requested by the Committee on Budget and Finance pursuant to paragraph 29 of the report on the work of its third session, August 2003, or those requested by the Assembly of States Parties".

ated the potential to reduce the oversight of the Court's institutional activities by the Assembly.

The stated intention of the Oversight Committee was to enhance cooperation between the organs and the OIA. However, the provisions in the Charter assigned a significant level of power to the heads of organs with respect to the focus, findings and reporting of the internal audits. Although the Charter was undertaken by the OIA in good faith, the use of the provisions by the heads of organs marked a negative turning point for the Office that contributed to undermining its full independence and curtailing the robust exercise of its mandate.

Simultaneously in 2005, as the Court was establishing the Oversight Committee, the External Auditor recommended the establishment of an independent Audit Committee.[149] This recommendation was echoed by the CBF.[150] It seems that the instigation of an Oversight Committee created by the heads of organs and the recommendation to establish an Audit Committee by the Auditor and CBF were on two separate tracks with distinct and different motivations. The former appears to have been intended to contain the work and scrutiny of the OIA, reduce its independence, and avert its ability to report to the ASP and the CBF on all of its findings. The intention of the latter appears to have been to strengthen the ICC's internal controls, add further expertise and independence, and to work with the OIA. This divergence led to an impasse between the ASP and the Court with respect to the independent functioning of the OIA, and the expertise required on the Oversight and Audit Committees to support these most fundamental and important components of the system of internal oversight.

As early as 2006, major tensions had reportedly arisen between the OIA and the heads of organs with the latter wanting to limit the OIA's ability to report major findings of its internal audits to the CBF and ASP.[151] Observing these tensions, the CBF noted that:

> While it was satisfied that the Office of Internal Audit had now fully assumed its functions as confirmed by a peer review carried out by the National Audit Office, the Committee could not escape the impression that the relationship between the Court and the Office of Internal Audit was adversely affected

---

[149] ICC-ASP/4/27, para. 13, see above note 107.

[150] *Ibid.*

[151] ICC-ASP/5/23, para. 26, see above note 108.

by a misunderstanding on both sides as to the role of internal oversight.[152]

According to the CBF, Court officials seemed "to be generally uneasy about the Internal Auditor's right and obligation to report major findings to the Committee and to the Assembly and would prefer the Office to be an exclusively internal controlling instrument".[153] The CBF also noted on the other hand that the OIA, "must not limit itself to detecting irregularities and uncovering administrative weaknesses, but should more strongly emphasize the goal of working in partnership with management to improve the overall performance of the Court".

Conscious of the tension, the CBF, "urged both sides to work for a better understanding of their respective roles. The Court's Internal Oversight Committee, in particular, was called upon to work towards that goal. The early inclusion of external experts in the Internal Oversight Committee would be helpful in that endeavour".[154]

A review of the OIA reports from this period does not appear to support the assessment of a one-sided focus on the detection of problems by the OIA without the intention to work together to improve the performance of the Court. On the contrary, the OIA reports appear to be even-handed, often encouraging and noted that the ICC was making progress. The reports also indicate that the OIA consistently demonstrated its willingness to work with the Court's management. In its first three years of operation, the Office made a number of recommendations aimed at, "assisting management to strengthen internal controls, operate more efficiently, realize potential cost savings and ensure compliance with governing authorities".[155] These activities appear to be strongly in line with the functions of an office responsible for internal audits.

In 2007, the relationship further deteriorated with limited responses from Court officials to the OIA's audit findings, as well as insufficient information provided by the ICC for the internal audits.[156] The heads of organs were also non-compliant in their interactions with the Office of the Controller and failed to provide this office with the required reports and

---

[152] *Ibid.*, para. 25.

[153] *Ibid.*, para. 26.

[154] *Ibid.*, para. 27.

[155] ICC-ASP/6/7, p.4, see above note 141.

[156] *Ibid.*, p. 5.

updates regarding their progress implementing substantive recommendations made by the External Auditor.[157]

In September 2007, the CBF raised concerns with the Court regarding the lack of implementation of the external audit recommendations and, "the pace of progress in appointing non-executive members [external members] to the Audit Committee, developing a risk management framework, and implementing a statement of internal control".[158]

At the CBF's meeting in September, it appears that the Committee acquiesced to the discomfort of the heads of organs regarding the independence of the OIA and its ability to report to the ASP. The Committee made critical decisions at this meeting that altered the independence of the OIA and curtailed its ability to scrutinize the Court. Firstly, it designated to the Audit Committee the ability to approve the annual work plan for the OIA, thus giving the heads of organs the ability to determine the areas and scope of the OIA's internal audits.[159]

Secondly, the CBF cut off the OIA's ability to submit reports about internal compliance and audits directly to the ASP for their review and consideration.[160] Instead, it required that the OIA report only to the CBF, which would then decide whether there were any issues it wished to draw to the ASP's attention. This placed significant power to vet and filter information in the hands of the CBF rather than these reports being considered by the wider membership of the ASP. It also curtailed the ability of the ASP to fully govern. To make matters worse, the CBF also declared that the OIA should report to it through the chair of the Audit Committee, which at that time was one of the principals of the Court operating within a committee dominated by all of the heads of organs.[161] Subsequently, the ICC Financial Regulations and Rules were amended specifying the change in this reporting line.[162]

---

[157] *Ibid.*

[158] ICC, Report of the Committee on Budget and Finance on the work at its ninth session, 28 September 2007, ICC-ASP-6/12, para. 21 ('ICC-ASP-6/12') (https://www.legal-tools.org/doc/1eamh2/).

[159] *Ibid.*, para. 22.

[160] *Ibid.*

[161] *Ibid.*

[162] ICC, Amendments to the Finance Regulations and Rules, Assembly of State Parties Resolution, adopted on 14 December 2007, ICC-ASP/6/Res.5 (https://www.legal-tools.org/doc/3a62e0).

Lastly, the CBF recommended that the OIA focus its work on providing the Registrar, as the ICC's accounting officer, with assurances and advice regarding the effectiveness of the management and control systems.[163] Combined with the other changes, this had the effect of pulling the OIA too close to the Registry and increasing the communication and eventual influence of the Registrar on the work of the OIA. In practice, the OIA came to 'report' to the Registrar by default, especially following the collapse of the Audit Committee between 2012 and 2016, and in the absence of effective oversight by the CBF. This further reduced the level of independence normally expected of an internal audit office.

These far-reaching changes were taken further by the Audit Committee in August 2008 when the heads of organs revised the Terms of Reference for the Audit Committee and established a model which according to the CBF "differed from the one recommended previously by the External Auditors, the ASP and the Committee on Budget and Finance" and ensured that the balance of power was firmly with the heads of organs.[164] Contradicting the 2006 recommendations from the Auditor and the CBF that the Audit Committee should be composed of a majority of external members and chaired by an external member, the Court insisted upon the composition of three Court members (the Principals) and two external members.[165] Going even further, the Court insisted that it would appoint the two external members.[166] In addition, whereas the model advocated by the CBF would provide "advice to management and add independent oversight to the audit function", according to the CBF the Audit Committee established by the Court, "'was a management committee with some external members".[167]

All of these changes appear to demonstrate a level of determination on the part of the principals, to strip the OIA of any independence and curb the activities, scope, findings and dissemination of its reports. The OIA was

---

[163] ICC-ASP-6/12, para. 22, see above note 158.

[164] ICC, Report of the Committee on Budget and Finance on the work of its eleventh session, 31 October 2008, ICC-ASP/7/15, para. 24 ('ICC-ASP/7/15') (https://www.legal-tools.org/doc/1q3lhk/).

[165] *Ibid.*, para. 25.

[166] ICC, Report of the Committee on Budget and Finance on the work of its tenth session, 26 May 2008, ICC-ASP/7/3, para. 19 (https://www.legal-tools.org/doc/oe4mh7/).

[167] ICC-ASP/7/15, para. 25, see above note 164.

the only internal mechanism providing any kind of oversight and acting as a control function within the Court until 2016.

Failure to safeguard the independence and impartiality of the OIA appears to have been one of the significant stumbling blocks for the ICC regarding its institutional integrity. Many of the unlawful and unethical issues it has faced may have been averted, and/or identified earlier had the full independence of the OIA been preserved. The harm caused to the Court by the patterns of impropriety, mostly by Court officials and senior managers, may have been reduced, and a culture of accountability could have been fostered, had the OIA been properly supported and enabled to fulfil its mandate.

The Audit Committee ceased to operate in 2012 and was formally terminated in 2014.[168] New Terms of Reference were drafted by an ad hoc Committee, and a new composition of membership was designed comprised of only external members and members of the CBF.[169] The Audit Committee was reconstituted in 2015 and became operational with a new charter in 2016.[170] Finally, after 13 years of ICC operations, the ASP instigated a dedicated entity with responsibilities for: governance; risk management; values and ethics; internal control framework; oversight of internal and external audit; and financial statements and public accountability reporting.[171]

With the restoration of a credible structure for the Audit Committee, the OIA now reports to this body.[172] In 2014, the OIA was elevated to a ma-

---

[168] ICC, Report of the Committee on Budget and Finance on the work of its twenty-third session, ICC-ASP/13/15, 18 November 2014, paras. 132–135 ('ICC-ASP/13/15') (https://www.legal-tools.org/doc/iv9xys/). It was subsequently disbanded on 13 February 2015 by Presidential Directive, ICC-ASP/PRESD/G/2015/001 (https://www.legal-tools.org/doc/75fbb6/).

[169] ICC, Report of the Committee on Budget and Finance on the work of its twenty-fifth, Charter of the Audit Committee, 9 November 2015, ICC-ASP/14/15, Annex IV, Section E, para. 10 ('ICC-ASP/14/15') (https://www.legal-tools.org/doc/575aqd/).

[170] Ibid., Section C, 2, paras. 140–141; ICC, Official Records of the Assembly of States Parties, ICC-ASP/14/20, vol. II, Part B, B.3 (https://www.legal-tools.org/doc/156059/).

[171] ICC, Charter of the Audit Committee, annexed to Report of the Committee on Budget and Finance on the work of its Twenty-Fifth session, 9 November 2015, ICC-ASP/14/15, Section B, paras. 2–3 (https://www.legal-tools.org/doc/575aqd/).

[172] ICC, Resolution on the Programme budget for 2016, the Working Capital Fund and the Contingency Fund for 2016, scale of assessments for the apportionment of expenses of the International Criminal Court and financing appropriations for 2016, 26 November 2015, ICC-

jor programme within the Court's budget with its own dedicated budget line, further underscoring its independence.[173] The Audit Committee approves and monitors implementation of the OIA's annual audit plans. In practice, the agreement of the head of organ is still required to enable the OIA to proceed with an audit into areas under their authority and leadership. Their co-operation with the audits is an important part of the process.

With the active oversight being exercised by the Audit Committee, the OIA has been directed to implement a significant backlog of urgent audit recommendations. Since its re-establishment, the Audit Committee has implored the Court to: provide the OIA with the timely information it needs to perform its mandate: co-operate with it in addressing the high number of unimplemented audit recommendations;[174] do more with respect to risk management;[175] and allow the OIA to attend decision-making meetings when issues of risk management and governance are discussed.[176] In response, the ICC has made some concessions but mostly declined these suggestions.

The Audit Committee has a critical role to play in raising the ethical standards of the ICC as an international public institution through the provision of impartial, principled and objective oversight. The challenge for the Committee will be in finding the right balance between respectful and open communication with Court officials in which it is sincerely receptive to the genuine challenges faced by the Court. At the same time, it is compelled to remain objective and impervious to the ongoing reluctance displayed by the ICC with respect to addressing issues of risk management, amongst other areas. It must also remain vigilant in exercising its own independent assessments rather than simply echoing or relying upon the CBF, given this Committee has acquiesced to the demands of Court officials on more than one occasion, whilst also recognizing the significant expertise of this Committee, its institutional knowledge and its proximity to the detail

---

ASP/14/Res.1, Section K, para. 1 ('ICC-ASP/14/Res.1') (https://www.legal-tools.org/doc/2c9828/).

[173] ICC-ASP/13/15, para. 131, see above note 168.

[174] See, for example, ICC, Report of the Committee on Budget and Finance on the work of its twenty-seventh session, 28 October 2016, ICC-ASP/15/15, Annex VII, Section II, C, paras. 32–37 ('ICC-ASP/15/15') (https://www.legal-tools.org/doc/12c964/).

[175] *Ibid.*, paras. 18 and 23.

[176] *Ibid.*, paras. 9 and 13.

of the budget issues. The Audit Committee's credibility and that of the Court are closely aligned.

8.6.2.2. Independent Oversight Mechanism

Complementing the OIA, is the IOM. Article 112(4) of the Rome Statute stipulates that:

> The Assembly may establish such subsidiary bodies as may be necessary, including an independent oversight mechanism for inspection, evaluation and investigation of the Court, to enhance the efficiency and economy.

First proposed in 2005 by the ASP President, Ambassador Prince Zeid Al-Hussein, a mandate establishing an IOM with investigative, evaluation and inspection functions was eventually adopted by the ASP at its eighth session in 2009.[177] However, it took until 2013 for the ASP to adopt a resolution establishing the operational components and parameters of its three-pronged mandate;[178] and until 2015 for the IOM to be operational with the hiring of a head of office. It took a further two years for the IOM to be fully operational with the hiring of all of its designated staff positions.[179] It was, therefore, not until 2017 that the ICC finally had in place a mechanism that could address issues of misconduct and serious misconduct allegedly committed by elected officials, staff, and contractors of the ICC.[180]

The primary initial obstruction to the creation of the IOM emanated from the OTP, specifically the Prosecutor, the Executive Committee, and senior policy staff. The OTP's opposition to the mechanism was active behind the scenes for several years before coming into full view at the eighth session of the ASP in 2009. As with earlier responses to oversight and accountability initiatives, the main reason for the OTP's opposition to the proposed mandate of the IOM related to concerns about potential infringements upon the independence of the office. Specifically, the OTP argued that: the IOM could interfere with the running of the Office and the Prosecutor's autonomy over its management; the IOM's *proprio motu* powers to

---

[177] ICC-ASP/8/Res.1, see above note 65.

[178] ICC, Independent Oversight Mechanism, 27 November 2013, ICC-ASP/12/Res.6 ('ICC-ASP/12/Res.6') (https://www.legal-tools.org/doc/64ebeb/).

[179] Report of the Committee on Budget and Finance on the works of its twenty-ninth session, 3 November 2017, ICC-ASP/16/15, para. 136 ('ICC-ASP/16/15') (https://www.legal-tools.org/doc/n4gove/).

[180] ICC-ASP/8/Res.1, para. 6(c), see above note 65.

---

open an investigation into allegations of misconduct against staff or elected officials should be constrained by the requirement for the approval from, or only initiated at the request of the relevant head of organ; and that the *proprio motu* powers of the IOM could be weaponized by "malicious third parties" against the OTP in an attempt to affect its operations.[181]

Given the concerns about the professional environment within the OTP and the perception of a high tolerance for behaviour ranging from 'bending the rules' to serious misconduct, some stakeholders supported the original proposal for the IOM mandate, including its ability to exercise its *proprio motu* powers to initiate an investigation without prior approval of the heads of organs, a proposal to which the Prosecutor was specifically opposed.[182] These actors viewed the intensity of the Prosecutor's objections as conforming with his persistent and ongoing aversion to checks and balances. Others genuinely shared most or several of the Prosecutor's concerns and joined the OTP's call for delaying the adoption of the operational mandate.[183] Both the ICC President and Registrar distanced themselves from the Prosecutor's opposition to the IOM and publicly stated their support for the mechanism, without further delays.[184] Despite a compromise being reached at the ninth session of the ASP whereby the procedures governing the exercise of the IOM's investigative capacity conformed to the

---

[181] For a discussion on these issues, see Max du Plessis and Christopher Gevers, "The Independent Oversight Mechanism Argument is not merely about Administration Functions, but is Situated in a Boarder Debate Over the Role of the Assembly of States Parties", *ICCForum*, 6 May 2011 (available on its web site); and ICCForum, Invited Experts on Oversight Question, May –September 2011 (available on its web site).

[182] Within civil society organizations, the American Coalition of NGOs for the ICC and the Women's Initiatives for Gender Justice were amongst the earliest, most vocal and most consistent supporters of the IOM. See, for example, Women's Initiatives for Gender Justice, *Gender Report Card on the International Criminal Court 2009*, p. 35; *Gender Report Card on the International Criminal Court 2010*, pp.71-72; *Gender Report Card on the International Criminal Court 2011*, pp. 339–340; *Gender Report Card on the International Criminal Court 2012*, pp. 285–287; *Gender Report Card on the International Criminal Court 2013*, pp. 17–24, 243-244; *Gender Report Card on the International Criminal Court 2014*, pp. 17–27, 269-270.

[183] See, for example, Human Rights Watch, "Memorandum for the Ninth Session of the ICC Assembly of States Parties", 16 November 2010, Section II, B; and International Federation for Human Rights ('FIDH'), "Position Paper Ninth Session of the ICC Assembly of State Parties", 30 November 2010, No. 551a, p. 18.

[184] du Plessis and Gevers, 2011, see above note 181. It was widely known amongst civil society advocates that the President and the Registrar did not support the OTP's position that the approval of a head of organ was necessary prior to the IOM initiating an investigation.

concerns of the Prosecutor, the OTP continued to obstruct the formation of the mechanism.[185]

The stonewalling was effective in delaying the overall establishment of the IOM for more than 10 years from the time it was first proposed until it was fully staffed and operational. It also led to the creation of a complicated approval process in order to open an IOM investigation and resulted in a lack of transparency regarding the results of such an investigation should it be activated by the head of an organ. In this scenario, it is possible that only the head of the requesting organ may receive the results of an IOM investigation and in theory he or she could decline to disclose the results to the President of the ASP, or to the internal or external auditors. Overall, the initial obstruction by the OTP, combined with long-term indifference by States Parties to establish and then fund the IOM, delayed the complete establishment of this critical statutory body.

In an almost inevitable twist of irony, the most public scandal to be investigated by the IOM to date involved two OTP staff members in relation to alleged breaches of their duties, with respect to their interactions and communication with the former Prosecutor, at his behest and after he had left office.[186] This incident led to discussions within the ICC and amongst States Parties regarding not only the need to strengthen accountability within the Court but also to consider possible mechanisms through which former Court officials could be held accountable for their conduct while in office, which may only come to light after they have left the ICC, or for misconduct committed after they have completed their terms.[187] An abiding obligation exists for former ICC officials to uphold or at least not to compromise the reputation and independence of the Court.

---

[185] Conversations with diplomats on file with the author.

[186] Becker, Blasberg and Pieper, 2017; EIC Network, 2017; Maupas, 2017; Thompson, 2017, see above note 18.

[187] Prosecutor's Briefing, 2020, paras. 40–42, 45-47, see above note 135; Independent Experts Review, 2020, paras. 256, R106, see above note 85.

8.6.3. Limited Infrastructure to Support and Ensure the Court's Institutional Integrity

In spite of having more than 1,400 staff members, contractors and interns,[188] the Court operates without an ethics and compliance office, an entity common in organizations of this size. There is not even a single compliance or ethics officer within the ICC. The Controller post formerly in the Registry was one of the first positions abolished in 2014 under the Registry's restructuring project, known as 'ReVision'.

According to the Audit Committee, the ICC also does not have an integrated Court-wide values and ethics framework applicable to all staff.[189] Best practice suggests that a framework alone is insufficient to ensure an ethical culture,[190] but the absence of this fundamental component is perhaps emblematic of the lack of priority given to these issues by States Parties, the Court and other stakeholders.

According to the Audit Committee, the ICC does not have a comprehensive risk management framework despite recommendations from the Auditor, echoed by the CBF, since August 2004 calling for greater consideration by the Court for "[implementing] risk management procedures in its operations and to ensure better planning and implementation of procurement".[191] Versions of this recommendation have been made repeatedly by Auditors over many years with little response from the ICC and insufficient oversight by the CBF and the ASP regarding the implementation of these requirements. According to the Audit Committee, the Court's approach to risk management "does not meet the international standards for comparable institutions",[192] despite the challenging environments the ICC is working in, as well as, its history of underestimating and mismanaging institutional risks.

---

[188] Report of the Committee on Budget and Finance on the work of its thirtieth session, 31 May 2018, ICC-ASP/17/5, Annex II, p. 43 ('ICC-ASP/17/5') (https://www.legal-tools.org/doc/3037jc/).

[189] ICC-ASP/16/15, Annex V, paras. 35,36, see above note 179; Report of the Committee on Budget and Finance on its work of the thirty-first session, 29 October 2018, ICC-ASP/17/15, Annex VI, para. 28 ('ICC-ASP/17/15') (https://www.legal-tools.org/doc/34xy2r/).

[190] See, for example, Lynn S. Paine, "Managing for Organizational Integrity", in *Harvard Business Review*, March-April 1994 Issue; Caterina Bulgarella, "Why good words can produce bad acts", in *The FCPA Blog*, 26 June 2018.

[191] ICC-ASP/3/18, para. 15, see above note 103.

[192] ICC-ASP/15/15, para. 198, see above note 174.

Some efforts have been undertaken by the Court; however, these have not always been strategic. In 2017, the ICC's first Administrative Instruction on Risk Management was promulgated by the Registrar and "takes into consideration International Standard ISO 31000:2009".[193] Unfortunately, this standard was updated by the International Organisation for Standardization in 2018.[194] Just as the ICC was starting to catch-up with some of the policy-related benchmarks in the practice of risk management, the field evolved and the standards changed, making the ICC's policy on this issue partially outdated within a year of its promulgation.

During 2018, a Risk Management Committee was established by the Court and the "owners" of "major risks" participated in training.[195] The Committee also developed and adopted its Terms of Reference. However, the Court still does not have a risk management unit, or even a post solely dedicated to this function. Within the Administrative Instruction, the role of co-ordinating risk management was designated to the Director of the Division of Management Services to oversee.[196] This role was ultimately assigned within the Division to an existing position as an add-on function where it was ultimately approved for reclassification by the CBF as an Administrative Officer and Risk Management Coordinator.[197] This marks a small but important development by the Court.

The ICC has never undertaken Court-wide ethics training for its mid-to-senior level managers, and according to the International Criminal Court Bar Association, its anti-fraud and whistle-blower policies have not been fully integrated into the legal framework of the Court.[198]

By any standards, this overall level of institutional architecture appears to be flimsy if not reckless. It evidently does not provide the Court with the solid anchor and ethical centre needed to hold it sure and steady,

---

[193] ICC Administrative Instruction, Risk Management, 31 March 2017, ICC/AI/2017/003 ('AI-Risk Management') (https://www.legal-tools.org/doc/e928d8).

[194] International Organization for Standardization (ISO), Risk management — Principles and guidelines, November 2009, ISO 31000:2009.

[195] ICC-ASP/17/15, Annex VI, Section B, para. 8, see above note 189.

[196] AI-Risk Management, para. 1.4, see above note 193.

[197] Report of the Committee on Budget and Finance on the work of its thirty-first session, 2 October 2018, ICC-ASP/17/15, Advance version, para. 93 (https://www.legal-tools.org/doc/oz48xe/); ICC-ASP/16/15, para. 196, see above note 179.

[198] International Criminal Court Bar Association, "Legal Analysis: ICC Internal Accountability Mechanisms and Policies", ICCBA Legal Advisory Committee, February 2018.

for it to return to as its integrity checkpoint to avert ethical dilemmas and to chart a course through turbulent waters when these challenges arise.

The Court's reluctance to develop a robust oversight system is matched by the reluctance of States Parties to insist upon and fund one. When the Court has attempted, in good faith, to strengthen its oversight and ethics capacity it has been forced to do so using existing resources, and to rely upon other Court personnel for advice and limited training.[199] The Court has also been asked to do more by States Parties without the support of additional funds for tasks, such as the development of an organizational manual, that may genuinely require resources beyond its approved budget.

At the same time, when States Parties have asked the Court to make more effort concerning risk management[200] or to develop Terms of Reference for the Coordination Committee of Heads of Organs,[201] the Court has delayed action, politely declined or made small gestures in some of these areas.

In addition, the existing internal control elements continue to be underfunded. One school of thought suggests that the budget for internal audit activities should represent approximately 0.5 to 1.0 per cent of the total annual budget of an organization.[202] Applying this to the ICC, the budget approved by the ASP for the OIA in 2019 of EUR 685,600 is only 0.47 per cent of the total budget of the Court, of EUR 144,550,000.[203] A review of the past five years of ICC budgets reveals that the OIA has been consistently under-resourced with an average annual funding of 0.48 per cent of the overall budget designated to support internal audit activities. It would appear that the continued underfunding of the ICC's institutional architecture may be one of the elements contributing to the Court's ongoing vulnerabilities with respect to its organizational integrity.

Between States Parties and the Court, there has been a leadership vacuum in relation to institutional integrity and the development of an eth-

---

[199] ICC-ASP/15/15, Annex VII, Section II, para. 22, see above note 174.

[200] *Ibid.*, para. 19.

[201] ICC-ASP/16/15, Annex V, Section II, paras. 11, 13, see above note 179.

[202] ICC-ASP/4/4, para. 9, see above note 141; ICC-ASP/5/5, para. 11, see above note 141.

[203] ICC, Assembly of States Parties, "Resolution of the Assembly of States Parties on the proposed programme budget for 2019, the Working Capital Fund for 2019, the scale of assessment for the apportionment of expenses of the International Criminal Court, financing appropriations for 2019 and the Contingency Fund", 12 December 2018, ICC-ASP/17/Res.4, para. 1 (https://www.legal-tools.org/doc/obysgj/).

ics-oriented culture. The most recent and most striking example of this leadership vacuum was with the Registry's restructuring project (ReVision) during which all three categories of ethical vulnerabilities were triggered simultaneously.

8.7. Case Study: ReVision

ReVision was officially launched on 1 January 2014 and was completed on 31 July 2015.[204] During this 18-month period, the project surpassed anything the Court had experienced before with respect to the volume and rapidity of regulatory violations and breaches of ethical standards. ReVision both exposed and took advantage of the weaknesses in the oversight and governance system and brought the Court's institutional integrity crisis to a head.

This section will examine the restructuring project through an ethics lens to assess whether the errors associated with ReVision were simply genuine mistakes made within the context of an ambitious project or rise to the threshold of institutional corruption.

The purpose of this case study is not to provoke paralysis or despondency. Rather, it is to provide a clear diagnosis of the current status of the ICC's institutional integrity as motivation for change and transformation and to highlight the urgency of these issues. The ICC deserves our forthright and sympathetic support as well as our candid and loyal criticism.

To examine this further, it is important to consider the tests of institutional corruption and the definitions available to evaluate its existence. Work in this relatively new field of research by ethicists and academics has largely focused on public institutions, specifically institutional corruption with respect to the legislative process of the US Congress,[205] as well as issues of campaign finance of Congressional leaders and their decision-making.[206]

---

[204] ICC, Audit Report of the ReVision Project of the International Criminal Court's Registry, 9 November 2016, ICC-ASP/15/27, para. 10 ('Audit Report of ReVision') (https://www.legal-tools.org/doc/80a7a5/); Comprehensive Report of the Reorganisation of the Registry of the ICC, August 2016, p. 29 ('Comprehensive Report') (https://www.legal-tools.org/doc/cbc6cc/).

[205] Dennis F. Thompson, *Ethics in Congress: From Individual to Institutional Corruption*, Washington, DC, The Brookings Institution, 1995.

[206] Lawrence Lessig, *Republic, Lost: How Money Corrupts Congress- And a Plan to Stop It*, Twelve publishers, 5 October 2011.

Dennis Thompson, whose foundational work on institutional corruption opened up this field of inquiry, argues strongly that institutional corruption is linked to the improper use of public office in contrast to the obligation of a public institution to always act for a public purpose and in the public good.[207] Thompson does not consider honest mistakes to be indicative of corruption, rather a public institution or process may be considered corrupt if the decision-making process involves a pattern of influence that is irrelevant to the deliberations.[208] In his view, people may act with "noble motives" but may still be "agents" of corrupt practices.[209] In other words, institutional corruption does not require an intention to corrupt.

In his research, Thompson found that an institution (Congress) acts for a public purpose, and is therefore not institutionally corrupt, in so far as it follows a deliberative decision-making procedure in which "members consider policies based on their merits; treats citizens and colleagues fairly; and is publicly accountable for their actions".[210] An institution that adheres to the above decision-making procedure can be considered to make justifiable decisions and therefore is not corrupt, irrespective of the quality or outcomes of those decisions or whether they proved to be erroneous. Building on this work, Lawrence Lessig's research on institutional corruption examines the effect that dependency on campaign donations has on the legislative activities of the US Congress. Lessig has summarized his definition of institutional corruption as: "[a]n economy of influence which weakens the purpose of the institution, especially by weakening public trust of that institution".[211]

Other researchers have examined concepts of corruption in the context of organizational integrity, the efficacy of compliance frameworks, and with respect to the distortion of professional independence for those in positions of trust.[212]

---

[207] Thompson, 1995, pp. 1–29, see above note 205.

[208] *Ibid.*, 20-21.

[209] *Ibid.*, p. 25.

[210] *Ibid.*, p. 20; Newhouse, 2014, p. 557, see above note 118.

[211] *Ibid.*, p. 554; Lessig, 2011, see above note 206.

[212] Garry C. Gray, "Insider Accounts of Institutional Corruption Examining the Social Organization of Unethical Behaviour", in *British Journal of Criminology*, vol. 53, no. 4, April 2013, pp. 533–551; Eberhard Schnebel, Margo A. Bienet, "Implementing Ethics in Business Organizations", in *Journal of Business Ethics*, Kluwer Academic Publishers, 2004, vol. 53, pp. 203–211; Kendra Cherry, "How to Recognize and Avoid Groupthink", in *verywell mind*, 29 August 2018; Edward J. Romar, "Virtue Is Good Business: Confucianism as a Practical

Some of the challenges acknowledged in this field are the difficulties in neatly applying the existing definitions of institutional corruption to a range of different private and public institutions, specifically with respect to the requirement to clearly identify the intended purpose of the institution. This difficulty is more prevalent for private companies than public institutions that are inherently tasked with acting on behalf of the public good.

In the case of the ICC, there is no such challenge in determining the purpose of the ICC and its obligatory mandate as a global public institution staffed by international civil servants in service to humanity for the sake of "present and future generations".[213] Its purpose and its obligation to act for the public good are clear.

Whilst a number of definitions are available, the components most commonly utilized to assess institutional corruption, are posited below as questions with respect to assessing ReVision through a corruption lens. These include:

- Were merit-based decision-making processes applied throughout ReVision?

- Were colleagues treated fairly?

- Were interests, other than the objectives of ReVision, the best interests of the ICC's mandate and the public interest, at play which influenced the decision-making process during ReVision?

- Were (public) accountability processes applied to those responsible for ReVision?

- Did ReVision weaken the trustworthiness of the ICC and thus compromise the efficacy of the Court?

Business Ethic", in *Journal of Business Ethics*, Kluwer Academic Publishers, 2002, vol. 38, pp. 119–131; Jan Tulberg, "Moral Compliance and the Concealed Charm of Prudence", in *Journal of Business Ethics*, 2009, vol. 89, pp. 599–612; and Lynn S. Paine, "Managing for Organizational Integrity", in *Harvard Business Review*, March-April 1994; Catherin Broadman and Vicki Klum, "Building Organisational Integrity", in Peter Larmour and Nick Wolanin (eds.), *Corruption and Anti-Corruption*, ANU, 2013, pp. 82–96; Peter Roberts, A.J. Brown and Jane Olsen, "Organisational Commitment", in Peter Roberts, A.J. Brown and Jane Olsen (eds.), *Whistling While they Work: A good-practice guide for managing internal reporting of wrongdoing in public sector organisations*, ANU Press, 2011, pp. 17–35.

213 ICC Statute, Preamble, see above note 2

The concept of transparency is a widely accepted component of trustworthy public institutions. The following examination of ReVision will, therefore, consider transparency as well as the above questions.

It is not necessary for violations of all of the above tests to occur for the conditions of institutional corruption to be met. Violations of any one of these would be indicative of corruption.

8.7.1. Background

Undertaking a restructuring of the Registry was widely supported by States Parties. A number of reports had been commissioned examining the functioning of the Registry that highlighted the need for some reform;[214] and, in 2013 the newly appointed Registrar had positioned himself during the recruitment process on a platform promising an ambitious restructuring agenda.[215] The intentions of the ReVision project were legitimate, laudable and worthwhile.

Shortly after taking office in April 2013, the narrative from the Registrar about the objectives of the restructuring process for the Registry was that it would increase efficiencies, find synergies with other organs where possible, and reduce costs.[216] The confidence of the Registrar was such that even before ReVision began, he recommended that the inevitable savings generated by the restructuring should be given to the OTP, which, in his view, needed more funding.[217]

The initial objectives of ReVision adopted by States Parties in November 2013, were for the project to reduce costs including a minimal structural reduction of 3 per cent, increase efficiencies, eliminate duplication and create synergies with other organs of the Court.[218] This was to be achieved within the budget envelope of EUR 42.9 million associated with

---

[214] Audit Report of ReVision, paras. 15(a-h) and 16, see above note 204.

[215] *Ibid.*, para. 17.

[216] Presentations by the Registrar to NGOs and States Parties; Conversations in 2013 with diplomats on file with the author; Report of the Committee on Budget and Finance on its work of its twenty-first session, 4 November 2013, ICC-ASP/12/15, para. 82 (https://www.legal-tools.org/doc/kdybms/).

[217] Presentations by the Registrar to NGOs and States Parties, respectively; conversations in 2013 with diplomats on file with the author.

[218] ICC, Assembly of States Parties Resolution to the Rome Statute of ICC, adopted at the twelfth plenary meeting on 27 November 2013, vol. I, part III, ICC-ASP/12/Res.1, Section H, para. 3 (https://www.legal-tools.org/doc/7a9071/).

staff costs and 560 staff positions approved for 2014.[219] According to the *Audit Report of the ReVision Project of the International Criminal Court's Registry* (the 'Audit Report') these objectives were changed at the following ASP in December 2014, when the Assembly renewed the authorization to reorganize the Registry but removed from the objectives, the intention to generate savings and the need to eliminate duplication, increase efficiencies and seek synergies with other organs.[220] That left, increasing efficiencies within the Registry as the only formal objective of the restructuring.

However, the Official Records of the ASP in 2014 explain the objectives differently and indicate that within the context of the restructuring, the Registrar was tasked with continuing to identify savings "throughout the [sic] 2014 and beyond", to find additional synergies, as well as efficiencies, and to report on these items, "after completion of the ReVision project".[221] In contrast with the Audit Report of ReVision, there is a clear indication in the Official Records that more than efficiencies were required and formed part of the objective of the restructuring process.

Ambiguity about the objectives was reinforced by the Registrar who at times asserted that savings were not a component of the ReVision project whilst also continuing to talk to States Parties about savings up until two months before the end of the project, including in the report on the results of the restructuring submitted to States Parties on 4 May 2015.[222] It was therefore understandable that most States Parties continued to expect savings as a result of the restructuring, [223] even though it was later claimed that it had been eliminated as one of the formal objectives.

After ReVision was completed, the Registrar along with members of his office, vehemently and repeatedly stated in meetings with NGOs and

---

[219] Audit Report of ReVision, para. 6, see above note 204. The Audit Report notes that there was a slight decrease in the approved budgets between 2014 (EUR 65,684,900,000) and 2015 (EUR 65,025,900,000). However, the critical figured approved by the ASP for the staff costs related to the restructuring process was EUR 42,900,000. For clarity, see ICC, Official Records, Fourteenth Session, ICC-ASP/14/20, 18-26 November 2015, vol. II, part B.2, para. 10.

[220] Audit Report of ReVision, paras. 6–8(a)(b), see above note 204.

[221] Official Records of the Assembly of States Parties to the Rome Statute of the ICC, 8-17 December 2014, ICC-ASP/13/20, vol. I, Annex IV, Section F, para. 28 (https://www.legal-tools.org/doc/8485ce).

[222] ICC, Report on the review of the organizational structure of the Registry, 4 May 2015, ICC-ASP/14/18, Executive Summary (https://www.legal-tools.org/doc/omfqht/).

[223] Conversations with diplomats in 2015 on file with the author.

States Parties, respectively, that savings in the Registry's budget had never been an objective of the restructuring.[224] Whilst a level of ambiguity about this objective may have emerged, it was not accurate to deny its existence, as indicated in the Official Records. In addition, the Registrar had actively kept this probability alive, and in the minds of many States Parties it remained a highly desirable expectation. Their assumptions on this issue were abruptly refocused when the Registry submitted its post-restructuring budget for 2016 requesting a 26 percent increase in funding to implement the new structure designed as a result of the re-organization.[225]

According to experts in the field of institutional corruption, setting ambiguous and confusing workplace objectives and/or unrealistic expectations can facilitate an environment in which those responsible for meeting the objectives may resort to exaggeration, carelessness or misrepresentation.[226]

The ambiguity of the objectives and the creation of confusing or unrealistic expectations by both States Parties and the Registrar was an important precursor, amongst other factors, with respect to the credibility of the process and the manner in which this project was implemented.

8.7.2. Examination

Three specific decisions provide compelling examples against which to apply the five test questions and transparency elements with respect to examining potential institutional corruption.

8.7.2.1. Decision 1: Circumventing Recruitment Policies

The Registrar established a Project Team comprised of three external members and five internal members, all from within the Registry.[227] Later

---

[224] Conversations with non-governmental organizations and diplomats on file with the author; Women's Initiatives for Gender Justice, "An Examination of the Registry's 2016 Budget and implications of the ReVision Project", 17 September 2015, p. 11 ('Examination of the Registry's 2016 Budget').

[225] ICC-ASP/14/15, para. 53, see above note 169.

[226] See Lynn S. Paine, "Managing for Organizational Integrity", in *Harvard Business Review*, 1994; David Lehman and Rangaraj, "Selectivity in Organisational Rule Violations", in *The Academy of Management Review*, 2009, vol. 34, no. 4, pp. 643–657; Newhouse, 2014, pp. 573–574, see above note 118.

[227] Audit Report of ReVision, para. 10, see above note 204.

in the project, the internal members were increased to nine and included staff from other organs of the Court.[228]

According to the Audit Report of ReVision, the mandate of the Project Team was to conduct audits of the structures and methods of the Registry.[229] In assessing the decision to establish a project team, the Audit Report noted that engaging an external audit or hiring a management consulting firm, rather than the structure selected by the Registrar, would "clearly have been better suited to a project as ambitious as ReVision whose terms of reference laid down a wide-ranging scope of objectives".[230] It also noted that "it would probably have been at least as expensive as the solution selected".[231]

According to the Audit Report, the Registrar considered several options and decided upon a hybrid model of a project team comprised of external experts and internal Registry staff.[232] The establishment of the project team was part of a deliberative merit-based decision-making process, and the model chosen was consistent with those utilised elsewhere for reorganization processes.[233] It may have been a regrettable decision and inadvisable, as indicated in the Audit Report,[234] but it was justifiable and not unlawful.

However, in hiring the three external members of the Project Team between November 2013 and January 2014, the Registrar violated the rules governing recruitment that require all positions to be made on a competitive basis. It also departed from the appropriate provision in the appendix to the Staff Regulations, which states that selection panels 'shall' be established.[235] Rather than complying with these well-established practices, all of the external members of the project team were appointed directly by the Registrar without "prior definition of role profiles, no call for applications and no selection procedure".[236]

---

[228] *Ibid.*

[229] *Ibid.*, para. 24.

[230] *Ibid.*, para. 31(b) and 32.

[231] *Ibid.*, para. 32.

[232] *Ibid.*, paras. 24, 25.

[233] *Ibid.*, para. 25.

[234] *Ibid.*, para. 32.

[235] ICC Staff Regulations, appendix, para. 5, see above note 32.

[236] Audit Report of ReVision, para. 25, see above note 204.

According to the Audit of ReVision, the Registrar's explanation for subverting the standard recruitment practice was the "urgency to start the project" and the time it takes to fulfil the standard recruitment process.[237] As noted in the constrained language of auditors, "[i]n light of the project's duration (a year and a half), the urgency invoked must be seen in its proper perspective. Spending more time on defining role profiles would have made it possible to construct a more rounded team".[238] Thus, the motivation of urgency was not perceived by the Auditors to be a compelling justification for violating the required recruitment procedure in the appointments of the three external members.

The implications of this course of action hampered the ReVision process. In effect, within weeks of initiating the restructuring project, aspects of its implementation were in violation of the rules and fell short of the desirable level of transparency necessary in a restructuring process. It appears that, before ReVision even got off the ground, it had run afoul of the standards required and critical elements of the restructuring project were in violation of ICC rules.

In addition to the manner in which the external members were appointed, it also transpired that these members did not have the experience or expertise needed to undertake a complex restructuring process. According to the Audit Report on ReVision, none of the external members of the team had experience in financial management, human resources or auditing,[239] skills highly relevant to undertaking a reorganization process. The external members also lacked significant prior experience with respect to undertaking major restructuring programmes.[240] The Team, described by the Registrar as providing "the crucial recommendations on the basis of which [he] and the senior Registry management were able to take the necessary decisions",[241] lacked the expertise required to undertake an effective and credible restructuring process.

---

[237] *Ibid.*, para. 28.

[238] *Ibid.*

[239] *Ibid.*, para. 29.

[240] Only one member of the Project Team had previous experience in organizational restructuring, and this was in relation to a relatively small re-organization project within a unit of the ICTY. Conversations with former ICTY staff members in 2015 on file with the author.

[241] Comprehensive Report, Foreword by the Registrar, pp. ix-x, August 2020, see above note 204.

The Audit Report notes, somewhat unconvincingly, that these "short-comings" were overcome by the skills of the internal members of the project team from within the Registry.[242] Although each internal member of the team possessed genuine expertise relevant to their substantive positions in the Registry, it is unclear that they had the depth of knowledge and level of technical expertise required for a restructuring process including specific and in-depth experience in auditing (of structures, methodologies and roles), as envisaged by the project.

The fact that the project team did not embody the necessary expertise or gravitas, understandably raised the concerns of Registry staff whose posts and livelihoods were in the hands of external experts, appointed through questionable means, and colleagues who did not have the experiential track record of making the "crucial recommendations"[243] upon which key decisions were allegedly made. This structure was not reassuring for staff and placed internal members of the project team in unenviable positions with their colleagues.

These specific features of the ReVision project do not appear to have utilised merit-based decision-making processes. This is clarified by the unlawfulness of the appointments of the external members and the absence of sufficient expertise within the project team as a whole. Given the risks involved, it could be considered brazenly irresponsible to fail to ensure that those involved in designing and implementing ReVision possessed the necessary competencies and expertise to undertake a process directly and indirectly affecting the 600 staff members of the Registry.

If the appointments of the external members were not based on the recruitment of those with the depth of experience and expertise required to undertake a complex restructuring project, then what was the basis for their appointments? The only commonality readily obvious is that all three were known to the Registrar either on a personal basis or as former colleagues at the Special Tribunal for Lebanon ('STL'), where he had previously served as Registrar before joining the ICC. Some of the external experts also knew each other as colleagues at the ICTY. Only one of the external experts was in a senior management position (P-5) at the time of being hired for ReVi-

---

[242] Audit Report of ReVision, para. 29, see above note 204.
[243] *Ibid.*

sion, another was recruited to the team from a junior post (P-2) at the ICTY, and the third was in a mid-level management position at the STL.[244]

Prior collegial relationships and other alliances may have also played a role in other key appointments as well, including the recruitment of three personnel within the Registry on the eve of, or early on in, the ReVision project. Appointees to positions of the Head of Human Resources, the Chief of the Legal Advisory Service Section and the Chief of Budget Section,[245] were all individuals with whom the Registrar had worked at the STL or was a fellow civil servant of the ministry of foreign affairs of the host State. Each of these posts would subsequently feature prominently in the restructuring process in roles that were instrumental to the project in the core areas within which the meritocracy of the decision-making appears to have been most questionable and the reliability of information least convincing. The legal advice, human resource data and budget assumptions with respect to ReVision are examined in the sub-sections ahead.

It is believed that questions were raised internally at the time of each of these selections regarding the basis of their appointments in terms of the prior professional experience and qualifications of the appointees.[246] Concerns were also expressed about perceived anomalies in the recruitment processes, including the extent to which, or whether, the Registrar had personally intervened in one or more of these appointments, possibly ignoring the recommendations of the recruitment panel(s), which may have deemed a candidate(s) unsuitable for interview.

---

[244] Conversations with former ICC and ICTY staff on file with the author. In terms of State representation on the team, the three external members were from Bulgaria, the Republic of Ireland and the Netherlands.

[245] The Budget Section was created as a result of the restructuring project. Prior to ReVision, the functions of budget and finance operated together within one section. It would appear that the appointment of Chief of Budget Section, whilst the restructuring was still underway may have subverted the 'priority candidate' provision outlined in the Principles and Procedures under which staff, whose posts were abolished, could apply for new positions created within the Registry as a result of the restructuring, as well as other posts available within the ICC. The Budget Section was a new section created by ReVision and similarly, the Chief of Budget Section was a new position emerging from the restructuring project. At the time of this appointment, the Registry was still undergoing the restructuring process and more than 110 staff were unaware that their posts would ultimately be abolished. This included staff with potentially relevant financial and budget-related experience. Some of these individuals may have qualified to apply for the Chief of Budget position but did not have the opportunity to contest this post because the position was filled before they were made aware that their own posts were to be abolished.

[246] Conversations with Registry staff on file with the author.

Circumventing the legal framework in the appointment of the external members of the project team immediately negates the possibility of the decision-making process embodying any merit. The extent of the prior relationships of the Registrar with the external members of the team and with those employed in three positions central to the implementation of the restructuring project, as well as the manner in which all of these appointments were made, provoked legitimate questions by staff. It also inevitably gave rise to mistrust in the process and of those responsible for the project. Ultimately, these decisions created significant financial and legal risks for the ICC.

8.7.2.2. Decision 2: Unlawful Promulgation of the Principles and Procedures

On 19 August 2014, the Registrar promulgated the *Principles and Procedures applicable to Decisions Arising from The ReVision Project* (the "Principles and Procedures", or the 'Principles').[247] These Principles were intended to "establish a framework for the implementation of decisions arising from the restructuring process, so that staff members can be confident that decisions affecting them are implemented according to a fair, transparent process and with full respect for their contractual rights".[248] Half way through the restructuring process, the Principles were amended and re-disseminated on 13 June 2015, 18 months into the project.[249] On both occasions, the Registrar promulgated the Principles through the use of an Information Circular.

The consideration of these issues by the ILOAT, with respect to ReVision, provides clarity on this aspect of the ICC's legal framework. In its Judgment No. 3907 related to ReVision, the ILOAT explains that the ICC's Presidential Directive ICC/PRESD/G/2003/001 "governs the promulgation of the ICC's three types of Administrative Issuances: Presidential Directives; Administrative Instructions; and Information Circulars".[250] Accord-

---

[247] ICC, Principles and Procedures Applicable to Decisions Arising from the ReVision Project, 19 August 2014, ICC/INF/2014/011 ('ICC/INF/2014/011') (https://www.legal-tools.org/doc/36d086).

[248] *Ibid.*, Article 5.

[249] ICC, Principles and Procedures Applicable to Decisions Arising from the ReVision Project, 13 June 2015, ICC/INF/2014/011 Rev.1 ('ICC/INF/2014/011 Rev.1') (https://www.legal-tools.org/doc/d7a314).

[250] ILOAT, Judgment No. 3907, para. 6, see above note 126.

ing to the ILOAT, the Registrar's decision to promulgate the Principles and Procedures by an Information Circular violated the Presidential Directive, making the principles and the decisions derived from the application of the principles "unlawful":

> As the promulgation of the Principles and Procedures by Information Circular was in violation of the Presidential Directive, they were without legal foundation and are, therefore, unlawful as are the decisions taken pursuant to the Principles and Procedures.[251]

In effect, ReVision in its entirety was found by the ILOAT to be illegal at its very foundations.

According to the same ILOAT judgment, the Principles and Procedures included provisions which effectively changed some of the articles of the ICC staff regulations and rules. Such significant policy changes are outside of the legal scope of an Information Circular.[252] The ICC asserted that the Principles did not denote a change in the staff rules and regulations and only applied to the Registry, and not to other ICC staff.[253] The ILOAT "rejected" this reasoning,[254] and noted that "a number of provisions within the Principles and Procedures involve[d] regulatory matters",[255] including several substantive changes to the Staff Regulations.[256] In other ReVision-related cases, the ILOAT also noted that several of the individual provisions contradicted the ICC Staff Regulations and/or did not meet the standards of existing ILOAT jurisprudence,[257] including: the extension of appointments;[258] the enhanced agreed separation package;[259] and the 'priority candidate' provision which did not meet the ICC's obligation to explore employment options prior to separation.[260]

In addition, the ILOAT found that the changes to the Staff Regulations outlined in the Principles, which were applicable only to decisions

---

[251] *Ibid.*, para. 26.

[252] *Ibid.*

[253] *Ibid.*, paras. 13–15.

[254] *Ibid.*, para. 16.

[255] *Ibid.*, para. 17.

[256] *Ibid.*, paras. 18–23.

[257] *Ibid.*, para. 13.

[258] *Ibid.*, para. 18.

[259] *Ibid.*, paras. 19–24.

[260] *Ibid.*, paras. 13–19.

arising from ReVision, unfairly advantaged staff impacted by the restructuring and "would result in unequal treatment not only for staff members outside the Registry but also for those Registry staff members not affected by the restructuring".[261]

The complainant in the case associated with Judgment No. 3907 submitted that the Chief of the Registry's Legal Advisory Services Section provided the Registrar with an outline of "the risks surrounding the promulgation of the Principles and Procedures by way of an Information Circular", and as such the promulgation of the Principles had not been cleared by the Section, as required in the Presidential Directive.[262] In response, the Registry argued that the legal advice provided by the Section supported the promulgation of the Principles via the Information Circular.[263] Ultimately, the ILOAT found that "in the absence of the requisite clearance, the Registrar lacked the authority to sign the Information Circular",[264] and as such the Principles "were without legal foundation and are, therefore, unlawful as are the decisions taken pursuant to the Principles and Procedures".[265]

The unlawful promulgation of the Principles through the incorrect administrative issuance created profound financial, legal, and reputational risks for the Court, which the Registrar was prepared to take. This decision abandoned a merit-based decision-making process and failed to meet the minimum standard of legal compliance, even though the legal requirements were both knowable and known.

The transparency in the communication of the Principles to Registry staff was also less than ideal. The Principles and Procedures were adopted by Registrar on 19 August 2014, eight and a half months after the restructuring process began.[266] As such, the Registry staff most affected by ReVision were not informed of the detail of the methodology to be employed by the project including the process of post assessments, work surveys and detailed functional analysis, the (re)classification process and the implications of having one's post abolished until late in the process and just two months before the first set of posts were terminated in October 2014. The

---

[261] *Ibid.*, para. 24.

[262] *Ibid.*, para. 25.

[263] *Ibid.*, para. 25.

[264] *Ibid.*, para. 25.

[265] *Ibid.*, para. 26.

[266] ICC/INF/2014/011, see above note 247.

Revised Principles were promulgated on 12 June 2015, three weeks before the second set of notices were issued to more than 110 staff informing them that their posts were to be abolished.[267] In addition to the concerns about the capacity of the project team, communication to staff at a late stage of the process regarding the methodology to be utilized for the restructuring and the components of the reclassification phase created further anxiety and stress for Registry staff.

The Principles and Procedures provided assurance to staff members that for "any proposal to abolish a position, there would be an underlying objective basis".[268] However, according to the same Principles and Procedures, one of the factors to be taken into account by the 'classification expert' in determining whether a substantial change had been made to a position and therefore could be abolished in its current form, was a review of staff "performance appraisal documents" and "mid-term reviews".[269] It is difficult to understand why the performance of the current individual in a post is relevant to assessing the objective role, responsibilities and tasks associated with that position, in the context of the overall functions of the Registry. Performance considerations and mid-term reviews are important and valuable assessments. However, arguably they should not have been relevant to a restructuring process that claimed to be based on objective criteria associated with reviewing the roles and tasks of positions.

There is insufficient information available to examine whether or to what extent decisions to abolish posts were driven by a desire to terminate the current post-holder for performance or any other reason or were based on objective assessments of the functions and responsibilities of the position. This appears to have been unclear for the External Auditor as well, whose report notes that if the Registrar had simply wanted to dispense with a dozen officials, "a targeted operation offering them enhanced separation indemnities would have been much less costly [than the cost of ReVision] (and allayed the stress, suffered by at least 120 people)".[270]

---

[267] Comprehensive Report, p. 32, see above note 204. The timeline also indicates that in early July, all Registry staff members were notified whether or not their post was to be abolished.

[268] ICC/INF/2014/011, para. 5, see above note 247; ICC/INF/2014/011 Rev.1, para. 5, see above note 249.

[269] *Ibid.*, para. 25.

[270] Audit Report of ReVision, para. 66(a), see above note 204.

8.7.2.3. Decision 3: Lack of Credible Oversight

The Registrar created a Project Board to assist in overseeing the ReVision project. According to the Principles and Procedures, the role of Project Board was to "advise and support the Registrar in the evaluation and decision-making process".[271] In the *Comprehensive Report of the Reorganisation of the Registry of the ICC* (the 'Comprehensive Report'), the important role of the Board is described as being designed to "oversee the execution of the ReVision project and to advise and support the Registrar in the overall direction and management of the project".[272] In addition, the Board "approved the opening and closing of each phase, verifying that the project was on track".[273]

The Board included: three external members[274] (a Defence Counsel representative and two others with experience in an international judicial institution); the staff through the President of the Staff Union Council; as well as three internal members who were representatives of the Registry's clients, specifically: the ASP; the Presidency; and the Office of the Prosecutor.[275]

The formation of a Board and the engagement of 'end-users' of the Registry's services on this Board were reasonable and sound decisions. However, according to the Audit Report on ReVision, the Registrar appointed all of the Board members, including the internal members, which had the effect of "reducing the Project Board's independence from the Registry".[276] On top of this, the Registrar also chaired the Board,[277] whose role

---

[271] ICC/INF/2014/011, para. 7, see above note 247; ICC/INF/2014/011 Rev.1, para. 7, see above note 249.

[272] Comprehensive Report, para. 49, see above note 204. This was reiterated in the *Presidency note on the issues raised relating to the ReVision project*, 24 July 2015, para. 1.

[273] *Ibid.*

[274] *Ibid.*, para. 50(b) and (d). There were three external members of the Board. Two of these experts were described in the Comprehensive Report as having leadership experience in international judicial institutions. It is known that at least one of these individuals had worked with the Registrar at the SCSL. Additionally, the third external expert on the Board was a Defence Counsel representative who was described as having significant experience before the SCSL as well as the ICTY and the STL. These are all tribunals where the Registrar had worked, including in the role as Registrar at the STL and SCSL. Some of the concerns with the Board rotated around the appearance of possible allegiance to and friendships with the Registrar. This raised questions regarding the ability of the Board to exercise objective evaluations of the ReVision project and the decisions of the Registrar.

[275] *Ibid.*, para. 50(a) and (c).; Audit Report of ReVision, para. 11, see above note 204.

[276] *Ibid.*, para. 22.

---

involved oversight of the execution of the project including, "monitoring the work of this [project] team and, in particular, authorising the project to transition from one phase to the next".[278]

With the Registrar appointing the Board members and chairing the Board, the structure lacked the appearance of transparency and, therefore, credibility. The design of the Project Board called into question its ability to provide genuine, objective scrutiny and oversight of the decisions associated with ReVision. With the co-operation of the Board, some of whose members, especially those external to the Court who may have been unaware of the legal violations and the lack of transparency embedded in the project, the Registrar was able to proceed through each of the restructuring phases with the 'legitimacy' of Board-confirmed decisions.

It is unclear whether the external Board members were provided with copies of the ICC's legal framework and other relevant material through which they could objectively consider and assess the decisions they were being asked to confirm.

However, it is clear that the senior ICC staff members on the Project Board were fully aware of the required legal framework. They would also have been aware of some of the serious concerns about the restructuring which had been raised internally. As Board members, one could also assume that they participated in discussions about decisions that enabled the occurrence of impropriety and violations as determined by the ILOAT and critiqued in this case study. As employees of the ICC, these Board members possessed a positive obligation to report patterns of anomalies and breaches of the legal framework,[279] and to exercise loyalty, first and foremost, to the institution.[280] These obligations are complemented by the standards of conduct expected of international civil servants.[281]

As revealed in the examination of the above three decisions, several deviations from a merit-based decision-making process occurred. It is self-evident that any meritorious qualities are immediately annulled for all deci-

---

[277] *Ibid.*, para. 11.

[278] *Ibid.*, para. 10.

[279] ICC Anti-Fraud Policy, Presidential Directive, 13 May 2014, ICC/PRESD/G/2014/002, paras. 4.1-4.5 (https://www.legal-tools.org/doc/a5168a).

[280] ICC Staff Regulations, Regulation 1.2(e), see above note 32.

[281] UN, Standards of Conduct for the International Civil Service, 2013, paras. 2–5, 13, 20, 23 ('Standards of Conduct for the International Civil Service') (https://www.legal-tools.org/doc/giezn9/).

sions that violate the relevant legal framework. The procedural and legal requirements were known, well established and available to the Registrar, his team and the Project Board before, during and after each of the decisions related to ReVision and at each of the six phases of the project.

8.7.3. Exercise of the Registrar's Authority

In light of the serial breaches in the decision-making processes associated with ReVision, it is relevant to consider the structure within which the Registrar functions. Article 43(2) of the Rome Statute states that:

> The Registry shall be headed by the Registrar, who shall be the principal administrative officer of the Court. The Registrar shall exercise his or her functions under the authority of the President of the Court.

The implementation of the restructuring project was, therefore, conducted by the Registrar under the authority and oversight of the President. Due to the conclusion of a presidential term during ReVision, two Presidents were in office for different stages of the restructuring process.[282] They were, therefore, each responsible for the Registrar's exercise of his functions in relation to the specific ReVision activities which occurred whilst they were in office.

The responsibility of the President of the ICC with respect to the administration of the Court is underscored in Article 38(3)(a) of the Rome Statute, which indicates that the President and the First and Second Vice-Presidents of the Court are responsible for the proper administration of the Court, with the exception of the Office of the Prosecutor.

On 24 June 2015, five Judges wrote to the Presidency expressing concerns about the restructuring project, including its legality, cost, the potential liability for the Court, the benefits of the exercise and the impact on staff morale, amongst other issues.[283] In the letter, the Judges requested that the project be suspended until these issues could be properly considered. On 24 July, the Presidency provided written reassurance to the Judges

---

[282] President Song Sang-hyun was in office from 11 March 2009 – 11 March 2015; and President Silvia Fernández de Gurmendi was in office from 11 March 2015 – 11 March 2018.

[283] ICC, Marc Perrin de Brichambaut, Sanji Monageng, Geoffrey Henderson, Chile Eboe-Osuji and Cuno Tarfusser, "Concerns expressed by Judges on the ReVision project and request for action to be taken", 24 June 2015. These judges included the Presidents of the three Judicial Divisions (Appeals, Trial and Pre-Trial); Audit Report of ReVision, para. 38, see above note 204.

in line with earlier material produced by the Registrar for States Parties, regarding the legality of the process as well as the size and cost of the new model of the Registry and reiterated the Registry's claims about the impact on the staff profile of the restructuring with respect to gender and geographical representation within the Registry.[284] The Presidency also shared this communication with civil society networks. It was assumed that this action was intended to inform and provide reassurance to a range of stakeholders, including more than 110 staff within the Registry who by that time had been notified that their posts were to be abolished in the second wave of the restructuring.

With this endorsement, it was widely accepted and believed that the process was legal. Despite questions about the legal underpinnings of the restructuring, the cost and the lack of merit-based decision-making in fundamental aspects of the project, ReVision was resoundingly supported by the Presidency, the senior leadership across the Court, as well as, resolutely promoted and defended by States Parties. It had the seal of approval from States Parties and the ICC President. Regardless of the questions and concerns raised during the process, most stakeholders, including Registry staff, assumed that the process must at least be legally compliant, even if it was not being managed and implemented in a transparent and competent manner. With the exception of the Registrar and the Chief of LASS, the extent of the legal risks and violations were likely to have been largely unknown to almost all other staff members and stakeholders until the issuance of ILOAT decision 3907 in January 2018.

With recognition that the Registrar exercises his or her functions under the authority of the President, and with presidential responsibility for the proper administration of the Court, the Presidency held a positive obligation to exercise oversight of the Registrar's management of the ReVision project. The mechanisms to do so existed. In addition to regular meetings and updates between the President/Presidency and Registrar, the President could have requested an IOM evaluation or investigation of the restructuring project at various stages, or the Presidency could also have invited, in

---

[284] ICC, *Presidency note on the issues raised relating to the ReVision project*, 24 July 2015, paras. 4–15, 41-50, p.15; Audit Report of ReVision, para. 38, see above note 204. The Audit Report of ReVision does not mention or address the Presidency's note in response to the judges' letter, although it does make reference to the concerns raised by the five judges. Examination of the Registry's 2016 Budget, 2015, pp. 2, 4, 8, 10, 11, 12, 14, 18, see above note 224.

co-operation with the CBF and/or the Audit Committee, an internal or external audit of the process. Utilizing one or more of these options may have been a more appropriate response to the specific concerns raised in 2015 by a number of fellow judges. It is unclear whether the President or Presidency were aware of the legal jeopardy for the Court regarding the Principles and Procedures, prior to the ILOAT decision of January 2018. In spite of the financial, legal and reputational risks, it seems evident that active steps to ensure the proper administration of the Court were not taken.

8.7.4.   Duty of Care and Treatment of Colleagues

States Parties were led to believe by the project team and in particular the Registrar, that the concerns being raised about ReVision by staff within the Registry were no more than the complaints and discomfort one would expect from employees going through a restructuring process. Substantive concerns from staff were largely dismissed, and those who continued to raise issues internally were problematized and ostracized. Most diplomats amongst The Hague-based States Parties were unable to or chose not to explore the concerns expressed by staff and did not seek verification of these issues from other sources. Staff welfare in relation to the restructuring process did not appear to be sufficiently or thoroughly considered in the discussions amongst either internal or external stakeholders. With respect to the treatment of Registry staff affected by ReVision, ILOAT judgments to date have determined that the restructuring project amounted to: unequal treatment for staff in general;[285] that the ICC had an obligation to deal fairly with staff who occupied abolished positions and fell short of what was required in specific areas;[286] subjected some individuals to specific experiences of unequal treatment;[287] and failed in their duty of care.[288]

Substantial concerns about ReVision including questions about the veracity of the information being provided to the Court and States Parties were often deflected by the Registrar and the States most closely involved with the restructuring process. According to the Registrar, "undertaking a reorganization doesn't always make you very popular in organisations".[289] Concerns raised, most of which have been subsequently vindicated by the

---

[285] ILOAT, Judgment No. 3907, para. 24, see above note 126.

[286] *Ibid.*, paras. 16 and 19.

[287] *Ibid.*, para. 20.

[288] *Ibid.*, para. 21.

[289] Video interview with the Robert H. Jackson Center, at 22:11 minutes.

ILOAT and other reviews, were perceived and bluntly filtered by the Registrar through a personal, rather than a professional, lens. Whilst the Registrar's statement holds some truth in a general sense that restructuring projects are often inherently unpopular, the concerns raised about ReVision, and later verified, were not about the popularity of the restructuring process but rather, they reflected fundamental questions about the integrity of the process and by implication, the institution.

8.7.5.   Internal Oversight System

How did the ICC's internal control system respond to ReVision? In the following sub-section, the role of three bodies will be sketched.

8.7.5.1.   Office of Internal Audit

The prior weakening of the OIA and its proximity to the Registrar in the absence of a functioning Audit Committee disempowered a key feature of the Court's minimalist internal control system. This had a significant impact during the ReVision Project.

According to the Audit Committee, the OIA deviated from its preapproved audit plan for 2015 "as a consequence of the Registry's reorganisation".[290] The purpose of the OIA's audit was to assess whether the ReVision project plan was robust and in line with best practices in project management with respect to the objective, planning, resources and the expected benefits. It is apparent that undertaking a process audit whilst the restructuring was ongoing would allow the project to incorporate findings and integrate any adjustments into the remainder of the process. This was a much-needed safety valve enabling corrective action to be taken, if required, to ensure that the project was compliant and on track to achieve its objectives. As with all internal audits, the OIA required the agreement of the Registrar, as the head of organ, to be able to proceed with its work in areas under their authority. On this occasion, it is clear from the Audit Committee Report that the Registrar prevented the OIA from undertaking an audit of ReVision; thus, it was forced to deviate from its preapproved plan. The External Audit of ReVision, undertaken in 2016 after the completion of the project, did not identify this revealing and critical fact. It was also not included in the Comprehensive Report on ReVision produced by the Registry.

---

[290]   ICC-ASP/15/15, Annex VII, para. 28, see above note 174.

Although primarily the responsibility of the Registrar, the President could have insisted upon the internal audit of ReVision proceeding, had he or she been aware that the Registrar had obstructed the OIA from carrying out its audit of the restructuring process. It is unclear whether the President was aware of this or inquired, independently, about the possibility of an internal audit for the project.

In addition, during ReVision, the OIA conducted internal audits, unrelated to the restructuring process, on issues that involved some of the staff members whose posts had already been earmarked to be abolished.[291] This involved staff members who were still considering the separation package and/or who were the subject of other forms of 'harassment' within the intimidating environment created by the restructuring. In the context of the Registry straining under the restructuring process, these audits appeared to contribute, intentionally or inadvertently, to the hostile and retaliatory climate that existed within the Registry at that time.

8.7.5.2. Independent Oversight Mechanism

Although it took over a decade to establish the IOM, in short-order its independence and impartiality were called into question. This was a result of statements made by the newly appointed head of the IOM regarding the non-applicability of its mandate to the restructuring project. Within a few months of taking office in 2015, the then head of the IOM informed a meeting of all senior managers in the Registry that there were no aspects of ReVision that would fall within the IOM's mandate.[292] This statement surprised many of those present at the meeting in light of the range of concerns that had already emerged with respect to the restructuring. It was also unexpected given the relatively limited period of time in which the new head of office had been in his position.[293] For some, it seemed premature for the head of the IOM to have been able to make such an assessment so quickly and without undertaking even a preliminary analysis of the project.[294]

The mandate of the IOM is to evaluate, inspect and investigate in order to enhance the efficiency and economy of the Court. ReVision was a

---

[291] Conversations in 2015 with Registry staff and managers, on record with the author.
[292] Ibid.
[293] Ibid., The Head of Office assumed his duties on 15 October 2015.
[294] Ibid.

project focused on efficiencies within the Registry and at least initially on potential savings, thus squarely within the purview of the IOM.

In addition, according to the IOM's operational mandate, the ASP and the Bureau can request the IOM to conduct inspections of Court processes as well as evaluations of any programme, project or policy.[295] It was, therefore, not up to, nor possible for, the IOM to foreclose its potential involvement in an evaluation of the ReVision process given the powers of the ASP Bureau to request it to do so at any given time.

The IOM announcement to managers within the Registry depleted staff confidence in the mechanism and raised questions about its independence. These concerns were raised by civil society representatives to the CBF who urged the Committee to better resource the IOM, to take action to safeguard its independence and avert any loss of credibility with respect to its perceived or actual impartiality.[296] In their view, the ability of the IOM to conduct its work "without fear or favour" was critical to its efficacy as a trusted feature of the Court's oversight framework and as a reliable mechanism of internal accountability for ICC staff and officials.[297]

8.7.5.3.   Committee on Budget and Finance

Not to be left out, the States Parties subsidiary body, the CBF, also failed to adequately examine several aspects of ReVision including, process management, compliance and financial implications as well as its potential impact on the Registry and the reputation of the Court as a whole.

Beyond being unable to avert the regulatory violations of the restructuring project, the CBF enabled the Registrar's use of Court funds, contradicting the advice of the External Auditor. To offset some of the cost blowouts associated with undertaking the ReVision Project, in 2015 the Registrar decided to utilize EUR 3.38 million from the Employee Benefits Liabilities ('EBL') Fund without the required prior authorization of the ASP, as

---

[295]   ICC-ASP/12/Res.6, paras. 16, 18, see above note 178.

[296]   Women's Initiatives for Gender Justice, Presentation to the Committee on Budget and Finance, pp. 7–8, September 2016.

[297]   *Ibid.*. Independent Expert Review, 2020, para. 285, see above note 85:

> The IOM does not as yet enjoy the full confidence and trust of all staff. There is a disinclination to make complaints freely and willingly about, and to report officially, alleged impeachable conduct, especially by elected or senior officials. In turn, this makes it more difficult to assess the real extent of the occurrences of misconduct and misbehaviour, and could be a significant factor in the underreporting of reprehensible conduct.

recommended by the External Auditor.[298] When questions were raised about the utilization of a considerable amount of unauthorized funds, the CBF provided justification for the use of the EBL Fund for ReVision,[299] thereby ignoring the External Auditor's advice, subverting the rules and shielding the Registrar from repercussions regarding his decision.

In the lead up to the fourteenth Session of the ASP in December 2015, States Parties were preparing to adopt a resolution in which they intended to express that they "seriously regret" the Registrar's use of the Fund without the required prior approval of the Assembly.[300] The original draft of the resolution also included language highlighting the individual responsibility of the Registrar regarding the use of the funds. During the first meeting about the resolution, there was significant support for such a statement amongst the diplomatic corp. However, when States Parties resumed their negotiations, several diplomats unexpectedly voiced their opposition to the use of the term "seriously regret" and insisted on the resolution only expressing "regret". They were also adamant in arguing for the deletion of any reference to the individual responsibility of the Registrar. As a result, any references to the responsibility of the Registrar regarding the use of the EBL funds were changed to refer in general to the responsibility of the Registry with respect to its use.[301] According to some of those involved in this resolution, prior to the resumed negotiations of the text, the Registrar, a national and former civil servant of the host State, and the Dutch Ministry of Foreign Affairs, contacted States Parties to request them to diminish the language in the ASP resolution reprimanding the Registrar.[302]

The pressure from the foreign ministry of the host State to soften the language and drop any reference to the personal responsibility of the Registrar was complicated for States Parties many of whom have valued bilateral relationships with the Netherlands. Legal advisors and States were concerned about broader implications for their relationships with the Netherlands either within the ICC context or in other political spheres including the European Union, the UN and other international bodies. The host State

---

[298] Audit Report of ReVision, para. 102, see above note 204.

[299] ICC-ASP/14/15, para. 57, see above note 169; ICC, Official Records, Fourteenth Session, ICC-ASP/14/20, 18-26 November 2015, vol. II, part B.2, para. 12.

[300] Conversations with diplomats on file with the author.

[301] ICC, Official Records, Fourteenth Session, ICC-ASP/14/20, 18-26 November, vol. I, part III, section C, para. 1.

[302] Conversations with diplomats on file with the author.

is a highly valued party to the ICC system and its ongoing co-operation with the Court is essential for the ease of some of its routine functions. It also provides conditions and courtesies to the Court's employees and civil society organizations working on ICC-related issues. Capitals did not want to strain their relationships and the host State appeared to be highly invested in assisting the Registrar, as a Dutch national, to deflect or avoid any negative repercussions. The pressure was effective, and, in the end, the ASP adopted a resolution addressing this issue in the weakest terms possible. [303]

The protective impulse of States to defend the actions of their citizens working as civil servants within global institutions was foreseen in the Standards of Conduct of the International Civil Service.

In reaching out to a government to seek their support in order to "block or reverse [an] unfavourable decision[s]" regarding his status, it is possible that the Registrar breached the Standards of Conduct of the International Civil Service (2013) specifically Article 29.[304] In coming to his assistance, the host State may have also breached the same article within the Standards, which require Governments to "safeguard the independence of the international civil service" and as such, "it is understood that Government representatives and members of legislative bodies will neither accede to such requests nor intervene in such matters".[305]

The abrogation's of duty and independence by the OIA, the IOM, the CBF and the Assembly, are laid bare in light of the ILOAT judgment which

---

[303] ICC-ASP/14/Res.1, para. 2, see above note 172: "*Regrets* that the Registry did not seek the formal authorization of the Assembly before resorting to the Employee Benefit Liability fund and *calls for* full transparency in any future such transactions and *recalls* the rules applying for such transactions".

[304] Standards of Conduct for the International Civil Service, UN Doc. A/RES/67/257, in effect as of 1 January 2013, Section A.3., para. 29:

It is entirely improper for international civil servants to lobby or seek support from Government representatives or members of legislative organs to obtain advancement either for themselves or for others or to block or reverse unfavourable decisions regarding their status. By adhering to the Charter and the constitutions of the organizations of the United Nations system, Governments have undertaken to safeguard the independence of the international civil service; it is therefore understood that Government representatives and members of legislative bodies will neither accede to such requests nor intervene in such matters. The proper method for an international civil servant to address such matters is through administrative channels; each organization is responsible for providing these.

[305] *Ibid.*

found the restructuring project to have been "unlawful" in its entirety,[306] the specifics of which could have been identified by a routine internal audit, an IOM investigation or process evaluation, with more thorough scrutiny by the Committee on Budget and Finance, and by proper oversight of the ASP.

The entire internal control system, ill-prepared for the range and scale of ethical and substantive violations committed during the ReVision process, faltered and failed.

8.7.6. Misleading Data

When the restructuring project did not produce the outcomes expected and promised, some of the data was manipulated to make it appear as if the process had been valid, and the results had been met. This included providing misleading information to States Parties about: the legality of the project; the fulfilment of the Court's duty of care to staff during the process; the negative impact on gender and geographical representation as a result of ReVision; and the size, cost and alleged savings of the new Registry structure. The following two sub-sections will address the latter aspects of the misleading data provided to States Parties.

8.7.6.1. Gender and Geographical Representation

Gender and geographical considerations are *live* issues at the ICC. They form part of the statutory requirements for the election of Court officials and, through a complicated formula, each State Party is allocated a certain number of nationals to professional posts within the Court. These data points hold great value for the sense of collective ownership and positive engagement by Member States within the ICC. Individual States and regions are attentive to the levels of representation and under-representation within the professional profile of the Court.

Through the Comprehensive Report produced after ReVision and a series of Q&A papers on gender and geographical issues disseminated to States Parties during the restructuring, the Registry sought to inform and reframe the emerging results with respect to the abolishment of posts and the subsequent appointments made to the new positions. This material included the provision of misleading information to States Parties in order to dilute the political impact of the restructuring process when it resulted in

---

[306] ILOAT, Judgment No. 3907, para. 26, see above note 126.

fewer women and fewer nationals from African States in leadership and management positions after ReVision than before the project. The provision of some of the data presented to States appeared to be intended to obscure and downplay the politically sensitive negative results.

The geographical aspect was particularly delicate given the Africa region had been the near exclusive focus of the Court's prosecutorial work until 2019 with the exception of its investigations in Iraq. Attention to the regional impact was also heightened because the position of Deputy Registrar (D-1), designated by the Rome Statute,[307] and at that time held by a national from an African State, had been abolished at the end of 2013 at the recommendation of the Registrar, in part as a cost-saving measure, in line with the publicly stated intentions of the Registrar to create savings and efficiencies. The abolition of this post was the first major change in the landscape of the Registry.

According to the Comprehensive Report on ReVision, there were more nationals from African States appointed to professional posts within the Registry after the restructuring, than before.[308] Reviewing the tables within the Report on ReVision it is clear that this is due to an alleged increase in the representation of African nationals in the most junior level professional positions (P-2).[309] This is the only category of professional posts in which there may have been an increase in the representation of nationals from African States. Unfortunately, the figures in the Report also misrepresent and reduce the number of nationals of African States in leadership and senior management posts (P-5) *before* ReVision.[310] The figures utilised in the Comprehensive Report also do not reflect the first set of posts abolished as part of the restructuring project in October 2014. In other words, a false picture was created through the selective and partial use of data or the omission of relevant information.

Overall, there were fewer nationals from African States Parties in management and leadership positions after ReVision than before the restructuring process. Although the numerical difference in representation at

---

[307] ICC Statute, Article 43(3), see above note 2: "The Registrar and the Deputy Registrar shall be persons of high moral character, be highly competent and have an excellent knowledge of and be fluent in at least one of the working languages of the Court".

[308] Comprehensive Report, para. 567, see above note 204.

[309] Audit Report of ReVision, para. 106, see above note 204; Examination of the Registry's 2016 Budget, 2015, pp. 5, 6, 19-30, see above note 224.

[310] *Ibid.*

the senior management level before and after ReVision is relatively small, the political sensitivities and relational context of these changes were keenly felt by African Member States whose distress and concerns appeared to be undervalued by the Registrar. This was exacerbated by the series of questionable human resource figures presented by the Registry and the denials of any adverse impact on the representational profile of African nationals as a result of the ReVision project.

Unlike geographical issues, few States Parties demonstrated any sustained interest in the implication of the restructuring on the representation of women in management, senior management and leadership positions within the Registry. There were significant decreases in the number of women in mid-level management positions (P-4) and a slight decrease in the number of women in P-5 posts as a result of ReVision. There was also a missed opportunity to appoint a woman, for the first time, to a head of division with the creation of the new External Relations Division. To date, no women have ever been appointed as a divisional head within the Registry. These posts continue to be dominated by males from the Western Europe and Others Region (WEOG). In the aftermath of ReVision, some States Parties have become animated by concerns about the under-representation of women in management and leadership positions within the ICC and are now championing these issues at the Court as well as across a range of multilateral organizations.[311] Whilst attention to these issues is always important, the depth of commitment to gender equality is unclear given the silence of almost all States during the restructuring process even when informed of the negative impact in real time on the representation of women at mid-level and senior positions. Since the restructuring process, the CBF has adjusted its approach to this issue by analysing more nuanced data regarding the representation of women in professional posts across the Court and has noted their specific concerns about the need for the Registry in particular to "narrow the gender gap".[312] In turn, the Independent Expert Review devoted attention to this issue in their report with the inclusion of numerous statements and recommendations urging the Court to address the significant under-representation of women in leadership posts.[313]

---

[311] ICC, "ICC hosts launch of International Gender Champions Network's New 'Den Haag Hub'", press release, 5 February 2019, ICC-CPI-20190205-PRI1437 (https://www.legal-tools.org/doc/a4a94c/).

[312] ICC-ASP/17/5, part F, section 3, paras. 97 and 98, see above note 188.

[313] Independent Expert Review, 2020, for example, paras. R15, R88, 138, 212.

The narrative about the gender and geographical issues promoted by the Registrar and his team, which the CBF, the ASP and the Presidency were willing to echo, seemed intended to provide political cover for the Registrar, for the Court as a whole and for diplomats, especially those from States Parties which genuinely profess a commitment to gender and geographical diversity and yet had overseen a restructuring process that had reduced the meaningful representation of both.

8.7.6.2. Determining the Data

The Registry's misleading figures and narratives about the staff profile following the restructuring was made possible through, a manipulation of the timeframes selected to determine the staff figures both before and after ReVision. For example, in the Comprehensive Report of ReVision, the Registry indicates 30 April 2015 as the date it utilized to count the staff profile prior to ReVision even though the project was launched 16 months before this time, on 1 January 2014.[314] By selecting April 2015, it negates the positions abolished in October 2014 under ReVision and to which the enhanced separation package applied. This enabled the Registry to produce misleading figures that downplayed the negative gender and geographical impact of the restructuring. The Report also indicates the date of 30 June 2016 to assess the staff profile after ReVision, although the project ended on 31 July 2015.

Arguably, more realistic dates for the staff profile of the Registry before ReVision would be 31 December 2013, given the restructuring project officially started on 1 January 2014. Or one might consider 31 July 2014, the final month before the promulgation of the first set of Principles and Procedures on 19 August 2014. Both of these dates would provide a reasonable and more accurate assessment of the staff profile of the Registry prior to the restructuring, inclusive of the first posts abolished in October 2014. The date to assess the staff figures after ReVision could be 30 August 2015, given the project officially ended on 31 July 2015 or alternately, one could consider 31 December 2015 to bring it into alignment with other ICC human resource reports and provide a clear two-year period for comparison between the start and the end of ReVision (31 December 2013–31 December 2015).

---

[314] Comprehensive Report, p. 26, see above note 204.

8.7.6.3.   The Cost of ReVision and Its 'Savings'

An area, which has yet to be fully reviewed, relates to the alleged cost of the new Registry structure. In particular, whether ReVision adhered to the envelope of EUR 42,929,500 and the staff level of 560 fixed-term posts set by the ASP for the restructuring, and generated savings of EUR 443,800, as claimed by the Registrar,[315] and confirmed by the Presidency.[316] In reviewing the Registry's projected budget for 2016, the CBF labelled the alleged savings contradictory,[317] and described the costs associated with the new structure as "lacking the necessary consistency, transparency and comparability".[318]

The CBF and the 2016 Audit of the ReVision project, both accepted that the Registry's figure for the total cost of the new structure was within the envelope and acknowledged the savings as reported by the Registry. The Audit Report also noted that the alleged savings of EUR 443,800 were quickly absorbed with the increase in staff numbers and other costs within the budget for 2016, based on the new model of the Registry.[319] The Audit Report found the savings in staff costs alleged within the 2016 budget to be "unconvincing".[320]

In its series of 18 "detailed reports"[321] produced on ReVision, the Registry has never provided information regarding how it arrived at the cost of the new structure.[322] It would be valuable to conduct a forensic financial examination to assess whether States Parties were provided with reliable information, and whether the costs and alleged savings of the new structure are verifiable, thereby ensuring that the Registry has a sound basis for future budget projections. Two aspects worthy of specific scrutiny are:

(a)   Whether all of the positions counted in the staff costs for the Registry budget before ReVision were also counted in the costs of the new structure. The information about the significant increase in the ICC's

---

[315]   *Ibid.*, para. 136.

[316]   Audit Report of ReVision, p. 8, see above note 204.

[317]   ICC-ASP/14/15, fn.11, see above note 169.

[318]   *Ibid.*, para. 58 and fn. 11.

[319]   Audit Report of ReVision, para. 127, see above note 204; ICC-ASP/14/15, fn. 11, see above note 169.

[320]   *Ibid.*, para. 126.

[321]   Comprehensive Report, p. 25, see above note 204.

[322]   Examination of the Registry's 2016 Budget, p. 11, see above note 224.

2016 budget request based on the new model, compared with the alleged savings in the new structure, do not seem strongly aligned. The challenges in reconciling contrasting budget figures with respect to ReVision was referred to in the Audit Report as "difficult to explain",[323] and that while the increase in staff numbers to adjust to the new premises was reasonable, the Registry's explanations justifying the effectiveness of the restructuring project, "warrant qualification".[324] It is relevant for the integrity of the budget, the verification of the alleged savings, and the claims of adherence to the financial envelope determined by States that all of the same positions (contractors, consultants, advisers, fellows, staff posts and so on) that were counted before the restructuring, were also included in the headcount related to the cost of the structure after ReVision. This question remains open and unanswered.

(b) Whether the standard practice utilized by the Registry of budgeting for each position based on the maximum cost of the post was applied to the new structure. The practice of budgeting for the ceiling costs per post ensures that, regardless of who is in the position, the post is properly and adequately addressed within the budget. For example, all of the professional posts at the ICC (P1-P5) have 13 steps in the salary structure. Under the standard budgeting practice, each post would be budgeted at Step 13 (the highest step) to ensure that the position is fully budgeted in case of changes in the post and the need to recruit a new person into the position. If the new person is more experienced than the previous holder of the post, the ICC is able to benefit from the additional experience by being able to offer the incoming appointee a higher step level than the previous occupant. If this standard practice was applied to the restructuring, then it has a sound budget. If not, and if instead the budget for ReVision deviated from the standard practice and was based on budgeting only for the actual step level of the incumbent, then the budget has been underestimated and misrepresented, and may not be reliable as the basis for budget projections in the long term. This issue speaks to both the integrity of the budget as well as the process.

---

[323] Audit Report of ReVision, para. 111, see above note 204.

[324] *Ibid.*, para. 114.

8.7.7. Governance

Despite their governance responsibilities, States Parties were consistently willing to forgo a critical analysis of the information they were provided as long as what they were being told about ReVision was compatible with what they wanted to hear, regardless of how unlikely or implausible it was. What they wanted to hear was that the new structure would deliver savings and efficiencies, and that the process was valid and complied with the legal framework. This narrative was closely adhered to by all Court principals, as well as States Parties, elected officials, and other stakeholders, with few exceptions, throughout the entire project.

As time went by and the role of States Parties in the mismanagement of ReVision began to surface, it was perhaps not in the interest of the States to probe further.

In reality, it was likely that some of the diplomats, especially those in small to mid-size embassies, were overworked and overwhelmed by their duties to simultaneously cover a number of Hague-based multilateral institutions, including the ICC, the ICTY, the International Court of Justice as well as the Organisation for the Prohibition of Chemical Weapons. Some embassies simply did not have the bandwidth to interrogate the voluminous restructuring information with which they were furnished by the Registrar and his team.[325] Many States appeared to passively go along with the process, whilst others seemed to be disengaged due to competing work priorities. Some may have overly relied on the assessment of the States that were actively involved in the restructuring process, and most seemed to assume that the Registrar and his team were competently managing the project, or at least ensuring that it was legally compliant.

During ReVision, the pressure experienced by individual diplomats to forgo dissent and to conform to the group narrative was clear and tangible. Legal advisors of States Parties who raised questions or expressed an alternative view about the restructuring were sometimes threatened by the Registrar with being reported to their capitals if they persisted.[326] This was a powerful disincentive. Diplomats on assignment do not like to be undermined to their capital or to have their reputations compromised. Inevitably, as a result of this pressure, most of the issues were quickly dropped. In effect, individual diplomats may have been pressured or harangued by the

---

[325] Conversations on file with the author.
[326] *Ibid.*

person whose work in the context of the Court as a whole they were responsible for overseeing as States Parties. Individual diplomats were reluctant or even afraid to express ideas that contradicted the Registrar and the other group members (States Parties), especially those whose national and individual reputations became entwined with the success of this reform process.

The pressure also went the other way with some Court officials reportedly urged by States Parties to be more vocal and visible in their support for ReVision and the Registrar.[327] As an elected official, a request from an influential State Party can quickly feel like a requirement.

The Registrar and States Parties were unwilling to consider or discuss discrepant or unsettling information about ReVision and were aggressive towards discordant critiques about the process. Any data or analysis that questioned or contradicted the group narrative was dismissed. Those providing the analysis were treated with suspicion and disdain or, alternatively, accused of threatening the reputation of the project.[328] The Registrar and personnel in his immediate office who, according to the Comprehensive Report, were responsible for external communication about ReVision[329] adopted a strategy of personally attacking those who critiqued ReVision as a way of discrediting their analysis. This strategy, a now familiar tool in the daily political discourse within the US, was not new to the ICC. But the personalized attacks targeting both internal and external stakeholders was unprecedented and as a tactic, it was effective in deflecting attention from the facts and the vulnerabilities within the ReVision process, at least in the short term.

It is reasonable for States Parties to expect civil servants to be candid, honest and transparent and that States will be provided with reliable information upon which they make significant decisions as the governing body. But when it became clear that some essential information about ReVision was questionable at best and warranted a more critical evaluation given what was at stake, States chose to remain with the group narrative and, by doing so, they knowingly colluded with being deliberately deceived.

This dynamic prevented States Parties from making fully informed decisions on issues affecting the overall budget of the Court and obstructed

---

[327] *Ibid.*

[328] *Ibid.*; Comprehensive Report, para. 567, see above note 204.

[329] *Ibid.*

States from being made aware of the serial and serious violations of Court rules and regulations as well as the breaches of the ICC's duty of care to its staff inherent within the restructuring project.

8.7.7.1. Decision-Making Processes

The factors that influence collective and deliberative decision-making processes can be subtle.

In the case of ReVision, the chance to undertake institutional reform of the Registry with 560 staff and with an annual budget of over EUR 60 million was ambitiously seductive for the Registry staff and diplomats most engaged in the restructuring process. In addition to the genuine intentions of the project and the legitimacy of the re-organization itself, there appeared to be a significant level of State- and self-interest associated with the opportunity to undertake an institutional reform process on this scale.

According to Thompson, one of the ways in which corruption of a public institution occurs, is when interests, irrelevant to its purpose, undermine the effective stewardship of the organization.[330] Personal ambition, the interests of States Parties, and the preservation of bilateral relationships are all legitimate and ethically neutral considerations. But each of these interests was irrelevant to either the objectives of ReVision (to enhance the efficiency of the Registry and generate savings) or to the mandate of the ICC. Yet, such considerations appeared to qualify and shape the engagement with and oversight of the project and facilitated the occurrence of a series of violations, without consequence or accountability. These were influences that appeared to undermine and compromise the internal control and oversight procedures of the Court. In the language of Lessig, these were interests, irrelevant to the objectives of ReVision, that formed an "economy of influence", which in this context, weakened the purpose of the restructuring, the trustworthiness of the institution and possibly the credibility of the Court.

In hindsight, it was profoundly unwise for States Parties to have proceeded with a restructuring project in the absence of a functioning and independent Audit Committee. The Committee was dissolved in 2014 but had not met since 2012. A credible Committee of external experts may

---

[330] Thompson, 1995, pp. 20–25, see above note 205; Newhouse, pp. 584, 576, fn. 122, see above note 118; Dennis F. Thompson, "Two Concepts of Corruption", in *Edmond J. Safra Centre for Ethics Working Papers*, no. 16, 1 August 2013.

have been able to provide the objectivity needed in this process and alerted States Parties and the ASP to anomalies, violations and non-compliance at an early enough stage of the process for corrective action to have been taken. Whether States Parties would have acted upon this information is unknown, but had it existed, it would have preserved some integrity for the institution.

The project suffered from a lack of preparation in advance of the restructuring to ensure mechanisms were in place to provide checks and balances throughout the process. States Parties enabled a system in which those responsible for ReVision could determine whether an internal audit of the project could proceed or not, thereby exposing the Court to significant risk and liability. The Presidency did not take steps to ensure the proper administration of the Court with an appropriate level of oversight of the Registrar during this process. When non-compliance with external Audit recommendations regarding the (mis)use of funds was discovered, the CBF was prepared to shroud it in justification and States Parties were unwilling to critique this conduct as improper, let alone address it as a potential violation of Court rules.

It is evident that the restructuring process did not adhere to merit-based decision-making processes and that there were serious violations of the ICC's legal framework leading to the unfair treatment of staff and the Court's failure to meet its duty of care. This was harmful for the staff and created significant liabilities for the ICC. It is also apparent that the structure and operating methods of the Project Board did not embody the necessary objectivity and credibility for the process and approved phases of the project that were inherently flawed. The restructuring suffered from a significant lack of transparency in almost all areas including within its decision-making procedures and in the communication with States Parties with key aspects of the information provided to States proving to be unreliable and lacking in veracity. Each one of these areas on their own, meets the definition of institutional corruption. That corruption is 'satisfied' in all of these aspects, is revealing of the widespread and deep-seated vulnerabilities within the internal and external control systems of the Court. It is also indicative of a lack of impartiality and critical evaluation in the exercise of governance by the ASP.

During this period at the Court, institutional dishonesty flourished at a rapid and voluminous pace. Most alarming was the ease with which this was accepted by States Parties, the ICC leadership and most independent stakeholders. The lack of discomfort at the assault on the integrity of the institution was disconcerting.

To date, ReVision has cost the Court over EUR 7,300,000, inclusive of the costs associated with undertaking this project (EUR 1,075,500),[331] the separation indemnities paid to staff (EUR 5,311,000 million),[332] along with the damages awarded by ILOAT to former staff members (EUR 1,000,000) whose posts were abolished.[333] More than five years after ReVision officially ended, the ICC is still mired in litigation with dozens more restructuring-related cases still to be resolved and adjudicated for individuals whose posts were illegally abolished.[334]

The sense of invulnerability for the Registrar and his team was reinforced every time a breach of rules, an unlawful act, false information or a perversion of transparency occurred without consequences for these violations.

To date, no one has yet been held accountable for ReVision. The mismanagement and institutional corruption within the process and the damage to the ICC's inherent trustworthiness as a public institution have largely been ignored. In reality, all of the key senior staff whose roles were central to the process within the Registry and on the Project Board, remain in their posts without any healthy accountability for the institution. Some of those involved in the restructuring process have sought higher office, others have been promoted. According to Dennis Thompson, in cases of institutional corruption, the actions of individuals implicate the institution but "it is still individuals who are the agents of institutional corruption and individuals who should be held accountable for it".[335]

The Registrar stood for re-election for a second term at the end of his five-year tenure. He ultimately withdrew from the process a month before the appointment was due to be made, immediately following the election of a new presidency.[336] This was perhaps not surprising given two-thirds of the incoming Presidency had been amongst the small group of judges who

---

[331] Audit Report of ReVision, para. 89, see above note 204.

[332] *Ibid.*, para. 95.

[333] Judgment No. 3907, see above note 126; ILOAT, *L. (No. 3) v. ICC*, Judgment No. 3908 (https://www.legal-tools.org/doc/dw2f4u/) and ILOAT, *B. v. ICC*, Judgment No. 4004 (https://www.legal-tools.org/doc/7d3c02/).

[334] ICC-ASP/17/5, paras. 147–153, see above note 188.

[335] Thompson, 1995, p. 7, see above note 205.

[336] Registrar Herman von Hebel withdrawal letter, 13 March 2018.

had earlier raised a number of concerns about the restructuring including its legality, efficacy and potential impact on the Court.

It is not yet clear that the ASP and its subsidiary bodies, the Audit Committee and the CBF, are taking seriously enough the systemic vulnerabilities exposed by the restructuring process, the extent of the damage inflicted upon the reputation and credibility of the Court, and the urgency with which it should be undertaking actions to restore trust and confidence in this publicly funded and correspondingly, publicly accountable international institution for justice. It is perhaps most important that the process begins by restoring the ICC's confidence and trust in itself.

The failure of ReVision to deliver on its objectives and the financial costs of the project have perhaps done significantly less harm to the ICC than the corruption that the management of the process injected into the heart of the Court and the culture of unethical behaviour that the process tapped into and accelerated across the ICC as a whole.

For the Court, ReVision was a painful example of the fragility of an institution untethered from a clear set of ethical values and practices, operating without the institutional safeguards needed to ensure its integrity. For States Parties, it was a devastating example of the impact of long-term institutional neglect, the result of not applying an ethics lens to their oversight functions, and emblematic of the limitations of budget-driven governance.

8.8. Conclusion

At this time in its history, the ICC is ethically discordant with the principles of the Rome Statute and the global inspiration that gave rise to this revolutionary treaty. Such contrast is the perfect invitation for new models of diplomacy and collective leadership to emerge.

The willingness of States Parties to hold themselves and each other accountable is central to the integration of ethical practices within their governance and decision-making activities. The continued readiness to overlook impropriety of elected ICC officials, the sparing of political blushes, the shielding of senior leaders from accountability processes by their respective States Parties, and diminishing and denying the harm inflicted upon the Court's institutional integrity, breeds more of the same. This has led to a crisis of trust and ethical integrity within the institution. The Independent Expert Review found that the ICC suffers internally from distrust and a culture of fear.[337] According to their report, concerns about ethics were identified as an important topic for all stakeholders during their consultation process and it noted the erosive effect of allegations of potential ethics violations on the Court's reputation, credibility and trust.[338] Professor Gregory Gordon has described this period in the field of international justice as "an existential crisis that calls for an ethical catharsis" and postures that it is this very crisis which "might be what ultimately saves it".[339]

Fortunately, the Court is constantly in the process of *becoming* the 'International Criminal Court' of the Rome Statute, in service to humanity, preserving the delicate mosaic of peoples united by common bonds, and providing accountability for the most serious crimes in order to foster peace and well-being.[340]

People in every country of the world, including the 2.5 billion who are currently citizens of States Parties to the ICC, are increasingly looking for institutions where conduct matches mission, and where institutional culture is aligned with the nobility of its mandate. Business, as usual, is no longer enough.

There is a growing global consciousness emerging that is impressed more by authenticity than status; seeks credibility, not perfection; and chooses courage over cynicism. These are the qualities needed in a new era of multilateral leadership to restore the integrity of the Court, expand public trust, and renew pride in this magnificent endeavour.

---

[337] Independent Expert Review, 2020, para. 62, see above note 85.

[338] *Ibid.*, para. 254

[339] Gregory S. Gordon, "Closing Remarks at the Peace Palace Conference on Integrity in International Justice", CILRAP, 2 December, at 2.34-2.50 minutes (www.cilrap.org/cilrap-film/181202-gordon-closing/).

[340] ICC Rome Statute, Preamble, see above note 2.

9

Effective Leadership, Management and Integrity in International Criminal Investigations

William H. Wiley[*]

9.1. Introduction

The offices of the prosecutor of the international courts and tribunals[1] established since 1993 have shown wildly disparate results with respect to the number of individuals brought to trial and convicted on some or all charges. The formative institutions of the modern era – the International Criminal Tribunals for the former Yugoslavia and for Rwanda ('ICTY' and 'ICTR') – sentenced 90 and 62 persons, respectively, for the perpetration of core international crimes.[2] Other bodies have registered lesser numbers of convictions. For instance, the Special Court for Sierra Leone ('SCSL') sentenced nine persons to custodial sentences for international offences,[3] and the Extraordinary Chambers in the Courts of Cambodia ('ECCC') have registered three convictions.[4] The Special Tribunal for Lebanon ('STL') has yet to issue a single judgement, although the investigative body which gave rise to the Tribunal commenced its work in 2005.[5] In a similar vein, the Kosovo Specialist Chambers ('KSC') and Specialist Prosecutor's Office has not at the time of writing brought its first charge, even though its inves-

---

[*] Dr. **William H. Wiley** is the founder and Executive Director of the Commission for International Justice and Accountability (CIJA). He started his career in the field of international criminal investigations with the Canadian war-crimes programme in 1997 and later served at the International Criminal Tribunal for the former Yugoslavia, International Criminal Tribunal for Rwanda, International Criminal Court, and the Iraqi High Tribunal.

[1] The use of the adjective 'international' in this context refers to bodies established under United Nations and international-treaty auspices as well as so-called hybrid institutions which bring together domestic and international laws and actors.

[2] International Residual Mechanism for Criminal Tribunals ('IRMCT'), "Infographic: ICTY Facts & Figures" and "The ICTR in Brief" (available on its web site).

[3] See the Residual Special Court for Sierra Leone's web site.

[4] Extraordinary Chambers in the Courts of Cambodia, "Who has been prosecuted" (available on its web site).

[5] The United Nations International Independent Investigation Commission ('UNIIIC') was established in April 2005 pursuant to United Nations Security Council resolution 1595.

---

tigations started in 2011.[6] The International Criminal Court ('ICC') has registered four convictions for the perpetration of core international crimes since the establishment of its Office of the Prosecutor ('OTP') in mid-2003.[7]

The mandates of the international courts and tribunals established since 1993 are unique and their annual budgets differ, or have differed, considerably. What is more, the investigative arms of these institutions have found themselves confronted by quite distinct geographical contexts presenting highly dissimilar physical risks to deployed personnel. For instance, ICTY investigators faced no meaningful physical risks whilst in the field, whereas ICC-OTP investigators cannot operate with any significant effect upon Libyan territory as well as that of a number of other ICC situation countries. Additionally, the political calculations of domestic actors frequently generate drag upon investigative efforts; this would go some distance towards explaining the dearth of prosecutorial output by the STL, the ECCC and the KSC. For these and other reasons, the number of persons prosecuted successfully by any given OTP serves as a poor guide to the quality of any particular institution, its leadership and management. Notwithstanding these caveats, might the number of successful prosecutions by all of the international courts and tribunals be tallied with an eye to their collective performance over the last quarter-century? The following question should be asked: is the conviction over 25 years of fewer than 200 perpetrators of core international crimes, involving the expenditure of several billion US dollars, suggestive of a highly functioning system of international investigations and prosecutions?

One thinks not.

What lies at the root of the underperformance of the system of international criminal justice since 1993? It is most certainly not insufficient funding; and, whilst one might rightly point to a lack of politico-diplomatic will in certain instances, in and of itself policy calculation does not explain

---

[6]   The Special Investigative Task Force, established in 2011, evolved into the Special Prosecutor's Office in 2016; see Kosovo Specialist Chambers and Specialist Prosecutor's Office, "Special Investigative Task Force" (available on its web site).

[7]   The four persons convicted at trial, at the time of writing, are Thomas Lubanga Dyilo, Germain Katanga, Ahmad al-Faqi al-Mahdi, and Bosco Ntaganda. Al-Mahdi pleaded guilty; appellate proceedings remain underway in the case of Ntaganda. This tally does not include Jean-Pierre Bemba, all of whose convictions for the perpetration of core international crimes were vacated by an ICC appellate panel.

the relative dearth of successful prosecutions. Nor do the physical risks presented by certain operational areas, not least as public institutions have always had the option of circumventing physical risk through the enlistment of non-public actors. Insufficiency of successful prosecutions is, first and foremost, a reflection of the uneven performance of the various international investigations divisions which are (or were, in the case of the now-closed ICTR and ICTY) subordinate to the offices of the prosecutor of the international courts and tribunals. In particular, since 1993, the overall quality of the leadership and management of the international offices of the prosecutor and their investigations divisions has frequently fallen short of the standards required to meet the evidentiary standards necessary for successful prosecutions consistently. Put simply, in a number of instances, the people in charge have not been up to the task. In noting as much, this chapter takes as its starting point the convincing arguments advanced by Morten Bergsmo regarding the frequent failure of the international community, as well as the courts and tribunals which it establishes, to foster institutional cultures built upon professional as well as personal integrity.[8]

This chapter draws on personal observations as the author was employed by the ICTY, the ICTR and the ICC on a continuous basis from May 2000 to August 2005. It is built around six issues, which are examined in turn: (1) the roots of international criminal investigative insufficiency; (2) the crucial distinction between leadership and management in the administration of international criminal justice; (3) the importance of institutional loyalty; (4) how failures of discipline serve to undermine the proper functioning of offices of the prosecutor and, most especially, their investigations divisions; (5) examples of successful as well as insufficient leadership witnessed at the OTPs of the ICTY, the ICTR and the ICC; and (6) the necessary intersection of strong leadership and professional integrity in the execution of effective international criminal investigations. Viewed as a whole, this chapter asserts that a great many poor staffing decisions have been made by the international community as well as the international offices of the prosecutor themselves, with a negative effect upon the proper functioning of the investigations divisions, most especially during the formative phase of the post-1993 era of international courts and tribunals. More specifically, the inconsistent approach taken towards the appointment

---

[8] Morten Bergsmo, "Revisiting Integrity in International Justice", FICHL Policy Brief Series No. 93 (2018), Torkel Opsahl Academic EPublisher, Brussels, 2018 (https://www.legal-tools.org/doc/e550f7).

of individuals to leadership and management positions has had a deleterious effect upon rank-and-file performance, integrity and, inevitably, investigative output. Whereas the overall quality of international criminal investigations has improved over the last 10 years, in a number of respects, the system of international criminal justice remains burdened by early errors as well as the lack of consensus, within the institutions and beyond, regarding their core objectives.

9.2. The Roots of International Criminal Investigative Insufficiency

Have the great and the good, in establishing the various international courts and tribunals, not least the ICC, believed themselves to be laying the legal foundations of judicial institutions with little purpose other than the investigation, prosecution and adjudication of persons suspected of having perpetrated core international crimes? Conversely, have they seen themselves as being engaged in processes of social experimentation *vis-à-vis* conflict-affected societies as well as the practice of international criminal law?

Notwithstanding their lofty preambles, the statutes which inform the relevant international bodies suggest that the international courts and tribunals have been envisioned by their politico-diplomatic authors as judicial institutions with missions not dissimilar to those of domestic justice systems. However, those tasked by the United Nations, the ICC Assembly of States Parties ('ASP'), as well as by smaller groups of States with giving concrete form to the institutions in question have often treated the building and operation of the offices of the prosecutor as a social rather than operational mission – or they have otherwise succumbed to external pressures to organize their affairs around such an understanding.

Police, prosecutors, judges and other servants of the law who ply their trades in the domestic realm might bask in the relative luxury of knowing that there exists a large degree of social consensus regarding the purpose of their respective labours. Broadly speaking, the actors in domestic criminal justice systems operate on the assumption, largely unspoken, that their work is designed to protect the citizenry from the threats posed thereto by persons who conduct themselves outside of the law. Put another way, domestic actors in the field of criminal justice see themselves as contributing to the protection of the populace through the preservation of the rule of law.

No such consensus exists in the field of international criminal justice. It is posited here that, were all of the men and women employed by the archipelago of international courts and tribunals to be canvassed regarding the purpose of their labours, a wide range of conflicting or otherwise difficult-to-reconcile priorities would be identified. Is the purpose of international criminal justice to provide a measure of redress for the victims of war and other forms of widespread or systematic violence? Conversely, is it the mission of international courts and tribunals simply to incarcerate offenders where the evidence warrants, thereby eradicating demonstrable threats to the vulnerable through the denial of freedom to the perpetrators of core international crimes? Or is the aim of international criminal justice to signal to would-be offenders that there shall be no impunity for those who violate international criminal and humanitarian law?

Perhaps international criminal justice is designed to serve all of these ends. What it manifestly cannot do is serve all of these ends in equal measure, for the budgets of the international courts and tribunals, whilst considerable, are finite. It therefore falls to the leaders of the institutions to establish priorities within the context of the available resources. Where, though, should an international chief prosecutor turn for guidance when establishing the said priorities? Quite obviously, the statutes of any given international court or tribunal would logically be the first point of reference. In the event, the lofty statements of purpose set out in the collected statutes are highly abstract; as such, they necessarily serve as an imperfect guide. External consultations are of little additional utility in this regard insofar as there exists in the wider world no international consensus – social or political – regarding the purpose or the desirability of international investigations and prosecutions. This absence of consensus might nonetheless be seen as a two-edged sword. On the one hand, the lack of agreement has generally served to create uncertainty within investigative-prosecutorial leadership cadres about how best to direct their subordinates to common ends. On the other hand, amorphous statements of purpose and the absence of wider accord regarding the objectives of international criminal justice leave considerable scope for leaders, with a clear sense of resolve as well as moral courage, to shape their missions as they see fit without having to face *well-founded* claims that they have violated the letter and spirit of the relevant statute.

The increasing and distressing tendency towards social experimentation in the field of international criminal justice is revealed in a number of practices. First and foremost, recruitment policies prioritizing gender parity and geographical representation over relevant experience and professional competence have given rise to all manner of leadership failures, managerial insufficiency and demonstrations of rank-and-file ineptitude. More specifically, over the last 25 years, the offices of the prosecutor of international courts and tribunals have retained an unconscionable number of personnel who have shown themselves to be unfamiliar with, and unable to conform to the exacting standards required by investigative and prosecutorial processes undertaken in the context of international criminal and humanitarian law. The objective of creating familiarity with international criminal and humanitarian law beyond its Western-centric practice through the demographic engineering of offices of the prosecutor might be characterized as being admirable in principle. However, to seek to foster a truly global understanding of the merits of international criminal justice through social engineering at a pace which undermines the proper development of a given institution – and by extension, the wider system – constitutes a self-defeating move by those whose first loyalty ought to be to the principle of institutional efficiency.

Secondly, the staff-*cum*-employment rules which govern the relevant institutions tend to render it difficult for leaders and managers to purge the institutions of under-performing and otherwise unessential personnel without risk to their own positions. This problem is exacerbated by State officials, from the developed as well as the developing world, who intervene directly with international courts and tribunals where one of their nationals is threatened with dismissal or whose services have otherwise been dispensed with. The ICC-ASP granted the last Registrar of the ICC, Mr. Herman von Hebel, what he believed to be a free hand to dismiss underperforming personnel as well as others who, oftentimes through no fault of their own, were holding positions and ranks that were superfluous to the needs of the Court. In the event, once the sackings started, Mr. von Hebel began to receive communications from diplomats interceding on behalf of the individuals effected by the reorganization, whilst still other ASP members failed to signal publicly their support for the reorganization which they had already approved by less-formal means. Ultimately, the complaints by various States Parties brought to a conclusion Mr. von Hebel's career at the Court – and leaders, as well as senior managers working in the field of international criminal and humanitarian law, will not have missed this abject lesson.

Thirdly, pressures placed upon international courts and tribunals by civil society groups, both directly and through advocacy efforts directed at the States funding these bodies, have increasingly had the effect of drawing limited resources away from the core investigative and prosecutorial functions. In turn, the resources have been spent upon relevant, albeit secondary tasks such as strategic communications, the protection (defined broadly and hopelessly imprecisely) of victims, who may or may not be witnesses, and other presumed stakeholders in the judicial process (save suspects and the accused). Under-explored to date by scholars and commentators,[9] the redirection of resources in this manner from the core functions weighs particularly heavily upon offices of the prosecutor. This phenomenon is particularly in evidence at the ICC, which the uncharitable might assert displays, at times, a tendency to place more focus upon the needs of victims than on the evidentiary requirements for a successful prosecution.

Finally, in this context, it will be observed that the professional performance of the managerial and, most importantly, the leadership cadres of the international courts and tribunals have, since 1993, proved to be uneven. The shortcomings witnessed over the last quarter-century are inseparable from the recruitment policies of the institutions which have employed (or otherwise promoted) men and women to leadership and management positions. More specifically, the assessment of individuals for senior leadership and managerial positions have not factored the qualities of institutional loyalty and moral courage into hiring processes, thereby exacerbating the problems which arise from the continued employment of unproductive personnel at lesser ranks as well as the frequent failure of offices of the prosecutor to resist external pressures to shift finite resources away from the core investigative and prosecutorial functions. Managerial and, most especially, leadership insufficiency encourages institutional rot, too often leading to the voluntary withdrawal of the most talented personnel to other places of employment. High rates of staff turnover – which characterized most especially the ICC-OTP during the suzerainty of chief Prosecutor Luis Moreno-Ocampo – have a concomitantly negative effect upon institutional memory. In turn, the degradation of the latter has a deleterious impact upon the proper functioning of international offices of the prosecutor, given the fact that the temporal parameters which frame the opening of a given investigation and the conclusion of appellate proceedings in the event of a conviction will span several years.

---

[9] The exception to this rule is Kjersti Lohne, *Advocates of Humanity: Human Rights NGOs in International Criminal Justice*, Ph.D. dissertation, Department of Criminology and Sociology of Law, University of Oslo, 2015.

As was noted at the outset of this chapter, Morten Bergsmo has distinguished himself in recent years as the most forceful advocate for the creation of a culture of integrity within the system of international criminal justice. Whilst it may be tempting for some to see his demands for uprightness and high moral character as nothing more than a rejoinder to the ethical lapses of Moreno-Ocampo, to do so would be to misconstrue the arguments advanced by Bergsmo as well as the pressing need for new approaches to personnel matters within the existing institutions charged with the application of international criminal and humanitarian law. It is the view taken here that, notwithstanding improvements witnessed over the last 10 years, there remains an urgent requirement for a root-and-branch reform of the flawed approach to leadership and management, which has been too often in evidence in the system of international criminal justice. Until such reforms are made, the overall prosecutorial record of the international courts and tribunals shall remain at levels incommensurate with their financial expenditures, thereby serving to call the entire system of international criminal justice into disrepute.

9.3. Leadership and Management in International Courts and Tribunals

Many of the problems plaguing the system of international criminal justice and the associated offices of the prosecutor can be traced to insufficient institutional leadership and management. As has been noted already, this state of affairs owes a great deal to the manner in which persons are appointed to positions of significant responsibility. Unsatisfactory leadership and management also reflect the fact that the distinction between leadership and management is poorly understood by those employed by international courts and tribunals, not least the very persons holding leadership and management appointments.

There exists a dizzying quantity of books, audio guides, seminars and the like which are designed to create effective leaders as well as managers in the world of business; these materials are mind-numbing, at least for those disinterested in matters of commerce. Highly professional military forces have their own approach to leadership and management, built respectively around the distinction between the officer and non-commissioned officer ranks, and the unique training regimens of each professional stream. In contrast, treatises which concern themselves with the practice of law are rarely, if ever, coupled with panegyrics on the importance of effective leadership and management. Omissions of this nature are understandable to the extent that law is perceived by its practitioners to be, and frequently is, an individual pursuit, even where a lawyer practises within a large private firm or a public prosecutor's office. Be that as it may, it is the culture of the practice of law which most influences international criminal courts and tribunals; perhaps as a consequence, the senior most positions in these institutions – president, chief prosecutor and registrar – are by design occupied by men and women drawn from the ranks of lawyers and judges.[10] In practice, this approach to the filling of senior positions within the system of international criminal justice has seen the appointment of a great many leaders and managers with an understanding of law – though not necessarily international criminal and humanitarian law – who rarely grasp the fundamentals of leadership, management and the distinction betwixt the two.

What, then, is the difference between leadership and management?

9.3.1. Leadership

The hallmark of effective leadership in an international criminal court or tribunal is – or ought to be – a capacity for long-term thinking which is woven around a clearly-defined vision which the leader is able to impart to his or her subordinates in terms which are understandable to the latter in the context of their respective professional functions. For this reason, leaders need to be effective communicators, that is, to be skilled at selling their vision on an ongoing basis to their subordinates as well as to external partners and stakeholders; in the field of international criminal justice, the gamut of stakeholders runs from international human rights organizations, through the United Nations Security Council, to key States and (in the case of the ICC) the ASP.

To ensure the effective implementation of the vision, a leader in the field of international criminal justice needs to be prepared to take risks. For the men and women leading international institutions, or component parts thereof such as the offices of the prosecutor, hazards present themselves where discipline must be imposed in order to bring recalcitrant and underperforming subordinates into line. The case of Mr. von Hebel, cited above,

---

[10] As far as this author is aware, the only non-practitioner of law (that is, neither a licensed lawyer nor a judge) to have held a senior most leadership position in the international system of criminal justice was Mr. Robin Vincent, a brilliant court administrator from England who served as Registrar of the SCSL and, later, the STL.

is instructive insofar as an example was made of this individual by various stakeholders when he resorted to mass redundancies in an effort to restore order to an unruly arm of the ICC which he inherited from his predecessors. Stakeholders – both real and imagined – pose a genuine threat to leaders in the field of international criminal law. This is particularly the case where States, acting individually or in concert with one another, to say nothing of civil society groups, seek to push offices of the prosecutor, most especially, in directions which are inconsistent with the vision of the leader and, or in the alternative, the effective functioning of that part of the institution for which the leader is responsible. By way of example, the United States and the United Kingdom engineered the removal of Ms. Carla Del Ponte from her post as chief Prosecutor of the ICTR when she refused to cease pursuing the investigation of core international crimes allegedly perpetrated during 1994 by Rwandan President Paul Kagame and his subordinate officers.

Identifying and responding effectively to risk demands, above and beyond all else, the exercise of moral courage. The latter might be defined as preparedness to place the interests of the institution as well as its mission before those of any given individual, including the leader him- or herself. It does not follow from the requirement for moral courage that the effective leader should be inflexible. On the contrary, the effective leader must stand ready to acknowledge where the vision has become unsustainable, in whole or more likely in part, owing to external factors which the leader is unable to control, for instance, the deterioration of the politico-military situation in a given operational area or an unanticipated paucity of financial resources. Returning for a moment to the investigation of Mr. Kagame *et al.*, Ms. Del Ponte might well have continued to pursue this course of action in her capacity as ICTR chief Prosecutor had she done so without broadcasting her intentions and, had a sufficiency of evidence for one or more indictments come to light, presented the opposition to this undertaking with a *fait accompli* in the form of unsealed indictments. In so doing, she could have continued to exercise her considerable moral courage whilst retaining the position of chief Prosecutor of the ICTR.

9.3.2. Management

Leaders are not managers; the functions of leaders and managers are, in most respects, distinct. Managers are responsible for ensuring, at the working level, the execution of the vision of the leader, generally in accordance with concrete objectives – for instance, effective case-building and prose-

cutions – set out by the leader and agreed to by his or her managers. Co-
ordination between leaders and managers to this end is of the utmost importance; it is correspondingly crucial that the leader ensure that his or her
time not be absorbed disproportionately by dealings with external stakeholders. The leader who has insufficient contact with his or her subordinates will, invariably, exercise poor command and control over the institution which he or she leads. As such, the leader needs to communicate regularly with subordinate leaders and managers, not least to ensure the execution of the vision in accordance with the goals which afford concrete shape
to that vision. Beyond such co-ordination efforts, competent managers
should be free to act with a certain autonomy, that is, to be free from micro-
management emanating from the leadership level. In large institutions,
where the leaders and managers know their jobs and are committed to the
successful execution of the agreed goals, it is incumbent upon managers to
report only that such-and-such goals have been accomplished within established temporal parameters or, where the latter is proving difficult, to request further direction. In the execution of the goals assigned to them,
managers may resort to innovative methods which are consistent with the
vision of the leader and, in the case of an investigative body, consistent
with any relevant procedural law. In this respect, innovation is a hallmark
of creative leadership as well as capable management.

9.3.3. OTP Leaders, Managers and Followers

It might logically be asked at this juncture what positions in an international office of the prosecutor are held by leaders and which roles are assumed
by managers.

The chief prosecutor in any given office of the prosecutor is indis-
putably a leader, as is his or her deputy chief prosecutor. The functionaries
who surround these individuals in the immediate office of a chief prosecutor are neither managers nor leaders, though persons so employed do on
occasion come to the erroneous conclusion that their proximity to the leadership lends them their own measure of executive authority.[11] Where mis-

---

[11] A long-ago spokesperson for chief Prosecutor Carla Del Ponte, who was situated in the immediate Office of the Prosecutor, was perceived by some within the OTP of harbouring such
delusions. In 2003, the author of this chapter was told by his senior trial attorney to embark
on a mission to Montenegro to speak to a valuable (in the view of the spokesperson) source.
When this author protested that any such mission was likely to constitute a waste of time
and money, it was explained to him that the direction had come from the said spokesperson

conceptions of this nature appear in evidence, the failure is that of the leader(s) rather than that of delusional subordinates, most especially where leaders use relatively inexperienced staff in their immediate office to give direction to senior managers. Office of the prosecutor leaders (that is, chief and deputy prosecutors) need to interact directly with their senior managers, that is, their chiefs of appeals, prosecutions[12] and investigations. Each of these senior managers will have sub-managers, most notably the senior prosecutors (in the case of a chief of prosecutions) and investigative team leaders (in the case of a chief of investigations).[13] These sub-managers have purely management functions. The same might be said of the senior managers, although the latter may, at their discretion and in agreement with the leadership cadre, take on certain of the characteristics of the leader, for instance, where they share with the leader responsibility for the communication of the institutional vision to subordinate ranks. All other personnel employed by an office of the prosecutor are effectively followers insofar as their primary task is to conform to the institutional vision by contributing, in accordance with their function, to the successful execution of the concrete goals communicated to them by their respective managers and sub-managers.

9.4. Institutional Loyalty

Capable leadership and management alone will not ensure the success of an international criminal court or tribunal and, most especially, its office of the prosecutor; there is an additional requirement for institutional loyalty which weighs upon every leader, manager and follower. Indeed, the effectiveness of any given court or tribunal will run parallel to the degree of institutional loyalty which is in evidence throughout the ranks of those employed therein. The fostering of a culture of institutional loyalty, not least

---

and could not, therefore, easily be challenged. It was not; and, as expected, the mission proved to be pointless.

[12] At the ICC-OTP, what was known as the Chief of Prosecutions in the *ad hoc* Tribunals is named the Prosecutions Coordinator.

[13] The chief of investigations at the ICC-OTP has a deputy who carries the title Investigations Coordinator. This arrangement would appear to work well, not least as the position has been held, since its creation, by a series of capable incumbents. At the ICTY-OTP, the equivalent position was known as Investigations Commander, there being four such posts when the author arrived at the OTP in 2000. Ms. Del Ponte ordered the posts to be abolished in 2001 on the grounds that they were superfluous to requirements although the incumbents ultimately retained their positions, albeit without substantial authority over investigative matters.

by example, is one of the greatest challenges facing leaders in the field of
international criminal justice because (as noted earlier in this chapter) the
practice of domestic law, which influences in a frequently deleterious manner the practice of international criminal law, is generally a largely individual or small-team pursuit. In contrast, successful international prosecutions
and, more so, the investigative processes which lead to convictions, are
built upon the work of oftentimes sizeable, interdisciplinary teams operating transnationally.

The requirement for institutional loyalty in the pursuit of international criminal justice can be identified in a number of legal instruments, regulations and rules. Admittedly, the term institutional loyalty *per se* does not
appear in the collected statutes of the international courts and tribunals.
However, a requirement for institutional loyalty can be inferred from certain of their provisions. For instance, at Article 44(2), the Rome Statute directs that the "Prosecutor and Registrar shall ensure the highest standards
of competency, efficiency and integrity" of the Court staff. Article 36(3) (a)
requires of judges "high moral character, impartiality and integrity". Likewise, Article 42(3) demands that the chief and Deputy Prosecutors be of
"high moral character". Furthermore, the Rome Statute indicates at various
points that the judges and chief Prosecutor should act independently – presumably from one another as well as external actors. For its part, the Statute of the ICTY states in Article 14 that the judges of that tribunal should
be "of high moral character, impartiality and integrity". Whereas a similar
demand is not imposed upon the ICTY chief Prosecutor, Article 16 states
that he or she should "act independently as a separate organ of the International Tribunal" and not "seek or receive instructions from any Government or from any other source". Like provisions can be found in the Statute
of the ICTR. The requirement that judges and prosecutors be of high moral
character and independent in the execution of their professional duties is
found in, amongst other statutes, those of the STL,[14] the SCSL[15] and the
ECCC.[16]

---

[14] Statute of the Special Tribunal for Lebanon, 30 May 2007, Articles 9(1), 11(2) and 11(3)
(https://legal-tools.org/doc/da0bbb).

[15] Statute for the Special Court for Sierra Leone, 29 July 2000, Articles 12(1), 13(1), 15(1) and
15(3) (https://legal-tools.org/doc/4768bc).

[16] Law on the Establishment of the Extraordinary Chambers, with inclusion of amendments as
promulgated on 27 October 2004, Articles 10, 19 and 25. Interestingly, the Statute of the
ECCC requires, at Article 31, that the Chief of Administration should likewise be of "high
moral character and integrity".

It will be noted additionally that personnel employed by international courts and tribunals operating under United Nations guidelines – which constitutes the majority of the international courts and tribunals established since 1993 – are bound by the United Nations Staff Regulations and Rules. The latter set out clearly at various junctures that the "international civil servant" shall conduct his- or herself with "integrity, independence and impartiality".[17] It is here, in the said Regulations and Rules, that the requirement for integrity is brought together with the concept of institutional loyalty. In particular, at Regulation 1.2(e), staff members "pledge themselves to discharge their functions and regulate their conduct with the interests of the Organization only in view. Loyalty to the aims, principles and purposes of the United Nations […] is a fundamental obligation of all staff members by virtue of their status as international civil servants". What is more, the requirement for institutional loyalty is set out in a written declaration which every staff member is required to sign upon retention by any and all of the myriad United Nations bodies.[18]

The United Nations Staff Regulations and Rules, cited above, offer a succinct definition of institutional loyalty whilst making it clear, at least implicitly, that institutional loyalty is something quite distinct from loyalty to one's self. The insufficiency of institutional loyalty in the international courts and tribunals, including their offices of the prosecutor, reflects the cultural influence of domestic legal practice (as has been noted already) along with the frequent failure of leaders within the relevant institutions to be seen to embody as well as demand institutional loyalty of all subordinate personnel, irrespective of rank. However, it does not follow from the requirement for institutional loyalty that individuals should not be free to pursue personal objectives such as promotion and professional development. Institutional loyalty and the pursuit of professional advancement by the individual might co-exist in a complementary manner. Such is particu-

---

[17] Staff Regulations and Rules of the United Nations, 1 January 2018, ST/SGB/2018/1, Regulation 1.2.

[18] *Ibid.*, Regulation 1.1:

I solemnly declare and promise to exercise in all loyalty, discretion and conscience the functions entrusted to me as an international civil servant of the United Nations, to discharge these functions and regulate my conduct with the interests of the United Nations only in view, and not to seek or accept instructions in regard to the performance of my duties from any Government or other source external to the Organization. I also solemnly declare and promise to respect the obligations incumbent upon me as set out in the Staff Regulations and Rules.

larly the case where the leadership of an institution demands institutional – as opposed to personal – loyalty of all subordinates whilst fostering an organizational culture which entreats with personnel on an individual basis, that is, with an eye to the proper execution of professional functions whilst recognizing the inherent desire of most professionals for recognition as well as career advancement. Where individual staff members are regarded from on high as no more than cogs in a mechanical wheel, they will tend to conform to a minimal standard of performance – or worse, where a flawed approach to the leadership and management of subordinate personnel is coupled with disciplinary procedures which are rarely enforced.

9.5. Failures of Discipline and Integrity at the ICTR, the ICTY and the ICC

The purpose of this chapter is not to recount in an exhaustive manner the disciplinary failures which have been too often in evidence in international offices of the prosecutor. However, a few examples of disciplinary failings dating from the formative years of the ICTR and the ICTY are set out in order to reinforce the broader argument – without, it is hoped, creating the impression that the majority of personnel employed by these bodies, during their youth and later, acquitted themselves in a dishonourable manner. In turn, the altogether better situation at the ICC-OTP – and some of the reasons therefore – shall be examined.

9.5.1. ICTR

At the ICTR-OTP, within which this author was employed as an investigator in Kigali, Rwanda during 2001 and 2002, all manner of grift – generally petty and sometimes more egregious – was in evidence. For instance, this author recalls with clarity his investigations team leader arriving before his desk one morning to collect monies to make good on this author's personal use of a United Nations vehicle; such use was permitted by the ICTR in exchange for a small, per-kilometre fee. As the present author had long before purchased his own car, and correspondingly did not use United Nations vehicles for personal business, he had no idea why he was being asked to pay what was, in fact, a trifling sum in relation to his income. As it turned out, another investigator – who had served in an exceedingly senior position in his national police force – had been entering this author's name into vehicle logs against what was, in fact, the personal vehicle usage of the forger. Other investigators were in the habit of returning nightly to sleep in their own homes in Kigali when they were supposed to be working in out-lying areas whilst pocketing the daily subsistence allowance ('DSA') paid by the United Nations for meals and accommodation. Although ultimately petty in nature, conduct of this nature constituted fraud in the strict sense – and in this context, it is worth recalling that the offenders of these and other indiscretions were criminal investigators employed by a law-enforcement body.

A further problem at the ICTR-OTP during its early years was that a great many of the investigators had a better grasp of the various privileges enjoyed by United Nations staff – in particular, the familial benefits to which those with dependent spouses and children were entitled – than they did of the case-files to which they had been assigned. Or such was the view formed by this author, who was on occasion called upon by fellow team members to interpret the relevant (to the latter) United Nations rules on the grounds he had studied law. Protestations by *de facto* counsel that he had studied international criminal and humanitarian law, not whatever law in-formed the United Nations rules, with which in any event he had no fiduci-ary interest as he had no dependents, fell upon deaf ears.

Far more serious offences against the integrity and proper function-ing of the ICTR-OTP were perpetrated during the early life of that institu-tion by the Deputy Prosecutor, Mr. Bernard Muna, who was likewise based in Kigali. He would arrive daily at the Investigations Division headquarters, seated in the back of a white Mercedes sedan which featured a small UN flag affixed to the bonnet. Upon exiting his vehicle at the main door of the building, whatever staff found themselves in the proximity of his arrival would engage in great displays of bowing and scraping as Mr. Muna made his way into the building and towards his office. The charitable might as-cribe the waves of genuflection to social mores. A less generous interpreta-tion of the grovelling would hold that Mr. Muna had created the impression in the minds of a great many of the personnel in the Kigali office that they served the United Nations only at his pleasure. Indeed, under the noses of chief Prosecutors Louise Arbour and, in turn, Carla Del Ponte, Mr. Muna had built an impressive patronage network which encompassed much of the Investigations Division management as well as its rank-and-file. No suggestion is made here that Mr. Muna realized fiduciary benefit from this arrangement, which is to observe that the purpose of the structure was un-clear. What is certain is that its effect was to control tightly the hiring of investigators recruited from African States as well as all decisions regarding internal promotion within the Investigations Division.

Mr. Muna was eventually sacked by Ms. Del Ponte, the latter having summoned him to the seat of the Tribunal (that is, Arusha) for this purpose, evidently without having provided Mr. Muna with any inkling of the fate which awaited him; his firing was observed, with considerable satisfaction, by several ICTR-OTP personnel.[19] In the event, the damage wrought by Mr. Muna was not undone by his removal from his leadership post to the extent that the African members of his patronage network remained in their positions. Most (and some would suggest that all) of these men – at that time, there were very few female investigators at the ICTR – were unsuited to the requirements of international criminal investigations. If nothing else, the overall work ethic of the Investigations Division remained appallingly poor even following the demise of Mr. Muna, presumably because there was no evident disincentive arising, in the way of disciplinary action, where an investigator failed to perform to minimal professional standards.

9.5.2. ICTY

The level of professionalism witnessed by this author at the ICTY Investigations Division during 2000–2001 and 2002–2003 was altogether better than that seen at the ICTR; the overall situation was, however, far from ideal.

Whilst outright grift was not in evidence at the ICTY-OTP Investigations Division, until the Investigations Division leadership was restructured in 2001, travel budgets were put under constant pressure by unnecessary – and unnecessarily lengthy – investigative missions. In the aforementioned year, Ms. Del Ponte sacked the Chief of Investigations, an Australian police officer, and concomitantly neutered the so-called investigations commanders, who sat metaphorically between the Chief of Investigations and the leaders of the nine investigative teams. The Chief of Investigations was replaced by a French investigative judge, Mr. Patrick Lopes-Terres, who was evidently instructed by Ms. Del Ponte to get (amongst other things) the travel budget under control. More than one investigator was soon heard moaning at a popular Investigations Division watering hole about the disappearance of what might be termed the margin on DSA payments,[20] that is,

---

[19] Or so this author was informed immediately after the fact by one of the persons present.

[20] The United Nations paid a fixed daily amount for accommodation, meals and incidentals for travel, in accordance with the relevant costs of temporary living at a given location; this ar-

the monies left over after one had met the actual cost of room and board whilst on mission. Plainly, a number of investigators had grown accustomed to supplementing their familial budgets by this means, which in fairness was not formally contrary to the applicable rules. It will be recalled nonetheless that these same rules afforded well-paid, lightly-taxed international public servants with all manner of education and housing grants with which to support dependent family members.

More troubling than needless mission travel was the practice, which was occasionally in evidence until the aforementioned reorganization of the Investigations Division, of exploiting the differential between the rates of DSA and mission subsistence allowance ('MSA'). DSA was paid for shorter missions, that is, for periods of travel of up to 30 continuous days. MSA was meant to cover lengthy deployments; it was paid at a lower rate on the assumption that long deployments in a fixed location would reduce accommodation costs markedly insofar as those so deployed could make longer-term housing arrangements whilst at the same time facilitating the preparation of one's own meals. The trick within the ICTY Investigations Division would see personnel deploying away from headquarters for temporal periods close to, though not exceeding the point at which DSA would become MSA. To avoid financial loss arising from the movement from DSA to MSA rates, a brief sojourn to The Hague would then be taken before DSA became MSA with, in turn, redeployment to the same location. Proceeding in this manner, DSA rates would be paid for lengthy, albeit not strictly continuous absences from The Hague.

Until the reorganization of the ICTY Investigations Division effected by Ms. Del Ponte, the more serious problem bedevilling the OTP was the tendency of Investigations Division managers to facilitate the hiring of their erstwhile colleagues in the domestic realm to rank-and-file investigator positions, without having undertaken a sufficient assessment of the suitability of each individual for the investigation of core international crimes. In this manner, the Investigations Division approach to recruitment to the

---

rangement was termed the daily subsistence allowance (or DSA, as indicated above). The production of receipts, beyond proof of presence in the given location, was not required. The DSA rates were very generous, particularly where the traveller was prepared to eschew traditional hotels for privately-hired accommodation; and, by the time this author arrived at the ICTY in 2000, a vast network of private accommodation options had been identified in the cities to which ICTY personnel travelled habitually (for instance, Sarajevo, Zagreb and later Belgrade, after the fall from power of Slobodan Milošević).

follower ranks, in a period of rapid OTP growth, served to reinforce the professional shortcomings of the Division, which were ultimately rooted in the employment at the start of a good many police officers whose investigative specialization lay in fields which did not translate readily into the building of international criminal case-files. The equivalent approach, in the hiring of trial counsel, would have seen the retention of non-litigators specializing in the fields of, say, intellectual property and contract law.

The problems created by the manner in which investigators were recruited to the OTP were compounded considerably by Investigations Division promotion practices, the tendency being to elevate internal candidates to management positions as opposed to seeking ostensible talent from outside the ICTY. Whereas certain of the investigative team leads at the ICTY-OTP were professionally suited to overseeing complex criminal investigations rooted in international criminal and humanitarian law – just as there were highly-competent, rank-and-file investigators – it is arguable that most of the managers retained were not ideally suited to the sort of investigations which the ICTY-OTP was mandated to execute. This is not to suggest that the vast majority of Investigations Division managers were not highly engaging in a social context. And indeed, ICTY Investigations Division promotion practices suggested strongly to a great many keen observers within the OTP that social adroitness – 'clubability', if one will – was prioritized over professional competence in the selection of individuals for management positions. In the event, just as the patronage network established by Mr. Muna survived the sacking of its patron, all of the investigative managers at the ICTY outlived the removal of the Chief of Investigations.[21] Instead of a comprehensive house-clearing, the problems arising from poor Investigations Division recruitment and promotion practices at the *ad hoc* Tribunals were resolved – to the extent that they were – by the appointment of senior trial lawyers to manage investigations from their formative stages. This change, along with a number of related reforms ordered by Ms. Del Ponte, shall be discussed at more length, below.

---

[21] It would be wholly false to assert that the Chief of Investigations oversaw patronage arrangements of the sort facilitated by Mr. Muna. The former is an honourable man whose professional capabilities were evidently deemed by Ms. Del Ponte to be incommensurate with his appointment as Chief of Investigations.

9.5.3. ICC

When this author served with the Investigations Division at the ICC during its formative period (2003–2005), rank-and-file self-discipline, as well as the quality of the Investigations Division leadership and management, were of a high order. During the said period, the ICC had two Deputy Prosecutors, one of whom, Dr. Serge Brammertz, oversaw the Investigations Division. In this role, Dr. Brammertz was assisted by a capable Chief of Investigations to whom the investigative team leaders reported. The latter oversaw the Democratic Republic of the Congo ('DRC') and Uganda (that is, Lord's Resistance Army) investigations; later, a Darfur team was established to deal with that situation. Presumably by design, given widespread knowledge in the field of international criminal and humanitarian law of the managerial deficiencies plaguing the investigations divisions of the *ad hoc* Tribunals, neither Dr. Brammertz nor any of the ICC investigative managers were recruited from or had any experience of the system of international criminal justice prior to joining the ICC-OTP. Perhaps for this reason, the initial ICC Investigations Division arrangements worked well, owing to the quality of the leadership, management, and the rank-and-file personnel, many of the latter having been hand-picked from the ICTY-OTP. Or rather, the leadership and management structure of the ICC Investigations Division worked well until such time as Mr. Moreno-Ocampo – who had no discernible grasp of either investigations or international criminal and humanitarian law – began to meddle in the day-to-day investigative work, roughly one year into his tenure.

The brazen manipulation of travel allowances and the like which characterized the conduct of a minority of investigators at the *ad hoc* Tribunals was not in evidence at the ICC Investigations Division. Aside from the high levels of professional motivation and institutional loyalty which were shown by the initial intake to the OTP as a whole (those overseeing this initial intake deserve recognition), there were no additional monies to be had insofar as investigative missions were undertaken, with rare exceptions, to locations with exceedingly spartan living arrangements and the DSA rates had accordingly been set at negligible levels. Indeed, the situation was such that those whose jobs required deployment to the field had to be equipped with sleeping bags, mosquito nets, medical kits and other bits of field gear as the quality of the hotels in many of the mission areas – where there were any hotels at all – invariably offered conditions only marginally better than those of the local prisons.

Finally, it will be noted that at the ICTR and the ICTY, intelligence organs with an interest in the course of particular investigations were believed, not without a good deal of *prima facie* evidence, to have developed informants within the offices of the prosecutor of those institutions. One refers, most especially, to Rwandan and Croatian security services. Quite obviously, acting as an informant for a foreign intelligence service whilst employed by the United Nations would constitute a grievous lapse of professional ethics running manifestly contrary to the applicable regulations and rules. Where the ICC-OTP was concerned, suggestions have been made that intelligence agents loyal to the then-President of the DRC, Mr. Joseph Kabila, developed a source within the ICC DRC Team as early as 2004. However, assertions of this nature must necessarily be characterized as unproven.[22]

9.6. Leadership at the OTPs of the ICTY, the ICTR and the ICC

From 2000 to 2005, as mentioned above, this author had the opportunity to observe and otherwise witness the ramifications of a range of OTP leadership styles across the ICTY, the ICTR and the ICC. The latter shall be considered here with an eye to illustrating the benefits which arise from effective leadership and the problems which invariably follow where it is insufficient.

9.6.1. ICTR

The deleterious effect upon the Investigations Division of the tenure of Mr. Muna has already been touched upon. What is left to consider, briefly, is the effect upon the Investigations Division of the ICTR-OTP of the leadership of Ms. Arbour and Ms. Del Ponte; they served as chief Prosecutor during the periods 1996–1999 and 1999–2003, respectively, with the terms of both chief Prosecutors being marked by the production of sub-standard investigative case-files.

Ms. Arbour and Ms. Del Ponte were highly-capable as well as ethical professionals who sought to execute their mandates in conformity with the ideals set out in the Statute of the ICTR. Whereas both of these chief Prosecutors were affable individuals, Ms. Arbour evidenced a clear ability to tolerate fools gladly, in marked contrast to Ms. Del Ponte, rendering the

---

[22] International offices of the prosecutor have been consistently loath to establish counter-intelligence capabilities. This reticence has led to endless breaches of security and constitutes the Achilles' heel of all existing witness-protection arrangements.

former the more popular of the two in the eyes of the Investigations Division management as well as the rank-and-file.

The leadership of Ms. Arbour over the Investigations Division of the ICTR might be regarded as a failure. Admittedly, she was poorly served by her Deputy Prosecutor, Mr. Muna, from his appointment in April 1997. What is more, the fact that Ms. Arbour was based several-thousand kilometres away in The Hague, as she was concomitantly chief Prosecutor of the ICTR as well as the ICTY, lent Mr. Muna a freer hand to wreak havoc in Kigali. The ICTR-OTP as a whole experienced immense growth in staffing numbers under Ms. Arbour, and it was during this period that the ranks of the Investigations Division came to be filled with investigators as well as managers who were, in the main, unsuited to the investigation of breaches of international criminal and humanitarian law.

In assessing the tenure of Ms. Arbour from the perspective of the ICTR-OTP Investigations Division, there are a number of mitigating factors to be considered: first, the requirement that she was required to oversee concomitantly the ICTY-OTP, which was likewise experiencing considerable expansion in its staffing numbers; and second, the stellar work undertaken by Ms. Arbour to ensure, through relations with external actors such as the UN Security Council as well as myriad States, a future for both of the *ad hoc* Tribunals. However, responsibility for a great many of the investigative shortcomings of the ICTR-OTP, most of which long outlived Ms. Arbour's tenure as chief Prosecutor, must be laid at her feet. If nothing else, the term of Ms. Arbour illustrates the point that even the most inspirational leader will fail where he or she does not remain in constant contact with his or her leadership and management teams or otherwise fails to control them effectively.

The record of Ms. Del Ponte is altogether positive when seen from the perspective of the necessity of carrying out effective investigations. First, she sacked Mr. Muna, albeit well into her term. Second, when sacking Mr. Muna, the chief Prosecutor placed trial lawyers in charge of investigations, thereby neutering, to an extent, the fact that the removal of Mr. Muna was not coupled with changes to the ranks of the investigative management cadre. In the event, the requirement that trial counsel oversee the investigative processes from the start served to improve the quality of the investigative output somewhat less than it might have done were geography not something of Ms. Del Ponte's enemy. One refers to the fact that, like Ms. Arbour, Ms. Del Ponte was (until 2003) concomitantly chief Prosecutor of the ICTY and therefore limited in the amount of time that she could spend in Arusha, never mind Kigali. A second problem was the bifurcation of the OTP between those cities, with the trial lawyers afforded responsibility for the building of individual cases (after the sacking of Mr. Muna) being based in Arusha, whilst the investigators were, logically enough, situated in Kigali. A third problem was that the quality of the trial lawyers available to Ms. Del Ponte remained uneven, despite the mass-sacking of a number of senior counsel earlier in her tenure.

In summary, Ms. Del Ponte took several (re-)organizational decisions which were badly needed, thereby laying the foundation for improvements in the quality of the ICTR investigative output. Ultimately, it was her successor, chief Prosecutor Hassan Jallow, who was left to capitalize upon these improvements. The view taken here is that Ms. Del Ponte showed considerable moral courage as well as institutional loyalty in reforming the investigative management arrangements of the ICTR, through the sackings of some and the neutering of the authority of others. For these and other reasons, based on personal observations, the leadership of Ms. Del Ponte of the ICTR-OTP can be assessed positively, not least given the highly unsuitable arrangements which had been bequeathed to her in 1999 by Ms. Arbour.

9.6.2. ICTY

During her tenure as ICTY chief Prosecutor, Ms. Del Ponte made important changes to the functioning of the Investigations Division, having inherited from Ms. Arbour a poorly functioning operation. The removal of the Chief of Investigations, with Mr. Lopez-Terres as his replacement, has already been noted. Additionally, Ms. Del Ponte would later sack her Deputy Prosecutor, Mr. Graham Blewitt, and Chief of Prosecutions, Mr. Michael Johnson, though the reason for their removal in 2004 was unrelated to the proper functioning of the Investigations Division.[23] As at the ICTR-OTP, ICTY-OTP trial counsel were placed in charge of the building of individual case-files, thereby circumventing, for the most part, the collective insufficiency of the management and rank-and-file membership of the Investigations Division.

---

[23] Mr. Blewitt and Mr. Johnson were removed from their posts after Ms. Del Ponte received evidence that they were advocating for the replacement of Ms. Del Ponte as ICTY chief Prosecutor.

The changes initiated in The Hague worked well for two reasons. First, the Investigations and Prosecutions Divisions were situated in the same building, not one thousand kilometres apart, as was the case with the ICTR. Second, the Investigations Division of the ICTY had at its disposal a large number of highly specialized as well as capable linkage analysts, situated within the Leadership Research and Military Analysis Teams ('LRT', 'MAT'). Analysts from these teams already worked closely and constructively with OTP trial counsel when cases came to trial. These linkage analyst–trial counsel relationships were generally predicated on the fact that, prior to the reform of the management of the investigative processes, more often than not, trial counsel found themselves commencing litigation with insufficient linkage evidence to secure a conviction on some or all of the offences alleged in any given indictment. Under the circumstances, when trial counsel assumed responsibility for case building during the investigative phase, rather than only at the start of trial – by which point investigations should, as a matter of professional ethics and procedural fairness have been all but complete – the analyst–counsel relationships of this nature served to inform positively the ICTY-OTP case-files developed from 2001.

9.6.3.   ICC

The paucity of disciplinary breaches and like failures by rank-and-file personnel at the ICC-OTP witnessed by this author during 2003–2005 owed much to a strong culture of institutional loyalty, effective management and, where Dr. Brammertz was concerned, effective leadership.

The difficulties experienced by the ICC-OTP in bringing consistently credible allegations against the accused and, in turn, securing convictions where allegations have given rise to charges has been examined *ad nauseum* elsewhere and need not be recounted here. What will be observed in this chapter is the fact that the initial recruitment effort of the OTP – which was in the enviable position of poaching top-drawer talent from elsewhere in the system of international criminal justice during a period of OTP reform at the *ad hoc* Tribunals – led to the retention of a great many highly-experienced investigators, analysts and lawyers with an inherent belief in the mission of the Court as this was set out in the language of the Rome Statute and in the carefully drafted vacancy announcements and job descriptions by the Preparatory Team. Likewise, the selection of investigative managers from outside of the field of international criminal justice was undertaken with considerable care. The bulk of the credit for the positive hir-

ing practices must go to Serge Brammertz and, before he was installed, to
the Senior Legal Adviser of the OTP, Morten Bergsmo, who had designed
the initial system of qualification requirements – setting proper standards –
already in 2002-2003.

It was not until Mr. Moreno-Ocampo began to engage personally in
the hiring of OTP personnel, for the most part not until the period 2004–
2005, that individuals ill-suited to employment in the field of international
criminal justice began to appear at the OTP. Prior to this point, Mr. Moreno-Ocampo had not concerned himself unduly with staffing matters, particularly where the latter impacted upon the Investigations Division. For
these and other reasons which have already been noted, the quality of the
initial OTP staff intake gave rise to a culture of institutional loyalty and
professional competence, which facilitated effective investigations centred
upon the eastern DRC and northern Uganda. At the same time, Mr. Moreno-Ocampo served, in his inimitable manner, as a powerful advocate internally for the mission of the Court. Or such was the case until, in 2004, the
chief Prosecutor began to micro-manage the Investigations Division personnel who, aside from their prior international service, brought a great
deal of experience from their domestic military, security-intelligence, police and prosecutorial organs – and concomitantly were quick to recognize
that the would-be emperor had no clothes.

Certain of the egregious ethical lapses of Mr. Moreno-Ocampo have
been well documented elsewhere, not least by the erstwhile chief Prosecutor himself, however unwittingly, through the release into the public domain of a great deal of his personal and professional correspondence. His
troublesome tenure as ICC chief Prosecutor was, it is here held based on
personal observations, informed by three phenomena.

First, Mr. Moreno-Ocampo evinced what might be termed a Louis
XIV tendency. Just as the Sun King had allegedly claimed, "l'état, c'est
moi", Moreno-Ocampo clearly believed that the Court did not, and perhaps
could not exist independently of his genius. In fairness, whilst Moreno-
Ocampo is not known to have proclaimed, "la cour, c'est moi", he most
certainly left his subordinates with the impression that this was his belief.

Secondly, Mr. Moreno-Ocampo displayed a self-confessed tendency
to micro-manage his subordinates at all levels, which had the effect of rob-
bing them – and by extension, the OTP as a whole – of the sort of individual initiative which is absolutely key to the resolution of complex problems,
the likes of which frequently confront international investigators grappling

with the challenges of *prima facie* evidence collection in hostile environments.

Thirdly, the ICC chief Prosecutor proved to be incapable of translating his vision for the OTP into concrete objectives to be assigned, in turn, to his deputies as well as the managerial cadre to execute over the medium- and longer-term without ongoing interference (or wholesale change of plan) emanating from the chief Prosecutor.

Finally, Mr. Moreno-Ocampo, perhaps for reasons of hubris, fancied himself a savvy politico-diplomatic operator, despite having arrived at the Court with no experience in this domain. His engagement on the politico-diplomatic level, in a manner clearly not foreseen by the drafters of Rome Statute, created opportunities for more seasoned, domestic operators to run metaphorical circles around the chief Prosecutor, with the result that the OTP was occasionally instrumentalized by self-interested States. The referral of the Libya situation to the Court by the United Nations Security Council as well as the arrest of Jean-Pierre Bemba, both of which occurred with the connivance of the chief Prosecutor despite the nakedly political objectives of the external parties pushing for these courses of action, transpired notwithstanding the fact that the OTP was ill-equipped to mount an effective criminal-investigative response in either case.

Recalling the circumstances of the Libya referral, amongst other cases, constitutes a reminder that institutional loyalty requires that leaders consider at all times the long-term health of the institutions which they lead, not least, to points beyond their own tenure. In this respect, additional to others, Mr. Moreno-Ocampo failed miserably, saddling as he did his successor with a great many investigative challenges which could not easily be resolved, if they could be resolved at all. The difficulties which have been experienced in attempting to undo the disastrous legacy of Mr. Moreno-Ocampo have, in this author's personal view, served to sap OTP staff morale whilst concomitantly giving rise to questions regarding the competence of the Court as a whole. In its entire history, the field of international criminal justice has never seen the likes of Mr. Moreno-Ocampo; and, if the system is to survive in anything approximating its current form, it would do well to avoid seeing his like again.

9.7. Leadership, Professional Integrity and Their Intersection with International Investigative Processes

The offices of the prosecutor of the international courts and tribunals have two core functions: (1) the building of case-files for prosecution (that is, investigations) and (2) litigation. Legal-analysis sections, units which serve victims, public-engagement and the like, whilst all necessary functions, constitute secondary duties whose sole function is, or ought to be, the provision of support to the investigative and litigative core. The proper execution of these central tasks requires the effective input of three categories of professionals: investigators, analysts and counsel. Although it is essential to the realization of the core mission that these professionals should work in harmony with one another, their respective responsibilities are distinct.

9.7.1. Investigators

Investigators are, in the main, of little use in the office, that is, they should be deployed as often as possible by those heading investigative teams with the aim of collecting information of evidentiary value, which will ultimately withstand the scrutiny of pre-trial, trial and appellate proceedings. The successful investigator must embody a measure of cunning in his or her approach to the collection of information, particularly in the search for *prima facie* linkage evidence. This assertion follows from the fact that a linkage case which has been properly constructed will rest heavily upon documentation generated by the perpetrating institutions, the acquisition of which shall, more often than not, require the exercise of considerable creativity on the part of the investigators involved in its acquisition. Additionally, the building of linkage cases will, in almost every case, lead to the recruitment of so-called insider witnesses, in particular, individuals who have served alongside the suspects-*cum*-accused within the perpetrating structures. It is something of an understatement to observe that the co-operation of witnesses of this nature is rarely driven by a disinterested commitment to the fundamental principles of justice. As such, insider witnesses need to be handled from the start with a great deal of psychological dexterity. Finally, to ensure the effective execution of their mission, investigators will necessarily avoid dubious collection methods which involve resort to low cunning, for instance, the offering of false inducements to putative witnesses. Conduct of this nature is at all times impermissible in order to maintain the reputation of the institutions for which investigators work and, more immediately, to avoid any violation of the rules of procedure and evidence which constitute the ultimate guide to investigative conduct insofar as inadmissible evidence is no evidence. For these reasons, investigators must excel at the art of followership whilst being carefully managed and led.

9.7.2. Analysts

Analysts tend to work from institutional headquarters, their primary function being to transform the information collected by investigators into evidence through analytical processes undertaken within the context of the applicable substantive law. As a general rule, analysts need not concern themselves with matters of procedural law, unless they suspect a violation of the same. However, it is imperative that they should remain alert at all times to any formal requirement to consider exculpatory evidence,[24] not least in order to ensure that any case brought to trial will withstand judicial scrutiny. The bulk of the analytical effort which goes into the case-building process is, like the work of investigators, focused upon the building of the linkage case, that is, establishing to a beyond-reasonable-doubt standard the connections between higher-level suspects and the physical authors of the underlying criminal acts. Broadly speaking, in the building of linkage cases, analysts are focused upon the command, control and communications arrangements of perpetrating structures; in this context, analysts resort to their intellect as well as an array of software which has been developed to link fact to law, for instance, CaseMap and the Case Matrix. Effective linkage analysis demands of the analyst – and, for that matter, the skilled investigator – the possession of a well-developed understanding of the modes of liability set out in international criminal and humanitarian law and the legal requirements thereof. For this reason, the profile of the average investigator and analyst has evolved markedly over the last 10 to 15 years, their ranks having come to include a substantial number of individuals with a legal education.

9.7.3. Counsel

Persons employed as counsel within international courts and tribunals tend to be, as in domestic jurisdictions, highly specialized in one of a number of

---

[24] For instance, in the Rome Statute of the International Criminal Court, 17 July 1998, Article 54(1)(a) (https://legal-tools.org/doc/9c9fd2), where the Prosecutor is required to "[i]n order to establish the truth, extend the investigation to cover all facts and evidence relevant to an assessment of whether there is criminal responsibility under this Statute, and, in doing so, investigate incriminating and exonerating circumstances equally".

sub-disciplines. The specialization of primary relevance to the case-building process is that of trial counsel.

Trial counsel prosecute cases before first-instance chambers and, as has been a general rule since the early 2000s, are integrated to a greater or lesser degree into the investigative and analytical processes. The principal role of trial counsel – acting as required with the support of appellate counsel as well as lawyers specialized in procedural law – is to ensure, as early in the case-building process as possible, that prosecution cases are (being) assembled in accordance with the applicable substantive law. As a matter of self-preservation, given that it is trial counsel who appear in court, they should be highly motivated in the use of quality-control measures geared towards the proper application of substantive and procedural law. Where evidence is insufficient or lacking, judges will – and should – hold trial counsel responsible. Lead prosecutors who blame trial judges for setbacks in court ought, as a general rule, to be encouraged by the leadership of offices of the prosecutor to seek employment elsewhere.

9.7.4. Case-Building Arrangements at the ICTY and the ICTR During Their Formative Years

When international criminal justice re-emerged in 1993 as a discipline for the first time since the late-1940s, the investigative culture of the Investigations Division stood up at the ICTY-OTP mirrored in a number of significant respects the investigative practices of several adversarial systems, in particular, those of Australia, Canada, New Zealand and the United Kingdom – the States from which the bulk of the investigators were recruited until several years after the turn of the century. What is more, only one of the many investigators employed by the ICTY-OTP during its first decade was not a police officer by profession, notwithstanding the fact that the substantive investigative work undertaken during the immediate post-1945 period was performed by military intelligence officers and lawyers.[25] More problematical still was the fact that until 2001, the ICTY-OTP Investigations Division management cadre had tended as a general rule to exclude counsel from the case-building process.

Whereas a great many analysts were employed by the ICTY from the 1990s, they had been used improperly by the Investigations Division man-

---

[25] Prior to joining the ICTY, the investigator in question was employed as an intelligence officer by a domestic security service.

agers and sub-managers until 2001. This was hardly surprising given that very few of the police officers employed by the ICTY during its first decade arrived at the OTP after having witnessed the sort of analytical input which informs the building of multifaceted criminal cases in which the investigative targets stand several organization layers above the physical perpetrators of the underlying criminal acts. As far as the casual observer could tell, the police officers retained by the OTP for most of its first decade hailed from the domains of routine domestic policing and (domestic) murder squads. One has no reason to doubt that the ICTY-OTP investigators had been highly proficient in these domestic realms. However, the difficulty with recruitment from these specializations was that what was needed were men and women with a grasp of complex fraud and transnational crime, insofar as the investigative methodology used in these areas approximates closely that of international criminal investigations.

The exclusion of trial counsel from investigative processes gave rise to a situation prior to 2001 in which the litigators tended to see the case-files assigned to them only on the metaphorical eve of trial, that is, after suspects had been rendered accused persons and, more often than not, already spent periods of time in pre-trial custody which would be unconscionable in the jurisdictions in which all concerned had worked domestically. Secondly, owing to the (mis-)recruitment and promotion practices within the Investigations Division, the files were invariably a mess at the outset of the trial. One erstwhile senior trial attorney likened what the trial lawyers were seeing – when they finally did see the case-files – as akin to "getting inundated with three filing cabinets full of statements and documents", which had not been assembled in any coherent manner.[26] Far worse than the poor organization of the case-files was the fact that a great many trials commenced with the prosecutors possessing insufficient linkage evidence to warrant a conviction – naturally enough raising questions regarding whether the accused ought to have been indicted and detained. The action taken by the ICTY-OTP in these situations would see the senior trial attorneys responsible for a case which was in disarray initiate as well as lead a proper linkage investigation, generally with one of the LRT or MAT linkage analysts working closely to hand, whilst concurrently leading the prosecution in court. Manifestly, an approach to investigations and prosecutions of this nature would never have been tolerated in any of the nation-

---

26 Quoted in John Hagan, *Justice in the Balkans: Prosecuting War Crimes in the Hague Tribunal*, University of Chicago Press, 2003, p. 224.

al justice systems from which the majority of ICTY investigators, analysts and counsel had been drawn.

Similar problems were witnessed at the ICTR, albeit for slightly different reasons. As with the ICTY, the majority of the investigators were police officers. However, the ranks of the ICTR-OTP Investigations Division included a handful of individuals with legal, military and intelligence backgrounds. Additionally, owing to the requirement for French-language skills in the Rwanda of that period, the bulk of the investigators had been drawn from inquisitorial systems which followed French criminal procedure, or some variation thereupon.[27] It followed from this arrangement that the culture of the Investigations Division at all phases of the investigative process was not in the least hostile to the input of counsel. Indeed, during the first decade of the life of the ICTR, the OTP had anywhere from 8 to 10 counsel based in Kigali, with the bulk of OTP lawyers working from the seat of the Tribunal in Arusha. Whilst investigators were formally responsible for the building of cases, this fact alone does not – given the presence of full-time counsel in the Kigali office – explain the generally poor quality of the files with which the litigators in Arusha were presented prior to trial. The insufficiency of most case-files on the eve of trial is a phenomenon better attributed to the dearth of analysts of any kind at the ICTR as well as the unacceptable number of professional incompetents infecting the ranks of the OTP as a whole in the view of this author – notwithstanding the fact that relatively early in her term as chief Prosecutor, Ms. Del Ponte had sacked an impressive number of senior OTP counsel. A cull of incompetent personnel on this scale had not – and has not since – been witnessed at any international office of the prosecutor, although the effort made by Ms. Del Ponte clearly constituted an insufficient tonic for the overall health of that investigative and prosecutorial body.

9.7.5.   Investigations Division Reforms at the *Ad Hoc* Tribunals

The problems which plagued the case-building process at the ICTR were ultimately resolved, to the extent that they were resolved, by improvements in the recruitment of trial counsel and their increasing engagement in the case-building process. As has been noted already, at the ICTY, Ms. Del Ponte sacked the police officer who was leading the Investigations Division

---

[27]   There were very few French investigators at the ICTR. Rather, the OTP had a great many investigators from former French colonies that had retained variants of French procedural law following independence.

in 2001, replacing him with a French investigative judge whilst concomitantly removing the authority of the investigations commanders, who sat between the investigative team leads and the chief of investigations. In their stead, ICTY-OTP senior trial attorneys were assigned to cases early in the case-building process.

What emerged from these changes was a two-track system which, intentionally or otherwise, incorporated a number of checks and balances, which served to improve over time the quality of ICTY case-files prior to indictment and, most especially, prior to trial. On the one hand, the core of the Investigations Division remained built around investigative teams constructed upon thematic lines, for instance, Bosnian-Serb crimes, Croatian criminality and Kosovo Liberation Army misconduct. At the same time, the investigative teams began to serve little more than administrative functions, akin to home-room or registration in a secondary school, that is, the assembly point at which attendance is taken and administrative instructions imparted, with the students otherwise moving between various lessons elsewhere in accordance with individual timetables. The OTP crime-base analysts remained with the investigative teams, although the nature of their output, before and after the reforms to the Investigations Division, was never evident to the OTP personnel who understood how to assemble a prosecution case. Additionally, the specialized linkage analysis teams remained intact – the LRT and the MAT – serving the 'home-room' function and as centres for a great deal of peer review; as with the investigative teams, their members were farmed out to the case-building and prosecution teams, in accordance with their thematic speciality. From 2001, the linkage analysts continued to work closely with the senior (or more seasoned) trial attorneys who were responsible for the prosecutorial and, after the aforementioned changes had been made, investigative processes. In summary, then, the Prosecutions Division of the ICTY assumed effective control over OTP investigations from the Investigations Division in 2001, drawing upon individual Investigations Division personnel as required, once it had been determined by Ms. Del Ponte that the Investigations Division management was not fit for purpose. This reformed approach to case building at the ICTY-OTP worked well by breaking down the divisions which had existed prior to 2001 between the investigative, analytical and legal functions. Where problems within the case-specific teams did arise, these were invariably a reflection of the insufficient competence shown by key personnel, in particular, the senior trial attorney and, equally, the senior linkage analyst serving within the case-specific team, generally (if the senior trial attorney had any sense) at his or her right hand.

9.7.6. The Effective Management of Case-Building Processes

It should not be inferred from the improved investigative practices of the OTPs of the ICTY and the ICTR that an effective case-building effort might be achieved only where a senior trial attorney serves in the lead role. Such an arrangement is desirable, given that prosecution cases, to be effective, require a clear understanding of the substantive law. However, the increasing number of legally trained, or otherwise legally aware investigators and analysts working in the system of international criminal justice points to the potential for an investigator or analyst to serve as a case-specific team manager, prior to a given case proceeding to trial. Where an investigator or analyst is assigned to the lead role in such situations, it remains necessary for trial counsel to remain close to hand to advise the case-specific team manager on questions relating to the intersection of evidence and law. By way of example, non-lawyers have served as investigative team leaders at what remains, to date, the only non-public international criminal and humanitarian law investigative body, that is, the Commission for International Justice and Accountability ('CIJA'). In particular, CIJA has, on occasion, appointed non-lawyers to the head of investigative teams, with a lawyer acting as the *de facto* second in command, generally where the day-to-day challenges of *prima facie* evidence collection in high-physical-risk environments exceed those posed in meeting the legal requirements of effective case building.[28] In a similar vein, the longstanding ICC-OTP Chief of Investigations is a former police officer, though his deputy (that is, the Investigations Coordinator) is a Portuguese prosecutor and the case-by-case investigations at the ICC-OTP are overseen for all intents and purposes by Prosecutions Division counsel.

9.8. Conclusion

It is the duty of States as well as the supranational institutions which support international criminal justice to ensure that qualified personnel are appointed to leadership positions within offices of the prosecutor and, equally, to engineer their prompt removal where their professional competence or

---

[28] For instance, the CIJA Da'esh Crimes Team has seen three team leaders since January 2014, each of whom brought to the position significant field experience in a military and intelligence capacity *vis-à-vis* non-State actors operating in areas of high-intensity armed conflict.

personal conduct falls below minimally-acceptable standards. If nothing else, this is a central point that informs this volume, in accordance with the concept note which serves as its foundation.[29] It is likewise the responsibility of those leading offices of the prosecutor to ensure that their prosecutions and investigations divisions are properly managed, with the goals established by the leaders being executed in a timely manner by the management cadre. Concomitantly, it falls to these leaders to foster organizational cultures which are characterized by, above all, professional competence and institutional loyalty. Personal and professional integrity – which are inseparable concepts – will follow naturally where the standards of conduct applicable to all personnel, not least chief and deputy prosecutors, are clear; and, where there is misconduct of any sort, leaders must ensure that disciplinary systems are in place and brought to bear. Where standards are permitted to slip, institutional rot shall set in quickly; and, where there is institutional rot, the investigative and prosecutorial output of the institution will be poor, not least because many of the high-performing personnel are likely to seek employment elsewhere.

Since 1993, international courts and tribunals have shown only a limited collective awareness of the simple prescription set out in the preceding paragraph; this fact is all the more shocking, because the core principles of leadership, management and followership are central to the proper performance of any institution, be it a commercial firm or a public-sector institution. It is appreciated here that there are unique pressures, political as well as social, frequently weighing heavily upon those bodies raised to deliver international criminal justice, not least their investigative and prosecutorial arms. However, the quality of office of the prosecutor leadership at any of the international courts and tribunals, particularly during the formative years of the post-1993 era, has proved itself to be uneven in a number of important respects. In part, these shortcomings have arisen from the monumental challenges inherent in the process of institution-building whilst under pressure. However, certain of the more egregious failings – those of Mr. Moreno-Ocampo and Mr. Muna, most especially – must be ascribed to personal unsuitability for international leadership appointments and insufficient professional competence for the task at hand.

A number of the chief and deputy prosecutors appointed since 1993 have absorbed, perhaps unconsciously, certain of the core principles of

---

[29] Bergsmo, 2018, see above note 8.

leadership identified in this chapter and, in turn, applied them to the offices of the prosecutor for which they have been entrusted with responsibility. The examples of Ms. Del Ponte and Dr. Brammertz have been cited in this chapter, though one hastens to add that there have been others. What has ultimately set apart the successful leaders from those who have come up short is their willingness to sack non-performing managers as well as rank-and-file personnel who ought never to have been retained – conduct which reflects, amongst other considerations, their understanding of the im-portance of ensuring excellence in the execution of the investigative and prosecutorial functions (that is, the core tasks) of an office of the prosecutor. However, until the principles of effective leadership and management in (most especially) the area of international criminal investigations are more widely discussed, the overall prosecutorial output of the system of interna-tional criminal justice shall continue to fall short of what might be expected as a reasonable return on the monies which are poured annually into this endeavour.

10

Decency as a Prerequisite to
Integrity in International Proceedings

Andrew T. Cayley[*]

Hans Holbein's portrait of Sir Thomas More graced the programme of the conference that gave rise to the papers in this volume. I expect his face to appear on the cover of the book. He was a man of principle and conscience at a time, in England, when that took very great courage indeed. In Robert Bolt's play, *A Man for all Seasons*, which depicts the last year of More's life, More says:

> I believe, when statesmen forsake their own private conscience for the sake of their public duties, they lead their country by a short route to chaos.[1]

10.1. Introduction

Decency should be a natural part of the private conscience. But it is one of those human qualities which is hard to define with absolute precision because all of us have such differing experiences and instincts shaped by the challenges we have met and the decisions we have made in the face of those challenges.

The American sociologist and civil rights activist, William E.B. Du Bois, wrote:

> How shall Integrity face Oppression? What shall Honesty do in the face of Deception, Decency in the face of Insult, Self-Defence before Blows? How shall Desert and Accomplishment meet Despising, Detraction, and Lies? What shall Virtue do to meet Brute Force? There are so many answers and so contradictory; and such differences for those on the one hand

---

[*] **Andrew T. Cayley** CMG QC is the United Kingdom's Director of Service Prosecutions and former Senior Prosecuting Counsel at the International Criminal Court and the International Criminal Tribunal for the former Yugoslavia. Between 2009 and 2013, he was the International Co-Prosecutor of the Extraordinary Chambers in the Courts of Cambodia. The chapter draws on judgments in cases on which he has worked or been closely associated with.

[1] Robert Bolt, *A Man for All Seasons*, 1954.

who meet questions similar to this once a year or once a decade, and those who face them hourly and daily.[2]

Here the author was confronting the responses of African Americans
in the face of extreme forms of discrimination and oppression – human virtue placed under the kind of immense strain that most of us never have to
endure in our daily lives. As the author points out, the response of an individual who has to regularly confront the worst aspects of human nature
may well be very different from someone who meets this test once a year
or once every ten years. And while experiences in the courtroom are generally not as powerful, dramatic or shameful as those to which Dubois refers,
the fact is that we have all encountered in our legal careers confrontations
between honesty and deception, clashes between decency and insult. And
we have had to calibrate a response to these clashes.

How legal counsel *should* conduct themselves is governed by the
rules which proscribe standards of professional conduct – mostly in terms
of the relationship between counsel and the court, and counsel and their
client. In the international courts, where rules of conduct are less ingrained
and less a part of a normative structure when compared to most domestic
systems, private conscience has tended to play a much more significant
role in the decisions made or the course that was set.

I could glibly discuss at great length what decency means to me and
how it has played its part in my legal career and court work. The truth is,
like everyone else, I have struggled with the rights and wrongs of conduct.
And beyond the most obvious examples of what is clearly decent conduct,
and what is not, I have no easy way of objectively and definitively evaluating the vast majority of conduct before the courts.

In terms of my own professional experience: in 2004, I refused to
draft an indictment for war crimes and crimes against humanity against an
individual where I believed there was an insufficiency of evidence, even
with a chief Prosecutor insisting on bringing such charges. I thought that
obviously wrong, and by 2012 the principal accused in that case had been
tried twice and acquitted twice. Later in 2007, I resigned from a job in the
international courts I loved because, eventually, my private conscience became so weighed down and exhausted that I simply had to go. In Southeast
Asia in 2011, I risked contempt proceedings to prevent what I saw as a
miscarriage of justice. These few examples do not place me beyond re-

---

[2] William .E.B. Du Bois, *The Ordeal of Mansart*, Kraus-Thomson, 1976, p. 275.

proach, but I think my reflexes are now well-tuned to what decency requires.

The English word 'decency' has its origins in the Ancient World. It is from the Latin present participle 'decere', meaning fitting or suitable. Decency in the courts is about trust and being honest in court proceedings. I approach this discussion as someone who has predominantly prosecuted before the courts. Of the international defence work I have done, I would readily accept that the duties affecting defence counsel are much more challenging, in particular balancing the interests of fearlessly defending a client against the overarching interests of the proper administration of justice. But in the end, whether prosecuting or defending, if the courts do not trust us as counsel, they are not going to believe us.

Decency, I would submit, may often require you, particularly when prosecuting, to act in a way that is not self-serving. It may require you to lose a point or argument in the courtroom.

Decency, you will find, is at the heart of almost all sets of regulations for the governance of counsel before domestic and international courts. To take my own legal system, that of England and Wales, as a straightforward example: counsel have ten core duties to comply with, and these duties apply to all counsel whatever the area of law in which they practice.[3] The duties are laid down by an organization called the Bar Standards Board, which is the independent regulator which governs the conduct of barristers in England and Wales.[4]

The ten core duties are:

1. You must observe your duty to the court in the administration of justice.
2. You must act in the best interests of each client.
3. *You must act with honesty, and with integrity.*
4. You must maintain your independence.
5. *You must not behave in a way which is likely to diminish the trust and confidence which the public places in you or in the profession.*
6. You must keep the affairs of each client confidential.

---

[3] "The Code of Conduct", *The Bar Standards Board Handbook*, fourth edition, 2019, part 2, sect. B, p. 22 ('The Core Duties').

[4] *Ibid.*, p. 9.

7. You must provide a competent standard of work and service to each client.

8. You must not discriminate unlawfully against any person.

9. You must be open and co-operative with your regulators.

10. You must take reasonable steps to manage your practice, or carry out your role within your practice, competently and in such a way as to achieve compliance with your legal and regulatory obligations.[5]

Article 24 of the Code of Professional Conduct for Counsel of the International Criminal Court ('ICC') sets out counsel's duties towards the Court:

> 24(1). Counsel shall take all necessary steps to ensure that his or her actions or those of counsel's assistants or staff are not prejudicial to the ongoing proceedings and do not bring the Court into disrepute.
>
> 24(2). Counsel is personally responsible for the conduct and presentation of the client's case and shall exercise personal judgement on the substance and purpose of statements made and questions asked.
>
> 24(3). *Counsel shall not deceive or knowingly mislead the Court.* He or she shall take all steps necessary to correct an erroneous statement made by him or her or by assistants or staff as soon as possible after becoming aware that the statement was erroneous.
>
> 24(4). Counsel shall not submit any request or document with the sole aim of harming one or more of the participants in the proceedings.
>
> 24(5). Counsel shall represent the client expeditiously with the purpose of avoiding unnecessary expense or delay in the conduct of the proceedings.[6]

The domestic regulations of England and Wales require of counsel a positive duty of decency. The ICC, an international court arguably sitting at the apex of the domestic criminal courts of the world, expresses the duty of decency in the negative – what you cannot do, not what you must do. And

---

5   See above note 3 (emphasis added).

6   ICC Code of Professional Conduct for Counsel, 2 December 2005, ICC-ASP/4/Res.1 (https://www.legal-tools.org/doc/f9ed33) (emphasis added).

that is surprising as you would think, because of complementarity, the ICC would want to lead the world in this vital area of counsel's conduct.

In the early days of the *ad hoc* tribunals, I recall that the formal attention paid to the professional conduct of counsel was fairly limited – both for prosecutors and defence counsel, although arguably all were subject to at least part of their own domestic rules.[7] The discussions that took place over counsel's duties, when such issues did arise, always seemed to default back to the national systems of those discussing the issue of concern at the time. At the International Criminal Tribunal for the Former Yugoslavia ('ICTY'), lawyers had been recruited from many different jurisdictions. And while national systems do all slightly differ on what is regarded as decent or indecent conduct, the fundamental principles seemed to me to be broadly the same.

At the ICTY, it was the defence bar who first published a code of professional conduct for counsel appearing before the court.[8] That was in June 1997. The Office of the Prosecutor took until September of 1999 to come up with a set of Standards of Professional Conduct for Prosecution Counsel.[9] And that was Prosecutor's Regulation No 2 of 1999. If you examine this set of prosecutors' rules, it reads broadly, like the English Bar Standards Board set of core principles. So, requirements of independence, integrity, good faith and, above all, a duty of candour and honesty to the Tribunal itself – that is, Rules 2(e) and 2(h). Prosecutors must tell the truth before the court, and if they find out they have not told the truth, which can happen whereby you believe something to be true and then later find out it is false, you have a duty to tell the court quickly and correct the position.

Judges too have duties to the court and the administration of justice. The decency required of them primarily centres around independence, impartiality and integrity. Fundamentally, they cannot be seen to be influenced in their decision-making by external factors, nor in any way biased

---

[7] See, for example, Solicitors Regulatory Authority Overseas Rules, 2013.

[8] International Criminal Tribunal for the former Yugoslavia ('ICTY'), Code of Professional Conduct for Counsel Appearing before the International Tribunal, 1997, IT/125 REV. 3 (https://www.legal-tools.org/doc/rtgkbb).

[9] ICTY and International Criminal Tribunal for Rwanda ('ICTR'), Standards of Professional Conduct for Prosecution Counsel, Prosecutor's Regulation No 2 (1999), 14 September 1999 (https://www.legal-tools.org/doc/d74c40).

in dealing with the parties. Judicial codes for the *ad hoc* tribunals and the ICC state broadly similar duties.[10]

As I have already discussed, decency can be an abstract concept so, for the purposes of this chapter, it is of value to give some concrete examples of how international courts have interpreted requirements of conduct for both counsel and judges.

10.2. *The Prosecutor v. Radislav Krstić*

Between 1999 and 2001, I was junior counsel in the *Krstić case*.[11] It was the first prosecution at the ICTY for the crime of genocide. It was a harrowing trial with evidence which garnered much public attention because of the nature of the principal charge. Krstić was convicted, after trial, of genocide, crimes against humanity and a war crime.[12] At first instance, he was sentenced to forty-six years imprisonment.[13]

During the trial, everyone felt the overwhelming weight and tragic nature of what took place. It had a profound impact on us all. To this day, nearly twenty years on, reading the first part of the trial judgment, I still sense this great outpouring of grief and righteous anger in the face of industrial killing. You can see in those paragraphs how the judges felt. They were deeply affected by what they had seen and heard, but they had to publicly express that any private indignation they felt had to be put out of their mind for the sake of a fair trial:

> The events of the nine days from July 10-19 1995 in Srebrenica defy description in their horror and their implications for humankind's capacity to revert to acts of brutality under the stresses of conflict. In little over one week, thousands of lives were extinguished, irreparably rent or simply wiped from the pages of history.... The Trial Chamber cannot permit itself the indulgence of expressing how it feels about what happened in Srebrenica, or even how individuals as well as national and international groups not the subject of this case contributed to the tragedy. This defendant, like all others, deserves individu-

---

[10] See, for example, ICTY, Code of professional conduct for the judges of the Tribunal, 6 July 2016, S/2016/976 (https://www.legal-tools.org/doc/55lsey); ICC, Code of Judicial Ethics, 2 January 2005, ICC-BD/02-01-05 (https://www.legal-tools.org/doc/383f8f).

[11] ICTY, *Prosecutor v. Krstić*, Trial Judgement, 2 August 2001, IT-98-33-T ('Krstić case') (https://www.legal-tools.org/doc/440d3a).

[12] *Ibid.*, paras. 687–689.

[13] *Ibid.*, para. 726.

---

alised consideration and can be convicted only if the evidence presented in court shows, beyond a reasonable doubt, that he is guilty of acts that constitute crimes covered by the Statute of the Tribunal ("Statute").[14]

The judges were conscious as we all were of the need to be fair to Krstić *a fortiori* in the face of such terrible crimes and such powerful evidence. But, in my own experience, human beings can sometimes struggle to be completely fair when the crimes are very grave. The bellowing cries for justice drown out those whispers for fairness.

On appeal, amongst other grounds, the Defence claimed that Krstić had not received a fair trial because the Prosecution had not, in a number of instances, acted decently or fairly. The assertions included that the Prosecution had withheld copies of exhibits for tactical reasons; had concealed a tape for later submission as evidence in cross-examination; and had violated Rule 68 (disclosure of exculpatory material).[15]

Prior to the trial, and pursuant to Rule 65*ter*(E) (as it then was) of the ICTY Rules of Procedure and Evidence ('ICTY Rules'), the Defence sought copies of exhibits upon which the Prosecution intended to rely at trial. The Prosecution refused to disclose these exhibits on the basis that it was not bound to do so absent a request for reciprocal disclosure under Rule 67(C) of the ICTY Rules which the Defence did not make.[16] This rule, at the time of *Krstić*, stated:

> If the defence makes a request pursuant to Sub-rule 66 (B), the Prosecutor shall be entitled to inspect any books, documents, photographs and tangible objects, which are within the custody or control of the defence and which it intends to use as evidence at the trial.[17]

Rule 66(B) of the ICTY Rules stated:

> The Prosecutor shall, on request, permit the defence to inspect any books, documents, photographs and tangible objects in the Prosecutor's custody or control, which are material to the preparation of the defence, or are intended for use by the

---

[14] *Ibid.*, para. 2.

[15] Krstić case, Appeals Judgment, 19 April 2004, IT-98-33-A, para. 152 ('Krstić appeal') (https://www.legal-tools.org/doc/86a108).

[16] *Ibid.*, para. 154.

[17] ICTY Rules of Procedure and Evidence, November 1999, IT/32/Rev. 17 ('ICTY Rules') (https://www.legal-tools.org/doc/mo8alp).

Prosecutor as evidence at trial or were obtained from or belonged to the accused.[18]

The issue of disclosure of exhibits was raised in a pre-trial conference, where the Defence was denied access to the documents in question.[19] The exhibits relied upon by the Prosecution were subsequently disclosed as the trial proceeded.[20]

In refusing to order the Prosecution to disclose all its exhibits prior to trial, the pre-trial Judge had held that if the Prosecution was obliged to communicate all of its exhibits to the Defence, in the absence of any reciprocal disclosure by the Defence under Rule 67(C), it would result in inequality of arms.[21] On appeal, the Defence argued that the pre-trial Judge was wrong in finding that the Prosecution was not obliged by Rule 65*ter* to disclose copies of exhibits to the Defence prior to the commencement of trial, and that Krstić, therefore, did not receive a fair trial.[22] Rule 65*ter* required in relevant part that the pre-trial Judge order the Prosecutor to file a list of exhibits for the benefit of the court and the Defence, but only a list and not the exhibits themselves.[23]

The Defence sought a re-trial as a remedy for the Prosecution's failure to disclose exhibits prior to trial.[24] The Defence argued in two parts. The first part relied on the reasoning set out in a decision in *Krajišnik and Plavšić*, delivered after the closure of arguments in the *Krstić* trial.[25] That decision held that Rule 65*ter*(E) obliged the Prosecution to disclose copies of exhibits to the Defence prior to trial.[26] The second part of the Defence submission relied upon an amendment to Rule 65*ter*(E), which was adopted by the Judges of the Tribunal on 13 December 2001.[27] That amendment altered the terms of Rule 65*ter*(E) so as to explicitly require the Prosecution to provide to the Defence copies of exhibits listed in pre-trial disclo-

---

[18] *Ibid.*

[19] Krstić appeal, para. 154, see above note 15.

[20] *Ibid.*

[21] *Ibid.*, para. 155.

[22] *Ibid.*, para. 156.

[23] ICTY Rules, rule 65 *ter* E(v), see above note 17.

[24] Krstić appeal, para. 156, see above note 15.

[25] *Ibid.*, para. 157.

[26] *Ibid.*, paras. 157 and 159.

[27] *Ibid.*, para. 158.

sure.[28] The Defence argued that this subsequent amendment demonstrated that the decision in *Krajišnik and Plavšić* was adopted by the entire Tribunal.[29] In contrast to the finding in the *Krstić* pre-trial conference, the Trial Chamber in *Krajišnik and Plavšić* held that the only way in which the Defence can properly prepare for trial is by having notice in advance of the materials on which the Prosecution intends to rely, including exhibits.[30]

So in *Krajišnik and Plavšić*, the Defence argued that, by not disclosing the documents prior to trial, the Prosecution placed the Defence in a position in which it was not able to properly prepare for trial; and it was this fact that would likely lead to a violation of the principle of equality of arms.[31] The Trial Chamber agreed and held that Rule 65*ter*(E)(iii) required the Prosecution to disclose the actual exhibits appearing in the list, irrespective of any reciprocal pre-trial disclosure of exhibits by the Defence under Rule 67.[32] The Trial Chamber in *Krajišnik and Plavšić* reasoned that, since Rule 65*ter*(E)(iii) referred to possible objections by the Defence to the authenticity of the exhibits, the Defence would need to have access to those exhibits in order to assess their authenticity.[33] The subsequent amendment of the Rule adopted this approach.[34]

At issue in *Krstić* was whether the amendment to Rule 65*ter* reflected a consensus as to the proper interpretation of the former Rule, and whether the Trial Chamber in *Krajišnik and Plavšić* accurately described that interpretation.[35] The Appeals Chamber rejected the argument by the Defence that the amendment to Rule 65*ter*(E) bound the Appeals Chamber to adopt the interpretation submitted by the Defence.[36] The Appeals Chamber said that it was common for the ICTY Rules to be amended from time to time where those Rules are shown through practice to require clarification or modification.[37] At most, the amendment of the Rule might cast light on the ambiguity of the former formulation of the Rule, but it did not nec-

---

28   *Ibid.*
29   *Ibid.*
30   *Ibid.*, para. 159.
31   *Ibid.*
32   *Ibid.*
33   *Ibid.*, para. 160.
34   *Ibid.*, para. 161.
35   *Ibid.*
36   *Ibid.*, para. 162.
37   *Ibid.*

essarily assist in the interpretation of it.[38] The new Rule 65*ter*(E) required the Prosecution to provide the Defence with access to copies of the Prosecution's exhibits prior to trial.[39] Before the amendment, however, the actual scope of the Rule was open to interpretation, as shown by the contrasting decisions of the *Krstić* pre-trial conference and of the Trial Chamber in *Krajišnik and Plavšić*.[40] The text of the former Rule 65*ter*(E) did not expressly require exhibits themselves to be disclosed but referred only to them being 'listed', suggesting that Rule 65*ter*(E) was not a means by which the disclosure of exhibits could be secured.[41] The subsequent amendment to the Rules suggested, however, that the judges of the Tribunal recognized that this practice might lead both the Defence and the Prosecution into difficulties when it comes to contesting the authenticity of exhibits.[42] Where the parties contested exhibits, delays to the trial could occur while adjournments are granted in order to permit the parties to investigate those exhibits as they are tendered.[43] As such, the subsequent amendment may have been a matter relevant to the efficient management of the trial itself, and not the result of any perceived unfairness to the Defence.[44]

Furthermore, in *Krstić*, the Prosecutor had reached an agreement with Defence Counsel – at the suggestion of the Trial Chamber – and established a regime for the disclosure of certain evidence.[45] In agreeing to the disclosure regime with the Defence, the Prosecution was, in fact, exceeding its obligations under the Rules in as much as those obligations had been determined pre-trial.[46] At trial, the Defence did not object to this agreement and made no complaint regarding the disclosure regime.[47] On appeal, the Prosecution argued that the Defence's acceptance of this regime meant that the Defence could not now claim that the regime was unfair.[48] The Appeals Chamber did not agree that initial compliance by the Defence with the dis-

---

38   *Ibid.*
39   *Ibid.*
40   *Ibid.*
41   *Ibid.*, para. 163.
42   *Ibid.*
43   *Ibid.*
44   *Ibid.*, para. 164.
45   *Ibid.*
46   *Ibid.*
47   *Ibid.*
48   *Ibid.*

closure regime could be a basis for refusing to allow the Defence to argue on appeal that it was unfair.[49] However, to succeed on this ground of appeal, the Defence would have to establish that it was prevented from properly investigating the authenticity of the exhibits by the Trial Chamber's interpretation of the Rule, and that it suffered prejudice as a result.[50] The Defence did not establish any prejudice. On the contrary, the Trial Chamber did permit adjournments which allowed the Defence the opportunity to contest the authenticity of various exhibits tendered by the Prosecution. The Appeals Chamber accordingly dismissed this ground of appeal.

During 1999 and 2000, there was an in-built tension in the ICTY Rules of Procedure and Evidence concerning disclosure. If the Defence invoked Rule 66(B), and sought inspection of exhibits and other real evidence in the custody and control of the Prosecutor and on which the Prosecutor would seek to rely at trial, the Prosecution could then invoke the same right against the Defence under Rule 67(C). The Defence often did not want to have to disclose its own documentary evidence before trial. If the truth were told, I think it was regularly the case that the Defence were unable to make disclosure of their own documents before the beginning of trial because they did not know what documents they would be seeking to rely on. This decision by the Appeals Chamber in *Krstić* centred around disclosure rights. It was technically absolutely correct in that you could not, at that time, circumvent reciprocal discovery rights by relying on rules around pre-trial preparation. That said, a fundamental internationally recognized right in any criminal trial, at the time of *Krstić*, was for an accused person "to be *informed promptly*, in a language which he understands and *in detail*, of the nature and cause of the accusation against him".[51]

The Appeals Chamber held that there was no impropriety by the Prosecution, as they had simply applied the ICTY Rules as they then existed. But, arguably, for Krstić to know the case against him *promptly and in detail*, all exhibits should have been disclosed prior to trial and not piecemeal as the case went along. The potential loss of reciprocal discovery was

---

[49]   *Ibid.*, para. 165.

[50]   *Ibid.*

[51]   European Convention on Human Rights, 3 September 1953, Article 6(3)(a) (emphasis added) (https://www.legal-tools.org/doc/8267cb). See also International Covenant on Civil and Political Rights, 23 March 1976, Article 14(3) (https://www.legal-tools.org/doc/2838f3); American Convention on Human Rights, 18 July 1978, Article 8(2)(b) (https://www.legal-tools.org/doc/1152cf).

tactically significant for the Prosecution, but the decision not to disclose exhibits to the Defence led to this rather unfortunate result of *prima facie* unfairness, even though the Defence could not show any prejudice.

During the presentation of the Defence's case at trial, the Prosecution introduced taped evidence that was played to Krstić during his cross-examination.[52] The existence of the taped evidence had not been disclosed to the Defence until after the closure of both the Prosecution's case and the evidence-in-chief of the accused, even though the Prosecution had been in possession of it for some time.[53] The Defence had, however, been aware of the contents of the tape prior to its introduction to the Trial Chamber, and had not objected to it being played at the time.[54] On appeal, the Defence submitted that a new trial should be ordered for two reasons: the alleged impossibility of the Trial Chamber ignoring the contents of the tape; and the Prosecution's employment of so-called 'sharp' trial tactics.[55]

The contents of the tape, if true, were devastating for Krstić:

> Intercepted and recorded on August 2 1995, it appears to refer to what action should be taken against Bosnian men who fled the massacre and were caught in the hills around Srebrenica.
>
> Krstić: Are you working down there?
>
> Obrenovic: We are working, indeed.
>
> K: Good.
>
> O: There are still a few, [they] got snared ...
>
> K: Yeah.
>
> O: ... either by guns or mines.
>
> K: Kill all in turn. Fuck their mothers!
>
> O: Everything is going according to plan.
>
> K: Don't leave a single one alive!
>
> O: What?
>
> K: Do not leave anyone alive!
>
> O: Everything is going according to plan. Everything.[56]

---

[52] Krstić appeal, para. 167, see above note 15.

[53] *Ibid.*

[54] *Ibid.*

[55] *Ibid.*, para. 168.

[56] *The Guardian*, "Serb major denies Bosnian genocide", 19 April 2001.

The Defence argued that, once the tape had been played to the Trial Chamber, it became impossible for the Trial Chamber to ignore its contents when deciding on the guilt and sentence of the accused, even though the Trial Chamber had excluded it from evidence.[57] The Appeals Chamber did not accept this argument. The Appeals Chamber stated that the role of Judges as arbiters of both fact and law was essential to the basic functioning of the Tribunal.[58] Judges were frequently required to disregard evidence from their deliberations, not only as an incident to their role as Judges but also as an acknowledged part of their judicial function in assessing the admissibility of evidence at trial.[59] The Defence had shown neither the existence of any prejudice resulting from the playing of the tape nor that the contents of the tape were taken into account or relied upon by the Trial Chamber in arriving at its conclusions.[60] There were no grounds to support the Defence's submission that the playing of the tape influenced the Judges, and therefore no re-trial was warranted.[61]

The Defence argued that the manner in which the tape was used constituted a 'sharp' trial tactic by the Prosecution and that the Appeals Chamber should deter future prosecutorial misconduct by granting the Defence a re-trial.[62] The Prosecution defended its conduct by arguing that there was no directly applicable Rule prohibiting parties from introducing evidence in the manner described.[63] The Defence suggested that the Prosecution deliberately declined to disclose the tape as an exhibit, deciding instead for tactical reasons to conceal it for use in cross-examination "so that the defence would not have an opportunity to explain it".[64] The Decision of the Trial Chamber to exclude the evidence, together with the nature of the evidence in question and the amount of time in which the Prosecution possessed it, supported the Defence's submission.[65] There appeared to be sufficient grounds in the circumstances to question the propriety of the Prosecution as

---

[57] Krstić appeal, para. 169, see above note 15.
[58] *Ibid.*, para. 170.
[59] *Ibid.*
[60] *Ibid.*, para. 171.
[61] *Ibid.*
[62] *Ibid.*, para. 172.
[63] *Ibid.*
[64] *Ibid.*, para. 173.
[65] *Ibid.*, para. 174.

regards the disclosure of this evidence.[66] The Appeals Chamber did not accept that a re-trial was necessary but instead concluded that where counsel had engaged in such misconduct, the appropriate sanctions were provided by Rule 46 (Misconduct of Counsel).[67] So here the Appeals Chamber regarded this disclosure decision by the Prosecution as professional misconduct – potentially a lack of integrity or dishonesty.

At the time, I did not understand the decision of the OTP not to rely on this evidence in its case-in-chief because it was potentially powerful evidence. Also, as a general rule in English law, all evidence on which the Prosecution intends to rely on as probative of guilt should be called before the close of their own case.[68] Subject to a number of limited exceptions, the Prosecution cannot call new evidence after the start of the Defence case.[69] So for me, at the time, the decision by the OTP to introduce this evidence for the first time in the accused's cross-examination by the OTP was ill-judged. I recall it went down badly with the Trial Chamber judges too and there was a strong sense at the time that they were disappointed by the conduct of the OTP. Since the evidence was excluded by the judges, it lost any value it might have had. On appeal, Krstić was found not to have genocidal intent. To this day, I wonder had we adduced this evidence in the normal fashion, in our own case, whether that outcome would have been different. We will never know.

The last issue I will address from the *Krstić* appeal was an alleged violation of Rule 68 of the ICTY Rules by the Prosecution.[70] I suspect Rule 68 was one of the most oft-quoted of the Rules of Procedure and Evidence. This Rule required the Prosecution to disclose to the Defence any material which, in the actual knowledge of the Prosecutor, suggested the innocence or mitigated the guilt of the accused or affected the credibility of Prosecution's evidence. So, the obligation to disclose exculpatory evidence to the Defence. This obligation goes to the heart of what decency means to a prosecutor because, of course, this obligation requires a prosecutor to be like a minister of justice and to ensure that the process of prosecution is a fair one, whereby the accused receives information known to the prosecu-

---

[66] *Ibid.*

[67] *Ibid.*

[68] United Kingdom, Court of Appeal, *R. v. Rice*, Judgment, 29 January 1963, [1963] 1 QB 857.

[69] David Ormerod and David Perry, *Blackstone's Criminal Practice*, Oxford University Press, 2019, pp. 2580–2585.

[70] Krstić appeal, para. 176, see above note 15.

tor which undermines the prosecutor's case or assists the accused's defence. Undoubtedly, in large complex international cases, it was not always clear what was exculpatory and what was not because it was not always apparent what defence or defences the accused was running. Defences often developed throughout a case. And I do not in any way, infer criticism of defence counsel for this uncertainty. Having done some international defence work myself, it was often hard to simply encapsulate what the defence was going to be and what constituted all the evidence which would be helpful to the client and was in the prosecutor's possession. So, the disclosure of exculpatory material, pursuant to Rule 68, led to many sleepless nights for prosecutors. It often provided for dramatic court encounters where such material was discovered late on in a trial and then disclosed to the defence, who would understandably shout foul and ask for sanctions to be applied to the prosecutor. Judges of the international courts, I think, became equally frustrated by the application of this Rule and the procedural mishaps that occurred around it.

In the *Krstić* case, the Defence argued that the Prosecution violated its disclosure obligations under Rule 68 by: failing to disclose a number of witness statements containing exculpatory material; failing to disclose exculpatory material amongst other evidence without identifying that material as exculpatory; preventing the Defence from taking copies of exculpatory materials, and instead requiring the Defence to view the materials at the offices of the Prosecution; and failing to make two disclosures as soon as practicable.[71]

So, the Defence argued that a number of interviews with witnesses, conducted by the Prosecution prior to the Trial Chamber delivering the Judgement, contained exculpatory evidence and that the failure of the Prosecution to disclose that material at that time constituted a breach of Rule 68.[72] The Prosecution conceded, at the time, that of the ten witness statements filed by the Defence in its first Rule 115 Motion, six "fall within the ambit of Rule 68", but argued that the other four statements did not fall within the Rule, and that, in any case, the Defence had been unable to establish prejudice resulting from the failure to disclose.[73]

---

[71] *Ibid.*

[72] *Ibid.*, para. 177.

[73] *Ibid.*

The Appeals Chamber recognized that the jurisprudence of the Tribunal mirrored the text of Rule 68 itself, and established that material fell within the ambit of Rule 68 if it tended to suggest the innocence or mitigate the guilt of the accused, or affected the credibility of Prosecution evidence.[74] The Tribunal held that material would affect the credibility of the Prosecution's evidence if it undermined the case presented by the Prosecution at trial;[75] material to be disclosed under Rule 68 was not restricted to material which is in a form which would be admissible in evidence.[76] Rather, it included all information which in any way tended to suggest the innocence or mitigate the guilt of an accused or might affect the credibility of Prosecution evidence, as well as material which might put an accused on notice that such material existed.[77] The Prosecution argued that any interpretation of Rule 68 should draw upon the practice of domestic jurisdictions with comparable disclosure regimes.[78] It relied heavily upon cases from the United States in arguing that, for a document to fall within Rule 68, it must be exculpatory "on its face".[79] The Prosecution was seeking on appeal to restrict the application of Rule 68. The Appeals Chamber rightly rejected this position and found the meaning and purpose of Rule 68 to be sufficiently clear, and it dismissed consideration of domestic provisions.[80] The disclosure of exculpatory material was fundamental to the fairness of proceedings before the Tribunal, and considerations of fairness were the overriding factor in any determination of whether the governing Rule had been breached.[81]

The Appeals Chamber was also aware of the obligation and burden placed on the Prosecution, both in terms of the volume of material to be disclosed, and the effort expended in determining whether the material is exculpatory. But it also recognized the pre-eminent importance of disclos-

---

[74] *Ibid.*, para. 178.
[75] *Ibid.*
[76] *Ibid.*
[77] *Ibid.*
[78] *Ibid.*, para. 179.
[79] *Ibid.*
[80] *Ibid.*
[81] *Ibid.*, para. 180.

ing exculpatory evidence to the Defence,[82] so it would be against the interests of a fair trial to limit the scope of Rule 68.[83]

The disputed evidence related to the statements of four protected witnesses submitted on appeal as additional evidence pursuant to Rule 115 of the ICTY Rules.[84] The Defence claimed that the evidence in the statements revealed a parallel chain of command of which Krstić was not a part and that those responsible for the mass killings were bypassing him in the chain of command. Moreover, the Defence claimed that they demonstrated Krstić had not had control of forces committing the massacres in and around Srebrenica and that documents showing he was a commander on a particular day did not mean he became commander on that day.[85] Interestingly, the Appeals Chamber found none of this potentially exculpatory evidence had any effect on the trial verdict at all, however, it still held to the extent that they had found that the Prosecution had failed in respect of its obligations under the ICTY Rules, those breaches fell to be addressed by the appropriate remedies, namely Rule 46 (Misconduct of Counsel) and Rule 68*bis* (Failure to Comply with Disclosure Obligations).[86] Where alleged breaches had no effect on the outcome of the trial, I question whether they justify a sanction. It seems questionable why should you be punished for lack of decency when the basis is an unsubstantiated allegation. That said, my position on Rule 68 disclosure was always if in doubt disclose it, because the consequences and fall-out from non-disclosure were often out all proportion to the weight and importance to the Defence of the evidence being disclosed late.

The Defence also submitted that some Rule 68 disclosures made during trial were buried beneath other material provided at the time, and that the failure of the Prosecution to identify the disclosed material as being disclosed under Rule 68 breached the spirit and letter of that Rule.[87] In response, the Prosecution argued that there was no specific requirement obliging it to indicate the provision in the Rules whereby disclosure of documents occurred, or to identify the specific material disclosed as excul-

---

[82]   *Ibid.*
[83]   *Ibid.*
[84]   *Ibid.*, para. 182.
[85]   *Ibid.*, paras. 183–186.
[86]   *Ibid.*
[87]   *Ibid.*, para. 189.

patory.[88] The Appeals Chamber agreed with the Prosecution that Rule 68 did not require the Prosecution to identify the material being disclosed to the Defence as exculpatory.[89] The jurisprudence of the Tribunal showed that, while some Trial Chambers had recognized that it would be fairer for the Prosecution to do so, there was no *prima facie* requirement, absent an order of the Trial Chamber to that effect, that it must do so.[90] However, the fact that there was no prima facie obligation on the Prosecution to identify the disclosed Rule 68 material as exculpatory did not prevent the accused from arguing, as a ground of appeal, that he suffered prejudice as a result of the Prosecution's failure to do so.[91] Here the Appeals Chamber had not been persuaded by the Defence that the failure of the Prosecution to identify exculpatory evidence it disclosed resulted in any prejudice to the Defence.[92] They found the Defence had both sufficient time in which to analyse the material, and the opportunity to challenge it during cross-examination.[93] This ground of appeal was dismissed. I confess I disagreed with this finding. My feeling was, while there was no obligation to identify specific sentences or paragraphs in documents which were potentially exculpatory, at least identifying single documents or groups of documents which were potentially exculpatory seemed to me to be the minimum that should be expected of the Prosecution. And I still believe that today.

Next, the Appeals Chamber had to consider whether Rule 68 required the Prosecution to allow the Defence to take copies of exculpatory material.[94] The Defence submitted that, in only being permitted to view copies of exculpatory evidence in the Prosecution's office, and being refused copies of the materials, the Prosecution breached Rule 68, as well as its obligation to act as a 'minister of justice' – so in effect with fairness and decency.[95] On a plain reading of Rule 68, the Prosecution was found to be merely obliged to disclose the existence of Rule 68 material, not to provide the actual material itself.[96] The Appeals Chamber found if the Defence had

---

[88] *Ibid.*
[89] *Ibid.*, para. 190.
[90] *Ibid.*
[91] *Ibid.*, para. 191.
[92] *Ibid.*, para. 192.
[93] *Ibid.*
[94] *Ibid.*, para. 194.
[95] *Ibid.*
[96] *Ibid.*, para. 195.

demonstrated that the preparation of its case had been prejudiced by only being able to view the Rule 68 material held by the Prosecutor, then it should have brought this prejudice to the attention of the Trial Chamber.[97] The Prosecution did disclose the existence of this material, and the Defence did not complain to the Trial Chamber, at the time, it was unable to make copies.[98] The Defence did not persuade the Appeals Chamber that it did indeed suffer any prejudice during the trial, and so this ground of appeal was dismissed.[99] Whatever the strict reading of the rule, one might question why the Prosecution would not provide copies of potentially exculpatory documents to the Defence to avoid later dispute? What advantage did they gain in this situation by not providing copies? I can see situations where the provider of a document, such as a government or international organization, might not wish copies of sensitive documents to be copied and distributed beyond the Prosecution, but I cannot see any advantage for the Prosecution here in not providing copies of Rule 68 material to the Defence.

Lastly, I want to consider the appellate finding in the *Krstić* appeal on whether two disclosures were made 'as soon as practicable'. Here the Defence submitted that certain disclosures were not made 'as soon as practicable', as required by Rule 68.[100] For example, disclosures of 25 June 2000 occurred over two years after the Prosecution came into possession of the evidence, and more than three months after the trial had begun.[101] Disclosures of 5 March 2001 occurred over three months after the Prosecution came into possession of the evidence.[102] The Defence also alleged that the Prosecution deliberately withheld evidence in order eventually to avail itself of the reciprocal discovery mechanism of Rules 67(B) and 67(C).[103]

I was aware in the year 2000 of the amount of material that was collectively in possession of the OTP, and the time it took to translate that material from Bosnian and Serbian into English and French. And then to study it and decide its importance, including whether it was exculpatory. The Appeals Chamber was sympathetic to the argument of the Prosecution that, in most instances, material requires processing, translation, analysis and iden-

---

[97] *Ibid.*

[98] *Ibid.*

[99] *Ibid.*

[100] *Ibid.*, para. 196.

[101] *Ibid.*

[102] *Ibid.*

[103] *Ibid.*

tification as exculpatory material.[104] They rightly found the Prosecution could not be expected to disclose material which – despite its best efforts – it had not been able to review and assess.[105] Nevertheless, the Prosecution did take an inordinate amount of time before disclosing material in *Krstić*, and had failed to provide a satisfactory explanation for the delay.[106] The Appeals Chamber found that the Prosecution had breached Rule 68 and that its submission that the Defence had enough time to consider the material, while allaying allegations of prejudice to the Defence's case, did not contradict the allegation that the Prosecution breached Rule 68 by not providing the material as soon as practicable.[107] The Defence could not demonstrate prejudice nor could they provide sufficient evidence to the Appeals Chamber for it to determine whether late disclosure was a trial tactic.[108] Late disclosure of exculpatory material as a deliberate trial tactic to force the Defence into reciprocal disclosure would have been dishonest and indecent.

The Appeals Chamber did find that the disclosures of 25 June 2000 and 5 March 2001 were not made as soon as practicable, and that the Prosecution had, as a result, breached Rule 68.[109] Again, a pre-requisite for the remedy sought on appeal for breaches of Rule 68 was proof of consequential prejudice to the Defence.[110] The Defence had not established any such prejudice from the delayed disclosures by the Prosecution, so the remedy sought was not justified.[111] The Appeals Chamber did again find that the Prosecution did not meet its obligations under the Rules. And the consequences again were governed by Rule 46 (Misconduct of Counsel) and Rule 68*bis* (Failure to Comply with Disclosure Obligations). Again, I do question potential sanctions for technical breaches of Rule 68 when no prejudice was suffered. I suppose such findings did have the result of encouraging prosecutors to be straightforward about these issues in other cases in order to avoid these kinds of appeals.

---

[104] *Ibid.*, para. 197.

[105] *Ibid.*

[106] *Ibid.*

[107] *Ibid.*

[108] *Ibid.*, para.198.

[109] *Ibid.*

[110] *Ibid.*, para.199.

[111] *Ibid.*

10.3. *The Prosecutor v. Nikola Šainović, Dragoljub Ojdanić, Nebojša Pavković, Vladimir Lazarević, Sreten Lukić and Milan Milutinović*

Moving to another case which concerned alleged violations of an accused's rights to a fair trial, this chapter turns next to the case *The Prosecutor v. Nikola Šainović*. In this case, it was the Presiding Judge accused of misconduct and bias. The trial judge concerned was a decent man of integrity with extensive judicial experience prior to the ICTY.

On 26 February 2009, Sreten Lukić had been convicted at trial of crimes against humanity and violations of the laws or customs of war.[112] The Trial Chamber had found that in 1999 there was a broad campaign of violence directed against the Kosovo Albanian civilian population in Kosovo conducted by the army and Interior Ministry police forces ('MUP'), under the control of the Federal Republic of Yugoslavia and Serbian authorities, who were responsible for mass expulsions of Kosovo Albanian civilians from their homes, as well as incidents of killing, sexual assault, and the intentional destruction of mosques.[113] The Trial Chamber found that these crimes were committed in the execution of a joint criminal enterprise, the purpose of which was to "use violence and terror to force a significant number of Kosovo Albanians from their homes and across the borders, in order for the state authorities to maintain control over Kosovo".[114] Lukić, as Head of the Ministry of Internal Affairs in Kosovo, was part of this joint criminal enterprise and sentenced to 22 years imprisonment.[115]

During his appeal, Lukić argued that on several occasions the Trial Chamber exhibited "personal bias" against him, thus violating his right to be heard by an independent and impartial tribunal.[116] In support of his assertion, Lukić noted that the Presiding Judge, Judge Iain Bonomy, was a judge in the trial of the former President of Yugoslavia, Slobodan Milošević, which shared many witnesses and subject-matter with his case.[117] Lukić also referred to several remarks made by Judge Bonomy which, in

---

[112] ICTY, *The Prosecutor v. Šainović et al.*, Trial Chamber, Judgement, 26 February 2009, IT-05-87-T, vol. 3, para. 1138 ('Šainović *et al.* case') (https://www.legal-tools.org/doc/d79e85).

[113] Šainović *et al.* case, Judgement Summary, 26 February 2009, p. 4 (https://www.legal-tools.org/doc/c75af2).

[114] *Ibid.*, p. 12.

[115] Šainović *et al.* case, para. 1212, see above note 112.

[116] Šainović *et al.* case, Appeals Chamber, Judgement, 23 January 2014, IT-05-87-A, para. 176 (https://www.legal-tools.org/doc/81ac8c).

[117] *Ibid.*

Lukić's view, showed "disparaging treatment" and argued that the pressure of the Tribunal's completion strategy coupled with Judge Bonomy's prior work in advocating the speeding-up of trials in Scotland, might have been the reason for such "prejudgement [or] bias".[118] Lukić alleged that as a result of this bias: (i) he received a significantly higher sentence compared to that of Ojdanić and Lazarević, and was sentenced to 22 years of imprisonment along with other co-accused who, unlike him, did not have circumstances in mitigation;[119] (ii) his voluntary surrender, unlike that of Lazarević, was not regarded as a mitigating factor;[120] (iii) Milutinović, who had attended the same meetings and had a similar level of knowledge of the crimes, was acquitted;[121] (iv) motions filed by Lukić for admission of documents from the bar table were dismissed by the Trial Chamber;[122] and (v) the evidence of defence witnesses was almost entirely disregarded in the Trial Judgement, thus suggesting that Lukić's Defence had not been considered.[123]

In response, the Prosecution submitted that Lukić had failed to demonstrate an appearance of bias and that the examples he alleged show, instead, the efforts of the Presiding Judge to ensure the fair and expeditious conduct of the proceedings.[124] The Prosecution argued that the Trial Chamber correctly distinguished the criminal responsibility of the individual co-accused, had valid reasons for denying the admission of certain evidence tendered by Lukić and provided detailed conclusions on the credibility of the defence witnesses.[125]

Lukić replied that the combination of the Trial Judgement's "openly hostile disposition" towards him, the difference in treatment he received compared to that received by Milutinović, Lazarević and Ojdanić, and the impugned remarks of the Presiding Judge established bias that invalidated the Trial Judgement.[126]

---

[118] *Ibid.*
[119] *Ibid.*
[120] *Ibid.*
[121] *Ibid.*
[122] *Ibid.*
[123] *Ibid.*
[124] *Ibid.*, para. 177.
[125] *Ibid.*
[126] *Ibid.*, para.178.

The Appeals Chamber in examining all the arguments in the case, naturally reiterated that the right to be tried before an independent and impartial tribunal was an integral component of the right to a fair trial and was enshrined in Article 21 of the ICTY Statute.[127] This fundamental guarantee was also reflected in Article 13 of the Statute, which provided that the Judges of the Tribunal "shall be persons of high moral character, impartiality and integrity". It is further reinforced by Rule 15(A) of the ICTY Rules, stipulating that "[a] Judge may not sit on a trial or appeal in any case in which the Judge has a personal interest or concerning which the Judge has or has had any association which might affect his or her impartiality".[128]

In the *Furundžija* Appeals Judgement, upon reviewing the interpretation of the impartiality requirement in a number of national legal systems and under the ECHR, the Appeals Chamber enunciated the principles that should guide the interpretation and application of this requirement under the Statute as follows:

1. A Judge is not impartial if it is shown that actual bias exists.

2. There is an unacceptable appearance of bias if:

   i) a Judge is a party to the case, or has a financial or proprietary interest in the outcome of a case, or if the Judge's decision will lead to the promotion of a cause in which he or she is involved, together with one of the parties. Under these circumstances, a Judge's disqualification from the case is automatic; or

   ii) the circumstances would lead a reasonable observer, properly informed, to reasonably apprehend bias. With regard to the 'reasonable observer' standard, the Appeals Chamber has held that a "reasonable person must be an informed person, with knowledge of all the relevant circumstances, including the traditions of integrity and impartiality that form a part of the background and apprised also of the fact that impartiality is one of the duties that Judges swear to uphold.[129]

The Appeals Chamber, therefore, had to determine whether the reaction of such a hypothetical fair-minded observer would be that a Judge

---

[127] *Ibid.*, para. 179.

[128] *Ibid.*

[129] *Ibid.*, paras. 180–181.

might not bring an impartial and unprejudiced mind to the issues arising in the case.[130] The Appeals Chamber emphasized that Judges enjoy a presumption of impartiality and that there is a high threshold to reach in order to rebut that presumption.[131] In this respect, the Appeals Chamber had held that:

> in the absence of evidence to the contrary, it must be assumed that the Judges of the Tribunal can disabuse their minds of any irrelevant personal beliefs or predispositions.[132] It is for the Appellant to adduce sufficient evidence to satisfy the Appeals Chamber that [the] Judge [...] was not impartial in his case. There is a high threshold to reach in order to rebut the presumption of impartiality.[133] As has been stated, disqualification is only made out by showing that there is a reasonable apprehension of bias by reason of prejudgement, and this must be firmly established.[134]

The Appeals Chamber pointed out that Lukić did not raise the question of Judge Bonomy's impartiality before the Trial Chamber.[135] The Appeals Chamber stated such an omission could constitute waiver of the right to raise the matter on appeal, but it had been the practice of the Appeals Chamber to treat the issue of bias as a special circumstance allowing it to address the merits of the challenge despite the waiver.[136] So the Appeals Chamber considered the merits of Lukić's challenges first, addressing Judge Bonomy's previous involvement in the *Milošević* case.

The Appeals Chamber noted that, following the resignation of Judge Richard May and pursuant to an order of the President of the Tribunal, on 10 June 2004 Judge Bonomy was assigned to Trial Chamber III, hearing the case of *Milošević*.[137] He performed the functions of a trial judge in that case until 14 March 2006 when, following the death of Milošević, the proceedings were terminated.[138] Lukić alleged that the *Milošević* case shared

---

[130] *Ibid.*, para. 181.

[131] *Ibid.*

[132] *Ibid.*

[133] *Ibid.*

[134] *Ibid.*, citing ICTY, *Prosecutor v. Anto Furundžija*, Appeals Chamber, Judgement, 21 July 2000, IT-95-17/1-A (https://www.legal-tools.org/doc/660d3f/).

[135] *Ibid.*, para. 182.

[136] *Ibid.*

[137] *Ibid.*, para. 183.

[138] *Ibid.*

many common witnesses with his case.[139] However, he had failed to present any arguments explaining how Judge Bonomy's involvement in the *Milošević* proceedings would lead a reasonable and informed observer to apprehend bias.[140] The Appeals Chamber pointed out that the Judges of the Tribunal often become involved in several trials which, by their very nature, concern issues that overlap and may be presented with witness testimony that was already admitted in another case.[141] The Appeals Chamber assumed, in the absence of evidence to the contrary that, by virtue of their training and experience, Judges will rule fairly on the issues before them, relying solely and exclusively on the evidence adduced in the particular case.[142] Lukić's generic contention falls short of rebutting this presumption of impartiality. His submission was therefore dismissed.[143]

Second, the Appeals Chamber addressed Judge Bonomy's prior work in advocating the speeding-up of trials in Scotland and the ICTY's completion strategy. Lukić submitted that Judge Bonomy "was known in Scotland for his work in advocating the speeding-up of the trial process".[144] He referred in this respect to a 142-page document entitled "Improving Practice: 2002 Review of the Practices and Procedure of the High Court of Justiciary" authored by Judge Bonomy.[145] Again, however, Lukić did not substantiate his contention nor provide any precise references to information in the document that would support the allegation of apprehension of bias.[146] He did not specify how the document was relevant to the work of the Tribunal and, in particular, to his case.[147] So the Appeals Chamber dismissed this argument on appeal too.[148]

Regarding Lukić's first appeal point on bias, candidly, I always had concerns about the judges' involvement in trials with overlapping factual bases. Not because such involvement went to their decency or integrity. Judges are credited with being able to do the mental gymnastics required to

---

[139] *Ibid.*, para. 184.
[140] *Ibid.*
[141] *Ibid.*
[142] *Ibid.*
[143] *Ibid.*
[144] *Ibid.* para. 185.
[145] *Ibid.*
[146] *Ibid.*
[147] *Ibid.*
[148] *Ibid.*

always be impartial and not predisposed, unless strong evidence demonstrates otherwise, but they are also human and being human sometimes mean these higher qualities attributed to you are not always infallible. ICTY cases were very long, indeed. Evidence was often heart-breaking and painful. The facts of these cases rested deeply with all of us.

Lukić's second point regarding Judge Bonomy's work in Scotland on speeding up the trial process was bogus, since prior work on more efficient trials has nothing to do with fairness.[149] Most likely one of the reasons Bonomy was put forward as a judge for the ICTY, at this particular time, was exactly because he would make trials and appeals more efficient – which, in fact, he did.

Lukić also argued that the pressure of the Tribunal's completion strategy was another factor contributing to the apprehension of bias. However, he again failed to substantiate his allegation, and the Appeals Chamber refused to address it any further.

Lukić argued that statements made by Judge Bonomy during trial had made his trial unfair. In scrutinizing these allegations, the Appeals Chamber was needlessly cautious, emphasizing that when examining allegations of apprehension of bias, extracts from transcripts had to be placed in their proper context so that the intent of the Judge who made the impugned remarks may be inferred.[150] Iain Bonomy was born in Motherwell in Scotland. He started his legal career as a corporate solicitor later becoming an advocate, then a Queen's Counsel, and finally a judge. He was unusual for a judge in that he lived not only fully in the law but also in the real world. By experience of the world, he was and is a straightforward man who spoke the truth bluntly in life and in trials.

Lukić argued that, during the cross-examination of Emin Kabashi, Judge Bonomy made a remark "essentially curtailing vigorous cross-examination by co-counsel for Appellant".[151] In particular, Lukić challenged the following statement made by Judge Bonomy in relation to a question put by Lukić's co-counsel to Kabashi: "Perry Mason probably once got somebody to break down and admit to that but let's move on".[152] In response, the Prosecution submitted that the Presiding Judge properly

---

[149] *Ibid.* para. 186.

[150] *Ibid.* para. 187.

[151] *Ibid.* para. 188.

[152] *Ibid.*

directed Lukić to proceed with another question.[153] The trial record indicated that, prior to the impugned remark, the Prosecution objected to the question put to the witness by Lukić's co-counsel and the Presiding Judge intervened, inquiring into its relevance. A hypothetical fair-minded observer, properly informed, would recognize that the Presiding Judge's allegoric remark was made in the context of an intervention, the purpose of which was to ensure that the mode of the witness examination was effective.[154] Accordingly, the Appeals Chamber found that no appearance of bias had been demonstrated in this case.

Lukić further claimed that on two occasions the Presiding Judge prevented him "from attempting to make a record and be heard".[155] Lukić referred to a statement of the Presiding Judge made on 14 February 2008:

> JUDGE BONOMY: Mr. Lukic, sit down, please. Mr. Mijatovic can answer questions[.][156]

He also refers to the following exchange which took place on 4 March 2008:

> JUDGE BONOMY: Sit down. You're just interfering with the cross-examination now. MR. IVETIC: I don't believe so, Your Honour. I think this is a very important point. JUDGE BONOMY: Sit down. MR. IVETIC: And I want it on the record. JUDGE BONOMY: Sit down and deal with it in re-examination.[157]

In response, the Prosecution argued that in both instances the intervention of the Presiding Judge was appropriate as, first, he directed Lukić's lead counsel not to give evidence on behalf of the witness, and, second, he overruled an unfounded objection by Lukić's co-counsel.[158]

As shown by the trial record, in the first instance, Lukić's lead counsel intervened when the Presiding Judge was seeking to elicit an answer from Miroslav Mijatovic concerning the reporting obligations of the Kosovo Secretariats of the Interior. A reading of the relevant section of the transcript showed that not only was Lukić's lead counsel not prevented from

---

[153] *Ibid.*
[154] *Ibid.*, para. 189.
[155] *Ibid.*, para. 190.
[156] *Ibid.*
[157] *Ibid.*
[158] *Ibid.*, para. 191.

having his objection recorded, but he engaged in an extensive discussion with the Presiding Judge, who invited counsel to address any possible concerns he may have during the re-examination of the witness.[159] Lukić does not claim that he was subsequently prevented from effectively re-examining the witnesses in question. In the second instance, Lukić's co-counsel attempted to intervene during the cross-examination of Danica Marinković by the Prosecution. The Presiding Judge instructed him to refrain from doing so and to pursue any clarification he deemed necessary during the re-examination of the witness.[160]

Thus, having considered Judge Bonomy's remarks in their proper context, the Appeals Chamber found that Lukić had failed to demonstrate that they would lead a reasonable and well-informed observer to apprehend bias.[161]

During the direct examination of Ljubivoje Joksić, Lukić asserted that the Presiding Judge made a statement "essentially curtailing consultations" between Lukić and his counsel, and constituting "a disparaging remark about both during a critical point of the proceedings".[162] In response, the Prosecution submitted that the Presiding Judge correctly instructed that only one person speak at a time, and that the impugned remark does not show any improper restriction upon communication between Lukić and his counsel.[163]

The impugned remark reads as follows: "I'd prefer just to hear from the puppet rather than the puppet master as well. One person at a time will be sufficient for our purposes".[164] When the court session resumed, the Presiding Judge made the following clarification:

> In reviewing the transcript [...] I was reminded of a hurried intervention when accused and counsel appeared to be speaking loudly at the same time when I made reference to puppetry. [I]t concerned me when I re-read it that it could be regarded as a general comment and not confined to that particular occasion, so [for the] avoidance of any doubt whatsoever, I want to say one thing. I hope, indeed I think, that counsel know that I

---

[159] *Ibid.*, para. 192.
[160] *Ibid.*
[161] *Ibid.*
[162] *Ibid.*, para. 193.
[163] *Ibid.*
[164] *Ibid.*, para. 194.

> appreciate the responsible way in which the proceedings have been handled in general by counsel and that the comment was one made in the heat of the moment.[165]

It is clear from the record that the impugned remark addressed a particular situation where the accused and his counsel were speaking loudly at the same time.[166] The Appeals Chamber considered that the impugned remark reflected the immediate reaction of Judge Bonomy to an unsatisfactory instance during the trial.[167] As illustrated above, shortly after making the impugned remark, Judge Bonomy clarified his statement to ensure that the parties fully understood that it was an immediate reaction to a specific incident and was not to be interpreted as a general comment regarding counsel's handling of the proceedings.[168] In these circumstances, the Appeals Chamber found that a reasonable and well-informed observer could not apprehend any bias in Judge Bonomy's statement.[169]

In the hearing of 4 March 2008, Lukić asserted that the Presiding Judge "attempt[ed] to prevent a record as to the serious complaints raised about the rush of the trial" expressed in Lukić's motion objecting to the trial sitting schedule.[170] In response, the Prosecution submitted that the Presiding Judge merely sought clarification as to whether Lukić intended to withdraw a comment according to which he alleged that the Trial Chamber viewed the trial as a formality and had already assumed Lukić's guilt. The Appeals Chamber considered that the Presiding Judge's impugned statement must be considered in its procedural context. The trial record shows that, on 11 February 2008, Lukić submitted a motion objecting to the trial sitting schedule and seeking an amendment thereof.[171] He stated, *inter alia*: "Surely, the Trial Proceedings themselves are of more substantive value than simply being a mere legal formality to be endured before a judgement is rendered (particularly in light of the requirement of the presumption of innocence)".[172] The Trial Chamber found Lukić's submission to be "unfounded and impertinent" in suggesting that the Trial Chamber disregarded

---

[165] *Ibid.*, citing Ljubivoje Joksić, 8 February 2008, T. 21925.

[166] *Ibid.*, para. 195.

[167] *Ibid.*

[168] *Ibid.*

[169] *Ibid.*

[170] *Ibid.*, para. 196.

[171] *Ibid.*, para. 197.

[172] *Ibid.*

the presumption of innocence.[173] It considered that, pursuant to Rule 46(A) of the Rules, Lukić's assertion could constitute conduct that is offensive and invited him to withdraw the relevant part of the motion. Lukić neither complied with nor sought leave to appeal the decision of the Trial Chamber. The matter was raised again by the Presiding Judge during the hearing of 4 March 2008, when he made the following impugned statement:

> [I]n that decision on the 20th of February we drew attention to a remark that had been made in the motion itself, which depending perhaps on how you interpret it, others might say perhaps not, might have constituted a comment that wasn't exactly appropriate. And we did indicate that you ought to consider whether that comment should be withdrawn or remain. Now, there's been no response from you to that. Do we take it from that that you have made a deliberate decision to take no action?[174]

In response to the Presiding Judge's impugned remark, Lukić clarified that the submission in question "was not meant as a criticism [...] or [...] as an accusation", and refused to proceed with its withdrawal. No further action was undertaken by the Trial Chamber in this regard.

When considered in its proper context, it is clear that Judge Bonomy's impugned statement at the hearing of 4 March 2008 was aimed at clarifying Lukić's position as to whether he intended to withdraw the submission in question. Rather than preventing Lukić from raising his concerns with respect to the pace of the trial, the trial record clearly shows that the true intention of the Presiding Judge was to elucidate Lukić's position on the matter. In these circumstances, the Appeals Chamber was not convinced that a reasonable and well-informed observer would apprehend any bias as a result of Judge Bonomy's statement.[175] Lukić's argument was dismissed.[176]

In Closing Arguments, Lukić asserted that Judge Bonomy rejected without consideration "the glaring misstatements/misrepresentations of evidence" in the Prosecution's Closing Brief, which he claimed were validly brought to the attention of the Trial Chamber.[177] In response, the Prosecu-

---

[173] *Ibid.*

[174] *Ibid.*

[175] *Ibid.*, para. 198.

[176] *Ibid.*

[177] *Ibid.*, para. 199.

tion submitted that the Presiding Judge's reaction to the allegation of dishonesty made by Lukić's co-counsel against the Prosecution during his Closing Arguments was appropriate, in that inaccuracies in the Prosecution's Closing Brief were not a sufficient basis for an accusation that the Prosecution purposefully sought to mislead the Trial Chamber.[178]

The impugned statement reads:

> Mr. Ivetic, I'm not prepared to sit back any longer and listen to allegations of lack of candour when there have been many instances in this trial when the *Lukic* briefs have been less than accurate without the allegation being made against you of lack of candour. Do you consider that what you're doing is an appropriate way to be addressing us in regard to matters which do not simply on the face of your assertion justify that claim?[179]

It is evident from the transcript that Judge Bonomy's remark was made in response to the following statement of Lukić's co-counsel:

> You cannot believe a word of what is contained in the [Prosecution's] brief because they make a mockery of candour and honesty in their citations.[180]

Lukić's co-counsel later recognized that "perhaps candour is a strong word", but maintained that the Trial Chamber should carefully examine the evidence cited by the Prosecution.[181] The Presiding Judge responded as follows:

> [Y]our actual remarks were that the Prosecution submissions make a mockery of candour and honesty, and that's just one of a series of remarks that bear the interpretation that there is a deliberate attempt on the part of the Prosecution to mislead the Bench. Now, we recognise the highly charged atmosphere which surrounds this stage in the proceedings; nevertheless, we regret that you have not had the courtesy to recognise that the language you've just used is not appropriate language for counsel appearing in any Tribunal. At this late stage in the proceedings, we choose to simply record that we do not accept

---

178 *Ibid.*

179 *Ibid.*, para. 200.

180 *Ibid.*

181 *Ibid.*

that there is a basis for claiming that the Prosecution deliberately set out to mislead the Bench.[182]

Considering Judge Bonomy's remark in its context, the Appeals Chamber did not find that a reasonable and well-informed observer would have apprehended bias on his part. The Presiding Judge did not suggest in any way that the evidence cited by the Prosecution would not be subject to scrutiny. Rather, he reproached Lukić's co-counsel for using inappropriate language, the legitimacy of which seems to have been recognized by the counsel himself. The Appeals Chamber, therefore, dismissed Lukić's argument.[183]

10.4. Conclusion

So, what is the worth of all this.

You can see with the judicial examples in *Lukić* that, in reality, this was a string of either false allegations or at best misperceptions framed as allegations and designed to draw attention away from the fact that the accused had a poor defence to the facts of the case. But still, the Judge had to be beyond any reproach whatsoever in order both to defend himself and ensure the trial was truly fair.

In *Krstić,* the Prosecution took a very robust approach at trial to defence lawyers, who I recall were honourable men largely inexperienced in adversarial trials before international courts. Where the Appeals Chamber found that prosecutorial conduct in the trial fell short, it generated needless criticism in what was otherwise an extremely well prosecuted and led case with absolutely overwhelming evidence.

Appropriate standards of professional and judicial conduct in international proceedings have had little attention by academics and commentators. One man who has taken a hard look at it, and written and spoken about it extensively, is Sir Geoffrey Nice QC, Senior and Principal Prosecuting Counsel at the ICTY and lead prosecutor on the *Slobodan Milošević* case, he was confronted with a number of challenges to his integrity, decency and sense of fairness while at the ICTY – in profoundly important cases. He never shrunk from those clashes nor waivered in doing what was right. He often found himself painfully isolated from colleagues in taking the

---

[182] *Ibid.*
[183] *Ibid.*, para. 201.

right course. And that is very hard. In his book, *Justice for All and How to Achieve It*, he wrote this about his time at the ICTY:

> The way in which any country's lawyers work can determine the fairness of a trial quite as much as the law itself does. The UK legal system historically depended for its integrity substantially on the independence of its barrister advocates – usually genuinely and completely independent practitioners – who earned fees on a case-by case basis and whose only saleable asset were their reputations. They knew that one obvious professional blunder or a breach of ethical standards could be terminal for reputation and career. Whatever their internal inclinations they were normally pushed by powerful vectors to behave honestly, honourably, openly and incompliance with professional standards. They had too much to lose if they didn't.[184]

Before coming to the ICTY in 1999, Geoffrey Nice had spent nearly thirty years as an independent practitioner at the English bar. His reputation came before him, and decency and fairness, for the reasons in the quoted passage above, were in his bones. I know because, as a young lawyer, I went to him for advice. The passage from his book succinctly demonstrates, that in the end, whatever the law says, decency depends on the strength and chosen direction of individuals. Most of us instinctively know what decency requires of us before the courts. There can be instances, certainly, where it is not clear regarding the right thing to do, but I would submit that these instances are rare indeed and that by and large, if there is uncertainty – say, for example, in whether to disclose material to the defence or not – it is always preferable to disclose unless there are compelling reasons not to disclose that material. And, then, the court should be consulted.

I would add here, too, that it is a lot easier on yourself to be straightforward and honest in a case because then you do not have to constantly keep reminding yourself of what you have most recently said or written. Your relations with the other parties and the judges are based on the trust and confidence that you are speaking candidly about the case, the evidence and the law. You are under much less strain, and you live longer.

In international criminal trials, there has been an historic risk that the nature of the cases and the terrible crimes required relentless and hard-

---

[184] Geoffrey Nice, *Justice for All and How to Achieve It*, Scala Arts & Heritage, London, 2017, p. 301.

nosed prosecutions. The success or failure in these cases is world news. Trials have been long, often years. The evidential base is usually huge. High-level defendants generally have not been proximate to the crimes themselves. This required reliance on complex legal theories of culpability such as joint criminal enterprise or common purpose. Evidence linking high-level defendants to the crimes on the ground is difficult to find and to adduce before the courts. So, these cases remain very demanding on all the counsel and judges involved. The stakes have always been very high.

With all this, my single observation over twenty years is prosecuting counsel go one of two ways. Some find reasons for the ends to justify the means and in the process detach themselves, either fully or partly, from what is right and decent. Other prosecutors in these charged cases, like Geoffrey Nice, worked twice as hard to ensure defendants benefited from every fundamental trial right even in the face of mass murder. Giving the Devil the benefit of the law takes great strength and courage, but it is the only way to ensure that such international trials survive the legal process and the scrutiny of history.

> William Roper: "So, now you give the Devil the benefit of law!"
>
> Sir Thomas More: "Yes! What would you do? Cut a great road through the law to get after the Devil?"
>
> William Roper: "Yes, I'd cut down every law in England to do that!"
>
> Sir Thomas More: "Oh? And when the last law was down, and the Devil turned 'round on you, where would you hide, Roper, the laws all being flat? This country is planted thick with laws, from coast to coast, Man's laws, not God's! And if you cut them down, and you're just the man to do it, do you really think you could stand upright in the winds that would blow then? Yes, I'd give the Devil benefit of law, for my own safety's sake!"[185]

---

[185] Robert Bolt, *A Man for All Seasons*, 1954.

11

Only the Best Should Prosecute and Judge in International Justice

Julija Bogoeva[*]

> I would like to leave behind me the conviction that if we maintain a certain amount of caution and organization we deserve victory [but] You cannot carry out fundamental change without a certain amount of madness. In this case, it comes from nonconformity, the courage to turn your back on the old formulas, the courage to invent the future. It took the madmen of yesterday for us to be able to act with extreme clarity today. I want to be one of those madmen. [...] We must dare to invent the future.[1]

11.1. Introduction

When the explosion of nationalism destroyed Yugoslavia primarily because Serbian chauvinists and their leader Slobodan Milošević wanted to make Serbia Great again, a prominent colleague journalist in Belgrade said to me: "these are hard times". In the Serbo-Croatian language, the word is the same for hard and heavy, so hard and heavy times. I think of this often because these are also hard and heavy times in, to quote one of the last presidents of Yugoslavia, "a strange and dangerous world".[2]

The world has always been strange (and fascinating and beautiful, if I may add), but it has never been more dangerous, or in greater peril, be-

---

[*] **Julija Bogoeva** holds a law degree from the University of Belgrade. As a journalist she reported from the ICTY the first four years. For thirteen years, she was a researcher at the ICTY Office of the Prosecutor. She is the co-editor of the book *Srebrenica – Ein Prozess*, and author of the analysis "The War in Yugoslavia in ICTY Judgements".

[1] Thomas Sankara, a man of integrity, President of Burkina Faso 1983-1987 (assassinated), in a 1985 interview with Swiss journalist Jean-Philippe Rapp: "Interview de Jean Philippe Rapp réalisé en 1985: 'Oser inventer l'avenir'" (available on the Thomas Sankara's web site).

[2] Janez Drnovšek, "Interview with the President of the Republic for radio Štajerski val", President of the Republic of Slovenia, 17 January 2007 (available on the President's archived web site).

cause of the real threat of nuclear war,[3] the existence of nuclear and other weapons of mass destruction, and because of the effects of human accelerated global warming.

This chapter is a personal reflection on the significance of integrity, with a focus on the International Criminal Tribunal for the former Yugoslavia ('ICTY') and the International Criminal Court ('ICC').

11.2. The Context: These Are Not Times of Integrity

At the outset, I would like to mention some elements more directly relevant to the very important topic here in the contemporary context.

These are *not* times of integrity in any meaning of the term, nor times of justice, equality, fraternity, and human dignity:

- The world population has never been more depressed, according to the latest research;[4] and no wonder.

- Finance and competition are religion, and money is God; market-based societies have led to repugnant forms of inequality being normalized,[5] while "a fundamental truth – that peace rests on social jus-

---

[3] UN Secretary-General António Guterres, "Remarks to the Conference on Disarmament", 25 February 2019, stating that "I will be blunt. Key components of the international arms control architecture are collapsing."; John Mecklin, "A new abnormal: It is *still* 2 minutes to midnight – 2019 Doomsday Clock Statement", *Bulletin of the Atomic Scientists*, 24 January 2019 (available on its web site); Scott Ritter, "One Minute to Midnight", *Truthdig*, 12 February 2019 (available on its web site), which states that "I disagree, however, with his use of the word 'slightly' to describe the situation we face, and I dissent from the bulletin's decision to stay the hands of the Doomsday Clock. Humanity is sleepwalking toward global annihilation, furthered by a collective amnesia about the threat posed by nuclear weapons, especially in an environment void of meaningful arms control [...] The world is on the edge of the nuclear abyss. It's one minute before midnight and we are acting as if we have time. We don't".

[4] Julie Ray, "World Took a Negative Turn in 2017", *Gallup*, 12 September 2018 (available on its web site); The Edelman Trust Barometer published global research in late 2017 showing that on average 53% of people worldwide felt the system they lived in was failing. Respondents expressed a "sense of injustice", "lack of hope", "lack of confidence" and "desire for change". In countries like France, Germany, Italy, US, Spain, the UK and the Netherlands, between 56% and 72% of the population described a meltdown of their trust in democratic society, see "2017 Edelman Trust Barometer", *Edelman*, 21 January 2017 (available on its web site).

[5] See Boaventura de Sousa Santos, *The End of the Cognitive Empire*, Duke University Press, Durham and London, 2018, Preface: Peter Phillips (author of *Giants: The Global Power Elite*, Seven Stories Press, New York, 2018) examines the roles and networks of the world's richest and most powerful in interview with *The Real News*, see "The Global Power Elite: A

Transnational Class", *The Real News Network*, 26 December 2018 (available on its web site). In the interview, Phillips said:

In that sixty, seventy year period now, we've seen a globalization of power and wealth in the world so that capital is concentrated in very, very few hands, the hands of what I call the giants, these are the transnational investment companies. Seventeen of them have over a trillion dollars in assets collectively, seventeen controlled forty-one trillion dollars in 2017. They represent and are the investment, literally the investment banks and investment advisers, for the two thousand plus billionaires and the thirty-six million millionaires in the world who put their money into investment capital where they want to get a return, annual return. And that's been concentrated, the wealth has concentrated even greater now, it's like eight people have control over half the wealth in the world. But what it boils down to is eighty percent of the people in the world live on less than ten dollars a day, half of the people in the world live on less than three dollars a day, and about a quarter live on less than two. So there's massive inequality. 30,000 people a day die from starvation and malnutrition, so there's this ongoing massacre of people. When there's more than enough food in the world, a third of it's thrown away because it's just not profitable to sell it. So this whole system is pretty much non-humanitarian, based upon gaining profit and capital concentration, and of those seventeen giant investment firms, there's only 199 people that manage those firms. So they're deciding how wealth will be invested, fifty trillion dollars worth now, and making those kinds of decisions. And their biggest problem is they've got more capital than they've got safe places to put it in.

Henry Girouw, "Resisting the Weaponization of Ignorance in the Age of Trump", *Truthout*, 12 February 2019 (available on its web site), where he wrote:

A morbid inequality now shapes all aspects of life in the United States. Three men – Jeff Bezos, Warren Buffett and Bill Gates – have among them as much wealth as the bottom half of U.S. society. In a society of pervasive ignorance, such wealth is viewed as the outcome of the actions and successes of the individual actors. But in a society in which civic literacy and reason rule, such wealth would be considered characteristic of an economy appropriately named casino capitalism. In a society in which 80 percent of U.S. workers live paycheck to paycheck, and 20 percent of all children live below the poverty line, such inequalities in wealth and power constitute forms of domestic terrorism – that is, state-initiated violence or terrorism practiced in one's own country against one's own people...We live in dangerous times and there is an urgent need for more individuals, institutions and social movements to come together in an effort to construct a new political and social imaginary. We must support each other in coming to believe that the current regimes of tyranny can be resisted, that alternative futures are possible and that acting on these beliefs will make radical change happen.

Richard Wolff, "Economic Update: Is U.S. Capitalism In Decline?", *The Real News Network*, 9 July 2019 (available on its web site), where he stated that "[i]n 2018 the average pay of an American CEO was – 238,000 dollars a week, the average pay of an American worker was – 752 dollars a week". Moreover, according to research of Jörg Wiegratz, Lecturer in Political Economy of Global Development at University of Leeds,

we are currently living in the age of fraud. Fraud has become mainstream; it is at high levels, institutionalized, at the core of "the system" and part and parcel of the (re)production of contemporary society. That applies to many societies, not just in the often discussed Global South but also in the Global North.

tice has been ushered out of our sight and consciousness", noted an author on the digital publication platform Social Europe.

- The principle of legality, democratic institutions and the rule of law are being undermined or openly abandoned.

- Trust between States, in national institutions and a rule-based order is at a breaking point, as stated by the United Nations Secretary-General ('UNSG').[6] Research tells us that trust in justice and the courts is low and that, in many countries of the global south and north, the military and the police are trusted more.[7] It also confirms that "[d]istrust in domestic judiciaries tends to go together with distrust in the international judiciary".[8]

Humanity seems to have lost moral compass:

- States are becoming more and more secretive, effectively ensuring impunity for the ruling class, including for core international crimes, while expanding their surveillance powers over everything and everyone.[9]

- Whole countries are being destroyed on false pretences in criminal wars with new levels of barbarity and violations of international hu-

---

The seven key characteristics of contemporary fraud in the global economy include: (i) fraud is at an industrial scale; (ii) it has become significantly routine; (iii) it is ever more blatant; (iv) it is spreading across the economy and society, that is, it is affecting new areas, such as education; (v) it produces staggering levels of social harm; (vi) it is co-produced by economic and state actors; and (vii) it implicates the most powerful members of society (the ruling class, transnational companies, top managers, top state officials, the rich and famous, celebrated role models, etc.). See Jörg Wiegratz, "The Age of Fraud: the Link Between Capitalism and Profiteering by Deception", *Counter Punch*, 26 September 2018 (available on its web site).

6   UN Secretary-General António Guterres, "Address to the General Assembly", 25 September 2018.

7   Courtney Johnson, "Trust in the Military Exceeds Trust in Other Institutions in Western Europe and U.S.", Pew Research Center, 4 September 2018 (available on its web site).

8   Erik Voeten, "Public Opinion and the Legitimacy of International Courts", in *Theoretical Inquires in Law*, 2013, vol. 14, no. 2, p. 425. It is notable that in Gallup's 2005 "Voice of the People" survey, the single broad comparative survey the author found that asked about the ICC, those with negative sentiments outnumbered those who were positive only in Austria, Croatia, Israel, Serbia and the United States.

9   William Binney, "Random Slaughter: 'The NSA Tracks Them and the CIA Whacks Them'", *Information Clearing House*, 8 August 2018 (available on its web site)

---

manitarian law, which have caused hundreds of thousands of deaths, based on conservative estimates.[10]

- Technology is posited as the definitive panacea for human problems, while technologies over which man no longer has control are being used for military purposes in an already overly militarized world.[11]

The question then is whether there is at all a place for international (criminal) justice in these hard and heavy times, these times of uncertainty? Is the entire project reversible? *Can* there be integrity in international (criminal) justice, just a piece of a whole, if the whole is so lacking of it? My answer to these three questions is *yes*, but the focus here is on integrity, which is essential, like never before.

11.2.1.1. Integrity Is Necessary More Than Ever

Delivering justice is synonymous with integrity in the common imagination. The sequence, in my view, is this: legality – legitimacy – integrity – independence – justice – credibility. If that order is correct, integrity is central to independence, to the delivery of justice, and to the credibility of international (criminal) justice. That means that only the best, only persons of integrity, should have a place at the helm in international (criminal) justice.

Integrity, in my understanding, is an all-encompassing human quality; it is indivisible, a way of being, a way of living. It means straightforward honesty, clear ethics, transparency of motives and behaviour. It includes moral, intellectual and professional integrity. It is the full consciousness of the meaning and importance of the mandate, of judicial responsibility as the ultimate protector of human dignity, and of one's role and duties in achieving the assigned purpose.

---

[10] Nicolas J.S. Davies, "How Many Millions of People Have Been Killed in America's Post-9/11 Wars? – Part One: Iraq", *Consortium News*, 22 March 2018 (available on its web site); Nicolas J.S. Davies, "How Many People Has the U.S. Killed in its Post-9/11 Wars? Part 2: Afghanistan and Pakistan", *Consortium News*, 3 April 2018 (available on its web site); Nicolas J.S. Davies, "How Many Millions Have Been Killed in America's Post-9/11 Wars? Part 3: Libya, Syria, Somalia and Yemen", *Consortium News*, 25 April 2018 (available on its web site); UN Assistance Mission in Afghanistan, "Civilian Deaths From Afghan Conflict in 2018 at Highest Recorded Level – UN Report", February 2019.

[11] "Addicted To Technology – Most People Don't Even Realize What's Coming", *Information Clearing House*, 10 August 2018 (available on its web site); António Guterres, "Remarks to the Conference on Disarmament", see above note 3. That technology is not the solution to man's troubles and tribulations was argued, for instance, decades ago by Erich Fromm, and today persuasively by James Bridle, *New Dark Age: Technology and the End of the Future*, Verso Books, London, 2018.

Individuals with integrity have a genuine, unwavering commitment to only one purpose – the fair and impartial administration of justice. There is no separate interest that they hope to achieve through their function. They are content with the benefits that come with their role. They are not driven by vanity or ambition to secure a place in history, to be seen as important or in the company of those deemed important, and certainly not by mere power and any material gain. "Court decisions help to create the basic value system of society and establish the character of our constitutional democracy. And every detail matters. [...] The objective is not to please or displease anyone, but to converse with as much rigour, integrity and awareness of our constitutional responsibilities as possible, with as wide an audience as can be imagined", wrote former Justice of the Constitutional Court of South Africa, Albie Sachs.[12] His words have a universal meaning applicable to international (criminal) justice.

Integrity implies a well-integrated, mature personality, a free individual. It usually goes in tandem with an open mind, a passion for knowledge and the broader meaning and potential of the law, as well as firm respect for the dignity of every human being. As expressed by a US federal judge, reminding of Aristotle's teaching that judges should be the very personification of justice:

> To me, the essential attribute of judicial integrity is a *passion* for justice informed by a deep and abiding morality, a *compassion* that propels the judge to a just conclusion even when the party or the issue before the bar is unpopular. I speak of those occasions when, as Justice Black so eloquently said, the 'courts stand against any winds that blow as havens of refuge for those who might otherwise suffer because they are helpless, weak, outnumbered, or because they are nonconforming victims of prejudice and public excitement'. When a judge has the courage of his convictions, a willingness to do *what his understanding of the law tells him is right,* (not the result that reading of the latest polls tells him will be the most popular), he can in my view properly be called a judge of integrity. [...] As a society, [we] must measure the worth, and the integrity, of the judiciary not by the extent to which its judgments are popular or accepted by some ephemeral majority, however defined, but rather by the extent to which the judgments of the

---

[12] Albie Sachs, *The Strange Alchemy of Life and Law*, Oxford University Press, 2009, pp. 148–149.

courts spare us from the disorders that otherwise inevitably result from injustice.[13]

A person possessing integrity has the will to be one's best and not to
falter. Such a person enables and contributes to institutional integrity by a
genuine interest in every aspect of the work process and the people involved. In practical terms, that should lead to timely improvement of internal processes and procedures, and importantly, to optimal tasking: match-
ing the right person with each assignment so that the highest quality is efficiently achieved in every phase and aspect of establishing the truth and doing justice.

Individuals of integrity recognize, and repel, attempts at the abuse of
their role and the court's functions, as well as all forms of corruption. In all
situations and relations, they act competently, honourably, and with respect,
upholding the dignity of the court. This may invite anger and frustration,
especially of the powerful, or hierarchically superior, but it can also generate respect and even admiration for the independence of the court and its
officers.

11.3. The Best Are Needed

In my view, judging fellow humans for criminal conduct is *the most unique
human activity*, and that in itself imposes the highest requirements of integrity. It is a formidable task to entrust a person with restoring the human
dignity of a victim of violent crime through a credible humanly-constructed
judicial proceeding that satisfies the victim's intense desire for justice, for
truth, for solidarity, a universal desire inherent to man. By renewing and
reaffirming the humanity of the victim and acknowledging the humanity of
the perpetrator through finding the truth and locating the responsibility,
through establishing the crime and deciding the punishment, the sanity and
humanity of the community and society disrupted by the criminal breach
are restored. One cannot but always ask anew – is it truly possible that human beings, in all their frailty, are capable of, and can actually perform
such a task. Yet they are, and they do. But in order to serve justice and deliver justice, they need to have, *sine qua non*, the high human qualities.
Otherwise, an apprehension would prevail: how can those who themselves
lack the conscience, the quality, the gravitas of integrity sit in judgment for

---

[13] Frank M. Johnson Jr., "Civilization Integrity, and Justice: Some Observations on the Function of the Judiciary in Honor of Judge Irving L. Goldberg", in *SMU Law Review*, 1989, vol.
43, pp. 650–651, 655.

the truth, the restoration of individual dignity and the reparation of the integrity of community and society.

In international (criminal) justice, people of integrity, the very best, are needed for attaining the highest standards of law, the best law,[14] the highest standards of uncovering the truth and of justice. They are needed because of the exceptional nature of the crimes, because of the extraordinary complexity and hostilities of the international environment in which they operate, and because it is only right that the best should judge the worst excesses of humanity, demonstrating fairness and advantages of justice over revenge.

Integrity entails incorruptibility, a particularly important element, which protects against instrumentalization; against the outside influence and internal pressures. It means speaking up and speaking out whenever that is called for without fear or calculation.

A 2018 Oxford University multi-disciplinary review of the definition of integrity in academic literature,[15] 40 journals across seven disciplines, including law, as well as books, found that virtue and ethical framework appears most productive for the grounding and understanding of the normative elements of integrity. It also stated that public integrity should be seen as a rational basis for trust; that it is explicitly concerned with the coherence of purposes, and the consistency of action with those stated purposes; that it is focused on the cultivation of ethical culture, not simply on rule compliance, and that it is not merely the absence of corruption.

The study shows that individual-centred conceptions of integrity are prevalent, but that there is also a growth in the academic literature on the integrity of institutions. The linking of integrity directly to institutions is considered a promising development, citing views that an institution will have integrity if it adheres to its publicly declared values, and that integrity

---

[14] Philip Allott opines that "lawyers have a duty to try to make the law as good as it can be. Nowhere is this more necessary than in international society [...] We must give to international law the true status and function of *law* in a society of all human beings and all human societies – an international society in which other human societies, including state-societies, play their part in serving the common human interest, that is to say, the survival and flourishing of all human beings". See Philip Allott, "How to Make a Better World: Human Power and Human Weakness", FICHL Policy Brief Series No. 75 (2016), Torkel Opsahl Academic EPublisher, Brussels, 2016 (https://www.legal-tools.org/doc/a35654).

[15] Thomas Robinson, Lucinda Cadzow and Nikolas Kirby, "Investigating Integrity: A Multi-Disciplinary Literature Review", in *Working Paper*, Blavatnik School of Government, University of Oxford, 2018.

pertains to the "relationship between an institution's performance and the truth".

Particularly important, in my view and experience, is the interest in the literature in "the coherence of individuals and institutions: what their values are and how do they cohere", "*the extent* to which individuals and institutions have remained true to those values – how they endure over time", and on the need for "internal coherence of one's purposes to be met with a consistency of action".

Equally relevant is the focus on 'an ethical climate' of an organization or institution, "the culture and ethical environment that the institution can promote to aid self-regulation and adherence to organizational purpose". These depend, based on my experience, in most part on the integrity of those in leadership positions.

The study observed that the relationship between integrity and corruption is being refined from simple misuse of public office for private gain towards how institutions diverge from their purpose, capturing problematic activity that conventionally would not be considered corrupt. The conception that "integrity is analytically distinct from the absence of negative behaviour, such as corruption or bribery" has, I would say, a particular value in international (criminal) justice where typical forms of corruption and bribery will be avoided. The main insight is that integrity is more than the absence of corruption, that it can mean "that an organization and its members strive to maintain a commitment to the organization's legitimate purpose".

I have had the privilege of seeing integrity at work in the ICTY Office of the Prosecutor – from staff in supporting roles, through investigators, analysts, junior lawyers and at the senior level. From tireless work that improved the technical abilities to conquer mountains of evidence despite unclear or misguided instructions and deadlines, through hard-fought battles for understanding the evidence and choosing the best evidence, to decisions at the most senior level that unfailingly upheld the integrity of the Office.

When I first interviewed former ICTY Prosecutor Louise Arbour,[16] I said to her that many people believe that she does what powerful politicians tell her to do or not do, but before I even finished she exclaimed: "No one tells me what to do". There was no doubt in my mind about that. Whenever I saw her at the Tribunal, I remember thinking: "Louise is here,

---

[16]   Chief ICTY Prosecutor 1996–1999.

we are safe". I believed in her and trusted her judgment. I have equal respect for Carla Del Ponte[17] who fended off all kinds of pressures, both external and internal, and was punished for attempting to pursue the so-called special investigations in Rwanda and other reasons.[18] When Serge Brammertz[19] became the Chief Prosecutor and was meeting the trial teams, the first thing he said to us was: "How can I help you?". The effect of such an attitude on team spirit and confidence in the fulfilment of the Office of the Prosecutor mission is immeasurable.

Thanks to the unmatched inspirational power of example, with people of integrity, the example of international (criminal) justice can do more for strengthening the rule of law and efforts at raising the quality of justice nationally than is imagined and can be measured.

The standards projected by the ICTY were so high that the international criminal trial was respected even by opponents not ideologically blinded or otherwise prejudiced. Professionals and laypeople alike in the former Yugoslavia, for example, were captivated by the solidity of the criminal justice process in The Hague, regardless of criticism and dilemmas arising from the differences between the domestic civil law system and the hybrid law and procedure of the ICTY. That, despite the incessant, vehement anti-ICTY propaganda. The confidence the ICTY process inspired was captured in anecdotes mentioned by Arbour at an event in Amsterdam while she was Chief Prosecutor. A surviving victim in Bosnia had been asked what she would do with the perpetrator. She replied that she would kill him, or better yet, go to "that woman judge in The Hague". The father of a Serbian victim in Kosovo replied to a similar question that he would want to see the perpetrator in the dock in The Hague. A number of the accused preferred the ICTY to domestic jurisdiction. A desire to attain high

---

[17] Carla Del Ponte, Chief ICTY Prosecutor 1999–2007.

[18] John Hooper, "I was sacked as Rwanda genocide prosecutor for challenging president, says Del Ponte", *The Guardian*, 13 September 2003 (available on its web site). Del Ponte's fight for the independence of the Prosecutor is reflected in *WikiLeaks* cables. Her mandate at the ICTY was renewed on 4 September 2003, but her Office was split. A veteran ICTY journalist Marliese Simons wrote in the *New York Times* on 28 July 2003: "With the quiet support of the United States, the Rwandan government has been campaigning to have Carla Del Ponte replaced as chief prosecutor for the tribunal dealing with the mass killing in Rwanda in 1994, Western diplomats and tribunal officials have said in recent days". See Marlise Simons, "Rwanda Is Said to Seek New Prosecutor for War Crimes Court", *New York Times*, 28 July 2003 (available on its web site).

[19] Serge Brammertz, Chief ICTY Prosecutor 2008–2017.

---

standards of administration of justice 'like in The Hague' was often mentioned by committed professionals from the former Yugoslavia in discussions about domestic circumstances and the national criminal justice system. That should come as no surprise. The dream of every true professional is to practice in a highly professional environment of individual and institutional integrity, "in a court of law, because that is where the real law is", as one of my professors used to say.

11.4. Impunity of the Most Powerful Must End

Integrity is also necessary because it is no longer possible to ignore that the most powerful States are responsible for grave international crimes and that their officials may be criminally liable. International criminal justice does not have a future if the most powerful violators enjoy impunity. Bringing the most powerful to justice requires integrity. It is a test of integrity and proof of integrity.

Persons of integrity in leadership positions should be expected to elevate contacts and relations between the international courts and State representatives to a completely different level and quality than that revealed by *WikiLeaks* and other releases; one that maintains integrity and independence of the courts, professionalism, and respectful diplomatic tact, never going beyond the law and what is appropriate. International (criminal) justice is not a matter of favour or favours by the powerful, it is not at their service and should not be presented, understood, practiced or seen as such.

11.4.1. Culture of Untruth and International Criminal Justice

There is, in my view, a fundamental contradiction between the truth, on the one hand, and the prevailing system and culture founded on the slogan of the free market but the *reality* of monopolies, reinforced by the internet and new technologies. The market generates false needs and values relentlessly promoting and utilizing perception as deception. Everything has been commodified, including the human being itself: we sell children, grown-ups, our bodies and body parts. The pressure for speed, a corollary of marketization and digital technology, has created a social vortex that is doing away with memory, history and everything permanent and certain. Truth is defined as relative and laughed away by the growing number of cynics as irrelevant, a remnant of bygone times. Truth equals opinion, is the publicly nurtured formula.

In the high-speed competition that prevails, everything must be instant, and hence is superficial. No time, and no need, for study, for depth, for nuance, for reflection, for listening and understanding. To be first is to be seen and heard. The newly imposed norm of fastness, of immediacy, works against (criminal) justice which, in particular at the international level, is inevitably slow. To follow and understand it require interest, time, study, reflection. Even some legal commentators, caught in the speed trap, publicize their views before a proper review of the subject-matter of their commentary; they act on the first ball. Today's unprofessional media instantly pick up their instant opinions on important issues of international law and international criminal justice. The result is the wide dissemination of misinformation, of opinion as fact, instead of information and clarification. This deeply troubling state of affairs is exemplified by the blitz reactions of legal pundits to the recent ICC Appeals Chamber judgement in the Jordan referral regarding the arrest of Al-Bashir, a decision of fundamental importance for international criminal law.

By all measures, it is an age of untruth.[20] A striking recent illustration came from a high official of a powerful government. On 15 April 2019, the former CIA Chief, now US Secretary of State Mike Pompeo, said at Texas A and M University: "What's the cadet motto at West Point? You will not lie, cheat, or steal, or tolerate those who do. I was the CIA director. We lied, we cheated, we stole. It's – it was like – we had entire training courses. It reminds you of the glory of the American experiment".[21]

International criminal justice is incompatible with the age of untruth. International crimes, by their nature, expose the essence of the prevailing system and culture, their lies and fallacies. At the national level only sometimes and some crimes reach that deep and touch that high, to the summit of power. National trials of such cases can more or less easily be influenced or prevented.

Hallmarks of integrity, such as an open mind, knowledge, intellectual honesty, are essential for grasping and revealing core international crimes in their intricate and intertwined local and global context, but also for confronting the reaction of the power structures that oppose the uncovering

---

[20] One such measure is a list of admitted false flag attacks, most of which are in the last 30 years. See George Washington, "The Ever Growing List of Admitted False Flag Attacks", *Zero Hedge*, 3 July 2017 (available on its web site).

[21] Tyler Durden, "I was the CIA Director, We Lied, We Cheated We Stole", *Information Clearing House*, 22 April 2019 (available on its web site).

and public unwrapping of their role. Steering an international criminal court with integrity in an age of untruth is as hard an endeavour as can be.

The problem is not theoretical. Some States which were vocally advocating for the establishment of the *ad hoc* tribunals are major violators of the laws of war and international law. They have long records of resenting the 'entanglements of the law' if it crosses the interest of their ruling classes. Time and again they have made clear that international (criminal) justice is for 'the other', 'the barbarians', not for them, despite their own role in the conflicts that attracted international criminal jurisdiction. Their position can be summarized in the words of a leading Serbian chauvinist and Milošević collaborator who said: "The crimes of the Serbs are in the realm of God and the crimes of the Croats in the realm of the Devil". The attitude of these States towards the ICC leaves no room for doubt. That includes States which have not openly disavowed the Court, States which nominally support it. In words, not consistently in deeds. Certainly not when they manoeuvre behind the scenes to direct the Court and not only through appointments of the highest officers.

The exact truth of the attempts of control should be established and made public.[22] Interference and obstruction need to stop. They should be condemned and banished from our culture. Judicial organs need to be independent in fact instead of on paper, in noble proclamations and opportunistic speeches.

Not long ago there was a renewed global confirmation "that the independence of the judicial system, together with its impartiality and integrity, is an essential prerequisite for upholding the rule of law and ensuring that there is no discrimination in the administration of justice". It was accompanied by a pledge and a recognition of the role of the ICC:

> We commit to ensuring that impunity is not tolerated for genocide, war crimes and crimes against humanity or for violations of international humanitarian law and gross violations of human rights law, and that such violations are properly investigated and appropriately sanctioned, including by bringing the perpetrators of any crimes to justice, through national

---

[22] See Muhamed Sacirbey, in "A Diplomatic "Hunting Party" – facts never published before by Ms. Hartmann – part 1", *Croatian World Network*, 16 September 2007, section "A Timeline of Evidence" (available on its web site); Christopher B. Mahoney, "The Justice Pivot: US International Law Influence Outside the Rome Statute", in *Georgetown Journal of International Law*, 2015, vol. 46, no. 4.

mechanisms or, where appropriate, regional or international mechanisms, in accordance with international law, and for this purpose we encourage States to strengthen national judicial systems and institutions.

We recognize the role of the International Criminal Court in a multilateral system that aims to end impunity and establish the rule of law [...] and call upon all States that are not yet parties to the Statute to consider ratifying or acceding to it, and emphasize the importance of cooperation with the Court.[23]

11.4.2. Full Protection for Whistle-Blowers

As a guarantee of integrity, international justice jurisdictions need to have procedures in place for whistle-blowers that include their full protection.

Whistle-blowers are "the bad conscience of our democracies", underscored Florence Hartmann in her latest book: "They are police, military, civil servants, executives who stand up against the state or the company that employs them to denounce illegal activities, abuses of power, serious threats to health, public safety or the environment".[24] They can also be judges, as occurred at the ICTY, which had no provisions for whistle-blowers. The judge who cried wolf was shown the door.[25]

The assault on truth and truth-tellers, a constant in history, has in the last two decades become an aggressive, concerted effort of the State apparatus as a tool of moneyed, military, intelligence and instrumentalized mainstream media interests. The obvious aim of this naked attack is to instil fear and keep a permanent lock on, or label as lies, fabrications or subversion, the facts and evidence about unlawful, immoral and outright criminal policies and actions, including core international crimes, of State officials and State proxies. The iron fist of the 'democratic' State has come down brutally on a long line of whistle-blowers culminating in the blatant abuse of the law at every twist of the ongoing persecution of journalist and

---

[23] Declaration of the high-level meeting of the General Assembly on the rule of law at the national and international levels, UN Doc. A/RES/67/1, 30 November 2012 (https://www.legal-tools.org/doc/d0qwyx/).

[24] Florence Hartman, *Lanceurs d'alerte. Les mauvaises consciences de nos démocraties*, Don Quichotte, 2014, p. 12.

[25] "Credibility of ICTY must be restored", Norwegian Helsinki Committee, 7 April 2016 (available on its web site).

co-founder of *WikiLeaks*, Julian Assange. His treatment was characterized as torture by the UN Special Rapporteur on torture Nils Melzer:

> In the course of the past nine years, Mr. Assange has been exposed to persistent, progressively severe abuse ranging from systematic judicial persecution and arbitrary confinement in the Ecuadorian embassy, to his oppressive isolation, harassment and surveillance inside the embassy, and from deliberate collective ridicule, insults and humiliation, to open instigation of violence and even repeated calls for his assassination. [...]
>
> 'The evidence is overwhelming and clear', the expert said. 'Mr. Assange has been deliberately exposed, for a period of several years, to progressively severe forms of cruel, inhuman or degrading treatment or punishment, the cumulative effects of which can only be described as psychological torture.
>
> I condemn, in the strongest terms, the deliberate, concerted and sustained nature of the abuse inflicted on Mr. Assange and seriously deplore the consistent failure of all involved governments to take measures for the protection of his most fundamental human rights and dignity,' the expert said. 'By displaying an attitude of complacency at best, and of complicity at worst, these governments have created an atmosphere of impunity encouraging Mr. Assange's uninhibited vilification and abuse.
>
> In 20 years of work with victims of war, violence and political persecution I have never seen a group of democratic States ganging up to deliberately isolate, demonise and abuse a single individual for such a long time and with so little regard for human dignity and the rule of law,' Melzer said. "The collective persecution of Julian Assange must end here and now!"[26]

The States Melzer refers to are, with one exception, States Parties to the Rome Statute and strong nominal supporters of the ICC. The irony and the duplicity are laid bare before the world.

Melzer also delivered a warning:

> [...] you may say, why spend so much breath on Assange, when countless others are tortured worldwide? Because this is

---

[26] "UN expert says 'collective persecution' of Julian Assange must end now", media release, 31 May 2019 (available on the UN Office of the High Commissioner for Human Rights's web site).

> not only about protecting Assange, but about preventing a precedent likely to seal the fate of Western democracy. For once telling the truth has become a crime, while the powerful enjoy impunity, it will be too late to correct the course. We will have surrendered our voice to censorship and our fate to unrestrained tyranny.[27]

It is worth recalling here the message of the German philosopher Karl Jaspers that peace is only possible through freedom, and freedom, in turn, through truth. Hence, untruth is the actual evil, annihilating all peace: untruth, from the untruthfulness of the individual to the untruthfulness of public affairs.

Of interest from the perspective of integrity in the current circumstances is that the legal profession has largely remained silent in the face of such crude, long-lasting, open and public trampling of a human being and the law. Moreover, a whole line of prosecutors and judges, acting as the face of the law and justice, are enablers of the criminal attack on Assange for publishing the truth, including about war crimes committed by forces of the most powerful States. Together with the corporate mainstream media, it is the legal profession, and in particular certain prosecutors and judges, that will be remembered as protagonists of this history of ignominy.

Judge Sérgio Fernando Moro, elevated to the Minister of Justice in Brazil, whose vigorous abuse of high legal office and the law was caught on tape and made public, is an exemplary antipode to integrity. The journalist who published the leaked evidence is being harassed by the Brazilian government and publicly threatened by the Head of State.

These, and other powerful negative examples, the corrosive pathology of hiding the truth at all costs and of propagandizing entire populations with lies presented as truth, has a direct bearing on international criminal justice: on its ability to perform its important truth-finding role, on the moral, intellectual and professional fortitude of its officers and staff, and on the preparedness and willingness of the public to trust in the integrity of international investigators, prosecutors and judges, and to have faith in the institutional integrity of international courts.

Under such circumstances, these courts are pressed between cynicism, malevolence and elevated scrutiny that requires of them to make not

---

[27] Nils Melzer, "Demasking the Torture of Julian Assange", *Medium*, 26 June 2019 (available on its web site).

a single mistake that may appear as a departure from the law and 'high moral character', from both individual and institutional integrity. To ensure the adherence to the highest standards of justice when relevant internal procedures are not, or cannot be set in motion, or prove to be ineffective, international courts need to provide full protection for whistle-blowers. Common sense and experience teach that it is best, or least harmful, to expose wrongdoing and malfeasance sooner than later, so that problems are solved instead of stored as family secrets which always have toxic effects and ultimately never remain in the family.

11.5. Without Integrity, International Justice Is a House of Cards

There is a simple fact that may be overlooked: every person working in international (criminal) justice forms an impression of the process and shares it with numbers of people who then pass that on to others. Each person working in international (criminal) justice is viewed with particular attention by everyone because the mandate is atypical, with expectations and suspicions attached. Hence, the words and deeds of *everyone* in international (criminal) justice determine the trust in its integrity.

Every lapse in integrity, however 'trivial' it may seem, has consequences that are not always obvious or predictable.[28] Each one causes disappointment and confusion: internally, it disrupts teamwork because it ruptures mutual trust, reliance and respect, and the compactness needed in the substantial team effort that international (criminal) justice requires. Lack of integrity at the highest levels leads to anxiety and a drop in mission confidence that infects the working atmosphere; externally, it affects any enthusiasm and support for international justice that there may be. Actions that compromise integrity hand control over the international justice project to

---

[28] Take as an example investigators getting drunk while on mission, or, intoxictated or not, boasting or denigrating the local officials and populace, or an investigator telling his colleagues that the international court they all work in is a 'kangaroo court' unlike his national jurisdiction. Even small lapses not related to integrity, like an unacknowledged courtesy, affect the way the courts, their officials and staff are viewed. I recall vividly the surprise and disappointment, expressed more in body language than words, of two prominent Belgrade defense attorneys of great integrity when they received not a word from the ICTY President for sending him books on Yugoslav law that he needed. The attorneys, one of whom was a former Supreme Military Court judge, had promptly answered my request to aid the ICTY President. In memory of that former Supreme Military Court judge, I want to record that early on in the Yugoslav crisis, he publicly proposed, with passionate argument, the formation of a Yugoslav war crimes court comprising the best Yugoslav judges from all the republics. Unfortunately, it was too late.

witnesses or beneficiaries of those compromising actions. That in itself is a reason to insist on the integrity of the highest officers in international (criminal) justice, but also of all involved.

In the States where the crimes were committed, the sceptics and opponents, including officials and public personalities involved in the crimes, usually believe, or preach, that international courts and their officials are corrupt, based on domestic practice and *Realpolitik*. Being corrupt themselves, they are usually acutely attuned to the hypocrisy and wheeling and dealing of politics and international relations, as they are subjected to them. They have only contempt for the powerful and their proclaimed righteousness. Their philosophy appears to be: we may be no good, but everyone else is worse. The possibility of the integrity of international (criminal) justice terrifies them the most. Any semblance, or potential evidence, of lack of integrity is used by such actors as definitive proof that international justice is a sham, as they claim all along. This must never be allowed to happen.

For individuals, groups and organizations in crime zones who believe in accountability and international (criminal) justice, who actually have a desperate need to trust international courts, and who take risks by supporting them, there is no worse setback than accusations and evidence of lack of integrity and independence. That needs to be emphasized – there is no worse setback, with serious consequences for the effectiveness of international criminal justice. Because the focus shifts away from the crimes, their causes and perpetrators, to the alleged or real lack of integrity of the courts, which calls into question the entire process and all its achievements. These advocates of accountability and the truth on the ground, where denial is usually the norm, are forced to defend the ideal of international (criminal) justice from international (criminal) justice as bad practice. How does one do that when there is a wholly mishandled case like, for example, the Šešelj case.

Internationally, the effects are essentially the same: skeptics and opponents are strengthened, and supporters are weakened, which breathes new life into the culture of impunity.

There can be not even a pretence of integrity when international judges are lobbying for re-election in New York, leaving the courtrooms empty for days. Or when they habitually invite young female interns to dinner and are rumoured to have an unsavoury reputation. Or when they exert pressure on fellow judges to ensure a certain kind of judgement. Or when they use a lecture to visiting national judges to insist that 'their own' particular judgement is superior being grounded more in civil law, which they take the time to laud as superior to common law. Or when prosecutors jeopardize a case by rivalries and personal ambitions and openly blame each other. Or when a prosecutor insists on absolute personal loyalty and creates an exclusive circle by surrounding himself with those who comply. Or when a prosecutor not on a case suddenly, at the last moment, requests the withdrawal of a signed indictment that is supported by rock-solid evidence. Such dramatic events affect everyone involved. It is even more damaging when a high profile international prosecutor repeatedly and publicly falsely accuses the chief prosecutor of an alleged deal with a government for concealing crucial evidence, or when judgments are manifestly unjust, being contrary to established facts and the law, but favourable for powerful States and interests.[29] Or when an unpersuasive decision fully aligns with the interests of a threatening superpower.[30]

It must not be forgotten that there is no greater injustice than injustice done by a court of law or its officers. The resulting harm is profound, and it cannot be undone. People will then tell you that they have lost all respect for the judges, the court and the law.

In order to ensure that persons of integrity, the best, are in leading positions in international (criminal) justice, it is essential to devise an optimal system for candidate selection. If all candidates satisfy merit and integrity criteria, and possess professional experience, the actual system of appointment or election is of secondary importance. Until a time when international judges and prosecutors are elected by an independent professional body, their election or appointment will remain politicized. Interests other than the interests of justice may be determinative. It is well known that international positions are used in domestic politics to reward loyalty, return favours or repay debts, to remove those considered undesirable, or to promote friends, family or partners, and, not least, to secure influence, inside information and control. It has become clear over the years that some

---

[29] Julija Bogoeva, "International Judges and Government Interests: The Case of President Meron", FICHL Policy Brief Series No. 48 (2016), Torkel Opsahl Academic EPublisher, Brussels, 2016 (https://www.legal-tools.org/doc/56a576).

[30] ICC, Situation in the Islamic Republic of Afghanistan, Pre-Trial Chamber, Decision Pursuant to Article 15 of the Rome Statute on the Authorisation of an Investigation into the Situation in the Islamic Republic of Afghanistan, 12 April 2019, ICC-02/17-33 (http://www.legal-tools.org/doc/2fb1f4/).

powerful States do not want their nationals at the highest positions in international criminal courts in order to avoid the attendant responsibilities and 'entanglements', but instead try to make use of all other avenues of influence and control.

It seems most purposeful to focus on ensuring that only quality candidates are in the running. They should be put forward at the national level by professional bodies, not governments and politicians. One way would be to establish a pool of candidates for domestic and international war crimes prosecutions at the State level. That would, as a matter of policy, give prominence to accountability for core international crimes, and incentivize and enable interested professionals to aim for qualifying for such a pool. The criteria would be merit and integrity based, transparent, and set by the legal profession. Maximum three members of a national pool at any given time could be included in such a pool at the international level. They would be chosen by a national professional body. Any candidates for the most senior positions in international justice, however, selected from such an international pool, and those finally elected or appointed, would have the necessary qualities, as a minimum guarantee of integrity and effectiveness of international (criminal) justice. But the aim should be higher, that the best in the pool become candidates for the top positions. That would require the will to have the best and to identify the best at every election or appointment of the most senior officers in international justice. The stimulating of this will, so that it takes root and can be fostered, is a primary task in creating a new culture of international justice, peace, human dignity and prosperity for all.

The simple slogan – "If you want peace, have justice" – of the global movement World Beyond War, encapsulates this new culture that, in fact, is being created by people of integrity around the globe. In cultivating the will to have only the best prosecute and judge in international justice, legal professionals of integrity will by no means be alone.

11.6. Conclusion

Due to lack of integrity and professional excellence of some of its (highest) officers, and apparent attempts to please the mighty and powerful, or in fear of their wrath, the still nascent international (criminal) justice project has faltered and has been endangered. Instead, by displaying individual and institutional integrity, organs of international (criminal) justice could prevail on the still sceptical and reluctant (States and the general public) that they are capable of impartially, fairly and independently fulfilling their task; that there will be no subservience, double standards and hypocrisy in the administration of international justice.

By earning respect based on integrity, international (criminal) justice could secure its non-dependence on the big powers of the day, enjoy wide confidence, and rest on genuine majority support. There is more than enough evidence that 'adjusting' to the wishes and whims of the powerful means serving the interests of the military-corporate-media complex, the war machine, which is vitally interconnected with the political class it has subordinated to its goals of profit and domination.[31] Serving such interests is directly opposite to the principle of legality, to morality, the notion of justice and the purpose of international (criminal) justice. It effectively renders the practice of international (criminal) justice senseless. That hard fact cannot be changed by any amount of theorizing, pragmatism, well-wishing, white-washing or propagandizing.

Viewed from any angle, therefore, integrity is key for international (criminal) justice. Integrity should be valued and acknowledged. Great importance and attention should be given to ensuring that persons of integrity are in the highest positions in international courts. Their qualities set the standard and the tone and determine the ethical atmosphere – the more they are respected and trusted for their integrity, the higher the morale, the work ethic, and the results. And the willingness to stand up for justice. And not least, it is very enriching and a pleasure to work with people of integrity. There are many such professionals. We should always look for them, find them, and stand by them.

The words of the great humanist Erich Fromm still hold true. The contemporary contradiction between an abundance of technical means for material satisfaction and the incapacity to use them exclusively for peace and the welfare of the people is soluble; it is not a necessary contradiction but one due to man's lack of courage and wisdom.

---

[31] William D. Hartung, "The Military-Industrial Complex on Steroids", *Information Clearing House*, 18 July 2019 (available on its web site), which states that "[a]s POGO's research has demonstrated, the infamous 'revolving door' that deposits defense executives like Esper in top national security posts swings both ways. The group estimates that, in 2018 alone, 645 senior government officials – mostly from the Pentagon, the uniformed military, and Capitol Hill – went to work as executives, consultants, or board members of one of the top 20 defense contractors".

The Role of Aesthetics in Furthering Integrity

Marina Aksenova[*]

12.1. Aesthetics, Integrity and the Internal Values of International Criminal Justice

International criminal law is a discipline that looks outwards by establishing the standards of behaviour upon which the international community agrees. There is a threshold of reprehensible conduct and anything below that threshold gets universally condemned. The discipline seeks to protect the core of life and dignity by outlawing abuses, which can hurt our shared humanity. The question is whether people directly involved in the process of administering international justice must embrace the values of international criminal law internally. This is when the integrity question becomes relevant. Is this a legal or an extra-legal consideration?

The policy brief underlying this volume refers to 'integrity' both as a legal term and a virtue term referring to the quality of a person's character.[1] For instance, Articles 36(3)(a) and 42(3) of the Rome Statute of the International Criminal Court ('ICC') refer to "high moral character" of the participants of an international criminal justice process. The term 'integrity' is simultaneously a virtue term for the purposes of this work. If one dwells on the virtue meaning of 'integrity', the policy brief mentions, among other

---

[*] **Marina Aksenova** is Professor of comparative and international criminal law at IE University, Madrid. She graduated with honours from the International University in Moscow. She holds an LL.M. in Public International Law from the University of Amsterdam and an M.Sc. in Criminal Justice and Criminology from the University of Oxford. Dr. Aksenova defended her Ph.D. entitled "Complicity in International Criminal Law" in 2014 at the European University Institute, in Florence. Prior to joining the IE Law School, she was as a postdoctoral research fellow at the Centre of Excellence for International Courts (iCourts), Faculty of Law, University of Copenhagen.

[1] Morten Bergsmo, "Revisiting Integrity in International Justice", FICHL Policy Brief Series No. 93 (2018), Torkel Opsahl Academic EPublisher ('TOAEP'), Brussels, 2018 (https://legal-tools.org/doc/e550f7). See, for more discussion of the legal meaning of integrity, the lecture by Olympia Bekou, "Integrity Standards in the Statutes of International Criminal Jurisdictions", Centre for International Law Research and Policy ('CILRAP') Films, 1 December 2018 (www.cilrap.org/cilrap-film/181201-bekou/).

definitions, the alignment of intention, speech and action.[2] It is important for operationalizing the discipline of international justice that those who are tasked with manifesting its values in specific cases and situations, do so based on their inner conviction. Any misalignment has the potential of damaging the system in the long run. How does one connect to the inner guidance or the inner moral compass of individuals working in the field of international criminal justice?

One way to promote better connection between inner guidance and outer norms propagated by international criminal law is through embracing the wider role of art or aesthetics. Here, it is important to note that the terms 'art' and 'aesthetics' are used interchangeably in this chapter. Art is understood broadly to encompass different forms of expression (visual, auditory, sensual) employed with the purpose of transmitting a certain message coloured by emotions. Aesthetics is the study of these processes.

To cover basic definitional concerns, it is useful for the present analysis to view art as a process of creative expression rather than as an outcome-driven activity. The work of Simon O'Sullivan is helpful in explaining this specific vision. In his article, "The Aesthetics of Affect: Thinking Art beyond Representation", O'Sullivan observes that art is not merely an object of knowledge to be studied from the perspective of representation, but something that produces affects.[3] O'Sullivan explains that seeing art from the 'representational' point of view traditionally means one of two things: either one speaks of the moment of art's production, which entails adopting the historical lens through which the object of art is viewed, or, alternatively, it means that one foregoes the historical explanation and resorts to the framework of deconstructivism. This latter position still refers to art as an object, which forms part of the representational discourse.[4] But even after the deconstruction exercise, the object of art remains and continues to produce affects. Affects are moments of intensity, a reaction in or on the body at the level of matter.[5]

This complex vision of art exposes art's dual function: to represent and interpret reality, and to create direct human experience connecting us to

---

2   *Ibid.* This approach to integrity also constitutes in part the Noble Eightfold Path to Happiness, which is one of the central teachings in Theravada Buddhism.

3   Simon O'Sullivan, "The Aesthetics of Affect: Thinking Art beyond Representation", in *Angelaki Journal of the Theoretical Humanities*, 2010, vol. 6, no. 3, pp. 125–135.

4   *Ibid.*, pp. 125–126.

5   *Ibid.*

ourselves through aesthetics. Art goes beyond language and even beyond the representation of meaning by creating a direct experience. It facilitates the channel of communication between the observer and the observed, dispensing with the dimensions of time and space.[6] In other words, art creates room in which the attention of the observer is manipulated so that he or she perceives the world in an unfamiliar way. To further demonstrate what is meant by the affective function of art, it is helpful to refer to the work of the art theorist John Dewey, who points out that art traditionally accompanied daily rituals, such as worship, hunting or law-making.[7] Originally, art was inseparable from the conditions of its creation, thereby bringing its affective function to the forefront: experience associated with the object of art was of utmost importance. For instance, the Greek Parthenon, which is regarded today as an art masterpiece, was originally designed and built as a place of civic commemoration.[8] Dewey further observes that it is only much later and through the process of industrialization that art became contextualized by being confined to specific places, such as museums or opera houses.[9] Such contextualization strengthened the representational vision of art.

The experiential aspect of art opens up the emotional channels for receiving the interpretative or representational message, while at the same time avoiding intransigence. In this way, the message is internalized by an individual, taking into account their subjective reality and experience of life. It is the process-oriented feature of art that invites contemplation and makes it possible to speak of the improved alignment of inner moral convictions and external action in individuals. Art and creative expression have the capacity to go beyond firm analytical structures, and surpass cognitive biases and other 'mental defences' to enhance clearer views of the specific situation calling for attention. Dewey's distinction between the 'thinker' and the 'artist' in the context of life cycles is helpful to explain this point.

Life, according to Dewey, goes in cycles reflective of an adaption to the environment by any living creature. There is constant adjustment and transformation of imbalance happening (for instance, satisfying hunger). Dewey calls this process the rhythm of loss of integration with the envi-

---

[6]   *Ibid.*

[7]   John Dewey, *Art as Experience*, Capricorn, 1958 [1934].

[8]   *Ibid.*, p. 4.

[9]   *Ibid.*, p. 6.

ronment and recovery of union with it.[10] This rhythm produces both intellectual and aesthetic work. The former is more concerned with the conflict or the situation in which the discord arose, while the latter focuses on the phase of experience where union is achieved. Hence both the 'thinker' and the 'artist' are ultimately concerned with the interaction of any living creature with its surroundings, simply with the emphasis put in different places. The intellectuals create solutions to the problem using language, symbols and mathematical signs, whereas the artists do their thinking in the very qualitative media they work in.[11]

Going back to the question of integrity in the field of international justice, this chapter argues that the time is ripe to rethink what we expect from international law. The premise is that there needs to be a better defined link between its 'outward' values and the 'inner' values of those tasked with imparting the 'outward' values. As a first step in this process, the chapter suggests reflecting on the vehicles to facilitate this reassessment process. Relying, among other frames of reference, on natural law theory, it insists on strengthening the persuasive authority of international law by referring to the list of basic human goods, including that of aesthetics. The contribution engages in particular with the work of John Finnis, who discusses basic human goods pursued by humans, such as aesthetic experience.[12] Justice is a way of distributing these goods in society, and law is a coercive instrument for such distribution. The question is whether law can also be a direct reflection of the basic goods and not just the 'enforcer' of them. This is particularly true for international (criminal) law, which relies strongly on persuasion. International law has the capacity to impose duties or to confer powers on State officials, thereby reducing arbitrariness in their decision-making; it creates causes of action.[13] How can instrumentalization be prevented and the universality of international law be preserved in these circumstances? The answer lies in strengthening its link with the underlying values it represents, including that of aesthetics.

John Finnis in his work on natural law identifies an exhaustive list of seven basic human goods pursued by humans: life, knowledge, play, aes-

---

[10]   *Ibid.*, p. 14.

[11]   *Ibid.*, p. 15.

[12]   John Finnis, *Natural Law and Natural Rights*, second edition, Oxford University Press, 2011, p. 85.

[13]   Basak Çali, *The Authority of International Law: Obedience, Respect, and Rebuttal*, Oxford University Press, 2015, p. 11.

thetic experience, sociability (friendship), practical reasonableness, and religion.[14] These elements comprise the notion of good and well-being. The list is exhaustive because, according to Finnis, the other goods will be the ways of pursuing or realizing one of the basic goods.[15] The idea of 'good' in formulating this list stems from man's natural inclination to good – a feature he or she shares with all the substances in nature – with the ultimate goal being self-preservation.[16] One seeks to attain these goods as an individual, but also as a member of the community. As Thomas Aquinas wrote:[17]

> since every part is ordained to the whole, as imperfect to perfect; and since one man is a part of the perfect community, the law must needs regard properly the relationship to universal happiness.

Justice, then, provides a framework for the realization of these goods in the community.[18]

The following section of the chapter dwells on the role of natural law theory and other theoretical frames of reference in explaining the role of aesthetics in promoting integrity in the field of international justice. Each sub-section discusses the role of art and creative expression in reclaiming the universal dimension of international law from a different theoretical standpoint. The third section of the chapter moves away from a purely theoretical analysis and discusses specific ways in which it is possible to engage with art in the field of international justice. It is argued that one can see international criminal law trials through the lens of aesthetics by viewing them as ritualistic performances. Secondly, it is possible to see art and creative expression as a method of scientific inquiry aimed at illuminating unseen elements of the discipline. Finally, one can explore and further develop the idea of engaging with art as a form of reparations practised by the ICC.

---

[14] Finnis, 2011, see above note 12.

[15] *Ibid.*, p. 90.

[16] Thomas Aquinas, *Summa Theologiae*, ST II.I.94:2.

[17] *Ibid.*, ST I.II.90:2.

[18] Robert Nozick conceptualizes State as a dominant protective association that reserves for itself the right to judge any procedure of justice to be applied to its clients. He understands justice in a procedural sense as a moral restriction on the use of force by the dominant association, that is, the State. According to this reasoning only the minimal State can be justified, for any State that is more extensive violates people's rights. See Robert Nozick, *Anarchy, State and Utopia*, Blackwell, 1974, pp. 101, 149.

12.2. Theoretical Frameworks for Discussing the Role of Aesthetics in Promoting Integrity

12.2.1. Natural Law Theory

The introduction alluded to the work of John Finnis that enumerates a list of goods towards which every human strives.[19] Finnis sees justice as a 'distributor' of these goods in society. It is always inter-subjective, or points to the direction of another person ('other-directedness'); it regulates duties owed to others and the corresponding rights; and it contains a measure for distributing the goods in a proportionate way.[20] Justice excludes arbitrary self-preference in pursuit of good.[21] Law is the instrument of justice; it is a force keeping the equilibrium in society by regulating the pursuit of human goods and thus contributing to a common good of the relevant community.

The coercive qualities of law are well-documented and extensively discussed.[22] The key question is whether, in addition to being the distributive force in societies, law can also embody the essence of the human goods themselves. This question is particularly relevant to international law, which lacks coercive powers and systemically applicable sanctions akin to those imposed by national States on its subjects. Take, for instance, the work of Thomas Hobbes on the coercive powers of law in the context of a State. He argued that law coerces us by arousing fears about evil consequences of disobedience.[23] The will to obey law is thus the result of a reasoned reflection on the implications of one's actions. The social contract is enforced without impeding on the individual's freedom, which, according to Hobbes, is only taken away by the identifiable acts of interference by external agents. We cannot be said to act un-freely when obeying law be-

---

[19] Finnis, 2011, see above note 12.

[20] *Ibid.*, pp. 161–63.

[21] *Ibid.*, p. 164.

[22] Hans Kelsen, *The Pure Theory of Law*, original German first edition 1934; second edition, 1960, translated to English by Max Knight (trans.), University of California Press, Los Angeles, 1967, p. 34; Dennis Lloyd, *The Idea of Law*, Penguin Books, Middlesex, 1970 [1964], p. 35 (in his index, the entry for coercion says, "See force, sanction"); Jacques Derrida, "Force of Law: The Mystical Foundation of Authority", in Drucilla Cornell, Michel Rosenfeld and David Gray Carlson (eds.), *Deconstruction and the Possibility of Justice*, Routledge, New York and London, 1992, chap. 1.

[23] Thomas Hobbes, *Leviathan*, Cambridge University Press, 1996, chap. 21, as cited by Quentin Skinner, in Bo Stråth (eds.), *States and Citizens: History, Theory, Prospects*, Cambridge University Press, 2003, pp. 15–16.

---

cause reasoned reflection produces the will to obey the law.[24] The same will to obey may not necessarily arise with the same strength when it comes to the norms of international law because the threat of sanctions is not as pronounced as in domestic orders.

The authority of international law is, to a large extent, persuasive and includes the capacity of law to impose duties or to confer powers on State officials.[25] Basak Çali explains that, in practice, it means State officials engage in a deliberative exercise comparing and contrasting the authority of domestic law and international law when responding to authority claims made by international law.[26] This is the manifestation of the persuasive power of international law: it contributes to the decision-making process by reducing arbitrariness. It thus protects common values, not so much through coercion, but rather through bestowing additional causes of action on those in power.

The enforcement deficit characteristic of general public international law is acutely felt in the specific sub-field of international criminal law, which is the focal point of this chapter. The problem of modern international criminal justice is that it is torn between its focus on the universal sense of morality and its high degree of dependence on political processes at international, State and individual levels. For instance, at the international level, there is no consensus on whether to bring the situation in Syria to the attention of the United Nations Security Council for its subsequent referral to the ICC.[27] At the State level, there is wariness by some States about what is perceived as interference by the international community in the domestic affairs of States through the activities of international courts and human rights bodies.[28] And at an individual level, some high-ranking State officials enjoy *de facto* impunity, even in the presence of an arrest warrant issued by the ICC.[29] These inconsistencies have a direct bearing on

---

[24] *Ibid.*

[25] Çali, 2015, see above note 13.

[26] *Ibid.*, p. 64.

[27] UN Security Council, "Referral of Syria to International Criminal Court Fails as Negative Votes Prevent Security Council from Adopting Draft Resolution", press release, 22 May 2014, UN Doc. SC/11407.

[28] For example, Reuters, "Philippines informs U.N. of ICC withdrawal, court regrets move", 16 March 2018.

[29] For example, International Criminal Court ('ICC'), Situation in Darfur, Sudan, *The Prosecutor v. Omar Hassan Ahmad Al Bashir*, Pre-Trial Chamber I, Warrant of Arrest for Omar Hassan Ahmad Al Bashir, 4 March 2009, ICC-02/05-01/09-1 (https://legal-tools.org/doc/814cca).

the question of integrity of those tasked with enforcing international criminal justice, making misalignment of the external ambitions and inner values more possible due to moral relativism, political constraints, and overall contradictions implicit in the project of international criminal justice.

How to address these inconsistencies? There is a powerful educational potential in international criminal law. Its strong moralistic embedment makes it a suitable platform for communicating values to a wider audience. It is not just about the prosecution of individuals but also about sharing the norms concerning the conduct not tolerated by the rest of humanity. Accountability efforts are dependent on the intensity and scale on which these core values are shared.[30] This is precisely the point where international (criminal) law needs to come in closer contact with the ultimate values it protects.

If the law seeks to regulate human conduct for the benefit of the entire community, then why not see it as a force capable of upholding the values more directly through its own authority? Indeed, law embodies its coercive power and serves as a force maintaining order when it comes to the value it aims to endorse. However, I argue, law in its operation also touches upon all basic human values, including that of aesthetics, and not only the one it directly protects. This is particularly relevant for international law, which relies on its persuasive authority. Section 12.3. of the chapter provides an example of how this theoretical vision can be applied to an international criminal trial.

12.2.2. Visual Methodology in the Age of the Digital Baroque

Natural law theory is just one framework that supports the use of art or aesthetics in promoting integrity. Jurisprudence provides for another fruitful paradigm to further support the claim of this chapter. Richard Sherwin, a scholar of contemporary jurisprudence, argues that there is an urgent demand for exploring visual methodology in legal science. The overproduction of imagery in our modern life is what Sherwin refers to as the age of the 'digital baroque'.[31] The term 'baroque' emphasizes the shifts in the

---

[30] Kathryn Sikkink, *The Justice Cascade: How Human Rights Prosecutions Are Changing World Politics*, W.W. Norton, 2011; Marina Aksenova, "Symbolism as a Constraint on International Criminal Law", in *Leiden Journal of International Law*, 2017, vol. 30, no. 2, pp. 475–499.

[31] Richard K. Sherwin, *Visualizing Law in the Age of the Digital Baroque: Arabesques and Entanglements*, Routledge, 2011, pp. 187.

dominant forms of communication, whereby images collected, for instance, through social media, create mediated reality.[32] The original concept depicted by an image fades away with the unfolding of the infinite representational forms amply supplied by the Internet. The digital baroque calls for a new mindfulness, one that integrates the affects of the body's senses with the mind's natural capacity to analyse and categorize.[33]

Sherwin argues for the exploration of the path of visual jurisprudence as a way to navigate the new forms of mediated reality.[34] In this new state of affairs, where the visual shapes our perception of reality, law in its purely analytical form retains its validity, but loses the significance.[35] This is where Sherwin finds clear scope for developing new visual rhetoric, integrating ethics and aesthetics.[36] His call is to cultivate visual literacy and to retrieve the core humanist ideals of creative intuition and eloquence in the service of ethical wisdom.[37] The wise 'lawyer-poet-statesman' finds a way to balance unruly passions and deceits cultivated in the age of visual baroque with the "tyranny of the rational systems of knowledge" to make civic life both secure and just.[38] Sherwin's philosophical and jurisprudential stance serves to demonstrate the timeliness of an aesthetic intervention in the development of law as a discipline.

The field of international criminal law is particularly susceptible to the reception of visual or aesthetic rhetoric at this point of its development. The discipline urgently requires rethinking and additional support to strengthen its highly moralistic claims. International criminal law was conceived in the aftermath of World War II as a project to individualize the responsibility of the senior Nazi leadership for aggression. It later spearheaded the accountability movements for mass atrocities in the 1990s, through the creation of the International Criminal Tribunal for the former Yugoslavia ('ICTY') and the International Criminal Tribunal for Rwanda ('ICTR'), accompanied by the rise of enthusiasm around the project of international criminal justice. The early 2000s, however, signified a shift to-

---

[32] *Ibid.*, p. 174.

[33] *Ibid.*, p. 113.

[34] In this regard, TOAEP's commitment to a wider use of the AV-recordings of conference lectures to support academic arguments in its publications is highly commendable.

[35] Sherwin, 2011, p. 177, see above note 31.

[36] *Ibid.*, p. 174.

[37] *Ibid.*, p. 187.

[38] *Ibid.*, p. 188.

wards a more critical perception of the field, leading up to what we now might call a legitimacy crisis stemming from the growing awareness of the field's own inherent limitations.[39]

The ICC is engaged in an ongoing battle to garnish support at the State level so that it can fully exercise its enforcement powers over individuals. Immi Tallgren articulately explains the difficulties implicit in the project of international criminal law, such as its propensity to overstate its own claims.[40] She refers to this field as "a truly illuminating package of ideas" dealing with existential questions of life and death, and choices between good and evil.[41] At the same time, Tallgren notes that the focus on individual criminal responsibility obfuscates complexity and context. Instead of discussing nuclear weapons, we discuss machete knives used in Rwanda. Instead of focusing on State responsibility for aggression, we focus on individual war crimes, such as rape or murder.[42] Another pertinent example is the problem of child soldiers.

At the time of writing, the ICC is trying Dominic Ongwen, who started as a child soldier in the Lord's Resistance Army in Uganda at the age of 10, subsequently rising in its ranks.[43] The moral ambiguity of prosecuting someone socialized into atrocities as a child certainly gets attention in the courtroom but is unlikely to get full expression in the eventual legal judgment.[44] The categories of victims and perpetrators are rather contained and fixed within the realm of international law, while the reality may be more complex: with time, child soldiers transition from the role of victims into the role of perpetrators.[45] Art, therefore, allows contextualization of law. Augmenting one's sense of empathy and positive sympathy may not only involve explaining the nature of an internationally recognized prohibi-

---

[39] Aksenova, 2017, see above note 30.

[40] Immi Tallgren, "The Sensibility and Sense of International Criminal Law", in *European Journal of International Law*, 2002, vol. 3, pp. 571, 572.

[41] *Ibid.*, p. 593.

[42] *Ibid.*, p. 594.

[43] ICC, Situation in Uganda, *The Prosecutor v. Dominic Ongwen*, Case Information Sheet, October 2018, ICC-02/04-01/15.

[44] Mark Drumbl, "The Ongwen Trial at the ICC: Tough Questions on Child Soldiers", Open Democracy, 14 April 2015 (available on its website).

[45] Erin Baines, *Buried in the Heart: Women, Complex Victimhood and the War in Northern Uganda*, Cambridge University Press, 2016, p. 3.

tion (of torture, for example) but also by creating a direct experience of what it means to be human with all its complexities and ambiguities.

There is thus a clear need for mediating noble claims of international criminal law as formulated in the Preamble of the Rome Statute of the ICC and what this field is actually able to achieve. It is argued here that artistic expression can assist with this exercise by adding an experiential dimension to the claims of international criminal justice. In addition to that, art then becomes a suitable medium for communicating complex truth. It is possible that re-orienting the rhetoric of international criminal justice towards visual jurisprudence may provide an additional layer of context and complexity, and thereby contribute to the integrity of the participants of an international justice process.

12.2.3. The Connection Between Ethics and Aesthetics

Admittedly, the study of integrity initially brings to mind the role of ethics and not that of aesthetics.[46] This is because ethics, as a branch of philosophy – and religion – deals with human actions and the general principles guiding these actions. Ethics is outcome-oriented – the goal is to apply generalized principles to a specific matter in order to attain the result aligned with a certain moral foundation. In contrast, aesthetics is process-oriented. It is less concerned with outcomes, but places values on the process through which certain action takes place. Aesthetics is, therefore, concerned with thoughtful contemplation. It is not focused on the general principles, but rather on the uniqueness of each experience.[47] Why study the role of aesthetics, one may ask, if it is ethics that supplies us with a 'code of conduct' that we may apply to the situations which require the alignment of inner guidance with the demands of external rules and values?

The work of Wittgenstein may provide an answer to this question. He argued that essentially ethics and aesthetics are two sides of the same coin. Just as they focus on different aspects of the same action (generality versus specificity; outcome versus process; acting versus experiencing), they do

---

[46] See, for instance, lectures by Dieneke de Vos, "Recent Developments in Ethics Standard-Setting and Mechanisms in the UN", CILRAP Films, 1 December 2018 (www.cilrap.org/cilrap-film/181202-vos/); Shannon E. Fyfe, "Integrity and Prosecutorial Ethics in International Criminal Justice", CILRAP Films, 1 December 2018 (www.cilrap.org/cilrap-film/181202-fyfe/).

[47] Diané Collinson, "Ethics and Aesthetics are one", in *The British Journal of Aesthetics*, 1985, vol. 25, no. 3, p. 266.

not imply a different set of underlying values. Rather they discuss the very same process from a different point of venture.[48]

In line with this position, this chapter does not denounce the role of ethics in promoting integrity, but rather suggests an alternative way of perceiving it. To give a concrete example, one may contemplate judicial impartiality. One way to look at this principle is through the lens of ethics that requires judges to apply the law without being influenced by personal convictions and biases. This is one of the fundamental elements of due process and is codified in a variety of human rights instruments as well as the statutes of international courts and tribunals.[49]

However, one may also see the application of the same principle as a process in each particular case. What are the elements inherent in an international criminal trial that promote judicial impartiality? One can suggest that certain procedures characteristic of an international trial – such as the swearing in of judges as they pledge to avoid representing a State or any other vested interests, their professionally worn attire as well as formalized conduct in the courtroom, including rising when the judges enter the room – all emphasize respect to the nature of judicial activity and remind judges of the need to uphold the principle of judicial independence. Is the process a trivial matter? Far from it, this chapter argues. Misalignment of inner guidance and the demands of justice can occur easily depending on the factual circumstances of the case, 'triggering' certain biases in a judge, which they may not even be conscious of.[50] There may also be situations of personal fatigue or general policy considerations of expediency of an international trial. All these factors may compromise judicial impartiality if it is only formulated as a general principle or a rule. The process whereby this rule is enforced in practice exists as a constant reminder of the need to uphold this principle in each specific case.

12.2.4. The Role of Art in Evoking the Truth-Content

Theodor Adorno, in the famous *Aesthetic Theory*, acknowledges the difficulty of defining art and chooses to describe it through dialectical exercises

---

[48] *Ibid.*

[49] For example, European Convention on Human Rights, 4 November 1950, Article 6 (https://legal-tools.org/doc/8267cb); Rome Statute of the International Criminal Court, 17 July 1998, Article 36(3)(a) (https://legal-tools.org/doc/7b9af9).

[50] For a recent example, see Kevin Jon Heller, "Judge Ozaki Must Resign — Or Be Removed", *Opinio Juris*, 29 March 2019 (available on its web site).

by resorting to contradictions, while simultaneously upholding the limit to these contradictions. Art has two elements: 'import' – art's form and content – and 'function' – the work's purpose.[51] He then dwells extensively on the contradiction between the components of import, emphasizing the essential nature of the 'truth-content' of art, or the way in which artwork simultaneously challenges the way things are and suggests how they could be.[52] Importantly, Adorno underlines the fluidity of art, which exists in relation to what it is not – historical origins of the production. Art's servitude to kings and amusement is not to be held against it as its original sin as "truth exists exclusively as that which has become".[53] These sets of identified contradictions give us a sense of the effects of art without necessarily providing a comprehensive definition. The inquiry into the nature of art would therefore require a separate study going far beyond the scope of the present chapter. It is rather the qualities art that can be known and discussed in conceptual terms.

The 'truth-content' of art, then, is an inalienable part of the art-object and the aesthetic experience of the art. Art reveals truth that is not so easily captured by formalized knowledge because experiences, such as suffering, remain foreign to knowledge.[54] Knowledge can subordinate them conceptually and provide means for improving certain states, such as amelioration of suffering, but it cannot express through its own means the experience without becoming itself irrational.[55] Art and knowledge are thus complementary in revealing the truth. Art cannot be reduced to rationalistic determinations, but it contains an implicit need for interpretation.[56] By demanding such interpretation, it invites philosophical reflection. According to Adorno, this alone is the justification of the discipline of aesthetics.[57]

It is therefore possible to see art as being complementary to international (criminal) law: suffering cannot be understood at the level of analytical categories, yet it can be described and ameliorated. It is the experiential dimension brought about by art that allows for deeper internalization of suffering. The pitfall in this process that Adorno identified in his other

---

[51]   Theodor W. Adorno, *Aesthetic Theory*, Continuum, 1970, pp. 100, 227.
[52]   *Ibid.*, p. 132.
[53]   *Ibid.*, p. 3.
[54]   Adorno, 1970, p. 18, see above note 51.
[55]   *Ibid.*
[56]   *Ibid.*, p. 128.
[57]   *Ibid.*

work is the challenge of aesthetic representation removing some of the horrors the depiction or production represents.[58]

12.3. Art as a Vehicle of Transformative Change

This section is exploratory in nature in that it investigates the possibilities of, firstly, viewing international proceedings from the aesthetics point of view, while examining the implications of this view. Secondly, it briefly touches upon the prospects of using art as a method of inquiry to gain more insight into the field of international justice and thus improving the integrity of its stakeholders. Finally, this section examines some practical examples of interjecting creative expression in the administration of international justice in the form of reparations.

12.3.1. Viewing International Criminal Proceedings as an Aesthetic Experience

This sub-section focuses on the application of Finnis's basic goods theory directly to an international criminal trial. As already mentioned, international criminal law is a sub-field of international law with a strong moral appeal. It endorses values shared by humanity as a whole by prohibiting the most heinous conduct in both war and peace. It is an attempt by the international community to foster a collective response to evil. A clear example of how basic human goods are reflected in international criminal law comes from the provision prohibiting genocide. For the completeness of the picture, it is important to provide a comprehensive account of how each basic good, not just aesthetics, discussed by Finnis is reflected in an international criminal trial. This is to emphasize the connections between different values.

The legal definition of genocide is found in Article II of the Genocide Convention[59] and is replicated in Article 6 of the Rome Statute of the

---

[58] Theodor W. Adorno, *Can One Live after Auschwitz? A Philosophical Reader*, Stanford University Press, 2003, p. 252.

[59] In the present Convention, genocide means any of the following acts committed with intent to destroy, in whole or in part, a national, ethnical, racial or religious group, as such:
1. Killing members of the group;
2. Causing serious bodily or mental harm to members of the group;
3. Deliberately inflicting on the group conditions of life calculated to bring about its physical destruction in whole or in part;
4. Imposing measures intended to prevent births within the group;
5. Forcibly transferring children of the group to another group.

ICC. This norm clearly protects life as a basic human value. The crime of genocide sits at the apex of the group of offences with highly traumatic connotations for future generations. It criminalizes the destruction of individuals as a collective entity, on the basis of their belonging to a group defined by certain characteristics. This act is particularly heinous for it attacks persons and denies them their right to exist as a group. Hannah Arendt referred to genocide as "an attack upon human diversity as such, that is, upon a characteristic of the 'human status' without which the very words 'mankind' or 'humanity' would be devoid of meaning".[60] The convoluted logic underlying acts of genocide threatens the whole of humankind due to its capacity to indoctrinate and turn humans against each other. The dangerous potential of genocide, historically tested, elevates it to the status of the most odious international crime.

Genocide is also an attack on sociability or the peaceful co-existence of humans. The process whereby genocide occurs consists of several steps.[61] It starts with the feelings of animosity, resentment and fear directed against individuals based on their belonging to a certain group. These sentiments are not endogenous, however, and are usually linked to the ideas planted 'from above' by the authority seeking control or power. One group is made to believe that the other group is threatening the well-being of the former. Sometimes, the feelings of mistrust and resentment are mutual between the groups. The ideology of hate is one of the ways to manipulate people and make them 'governable'. As a result of indoctrination, the culture of blaming others for personal grievances with the potential of escalating into violence is thus created.

Even if somebody, based on their flawed practical reasonableness, decides to destroy a group as such for the sake of pursuing other goods, law would stand in their way as a deterrent. In this case, law overtakes individual practical reasonableness and becomes a manifestation of the same value at the community level. Finnis defines practical reasonableness as bringing intelligence and order into one's own actions and habits.[62] However, one's internal order and decision-making process may come into conflict with the

---

[60] Hannah Arendt, *Eichmann in Jerusalem: A Report on the Banality of Evil*, Viking Press, 1965, pp. 268, 269.

[61] For more discussion, see, for example, Bert Ingelaere, Stephan Parmentier, Jacques Haers and Babara Segaert (eds.), *Genocide, Risk and Resilience: An Interdisciplinary Approach*, Palgrave, 2013.

[62] Finnis, 2011, p. 88, see above note 12.

common good. In specific instances of criminality, the emotional state may overtake an individual, leading to actions misaligned with practical reasonableness. Eric Posner, in his work on "Law and the Emotions", points to the neglected role of emotions in legal theory. He contends that people's preferences differ depending on whether they are in the 'calm' state or affected by emotions. He upholds rationality in both states but claims that this rationality is consistent with the internal order of preferences dictated by the emotional state.[63] In such situations, law serves as a 'common denominator' for collective intelligence. It remedies internal misalignment with the external common good.

If the deterrent effect of law for whatever reason does not take effect and genocide occurs, international criminal law then, in theory and subject to its multiple limitations, provides for remedies, such as trial and punishment of the responsible person. In this case, law is by no means devoid of the emotional component. It can be said to express anger as an emotional response to the violation of community values. Thomas Aquinas in his teachings insisted that anger does not always lead us astray and can very well be the consequence of reason. Anger, according to him, can be the instrument of virtue when it requires judgment on the nature and degree of punishment of the offender and an appropriate emotive stance towards him or her.[64] Law is thus once again relevant to sociability, as an international criminal trial for the crime of genocide provides for a sense of community and justice, which are meted out on behalf of international society as a whole as "a passionate reaction graduated in its intensity".[65]

Criminal trials are instruments of generating knowledge, as one of their purposes is ascertaining the truth about what happened. Establishing individual criminal responsibility beyond reasonable doubt is premised on the sufficiency of evidence and the scrupulous analysis of facts. There is a certain distinction between ordinary criminal trials focusing on individual responsibility and legal proceedings targeting mass atrocities, such as genocide. The latter shape collective memory by looking at a broader picture of events and contrasting conflicting accounts embedded in political, social

---

[63] Eric A. Posner, "Law and the Emotions", University of Chicago, John M. Olin Law and Economics Working Paper No. 103, September 2000, pp. 2–5.

[64] Gregory M. Reichberg, *Thomas Aquinas on War and Peace*, Cambridge University Press, 2016, p. 92.

[65] Émile Durkheim, *The Division of Labour in Society*, 1893, p. 52.

and religious frameworks.[66] The knowledge produced by international trials is thus of a broader nature.

It is thus possible to conceptualize international criminal trials as ritual-like social performances.[67] Such vision of justice resonates with the basic human good of play. Play is understood here as a process. Jeffrey Alexander's conceptualization of social performances is useful to explain this point.[68] He argues that a social performance consists of a number of elements, including actors, scripts, background representations, and audience. In simpler societies, these elements are fused, or tightly linked to each other. Religious rituals are examples of social performances when the audience does not need to be convinced because it already shares the beliefs that the actors are transmitting. With increasing social complexity, the elements of any social performance become de-fused. The successful social performance re-fuses the elements by bringing them together in a coherent fashion. Failure to do so may render the social performance unconvincing, thus obstructing the delivery of the symbolic integrative message indented by the cultural practice in question.[69]

The first international prosecutions of genocide at the ICTY and the ICTR were undoubtedly social performances carrying a strong message of condemnation and giving effect to the values agreed upon internationally.[70] Criminal punishment resulting from this process is a manifestation of the other-directedness of justice in a sense that it remedies the situation from the other end by evoking retribution aimed at atonement. The administration of justice, especially at the international level, is a highly regulated and highly emotive performance that relies on actors, script and audience.

The connection between the prohibition of genocide and religion as a basic human value is rather straightforward. The divinity of life has been one of the reasons for the initial criminalization of murder in the context of ordinary criminal law. Genocide as an attack on diversity with the potential

---

[66] Ruti G. Teitel, *Transitional Justice*, Cambridge University Press, 2010, p. 72.

[67] Marina Aksenova, "The Role of ICT in Historical Accounts of Genocide", in Uladzislau Belavusau and Aleksandra Gliszczyńska-Grabias (eds.), *Law and Memory: Towards Legal Governance of History*, Cambridge University Press, 2017, p. 57.

[68] Jeffrey C. Alexander, "Cultural Pragmatics: Social Performance between Ritual and Strategy", in Jeffrey C. Alexander, Bernhard Giesen and Jason L. Mast (eds.), *Social Performance: Symbolic Action, Cultural Pragmatics and Ritual*, Cambridge University Press, 2006, p. 32.

[69] For more on this topic, see Aksenova, 2017, see above note 67.

[70] Alexander, 2006, p. 58, see above note 68.

of the destruction of the whole portion of the population magnifies the harm of murder. In terms of functionality, one can also see clear parallels between a criminal trial and a religious ritual. Émile Durkheim, looking for moral foundations of the legal order, turned to religion as a system of communication of ideas and sentiments. For Durkheim, religion consists of acts that have the object of perpetually making and remaking the souls of the collectivity and of individuals; thus, its function is to strengthen the bonds attaching the individual to society.[71] International criminal trials, although secular in nature, also promote a similar value-based system and serve as a glue for individuals across countries, who share their moral outrage at the crime of genocide.

Finally, there is a powerful interaction between aesthetics and the legal prohibition of genocide. It is clear that international criminal trials embody a very strong sense of aesthetics, which becomes apparent if one looks at the attributes of an international criminal trial. Procedurally speaking, they run according to a strict script, which approximates them to a theatrical performance. The judges wear carefully designed robes. The ICC's physical premises were constructed with the idea of justice and transparency in mind.[72] All of the participants in the process rely on powerful emotive rhetoric in their arguments. For instance, the ICTY judges reserved particularly strong statements for genocide as compared to other crimes in the Statute. The judgment against Radoslav Krstić – the first person convicted of genocide at the ICTY – delivers a powerful message of condemnation of this crime pointing to its particular heinousness: "[a]mong the grievous crimes this Tribunal has the duty to punish, the crime of genocide is singled out for special condemnation and opprobrium".[73]

These aesthetical attributes of international criminal law do not only serve the practical purpose of bringing order to the process of the administration of justice, but also stress the importance of the values claimed by the discipline. This point of view of international criminal justice allows strengthening integrity of its stakeholders by highlighting the elements that

---

[71] Émile Durkheim, *The Elementary Forms of the Religious Life*, George Allen & Unwin, London, 1912, p. 471.

[72] ICC, "The ICC has moved to its permanent premises", press release, 14 December 2015, ICC-CPI-20151214-PR1180.

[73] International Criminal Tribunal for the former Yugoslavia ('ICTY'), *Prosecutor v. Radislav Krstić*, Appeals Chamber, Judgement, 19 April 2004, IT-98-33-A, para. 36 (https://legal-tools.org/doc/86a108).

comprise the system and make it operational. This view serves as a reminder of why international criminal law exists in the first place and what its overall objectives are.

Moreover, the strong aesthetic element embedded in the field of international criminal justice complements the production of knowledge by the courts through judgments and decisions. Aesthetics allows revealing an additional layer of truth about suffering through artistic expression. As discussed in the previous section, truth-content is an inalienable part of the art-object and the aesthetic experience of the art, according to Adorno.

12.3.2. Methodological Advantages of Using Art in the Field of International Justice

From a methodological perspective, art may serve as a method of inquiry with the purpose of illuminating aspects of the field of international justice currently concealed from view.

The thought of exploring the instrumental dimension of art is not new, as art has been used for educational purposes since as early as in the times of the Renaissance. In the field of politics, art is frequently employed to question dogmatic ideas and reach out to diverse segments of the population. For instance, Chinese artist AI Wei Wei drew attention to the refugee crisis by wrapping a Florentine Palazzo in orange lifeboats during his 2016 exhibition there. In addition to that, visual methods are used in discourse analysis, which can be studied through documentary or historical images with other forms of data.[74] More generally, sociology has started taking the 'visual' more seriously with the ongoing research on the promise of visual methodology as an alternative way of scientific inquiry.[75]

Such a turn has not yet occurred in the study and practice of law, a discipline which remains focused entirely on texts and the written word. One can imagine, however, how undertaking art projects aimed at promoting international (criminal) law values, such as integrity, can contribute to the study of the discipline as such. Creative expression can bring to light the aspects of this field long ignored by traditional approaches. For instance, an exhibition dedicated to the work of the ICC may evoke responses in the general public indicative of the new solutions to practical prob-

---

[74] Gillian Rose, *Visual Methodologies: An Introduction to Researching with Visual Materials*, third edition, Sage, 2012.

[75] *Ibid.*

lems faced by the Court. The ICC took its first steps in this direction in 2018 by partnering with the *National Geographic* photographer Marcus Bleasdale in organizing an exhibition entitled "Healing, Trauma and Hope". The exhibition took place on the ICC premises in The Hague and at the United Nations Headquarters in New York and is available online at the time of writing.[76] It is important to note, however, that precise impact of such creative outreach activities has not yet been fully studied.[77]

12.3.3. Practical Example of Using Art in International Criminal Law

This sub-section explores the practical ways in which art and creative expression can be interjected in the process of administration of international justice. International criminal law and its emerging system of reparations is chosen to illustrate the point. In this example, the ultimate goal of engaging with art is promoting reconciliation in the affected communities.[78] While the purpose of strengthening integrity is not directly covered in the following discussion, it is fair to assume that exploring the ways of enhancing international justice through alternative means has direct impact on the integrity of its actors. As discussed in the introduction, lack of integrity often stems from the lack of alignment of inner values and their outer expression. Arguably, the more instruments international justice has at its disposal, the more clarity its various stakeholders will benefit from. Seeing positive change in the communities and focusing on the core values of the discipline can facilitate better judgment in individuals.

The practice of reparations is one clear entry point where international justice starts accepting the deployment of creative expression. While the old generation of international criminal courts and tribunals placed little emphasis on reparations and victim participation, the ICC together with Extraordinary Chambers in the Courts of Cambodia ('ECCC') are pioneering the idea of inclusivity of victims' concerns in international criminal proceedings. Pursuant to Article 75(1) of the Rome Statute of the ICC, the Court may order reparations to victims, in the form of restitution, compensation and rehabilitation. This list is not exhaustive as the Court may select

---

[76] ICC, "Trauma, healing and hope" (available on its web site).

[77] Fiana Gantheret, "The Use of Artistic Productions as a Transitional Justice Mechanism in the Context of International Criminal Justice and the Misuse of International Tribunals' Mandates", *Art and International Justice Blog*, 1 July 2019.

[78] Rachel Kerr, "The 'Art' of Reconciliation', FICHL Policy Brief Series No. 78 (2017), TOAEP, Brussels, 2017 (http://www.toaep.org/pbs-pdf/78-kerr/).

reparations with symbolic, preventative and transformative value.[79] Reparations give victims a chance to reclaim their story and their dignity. In the practice of reparations, criminal law is called upon to fulfil its secondary functions, that is, to bring back the equilibrium not through pure coercion but also through its persuasion. The clear challenge, of course, is how to repair the irreparable

Reparations have thus potential to become one of the vehicles of reconciliation as the ICC orders symbolic reparations to honour the losses suffered by the community and individuals. Symbolic reparations therefore do not aim to bring back what has been forever lost, but rather acknowledge the importance of the values harmed by the crimes. Implementation of such orders will be, to a large extent, an artistic exercise. It is through these symbolic measures, with artistic underpinnings, that the layer of truth about suffering can reveal itself.

Two reparation orders issued by the ICC clearly demonstrate the link between reparations and reconciliation. Firstly, in *Lubanga* – the case dealing with the recruitment of child soldiers – the judges expressly acknowledged that the objectives of rehabilitation, reconciliation, and reintegration of former child soldiers might be accomplished through symbolic and transformative reparations.[80] The *Lubanga* order on reparations explicitly states that "reparations should aim at reconciling the victims with their families and the affected communities".[81] The Trust Fund for Victims – the ICC body tasked with implementing reparations orders – now faces a real challenge in explaining how reconciliation and reintegration should be understood for the purposes of symbolic reparations initiatives in the specific context of this case. Based on their work in the affected communities, the experts concluded that crimes against children are often committed with the acceptance of the broader community. Thus, what is really needed in terms of memorialization or any other symbolic initiative is awareness-

---

[79] ICC, Situation in the Democratic Republic of Congo, *The Prosecutor v. Germain Katanga*, Trial Chamber, Order for Reparations Pursuant to Article 75 of the Statute, ICC 01/04-01/07, 24 March 2017, para. 297 (https://legal-tools.org/doc/63d36d).

[80] ICC, Situation in the Democratic Republic of Congo, *The Prosecutor v. Thomas Lubanga Dyilo*, Appeals Chamber, Order for Reparations (amended), 3 March 2015, ICC-01/04-01/06-3129-AnxA, para. 67 (https://legal-tools.org/doc/df2804).

[81] *Ibid.*, para. 46.

raising within this broader community about the harm inflicted on children as a result of their inscription in the armed forces.[82]

The use of symbolic rehabilitative measures can also be seen in the *Al Mahdi* case, in which the ICC pronounced on the appropriate reparations in cases of the destruction of cultural heritage. This case is unique because artistic expression is not only a tool for reparations, but also the value protected by the principles of international criminal law. The reparations order, issued in August 2017, found Mr. Al Mahdi, who orchestrated the demolition of ten shrines of historical and cultural significance in Timbuktu, Mali,[83] liable for EUR 2.7 million for damage caused by the attack.[84] The Court emphasized the emotional distress caused to the Timbuktu community as a whole by the destruction of the shrines.[85] The ICC further stressed the inherent, unique and sentimental value of most cultural property and cultural heritage because of their purpose and symbolism.[86]

Thus, the mental anguish caused by its obliteration is addressed on an individual level by compensation and on a collective level by symbolic rehabilitative measures, such as memorial, commemoration or forgiveness ceremony. The aim is to grant public recognition to the harm suffered by the Timbuktu community.[87] The Court also focused on Mr. Al Mahdi's apology, which it found to be "genuine, categorical and empathetic".[88] As a symbolic measure with potential reconciliatory impact, the judges ordered the excerpt from the trial containing an apology be put on the Court's web

---

[82] ICC, Situation in the Democratic Republic of Congo, *The Prosecutor v. Thomas Lubanga Dyilo*, Trial Chamber II, Public Redacted version of Filing regarding symbolic collective reparations projects with Confidential Annex: Draft Request for Proposals, ICC-01/04-01/06-3223-Conf, 19 September 2016, ICC-01/04-01/06 (https://legal-tools.org/doc/401740).

[83] Marina Aksenova, "The Al Mahdi Judgment and Sentence at the ICC: A Source of Cautious Optimism for International Criminal Justice", *EJIL: Talk!*, 13 October 2016 (available on its web site).

[84] ICC, Situation in the Republic of Mali, *The Prosecutor v. Ahmed Al Faqi Al Mahdi*, Trial Chamber, Reparations Order, 17 August 2017, ICC-01/12-01/15, para. 134 (https://legal-tools.org/doc/02d1bb).

[85] *Ibid.*, para. 90.

[86] *Ibid.*, para. 22.

[87] *Ibid.*, para. 90.

[88] *Ibid.*, para. 70 (citing Trial Judgment, paras. 103–05).

site accompanied by the corresponding transcript translated into the primary local languages.[89]

In the same vein, the ECCC accepted as a form of reparations a classical dance production and a related exhibition addressing the crime of forced marriage committed during the Khmer Rouge regime.[90] Courts and tribunals are thus now beginning to acknowledge the reconciliatory potential of art and creative expression explicitly, yet further research is needed to understand how art can be used to achieve these goals.

12.4. Conclusion

This chapter argued that art and aesthetic studies are useful tools in promoting integrity in international justice because of their process-oriented nature and focus on subjectivity. Contemplative reflection inherent in aesthetics increases mindfulness and invites self-inquiry. More specifically, this contribution focused on the function of art as the 'connector' of inner values and external action. It is possible to justify the study of aesthetics in the field of international justice by relying on a number of theoretical frameworks, including visual jurisprudence and natural law theory. Furthermore, there are several concrete ways in which art can be integrated into the study of international justice. One possibility is viewing international (criminal) trials as ritualistic performances, unfolding based on a certain script. The robes worn by the participants in the process, the public nature of a hearing, the dramatic undertones are all there to serve as a reminder of the values at stake. Aesthetics becomes a bridge connecting the physical manifestation of a criminal trial with what it is supposed to represent. It is also the language spoken by those involved in the process.

---

[89] *Ibid.*, paras. 70–71.

[90] Extraordinary Chambers in the Courts of Cambodia, *The Prosecutor v. Nuon Chea and Khieu Samphan*, Trial Chamber, Civil Party Lead Co-Lawyers' Final Claim for Reparation in Case 002/02 with Confidential Annexes, 30 May 2017, E457/6/2/1, para. 30 (https://legal-tools.org/doc/876df7).

PART III:
ROLE OF INTERNATIONAL ORGANIZATIONS AND STATES

13

Institutional Ethics, Individual Integrity, and Sexual Harassment:
Recent Developments in Ethics Standard-Setting and Mechanisms at the United Nations

Dieneke T. de Vos[*]

13.1. Introduction

Questions of ethics and integrity should be at the core of justice institutions, whether at a national or international level, yet they are often either neglected or, more likely, simply presumed to exist. Integrity is often seen as something one simply 'has' (or 'has not'). Yet, when asked what it means to 'have' integrity, various definitions are likely to be offered, depending on one's viewpoint or the nature of the institution.

For example, during discussions in 1998 around revisions to the United Nations Staff Regulations and Rules and the possible adoption of a United Nations ('UN') Code of Conduct, one UN representative stated that of the three staff requirements set out in Article 101 of the UN Charter (efficiency, competence and integrity), integrity "was the most difficult to measure in relative terms" and as such needed further definition.[1] Contrastingly, other representatives stated that "Member States would not propose candidates lacking in integrity" and that as such, "there was no need" for these regulations to expand upon this term.[2] In other words, integrity

---

[*] **Dieneke T. de Vos** is currently Integrity Lead with Oxfam Novib, where she heads the organization's integrity unit, which is responsible for the prevention of and response to allegations of sexual harassment, sexual exploitation and abuse, child abuse, and corruption misconduct. Dr. de Vos was previously an Ethics Officer with the United Nations and has worked for various other international organizations in the field of international justice. Dr. de Vos received her Ph.D. in international criminal law from the European University Institute. All views expressed in this chapter are the author's own, and do not necessarily represent those of her current or past employers.

[1] Comments of the International Civil Service Commission on the report of the Secretary-General entitled "Proposed United Nations Code of conduct" (A/52/488), Addendum to Report of the International Civil Service Commission for the year 1997, UN Doc. A/52/30/Add.1, 20 May 1998, para. 28 (https://www.legal-tools.org/doc/7fp24a/).

[2] *Ibid.*, para. 34.

was simply presumed to exist, an inherent quality of those deemed suitable for the international civil service. Similarly, while the Rome Statute provides that its senior officials, such as the Prosecutor, the Deputy Prosecutor, and the Judges, must be of "high moral character",[3] it fails to actually define the criteria that should be used to asses one's moral suitability for the job, thus leaving the meaning of integrity, or high-moral character, open to interpretation.[4]

While the focus of the conference preceding the publication of this book was understandably on the integrity of individual actors within international justice institutions, this chapter argues that distinguishing 'individual' integrity from 'institutional' integrity is somewhat arbitrary. Of course, the institutions we study and speak of are made up of those very individuals to whom we seek to ascribe this superior quality of integrity or high moral character; the integrity with which these individuals perform their duties thus undoubtedly affects and shapes the (perceived) integrity of the institutions these individuals serve. Yet, how such individual integrity manifests itself or what it is understood to mean is ultimately shaped by the integrity of the institution, and in particular by the institutional mechanisms and structures (the "ethics infrastructure"[5]) put in place to ensure individu-

---

[3]   Rome Statute of the International Criminal Court, 17 July 1998, Articles 33(3)(a), 42(3), 43(3) and 44(2) ('ICC Statute') (http://www.legal-tools.org/doc/3758e4/).

[4]   The interpretation of the 'high moral character'-requirement has gained particular prominence during the 2020 election of the third chief Prosecutor of the International Criminal Court. See, for example, Eric Witte, "By Failing to Screen ICC Prosecutor Candidates for Sexual Misconduct, States Put Court at Risk", *International Justice Monitor*, 9 March 2020 (available on its web site).

[5]   The term 'ethics (or ethical) infrastructure' was first coined by Ted Schneyer in his work on the legal profession in the United States. He focused primarily on understanding 'law firm discipline', which was defined as a system of compliance with professional conduct rules: a set of organizational systems, procedures, policies and incentives that promote desirable behaviour and discourage unethical conduct. See, for example, Ted Schneyer, "Professional Discipline for Law Firms?", in *Cornell Law Review*, 1991, vol. 77, no. 1, pp. 1–46; Ted Schneyer, "A Tale of Four Systems: Reflections on How Law Influences the Ethical Infrastructure of Law Firms", in *South Texas Law Review*, 1998, vol. 39, pp. 245–277. This chapter, however, follows Parker *et al.* (2008) in arguing for a broader understanding of the term 'ethics infrastructure' that "incorporates informal management policies and work cultures (not just formal management policies) and the promotion of ethical dialogue and values (not just compliance with professional conduct rules)". Christine Parker, Adrian Evans, Linda Haller, Suzanne Le Mire and Ried Mortensen, "The Ethical Infrastructure of Legal Practice in Larger Law Firms: Values, Policy and Behaviour", in *UNSW Law Journal*, 2008, vol. 13, no. 1, p. 160 (fn. 6).

---

als within those institutions understand what it means to act with the required integrity in that particular institutional context.

This chapter thus focuses on this linkage between the institution and the individual by examining the ethics infrastructure of the UN. The first part will set out the UN's regulatory framework around (individual) conduct and behaviour. This section thus focuses on what individual integrity means in a UN institutional context, and how it is shaped by and given meaning through established rules and regulations. It will try to answer the question: what does it mean for international civil servants to 'have' integrity under the UN's 'regulatory' ethics infrastructure? The second part of this chapter will then turn its focus to some of the institutional mechanisms developed to help shape and ultimately enforce the UN's standards around individual integrity – the UN's 'institutional' ethics infrastructure. In particular, this section will seek to understand the function of the UN Ethics Office in safeguarding both the integrity of the institution itself and the integrity of its individual staff members and will illustrate a number of concrete institutional mechanisms established by and/or under the guardianship of the UN Ethics Office.

However, as the third and final part of this chapter argues, examining the UN's regulatory and institutional ethics infrastructure presents an incomplete picture. Sections 13.1. and 13.2. of this chapter illustrate that the UN has a range of rules and regulations, and enforcement and compliance mechanisms around expected standards of behaviour of international civil servants *vis-à-vis* external parties linked to organizational and reputational risks. Fewer structures, exist, however, to address interpersonal conduct *within* the organization. The UN's ethics infrastructure has prioritised rules, systems and structures to address unethical behaviour that constitute misconduct against the institution, that is, violations against the organization's (public or financial) interests such as fraud and corruption, over unethical actions that firstly harm individuals and harm the institution secondarily (such as sexual harassment, bullying and discrimination). The third and final part of this chapter thus focuses on this gap in the UN's ethics infrastructure, which has gained increased attention in the past years: sexual harassment as a serious breach of both individual and institutional integrity. It argues that an organizational ethics infrastructure designed to give meaning to, and shape, individual integrity must be inclusive of systems and structures to address interpersonal (mis)conduct.

Ultimately, this chapter argues that integrity in international justice institutions (or in any organizational context) requires more than the existence of a regulatory framework and an institutional structure built around those regulations to encourage ethical behaviour. It requires accountability for all types of unethical behaviour to exist, not simply on paper, but to be seen and experienced in the daily reality of institutions, among its staff and those they interact with. Advancing institutional ethics and individual integrity thus requires an ethics infrastructure that is value-based, and that supports and encourages ethical behaviour through "formal and informal management policies, procedures and controls, work team cultures, and habits of interaction and practice".[6] Such ethical behaviour must become part of the DNA of an organization, so that the answer to the question what it means to 'have' integrity is rooted both in (1) how individual staff members conduct themselves *vis-à-vis* those outside that organization, and thus uphold the organization's external reputation, *and* in (2) how individuals treat each other, in line with the values for which international justice organizations strive in their substantive work. Ultimately, as the last section of this chapter argues, this requires critically examining, challenging and changing unequal distributions of power, and associated workplace culture and practices, within an organization.

13.2. The UN's 'Regulatory' Ethics Infrastructure

Integrity represents one of three core values of the UN (the others being professionalism and respect for diversity) and constitutes a "paramount consideration" in the appointment of its staff.[7] In defining what such integrity means in the UN's institutional context, reference is frequently made to Dag Hammarskjöld, the UN's second (and possibly most influential[8]) Secretary-General who served from 1953 until his death in 1961. His success

---

[6] Parker *et al.*, 2008, p. 172, see above note 5.

[7] Charter of the United Nations, 26 June 1945, Article 101(3) (https://www.legal-tools.org/doc/6b3cd5): "The paramount consideration in the employment of the staff [...] shall be the necessity of securing the highest standards of efficiency, competence, *and integrity*" (emphasis added).

[8] Some argue that Dag Hammarskjöld best personified and personally helped define, or even gave birth to, what it means to be an international civil servant today. See, for example, *The Ethics of Dag Hammarskjöld*, Dag Hammarskjöld Foundation, Uppsala, 2010, p. 4 (available on its web site): "[He] shaped a lasting concept of the role and responsibilities of the international civil servant, creating standards against which his successors continue to be measured".

is often ascribed to his 'high moral character',[9] characterised by the impartiality and independence with which he exercised his duties. Such impartiality and independence, particularly from governments and other outside entities, has come to be seen as the backbone of the international civil service. Notably, the UN Charter stipulates that neither UN staff members nor the Secretary-General may seek or accept instructions from any government, person or entity external to the organization and that their conduct must reflect that independence. Additionally, the international civil service, by virtue of its international nature, is precisely that: international civil servants must be *international* in the discharge of their duties, and, as such, must be responsible and loyal only to the organization they serve, not to any national, local or personal interests or entity.[10] The individual integrity of international civil servants is, in other words, first and foremost shaped by the independent and impartial (international) character of the mandate they hold, whereby they must place the values, principles and interests of the UN above their own.

But what exactly does such 'integrity', characterised by independence and impartiality, mean for international civil servants? Examining integrity in public administration, Armstrong argues that "integrity refers to 'honesty' or 'trustworthiness' in the discharge of official duties, serving as an antithesis to 'corruption' or 'the abuse of office'".[11] Similarly, the UN Staff Regulations provide that the concept of integrity for UN staff members "includes, but is not limited to, probity, impartiality, fairness, honesty and truthfulness in all matters affecting their work and status".[12] Accordingly, it is generally understood that integrity relates to the (exemplary) conduct or behaviour that is expected of (international) civil servants at all

---

[9] Guy Fiti Sinclair, "The International Civil Servant in Theory and Practice: Law, Morality, and Expertise", in *European Journal of International Law*, 2015, vol. 26, no. 3, pp. 755–756.

[10] Staff Regulations and Rules of the United Nations, Secretary General's Bulletin ST/SGB/2018/1, 1 January 2018, Staff Regulation 1.1(a) ('ST/SGB/2018/1') (https://www.legal-tools.org/doc/zn5lba/).

[11] Elia Armstrong, "Integrity, Transparency and Accountability in Public Administration: Recent Trends, Regional and International Developments and Emerging Issues", *United Nations Department of Economic and Social Affairs*, August 2005, p. 1.

[12] ST/SGB/2018/1, Staff Regulation 1.2(b), see above note 10. See also, para. 5 of the 2013 Standards of Conduct, which provide that the concept of integrity "embraces all aspects of behaviour of an international civil servant, including such qualities as honesty, truthfulness, impartiality and incorruptibility". Standards of Conduct of the International Civil Service, International Civil Service Commission, July 2013.

times. However, simply requiring international civil servants to always act with such 'integrity' without further definition or guidance is likely to mean different things to different people in different contexts, particularly in an organisation like the UN, where its staff come from a multitude of different backgrounds, cultures and countries, and often work in countries and cultures different from their own. The integrity expected of international civil servants has thus been further defined through various rules and regulations: the UN's regulatory ethics infrastructure.

The Standards of Conduct for the International Civil Service (hereinafter 'Standards of Conduct') were first drafted in 1954 and are intended as a behavioural and ethical guide for international civil servants that is based on shared values and principles that must underpin their conduct at all times, such as incorruptibility, mutual respect, loyalty, independence and the avoidance of conflicts of interest.[13] In turn, the UN Staff Regulations, Staff Rules and other administrative instruments set out the obligations – rights *and* responsibilities – that derive from these broader values and principles.[14] These institutional rules and regulations defining (individual) in-

---

[13] The Standards of Conduct for the International Civil Service were first drafted by the International Civil Service Advisory Board in 1954. They have since been revised by the International Civil Service Commission in 2001, and most recently in 2013. The 2013 Standards of Conduct, which remain in force today, were approved, with effect from 1 January 2013, by the General Assembly through resolution 67/257 of 12 April 2013 (https://www.legal-tools.org/doc/y77yzh/). The Standards of Conduct set out the principles that must define the relationship between staff members and their organisations (for example, loyalty, mutual respect, and an enabling environment), the relationship between international civil servants and outside entities, in particular governments (for example, independence, neutrality and incorruptibility), and the principles underpinning staff members' personal conduct (for example, respect for different cultures, avoiding conflicts of interest, and not abusing their power).

[14] See, in particular ST/SGB/2018/1, Chapter I of the Staff Regulations (Regulation 1.2) and Chapter I of the Staff Rules (Rule 1.2), see above note 10. The UN Staff Regulations and Staff Rules, like the UN Charter, are applicable to all UN staff members, including those of the separately administered funds and programmes. For other categories of personnel who do not fall within the scope of the Staff Regulations and Rules, such as experts on mission, separate policies have been adopted setting out similar conduct requirements. See, for example: "Regulations Governing the Status, Basic Rights and Duties of Officials other than Secretariat Officials, and Experts on Mission", Secretary-General's Bulletin ST/SGB/2002/9, 17 June 2002, Regulation 2 ('ST/SGB/2002/9') (https://www.legal-tools.org/doc/abt35z/); "Consultants and individual contractors", Administrative Instruction ST/AI/2013/4, 19 December 2013, Sections 5.5-5.6 ('ST/AI/2013/4') (https://www.legal-tools.org/doc/k3vfax/); "Gratis personnel", Administrative Instruction ST/AI/1999/6, 28 May 1999, Section 11 ('ST/AI/1999/6') (https://www.legal-tools.org/doc/lsqcgc/); "The UN internship programme", Administrative Instruction ST/AI/2014/1, 13 January 2014, Section 6.2

tegrity can generally be divided into two categories. Firstly, the rules and regulations that define international civil servants' impartiality and independence from outside entities, in particular, governmental or other political actors; and, secondly, the rules and regulations governing the private affiliations and personal conduct of international civil servants. This regulatory ethics infrastructure thus delineates the behaviour expected of international civil servants because of their status, including the limitations that attach thereto, in particular in their engagement with outside entities.

Most of the Staff Rules and Regulations prescribing staff members' independence and impartiality revolve around the principle that international civil servants are not, in any way, representatives of governments or other outside entities, nor are they proponents of their policies.[15] As the Standards of Conduct explain, their impartiality requires international civil servants to act with the greatest tact and discretion. Moreover, it implies tolerance and restraint in expressing opinions particularly on controversial, political or religious matters as "international civil servants do not have the freedom of private persons to take sides or to express their convictions publicly on controversial matters, either individually or as members of a group, irrespective of the medium used".[16]

As a result, there are certain things one must leave at the door when entering the international civil service. Notably, while the UN respects the inviolability of staff members' personal opinions, including political or religious, as international civil servants, UN staff members must not act in a manner that could reflect adversely upon the interests of the organization or upon the independence, impartiality and integrity required by their status as international civil servants.[17] Accordingly, while UN staff members may exercise their right to vote, may be a member of a political party or make normal financial contributions to political parties, they may not stand for election and their participation in certain activities, such as making public pronouncements on controversial issues in a personal capacity, or campaigning or fundraising on behalf of a political party, individual or outside

---

('ST/AI/2014/1') (https://www.legal-tools.org/doc/7arli8/); and the UNV Code of Conduct provided in sections 2 and 3, respectively, of the Conditions of Service of International UN Volunteers and of National UN Volunteers (available on UN Volunteers web site).

[15] Standards of Conduct for the International Civil Service, para. 8, see above note 12.

[16] *Ibid.*, para. 9.

[17] ST/SGB/2018/1, Staff Regulation 1.2(f), see above note 10.

entity are restricted or prohibited.[18] UN staff members must not criticise or try to discredit a particular government, and are required at all times to avoid any action that might impair the organization's relationship with governments.[19]

Pursuant to their oath of office, UN staff members pledge to discharge their functions and regulate their conduct with the interests of the organization only in view and they accept that loyalty to the aims, principles and purposes of the UN, as set forth in its Charter, is a fundamental obligation.[20] Accordingly, staff members shall not engage in any activity in their private lives that is incompatible with the proper discharge of their duties with the UN. A reputational risk may, for example, arise in situations in which the policies, positions and specific actions of an outside entity, or its affiliated entities or personnel, are not consistent with or contrary to those of the UN. A UN staff member's affiliation with such an entity may then reflect adversely upon the UN and thus on their required integrity. For this reason, UN staff members must seek the Secretary-General's prior approval to engage in any outside (that is, non-UN) occupation or employment or any outside activity that relates to the purpose, activities or interests of the organization. The latter includes, but is not limited to, accepting speaking engagements, submitting articles, books or other written material for publication, issuing statements to the press or taking part in radio or TV productions.[21] For example, the participation in an academic conference such as the one preceding the publication of this book, or the publication of a paper on peace and justice, would require the Secretary-General's prior approval for UN staff members because "publicly available statements of United Nations officials, even in their private capacity, may have a significant impact on the image and reputation of the Organization".[22]

---

[18] *Ibid.*, Staff Regulation 1.2(f), (h), Staff Rule 1.2(u); "Charter of the United Nations and the Convention on the Privileges and Immunities of the United Nations: provisions relating to the status, basic rights and duties of United Nations staff members, with commentary", Secretary-General's Bulletin ST/SGB/2016/9, 21 July 2016 ('Commentary to the Staff Rules and Regulations') (https://www.legal-tools.org/doc/mjxin2/). See also Standards of Conduct for the International Civil Service, paras. 48–49, see above note 12.

[19] *Ibid.*, para. 33.

[20] The UN Declaration (or Oath) of Office is set out in ST/SGB/2018/1, Staff Regulation 1.1(b), see above note 10.

[21] *Ibid.*, Staff Regulation 1.2(o) and (p); Staff Rule 1.2(s), (t), and (v), see above note 10.

[22] Commentary to the Staff Rules and Regulations, Staff Rule 1.2(t), see above note 18.

Although there is no blanket prohibition on outside employment as such, the Staff Regulations specify that any such outside employment may only be authorised if: it does not conflict with staff members' official functions or their status as international civil servants; it is not against the interests of the UN; and it is permitted by local law.[23] For example, the Commentary to the Staff Regulations explain that "no approval is possible for outside occupation or employment in governmental service in a political office, in a diplomatic or other representational post or in any other function not compatible with the staff member's continued status as an international civil servant".[24] As such, (political) outside employment would conflict with a staff member's (perceived) independence and impartiality and thus their integrity.

Besides their independence and impartiality, the integrity of international civil servants also requires their absolute incorruptibility. For this reason, the receipt of gifts, honours, decorations, favours or remuneration from outside sources is strictly regulated in the Staff Regulations and Rules. The general rule, subject only to very few exceptions, is that UN staff members must decline any gifts, honours, decorations or favours, regardless of value, that may be offered to them while in the service of the UN,[25] especially where such gifts are presented to them by a source having or seeking to have a contractual relationship with the organization,[26] or by a governmental source.[27] On the other hand, staff members may, in certain exceptional circumstances, request the Secretary-General's prior approval to receive gifts, honours, decorations or favours from *non*-governmental sources.[28] For example, staff members may generally receive honorary de-

---

[23] ST/SGB/2018/1, Staff Regulation 1.2(p), see above note 10.

[24] Commentary to the Staff Rules and Regulations, Staff Regulation 1.2(c), see above note 18.

[25] ST/SGB/2018/1, Staff Regulation 1.2(j), (k) and (l) and Staff Rule 1.2(l), (m), (n), (o) and (p), see above note 10; see also, Standards of Conduct for the International Civil Service, paras. 50–51, see above note 12. The procedure for seeking approval and/or for reporting unanticipated gifts can be found in: "Reporting, retaining and disposing of honours, decorations, favours, gifts or remuneration from governmental and non-governmental sources", Administrative Issuance ST/AI/2010/1, 14 January 2010 ('ST/AI/2010/1') (https://www.legal-tools.org/doc/5if6za/). The separately funded agencies, funds and programmes, such as UNICEF, the United Nations Population Fund ('UNFPA') or the United Nations Development Programme ('UNDP'), may have their own procedures for requesting such approval, although the same requirements apply.

[26] ST/SGB/2018/1, Staff Rule 1.2(p), see above note 10.

[27] *Ibid.*, Staff Regulation 1.2(j) and (k), and Staff Rule 1.2(l).

[28] *Ibid.*, Staff Regulation 1.2(l); Staff Rule 1.2(m) and (n).

grees from recognised academic institutions,[29] provided that they request the Secretary-General's prior approval and that such acceptance is not incompatible with their status as international civil servants. Again, as with outside engagements, such approval is required to ensure that no conflicts of interest or other reputational risks, including to the individual staff member and the institution's (perceived) integrity, independence and impartiality and in particular their incorruptibility, could arise from the acceptance of any such honours, gifts or degrees.

While staff members may thus receive certain gifts, honours or decorations from *non*-governmental sources in exceptional circumstances, the Staff Regulations are clear that there is no basis for the Secretary-General to grant any such exception for gifts, honours, decorations or favours from *governmental* sources.[30] Accordingly, staff members are required to decline any such items that may be offered to them by representatives of governments. Staff may only receive such items from governmental sources in highly exceptional circumstances, namely where a staff member is presented with an *unanticipated* gift from a governmental source and refusal of which would cause embarrassment to the organization; in such instances, they may receive the item only and expressly on behalf of the organization and any such items would then have to be reported and entrusted to the Secretary-General "who will either retain it for the Organization or arrange for its disposal for the benefit of the Organization or for a charitable purpose".[31]

---

[29] *Ibid.*, Staff Rule 1.2(n). The Commentary to Staff Rule 1.2(n), explains: "the Secretary-General would normally grant authorization to accept an honorary degree or certificate from any university or related institution that is recognized as an academic institution by the Secretary-General. For example, no approval would be granted for honours from so-called "diploma mills" or institutions not recognized by a competent national authority". Commentary to the Staff Rules and Regulations, see above note 18.

[30] Commentary to Staff Regulation 1.2(j): "Staff regulation 1.2 (j) stresses the importance of the appearance of strict independence and impartiality of staff and thus reaffirms the absolute prohibition on acceptance of benefits from Governments. No exception to this prohibition beyond staff regulation 1.2 (k) [...] is foreseen, *and there is no basis for the Secretary-General to grant approval for acceptance*" (emphasis added). *Ibid.*

[31] ST/SGB/2018/1, Staff Regulation 1.2(k), and Staff Rule 1.2(l), see above note 10. See also the Commentary to the Staff Regulations and Rules, see above note 18. The Secretary-General may then decide to display such received items in any of the UN's premises for educational or symbolic purposes. "Preservation and Disposition of Gifts and Historical Items", Secretary-General's Bulletin ST/SGB/136, 1 February 1971, provides that articles or items (including archival or documentary materials) may be displayed or exhibited for educational, informational and decorative purposes in UN premises or elsewhere. See also, ST/AI/2010/1,

Another key aspect of international civil servants' incorruptibility, and thus their integrity, is the requirement to place the organization's interests above their own and to avoid at all times any actual, possible or perceived conflict of interest. For instance, staff members may not use their office "or the knowledge gained from their office" for private gain, financial or otherwise, or the private gain of third parties, including friends, family or those they favour.[32] This includes using confidential or non-public information for one's own private advantage or the advantage of a third party. Quite clearly, sharing (confidential) procurement information about an upcoming bidding process with a family member or friend to help their business gain a contract with the UN would be highly inappropriate. The Commentary to the Staff Regulations explains that the terms 'family' or 'friend' in this regard "are broad and intended to encompass not only family members and friends as normally understood, but also relationships that are not recognized by the Staff Regulations and Rules as creating a dependency".[33] Additionally, although giving presents between colleagues is not in itself prohibited, such gifts may only be offered provided they do not come with a request or promise to act in a certain way, or to fail to perform or delay the performance of any official act.[34]

Ultimately, key to international civil servants' incorruptibility is the avoidance of (even the appearance of) impropriety, including conflicts of interest. It should be noted that a conflict of interest, as defined in the UN Staff Regulations and Rules, is not limited to a situation in which a staff member's personal interest conflicts with (or is perceived to conflict with) the interests of the UN or the performance of their duties. It includes a situation in which a staff member's personal interest conflicts with (or is perceived to conflict with) *their required independence, impartiality and in-*

---

above note 25, and "Honours, gifts or renumeration from outside sources", Information Circular, 16 August 2006, ST/IC/2006/31 (https://www.legal-tools.org/doc/j19d4l/).

[32] ST/SGB/2018/1, Staff Regulation 1.2(g), see above note 10.

[33] Commentary to the Staff Rules and Regulations, Staff Regulation 1.2(g), see above note 18.

[34] ST/SGB/2018/1, Staff Rule 1.2(k), see above note 10: "Staff members shall neither offer nor promise any favour, gift, remuneration or any other personal benefit to another staff member or to any third party with a view to causing him or her to perform, fail to perform or delay the performance of any official act. Similarly, staff members shall neither seek nor accept any favour, gift, remuneration or any other personal benefit from another staff member or from any third party in exchange for performing, failing to perform or delaying the performance of any official act".

tegrity.[35] Conflicts of interest, whether actual, possible or perceived, can occur in relation to staff members' engagement in outside activities, family relationships, the receipt of gifts or honours, personal investments and assets, post-employment restrictions, personal references, campaigning for elected office, and *pro bono* goods and services.[36] All staff members are required to disclose any actual or possible conflict of interest, which must be resolved in favour of the interests of the organization.[37] For example, where a staff member's affiliation with an outside entity, such as a proposed board membership of an NGO, is deemed to reflect adversely upon their required independence and impartiality, a staff member may be required to relinquish that outside engagement while in the service of the UN to preserve their integrity.

While the UN encourages staff members' personal development outside their work and their engagement with the communities in which they live, any such engagement with outside entities must not call into question the UN's independence and impartiality, or otherwise reflect adversely on the UN or staff members' status as international civil servants. These rules thus seek to instil in staff members the need for exercising discretion in their engagement with or support for outside entities, in recognition of the fact that even when they act in a private capacity, they remain representatives of the UN, subject to its Rules and Regulations, and that even their private conduct may reflect adversely upon the UN and their status as international civil servants. In other words, the UN's regulatory ethics infrastructure focuses on circumscribing the individual conduct and behaviour of individual staff members *vis-à-vis* outside entities as required by their status as international civil servants: they must put the organization and its interests above everything else, including their personal convictions, loyalties, affiliations or ideological preferences, and must not be perceived as being partial to and/or a proponent of any one particular policy, except the policies of their organization. Indeed, for international civil servants to act with the required integrity, as characterised by their independence and impartiality, means that "they must at all times maintain a broad international outlook and an understanding of the international community as a

---

[35] *Ibid.*, Staff Regulation 1.2(m) and Staff Rule 1.2(q).

[36] Activities of the Ethics Office, Report of the Secretary General, 8 June 2018, UN Doc. A/73/89, para. 17 ('UN Ethics Office Annual Report 2017') (https://www.legal-tools.org/doc/z8uoqo/).

[37] ST/SGB/2018/1, Staff Regulation 1.2(m) and Staff Rule 1.2(q), see above note 10.

whole".[38] Viewed this way, these integrity requirements ultimately serve to protect the institutional integrity of the organization by guaranteeing the incorruptibility and impartiality of its staff members.

Given the multinational, multicultural, multi-ethnic and multi-generational make-up of the workforce of the UN, however, even with the existence of a detailed set of rules and regulations around conduct and be-haviour, the UN cannot simply assume that all staff members have the same understanding of these requirements of independence, impartiality and integrity. As such, as important as the existence of regulatory ethics infrastructure is, investment should also be made in establishing organiza-tional systems of compliance that reward ethical behaviour and discourage unethical behaviour: an 'institutional' ethics infrastructure.

13.3. The UN's 'Institutional' Ethics Infrastructure

In the early 2000s, the UN faced what some have called the biggest corrup-tion scandal in the organization's history: the oil-for-food scandal.[39] This illustrated that the existence of anti-corruption rules circumscribing indi-vidual integrity was not sufficient alone to ensure the institution and its civ-il servants acted with the integrity required of them. This thus prompted a number of management and other institutional oversight reforms with a view towards bolstering the organization's institutional ethics infrastructure. This included the establishment in 2005 of the UN Ethics Office by then-

---

[38] Standards of Conduct of the International Civil Service, para. 10, see above note 12.

[39] The Oil for Food programme was established in 1995 under Security Council resolution 986 to alleviate "the serious nutritional and health situation of the Iraqi population". The pro-gramme sought to allow the purchase by Iraq of "medicine, health supplies, foodstuffs, and materials and supplies for essential civilian needs" through the controlled sale of oil from Iraq through an escrow system. Security Council resolution 986, "authorization to permit the import of petroleum and petroleum products originating in Iraq, as a temporary measure to provide for humanitarian needs of the Iraqi people", 14 April 1995, UN Doc. S/RES/986 (https://www.legal-tools.org/doc/502a28/). However, following the programme's official closure in 2003, in January 2004, serious allegations were made that around 270 persons and companies sympathetic to Saddam Hussein paid bribes and agreed to pay substantial kick-backs to the Iraqi government in exchange for their participation in this scheme. A subse-quent investigation found "a range of lapses, negligence and corrupt practices that allowed Saddam [Hussein]'s regime to earn as much as $11 billion while under sanctions": Robert McMahon, "The Impact of the UN Oil-for-Food Scandal", *Council for Foreign Relations*, 2006 (available on its web site). It also pointed to deep flaws in the UN's oversight of the administration of the programme.

Secretary-General Kofi Annan.[40] The UN Ethics Office is an independent office within the UN Secretariat, whose function is to cultivate and nurture a culture of ethics, integrity and accountability, and thereby to enhance the trust in, and the credibility of, the UN, both internally and externally. In doing so, the UN Ethics Office provides five lines of service: (i) providing confidential ethics advice to staff members; (ii) conducting ethics aware-ness, outreach and training; (iii) administering the UN financial disclosure programme; (iv) administering the UN's policy for the protection against retaliation for reporting misconduct or for cooperating with an audit or in-vestigation; and (v) promoting coherence and common ethics standards across the UN family.[41] It is beyond the scope of this chapter to provide a comprehensive review and analysis of each aspect of the mandate of the UN Ethics Office. Instead, this section will seek to highlight a number of specific initiatives that may provide food for thought as to how to (better) cultivate an organizational culture of ethics and integrity in other institu-tional contexts, such as international justice institutions like the Interna-tional Criminal Court ('ICC').

The primary objective of the UN Ethics Office is to assist the Secre-tary-General in ensuring that all staff members observe and perform their functions "consistent with the highest standards of integrity required by the Charter of the United Nations".[42] As an independent office, the UN Ethics

---

[40] "Ethics Office – establishment and terms of reference", Secretary-General's Bulletin ST/SGB/2005/22, 30 December 2005 ('ST/SGB/2005/22') (https://www.legal-tools.org/doc/a8gm8e/). Several of the separately funded agencies and programmes, such as the UNFPA, UNICEF, UNDP and the United Nations High Commissioner for Refugees ('UNHCR'), have since also established their own Ethics Offices. Rather than canvassing the entire spec-trum of work of these different Ethics Offices in the UN system, this chapter will focus on the UN Ethics Office established within the UN Secretariat. The Director of the UN Ethics Office chairs the Ethics Panel of the United Nations ('EPUN'), which is comprised of the Directors of the various ethics offices of the UN system (UNDP, UNICEF, UNFPA, UN-HCR, the United Nations Office for Project Services, the World Food Programme and the United Nations Relief and Works Agency for Palestine Refugees in the Near East) and is charged with ensuring coherence and harmonization in ethics standard setting across the UN family. The UN Ethics Office continues to provide ethics services to entities which have not appointed an ethics officer and/or established an ethics office, in accordance with: "United Nations system-wide application of ethics: separately administered organs and programmes", Secretary-General's Bulletin ST/SGB/2007/11, 30 November 2007 ('ST/SGB/2007/11') (https://www.legal-tools.org/doc/te040l/). See also the web site of the UN Ethics Office for more information about EPUN (formerly the UN Ethics Committee).

[41] ST/SGB/2005/22, para. 3.1, see above note 40.

[42] UN Ethics Office Annual Report 2017, para. 2, see above note 36.

Office serves the best interests of the organization, seeking to advance the integrity of both the institution and that of its staff members. While the UN Ethics Office provides five lines of service, requests for confidential ethics advice, in particular on the management and mitigation of conflicts of interest and other reputational risks, constitutes the majority of its work: in 2019, 44 per cent of the requests for service submitted to the UN Ethics Office were requests for ethics advice.[43] Importantly, requests for ethics advice are confidential,[44] which allows staff to seek advice and guidance in confidence concerning ethical dilemmas they may face. By providing advice to staff members on concrete ethics questions, the Ethics Office helps staff and the organization proactively and preventatively manage and mitigate conflict-of-interest risks and potential reputational harm, and thus helps safeguard the integrity of both individual civil servants and of the institution as a whole. In other words, through its advisory function, the UN Ethics Office constitutes an important institutional mechanism that gives meaning to and helps shape the interpretation of the UN's regulatory ethics infrastructure, including its individual integrity requirements.

In addition to the advice provided at the request of staff members and/or to management on the mitigation of conflict-of-interest risks or related ethics concerns, the UN Ethics Office also administers the UN Financial Disclosure Programme ('UNFDP'). The UNFDP requires the disclosure of personal assets and affiliations by selected staff members on an annual basis with a view towards assisting staff members and the organization in identifying, mitigating and managing personal conflict-of-interest risks. Participation in the UNFDP is determined based on a staff member's seniority or the substantive nature of their position. Initially, only staff members at the Assistant Secretary-General level and above were required to file financial disclosure statements.[45] However, the financial disclosure programme was reviewed and expanded significantly in 2006, in part as a

---

[43] Activities of the Ethics Office, Report of the Secretary General, 30 April 2020, UN Doc. A/75/82, paras. 8, 13 ('UN Ethics Office Annual Report 2019').

[44] The mandate of the Ethics Office specifically protects the confidentiality of its ethics advice: "In respect of its advisory functions as set out in section 3.1(c) above, the Ethics Office shall not be compelled by any United Nations official or body to testify about concerns brought to its attention". ST/SGB/2005/22, para. 3.4, see above note 40.

[45] See "Financial Disclosure Programme", Secretary-General's Bulletin ST/SGB/1999/3, 28 April 1999 ('ST/SGB/1999/3') (https://www.legal-tools.org/doc/wnk1hh/).

result of the oil-for-food scandal,[46] and now covers: all senior staff members at Director (D-1) level and above; all staff members who are procurement officers or whose principal duties relate to the procurement of goods or services for the UN; all staff members whose principal duties relate to the investment of the assets of the UN; other staff members with direct access to confidential procurement or investment information; and, all staff members of the UN Ethics Office.[47] Participation in the UNFDP is mandatory; failure to comply may constitute misconduct and will be referred to the Office of Human Resources Management for possible disciplinary action.[48]

Staff members required to participate in the UNFDP must disclose in relation to themselves and their spouse and/or dependent children (if any) their assets, profits, non-UN income, stock options, gifts and liabilities (above a certain threshold) in addition to their private affiliations such as outside activities, leadership or policy-making positions with non-UN entities, relatives employed within the UN system, or any other activity that may reflect upon their integrity.[49] In addition, staff members serving on a "When Actually Employed" (WAE) basis, on a one-dollar-per-year (symbolic) appointment,[50] or on appointments of a short duration must file a

---

[46]   The UN's financial disclosure programme was first established in 1999 to implement the requirements set out in Staff Regulations 1.2(m) and (n). It was subsequently expanded in 2005 following the conclusions of the Volcker Report about the Oil-for-Food scandal, and again amended in 2006 following the establishment of the UN Ethics Office. For the relevant administrative documents, see *ibid.*, ST/SGB/1999/3; "Financial Disclosure and Declaration of Interest Statements", Secretary-General's Bulletin ST/SGB/2005/19, 25 November 2005 ('ST/SGB/2005/19') (https://www.legal-tools.org/doc/th9lb9/), and "Financial Disclosure and Declaration of Interest Statements", Secretary-General's Bulletin ST/SGB/2006/6, 10 April 2006 ('ST/SGB/2006/6') (https://www.legal-tools.org/doc/58es6q/). The latter remains in force at the time of writing.

[47]   *Ibid.*, para. 2.1.

[48]   In its 2017 Annual Report, the UN Ethics Office notes that during the 2017 filing cycle, two filers failed to submit their statements and were referred to the Office of Human Resources Management ('OHRM'). See UN Ethics Office Annual Report 2017, para. 26, see above note 36.

[49]   ST/SGB/2006/6, paras. 3.1 and 3.2, see above note 46.

[50]   WAE and One-Dollar-A-Year contracts are granted only in exceptional circumstances and are limited to high-level appointments, such as at the level of Assistant-Secretary-General, Under-Secretary-General, Special Representative, or Special Envoy. See UN General Assembly resolution 67/255 'Human Resources Management', UN Doc. A/RES/67/255, 23 May 2013, para. 63 (https://www.legal-tools.org/doc/zq330a/); "Use of 'When Actually Employed' contracts for special representatives, envoys and other special high-level positions",

declaration of interest statement, which requires them to disclose their out-side interests in relation to entities with which they may be required to en-gage in their UN role, leadership or policy-making positions in external entities, relatives employed within the UN system, as well as other activi-ties that may reflect upon their integrity.[51] Financial disclosure and declara-tion of interest statements must be filed upon entry upon duty, and annually thereafter for as long as a staff member falls within the categories of staff required to file such statements. In 2019, 6,157 staff members participated in the UNFDP (compared to around 1,700 filers in 2006).[52] Although some UN entities administer their own financial disclosure programme, others have opted to participate in the UNFDP administered by the UN Ethics Of-fice on a cost-sharing basis.[53] This also ensures a harmonised interpretation of the financial disclosure requirements and management of conflicts of interest across all UN entities participating in the UNFDP. The ICC's fi-nancial disclosure programme for designated staff members, while separate from the UN, has also been administered by the UN Ethics Office since 2015.[54]

As mentioned, the main purpose of the UNFDP is to assist with the management and mitigation of conflicts of interest. Additionally, it is an honour-based system, and staff are expected, in line with their required in-tegrity, to provide honest, truthful and complete statements to assist the or-ganization in identifying and managing conflicts of interest. Once state-ments have been reviewed, which is done by an independent external ser-vice provider under the general guidance of the UN Ethics Office,[55] and where conflicts of interest have been identified, staff members will receive recommendations to manage and mitigate the identified conflict(s) of inter-est.[56] Ultimately, the purpose is to reinforce the highest standards of ethics

---

Secretary-General's Bulletin ST/SGB/283, 29 August 1996; OHRM Guidelines on Use of One-Dollar-Per-Year Contracts (available on UN's web site).

[51] ST/SGB/2006/6, para. 2.3, see above note 46.

[52] UN Ethics Office Annual Report 2019, para. 22, see above note 43.

[53] *Ibid.*, para. 26.

[54] See Administrative Instruction ICC/AI/2015/005 of 6 October 2015, implementing Section 6.1 of Presidential Directive ICC/PRESD/G/2014/002 of 13 May 2014 (the 'ICC's Anti-Fraud Policy').

[55] "Activities of the UN Ethics Office", Report of the Secretary-General, UN Doc. A/71/334, 16 August 2016, para. 23 (https://www.legal-tools.org/doc/uux6c1/) ('UN Ethics Office An-nual Report 2016'); UN Ethics Office Annual Report 2017, para. 25, see above note 36.

[56] For more information, see the web site of the UN Ethics Office.

and integrity in their personal and professional conduct as required by the UN Charter. This, in turn, reinforces the integrity of the institution itself. The UNFDP thus represents another important component of the UN's 'institutional' ethics infrastructure aimed at safeguarding the organization's integrity, and thus maintaining and enhancing public trust in the institution, through managing individual compliance with the UN's 'regulatory' ethics infrastructure.

In recognition of the importance of ethical leadership,[57] a number of additional institutional ethics structures exist to encourage ethical behaviour, particularly among senior-level UN officials. For instance, in July 2016, the Secretary-General introduced a pre-appointment declaration-of-interest form for candidates under consideration for positions at the Under-Secretary-General and Assistant Secretary-General levels; since July 2017, this form has also been applied to other senior-level staff in the field such as force or police commanders.[58] This pre-appointment review is different to and completely separate from general background checks – rather, it is an institutional ethics mechanism created to enable the organization to proactively manage conflict-of-interest risks before the entry upon duty of senior officials. This pre-appointment conflict-of-interest vetting conducted by the UN Ethics Office has assisted the organization in pre-emptively identifying, managing and mitigating conflicts of interests, and ensures that senior officials enter the service of the UN responsible only to the organization.[59] Newly appointed senior officials are also provided with personalised ethics briefings by the UN Ethics Office to ensure the right 'tone at the top'.[60] Such personalised ethics briefings are important opportunities to instil in the organization's leadership the importance of ethical leadership

---

[57] Research has shown that employees who believe their manager behaves ethically are more likely to behave ethically themselves, are happier in their work, are more committed to their work, and are more likely to help others. See, for example, David M. Mayer, Karl Aquino, Rebecca L. Greenbaum and Maribeth Kuenzi, "Who displays ethical leadership and why does it matter? An examination of antecedents and consequences of ethical leadership", in *Academy of Management Journal*, 2012, vol. 55, no. 1, p. 167.

[58] UN Ethics Office Annual Report 2017, paras. 15–16, see above note 36. It should be noted that UNDP's Ethics Office makes reference to the development and adoption of a Conflict of Interest Declaration Form for newly recruited staff members already in its 2014 Annual Report. Activities of the UNDP Ethics Office in 2013: Report of the Ethics Office, DP/2014/17, 25 March 2014, para. 4 (https://www.legal-tools.org/doc/4t9ohx/).

[59] UN Ethics Office Annual Report 2017, para. 15, see above note 36.

[60] *Ibid.*, para. 62.

and to strengthen their familiarity with the organization's ethics infrastructure. This is important because, as Mayer *et al.* (2012) found, "leaders set the ethical tone of an organization and are instrumental in encouraging ethical behaviour and reducing interpersonal conflict from their subordinates".[61]

In addition to the abovementioned (internal) institutional ethics mechanisms, a number of public measures have also been implemented to increase public trust and confidence in the integrity of the UN. Notably, in 2007, the Secretary-General launched the Voluntary Public Disclosure Initiative ('VPDI'), pursuant to which the Secretary-General encourages senior leaders in the organization at the Assistant-Secretary-General level and above to publish a publicly redacted version of their financial disclosure or declaration of interest statement.[62] Contrary to their participation in the UNFDP, which is mandatory in accordance with the applicable regulatory framework, participation in the VPDI, as its name suggests, is voluntary. As the UN acknowledges, participation in the VPDI is an important measure to demonstrate the personal commitment of senior leaders in the UN to ethical conduct and principles of integrity; however, the multi-cultural and often security-sensitive environment in which UN officials operate may not always make it possible for officials to participate in the VPDI.[63] Nonetheless, each year, around 70 per cent of senior officials opt to publish a public version of their confidential disclosure statement (note that this also includes senior officials of the ICC).[64] Similarly, while not required, since 2016, the President of the UN General Assembly also makes public a redacted summary of her/his disclosure statement.[65]

The focus of these last two initiatives is on the organization's senior leadership; this is understandable given, as mentioned, the importance of

---

[61] Mayer *et al.*, 2012, p. 167, see above note 57.

[62] See the Policy on Voluntary Public Disclosure by UN staff members of Financial Disclosure and Declaration of Interest Statements (available on UN's web site).

[63] See the web site of the Voluntary Public Disclosure.

[64] UN Ethics Office Annual Report 2017, para. 39, see above note 36: "In 2016, of the 163 senior officials eligible to participate in the voluntary public disclosure initiative, 115 (or 70.6 per cent) did so. In 2017, 95 of the 142 eligible senior officials (or 66.9 per cent) participated. Overall participation rates remained largely in line with those in previous years". In 2019, a little more than 75 per cent of eligible officials participated. UN Ethics Office Annual Report 2019, para. 29, see above note 43.

[65] H.E. President María Fernanda Espinosa Garces (the seventy-third President of the UN General Assembly) is the second President to do so (available on UN's web site).

ethical leadership for the integrity of an institution. However, the ethics and integrity requirements, of course, apply to all staff members, regardless of their seniority within an organization. All UN staff members are required to disclose possible, potential and actual conflicts of interest and are required to proactively seek advice from the Ethics Office when they are in doubt.[66] This ensures a certain degree of consistency in the application and interpretation of the UN's regulatory ethics infrastructure.[67] It also seeks to ensure conflicts of interest are increasingly identified before they occur, thus proactively managing and mitigating any such reputational risks.

To facilitate a broader understanding of the ethics and integrity requirements across the UN, since 2013, the Executive Office of the Secretary-General jointly with the UN Ethics Office each year launches what are called the 'Leadership Dialogues'. The Leadership Dialogues provide a structured framework around a specific theme for managers to discuss ethics questions with their staff at a dedicated time. The theme, while different every year, focuses on further developing staff member's understanding of their required integrity. For example, the 2017 Leadership Dialogue was entitled: *"Standards of Conduct: What's expected of me?"*.[68] It focused on the UN standards of conduct and what they mean for being accountable for one's actions, making decisions in the best interests of the organization, and adhering to the organizational regulations, rules and policies in this regard. Topics covered included organizational priorities relating to the prevention of sexual exploitation, abuse and harassment, conflicts of interest, the rules around gifts, and staff members' participation in political activities. In 2019, the Leadership Dialogue was entitled *"Conflicts of interest: why do they matter?"*.[69] All managers are required to undertake this structured 1.5-hour dialogue session on an annual basis with their direct reports. Starting with the Secretary-General, who undertakes the session with his Under-Secretary-Generals, the Leadership Dialogue thus cascades through

---

[66] Whereas all UN Secretariat staff members are expected and encouraged to seek advice from the UN Ethics Office when in doubt, in UNDP, staff members are *required* to first seek ethics clearance from the UNDP Ethics Office before seeking approval from their management to engage in outside activities. See, "Operating with Unwavering Integrity", UNDP Code of Ethics, October 2017, p. 12 (available on UNDP's web site).

[67] The consistency of ethics standards and policies is further strengthened through regular EPUN meetings and consultations on particularly complex cases or issues having UN-wide implications. See further note 40, above.

[68] See the website of the Leadership Dialogues (available on UN's web site).

[69] *Ibid.*

---

the organization and across teams, departments and countries. The UN Ethics Office monitors compliance and is available for further support and advice as teams embark on their annual Leadership Dialogue exercise.[70] Such initiatives, which allow managers dedicated time to discuss ethics and integrity questions with their direct reports, provide an important impetus for further developing and enhancing the organization's collective understanding of the ethical challenges that occur in the context of its work, and the different viewpoints that may exist on how to resolve such challenges. Such regular conversations form an important part of an organization's ethics learning, and a deeper "moral learning process",[71] another important component of establishing and reinforcing a culture of organizational ethics and individual integrity.

In other words, a number of institutional mechanisms have been established over the years to further enhance understanding of and ensure compliance by its staff members with the UN's regulatory ethics infrastructure, which in turn seek to enhance public trust and confidence in (the integrity of) the institution itself. More importantly, through its advisory, reputational risk management, and outreach initiatives, the UN Ethics Office aims to contribute to creating an organizational culture where every staff member understands and fulfils the requirements of independence, impartiality and integrity, treats everyone with respect and dignity, and fosters a safe and inclusive working environment for all.

However, as important as regulatory and institutional ethics infrastructures are, research has shown that the single best predictor of unethical behaviour is organizational culture,[72] and in particular organizational *tolerance*. Where unethical behaviour is seen to be tolerated (such as where there are no repercussions or where those repercussions are not publicly communicated as accountability standards), the overall impact of regulatory or institutional ethics infrastructure on strengthening the (perceived) in-

---

[70]   *Ibid.*

[71]   On the 'moral learning process', see, for example, Dr. Julien Topal, "Installing a Moral Learning Process: Integrity Beyond Traditional Ethics Training", *Columbia Center for the Advancement of Public Integrity*, 2017 (available on its web site).

[72]   See, for example, Azish Filabi and Caterina Bulgarella, "Organizational Culture Drives Ethical Behaviour: Evidence From Pilot Studies", 2018 OECD Anti-Corruption and Integrity Forum (available on OECD web site); Paula A. Johnson, Sheila E. Widnall and Frazier F. Benya (eds.), *Sexual Harassment of Women: Climate, Culture, and Consequences in Academic Sciences, Engineering, and Medicine*, The National Academies Press, Washington, D.C., 2018.

tegrity of either individual staff members or the institution as a whole will be limited. An area where this has been highlighted most prominently in recent years is in relation to interpersonal (prohibited) conduct and, in particular, the way in which ethics infrastructures have not focused (sufficiently) on (sexual) harassment as a breach of institutional ethics and individual integrity. Indeed, as the next section will show, the UN's ethics infrastructure is only just beginning to grapple with how to better address the interpersonal, yet systemic, integrity violations exemplified by sexual harassment.

13.4. Ethics Infrastructure and Sexual Harassment

Just like other institutions, businesses, and entities, the UN is, unfortunately, not immune to sexual misconduct committed by its staff members. It has long struggled and continues to struggle, with allegations of sexual exploitation and abuse by peacekeepers of communities and beneficiaries of UN assistance.[73] Additionally, in recent years, there has been increased recognition that sexual exploitation and abuse are not restricted to peacekeeping personnel but are also committed by civilian personnel.[74] Similarly, in large part due to the #MeToo and #AidToo movements and the courage of many women and a few men to speak up about the sexual harassment they have

---

[73] Although allegations of sexual exploitation by aid workers first surfaced in 1992 in the context of the UN Mission in Cambodia, the issue was not formally recognised until a 2002 report by Save the Children and UNHCR highlighted widespread sexual abuse of populations by UN peacekeepers and NGO personnel in West Africa. Accusations included: sexual assault, rape, sex trafficking, organized prostitution rings, abduction, child pornography, and sex in exchange for food, medicine, employment, and protection. See, Save the Children and UNHCR, "Sexual Violence and Exploitation: The Experience of Refugee Children in Guinea, Liberia and Sierra Leone", 1 February 2002. See also, Melanie O'Brien, *Criminalising Peacekeepers: Modernising National Approaches to Sexual Exploitation and Abuse*, Palgrave MacMillan, 2017; Rosa Freedman, "UNaccountable: A New Approach to Peacekeepers and Sexual Abuse", in *European Journal of International Law*, 2018, vol. 29, no. 3, pp. 961–985; Jasmine-Kim Westendorf, *Violating Peace: Sex, Aid and Peacekeeping*, Cornell University Press, 2020.

[74] For instance, in 2018, of the 55 allegations of sexual exploitation and abuse reported to the UN peacekeeping operations and special political missions, 38 were against military personnel, 4 against police, and 13 against civilian personnel. Additionally, a further 94 allegations were reported involving UN staff and related personnel of UN entities other than peacekeeping operations and special political missions. See, "Special measures for protection from sexual exploitation and abuse", Report of the Secretary-General, UN Doc. A/73/744, 14 February 2019 (and annexes) (https://www.legal-tools.org/doc/e5i9ma/). The United Nations publishes quarterly updates on allegations of sexual exploitation and abuse and maintains an up-to-date online database of allegations (available on its web site).

experienced in the UN institutional context, there is now also increased attention for sexual misconduct arising within the workplace and between UN colleagues, interns, volunteers, and others. Notably, in January 2019, the results of an internal UN staff survey showed that one in three staff members reported having been sexually harassed during the preceding two years.[75] Only one in three respondents who experienced sexual harassment, however, said they took action, such as reporting the misconduct, pointing to a lack of trust in formal reporting systems and perceptions of inaction and impunity for offenders.

These UN statistics do not stand in isolation; similar data and allegations have arisen in recent years in the wider humanitarian, development and human rights context, such as at Oxfam,[76] Amnesty International[77] and in law firms, as evidenced by the global survey conducted by the International Bar Association, the results of which were published in May 2019.[78] This latter survey illustrated that in the legal profession, one in three women and one in fourteen men had been subjected to some form of sexual harassment. Respondents reported they had experienced a broad range of sexually harassing behaviours, including sexist or sexually suggestive comments, inappropriate physical contact, such as patting, pinching or brushing up against someone, sexual propositions, invitations or other pressure for sex, and demands for sex in exchange for employment or career advancement opportunities.[79] Since writing this chapter, in 2020, allegations of sexual harassment were also raised in the context of the election of the next

---

[75] "Safe Space Survey on Sexual Harassment in the Workplace Report", *Deloitte* (for the United Nations), January 2019 (available on Code Blue Campaign's web site) ('Safe Space Survey Report'). See also, "One in three UN workers say they have been sexually harassed in past two years", *The Guardian*, 16 January 2019 (available on its web site).

[76] In February 2018, allegations surfaced in the media about the abuse of vulnerable women by senior Oxfam officials in Haiti in 2011. Oxfam announced a Ten Point Action Plan to address sexual misconduct and accountability, which included the establishment of an Independent Commission. The Commission's Interim Report was published in January 2019 and its final report in June 2019 (available on its web site).

[77] Amnesty International commissioned an external, independent investigation into the circumstances following the deaths of two staff members who had taken their own lives while in the service of the organization. The external investigation report was published in January 2019. "Staff Wellbeing Review", Amnesty International, January 2019 (available on its web site) ('Amnesty International Report').

[78] Kieran Pender, "Us Too? Bullying and Harassment in the Legal Profession", *International Bar Association*, May 2019 (available on its web site) ('IBA Report').

[79] *Ibid.*, pp. 55–56.

chief Prosecutor of the ICC.[80] This emerging data shows very clearly that much more work needs to be done not only to improve existing policy frameworks around sexual harassment to recognise the full spectrum of behaviours that occur, but also to invest in stronger compliance, regulatory and institutional ethics infrastructure to address sexual harassment.[81] This section will thus focus on recent developments at the UN in relation to this under-researched and emerging area in ethics research and scholarship.

I deliberately call this an 'emerging area' because most scholarship and other ethics research has focused on conflicts of interest, reputational risk management and other anti-corruption measures as encompassing 'ethics' or 'ethics infrastructure'. For instance, the Organisation for Economic Co-operation and Development has conducted a number of research projects and developed various concept papers on governance in public institutions, which define integrity as anti-corruption.[82] Likewise, scholarship on ethics in the legal profession thus far has focused mostly on inappropriate and corrupt conduct by lawyers *vis-à-vis* their clients or the law and courts more generally.[83] Arguably, even the UN's ethics infrastructure discussed above is similarly focused (more) on anti-corruption; notably, the UN Ethics Office's mandate defines 'ethical issues' as "conflicts of interest".[84] This is perhaps not surprising as the UN Ethics Office, was created *in direct response to* a corruption scandal. This has, however, meant that the

---

[80] Danya Chaikel, "ICC Prosecutor Symposium: The Next ICC Prosecutor Must Embody Integrity in the #MeToo Era", in *Opinio Juris*, 16 April 2020 (available on its web site). See also, the April 2020 ATLAS Statement to the Committee on the Election of the Prosecutor and States Parties to the Rome Statute of the International Criminal Court calling for a fair, transparent and safe procedure for receiving and assessing complaints of misconduct against candidates for ICC Prosecutor (available on its web site).

[81] This section largely focuses on frameworks to address sexual harassment as opposed to other sexual misconduct such as sexual exploitation and abuse (SEA) by aid workers of the populations they are working for/with, which has been extensively covered elsewhere. The author recognizes that this is distinction is arbitrary as sexual harassment, exploitation and abuse are part of a continuum of sexual violence. For more on SEA, see sources above in note 73.

[82] See, for example, the 2005 OECD policy document, "Public Sector Integrity – A Framework for Assessment" or its 2018 research paper by Azish Filabi and Caterina Bulgarella, "Organizational Culture Drives Ethical Behaviour: Evidence from Pilot Studies", *2018 OECD Global Anti-Corruption and Integrity Forum*, 27 March 2018.

[83] For an overview, see, for example, Parker *et al.*, 2008, pp. 161–163, see above note 5.

[84] ST/SGB/2005/22, Section 3.1, see above note 40: "(c) Providing confidential advice and guidance to staff *on ethical issues (e.g., conflict of interest)*, including administering an ethics helpline" (emphasis added).

---

organization has prioritised creating systems and structures to address un-ethical behaviour that constitute misconduct against the institution, that is, violations against the organization's (public or financial) interests such as fraud and corruption, over unethical actions that firstly harm individuals and harm the institution secondarily (for instance, sexual harassment, bullying and discrimination). These latter violations are still too often seen as private or personal issues. This is not unlike the public-private divide that has been criticised by feminist scholarship in many other areas.[85]

Nonetheless, the *Standards of Conduct for the International Civil Service* do include various provisions on personal conduct by staff members *vis-à-vis* their colleagues[86] and a number of policies have been adopted over the years to (start to) address sexual exploitation, abuse, and harassment.[87] Contrary to financial misconduct matters, such as fraud, corruption or conflicts of interest, however, (sexual) harassment, bullying and discrimination have primarily been understood as constituting management issues, as opposed to issues of ethics and integrity. For instance, until the adoption of its updated policy in 2019, the UN's policy on the prohibition of discrimination, harassment, including sexual harassment, and abuse of authority (ST/SGB/2008/5) placed all responsibility for dealing with (sexual) harassment with individual managers and the UN Office of Human Resources Management.[88]

---

[85] See, for example, Carole Pateman, "Feminist Critiques of the Public/Private Dichotomy", in Stanely I. Benn and Gerald F. Gaus (eds.), *Public and Private in Social Life*, St. Martin's Press, New York, 1983; Hilary Charlesworth, "The Public/Private Distinction and the Right to Development in International Law", *Australian Year Book of International Law*, 1988, vol. 12, pp. 1902–04; Hilary Charlesworth, "Feminist Methods in International Law", in *The American Journal of International Law*, 1999, vol. 93, no. 2, pp. 3793–94; Christine Chinkin, "A Critique of the Public/Private Dimension", in *European Journal of International Law*, 1999, vol. 10, no. 2, pp. 3873–95.

[86] Standards of Conduct for the International Civil Service, paras. 21 and 22, see above note 12.

[87] "Special measures for protection from sexual exploitation and sexual abuse", Secretary-General's Bulletin ST/SGB/2003/13, 9 October 2003 ('ST/SGB/2003/13') (https://www.legal-tools.org/doc/ftozsr/); "Prohibition of discrimination, harassment, including sexual harassment, and abuse of authority", Secretary-General's Bulletin ST/SGB/2008/5, 11 February 2008 ('ST/SGB/2008/5') (https://www.legal-tools.org/doc/ibc9oq/). Since the writing of this chapter, the UN Secretariat has adopted an updated policy on discrimination, harassment, including sexual harassment, and abuse of authority: Secretary-General's Bulletin ST/SGB/2019/8, 10 September 2019.

[88] Until 2019, under the UN's policy on (sexual) harassment, senior managers were responsible for addressing complaints of sexual harassment by establishing a fact-finding panel "of at least two individuals from the department, office or mission concerned who have been

Sexual harassment is still too often seen as an issue affecting only individuals, not the institution as a whole, which has predetermined the way in which it has been addressed (not only at the UN, but in many other contexts). Yet, as the #MeToo movement has clearly demonstrated, sexual harassment is rooted in systemic structures of power imbalance and gender inequality, and is symptomatic of a broader workplace culture that silences certain truths, experiences and stories. It has become clear that policy frameworks that emphasise informal or management solutions to individual cases between affected parties or other individualised management responses are insufficient to address and redress these structural dimensions of power and inequality that underpin almost all forms of (sexual) harassment.

The UN has been heavily criticised for the way in which it has addressed sexual harassment committed by its officials, including in a number of recent high-profile cases that led to the resignation, and in one case dismissal, of senior officials. At the end of February 2018, then-Deputy Director of UNICEF, Justin Forsyth, resigned following controversy over allegations that he engaged in inappropriate behaviour, including sexual harassment, in his previous position with Save the Children.[89] That same month, Luiz Loures, then-Deputy Executive Director at UNAIDS, announced that he would not seek renewal of his mandate in March 2018.[90] This followed an outcry over the way in which UNAIDS had handled sexual harassment allegations brought against Mr. Loures in November 2016. An independent review of the agency's handling of the case was subsequently conducted, which heavily criticised the agency's senior management. The report, which was published in December 2018, called for a change in leadership and criticised in particular Executive Director Michel

---

trained in investigating allegations of prohibited conduct or, if necessary, from the Office of Human Resources Management roster". See ST/SGB/2008/5, section 5. Although a full critique of the UN's policy framework around sexual harassment is beyond the scope of this chapter, it should be noted that best practice in addressing integrity violations is for such allegations to be investigated by independent investigators. Individuals who work closely with the alleged offender of sexual harassment, or with the person targeted, are not generally deemed to be sufficiently impartial and independent to allow for the fair and transparent decision-making on such matters. As such, the appointment of a fact-finding panel of individuals from *within* a department, office or mission, depending on the size of that department, office or mission, can be problematic.

[89] "Charity boss Justin Forsyth resigns from Unicef", *BBC News*, 22 February 2018.

[90] "Top UN official accused of sexual harassment stands down", *The Guardian*, 23 February 2018.

Sibidé's "personalised, patriarchal leadership style [that] has [...] come at a significant cost to transparent due process within the UNAIDS Secretariat and enabled a culture of harassment, including sexual harassment, bullying, and abuse of power".[91] In response, Mr. Sibidé, who was due to hold office until January 2020, offered to resign in June 2019;[92] in May 2019, however, he unexpectedly announced his resignation with immediate effect.[93] In December 2018, the Chairman of the International Civil Service Commission, Kingston Rhodes, also resigned after or during an internal inquiry into allegations of sexual harassment against him (the results of that investigation remain unclear).[94] In September 2018, UN Women dismissed a senior staff member after an investigation substantiated allegations of sexual misconduct committed by him against younger male staff members in his office.[95] These cases, and the critiques they elicited, illustrate the UN still has a long way to go to better respond to and ultimately prevent sexual harassment.

Yet, some important first steps have also been made since 2018. In February 2018, the UN Secretary-General announced a Five Point Plan to address sexual harassment. The implementation of the plan saw the launch of a 24-hour Speak Up helpline accessible to staff and non-staff personnel (for example, interns, consultants and volunteers) to confidentially seek support when faced with sexual harassment,[96] additional mandatory (online) training modules on a respectful workplace and the prevention of sexual harassment, and the appointment of a senior-level task force to spearhead reforms around sexual harassment policies and procedures.[97] These reforms included the adoption of a uniform definition of sexual harassment to be

---

[91] "Report on the work of the Independent Expert Panel on Prevention of and response to harassment, including sexual harassment; bullying and abuse of power at UNAIDS Secretariat", Doc. No. UNAIDS/PCB (43)/CRP1, 7 December 2018, para. 61 ('UNAIDS Report').

[92] "Under-fire UNAIDS chief offers to resign in June", in *France 42*, 13 December 2018.

[93] "Damaged in Scandal, Head of U.N. AIDS Agency Resigns Suddenly", *New York Times*, 8 May 2019.

[94] "Another UN Harassment Case Quietly Disappears", *PassBlue*, 6 January 2019.

[95] "Statement: Final decision on the sexual misconduct investigation at UN Women", *UN Women*, 18 September 2018 (available on its web site); "Exclusive: Senior UN Official Fired, Referred to Criminal Authorities for Alleged Sexual Misconduct", *News Week*, 17 September 2018.

[96] As provided in the UN's updated policy on (sexual) harassment, the helpline can be reached at +1 917 367 8910 or, from peacekeeping missions, at +1212 78910. The helpline can also be reached at speakup@un.org. See ST/SGB/2019/8, above note 87.

[97] In November 2017, a senior level taskforce within the UN's Chief Executives Board was created to improve the UN system organizations' responses to sexual harassment.

used across the UN family, which subsequently formed the basis of a UN System Model Policy on Sexual Harassment adopted by the Chief Executives Board in October 2018.[98] Additionally, recognising the importance of accountability for sexual harassment, and thus a need to strengthen systems to ensure perpetrators of sexual misconduct are not able to move from one job to another undetected, in June 2018, the UN launched a system-wide screening database called 'ClearCheck' to avoid the re-hiring of individuals whose working relationship with an organization ends because of a finding they had perpetrated sexual harassment. As of October 2018, UN system entities may also opt to include individuals in this database who left an organization before an investigation or disciplinary process was completed.[99]

The UN Model Policy on Sexual Harassment, defines sexual harassment as follows:

> Sexual harassment is any unwelcome conduct of a sexual nature that might reasonably be expected or be perceived to cause offense or humiliation, when such conduct interferes with work, is made a condition of employment, or creates an intimidating, hostile or offensive work environment. Sexual harassment may occur in the workplace or in connection with work. While typically involving a pattern of conduct, sexual harassment may take the form of a single incident. In assessing the reasonableness of expectations or perceptions, the perspective of the person who is the target of the conduct shall be considered.[100]

In its explanatory notes, the model policy further recognises sexual harassment as "the manifestation of a culture of discrimination and privi-

---

[98] See Annex 4 to "CEB Taskforce on Addressing Sexual Harassment within the Organizations of the UN system – Progress Report", UN Doc. CEB/2018/HLCM/14, 3 October 2018 ('CEB/2018/HLCM/14'). See also, the UN Secretariat's updated policy ST/SGB/2019/8, above note 87. Additionally, in July 2019, jointly with member states, the UN launched a Model Code of Conduct to Prevent Harassment, Including Sexual Harassment, at UN System Events. The International Bar Association in May 2019 announced that it would also develop a harassment policy specifically applicable to the events and conferences it organizes around the world each year. IBA Report, May 2019, p. 101, see above note 78.

[99] CEB/2018/HLCM/14, paras. 22–30, see above note 98. Efforts are also ongoing in the broader humanitarian and development sector to set up similar misconduct disclosure systems at an inter-agency level. For more information on this Inter-Agency Misconduct Disclosure Scheme, see the website of the Steering Committee for Humanitarian Response.

[100] CEB/2018/HLCM/14/Add.1, Annex 4, p. 13, see above note 98.

---

lege based on unequal gender relations and other power dynamics".[101] It also acknowledges the intersectional nature of identities, noting that "power imbalances based on gender, workplace or educational status, racial or ethnic backgrounds, age, disability, sexual orientation or economic class could impact on sexual harassment".[102] This recognition of sexual harassment as an expression of power inequality is important as it is still too often underrecognized: sexual harassment (most often) has very little to do with sex and everything to do with power. Although sexual harassment does not always constitute an abuse of authority in the professional misconduct understanding of the word (such as a senior manager abusing their position of authority to gain sexual favours from junior staff, as the behaviour can also occur between individuals of similar 'rank' in an organizational hierarchy), sexual harassment always constitutes an abuse of relative or social power, as it expresses and reinforces existing (gendered and other) power imbalances and inequalities.[103]

The UN's Model Policy on sexual harassment also acknowledges that sexual harassment can be verbal, non-verbal and physical, and can occur between people of the same and of different genders. Importantly, the policy emphasises the need for support to victims and a victim-centred approach as well as work on prevention. Involving victims or survivors in the response to sexual harassment in a meaningful way is one way to equalize the unequal power dynamic that harmed them in the first place. This includes allowing victims/survivors to remain meaningfully engaged and involved in decisions about a process that influences and affects them, including the power to decide the extent to which they wish to remain involved (if at all) in any disciplinary investigation.[104] Although the meaning of such a survivor or victim-centred approach to sexual harassment is not specifically spelled out in the Model Policy, and thus requires further definition in the UN's practices, the recognition that a process must be survivor

---

[101] *Ibid.*

[102] *Ibid.*, p. 14

[103] "Towards an End to Sexual Harassment: The Urgency and Nature of Change in the Era of #MeToo", in *UN Women*, November 2018, p. 10: "Sexual harassment expresses and reinforces inequalities of power" ('UN Women Report'). See also, Catharine A. MacKinnon, *Sexual Harassment of Working Women*, Yale University Press, New Haven, 1979.

[104] Lyndsey Jones-Renaud, "What does a Survivor-Centered Approach to Workplace Harassment Look Like?", in *Medium*, 29 November 2018.

or victim-centred is a first step towards equalizing inherently unequal power dynamics.

The Model Policy has, however, also been criticised for continuing to emphasise offensiveness and humiliation in its definition of sexual harassment, which some argue trivializes the issue, displays moral judgment, and engages in "demeaning psychologizing".[105] Furthermore, it is expected that all UN entities use this Model Policy on Sexual Harassment to further strengthen and reform their own policy documents to align with their respective institutional and legal frameworks. As it continues to allow for the adoption of diverse policy frameworks by different UN entities, it leaves the door open to diverse interpretations of its provisions. As the policy, and thus the definitions set out therein, were the result of negotiations and compromise between a large number of UN entities, the result is ultimately imperfect.[106] Nonetheless, the commitment to adopt a uniform definition of sexual harassment, and the setting of minimum standards and core policy principles, is an important (first) step towards a more harmonised approach to sexual harassment. It opens possibilities for very necessary discussions and reflections on the scope of sexual harassment policy frameworks at the UN and beyond. This is important not least because other organisations in the human rights, humanitarian, and development fields tend to use UN definitions in the development of their own internal policies.[107] As data gathering on the range of misconduct that occurs within a workplace continues, at the UN and elsewhere, it would be important to ensure that the policy framework captures the full scale of behaviours that may constitute sexual violence within the workplace.

---

[105] UN Women Report, November 2018, p. 8, see above note 103: "Define sexual harassment as what it is: a human rights violation of gender-based discrimination, regardless of sex, in a context of unequal power relations such as a workplace and/or gender hierarchy. It can take the form of various acts including rape, other aggressive touching, forced viewing of pornography, taking and circulation of sexual photographs, as well as verbal sexual conduct. Definitions should define, not trivialize (for example, refer to 'annoyance'), make moral judgments ('offensiveness'), or engage in demeaning psychologizing ('humiliation')".

[106] On the wins and losses of the new policy, see also: Priyanka Chirimar, "UN's New Harassment Policy: You win some, you lose some", *Action against Prohibited Conduct (AAPC)*, 25 September 2020 (available on its web site).

[107] For instance, Oxfam has adopted UN definitions of sexual harassment, sexual exploitation, and sexual abuse. See Oxfam, "One Oxfam Policy on Protection from Sexual Exploitation and Abuse", December 2018 (available on its web site). See also, the definitions adopted in the CHS Alliance's PSEAH Quick Reference Handbook, revised version 2020 (available on its web site).

Work on other areas, such as better data collection to inform evidence-based policy making and strengthening investigative capacity, both of which are important to strengthen organizational responses to sexual harassment,[108] remains ongoing. For instance, in February 2018, the Secretary-General announced that the Office of Internal Oversight Services would assume responsibility for investigating all complaints of sexual harassment.[109] A specialised team of investigators, for which the UN prioritised the recruitment of female investigators, would implement a fast-tracked procedure to review, process and investigate complaints of sexual harassment.[110] Before this decision was made, sexual harassment allegations, if they were addressed through a formal process at all, were either addressed through informal mediation procedures, or through the establishment of an inquiry conducted by a panel of peers.[111] The move towards ensuring sexual harassment allegations are investigated by professional investigators with specific expertise in investigating these types of allegations is a welcome step. However, it would be important to equally invest in building the capacity of senior decision-makers (such as Heads of Department, Under-Secretary-Generals and/or members of the Office of Human Resources Management) in better understanding the context, consequences and structures that enable sexual harassment. They are generally tasked with interpreting investigation reports and translating these into the appropriate disciplinary action, as well as with taking measures to promote a workplace culture that prevents and does not tolerate sexual harassment and other similar integrity violations.

Earlier in 2017, the UN also strengthened its protection against retaliation policy. Protection against retaliation policy – also sometimes referred to as a 'whistle-blower policy'– is an important organizational measure to encourage staff to speak up about misconduct they witness or become aware of. The UN's protection against retaliation policy now applies not just to staff members, interns and UN volunteers, but also to individual

---

[108] See also, the recently adopted Convention and Recommendation by the International Labour Organization on violence and harassment in the workplace (available on its web site).

[109] It should be noted, however, that in its updated policy, while OIOS retains primary responsibility for investigating cases of sexual harassment, OIOS may also refer cases (back) to responsible officials for action, which may include investigative actions by an investigative panel of staff. ST/SGB/2019/8, section 5, see above note 87.

[110] "UN launches 24-hour hotline for staff to report sexual harassment", *UN News*, 26 February 2018.

[111] See above note 88.

contractors and consultants.[112] The policy defines retaliation as "any direct or indirect detrimental action that adversely affects the employment or working conditions of an individual, where such action has been recommended, threatened or taken for the purpose of punishing, intimidating or injuring an individual because that individual engaged in" a protected activity.[113] Such a 'protected activity', however, is narrowly defined to cover reporting misconduct through established reporting channels[114] and/or cooperating with a duly authorised audit or investigation. While protection against retaliation for reporting misconduct is an important part of a functioning ethics infrastructure to encourage staff members and others to speak up about concerns of misconduct, through the adoption of such a formal definition, it fails to address more informal ways in which retaliation manifests, in particular in cases of sexual harassment. For example, women have reported that they were denied promotions, have been excluded from meetings or duty travel, and were denied training opportunities, projects, assignments or other work to advance their career merely for rebuffing sexual advances from senior officials.[115] Such retaliatory behaviour often already occurs before a complainant submits a report of misconduct through the appropriate reporting channel (if they do at all), and as such, would likely fall outside the formal scope of the UN's protection against retaliation policy. In other words, these other forms of retaliatory behaviour,

---

[112] "Protection against retaliation for reporting misconduct and for cooperating with duly authorized audits or investigations", Secretary-General's Bulletin ST/SGB/2017/2/Rev.1, 28 November 2017 ('ST/SGB/2017/2/Rev.1') (https://www.legal-tools.org/doc/opkf43/). Section 2.1. now provides that protection against retaliation applies to any staff member (regardless of the type of appointment or its duration), intern, United Nations volunteer, individual contractor or consultant who engages in a protected activity. A protected activity is defined as reporting misconduct through established reporting channels and/or cooperating with a duly authorised audit or investigation. Previously, the policy only covered UN staff members, interns and UN volunteers. Note, the UNDP protection against retaliation policy already covered non-staff personnel such as contractors, interns and UNVs serving in UNDP or another UNDP administered fund, programme or agency since July 2012. The revised policy also introduced protection of individuals who choose to report wrongdoing to an external entity in limited circumstances, allows for recommending transfer of the alleged retaliator, and explicitly prohibits retaliation against outside parties.

[113] *Ibid.*, Section 1.4.

[114] The established reporting channels are set out in: "Unsatisfactory conduct, investigations and the disciplinary process", Administrative Instruction ST/AI/2017/1, 26 October 2017 (https://www.legal-tools.org/doc/vzfumy/).

[115] *PassBlue*, January 2019, see above note 94.

---

much more common than retaliation as defined in the policy, still remain subject only to other, more informal resolution mechanisms.

The various measures taken by the UN since 2018 are important first steps towards addressing sexual harassment. But they are simply that: *first* steps. Their true test will lie in their implementation and, in particular, in their impact upon changing structural dimensions of inequality that have manifested in an organizational culture that has long silenced and ignored sexual harassment (in the UN and beyond, as illustrated by the #MeToo movement). The UN and NGO surveys on (sexual) harassment that have followed each other in relatively quick succession in the first six months of 2019, confirm the importance of workplace culture, and in particular unequal power dimensions and structures of privilege that protect those in positions of power, as a predictor for incidents of (sexual) harassment and other forms of gender-based violence in the workplace.[116] What these reports ultimately illustrate is that having regulatory and institutional ethics infrastructure is simply not enough when the values underpinning that ethics framework are not lived as a reality by staff and reflected in the management practices of institutions.

Ultimately, to address systemic integrity breaches such as sexual harassment, whether in the UN or elsewhere, requires addressing the pervasive male-dominated power structures that exist, and challenging the distributions of power within the workforce and therefore the nature of the workforce. Research has shown that sexual harassment is much more likely to occur in workplace contexts "where men outnumber women, where leadership is male-dominated, [...] where the power structure is hierarchical, where lower-level employees are largely dependent on superiors for advancement, and where power is highly concentrated in a single person".[117] Another key determining factor is organizational climate, and, in particular, "organizational tolerance".[118] In other words, organizations with

---

[116] UNAIDS Report, December 2018, see above note 91; Safe Space Survey Report, January 2019, see above note 75; Amnesty International Report, January 2019, see above note 77; IBA Report, May 2019, see above note 78; Oxfam interim and final report of Independent Commission, June 2019, see above note 76.

[117] Nancy Gertner, "Sexual Harassment and the Bench", in *Stanford Law Review Online*, 2018, vol. 71, p. 91.

[118] UN Women Report, November 2018, p. 16, see above note 103; Chloe Hart, Alison Dahl Crossley and Shelley Correll, "Study: When Leaders Take Sexual Harassment Seriously, So Do Employees", in *Harvard Business Review*, 14 December 2018 (available on its web site); Paula A. Johnson, 2018, see above note 72.

diversified leadership, including but not limited to gender diversity, are likely to have fewer sexual harassment instances and a different, more inclusive organizational culture.[119] The Secretary-General's gender parity strategy[120] is an important first step in that direction. But equally, it requires consistent and unequivocal messaging from leadership, and swift, decisive action when confronted with integrity breaches such as sexual harassment. Real accountability must exist and be seen to exist at all levels in the hierarchy, with no exceptions. While a lot of attention has been paid since the establishment of the UN to how to ensure the independence and impartiality of international civil servants *vis-à-vis* the 'outside world', to truly understand the meaning of and to improve the integrity of international justice institutions and of individual justice actors, requires critically examining our own institutions and reflect internally on what integrity means within our workforces. That requires asking the awkward questions, exposing and changing structures of (predominantly male) power, and redefining ethical leadership based on feminist principles.[121]

13.5. Conclusion: Redistributing Power and Culture Change

Unfortunately, today's world continues to be inherently unequal, where people are continuously discriminated against based on their sex, gender, ethnicity, age, religion or sexual orientation (or any other protected ground), where power is abused on a daily basis, and where injustices are present every day. It is easy to forget that the staff members who make up the UN are not super-humans who live and breathe only the higher ideals of the international civil service; rather, they bring with them their personal values, experiences, backgrounds and cultures that are based in that inherently unequal world (with some being more unequal than others). Personal values play an important part in navigating an individual's personal and professional lives, and there may be times when those personal values come into conflict with organizational values. Indeed, diversity in an institution like the UN or the ICC is what gives these institutions their strength, but at the same time can also become their biggest weakness. In such contexts,

---

[119] See, for example, Nancy Gertner, 2018, p. 91, see above note 117; IBA Report, May 2019, p. 14, see above note 78.

[120] UN System-Wide Strategy on Gender Parity, October 2017 (available on UN web site).

[121] See, for an example of Feminist Leadership Principles, Shawna Wakefield, "Transformative and Feminist Leadership for Women's Rights", *Oxfam America Research Backgrounder Series*, 23 January 2017 (available on its web site).

there is always a risk that organizational culture and practices reflect those same injustices and inequalities these organisations were designed to fight.[122] For this reason, many organisations, like the UN, have adopted Codes of Conduct and other regulatory ethics infrastructure to provide their staff members with a framework or moral compass to guide decisions they are making on a daily basis. Such ethics and integrity frameworks thus often focus on delineating both desirable and undesirable behaviour in line with an organization's core values.

However, as Parker *et al.* (2008) have demonstrated,

> ethical infrastructures will only be useful if everyone […] is explicitly encouraged to raise ethical issues so that ethical problems can be identified, discussed and resolved – and people are not punished for raising them in the first place.[123]

In other words, successful ethics infrastructures require not only the existence of rules and regulations, and mechanisms to enforce compliance and mete out sanctions for transgressions, but a deeper engagement with ethics and integrity by an institution and its staff on a day-to-day basis, both externally and internally. Integrity and its associated ethics infrastructure must become part and parcel of an organization's informal workplace practices, cultures and expectations. Otherwise, "there is a danger that ethical infrastructure will simply amount to formal ethical structures that do not connect with informal work team cultures and individual [staff members'] values in practice".[124] A workplace culture that privileges and is per-

---

[122] In 2010, David La Piana described what he called the 'Non-Profit Paradox': "Nonprofits tend to recreate within their own organizational cultures the problems they are trying to solve in society". He explains that organizations that are highly value-driven, such as nonprofits, employ individuals who are also highly value and mission-driven. Yet this mission-drive and their commitment to progressive social values, he explains, "can drive dysfunctional organizational behaviour by blinding workers to their own faults". Additionally, he also observed that "values-driven people sometimes feel that their ethical activities entitle them to act less morally". The irony, then, is that such value-driven individuals who often observe or interact with human rights abusers may (unintentionally) start exhibiting those same abusive behaviours in their interaction with others, most notably with their peers and colleagues. At the same time, value-driven individuals in less powerful positions tend to become particularly sensitive to possible abuses of power, and thus to feel oppressed by those in positions of power. See David La Piana, "The Nonprofit Paradox: Why organizations are so often plagued by the very ills they aim to cure", in *Stanford Social Innovation Review*, 2010.

[123] Parker *et al.*, 2008, p. 183, see above note 5.

[124] *Ibid.*, p. 161.

ceived to protect individuals who engage in misconduct is much more damaging than the absence of an ethics infrastructure altogether. The added value of addressing these deeper structures may not be seen in the immediate short term, but institutions that put in place ethics mechanisms coupled with cultural change practices will reap long term benefits.

14

Sexual Harassment

Matthias Neuner[*]

This chapter discusses the United Nations' ('UN') decades-long and ongoing effort to preserve and defend the integrity of its staff by defining sexual harassment[1] and investigating as well as judicially pursuing those who are alleged to have engaged in such illegal behaviour. Personal conduct in this area is at the very centre of the notion of 'integrity' of those who serve international organisations. It is a topic that has only become more important in recent years, especially after the global #metoo movement.

Twenty-six years after the enactment of the first administrative definition of sexual harassment, the Chief Executive Board for Coordination ('CEB') of the UN observed in 2018 that "sexual harassment results from a culture of discrimination and privilege, based on unequal gender relations and power dynamics. It creates hostile workplaces, which limit the target/victim/affected individual's ability to thrive".[2]

---

[*] **Matthias Neuner** is Trial Counsel, Office of the Prosecutor, Special Tribunal for Lebanon. The views expressed in this chapter are those of the author and do not necessarily reflect the views of the Tribunal.

[1] This chapter exclusively focuses on sexual harassment and covers *neither* sexual exploitation *nor* sexual abuse. Sexual exploitation means "any actual or attempted abuse of a position of vulnerability, differential power, or trust, for sexual purposes, including, but not limited to, profiting monetarily, socially or politically from the sexual exploitation of another", similarly, the term 'sexual abuse' means the "actual or threatened physical intrusion of a sexual nature, whether by force or under unequal or coercive conditions". Secretary-General's Bulletin, Special measures for protection from sexual exploitation and sexual abuse, UN Doc. ST/SGB/2003/13, 9 October 2003, section 1 (https://www.legal-tools.org/doc/ftozsr/). For the UN Organization Mission in the Democratic Republic of Congo, a 'Code of Conduct on Sexual exploitation and sexual abuse' has been published, which refers to ST/SGB/2003/13 and ST/SGB/1999/13. Section 7.2 of the latter instrument prohibits that UN forces commit against civilians and persons *hors de combat* "rape, enforced prostitution, any form of sexual assault and humiliation and degrading treatment". Secretary-General's Bulletin, Observance by United Nations forces of international humanitarian law, UN Doc. ST/SGB/1999/13, 6 August 1999 (https://www.legal-tools.org/doc/kbgmi6/). This chapter does *not* discuss any of the criminal offences mentioned in section 7.2 of ST/SGB/1999/13.

[2] UN Chief Executives Board, System Model Policy on Sexual Harassment, London, 3-4 May 2018 ('UN model policy on sexual harassment'), section II (policy statement), para. 1.

The definition of sexual harassment has evolved over time. Various UN agencies adopted distinct definitions containing slight variations. However, in 1992 and 2008, the UN Secretariat issued two bulletins which bound the UN common system, including most of its sub-agencies. The 2008 instrument defines sexual harassment as

> any unwelcome sexual advance, request for sexual favour, verbal or physical conduct or gesture of a sexual nature, or any other behaviour of a sexual nature that might reasonably be expected or be perceived to cause offence or humiliation to another, when such conduct interferes with work, is made a condition of employment or creates an intimidating, hostile or offensive work environment.[3]

14.1. Impact on Target's Health and Thus on Work Environment

At the heart of defining and banning sexual harassment stands the conviction that such behaviour conflicts with the principle of equal treatment and interferes with productivity because it affects the target's health by undermining morale, causing anxiety, stress and, if no timely intervention occurs, can lead to the affected individual's absence from work, higher labour turnover combined with long term damage of career prospects as the affected person chooses to avoid the damaging situation by changing jobs.[4]

The case of *Cateaux v. Secretary-General* ('S-G') is exemplary of how sexual harassment can affect its target. Cateaux, a UN staff member, had entertained a relationship with a married man. After this relationship had ended the man sent from his wife's email-account a message containing various swear words and attached two nude pictures of Cateaux. Recipients were various persons including Cateaux, family members of Cateaux and other UN staff. The former described the effect the sending of this email had:

> I was shocked. I really lost my mind. This was overwhelming. I was completely demoralised. The only solution was to commit suicide. I did not see people. Everyone called to ask me what kind of problem you could have with someone like this.

---

[3] UN Secretary-General's ('S-G') bulletin, Prohibition of discrimination, harassment, including sexual harassment, and abuse of authority, 11 February 2008, ST/SGB/2008/5, Article 1.3 ('2008-UN-AI') (https://www.legal-tools.org/doc/ibc9oq/).

[4] Michael Rubenstein, *Dignity of women at work – A Report on the Problem of Sexual Harassment in the Member States of the European Communities*, Office for Official Publications of the European Communities, 1988, paras. 1.5, 1.7, 12.1 ('Rubenstein report').

I was not myself. I did not know what to do. [...] I felt very embarrassed. [...] It was difficult to go to work every day [...] [E]veryone was looking at me. I stayed indoors the whole time. I did not speak to anyone.[5]

14.2. History

Sexual harassment was first discussed and defined domestically, namely in the United States of America ('US') in the late seventies and early eighties. With regards to international organisations, sexual harassment was mentioned in a UN document in 1979, discussed by the European Communities ('EC') in the eighties and, in the early nineties, first defined by the EC and, shortly thereafter, by the United Nations. In this section, these developments will be traced chronologically.

14.2.1. International and Domestic Efforts to Define Sexual Harassment

Article 8 of the UN Charter ('Charter') directs the UN to "place no restrictions on the eligibility of men and women to participate in any capacity and under conditions of equality in its [...] organs". In addition, Article 101(3) of the Charter refers to the "highest standards of efficiency, competence, and integrity" of UN staff.[6] Integrity was initially not understood to encompass sexual harassment, as this concept was developed only later, in the seventies. In 1954, when the International Civil Advisory Board prepared standards, which gave meaning to equality in Article 8 and "integrity" in Article 101 of the Charter, these mentioned that UN staff should cultivate "social relations with colleagues of different races, religions and cultural backgrounds" and the "conduct of superiors must be free of intimidation".[7] However, harassment and in particular sexual harassment were omitted.

In the seventies, discussions in the US resulted in the adoption of domestic administrative regulations and judicial recognition that sexual harassment is unlawful sex discrimination.[8]

---

[5] United Nations Dispute Tribunal ('UNDT'), *Cateaux v. S-G*, UNDT/NBI/2010/066, Judgment, 21 February 2013, UNDT/2013/027, paras. 40, 41 (https://www.legal-tools.org/doc/exsyrw/).

[6] Charter of the United Nations, 26 June 1945 (https://www.legal-tools.org/doc/6b3cd5/).

[7] International Civil Advisory Board, *Report on Standards of Conduct in the International Civil Service*, 1954, paras. 11, 13 (https://www.legal-tools.org/doc/d94c61/).

[8] Rubenstein report, 1988, p. 1, paras. 1.1, 1.2, see above note 4.

Independent thereof the Administrative Tribunal of the UN ('UN-AdminT') decided its first court case regarding allegations of harassment in 1974.[9]

14.2.1.1. UN Information Circular on 'International Women's Day' 1979

On 8 March 1979, on international women's day, the UN Secretariat published an information circular:

> Sexual harassment of either sex is unacceptable. Sexist remarks, jokes and innuendos are inappropriate in any circumstance.[10]

This was a step forward as the UN had used the term 'sexual harassment' for the first time in an official document that went public. However, the first sentence, while using the phrase sexual harassment, did not define it. The second sentence appeared to restrict sexual harassment to mere *verbal* conduct, namely remarks, jokes and innuendos. However, physical conduct such as touching would be equally unacceptable or inappropriate but was *not* encompassed.

Further, the examples provided in the second sentence coupled with the phrase "inappropriate *in any circumstance*" rendered the UN's message as too broad. Generally, sexist remarks, jokes and innuendos are indeed inappropriate, but not "in any circumstance". This phrase misses the crucial legal element of the definition of sexual harassment, namely that conduct must be "unwelcome" (or unwanted) to constitute sexual harassment. For example, sexual innuendo between partners, both of which work at the UN, might be deemed as "welcome". The statement advanced by the UN on international women's day omitted the legal requirement of "unwelcome" conduct completely by qualifying all sexist remarks, jokes and innuendos, regardless of these being welcome or not, as "inappropriate in any circumstance". Paul rightly observed that the "gravamen" of sexual harassment claim is that the sexual advances are "unwelcome".[11]

---

[9] Administrative Tribunal of the United Nations ('UN-AdminT'), *Ho v. S-G*, Judgment no. 189, 7 October 1974 (https://www.legal-tools.org/doc/3m78i2/).

[10] UN Secretariat, Information circular from the Under-S-G for Administration and Management, Guidelines for promoting equal treatment of men and women in the Secretariat, 8 March 1979, ST/IC/79/17, para. 9.

[11] Ellen Frankel Paul, "Sexual Harassment as Sex Discrimination: A Defective Paradigm", in *Yale Law and Policy Review*, 1990, p. 344.

Further, due to the aforementioned shortcomings, this first UN statement failed to provide a precise legal and actionable definition. It also omitted any reference to disciplinary proceedings and sanctions. The status of the document was a mere 'information circular' instead of an administrative instruction that would at least make reference to 'disciplinary measures' and announce an investigation or sanction in case such behaviour occurs. Rather, paragraph 15 of the UN's information circular issued on international women's day clarified that the document would constitute mere "guidelines". The document issued with the best intentions on international women's day in 1979 was less legal but rather political in nature.

14.2.1.2. Domestic Legislation Defines Sexual Harassment First

Half a year after the UN had issued its information circular on international women's day, Catharine MacKinnon published the book *Sexual harassment of Working Women*.[12] She defined sexual harassment as "the unwanted imposition of sexual requirements in the context of a relationship of unequal power".[13] Unlike the UN in its information circular months before, MacKinnon emphasized that conduct has to carry the element of 'unwanted' to constitute sexual harassment. MacKinnon described two types of sexual harassment: the first consisting of an exchange of sexual compliance in exchange for an employment opportunity (*quid pro quo*) and the second when sexual harassment is a persistent condition of work.[14]

14.2.1.2.1. Equal Employment Opportunity Commission

Months later, in the US the Equal Employment Opportunity Commission ('EEOC') observed regarding the US that "sexual harassment continues to be especially widespread".[15] In April 1980, the EEOC suggested adding a provision defining sexual harassment as physical or verbal in nature. Sexual harassment was seen as conduct to which the target submits as a term or condition or basis of employment,[16] and was defined as

---

[12] Catharine A. MacKinnon, *Sexual Harassment of Working Women – A Case of Sex Discrimination*, Yale University Press, 1979.

[13] *Ibid.*, p. 1.

[14] *Ibid.*, pp. 32–42.

[15] Equal Employment Opportunity Commission ('EEOC'), *Interim Guidelines on Sexual Harassment*, 11 April 1980, p. 25024 ('EEOC interim guidelines 1980').

[16] *Ibid.*

> [u]nwelcome sexual advances, requests for sexual favors, and other verbal or physical conduct of a sexual nature when (1) submission of such conduct is made either explicitly or implicitly a term or condition of an individual's employment, (2) submission to or rejection of such conduct by an individual is used as a basis for employment decisions affecting such individual, or (3) such conduct has the purpose or effect of substantially interfering with an individual's work performance or creating an intimidating, hostile, or offensive working environment.[17]

Firstly, unlike the UN's 1979 information circular, the US definition also included *physical* conduct. Secondly this domestic definition introduced the concept of "unwelcome" conduct. Excluding welcome advances, the definition only prohibited conduct which was 'unwelcome'. The EEOC did not specifically adopt the 'unwanted' element MacKinnon had proposed, but the 'unwelcome' element was at least similar. Thirdly, the definition contained three variants, with the first two including conduct of a sexual nature in relation to hiring of staff for *future* or existing employments,[18] and the third relating to conduct relating to existing employment.

Following a public consultation process, the EEOC refined this definition some seven months later:

> Unwelcome sexual advances, requests for sexual favors, and other verbal or physical conduct of a sexual nature constitute sexual harassment when (1) submission to such conduct is made either explicitly or implicitly a term or condition of an individual's employment, (2) submission to or rejection of such conduct by an individual is used as the basis for employment decisions affecting such individual, or (3) such conduct has the purpose or effect of unreasonably interfering with an individual's work performance or creating an intimidating, hostile, or offensive working environment.[19]

---

[17] *Ibid*, p. 25025, § 1604.11.

[18] Often referred to as *quid pro quo* (compare UN-AdminT, *Applicant v. S-G*, Judgment, 30 January 2009, No. 1423, pp. 3, 6 (section II), 10 (section XVIII) (https://www.legal-tools.org/doc/uhsmw3/)); Paul, 1990, p. 333, see above note 11.

[19] Equal Employment Opportunity Commission ('EEOC'), *Guidelines on Discrimination Because of Sex*, 10 November 1980, § 1604.11.

Regarding the third variant, this amended definition dropped the requirement for 'substantial' interference with an individual's work performance, substituting it with 'unreasonable' interference.

14.2.1.2.2. US Supreme Court

In 1986, the Supreme Court of the US decided the case *Meritor Savings Bank v. Vinson*. The judges accepted the definition advanced by the EEOC[20] and further held that a 'hostile environment' sexual harassment is a form of sex discrimination.[21] The judges found that sexual harassment occurs when it is "sufficiently severe or pervasive 'to alter the conditions of [the affected individual's] employment and create an abusive working environment [...]'".[22]

14.2.1.2.3. The EC's Efforts to Define Sexual Harassment until 1991

In the mid-eighties, the European Parliament and the Council of Ministers, in a series of resolutions, recognised sexual harassment as a problem affecting the dignity and rights of women at work.[23] Still, by 1988 the Rubenstein report observed that no Member States of the EC "has any express legal prohibition of sexual harassment".[24] European legislation had been dormant. Rubenstein's report sent a wakeup call to the EC in Brussels and to other capitals of European States, resulting in a delayed effort to catch up with the legislative developments in the US on defining and prohibiting sexual harassment at work.

On 20 June 1988, the EC's Advisory Committee on Equal Opportunities for Women and Men suggested adopting a recommendation and a

---

[20] US Supreme Court, *Meritor Savings Bank v. Vinson*, Judgment, 19 June 1986, No. 84-1979, p. 57 (65).

[21] *Ibid.*, p. 57, section 1, pp. 66, 67.

[22] *Ibid.*, p. 67, quoting US Court of Appeals, 11th Circuit, *Henson v. City of Dundee*, Judgment, 9 August 1982, No. 80-5827, 682 F.2d 897 (1982).

[23] Rubenstein report, para. 1.2, see above note 4, referring, among others, to a "series of resolutions" of the European Parliament and the European Council resolution of 13 December 1984 on the promotion of positive action for women (Council Recommendation of 13 December 1984 on the promotion of positive action for women, 84/635/EEC, in *Official Journal of the European Communities*, 19 December 1984, no. L 331/34, op. para. 4, second point; also compare European Parliament, Recommendation to member states on 25 October 1984, in *Official Journal of the European Communities*, 26 November 1984, no C 315/77.

[24] Rubenstein report, paras. 1.6, 12.3, and chapter IV, see above note 4.

code of conduct on sexual harassment in the workplace.[25] Following up on the Rubenstein report, the Commission of the EC adopted on 27 November 1991 a Code of Practice on measures to combat sexual harassment which defined:

> Sexual harassment means unwanted conduct of a sexual nature or other conduct based on sex affecting the dignity of women and men at work. This can include unwelcome physical, verbal or non-verbal conduct.[26]

This definition was inclusive in that verbal, non-verbal or physical conduct sufficed. The definition further distinguished, similar to MacKinnon in her book, between wanted and 'unwanted' conduct. 'Unwanted' was an intentional element comparable to the 'unwelcome' element in the definition advanced in the US. The Commission of the EC excluded conduct from constituting sexual harassment when wanted by the target. Only unwanted conduct was prohibited, similar to the American approach which targeted conduct 'unwelcome' by the affected individual.

14.2.1.2.4. The UN's First Legal Definition in 1992

Less than a year later, the UN Secretariat adopted its first administrative instruction prohibiting sexual harassment. Referring to Articles 8 and 101(3) of the Charter, the S-G stated that

> [a]ny form of harassment, particularly sexual harassment, at the workplace in connection with work is contrary to the provisions of the Charter and, consequently, to the policy of the organisation; it is a violation of the standards of conduct expected of every international civil servant and may lead to disciplinary action.[27]

On the same day, an administrative instruction was issued which defined sexual harassment as:

---

[25] European Communities, Commission Recommendation of 27 November 1991 on the protection of the dignity of women and men at work, 27 November 1991, 92/131/EEC, in *Official Journal of the European Communities*, 4 February 1992, no. L 49/1 ('EC Commission Recommendation 1991').

[26] *Ibid.*, annex, "Protecting the dignity of women and men at work: code of practice on measures to combat sexual harassment", section 2, para. 1.

[27] UN, Promotion of equal treatment of men and women in the secretariat and prevention of sexual harassment, 29 October 1992, ST/SGB/253, para. 1 ('ST/SGB/253') (https://www.legal-tools.org/doc/11e3wb/).

[A]ny unwelcome sexual advance, request for sexual favours or other verbal or physical conduct of a sexual nature, when it interferes with work, is made a condition of employment or creates an intimidating, hostile or offensive work environment.[28]

Unlike the 1979 information circular issued on international women's day, the UN introduced, for the first time in 1992, the legal requirement that conduct must be 'unwelcome'. A comparison of the definitions advanced by the Commission of the EC and the UN reveals large overlaps. Both definitions demand (1) an unwelcome,[29] (2) conduct of a sexual nature, (3) in verbal or physical form which (4) occurs in relation to, or interferes with work, including by creating a negative work environment.

Regarding the third element, the EC definition is clearer and possibly wider, as it clarifies that also "non-verbal" conduct suffices. In relation to the fourth element, the UN definition is wider: while the EC definition requires that the violation affects the dignity of the target at work, does the UN definition not require dignity to be affected, and also prohibits conduct which "is made a condition of employment".[30] This would prohibit a *quid pro quo* request for sexual favour expressed by a hiring agent at a point in time when no working relationship exists between the applicant and the UN. By contrast, the EC definition appears narrower as the conduct must affect the target 'at work'.

Unlike in 1979, when the UN Secretariat had first used the concept of sexual harassment in a political context without defining and accompanying it by sanctions, now, in October 1992, it provided a legal definition. Further, a written complaint on sexual harassment the "Office of Human Resources Management will promptly conduct [...] the initial investigation and fact-finding" which "may lead to disciplinary action".[31] This step meant that the UN administration had adopted a legal definition of sexual harassment which qualified the prohibited conduct as a breach of discipline that incurred sanctions. This step opened the doors for affected individuals

---

[28] UN, Administrative Instruction: Procedures for dealing with sexual harassment, 29 October 1992, ST/AI/379, para. 2 ('1992-UN-AI') (https://www.legal-tools.org/doc/juboyq/).

[29] The EC definition interchangeably uses 'unwelcome' and 'un*wanted*'.

[30] Compare the first variant of the definition of US law on the prohibition of sexual harassment (EEOC interim guidelines 1980, page 25025, § 1604.11 under (1)).

[31] 1992-UN-AI, para. 9, see above note 28; ST/SGB/253, para. 1, ST/SGB/253, see above note 27.

to report these allegations, for the administration to initiate fact-finding and investigation processes in order to sanction offenders and, in case of legal disputes, for the UN Administrative Tribunals to adjudicate them.

14.2.2. Standard-Setting Phase

After the UN Secretariat had defined sexual harassment and prohibited such conduct, the various organs and sub-agencies within and associated to the UN adopted administrative instructions defining the prohibited conduct as well as the procedures to be followed if the victim reported such conduct. Table 1 lists some of the main instruments containing definitions of sexual harassment in chronological order.

Date	Entity	Instrument
29 Oct. 1992	Under-Secretary-General for Administration and Management	Nr. 2, ST/AI/379
18 May 1993	United Nations Development Programme ('UNDP')	UNDP/ADM/93/26, policy on sexual harassment
16 Jan. 1995	UNDP	Circular UNDP/ADM/95/6, policy on sexual harassment
30 Jun. 1995	Word Food Program ('WFP')	Section 6, WFP Circular N. 95/004: Policy on the Prevention of Sexual Harassment and the Resolution of Problem Cases
19 Feb. 1999	WFP	Section 6, WFP Policy on the Prevention of Harassment
14 Jul. 2005	International Criminal Court	Administrative Instruction ICC/AI/2005/005, section 2.2
16 Dec. 2005	UNICEF	Para. 8, CF/AI/2005-017 (UNICEF)
11 Feb. 2008	UN S-G	Article 1.3 ST/SGB/2008/5; S-G bulletin
2010	UN Relief and Works Agency ('UNRWA')	Paragraph 6, UNRWA General Staff Circular No. 6/2010 on Prohibition of Discrimination, Harassment – including Sexual Harassment – and Abuse Power
23 May 2013	Special Tribunal for Lebanon	Section 2.3, AI prohibition of discrimination, harassment, including sexual harassment and abuse of authority

Date	Entity	Instrument
15 Jan. 2015	Food and Agricultural Organisation	12 f), FAO Policy on the Prevention of Harassment, Sexual Harassment and Abuse of Authority
3 May 2018	CEB	Section I, UN model policy on sexual harassment

Table 1: Main instruments containing definitions of sexual harassment.

With sexual harassment being defined, the first cases were reported and formal procedures were initiated to determine whether allegations of sexual harassment could be substantiated. Some disciplinary proceedings involving sexual harassment resulted in the imposition of sanctions on certain offenders. Some of these cases were then litigated in front of the UN administrative tribunals. In the following, a cursory overview of some of the 43 judgements issued by the UNAdminT, the UN Dispute Tribunal ('UNDT') and the UN Appeals Tribunal ('UNAT') is provided. The following graphs distilling key facts of the 43 cases provide some important information and context.

The gender breakdown of the alleged offenders was:

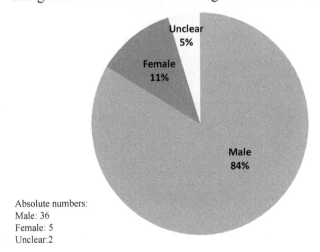

Absolute numbers:
Male: 36
Female: 5
Unclear: 2

Graph 1: Alleged offenders by gender (in percentage).

The term 'unclear' in the above signals that due to the gender-neutral language used throughout the judgment it was not possible to determine the gender of the alleged perpetrator.

The gender breakdown of the affected individuals was:

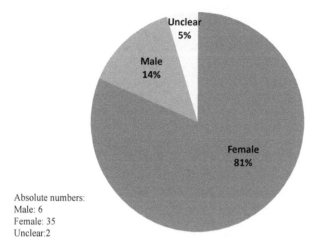

Absolute numbers:
Male: 6
Female: 35
Unclear:2

Graph 2: Alleged victims by gender (in percentage).

The alleged male offenders targeted:

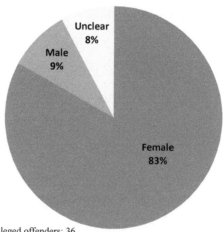

*Number of male alleged offenders: 36

Graph 3: Targets of male alleged offenders* by gender (in percentage).

Already in 1988, Rubenstein observed that sexual harassment is "frequently a function of power. Because women rarely have power over men, sexual harassment at work is mainly a problem affecting women, although men, as well as women, can be sexually harassed".[32]

For cases where the alleged offender is a female, the gender breakdown of the target is as follows:

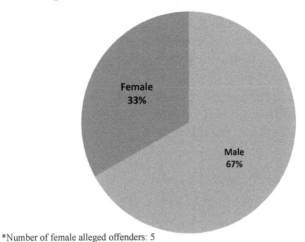

*Number of female alleged offenders: 5

Graph 4: Targets of female alleged offenders* by gender (in percentage).

Also, the growing sexual liberation of society has led to more individuals identifying themselves as lesbian, gay, bisexual or queer. Thus, the aforementioned male–female dichotomy has become a little bit simplistic and therefore outdated. Indirectly acknowledging these developments, the nuances in the CEB's statement become obvious: "sexual harassment is the manifestation of a culture of discrimination and privilege based on unequal gender relations and other power dynamics".[33]

This statement replaces the outdated male/female dichotomy and highlights instead discrimination and privilege, which are exercised against a background of gender relations and other power dynamics.

For example, 11 of the cases reviewed were related to 'power dynamics' involving a person in superior capacity.[34] Furthermore, at least

---

[32] Rubenstein report, para. 1.5, see above note 4.

[33] UN model policy on sexual harassment, section II, para. 1, see above note 2.

[34] UN-AdminT, *Claxton v. S-G*, Judgement, 30 June 1992, No. 560 (https://www.legal-tools.org/doc/iujb1v/); UN-AdminT, *van der Graaf v. S-G*, Judgement, 23 July 2001, AT/DEC/997 ('van der Graaf v. S-G') (https://www.legal-tools.org/doc/fyqtk7/); UN-AdminT, *Al-Fahoum v. S-G*, Judgement, 20 November 2001, AT/DEC/1018 (https://www.legal-

three cases related to 'gender relations' involving questioning of homosexuality, and allegations of sexual harassment and sexual assault.[35] Two of the latter three cases did *not* involve a perpetrator in a senior capacity.[36]

14.3. Evolution of the Definition of Sexual Harassment

According to the 1992 UN definition sexual harassment consists of three elements: (1) an advance with, request for, or conduct of a sexual nature which (2) is unwelcome, and (3) negatively interferes with the work environment or is made a condition of employment.

The following section describes the evolution of the first and second elements of this definition through the jurisprudence of the UN Administrative tribunals and the subsequent administrative instruction which was enacted in 2008.[37]

14.3.1. First Element: Twofold Evolution

The first element of the definition of sexual harassment evolved in a twofold way. An objective test was added and it was clarified that non-verbal conduct may constitute sexual harassment.

---

tools.org/doc/oeq66n/); UN-AdminT, *Rahman v. S-G*, Judgement, 23 November 2001, AT/DEC/1032 (https://www.legal-tools.org/doc/t24vxz/); UNDT, *Pandey v. S-G*, Judgment, 30 June 2011, UNDT/2011/117 (https://www.legal-tools.org/doc/v9o51d/); UNAT, *Perelli v. S-G*, Judgment, 28 March 2013, 2013-UNAT-291 ('UNAT Perelli judgment') (https://www.legal-tools.org/doc/e5ss3z/); UNDT, *Perelli v. S-G*, Judgment, 9 March 2012, UNDT/2012/034 ('UNDT Perelli judgment') (https://www.legal-tools.org/doc/f24e3o/); UNDT, *Khan v. S-G*, Judgment, 12 November 2013, UNDT/2013/140 ('UNDT – judgment Khan') (https://www.legal-tools.org/doc/chrhfp/); UNDT, *Portillo Moya v. S-G*, Judgment, 24 February 2014, UNDT/2014/021 ('UNDT judgment Portillo Moya') (https://www.legal-tools.org/doc/sop09m/); UNDT, *Michaud v. S-G*, Judgment, 12 October 2016, UNDT/2016/184 ('UNDT judgment Michaud') (https://www.legal-tools.org/doc/3t7p19/); UNAT, *Michaud v. S-G*, Judgment, 14 July 2017, 2017-UNAT-761 ('UNAT judgment Michaud') (https://www.legal-tools.org/doc/22fi7z/); UNAT, *Bagot v. Commissioner-General of the United Nations Relief and Works Agency for Palestine Refugees in the Near East*, Judgment, 31 March 2017, 2017-UNAT-718 ('UNAT Bagot judgment') (https://www.legal-tools.org/doc/f6ksww/); Dispute Tribunal of the United Nations Relief and Works Agency for Palestine Refugees in the Near East ('UNRWA'), *Bagot v. Commissioner-General UNRWA*, Judgment, 19 May 2016 ('UNRWA Bagot judgment') (https://www.legal-tools.org/doc/r2ja0m/);UN-AdminT, *Applicant v. S-G*, Judgment, 30 September 2009, AT/DEC/1449 (https://www.legal-tools.org/doc/sg3dk1/).

[35] Van der Graaf v. S-G, see above note 34; UNDT, *Applicant v. S-G*, Judgment, 18 April 2012, UNDT/2012/054 (https://www.legal-tools.org/doc/owtw59/) ('Applicant v. S-G').

[36] *Applicant v. S-G*, see above note 35.

[37] AI ST/SGB/2008/5.

14.3.1.1. Non-Verbal Conduct

The 1992 UN Administrative Instruction had defined the prohibited conduct as "any unwelcome sexual advance, request for sexual favours or other verbal or physical conduct of a sexual nature". As pointed out earlier, this first UN definition was slightly narrower than the EU definition as it was unclear whether it would also include *non-verbal* conduct. In 2008, the General Secretariat clarified that also non-verbal conduct is included by adding language that "any other behaviour" suffices as long as it is "of a sexual nature".[38]

14.3.1.2. Adding an Objective Test: Reasonably Expected

The first element of sexual harassment as defined by the 1992 UN Administrative Instruction further evolved through the issuance of other administrative instructions by other UN entities: in 1999, the WFP added a new nuance to the definition, prohibiting conduct of a sexual nature that might *reasonably* be expected to cause offence or humiliation to another or others; or that another or others might *reasonably* perceive as placing a condition of a sexual nature on employment, or on conditions of employment.[39]

In 2005 the UN High Commissioner on Refugees ('UNHCR') also added in its definition of sexual harassment a 'reasonable-test',[40] requiring behaviour of a sexual nature that might *reasonably* be expected or be perceived to cause offence or humiliation.

The General Secretariat of the UN issued the 2008 UN Administrative Instruction, and followed the developments on the prohibition of sexual harassment at the WFP and UNHCR by adding an objective test to sexual harassment: only conduct which "might reasonably be expected or be perceived to cause offence or humiliation" was prohibited.[41] This phrase is repeated *verbatim* in the 2008 UN Administrative Instruction for harassment.[42]

---

[38] 2008-UN-AI, para. 1.3, see above note 3.

[39] World Food Programme ('WFP'), Policy on the Prevention of Harassment, 19 February 1999, HR 99/002, para. 6.

[40] UNHCR, Policy on Harassment, Sexual Harassment, and Abuse of Authority, para. 2 (https://www.legal-tools.org/doc/y9vlxr/).

[41] 2008-UN-AI, para. 1.3, see above note 3.

[42] *Ibid.*, para. 1.2.

Dealing with harassment, the UNDT found in *Belkhabaz v. S-G* that this phrase

> very clearly sets out an objective test for establishing harass-
> ment in stating that 'the conduct *might reasonably be expected
> or be perceived* to cause offence or humiliation' (emphasis
> added). The test focusses on the conduct itself and requires an
> examination as to whether it would be expected or be per-
> ceived to cause offence or humiliation to a reasonable per-
> son.[43]

14.3.1.3. Intention of the Alleged Offender

The UNDT ruled it is not necessary to establish that the alleged offender was ill-intended and, to that extent, the motivation of the alleged offender is not directly relevant for establishing harassment.[44]

14.3.1.4. Expectations and Perceptions of the Target

The UN model policy on sexual harassment requires that "[i]n assessing the reasonableness of expectations or perceptions, the perspective of the person who is the target of the conduct shall be considered".[45]

In *Michaud v. S-G*, a dispute arose out of an email exchange contain-ing inappropriate suggestive wording. The supervisor's comments suggest-ed sexual interest towards a subordinate who had days before joined an in-vestigation in Afghanistan. The UNAT, noting the superior failed to see the higher level of sensitivity, analysed the perspective of the affected individ-ual who "indeed f[ou]nd the advances and comments inappropriate. But the precise degree of offence [the target] took is inconsequential".[46]

In *Cooke v. S-G*, the UNDT extensively considered the views and perceptions of the affected *Michaud v. S-G* individual. The alleged offender, a person of senior status, had implicated at least three women. The first woman had signalled her intention to progress professionally to her super-visor. The alleged offender then pointed to a photograph depicting senior

---

[43] UNDT, *Belkhabaz v. S-G*, Judgment, 5 February 2018, UNDT/2018/016/Corr.1, para. 141 ('UNDT – judgment Belkhabaz') (https://www.legal-tools.org/doc/jnftsy/); United Nations Appeals Tribunal ('UNAT'), *Belkhabaz v. S-G*, Judgment, 26 October 2018, 2018-UNAT-873, para. 31 (https://www.legal-tools.org/doc/lra752/).

[44] UNDT – judgment Belkhabaz, para. 141, see above note 3.

[45] UN model policy on sexual harassment, section I, see above note 2.

[46] UNAT judgment Michaud, para. 61, see above note 34.

women in the organisation and responded that it was not just their brains that got them to where they were, but that they all had to do a bit of something else to get there. She had to be prepared to do something and that her future lay in his hands.[47] The subordinate felt uneasy about these "comments and that it seemed that he inferred she had to sell her body to progress".[48]

Though the UNDT finally denied the contested behaviour had amounted to sexual harassment, it extensively considered the expectations and perceptions of the individual affected by these words:

    a. Did Female 1 ask the [alleged offender] what he meant when he allegedly told her that she had "to be prepared to do something and your future lies in my hands"? The evidence is that she did not and merely assumed that by this vague remark, he was referring to sexual favours and consequently felt degraded.

    b. Granted that her version of the facts are to be believed rather than that of the [alleged offender], was it not possible that in saying that her future lay in his hands, the [alleged offender] had other ideas of what he expected of her rather than a sexual relationship? There is no evidence that the words allegedly spoken by the [alleged offender] were accompanied by any suggestive actions or gestures as to lead to the singular conclusion that he wanted sexual favours from Female 1.

    c. Was the fact of Female 1's assumption as to what the [alleged offender] meant and her feelings of being upset and degraded as a result thereof sufficient to establish that sexual harassment had occurred in this alleged singular encounter with the [alleged offender]? My answer to this is No.

    d. Assuming yet again that the account of Female 1 is to be preferred over the explanations of the [alleged offender], was the remark such that it would reasonably be expected or perceived to cause offence or humiliation? The alleged remark is so vague and unclear that any ordinary person may wonder at what the [alleged offender] meant but

---

[47] UNDT, *Cooke v. S-G*, Judgment, 19 October 2012, UNDT/2012/154, para. 83 (https://www.legal-tools.org/doc/94bml2/).

[48] *Ibid.*, para. 84.

would not feel degraded merely by the words spoken. It must be borne in mind that the standard of reasonableness to be adopted is the standard of the ordinary, reasonable man or woman on the United Nations corridors.[49]

14.3.1.5. The Ordinary, Reasonable Person Test

But what is an ordinary, reasonable person on the UN corridors, so to speak?

The UNAT explained in *Applicant v. S-G* that the "test is not if [the contested] actions and behaviour can be explained but the perception of [t]his behaviour by a *reasonable* person within a multicultural environment".[50]

This approach refers to a hypothetical, ordinary and reasonable person on the UN corridors. This reference to a hypothetical person resembles an approach taken by English courts since the Victorian era. In *McQuire v. Western Morning News* the court referred to the "ordinary reasonable man, the man on the Clapham omnibus".[51]

In *Michaud v. S-G*, the UNAT had to assess an email exchange, which led to a dispute between both sides of the conversation. Having briefly touched upon possible interpretations of the sender and receiver of these emails exchanged by staff on the working level, the UNAT assumed the perspective of the employer for whom both sides of the dispute worked: "Regardless of how the comments were received, an employer [...] might *reasonably* expect that such comments should not be made at all to a recently employed subordinate by a senior misconduct investigator".[52] Here, the UNAT interpreted the superior's written words from the perspective of his employer's reasonable expectations.

14.3.1.6. Other UN Institutions Follow

Before the UN Secretariat issued the 2008 UN Administrative Instruction, some instruments on sexual harassment of other UN agencies did not *yet* contain the requirement that conduct must reasonably be expected or be

---

[49]   *Ibid.*, para. 102.

[50]   UNAT, *Applicant v. S-G*, Judgment, 16 March 2012, 2012-UNAT-209, para. 54 (https://www.legal-tools.org/doc/9cztvz/).

[51]   English Court of Appeal, *McQuire v Western Morning News*, Judgment, 11 May 1903, 2 K.B. 100 at 109 per Collins M.R.

[52]   UNAT judgment Michaud, para. 61, see above note 34 (emphasis added).

perceived to cause offence and humiliation.[53] Following the enactment of the 2008 UN Administrative Instruction, other UN agencies followed and enacted the objective test by making explicit reference to "reasonable" or "reasonably".[54]

14.3.1.7. Comparison Between UN and US Jurisprudence

Overall, it can be concluded that at the UN, the assessment of whether a conduct constitutes sexual harassment evolved towards a 'reasonable' standard, whether it is the perspective of a reasonable person or if it involves the conduct of a superior, the reasonable expectations of the employer. Though this test is objective, the UN jurisprudence reveals that judges also take the perspectives of the target of the conduct into consideration.

This UN approach developed in a direction somewhat similar and somewhat different than in the US, where the Supreme Court settled in 1993 a harassment case about the standard of whether the conduct in a work environment was 'abusive' or not. In *Harris v. Forklift Systems*, the Supreme Court held that "this standard requires an objectively hostile or abusive environment – one that a *reasonable* person would find hostile or abusive – *as well as the victim's subjective perception* that the environment is abusive".[55] The Supreme Court created a double, objective *and* subjective, standard. Both the target's 'subjective' impressions of the experiences

---

[53] ST/SGB/253, see above note 27; United Nations Children's Fund ('UNICEF'), Sexual Harassment in the UNICEF Workplace, 11 March 1994, CF/AI/1994-005 (https://www.legal-tools.org/doc/unou0n/); International Criminal Court, Administrative Instruction ICC/AI/2005/005, 14 July 2005, section 2.2 (https://www.legal-tools.org/doc/hyvqzp/); World Food Programme, Policy on Harassment, Sexual Harassment and Abuse of Authority, 14 February 2007, ED2007/003, para. 7 ('WFP policy on sexual harassment') (https://www.legal-tools.org/doc/x3j9ng/).

[54] Food and Agriculture Organisation, Policy on the prevention of harassment, sexual harassment and abuse of authority, 15 January 2015, no. 2015/03, para. 12(f) (https://www.legal-tools.org/doc/bflryf/); UNICEF, Prohibition of harassment, sexual harassment and abuse of authority, 10 October 2008, CF/EXD/2008- 004, section 1.1(b) (https://www.legal-tools.org/doc/1g2arj/); UNICEF, Prohibition of discrimination, harassment, sexual harassment and abuse of authority, 30 November 2012, CF/EXD/2012-007, section 1.1(b) or (c); UN Development Program, "Duties and Responsibilities", in *HR User Guide*, January 2010, section I para. 5; United Nations Relief and Works Agency ('UNRWA'), Prohibition of Discrimination, Harassment – including Sexual Harassment – and Abuse of Power, General Staff Circular No. 06/2010, para. 6(c).

[55] US Supreme Court, *Harris v. Forklift Systems, Inc.*, Judgment, 9 November 1993, No. 92-1168, pp. 17, 21 (emphasis added).

as well as the specific objective environmental conditions that a 'reasonable person' would find intimidating or offensive are taken into account.[56]

14.3.2. Second Element: Unwelcome

The element that behaviour must be 'unwelcome' is the core element of the definition of sexual harassment. Even if a certain conduct, when applying the objective test, amounts to sexual harassment according to a reasonable person's perception, it can lose its harassing nature (and thus its qualification as prohibited conduct) if the target of the conduct welcomes it. For example, let us consider a male colleague who, during office hours, intrudes the sphere of privacy of his sitting female colleague by massaging her neck. Generally, such behaviour would be perceived by a reasonable person as constituting sexual harassment. However, if the colleague reacts to the skin contact and massage by saying "thank you, this relieves my pain" or "that is exactly what I had asked from you earlier" then such a reaction is indicative that the conduct of the office mate was probably welcomed by her. For instance, regarding the putting of a colleague's toe and thumb in the mouth by another co-worker and causing pain by biting, as it happened in the case detailed in Section 14.4.4., the UNAT pointed out that "no conduct automatically rises to the level of sexual harassment merely on the basis of its sexual overtones and lack of 'appropriateness' [...]".[57]

To determine whether a certain conduct satisfies the objective test of sexual harassment, the 'welcome' or rather 'unwelcome' determination is therefore key. The UNDT held that

> [i]n every definition or examination of the subject of sexual harassment, it is the unwelcome and unwanted nature of the conduct on the part of the recipient which makes it prohibited conduct capable of constituting misconduct on the part of the staff member engaging in such conduct.[58]

Analysis of the jurisprudence of UNAdminT reveals that judges in the first and second instances occasionally differ, whether contentious conduct in question was indeed 'unwelcome'. The UNAT overturned cases[59]

---

[56] Christopher Uggen and Amy Blackstone, "Sexual Harassment as a Gendered Expression of Power", in *American Sociological Review*, 2004, vol. 69, no. 1, p. 64 (65).

[57] UNAT Bagot judgment, para. 62, see above note 34.

[58] UNDT, *Applicant v. S-G*, Judgment, 23 June 2011, UNDT/2011/106, para. 43 ('UNDT – judgment on friendship gone cold') (https://www.legal-tools.org/doc/2rkaem/).

[59] UNAT Bagot judgment, see above note 34; UNAT Perelli judgment, see above note 34.

because the judges disagreed with the assessment of the first instance courts whether certain conduct was 'unwelcome' or not.

14.3.2.1. Welcome or Unwelcome Conduct

At the core of many sexual harassment cases lies the disagreement of the alleged offender and target about whether certain conduct was unwelcome or not. While the target will claim that behaviour was certainly 'unwelcome', the alleged offender will claim the exact opposite. Thus, as both sides find themselves involved in disciplinary proceedings, one as the alleged offender and the other as the target, they are bound to disagree on this key element.

The UN jurisprudence adopts a conservative stance on which perspective, the one of the alleged offender or the affected individual, is ultimately decisive for determining whether a conduct was welcome or not. The UNAT, by requiring that "the alleged offender should reasonably be able to understand that his advances are not welcome",[60] appears to emphasize the perspective of the alleged offender. Only if the alleged offender was reasonably able to understand or should reasonably have known[61] that the conduct was unwelcome, then this conduct may amount to sexual harassment.

In conclusion, the judges do not rely on the perspective of the target, but rather on one of the alleged offender to determine whether conduct is 'unwelcome'. One can interpret this phrase to point out that the burden of proof that the alleged offender was "reasonably able to understand" lies squarely with the administration or the alleged target.[62] The administration, which usually intends to implement the zero-tolerance[63] approach on sexual harassment by pursuing the alleged offender, has to prove that the person who engaged in the contested conduct disregarded certain 'sign-posts' or 'signals' which would have enabled a *reasonable* person to conclude that

---

[60] UNAT Bagot judgment, para. 52, see above note 34.

[61] UNAT Perelli judgment, para. 105, see above note 34.

[62] UNAdminT, *Belas-Gianou v. S-G*, Judgment, 28 July 1995, Judgement No. 707, p. 30 ('UNAdminT judgment Belas-Gianou') (https://www.legal-tools.org/doc/cbcpj7/). "It is, of course the responsibility of the person alleging sexual harassment [...] to produce convincing evidence in support of the allegations".

[63] UN Chief Executives Board for Coordination ('CEB'), Summary of deliberations, 24 July 2018, CEB/2018/1, Annex I, pp. 17, 18 ('CEB First deliberations 2018') (https://www.legal-tools.org/doc/g4iqls/); CEB, Summary of deliberations, 18 January 2019, CEB/2018/2, para. 53(a) ('CEB Second deliberations 2018') (https://www.legal-tools.org/doc/hfwl5d/).

an advance was not welcome. For behaviour to be 'unwelcome', the alleged offender should "reasonably be able to understand" that such conduct is not welcome.[64] This means that the alleged offender must have had actual knowledge or, lacking thereof, at least constructive knowledge that certain conduct was unwelcome.[65]

Actual knowledge can be inferred if the alleged offender continues with his or her sexual behaviour despite the target or affected individual indicating clearly that the conduct is unwelcome.[66]

14.3.2.2. Boundaries

To distinguish between an unwelcome and a welcome conduct, the administrative jurisprudence focuses on the concept of boundaries. If the behaviour and expressions of the target demonstrate it had set boundaries in place before the conduct occurred, and nevertheless the alleged offender crossed these, then this indicates that the offender indeed transgressed and that the behaviour was "unwelcome".

Both principal administrative instructions of the UN encourage the affected individual to inform the alleged offender:

The 1992 UN Administrative Instruction stated "[i]ndividuals who believe that they are being [sexually] harassed are encouraged to notify the offender that his or her behaviour is unwelcome".[67] Again, the 2008 UN Administrative Instruction encourages aggrieved persons to inform the offender, but voices also understanding if this does not occur:

> Aggrieved individuals are encouraged to notify the offender of their complaint or grievance and ask him or her to stop as, in some instances, the alleged offender may not be aware that his or her behaviour is offensive. However, the disparity in power, [authority] or status or other considerations may make direct confrontation difficult, and aggrieved individuals are not required to confront the offender.[68]

It is the latter cases in which an aggrieved person has boundaries in place, and chooses not to inform the alleged offender to avoid confronta-

---

[64] UNAT Bagot judgment, para. 52, see above note 34.

[65] UNDT Perelli judgment, paras. 102–104, see above note 34.

[66] *Ibid.*, para. 103.

[67] 1992-UN-AI, section 3, see above note 28.

[68] 2008-UN-AI, section 5.5, see above note 3; UNDT Perelli judgment, para. 104, see above note 34.

tions, that make it difficult to decide whether certain conduct was unwelcome.

If the affected individual claims boundaries and that these were transgressed, then the alleged offender can raise the defence that a reasonable person was unable to note these boundaries. The alleged offender then claims a subjective deficit: to be *unaware* of the existence of boundaries because a reasonable person in the same shoes would have been unaware too.

14.3.2.3. Constructive Knowledge

In response to a defence that the alleged offender could have reasonably been unaware and was thus unable to notice the boundaries, the jurisprudence analyses whether the specific circumstances of each situation create *constructive* knowledge of the alleged offender that conduct was unwelcome.[69] Constructive knowledge "ensures accountability for sexual harassment that is conducted out of thoughtlessness or irresponsibility but nevertheless creates problems for affected staff members".[70]

The UNAT required in *Bagot v. S-G* that it should be established in a "clear and unambiguous way that [the alleged offender] had constructive knowledge of the unwelcome nature of his actions".[71]

Constructive knowledge can flow from a variety of sources. For example, after a former male colleague expressed to a female co-worker in an email that he could "help her getting pregnant" the target of this sexual advance responded "if I will be ever in a position to share a room one of us must sleep on the floor".[72] The same target of this advance also sent another email clarifying "I do not want to give you any false hope because I do not want to have sex with you. I never wanted that".[73] Both emails set a boundary, regardless of an otherwise longstanding close friendship with sexual overtones, constituting at least constructive knowledge that further sexual advances are 'unwelcome' in case the colleague chooses to engage in further innuendos.

---

[69] UNDT Perelli judgment, para. 104, see above note 34.

[70] *Ibid.*

[71] UNAT Bagot judgment, para. 60, see above note 34.

[72] UNAT, *Applicant v. S-G*, Judgment, 28 March 2013, 2013-UNAT-280, para. 45 ('UNAT – judgment on friendship gone cold') (https://www.legal-tools.org/doc/6ivbku/).

[73] *Ibid.*, para. 46.

14.4. Case Law on Sexual Harassment

This section presents a brief overview of relevant case law on sexual harassment. In the following, a number of judgments by different international tribunals will be presented in turn.

14.4.1. First Judgment on Sexual Harassment at the UN

The events leading to the case *Belas-Gianou v. S-G* occurred between July and November 1991, before the UN had formally defined and implemented the definition of sexual harassment through ST/AI/379 in October 1992. However, this instrument was used as a reference by the administration and during the appeals proceedings.[74] The affected individual claimed that the supervisor had entered the office without knocking, expressing pleasure at the thought that, due to a colleague's absence, the supervised staff member would work alone with him. The supervisor then came for unduly long periods to his staff's office complaining about his wife, stating he would be unhappily married, addressing the staff member as 'darling' or 'dearest', making sexual innuendos in Arabic which the affected staff member did not understand and could therefore not substantiate further.[75] The target reacted embarrassed and, being fearful of possible consequences, did not object to the supervisor.[76]

The UNAdminT denied sexual harassment had occurred, emphasizing the absence of some indication that the alleged offender was either on notice or "should reasonably have realized from the circumstances that the conduct was unwelcome, might be viewed as being of a sexual nature and as creating an offensive working environment".[77] The judges stressed that it is important that the aggrieved person makes a clear and unequivocal complaint promptly, if unable to stop the interaction immediately by less formal means.[78]

The judges' analysis of the conduct in question considered the views of the target, but with caution. The judges held that a

> belief in good faith that one has been the victim of sexual harassment, however strongly held, does not automatically mean,

---

[74] UNAdminT judgment Belas-Gianou, para. 63, see above note 62.

[75] *Ibid.*, p. 31, section VI.

[76] *Ibid.*, p. 31, section VI(e) and p. 33, section VIII.

[77] *Ibid.*, p. 34, section IX.

[78] *Ibid.*, p. 35, section X.

without more, that sexual harassment occurred. [...] The enumerated items are at most either ambiguous, or the possibility of a relationship between them and conduct of a sexual nature is both tenuous and remote.[79]

14.4.2. A Close Friendship with Sexual Overtones Went Cold

This case centred around a five-year-long close and intimate friendship with sexual overtones between a superior and a subordinate, both married to other partners, which escalated into sexual harassment claims after the superior had sent a picture of his genitalia to the subordinate and had tried to kiss her.[80]

Having entertained a close friendship at one duty station, the alleged offender had expressed sexual advances towards the target months before the latter joined the alleged offender at a new duty station. The alleged offender wrote less than a year before the target resumed duties:

> Over the years you have resolutely resisted all my advances [...] I just had and still [missing word] overriding desire to make love to you and be inside you. I know you didn't want [word indecipherable] and, of course, I accept your view. I just wish we could be together here in East Timor.[81]

Shortly before the target of this advance resumed duties at the UN the alleged offender wrote "You could always get pregnant early if you are worried, maybe I could help with that!" and received the following response from the target of this new advance

> Wooow, Eih, hold on!!! [...] And if I will ever be in a position to shar [sic] your room, one of us must sleep on the floor!!! Punto. :) P.S.: I note that we are now joking only, we are really good friends and there is nothing that can change that (just do not mention sex or sleeping ina [sic] same room and everything will be fine). :)[82]

The next day, the affected individual wrote

---

[79] *Ibid.*, p. 34, section X. Compare also p. 40, section XIX: "In essence, the Applicant's claims of sexual harassment [...] find support only in her own statements to the Tribunal and to others to whom she says she conveyed them".

[80] UNDT – judgment on friendship gone cold, paras. 42, 44, 47, 134, 135, see above note 58; UNAT – judgment on friendship gone cold, para. 39, see above note 72.

[81] *Ibid.*, para. 41.

[82] *Ibid.*, para. 45.

> But I do not wont [sic] to give you any false hope becouse [sic] I do not wont [sic] to have sex with you. I never wonted [sic] that and morre [sic] correct I do not wont [sic] to have sex with anybody at all. I do not joke now.[83]

Four weeks after the target had resumed duties at the duty station, the alleged offender sent via email a photo of his genitalia to the subordinate who responded

> I simply cannot belive [sic] that you have sent me this photo. I have not seen your intimate part before definetly [sic] and I truly hope you are joking only. What on earth made you to take this kind picture of your exposed body and send it to me [...] I can forgive you only if you were drunk completely [sic] when done so.[84]

However, the next morning, the affected individual joked with the superior that "it was well shaved".[85] About two weeks later, the targeted person moved out of the hotel in which the alleged offender was also staying, in a separate room.[86]

The first instance court and the UNAT disagreed whether the conduct of the superior who had sent a photo of his genitalia was 'unwelcome' pursuant to 1992 UN Administrative Instruction.

14.4.2.1. UNDT

The UNDT focused on the overall behaviour displayed between the superior and the subordinate by claiming:

> The charge of sexual harassment against the Applicant cannot be sustained in the circumstances. To the extent that [the affected individual] was willing and happy to engage in sex talk via emails, telephone, text messages and in-person with the [alleged offender], the [affected individual] cannot blow hot and cold deciding after the fact and several months later after other disagreements that [the affected individual] was sexually harassed based on incidents [the affected individual] had at the time they occurred joked about.[87]

---

[83] *Ibid.*, para. 46.

[84] *Ibid.*, para. 50.

[85] UNDT – judgment on friendship gone cold, para. 67, see above note 58.

[86] *Ibid.*, paras. 44, 65; UNAT – judgment on friendship gone cold, para. 51, see above note 72.

[87] UNDT – judgment on friendship gone cold, para. 187, see above note 58 (compare also paras. 64, 65).

In essence, the UNDT argued that the alleged conduct was *not* unwelcome.[88] The UNDT found that what happened between the affected individual and the alleged offender was "a personal and intimate feud between two consenting adult staff members".[89]

14.4.2.2. UNAT

The UNAT disagreed, finding the conduct was 'unwelcome': From the outset the affected individual "did not share the [alleged offender's] desire to pursue a sexual relationship".[90] The judges held that the target had set boundaries while being recruited by the alleged offender for a post under his supervision:

> The transmission by the [offender] of a photograph of his genitalia to a female colleague, much less a female colleague under his direct supervision, irrespective of whether the photograph was sent within or outside work hours, can at its best [...] 'be characterised as outrageous, and most probably unwanted'. In the present case, there was no "probability" surrounding the issue as to whether this action was unwanted or unwelcome, given the boundaries which the [target] had set in her correspondence of January 2005. [...] The fundamental basis of the [alleged offender's] and [target's] relationship, from 15 February 2005 onwards, was that of supervisor and supervisee. Given the unequal nature of this relationship and the boundaries which the [target] had attempted to establish, together with the [alleged offender's] breach of those boundaries, [...] the [offender's] very graphic conduct on 15 March 2005 and its unwelcome nature rendered the [target's] work environment "offensive" within the meaning of ST/AI/379.[91]

The judges continued that the offender's

> approaches to the [target] remained sexual in nature, notwithstanding the absence of overt sexual comments or entreaties

---

[88] Compare *ibid.*, para. 67: "It can be deduced also from later communication between [the affected individual and alleged offender] that their friendship continued nevertheless and that [the affected individual] did not find the photograph [of the penis] unwelcome or offensive". Further, the judge observed in this same case, with regards to workplace harassment: "Such conduct must be unwelcome in the sense that the alleged victim did not solicit, incite or court the conduct and regarded it as undesirable and offensive" (compare also para. 59).

[89] *Ibid.*, para. 181.

[90] *Ibid.*, para. 59.

[91] UNAT – judgment on friendship gone cold, para. 60, see above note 72.

on the part of the [offender]. It is apparent from the [targets] responses to the [offenders] communications and notwithstanding any concessions [the target] made to the friendship they had, that the sexual context of the [offenders] conduct and the jealousy and possessiveness it gave rise to remained unwelcome to the [target]. Moreover, we are satisfied that the totality of the circumstances in which the [target] found [it]self in the period from February to May 2005 constituted circumstances which could reasonably [...], under any standard, [be] unwelcome to the [target] as well as an offensive, and on occasions intimidating, work environment for the [target].[92]

[T]he UNDT failed manifestly to attach sufficient weight to the unequal nature of the respective positions of the target and the offender within the Organisation [and] [...] to the strength of the [target's] rejection of the [offender's] desire for an intimate sexual relationship with [the affected individual]. Thus, we regard as manifestly unreasonable the Dispute Tribunal's finding that the [target] 'was a consenting partner in an intimate adult relationship where no holds were barred as far as topics for discussions were concerned,' particularly since the target, as evident from [his/her] e-mails, had set out in clear terms for the [offender] the parameters of [his/her] non-sexual relationship with [him/her].[93]

14.4.3. UNHCR Case in Budapest

Another case related to a senior UNHCR staff member who had arrived in Budapest and had received telephone numbers from local staff members to assist him. A dynamic ensued in which the senior sent numerous SMSs and emails asking staff out, including to come to the senior's apartment to hang curtains. The superior mentioned massages in the office and finally faced three allegations of inappropriate physical touching, including once during a salsa evening and twice in the office, specifically once on the leg, and on the other occasion by giving a brief massage on a subordinate's neck.[94]

The UNDT found that, if established as true, the conduct could be described as sexual harassment, it would have been offensive and unwel-

---

[92] *Ibid.*, para. 62.

[93] *Ibid.*, para. 63.

[94] UNDT, *Applicant v. S-G*, Judgment, 16 March 2011, UNDT/2011/054, paras. 123, 124 (https://www.legal-tools.org/doc/c4yvag/).

come and, at the very least, would have made the subordinates uncomfortable in his presence, and impacted on staff members' relationship to the superior.[95] The superior was not denying that he had spoken about massages, had sent numerous messages, had touched his staff and talked with one subordinate about marriage, but emphasised that he was also asked a lot of questions by the staff concerned about his own mixed cultural upbringing and therefore neither the conversations nor actions would have had a sexual connotation.[96]

Having listened to the superior, the UNDT observed that at least one witness also reported about email interactions which were not unwelcome, and that the superior acknowledged discussions about massages and other topics which one could interpret "in more than one way".[97] Overall, the UNDT emphasised that the investigation leading to the summary dismissal of the superior was not conducted properly, and was "one-sided".[98] This left the judge with two possibilities: either the subordinated staff, having learned from each other, brought their genuine and serious concerns jointly about the alleged offender to the attention of senior management, or the subordinates did not like his management style and elevated some concerns to engineer his removal.[99] As the investigation and disciplinary proceedings failed to clarify which of both options applied, the UNDT set aside the summary dismissal of the superior.[100]

This case demonstrates how crucial a proper investigation is. The investigation should not only touch upon the facts constituting sexual harassment, but also cover the perceptions of both sides of the contested conduct, and the overall dynamic the conduct has at the workplace. Due to the UN's zero-tolerance policy, allegations of sexual harassment, if proven at the end of a proper investigation, are likely to result in the removal of the alleged offender. Thus, the facts must be proven to the 'clear and convincing' evidence standard required for dismissal.[101]

---

[95] *Ibid.*, para. 125.

[96] *Ibid.*, paras. 131–133, 135.

[97] *Ibid.*, paras. 128–132.

[98] *Ibid.*, para. 141.

[99] *Ibid.*, paras. 140, 139.

[100] *Ibid.*, paras. 143, 144.

[101] UNAT, *Molari v. S-G*, Judgment, 21 October 2011, 2011-UNAT-164, para. 2 ('UNAT judgment Molari') (https://www.legal-tools.org/doc/6r0pmm/).

14.4.4. *Bagot v. S-G*

In this case, the alleged offender was a director within the department of internal oversight in Amman in Jordan, and the target was a contractor. On a work-free day both went first to a restaurant and to the director's apartment where they discussed personal matters ending in the director massaging the contractor until, at some point, the director took the target's toe and thumb in the mouth and bit, causing pain.[102] The target feigned an emergency at home as an excuse to leave, declined the offer to be driven home, and left alone.[103] The alleged offender then contacted the target via SMS to learn its current location, drove there, repeatedly contacting the target from there, and finally reached the affected individual with whom the director then phoned for 17 minutes.[104] Over the phone, the target suggested the alleged offender "should go home, don't trouble yourself, I am ok" to which the alleged offender stated "we are meant to be together, we are soul mates, we are destined to be together, the universe had this plan, [...] this is the way the universe is giving you a choice and the choice is yours but you have to make the choice tonight".[105]

The alleged offender insisted he would stay "outside the target's house for 2, 3, 4, hours, however long it takes" and was told to "go home".[106] The alleged offender returned to the apartment, sent two more unanswered text messages, and, in the early morning of the following day, apologized by SMS, subsequently calling again with getting an answer.[107]

The first and second instance courts disagreed whether the conduct of the alleged offender was 'unwelcome'.

14.4.4.1. UNRWA Dispute Tribunal

The Dispute Tribunal of the UNRWA argued the conduct of the alleged offender was welcome throughout the lunch and in the apartment, as the affected individual initially did not object to the physical contact (the massage) up to the point of putting the toe and thumb into the mouth and the

---

[102] UNAT Bagot judgment, paras. 2, 3, see above note 34.

[103] *Ibid.*, paras. 3, 54, 55.

[104] *Ibid.*, paras. 3, 55.

[105] *Ibid.*, para. 55.

[106] *Ibid.*, para. 3.

[107] *Ibid.*

subsequent biting.[108] The Dispute Tribunal pointed out that until the target objected (following the biting), the alleged offender who then stopped could reasonably consider that the behaviour until then was not unwelcome.[109] However, following the target abruptly leaving the apartment and having declined the offer to be driven home, the first instance judge found that "no reasonable person could have doubted that the emergency situation was only an excuse to leave his apartment and that any other action on his part would be unwelcome".[110] Thus, in these circumstances, all subsequent calls and text messages constituted sexual harassment:

> In view of the manner in which the meeting at the apartment had ended,[…] [I]t was obvious that [the affected individual] did not want to talk to the [alleged offender] any further. Therefore, the [alleged offender's] actions in calling [the target] six times between 6:06 p.m. and 6:29 p.m. and sending […] three text messages between 6:26 p.m. and 9:20 p.m. certainly constituted unwelcome conduct. Furthermore, the content of the 17-minute conversation […] does constitute sexual harassment. The sexual harassment continued [the next day] when the Applicant sent a text message to [the target] at 5:47 a.m. and attempted to call […] at 3:26 p.m.[111]

14.4.4.2. UNAT

The UNAT disagreed with this assessment and doubted that the conduct of the alleged offender following the biting was unwelcome, at least the alleged offender had no constructive knowledge of it.

The Appeals judges pointed out that the reasoning of the UNRWA's judges "does not reveal in a clear and unambiguous way that [the alleged offender] had constructive knowledge of the unwelcome nature of his actions".[112] For the contested conduct to amount to sexual harassment,

> it is not enough to be found 'inappropriate.' No conduct automatically rises to the level of sexual harassment merely on the

---

[108] UNRWA Bagot judgment, paras. 104–110, see above note 34; compare UNAT Bagot judgment, paras. 49, 51, 52, see above note 34.

[109] *Ibid.*, para. 110.

[110] *Ibid.*, para. 112.

[111] *Ibid.*, para. 114.

[112] UNAT Bagot judgment, para. 60, see above note 34.

basis of its sexual overtones and lack of 'appropriateness' [...] on foot of its 'inappropriate' character.[113]

The judges observed that it was

> not evident that [the target] had set out boundaries in clear terms for [the alleged offender] at this time. In any case, when [the affected individual] did, as happened in the apartment, when [the alleged offender] 'bit her toe and thumb', [the alleged offender] immediately complied with her request to stop. [...] neither the manner in which the meeting at the apartment had ended, nor the unanswered phone calls, made by [the offender] between 6:06 p.m. and 6:29 p.m. [on the day of the incident] or the text message to [the target] at 5:47 a.m. and the attempts to call her at 3:26 p.m. [the next day] made it obvious that [the alleged offenders] conduct was unwelcomed [...] in view of the fact that the latter answered his phone call at 6:29 p.m. [on the day of the incident] and talked with him for 17 minutes without objecting to his calling. As for the content of the 17-minute conversation [...], it cannot be considered as per se constituting sexual harassment. These facts do not constitute clear and convincing evidence of misconduct.[114]

14.4.5. *Perelli v. S-G*

Similarly, in this case the first and second instance judges disagreed on whether the conduct of Perelli was unwelcome and whether the alleged offender had constructive knowledge of it.

Perelli was a director in a division of the UN. An external management review revealed numerous managerial shortcomings. An investigation found that a persistently sexually charged atmosphere existed within the unit headed by Perelli: [115] "crude language, sexual jokes and references/innuendo to [Perelli's] sex life and inquiries/references to staff's sexual habits, often in front of others" and "two instances of overt sexual harassment on the part of [...] Perelli" occurred.[116] Perelli routinely used coarse and profane language, made references to sexual matters and used sexual innuendo, on a number of occasions referred to bottoms of male staff members and engaged at least in one instance of inappropriate physi-

---

113 *Ibid.*, para. 62.

114 *Ibid.*, paras. 63, 64.

115 UNAT Perelli judgment, paras. 2, 3, 6, see above note 59.

116 *Ibid.*, paras. 6, 8b.

cal contact with a male subordinate;[117] overall some staff members believed in good faith that the offensive, hostile or intimidating environment
in the unit was created or further aggravated by Perelli.[118]

The alleged offender argued that in seven years at the UN, no staff
member ever complained to management about sexual harassment by
Perelli.[119]

14.4.5.1. UNDT

The UNDT argued that Perelli was

> a senior manager and head of [a] division in a multicultural
> organisation. The workplace of the UN is governed by stand-
> ards of conduct set by the Charter, staff regulations, rules and
> policies. Staff members have at least presumptive knowledge
> of these exacting standards, and, particularly given the posi-
> tion of seniority, the alleged offender should have been aware
> that such conduct breached them. It was the alleged offender's
> responsibility to ensure that the workplace Perelli managed
> was free of sexually explicit behaviour and that Perelli did not
> contribute to or encourage it.[120]

14.4.5.2. UNAT

The UNAT was aware that Perelli was not on actual notice about the unwelcome nature of the conduct. The court therefore focused on the issue,
whether the UNDT's conclusion that Perelli had no constructive knowledge
of the unwelcome nature of one's own actions, is factually and legally sustainable.

The UNAT referred to a report of the Joint Disciplinary Committee
that found: 1) Perelli did not introduce coarse language and profanity in the
unit as such conduct existed there before, 2) subordinates issued no warning or request about Perelli's behaviour during the six years tenure as Director, 3) body language was insufficient to demonstrate that Perelli was
put on notice; and 4) if oral complaints reached Perelli and other senior officials, then these related to management issues and not sexual harassment

---

[117] UNDT Perelli judgment, para. 95, see above note 34; compare UNAT Perelli judgment,
para. 55, see above note 59.

[118] *Ibid.*

[119] *Ibid.*, para. 106.

[120] *Ibid.*, para. 107.

issues.[121] The panel found that Perelli's contention was credible: having received no clear warning signals from staff that her conduct was seen as offensive and/or inappropriate, Perelli was unaware that her own conduct was considered by some as inappropriate and unwelcome; in such circumstances, a reasonable person would *not* necessarily have been aware, given the existing differences in cultural backgrounds and professional work experiences.[122] The appeals judges concurred with the panel's assessment and found that Perelli had *no* constructive knowledge that her own conduct was unwelcome by staff.

14.5. Superiors

By virtue of their position, perceived and real power, superiors can greatly influence the careers and well-being of staff. Thus, they are expected to set the example of the highest standards of behaviour. As they are expected to perform a role model function, their entails not only to refrain from engaging in any conduct potentially amounting to sexual harassment, but also to inform staff about their rights, including the possibility to report misconduct, and, if reports are then made, to react to allegations in a prompt, impartial and fair manner.

The evolution of these functions of superiors should be briefly sketched out. The UN Administrative Instructions moved from vague to specific in this regard. The 1992 UN Administrative Instruction simply referred to "senior member of the department or office"[123] without clarifying whether this person is the direct supervisor, a mid-level manager or top manager in the office. By contrast, the 2008 UN Administrative Instruction introduces a distinction between managers and supervisors[124] on the one hand and "heads of department/office/mission" on the other hand.[125]

14.5.1. Acting Twofold upon Receiving Information

Both UN Administrative Instructions from 1992 and 2008 provide that superiors exercise a twofold function in relation to informal and formal settlement of situations arising out of allegations of sexual harassment. The 1992 UN Administrative Instruction leaves it to the discretion of the ag-

---

[121] *Ibid.*, para. 64.

[122] *Ibid.*

[123] 1992-UN-AI, section 6, see above note 28.

[124] 2008-UN-AI, section 3.2, see above note 3.

[125] *Ibid.*, section 3.3.

grieved individual whether to seek advice from a "senior member of the department or office". If informed, this 'senior member' could then either discuss the matter discreetly with both sides of the allegation of sexual harassment to achieve an informal resolution[126] or, if the reported conduct "may constitute misconduct", this senior will report the matter up in the chain of command.[127] Thus, the "senior member" envisaged by the 1992 UN Administrative Instruction had discretion ("where appropriate") to pursue an informal settlement and, if allegations of misconduct were involved, was bound ("will be reported") to inform the higher echelons.

A senior member's report on allegations of sexual harassment has the same effect and function as a formal complaint of the aggrieved individual in that both enable the UN Office of Human Resources Management to trigger an initial investigation and fact-finding.[128] Thus, the 1992 UN Administrative Instruction provided a twofold role of a senior member: if suitable, the superior conducts an informal settlement and/or files a report of sexual harassment to have the higher echelons trigger a formal procedure of fact-finding and investigation.

The 2008 UN Administrative Instruction repeated the above functions, including the superior's and supervisor's possible involvement in the informal settlement of the situation arising out of sexual harassment allegations.[129] However, in a list of several possible entities carrying out an informal settlement, the 2008 UN Administrative Instruction listed the supervisor only as the last option.[130]

In 2018, the UN model policy on sexual harassment provided three variants of settlement: informal settlement, formal reporting to trigger fact-finding/investigation, or involving an ombudsman. Regarding the role of superiors, the UN model policy on sexual harassment specifically sketches

---

[126] 1992-UN-AI, section 6, see above note 28.

[127] *Ibid.*, section 7.

[128] *Ibid.*, section 9.

[129] 2008-UN-AI, sections 5.3., 5.6(j), 5.7, 5.9, 5.11, see above note 3, namely the second sentence referring indirectly to the superior as the "third party who has direct knowledge of the situation".

[130] *Ibid.*, section 5.6(j). Compare also 1992-UN-AI, see above note 28, which mentions, in section 5, several persons able to conduct informal settlements before mentioning, in section 6, first the Personnel Officer and, finally, the "senior member of the department".

out how a 'managerial intervention' to assist an affected individual should occur:[131]

> Targets may choose to raise allegations of sexual harassment with their superiors who then should inform about the responsible office which provides confidential advice. Further, managers themselves should provide advice, assistance, information and support in a timely, sensitive and impartial manner. Managerial intervention is thereby one of several options with alternative options being the filing of a formal complaint or seeking the service of an ombudsman.[132]

14.5.2. Training in Informal Mediation to Become A 'Role Model'

The 2008 UN Administrative Instruction obliges superiors to participate in online training courses on preventing (sexual) harassment and also to receive targeted training in informal and formal resolution techniques as a requirement for advancement.[133] The latter obligation enables superiors to understand the role they would have to play in an informal settlement before allegations of sexual harassment being brought to their attention. In 2018, the CEB created a common guide for managers on prevention of and response to sexual harassment in the workplace.[134]

Furthermore, 2008 Administrative Instruction puts all managers and supervisors under the

> duty to take all appropriate measures to promote a harmonious work environment, free of intimidation, hostility, offence and any form of prohibited conduct. They must act as role models by upholding the highest standards of conduct.[135]

The case *Portillo Moya v. S-G*, which involved the supervisor of a warehouse of the WFP, demonstrates how a superior failed to meet and repeatedly violated this standard. Portillo Moya had made sexual jokes, had used offensive words and nicknames in the Portuguese language, including but not limited to *mierdosa* ('piece of shit') and *penderja* ('dumb') to address a colleague about whose intimate life the offender had sent emails to

---

[131] UN model policy on sexual harassment, section IV, sub-paras. 2–4, see above note 2.

[132] *Ibid.*, p. 6, explanatory notes.

[133] *Ibid.*, sections 4.2, 4.3.

[134] CEB First deliberations 2018, para. 49, see above note 63; CEB Second deliberations 2018, para. 52(d), see above note 63.

[135] *Ibid.*, section 3.2.

another staff member.[136] On other occasions, Portillo Moya had used the swear words *puta* ('fuck'), *hijueputa* (a shorter form of 'son of a bitch') claiming not to have meant her colleagues, but to address one's frustration.[137]

The administration informed Portillo Moya to have displayed a standard of conduct, which was below that required in international civil service.[138] Particularly, section 13 of the applicable WFP's Directive states "[e]mployees with supervisory and/or management responsibilities are responsible for: maintaining a high standard of personal conduct in dealing with all employees, and leading by example in maintaining the personal dignity of employees [...]".[139] The administration imposed the sanction 'separation from service' on Portillo Moya.[140]

14.5.3. Senior Position Demands a Higher Level of Sensitivity

The UNAT held in *Michaud v. S-G* that a senior position demands and justifies a higher level of sensitivity. Among investigators in the UN's Office of International Oversight, a dispute arose out of an email exchange occurring between a superior and subordinate about ten days after the latter had joined an investigative mission in Afghanistan.[141] The UNAT observed "the e-mails speak for themselves and invite admonition, if not censure, without further ado"[142] because they are inappropriately suggestive and contain comments of the superior intended to suggest sexual interest.[143] Both the UNDT and the UNAT agreed that the sanction of written reprimand imposed by the administration was appropriate.[144] The UNAT admitted that the words contained in the emails would be

---

[136] UNDT judgment Portillo Moya, paras. 7, 31(d), 38, see above note 34. Translations supplied in the source.

[137] *Ibid.*, paras. 7, 38.

[138] *Ibid.*, para. 8.

[139] WFP policy on sexual harassment, p. 3, para. 13, see above note 53.

[140] UNDT judgment Portillo Moya, paras. 74, 75, 8, 10, 25, see above note 34.

[141] For the content of the email exchange see UNDT judgment Michaud, paras. 4–7, see above note 34.

[142] UNAT judgment Michaud, para. 60, see above note 34.

[143] *Ibid.*, para. 61.

[144] UNDT judgment Michaud, para. 70, see above note 34; UNAT judgment Michaud, paras. 63, 61, see above note 34.

low on the bar of sexual harassment and legitimately may be seen as flirtatious and relatively innocent. They assume greater impropriety, however, because they emanate from a senior investigator with specific responsibility under his job description to investigate the misconduct of others.[145]

14.5.4. Heads of Department, Office or Mission

While 1992 UN Administrative Instruction had created regarding superiors a conscious ambiguity by introducing the category of 'senior member of the department or office', the 2008 UN Administrative Instruction changed this approach by introducing a distinction between ordinary and top managers. In Sections 14.5.1 to 14.5.3, the rules applicable to ordinary managers, which 2008 UN Administrative Instruction introduces as "managers and supervisors",[146] have been discussed. This section introduces the additional rules and responsibilities applicable to the heads of department, office, or mission. The most senior staff members are responsible for the overall implementation of the prohibition of sexual harassment, including by "holding all managers and other supervisory staff accountable for compliance".[147]

As heads provide performance appraisals to subordinated managers, they are also to include whether and how subordinated managers discharged their obligation to promptly, impartially, and fairly address complaints of sexual harassment.[148] Further, they should ensure that subordinated staff undertakes the required mandatory training to prevent sexual harassment.[149]

At least two cases adjudicated by the UN administrative tribunals address allegations of sexual harassment surrounding heads of offices, which are briefly outlined below.

14.5.4.1. *Khan v. S-G*

Khan, then head of a WFP Sub-Office in Quetta, Pakistan, had offered two administrative assistants his "friendship", which was refused. Khan continued to subject one assistant to unwelcome sexual comments, touching, re-

---

[145] UNAT judgment Michaud, para. 61, see above note 34.

[146] 2008-UN-AI, section 3.2, see above note 3.

[147] *Ibid.*, section 3.3.

[148] *Ibid.*, section 3.2.

[149] *Ibid.*, section 4.4 in connection with section 4.2.

questing for sex, and kissing the aggrieved individual on the face.[150] Another staff member whose contract was expiring understood Khan's actions as requesting sexual favours.[151] The WFP's policy clarifies, "When this [sexual] harassment is committed by a person in a position to influence the career or employment conditions of the victim, the sexual harassment is more offensive as it may also constitute abuse of authority".[152]

The UNDT found Khan's conduct constituted sexual harassment[153] and that the

> Head of the Sub-Office [...] was required to respect high professional and moral standards, [...]had direct responsibility to both prevent and ensure that the workplace [the head] managed was free of offensive and harmful behaviour. Contrary to his obligations, [the head] not only disregarded the interest of the staff members in his office but [...] was actually directly responsible for creating a hostile working environment.[154]

These acts were aggravated because the position of head of a sub-office means the superior can influence the employment conditions of the staff.[155]

14.5.4.2. *Perelli v. S-G*

The case *Perelli v. S-G* has been already discussed.[156] It related to a director of a division who had found a persistently sexually charged atmosphere when taking up office[157] and who did little, if anything, to change this. Indeed, insufficient proof existed that this head of the division had *constructive* knowledge satisfying the "clear and convincing"[158] evidence standard required for dismissal that subordinates felt sexually harassed. It is under-

---

[150] UNDT – judgment Khan, paras. 59, 69, see above note 34.

[151] *Ibid.*, para. 65.

[152] WFP policy on sexual harassment, p. 13, see above note 53.

[153] UNDT – judgment Khan, para. 76, see above note 34.

[154] *Ibid.*, para. 110.

[155] *Ibid.*, para. 111.

[156] See Section 14.4.5. above.

[157] UNAT Perelli judgment, paras. 6, 34, 64, see above note 59: "Perelli did not introduce coarse language and profanity in [this office]; such conduct existed before [the alleged offender] joined the Division"; UNDT Perelli judgment, para. 26, see above note 34.

[158] UNAT Perelli judgment, paras. 66, 55, see above note 59, in footnote 10 referring to UNAT judgment Molari, para. 2, see above note 101; UNAT, *Aqel v. Commissioner-General of the UNRWA*, Judgment, 1 July 2010, 2010-UNAT-040, para. 27 (https://www.legal-tools.org/doc/57k511/).

standable that the UNAT set aside the UNDT's judgment supporting summary dismissal of Perelli. On the other hand, this director was neither fully ignorant nor just indifferent to the sexually charged atmosphere in the workplace directed. Rather, the director appeared to have at least 'played along', possibly even actively contributed to the sexually charged atmosphere: the investigation panel's report revealed that

> [m]any referred to [Perelli's] use of crude language, sexual jokes, references and innuendo about [the director's] sex life, as well as inquiries and references to staff's sexual habits, *often in front of others*. None of the staff had directly complained about these matters to [Perelli], although *some had indicated to [Perelli] that they felt uncomfortable in these situations*.[159]

So the staff at least mentioned to Perelli that they felt 'uncomfortable' about the atmosphere. There was no higher person to whom complaints could have been addressed within this division, as Perelli assumed the highest post.

This raises two questions: how did Perelli use her own position as head of department to 'act as role model by upholding the highest standards of conduct'? And, did Perelli indeed discharge the superior's 'duty to take all appropriate measures to promote a harmonious work environment, free of intimidation, hostility, offence and any form of prohibited conduct' pursuant to section 3.2 of 2008 UN Administrative Instruction? The UNDT suggests that Perelli did not, because the outcome of the investigation into the allegations revealed

> […] it was more likely than not that there was at least one instance of physical contact with Mr A, a […] staff member. The contact was non-consensual. […]. [I]t was supported by 'credible corroborating testimony [by two staff members] and less than categorical denial by [Perelli].' This inappropriate physical contact was described as [Perelli] leaning over Mr A while he was sitting at his computer and touching his body with her breasts.[160]

The balance of probability standard ('more likely than not') is too low to form a basis for summary dismissal of Perelli. Dismissals can be based only on the standard of 'clear and convincing' evidence. However,

---

[159] UNDT Perelli judgment, para. 26, see above note 34 (emphasis added).
[160] UNDT Perelli judgment, para. 54, see above note 34.

the Perelli case is not only about the question of the legality of her summary dismissal, but also about how the UN regulations for superiors function in practice regarding the prohibition of sexual harassment. To assess whether Perelli satisfied the obligations the 2008 UN Administrative Instruction created for heads of divisions, the balance of probability standard is enough. Two corroborating statements existed about this incidence which, together, suggest that Perelli neither acted as a role model nor ensured "the highest standards of conduct" as section 3.2 of the 2008 UN Administrative Instruction required of managers and superiors. Furthermore, Perelli was no ordinary manager or superior, but was, as the head of division, *above* this level and thus expected to "hold all managers and other supervisory staff accountable for compliance" with the 2008 UN Administrative Instruction.[161] The alleged and corroborated incident renders it nearly impossible that Perelli could have performed the role of head of office as envisaged by section 3.3 of the 2008 UN Administrative Instruction.

Nevertheless, the UNAT was correct in pointing out that Perelli's constructive knowledge of other allegations of sexual harassment by subordinates in her department had not been proven to the 'clear and convincing' standard required. However, the signal sent to the affected individuals in Perelli's unit was at least irritating, because the UNAT not only reversed the UNDT's judgment which had upheld the UN Administration's dismissal, but also "order[ed] Ms Perelli's reinstatement or, if the Administration so chooses, the award to her of two years' net base salary".[162]

14.6. Conclusion

The efforts within the UN to ban, investigate, and adjudicate cases of sexual harassment are decades-long and ongoing. In comparison to the US, the UN commenced these belated efforts in 1992; but since then, it persistently pursues its approach of 'zero-tolerance'[163] regarding such conduct.

Since 2018, the UN created a system-wide database in which it registers offenders who have engaged in sexual harassment to avoid rehiring them.[164] A mechanism for UN system-wide collection and analysis of data

---

[161] 2008-UN-AI, section 3.3, see above note 3.
[162] UNAT Perelli judgment, para. 70, see above note 59.
[163] CEB Second deliberations 2018, para. 53 (a), see above note 63.
[164] *Ibid.*, para. 52(b), see above note 63; CEB First deliberations 2018, para. 48 and Annex I, p. 18, see above note 63.

has been set up.[165] The most senior heads of the organisation have pledged to strengthen the UN's capacity to investigate[166] sexual harassment to improve the quality of investigations of sexual harassment including, but not limited to, through specific training and selection suitable staff. Apart from boosting psychological and other support for the direct targets of sexual harassment, the UN also makes efforts to address the witnesses of sexual harassment and enhance the protection of whistle-blowers.[167]

---

[165] CEB Second deliberations 2018, para. 52(c), see above note 63.

[166] *Ibid.*, para. 52(e).

[167] CEB First deliberations 2018, Annex 1, p. 17, see above note 63; Eileen A. Cronin and Aicha Afifi, Review of whistle-blower policies and practices in United Nations system organizations, 2018, JIU/Rep/2018/4, paras. 112, 156; UN News, "Secretary-General Guterres approves updated UN whistleblower protection policy", 23 January 2017 (available on its web site).

15

Integrity and the Work of
the European Ombudsman

Marta Hirsch-Ziembinska and Vieri Biondi[*]

15.1. Introduction

The principle of integrity has a twofold importance for Ombudsman institutions. It is, at once, a precondition for their functioning and the goal that many of their inquiries are aimed at achieving. The scope of this chapter is to describe the role that the principle of integrity plays in the work and the functioning of the European Ombudsman.

The chapter will describe how the principle of integrity is an integral part of the right to good administration established in Article 41 of the European Charter of Fundamental Rights[1] and how the European Ombudsman has addressed it in practice, from which lessons for other international justice institutions may be drawn. The work of the European Ombudsman that will be presented in this chapter shows how a direct relationship exists between integrity and transparency and how improving the transparency of public institutions directly improves their integrity.

15.2. Ombudsmen Institutions and the Principle of Integrity

The first Ombudsman institution originated in Sweden in 1809 following the deposition of King Gustav IV Adolf. The legislator set up a body (Riksdagens Ombudsmän) to allow the Parliament (the 'Riksdag') to exercise a certain degree of control over the executive power. However, it is

---

[*] **Marta Hirsch-Ziembinska** is the Principal Adviser of the European Ombudsman, formerly Head of Complaints and Inquiries Unit and ICT. **Vieri Biondi** works as case handler at the European Ombudsman. The views and opinions expressed in this chapter are those of the authors and do not necessarily reflect the official policy or position of the European Ombudsman.

[1] Charter of Fundamental Rights of the European Union, 7 June 2016, 2016/C 202/02 (https://www.legal-tools.org/doc/j00z87/).

only in the second half of the twentieth century that Ombudsman institutions spread in most European countries.[2]

The role and structure of Ombudsman institutions may vary from country to country. However, certain goals are common to all of them, particularly ensuring and promoting the principle of integrity in the public sector. The importance that Ombudsmen have in ensuring integrity in public administrations is also recognized in a working paper of the Organisation for Economic Co-operation and Development ('OECD').[3]

However, Ombudsman institutions have to deal with the principle of integrity not only in the framework of their inquiries; it is of the utmost importance for Ombudsmen to ensure the integrity of their own institutions before engaging in their core activities. This is due to the nature of Ombudsman institutions, which do not have the power to issue binding decisions. Ombudsmen rely on their moral authority to have their recommendations accepted and their suggestions followed by the institutions that are the object of their investigations. The authority of Ombudsmen is not inherent to these institutions; it is directly linked to the moral authority of the office-holders. For this reason, Ombudsmen need to maintain their impartiality and independence, and to conform their actions to the highest ethical standards to be able to ensure the effective functioning of their institution and their credibility when addressing the shortcomings of other bodies. This is why Ombudsmen, although usually appointed by a political body, tend to be very cautious in trying not to politicize their institutions. An Ombudsman perceived as politicized would lose moral authority over other institutions and would simply become one of the many actors on the political level.

15.3. The European Ombudsman

The European Ombudsman was established in 1992, at the same time as European citizenship, with the Maastricht Treaty[4] to act as a bridge between the European Union ('EU') and its citizens. The first European Om-

---

[2] Nicholas Copeland, "National Ombudsmen in the EU", *EPRS Library Briefing*, 23 September 2010 (available on its web site).

[3] Organisation for Economic Co-operation and Development ('OECD'), "The Role of Ombudsman Institutions in Open Government", in *OECD Working Paper on Public Governance*, 2018, p. 12.

[4] Treaty on European Union, 7 February 1992, 92/C 191/01, Article 138e (https://www.legal-tools.org/doc/806147/).

budsman, Jacob Söderman, was elected by the European Parliament in July 1995.

The European Ombudsman was created as an independent office to which citizens or businesses can submit complaints against institutions, bodies and agencies of the Union when they are faced with instances of poor administration. The role of the European Ombudsman is to safeguard the citizens' right to good administration, which is an open-ended principle enshrined in the EU Charter of Fundamental Rights. The mission of the European Ombudsman is to uncover instances of maladministration and its role reflects that of national Ombudsmen to whom citizens can turn to complain about the administration of their Member States. Upon request of the European Parliament, the first Ombudsman elaborated a definition of maladministration, which is still relevant today. After having requested national Ombudsmen to inform him of the meaning given to the concept of maladministration in their own countries, Söderman concluded that "maladministration occurs when a public body fails to act in accordance with a rule or principle which is binding upon it".[5]

Today, the rules governing the work of the European Ombudsman can be found in Article 228 of the Treaty on the Functioning of the European Union[6] and the Statute of the European Ombudsman.[7] It is clear that the powers of the European Ombudsman draw inspiration from those of national Ombudsmen. The European Ombudsman is not limited to acting upon complaints received, but can also be proactive and launch inquiries at his or her own initiative. In this way, the Ombudsman plays an educational role aimed at improving the administrative standards of a particular European institution, body or agency without having to rely on a formal complaint.

Under the guidance of Söderman and on a proposal of Roy Perry, Member of the European Parliament, the European Ombudsman's Office developed the European Code of Good Administrative Behaviour (herein-

---

[5]   European Ombudsman, Annual Report for 1997, 20 April 1998 (https://www.legal-tools.org/doc/zu9e1m/).

[6]   Consolidated version of the Treaty on the Functioning of the European Union, 7 June 2016, 2016/C 202/01 (https://www.legal-tools.org/doc/15b8be/).

[7]   Decision of the European Parliament amending Decision 94/262/ECSC, EC, Euratom on the regulations and general conditions governing the performance of the Ombudsman's duties, 18 June 2008, 2008/587/EC, Euratom (https://www.legal-tools.org/doc/rkj24h/).

after the 'Code'),[8] which was approved by the European Parliament by a resolution in 2001.[9] The Code is intended to provide a practical explanation of what the right to good administration means in practice.[10] As the second Ombudsman, Nikiforos Diamanduros, noted, the Code has a dual function: while it serves the Ombudsman when assessing whether an institution committed maladministration, it also works as a guide for civil servants by helping them to behave according to the highest ethical standards.[11]

By reading the Code, it is possible to understand how the principle of integrity permeates the work of the European Ombudsman. First, 'integrity' is one of the five 'public service principles' established by Diamanduros, which are now an integral part of the Code and which can be considered as the foundation of the Code's detailed provisions.[12] In addition, several of the Code's articles, such as Article 8 about "impartiality and independence" and Article 11 concerning "fairness" are direct expressions of the application of the principle of integrity into practice.

As briefly discussed above, the effective functioning of Ombudsman institutions is directly linked to the moral authority of the office-holder. This clearly applies also to the European Ombudsman. In 2015, the current Ombudsman, Emily O'Reilly, took a significant step to increase the transparency of her role and, consequently, the image of integrity of the European Ombudsman's Office. O'Reilly introduced an *ad hoc* Code of Conduct to clarify the Ombudsman's expected conduct and obligations and to promote high ethical standards of conduct, in line with the public service principles.[13] The Code of Conduct addresses several practical issues such as "financial interests, assets and declaration of interests", "outside activities" and "gifts", also providing instructions on how to best handle these situations. This Code of Conduct is a clear example of how a controlling body such as the European Ombudsman aims at applying the highest administra-

---

[8] European Ombudsman, The European Code of Good Administrative Behaviour, 2015 (the 'Code') (https://www.legal-tools.org/doc/uut88i/).

[9] European Parliament resolution on the European Ombudsman's Special Report to the European Parliament following the own-initiative inquiry into the existence and the public accessibility, in the different Community institutions and bodies, of a Code of Good Administrative Behaviour, 6 September 2001, C5-0438/2000 - 2000/2212 (COS), pp. 331–336 (https://www.legal-tools.org/doc/iznb55/).

[10] *Ibid.*, p. 4.

[11] European Ombudsman, The European Code of Good Administrative Behaviour, 2005, p. 4.

[12] The Code, p. 8–10, see above note 8.

[13] European Ombudsman, "Code of Conduct for the European Ombudsman", 2015.

tive standards internally in order to be in the position to be credible when criticizing the behaviour of other institutions.

15.4. Fostering the Integrity of EU Administration

Since the establishment of the European Ombudsman, ensuring the integrity of civil servants' behaviour and promoting ethical standards have been a priority. This is because ensuring integrity is essential to safeguarding citizens' trust in the Union. Indeed, it is the trust of the citizens that ensures the legitimacy of the Union, which would otherwise be just a supranational organization distant from those whom it represents. Through its inquiries, the European Ombudsman called upon institutions, bodies and agencies of the Union to elaborate codes of conduct and to develop guidance and instructions for their staff aimed at explaining how to ensure high ethical standards in practice. The provision of guidance to staff, which is of the utmost importance in any public institution, assumes a crucial role in the reality of the Union. Civil servants working for the Union come from different backgrounds and realities, and do not necessarily share the same understanding of what behaviour is the most appropriate in a certain situation. As they might not have uniform ethical standards, they need clarification and guidance about what is expected from them.

As this section will show, the current European Ombudsman has been very active in trying to make the work of the European institutions more transparent and more accountable to the citizens. Actions carried out in this area do not only allow citizens to have a clear view of what happens at the European level, but they also directly benefit the integrity of the institutions and their staff. A transparent environment has a crucial role in promoting ethical behaviour and in ensuring compliance with the principle of integrity. Individuals who know that their actions might be made public are discouraged from engaging in unethical activities. The same reasoning can be applied to institutions. Where institutions are fully transparent, the public and the media can act as watchdog and help uncover unethical behaviour. Promoting a transparent institutional environment has a double effect. For one, it encourages civil servants to follow high ethical standards; further, it allows the public to supervise the action of the institution and to denounce unethical behaviour. Thus, it could be argued that in a transparent environment, the principle of integrity is self-enforced.

The link between transparency and integrity is evident in the European Ombudsman's inquiries that will be analysed in this section. All inquiries addressed the principle of integrity from the point of view of a conflict of interest, as defined by the OECD,[14] and keeping in mind the distinction between an apparent, potential and actual conflict of interest.[15]

15.4.1. The So-Called Revolving Doors Phenomenon

The expression 'revolving doors' refers to the situation of EU civil servants who leave the Union for a job in the private sector and of people joining the Union from the private sector. While it is clearly legitimate for professionals working in the private or in the public sector to change their jobs, the above situations present certain risks that the institutions have to keep in mind when dealing with them.

In the case of former EU civil servants who move to the private sector, the risk is that they may use confidential information obtained while working for the EU in their new positions. In addition, there is a concrete risk that these individuals might take advantage of their contacts within EU institutions to lobby, directly or indirectly, their former colleagues. When workers join the Union from the private sector, the risk is that a conflict of interest may arise in case they have to work on files which relate to their previous employment.

In addition to the risks described above, the public might perceive this movement of high-level civil servants from the Union to the private sector as unethical, regardless of the behaviour of the individuals concerned. Thus, in order to safeguard the public trust in the Union, it is of the utmost importance to ensure that the procedures in place are effective and that they are strictly followed.

The European Ombudsman, while always being conscious of the fundamental right to work,[16] follows revolving doors situations very closely, especially when they concern senior high-level staff of the EU.

In September 2016, the European Ombudsman took a decision on two complaints submitted by a number of non-governmental organizations concerning the European Commission's handling of the revolving doors phenomenon.[17] In the context of her inquiry, the Ombudsman issued rec-

---

[14] OECD, *Bribery in Public Procurement: Methods, Actors and Counter-Measures*, OECD Publishing, 2007, p. 33.

[15] Code of Conduct for the European Ombudsman, see above note 13.

[16] Charter of Fundamental Rights of the European Union, Article 15, see above note 1.

[17] European Ombudsman, Decision of the European Ombudsman closing the inquiry based on complaints 2077/2012/TN and 1853/2013/TN concerning the European Commission's han-

ommendations and provided guidelines for the Commission to ensure that all its decisions in this area are correct, well-reasoned and well-documented, and that the decision-making process is transparent.[18] The Ombudsman closed her inquiry acknowledging the steps forward made by the Commission and making four suggestions for improvement, on which she then followed up with an own-initiative strategic inquiry in 2017. This inquiry moved from the assumption that the Union can benefit from recruiting staff members with experience in the private sector and that for former civil servants the restriction to the right to work in the private sector, as it concerns a restriction of a fundamental right, must be necessary and proportionate. The Ombudsman found that, since the closure of her previous inquiry, the Commission had improved the technical handling of the revolving doors phenomenon.[19] Nevertheless, she identified certain areas that could be further improved. In particular, the Ombudsman suggested to the Commission to take a more robust approach to the issue with regard to senior officials and encouraged the Commission to also consider the option of forbidding the new activity when it could conflict with the legitimate interests of the European Commission. The Ombudsman also called on the Commission to adopt a more ambitious approach to the transparency of potential lobbying or advocacy bans issued in the context of approving the transfer of senior staff to the private sector. She suggested the Commission to publish these bans directly on the Transparency Register under the entries of the former officials' new employers. The Ombudsman also made several detailed suggestions for improvement to the Commission.

In parallel to these inquiries on the general functioning of the system, the Ombudsman also dealt with individual revolving doors situations. The best known of these inquiries is the one concerning the Commission's handling of post-mandate employment of the former President of the Commission, José Barroso. The Ombudsman found that the Commission's failure to take a specific decision on Mr. Barroso's situation constituted maladministration and recommended the Commission to refer the case back to the

---

dling of the 'revolving doors' phenomenon, 9 September 2016 (https://www.legal-tools.org/doc/oacxg9/).

[18] Draft recommendation of the European Ombudsman in the inquiry based on complaints 2077/2012/TN and 1853/2013/TN against the European Commission, 22 September 2014 (https://www.legal-tools.org/doc/y02w2c/).

[19] European Ombudsman, Decision of the European Ombudsman in her strategic inquiry OI/3/2017/NF on how the European Commission manages 'revolving doors' situations of its staff members, 28 February 2019 (https://www.legal-tools.org/doc/qy7qjc/).

Ethics Committee and to evaluate the opportunity of imposing a lobbying ban on Mr. Barroso for a certain number of years.[20] Even if the Commission did not accept the Ombudsman's recommendation in its immediate reply, the Ombudsman's inquiries led to the adoption of a Code of Conduct for Commissioners in 2018. This code extends the existing lobbying cooling-off period, from eighteen months to two years for former Commissioners and to three years for the Commission's President.[21]

15.4.2. The Transparency of the Expert Groups Advising the European Commission

The 'expert groups' are consultative bodies, which provide the Commission with high-level expertise and advice in a given policy area. The groups are composed of public and/or private sector members and they meet more than once.[22] Overall, there are over 800 expert groups, which are divided between permanent and temporary ones and can be either formal or informal. The formal groups are established by a decision of the Commission, while the informal ones are set up by individual Commission departments with the agreement of the relevant Commissioner and Vice-President and of the Secretariat-General of the Commission.

As the expert groups play a crucial role in advising the European Commission, they also have a clear part in indirectly shaping EU policy. On many occasions, the European Ombudsman expressed her view that promoting the transparency and the integrity of these groups is crucial to ensure the accountability of the institutions and the legislative process of the EU.[23]

---

[20] Recommendations of the European Ombudsman in the joint inquiry into complaint 194/2017/EA, 334/2017/EA, and 543/2017/EA on the European Commission's handling of post-mandate employment of former Commissioners, a former Commission President and the role of its 'Ethics Committee', 20 July 2018 (https://www.legal-tools.org/doc/eu1t29/).

[21] European Union, Commission Decision of 31 January 2018 on a Code of Conduct for the Members of the European Commission, 31 January 2018, Article 11 (https://www.legal-tools.org/doc/dwjlw0/).

[22] European Commission, Decision of 30 May 2016 establishing horizontal rules on the creation and operation of Commission expert groups, 30 May 2016, C (2016) 3301 final (https://www.legal-tools.org/doc/fhziyq/); European Commission, Communication to the Commission Framework for Commission Expert Groups: Horizontal Rules and Public Register, 30 May 2016, C (2016) 3300 final (https://www.legal-tools.org/doc/01v7ek/).

[23] Emily O'Reilly, Introductory Address for a dialogue with the Civil Society Europe Annual General Assembly, Brussels, 26 April 2018.

The issue of integrity was submitted to the European Ombudsman for the first time in 2010. The Ombudsman received a complaint concerning the functioning and the transparency of the expert groups. The Ombudsman's inquiry led to a friendly solution being proposed to the Commission.[24] The Ombudsman asked the Commission to define criteria for categorizing the different entities represented in the groups and to ensure that all the groups and all the experts are correctly registered in the Register. The Ombudsman added that the Register should provide a sufficiently detailed account of the minutes and of the reports of the groups' meetings. The Ombudsman also proposed to the Commission to consider ensuring a balanced representation of all areas of expertise and interest in the expert groups. The inquiry was closed with the conclusion that the Commission had accepted the Ombudsman's friendly solution proposal.[25]

In 2014, the European Ombudsman decided to open an own-initiative strategic inquiry to follow up on her previous findings and to monitor the transparency and the composition of the expert groups. After having carried out a public consultation on the matter,[26] the Ombudsman made two recommendations to the Commission concerning the content of the published minutes of the experts' meetings and the transparency of the groups' deliberations.[27] The Ombudsman also made a number of suggestions to the Commission aimed in particular at improving the composition of the groups, the synergies between the expert groups register and the Transparency Register, the calls for applications in this area, and the conflict of interest policy for individual experts. The Ombudsman found that

---

[24] An overview of the Ombudsman's solution proposal can be found in the Decision of the European Ombudsman closing her inquiry into complaint 1682/2010/(ANA)BEH against the European Commission, 19 December 2013, para. 144 (https://www.legal-tools.org/doc/gx5bbj/).

[25] *Ibid.*

[26] European Ombudsman, "European Ombudsman launches public consultation concerning the composition of European Commission expert groups", 14 May 2014 (available on European Ombudsman's web site).

[27] European Ombudsman, Recommendation of the European Ombudsman in her strategic inquiry OI/6/2014/NF concerning the composition of Commission expert groups, 29 January 2016 (https://www.legal-tools.org/doc/uxi25m/).

the Commission had reformed the expert groups system and closed the inquiry considering that its purpose had been achieved.[28]

15.4.3. Lobbying

Lobbying is an extremely delicate topic as the public might perceive the fact that civil servants meet with interest representatives as inappropriate. Citizens might thus question the integrity of the civil servants involved in these meetings and consequently that of the institution that they represent. At the same time, lobbying is an essential tool of our democracies, as seeking the views of interest representatives allows policy-makers to receive precious input, allowing them to better understand the practical consequences of their decisions.

Lobbying activities are common and widespread in the Brussels' reality. The European Ombudsman has consistently maintained that transparent and well-regulated lobbying is an activity carried out in the public interest, as it allows the EU administration to be informed of the global impact of its proposed policies.[29] On the contrary, non-transparent lobbying is a dangerous activity which might jeopardize the public trust in the European Union's institutions and should thus be avoided. Hence, it is evident that it is of the utmost importance that civil servants behave in accordance with the highest ethical standards when meeting with interest representatives.

In 2011, the European Commission and the Parliament set up the Transparency Register to ensure public oversight on the activities of interest representatives who meet with EU civil servants. While the Registry is already a very advanced model, certain of its aspects would need further improvement. In the framework of a public consultation launched by the European Commission in 2016, the Ombudsman opened a 'strategic initiative' to contribute to the debate. As a result, the Ombudsman made nine suggestions to the Commission on how to further improve the Transparency Registry.[30] These suggestions concerned different issues such as making the Registry common to all institutions and agencies, including information

---

[28] European Ombudsman, Decision of the European Ombudsman in her strategic inquiry OI/6/2014/NF concerning the composition and transparency of European Commission expert groups, 14 November 2017 (https://www.legal-tools.org/doc/6wn5vz/).

[29] Emily O'Reilly, Address to Transparency International/EPACA conference, Brussels, 13 November 2019 ('Introductory Speech').

[30] Emily O'Reilly, "Efforts to improve the EU Transparency Register", 25 May 2016 (available on European Ombudsman's web site).

on the source of funding of interest representatives, introducing suspension from the Registry for organizations which do not respect the rules applicable to revolving doors situations, and proactive transparency in relation to meetings with tobacco lobbyists. The Ombudsman was overall satisfied with the steps taken to improve transparency in this area. However, the Transparency Register has not yet been made applicable to all EU lawmaking bodies and, especially, to the Council of the European Union. This is a significant lack in the European effort of ensuring fully transparent and ethical lobbying and the Ombudsman has been consistently calling for the extension of the scope of application of the Register.[31]

In the context of this strategic initiative, the European Ombudsman also published a list of Dos and Don'ts meant as a guide for civil servants interacting with interest representatives.[32] The list places great importance on the need to meet with lobbyists registered in the Transparency Register, to avoid conflict of interest and to keep transparent records of any meeting. This tool has the merit of being extremely short and practical, and it can thus be easily circulated among all EU staff to inform them of how they should behave in this sensitive area.

15.5. Conclusion

As Thomas Jefferson said already in the early nineteenth century, "when a man assumes a public trust, he should consider himself as public property".[33] It is with this spirit and keeping in mind that they are serving the public good that civil servants should approach their daily work.

When acting in the public interest, individuals should always respect the law applicable to their actions. However, while the legality of an action is clearly a precondition for its integrity, merely acting within the law is not enough to ensure the respect of such principle. Civil servants are expected to adopt more stringent standards than those set out by the law and to follow the highest ethical principles.

As it has been described in this chapter, the European Ombudsman places the respect of the principle of integrity at the very basis of the concept of good administration. Hence, in case of a breach of the principle of

---

[31] Introductory Speech, see above note 29.

[32] European Ombudsman, "Practical recommendations for public officials' interaction with interest representatives", 24 May 2017 (available on European Ombudsman's web site).

[33] Thomas Jefferson, personal correspondence with Baron von Humboldt, 1807, B.L. Rayner, "Life of Jefferson (1834)", in *Oxford Essential Quotations*, Oxford University Press, 2017.

integrity, the Ombudsman will find an instance of maladministration and will issue a recommendation aimed at resolving the issue and at avoiding that a similar situation might happen again in the future. However, the Ombudsman's role in ensuring the integrity of EU institutions is not limited to being reactive. As the inquiries described in this chapter show, also when investigating issues that are not immediately related to integrity, the Ombudsman can indirectly safeguard the respect of such a principle.

However, it is essential to be aware that soft and hard laws (even when supported by strong and reliable accountability mechanisms) are not enough to ensure the full integrity of civil service. Civil service has a human dimension, which cannot be forgotten: it is mainly about the people and, regardless of how clear the instructions and how stringent the obligations can be, integrity can be ensured only if the institutions are made up of honest individuals who are willing to follow them.

16

On Whistle-Blowing and
Inquiry in Public Institutions

Jan Fougner[*]

16.1. Introduction

Given that ensuring integrity in international justice is the desired end, the predominant questions are which means are suitable to achieve such an end and how must these institutions apply such means.

International justice institutions are ultimately defined by persons – judges, prosecutors, administrative employees, bureaucrats, management *et al.* – and the institutions must, therefore, establish a framework within which these persons can avoid misconduct and pursue integrity. Further, in the event of non-compliance within such a framework, impartial inquiries should be considered a means through which one may hold the perpetrator of misconduct responsible and thus re-establish integrity.

Whereas whistle-blowing may be conducive to eradicating misconduct by introducing a culture of transparency, and freedom of expression and from oppression, impartial inquiries may impede concealment, place responsibility, and suggest effective measures to prevent future misconduct. These two mechanisms, namely whistle-blowing and inquiries, represent proactive and reactive approaches, symbiotically, inculcating the virtue of integrity in an institution.

Both nationally and internationally, great efforts have been made to ensure transparency and disclosure in order to drive us towards integrity. Several countries have introduced new legislation on whistle-blowing,[1] and

---

[*] **Jan Fougner** is Partner in the leading Norwegian law firm Wiersholm (whose employment practice he leads), and Professor at BI Norwegian Business School. He has led a number of high-profile inquiries involving problems of integrity (including in the police) and is an expert on whistle-blowing. He holds the Cand. jur. from the University of Oslo and a doctoral degree from the University of Aarhus.

[1] France, Loi relative à la transparence, à la lutte contre la corruption et à la modernisation de la vie économique, 9 December 2016 ('Sapin II'); Norway, Lov om arbeidsmiljø, arbeidstid og stillingsvern m.v. (arbeidsmiljøloven) (Act relating to working environment, working hours and employment protection, etc. (Working Environment Act)), 17 June 2005, Chapter 2A; UK Financial Conduct Authority, Accountability and Whistleblowing Instrument 2015,

surely, the EU Directive on this matter is a sign of progress.[2] For the same reason, inquiries have been undertaken, for instance concerning the governments' implication in Iraq and Libya,[3] the Mueller investigation in the United States ('US'), the Sarkozy affair in France,[4] and the inquiries into the Khashoggi affair and the North-Korean missile programme and facilities.[5]

It is conspicuous that the legislation on whistle-blowing and inquiries do not pinpoint the judiciary as such. Even though some inquiries, such as 'kids for cash' in the US, suggest a certain interest in questions regarding justice and corruption, one might wonder whether we perceive the judicial system as being less flawed by corruption than other institutions. One might ask whether the judiciary is *per se* transparent and righteous without the same need to implement measures to safeguard integrity.

There are those challenging such a viewpoint. As an example, the International Criminal Court ('ICC') has been confronted with stark criticism regarding immoral behaviour (from both the Helsinki Committee, Bolton and representatives of Burundi and the Philippines). An Independent Expert Review submitted a comprehensive, critical report on 30 September

---

24 September 2015; and EU, Protection of persons reporting on breaches of Union law, 16 April 2019.

[2] See Directive (EU) 2019/1937 of the European Parliament and of the Council of 23 October 2019 on the protection of persons who report breaches of Union law, PE/78/2019/REV/1.

[3] The UK and Norway, respectively.

[4] For instance, the Libya investigation in Norway is an example of this purpose of an investigation. A few years ago, the Norwegian Parliament asked the executive branch to initiate an investigation of the Norwegian military as well as civilian participation in operations in Libya in 2011. More specifically, the purpose was to draw lessons from the participation in Libya as to how to improve future participation in international operations.

As for the Chilcot report concerning the United Kingdom's participation in an opposed invasion and full-scale occupation of the sovereign State of Iraq, it was also aimed at enlightening the public and elucidating an event rather than causing prosecutions. The Chilcot report concluded that the there was no "imminent threat from Saddam Hussein" and that by supporting the war, the UK was in fact "undermining the Security Council's authority".

There is yet another example of such investigations, which is even more prominent: the Mueller investigation in the US, assessing potential Russian meddling during the 2016 presidential election race between Donald Trump and Hillary Clinton.

[5] Deirdre Shesgreen, "North Korea running at least 13 secret operating bases for ballistic missile program, new study shows", in *USA Today*, 12 November 2018.

2020.[6] Concerning national judicial systems, we might mention that the citizens of Peru or Venezuela, Burkina Faso,[7] France and recently the US[8] all seem to be opposed to the idea of an incorruptible and virtuous judiciary. On the contrary, they seem to view the judicial system as transcendent, lacking transparency.[9] In fact, there is evidence of misconduct and unethical behaviour in the judiciary, righteously giving rise to the question of how to fight it.

Thus, the international justice institutions must, like all other public institutions, implement appropriate mechanisms in order to combat corruption and violations of professional and ethical standards and consequently preserve integrity.

16.2. Do Whistle-Blowing Procedures and Inquiries Constitute Means to Guarantee Integrity?

Historically, white-collar crime and other similar misconduct have been near impossible to expose because none of the perpetrators, the beneficiaries, or the broad mass of people constituting the victims of such crimes have an incentive to reveal it.[10] Furthermore, white-collar criminality primarily constitutes a *violation of trust*[11] traditionally viewed as a less serious crime.[12] However, fraudulent practices and corruption do endanger public welfare, stability and security. They undermine the institutions and values of democracy and justice. The links between corruption and other forms of crime, including organized and economic crime, are furthermore not only costly, placing a greater tax burden on citizens,[13] but they create an even

---

[6] See Independent Expert Review, Independent Expert Review of the International Criminal Court and the Rome Statute System: Final Report, 30 September 2020 (https://www.legal-tools.org/doc/cv19d5/).

[7] RFI, "Burkina Faso: 37 magistrats épinglés pour des cas de corruption", 9 July 2017.

[8] The 'Kids for cash' scandal in Philadelphia and Brett Kavanaugh, who is now judge of the Supreme Court.

[9] Jacques Commaille, *À quoi nous sert le droit ?*, Gallimard, Paris, 2015, Introduction.

[10] Edwin H. Sutherland, "White-Collar Criminality", in *American Sociological Review*, 1940, vol. 5, no. 1, pp. 1–12.

[11] Donald J. Newman, "White-Collar Crime", in *Law and Contemporary Problems*, 1958, vol. 23, no. 4, p. 738.

[12] Sutherland, 1940, see above note 10.

[13] "The History Of Whistleblowing in America", in Whistleblowers International (available on its web site).

more pronounced mistrust in the governmental body concerned.[14] Consequently, when public investigations conducted by police forces have proven insufficient to combat such crimes, other measures must be employed.

The Organisation for Economic Co-operation and Development (OECD)[15] and the United Nations ('UN')[16] view whistle-blowing and inquiries as effective measures to combat white-collar crime. The UN has held that "public inquiries into major disasters and scandals have shown that a workplace culture of silence in the face of malpractices can cost lives, damage livelihoods, cause jobs to be lost and undermine public confidence in major institutions",[17] illustrating the importance of *both* creating an institutional culture of transparency in order to ensure integrity and to launch public inquiries if integrity is compromised. The UN advocates for stronger whistle-blowing protection, including prohibition and sanctions of retaliation and clear reporting channels, both external and internal.[18] Several countries have followed suit. Examples are the Norwegian Employment Act,[19] the French law Sapin II, the United Kingdom's law on Accountability and Whistleblowing Instrument of 2015,[20] and the aforementioned EU Directive of 2019.[21]

Today, whistle-blowing is primarily associated with the disclosure of illegal, immoral or illegitimate practices by *organization members*.[22] Con-

---

[14] United Nation Convention against Corruption, 31 October 2003, Preamble ('UNCAC') (http://www.legal-tools.org/doc/7640fb/).

[15] OECD, *Study on Whistleblower Protection Frameworks, Compendium of Best Practices and Guiding Principles for Legislation*, 2011 (available on its web site).

[16] UNCAC, see above note 14.

[17] Natalie Christelis *et al.*, in Petter Langseth (ed.), *United Nations Handbook on Practical Anti-Corruption Measures for Prosecutors and Investigators*, UN Office on Drugs and Crime, Vienna, September 2004, p. 75 (https://www.legal-tools.org/doc/zw3xvs/):

> public inquiries into major disasters and scandals have shown that a workplace culture of silence in the face of malpractices can cost hundreds of lives, damage thousands of livelihoods, cause tens of thousands of jobs to be lost and undermine public confidence in major institutions. In some cases, victims may be compensated but no one held accountable for what has happened.

[18] European Commission, "Whistleblower protection", 23 April 2018.

[19] Chapter 2A, see above note 1 (which is being revisited now).

[20] Which established a robust regime of whistle-blower protections from unfair treatment that went into effect in 2016, see above note 1.

[21] Protection of persons reporting on breaches of Union law, see above note 1.

[22] Janet P. Near and Marcia P. Miceli, "Organizational Dissidence: The Case of Whistle-blowing", in *Journal of Business Ethics*, 1985, vol. 4, no. 1, p. 4: "the disclosure by organi-

versely, the *concept* of whistle-blowing dates back to the notion of *qui tam* in seventh century England[23] and the *term* to the police officers who blew their whistles in order to alert the public.[24] The origin of the concept and the term emphasizes the importance of external actors as whistle-blowers in order to combat weak internal control, the fact that no one questions disloyal behaviour, or the dissimulation of misconduct.[25] Both internal procedures and the embracement of external whistle-blowers are, at present, some of the most important instruments to safeguard transparency, compliance and anti-corruption through which integrity might be achieved.

While whistle-blowing discloses misconduct and ultimately aims at creating a *culture* of openness, inquiries are non-trial examinations clarifying the course of events and assessing whether human mistakes, omission or maladministration have caused issues for which a person should be held liable. Such inquiries may be internal or conducted by external parties, and usually, one might be preferred to the other depending on the circumstances. In general, external parties, whilst more expensive and usually more burdensome for the organization, tend to be impartial, and provide a fresh approach and inspire trust among the public and the media. As for external whistle-blowers, this might be particularly necessary when the internal control has proven insufficient or dissimulation of misconduct has taken place.

---

zation members of illegal, immoral or illegitimate practices under the control of their employers, to persons or organizations that may be able to effect action"; cited in Varslingsutvalget, in Departementenes sikkerhets- og serviceorganisasjon (ed.), *Varsling – verdier og vern: Varslingsutvalgets utredning om varsling i arbeidslivet*, Oslo, 2018, NOU 2018:6.

[23] The concept was described by the term *qui tam*, which became "synonymous with whistle-blowers who sue corrupt companies on behalf of their government", see "The History Of Whistleblowing in America", see above note 13.

[24] Marion A. Hersh, "Whistleblowers – heroes or traitors?: Individual and collective responsibility for ethical behaviour", in *Annual Reviews in Control*, 2002, vol. 26, no. 2, p. 243; reference to Kent D. Strader, "Counterclaims against Whistleblowers: Should Counterclaims against Qui Tam Plaintiffs Be Allowed in False Claims Act Cases", in *University of Cincinnati Law Review*, 1993, vol. 62, p. 713 (1 Hersh (2002), p. 243 with further reference to Strader (1993)).

[25] Erling Grimstad, *Granskning: ved mistanke om korrupsjon og andre former for økonomisk kriminalitet i arbeidsforhold*, Gyldendal juridisk, 2015, p. 21.

16.3. How May Such Means *Effectively* Achieve the End of Inculcating the Virtue of Integrity in Justice Institutions?

The implementation of whistle-blowing procedures depends on the willingness of the institution to ensure these. In Norway, different governmental departments apply such procedures, including internal and external reporting channels and procedures for successive investigations.[26] These may be employed in international justice systems as well.

It may be more challenging to institute inquiries because the revelation of the course of events, the finding of a causal link between a phenomenon and an action, as well as the provision of an analysis of a problem in the institution might generate *a feeling of being under attack*. Generally, one should not throw caution to the wind and initiate external inquiries for all misconduct. An employee's minor misconduct should principally be investigated internally. Inquiries by external parties are expensive and burdensome for those implied, but indeed a more powerful tool when used correctly.

If the misconduct is serious and committed by a superior, inquiries by external experts will usually be more fitting. The superior will be disqualified as partial and any direct subordinate in the same administration must, based on the general notion on impartiality,[27] usually be considered partial as well. Hence, if a superior has engaged in misconduct, all of the subordinates are, in a legal context, partial and inquiries by external parties seem like the most suitable approach.

Additionally, the psychological factor of feeling under attack must be taken seriously. Gross misconduct committed by a superior will usually be

---

[26] The Ministry of Foreign Affairs, Norway, and now the Ministries of Justice and of Customs follow.

[27] This notion derives from, among others, the International Covenant on Civil and Political Rights, 16 December 1966, which in its Article 14(1) states that "all persons shall be equal before the courts and tribunals", and that "in the determination of any criminal charge against him, or of his rights and obligations in a suit of law, everyone shall be entitled to a fair and public hearing by a competent, *independent and impartial* tribunal established by law" (emphasis added) (http://www.legal-tools.org/doc/2838f3/). The UN Human Rights Committee has unambiguously held the same, as well as the African Charter on Human and Peoples' Rights, 21 October 1986, Article 7(1) (http://www.legal-tools.org/doc/f0db44/), and the American Convention on Human Rights, 22 November 1969, Article 8(1) (http://www.legal-tools.org/doc/1152cf/). Lastly, this is specified in Article 6(1) of the European Convention on Human Rights, 4 November 1950 (http://www.legal-tools.org/doc/8267cb/), as well as in the Rome Statute of the International Criminal Court, 17 July 1998, Article 36(3)(a) (http://www.legal-tools.org/doc/7b9af9/).

perceived as an attack on the organization as such, and thus on all employees who identify themselves with it. Regardless of the feeling of being under attack, a subordinate rarely wants to harm the employer or the institution in which he or she works. Further, there might be established a link between an external revelation of misconduct, which is evidence of low or non-existent internal control, and the need for external experts to investigate and assess the misconduct. In such events, the organization will be ill-equipped or unable, to properly conduct the necessary investigations and analysis. Moreover, if the issue at hand may be emblematic of an underlying cultural problem, external and independent experts might ensure that the inquiry is legitimate and independent, as well as perceived as such. For an external and independent expert to conduct an independent inquiry, the mandate needs to be delimited clearly and supported by the Board of Directors or the highest executive organ of the institution.

By virtue of the private investigation's character – approaching that of ordinary investigations (even though there is no prosecution following from it) – it is important to secure the right to liberty and security,[28] the right to fair proceedings,[29] respect regarding the presumption of innocence, protection against self-incrimination[30] as well as the right and respect of private and family life.[31] These principles are all enshrined, for example, in the Norwegian code of conduct for private inquiries,[32] providing the investigator with a clear framework for its work, and might be worth looking at when launching an inquiry.

Since information obtained through an investigation and set forth in a report may be used in an upcoming public investigation, everyone implied, particularly the parties to the inquiry, must receive legal advice and help. The report concluded by the external experts may have judicial or factual consequences for those subject to investigation, even though it is *per se* extra-judicial. Sometimes, the publication of an investigative report might even entail a greater burden on those implied due to ample media coverage and exposure.

---

[28] European Convention on Human Rights, Article 5, see above note 27.

[29] *Ibid.*, Article 6.

[30] *Ibid.*

[31] *Ibid.*, Article 8. See also the International Covenant on Civil and Political rights.

[32] Norway, Advokatforeningens retningslinjer for private granskninger, 4 March 2011, part 2, sections 3.2, 5.1, 5.2, 6 and 6.3 (https://www.legal-tools.org/doc/kn9t3j/).

Recognizing that integrity is the ultimate end, the report should be rightful and disclosed in its entirety. To ensure full transparency, no summaries should be distributed. Following the release of a report, responsibility must be attributed and internal procedures revisited. For the re-establishment of confidence, one must recognize that everyone makes mistakes, and admitting a mistake requires fortitude. Admitting wrong-doings is a most dignifying act and does not, based on my experience, endanger a position of power, but rather gives rise to authority.

With reference to the ICC, independent investigations in the event of serious misconduct are key to safeguarding all stakeholders' interests and not undermining the court's role as a guardian of justice. The report of the Independent Expert Review is a comprehensive systemic *review*, but this is not the same as an *inquiry* into specific allegations of individual wrong-doing.

16.4. Closing Remarks

Both proactive and reactive measures, including whistle-blowing procedures and inquiries, are appropriate in order to achieve integrity in international justice institutions.

However, the virtue of integrity will not become a reality prior to our *choosing* it. The responsibility of selecting and implementing mechanisms appropriate to the end sought lays within the institution itself.

Having regard to the role of the judicial institutions – which entails a great responsibility to ensure full transparency, to inspire confidence, and embody integrity – such measures must be employed for three reasons. First, in order to hold others accountable, one must not oneself fear accountability. Second, in order to combat impunity, one must not expect impunity for oneself. Third, the judiciary is indivisible from law, meaning that law constitutes both the framework in which it operates as well as the instrument by which it provides justice. The judiciary is thus an incarnation of law, a protector of rights and freedoms given to the people, and it must not violate these itself.

Especially for the ICC, maintaining integrity is of great importance for both *practical* and *moral* reasons. It is effectively the only way to maintain support. The Court does not have its own police force, it is funded by the States Parties, and dilutes sovereignty, based on the principle of complementarity. It must therefore uphold a particularly high ethical standard in order to preserve its members, funding and legitimacy. Morally, the

Court has a duty to fight abuse of power, corruption and misconduct because it is a guardian of freedom from harm against fundamental common values. Remembering the Machiavellian maxim, whistle-blowing mechanisms, as well as impartial and independent inquiries, may impede absolute power and therefore hinder corruption, ultimately establishing, or re-establishing, the virtue of integrity.

17

Private International Criminal Investigations and Integrity

Alexander Heinze[*]

17.1. Introduction

Private investigators have always created a certain admiration and fascination. In fact, informed by famous writers such a Sir Arthur Conan Doyle, in the eyes of their readers – and the public in general – private investigators are the real heroes of crime novels, usually solving a case that eventually brings fame not to themselves but to the police detective they are working with. Thus, Inspector Lestrade has Sherlock Holmes and Leland Stottelmeyer has Adrian Monk. Not to forget all those private investigators who generally assist the local police, such as Jane Marple and Hercule Poirot. And then there are those who conduct 'investigations' in a broad sense, even though it seems counter-intuitive to classify them as private investigators: Bruce Wayne aka Batman; John Shaft; the A-Team; Christian Wolff aka "The Accountant"; Tintin, the young Belgian reporter; Mikael Blomkvist, journalist and the main character in Stieg Larsson's Millennium series; and April O'Neil, anchor-woman for Channel 6 News in the 1987-1996 animated Teenage Mutant Ninja Turtles series.

The appeal of private investigations has now reached the field of international criminal justice. For instance, the work of the Commission for International Justice and Accountability ('CIJA') has attracted some attention, also in connection with recent universal jurisdiction cases concerning Syria. Of course, investigatory work done by private non-State agencies is

[*] **Alexander Heinze** is an Assistant Professor of Law at the University of Göttingen, Germany. He holds a Ph.D. in International Criminal Law (with honours), received his Master's in International and Comparative Law from Trinity College Dublin, Ireland, with distinction and published various papers on topics such as international criminal law and procedure, media law, comparative criminal law, human rights law and jurisprudence. His book *International Criminal Procedure and Disclosure* (Duncker & Humblot, 2014) won three awards. He is a member of the ILA's Committee on Complementarity in ICL, co-editor of the *German Law Journal*, book review editor of the *Criminal Law Forum*, and worked for the Appeals Chamber of the ICC as a visiting professional. The author would like to thank the editors for their valuable comments.

not novel as there are countless non-governmental organisations ('NGOs') and inter-governmental organizations ('IGOs') who collect evidence to be used before international(ised) criminal tribunals ('ICTs') or before a national court trying international crimes. Investigative staff at the International Criminal Court ('ICC') and other ICTs are dependent on the field-work undertaken by human rights monitors as fact-finders, employed by IGOs, NGOs, and, in some cases, by governmental agencies.[1] Especially, personnel "not serving with a belligerent party" proved valuable to the investigative staff of ICTs and were sometimes later called to testify at trial.[2] Private investigations are indispensable at the international level, and privately funded international human rights organisations have been crucial to hold perpetrators of international crimes accountable.[3]

Considering the importance of private investigators for the administration of ICTs, the potential dangers of such cooperation easily take a backseat in a car that is driven by the anti-impunity agenda. Prosecutors of both national courts and ICTs become taciturn when confronted with illegal

---

[1] See, for instance, ICC, Office of the Prosecutor, Nineteenth report of the Prosecutor of the International Criminal Court to the United Nations Security Council pursuant to UNSCR 1970 (2011), 5 May 2020, para. 35 (https://www.legal-tools.org/doc/6z4snc/): "The Office also benefits from assistance provided by a range of international and regional organisations, civil society groups, and private individuals. As always, the Office invites submissions from any group or individual in possession of credible and reliable information pertaining to the alleged commission of Rome Statute crimes in Libya since 15 February 2011. The Office regularly receives such submissions of information from a variety of sources". See generally Morten Bergsmo and William H. Wiley, "Human Rights Professionals and the Criminal Investigation and Prosecution of Core International Crimes", in Norwegian Centre for Human Rights (ed.), *Manual on Human Rights Monitoring – An Introduction for Human Rights Field Officers*, 2008, p. 1 (https://www.legal-tools.org/doc/8362d5/); Barry de Vries, "Could International Fact-Finding Missions Possibly Render a Case Inadmissible for the ICC?: Remarks on the Ongoing Attempts to Include International Criminal Law in Fact-finding", in *Journal of Conflict and Security Law*, 2019, vol. 24, p. 600; Marina Aksenova, Morten Bergsmo and Carsten Stahn, "Non-Criminal Justice Fact-Work in the Age of Accountability", in Morten Bergsmo and Carsten Stahn (eds.), *Quality Control in Fact-Finding*, second edition, TOAEP, Brussels, 2020, pp. 9–12. For an instructive overview of the practicalities of NGO fact-finding see Wolfgang Kaleck and Carolijn Terwindt, "Non-Governmental Organisation Fact-Work: Not Only a Technical Problem", *ibid.*, pp. 417 ff. Generally, about the cooperation of international organisations and NGOs Wolfgang Graf Vitzthum, "Begriff und Geltung des Völkerrechts", in Wolfgang Graf Vitzthum and Alexander Proelß (eds.), *Völkerrecht*, 8th edition, De Gruyter, Berlin, 2019, mn. 19.

[2] Bergsmo and Wiley, 2008, p. 12, see above note 1.

[3] Beth Stephens, "Accountability for International Crimes: The Synergy between the International Criminal and Alternative Remedies", in *Wisconsin International Law Journal*, 2003, vol. 21, p. 527 (528).

behaviour by their most important aids. At most, they refer to their supervision and the fact that all witness statements have to be repeated in front of them anyway, let alone that evidence collected by private investigators is merely used as lead evidence. Yet, once the cooperation between an ICT and private individuals[4] in the collection of evidence becomes public, which is usually the case when something went wrong, reality speaks a different language. In the *Lubanga* case before the ICC, the suspicion arose that certain so-called intermediaries had bribed various persons to prepare false evidence for alleged former child soldiers. In another instance, in the same case, the Office of the Prosecutor ('OTP') was supposed to use certain material as lead evidence only, but did the opposite.

This chapter is about these instances; it is about illegal conduct of private investigators; and it is eventually about the proposal of a compass for private investigators.

The chapter is structured into four main sections. It starts with a stocktaking endeavour, describing the occurrence of private investigations in the former Yugoslavia and Rwanda, in Kosovo, Sierra Leone, Cambodia and, especially, Syria (17.2.). Following a brief delineation of the advantages of private investigations (17.3.) and some terminological remarks (17.4.), the focus turns to the main section on private investigations as a matter of ethics and integrity (17.5.).

The chapter will demonstrate that the idea of the 'integrity' or 'legitimacy' of the trial as a distinctive kind of legal process can serve as an important, if not the only compass for private conduct in the collection of evidence. Concretely, let us suppose a private investigator offers money to a witness in return for information about a suspect and his or her criminal activities.[5] After all, it has become public that the OTP of the Special Court for Sierra Leone had an extensive practice of paying both informants and

---

[4]   I prefer the term 'individual' over 'actor', since the focus of this chapter is on *private* conduct. I use the term 'actors' to describe agents acting for or on behalf of certain institutions and organisations. Individual actors – or individuals – have the ability to act reflexively but in doing so "they are significantly constrained by the structures in which they operate" (Nerida Chazal, *The International Criminal Court and Global Social Control*, Routledge Taylor & Francis, Abingdon, 2016, p. 4).

[5]   Other examples, convened by Robertson for the context of interviews: leading questions, "brainwashing" the witness, persuasion, the private investigator is a national of the State under investigation, see Geoffrey Robertson, "Human Rights Fact-Finding: Some Legal and Ethical Dilemmas", in Morten Bergsmo and Carsten Stahn (eds.), *Quality Control in Fact-Finding*, second edition, TOAEP, Brussels, 2020, pp. 491–507.

witnesses in return for information and statements.[6] The scenario is thus real and can be transferred to the private level. Or even more extreme: a person tasked with investigating tortures that witness to get the desired information. Does 'integrity' provide a guideline for this investigator to refrain from his or her activities?

The term 'integrity' will be approached as a semantic concept in the first place, and only secondarily as a philosophical concept. It will unfold in three perspectives: object, subject and context. Using these perspectives, the analysis will focus on illegally obtained evidence. Integrity, as an element and value in the different decisions about illegally obtained evidence by private individuals, may lead to several consequences. For the sake of better following the arguments, I will single out the example of the exclusion of evidence as a consequence of a violation of the integrity element (in whatever form). Exclusion is understood broadly, encompassing both the exclusion of material *per se* and its nullity.[7] Rules regulating such an exclusion may safeguard individual rights, protect the integrity of procedures, achieve reliable fact-finding, and deter police misconduct.[8] Other consequences will be described at the end of the chapter.

There are different investigatory contexts when private individuals collect evidence that may eventually be used before an ICT: the inter-investigatory context (international investigation – domestic investigation); the intra-investigatory context (internal investigation by a private individual); and the extra-investigatory context (collection of evidence by a private individual outside any investigation). I will raise the question whether the procedural regime, especially exclusionary rules, may be applicable in these three contexts. The inter-investigatory context is the least problematic. In the intra-investigatory context, there is an attribution of the private individual to an organ of the ICT (usually, the OTP) that may occur rather openly through the utilisation of the individual in the collection process, that is, *ab initio*, or through an *ex post*-attribution, when the individual acted in the interest of the organ. In the latter, a person acts independently of

---

[6] In detail the eye-opening account of Wayne Jordash, "Insiders: The Special Court for Sierra Leone's Dirty Laundry", *Justiceinfo.net*, 30 April 2020.

[7] About the semantic difference between those two in more detail, albeit misleadingly described as "linguistics", Dimitrios Giannoulopoulos, *Improperly Obtained Evidence in Anglo-American and Continental Law*, Hart, Oxford, 2019, pp. 6–7.

[8] Sabine Gless and Laura Macula, "Exclusionary Rules – Is It Time For Change?", in *IUS Gentium*, 2019, vol. 74, p. 349 (350).

an ICT-organ and outside an investigation. It is the extra-investigatory context that is the neuralgic point of exclusionary rules applied before ICTs. What seems to be a rather simple question – do exclusionary rules apply in this setting? – will unfold into an analysis that enters the depth of procedural law theory. Through norm-theory (Dan-Cohen) and systems theory (Luhmann and Teubner), combined with procedural theory (Packer), the playing field of the rather wide-ranging controversy about the addressees of procedural rules will be entered. I will render the common bipolar legislator-addressee relationship fruitless, and approach the process as a system instead.

Finally, integrity will be identified in the remedies of exclusion, a stay of proceedings, integrity testing and integrity units.

17.2. The Occurrence of Private Investigations in International Criminal Justice

17.2.1. Historical Observations

Both the International Criminal Tribunal for the former Yugoslavia ('ICTY') and the International Criminal Tribunal for Rwanda ('ICTR') relied heavily upon materials published by IGOs and NGOs.[9] They have provided the prosecutors' offices with 'background information' on the commission of international crimes, and on the willingness of States to investigate or prosecute alleged crimes.[10] They have also shifted the focus from state responsibility to individual criminal responsibility, which had a considerable impact on the way evidence was collected and eventually handled.[11]

17.2.1.1. The Former Yugoslavia and Rwanda

More concretely, Human Rights Watch ('HRW') placed a 'permanent representative' in the former Yugoslavia during the conflict,[12] and reported

---

[9]   Bergsmo and Wiley, 2008, p. 9, see above note 1.

[10] Mark S. Ellis, "The contribution of non-governmental organizations to the creation of international criminal tribunals", in Bartram S. Brown (ed.), *Research Handbook on International Criminal Law*, Edward Elgar, Cheltenham, 2011, p. 143 (156).

[11] De Vries, 2019, p. 602, see above note 1.

[12] Ellis, 2011, p. 143, see above note 10. See also William Korey, *NGOs and the Universal Declaration of Human Rights*, Palgrave, New York, 1998, p. 320: "[HRW] had at least one or more staffers present in Bosnia and other parts of Former Yugoslavia throughout all of 1992 and 1993. These virtually full-time representatives of the New York-based NGO had maintained contacts with local human rights activists and a variety of sources within the various levels of governments and media in the area".

human rights abuses in the region by conducting investigations and interviewing witnesses.[13] In 1992, HRW published "War Crimes in Bosnia-Herzegovina," its first report on violations of the laws of war[14] and a "call for action, for accountability",[15] followed by a second report that was used by the ICTY.[16] HRW's investigatory agenda was certainly underlined by its report "Prosecute Now!", where Helsinki Watch, a division of HRW, presented "summaries of eight cases that, with immediate investigation, will be strong candidates for prosecution".[17]

The report provided the "legal basis and potential evidence necessary to prosecute those first cases before the Tribunal".[18] And indeed, despite separate investigations by the ICTY-Prosecution, the eight cases selected by HRW and Helsinki were among the very first cases that the Office investigated.[19]

Apart from HRW, Physicians for Human Rights ('PHR') conducted "multiple mass grave investigations across the former Yugoslavia in the 1990s for the Tribunal",[20] which provided important. PHR called those persons "investigators" that "exhumed and identified remains in several large mass graves and gathered evidence showing the victims were executed".[21] They established "teams of forensic scientists to locate mass gravesites, exhume bodies, conduct autopsies and report the evidence and findings to

---

[13] Emma Daly, "Beyond Justice: How the Yugoslav Tribunal Made History", in *Human Rights Watch*, 19 December 2017 (available on its web site). See also Ellis, 2011, p. 143, see above note 10.

[14] Human Rights Watch, "War Crimes in Bosnia-Hercegovina", 1 August 1992 (available on its web site).

[15] Daly, 2017, see above note 13.

[16] Ellis, 2011, p. 143, see above note 10; Korey, 1998, p. 322, see above note 12.

[17] Helsinki Watch, *Prosecute Now!*, 1 August 1993.

[18] Ellis, 2011, p. 144, see above note 10.

[19] Korey, 1998, p. 325, see above note 12.

[20] Physicians for Human Rights ('PHR'), "Bosnian Serb Commander Ratko Mladic Convicted of Genocide, War Crimes, Crimes Against Humanity", 22 November 2017 (available on its web site).

[21] PHR, "Mass Grave Investigations | Mass Crimes in Srebrenica", undated (available on its web site).

the tribunals".[22] The Former Director of the PHR's International Forensic Program, William Haglund, testified in the trial of Radovan Karadzic.[23]

NGOs, IGOs and the media also played an important part in the initial investigations into the genocide that occurred in Rwanda in 1994. It is no exaggeration to contend that the creation of the ICTR was also – amongst other factors – the result of their work on the ground.[24] As former ICTR Prosecutor Jallow states:

> Reports from NGOs proved very helpful in enabling the OTP to gather pertinent, substantiated data. Though NGOs are not in essence investigatory bodies the extent of the investigations underlying these reports and the level of analysis they achieved indicated a true effort and genuine commitment by many such organizations to produce verifiable facts. Witness interviews, for instance, were very useful not only for learning about the incidents they described but also for corroborating other events and reports.[25]

17.2.1.2. Kosovo

In Kosovo, too, evidence about the forced expulsion, arbitrary killings, torture and sexual assault of the Albanians was gathered by NGOs.[26] Journalists and human rights researchers have investigated, documented and reported many individual accounts of human rights violations taking place in Kosovo.[27]

PHR and the Program on Forced Migration and Health of Columbia University's Joseph L. Mailman School of Public Health designed a study to "establish patterns of human rights violations among Kosovar refugees by Serb forces using a population-based approach".[28] The study "randomly

---

22 Ellis, 2011, p. 156, see above note 10.

23 PHR, "Forensic science is applied in nearly every area of our work and is crucial to document mass crimes", undated (available on its web site).

24 In the same vein, see Hassan B. Jallow, "Challenges of Investigating and Prosecuting International Crimes", in Emmanuel Decaux, Adama Dieng and Malick Sow (eds.), *From Human Rights to International Criminal Law*, Martinus Nijhoff, Leiden, Boston, 2007, p. 437 (438).

25 *Ibid.*, p. 438.

26 Ellis, 2011, p. 156, see above note 10.

27 PHR, "War Crimes in Kosovo – A Population-Based Assessment of Human Rights Violation Against Kosovar Albanians", 1 August 1999, p. 1 (available on its web site).

28 *Ibid.*

sampled 1,209 Kosovar refugees in 31 refugee camps and collective centers in Albania and Macedonia between April 19, 1999 and May 3, 1999. The survey assessed human rights abuses among 11,458 household members while living in Kosovo".[29] Furthermore, the Independent Law Commission asked the American Bar Association's Central European and Eurasia Initiative ('ABA-CEELI') to "establish a team of experts to review this information and compile data from other NGOs concerning the human rights violations in Kosovo".[30] ABA-CEELI conducted comprehensive statistical studies to add clarity and precision to the potential evidence.[31] ABA-CEELI established the Kosovo War Crimes Documentation Project (led by Executive Director Mark Ellis)[32] to interview refugees and provide victim statements to the ICTY, collaborating with a coalition of Albanian NGOs called the Center for Peace Through Justice to gather critical refugee interviews.[33] Between April and October 1999, ABA-CEELI volunteers in Albania, Macedonia, Kosovo, Poland, and Ft. Dix, New Jersey, worked with translators and local investigators to assemble accounts of Kosovar refugees.[34] Apart from NGOs such as the previously mentioned HRW and PHR, the American Association for the Advancement of Science ('AAAS') – with members of the Human Rights Data Analysis Group ('HRDAG') – wrote several reports on the conflict.[35] Employing the statistical expertise of the AAAS and HRDAG, NGO-investigations collected evidence of ethnic cleansing against Kosovar Albanians.[36] In its report "Political Killings in Kosova/Kosovo, March-June 1999", ABA-CEELI and the Science and Human Rights Program of the AAAS concluded that "approximately 10,500 Kosovar Albanians were killed between March 20 and June 12, 1999, with a 95 percent confidence interval from 7,449 to

---

[29] *Ibid.*

[30] Ellis, 2011, p. 156, see above note 10.

[31] See, for instance, American Bar Association and Central and East European Law Initiative ('ABA-CEELI'), *An Introduction to the Human Trafficking Assessment Tool*, December 2005 (available on its web site). See also Ellis, 2011, p. 156, see above note 10.

[32] ABA-CEELI, American Association for the Advancement of Science ('AAAS'), *Political Killings in Kosova/Kosovo, March-June 1999*, 2000, p. xi (available on its web site).

[33] Ellis, 2011, p. 157, see above note 10; ABA-CEELI, AAAS, 2000, p. xi, see above note 32.

[34] *Ibid.*

[35] See Human Rights Data Analysis Group ('HRDAG'), "Kosovo" (available on its web sitehttps://hrdag.org/kosovo/).

[36] Ellis, 2011, p. 157, see above note 10.

13,627".[37] This analysis was used by the ICTY-OTP in the trial of Slobodan Milošević to refute the argument that the killings were simply a consequence of battles between the Kosovo Liberation Army and Serbian forces.[38]

17.2.1.3. Sierra Leone, Cambodia, Liberia, MH17

In Sierra Leone, No Peace Without Justice ('NPWJ') initiated a Conflict Mapping Program, namely

> the reconstruction of the chain of events during the ten-year war through the scrupulous selection and debriefing of key individuals throughout the country whose profession, role in their community or in the forces involved in the conflict, placed them in a position to follow events as they unfolded.[39]

NPWJ's analysis was "based on testimonial and other data overlaid with order of battle and command structures of the various forces as they evolved over time and space".[40] The mapping aimed at establishing the "chain of command within the armed forces operating in Sierra Leone and assembling these disparate pieces of information to create the bigger picture of the decade-long conflict in Sierra Leone" to demonstrate "direct and command responsibility for crimes committed during the conflict".[41]

As in Kosovo, in 1999, the ABA established a Sierra Leone War Crimes Documentation Project aimed at contributing to the documentation of the war crimes committed in Sierra Leone between 1991 and 2002, and,

---

[37] ABA-CEELI, AAAS, 2000, p. xi, see above note 32.

[38] The International Criminal Tribunal for the former Yugoslavia ('ICTY'), *Prosecutor v. Slobodan Milosevic*, Transcript, IT-02-54, 14 March 2002, p. 2256:

> During the break, I checked some assertions that you denied, and I would like to ask you a few questions about this. Namely, I asked about your cooperation and adjustment of data to the data of the International Crisis Group, and you said that was not true. However, on the website of your AAA association, and that is website hrdataaas.org/kosovo/index/html [as interpreted], titled "Political Killings in Kosovo from March to June 1999," in the column called "Statistical Analysis of Data," it says: The method of killing people in Kosovo coincides with migrations, and this claim corresponds to the data obtained from the International Crisis Group; and then others are enumerated as well.

[39] No Peace Without Justice ('NPWJ'), "Conflict Mapping in Sierra Leone: Violations of International Humanitarian Law 1991 to 2002", Preface, p. III (available on its web site).

[40] *Ibid.*, p. VII.

[41] *Ibid.*, p. VIII.

---

thereby, strengthening the ongoing truth and reconciliation process.[42] In Cambodia, the International Crisis Group, in partnership with NPWJ[43] and the Documentation Centre of Cambodia,[44] has created similar successful documentation projects for the Extraordinary Chambers in the Courts of Cambodia ('ECCC').

In Liberia, the Swiss NGO Civitas Maxima and the Global Justice and Research Project had documented crimes allegedly committed by Martina Johnson and the National Patriotic Front of Liberia of Charles Taylor.[45] The information collected by both organisations was eventually used by Belgian authorities in the arrest and prosecution of Johnson. Last but not least, a major breakthrough of the Dutch-led Joint Investigation Team in the investigation into the downing of flight MH17 was the identification of a key suspect by the research and investigation network Bellingcat.[46]

17.2.2. Special Focus: Private International Criminal Investigations in Syria

Despite growing expectation, the international criminal community has remained largely unable to stop the alleged commission of international crimes in Syria. Russia vetoed 12 UN Security Council resolutions regarding the conflict. As a result, alternative ways to bring perpetrators to justice were pursued, *inter alia*:

First, the Organisation for the Prohibition of Chemical Weapons installed a fact-finding mission[47] and decided

> that the Secretariat shall put in place arrangements to *identify the perpetrators* of the use of chemical weapons in the Syrian Arab Republic by identifying and reporting on all information

---

[42] AAAS, "Partnership 8: Surveying Human Rights Abuses in Sierra Leone" (available on its web site).

[43] See International Crisis Group, *Reality Demands: Documenting Violations of International Humanitarian Law in Kosovo 1999*, 27 June 2000 (available on its web site); Ellis, 2011, p. 157, see above note 10.

[44] See Documentation Centre of Cambodia, "Documentation" (available on its web site).

[45] See Civitas Maxima, "Our Work" (available on its web site).

[46] See Bellingcat, "Key MH17 Figure Identified As Senior FSB Official: Colonel General Andrey Burlaka", 28 April 2020 (available on its web site).

[47] See Organisation for the Prohibition of Chemical Weapons, "Fact-Finding Mission" (available on its web site). In more detail Rebecca Barber, "Uniting for Peace Not Aggression: Responding to Chemical Weapons in Syria Without Breaking the Law", in *Journal of Conflict and Security Law*, 2018, vol. 24, no. 1, p. 74.

potentially relevant to the origin of those chemical weapons [...].[48]

Second, Syrian civil society organisations and a few innovative NGOs have been working to document and build cases against those most responsible in Syria.[49] Third, a test of a completely new and unique form of international criminal investigations was put in place: after the Security Council remained inactive, to ensure accountability for international crimes committed in the war in Syria, on 21 December 2016, the UN General Assembly ('UNGA') created the "International, Impartial and Independent Mechanism to Assist in the Investigation and Prosecution of Those Responsible for the Most Serious Crimes under International Law Committed in the Syrian Arab Republic since March 2011" ('IIIM') with Resolution 71/248.[50] The Syria Mechanism is a subsidiary organ of the UNGA and not a prosecutorial body but "quasi-prosecutorial", meaning that it is required to

> prepare files to assist in the investigation and prosecution of the persons responsible and to establish the connection between crime-based evidence and the persons responsible, directly or indirectly, for such alleged crimes, focusing in particular on linkage evidence and evidence pertaining to mens rea and to specific modes of criminal liability.[51]

---

[48] Organisation for the Prohibition of Chemical Weapons, Addressing the threat from Chemical Weapons Use, 27 June 2018, C-SS-4/DEC.3, para. 10 (https://www.legal-tools.org/doc/lmqyd4/).

[49] Ingrid Elliott, "'A Meaningful Step towards Accountability'? A View from the Field on the United Nations International, Impartial and Independent Mechanism for Syria", in *Journal of International Criminal Justice*, 2017, vol. 15, no. 2, p. 240; Michael P. Scharf, Milena Sterio, and Paul R. Williams, *The Syrian Conflict's Impact on International Law*, Cambridge University Press, Cambridge, 2020, pp. 4 ff.

[50] United Nations General Assembly, International, Impartial and Independent Mechanism to Assist in the Investigation and Prosecution of Those Responsible for the Most Serious Crimes under International Law Committed in the Syrian Arab Republic since March 2011, UN Doc. A/RES/71/248, 11 January 2017 (https://www.legal-tools.org/doc/fecaf0/). See also Christian Wenaweser and James Cockayne, "Justice for Syria? The International, Impartial and Independent Mechanism and the Emergence of the UN General Assembly in the Realm of International Criminal Justice", in *Journal of International Criminal Justice*, 2017, vol. 15, no. 2, pp. 211–230; Elliott, 2017, pp. 239–256, see above note 49; Alex Whiting, "An Investigation Mechanism for Syria. The General Assembly Steps into the Breach", in *Journal of International Criminal Justice*, 2017, vol. 15, no. 2, pp. 231–237.

[51] United Nations General Assembly, Implementation of the resolution establishing the International, Impartial and Independent Mechanism to Assist in the Investigation and Prosecution of Persons Responsible for the Most Serious Crimes under International Law Commit-

It is headed by Catherine Marchi-Uhel, former Judge at the ECCC and former Senior Legal Officer and Head of Chambers at the ICTY.[52] In general, at the UN-level, the following measures have been taken to investigate international crimes: UN Fact-Finding Missions ('FFMs'), Commissions of Inquiry ('CoIs'), and the mentioned novel investigative mechanisms.[53] These bodies do not only include legal advisers and coordinators but also (partly experienced) investigators – despite the fact that they are not always perceived to have a criminal accountability mandate.[54]

In addition, CIJA is collecting information that could eventually be used to hold perpetrators of international humanitarian law violations accountable. CIJA's private actions amidst the ongoing conflict in Syria represent a departure from the practice of conducting international criminal investigations under the aegis of public institutions. Burgis-Kasthala calls this "entrepreneurial justice".[55] CIJA has developed organisationally into a not-for-profit that is funded by a number of States and organisations, including the United Kingdom, the European Union, Canada and Germany.[56] CIJA "has 130 specialist personnel investigating, gathering and preserving evidence, analysing and building case files and indictments against those most responsible in Syria (and Iraq in terms of Da'esh crimes)".[57] It "combines international expertise with local on the ground capacity building

---

ted in the Syrian Arab Republic since March 2011, UN Doc. A/71/755, 19 January 2017 (https://www.legal-tools.org/doc/a0cd85/). See also Elliott, 2017, pp. 239–256, see above note 49.

[52] United Nations, "Secretary-General appoints Catherine Marchi-Uhel of France to head International Impartial Independent Mechanism Investigating Serious Crimes in Syria", 3 July 2017, SG/A/1744-BIO/4979-DC/3720 (available on the UN's web site); Nick Cumming-Bruce, "Ex-judge chosen by U.N. to Gather Evidence of Syria War Crimes", *The New York Times*, 4 July 2017.

[53] An instructive overview can be found on the UN Human Rights Council's website: https://www.ohchr.org/EN/HRBodies/HRC/Pages/COIs.aspx.

[54] Sareta Ashraph and Federica D'Alessandra, "Structural Challenges Confronted by UN Accountability Mandates: Perspectives from Current and Former Staff (Part II)", *OpinioJuris*, 14 October 2020.

[55] Michelle Burgis-Kasthala, "Entrepreneurial Justice: Syria, the Commission for International Justice and Accountability and the Renewal of International Criminal Justice", in *European Journal of International Law*, 2020, vol. 30, no. 4, pp. 1174 ff. with a very detailed and instructive account of CIJA, its protagonists and work on pp. 1176 ff.

[56] Melinda Rankin, "Investigating Crimes against Humanity in Syria and Iraq: The Commission for International Justice and Accountability", in *Global Responsibility to Protect*, 2017, vol. 9, no. 4, pp. 400–401.

[57] Elliott, 2017, p. 245, see above note 49.

which effectively develops a local Syrian civil society response. CIJA works with trained and mentored Syrian investigators with access to areas across Syria".[58]

Even though CIJA is not meant to replace public institutions involved in criminal investigations, but rather complement them, it symbolises a trend of the international criminal community towards private investigations, once political leaders display a lack of will to officially investigate the commission of core international crimes.

17.3. Advantages of Private International Criminal Investigations

The advantages of investigations conducted by private entities in the international field are obvious – even when there is, at a later moment, an official investigation. Members of those entities are often among the first persons to view crime scenes. Investigators of Prosecutor's Offices of ICTs rarely have the opportunity to inspect a crime scene until well after the underlying conduct has been perpetrated.[59] Consequently, in the 2016-2018 Strategic Plan, the ICC OTP explains:

> Preliminary examinations are critical to the Office in its determination of whether to open an investigation. They also greatly facilitate the Office's investigative work in various ways, such as: e.g. by systematically capturing and exploiting open source data; and building networks of cooperation partners and contacts for handover for investigative activities; and identifying potential cases for future investigations.[60]

As an interesting side note, the reference to open-source[61] data disappeared in the 12019-2021 Strategic Plan.[62] Furthermore, the OTP declared that it

---

[58] *Ibid.*

[59] Bergsmo and Wiley, 2008, p. 4, see above note 1.

[60] ICC Office of the Prosecutor ('OTP'), *Strategic Plan 2016-2018*, 16 November 2015, p. 20 (https://www.legal-tools.org/doc/2dbc2d/).

[61] Stressing its importance: Nikita Mehandru and Alexa Koenig, "ICTs, Social Media & the Future of Human Rights", in *Duke Law & Technology Review*, 2019, vol. 17, no. 1, pp. 129–145; for a nuanced and differentiated account, weighing advantages and risks of open source information in international fact finding, see Yvonne McDermott, Daragh Murray and Alexa Koenig, "Digital Accountability Symposium: Whose Stories Get Told, and by Whom? Representativeness in Open Source Human Rights Investigations", *OpinioJuris*, 19 December 2019. The authors are part of a larger team that initiated the project "Using open source research to transform the discovery and documentation of Human Rights Violations", see OSR4Rights, "Using open source research to transform the discovery and documentation of Human Rights Violations" (available on its web site).

"will also react promptly to upsurges or serious risks of violence by reinforcing its early interaction with States, international, regional organisations and NGOs in order to fine-tune its assessment and coordinate next steps".[63] In its current Strategic Plan, the OTP explicitly observed that "more individuals and civil society actors are collecting relevant information as events unfold".[64] Last but not least, according to Article 44(4) of the ICC Statute, the ICC

> may, in exceptional circumstances, employ the expertise of gratis personnel offered by States Parties, intergovernmental organizations or nongovernmental organizations to assist with the work of any of the organs of the Court. The Prosecutor may accept any such offer on behalf of the Office of the Prosecutor.

Bergsmo and Wiley also identify "preliminary analysis of open-source materials, operational planning and liaison with personnel employed by IGOs, NGOs, governmental and other organisations who have prepared reports of particular interest to the investigative body" as one of their four broad phases of investigation services of international criminal jurisdictions:.[65] As to the components of an investigation, they highlight especially two: "(a) the work to establish the so-called crime base of the case; and (b) the process to develop information on the link between the suspect and the actual perpetration of the crimes in question".[66]

CIJA has preserved and analysed over 600,000 pages of original documentation, including regime military and intelligence documents,[67] and focused on the linkage evidence in order to build leadership cases and indictments.[68] As Elliott describes, "it has a 'names database' with over one million entries, and three indictments or pre-trial files against 25 top regime officials including Assad, and a further three indictment or case files against over 35 Da'esh operatives in Syria and Iraq". The explicit purpose

---

[62] ICC OTP, *Strategic Plan 2019-2021*, 17 July 2019 (https://www.legal-tools.org/doc/7ncqt3/).

[63] ICC OTP, 2015, p. 21, see above note 60.

[64] ICC OTP, 2019, p. 21, see above note 62.

[65] Bergsmo and Wiley, 2008, pp. 12–13, see above note 1.

[66] *Ibid.*, p. 8.

[67] Seema Kassab, "Justice in Syria: Individual Criminal Liability for Highest Officials in the Assad Regime", in *Michigan Journal of International Law*, 2018, vol. 39, no. 2, p. 283 (287); Elliott, 2017, p. 239, see above note 49.

[68] Kassab, 2018, p. 287, see above note 67.

of CIJA is to assist national and international prosecutions.[69] This assistance proved to be quite effective in Germany: as the weekly magazine *Der Spiegel* reported on 8 June 2018, the German Federal Prosecutor issued an internationalised arrest warrant for Jamil Hassan, head of Syria's Air Force Intelligence Directorate on charges of war crimes and crimes against humanity.[70] On 29 October 2019, the German Federal Prosecutor announced that it charged two Syrians, Anwar R. and Eyad A., whom he believed to be former secret service officers, with crimes against humanity.[71] The European Center for Constitutional and Human Rights ('ECCHR'), by their own account an "independent, non-profit legal and educational organization",[72] supported witnesses whose testimony led, among other things, to the charging decision of the German Federal Prosecutor.[73] In a decision of 6 March 2020, the Higher Regional Court of Koblenz confirmed the charges and committed Anwar R. and Eyad A. for trial.[74] The start of the trial on 23 April 2020 was viewed by observers as a "historic step" towards accountability of perpetrators in Syria.[75]

Where an initial threshold of suspicion is met, and the case has some link to Germany, German authorities will open a so-called '*Strukturverfahren*' or a background investigation.[76] As the ECCHR describes,

---

[69] See Chris Engels, Written Testimony before the Commission on Security and Cooperation in Europe, 22 September 2016; Elliott, 2017, p. 245, see above note 49.

[70] See Jörg Diehl, Christoph Reuter, and Fidelius Schmid, "Die Jagd", in *Der Spiegel*, 8 June 2018, pp. 40–42; Boris Burghardt, "Endlich! – Erster Haftbefehl gegen einen ranghohen Vertreter des syrischen Assad-Regimes", in *Völkerrechtsblog*, 11 June 2018.

[71] Generalbundesanwalt, "Anklage gegen zwei mutmaßliche Mitarbeiter des syrischen Geheimdienstes wegen der Begehung von Verbrechen gegen die Menschlichkeit u.a. erhoben", 29 October 2019 (available on its web site). See also Philip Oltermann and Emma Graham-Harrison, "Germany charges two Syrians with crimes against humanity", *The Guardian*, 29 October 2019 (available on its web site).

[72] See European Center for Constitutional and Human Rights ('ECCHR'), "Who we are" (available on its web site).

[73] ECCHR, "With the Frist Criminal Trial Worldwide on Torture in Syria, German Courts to Set International Precedent", 29 October 2019 (available on its web site).

[74] Oberlandesgericht Koblenz, Beschluss v. 6.3.2020, 1 StE 9/19.

[75] See, for instance, Amnesty International, "Syria: Torture trial in Germany a 'historic step' towards justice", 22 April 2020. See the instructive comment of Elisabeth Baier, "A puzzle coming together – The henchmen of Assad's torture regime on trial in Germany", in *Völkerrechtsblog*, 23 April 2020.

[76] See the recent account of Christian Ritscher, "Aktuelle Entwicklung in der Strafverfolgung des Generalbundesanwalts auf dem Gebiet des Völkerstrafrechts", in *Zeitschrift für Internationale Strafrechtsdogmatik*, 2019, pp. 599 ff.

> [t]hese proceedings qualify as investigations as defined in the German Code of Criminal Procedure and can thus involve criminal justice mechanisms such as the hearing of witness testimony. They are comparable to 'situations' under scrutiny at the ICC. Over the course of these proceedings, individual suspects may be identified. Further investigations are then pursued against these suspects in separate proceedings.[77]

While early *Strukturverfahren* focused – among other things – on Rwanda and Congo, it has now centred to a great extent on Syria, Iraq and Sri Lanka.[78] The strong suspicion that the suspects had carried out the alleged crimes is based – to a considerable extent – on evidence that has been collected by private individuals and entities. First, the photographs taken by "Caesar", the code name of a former Syrian military photographer who brought over 50,000 photographs out of the country, 28,000 of which show detainees in Syrian prisons killed by torture, outright execution, disease, malnutrition or other ill-treatment.[79] Second, the assistance of the ECCHR, which provided the testimony from six survivors of torture in Al Khatib detention centre in Damascus.[80] Third, CIJA, who provided documentary evidence against one of the two former secret service officers.[81] Nerma Jelačić, CIJA's Deputy Director, announced on Twitter: "#CIJA is proud to have supported the #German prosecutor's investigation and arrest of the first high-ranking Syrian regime official".[82]

In addition, an earlier call for an international criminal trial in Germany was made in November 2016, when six German lawyers filed a criminal complaint against the Syrian President Bashar al-Assad for his involvement in the commission of war crimes and crimes against humanity

---

[77] ECCHR, *Universal Jurisdiction in Germany? – The Congo War Crimes Trial: First Case under the Code of Crimes against International Law*, 8 June 2016, p. 7 (available on its web site).

[78] Cf. Christian Ritscher, "'Foreign Fighters' und Kriegsvölkerstrafrecht", in *Zeitschrift für Internationale Strafrechtsdogmatik*, 2016, vol. 11, pp. 807 (807 f.); Ritscher, 2019, p. 600, see above note 76; Kai Ambos, *Internationales Strafrecht*, fifth edition, C.H. Beck, München, 2018, § 6 mn. 40.

[79] See Sara Afshar, "Assad's Syria recorded its own atrocities. The world can't ignore them", *The Guardian*, 27 August 2018; Ritscher, 2019, p. 600, see above note 76.

[80] See Nick Cumming-Bruce, "Germany Arrests Syrian Intelligence Officers Accused of Crimes Against Humanity", *The New York Times*, 13 February 2019.

[81] See Diehl, Reuter and Schmid, 2018, p. 41, see above note 70.

[82] Nerma Jelačić, "Tweet", *Twitter*, 13 February 2019.

between 26 April and 19 November 2016 in the Syrian town of Aleppo.[83] The evidence was mainly collected by NGOs such as Amnesty International, HRW and Physicians for Human Rights. A reporter of the weekly magazine *Die Zeit* argues that Germany is the appropriate place to hold a trial against Assad, since the country has accepted over half a million Syrian refugees within the last six years, the highest number in Europe.[84] These refugees could be used as potential witnesses.[85] As to the quality of CIJA's work, Stephen Rapp, who led the prosecutions at the ICTR and in Sierra Leone, claimed that CIJA's documentation was "much richer than anything I've seen, and anything I've prosecuted in this area".[86]

17.4. Terminological Remarks

In national jurisdictions, private investigations are nothing unusual, as I have demonstrated elsewhere.[87] Nevertheless, it is hard to find a comprehensive definition of private investigators, probably due to their diverse occurrence.[88]

The term "investigator" has roots in the Latin noun *vestigium*, meaning 'sole of the foot', 'footprint' or, more figuratively, 'something lost' or 'that has passed before'.[89] Gill and Hart therefore conclude: an investigator is "someone who "tracks" or "traces out" something that is missing; something that has occurred, or something that was or is known by someone but remains hidden"; and a private investigator is someone who "either runs or is employed by a business which provides investigative services for a fee".[90] An even broader definition seems to be employed by Bockemühl, who implicitly defines 'private investigation' as every investigation not

---

[83] Reported in Kristin Helberg, "Der Kriegsverbrecher Assad gehört vor Gericht", *Zeit Online*, 28 November 2016.

[84] *Ibid.*

[85] *Ibid.*

[86] Ben Taub, "The Assad Files", *The New Yorker*, 18 April 2016 (available on its web site). See also Kassab, 2018, p. 289, see above note 67.

[87] Alexander Heinze, "Private International Criminal Investigations", in *Zeitschrift für internationale Strafrechtsdogmatik*, 2019, pp. 173–174.

[88] *Ibid.*, p. 174.

[89] Martin Gill and Jerry Hart, "Exploring Investigative Policing: A Study of Private Detectives in Britain", in *The British Journal of Criminology*, 1997, vol. 37, no. 4, p. 550 with fn. 1.

[90] *Ibid.*

conducted by the prosecution.[91] Thus, these broad definitions are subject to all sorts of qualifications and refinements. Prenzler uses "private investigators", "inquiry agents" and "private agents" interchangeably.[92] In his view, "[t]he term 'private investigator' has both generic and specific legal definitions. In its broadest terms it relates to any person who conducts enquiries for a customer or employer. This may include serving summonses after locating a person, as well as repossessing property".[93] Button blames the diversity of the branch for the impossibility to define private investigators: "[T]here are other occupations that compete with and undertake similar activities".[94] Fraud investigations, for instance, can be conducted by private investigators but also by "accountants" and "specialized forensic accountants".[95] Who can tell the difference between an accountant and a private detective after having watched "The Accountant", starring Ben Affleck, a movie about the forensic accountant Christian Wolff, who – living with a high functioning form of autism – discovers that 61 million dollars have been embezzled from the company who hired him? Investigative journalists and solicitors are also performing acts that could be assigned to a private investigator,[96] not to mention corporate compliance and internal investigations,[97] which include the screening of documents; the monitoring of

---

[91] Jan Bockemühl, *Private Ermittlungen im Strafprozeß*, Nomos: Baden-Baden, 1996, pp. 15 ff., reviewed by André Klip, "Private investigations in criminal proceedings, a contribution to the concept of inadmissible evidence (in German)", in *European Journal of Crime, Criminal Law and Criminal Justice*, 1998, vol. 6, p. 83.

[92] Tim Prenzler, *Private Investigators in Australia: Work, Law, Ethics and Regulation*, Report to the Criminology Research Council, 2001, p. 5 (available on the web site of the Australian Criminology Research Council).

[93] *Ibid.*, p. 7. See also Johnston, "Private Investigation", in Tim Newburn, Tom Williamson and Alan Wright (eds.), *Handbook of Criminal Investigation*, Willan Publishing, Abingdon and New York, 2007, p. 278.

[94] Mark Button, "Beyond the Public Gaze — The Exclusion of Private Investigators from the British Debate over Regulating Private Security", in *International Journal of the Sociology of Law*, 1998, vol. 26, no. 1, p. 2.

[95] *Ibid.*, p. 2.

[96] *Ibid.*

[97] See, generally, Laura Christiane Nienaber, *Umfang, Grenzen und Verwertbarkeit compliancebasierter unternehmensinterner Ermittlungen*, Schriften zu Compliance, vol. 14, Nomos, Baden-Baden, 2019. Internal investigation can be defined as "an inquiry performed by a company or its agent after the company is made aware of a serious and reasonably plausible allegation of corporate misconduct", see Abraham Gitterman, "Ethical Issues and Practical Challenges Raised by Internal Investigations in the Life Sciences Industry", in *Defense Counsel Journal*, 2013, vol. 80, no. 4, p. 374. They are especially employed in the context of Deferred Prosecution Agreements, where the company shares interview memoranda and

snail mail and email communication, and of phone conversations; and the audio-visual observation of the work place.[98] Internal investigators regularly even conduct 'interviews' with employees of the company.[99] The list of those resembling activities – store detectives, solicitors and even psychics – is long.[100] George and Button, therefore, use a more complex definition, reproduced by Johnston: private investigators are

> [i]ndividuals (whether in house or contract) and firms (other than public enforcement bodies) who offer services related to the obtaining, selling or supplying of any information relating to the identity, conduct, movements, whereabouts, associations, transactions or character of any person, groups of persons or association, or of any other type of organization.[101]

The narrowest definition would reduce private investigators to "work either for the victim or for the defendant or his attorney in criminal proceedings".[102] Dörmann provides a slightly broader definition:

> Usually, private investigators working in the criminal justice field do so on behalf of the defence, checking the accuracy of police evidence and looking for witnesses who might undermine the case for the prosecution. By contrast, criminal investigations for private companies usually aim to establish the causes of loss and of any guilt associated with such loss.[103]

The difficulty to define the term 'private investigator' or 'private investigations' is increased on the international level. Here, too, many actors carry out the work of investigators, such as journalists or the media in general, as the above-mentioned 'Caesar' photos illustrate.[104] But even when

---

other materials generated in an internal investigation, see Federico Mazzacuva, "Justifications and Purposes of Negotiated Justice for Corporate Offenders: Deferred and Non-Prosecution Agreements in the UK and US Systems of Criminal Justice", in *Journal of Criminal Law*, 2014, vol. 78, no. 3, p. 258.

[98] Werner Leitner, "Unternehmensinterne Ermittlungen im Konzern", in Klaus Lüderssen *et al.* (eds), *Festschrift für Wolf Schiller: zum 65 Geburtstag am 12 Januar 2014*, Nomos, Baden-Baden, 2014, p. 433.

[99] *Ibid.*

[100] Button, 1998, p. 2, see above note 94.

[101] Bruce George and Mark Button, *Private Security*, vol. 1, Palgrave MacMillan, London, 2000, p. 88.

[102] Rory J. McMahon, *Practical Handbook for Private Investigators*, CRC Press, Boca Raton, London, New York, Washington, DC, 2001, p. 22.

[103] Johnston, 2007, p. 285, see above note 93.

[104] Afshar, 2018, see above note 79.

the term 'private investigator' is narrowed down to IGOs or NGOs, the nature of these organisations is often unclear. Thus, any definition would be arbitrary.[105] The only suggestion I would make is to dispense of the term 'private', since it is too broad and seems to be rather occupied by a domestic understanding. I also recommend avoiding the term 'human rights', since agencies such as CIJA do investigative work without human rights monitoring. Therefore, the best term to use would therefore be 'third party investigations', which goes back to Bergsmo and Wiley's description of personnel "not serving with a belligerent party".[106]

17.5. Private Investigations: A Matter of Ethics and Integrity

17.5.1. The Ethical Problem with Private Investigations

Lawyers are expected to abide by laws, professional rules, and informal professional norms, and in many jurisdictions, they are also required to abide by a professional code of conduct.[107] Professional legal ethics involve recognising that lawyers are often confronted with ethical dilemmas. Criminal lawyers, in particular, face "conflicting values, aims and interests".[108] They are expected, however, to separate the "morality of the[ir] representation" from the "morality of the client's cause".[109] A criminal lawyer is expected to vigorously argue for her side of the case, whether as a defence lawyer or a prosecution lawyer, and whether or not she thinks that she in fact has the most compelling argument. But this vigour remains limited by ethical constraints, such as the moral requirement to respect the dignity of all persons involved in a criminal trial, and the moral prohibition of lying to advance a client's interests. While a defence lawyer may have less control over criminal justice proceedings other than determining how best to advocate for his client, a prosecutor has additional ethical obliga-

---

[105] In the same vein for the national level, see Johnston, 2007, p. 278, see above note 93.

[106] Bergsmo and Wiley, 2008, p. 12, see above note 1.

[107] See Donald Nicolson, "Making Lawyers Moral? Ethical Codes and Moral Character", in *Legal Studies*, 2005, vol. 25, no. 4, pp. 601–26; Liz Campbell, Andrew Ashworth and Mike Redmayne, *The Criminal Process*, fifth edition, Oxford University Press, 2019, pp. 60 ff.

[108] Richard Young and Andrew Sanders, "The Ethics of Prosecution Lawyers", in *Legal Ethics*, 2004, vol. 7, no. 2, pp. 190–209.

[109] David Luban, *Legal Ethics and Human Dignity*, Cambridge University Press, 2007, p. 20.

tions due to her ability to select defendants for trial and determine the scope of the criminal justice process.[110]

The normative foundations of prosecutorial ethics consist of two main concepts: a prosecutor's general duty to seek justice,[111] and the moral theories that inform the corresponding, specific ethical obligations of the prosecutor. In both adversarial and inquisitorial systems of law,[112] regardless of other specific duties, the prosecutor is expected to seek justice.[113] While the particular features of what constitutes justice vary between, and sometimes within, criminal legal systems, it is always tied to the concept of fairness.[114]

---

[110] This of course applies more to the criminal justice process in the legal tradition of the common law than to a civil law criminal process, cf. Alexander Heinze, *International Criminal Procedure and Disclosure*, Duncker & Humblot, Berlin, 2014, pp. 107 ff. See also Alexander Heinze and Shannon Fyfe, "Prosecutorial Ethics and Preliminary Examinations at the ICC", in Morten Bergsmo and Carsten Stahn (eds.), *Quality Control in Preliminary Examination: Volume 2*, Torkel Opsahl Academic EPublisher ('TOAEP'), Brussels, 2018, pp. 5–6 (https://www.legal-tools.org/doc/dff594/).

[111] See Fred C. Zacharias, "Structuring the Ethics of Prosecutorial Trial Practice: Can Prosecutors Do Justice?", in *Vanderbilt Law Review*, 1991, vol. 44, no. 1, pp. 45 ff.

[112] About the meaning of terms 'inquisitorial' and 'adversarial' in more detail, see Heinze, 2014, pp. 117 ff., see above note 110; Kai Ambos and Alexander Heinze, "Abbreviated Procedures in Comparative Criminal Procedure: A Structural Approach with a View to International Criminal Procedure", in Morten Bergsmo (ed.), *Abbreviated Criminal Procedures for Core International Crimes*, TOAEP, Brussels, 2017, pp. 27, 28 ff. (https://www.toaep.org/ps-pdf/9-bergsmo).

[113] Shawn Marie Boyne, *The German Prosecution Service: Guardians of the Law*, Springer, Berlin, Heidelberg, 2014, p. 5 ("[P]rosecutors possess an ethical obligation to pursue justice"). The fact that the search for truth in inquisitorial systems is a constitutive feature (Heinze, 2014, p. 107, see above note 110) does not render justice as an ethical obligation of the prosecutor less relevant. In inquisitorial systems too truth is a means to the end of justice, as Karl Peters famously pointed out in his seminal work about the German criminal process (Karl Peters, *Strafprozeß*, C.F. Müller, Heidelberg, 1985, p. 82 ("Das Strafverfahren kann das Ziel der Gerechtigkeit nur erreichen, wenn es die Wahrheit findet").) In the same vein, see Theodore L. Kubicek, *Adversarial Justice: America's Court System on Trial*, Algora, New York, 2006, p. 37 with further references. See also Barton L. Ingraham, *The Structure of Criminal Procedure*, Greenwood Press, New York *et al.*, 1987, p. 13.

[114] See, for example, ICC, Situation in the Democratic Republic of the Congo, *The Prosecutor v. Thomas Lubanga Dyilo*, Appeals Chamber, Judgment on the Appeal of Mr. Thomas Lubanga Dyilo against the Decision on the Defence Challenge to the Jurisdiction of the Court pursuant to article 19 (2) (a) of the Statute of 3 October 2006, 14 December 2006, ICC-01/04-01/06-772, para. 37 ('Lubanga, 2006') (http://www.legal-tools.org/doc/1505f7/): "Where fair trial becomes impossible because of breaches of the fundamental rights of the suspect or the accused by his/her accusers, it would be a contradiction in terms to put the person on trial. Justice could not be done. A fair trial is the only means to do justice. If no fair trial can be

Deontological constraints are especially well suited to play the primary role in shaping prosecutorial or investigatory ethics and promoting fair trials. Danner has argued that prosecutorial decisions, for instance, will be both legitimate and perceived as such if they are taken in a principled, reasoned, and impartial manner.[115] The ICC's OTP has adopted this approach in several policy papers. The duty to treat every individual as an end in him- or herself and, thus, apply the same rules without bias or concern about outcomes lends itself to ensuring procedural fairness. The prosecutor is constrained by "rules which apply in an all-or-nothing, categorical manner without reference to the particular context or consequences of the prohibited or required behaviour".[116] The impartiality demanded by deontological constraints applies "separately to every relation between persons", which means that no one's rights may be violated, even if the violation could be "offset by benefits that arise elsewhere" in the justice system.[117]

This is not the place to go too deep into the matter of prosecutorial ethics, I have done this elsewhere with Shannon Fyfe.[118] One aspect of the procedural fairness mentioned above is that investigative staff employed by international criminal jurisdictions are ethically bound to search for inculpatory as well as exculpatory evidence from the start of an inquiry.[119] It is doubtful whether staff employed by CIJA abides by the same ethical obligations. This does not mean that NGOs or IGOs can never be trusted to comply with certain ethical obligations. In fact, human rights organisations are more concerned with issues of monitoring[120] and protection through

---

held, the object of the judicial process is frustrated and the process must be stopped". See also Catherine S. Namakula, "The Human Rights Mandate of a Prosecutor of an International Criminal Trial", in *International Criminal Law Review*, 2017, vol. 17, no. 5, pp. 935, 936. About the meaning of fairness in that context Heinze and Fyfe, 2018, pp. 6–8, see above note 110.

[115] Allison M. Danner, "Enhancing the Legitimacy and Accountability of Prosecutorial Discretion at the International Criminal Court", in *The American Journal of International Law*, 2003, vol. 97, no. 3, pp. 536–37.

[116] Nicolson, 2005, p. 606, see above note 107.

[117] Daniel Markovits, *A Modern Legal Ethics: Adversary Advocacy in a Democratic Age*, Princeton University Press, New York, 2010, p. 7.

[118] Heinze and Fyfe, "The Role of the Prosecutor", in Kai Ambos *et al.* (eds.), *Core Concepts in Criminal Law and Justice*, vol. 1, Cambridge University Press, 2020, pp. 344 ff.; Heinze and Fyfe, 2018, pp. 3 ff., see above note 110.

[119] Bergsmo and Wiley, 2008, p. 2, see above note 1.

[120] A definition of human rights monitoring is provided in Anette Faye Jacobsen (ed.), *Human Rights Monitoring*, Martinus Nijhoff, Leiden, Boston, 2008, p. 1:

---

advocacy.[121] The problem lies in entities, such as CIJA, which do mainly investigatory work and have donors at the same time.[122] Here, concerns about the substantive outcomes of investigations and criminal trials, the overall performance or record of an investigator or prosecutor, or the social and political impacts of criminal trials, will likely involve more consequentialist considerations.[123] From a psychological perspective, competition in that sense regularly leads to role-induced bias or what Simon *et al.* labelled the "myside bias".[124]

This is most visible at the national level. In meeting the needs of their clients, private investigators pursue instrumental ends.[125] As Johnston describes:

> Unlike police detectives, who collect evidence for constructing cases within a system of public justice, private investigators aim only to minimize the economic, social or personal losses of their clients. Instrumentalism is driven by a proactive, risk-based mentality, the object of which is to anticipate, rec-

---

Human rights monitoring can be defined as the systematic collection, verification, and use of information to address human rights problems or compliances. The compiled data will have to be analyzed against agreed standards. These standards primarily entail the human rights obligations and commitments that the State is a party to, and thus has committed itself to live up to; as well as additional human rights provisions which have come to be recognized as customary law applicable to all authorities regardless of the State's formal acknowledgement [...].

[121] Bergsmo and Wiley, 2008, p. 2, see above note 1.

[122] See also Burgis-Kasthala, 2020, p. 1173, see above note 55.

[123] Frédéric Mégret, "International Prosecutors: Accountability and Ethics", in *Leuven Centre for Global Governance Studies*, Working Paper No. 18, 2008, p. 8. Surely, consequentialist considerations also play an important role in prosecutorial decision making, especially at the ICC, as I have argued – together with Kai Ambos – in *amicus curiae* observation, see ICC, *Situation in the Islamic Republic of Afghanistan*, Written Submissions in the Proceedings Relating to the Appeals Filed Against the "Decision Pursuant to Article 15 of the Rome Statute on the Authorisation of an Investigation into the Situation in the Islamic Republic of Afghanistan" Issued on 12 April 2019 (ICC-02/17-33) and Pursuant to "Decision on the participation of amici curiae, the Office of Public Counsel for the Defence and the cross-border victims" Issued on 14 October 2019 (ICC-02/17-97), 14 November 2019, *Ambos and Heinze*, ICC-02/17-108 (https://www.legal-tools.org/doc/5v8d2b/) and Annex (https://www.legal-tools.org/doc/7m3bj2/).

[124] Dan Simon *et al.*, "The Adversarial Mindset", in *Psychology, Public Policy, and Law*, 2020, vol. 26, pp. 354 ff.

[125] Johnston, 2007, p. 280, see above note 93.

ognize and appraise risks and, having done so, to initiate actions that will help to minimize their impact on clients.[126]

Prenzler, in his previously mentioned study, found that "the large majority [of interviewees] also felt that anecdotal reports of misconduct were of sufficient gravity to justify greater control and scrutiny of the industry by government".[127] The investigators he interviewed particularly nominated "privacy as the area where their profession posed the greatest danger to the public".[128] Privacy is especially problematic in the case of social media evidence. Take, for instance, the investigations in Myanmar, where the Human Rights Council recently created another investigative mechanism.[129] Human Rights Council resolution 34/22 mandated the Mission

> to establish the facts and circumstances of the alleged recent human rights violations by military and security forces, and abuses, in Myanmar, in particular in Rakhine State, including but not limited to arbitrary detention, torture and inhuman treatment, rape and other forms of sexual violence, extrajudicial, summary or arbitrary killings, enforced disappearances, forced displacement and unlawful destruction of property, with a view to ensuring full accountability for perpetrators and justice for victims.[130]

---

[126] *Ibid.*

[127] Prenzler, 2001, p. 6, see above note 92.

[128] *Ibid.*, p. 36.

[129] Global Justice Center, "Statement on the Creation of the IIIM for Myanmar", press release, 27 September 2018 (available on its web site); International Commission of Jurists, "Myanmar: creation of UN mechanism a step toward accountability", 27 September 2018 (available on its web site). See generally Neriah Yue, "The 'Weaponization' of Facebook in Myanmar: A Case for Corporate Criminal Liability', in *Hastings Law Journal*, 2020, vol. 71, pp. 816 ff.; Emma Palmer, *Adapting International Criminal Justice in Southeast Asia: Beyond the International Criminal Court*, Cambridge University Press, Cambridge, 2020, pp. 159 ff.; Derek Tonkin, "Mission Creep Untrammelled: The UN Fact-Finding Mission on Myanmar", FICHL Policy Brief Series No. 102 (2020), Torkel Opsahl Academic EPublisher, Brussels, 2020 (http://www.toaep.org/pbs-pdf/102-tonkin).

[130] Human Rights Council, Report of the detailed findings of the Independent International Fact-Finding Mission on Myanmar, UN Doc. A/HRC/39/CRP.2, 17 September 2018, para. 4 (https://www.legal-tools.org/doc/0c0c69/). See also https://iimm.un.org/mandate-and-establishment/. In more detail Heinze, 2019, pp. 171–172, see above note 87; Aksenova, Bergsmo and Stahn, 2020, pp. 10 ff., see above note 1, with a list of "International Fact-Finding Mandates 1992-2020" at pp. 32–44. Generally about fact-finding by the Special Procedures of the Human Rights Council Martin Scheinin, "Improving Fact-Finding in Treaty-Based Human Rights Mechanisms and the Special Procedures of the United Nations Human Rights Council", in Morten Bergsmo and Carsten Stahn (eds.), *Quality Control in Fact-*

Apart from 875 in-depth interviews the mission conducted,[131] it also emphasised the important role of social media information.[132] It reported, among other things:

> The Mission has seen a vast amount of hate speech across all types of platforms, including the print media, broadcasts, pamphlets, CD/DVDs, songs, webpages and social media accounts. For example, the Mission encountered over 150 online public social media accounts, pages and groups that have regularly spread messages amounting to hate speech against Muslims in general or Rohingya in particular.[133]

In another study, Prenzler and King reported that according to "one-third of the respondents, non-compliance [with ethical boundaries] was fairly widespread", while others felt that instances of non-compliance were rather isolated.[134] Button describes that "there are many examples of illegal and unethical behaviour. There have been many alleged and reported incidents of private investigators bugging premises, breaking and entering, kidnapping or gaining confidential information from the police".[135]

As previously remarked, investigators are expected to separate the "morality in their representation" from the "morality of the client's cause".[136] This may lead to a moral dilemma when investigators who comply with ethical standards are asked by their clients to ignore these. Gill and Hart describe that "there is a demand for services that can only be considered to be of dubious legitimacy".[137] All investigators interviewed

---

Finding, second edition, Brussels, TOAEP, 2020, pp. 75 ff. About the question whether information collected by human rights bodies and "human rights investigators" can generally be admitted as direct evidence at ICTs, see Lyal S. Sunga, "Can International Criminal Investigators and Prosecutors Afford to Ignore Information from United Nations Human Rights Sources?", *ibid.*, pp. 409 ff.

[131] *Ibid.*, para. 19.

[132] *Ibid.*, paras. 515, 744. See also Emma Irving, "The Role of Social Media is Significant: Facebook and the Fact Finding Mission on Myanmar", *Opinio Juris*, 7 September 2018.

[133] Human Rights Council, 2018, para. 1310, see above note 130.

[134] Timothy Prenzler and Michael King, *The Role of Private Investigators and Commercial Agents in Law Enforcement, Australian Institute of Criminology*, August 2002, p. 5 (available on the repository of Griffith University).

[135] Button, 1998, p. 10, see above note 94. See also Johnston, 2007, see above note 93.

[136] Luban, 2007, p. 20, see above note 109.

[137] Martin Gill and Jerry Hart, "Private Security: Enforcing Corporate Security Policy Using Private Investigators", in *European Journal on Criminal Policy and Research*, 1999, vol. 7, p. 255.

could cite instances when clients, including members of the legal profession, had directly asked them to perform illegal or unethical actions. While some cited occasions when they had been asked to organise a serious offence, such as murder or serious assault, these most commonly included gaining unlawful access to confidential information, such as criminal records, medical histories and bank account details.[138]

Similar ethical problems are expected at the international level. Leaders and members of NGOs have private interests, such as financial interests, the increase of group membership, personal career motivations, or simply personal relationships.[139] Entities such as CIJA investigate and collect material without the permission of the UNSC or an international treaty body.[140] Thus, the investigations undertaken by third parties have not only been applauded.[141] It comes to no surprise that tribunals often impose limits upon investigatory NGOs. For example, the ICTY-OTP has cautioned NGOs not to conduct in-depth interviews with potential witnesses and have established strict guidelines for collecting evidence.[142]

Of course, it is emphasised that "CIJA adheres to international standards of ethical conduct and evidence management".[143] Rankin, however, paints a too optimistic picture when she remarks: "CIJA's objectives require an extraordinary degree of individual responsibility at all ranks of the organisation, for example many Syrian investigators share a personal responsibility to collect the material in an effort to establish the truth, and share a sense of public duty to investigate".[144] The question is thus how evidence that was obtained by private individuals who, in whatever form, acted illegally or unethically, is and should be treated.

---

[138] Gill and Hart, 1999, p. 255, see above note 137.

[139] Michael J. Struett, "The Politics of Discursive Legitimacy: Understanding the Dynamics and Implications of Prosecutorial Discretion at the International Criminal Court", in Steven C. Roach (ed.), *Governance, Order, and the International Criminal Court*, Oxford University Press, 2009, p. 115.

[140] Rankin, 2017, p. 414, see above note 56.

[141] Cheryl Hardcastle for instance, Windsor-Tecumseh Minister for Canadian Parliament, highlighted: "We do know in the international community that some people have criticized the privatizing of international criminal investigations", cited in *ibid.*, p. 405, fn. 39.

[142] See Danner, 2003, p. 532, see above note 115; Ellis, 2011, p. 156, see above note 10.

[143] Rankin, 2017, p. 414, see above note 56.

[144] *Ibid.*

17.5.2. Integrity as the Central Value for Private Investigators

To view the work of private investigators solely from a perspective of fairness and truth does not grasp the complexities of the matter. Instead, it is the idea of the 'integrity' or 'legitimacy' of the trial as a distinctive kind of legal process that should be focused on.[145] The question is: can integrity be the value that provides guidance for a private individual conducting an investigation? To be concrete, let us suppose that a private investigator offers money to witness in return for information about a suspect and his or her criminal activities. Does 'integrity' provide a guideline for this investigator to refrain from such activities?

17.5.2.1. Integrity Defined

Integrity as a jurisprudential concept has roots that reach into the nineteenth century. There are countless English cases that recur to integrity in relation to personal or professional honesty, good character or witness credibility.[146]

To define integrity, I will do what seems methodologically superficial and consult – at least initially – a dictionary. To be clear, this does have a methodological reason. Integrity as a term shall first and foremost be defined pragmatically,[147] that is, how it *is* used,[148] and not so much how it *should* be used or can be used (the latter semantic dimension does a play a role, though). Thus, I approach integrity as a semantic concept in the first place, and only secondarily as a philosophical concept. The reason for this methodological decision is twofold: First, integrity especially as an evidentiary concept has a strong pragmatic connotation. In other words, decision-makers expect a certain degree of practicability from a definition of integrity, despite its apparent vagueness. Second, integrity as a philosophical concept is covered elsewhere in this volume – in manifold ways and by scholars who could do it better than I ever could.

---

[145] Antony Duff *et al.*, *The Trial on Trial: Volume 3, Towards a Normative Theory of the Criminal Trial*, Hart, Oxford and Portland, Oregon, 2007, p. 108.

[146] Paul Roberts *et al.*, "Introduction: Re-examining Criminal Process Through the Lens of Integrity", in Paul Roberts *et al.* (eds.), *The Integrity of Criminal Process*, Hart, Oxford and Portland, 2016, p. 4 with further references.

[147] About the pragmatical turn in textual interpretation, see Umberto Eco, *Die Grenzen der Interpretation*, Hanser, München, 1992, pp. 350 ff.

[148] About the usage of words see already Wittgenstein, *Philosophische Untersuchungen*, posthum second edition, Blackwell, Malden, 1958, reprint 1999, p. 20.

According to a lexical definition, integrity is "[t]he condition of having no part or element taken away or wanting; undivided or unbroken state; material wholeness, completeness, entirety".[149] In addition, integrity is also equated with "soundness", meant "[i]n a moral sense", as an "[u]nimpaired moral state; freedom from moral corruption; innocence, sinlessness".[150] Last but not least, from a lexical perspective, 'integrity' is understood as "[s]oundness of moral principle; the character of uncorrupted virtue, esp. in relation to truth and fair dealing; uprightness, honesty, sincerity".[151] The different lexical definitions underline the different perspectives 'integrity' can be viewed from: a) from the perspective of the suspect or witness ("having no part or element taken away or wanting"); b) from the perspective of the investigator ("soundness", "the character of uncorrupted virtue, esp. in relation to truth and fair dealing; uprightness, honesty, sincerity"; and c) from the perspective of the entire process ("undivided or unbroken state"; "material wholeness, completeness, entirety"). I call those the 'object', 'subject' and 'context' perspectives of integrity. It goes without saying that the perspectives do not unfold in a vacuum but are somewhat intertwined.

17.5.2.1.1. Integrity from the Perspective of the Person Interrogated or Interviewed: The Object Perspective

Let us start with integrity as "[t]he condition of having no part or element taken away or wanting; undivided or unbroken state; material wholeness, completeness, entirety".[152] During an interrogation or an interview, suspects have certain rights: the right not to be physically or mentally injured or otherwise mistreated, the privilege against self-incrimination and a number of ancillary procedural rights, such as the right to consult a lawyer.[153] This rather cursory description must suffice at this point, I will return to the rights question in due course. The integrity of the individual is a cornerstone of these rights.[154] The physical and mental integrity of the sus-

---

[149] John A. Simpson and Edmund S.C. Weiner, *The Compact Oxford English Dictionary*, Clarendon Press, Oxford University Press, Oxford, 1989 and 2002, p. 860 [1066].

[150] *Ibid.*, p. 860 [1066].

[151] *Ibid.*

[152] *Ibid.*

[153] Adrian A.S. Zuckerman, "Coercion and the Judicial Ascertainment of Truth", in *Israel Law Review*, 1989, vol. 23, no. 2-3, p. 357.

[154] *Ibid.*

pect must not be violated.[155] Here, the notion of integrity is closely connected to human dignity,[156] as enshrined in various human rights instruments.[157] Understood this way, integrity is often equated with autonomy, individuality, independence, responsibility, and self-knowledge.[158] As Gerald Dworkin puts it: "Individuals have the right to be treated as persons, as masters of their own body, as responsible for their decisions, as makers of choices".[159] The Kantian footprint (namely: Kant's Categorical Imperative)[160] is obvious here. This supreme principle of ethics aims at the motivation (or reasons) for acting; any consideration of external behaviour is absent.[161] Kant's Categorical Imperative illustrates that dignity is "intrinsic, deontological and non-negotiable (replaceable), it is the basis of the individuality and the mutual recognition (inter-personal relationship) of the members of a society".[162] By contrast, the principle of Kant's legal philos-

---

[155] Israel, Supreme Court, *Abu Midjam v. State of Israel*, 1980, P.D. 34(4) 533, p. 539 – about the case, see Rinat Kitai Sangero and Yuval Merin, "Israel: The Supreme Court's New, Cautious Exclusionary Rule", in Stephen C. Thaman (ed.), *Exclusionary Rules in Comparative Law*, Springer, Dordrecht, 2013, p. 105. See also Eliahu Harnon, "Criminal Procedure and Evidence", in *Israel Law Review*, 1990, vol. 24, no. 3-4, p. 592 (603).

[156] Directive 2013/32/EU of the European Parliament and of the Council of 26 June 2013 on common procedures for granting and withdrawing international protection (recast), 29 June 2013, OJ L. 180/60, Article 13 ('Procedures Directive') (https://www.legal-tools.org/doc/7ijsc2/).

[157] See, for instance, Charter of Fundamental Rights of the European Union, 14 December 2007, 2007/C 303/01, Article 1 (https://www.legal-tools.org/doc/715d2e/). See also Galina Cornelisse, "Protecting human dignity across and within borders: the legal regulation of international migration in Europe", in Logi Gunnarsson, Ulrike Mürbe, and Norman Weiß (eds.), *The Human Right to a Dignified Existence in an International Context: Legal and Philosophical Perspectives*, Nomos, Baden-Baden, 2019, pp. 97–98.

[158] Gerald Dworkin, *The Theory and Practice of Autonomy*, Cambridge University Press, 1988 and 1997, p. 6.

[159] *Ibid.*, p. 103.

[160] "I ought never to act except in such a way that I could also will that my maxim should become a universal law", Immanuel Kant, *Groundwork of the Metaphysics of Morals*, Mary J. Gregor (ed., trans.), Cambridge University Press, 1997, p. 15 [402].

[161] Luke J. Davies, "A Kantian Defense of the Right to Health Care", in Reidar Maliks and Andreas Føllesdal (eds.), *Kantian Theory and Human Rights*, Routledge, London, 2014, p. 82; Wilfried Küper, "Das Strafgesetz ist ein kategorischer Imperativ: Zum 'Strafgesetz' in Kants Rechtslehre", in Michael Hettinger and Jan Zopfs (eds.), *Wilfried Küper – Strafrechtliche Beiträge zu Rechtsgeschichte und Rechtsphilosophie*, Mohr Siebeck, Tübingen, 2017, pp. 397 ff.

[162] Marie E. Newhouse, "Two Types of Legal Wrongdoing", in *Legal Theory*, 2017, vol. 22, no. 1, pp. 59 ff.; Ulfried Neumann, "Das Rechtsprinzip der Menschenwürde als Schutz elementarer menschlicher Bedürfnisse: Versuch einer Eingrenzung", in *Archiv für Rechts- und*

ophy, the Universal Principle of Right,[163] "transposes the categorical imperative to the sphere of external action".[164] Freedom referred to by the Universal Principle of Right is "external freedom", it "bars considerations of internal motivation".[165] The distinction between external and internal freedom is Kant's

> most profound statement on the relationship between an autonomous morality and political practice. By reconstructing Kant's arguments in favor of their distinction, we see the dynamics behind his theory of justice: The pure practical reason of morality (inner freedom) informs – and thereby subordinates – the structure of outer freedom and the political reality with which it is associated.[166]

Taking Kant's Categorical Imperative and the Universal Principle of Right as a basis, the 'object perspective' is not only a semantic description but at the same time an evaluation, since the infringement of the suspect's rights turns this suspect into an object,[167] up to a dehumanisation.[168]

Sozialphilosophie, 2017, vol. 103, no. 3, p. 293; Julian A. Sempill, "Law, Dignity and the Elusive Promise of a Third Way", in *Oxford Journal of Legal Studies*, 2018, vol. 38, no. 2, p. 228.

[163] Any action is *right* if it can coexist with everyone's freedom in accordance with a universal law, or if on its maxim the freedom of choice of each can coexist with everyone's freedom in accordance with a universal law. See Immanuel Kant, *The Metaphysics of Morals*, Mary J. Gregor (trans.), Cambridge University Press, 1991, p. 57 [231] (http://www.legal-tools.org/doc/cb8e1e/). See also Kai Ambos, "Punishment without a Sovereign? The *Ius Puniendi* Issue of International Criminal Law", in *Oxford Journal of Legal Studies*, 2013, vol. 33, no. 2, pp. 293, 305.

[164] Benedict Vischer, "Systematicity to Excess – Kant's Conception of the International Legal Order", in Stefan Kadelbach, Thomas Kleinlein and David Roth-Isigkeit (eds.), *System, Order, and International Law*, Oxford University Press, Oxford, 2017, p. 306: "[W]hile the categorical imperative requires the universalizability of the voluntary maxim, the principle of right merely demands that the action – irrespectively of the agents' motive – conforms to a universal law". About the different interpretations of Kant's external action, see Dietmar von der Pfordten, "On Kant's Concept of Law", in *Archiv für Rechts- und Sozialphilosophie*, 2015, vol. 101, no. 2, pp. 193 ff.

[165] Davies, 2014, p. 82, see above note 161.

[166] Antonio Franceschet, *Kant and Liberal Internationalism*, Palgrave Macmillan, New York, 2002, pp. 23–24.

[167] Cf. Jacob Bronsther, "Torture and Respect", in *Journal of Criminal Law and Criminology*, 2019, vol. 109, no. 3, p. 423 (431, albeit with regard to "penal rape").

[168] Peters, 1985, p. 82, see above note 113.

17.5.2.1.2. Integrity from the Perspective of the Interrogator or Interviewer: The Subject Perspective

As previously mentioned, according to a lexical definition, integrity is understood as "[s]oundness of moral principle; the character of uncorrupted virtue, esp. in relation to truth and fair dealing; uprightness, honesty, sincerity".[169] In the words of Roberts: "integrity conveys the impression of being almost unequivocally laudable, right and good".[170] In this way, integrity is connected to authenticity, reliability, constancy, fair dealing and sound judgement.[171] For Roberts: "A person of integrity treats others in accordance with her deepest enduring convictions about how people ought to be treated; she is true to her values and true to herself".[172] This definition illustrates that integrity and acting according to one's perceived moral duties are not necessarily the same. What about a person leading a terror regime (Nazi perpetrators, for instance)? Killing hundreds of thousands of people as a perceived act of self-defence of an allegedly higher race might comply with his or her perceived moral duties. Yet, is this person eligible for ascriptions of integrity?[173] The same example could be construed around a private investigator who offers money to his or her only witness so this witness provides the necessary proof that may lead to the prosecution of warlord X or Y. For Lenta, the same even holds true "of individuals whose moral beliefs are not wicked but are unreasonable or unintelligible".[174] As a result, McFall distinguishes between *personal* integrity and *moral* integrity: personal integrity "requires that an agent (1) subscribe to some consistent set of principles or commitments and (2), in the face of temptation or challenge, (3) uphold these principles or commitments, (4) for what the agent takes to be the right reasons".[175] To have moral integrity, by contrast, "it is natural to suppose that one must have some lower-order moral commitments; that moral integrity adds a moral requirement to personal integrity".[176] Thus, there are cases "in which we would want to grant

---

[169] Simpson and Weiner, 1989 and 2002, p. 860 [1066], see above note 149.
[170] Roberts *et al.*, 2016, p. 10, see above note 146.
[171] *Ibid.*
[172] *Ibid.*
[173] In the same vein, see Patrick Lenta, "Freedom of Conscience and the Value of Personal Integrity", in *Ratio Juris*, 2016, vol. 29, no. 2, pp. 247–248.
[174] *Ibid.*
[175] Lynne McFall, "Integrity", in *Ethics*, 1987, vol. 98, no. 1, p. 5 (9).
[176] *Ibid.*, p. 14.

that someone had *personal* integrity, even if we were to find his ideal morally abhorrent".[177] In reaction to this, it is questioned whether personal integrity has value whatsoever. In Lenta's words: "One might think that personal integrity is valueless since an individual's possessing personal integrity is compatible with his being wicked. In the case of the genocidal Nazi
who possesses personal integrity it may well be better if he lacked personal
integrity".[178]

The integrity of those who collect evidence has long been recognised
as a central value and qualification. Take, for instance, the Oath of Honor
of the International Association of Chiefs of Police: "On my honor, I will
never betray my badge, my integrity, my character, or the public trust. I
will always have the courage to hold myself and others accountable for our
actions. I will always uphold the Constitution, my community, and the
agency I serve".[179] Similarly, prosecutors "are meant to hold their professional integrity" and expected to have an "ethical compass".[180] Corrigan
goes even further: "The first, best, and most effective shield against injustice for an individual accused [person], or society in general, must be found
not in the persons of defense counsel, trial judge, or appellate jurist, but in
the integrity of the prosecutor".[181] The ICC, per its Statute, requires the
staff of the OTP and Registry to have "the highest standards of efficiency,
competency and integrity".[182]

17.5.2.1.3. Integrity from the Perspective of the Process: The Context Perspective

As previously mentioned, according to a lexical definition, 'integrity' also
means "undivided or unbroken state"; "material wholeness, completeness,
entirety". Integrity, thus, also implies normative coherence juxtaposed to
fragmentation. For the current purpose, this refers to the "material whole-

---

[177] *Ibid.* (emphasis in the original).

[178] Lenta, 2016, p. 248, see above note 173.

[179] The International Association of Chiefs of Police ('IACP'), "The Oath of Honor" (available
on its web site). See also Joycelyn M. Pollock, *Ethical Dilemmas and Decisions in Criminal
Justice*, tenth edition, Cangage, Boston, 2019, p. 129.

[180] Brent E. Turvey and Craig M. Cooley, *Miscarriages of Justice*, Elsevier, Amsterdam *et al.*,
2014, p. 286.

[181] Carol A. Corrigan, "On Prosecutorial Ethics", in *Hastings Constitutional Law Quarterly*,
1986, vol. 13, no. 3, p. 537.

[182] Rome Statute of the International Criminal Court, 17 July 1998, Article 44(2) ('ICC Statute')
(http://www.legal-tools.org/doc/7b9af9/).

ness, completeness, entirety" of the criminal process.[183] One proponent of the integrity as coherence of the criminal process is Andrew Ashworth, labelling it the "unity of the criminal justice system".[184] For Ashworth, a bribe by an interrogator does not only put in question the interrogator's integrity (depending on the definition of integrity, see above); it would also damage the integrity of the criminal justice system "if the courts were to act on the fruits of that investigation".[185] Criminal justice "must carry moral authority and legitimacy, and this would be significantly compromised if courts were able to convict citizens for acts which originated in an official error or other official misconduct".[186] In a chameleonic fashion, integrity from a 'context perspective' takes several forms here, and might appear as legitimacy, moral authority or, "integrity as integration". The latter was proposed by Duff *et al.*:

> Integrity as moral coherence is the principle that a criminal justice system which lacks moral coherence will lack the standing to call the defendant to account for his conduct. Integrity as integration is the idea that, in assessing the standing of the criminal process to call the defendant to answer the charge and account for his conduct, different parts of the criminal process cannot be isolated from each other. In particular, the criminal trial cannot claim that its moral integrity is intact in isolation, where there have been failings at an earlier stage in the criminal process.[187]

I will return to 'integrity as integration', as it will become a pillar of the reaction to illegally obtained evidence.[188]

---

[183] David Dixon, "Integrity, Interrogation and Criminal Justice", in Paul Roberts *et al.* (eds.), *The Integrity of Criminal Process*, Hart, Oxford and Portland, 2016, p. 79.

[184] Andrew Ashworth, "Testing Fidelity to Legal Values: Official Involvement and Criminal Justice", in Stephen Shute and Andrew P. Simester, *Criminal Law Theory: Doctrines of the General Part*, Oxford University Press, 2002, p. 308.

[185] *Ibid.*, p. 309.

[186] *Ibid.*

[187] A. Duff *et al.*, 2007, p. 226 see above note 145. See also See Andrew Ashworth, "Exploring the Integrity Principle in Evidence and Procedure", in Peter Mirfield and Roger Smith (eds.), *Essays for Colin Tapper*, LexisNexis, London, 2003, pp. 113–115.

[188] See below Section 17.5.2.3.2.3.

17.5.2.2. The Role of Integrity in Illegally Obtaining Evidence in an Official Investigation

Wrongfully obtained evidence could potentially undermine the "fairness of the proceedings," bring "the administration of justice into disrepute," or damage "the integrity of the proceedings".[189] As mentioned at the outset,[190] the exclusion of that evidence is the focus of the chapter, albeit not the only possible consequence.

Let us first assume that a *State actor* illegally obtains evidence during an *official investigation*. In such a situation, what role does integrity play?

Illegally obtained evidence is of concern for the person who obtains it, the person from it is obtained and for the process as a whole. As Ambos puts it:

> [P]rohibitions of evidence have not only an *individual component* – safeguarding individual rights and vindicating their violation by the exclusion of illegally obtained evidence against the accused. They also possess a *collective dimension* – upholding the *constitutional integrity* of the legal order, especially through the guarantee and realization of a fair trial.[191]

Various rationales have been advanced with respect to the question of how to address procedural violations committed in the pre-trial phase of criminal proceedings: the 'reliability' rationale, the 'disciplinary' rationale, the 'protective' (or 'remedial') rationale, and the 'integrity' rationale(s).[192]

---

[189] HO Hock Lai, "Exclusion of Wrongfully Obtained Evidence: A Comparative Analysis", in Darryl K. Brown *et al.* (eds.), *The Oxford Handbook of Criminal Process*, Oxford University Press, 2019, p. 834.

[190] See above Section 17.1.

[191] Kai Ambos, "The Transnational Use of Torture Evidence", in *Israel Law Review*, 2009, vol. 42, no. 2, p. 366 (emphasis in the original, fn. omitted).

[192] Kelly Pitcher, *Judicial Responses to Pre-Trial Procedural Violations in International Criminal Proceedings*, Asser Press, Springer, Berlin, Heidelberg, 2018, p. 185; John Jackson, "Human Rights, Constitutional Law and Exclusionary Safeguards in Ireland", in Paul Roberts and Jill Hunter (eds.), *Criminal Evidence and Human Rights*, Hart, Oxford and Portland, Oregon, 2012, p. 119 (121). For reviews of the various rationales, see Peter Mirfield, *Silence, Confessions and Improperly Obtained Evidence*, Clarendon Press, Oxford, 1997, chaps. 2 and 6; Ian H. Dennis, *The Law of Evidence*, seventh edition, Sweet & Maxwell, Thomson Reuters, London, 2020, mn. 3-041–3.046; Paul Roberts and Adrian Zuckerman, *Criminal Evidence*, second edition, Oxford University Press, Oxford, 2010, pp. 179 ff.

17.5.2.2.1. Integrity from the Subject Perspective: The Deterrence Theory

One of the most common rationales for exclusionary rules is the deterrence theory (also known as the "disciplinary rationale"),[193] a policy-based, and forward-looking[194] theory that justifies exclusion in terms of its impact on future police behaviour.[195] The US Supreme Court, for instance, emphasised the deterrent effect of excluding wrongfully obtained evidence ("policing the police").[196] In *Terry v. Ohio*, for instance, it remarked:

> Ever since its inception, the rule excluding evidence seized in violation of the Fourth Amendment has been recognized as a principal mode of discouraging lawless police conduct. [...] Thus, its major thrust is a deterrent one, [...] and experience has taught that it is the only effective deterrent to police misconduct in the criminal context, and that, without it, the constitutional guarantee against unreasonable searches and seizures would be a mere 'form of word'.[197]

As LIU reports, Japanese courts too relied on the deterrence theory as a rationale for excluding evidence.[198] Furthermore, the exclusionary rule of the fruit of the poisonous tree is established based on the deterrence theory.[199] On this rationale, "the effect and purpose of exclusion coincide. But,

---

[193] Peter Duff views the deterrence rationale (calling it "disciplinary rationale") as part of the "integrity of the process", see Peter Duff, "Admissibility of Improperly Obtained Physical Evidence in the Scottish Criminal Trial: The Search for Principle", in *Edinburgh Law Review*, 2004, vol. 8, no. 2, p. 152 (160).

[194] Roberts and Hunter, 2012, p. 121, see above note 192 ("Another argument often advanced is that the prohibition on the use of evidence serves as a deterrent to investigators and prosecutors from repeating their improper conduct in the future"); Adrian A.S. Zuckerman, "Illegally-Obtained Evidence—Discretion as a Guardian of Legitimacy", in *Current Legal Problems*, 1987, vol. 40, no. 1, pp. 56–57.

[195] HO, 2019, p. 824, see above note 189; Roberts and Zuckerman, 2010, p. 185, see above note 192.

[196] Stephen C. Thaman and Dominik Brodowski, "Exclusion or Non-Use of Illegally Gathered Evidence in the Criminal Process: Focus on Common Law and German Approaches", in Kai Ambos *et al.* (eds.), *Core Concepts in Criminal Law and Justice*, vol. 1, Cambridge University Press, 2020, p. 458.

[197] United States, Supreme Court ('US SC'), *Terry v. Ohio*, 1968, 392 US 1, p. 12. See also US SC, *Mapp v. Ohio*, 1961, 367 US 643, p. 655.

[198] LIU Jingkun, *The Exclusionary Rule of Illegal Evidence in China*, Springer, Law Press China, Beijing, 2019, p. 44.

[199] *Ibid.*

conceptually, the two are distinct. In many other jurisdictions, deterrence is not the (primary) purpose of exclusion".[200]

As the prominence of the deterrence grew, so did the criticism against this rationale of excluding wrongfully obtained evidence. With regard to the theory itself, Duff *et al.* pointed out that "the relevant comparator in terms of deterrent effect is not failing to respond to the wrong, but rather using alternative sanctions for the wrong".[201] Especially in the eyes of the public, the rationale has an ironic connotation. It at least requires an extensive line of justification why citizens should be protected from police misconduct by letting the (alleged) guilty go free.[202] The criticism of a lack of correlation between the exclusionary rule and the purpose to discipline the State actor is well known.[203]

The strongest objection is – this probably applies to every deterrence argument within the realm of criminal justice – that there is no valid empirical research at present.[204] A possible assessment of how law enforcement officials respond to exclusionary rules is difficult to make and past studies "have asserted that empirical data has been unable to substantiate or refute a deterrent effect".[205] Second, there are other forms to 'police the police', such as disciplinary proceedings or criminal prosecution of law enforcement officials.[206] It is doubtful whether the exclusion of evidence is really the best vindication for police wrongdoing, especially when the individual officer is more concerned with his or her own safety,[207] the expectations of peers,[208] or in making an arrest and/or has no personal interest in a convic-

---

[200] HO, 2019, p. 824, see above note 189.

[201] A. Duff *et al.*, 2007, p. 228, see above note 145.

[202] Zuckerman, 1987, p. 59, see above note 194; Roberts and Zuckerman, 2010, p. 27, see above note 192; P. Duff, 2004, p. 161, see above note 193: "are we really justified in letting the guilty go free in order that we can protect the public from the police?".

[203] See, for example, Luis Greco, "Warum gerade Beweisverbot? Ketzerische Bemerkungen zur Figur des Beweisverbots", in Ulrich Stein *et al.* (eds.), *Systematik in Strafrechtswissenschaft und Gesetzgebung, Festschrift für Klaus Rogall zum 70. Geburtstag am 10. August 2018*, Duncker & Humblot, 2018, pp. 485–515 (507 ff.).

[204] HO, 2019, p. 825, see above note 189; Gless and Macula, 2019, p. 355, see above note 8.

[205] Gless and Macula, 2019, p. 355, see above note 8.

[206] As it the case in Germany, Thaman and Brodowski, 2020, p. 458, see above note 196.

[207] Zuckerman, 1987, p. 59, see above note 194.

[208] *Ibid.*

tion.[209] Third, in many criminal justice systems, officials who violate an exclusionary rule never learn whether or not the evidence they obtained is excluded.[210] A fourth point is made by HO:

> To deter the police from breaking rules on evidence gathering, they must know what the rules are. It is questionable whether they do possess adequate knowledge. Exclusion will have little signaling and disincentivization impact if there is no communication channel that keeps the police in the loop every time the court rejects the evidence that they have collected.[211]

Ambos would not go so far to reject the deterrence rationale altogether but downgrade it to a "positive side-effect".[212]

17.5.2.2.2. Integrity from Object Perspective: The Theory of Remedies

The theory of remedies (also known as the "rights thesis",[213] 'vindication', 'remedial' or 'protective' theory[214]) focuses on the person interrogated and – more specifically – on his or her rights. Evidence ought to be excluded because legal (subjective) rights have been infringed.[215] The idea behind this rationale is that trials can and should protect citizens against the arbitrary exercise of State power.[216] If rights have been violated, the victim of the violation is entitled to a remedy (hence the name).[217] Human rights in the structure of criminal procedure vest the accused with legal rights which he or she can use to oppose State repression in the investigation and prosecution of a crime.[218] This defensive role is denoted in legal theory as the shield function of human rights law.[219] A criminal trial has a particularly

---

[209] Thaman and Brodowski, 2020, p. 458, see above note 196; Gless and Macula, 2019, p. 355, see above note 8; Zuckerman, 1987, p. 59, see above note 194.

[210] Gless and Macula, 2019, p. 355, see above note 8.

[211] HO, 2019, p. 825, see above note 189 (fn. omitted). In the same vein, albeit with regard to search and seizure, see Zuckerman, 1987, p. 59, see above note 194.

[212] Ambos, 2009, p. 366, see above note 191.

[213] A. Duff *et al.*, 2007, p. 230, see above note 145.

[214] Zuckerman, 1987, pp. 56–57, see above note 194; P. Duff, 2004, p. 164, see above note 193.

[215] About the "rights perspective" in general Campbell, Ashworth, and Redmayne, 2019, p. 46, see above note 107; see also P. Duff, 2004, p. 155, see above note 193.

[216] A. Duff *et al.*, 2007, p. 227, see above note 145.

[217] *Ibid.*, p. 230.

[218] Krešimir Kamber, *Prosecuting Human Rights Offences*, Brill, Leiden, 2017, p. 7.

[219] *Ibid.*

negative effect for the (alleged) offender's rights such as his or her reputation, financial position, personal liberty, and even life.[220] Thus, human rights protection ensures that the individual is shielded from the State's abuse of the *ius puniendi*.[221] Of course, human rights law also mandates the State to criminalise, investigate, prosecute and, if appropriate, punish criminal attacks on human rights.[222] This role can be descriptively denoted as the sword function of human rights law.[223] If failing to convict the defendant "where there is a powerful epistemic case against him is a serious abrogation of responsibility by the state, it will need powerful justification in terms of deterrence, a justification which we suspect will not be forthcoming".[224]

Duff *et al.* integrate this shield function of human rights in a trial into a more general communicative theory of the criminal trial.[225] In the spirit of this communicative theory of the trial, "state power must be justified to the defendant through the appropriate kind of communicative process, treating him as a responsible agent".[226] The combination of the remedy rationale and communicative theory is particularly appealing for international investigations, as I will demonstrate below.[227]

The remedial theory "is rights-based, and backward-looking, and defends exclusion as a direct response to the specific wrong committed by the police in getting the evidence".[228] Yet, unlike the deterrence theory, which

---

[220] Stefan Trechsel, *Human Rights in Criminal Proceedings*, Oxford University Press, 2005) pp. 6 ff. ("An individual's reputation, financial position, personal liberty, even life [...] is at stake"); Julia Geneuss, "Obstacles to Cross-fertilisation: The International Criminal Tribunals' 'Unique Context' and the Flexibility of the European Court of Human Rights' Case Law", in *Nordic Journal of International Law*, 2015, vol. 84, no. 3, pp. 410–411.

[221] Geneuss, 2015, pp. 410–411, see above note 220.

[222] Inter–American Court of Human Rights, *Case of Velásquez Rodríguez v. Honduras*, Merits, Judgment, 29 July 1988, Series C, No. 4, para. 176:

> The State is obligated to investigate every situation involving a violation of the rights protected by the Convention. If the State apparatus acts in such a way that the violation goes unpunished and the victim's full enjoyment of such rights is not restored as soon as possible, the State has failed to comply with its duty to ensure the free and full exercise of those rights to the persons within its jurisdiction.

[223] Kamber, 2017, p. 7, see above note 218.

[224] A. Duff *et al.*, 2007, p. 229, see above note 145.

[225] *Ibid.*, p. 227.

[226] *Ibid.*

[227] See below Section 17.5.2.3.2.3.1.

[228] HO, 2019, p. 824, see above note 189.

---

focuses on deterring the police's illegal behaviours, the theory of remedies concentrates on the vindication of rights of defendants suffered from an illegal investigation.[229] It is thus an all-or-nothing theory that leaves considerable room for balancing.[230] Furthermore, the remedy rationale has a correlation problem: critics argue that there is no correlation between the wrongdoing (police misconduct) and its legal consequence (exclusion of evidence up an acquittal of the accused).[231] It is argued that other remedies seem more convincing: disciplinary measures against the public official, the application of substantive criminal law to the person who violated the right of the suspect,[232] and so on.[233]

17.5.2.2.3. Integrity from Context Perspective: The Integrity of the Process

When evidence is wrongfully obtained, its exclusion is also justified by reference to integrity, with increasing popularity[234] (at least amongst common law systems). In the words of Peter Duff: "the justification for excluding improperly obtained evidence cannot – and should not – be based on 'internal' concerns about the reliability of the evidence but must be based on 'external' concerns relating to the integrity of the process and the broader public interest".[235] However, the utilisation of integrity varies.

---

[229] Roberts and Hunter, 2012, p. 121, see above note 192. See especially Andrew Ashworth, "Excluding Evidence as Protecting Rights", in *Criminal Law Review*, 1977, p. 723.

[230] LIU, 2019, p. 50, see above note 198.

[231] Zuckerman, 1987, p. 58, see above note 194:

> In a criminal trial exclusion of evidence of guilt amounts to a contribution towards the acquittal of a person who may be guilty. It is by no means self-evident that acquittal of the guilty is an appropriate response to earlier police transgressions. Nor is a blanket exclusion capable of achieving a balance between the seriousness of the infringement and the benefit to the accused.

[232] "There are far stronger grounds for punishing an officer who deliberately broke the rules or tricked the accused than where there has been mere inadvertence", P. Duff, 2004, p. 161, see above note 193.

[233] See also *ibid.*, p. 164.

[234] *Ibid.*, p. 171.

[235] *Ibid.*, p. 159.

17.5.2.2.3.1. Integrity as Moral Authority of the Verdict and Integrity as Legitimacy

One argument is that wrongfully obtained evidence endangers the moral authority of the verdict.[236] It is concerned with the "determination of moral blame, as well as of legal liability, which may in turn justify the infliction of suffering and humiliation on an individual".[237] The argument usually appears under different names: it may also be labelled the theory of fair trial or (moral) legitimacy[238] of the trial.[239] Legitimacy, in this sense,

> refers to a larger concept, of which factual accuracy is a major part, but which includes additional notions of moral authority and expressive value. In essence, legitimacy signifies an aspiration that an adjudicative decision should as far as possible be factually accurate and also consistent with other fundamental moral and political values embedded in the legal system. The objective is that the decision should claim not only to be factually accurate, thus fulfilling the truthfinding aim of the legal process, but also to be morally authoritative, and to express the value of the rule of law.[240]

I will address these elements in detail in the course of this chapter. One aspect of this argument is the hypothesis that the public would hold a critical attitude towards the fairness of the trial, and argue that the courts fail to uphold procedural justice if wrongfully obtained evidence would be admitted in every case and without scrutiny.[241] This is, at the same time, the legitimacy aspect of the argument: the government "is to have legitimacy in the sense of drawing (and being deserving of) public confidence and respect".[242] This legitimacy argument has been the driving force behind exclusionary rules in the US prior to the advancement of the deterrence theo-

---

[236] Roberts and Hunter, 2012, p. 121, see above note 192.

[237] Zuckerman, 1987, p. 56, see above note 194.

[238] In detail, see Dennis, 2020, mn. 2-022, see above note 192.

[239] LIU, 2019, p. 46, see above note 198.

[240] Dennis, 2020, mn. 2-022, see above note 192.

[241] Zuckerman, 1987, p. 56, see above note 194; Roberts and Zuckerman, 2010, p. 16, see above note 192; LIU, 2019, p. 45, see above note 198; P. Duff, 2004, p. 155, see above note 193: "[M]ost people would agree that it would not reflect well upon a criminal justice system if it were prepared to admit incriminating statements which had been tortured out of the accused by the police".

[242] HO, 2019, p. 830, see above note 189.

ry.[243] As HO puts it: "To preserve judicial legitimacy, and to avoid being tainted by the executive's dirty hands, the court has to renounce and disassociate itself from the police illegality by refusing to accept and act on the product of the illegality".[244] In the Rothman case before the Supreme Court of Canada,[245] Judges Laskin and Estey stated in their dissent:

> The basic reason for the exclusionary confession rule is a concern for the integrity of the criminal justice system. The support and respect of the community for that system can only be maintained if persons in authority conduct themselves in a way that does not bring the administration of justice into disrepute.[246]

The consideration of the public attitude is a double-edged sword: it appears doubtful that the public, especially the victims, would accept the decision of excluding key evidence only due to a relatively minor violation of legal procedure. Thus, the argument of legitimacy allows for a considerable exercise of balancing. The theory of fair trial is an important basis of the exclusionary rule in England. Section 78 (1) of the Police and Criminal Evidence Act 1984 stipulates that

> In any proceedings the court may refuse to allow evidence on which the prosecution proposes to rely to be given if it appears to the court that, having regard to all the circumstances, including the circumstances in which the evidence was obtained, the admission of the evidence would have such an adverse effect on the fairness of the proceedings that the court ought not to admit it.

Amongst the rationales of exclusionary rules, the moral legitimacy rationale receives increasing popularity,[247] while it carries some inherent dangers: "public opinion in these matters is likely to mirror the 'populist

---

[243] *Ibid.*

[244] *Ibid.*, with further references.

[245] Canada, Supreme Court, *Rothman v. The Queen*, [1981] 1 SCR 640 (available on its web site).

[246] *Ibid.*, p. 642.

[247] P. Duff, 2004, p. 173, see above note 193: "A further response might be that the moral legitimacy rationale provides a better explanation of what it is that the courts actually do, even if they do not always fully recognise or articulate their reasoning".

punitiveness' expressed in the tabloid press and by 'law and order' politicians".[248]

17.5.2.2.3.2. Integrity as Reliability

The rational that provides most flexibility is the reliability theory: evidence may be unreliable because of how it was obtained.[249] See, for instance, Section 76(2)(b) of the Police and Criminal Evidence Act of 1984 reads:

> If, in any proceedings where the prosecution proposes to give in evidence a confession made by an accused person, it is represented to the court that the confession was or may have been obtained [...] in consequence of anything said or done which was likely, in the circumstances existing at the time, to render unreliable any confession which might be made by him in consequence thereof, the court shall not allow the confession to be given in evidence against him except in so far as the prosecution proves to the court beyond reasonable doubt that the confession (notwithstanding that it may be true) was not obtained as aforesaid.[250]

Two aspects render the reliability rationale an integrity concept: First, excluding evidence that has been wrongfully obtained would advance the search for truth, since the use of unreliable evidence "increases the risk of error in fact-finding".[251] As previously argued, the search for truth is a means to the end of justice and thus a vital part of the integrity of a trial. Second, a guilty verdict that is based on unreliable evidence is an unfair verdict.[252] An unfair verdict lacks – as already mentioned – legitimacy. Accordingly, the reliability and legitimacy theory are intertwined. The connection between reliability and fairness is also underlined by the European

---

[248] *Ibid.*, p. 175, citing Ashworth, 2003, p. 111, see above note 187. P. Duff borrows the term "public punitiveness" from Anthony Bottoms, "The philosophy and politics of punishment and sentencing", in Chris Clarkson and Rod Morgan (eds.), *The Politics of Sentencing Reform*, Clarendon Press, Oxford, 1995, pp. 39–41.

[249] Roberts and Hunter, 2012, p. 121, see above note 192.

[250] UK, Police and Criminal Evidence Act 1984, 31 October 1984, s. 78 (https://www.legal-tools.org/doc/b52ec0/). Emphasis added.

[251] HO, 2019, p. 828, see above note 189; P. Duff, 2004, p. 154, see above note 193: "The first reason for excluding evidence is the fear that it may adversely affect the accuracy of the outcome of the trial. This may be because the evidence is, quite simply, inherently unreliable or because the evidence, even if factually accurate, is likely for other reasons to distort the decision-making process, thus affecting the reliability of the outcome".

[252] HO, 2019, p. 832, see above note 189.

Court of Human Rights in the *Gäfgen* case, where evidence was obtained by way of torture:[253]

> [T]he quality of the evidence must be taken into consideration, as must the circumstances in which it was obtained and whether these circumstances cast doubts on its reliability or accuracy. While no problem of fairness necessarily arises where the evidence obtained was unsupported by other material, it may be noted that where the evidence is very strong and there is no risk of its being unreliable, the need for supporting evidence is correspondingly weaker.[254]

17.5.2.2.3.3. Integrity as Rule of Law

Especially in legal systems relying on the civil law tradition, one of the main rationales for excluding or not admitting evidence is the rule of law principle. Displaying all the different meanings of this principle goes beyond the scope of this chapter. One of the earlier and more prominent definitions[255] is provided by Dicey, who assigns to the rule of law "at least three distinct though kindred conceptions":[256] First,

> that no man is punishable or can be lawfully made to suffer in body or goods except for a distinct breach of law established in the ordinary legal manner before the ordinary courts of the land. In this sense the rule of law is contrasted with every system of government based on the exercise by persons in authority of wide, arbitrary, or discretionary powers of constraint.[257]

Second,

---

[253] European Court of Human Rights, *Gäfgen v. Germany*, Judgment, 1 June 2010, 22978/05; John D. Jackson and Sarah J. Summers, *The Internationalisation of Criminal Evidence*, Cambridge University Press, Cambridge *et al.*, 2012, p. 158; Jamil Ddamulira Mujuzi, "The Admissibility of Confessions and Real Evidence Obtained in Violation of Human Rights in Criminal Trials in European Countries: Analysing the Jurisprudence of the European Court of Human Rights", in *European Criminal Law Review*, 2019, vol. 9, no. 3, pp. 340–345.

[254] *Gäfgen v. Germany*, 2010, para. 164, see above note 253.

[255] It should be stressed, though, that the concept of a Rule of Law goes back to Plato and Aristotle, see in more detail the account of Erhard Denninger, "Rechtsstaat", in *id.* and Klaus Lüderssen (eds.), *Polizei und Strafprozeß im demokratischen Rechtsstaat*, Suhrkamp, Frankfurt a.M., 1978, pp. 67–72.

[256] Albert Venn Dicey, *Introduction to the Study of the Law of the Constitution*, tenth edition, MacMillan, London, 1886 (reproduced in 1979), pp. 188 ff.

[257] Dicey, 1886 and 1979, p. 188, see above note 256.

> that here every man, whatever be his rank or condition, is sub-
> ject to the ordinary law of the realm and amenable to the ju-
> risdiction of the ordinary tribunals.[258]

The two elements described so far can certainly be named as the two main elements of the rule of law, independent of the legal system.[259] The third element is one that needs to be read against the historical context:

> There remains yet a third and a different sense in which the
> 'rule of law' or the predominance of the legal spirit may be
> described as a special attribute of English institutions. We may
> say that the constitution is pervaded by the rule of law on the
> ground that the general principles of the constitution (as for
> example the right to personal liberty, or the right of public
> meeting) are with us the result of judicial decisions determin-
> ing the rights of private persons in particular cases brought be-
> fore the courts [...].[260]

Defining the rule of law principle is not only beyond the scope of this chapter, but it is also methodologically questionable.[261] I follow MacCormick, student of H.L.A. Hart, in his seminal account of the meanings of the terms 'rule of law' and '*Rechtsstaatsprinzip*':[262] Every attempt to define terms like this is problematic, since they are neither open to a descriptive analysis nor a conventional determination. Instead, such an attempt needs to take account of the historical context, translated into a normative princi-

---

[258] *Ibid.*, p. 193.

[259] Erhard Denninger, "'Rechtsstaat' oder 'Rule of Law' – was ist das heute?", in Cornelius Prittwitz *et al.* (eds.), *Festschrift für Klaus Lüderssen*, Nomos, Baden-Baden, 2002, p. 43.

[260] Dicey, 1886 and 1979, p. 193, see above note 256.

[261] See also Matthias Klatt, "Der Begriff des Rechtsstaats", in Eric Hilgendorf and Jan C. Joerden (eds.), *Handbuch Rechtsphilosophie*, J.B. Metzler, Stuttgart, 2017, pp. 390 ff.; Eberhard Schmidt-Aßmann, "§ 26 – Der Rechtsstaat", in Josef Isensee and Paul Kirchhof (ed.), *Handbuch des Staatsrechts der Bundesrepublik Deutschland, Bd. II: Verfassungsstaat*, C.F. Müller, Heidelberg 2004, mn. 1.

[262] Neil MacCormick, *Questioning Sovereignty*, Oxford University Press, Oxford, 1999-2002, p. 43. About the difference between rule of law and Rechtsstaatsprinzip Oliver Lepsius, *Verwaltungsrecht unter dem Common Law. Amerikanische Entwicklungen bis zum New Deal*, Mohr Siebeck, Tübingen, 1997, pp. 207 ff. Denninger stresses that Rule of Law and *Rechtsstaatsprinzip* have conceptually different roots: While the Rule of Law is political, the *Rechtsstaatsprinzip* is apolitical. In England, for instance, subjective rights have always been closely connected to a functioning process of democratic political participation. The roots of the *Rechtsstaatsprinzip*, by contrast, are a reaction to the failed attempt at democracy in 1848 and 1849 and are thus apolitical and individualistic, Denninger, 1978, p. 68, see above note 255.

---

ple.[263] The rule of law could thus well be categorised as what Popper famously labelled as one of the "mere puzzles arising out of the misuse of language".[264]

A central idea of the rule of law is that the government should be subject to and accountable under the law.[265] A core value for achieving this is the separation of powers.[266] In Germany, for instance, any State activity infringing the rights of citizens requires a clear statutory legal basis.[267] The criminal trial is an important platform in this system. The court's role is to scrutinise unlawfulness on the part of the executive – eventually to preserve the integrity of the criminal process.[268] Courts make sure that the truth in a criminal trial is not sought at any price but that there are legal limitations on ascertaining it with the constitutional rights being protected. Truth has an integrity component.[269] Thus, the executive must be prevented

---

[263] Neil MacCormick, "Der Rechtsstaat und die rule of law", in *Juristenzeitung*, 1984, p. 65 (67) (author's translation). As a result, Denninger expressly emphasizes that he attempts to "describe" the essential, i.e. functional-necessary elements of the "invention" rule of law, which is supposed to be ahistorical, see Denninger, 2002, p. 43, see above note 259 ("Der folgende Versuch einer Beschreibung der 'wesentlichen', das heißt funktionsnatwendigen Elemente der ,Erfindung' rule of law ist also auf die Bewältigung gegen— wärtiger und absehbarer zukünftiger Probleme gerichtet. Er ist damit bewusst „unhistorisch" […]."). Klatt recognises three phases of the development of a Rechtsstaat-definition, see in more detail Klatt, 2017, pp. 390 ff., see above note 261.

[264] Karl Popper, *Unended Quest*, Routledge, London and New York, 2005, p. 11.

[265] Friedrich August von Hayek, *The Road to Serfdom*, Dymock's Book Arcade, Sydney, 1944, p. 54; Roberts and Zuckerman, 2010, p. 17, see above note 192.

[266] Ralf Dreier, "Der Rechtsstaat im Spannungsverhältnis zwischen Gesetz und Recht", in *Juristenzeitung*, 1985, vol. 40, no. 8, p. 353.

[267] See German Federal Constitutional Court, Judgment of 12 Apr. 2005 – 2 BvR 581/01 = BVerfGE 112, 304, 315 for the area of criminal procedure, and generally German Federal Constitutional Court, Judgment of 21 Dec. 1977 – 1 BvL 1/75, 1 BvR 147/75 = BVerfGE 47, 46, 78–9; Thaman and Brodowski, 2020, p. 429, see above note 196.

[268] See Pitcher, 2018, p. 117, see above note 192.

[269] Richard L. Lippke, "Fundamental Values of Criminal Procedure", in Darryl K. Brown *et al.* (eds.), *The Oxford Handbook of Criminal Process*, Oxford University Press, Oxford, 2019, p. 31:

I believe that it is useful to identify two subsidiary values in the service of truth. The first is integrity, according to which the various state agents tasked with arresting, investigating, and charging individuals with crimes, and seeing to the adjudication of charges, must respect and consistently abide by procedures that are reliable and evidence-driven.

"from using evidence that it had acquired unlawfully to support a criminal prosecution".[270]

Ideally, the 'law' in 'rule of law' incorporates the integrity rationale: that is, the moral authority of the verdict, legitimacy, fair trial and reliability. As Finnis famously pointed out, the rule of law "is to secure to the subjects of authority the dignity of self-direction and freedom from certain forms of manipulation. The rule of law is thus among the requirements of justice or fairness".[271] Hence, when the Court of Appeals in England and Wales held that a criminal prosecution should have been stayed when the accused had been entrapped by State agents into committing the offence for which he or she was standing trial, the rationale resembles the rationales mentioned above:

> [T]he judicial response to entrapment is based on the need to uphold the rule of law. A defendant is excused, not because he is less culpable, although he may be, but because the police have behaved improperly. Police conduct which brings about, to use the catch-phrase, state-created crime is unacceptable and improper. To prosecute in such circumstances would be an affront to the public conscience [...]. In a very broad sense of the word, such a prosecution would not be fair.[272]

The main similarity between the rule of law and integrity, however, is coherence.[273] Thus, when the separation of powers is identified as the most prominent element of the rule of law, it merely describes the means to an end, that is, the coherence of the law and its application.[274] At the same time, integrity complements the rule of law. An authoritarian regime that makes sure that the law is applied correctly, basically ensures legality, but not the rule of law. As MacCormick rightly points out, the rule of law can never be fully implemented by positive law.[275] MacCormick's reasons as follows: First, the rule of law is the formal guideline ("formale Leitlinie")

---

[270] See, for example, HO Hock Lai, "The Criminal Trial, the Rule of Law and the Exclusion of Unlawfully Obtained Evidence", in *Criminal Law and Philosophy*, 2016, vol. 10, no. 1, p. 109; HO, 2019, p. 833, see above note 189.

[271] John Finnis, *Natural Law and Natural Rights*, second edition, Oxford University Press, 2011, p. 273.

[272] United Kingdom, House of Lords ('UK HL'), *R v. Looseley*, [2001] UKHL 53, [2001] WLR 2060.

[273] See also Klatt, 2017, pp. 391–392, see above note 261, with further references.

[274] See already MacCormick, 1984, p. 69, see above note 263.

[275] *Ibid.* (author's translation).

of a rational practice of law on both the level of legislation and adjudication. This guideline is the direct result of the demand that legal norms are both enacted and applied according to the requirement of 'reasonableness', regardless of the acceptance of their actual content.[276] Second, the rule of law is closer to the natural law[277] than to the positive law and is thus customary law.[278] This interpretation of the rule of law might be the result of MacCormick's affinity for the common law tradition, what he admits when referring to Dicey's elements of the rule of law mentioned above. The natural law dimension of the rule of law principle is indeed a neuralgic point that caused some controversy.[279] For the purpose of this chapter, it suffices to say that this dimension is in fact due to the element of integrity that lies within the rule of law. Consequently, a positivist understanding of the rule of law,[280] or at least the full rejection of its naturalistic connotation, is hard to reconcile with the element of integrity as I defined it earlier (coherence, moral authority, legitimacy, fairness). In this vein, Denninger opines that 'law' in the rule of law is comprised of the two elements, rationality and normativity,[281] which corresponds with Fuller's "inner morality of law". The "inner morality of law" is defined by the "congruence between official action and the law".[282] The element of congruence is the common denominator of morality and integrity. Thus, Fuller explains:

---

[276] *Ibid.*: "Zum einen sind sie [die Prinzipien der Rechtstaatlichkeit] formale Leitlinien einer vernünftigen Rechtspraxis auf Gesetzes- und Gesetzesanwendungsebene; sie gebe der Forderung Ausdruck, daß Rechtsnormen unabhängig von der Akteptabilität ihrer Inhalte in Übereinstimmung mit den Erfordernissen von formal verstandener 'reasonableness' erlassen und angewandt werden müssen" (author's translation).

[277] In fact, MacCormick uses the term "überpositives Vernunftrecht". About the difference between Naturrecht and überpositivem Recht, Frank Dietrich, "Rechtsbegriffe", in Eric Hilgendorf and Jan C. Joerden (eds.), *Handbuch Rechtsphilosophie*, J.B. Metzler, Stuttgart, 2017, p. 2 (6).

[278] MacCormick, 1984, p. 69, see above note 263: "Zum anderen sind diese Prinzipien eher dem überpositiven Vernunftrecht als dem geschriebenen Recht zugehörig – einem Vernunftrecht, wie es die Rechtsphilosophie und Staatslehre im Laufe der Jahrhunderte in kritischer Auseinandersetzung mit bestehenden Rechtsordnungen entwickelt haben. Insofern sind sie gewohnheitsrechtlich verankert" (author's translation).

[279] For references see *ibid.*

[280] In this vein, see Denninger, 2002, pp. 44–45, see above note 259: "'Recht', und das heißt in einer entwickelten industriellen und postindustriellen Gesellschaft fast ausschließlich: gesetztes, 'positiviertes', damit auch änderbares Recht, also 'Gesetz'".

[281] *Ibid.*, p. 46.

[282] Lon L. Fuller, *The Morality of Law*, revised edition, Yale University Press, New Haven, 1969, p. 81.

> This congruence may be destroyed or impaired in a great variety of ways: mistaken interpretation, inaccessibility of the law, lack of insight into what is required to maintain the integrity of a legal system, bribery, prejudice, indifference, stupidity, and the drive toward personal power.[283]

Fuller also explicitly mentions integrity as fairness:

> Just as the threats toward this congruence are manifold, so the procedural devices designed to maintain it take, of necessity, a variety of forms. We may count here most of the elements of 'procedural due process,' such as the right to representation by counsel and the right of cross-examining adverse witnesses.[284]

In addition to Fuller's account, MacCormick adds – among other things – "reasonable consistency among laws (for contradictory laws afford no real guidance)".[285] Applied to actors such as the police or prosecutors, there is thus "an expectation of consistency in the attitudes" they display.[286] Fuller's eight principles of the rule of law are developed further by Finnis and Raz, including the principle of proportionality.[287]

Finally, the formal understanding of the rule of law (consistency, coherence, and so forth) is supplemented by a substantive element.[288] As MacCormick points out with reference to Kelsen:

> Where there is a constitutional separation of powers, with checks and controls on arbitrary discretion, and a requirement that government be conducted under clear and pre-announced laws, and above all when these laws include a justiciable catalogue of fundamental rights that limit governmental power, the *Rechtsstaat* in a substantive, not merely a formal sense, exists.[289]

---

[283] *Ibid.*

[284] *Ibid.*

[285] MacCormick, 1999 and 2002, p. 45, see above note 262.

[286] HO, 2016, pp. 119–120, see above note 270.

[287] Joseph Raz, *The Authority of Law – Essays on Law and Morality*, Oxford University Press, 1979, pp. 208 ff.; Finnis, 2011, pp. 270 ff., see above note 271; Klatt, 2017, pp. 391–392, see above note 261; Schmidt-Aßmann, 2004, mn. 4, see above note 261.

[288] Cf. Hasso Hofmann, "Geschichtlichkeit und Universalitätsanspruch des Rechtsstaats", in *Der Staat*, 1995, vol. 34, no. 1, p. 1 (12); Schmidt-Aßmann, 2004, mn. 19, see above note 261; Klatt, 2017, p. 391, see above note 261.

[289] MacCormick, 1999 and 2002, p. 43, see above note 262.

In other words, the rule of law incorporates basic civil and political rights.[290] It protects the dignity, integrity and moral equality of persons and groups.[291] Dworkin's theory of law as 'integrity' goes into the same direction, reflecting a broad and substantive conception of the rule of law,[292] so does Habermas' *Diskurstheorie*.[293] Thus, the substantive element of the rule of law combines the two dimensions of integrity: the systemic dimension and the deontological. It also includes the remedy rationale of exclusionary rules.[294]

17.5.2.2.4. Intermediate Conclusion

In this section, I have displayed the rationales for the exclusion of evidence illegally obtained by State officials to answer the question whether integrity should be the value that provides guidance for a private individual conducting an investigation. Within these rationales, I have identified the role of integrity and connected it to the three perspectives of integrity introduced at the outset of the section. The 'remedy rationale' corresponds with the 'object perspective', the 'deterrence rationale' with the 'subject perspective' and the 'integrity of the process rationale' with the 'context perspective'. The latter has three variants: integrity as moral authority of the verdict and integrity as legitimacy; integrity as reliability; and integrity as the rule of law. Integrity as the rule of law may incorporate all other elements

---

[290] *Ibid.*, p. 46. Critically Raz, 1979, pp. 208 ff., see above note 287; Ernst-Wolfgang Böckenförde, "Grundrechte als Grundsatznormen – Zur gegenwärtigen Lage der Grundrechtsdogmatik", in Ernst-Wolfgang Böckenförde (ed.), *Staat, Verfassung, Demokratie. Studien zur Verfassungstheorie und zum Verfassungsrecht*, Suhrkamp, Frankfurt a. M., 1991, pp. 190, 197 ff.

[291] Martin Krygier, "Rule of Law (and *Rechtsstaat*)", in James R. Silkenat, James E. Hickey, Jr., and Peter D. Barenboim (eds.), *The Legal Doctrines of the Rule of Law and the Legal State (Rechtsstaat)*, Springer, Cham, 2014, p. 52.

[292] Ronald Dworkin, *Law's Empire*, The Belknap Press of Harvard University Press, Cambridge, Massachusetts, 1986, 176 ff. See also T.R.S. Allan, "Freedom, Equality, Legality", in James R. Silkenat, James E. Hickey, Jr., and Peter D. Barenboim (eds.), *The Legal Doctrines of the Rule of Law and the Legal State (Rechtsstaat)*, Springer, Cham, 2014, p. 155 (169). In the same vein, see Jürgen Habermas, *Faktizität und Geltung*, fourth edition, Suhrkamp, Frankfurt am Main, 1994, p. 272: "Denn der Gesichtspunkt der Integrität, unter dem der Richter das geltende Recht rational rekonstruiert, ist Ausdruck einer rechtsstaatlichen Idee, die die Rechtsprechung zusammen mit dem politischen Gesetzgeber dem Gründungsakt der Verfassung und der Praxis der am Verfassungsprozeß beteiligten Staatsbürger *bloß entlehnt*" (emphasis in the original).

[293] *Ibid.*, p. 250.

[294] See above Section 17.5.2.2.2.

---

of the 'context perspective', namely, the moral authority of the verdict, legitimacy (fair trial) and reliability. The natural law dimension of the rule of law is crucial for this umbrella function.

17.5.2.3. The Role of Integrity in Illegally Obtaining Evidence in a Private Investigation

The distinction between the various perspectives mentioned above – put differently: the individual-collective approach[295] – can be upheld on the international level, albeit not without a determination of preceding issues. Those issues are the nature of investigations under consideration in this chapter and the different notions of fairness.

17.5.2.3.1. Investigatory Contexts

It lies within the nature of international criminal proceedings that the roots of certain pieces of information can be traced back to other investigatory contexts. This investigatory context can be non-existent – this is the situation this chapter is about: a private individual collects evidence that is then offered to an ICT. The evaluation of the context as 'non-existent' stems from the (albeit semantic, not necessarily conceptual) premise that an investigation is always conducted by State authorities, while a private person could only conduct an 'examination'[296] or make an 'inquiry'.[297] What seems to be a tempting way to separate already, through semantics and taxonomy, the collection of evidence by a State actor on the one hand, and by a private person on the other hand, is problematic in two ways. First, the solution of conceptual puzzles through semantics and taxonomy has always an arbitrary after taste. In other words, the problem is merely shifted to another level. Second, as I will demonstrate, a systemic understanding of 'in-

---

[295] Ambos, 2009, p. 366, see above note 191.

[296] In this vein, see Nienaber, 2019, pp. 47–48, see above note 97.

[297] In this vein, see Ulrich Eisenberg, *Beweisrecht der StPO – Spezialkommentar*, tenth edition, C.H. Beck, München, 2017, mn. 395 ("Nachforschungen"). De Vries provides a rather broad interpretation of term 'investigation' that seems to be based on the functional reading of decisions of regional human rights courts, albeit ignoring the procedural context of the decisions, see De Vries, 2019, p. 605, see above note 1 ("capable of leading to the identification and punishment of those responsible"). For a definition of the term "fact-finding" – albeit from an epistemological perspective and not from an institutional one – Simon De Smet, "Justified Belief in the Unbelievable", in Morten Bergsmo and Carsten Stahn (eds.), *Quality Control in Fact-Finding*, second edition, TOAEP, Brussels, 2020, pp. 83 ff. Several forms of fact-finding exercises are listed by Robertson, 2020, pp. 480–482, see above note 5.

vestigation' can and even must include the conduct of everyone acting within that system, namely, both State and private actors.

Moreover, the context can also be a domestic investigation, for example, evidence obtained legally under domestic law would be obtained illegally under the law of the ICT; entrapment by a law enforcement official of another jurisdiction[298] – or even an international investigation, where a third party working for an organ of the respective ICT (UN peace-keeping forces, for instance) obtains evidence through illegal means. I will call these contexts the inter-investigatory context (international investigation – domestic investigation); the intra-investigatory context (internal investigation by a private individual or another third actor); and the extra-investigatory context (collection of evidence by a private individual outside any ICT-investigation). Spatial restrictions dictate a dietary approach to those contexts.

17.5.2.3.1.1. The Inter-Investigatory Context

The inter-investigatory context has indeed been dealt with by ICTs in the past when national authorities obtained evidence in violation of the suspect's rights applicable before the Tribunals. In one instance, at the trial against *Mucić*, the Defence contended that Austrian authorities denied then suspect Mucić the right to counsel, the right to remain silent, and induced him to make a confession.[299] At that time, Austrian law did not provide for a right to counsel during questioning, which the ICTY evaluated as "not strange and not in violation of fundamental human rights or the European Convention on human rights".[300] I will go into the relevant provisions on a possible exclusion or admission of the evidence in a moment. Right now, for the description of the inter-investigatory context it suffices to say that the ICTY felt – unsurprisingly – that it was not bound by the law of a different investigatory context.[301] It is in the discretion of the Chamber, though, whether it "may apply such rules".[302] As a result, the Trial Cham-

---

[298] A. Duff *et al.*, 2007, p. 242, see above note 145.

[299] ICTY, *Prosecutor v. Delalić et al.*, Trial Chamber, Decision on Zdravko Mucic's Motion for the Exclusion of Evidence, 2 September 1997, IT-96-21-T, para. 8 ('Delalić *et al.*') (https://www.legal-tools.org/doc/afbced/). See also the analysis in Pitcher, 2018, p. 289, see above note 192.

[300] Delalić *et al.*, 1997, para. 46, see above note 299.

[301] *Ibid.*, para. 49: "The Trial Chamber is not bound by national rules of evidence – Sub-rule 89(A)".

[302] *Ibid.*

ber held that the Austrian procedure was in breach of the right to counsel according to Article 18(3) ICTY Statute and therefore the statement before the police was inadmissible at trial.[303] A similar situation occurred before the ICTR. On 15 April 1996, the authorities of Cameroon arrested and detained Barayagwiza and several other suspects on suspicion of having committed genocide and crimes against humanity in Rwanda in 1994.[304] Barayagwiza later argued that his pre-trial detention in Cameroon was excessive and that he was not promptly informed of the charges brought against him. This rendered his otherwise lawful arrest unlawful and constituted an obstacle to the Tribunal's personal jurisdiction on the basis of the "abuse of process doctrine".[305]

In the ICC Statute, the inter-investigatory context was taken into account via Article 69(8): "When deciding on the relevance or admissibility of evidence collected by a State, the Court shall not rule on the application of the State's national law". The provision clarifies a rather simple insight: that the ICC is supposed to apply its own law when deciding upon the admissibility of evidence.[306] Article 69(8) is thus a concretisation of Article 10: "Nothing in this Part shall be interpreted as limiting or prejudicing in any way existing or developing rules of international law for purposes other than this Statute". On its face, the provision applies to Part 2 of the Statute, namely, Articles 5–21.[307] Nevertheless, the drafting process of the provision indicates that it may also apply to Articles outside Part 2.[308] And since it includes Article 21, it certainly applies when internationally recognised human rights are concerned. Even though Article 10 exists to clarify that the Statute does not bar outside development, it cuts both ways and also stresses the differences between the text in the Statute and other instruments, including national law.[309] The purpose of Article 10 appears as a kind of reservation clause and clarifies that all articles in Part 2 are limited

---

[303] *Ibid.*, para. 52.

[304] International Criminal Tribunal for Rwanda ('ICTR'), *Prosecutor v. Barayagwiza*, Decision, 3 November 1999, ICTR-97-19-AR72, Introduction, para. 5 ('Barayagwiza decision') (https://www.legal-tools.org/doc/ee7411/).

[305] *Ibid.*, Introduction, paras. 13 *et seq.*

[306] Pitcher, 2018, p. 325, see above note 192.

[307] Alexander Heinze, "Article 10", in Kai Ambos (ed.), *Rome Statute of the International Criminal Court – A Commentary*, fourth edition, C.H. Beck, Hart, Nomos, München *et al.*, 2021, p. 775, mn. 16.

[308] *Ibid.*, mn. 12.

[309] *Ibid.*, p. 655, mn. 16.

to the purpose of building an agreement between the States Parties and shall have no binding effect going beyond the subject matter and the scope of the Statute and the State Party's agreements.[310] The Statutes for the ICTY and the ICTR are without a corresponding regulation.

The inter-investigatory context at the ICC played a role in the case against *Katanga and Ngudjolo*: the Defence argued that one of Katanga's statements was taken in violation of his right to remain silent, "insofar as it is alleged that Mr Katanga was not informed of his right to have counsel present during the interrogation" and pointed out "that Mr Katanga had such a right under the Statute, under existing norms of internationally recognized human rights and under the Constitution of the DRC".[311] As a result, the Defence claimed that "the admission of the *procès-verbal* would be antithetical to, and would seriously damage, the integrity of the proceedings".[312] Drawing on Article 69(7) , the Chamber emphasised "that the provisions of the DRC Constitution cannot apply in the context of admissibility decisions" and that

> the violation has to impact on international, as opposed to national, standards on human rights. [...] Therefore, evidence obtained in breach of national procedural laws, even though those rules may implement national standards protecting human rights, does not automatically trigger the application of Article 69(7) of the Statute.[313]

17.5.2.3.1.2. The Intra-Investigatory and Extra-Investigatory Context

Evidence collected by private individuals that enters a trial before ICTs may involve both the intra-investigatory and the extra-investigatory contexts. In the former, there is a perceived attribution of the private individual to an organ of the ICT (usually the OTP). That may occur rather openly through the utilisation of the individual in the collection process, that is, *ab initio*; or through an *ex post*-attribution, when the individual acted in the

---

[310] *Ibid.*, p. 648, mn. 6.

[311] ICC, *Prosecutor v. Katanga and Ngudjolo*, Decision on the Prosecutor's Bar Table Motions, 17 December 2010, ICC-01/04-01/07-2635, para. 55 (fn. omitted) ('Katanga and Ngudjolo, 2010') (https://www.legal-tools.org/doc/7710b6/).

[312] *Ibid.*, para. 56 (fn. omitted, emphasis in the original).

[313] *Ibid.*, para. 58 (fn. omitted).

interest of the organ.[314] In the latter, the person acts independently of a tribunal organ and outside an investigation. As described at the outset of this chapter, the extra-investigatory context is of relevance for the purpose of the chapter.[315]

17.5.2.3.1.2.1. Procedural Rules and the Extra-Investigatory Context

The particularity here lies in the lack of an investigatory context and the ensuing lack of rules that regulate the collection of evidence in such a context. But let us pause for a moment here: the lack of investigatory rules in an extra-investigatory context is not as clear as it seems at first sight. First, as already mentioned,[316] legislators may decide to regulate private conduct in an extra-investigatory context. Second, the inapplicability of procedural rules to private conduct requires an explanation. It goes to nothing less than the question of whom procedural rules are addressed to. The source of exclusionary rules can be constitutions, codes or case law, and, in the words of Thaman and Brodowski, "can be formulated in absolute terms, strictly requiring the exclusion of any evidence gathered in violation of 'the law' or of certain constitutional or fundamental rights, or can be formulated so as to allow judges discretion in deciding whether to admit or exclude illegally gathered evidence".[317] Take, for instance, § 136a(3) cl. 2 of the German Code of Criminal Procedure (*Strafprozessordnung*, 'StPO'), barring the use of evidence obtained through prohibited methods of examination (such as "physical interference, administration of drugs, torment, deception or hypnosis").

Already in 1952 the German Higher Regional Court (*Oberlandesgericht*, 'OLG') of Oldenburg decided that § 136a StPO only addressed State organs.[318] This is also the prevailing view in German legal litera-

---

[314] German scholars want to apply exclusionary rules when the private investigation was initiated by a state organ, see Martina Matula, *Private Ermittlungen*, Kovac, Hamburg, 2012, p. 101 with further references.

[315] About the intra-investigatory context: P. Duff, 2004, pp. 163–164, see above note 193, with case examples from Scotland.

[316] See above Section 17.5.1.

[317] Thaman and Brodowski, 2020, p. 437, see above note 196 (fn. omitted).

[318] Higher Regional Court (*Oberlandesgericht*, 'OLG') Oldenburg, in *Neue Juristische Wochenschrift*, 1953, p. 1237; Matula, 2012, p. 97, see above note 314. The German Code of Criminal Procedure is available in the ICC Legal Tools Database (https://www.legal-tools.org/doc/wc2l2a/).

---

ture.[319] Illegally obtained evidence by private individuals can generally be admitted and is not automatically excluded.[320] The German Federal Court of Justice (*Bundesgerichtshof*, 'BGH') confirmed this view.[321] Once a private individual obtains evidence and hands it over to a State agency, the Federal Court of Justice sees no reason to exclude that evidence.[322] The Court justifies this with reference to the search for truth.[323] It does not even suggest that the illegally obtained evidence may be treated with caution or may have lower probative value, as the OLG of Oldenburg did.[324]

The question of whom procedural rules are addressed to is crucial. If addressed merely to State organs but not individuals, the exclusion of illegally obtained evidence by private individuals is harder to justify than in the latter case. Thus, it is at least surprising how quickly German courts came to the conclusion that § 136a StPO is not addressed to private individuals.

17.5.2.3.1.2.2. Addressees of Procedural Rules

The question of who is addressed by a legal text is first and foremost a question of definition. Strictly speaking, the drafters of the text determine its addressees. Yet, laws are rarely very informative when it comes to the addressees. In fact, they are rather vague. Thus, it is left to the addressees themselves to determine whether they are indeed addressed by a certain law. Unsurprisingly, attempts to determine the addressee of a law in general terms remain controversial: from the "interested lay person" (Krüger),[325] to the person affected by the law (Noll, probably the broadest category of ad-

---

[319] Rainer Gundlach, "§ 136a StPO", in Rudolf Wassermann (ed.), *Kommentar zur Strafprozessordnung*, Reihe Alternativkommentare, vol. 2.1, Luchterhand, Neuwied, 1992, mn. 13; Matula, 2012, p. 100, see above note 314, with further references; Werner Leitner, "Unternehmensinterne Ermittlungen im Konzern", in Klaus Lüderssen *et al.* (eds), *Festschrift für Wolf Schiller: zum 65 Geburtstag am 12 Januar 2014*, Nomos, Baden-Baden, 2014, p. 432.

[320] *Ibid.*, p. 97.

[321] German Federal Supreme Court, Decisions in Criminal Matters, (*Bundesgerichtshof, Entscheidungen in Strafsachen*, BGHSt), vol. 27, p. 357; vol. 34, p. 52; Matula, 2012, p. 97, see above note 314.

[322] Bundesgerichtshof ('BGH'), in *Neue Juristische Wochenschrift*, 1989, p. 843 (844); Matula, 2012, p. 97, see above note 314.

[323] BGH, 1989, p. 845, see above note 322.

[324] OLG Oldenburg, 1953, p. 1237, see above note 318; also OLG Celle, in *Neue Juristische Wochenschrift*, 1985, p. 641.

[325] Uwe Krüger, *Der Adressat des Gesetzgebers*, Duncker & Humblot, Berlin, 1969.

dressees)[326] to those who potentially 'use' the law, that is, the decision makers (Baden),[327] the arguments are manifold. Therefore, it seems more like a claim than a justified argument that an exclusionary rule – such as § 136a StPO – is directed at State organs. The larger issue that looms behind the question whom exclusionary rules are addressed to is the question of what procedural rules are (compared to rules of substantive criminal law). Space restrictions again pose limits to an in-depth-elaboration.

17.5.2.3.1.2.2.1. The Relationship Between Procedural and Substantive Law

Compared to substantive law, procedural law has famously been classified as "imperative law" *vis-à-vis* "punitory law",[328] "secondary rules" *vis-à-vis* "primary rules"[329] or as "decision rules" *vis-à-vis* "conduct rules".[330] Even today, some reduce the function of criminal procedure to merely execute substantive criminal law,[331] on the basis that substance was logically anterior to procedure.[332] However, a clear (hierarchical) division between substantive criminal law and procedure is neither possible nor desirable in a legal system.[333] It may even be viewed as a mere semantic distinction – not

---

[326] Peter Noll, *Gesetzgebungslehre*, Rowohlt, Reinbek bei Hamburg, 1973, pp. 172 ff.

[327] Eberhard Baden, *Gesetzgebung und Gesetzesanwendung im Kommunikationsprozeß*, Nomos, Baden-Baden, 1977, p. 69.

[328] Jeremy Bentham, *An Introduction to the Principles of Morals and Legislation*, Batoche Books, Kitchener, 2000 [1781], p. 241.

[329] Herbert L.A. Hart, *The Concept of Law*, second edition, Clarendon Press, Oxford, 1994, pp. 79–99.

[330] Meir Dan-Cohen, "Decision Rules and Conduct Rules: On Acoustic Separation in Criminal Law", in *Harvard Law Review*, 1984, vol. 97, no. 3, pp. 625–677.

[331] Karel De Meester, *The Investigation Phase in International Criminal Procedure* (Intersentia, Cambridge, Antwerp, Portland, 2015, p. 100; Gunther Arzt, "Der Internationale Strafgerichtshof und die formelle Wahrheit", in Jörg Arnold *et al.* (eds.), *Festschrift für Albin Eser*, C.H. Beck, München, 2005, pp. 691–692 with further references.

[332] Herbert L. Packer, "Two Models of the Criminal Process", in *University of Pennsylvania Law Review*, 1964, vol. 113, no. 1, pp. 1–69 (1, 3); Joshua Dressler, Alan C. Michaels, and Ric Simmons, *Understanding Criminal Procedure, Volume One: Investigation*, third edition, Carolina Academic Press, Durham, 2017, § 1.01.

[333] In a similar vein Heike Jung, "Anmerkungen zum Verhältnis des materiellen Strafrechts zum Strafverfahrensrecht", in *Golddammer's Archiv für Strafrecht*, 2019, pp. 259 ff. In fact, most legal systems "are more concerned about procedural rights than about rights to a substantive law", George P. Fletcher, *Basic Concepts of Criminal Law*, Oxford University Press, 1998, p. 9.

---

more and not less.[334] This is especially true at the international level, where the concept of international criminal justice is still controversial, especially amongst the Realist school.[335] Moreover, there is not even a coherent definition of "international criminal law",[336] which "has not evolved in a linear, cohesive, consistent, or logical fashion"[337] and inevitably leads to an amalgamation of international criminal law and international criminal justice. The retributive or deterrent effect of punishment in international criminal law has always been dependent on the perception of international criminal trials.[338] Another telling example of the maceration of the substance-procedure divide at the international level is the application of the principle of non-retroactivity (*nullum crimen, nulla poena sine lege praevia*)[339] to procedural rules. While at the domestic level, this rule is usually only applied to matters of substance rather than procedure,[340] the ICC Statute ex-

---

[334] Klaus Volk, *Prozeßvoraussetzungen im Strafrecht*, Verlag Rolf Gremer, Ebelsbach, 1978, p. 4.

[335] Paul Roberts, "Comparative Law for International Criminal Justice", in David Nelken and Esin Örücü (eds.), *Comparative Law – A Handbook*, Hart Publishing, Oxford and Portland, Oregon, 2007, p. 341; Andreas Werkmeister, *Straftheorien im Völkerstrafrecht*, Nomos, Baden-Baden, 2015, p. 31; M. Cherif Bassiouni, "The Discipline of International Criminal Law", in M. Cherif Bassiouni (ed.), *International Criminal Law*, vol. 1, third edition, Martinus Nijhoff, Leiden, 2008, p. 26, all with further references.

[336] Roberts, 2007, p. 342, see above note 335; Jackson and Summers, 2012, p. 112, see above note 253.

[337] Bassiouni, 2008, pp. 17–18, see above note 335.

[338] Francis Biddle, *In Brief Authority*, Greenwood Press, Westport, 1962/1972, p. 372; Patricia M. Wald, "Running the Trial of the Century", *Cardozo Law Review*, 2005–6, vol. 27, pp. 1559, 1574; Geoffrey Lawrence, "Nuremberg Trial", in Guénaël Mettraux (ed.), *Perspectives on the Nuremberg Trial*, Oxford University Press, 2008, pp. 290, 292; Margaret M. de Guzman and Timothy Kelly, "The International Criminal Court is Legitimate Enough to Deserve Support", in *Temple International and Comparative Law Journal*, 2019, vol. 33, p. 402.

[339] Claus Roxin and Luis Greco, *Strafrecht Allgemeiner Teil*, vol. 1, fifth edition, C.H. Beck, München, 2020, § 5 mn. 10.

[340] Bruce Broomhall, "Article 51", in Kai Ambos (ed.), *Rome Statute of the ICC – A Commentary*, fourth edition, C.H. Beck, Hart, Nomos, München *et al.*, 2021, pp. 1592–1613, mn. 33; Alexander Heinze, "Tor zu einer anderen Welt", in Bock *et al.* (eds), *Strafrecht als interdisziplinäre Wissenschaft* (Nomos, Baden-Baden, 2015, p. 199 with further references. A retroactive application of procedural rules is usually nevertheless prohibited through the rule of law, see *ibid.* pp. 199–200.

plicitly[341] prohibits the retroactive application of amendments to the Rules of Procedure and Evidence ('RPE').[342]

That being said, the traditional separation between substantive and procedural law (and the ensuing question of whom they are addressed to) is particularly fruitless in the face of exclusionary rules. Malcai and Levine-Schnur made this point very well: "The court's decision on a procedural question may be necessary as a logical requirement for the adjudication of the substantive issue. For example, it will never be the case that a court will announce the verdict first and then rule on the (in)admissibility of evidence on which the verdict relies".[343] This is an argument Schreiber already made in 1968: procedural rules, especially rules of evidence, have a considerable impact on the substantive issue of punishment.[344] And yet, inadmissibility due to a violation of a person's rights might still be ignored, since it is morally justified not to acquit the defendant.[345] It touches upon the balancing exercise many courts in the world carry out between the severity of the rights violation and the alleged crime the accused is charged with.[346] It also hints at the integrity and morality of a judgment as described above;[347] and

---

[341] ICC Statute, Article 51(4), see above note 182. In the same vein, but less explicit, see ICTY, Rules of Procedure and Evidence, 8 July 2015, IT/32/Rev.50, Rule 6(D) ('ICTY RPE') (https://www.legal-tools.org/doc/30df50/); ICTR, Rules of Procedure and Evidence, 13 May 2015, Rule 6(c) ('ICTR RPE') (https://www.legal-tools.org/doc/c6a7c6/) and Special Tribunal for Lebanon ('STL'), Rules of Procedure and Evidence, 20 March 2009, Rule 5(H) ('STL RPE') (https://www.legal-tools.org/doc/3773bf/). See, generally, Philipp Ambach, "The 'Lessons Learnt' process at the ICC – a suitable vehicle for procedural improvements?", in *Zeitschrift für Internationale Strafrechtsdogmatik*, 2016, vol. 11, p. 855.

[342] Albeit with the qualification "to the detriment of the person who is being investigated or prosecuted or who has been convicted" (ICC Statute, Article 51(4), see above note 182), which allows the retroactive application of amendments to the RPE in exceptional cases, as it has been passionately discussed in the context of the application of the amended Rule 68, ICC RPE ("Prior recorded testimony") in the case against *Ruto* and *Sang* before the ICC, see in more detail Kai Ambos, *Treatise on International Criminal Law: Volume III: International Criminal Procedure*, Oxford University Press, 2016, pp. 497–499.

[343] Ofer Malcai and Ronit Levine-Schnur, "When Procedure Takes Priority: A Theoretical Evaluation of the Contemporary Trends in Criminal Procedure and Evidence Law", in *Canadian Journal of Law and Jurisprudence*, 2017, vol. 30, no. 1, p. 194.

[344] Hans-Ludwig Schreiber, "Die Zulässigkeit der rückwirkenden Verlängerung von Verjährungsfristen früher begangener Delikte", in *Zeitschrift für die gesamte Strafrechtswissenschaft*, 1968, vol. 80, p. 366; see also Volk, 1978, p. 56, see above note 334.

[345] Malcai and Levine-Schnur, 2017, p. 201, see above note 343.

[346] Campbell, Ashworth, and Redmayne, 2019, pp. 42 ff., see above note 107.

[347] See above Section 17.5.2.2.3.1.

the remedy theory.[348] Malcai and Levine-Schnur call this the *"ex-post* and *ex-ante* perspectives" of "substance-procedure dilemmas", which is in the case of exclusionary rules: "creating significant incentives to avoid the violation of rights without making the substantive outcome of trial strictly conditional on the legality or constitutionality of the (probative) evidence".

German courts have addressed this dilemma by embracing it and drawing (or, at least, attempting to draw) a clear line between procedure and substance. In that line, the main reason for a rejection of any exclusionary rule in the case of private acts is a plain reference to the fact that private individuals who act illegally against other persons commit crimes.[349] Thus, there would be no need for other means of sanctions. This argument, however, cannot be transferred to the situation at hand, namely private individuals, non-official investigations, and the international context. First, because the international or transnational context makes the identification of the respective criminal offense considerably difficult. Second, and more importantly, what this view lays bare is the premise – probably influenced by German dogmatic – of a clear distinction between substantive and procedural law.[350] In reality, the argument goes like this: we have a sanction from substantive law, why apply a procedural one? This distinction, however, is not only domestically controversial, but even more at the international level, as I have shown.

17.5.2.3.1.2.2.2. Exclusionary Rules: Conduct Rules, Decision Rules or Both?

A conceptual visualisation of these dilemmas is provided by Meir Dan-Cohen's (albeit controversial)[351] distinction between "decision rules" *vis-à-vis* "conduct rules". Drawing on previous dichotomies (or, less strictly, distinctions), for Dan-Cohen there are laws addressed to the general public – the citizens – that are designed to shape people's behaviour (conduct control) and laws that are addressed to officials that provide guidelines for

---

[348] See above Section 17.5.2.2.2.

[349] Matula, 2012, p. 150, see above note 314, with further references.

[350] In that vein, see Theodor Kleinknecht, "Die Beweisverbote im Strafprozeß", in *Neue Juristische Wochenschrift*, 1966, p. 1542.

[351] See the critical comments of Kyron Huigens, Samuel W. Buell, Anne M. Coughlin, Luís Duarte d'Almeida, Adil Ahmad Hague, Eric J. Miller and Malcolm Thorburn, in Paul H. Robinson, Stephen P. Garvey and Kimberly Kessler Ferzan (eds.), *Criminal Law Conversations*, Oxford University Press, 2009, pp. 12 ff.

their decisions. The former, imply instructing the public about the required conduct and by issuing threats to secure compliance. The latter are made 'with respect' to members of the general public. They are designed to authorise, constrain, or otherwise guide officials in the wielding of the State's power ("power control"). Dan-Cohen emphasises that "communicating to legally trained officials suggests a different style than communicating to the legally untutored general public". Thus, the guidelines "may be enhanced by the use of a technical, esoteric terminology that is incomprehensible to the public at large".

Taking these characteristics of decision rules together, on its face, rules of procedure and evidence fall into the category of decision rules, "on the grounds that they concern the basis for the legal conduct of trials as interpreted by judges and lawyers".[352] If this were the case, procedural rules would not be addressed to private individuals. Yet, this general observation might be ill-suited for exclusionary rules, since those do regulate conduct. The question is whether exclusionary rules are addressed to public officials, regardless of their conduct regulation – in that case, they are decision rules, or whether they regulate a conduct, regardless of their nature as procedural rules that generally address public officials – in that case, they are conduct rules. To be fair, upon application of Dan-Cohen's theoretical model, the characteristics of exclusionary rules overwhelmingly seem to point in the direction of decision rules. Yet, Dan-Cohen himself admits that his dichotomy is theoretical, and unfolds in a more nuanced fashion in the 'real world'. Thus, the question of whether exclusionary rules are conduct rules or decision rules might not have a clear answer after all. As Dan-Cohen puts it: "Any given rule may be a conduct rule, a decision rule, or both. The mere linguistic form in which a legal rule is cast does not determine the category to which it belongs".[353]

A central element for the differing appearance of both conduct rules and decision rules is what Dan-Cohen calls "acoustic separation", which – at least theoretically – "ensures that conduct rules cannot, as such, affect decisions; similarly, decision rules cannot, as such, influence conduct".[354] This is different in the real world:

---

[352] A. Duff *et al.*, 2007, p. 276, see above note 145.

[353] Meir Dan-Cohen, "Decision Rules and Conduct Rules – On Acoustic Separation in Criminal Law", in Paul H. Robinson, Stephen P. Garvey, Kimberly Kessler Ferzan (eds.), *Criminal Law Conversations*, Oxford University Press, 2009, p. 4.

[354] *Ibid.*, p. 4.

> Here, officials are aware of the system's conduct rules and may take them into account in making decisions, and individuals may consider decision rules in shaping their conduct. Real-world decision rules are accordingly likely to have conduct side effects, and real-world conduct rules are likely to have decisional side effects.[355]

This is true with (real world) exclusionary rules: they are addressed to the courts as guidelines for decision making, and to the person conducting – for instance – the interview, to prescribe a certain behaviour. Whether this person must be a public official, still remains unanswered. Applying Dan-Cohen's model, Malcai and Levine-Schnur decide affirmatively.[356] Yet, to follow from the design of a rule (technical, power control, and so on) and the relationship among rules (acoustic separation) to an addressee seems to put the cart before the horse. It is presumably also not what Dan-Cohen envisaged. In fact, he himself acknowledged the difficulty to apply his model in reality (or "the real world", as he expressed it):

> Societies differ in their degree of acoustic separation. But just as we would be hard pressed to locate a society displaying complete acoustic separation, we would find it equally difficult to identify a society in which such separation was wholly absent. We are also likely to discover that, within any given society, the degree of acoustic separation varies with respect to different groups of the population and different issues.[357]

It is especially true at the international level. As I have illustrated elsewhere,[358] though applying the law, a procedural question before the ICC can be decided differently by different Chambers. The reason for this phenomenon is that the drafters of the ICC Statute relied on the "constructive ambiguity" of legal texts.[359] In the words of Safferling: "A procedural system, which is so complex that the rules could be interpreted in a purely positivistic way, does not exist at the international level".[360] Since the ICC Statute leaves room for interpretation, it apparently has become *en vogue* to

---

[355] *Ibid.*

[356] Malcai and Levine-Schnur, 2017, p. 201 with fn. 55, see above note 343.

[357] Dan-Cohen, 1984, pp. 634–635, see above note 330.

[358] Heinze, 2014, pp. 34 ff., see above note 110.

[359] Christoph Safferling, *International Criminal Procedure*, Oxford University Press, 2012, p. 112.

[360] *Ibid.*

decide procedural matters on a so-called case-by-case basis.[361] The ICC OTP, in particular, seems to accommodate such an approach.[362] In its policy paper on the interests of justice of September 2007, it declares that the paper's scope would only "offer limited clarification in the abstract" as "the particular approach then will necessarily have to depend on the facts and circumstances of the case or situation".[363] Thus, international criminal procedure at the ICC highly depends on the persons involved.[364] As I have illustrated, the composition of the chamber can play an important role in determining how the Statute and the Rules are interpreted.[365] Issues arising in different chambers may be resolved in slightly different ways.[366] That the creation of international procedural law very often lies in the hands of international judges might indicate that it is composed of decision rules, addressed to public officials, that is, the judges themselves. As a matter of fact, governments prefer to leave judges to determine for themselves how the court will operate.[367]

Thus, the classification of exclusionary rules as decision rules does not exclude the possibility that they are also conduct rules that are only addressed both to public officials and citizens. This is what Duff *et al.* realised, too, when they point out that the categorisation of procedural rules as decision rules

---

[361] In the same vein, see Swoboda, *Verfahrens- und Beweisstrategien*, Nomos, Baden-Baden, 2013, p. 203, seeing no alternative to a case-by-case approach.

[362] Safferling, 2012, p. 110, see above note 359.

[363] ICC OTP, *Policy Paper on the Interests of Justice*, 1 September 2007, p. 7, fn. 9 (https://www.legal-tools.org/doc/bb02e5/).

[364] Safferling, 2012, p. 111, see above note 359.

[365] Kristina D. Rutledge, "Spoiling Everything – But for Whom? Rules of Evidence and International Criminal Proceedings", in *Regent University Law Review*, 2003-2004, vol. 16, no. 1, pp. 151–189 (162–163).

[366] Robert Christensen, "Getting to Peace by Reconciling Notions of Justice: The Importance of Considering Discrepancies Between Civil and Common Legal Systems in the Formation of the International Criminal Court", in *UCLA Journal of International Law and Foreign Affairs*, 2001-2002, vol. 6, p. 414.

[367] Daniel Terris, Cesare P.R. Romano, Leigh Swigart, *The International Judge*, Oxford University Press, Oxford, 2007, pp. 104–105. See, for instance, the "Judge-Legislator" model known from the ad hoc Tribunals, see Fabricio Guariglia, "The Rules of Procedure and Evidence for the International Criminal Court: A New Development in International Adjudication of Individual Criminal Responsibility", in Antonio Cassese, Paola Gaeta and John R.W.D. Jones (eds.), *The Rome Statute of the International Criminal Court; A Commentary*, vol. II, Oxford University Press, 2002, p. 1116.

does not imply, however, that such rules need not be comprehensible to citizens; indeed, the comprehensibility of the proceedings is still a precondition of a just public trial. If the trial is to address citizens in legal and moral terms which they can understand, the rules for courts must also be rules for citizens, in that they must be articulated in a way that connects appropriately with the ethical language of participants in the trial.[368]

Methodically, Duff *et al.* evade a by-effect of the application of Dan-Cohen's models: to miss the forest for the trees. It is so tempting to dive into the theoretical characteristics of decision rules and conduct rules that it is very easy to lose sight of what procedural law is really about: to regulate conduct during the proceedings and a trial respectively. The question of *whom* procedural rules are addressed to cannot therefore be answered without the question of *what* procedural rules are concerned with. It is unconvincing to rely on a principle according to which "the legal process should signify its insistence that those who enforce the law should also obey the law".[369] The *argumentum a contrario* that those who do *not* enforce the law are *not* obliged to obey the law demonstrates the fallacy of the principle, and calls for a holistic view on the addressee-issue.

17.5.2.3.1.2.2.3. The Holistic View: The Criminal Process as a System

This holistic view on the addressee-issue has roots in Luhmann's systems theory, which has a threefold effect. First, procedural law does not just delineate a bipolar relationship between the law and its addressees, but is a system. Especially the late Luhmann promoted the idea of sociological systems, where communication is a central feature.[370] Luhmann relied on theories of systems, as they had developed within biology and cybernetics. Law, within this theory, is one of society's sub-systems.[371] Teubner has taken this further, drawing on Luhmann's version of systems theory, to the autopoiet-

---

[368] A. Duff *et al.*, 2007, p. 276, see above note 145.

[369] Per Lord Griffiths in UK HL, *R v. Horseferry Road Magistrates' Court, ex parte Bennett,* [1994] 1 AC 42; Ashworth, 2002, p. 318, see above note 184.

[370] Niklas Luhmann, *Einführung in die Systemtheorie*, Dirk Baecker (ed.), fourth edition, Carl-Auer, Heidelberg, 2008, pp. 100 ff.; Richard Nobles, and David Schiff, "Taking the Complexity of Complex Systems Seriously", in *The Modern Law Review*, 2019, Advance Article, p. 2.

[371] *Ibid.*; Dietmar Braun, "Rationalisierungskonzepte in der Systemtheorie Niklas Luhmanns und in der Handlungstheorie Hartmut Essers: Ein Theorienvergleich", in Rainer Greshoff and Uwe Schimank (eds.), *Integrative Sozialtheorie? Esser – Luhmann – Weber*, VS Verlag, Wiesbaden, 2006, p. 377 with fn. 13.

ic systems theory to observe a wide range of linked legal or potentially legal issues, such as juridification, pluralism, transnational law, justice, the role of law in inter-social sub-system conflict, among others.[372] Applying Luhmann's systems theory, laws are not so much addressed to individuals but to closed systems – systems that cannot be influenced but merely motivated by external factors.[373] According to Luhmann, "the social system consists of meaningful communications— only of communications, and of all communications",[374] and "the legal system, too, consists only of communicative actions which engender legal consequences".[375] Understood this way, the addressees of exclusionary rules are not so much either public officials or private citizens, or both, but are all those who factually conducts an investigation.

The procedural, investigatory context is the closed system. At the same time, the criminal process is part of the (broader) criminal justice system.[376] Luhmann also admitted that there are communications that transgress a closed system.[377] Hamel has taken this point further and demonstrated that the judgment, as a form of speech act, is the autopoietic operation of the system criminal justice that – through its effects, especially the *res iudicata* – communicates to society and thereby transgresses the closed system.[378] This is nothing less than the connection between a judgment of a criminal court and the expressive or communicative effects of punishment. Concretely, a judgment that is based on illegally obtained evidence, and has therefore a questionable moral authority, might also have an impact on the

---

[372] See, for example, Gunther Teubner, "Altera pars audiatur: Law in the Collision of Discourses", in Richard Rawlings (ed.), *Law, Society and Economy*, Oxford University Press (Clarendon Press), Oxford, 1997, chap. 7.

[373] Niklas Luhmann, *Das Recht der Gesellschaft*, Suhrkamp, Frankfurt am Main, 1993-1997, p. 43; Theresa F. Schweiger, *Prozedurales Strafrecht: Zur Bedeutung von Verfahren und Form im Strafrecht*, Studien zum Strafrecht, vol. 91, Nomos, Baden-Baden, 2018, p. 113.

[374] Gunther Teubner, "Evolution of Autopoietic Law", in Gunther Teubner (ed.), *Autopoietic Law: A New Approach to Law and Society*, Walter de Gruyter, Berlin and New York, 1988, p. 17.

[375] *Ibid.*, p. 18; Mark van Hoecke, *Law as Communication*, Hart, Oxford and Portland, 2012, p. 117.

[376] Campbell, Ashworth, and Redmayne, 2019, pp. 2, 11-12, see above note 107; Heinze, 2014, pp. 114 ff., see above note 110; Alexander Heinze, "Bridge over Troubled Water – A Semantic Approach to Purposes and Goals in International Criminal Justice", in *International Criminal Law Review*, 2018, vol. 18, no. 6, p. 937.

[377] Luhmann, 1993-1997, p. 34, see above note 373.

[378] Roman Hamel, *Strafen als Sprechakt*, Duncker & Humblot, Berlin, 2009, pp. 81–82.

expressive function of punishment. I will get back to this a little later, since this connection becomes vital in international criminal law.

When taking the procedural system and the investigatory process as a closed system,[379] where everyone is addressed by the relevant rules, the next step would be to determine the parameters of such a system. I have done this elsewhere, not only with regard to national systems of criminal procedure[380] but, especially, with a view to international criminal procedure. Thus, I will limit myself to some brief remarks. The relevant attempts to model a procedural system can generally be divided into descriptive and normative models, although not all of them fit into this distinction and many of them seem to have an overlap between a rather descriptive or normative take.[381] The most prominent example of the descriptive model are Packer's Crime Control and Due Process Models. Packer's bifurcated approach focuses, on the one hand, on the efficient suppression of crime and, on the other, on fair trial rights and the concept of limited governmental power.[382] While under "crime control" speed, efficiency and finality are the overriding values, and any rule or measure compromising such values is deemed inappropriate,[383] "due process" aims at the protection of the "most disadvantaged" and thus demands equal treatment regardless of wealth or social status.[384] Under Packer's crime control model, the authority of the criminal justice system is derived from the laws passed by legislatures, whereas under his due process model authority is derived from the Supreme Court.

---

[379] About procedural law (more concretely, evidence law) as a system, see Roberts and Zuckerman, 2010, chap. 1 and p. 188, see above note 192.

[380] Heinze, 2014, pp. 92 ff., see above note 110.

[381] In more detail, see *ibid.*, pp. 133 ff.

[382] Herbert L. Packer, *The Limits of the Criminal Sanction*, Stanford University Press/Oxford University Press, Stanford, California and Oxford, 1969, pp. 149–53; see also the accounts of Yvonne McDermott, *Fairness in International Criminal Trials*, Oxford University Press, Oxford, 2016, pp. 9–10; Katja Šugman Stubbs, "An Increasingly Blurred Division between Criminal and Administrative Law", in Bruce Ackerman, Kai Ambos, and Hrvoje Sikirić (eds.), *Visions of Justice – Liber Amicorum Mirjan Damaška*, Duncker & Humblot, Berlin, 2016, pp. 351–370, 353; Campbell, Ashworth, and Redmayne, 2019, pp. 39 ff., see above note 107.

[383] Cf. Heinze, 2014, p. 134, see above note 110.

[384] See Packer, 1969, p. 168, see above note 382.

17.5.2.3.1.2.2.3.1. Parameters of the Criminal Process System: Crime Control

It would be within the spirit of Packer's Crime Control Model to admit illegally obtained evidence by private individuals and not apply exclusionary rules. In fact, the model would even admit illegally obtained evidence by public officials. In Packer's words:

> In theory the Crime Control Model can tolerate rules that forbid illegal arrests, unreasonable searches, coercive interrogations, and the like. What it cannot tolerate is the vindication of those rules in the criminal process itself through the exclusion of evidence illegally obtained or through the reversal of convictions in cases where the criminal process has breached the rules laid down for its observance.[385]

Moreover, according to this model, illegally seized evidence should also be admissible at trial. Unlike coerced confessions, guns, drugs and stolen property reveal the truth regardless of how the police obtained them.[386]

Under Packer's Crime Control Model, the authority of the criminal justice system is derived from the laws passed by legislatures.[387] This legislature, as opposed to the courts, is the model's "validating authority". A criminal sanction is suggested to be "a positive guarantor of social freedom" and necessary for the maintenance of "public order".[388] In the Crime Control Model, the police have an important role. They are concerned with "factual guilt" in the sense that the accused probably committed the criminal act,[389] and carry out most of the fact-finding.[390] Because it treasures "speed and finality",[391] the Crime Control Model allows the police and prosecutors to screen out the innocent and secure "as expeditiously as pos-

---

[385] *Ibid.*, pp. 167–168.

[386] *Ibid.*, p. 199.

[387] *Ibid.*, p. 173.

[388] *Ibid.*, p. 158.

[389] As opposed to "legal guilt" that could be established beyond a reasonable doubt through admissible evidence and after considering all the rights and defences of the accused.

[390] But see Peter L. Arenella, "Rethinking the Functions of Criminal Procedure: The Warren and Burger Courts' Competing Ideologies", in *Georgetown Law Journal*, 1983, vol. 72, no. 2, pp. 185–248.

[391] Packer, 1969, p. 159, see above note 382.

sible, the conviction of the rest, with a minimum of occasions for challenge, let alone post-audit".[392]

It is important to clarify that Packer's Crime Control Model in no sense authorises broad police abuse, as some authors assert.[393] It is quite the opposite: Packer's Crime Control model even imposes ordinary law for State officials in line with Dicey's idea of the rule of law.[394] However, it is fair to say that what the model most fears is a criminal going free just because of (procedural) mistakes done by the police.[395]

17.5.2.3.1.2.2.3.2. Parameters of the System Criminal Process: Due Process

The Due Process Model, by contrast, is not concerned with "factual guilt" but with "legal guilt".[396] This seems to touch upon different understandings of fairness, on which I will elaborate in the next section. The Due Process Model aims at the protection of the "most disadvantaged" and thus demands equal treatment regardless of wealth or social status.[397] It places much less emphasis on efficiency and guilty pleas than the Crime Control Model and strives to avoid police abuses.[398] Procedural rights like the right to remain silent and the right to contact counsel are seen as most important.[399] Unlike the Crime Control Model, the Due Process Model does not allow separate civil, disciplinary, or criminal actions in cases of prosecutorial or police abuses.[400] Therefore, the model provides for "prophylactic and deterrent"[401] exclusionary rules because much police abuse will

---

[392] *Ibid.*, p. 160.

[393] Kent Roach, "Four Models of the Criminal Process", in *Journal of Criminal Law & Criminology*, 1999, vol. 89, no. 2, pp. 671–716.

[394] Cf. Dicey, 1886 and 1979, pp. 188 ff., see above note 256.

[395] United States, New York Court of Appeals, *People v. Defore*, 12 January 1926, 150 N.E. 585, 587.

[396] Packer, 1969, p. 167, see above note 382.

[397] *Ibid.*, p. 168.

[398] *Ibid.*, p. 180.

[399] *Ibid.*, p. 191: "The rationale of exclusion is not that the confession is untrustworthy, but that it is at odds with the postulates of an accusatory system of criminal justice in which it is up to the state to make its case against a defendant without forcing him to co-operate in the process, and without capitalizing on his ignorance of his legal rights".

[400] *Ibid.*, p. 180. About disciplinary sanctions with respect to disclosure failures, see Heinze, 2014, pp. 421 ff., above note 110.

[401] *Ibid.*, p. 168.

never reach the stage of a criminal trial.[402] Under the Crime Control Model, anything that exhausts resources must be avoided, that is, a criminal trial. This can be done through guilty pleas and plea-bargaining arrangements. The opposite is the case in the Due Process Model. A criminal trial "should be viewed not as an undesirable burden but rather as the logical and proper culmination of the process".[403] Thus, guilty pleas are not encouraged;[404] the criminal trial – conceivably based on Luhmann[405] – has an intrinsic value and is detached from substantive law.[406] The Luhmannesque notion of a trial (and of proceedings) renders it possible that within the confines of the Due Process Model, exclusionary rules also apply when evidence was illegally obtained by private individuals.

Packer's categorisation served as a basis for further elaborations, for example, taking into account rehabilitation and societal stability,[407] focusing on cases that never reach the courtroom,[408] emphasising more strongly the protection of innocents,[409] and the interests of victims.[410] Damaška, in

---

[402] *Ibid.*, p. 180.

[403] *Ibid.*, p. 224.

[404] *Ibid.*

[405] Niklas Luhmann, *Legitimation durch Verfahren*, Suhrkamp, Frankfurt a. M., 1983 [first edition published by Hermann Luchterhand Verlag in 1969], pp. 30–31 ("Verfahren finden eine Art generelle Anerkennung, die unabhängig ist vom Befriedigungswert der einzelnen Entscheidung, und diese Anerkennung zieht die Hinnahme und Beachtung verbindlicher Entscheidungen nach sich"); see also Gerson Trüg, "Die Position des Opfers im Völkerstrafverfahren vor dem IStGH – Ein Beitrag zu einer opferbezogenen verfahrenstheoretischen Bestandsaufnahme", in *Zeitschrift für die gesamte Strafrechtswissenschaft*, 2013, vol. 125, no. 1, p. 78.

[406] See Packer, 1969, p. 217, sees above note 382 ("Many of the limitations on substantive criminal enactments safeguard us against being punished for a mere propensity to commit crime").

[407] John Griffiths, "Ideology in Criminal Procedure or A Third 'Model' of the Criminal Process", in *Yale Law Journal*, 1969-1970, vol. 79, no. 3, pp. 359–417.

[408] Satnam Choongh, "Policing the Dross – A Social Disciplinary Model of Policing", in *British Journal of Criminology*, 1998, vol. 38, no. 4, p. 625.

[409] Keith A. Findley, "Toward a New Paradigm of Criminal Justice: How the Innocence Movement Merges Crime Control and Due Process", in *Texas Tech Law Review*, 2008-2009, vol. 41, pp. 141 ff.

[410] Kent Roach, 1999, p. 672, see above note 393; Hadar Aviram, "Packer in Context: Formalism and Fairness in the Due Process Model", in *Law and Social Inquiry*, 2011, vol. 36, no. 1, p. 241. See also Trüg, 2013, p. 79, see above note 405, who however neglects existing procedural models which take the role of the victim into consideration. See, generally, Ambos, 2016, p. 7, see above note 342.

---

his seminal *The Faces of Justice*,[411] developed a set of models based on attitudes towards State authority and on concepts of government.[412] It goes beyond the scope of this chapter to also apply those to the question of exclusionary rules.

17.5.2.3.1.3. Intermediate Conclusion

There are different investigatory contexts when private individuals collect evidence that eventually may be used before an ICT. The inter-investigatory context (international investigation – domestic investigation); the intra-investigatory context (internal investigation by a private individual); and the extra-investigatory context (collection of evidence by a private individual outside any investigation). I raised the question whether the procedural regime, especially exclusionary rules, maybe applicable in the inter-investigatory, intra-investigatory and extra-investigatory contexts. The inter-investigatory context turned out to be the least problematic. In the intra-investigatory context, there is an attribution of the private individual to an organ of the ICT (usually, the OTP) that may occur rather openly through a utilisation of the individual in the collection process, that is, *ab initio*; or through an *ex post* attribution, when the individual acted in the interest of the organ. In the latter, a person acts independently of an ICT-organ and outside an investigation. It is the extra-investigatory context that is the neuralgic point of exclusionary rules applied before ICTs. This section was merely concerned with the admittedly rather simple question of whether exclusionary rules apply in this setting. As I have demonstrated, the allegedly simple question unfolded into an analysis that entered the depth of procedural law theory. Through norm theory (Dan-Cohen) and systems theory (Luhmann and Teubner), combined with procedural theory (Packer), I have laid bare a wide-ranging controversy about the addressees of procedural rules. I conclude that a bipolar legislator-addressee relationship is fruitless. Instead, the addressee of procedural law is the process as a

---

[411] "[A] key work in the field of comparative procedure", Steven G. Calabresi, "The Comparative Constitutional Law Scholarship of Professor Mirjan Damaška: A Tribute", in Bruce Ackerman, Kai Ambos, and Hrvoje Sikirić (eds.), *Visions of Justice – Liber Amicorum Mirjan Damaška*, Duncker & Humblot, Berlin, 2016, p. 107.

[412] Mirjan Damaška, *The Faces of Justice and State Authority*, Yale University Press, New Haven and London, 1986, pp. 8–12. For a comprehensive overview of the reviews of this book see Izhak England, "The Faces of Justice and State Authority: A Review of the Reviews", in Bruce Ackerman, Kai Ambos, and Hrvoje Sikirić (eds.), *Visions of Justice – Liber Amicorum Mirjan Damaška*, Duncker & Humblot, Berlin, 2016, pp. 199–211.

system. Rules apply to everyone within that system – and might even apply beyond that system through transgressive communication (just as the judgment communicates not only with the accused and victim but with society as a whole). Even when we divide the procedural law into a Crime Control and Due Process function, with the former addressing the police and prosecution, the latter applies to everyone that is involved in the investigatory process when this involvement eventually has an impact on due process. Understood this way, the exclusionary rules also apply to private conduct.

17.5.2.3.2. Rationales for the Exclusion of Illegally Obtained Evidence Before International Criminal Tribunals in the Face of Private Conduct

Due to the controversy around the application of exclusionary rules to the extra-investigatory context, the rationales for exclusionary rules again become the focus of attention – on its face because of the theoretical gap left by the controversy concerning the application of exclusionary rules. It is worth mentioning that this gap is larger in the civil law tradition than in the common law tradition. In the former, the application of legal principles is normally derived from or based on written law.[413] Thus, the exclusion of evidence must be based on written exclusionary rules. The generality of legal rules is high—codes in the civil law tradition are said to be rather a collection of abstract principles than specific rules for particular situations or even concrete cases.[414] Unsurprisingly, in Germany, most recent works about the exclusion of illegally obtained evidence by private individuals

---

[413] Brianne McGonigle Leyh, *Procedural Justice? Victim Participation in International Criminal Proceedings*, Intersentia, Cambridge *et al.*, 2011, p. 70; Michael Bohlander, "Language, Culture, Legal Traditions, and International Criminal Justice", in *Journal of International Criminal Justice*, 2014, vol. 12, no. 3, pp. 494 ff.; on the importance of truth-seeking, see, for example, Michèle-Laure Rassat, *Traité de procedure pénale*, Presses Univ. de France, Paris, 2001, p. 297; Frédéric Desportes and Laurence Lazerges-Cousquer, *Traité de procédure pénale*, fourth edition, Economica, Paris, 2016, mn. 550; Hans-Heiner Kühne, *Strafprozessrecht*, ninth edition, C.F. Müller, Heidelberg, 2015, mn. 1, 628, 751; Peters, 1985, pp. 16, 82–83, see above note 113.

[414] Joseph Sanders, "Law and Legal Systems", in Edgar F. Borgatta and Rhonda J.V. Montgomery (eds.), *Encyclopedia of Sociology*, vol. III, second edition, Macmillan, New York *et al.*, 2000, pp. 1544, 1546; Heinze, 2014, p. 109, see above note 110. For a German perspective, see Michael Bohlander, "Radbruch Redux: The Need for Revisiting the Conversation between Common and Civil Law at Root Level at the Example of International Criminal Justice", in *Leiden Journal of International Law*, 2011, vol. 24, no. 2, pp. 393–410, 402.

revolve around the question whether § 136a StPO, as written law, is applicable[415] – and not so much about what could be the rationale for excluding or admitting such evidence. While the civil law tradition emphasises codification, the chief source[416] of law in common law legal systems is the case law of the courts.[417] Procedural rules are especially set forth in the case law in a direct (or indirect) application of the constitution (if there is one).[418] As a result, the rationales for exclusionary rules have a much more prominent position in common law than in civil law. Yet, here too, the temptation is high to deny those rationales practical relevance, since they do not allow for a mechanical application of exclusionary rules. Roberts and Zuckerman made a similar observation and expressed it more eloquently:

> the impact of foundational principles on the day-to-day practice of the courts has been blunted by common lawyers' excessive preoccupation with technical legal definitions. The traditional textbook treatment of the Law of Evidence may allude to the rationale underpinning particular rules, but discussion then tends to proceed as though it can be assumed that the rules are either self-actuating, internally coherent, and ex-

---

[415] See, for example, Sebastian Eckhardt, *Private Ermittlungsbeiträge im Rahmen der staatlichen Strafverfolgung*, Peter Lang, Frankfurt a.M. *et al.*, 2009, pp. 14 ff.; Anja Bienert, *Private Ermittlungen und ihre Bedeutung auf dem Gebiet der Beweisverwertungsverbote*, Shaker, Aachen, 1997, pp. 11 ff.

[416] Many observers from the civil law system still ignore that the common law in the respective legal system has often been replaced by statutory law, see, in the same vein, Massimo Donini, "An impossible exchange? Versuche zu einem Dialog zwischen civil lawyers und common lawyers über Gesetzlichkeit, Moral und Straftheorie", in *Jahrbuch der Juristischen Zeitgeschichte*, 2017, vol. 18, no. 1, p. 342. See also Geoffrey Samuel, *A Short Introduction to Judging and to Legal Reasoning*, Edward Elgar, Celtenham, Northampton, MA, 2016, p. 31: "The common law has of course traditionally been regarded as being based upon cases and precedents. Before the 19th century this was largely true, but today the position is dramatically different. By far the most important source of law in England is legislation and the great majority of cases decided by the courts involve the interpretation and application of a legislative text"; Carissa Byrne Hessick, "The Myth of Common Law Crimes", in *Virginia Law Review*, 2019, vol. 105, no. 5, pp. 965–1024.

[417] Michael Zander, "Forms and Functions of the Sources of the Law from a Common Law Perspective", in Albin Eser and Christiane Rabenstein (eds.), *Neighbours in Law – Are Common Law and Civil Law Moving Closer Together?*, Papers in Honour of Barbara Huber on her 65th Birthday, Edition iuscrim, Freiburg i. Br., 2001, pp. 32, 43; Heinze, 2014, p. 111, see above note 110.

[418] David Alan Sklansky, "Quasi-Affirmative Rights in Constitutional Criminal Procedure", in *Virginia Law Review*, 2002, vol. 88, no. 6, pp. 1229–1300; Jerold H. Israel and Wayne R. LaFave, *Criminal Procedure*, seventh edition, Thomson West, St. Paul, Minnesota, 2006, pp. 3 ff.; Matthew Lippman, *Criminal Procedure*, second edition, Sage, London, 2014, p. 5.

haustive, or else inexplicably self-contradictory. No further reference to deeper rationalization or justification is thought necessary.[419]

This argument, that builds on the flawed premise that individual decisions can only be derived from rules,[420] ignores that judges have discretion[421] and that "criminal evidence is developing into a branch of constitutional criminal jurisprudence".[422]

17.5.2.3.2.1. Integrity from the Subject Perspective: The Deterrence Theory Within the Extra-Investigatory Context

As described in detail, the deterrence theory assigns to exclusionary rules a deterrent effect on future behaviour of the person collecting evidence. Apart from the theoretical doubts that are voiced as to the justification of such a deterrence theory, it is even more questionable whether this theory may have any effect in the extra-investigatory context. Before going into the four arguments against the utility of the deterrence theory in the extra-investigatory context, however, one popular argument needs to be refuted *ab initio*: "If the exclusionary discretion is based on a disciplinary rationale, there is no reason for not admitting this evidence [that is, evidence a civilian obtained]. The authorities have done nothing wrong and the public interest in admitting the evidence may be very great".[423] The remark that 'authorities have done nothing wrong' in cases when private individuals illegally obtained evidence somehow insinuates that exclusionary rules are exclusively addressed to those authorities. Any argument that goes like this carries the requirement to elaborate on the addressee-question of procedural rules. I have demonstrated in detail why exclusionary rules do in fact apply in an extra-investigatory context.

More convincing arguments to question the utility of the deterrence rationale within an extra-investigatory context are the following:

First, even in the case of police conduct, it was remarked that there are other forms to 'police the police', such as disciplinary proceedings or criminal prosecution of law enforcement officials.[424] When private individ-

---

[419] Roberts and Zuckerman, 2010, p. 25, see above note 192.

[420] In the same vein, see Zuckerman, 1987, p. 59, see above note 194.

[421] Roberts and Zuckerman, 2010, pp. 27, 29 ff., see above note 192.

[422] *Ibid.*, p. 31.

[423] P. Duff, 2004, p. 162, see above note 193.

[424] As is the case in Germany, Thaman and Brodowski, 2020, p. 458, see above note 196.

uals act, the criminal prosecution option becomes even more relevant, as is one of the prevailing objections against exclusionary rules in an extra-investigatory context in Germany. However, the criminal prosecution argument needs to be treated with caution at the international level – as argued earlier.[425]

Second, it is doubtful whether the exclusion of evidence is really the best vindication for police wrongdoing, especially when the individual officer is more concerned with making an arrest and/or has no personal interest in a conviction.[426] This counter-argument is even stronger at the international level, considering the individual motivations of private investigators, often acting in the interests of their donors. Third, in many criminal justice systems, officials who violate an exclusionary rule never learn whether or not the evidence they obtained is excluded.[427] This argument is especially true at the international level – for instance, when CIJA collects evidence and it is unclear before which national or international court this evidence might be used.[428] This leads to the fourth counter-argument: if it is doubtful whether public officials know in fact the exclusionary rule that might apply. This is all the more true in a context where it is unclear where the evidence might be admitted.

ICTs have reacted to the weakness of the deterrence theory, albeit in the inter-investigatory context. In *Brđanin*, the Trial Chamber admitted transcripts of illegally intercepted telephone conversations by the security forces of Bosnia and Herzegovina with the argument that the "function of this Tribunal is not to deter and punish illegal conduct by domestic law enforcement authorities by excluding illegally obtained evidence".[429]

---

[425] See above Section 17.5.2.3.1.2.2.1.

[426] Thaman and Brodowski, 2020, p. 458, see above note 196; Gless and Macula, 2019, p. 355, see above note 8.

[427] *Ibid.*

[428] In more detail Heinze, 2019, pp. 171 ff., see above note 87; William H. Wiley, "International(ised) Criminal Justice at a Crossroads: The Role of Civil Society in the Investigation of Core International Crimes and the 'CIJA Model'", in Morten Bergsmo and Carsten Stahn (eds.), *Quality Control in Fact-Finding*, second edition, TOAEP, Brussels, 2020, pp. 547 ff.

[429] See ICTY, *Prosecutor v. Radoslav Brđanin*, Decision on the Defence "Objection to Intercept Evidence", 3 October 2003, IT-99-36-T, para. 63 (https://legal-tools.org/doc/7efabf/); see also ICTY, *Prosecutor v. Kordić & Čerkez*, Transcript, 2 February 2000, IT-95-14/2-T, 13671 (https://www.legal-tools.org/doc/298d4d/): "It's not the duty of this Tribunal to discipline armies or anything of that sort". Pitcher, 2018, p. 291, see above note 192, with further references.

17.5.2.3.2.2. Integrity from Object Perspective: The Theory of Remedies in the Extra-Investigatory Context

The first rationale that does provide useful guidance for the collection of evidence by private individuals at the international level is the theory of remedies. This rationale is tailored – so to say – for the irrelevance of the interrogator's status. As George Christie remarks, "a right to one's bodily integrity, either against the state or against private persons, is only a right that neither state officials nor private persons may invade one's bodily integrity; and, if they do, that the law will give one a remedy against them".[430]

17.5.2.3.2.2.1. The Punishment Remedy

One possible remedy is a punishment of the interrogator according to substantive criminal law. To reiterate the Kantian footprint in the remedy theory: Kant remarks that "if a certain use of freedom is itself a hindrance to freedom in accordance with universal laws (i.e., wrong), coercion that is opposed to this (as a *hindering of a hindrance to freedom*) is consistent with freedom in accordance with universal laws, that is, it is right".[431] In other words, "[c]oercion is in general unjust because it is a hindrance of freedom, but *state* coercion following on an unjust hindrance of freedom is just, for it is a hindrance of a hindrance of freedom, which is consistent with universal freedom".[432] Coercion is morally justified "when used to protect rational agency from standard threats to its existence and flourishing".[433] Thus,

> the use of coercion by the state to restrain the thief is right, even though it is a hindrance to the thief's freedom, because the thief is using *his* freedom to restrain the victim's freedom under a universal law (in this case, the victim's peaceful enjoyment of his possession).[434]

---

[430] George C. Christie, *Philosopher Kings? The Adjudication of Conflicting Human Rights and Social Values*, Oxford University Press, Oxford, 2011, p. 15.

[431] Kant, 1991, p. 57 [231], see above note 163.

[432] Alan W. Norrie, *Law, Ideology and Punishment*, Kluwer, London, 1991, p. 51 (emphasis in the original).

[433] Brian Orend, "Kant on International Law and Armed Conflict", in *Canadian Journal of Law and Jurisprudence*, 1998, vol. 11, no. 2, p. 335.

[434] Fernando R. Teson, "Kantianism and Legislation", in *Annual Review of Law and Ethics*, 2008, vol. 16, p. 283.

Yet, I have previously shown that shifting the remedial possibilities of the suspect to substantive law presupposes a clear difference between substantive and procedural law, which is at least questionable at the international level.

17.5.2.3.2.2.2. Human Rights as Sword and Shield

Rogall refers to the State's obligation to protect individuals.[435] This is the shield function of human rights I have previously referred to.[436] This State obligation would be incomplete if it did not apply when private individuals obtain illegal evidence.[437] At the same time, the shield function of human rights collides with its sword function. The State is also obliged to ensure that justice is done and – indirectly – that the human rights of potential victims are protected.[438]

The argumentative force and even effectiveness of the remedy theory at the international level is underlined by the central role of human rights. Even though human rights have a dual character as constitutional norms and super-positive value,[439] they first took on concrete form as basic rights within constitutions or constitutional instruments.[440] As Habermas explains about human rights and basic rights:

> As constitutional norms, human rights have a certain primacy, shown by the fact that they are constitutive for legal order as such and by the extent to which they determine a framework within which normal legislative activity is possible. But even among constitutional norms as a whole, basic rights stand out. On the one hand, liberal and social basic rights have the form

---

[435] Klaus Rogall, "§ 136a StPO", in Hans-Joachim Rudolphi *et al.* (eds.), *Systematischer Kommentar zur Strafprozessordnung*, vol. II, §§ 94–136a StPO, fifth edition, Wolters Kluwer (Carl Heymanns), Köln, 2016, mn. 13.

[436] See above Section 17.5.2.2.2.

[437] Rogall, 2016, mn. 13, see above note 435.

[438] *Ibid.*, mn. 14.

[439] Jürgen Habermas, "Kant's Idea of Perpetual Peace with the Benefit of 200 Years' Hindsight", in James Bohman and Matthias Lutz-Bachmann (eds.), *Perpetual Peace – Essays on Kant's Cosmopolitan Ideal*, MIT Press, Cambridge, 1997, p. 137 ("as constitutional norms they enjoy a positive validity (of instituted law), but as rights they are attributed to each person as a human being they acquire a above positive value").

[440] *Ibid.*

of general norms addressed to citizens in their properties as "human beings" and not merely as member of a polity.[441]

Article 21(3) of the ICC Statute forms part of the provisions that identify the applicable law of the Court. It states that the

> application and interpretation of law [...] must be consistent with internationally recognized human rights, and be without any adverse distinction founded on grounds such as gender [...],[442] age, race, colour, language, religion or belief, political or other opinion, national, ethnic or social origin, wealth, birth or other status.[443]

Therefore, ICC judges draw from a large body of human rights law with ample discretion to guarantee the most basic and important protections.[444] Article 21(3) thus reflects support for the view "that the nature of human rights is such that they may have a certain special status or, at a minimum, a permeating role within international law".[445]

---

[441] *Ibid.*

[442] As defined in the ICC Statute, Article 7(3), see above note 182, the term 'gender' "refers to the two sexes, male and female, within the context of society" (fn. added).

[443] *Ibid.*, Article 21(3).

[444] See also Adriaan Bos, "1948–1998: The Universal Declaration of Human Rights and the Statute of the International Criminal Court", in *Fordham International Law Journal*, 1998–99, vol. 22, no. 2, pp. 229, 234.

[445] Rebecca Young, "'Internationally Recognized Human Rights' Before the International Criminal Court", in *International and Comparative Law Quarterly*, 2011, vol. 60, no. 1, pp. 189–90; Michael Reisman, "Sovereignty and Human Rights in Contemporary International Law", in *American Journal International Law*, 1990, vol. 84, no. 4, pp. 866, 872: "The international human rights program is more than a piecemeal addition to the traditional corpus of international law, more than another chapter sandwiched into traditional textbooks of international law. By shifting the fulcrum of the system from the protection of sovereigns to the protection of people, it works qualitative changes in virtually every component."; James D. Fry, "International Human Rights Law in Investment Arbitration: Evidence of International Law's Unity", in *Duke Journal of Comparative & International Law*, 2007–08, vol. 18, no. 1, p. 123: "The possibility exists that the field of human rights is an extra-special type of specialized regime that impacts all aspects of international law, and should not be seen as just another specialized body of law that other specialized bodies might use to reinterpret their own rules in its light, but is one that requires other specialized bodies to be reinterpreted in its light"; Dinah Shelton, "Normative Hierarchy in International Law", in *American Journal International Law*, 2006, vol. 100, no. 2, pp. 291, 294; Stefanie Schmahl, "Human Dignity in International Human Rights, Humanitarian and International Criminal Law: A Comparative Approach", in Eric Hilgendorf and Mordechai Kremnitzer (eds.), *Human Dignity and Criminal Law*, Duncker & Humblot, Berlin, 2018, p. 101; Yvonne McDermott, "The Influence of International Human Rights Law on International Criminal Procedure", in

Within the context of the ICC Statute, human rights reached the status of basic rights. In this context, human rights violations "are no longer condemned and fought from the moral point of view in an unmediated way, but are rather prosecuted as criminal actions within the framework of state-organised legal order according to the institutionalised legal procedures".[446] The Statute translates general human rights norms "into the language of criminal law", not only by defining the core international crimes, but also by providing procedural guarantees and a canonical formulation of the role of internationally recognised human rights.[447] The Appeals Chamber of the ICC has ruled, concerning the role of human rights in the interpretation of the Statute, that

> [h]uman rights underpin the Statute; every aspect of it […]. Its provisions must be interpreted, and more importantly applied in accordance with internationally recognized human rights; first and foremost, in the context of the Statute, the right to a fair trial, a concept broadly perceived and applied, embracing the judicial process in its entirety.[448]

In other words, human rights can certainly be seen as the mainstay of the ICC Statute.[449] The mere existence and work of the Court help to promote human rights by: creating a historical record for past wrongs;[450] offering a forum for victims to voice their opinions and receive satisfaction and compensation for past violations;[451] creating judicial precedent; and deter-

---

Philipp Kastner (ed.), *International Criminal Law in Context*, Routledge, London, New York, 2018, p. 288.

[446] Habermas, 1997, p. 140, see above note 439.

[447] ICC Statute, Article 21(3), see above note 182: "The application and interpretation of law pursuant to this article must be consistent with internationally recognized human rights".

[448] *Lubanga*, 2006, para. 37, see above note 114. The ICC Pre-Trial Chamber I referred to that Judgment in *Prosecutor v. Laurent Gbagbo*, Pre-Trial Chamber I, Decision on the fitness of Laurent Gbagbo to take part in the proceedings before this Court, 2 November 2012, ICC-02/11-01/11-286-Red, para. 45 (http://www.legal-tools.org/doc/4729b8/).

[449] Benjamin Perrin, "Searching for Law While Seeking Justice: The Difficulties of Enforcing International Humanitarian Law in International Criminal Trials", in *Ottawa Law Review*, 2007–08, vol. 39, no. 2, p. 398.

[450] United Nations Security Council, Statement of Judge Claude Jorda, UN Doc. S/PV.4161, 20 June 2000, p. 3 (http://www.legal-tools.org/doc/365c3f/); Jens David Ohlin, "A Meta-Theory of International Criminal Procedure: Vindicating the Rule of Law", in *UCLA Journal of International Law & Foreign Affairs*, 2009, vol. 77, no. 1, pp. 86 ff. For more detail, see Heinze, 2014, pp. 218 ff., see above note 110.

[451] Ben Swart, "Foreword", in *Journal of International Criminal Justice*, 2008, vol. 6, no. 1, pp. 87, 100; Minna Schrag, "Lessons Learned from ICTY Experience", in *Journal of Inter-*

ring potential violators of the gravest crimes[452] while punishing past offenders.[453] Thus, human rights norms in the Statute "provide a blueprint for
the common good of a community" in the Aristotelian sense[454] – which is,
at the same time, the link to Habermas's interpretation of Republicanism.[455]
Kant laid the foundations for all current conceptions of human dignity and
world peace. For Kant, a permanent peace is predicated on the recognition
and respect for human rights, and gross human rights violations rights must
be stigmatised as serious wrongs and punished.[456] Kant's language in this
regard resonates in the following statement by the ICTY Appeals Chamber:

> A State-sovereignty-oriented approach has been gradually
> supplanted by a human-being oriented approach. Gradually
> the maxim of Roman law *hominum causa omne jus constitu-*
> *tum est* (all law is created for the benefit of human beings) has
> gained a firm foothold in the international community as well.
> It follows that in the area of armed conflict the distinction be-
> tween interstate wars and civil wars is losing its value as far as
> human beings are concerned. Why protect civilians from bel-
> ligerent violence, or ban rape, torture or the wanton destruc-
> tion of hospitals, churches, museums or private property, as
> well as proscribe weapons causing unnecessary suffering
> when two sovereign States are engaged in war, and yet refrain
> from enacting the same bans or providing the same protection
> when armed violence has erupted "only" within the territory

---

national Criminal Justice, 2004, vol. 2, no. 2, pp. 427–28. For Ralph, this helps to constitute
a world society: see Jason Ralph, "International Society, the International Criminal Court
and American Foreign Policy", in *Review of International Studies*, 2005, vol. 31, no. 1,
pp. 27 (39).

[452] Kai Ambos, *Treatise on International Criminal Law*, vol. I, Oxford University Press, Oxford,
2013, p. 71.

[453] ICTR, *The Prosecutor v. Omar Serushago*, Trial Chamber, Sentence, 5 February 1999,
ICTR-98-39-S, para. 20 (http://www.legal-tools.org/doc/e2dddb/); ICTR, *The Prosecutor v.*
Georges Anderson Nderubumwe Rutaganda, Trial Chamber, Judgement and Sentence, 6 De-
cember 1999, ICTR-96-3-T, para. 455 (http://www.legal-tools.org/doc/f0dbbb/); ICTR, *The*
Prosecutor v. Emmanuel Ndindabahizi, Trial Chamber, Judgement and Sentence, 15 July
2004, ICTR-2001-71-I, para. 498 (http://www.legal-tools.org/doc/272b55/); ICTR, *The*
Prosecutor v. François Karera, Trial Chamber, Judgement and Sentence, 7 December 2007,
ICTR-01-74-T, para. 571 (http://www.legal-tools.org/doc/7bc57f/).

[454] John M. Czarnetzky and Ronald J. Rychlak, "An Empire of Law: Legalism and the International Criminal Court", in *Notre Dame Law Review*, 2003, vol. 79, no. 1, pp. 55, 110.

[455] Fernando H. Llano, "European Constitutional Patriotism and Postnational Citizenship in
Jürgen Habermas", in *Archiv für Rechts- und Sozialphilosophie*, 2017, vol. 103, no. 4, p. 506.

[456] Ambos, 2013, pp. 293, 306, see above note 452.

---

of a sovereign State? If international law, while of course duly safeguarding the legitimate interests of States, must gradually turn to the protection of human beings, it is only natural that the aforementioned dichotomy should gradually lose its weight."[457]

The human rights language of Article 21(3) of the ICC Statute is translated into the admissibility provision of Article 69. Here, integrity from the perspective of the suspect is visibly enshrined in paragraph 7: "Evidence obtained by means of a violation of this Statute *or internationally recognized human rights* shall not be admissible if [...] [t]he admission of the evidence would be antithetical to and would seriously damage the *integrity of the proceedings*".[458] At the same time, the integrity of the person as "internationally recognized human rights" is interlocked with integrity from the perspective of the process.

Taken the strong stance of human rights at the ICC, combined with a Kantian vision of human dignity protection, some scholars in my jurisdiction, Germany, make an exception of the general admissibility of illegally obtained evidence by private individuals when the constitutional right to human dignity has been infringed,[459] or when the collection of evidence "is flawed with an extreme violation of rights".[460]

17.5.2.3.2.3. Integrity from the Context Perspective: The Integrity of the Process in the Extra-Investigatory Context

At the heart of exclusionary rules within the extra-investigatory context lies the integrity of international criminal procedure itself. Illegally obtained evidence by private individuals questions the moral authority of the verdict and its legitimacy. The evidence may be unreliable. Admitting such evidence might violate the rule of law. So much about the raw claims. The ba-

---

[457] ICTY, *Prosecutor v. Duško Tadić*, Appeals Chamber, Decision on the Defence Motion for Interlocutory Appeal on Jurisdiction, IT-94-1-AR72, 2 October 1995, para. 97. For an analysis, see Luigi D.A. Corrias and Geoffrey M. Gordon, "Judging in the Name of Humanity: International Criminal Tribunals and the Representation of a Global Public", in *Journal of International Criminal Justice*, 2015, vol. 13, no. 1, pp. 100–1.

[458] Emphasis supplied.

[459] Kleinknecht, 1966, p. 1543, see above note 350; Herbert Diemer, "§136a StPO", in Rolf Hannich (ed.), *Karlsruher Kommentar zur Strafprozessordnung*, eighth edition, C.H. Beck, München, 2019, mn. 3 *in fine*; Matula, 2012, p. 101, see above note 314.

[460] Kleinknecht, 1966, p. 1543, see above note 350; Karl-Heinz Nüse, Zu den Beweisverboten im Strafprozeß, in *Juristische Rundschau*, 1966, p. 281 (285); Diemer, 2019, mn. 3, see above note 459.

sis of the integrity of the process is fairness. I have elaborated on this elsewhere with Shannon Fyfe.[461]

The interrelationship between criminal justice and fairness is obvious. A judicial or administrative body is tasked with serving the public, and in serving the public, a government body's most important higher-order goal is to treat every member of the public fairly. Especially the juxtaposition of procedural and substantive fairness is vital for private investigations. Procedural fairness can be assessed based on a system's rules[462] and will be translated into integrity from the perspective of the process. Rights that are guaranteed by procedures "allow for a system of law to emerge out of a set of substantive rules and [...] minimize arbitrariness".[463] If the same established rules and procedures are applied to all defendants and suspects (or potential suspects) without bias, then a system can be said to be procedurally fair, regardless of outcomes. To provide an extreme example: the accused is acquitted due to illegally obtained evidence, even though this evidence proofs his guilt beyond reasonable doubt – a popular counterargument against the remedy rationale.[464] However, "equal treatment involves at one extreme the impartial application of existing rules and procedures, regardless of the outcome (procedural justice), and at the other, the idea that any policies or procedures that have the effect of punishing or controlling a higher proportion of one social group than another are unjust".[465] One might argue, then, "that law and social policy should be adjusted so as to achieve equal outcomes".[466] This is distributive fairness, which shall be neglected in this chapter. Substantive fairness involves the protection of substantive rights, such as the right to bodily autonomy, liber-

---

[461] Heinze and Fyfe, 2020, pp. 345 ff., see above note 118; Heinze and Fyfe, 2018, pp. 3 ff., see above note 110.

[462] See, for example, Fuller, 1969, see above note 282; McDermott, 2016, see above note 382.

[463] Larry May, *Global Justice and Due Process*, Cambridge University Press, 2011, p. 52.

[464] Zuckerman, 1987, p. 58, see above note 194 ("It is by no means self-evident that acquittal of the guilty is an appropriate response to earlier police transgressions. Nor is a blanket exclusion capable of achieving a balance between the seriousness of the infringement and the benefit to the accused").

[465] Loraine Gelsthorpe and Nicola Padfield, "Introduction", in Loraine Gelsthorpe and Nicola Padfield (eds.), *Exercising Discretion: Decision-making in the criminal justice system and beyond*, Willian Publishing, New York, 2003, p. 12. See also Rebecca E. Hollander-Blumoff, "Fairness Beyond the Adversary System", in *Fordham Law Review*, 2017, vol. 85, no. 5, pp. 2081–2095.

[466] Gelsthorpe and Padfield, 2003, p. 12, see above note 465.

ty from confinement, or a trial that does not result in a mistaken conviction.[467] A trial that results in an absurd outcome or one that is intuitively immoral would be considered substantively unfair.[468]

The public generally thinks about fairness in terms of substantive justice, meaning that a just result of a trial is one in which the guilty are convicted, and the innocent acquitted. Law enforcement officers, for instance, "have the obligation to convict the guilty and to make sure they do not convict the innocent. They must be dedicated to making the criminal trial a procedure for the ascertainment of the true facts surrounding the commission of the crime".[469] Yet, this result-based, substantive view of fairness can also be hard to achieve, depending on the availability and admissibility of evidence. Transferred to the debate around illegally obtained evidence and the rationale for its exclusion, this evidence might not only be procedurally unfair but – it might also have low reliability and could put a conviction based merely on this piece of evidence in question with regard to the fairness of its outcome. This is an argument similar to those brought forward by the reliability rationale.[470] A conviction that is based on unreliable evidence is not substantially fair. Strictly speaking, substantive fairness has a truth component, a fact that lays bare the common conceptual denominator of the juxtapositions 'substantive fairness vs. procedural fairness' and 'substantive truth vs. procedural truth'.[471] In an inquisitorial or policy-implementing[472] system like Germany, the criminal justice system seeks the truth, and all parties to the legal proceedings share this aim. Here, truth in the context of criminal procedure is only a "subgoal" of the goal "peace under the law".[473] A complete analysis of the role of truth-finding in the

---

[467] See, for example, Larry Alexander, "Are Procedural Rights Derivative Substantive Rights?", in *Law and Philosophy*, 1998, vol. 17, no. 1, p. 19.

[468] See Fuller, 1969, see above note 282.

[469] US SC, *US v. Wade*, 1967, 388 US 218, pp. 256–58; Corrigan, 1986, p. 538, see above note 181.

[470] See above Section 17.5.2.2.3.2. and below Section 17.5.2.3.2.3.2.

[471] In a similar vein, see HO Hock Lai, *A Philosophy of Evidence Law*, Oxford University Press, Oxford, 2008, p. 49: "Various writers have cautioned against the tendency to explain and justify the law of evidence in strictly instrumental terms. They have argued persuasively that some evidential rules, principally those traditionally regarded as side-constraints on the main task of truth determination, are grounded in values that are intrinsic to the fairness, legitimacy, or integrity of the trial".

[472] For a categorisation of procedural models, see Heinze, 2014, pp. 104 ff., see above note 110.

[473] See Ralf Peter Anders, "Straftheoretische Anmerkungen zur Verletztenorientierung im Strafverfahren", in *Zeitschrift für die gesamte Strafrechtswissenschaft*, 2012, vol. 124, no. 2,

criminal process (and status afforded to the concept of 'truth' altogether) is outside the scope of this chapter. In Germany, a distinction is made between procedural truth and substantive truth, which largely corresponds with the distinction between procedural fairness and substantive fairness.[474] As Weigend notes, "[i]f truth-finding connotes the revelation (or discovery) of an objective reality, it is the result that legitimizes the process. The judicial process is only the means to discover the hidden, 'objective' reality and should be organized to optimize the chances of finding the 'piece of gold'".[475] He goes on to distinguish this substantive view of truth from procedural truth, which is "whatever emerges from a fair and rational discourse among the parties', and 'the content of the rules that determine the process [are] more important than the outcome itself, and adherence to these rules acquires paramount importance for truth-finding".[476] Interestingly, the BGH has explicitly underlined the role of procedural truth in criminal procedure:

> [a]cceptance and legitimacy of criminal judgments are not based on the trust in a 'correctness', understood as a material truth that is discovered in the course of a criminal trial. Instead, trust in the 'procedural truth' it is both necessary and sufficient. The 'procedural truth' is created through a trial that

---

p. 393. However, it should be stressed that the goals of criminal procedure in Germany and their relationship are highly disputed, see Dieter Dölling, "Über das Ziel des Strafverfahrens", in Christian Fahl *et al.* (eds.), *Festschrift für Werner Beulke zum 70 Geburtstag*, C.F. Müller, Heidelberg, 2015, pp. 679–87. About the divergent meanings of 'truth' in criminal procedure Edda Weslau, "Wahrheit und Legenden: die Debatte über den adversatorischen Strafprozess", in Roland Hefendehl, Tatjana Hörnle and Luis Greco (eds.), *Festschrift für Bernd Schünemann zum 70 Geburtstag*, De Gruyter, Berlin, 2014, pp. 1002–1005.

[474] In that vein Edda Weßlau, *Das Konsensprinzip im Strafverfahren – Leitidee für eine Gesamtreform?*, Nomos, Baden-Baden, 2002, p. 20.

[475] See Thomas Weigend, "Should We Search for the Truth, and Who Should Do it?", in *North Carolina Journal of International Law and Commercial Regulation*, 2011, vol. 36, no. 2, p. 389 (fn. omitted).

[476] See *ibid.*, p. 389 (fn. omitted). Weigend cites Jacqueline Hodgson, "Conceptions of the Trial in Inquisitorial and Adversarial Procedure", in Antony Duff *et al.* (eds), *The Trial on Trial – Volume 2: Judgment and calling to account*, Hart, Oxford, 2006, p. 225–226. For a general analysis, see A. Duff *et al.*, 2007, pp. 61 ff., see above note 145. See also Safferling, 2012, p. 55, see above note 359. From the perspective of communication- and discourse-theory, see Klaus Rolinski, "Der Grundsatz der Unmittelbarkeit: Garant der Wahrheitsfindung?", in Robert Esser *et al.* (eds.), *Festschrift für Hans-Heiner Kühne*, C.F. Müller, Heidelberg, 2013, p. 311; Mariana Sacher, "Diskurstheorie als Legitimation für die Absprachen im Strafverfahren?", in Roland Hefendehl, Tatjana Hörnle, and Luis Greco, *Festschrift für Bernd Schünemann zum 70. Geburtstag*, De Gruyter, Berlin, 2014, pp. 959–960.

complies with both the substantial and procedural law and is therefore fair.[477]

Thus, while both the Article 20(3) of the German Basic Law (Grundgesetz, 'GG') – in conjunction with Article 2(1) GG – and Article 6 of the European Convention on Human Rights,[478] ensure the right to a fair trial and other protections for the accused, a primary aim of the German criminal justice system is to seek the truth, or to seek the substantively fair result. The US criminal justice system, to take an example from the common law tradition, purports to be aimed at procedural fairness. The Fourteenth Amendment of the US Constitution states that no State shall "deprive any person of life, liberty, or property, without due process of law; nor deny to any person within its jurisdiction the equal protection of the laws".[479] The Fourth, Fifth, Sixth, and Eighth Amendments also provide protections for accused individuals.[480] Yet it remains the case that in an adversarial system like the US, the judge is responsible for protecting the accused's due process rights, or procedural fairness, and the prosecutor is responsible for obtaining a substantively fair result within the parameters set by the judge (albeit through the adversarial process rather than a pure truth-seeking process). The same applies to the Crown Prosecution Service in England and Wales, which searches for an "*approximation* of 'the truth'", understanding "truth *as* proof",[481] which appears to fall within the concept

---

[477] See BGH, Judgment from 10 June 2015 – 2 StR 97/14, in *Neue Zeitschrift für Strafrecht (NStZ)* 2016, 52, 58 (author's translation). The original quote reads:

Akzeptanz und Legitimation strafrichterlicher Urteile werden nicht durch das Vertrauen auf 'Richtigkeit' im Sinne einer im Verfahren gefundenen materiellen Wahrheit begründet. Ausreichend aber auch erforderlich ist das Vertrauen in die 'prozessuale Wahrheit', die vermittelt wird durch ein rechtsrichtiges, prozessordnungsgemäßes und daher unter anderem faires Verfahren.

[478] Claus Roxin and Bernd Schünemann, *Strafverfahrensrecht*, twenty-ninth edition, C.H. Beck, München, 2017, § 11 mn. 4; Bertram Schmitt, "Introduction", in Lutz Meyer-Goßner and Bertram Schmitt (eds.), *Kommentar zur Strafprozessordnung*, sixty-third edition, C.H. Beck, München, 2020, mn. 19; Klaus Geppert, "Zum ,fair-trial-Prinzip' nach Art. 6 Abs. 1 Satz 1 der Europäischen Menschenrechtskonvention", in *Juristische Ausbildung*, 1992, pp. 597–604 (597); Robert Esser, *Auf dem Weg zu einem europäischen Strafverfahrensrecht*, de Gruyter, Berlin, 2002, p. 401.

[479] United States, Constitution of the United States of America, 1787, amendment XIV (https://www.legal-tools.org/doc/bc3d56/).

[480] *Ibid.*, amends. IX, X, XI, XIII.

[481] Gary Slapper and David Kelly, *The English Legal System*, eighth edition, Routledge, London, New York, 2017, p. 394 (emphasis in the original). Cicchini argues that the truth as proof-model is now also applied by prosecutors in the US, see Michael D. Cicchini, "Spin

of 'procedural truth' rather than 'substantive truth'.[482] In the international arena, too, substantive fairness has received particular emphasis.[483] At the same time, however, especially at the *ad hoc* Tribunals, procedural fairness could outweigh substantive fairness: "A Chamber may exclude evidence if its probative value is substantially outweighed by the need to ensure a fair trial".[484]

17.5.2.3.2.3.1. Integrity as Moral Authority of the Verdict, and Integrity as Legitimacy

As remarked earlier, the public would hold a critical attitude towards the fairness of the trial and argue that the courts fail to uphold procedural justice if wrongfully obtained evidence would be admitted in every case and without scrutiny.[485] What this sentence incorporates is a combination of substantive fairness and the communicative effect of a judgment. In the words of Duff *et al.*:

> The communicative process is essential in order that verdicts reflect not only the epistemic standards appropriate to the criminal law, but also the court's moral standing to condemn the defendant for committing a public wrong. Such moral standing, we suggest, is only secure if the defendant is treated as a full citizen who is entitled to participate in a criminal process which he could accept as legitimate.[486]

This combination has turned out to be one of the theoretical bases of international criminal law.[487]

Doctors: Prosecutor Sophistry and the Burden of Proof", in *University of Cincinnati Law Review*, 2018, vol. 87, no. 2, p. 491.

[482] See in more detail Heinze and Fyfe, 2020, p. 348, see above note 118.

[483] Pitcher, 2018, p. 281, see above note 192 ("is concerned with the need to ensure a fair trial; specifically, it appears to be linked to a chamber's truth-finding task, i.e. the ability of a chamber to determine the guilt or innocence of accused accurately, or otherwise to 'trial fairness'") with further references.

[484] ICTY RPE, Rule 89(D), see above note 341.

[485] See above Section 17.5.2.2.3.1.

[486] A. Duff *et al.*, 2007, p. 236, see above note 145.

[487] The following part is, albeit in modified form, taken from Alexander Heinze, "The Statute of the International Criminal Court as a Kantian Constitution", in Morten Bergsmo and Emiliano J. Buis (eds.), *Philosophical Foundations of International Criminal Law: Correlating Thinkers*, TOAEP, Brussels, 2018, pp. 351–428.

At the international level, retribution is clothed in an expressivist[488] and communicative[489] appearance,[490] that is, as the expression of condemnation and outrage of the international community, where the international community in its entirety is considered one of the victims.[491] The stigmatisation and punishment for gross human rights violations in service of the confirmation and reinforcement of fundamental human rights norms can justify a right to punish of an international criminal tribunal that lacks the authority of a State. Given this justification of punishment, what the world community is trying to achieve through international criminal trials is a communicative effect: to show the world that there is justice at an international level, and that no perpetrator of grave international crimes can es-

---

[488] See for a definition and in more detail Heinze, 2018, pp. 417 ff., see above note 487. On the different forms of expressivism in ICL Sander, LJIL, 32 (2019), 851 ff.; Carsten Stahn, *A Critical Introduction to International Criminal Law*, Cambridge University Press, Cambridge, 2019, pp. 181–182; on the limits of expressivism Barrie Sander, "The Expressive Limits of International Criminal Justice: Victim Trauma and Local Culture in the Iron Cage of the Law", in International Criminal Law Review, 2019, vol. 19, pp. 1014 ff.; Daniela Demko, "An Expressive Theory of International Punishment for International Crimes", in Florian Jeßberger and Julia Geneuss (eds.), *Why punish perpetrators of mass atrocities? Purposes of punishment in international criminal law*, Cambridge University Press, 2020, pp. 176 ff.

[489] Heinze, 2018, pp. 417 ff., see above note 487; Klaus Günther, "Positive General Prevention and the Idea of Civic Courage in International Criminal Law", in Florian Jeßberger and Julia Geneuss (eds.), *Why punish perpetrators of mass atrocities? Purposes of punishment in international criminal law*, Cambridge University Press, 2020, pp. 213 ff.

[490] Mark A. Drumbl, *Atrocity, Punishment, and International Law*, Cambridge University Press, Cambridge, 2007, pp. 173 ff.; Mark A. Drumbl, "International Punishment from 'Other' Perspectives", in Róisín Mulgrew and Denis Abels (eds.), *Research Handbook on the International Penal System*, Edward Elgar Publishing, Northampton, 2016, p. 386; Jonathan H. Choi, "Early Release in International Criminal Law", in *Yale Law Journal*, 2014, vol. 123, no. 6, p. 1810; Robert D. Sloane, "The Expressive Capacity of International Punishment", in *Stanford Journal of International Law*, 2007, vol. 43, no. 1, p. 44; Kirsten J. Fisher, *Moral Accountability and International Criminal Law*, Routledge, London, 2012, pp. 51, 56–63, 65; Carsten Stahn, "Between 'Faith' and 'Facts'", in *Leiden Journal of International Law*, 2012, vol. 25, no. 2, pp. 251, 279–80; Larry May, *Aggression and Crimes Against Peace*, Cambridge University Press, Cambridge, 2008, pp. 329 ff. From a German perspective, see also Klaus Günther, "Criminal Law, Crime and Punishment as Communication", in Andrew P. Simester *et al.* (eds.), *Liberal Criminal Theory*, Hart, Oxford, 2014, pp. 123 ff. About the communicative function within the (new) retributivist theories, see Michael Pawlik, "Kritik der präventionstheoretischen Strafbegründungen", in Klaus Rogall *et al.* (eds.), *Festschrift für Rudolphi*, Luchterhand, Neuwied, 2004, p. 229.

[491] Kai Ambos, "Review Essay: Liberal Criminal Theory", in *Criminal Law Forum*, 2017, vol. 28, no. 3, pp. 589, 601.

---

cape it.[492] That is why international criminal law seeks to achieve retributive and deterrent effects of punishment through creating a certain perception of international criminal trials. It is also why the protection of due process rights is perceived as crucial in order to restore international peace, and strengthen the trust of the international society in legal norms (procedure "as an end in itself"[493]), and is the reason why Nazi perpetrators were not executed without trial. Instead, the former President of the US, Harry S. Truman, remarked at the start of the trials before the International Military Tribunal at Nuremberg in 1945: "The world should be impressed by the fairness of the trial. These German murderers must be punished, but only upon proof of individual guilt at a trial".[494]

It would be detrimental to the expressivist and communicative function of a public trial, if a conviction rendered by an ICT was based on illegally obtained evidence – irrespective of the status of the person who obtained the evidence. Rogall makes a similar general-preventive, or expressivist argument: trials and judgments respectively have a general-preventive effect. This effect would be circumvented, if evidence that is illegally obtained by private individuals could generally be admitted.[495] Rogall combines this argument with an empirical premise: private investi-

---

[492] International criminal law is also "educating society about its past" through the truth-telling function of international criminal trials, see Mina Rauschenbach, "Individuals Accused of International Crimes as Delegitimized Agents of Truth", in *International Criminal Justice Review*, 2018, Advance Article, p. 3 with further references.

[493] Jonathan Hafetz, *Punishing Atrocities Through a Fair Trial*, Cambridge University Press, 2018, p. 109.

[494] Cited in Francis Biddle, *In Brief Authority*, Greenwood Press, Westport, 1962/1972, p. 372; Patricia M. Wald, "Running the Trial of the Century", in *Cardozo Law Review*, 2005–6, vol. 27, no. 4, pp. 1559, 1574. US Chief prosecutor Jackson famously argued: "Unless we write the record of this movement with clarity and precision, we cannot blame the future if in days of peace it finds incredible the accusatory generalities uttered during war. We must establish incredible events by credible evidence.", see Telford Taylor, *The Anatomy of the Nuremberg Trials*, Back Bay Books, Boston, 1992, p. 54; Henry T. King, "The Spirit of Nuremberg—Idealism", in Beth A. Griech-Polelle (ed.), *The Nuremberg War Crimes Trial and its Policy Consequences Today*, 2nd edn., Nomos, Baden-Baden 2020, p. 5. Or, in the words of British International Military Tribunal Judge Geoffrey Lawrence, one wanted to punish "those who were guilty", to establish "the supremacy of international law over national law" and to prove "actual facts, in order to bring home to the German people and to the peoples of the world, the depths of infamy to which the pursuit of total warfare had brought Germany", see Geoffrey Lawrence, "Nuremberg Trial", in Guénaël Mettraux (ed.), *Perspectives on the Nuremberg Trial*, Oxford University Press, 2008, pp. 290, 292.

[495] Rogall, 2016, mn. 13, see above note 435.

gations are aimed at the production of evidence. Thus, private individuals in such a context show a reduced willingness to abide by procedural law or due process, due to a case of what Rogall calls "evidentiary emergency".[496] Excluding the evidence has the purpose of demonstrating the illegality of an individual taking justice in his or her own hands – a purpose that is generally assigned to an expressivist theory of punishment. This is especially underlined upon viewing the criminal process as a system: if evidence, based on an infringement of rights and a violation of rules, is used in a trial, the public loses confidence in the *system* of rules and their effectiveness – and not so much in a particular rule. It is of secondary importance who in fact broke the rules and violated the rights, whether a public official or a private individual. The public's trust in the system of rules is different from its expectation to be protected by the State against rights violations. The latter is what I have previously described as the sword function of human rights,[497] or *Strafanspruch*.[498] The former touches upon the expressivist and communicative function of a trial and the judgment.[499] More concretely: norms are recognised by society *as a whole* and determine the contents of social communication[500] – an argument put forward by Jakobs. He draws attention to the "validity" (*Geltung*) of a norm and its affirmation

---

[496] *Ibid.*

[497] See above Section 17.5.2.2.2.

[498] Henning Radtke, "Beweisverwertungsverbote in Verfahrensstadien vor der Hauptverhandlung und die sog. Widerspruchslösung", in Stephan Barton *et al.* (eds.), *Festschrift für Reinhold Schlothauer zum 70. Geburtstag*, C.H. Beck, München, 2018, pp. 461 ff.; Hilde Kaufmann, *Strafanspruch Strafklagerecht*, Otto Schwartz, Göttingen, 1968), pp. 9 ff.; Klaus Günther, "Falscher Friede durch repressives Völkerstrafrecht?", in Werner Beulke *et al.* (eds.), *Das Dilemma des rechtsstaatlichen Strafrechts*. Berliner Wissenschafts-Verlag, Berlin, 2009, p. 89 ("Parallel zum öffentlichen Strafanspruch beim nationalstaatlichen Strafrecht wird auch der völkerrechtliche Strafanspruch nicht im Namen der Verletzten erhoben, sondern im Namen der Völkergemeinschaft oder im Namen eines Staates, der auf der Grundlage des Universalitätsprinzips ein Völkerrechtsverbrechen verfolgt"). In detail Kai Ambos, "Strafrecht und Verfassung: Gibt es einen *Anspruch* auf Strafgesetze, Strafverfolgung, Strafverhängung?", in Jan Christoph Bublitz *et al.* (eds.), *Recht – Philosophie – Literatur. Festschrift für Reinhard Merkel zum 70. Geburtstag*, Berlin, Duncker & Humblot, 2020, pp. 565 ff. About a critique of the term 'Strafanspruch' Jung, 2019, pp. 265–266, see above note 333.

[499] See above notes 488 and 489 with main text.

[500] Günther Jakobs, "Strafrechtliche Zurechnung und die Bedingungen der Normgeltung", in Ulfried Neumann and Lorenz Schulz (eds.), *Verantwortung in Recht und Moral. ARSP-Beiheft*, vol. 74, Franz Steiner Verlag, Stuttgart, 2000, pp. 58–59; Günther Jakobs, "Das Strafrecht zwischen Funktionalismus und „alteuropäischem" Prinzipiendenken", in *Zeitschrift für die gesamte Strafrechtswissenschaft*, 1995, vol. 107, no. 4, pp. 843 ff. In detail Ambos, 2013, p. 300, see above note 163.

(*Bestätigung*).[501] Dennis combines these elements under the umbrella of legitimacy.[502] Understood this way, legitimacy has both a descriptive and normative element: descriptive, because it "refers to social facts concerning actors' beliefs about the legitimate authority" of an ICT; normative due to the "motivating force" behind an ICT's judgment (as implementation of international criminal justice goals).[503] What becomes visible upon reading these arguments is a close interrelationship between the goals and purposes of substantive criminal law[504] and procedural law – and underlines, again, the synchronisation between the two.[505] I have made this argument else-where: punishing perpetrators of international crimes will not work without the admission of relevant evidence. Thus, the goal of the admission of rele-vant evidence for guilt or not is at the same time the goal of punishing per-petrators of international crimes, which becomes a purpose of international criminal procedure.[506] Moreover, the admission of relevant evidence as a goal of international criminal procedure is also connected to the purpose of punishment "in such a way that it will increase the likelihood that the guilty will be punished and the innocent will go free".[507]

---

[501] Günther Jakobs, *Strafrecht, Allgemeiner Teil*, second edition, Walter de Gruyter, Berlin, New York, 1991, pp. 34 ff. See also Andrew P. Simester, Antje Du Bois-Pedain, and Ulfried Neumann, *Liberal Criminal Theory: Essays for Andreas von Hirsch*, Hart Publishing, Oxford, 2014, p. 25.

[502] Dennis, 2020, mn. 2-022, see above note 192.

[503] The definitions are taken from Andreas Føllesdal, "The Legitimacy of International Courts", in *Journal of Political Philosophy*, 2020, Advance Article, p. 5. See generally with an in-structive overview Cesare P.R. Romano, "Legitimacy, Authority, and Performance: Contem-porary Anxieties of International Courts and Tribunals", in *American Journal of Interna-tional Law*, 2020, vol. 114, pp. 149–163. About the legitimacy of International Criminal Jus-tice, combined with expressivism, Tom Dannenbaum, "Legitimacy in War and Punishment", in Kevin Jon Heller, et al. (eds.), *The Oxford Handbook of International Criminal Law*, Ox-ford University Press, Oxford, 2020), pp. 136 ff.

[504] In detail, see Heinze, 2018, pp. 929–957, see above note 376.

[505] In a similar vein, see Volk, 1978, p. 173, see above note 334.

[506] As clarified throughout the chapter, its research object is illegally obtained evidence. It goes without saying that the sentence to this footnote in the main text applies *mutatis mutandis* also to the rationale of disclosing exculpatory evidence and other procedural safeguards. Af-ter all, the goal of punishing perpetrators of international crimes also strives to punish only those perpetrators who are perceived to be guilty beyond reasonable doubt.

[507] Jens David Ohlin, "Goals of International Criminal Justice and International Criminal Pro-cedure", in Göran Sluiter *et al.* (eds.), *International Criminal Procedure*, Oxford University Press, 2013, p. 61.

Yet, it would have a similar detrimental effect, if the decision of excluding crucial evidence was only due to a relatively minor violation of legal procedure. The ICTY Appeals Chamber in *Karadžić* highlighted this imbalance by recalling

> that the Appellant is charged with genocide, crimes against humanity and war crimes. The public interest in the prosecution of an individual accused of such offences, universally condemned, is unquestionably strong. Against the legitimate interest of the international community in the prosecution of the Appellant for Universally Condemned Offences stands the alleged violation of the Appellant's expectation that he would not be prosecuted by the Tribunal, pursuant to the alleged Agreement.[508]

Here again, the two dimensions of fairness – procedural fairness (the accused go free, since procedural rules have been violated) vs. substantive fairness (the accused are convicted despite the violation of procedural rules, since they have been found guilty beyond reasonable doubt) – affect a judgment like two parents their child. Within this rationale, integrity becomes a "proxy, synonym or placeholder" for procedural values such as fairness, due process, natural justice or judicial legitimacy.[509]

17.5.2.3.2.3.2. Integrity as Reliability

Substantive fairness in international criminal law is also the objective behind integrity as reliability, since the use of unreliable evidence "increases the risk of error in fact-finding".[510] The interrelationship – almost interchangeability – of substantive fairness and substantive truth becomes most visible here, since excluding wrongfully obtained evidence would even *advance* the search for truth. As pointed out earlier, integrity as reliability is informed by the expressivist notion of integrity as moral authority of the verdict. Rogall expressly refers to a forward-looking evaluation of the illegally obtained evidence and requires the courts to take into account the "normative" (read as general-preventive, expressive) effect that the admission of the evidence might have.[511] Thus, the question of whether or not to

---

[508] ICTY, *Prosecutor v. Karadžić*, Decision on Karadžić's Appeal of Trial Chamber's Decision on Alleged Holbrooke Agreement, 12 October 2009, IT-95-5/18-AR73.4, para. 49 (https://www.legal-tools.org/doc/a1da0d/). See also Pitcher, 2018, p. 277, see above note 192.

[509] Roberts *et al.*, 2016, p. 5, see above note 146.

[510] HO, 2019, p. 828, see above note 189.

[511] Rogall, 2016, mn. 14, see above note 435.

exclude illegally obtained evidence by private individuals is a balancing exercise,[512] where the search for truth, and "indirectly, society's interest in criminal enforcement", is pit against "the respect for the rights of criminal defendants and, indirectly, of the entire civilian population, which have been declared to be so important to the legal order that they have been enshrined in human rights conventions and national constitutions".[513] Considering this balancing exercise, Haffke sees a prevalence of the search for truth.[514]

For ICTs, a reason not to admit – otherwise admissible – evidence is that the use of illicit methods would negatively affect the reliability of the evidence.[515] Article 69(7) of the ICC Statute – *lex specialis* to the general admissibility rule of paragraph (4) of the same article – repeats the (new) Rule 95 of the ICTY and ICTR Statutes stating: "Evidence obtained by means of a violation of this statute or internationally recognized human rights shall not be admissible if: [...] The violation casts substantial doubt on the reliability of the evidence". The integrity as reliability rationale becomes even more visible in the ICTY's framework (now MICT's respectively): a Chamber "may exclude evidence if its probative value is substantially outweighed by the need to ensure a fair trial"[516] or "if obtained by methods which cast substantial doubt on its reliability or if its admission is antithetical to, and would seriously damage, the integrity of the proceedings".[517]

---

[512] *Ibid.*, mn. 15.

[513] Thaman and Brodowski, 2020, p. 437, see above note 196.

[514] Bernhard Haffke, "Schweigepflicht, Verfahrensrevision und Beweisverbot", in *Goltdammer's Archiv für Strafrecht*, 1973, p. 83.

[515] ICC Statute, Article 69(7)(a), see above note 182; also ICTY RPE, Rule 95(1), see above note 341; ICTR RPE, Rule 95(1), see above note 341 and Mechanism for International Criminal Tribunals ('MICT'), Rules of Procedure and Evidence, 8 June 2012, MICT/1, Rule 117(1) ('MICT RPE') (https://www.legal-tools.org/doc/cef176/).

[516] ICTY RPE, Rule 89(D), see above note 341 and MICT RPE, Rule 105(D), see above note 515 (emphasis added).

[517] ICTY RPE, Rule 95, see above note 341; ICTR RPE, Rule 95, see above note 341 and MICT RPE, Rule 117, see above note 515; also Special Court for Sierra Leone ('SCSL'), Rules of Procedure and Evidence, 31 May 2012, Rule 95 ('SCSL RPE') (https://www.legal-tools.org/doc/4c2a6b/) (exclusion if "admission would bring the administration of justice into serious disrepute").

17.5.2.3.2.3.3. Integrity as Rule of Law

As I have demonstrated above in detail, one of the main rationales for excluding or not admitting evidence is the rule of law principle. Ideally, the 'law' in rule of law incorporates the integrity rationale, that is, the moral authority of the verdict, legitimacy, fair trial and reliability.[518] The question that remains to be answered is whether the rule of law principle applicable to both the extra-investigatory context and the international level?

17.5.2.3.2.3.3.1. Applicability of the Rule of Law to the Extra-Investigatory Context

I have previously opined that the question of *whom* a procedural rule is addressed to cannot be answered without the question of *what* procedural rules are concerned with. Applying Luhmann's systems theory, laws are not so much addressed to individuals but to closed systems – systems that cannot be influenced but merely motivated by external factors. I concluded that the addressee of procedural law is the process as a system. Rules apply to everyone within that system – and might even apply beyond that system through transgressive communication (just as the judgment communicates not only with the accused and victim but with society as a whole). Even when we divide the procedural law into Crime Control and Due Process functions, with the former being addressed to the police and prosecution, the latter applies to everyone that is involved in the investigatory process when this involvement eventually has an effect on Due Process. Understood this way, the exclusionary rules also apply to private conduct.

In this extra-investigatory context, where exclusionary rules still apply, the rule of law principle – and with it, integrity – is vital. In fact, it is the benchmark for every conduct within a procedural system. In the words of Turvey and Cooley, "The credibility of the criminal justice system relies heavily on the integrity of those who work *in* the system".[519] Due to the above-mentioned understanding of 'law', which incorporates integrity, the rule of law becomes a "proxy" (a term borrowed from Paul Roberts) for integrity and procedural values such as fairness, due process, natural justice

---

[518] Dennis, 2020, mn. 2-022, see above note 192. In a similar vein Allen Buchanan, "The Complex Epistemology of Institutional Legitimacy Assessments, As Illustrated by the Case of the International Criminal Court", in *Temple International and Comparative Law Journal*, 2019, vol. 33, p. 332-333.

[519] Turvey and Cooley, 2014, p. 164, see above note 180 (emphasis added).

or judicial legitimacy.[520] In a similar, albeit more restrictive fashion, some scholars in Germany make an exception of the general admissibility of illegally obtained evidence by private individuals when the State intends to make use of such evidence.[521] They argue that this might violate the rule of law, the legal order, or the constitution.[522]

Rogall refers to the rule of law that is also applicable in the case of evidence obtained by private individuals.[523] This goes to what Postema famously underlined through his "reflexive dimension" of the rule of law, while referring to Bentham: "Those in power as well as those subject to that power must be subject to the law".[524]

17.5.2.3.2.3.3.2. Criminal Procedure's Sub-systems

Every endeavour of applying the systems-theory by Luhmann and Teubner eventually passes over to the bifurcated decision of how narrow the systems and sub-systems should be. The criminal process with its various stages[525] is especially prone to such an endeavour. Strictly speaking, the investigatory context (sub-system 1) could easily be (and often is) separated from the trial process (sub-system 2).

17.5.2.3.2.3.3.2.1. Separating Investigatory System and Trial System: *Beweiserhebung* vs. *Beweisverwertung*

Separating the investigatory and trial contexts has the advantage of separating the effects violations may have within these systems. Let us assume, for a moment, that both systems are closed systems. They could thus be hermetically sealed to avoid that a violation of the integrity of one system affects the other system. This way, the advantages of sanctioning illegally obtained evidence could be enjoyed without risking the rupture of the en-

---

[520] Roberts *et al.*, 2016, p. 5, see above note 146.

[521] Matula, 2012, p. 101, see above note 314.

[522] Rogall, 2016, mn. 11 with further references in fn. 63, see above note 435.

[523] *Ibid.*, mn. 13: "Nach unserer verfassungsmäßigen Ordnung hat der Staat die Rechtsordnung so zu gestalten (vgl. Art. 1 Abs. 1 Satz 2, Abs. 3, 20 Abs. 3 GG), dass eine Verletzung der Grundrechte, namentlich der Menschenwürde, verhindert wird. Diese staatliche Schutzverpflichtung besteht dabei auch gegenüber Angriffen Privater".

[524] Gerald J. Postema, "Law's Rule: Reflexivity, Mutual Accountability, and the Rule of Law", in ZHAI Xiaobo and Michael Quinn (eds.), *Bentham's Theory of Law and Public Opinion*, Cambridge University Press, 2014, p. 56.

[525] Heinze, 2014, pp. 264 ff., see above note 110.

tire trial and eventually putting into question the substantive fairness of an acquittal (when it is almost certain, for instance, that the accused is guilty).

What sounds like a viable but almost artificial compromise is a reality in German criminal procedure. German courts differentiate between rules prohibiting the *obtaining or taking* of evidence (*Beweiserhebungsverbote*), and rules prohibiting the *use* of evidence by the court in its assessment of the defendant's guilt (*Beweisverwertungsverbote*).[526] How radically separated the two stages, or put differently: how closed the two subsystems are, is a matter of controversy, with the strictest separation-theory probably brought forward by Jäger ("Separation- and Abstraction Principle").[527] Distinguishing between the obtaining of evidence and its actual use at trial is *Janus*-faced. This works in both ways: not every illegally obtained piece of evidence necessarily leads to its exclusion.[528] And not all evidence obtained legally may later be used as evidence.[529] The separation of the two stages and the focus on the short- and long-term effects of a procedural violation creates a chain reaction of exclusionary rules: those rules may address a) the "re-use"[530] of the (same) evidence *as evidence* in further proceedings against the same or other defendants; b) a possible effect of illegally obtained evidence on a fresh investigation; and c) whether further evidence taken on the basis of excluded evidence needs to be excluded as well ("fruit of the poisonous tree"; "*Fernwirkung*").[531]

Separating the two stages in the scenario that this chapter is about (illegally obtained evidence in the extra-investigatory context at the international level), ICTs could declare that illegally obtained evidence must be

---

[526] In detail, see Thaman and Brodowski, 2020, pp. 434–435, see above note 196.

[527] Christian Jäger, *Beweisverwertung und Beweisverwertungsverbote im Straprozess*, C.H. Beck, München, 2003, pp. 137–138 (author's translation, original terminology: "Trennungs- und Abstraktionsprinzip").

[528] See German Federal Constitutional Court, Decision of 20 09 2018 – 2 BvR 708/18 –, para. 40; *idem*, Decision of 16.02.2006 – 2 BvR 2085/05 = BVerfG NStZ 2006, 46, 47; *idem*, Decision of 02.07.2009 – 2 BvR 2225/08 = NJW 2009, 3225; German Federal Court of Justice, Judgment of 13.01.2011 – 3 StR 332/10 = BGHSt 56, 127, para. 13; Kai Ambos, *Beweisverwertungsverbote*, Duncker & Humblot, Berlin, 2010, p. 22; Jäger, 2003, p. 135, see above note 527; Matthias Jahn, *Beweiserhebung und Beweisverwertungsverbote im Spannungsfeld zwischen den Garantien des Rechtsstaates und der effektiven Bekämpfung von Kriminalität und Terrorismus, Gutachten C, 67. Deutscher Juristentag*, C.H. Beck, München, 2008, p. 36.

[529] Thaman and Brodowski, 2020, p. 436, see above note 196.

[530] Translation by *ibid.*, p. 458.

[531] Generally, see *ibid.*, p. 436.

excluded from trial (non-use, or *Verwertungsverbot*), but it could still be eventually *used in the pre-trial stage as lead evidence*. In other words, evidence could be illegally obtained, but only lead to other evidence, and not be used in court.[532] An exclusionary rule would thus only address the non-use of evidence in court, and requires balancing that allows for the obtainment of the evidence (even though it was illegally obtained). To provide an example: in the case against Ieng Thirith before the ECCC, a statement was made under torture. The Defence requested the co-investigating judges not only to hold this statement inadmissible, but also to decide against its use as 'lead evidence'. With regard to the latter request, that is of interest at this point, the judges decided:

> there is nothing objectionable in using the information contained in confessions as investigative leads to other sources of information, even if the information within the confession is ultimately deemed unreliable. A great deal of 'lead evidence' used in investigations is inherently unreliable and as such, would not be relied on in the Closing Order. However, during the course of the investigation, the Co-Investigating Judges need not rule out any hypothesis and it is not necessary for them to believe the assertions in the confessions to be true in order to use them to develop new avenues for searching out the truth, without this affecting the integrity of the proceedings.[533]

Another emanation of the separation hypothesis is the amended Rule 95 of the ICTY RPE. The former rule provided that evidence shall not be admissible "*if obtained by methods* which cast substantial doubt on its reliability or if its admission is antithetical to, and would seriously damage, the integrity of the proceedings".[534] As Calvo-Goller analysed, this rule "had the merit to discourage human rights violations in the gathering of evidence *ab initio*".[535] The rule is reminiscent of the German '*Beweismethoden-*

---

[532] About lead evidence, see Heinze, 2014, p. 455, see above note 110.

[533] Extraordinary Chambers in the Courts of Cambodia ('ECCC'), Office of the Co-Investigating Judges, *Prosecutor v. Ieng Thirith*, Order on use of statements which were or may have been obtained by torture, 28 July 2009, C002/19-09-2007-ECCC-OCIJ, para. 26 (https://www.legal-tools.org/doc/6uqmcu/). See also Fergal Gaynor *et al.*, "Law of Evidence", in Göran Sluiter *et al.* (eds.), *International Criminal Procedure*, Oxford University Press, 2013, p. 1029.

[534] Emphasis added.

[535] Karin N. Calvo-Goller, *The Trial Proceedings of the International Criminal Court*, Martinus Nijhoff, Leiden, Boston, 2006, p. 97 (emphasis in the original).

verbote', prohibiting certain *methods* of obtaining evidence. In 1995, on the basis of proposals from the governments of the United Kingdom and the US,[536] the rule was amended to add "which constitute a serious violation of internationally protected human rights" after methods. The significance of this amendment cannot be overstated: from now on, evidence obtained by an illegal method could still be admitted at trial, unless it "seriously" damaged the integrity of the proceedings.[537] Since Article 69(7) of the ICC Statute is based on the amended Rule 95 of the ICTY RPE, the same applies regarding the former provision, as the *Lubanga* Trial Chamber confirmed:

> Some scholars have suggested that any violation of internationally recognized human rights will necessarily damage the integrity of proceedings before the ICC. This argument does not take into account the fact that the Statute provides for a "dual test", which is to be applied following a finding that there has been a violation. Therefore, should the Chamber conclude that the evidence had been obtained in violation of the Statute or internationally recognized human rights, under Article 69(7) it is always necessary for it to consider the criteria in a) and b), *because the evidence is not automatically inadmissible*. It is important that artificial restrictions are not placed on the Chamber's ability to determine whether or not evidence should be admitted in accordance with this statutory provision.[538]

However, the dual test of Article 69(7) of the ICC Statute has not always been envisaged for the Court's exclusionary rules. In fact, in what arguably became "the most important basis for the Rome negotiations",[539] the *Zutphen Report*, the exclusionary rule was proposed without the second

---

[536] Second Annual Report of the International Tribunal for the Prosecution of Persons Responsible for Serious Violations of International Humanitarian Law Committed in the Territory of the Former Yugoslavia since 1991, reprinted in ICTY Yearbook, p. 287, U.N. Doc. S/1995/728, 23 August 1995 (https://www.legal-tools.org/doc/9a66a1/). For the amendment see ICTY, Rules of Procedure and Evidence, 6 October 1995, IT/32/REV.6 (https://www.legal-tools.org/doc/rkps3b/).

[537] Calvo-Goller, 2006, p. 97, see above note 535; Ambos, 2009, p. 370, see above note 191.

[538] ICC, *Prosecutor v. Lubanga*, Decision on the admission of material from the "bar table", 24 June 2009, ICC-01/04-01/06-1981, para. 41 (fn. omitted, emphasis added) (https://www.legal-tools.org/doc/c692ec/).

[539] Ambos, 2013, p. 24, see above note 452.

prong, allowing for the exclusion *ab initio* (the dual test was provided in brackets, though):

> Evidence obtained by means of violation of this Statute or of other rules of international law [or by means which cast substantial doubt on its reliability] [or whose admission is antithetical to, and would seriously damage, the integrity of the proceedings] [or by means which constitute a serious violation of internationally protected human rights] [or which have been collected in violation of the rights of the defence] shall not be admissible.[540]

In other instances, an ICT might find a violation grave enough to find that the illegally obtained evidence can neither be admitted in court nor lead to other evidence. Thus, the separation hypothesis provides a tool to disentangle the Gordian knot of procedural vs. substantive fairness.

17.5.2.3.2.3.3.2.2. Disclosure System

The separation hypothesis is a familiar basis for another evidentiary problem that provides useful guidance for the matter at hand: disclosure violations. An appellate court in England, for instance, referred to the "integrity of the discovery process", albeit in a civil case.[541] I have pointed this out elsewhere: the position of a human rights non-governmental organisation with respect to the confidentiality of witnesses and the information collected from them is troubling.[542] This created a problem that became visible at the ICC: in the *Lubanga* case, the Prosecution obtained evidence from the UN and certain NGOs pursuant to confidentiality agreements made under Article 54(3)(e) of the ICC Statute.[543] Basically, there was nothing wrong

---

[540] Article 62(5) Zutphen Draft, in M. Cherif Bassiouni and William A. Schabas (eds.), *The Legislative History of the International Criminal Court*, vol. 2, second edition, Brill Nijhoff, Leiden, Boston, 2016, pp. 620–621.

[541] UK HL, *Taylor & Anor. v. Director of the Serious Fraud Office & Ors.*, 29 October 1998, [1998] 3 W.L.R. 1040, [1999] 2 A.C. 177, p. 191.

[542] Bergsmo and Wiley, 2008, p. 18, see above note 1.

[543] Article 18(3) of the ICC–UN Relationship Agreement provides that "the United Nations and the Prosecutor may agree that the United Nations provide documents or information to the Prosecutor on condition of confidentiality and solely for the purpose of generating new evidence and that such documents shall not be disclosed to other organs of the Court or third parties, at any stage of the proceedings or thereafter, without the consent of the United Nations", cited in *Prosecutor v Lubanga*, Decision on the consequences of non-disclosure of exculpatory materials covered by Article 54(3)(e) agreements, 15 June 2008, ICC-01/04–01/06-1401, para. 93 ('Lubanga, 2008') (https://www.legal-tools.org/doc/e6a054/). The same rule applies to the UN peacekeeping mission, MONUC, in the Democratic Republic of

---

with that. As long as the amount of evidence obtained this way is relatively minor, and the documents or information were received on a confidential basis "solely for the purpose of generating new evidence" (lead evidence), the Prosecution was allowed to do this.[544] It had no effect on the trial phases, and thus paid tribute to the separation hypothesis. In other words, a few documents and pieces of information can be obtained, coupled with an agreement for non-disclosure, as long as the only purpose of receiving this material is that it leads to other evidence. However, this was far from what the Prosecution did. First, the Prosecution obtained more than fifty per cent of its evidence on the basis of confidentiality agreements with NGOs.[545] The Prosecution itself admitted that its use of Article 54(3)(e) of the ICC Statute to obtain evidence "may be viewed as excessive" and that "an excessive use of Art. 54(3)(e) would be problematic".[546] Second, a great amount of these documents were exculpatory material relevant to defence preparation.[547] These documents usually have to be turned over to the defence.[548] Third, and most importantly, the Prosecution did not use the Article 54(3)(e)-agreements only for the purpose to obtain other evidence, for example, as "springboard or lead potential".[549] In fact, the Prosecution did quite the opposite, as the Trial Chamber described:

Congo by way of Article 10(6) of the MONUC Memorandum of Understanding with the ICC, which reads: "Unless otherwise specified in writing [...], documents held by MONUC that are provided by the United Nations to the Prosecutor shall be understood to be provided in accordance with and subject to arrangements envisaged in Article 18, paragraph 3, of the Relationship Agreement", cited in Kai Ambos, "Confidential Investigations (Article 54(3)(e) ICC Statute) vs. Disclosure Obligations: The Lubanga Case and National Law", in *New Criminal Law Review*, 2009, vol. 12, no. 4, p. 550. Generally, see Heinze, 2014, p. 454, see above note 110.

[544] Lubanga, 2008, para. 93, see above note 543.

[545] ICC, *Prosecutor v. Lubanga*, Hearing Transcript, 13 March 2008, ICC-01/04-01/06-T-79, pp. 5–6 (https://www.legal-tools.org/doc/bdf4aa/).

[546] Cf. Lubanga, 2008, para. 32, see above note 543.

[547] *Ibid.*, para. 63 ("In this case over 200 documents, which the prosecution accepts have potential exculpatory effect or which are material to defence preparation, are the subject of agreements of this kind. On 10 June 2008, the Chamber was told that there are 'approximately' 95 items of potentially exculpatory material and 112 items which are 'material to defence preparation', pursuant to Rule 77, making a total of 207 items of evidence. Of these 207 items, 156 were provided by the UN", fn. omitted). See also Heinze, 2014, p. 455, see above note 110.

[548] See *ibid.*, pp. 344 ff.

[549] Cf. Lubanga, 2008, para. 72, see above note 543.

> the prosecution's general approach has been to use Article 54(3)(e) to obtain a wide range of materials under the cloak of confidentiality, in order to identify from those materials evidence to be used at trial (having obtained the information provider's consent). This is the exact opposite of the proper use of the provision, which is, exceptionally, to allow the prosecution to receive information or documents which are not for use at trial but which are instead intended to 'lead' to new evidence.[550]

As a result of this, the Chamber opted for a stay of proceedings because of an abuse of process.[551] I will go into this in detail in a moment. For now, it suffices to say that the exclusion of evidence as a result of non-disclosure, as it is the law in England,[552] was never even an option at the ICC and the "drastic" and "exceptional" stay of the proceedings turned into the hot potato of (*Lubanga*) case law.[553] More importantly, the Lubanga-disclosure-scenario casts doubts on the practicability of the condition to only use illegally obtained evidence as lead evidence: this condition is very much dependant on the *bona fide* conduct of both prosecutors and investigators. It might not be taken seriously when a court – as the ICC did – is reluctant to follow through with an effective remedy, namely a stay of proceedings.

17.5.2.3.2.3.3.2.3. The Conceptual Flaw of the Separation Hypothesis

If the separation hypothesis provides a tool to disentangle the Gordian knot of procedural vs. substantive fairness, this tool is indeed a sword (as in the original legend involving Alexander the Great) rather than a sophisticated strategy. As I see it, the separation hypothesis is a radical conceptual measure that comes at a price. This price is: a) the artificial separation of proce-

---

[550] *Ibid.*, para. 73.

[551] Jenia Iontcheva Turner, "Policing International Prosecutors", in *New York University Journal of International Law & Policy*, 2012, vol. 45, pp. 194 ff.: "The balancing approach recognizes that remedies such as dismissal, stay, retrial, and exclusion may impose significant burdens on third parties and on the justice system, and it takes these burdens into consideration when determining the optimal remedy".

[552] UK, Police and Criminal Evidence Act 1984, s. 78, see above note 250.

[553] ICC, *Prosecutor v. Lubanga*, Appeals Chamber, Judgment on the appeal of the Prosecutor against the decision of Trial Chamber I of 8 July 2010 entitled "Decision on the Prosecution's Urgent Request for Variation of the Time-Limit to Disclose the Identity of Intermediary 143 or Alternatively to Stay Proceedings Pending Further Consultations with the VWU", 8 October 2010, ICC-01/04-01/06-2582, para. 55 (https://www.legal-tools.org/doc/8f3b61/); in more detail Heinze, 2014, pp. 443 ff., see above note 110.

dural stages that can easily be viewed as a unified system; and b) the false premise that these stages are in fact closed.

Employing Damaška's models of criminal procedure, the criminal process needs to be viewed first and foremost holistically, independent of its stages. Just because a procedural stage might appear in a certain setting does not change the characterisation of the process as a whole, but quite the contrary: procedural stages are usually "assigned methodological subtasks" that differ from each other: "One stage can be devoted to the gathering and organization of relevant material, another to the initial decision, still another to hierarchical review, and so on, depending on the number of levels in the pyramid of authority".[554] At first sight, this argument appears to resemble the familiar argument that different procedural stages may have different "objectives and procedural influences".[555] However, a procedural stage does not present some sort of autonomous, closed, Luhmannesque[556] system.[557] Damaška too doubted the autonomy of procedural stages by acknowledging that a) in the hierarchical ideal procedural stages are just part of a multi-layered hierarchy[558] (and are therefore – as already mentioned – assigned to "methodological *sub*tasks");[559] and b) the existence of procedural stages *per se* and the extent of their integration into the proceedings are already characteristics of a certain procedural model.[560] Thus, to treat procedural stages separately with regard to their objectives and characteristics is already constitutive of a certain procedural model. To do so would

---

[554] Damaška, 1986, pp. 47–48, see above note 412.

[555] See, for example, Mark Klamberg, *Evidence in International Criminal Trials*, Martinus Nijhoff, Leiden, Boston, 2013, p. 499.

[556] See Niklas Luhmann, *Soziologische Aufklärung 1: Aufsätze zur Theorie sozialer Systeme*, eighth edition, Springer, Cham, 2009, p. 226; Gunther Teubner, *Recht als autopoietisches System*, Suhrkamp, Frankfurt am Main, 1989; Niklas Luhmann, "Introduction to Autopoietic Law", in Niklas Luhmann (ed.), *Autopoietic Law: A New Approach to Law and Society*, De Gruyter, Berlin, 1988, pp. 1, 3; Luhmann, 2008, pp. 50 ff. (sixth edition, 2011, p. 111), see above note 370; Brian H. Bix, *Legal Theory*, Oxford University Press, 2004, p. 18; Roger Cotterrell, "Law in Social Theory and Social Theory in the Study of Law", in Austin Sarat (ed.), *The Blackwell Companion to Law and Society*, Blackwell, Malden, 2007, pp. 16, 22; Clemens Mattheis, "The System Theory of Niklas Luhmann and the Constitutionalization of the World Society", in *Goettingen Journal of International Law*, 2012, vol. 4, no. 2, pp. 626 ff.

[557] In a similar vein, see Campbell, Ashworth, and Redmayne, 2019, p. 10, see above note 107.

[558] Damaška, 1986, pp. 47–48, see above note 412.

[559] Emphasis added.

[560] See Damaška, 1986, p. 57, see above note 412.

somehow beg the question. Think of the perception of the criminal process in civil law *vis-á-vis* common law systems: it is certainly fair to say that all domestic legal systems within the common law or civil law tradition contain concentrated and 'continuous' proceedings, but they reach this concentration differently. In proceedings of the civil law tradition, the trial is the cumulation of a continuing criminal process, whereas many common law legal systems conceive the trial as "a discrete and continuous event" and differentiate more sharply between the trial and pre-trial phases of criminal proceedings.[561] A good illustration for this difference is the fact, that Franz Kafka's "Der Prozess" is still translated as "The Trial" in English, instead of "The Proceedings", which would certainly be more accurate.[562]

Furthermore, the ICC provides a reality check to the separation hypothesis, since the investigation phase (read as formal investigations)[563] and the trial phase can hardly be separated. As I have commented on elsewhere,[564] the ICC Appeals Chamber held that "the Prosecutor must be allowed to continue his investigation beyond the confirmation hearing, if this is necessary in order to establish the truth".[565] The Appeals Chamber based this decision on Article 54(1)(a) of the ICC Statute, which lays down that the Prosecutor shall, "[i]n order to establish the truth, extend the investigation to cover all facts and evidence relevant to an assessment of whether there is criminal responsibility under this Statute, and, in doing so, investigate incriminating and exonerating circumstances equally".[566] The Appeals Chamber further recognised that "ideally, it would be desirable for the investigation to be complete by the time of the confirmation hearing" but this

---

[561] Roberts and Zuckerman, 2010, p. 55, see above note 192.

[562] Mirjan Damaška, "Models of Criminal Procedure", in *Zbornik Pravnog Fakulteta u Zagrebu*, 2001, vol. 51, p. 490.

[563] Ambos, 2016, pp. 342 ff., see above note 342.

[564] Heinze, 2014, pp. 524 ff., see above note 110.

[565] ICC, *Prosecutor v. Thomas Lubanga Dyilo*, Appeals Chamber, Judgement on the Prosecutor's Appeal Against the Decision of Pre-Trial Chamber I entitled Decision Establishing General Principles Governing Applications to Restrict Disclosure Pursuant to Rule 81(2) and (4) of the Rules of Procedure and Evidence, 13 October 2006, ICC-01/04-01/06-568, para. 52 ('Lubanga, 2006') (https://www.legal-tools.org/doc/7813d4/). This view has been adopted by Trial Chamber IV in the case against Nourain and Jerbo Jamus, see ICC, *Prosecutor v. Abdallah Banda Abakaer Nourain and Saleh Mohammed Jerbo Jamus*, Trial Chamber, Prosecution's Response to the Defence's Oral Application of 19 April 2011, 4 May 2011, ICC-02/05-03/09-140, para. 7 (https://www.legal-tools.org/doc/e5a6ea/).

[566] Lubanga, 2006, para. 52, see above note 565.

was "not a requirement of the Statute".[567] It, therefore, accepted the argument of the Prosecutor

> that in certain circumstances to rule out further investigation after the confirmation hearing may deprive the Court of significant and relevant evidence, including potentially exonerating evidence – particularly in situations where the ongoing nature of the conflict results in more compelling evidence becoming available for the first time after the confirmation hearing.

As a consequence, the Prosecution may investigate as long as the trial has not been concluded. I have expanded on this argument elsewhere.[568] The rights of the defence to have adequate time and facilities for the preparation of the trial could be safeguarded even if the investigation continues beyond the confirmation of the charges.[569]

This does not mean that viewing procedural stages separately to decide about the admission or exclusion of evidence could not be a practical compromise. Yet, this compromise comes at the price of dissolving the criminal process as a system. As I have demonstrated, it is also questionable whether the separation hypothesis may work at the international level in the face of the growing popularity of private investigations. Even the OTP in the *Lubanga* case deliberately violated procedural rules to ensure the success of its investigation. It can only be speculated that the Office was probably rather certain that the ICC could not afford excluding the evidence and eventually acquit Lubanga – for reasons of substantive fairness. *Argumentum a majore ad minus*, a similar motivation might drive private investigators. Duff *et al.* take this argument conceptually even further. They distinguish two types of integrity (both types have been elaborated on earlier in a different context):[570]

> First, a defendant might claim that it would be inconsistent to continue the prosecution given the State's conduct at the pre-trial stage. Secondly, a defendant might claim that the moral standing of the trial would be undermined by the prosecution

---

[567] *Ibid.*, para. 54.

[568] In more detail Heinze, 2014, pp. 524 ff., see above note 110.

[569] Cf. Lubanga, 2006, para. 55, see above note 565.

[570] See above Section 17.5.2.2.

> through the association between the trial and the wrongful conduct pre-trial.[571]

While the former "focuses in particular on conduct of state officials",[572] the latter addresses

> wrongful behaviour without emphasising the need for that conduct to be perpetrated by state officials. We have already seen some examples of the latter claim where the former is not at issue: there might be cases of private torture where the rights of D are not violated by the state itself. Despite this, there seem good grounds to exclude the evidence obtained, even if those grounds are not as strong as cases in which torture is perpetrated by state officials.[573]

Duff *et al.* call this "integrity as integration": "the defendant must be treated as a citizen not only at trial, but throughout the criminal process, and that the normative validity of the trial rests on the validity of the state's conduct pre-trial".[574] They too argue against the separation hypothesis, meaning "that each part of the criminal justice process can be considered independently. According to this thesis, faults at one stage of the process need not infect decisions taken at later stages as long as there are independent remedies for those earlier faults".[575]

The rejection of the separation-hypothesis and the ensuing holistic view on the process (for Duff *et al.*, integrity as integration) is the continuation of the holistic view on the addressee-issue.[576] Integrity as integration, combined with the presumption that procedural rules are not merely addressed to actors but to systems and sub-systems respectively, allow for the application of exclusionary rules to private conduct. The status of the person collecting the evidence is not relevant for exclusionary rules, but the investigatory context is (within which both public officials and private individuals act). More concretely: whether exclusionary rules apply does not

---

[571] A. Duff *et al.*, 2007, p. 234, see above note 145.

[572] *Ibid.* ("It rests on the identification between the state and the actions of its officials such that actions by officials in the course of investigation are to be treated as actions by the state, which then have implications for the justification of future state actions").

[573] *Ibid.*

[574] *Ibid.*, p. 236.

[575] *Ibid.*

[576] See above Section 17.5.2.3.1.2.2.3.

depend on the *investigator* but on the existence of an *investigation*.[577] In the words of Duff *et al*.: "Integrity as moral coherence involves the moral coherence of treating certain actions, be they of officials or private citizens, as part of the investigation of D".[578] To separate trial and judgment as one sub-system from the investigation as another sub-system is thus not only artificial, it also betrays the communicative, moral and normative standards of a trial that I described above.[579] The umbrella that protects a trial from failing on legitimacy grounds is integrity, and eventually the rule of law with its coherence and consistency elements. It applies to both private actions and actions of public officials.[580] The integrity principle "suggests that there is normative continuity between the investigatory stage and the criminal trial".[581]

Admittedly, the holistic view misses the practicability[582] advantage of the separation-hypothesis. Yet, it is no less practical in the face of private investigators and possible rights violations at the international level. By simply asking whether there is an official investigation or not, it circumvents the somewhat Sisyphean task of categorising investigators into private, public and so forth, which is especially useful in the face of an increasing number of private investigators, security companies and so on.[583] This investigatory context can be as broad as the IIIM.[584]

---

[577] In a similar vein, see A. Duff *et al*., 2007, p. 239, see above note 145: "What distinguishes the cases of private torture, private entrapment, private phone-tapping and the like from this case is that those cases are investigatory".

[578] *Ibid.*

[579] See above Sections 17.5.2.2.3.1. and 17.5.2.3.2.3.1. In the same vein, see *ibid.*

[580] *Ibid.* ("[E]ven as far as private citizens are concerned, use of evidence wrongfully obtained involves treating the actions of those private citizens as part of the investigation. The argument on this view is that the integrity principle, the principle that the trial cannot be detached from the investigation in normative terms, applies to private actions as well as actions of public officials").

[581] *Ibid.*, p. 243.

[582] About practicability as an important value in evidence law, see Volk, 1978, p. 3, above note 334.

[583] See above Section 17.5.1.

[584] See above Section 17.2.2.

17.5.2.3.2.3.3.3. Applicability of the Rule of Law to the International Level

To justify the applicability of the rule of law at the international level, a recourse to Kant is anew fruitful.

Kant's conception of human dignity is complemented by his vision of a 'perpetual peace'. I have disentangled the structure of Kant's work *Toward Perpetual Peace* elsewhere.[585] In this vein, Kant's Definitive Articles:

1. The Civil Constitution of Every State shall be Republican (principle of civil right);

2. The Right of Nations shall be based on a Federation of Free States (principle of international right);

3. Cosmopolitan Right shall be limited to Conditions of Universal Hospitality (principle of cosmopolitan right).

Perpetual Peace, p. 98.

The conceptual novelty of Kant's doctrine of cosmopolitanism is that he recognised "three interrelated but distinct levels of 'right', in the juridical senses of the term".[586] Of interest for the rule of law[587] is the third level, a world citizen law (*Weltbürgerrecht*) which entails the "right of hospitality" (*Recht der Hospitalität*), that is, that each citizen must not be treated in a hostile way by another State.[588] With regard to the term hospitality, Kant himself notes the oddity of the term in this context, and therefore remarks that "it is not a question of philanthropy but of right".[589] In other writings, Kant clarified that the notion of hospitality and cosmopolitan right included a wider range of rights, including "the right of citizens of the world *to try to* establish community with all",[590] "engage in commerce with any other,

---

[585] Heinze, 2018, pp. 356 ff., see above note 487.

[586] Seyla Benhabib, *Another Cosmopolitanism*, Oxford University Press, 2006, p. 21.

[587] In more detail Denninger, 1978, p. 69, see above note 255.

[588] Ambos, 2013, pp. 293, 305–6, see above note 163.

[589] Immanuel Kant, *Toward Perpetual Peace and Other Writings on Politics, Peace, and History*, Yale University Press, New Haven, 2006, p. 105; Benhabib, 2006, pp. 21–22, see above note 586. For a detailed analysis see Jasmine K. Gani, "The Erasure of Race: Cosmopolitanism and the Illusion of Kantian Hospitality", in *Millennium*, 2017, vol. 45, no. 3, pp. 425 ff.; Pauline Kleingeld, "Kant's Cosmopolitan Law: World Citizenship for a Global Order", in *Kantian Review*, 1998, vol. 2, p. 75.

[590] Kant, 1991, p. 158, see above note 163 (emphasis in the original); Wade L. Huntley, "Kant's Third Image", in *International Studies Quarterly*, 1996, vol. 40, no. 1, p. 51.

and each has a right to make this attempt without the other",[591] and a free "public use of man's reason".[592] For Benhabib, therefore, human rights covenants can be qualified as cosmopolitan norms.[593] Günther follows from Kant's Third Definitive Article, that the application of public human rights is a necessary precondition for a permanent peace.[594] In sum, with this conception, Kant laid the foundations for all current conceptions of human dignity and world peace, an "international rule of law".[595] Even though according to the Second Definitive Article, international law is created through treaty obligations between States, cosmopolitan norms move the individual as a moral and legal person in a worldwide civil society into the centre of attention.[596]

17.5.2.3.2.4. Intermediate Conclusion

In this section, the rationales for exclusionary rules were applied to the extra-investigatory context. After questioning the usefulness of the deterrence theory, both remedy theory and the integrity of the process provide an im-

---

[591] Kant, 1991, p. 158, see above note 163 (fn. omitted).

[592] Immanuel Kant, "An Answer to the Question: What is 'Enlightenment?'", in Hans Reiss (ed.), *Immanuel Kant, Political Writings*, H.B. Nisbet (trans.), Cambridge University Press, 1991, p. 55; Garrett Wallace Brown, "Kantian Cosmopolitan Law and the Idea of a Cosmopolitan Constitution", in *History of Political Thought*, 2006, vol. 27, no. 4, pp. 661, 664; Gani, 2017, p. 431, see above note 589; Jürgen Habermas, *Politische Theorie*, Philosophische Texte, vol. 4, Suhrkamp, Frankfurt am Main, 2009, p. 321: "Die Gefahr des Despotismus, die in allen von der Obrigkeit bloß auferlegten Gesetzen brütet, kann einzig durch das republikanische Verfahren einer fairen Meinungs- und Willensbildung aller potentiellen Betroffenen vorgebeugt werden".

[593] Seyla Benhabib, "Claiming Rights across Borders", in *American Political Science Review*, 2009, vol. 103, no. 4, pp. 691, 696. Against this view with a narrow reading of hospitality, Vischer, 2017, p. 325, see above note 164: "Kant's cosmopolitan law is far from proclaiming a firm catalogue of human rights or even a world constitution. It only asserts in a rather moral than legal tone a minimal guarantee of peaceful intercourse, and explicitly presumes the ongoing asymmetry of host and visitor".

[594] See also Günther, 2009, p. 84, see above note 498. About Kant's two-step-justification see Heinze, 2018, p. 371, see above note 487.

[595] Huntley, 1996, pp. 45, 49, see above note 590; Alec Stone Sweet, "A Cosmopolitan Legal Order: Constitutional Pluralism and Rights Adjudication in Europe", in *Global Constitutionalism*, 2012, vol. 1, no. 1, pp. 53 (58); Jorrik Fulda, "Eine legitime Globalverfassung? Die US-Hegemonie und die weltgesellschaftlich gerechte Vollendung des Kantischen Projektes", in *Archiv des Völkerrechts*, 2016, vol. 54, no. 3, pp. 334, 345. About the role of human dignity in international human rights law and international criminal law, see Schmahl, 2018, pp. 79 ff., above note 445.

[596] Benhabib, 2009, pp. 691, 695, see above note 593.

portant theoretical basis for the exclusion of illegally obtained evidence in the extra-investigatory context. The argumentative force and even effectiveness of the remedy theory at the international level are underlined by the central role of human rights. The human rights language of Article 21(3) of the ICC Statute is translated into the admissibility provision of Article 69. Here, integrity from the perspective of the suspect is visibly enshrined in paragraph 7: "Evidence obtained by means of a violation of this Statute *or internationally recognized human rights* shall not be admissible if [...] [t]he admission of the evidence would be antithetical to and would seriously damage the *integrity of the proceedings*".[597] At the same time, the integrity of the person ('internationally recognized human rights') is interlocked with integrity from the perspective of the process.

Yet, at the heart of exclusionary rules within the extra-investigatory context lies the integrity of international criminal procedure itself. Illegally obtained evidence by private individuals questions the moral authority of the verdict and its legitimacy. The evidence may be unreliable. Admitting such evidence might violate the rule of law. The basis of the integrity of the process is fairness. Especially the juxtaposition of procedural and substantive fairness is vital for private investigations. A conviction that is based on unreliable evidence is not substantially fair. The two dimensions of fairness – procedural fairness vs. substantive fairness – affect a judgment like two parents their child. Within this rationale, integrity becomes a "proxy, synonym or placeholder"[598] for procedural values such as fairness, due process, natural justice or judicial legitimacy. Moreover, it would be detrimental to the expressivist and communicative function of a public trial, if a conviction rendered by an international tribunal was based on illegally obtained evidence – irrespective of the status of the person who obtained the evidence.

Every endeavour of applying the systems theory by Luhmann and Teubner eventually passes over to the bifurcated decision of how narrow the systems and sub-systems should be. The criminal process with its various stages is especially prone to such an endeavour. Strictly speaking, the investigatory context (sub-system 1) could easily be, and is often, separated from the trial process (sub-system 2). This separation hypothesis has practical advantages on the international level: ICTs could, if they found that

---

[597] Emphasis supplied.
[598] Roberts *et al.*, 2016, p. 5, see above note 146.

evidence had been illegally obtained, declare that, even if this evidence must be excluded from trial, it could still be obtained and eventually be *used in the pre-trial stage as lead evidence*. An exclusionary rule would thus only address the non-use of evidence in court and requires balancing that allows for obtainment of the evidence (even though it was illegally obtained).

Yet, the separation hypothesis must be rejected on the international level. It artificially separates procedural stages that can easily be viewed as a unified and is based on the false premise that procedural stages are in fact closed. The rejection of the separation-hypothesis and the ensuing holistic view on the process (Duff *et al.*'s integrity as integration) is the continuation of the holistic view on the addressee-issue. Integrity as integration, combined with the presumption that procedural rules are not merely addressed to actors but to systems and sub-systems respectively, allow for the application of exclusionary rules to private conduct. Whether exclusionary rules apply does not depend on the *investigator* but on the existence of an *investigation*.[599]

Last but not least, the *Lubanga* disclosure scenario casts doubt on the practicability of the condition to only use illegally obtained evidence as lead evidence: this condition is very much dependant on the *bona fide* conduct of both prosecutors and investigators. It might not be taken seriously when a court is reluctant to follow through with an effective remedy, that is, a stay of proceedings, as the ICC declared. These remedies and consequences and their effectiveness to ensure the integrity of the process shall be briefly analysed in the following section.

17.5.2.4. Consequences and Remedies: Exclusion vs. Other Remedies

As mentioned at the outset, integrity as an element and value in the decision about illegally obtained evidence by private individuals may lead to several consequences. For the sake of better following the arguments, I have decided to single out – by way of example – the exclusion of evidence as the consequence for a violation of the integrity element (in whatever form). It goes without saying that there are other consequences. Their mere existence has a considerable influence on the decision about whether to

---

[599] In a similar vein, see A. Duff *et al.*, 2007, p. 239, above note 145: "What distinguishes the cases of private torture, private entrapment, private phone-tapping and the like from this case is that those cases are investigatory".

exclude evidence from a trial or not. Rogall[600] and others[601] have made this point concerning the balancing exercise within the exclusion decision: the exclusion or non-use of evidence is *one*, but not necessarily the most apt reaction to an illegal gathering of evidence. According to them, whether this response is the appropriate remedy depends more on systemic aspects than on the individual situation of the accused. Thus, integrity can also be used to rationalise a stay of proceedings. It is the broader question of how to address procedural violations committed in the pre-trial phase of the proceedings. I will provide a brief sketch of those judicial responses, since there are others who have provided profound studies of the matter, especially recently Pitcher.[602] Other remedies involve financial compensation,[603] sentence reductions,[604] integrity testing and integrity units. Financial compensation and sentence reductions provide enough material for another chapter and will thus be neglected altogether. Integrity testing and integrity units need to be illuminated briefly since their existence is indeed an important check for both prosecutors and persons working in law enforcement.

Some prosecutors have set prosecution integrity units within their offices, to provide an internal review when they believe it is warranted.[605] The units usually work closely together with innocence projects. Some states in the US have created so-called 'integrity testing', where a police officer "is placed in a position where he or she might be tempted to break a rule or a law and monitored to see what he or she will do".[606] As Pollock explains: "Integrity testing is like undercover work in that unsuspecting

[600] Klaus Rogall, "Gegenwärtiger Stand und Entwicklungstendenzen der Lehre von den strafprozessualen Beweisverboten", in *Zeitschrift für die gesamte Strafrechtswissenschaft*, 1979, pp. 31–35; see also Klaus Rogall, "Über die Folgen der rechtswidrigen Beschaffung des Zeugenbeweises im Strafprozeß", in *Juristenzeitung*, 1996, 947–948; for a further summary see Thaman and Brodowski, 2020, p. 451, see above note 196.

[601] See Jürgen Wolter, "Beweisverbote und Umgehungsverbote zwischen Wahrheitserforschung und Ausforschung", in Claus Wilhelm Canaris *et al.* (eds.), *50 Jahre Bundesgerichtshof, Festgabe aus der Wissenschaft, Band IV*, C.H. Beck, München, 2000, pp. 963, 985–986; Greco, 2018, pp. 512 ff., see above note 203; see, generally, Thaman and Brodowski, 2020, p. 451, see above note 196.

[602] Pitcher, 2018, see above note 192.

[603] *Ibid.*, pp. 298 ff.

[604] *Ibid.*, pp. 302 ff.

[605] Turvey and Cooley, 2014, p. 368, see above note 180.

[606] Pollock, 2019, p. 204, see above note 179.

officers are tempted with an opportunity to commit an illegal or corrupt act, such as keeping a found wallet or being offered a bribe".[607]

17.5.2.4.1. Exclusion: Balancing

A decision about the exclusion of evidence is never a black and white decision. The entire criminal process is about balancing rights and interests[608] and so is the decision about excluding evidence. In fact, the exclusion of evidence is perceived "as playing an integral role in ensuring constitutional and judicial integrity in the criminal justice system as a whole, as well as promoting constitutional compliance by the police and prosecutorial services".[609] It is especially this decision that requires a specific justification for the exclusion of evidence. As I have illustrated, this is easier said than done – especially because it seems all too easy to let the goals of International Criminal Justice outweigh an alleged minor rights violation committed by a private individual.[610] Thus, even the law at ICTs is fragmented in that regard: the law of the *ad hoc* Tribunals provides explicitly for exclusionary rules in case of serious fair trial violations, while the ICC regime only takes such considerations into account with regard to admissibility and relevance of the respective evidence or generally as an admissibility criterion.[611] Last but not least, there are instances where the Chamber is obliged to 'exclude' ("not consider") the evidence ("shall")[612] and where this is within its discretion ("may").[613] Especially in the latter case, recourse to rationales of exclusionary rules is useful. Yet, the rationales themselves must not be taken as a dogma.[614] After all, they are theories.[615] For instance, the remedy rationale, taken in its pure form, can be

---

[607] *Ibid.*

[608] Dennis, 2020, mn. 2-009, see above note 192.

[609] Roberts and Hunter, 2012, p. 49, see above note 192.

[610] Lüderssen made this argument, albeit on a more conceptual level, see Klaus Lüderssen, "Was ist das – ein 'Rechtsstaat'?", in Erhard Denninger and Klaus Lüderssen (eds.), *Polizei und Strafprozeß im demokratischen Rechtsstaat*, Suhrkamp, Frankfurt a. M., 1978, p. 95.

[611] Cf. ICC Statute, Article 69(7), see above note 182: "shall not be admissible".

[612] Cf., for example, ICTY RPE, Rule 95, see above note 341; MICT RPE, Rule 117, see above note 515 and ICC Statute, Article 69(7), see above note 182.

[613] Cf., for example, ICTY RPE, Rule 89(D), see above note 341 and MICT RPE, Rule 105(D), see above note 515 and ICC Statute, Article 69(4), see above note 182.

[614] The value of a dogma is that it applies to a wide range of cases and instance. Those cases and instance thus do not have to be rationalized de novo, every time they occur, see Volk, 1978, p. 54, see above note 334.

a very crude tool, effectively allowing the court no discretion to vary the remedy according to the harm done to the accused. The remedy is either granted – and the evidence thus excluded – or the remedy is refused – and the evidence is admitted. There is no scope for adjusting the remedy according to the circumstances of the case, as in the case of a civil wrong, for instance, where there is scope for infinite variation of the damages awarded.[616]

As a result, national courts have developed sophisticated balancing exercises to be used upon an exclusionary decision. Thaman and Brodowski, in a recent and illuminating study, have summarised these factors with a special view to the US and Germany:[617]

the gravity of *objective* and *subjective misconduct*, such as the clear lack of a (sufficient) legal basis for the specific act of gathering evidence; a wilful, widespread and/or arbitrary misuse of state powers, or a wilful, widespread and arbitrary circumvention of a requirement of ex-ante judicial authorization [...] the *ratio legis* of the protected norm, including whether the "legally protected sphere" of the defendant has been affected; the *quality of the evidence* in light of the misconduct, the existence of *supporting evidence*; and a *hypothetical clean path* doctrine (i.e., whether the evidence could have been gathered legally); the *gravity* of the crime being prosecuted, in particular based on the guilt of the defendant and the expected punishment; and *systemic effects* on society's trust in criminal justice *and* in the lawfulness of state actions.

It needs to be emphasised that Thaman and Brodowski's criteria are descriptive and not prescriptive. It is also not surprising that Article 69(7)(b) of the ICC Statute does not require any degree of "damage" to the integrity of the proceedings; instead, this integrity must be "seriously" damaged, which thus involves a judgment of degree by the respective judge(s).[618]

---

[615] Canaris perceives the use of a 'theory' as a rather classifying and semantic exercise, see Claus-Wilhelm Canaris, "Funktion, Struktur und Falsifikation juristischer Theorien", in *Juristenzeitung*, 1993, p. 379: "[Theorie] ermöglicht die begriffliche und/oder dogmatische Einordnung der einschlägigen Problemlösung(en)").

[616] P. Duff, 2004, p. 165, see above note 193.

[617] Thaman and Brodowski, 2020, pp. 451–452, see above note 196 (fn. omitted, emphasis in the original). See also Jahn, 2008, pp. 46–47, see above note 528.

[618] Pitcher, 2018, p. 327, see above note 192.

Drawing on my argument about integrity as integration (following Duff *et al.*), the same test applies to the extra-investigatory context. Surely, it is fair to say that there is a stronger reason to exclude evidence once a State authority committed the rights violation.[619] Yet, this is more of a yardstick than a rule set in stone. Generally, what applies to State authorities also applies to private individuals in the context of obtaining evidence: "the trial provides the normative standards that ought to govern the investigation of public wrongs. In using evidence wrongfully obtained by private citizens in their investigations of public wrongdoing, the trial cannot distance itself from those wrongs".[620]

17.5.2.4.2. Stay of Proceedings

The most drastic consequence of illegally obtained evidence is a stay of proceedings.[621] As Roberts eloquently puts it: "Even more closely than its natural affinity with evidentiary exclusion, judicial integrity-talk is bound up with permanent stays of proceedings on the grounds of abuse of process".[622] In a seminal decision that became a yardstick for cases that followed, the ICTR Appeals Chamber in *Barayagwiza* recognised that a stay of proceedings may be imposed, among other things, "where in the circumstances of a particular case, proceeding with the trial of the accused would contravene the court's sense of justice, due to pre-trial impropriety or misconduct".[623] The "sense of justice" can be understood as the notions of fairness as previously defined. It could even easily be categorised as 'substantive fairness', if the Chamber had merely formulated "sense of justice". Yet, it clarified "the court's sense of justice". Thus, the criterion seems just to be a reformulation of the integrity concept. This reading is supported by a stay of proceedings decision at the ICTY in the case of *Stanišić and Župljanin*, where the Appeals Chamber remarked:

> The doctrine of "abuse of process" allows a court to decline to exercise jurisdiction either because it will be impossible to give the accused a fair trial or because it offends the court's sense of justice and propriety to try the accused in the circum-

---

[619] A. Duff *et al.*, 2007, p. 239, see above note 145.

[620] *Ibid.*

[621] About the difference between a permanent and a conditional stay of proceedings Pitcher, 2018, pp. 305 ff., see above note 192.

[622] Roberts *et al.*, 2016, p. 6, see above note 146.

[623] Barayagwiza decision, 1999, Introduction, para. 77, see above note 304.

stances of a particular case. The question in cases of abuse of process is not whether it is "necessary" for a court to issue an interlocutory decision terminating proceedings [...], but whether a court should continue to exercise jurisdiction over a case in light of serious and egregious violations of the accused's rights that would prove detrimental to the court's integrity. The discretionary power of a court to stay or terminate proceedings by reason of abuse of process applies during the trial phase of a case, and is mostly concerned with prosecutorial misconduct, since its main purposes are to prevent wrongful convictions and preserve the integrity of the judicial system.[624]

The ICC Chambers have had several opportunities to comment on the abuse of process doctrine.[625] On the one hand, they have recognised that the principle of abuse of process leading to the court's authority to stay proceedings is not provided for in the Statute, nor is it "generally recognised as an indispensable power of a court of law".[626] On the other hand, however, they have stated that the ICC Statute safeguards the rights of the suspect and the accused, especially under Articles 55 and 67 of the ICC Statute. Drawing on Article 21(3) of the ICC Statute,[627] the Appeals Chamber in *Lubanga* pointed out that "if no fair trial can be held, the object of the judicial process is frustrated and the process must be stopped".[628] However, not every breach of the rights of the suspect and/or the accused is tantamount to an abuse of process entailing the need to stay the proceed-

---

[624] ICTY, *Prosecutor v. Stanišić and Župljanin*, Decision on Mićo Stanišić's Motion Requesting a Declaration of Mistrial and Stojan Župljanin's Motion to Vacate Trial Judgement, 2 April 2014, IT-08-91-A, para. 35 (fn. omitted) (https://www.legal-tools.org/doc/494e31/).

[625] ICC, *Prosecutor v. Callixte Mbarushimana*, Pre-Trial Chamber, Decision on the "Defence request for a permanent stay of proceedings", 1 July 2011, ICC-01/04-01/10-264, p. 4, with further references ('Mbarushimana, 2011') (https://www.legal-tools.org/doc/27c6ab/); ICC, *Prosecutor v. Abdallah Banda Abakaer Nourain and Saleh Mohammed Jerbo Jamus*, Trial Chamber, Decision on the defence request for a temporary stay of proceedings, 26 October 2012, ICC-02/05-03/09-410 (https://www.legal-tools.org/doc/414cc4/). Recently ICC, *Prosecutor v. Ali Muhammad Ali Abd-Al-Rahman ("Ali Kushayb")*, Decision on Defence Request for a Stay of Proceedings, 16 October 2020, ICC-02/05-01/20-186, paras. 7 ff. (https://www.legal-tools.org/doc/1nq46m/).

[626] Lubanga, 2006, para. 35, see above note 114; Mbarushimana, 2011, p. 4, see above note 625.

[627] Lubanga, 2006, paras. 36–37, see above note 114; Mbarushimana, 2011, p. 4, see above note 625.

[628] Lubanga, 2006, para. 37, see above note 114.

ings.[629] Only gross violations, which make it impossible for the accused "to make his/her defence within the framework of his rights" justify the proceedings being stayed.[630] Thus, as has been stated in the case law of the Court,[631] behaviours which may trigger a stay of proceedings are those that entail unfairness of such a nature that it cannot be resolved, rectified or corrected in the subsequent course of the proceedings.[632]

One form of this 'behaviour' has included disclosure violations by the Prosecution. The Trial Chamber imposed a stay of proceedings because of an abuse of process relating to disclosure violations in connection with Article 54(3)(e) of the ICC Statute.[633] The Chamber imposed the stay of proceedings because of an abuse of process, also labelled as the "balancing approach".[634] It stated that "[t]he prosecution's approach constitutes a wholesale and serious abuse, and a violation of an important provision which was intended to allow the prosecution to receive evidence confidentially, in very restrictive circumstances".[635] Thus, the Trial Chamber issued a stay of the proceedings, because "the trial process has been ruptured to such a degree that it is now impossible to piece together the constituent elements of a fair trial"[636] and this "right to a fair trial – which is without doubt a fundamental right – includes an entitlement to disclosure of exculpatory material".[637] The Appeals Chamber later confirmed the stay,[638] but

---

[629] Mbarushimana, 2011, p. 4, see above note 625.

[630] Lubanga, 2006, para. 39, see above note 114; Mbarushimana, 2011, pp. 4–5, see above note 625.

[631] See, for example, Lubanga, 2008, para. 89, see above note 543.

[632] Mbarushimana, 2011, p. 5, see above note 625.

[633] See above Section 17.5.2.3.2.3.3.2.2. See, generally, Heinze, 2014, pp. 458 ff., see above note 110.

[634] Turner, 2012, see above note 551.

[635] Lubanga, 2008, para. 73, see above note 543; see, generally, Turner, 2012, pp. 179 ff., above note 551.

[636] Lubanga, 2008, para. 93, see above note 543.

[637] *Ibid.*, para. 77. With ponderous words, the Chamber continued (para. 91):

This is an international criminal court, with the sole purpose of trying those charged with the 'most serious crimes of concern to the international community as a whole' and the judges are enjoined, in discharging this important role, to ensure that the accused receives a fair trial. If, at the outset, it is clear that the essential preconditions of a fair trial are missing and there is no sufficient indication that this will be resolved during the trial process, it is necessary – indeed, inevitable – that the proceedings should be stayed.

[638] ICC, *Prosecutor v. Lubanga*, Appeals Chamber, Judgment on the appeal of the Prosecutor against the decision of Trial Chamber I entitled "Decision on the consequences of non-

made clear that the Trial Chamber "intended to impose a stay that was conditional and therefore potentially only temporary".[639]

17.5.2.4.2.1. The Intra-Investigatory Context: Lubanga and Intermediaries

Even more relevant for the purpose of this chapter is an instance where another stay was imposed: when during the proceedings against *Lubanga* the suspicion arose that certain so-called intermediaries had bribed various persons to prepare false evidence for alleged former child soldiers.[640] Intermediaries are "local organisations and/or private persons supporting the OTP by assisting in the collection of evidence and communication with potential witnesses, given their familiarity with the cultural, geographic and other characteristics of the region where alleged crimes took place".[641] In the case against *Lubanga* about twenty-three intermediaries assisted the OTP, seven of whom were used to contact approximately half of the witnesses the OTP called to give evidence against *Lubanga*.[642] Usually, both the cooperation with intermediaries and their use to create incriminating evidence are common and perfectly legal. Moreover, the Chamber deemed it appropriate that the identities of the intermediaries would not have to be dis-

---

disclosure of exculpatory materials covered by Article 54(3)(e) agreements and the application to stay the prosecution of the accused, together with certain other issues raised at the Status Conference on 10 June 2008", 21 October 2008, ICC-01/04-01/06-1486 (https://www.legal-tools.org/doc/485c2d/).

[639] *Ibid.*, para. 75, continuing: "The Trial Chamber acknowledged, however, that circumstances might change, in particular should the information providers alter their position and give their consent to the disclosure of the documents in question."

[640] ICC, *Prosecutor v. Thomas Lubanga Dyilo*, Trial Chamber, Transcript of hearing, 13 March 2009, ICC-01/04-01/06-T-146-Red-ENG, p. 3, lines 11-18 (https://www.legal-tools.org/doc/b0e64b/) ("[…] the Defence explained that they wished to explore the possibility that certain people have participated in preparing false evidence for alleged former child soldiers, and in this case that [143] helped the witness to invent a false story or a false identity, or both."), cited in *Prosecutor v. Thomas Lubanga Dyilo*, Redacted Decision on Intermediaries, 31 May 2010, ICC-01/04-01/06-2434-Red2, para. 16 ('Lubanga, 2010') (https://www.legal-tools.org/doc/8b5694/).

[641] See ICC Monitor, no. 41, November 2010 – April 2011, p. 9; Ambos, 2016, p. 122, see above note 342; Ambos, 2013, p. 31, see above note 452. The ASP broadly defines an intermediary "as an individual or entity that facilitates contact between the Court and a witness, victim or other source of information.", see ASP, Resolution ICC-ASP/9/Res.5, Adopted at the 5th plenary meeting, 10 December 2010, Annex, para. 2 with fn. 3 (https://www.legal-tools.org/doc/a399fa/).

[642] Lubanga, 2010, para. 3, see above note 640.

---

closed to the Defence, if particular material required protection and if the statement or document, in its redacted form, is sufficiently comprehensible for the purposes of dealing with trial issues.[643] Yet, once intermediaries commit illegal acts, there is an issue of illegally obtained evidence in an intra-investigatory context.

On 15 March 2010, the Chamber indicated that the Defence was entitled to know the names of certain intermediaries.[644] Balancing the need for intermediary-protection on the one hand and the rights of the accused on the other, the Trial Chamber adopted an approach under which, among other things, the intermediary's identity is disclosable under Rule 77 of the ICC RPE[645] (if "prima facie grounds have been identified for suspecting that the intermediary in question had been in contact with one or more witnesses whose incriminating evidence has been materially called into question, for instance by internal contradictions or by other evidence").[646] Be-

---

[643] Cf. *ibid.*, para. 6.

[644] ICC, *Prosecutor v. Thomas Lubanga Dyilo*, Transcript of hearing, 15 March 2010, ICC-01/04-01/06-T-261-Red3-ENG, p. 6, line 18 to p. 7, line 8 (https://www.legal-tools.org/doc/d5ee58/) cited in *ibid.*, para. 41.

[645] About ICC, Rules of Procedure and Evidence, 9 September 2002, Rule 77 ('ICC RPE') (https://www.legal-tools.org/doc/8bcf6f/); see Heinze, 2014, pp. 355 ff., above note 110.

[646] Lubanga, 2010, para. 139, see above note 640. The entire approach is:

    a. Given the markedly different considerations that apply to each intermediary (or others who assisted in a similar or linked manner), disclosure of their identities to the defence is to be decided on an individual-by-individual basis, rather than by way of a more general, undifferentiated approach.

    b. The threshold for disclosure is whether prima facie grounds have been identified for suspecting that the intermediary in question had been in contact with one or more witnesses whose incriminating evidence has been materially called into question, for instance by internal contradictions or by other evidence. In these circumstances, the intermediary's identity is disclosable under Rule 77 of the Rules. [...]

    c. The identities of intermediaries (or others who assisted in a similar or linked manner) who do not meet the test in b. are not to be disclosed.

    d. Disclosure of the identity of an intermediary (or others who assisted in a similar or linked manner) is not to be effected until there has been an assessment by the VWU, and any protective measures that are necessary have been put in place.

    e. The identities of intermediaries who did not deal with trial witnesses who gave incriminating evidence are not to be revealed, unless there are specific reasons for suspecting that the individual in question attempted to persuade one or more individuals to give false evidence or otherwise misused his or her position. Applications in this regard will be dealt with by the Chamber on an individual basis.

    f. The threshold for calling intermediaries prior to the defence abuse submissions is that there is evidence, as opposed to prima facie grounds to suspect, that the individual in question attempted to persuade one or more individuals to give false evidence.

cause "some intermediaries may have attempted to persuade individuals to give false evidence", those *prima facie* grounds have been identified. As a consequence, the Trial Chamber ordered the Prosecution to disclose confidentially to the Defence the identity ("names and other identifying information" plus the "professional background") of certain intermediaries.[647]

That the proceedings had to be stayed did not – at least not directly – result from the mere fact that the Chamber discovered that certain intermediaries, whose identity did justifiably not have to be revealed, had bribed witnesses to give false testimony. Instead, it resulted from the non-compliance of the Prosecution with the disclosure order just mentioned.[648] The Prosecution quite frankly remarked, after having missed the deadline by the Trial Chamber to comply with the order: "The Prosecution consider [sic] that it cannot disclose the information in the current circumstances, but will consult with the VWU as to whether the security situation allows for disclosure now". They continued: "The Prosecution is bound by autonomous statutory duties of protection that it must honour at all times".[649]

From the perspective of remedies, the refusal of the Prosecution to implement the Court's order is the fact that distinguishes this stay of proceedings from the earlier stay caused by an incorrect reading of Article 54(3)(e) of the ICC Statute. This refusal had – in the view of the Court – a twofold impact: first, it had an impact on the assessment of evidence by the Court, and second, it had an impact on the administration of justice. Both impacts were described and provided with an explicit warning by the – noticeably enraged – Chamber in sharp language. With regard to the former, the Chamber warned: "However, if the identifying information for 143, despite the orders of the Chamber, is not disclosed to the defence, then the Chamber will need to scrutinize the impact of this eventuality in the context of its *overall assessment of the evidence in the case*, and the fairness of

---

[647] Lubanga, 2010, para. 150, see above note 640.

[648] ICC, *Prosecutor v. Thomas Lubanga Dyilo*, Trial Chamber, Redacted Decision on the Prosecution's Urgent Request for Variation of the Time-Limit to Disclose the Identity of Intermediary 143 or Alternatively to Stay Proceedings Pending Further Consultations with the VWU, 8 July 2010, ICC-01/04-01/06-2517-RED, paras. 12, 13 ('Decision on the Prosecution's Urgent Request') (https://www.legal-tools.org/doc/cd4f10/).

[649] ICC, *Prosecutor v. Thomas Lubanga Dyilo*, Trial Chamber, Prosecution's Urgent Request for Variation of the Time-Limit to Disclose the Identity of Intermediary 143 or Alternatively to Stay Proceedings Pending Further Consultations with VWU, 7 July 2010, ICC-01/04-01/06-2515, paras. 1, 3 (https://www.legal-tools.org/doc/5e2ba5/), cited in *ibid.*, para. 13.

the proceedings against the accused".[650] This is an astonishing statement. The warning that the Chamber "will need to scrutinize the impact of this eventuality in the context of its *overall assessment of the evidence in the case*" mirrors the language of exclusionary rules. As I have shown elsewhere,[651] in England and Wales s. 87 PACE provides for the exclusion of evidence as a remedy for non-disclosure "if it appears to the court that, having regard to all the circumstances, including the circumstances in which the evidence was obtained, the admission of the evidence would have such an adverse effect on the fairness of the proceedings that the court ought not to admit it".[652] The use of intermediaries by the Prosecution qualifies this context as an intra-investigatory one.

17.5.2.4.2.2. The Extra-Investigatory Context: Nikolić and Tolimir

A situation of illegal actions of private individuals in the extra-investigatory context[653] occurred before the ICTY in the case against Nikolić. The accused, living in what was then the Federal Republic of Yugoslavia, "was taken forcibly and against his will and transported into the territory of Bosnia and Herzegovina [...] by unknown individuals having no connection with SFOR and/or the Tribunal".[654] In Bosnia and Herzegovina, Nikolić was then arrested and detained by the Stabilisation Force ('SFOR'), and delivered to the ICTY.[655] In its evaluation of the situation, the Appeals Chamber invoked the test in *Barayagwiza* previously mentioned.[656] It also stressed that, just because the unknown individuals could not be attributed to SFOR or the Prosecution, it "does not mean that such acts do not raise concerns with the Chamber".[657] And indeed, it remarked with rather clear words:

> [T]he Chamber holds that, in a situation where an accused
> [person] is very seriously mistreated, maybe even subjected to

---

[650] Decision on the Prosecution's Urgent Request, para. 20, see above note 648 (emphasis added).

[651] Heinze, 2014, pp. 437 ff., see above note 110.

[652] See *ibid.*, pp. 443 ff.

[653] For more examples see Aksenova, Bergsmo and Stahn, 2020, pp. 9 ff., see above note 1.

[654] ICTY, *Prosecutor v. Nikolić*, Decision on Defence Motion Challenging the Exercise of Jurisdiction by the Tribunal, 9 October 2002, IT-94-2-PT, para. 21 (https://www.legal-tools.org/doc/352e8c/).

[655] *Ibid.*, para. 21.

[656] *Ibid.*, para. 111.

[657] *Ibid.*, para. 113.

inhuman, cruel or degrading treatment, or torture, before being handed over to the Tribunal, this may constitute a legal impediment to the exercise of jurisdiction over such an accused [person]. This would certainly be the case where persons acting for SFOR or the Prosecution were involved in such very serious mistreatment. *But even without such involvement this Chamber finds it extremely difficult to justify the exercise of jurisdiction over a person if that person was brought into the jurisdiction of the Tribunal after having been seriously mistreated.*[658]

Citing *Barayagwiza*, the Chamber decided that it was thus "irrelevant which entity or entities were responsible for the alleged violations of the Appellant's rights".[659] In a twofold way, this decision confirms what has been elaborated earlier. First, that the rule of law with its integrity prong applies to the acts of individuals in an extra-investigatory context; and second, that this, however, does not relieve the Chamber from a balancing exercise between substantive and procedural fairness. The Chamber required not just any rights violation but an "egregious" violation,[660] which seems a too strict requirement that contradicts the equal treatment of investigatory context. A similar situation occurred in the *Tolimir* case, where the Chamber referred to *Nikolić*.[661]

17.5.3. Consequences for Private Investigators at the International Level

The aim of a private investigator is to answer the questions who, what, when, where, how, and why.[662] Investigators – whether private or public – use observation, inquiry, examination and experimentation to obtain evidence and factual information that can be used – if necessary – in court.[663] More concretely, a criminal investigation "is the systematic process of identifying, collecting, preserving, and evaluating information for the pur-

---

[658] *Ibid.*, para. 114 (emphasis added).

[659] *Ibid.* (emphasis added).

[660] *Ibid.* (emphasis added). See, in detail, the analysis in Pitcher, 2018, p. 273, see above note 192.

[661] ICTY, *Prosecutor v. Tolimir*, Trial Chamber, Decision on Preliminary Motions on the Indictment pursuant to Rule 72 of the Rules, 14 December 2007, IT-05-88/2-PT, para. 8 (https://www.legal-tools.org/doc/014693/).

[662] McMahon, 2001, p. 16, see above note 102.

[663] *Ibid.*

pose of bringing a criminal offender to justice".[664] McMahon mentions the "three I's": information, interrogation, and instrumentation.[665] By applying the three I's, "the investigator gathers the facts that are necessary to establish the guilt or innocence of the accused in a criminal trial".[666] The private investigator is often the "last hope for many people"[667] and it is certainly fair to say the same applies to CIJA's investigations in Syria.

This is the reason why the information that organizations like CIJA collect must be admissible in court as evidence[668] – and exactly that is unclear.[669] For CIJA's material to be admissible, its work must satisfy international standards of an evidentiary nature.[670] Here, these 'standards' might actually work in favour of CIJA in two ways. First, the evidence law of international criminal tribunals is governed by the principle of the free assessment of all evidence.[671] This means that Trial Chambers have "maxi-

---

[664] *Ibid.*, p. 138.

[665] *Ibid.*, p. 144.

[666] *Ibid.*

[667] *Ibid.*, p. 16.

[668] About term "evidence" *vis-à-vis* "material" and "information", see Ambos, 2016, pp. 446–447, see above note 342.

[669] In a similar vein, see Rankin, 2017, p. 402, see above note 56.

[670] *Ibid.*, p. 403.

[671] Ambos, 2016, p. 447, see above note 342. Cf. ICC RPE, Rule 63(2), see above note 645 ("assess freely all evidence"); for the case law, for example, see ICC, *Prosecutor v. Bemba et al.*, Appeals Chamber, Public Redacted Judgment on the appeals of Mr Jean-Pierre Bemba Gombo, Mr Aimé Kilolo Musamba, Mr Jean-Jacques Mangenda Kabongo, Mr Fidèle Babala Wandu and Mr Narcisse Arido against the decision of Trial Chamber VII entitled "Judgment pursuant to Article 74 of the Statute", 8 March 2018, ICC-01/05-01/13-2275-Red, paras. 93, 554 (https://www.legal-tools.org/doc/56cfc0/) ("'[d]eferring these assessments is also more consonant with' the right and duty to assess freely, according to Rule 63(2) of the Rules, all evidence submitted"), 585, 591; previously ICC, *Prosecutor v. Lubanga*, Trial Chamber I, Decision on the admissibility of four documents, 13 June 2008, ICC-01/04-01/06-1399, paras. 24, 32 ('Lubanga Decision on admissibility') (https://www.legal-tools.org/doc/2855e0/); ICC, *Prosecutor v. Ruto and Sang*, Trial Chamber V(A), Public redacted version of Decision on the Prosecution's Application for Addition of Documents to Its List of Evidence, 3 September 2014, ICC-01/09-01/11-1485-Red2, para. 28 (https://www.legal-tools.org/doc/342ede/) ("The Prosecution notes that there is a principle that the Chamber should have the ability to freely assess the evidence before it rather than seek to limit the use of evidence at the outset"); ICC, *Prosecutor v. Ongwen*, Pre-Trial Chamber II, Decision on Prosecution Request in Relation to its Mental Health Experts Examining the Accused, 28 June 2017, ICC-02/04-01/15-902, para. 6 (https://www.legal-tools.org/doc/80f3dc/).

---

mum flexibility"[672] and "broad discretion" when deciding on the admissibility.[673] The admissibility decision of the ICC, for instance, depends on the "relevance"[674] and "probative value"[675] of the evidence[676] and the absence of any serious rights violation.[677] Thus, as long as CIJA investigators do not commit a (serious) rights violation, it could be speculated that their information will at least not be ruled inadmissible prior to a judgment.[678] Espe-

---

[672] Gideon Boas *et al.*, *International Criminal Procedure*, International Criminal Law Practitioner Library Series, vol. III, Cambridge University Press, 2011, p. 336; Ambos, 2016, p. 447, see above note 342.

[673] Cf. Lubanga Decision on admissibility, para. 23, see above note 671; *Prosecutor v. Bemba*, Trial Chamber III, Judgment pursuant to Article 74 of the Statute, 21 March 2016, ICC-01/05-01/08-3343, para. 222 (https://www.legal-tools.org/doc/edb0cf/) ("In deciding on the admission of the various items, [...] the Chamber is afforded a measure of discretion".); for the same position at the *ad hoc* Tribunals and other ICTs, see ICTY, *Prosecutor v. Aleksovski*, Appeals Chamber, Decision on Prosecutor's Appeal on Admissibility of Evidence, 16 February 1999, IT-95-14/1-AR73, para. 15 (https://www.legal-tools.org/doc/168b25/); ICTY, *Prosecutor v. Kordić and Čerkez*, Appeals Chamber, Decision on Appeal Regarding Statement of a Deceased Witness, 21 July 2000, IT-95-14/2-AR73.5, para. 20 (https://www.legal-tools.org/doc/da3903/); ICTY, *Prosecutor v. Aleksovski*, Appeals Chamber, Judgment, 24 March 2000, IT-95-14/1-A, para. 63 (https://www.legal-tools.org/doc/176f05/); ICTR, *Prosecutor v. Musema*, Appeals Chamber, Judgment, 16 November 2001, ICTR-96-13-A, paras. 37–8 (https://www.legal-tools.org/doc/fba4cc/); SCSL, *Prosecutor v. Norman et al.*, Trial Chamber I, Appeal against Decision Refusing Bail, 11 March 2005, SCSL-04-14-AR65, para. 26 (https://www.legal-tools.org/doc/5f388e/) (purpose of Rule 89(C) "to avoid sterile legal debate over admissibility"). For the literature see, for example, Ambos, 2016, pp. 447 ff., see above note 342 with further references.

[674] ICC Statute, Articles 64(9)(a) and 69(4), see above note 182 (authorising the Trial Chamber to "rule" on the "relevance" of evidence), ICC RPE, Rule 63(2), see above note 645; see also ICTY RPE, Rule 89(C), see above note 341; ICTR RPE, Rule 89(C), see above note 341; SCSL RPE, Rule 89(C), see above note 517 and MICT RPE, Rule 105(C), see above note 515 (referring to "relevant" evidence); Ambos, 2016, p. 448, see above note 342.

[675] ICC Statute, Article 69(4), see above note 182, ICC RPE, Rule 72(2), see above note 645; see also ICTY RPE, Rule 89(C), see above note 341; ICTR RPE, Rule 89(C), see above note 341 and MICT RPE, Rule 105(C), see above note 515. Cf. SCSL, *Prosecutor v. Taylor*, Appeals Chamber, Decision on "Prosecution Notice of Appeal and Submissions Concerning the Decision Regarding the Tender of Documents", 6 February 2009, SCSL-03-01-T-721, para. 37 (https://www.legal-tools.org/doc/453718/); also Boas *et al.*, 2011, p. 340, see above note 672, with further references in fn. 18.

[676] In more detail Ambos, 2016, pp. 449–450, see above note 342.

[677] ICC Statute, Article 69(4), see above note 182, ICC RPE, Rule 72(2), see above note 645; see also ICTY RPE, Rule 89(D), see above note 341 and MICT RPE, Rule 105(D), see above note 515. Cf. Katanga and Ngudjolo, 2010, paras. 13 *et seq.*, see above note 311.

[678] In a similar vein Donald K. Piragoff and Paula Clarke, "Article 69", in Kai Ambos (ed.), *Rome Statute of the International Criminal Court – A Commentary*, fourth edition, C.H. Beck, Hart, Nomos, München *et al.*, 2021, p. 2093, mn. 95.

---

cially considering the ICC's practice, and, more concretely, the *Ongwen* Trial Chamber[679] – which rejected the Chambers' previous practice[680] of deciding on admissibility issues at the moment of submission (the 'admission approach') and promoted an alternative approach (authorised by the *Bemba* Appeals Chamber)[681] to defer the admissibility decision "until the end of the proceedings" (the 'submission approach').[682] The submission approach was recently adopted by Trial Chamber X in the Al Hassan case,[683] and by Trial Chamber V in the *Yekatom and Ngaissona* case.[684] However, if private investigators commit a rights violation while collecting evidence, exclusionary rules apply – irrespective of whether the investigators worked on behalf of an ICT-organ or *proprio motu*.

Second, on the international level, the importance of documentary evidence cannot be overstated.[685] Especially photography and visual media

---

[679] ICC, *Prosecutor v. Ongwen*, Initial Directions on the Conduct of the Proceedings, 13 July 2016, ICC-02/04-01/15-497, paras. 24 *et seq.* (https://www.legal-tools.org/doc/60d63f/); Decision on Request to Admit Evidence Preserved Under Article 56 of the Statute, 11 August 2016, ICC-02/04-01/15-520, para. 7 (https://www.legal-tools.org/doc/c47593/). In the same vein, see Fabricio Guariglia, "'Admission' v. 'Submission' of Evidence at the International Criminal Court", in *Journal of International Criminal Justice*, 2018, vol. 16, no. 2, p. 321 (who, however, cites the wrong decision in fn. 20).

[680] See, for example, Katanga and Ngudjolo, 2010, para. 15, see above note 311. For a similar approach at the ICTY, see Christine Schuon, *International Criminal Procedure, A Clash of Legal Cultures*, T.M.C. Asser Press, The Hague, 2010, pp. 137–8 (shift from admissibility to weight/reliability). See, generally, Ambos, 2016, p. 449, see above note 342.

[681] ICC, *Prosecutor v. Bemba*, Appeals Chamber, Judgment on the Appeals of Mr. Jean-Pierre Bemba Gombo and the Prosecutor against the Decision of TC III entitled "Decision on the admission into evidence of materials contained in the prosecution's list of evidence", 3 May 2011, ICC-01/05-01/08-1386, paras. 37, 41-2, 52-7 (http://www.legal-tools.org/doc/7b62af/).

[682] *Ibid.*, para. 37; in the same vein, see *Prosecutor v. Bemba et al.*, Decision on Prosecution Requests for Admission of Documentary Evidence, 24 September 2015, ICC-01/05-01/13-1285, para. 9 (https://www.legal-tools.org/doc/5a06b3/). See, generally, Guariglia, 2018, p. 315, see above note 679.

[683] ICC, *Prosecutor v. Al Hassan*, Annex A to the Decision on the conduct of proceedings, 6 May 2020, ICC-01/12-01/18-789-AnxA, paras. 29 *et seq.* (https://www.legal-tools.org/doc/jk54h9/).

[684] ICC, *Prosecutor v. Alfred Yekatom and Patrice-Edouard Ngaïssona*, Initial Directions on the Conduct of the Proceedings, 26 August 2020, ICC-01/14-01/18-631, paras. 52–59 (https://www.legal-tools.org/doc/ubfjw1/).

[685] Ambos, 2016, p. 487, see above note 342. Cf. Gaynor *et al.*, 2013, pp. 1045–1046, see above note 533. But see also Nancy Amoury Combs, *Fact-Finding Without Facts*, Cambridge University Press, 2010, pp. 6, 12–14, finding that the ICTR, the SCSL, and the SPSC basically relied on witness testimony with only the latter also receiving significant forensic evidence.

---

is gaining increasing importance and relevance before both ICTs and national courts trying international crimes.[686] Unsurprisingly, Wiley, CIJA's Director, maintained: "The queen and king of evidence in any criminal investigation is a document. It isn't cross-examined because it is factual".[687] As to the admissibility of documentary evidence the same general principles apply, that is, it depends on its relevance and probative value (reliability).[688] A document can only be reliable if it is authentic since "the fact that the document is what it purports to be enhances the likely truth of the contents thereof".[689] Thus, authenticity speaks to the probative value of a document, be it in the form of reliability or its evidentiary weight.[690] Furthermore, the 'chain of custody', that is, the document's production process from its creation to the submission to a Chamber, is to be considered.[691] The demonstration of that chain of custody is certainly one of the main challenges for the work of CIJA-investigators.[692]

---

[686] See Section 17.3 for the impact the Group Caesar had on German proceedings. See also Aoife Duffy, "Bearing Witness to Atrocity Crimes: Photography and International Law", in *Human Rights Quarterly*, 2018, vol. 40, no. 4, pp. 798 ff.

[687] Rankin, 2017, p. 409, see above note 56.

[688] See also ICTY, *Prosecutor v. Brđanin and Talić*, Standards Order, 15 February 2002, IT-99-36-T, para. 18 (https://www.legal-tools.org/doc/005043/); ICTR, *Prosecutor v. Musema*, Appeals Chamber, Judgement, 16 November 2001, ICTR-96-13-A, para. 56 (https://www.legal-tools.org/doc/6a3fce/); *Katanga and Ngudjolo*, 2010, paras. 13 *et seq.*, see above note 311; ICC, *Prosecutor v. Ruto and Sang*, Decision on the Prosecution's Request for Admission of Documentary Evidence, 10 June 2014, ICC-01/09-01/11-1353, paras. 13 *et seq.*, 37 (https://www.legal-tools.org/doc/e1a55f/). See, generally, Ambos, 2016, p. 487, see above note 342.

[689] ICC, *Prosecutor v. Bemba*, Public Redacted Version of Decision on the Prosecution's Application for Admission of Materials into Evidence Pursuant to Article 64 (9) of the Rome Statute of 6 September 2012, 8 October 2012, ICC-01/05-01/08-2299-Red, para. 9 (https://www.legal-tools.org/doc/13ca4b/); see also Ambos, 2016, p. 501, see above note 342.

[690] ICTY, *Prosecutor v. Blaškić*, Trial Chamber, Decision on the Defence Motion for Reconsideration of the Ruling to Exclude from Evidence Authentic and Exculpatory Documentary Evidence, 30 January 1998, IT-95-14-T (https://www.legal-tools.org/doc/vdkn6i/) ("the weight to be ascribed to it will depend on the additional elements which will have, if necessary, been provided and which permit attesting to its authenticity"). See also Boas *et al.*, 2011, p. 341, see above note 672.

[691] ICC, *Prosecutor v. Lubanga*, Judgment pursuant to Article 74 of the Statute, 5 April 2012, ICC-01/04-01/06-2842, para. 109 (https://www.legal-tools.org/doc/677866/); *Prosecutor v. Katanga*, Judgment pursuant to article 74 of the Statute, 7 March 2014, ICC-01/04-01/07-3436-tENG, para. 91 (https://www.legal-tools.org/doc/f74b4f/).

[692] Rankin, 2017, p. 401, see above note 56.

17.6. Conclusion

Considering the current political landscape of anti-multilateralism and the politically impotent UN Security Council, it was long overdue that the international community became more creative in its fight against impunity. The IIIMs in both Syria and Myanmar are the first step, CIJA is another. In an instructive short article about private investigations in Austria and Germany, Maier listed three reasons for the initiation of private investigations.[693] First, when public authorities are unwilling or unable to investigate; second, when the investigations of public authorities are ineffective and badly done; and third, when the victim does not want public authorities to investigate. The first and second requirements are met in the situation of Syria: the ICC (or any other ICT) cannot investigate, and investigations on the ground are fruitless. Private investigations are without an alternative, so to say, and there is nothing wrong with that. Despite the rich history and impressive success of private investigations in domestic contexts, private investigators still feel that "their role within society, the value of their services and the problems they faced, have been overlooked and undervalued for too long".[694] In fact, the perception of private investigators does not mirror the admiration readers identify with Sherlock Holmes and Miss Marple. Many private investigators are still viewed as "cowboys" and "dodgy characters".[695] This does not do justice to their work – at the international level, it is likely that they will be the future, and the next ICC Prosecutor is certainly aware of that. After all, human rights organisations and entities such as CIJA on the one hand, and the investigative arms of ICTs on the other, share one goal: the desire to end impunity.[696] This goal, however, is a double-edged sword: it makes the use of evidence collected by private individuals both necessary and dangerous; without it, perpetrators of international crimes can hardly be convicted – when illegally obtained, a conviction becomes less likely. It is thus past time for a framework for private conduct in investigatory contexts at the international level. One way to establish such a framework is regulation. Countries such as the US, Canada, Australia, New Zealand, Belgium, the Netherlands, Germany, Finland or Spain, have a statutory framework for regulating private investi-

---

[693] Bernhard Maier, "Verbrechensaufklärung durch Privatdetektive", *Kriminalistik*, 2001, pp. 670–672 (670).

[694] Gill and Hart, 1999, p. 246, see above note 137.

[695] *Ibid.*

[696] Bergsmo and Wiley, 2008, p. 2, see above note 1.

gators.[697] However, regulation cannot go at the detriment of the nature of those investigations. In other words, overregulation will eventually deprive private investigators of the advantages they have *vis-à-vis* public investigators. Thus, until today Britain has not regulated private investigations.[698] At the international level, regulation is unlikely. This is where 'integrity' can be employed. As an element of the rule of law, it is the umbrella that protects a trial from failing on legitimacy grounds. It applies to both private actions and actions of public officials. Understood this way, integrity becomes a proxy, synonym or placeholder for procedural values such as fairness, due process, natural justice or judicial legitimacy. All those values are the DNA of the ICC Statute. The integrity of the Statute is thus a crucial part in the fight against impunity. To close this chapter with the Declaration of the Statute's Review Conference in Kampala 2010:

> We, high-level representatives of States Parties to the Rome Statute of the International Criminal Court [...] [r]eaffirm our commitment to the Rome Statute of the International Criminal Court and its full implementation, as well as to its universality and *integrity*.[699]

---

[697] Johnston, 2007, p. 288, see above note 93.

[698] Gill and Hart, 1999, p. 248, see above note 137; Johnston, 2007, p. 288, see above note 93.

[699] ICC ASP, Review Conference of the Rome Statute of the International Criminal Court, Declaration RC/Decl.1, 1 June 2010 (https://www.legal-tools.org/doc/146df9-1/), emphasis added.

PART IV:
ROLE OF INTERNATIONAL COURTS

18

Codes of Judicial Ethics:
An Emerging Culture of
Accountability for the Judiciary?

Bettina Julia Spilker[*]

> Public confidence in the administration of justice is one of the
> essential components of a democracy. This involves not only
> the respect for independence, impartiality, efficiency and qual-
> ity, but also relies on the quality of the individual behaviour of
> judges. Respect by judges of ethical requirements is a duty
> which comes with their powers.[1]

18.1. Introduction

Establishing a culture of accountability for every actor participating in judicial proceedings is a crucial element in strengthening the integrity of such
proceedings, and ultimately of a judicial institution. In the same vein, the
foundational documents of each international or internationalised court and
tribunal profess that the qualifications of the judges, key actors in judicial
proceedings, must include integrity. However, it is only of late that judges
are themselves subjected to some form of accountability, with recent years
seeing the adoption of numerous codes of judicial ethics ('CoJEs') before
international and internationalised courts and tribunals ('ICTs'), some of
which include disciplinary procedures. Prior to such developments, judges
could only be subject to case-specific motions for disqualification with limited effect, and the result of which could never lead to their overall removal
from their positions. The adoption of these various CoJEs may thus be seen

---

[*] **Bettina Julia Spilker** is Legal Officer, International, Impartial and Independent Mechanism
(Syria). The views expressed in this article are those of the author alone and do not necessarily reflect the views of the International, Impartial and Independent Mechanism (Syria) or
of the United Nations. The author is grateful to Guénaël Mettraux, Kinga Tibori-Szabó and
Simon Meisenberg for their invaluable comments on earlier drafts.

[1] Judges: Independence, Efficiency and Responsibilities, Recommendation and Explanatory
Memorandum, adopted by the Committee of Ministers of the Council of Europe on 17 November 2010, CM/Rec(2010)12, para. 69 ('Recommendation of Committee of Ministers')
(https://www.legal-tools.org/doc/8r16ac/).

as a significant step towards guaranteeing the integrity of the judiciary in ICTs, and thus ultimately of proceedings in these jurisdictions in a most exhaustive manner. The question may, therefore, be posed as to whether such CoJEs constitute effective institutional measures to give proper effect to the 'integrity standard'.[2]

In order to respond to this query, the first section of this chapter will examine rules and procedures in place before the adoption of these CoJEs and relevant decisions in this respect, as well as their effectiveness – or lack thereof – in ensuring the integrity of proceedings (Section 18.2.). This will be followed by a comparative analysis of CoJEs adopted by ICTs, focussing on the various principles described therein and any jurisprudence developed thereon (Section 18.3.). The next section will provide a review and comparison of the three disciplinary procedures adopted in respect of these CoJEs – namely at the International Criminal Court ('ICC'), the Kosovo Specialist Chambers ('KSC'), and the International Residual Mechanism for Criminal Tribunals ('IRMCT') – in order to identify whether and how these procedures foster a culture of accountability for the judiciary, ultimately strengthening the integrity of proceedings, or whether they need to be developed further (Section 18.4.). Then, this chapter will close with some final remarks with respect to the questions posed at the beginning as well as an outlook on the future of CoJEs (Section 18.5.).

18.2. Regulation of Judicial Ethics – A Beginning

Whilst some ICTs never adopted any CoJE, the majority of those which have, did so several years after their establishment (see Table 1). The following ICTs will be examined: the International Criminal Tribunal for the former Yugoslavia ('ICTY'), the International Criminal Tribunal for Rwanda ('ICTR'), the ICC, the Special Court for Sierra Leone ('SCSL'), the Extraordinary Chambers in the Courts of Cambodia ('ECCC'), the Special Tribunal for Lebanon ('STL'), the IRMCT, and the KSC.

---

[2] See Morten Bergsmo, "Revisiting Integrity in International Justice", FICHL Policy Brief Series No. 93 (2018), Torkel Opsahl Academic EPublisher, Brussels, 2018, pp. 2–3 ("4. Institutional 'Integrity' Measures Available to International Courts") (https://www.toaep.org/pbs-pdf/93-bergsmo/).

	Establishment	Appointment of First Judges	Adoption of CoJE
ICTY	1993	1994	2016[3]
ICTR	1994	1995	n/a
ICC	1998	2003	2005[4]
SCSL	2002	2002	n/a
ECCC	2003	2006	2008[5]
STL	2007	2009	2016[6]
IRMCT	2010	2012	2015;[7] revised 2018;[8]
KSC	2015	2017	2017[9]

Table 1: Years of establishment, appointment of first judges and adoption of CoJEs of various ICTs.

In any case, every foundational document of each ICT includes a provision regarding the necessity for the integrity and impartiality of its judges.[10] However, this provision itself is not further fleshed out in any of these foundational legal texts.

---

[3] ICTY, Code of professional conduct for the judges of the Tribunal, adopted on 6 July 2016 ('ICTY CoJE') (https://www.legal-tools.org/doc/55lsey/).

[4] ICC, Code of Judicial Ethics, adopted on 9 March 2005 ('ICC CoJE') (https://www.legal-tools.org/doc/383f8f).

[5] ECCC, Code of Judicial Ethics, adopted on 31 January 2008 ('ECCC CoJE') (https://www.legal-tools.org/doc/5dys4p/).

[6] STL, Code of Professional Conduct for the Judges of the Special Tribunal for Lebanon, adopted on 27 September 2016 ('STL CoJE') (https://www.legal-tools.org/doc/oird6k/).

[7] IRMCT, Code of Professional Conduct for the Judges of the Mechanism, adopted on 11 May 2015 (https://www.legal-tools.org/doc/23cc92).

[8] IRMCT, Code of Professional Conduct for the Judges of the Mechanism, adopted on 9 April 2018 ('IRMCT CoJE') (https://www.legal-tools.org/doc/5deknw/).

[9] KSC, Code of Judicial Ethics for Judges Appointed to the Roster of International Judges of the Kosovo Specialist Chambers, adopted on 14 March 2017 ('KSC CoJE') (https://www.legal-tools.org/doc/wl7m65/).

[10] Updated Statute of the International Criminal Tribunal for the former Yugoslavia, 25 May, 1993, Article 13 ('ICTY Statute') (https://www.legal-tools.org/doc/b4f63b); Statute of the International Criminal Tribunal for Rwanda, 8 November 1994, Article 12 ('ICTR Statute') (https://www.legal-tools.org/doc/8732d6); Rome Statute of the International Criminal Court, 17 July 1998, Article 36(3)(a) ('ICC Statute') (https://www.legal-tools.org/doc/7b9af9);

Prior to the adoption of CoJEs, judges were therefore not subject to any form of accountability within their respective institutions. Indeed, not being staff members but rather appointed officials, they did not fall within the scope of disciplinary mechanisms of their respective institutions, since any relevant staff rules and attached disciplinary procedures only applied to staff members[11] – and hence not to them. In most cases, appointed by the United Nations ('UN') Secretary-General, a particular regime would apply to judges, including confidential terms of references or similar regulatory documents, which however did not provide for any disciplinary provisions or mechanisms.

In order to appreciate the necessity for the adoption of a sound ethical framework for the judiciary in ICTs, it is necessary to understand the context in which these institutions operate and the particularities which make such requirements all the more necessary. Importantly, judges in ICTs come from various legal cultures, which necessarily include different regulations of ethical duties. Added thereto, it is recalled that judges do not necessarily need prior judicial experience in order to be selected. More often than not, selection criteria for judges before ICTs are not or only very cursorily regulated. Some Statutes merely require that candidates must possess "the qualifications required in their respective countries for appointment to the highest judicial offices".[12] Notably, it is not required that candidates bring with them actual experience as judges, thus making them less likely to be familiar with ethical regulations for the judiciary. The most striking example thereof is the so-called List B of candidates for the ICC: pursuant to Article 36(3)(b)(ii) of the ICC Statute, it allows for candidates to apply to become ICC judges where they have "established competence in relevant areas of international law [...], and extensive experience in a profes-

---

Statute of the Special Court for Sierra Leone, 14 August 2000, Article 13 ('SCSL Statute') (https://www.legal-tools.org/doc/aa0e20); Statute of the Special Tribunal for Lebanon, 30 May 2007, Article 9(1) ('STL Statute') (https://www.legal-tools.org/doc/da0bbb); Statute of the International Residual Mechanism for Criminal Tribunals, 22 December 2010, Article 9(1) ('IRMCT Statute') (https://www.legal-tools.org/doc/30782d).

[11] For example, ICTY staff members were subject to the UN Staff Rules and Regulations, which detailed provisions on disciplinary misconduct and any proceedings attached thereto (see Rules 10.1-10.4). However, they are only applicable to staff members. Staff Regulations and Rules of the United Nations, UN Doc. ST/SGB/2018/1, 1 January 2018 (https://www.legal-tools.org/doc/zn5lba/).

[12] See, for example, ICTY Statute, Article 13; ICTR Statute, Article 12; SCSL Statute, Article 13(1), see above note 10.

sional legal capacity which is of relevance to the judicial work of the Court". This List is an alternative to Article 36(3)(b)(i), pursuant to which candidates shall bring with them "necessary relevant experience, whether as judge, prosecutor, advocate or in any other similar capacity, in criminal proceedings". The ICC Statute thus clearly foresees that some of its judges will not have any experience as domestic judges. As will be further exposed below, for many ICTs, the entire system is ultimately controlled by the judges themselves, rather than by independent external bodies. In many instances, judges are the rule-makers of their own standards, as those adopting the rules applicable to themselves. Further, the size and magnitude of cases before ICTs also make strict ethical standards necessary. Where ethical problems arise, implications in terms of judicial – and ultimately, financial – resources are significant. Added thereto is the fact that proceedings before ICTs generally take place in particularly sensitive political environments, where ethical flaws may be exploited. Overall, it is thus clear that the particularities of ICTs make the adoption of strong ethical requirements for the judiciary a serious necessity.

However, until recently, in the context of ICTs, the only mechanism to question the impartiality or integrity of a judge was the possibility of requesting his or her disqualification through motions under the applicable Rules of Procedure and Evidence ('RPE'). Whilst the wording of the relevant rules varies slightly, in essence, a judge may not sit in any case in which he or she has a personal interest, or concerning which he or she has or has had any association which might affect or appear to affect the judge's impartiality. If this is the case, a judge shall withdraw, or a party may apply to the president for the disqualification and withdrawal of a judge upon these grounds.[13] Article 41(2)(a) of the ICC Statute is the only regulatory document which provides additional details on this matter. Impartiality, in this respect, must be seen as a fundamental principle applica-

---

[13]   See, for example, ICTR, Rules of Procedure and Evidence, 29 June 1995, Rule 15 ('ICTR RPE') (https://www.legal-tools.org/doc/0b0d43/); ICTY, Rules of Procedure and Evidence, 11 February 1994, Rule 15 ('ICTY RPE') (https://www.legal-tools.org/doc/30df50/); SCSL, Rules of Procedure and Evidence, 16 January 2002, Rule 15 ('SCSL RPE') (https://www.legal-tools.org/doc/b36b82/); STL, Rules of Procedure and Evidence, 20 March 2009, Rule 25 ('STL RPE') (https://www.legal-tools.org/doc/3773bf/); IRMCT, Rules of Procedure and Evidence, 8 June 2012, Rule 18 ('IRMCT RPE') (https://www.legal-tools.org/doc/cef176/).

ble to all judges, as per the respective Statutes of ICTs[14] – a principle intrinsically linked to each judge's integrity. The jurisprudence developed in respect of disqualification requests is instructive – it primarily focusses on issues of impartiality, rather than integrity, although it is clear that there is some overlap between these concepts.

Early ICTY Appeals Chamber jurisprudence in *Furundžija* determined that "there is a general rule that a Judge should not only be *subjectively* free from bias, but also that there should be nothing in the surrounding circumstances which *objectively* gives rise to an appearance of bias".[15] It was thus determined that the requirement of impartiality is violated not only where a judge is actually biased, but also where there is an appearance of bias.[16]

On that basis, the following principles were developed:

1. A judge is not impartial if it is shown that actual bias exists.

2. There is an unacceptable appearance of bias if:

   a. a judge is a party to the case, or has a financial or proprietary interest in the outcome of a case, or if the judge's decision will lead to the promotion of a cause in which he or she is involved, together with one of the parties. Under these circumstances, a judge's disqualification from the case is automatic; or

   b. the circumstances would lead a reasonable observer, properly informed, to reasonably apprehend bias.[17]

---

[14] See, for example, ICTY Statute, Article 13; ICTR Statute, Article 12; ICC Statute, Article 36(3)(a); SCSL Statute, Article 13; STL Statute, Article 9(1); IRMCT Statute, Article 9(1), see above note 10.

[15] ICTY, *Prosecutor v. Furundžija*, Appeals Chamber, Judgement, 21 July 2000, IT-95-17/1-A, para. 189 (emphasis added) ('Furundžija Appeal Judgement') (https://www.legal-tools.org/doc/660d3f).

[16] ICTR, *The Prosecutor v. Karemera et al.*, Trial Chamber, Decision on Joseph Nzirorera's Motion for Disqualification of Judges Byron, Kam, and Joensen, 7 March 2008, ICTR-98-44-T, para. 4 ('Karemera et al. Decision of 7 March 2008') (https://www.legal-tools.org/doc/6003e9/), referring to Furundžija Appeal Judgment, paras. 181–188; ICTY, *Prosecutor v. Brđanin and Talić*, Trial Chamber, Decision on Application by Momir Talić for the Disqualification and Withdrawal of a Judge, 18 May 2000, IT-99-36-T, paras. 9–14 ('Brđanin and Talić Decision of 18 May 2000') (https://www.legal-tools.org/doc/44e03e).

[17] Furundžija Appeal Judgement, para. 189, footnote 257, see above note 15, recalling that in *Talić*, it was found that the test on this prong is "whether the reaction of the hypothetical fair-minded observer (with sufficient knowledge of the actual circumstances to make a rea-

The test of the reasonable observer, properly informed, refers to "an informed person, with knowledge of all the relevant circumstances, including the traditions of integrity and impartiality that form part of the background and apprised also of the fact that impartiality is one of the duties that Judges swear to uphold".[18] This jurisprudence is demonstrative of the close link between a judge's integrity and impartiality. The apprehension of bias test further reflects the maxim that "justice should not only be done but should manifestly and undoubtedly be seen to be done"[19] and is founded on the need to ensure public confidence in the judiciary.[20] The decisive question is whether a perception of lack of impartiality is objectively justified,[21] based on knowledge of all the relevant circumstances.[22]

Early in its jurisprudence, the ICTR Appeals Chamber in *Kayishema and Ruzindana* made the following finding:

---

sonable judgement) would be that [the judge] … might not bring an impartial and unprejudiced mind"; Brđanin and Talić Decision of 18 May 2000, para. 15, see above note 16.

[18]   *Ibid.*, para. 190, referring to Supreme Court of Canada, *R.D.S. v. The Queen*, 27 September 1997; see also ICTR, *The Prosecutor v. Nahimana et al.*, Appeals Chamber, Judgement, 28 November 2007, ICTR-99-52-A, para. 50 ('Nahimana *et al.* Appeal Judgment') (https://www.legal-tools.org/doc/04e4f9/); ICTY, *Prosecutor v. Galić*, Appeals Chamber, Judgement, 30 November 2006, IT-98-29-A, para. 40 (https://www.legal-tools.org/doc/c81a32/); ICTR, *The Prosecutor v. Rutaganda*, Appeals Chamber, Judgement, 26 May 2003, ICTR-96-3-A, para. 40 (https://www.legal-tools.org/doc/40bf4a/); *Prosecutor v. Delalić et al.*, Appeals Chamber, Judgement, 20 February 2001, IT-96-21-A, para. 682 ('Delalić *et al.* Appeal Judgment') (https://www.legal-tools.org/doc/051554/).

[19]   Karemera *et al.* Decision of 7 March 2008, para. 5, see above note 16, referring to *Furundžija* Appeal Judgment, para. 195; Brđanin and Talić Decision of 18 May 2000, para. 9, see above note 16; SCSL, *Prosecutor v. Sesay*, Decision on Defence Motion Seeking the Disqualification of Justice Robertson from the Appeals Chamber, 13 March 2004, SCSL-04-15-A, para. 16 (https://www.legal-tools.org/doc/d83edd/); ICTR, *The Prosecutor v. Ntahobali*, The Bureau, Decision on Motion for Disqualification of Judges, 7 March 2006, ICTR-97-21-T, para. 9 ('Ntahobali Decision of 7 March 2006') (https://www.legal-tools.org/doc/69f139/).

[20]   ICTY, *Prosecutor v. Stanišić and Župljanin*, Appeals Chamber, Judgement, 30 June 2016, IT-08-91-A, para. 43 (https://www.legal-tools.org/doc/e414f6/), referring to Delalić *et al.* Appeal Judgment, para. 707, see above note 18; ICTR, *The Prosecutor v. Karemera et al.*, Decision on Joseph Nzirorera's Motion for Disqualification of Judge Byron and Stay of Proceedings, 20 February 2009, ICTR-98-44-T, para. 6 (https://www.legal-tools.org/doc/f27eb3/).

[21]   Karemera *et al.* Decision of 7 March 2008, para. 5, see above note 16, referring to Ntahobali Decision of 7 March 2006, para. 9, see above note 19; Furundžija Appeal Judgement, para. 185, see above note 15.

[22]   *Karemera et al.* Decision of 7 March 2008, para. 5, *ibid.*

As a rule, a fair trial requires that a set of procedural rules be established to ensure equality between the parties to the case and guarantee the independence of the Tribunal and the impartiality of the judges. A judge is presumed to be impartial until proven otherwise. This is a subjective test: impartiality relates to the judge's personal qualities, his intellectual and moral integrity. A judge is bound only by his conscience and the law. That does not mean that he rules on cases subjectively, but rather according to what he deems to be the correct interpretation of the law, ensuring for an unbiased and knowledgeable observer that his objectivity does not give the impression that he his [*sic*] impartial, even though, in fact, he is. Moreover, before taking up his duties, each judge makes a solemn declaration obliging him to perform his duties and exercise his powers as a judge "honourably, faithfully, impartially and conscientiously."[23]

Importantly for the purpose of this chapter, judges of ICTs enjoy a "presumption of impartiality, based on their oath of office and the qualifications for their selection",[24] which cannot be easily rebutted.[25] In the absence of evidence to the contrary, it must be assumed that the judges "can disabuse their minds of any irrelevant personal beliefs or predispositions".[26] A 'high threshold' has thus been placed on the moving party to displace this presumption – justified as follows: while any real or apparent bias on the part of a judge undermines confidence in the administration of justice, "it would be equally a threat to the interests of the impartial and fair

---

[23] ICTR, *The Prosecutor v. Kayishema and Ruzindana*, Appeals Chamber, Judgment (Reasons), 1 June 2001, ICTR-95-1-A, para. 55 (https://www.legal-tools.org/doc/9ea5f4/), referring to Furundžija Appeal Judgement, paras. 196–197, see above note 15; ICTR, *The Prosecutor v. Akayesu*, Appeals Chamber, Judgment, 1 June 2001, ICTR-96-4-A, paras. 90 *et seq.* ('Akayesu Appeal') (https://www.legal-tools.org/doc/c62d06/); Delalić *et al.* Appeal Judgment, paras. 682 *et seq.* and 698 *et seq.*, see above note 18.

[24] Karemera *et al.* Decision of 7 March 2008, para. 6, see above note 16.

[25] ICTR, *The Prosecutor v. Nyiramasuhuko et al.*, Appeals Chamber, Judgement, vol. II, 14 December 2015, ICTR-98-42-A, para. 2843 (https://www.legal-tools.org/doc/93cee1/), referring to ICTR, *The Prosecutor v. Karemera et al.*, Appeals Chamber, Judgement, 29 September 2014, ICTR-98-44-A, para. 24 (https://www.legal-tools.org/doc/372a64/); ICTR, *The Prosecutor v. Hategekimana*, Appeals Chamber, Judgement, 8 May 2012, ICTR-00-55B-A, para. 16 (https://www.legal-tools.org/doc/885b2c/); Nahimana *et al.* Appeal Judgment, para. 48, see above note 18; Akayesu Appeal, para. 91, see above note 23; Furundžija Appeal Judgement, para. 197, see above note 15.

[26] Nahimana *et al.* Appeal Judgment, para. 48, see above note 18, referring to Furundžija Appeal Judgement, para. 197, see above note 15.

---

administration of justice if judges were to be disqualified on the basis of unfounded and unsupported allegations of bias".[27]

Throughout the existence of ICTs, rare were the occasions where bias, or an appearance of bias, was established. At the ICTR, in the *Karemera et al.* case, the Appeals Chamber determined that

> the admitted association and cohabitation [of Judge V with Prosecution counsel on the same case], the fact that [Judge V] did not disclose these facts until Defence counsel expressly raised the matter in court and that she withdrew from the case after Defence lodged applications for her disqualification on this basis and before the Bureau decided the disqualification motions [...] could well lead a reasonable, informed observer to objectively apprehend bias.[28]

However, even in such the circumstances – which could be deemed evident from the point of view of an objective observer – the ICTR Appeals Chamber emphasised that this was "not a finding of actual bias on the part of [Judge V], but rather a finding, made in the interests of justice, that the circumstances of the case gave rise to an *appearance* of bias".[29] It is noteworthy in this respect that the Appeals Chamber found that this appearance also extended to the remaining two judges because, although aware of the circumstances of Judge V's association with the Prosecution counsel, they acquiesced in rejecting a Defence motion for Judge V's recusal and, therefore, in continuing the trial with the Judge on the bench.[30]

In a now infamous case before the ICTY, the Judge in question – in a letter, later widely published in the media – referred to "what he perceived as a 'set practice' of convicting military commanders and ma[de] clear his dissatisfaction with his perceived change in the Tribunal's direction in this

---

27 Karemera *et al.* Decision of 7 March 2008, para. 6, see above note 16, referring to Ntahobali Decision of 7 March 2006, para. 9, see above note 19; Delalić *et al.* Appeal Judgment, para. 707, see above note 18.

28 ICTR, *The Prosecutor v. Karemera et al.*, Reasons for Decision on Interlocutory Appeals Regarding the Continuation of Proceedings with a Substitute Judge and on Nzirorera's Motion for Leave to Consider New Material, 22 October 2004, ICTR-98-44-AR15bis.2, para. 67 ('Karemera *et al.* Decision of 22 October 2004') (https://www.legal-tools.org/doc/7e9d02/).

29 *Ibid.*, para. 67.

30 *Ibid.*, para. 69.

regard".[31] In adjudicating upon a motion on the Judge's disqualification, the Majority considered that:

> By referring to a 'set practice' of convicting accused persons without reference to an evaluation of the evidence in each individual case, [...] there are grounds for concluding that a reasonable observer, properly informed, would reasonably apprehend bias on the part of [Judge H] in favour of a conviction. [...] [T]his appearance of bias is further compounded by [Judge H's] statement that he is confronted by a professional and moral dilemma, which in the view of the Majority, is a clear reference to his difficulty in applying the current jurisprudence of the Tribunal. In the circumstances, the Majority considers that the Letter, when read as a whole, rebuts the presumption of impartiality.[32]

Of importance for the present purposes, a dissent was filed alongside the above decision, in which the dissenting Judge very clearly stated that he

> consider[ed] a letter of this kind to be undoubtedly improper in various respects for a Judge in [Judge H's] position. In the Letter, [Judge H] sets forth an inarticulate critique of the recent jurisprudence of the Tribunal based on unsubstantiated speculations and insinuations of improper conduct by other colleagues in a fashion that is unbefitting of a Judge.[33]

Overall, however, the dissenting Judge disagreed with the Majority and, in doing so, he noted that

> in applying the test of a 'reasonable observer', the Majority fail[ed] to adequately take into account and address *all of the surrounding circumstances* that an informed observer is assumed to know in order to assess whether there is a reasonable apprehension of bias. [...] Such circumstances include, for example, the high eligibility standard for Judges of the Tribunal as embodied in Article 13 of the Statute, the oath taken by judges to exercise their powers 'honourably, faithfully, impar-

---

[31] ICTY, *Prosecutor v. Šešelj*, Decision on Defence Motion for Disqualification of Judge Frederik Harhoff and Report to the Vice-President, 28 August 2013, IT-03-67-T, para. 12 ('Šešelj Decision of 28 August 2013') (https://www.legal-tools.org/doc/5b4aa1/).

[32] *Ibid.*, para. 13.

[33] *Ibid.*, Dissenting Opinion of Judge Liu, para. 2.

tially and conscientiously', and a judge's professional experience.[34]

In the dissenting Judge's view,

> had the Majority considered [Judge's H's experience as a Judge of the Tribunal and a professor of law], it would have found that [his] statements do not demonstrate an appearance of bias towards conviction of accused before the Tribunal as to overcome the presumption of impartiality.[35]

This approach deserves particular scrutiny – mostly because the argument can readily be turned on its head. Indeed, should it not be the case that precisely *because* of Judge H's position as an ICTY judge and a professor of law and *because* of the oath he took, a reasonable observer should be even stricter in his determination of whether an appearance of bias towards a conviction of an accused person has been established? Should it not be the case that someone in this position should be even less likely to make such statements – rather than justifying such statements by the fact that, even though 'unbefitting' of a judge, they do not demonstrate bias?

The above demonstrates that the jurisprudence regarding the disqualification of judges in cases of lack of impartiality is less than satisfactory in holding judges accountable in instances which could be qualified as having the potential of seriously affecting the integrity of proceedings. In addition, it must be stressed that the purpose of motions for disqualification is to ensure the integrity of proceedings. CoJEs, on the other hand, serve a different aim, namely ensuring the professional integrity of the judiciary and providing for accountability mechanisms in this respect.

In the light of this, the adoption of appropriate CoJEs, with disciplinary proceedings attached thereto, may be seen as a necessity in order to guarantee such accountability and to ensure that judges abide by the standards they swear an oath to.

18.3. Codes of Judicial Ethics – Applicable Standards

The following section will look into the respective preamble and legal basis of each CoJE to ascertain the considerations underlying their adoption, and whether the judges, in adopting these CoJEs, were provided with, or provided themselves with, a sound legal basis for this purpose. This will be

---

[34] *Ibid.*, para. 8.
[35] *Ibid.*, para. 9.

followed by a comparative analysis of the various principles set out in each CoJE. Finally, this section will close with a comparison of the disciplinary proceedings attached to the CoJEs of the ICC, the KSC and the IRMCT – as the only CoJEs including such proceedings.

18.3.1. Preamble and Legal Basis

From a comparative perspective, it is interesting to look at the preamble and the legal basis for each CoJE. Indeed, the foundational documents of most ICTs provide judges with powers to regulate their own proceedings. With the exception of the ICC, the most poignant example thereof is their competence, as per their respective foundational documents, to adopt their own RPE.[36] Judges of ICTs have taken a broad approach to this competence in adopting RPE which provide for additional competences to further regulate detailed aspects of the conduct of proceedings – often through the president of a respective institution, in consultation with the judges and other internal stakeholders.[37] This demonstrates the emergence of a culture, in ICTs, in which the judges of each institution have adopted a practice of providing themselves or their respective president with broad powers to regulate a range of matters regarding the internal functioning of their respective institutions. This, in turns, means that it was only upon the initiative of the judges themselves that a CoJE could be adopted – and this practice could thus only emerge through a change of approach, an awareness by the judges themselves that there was a necessity for accountability.

18.3.1.1. ICC (2005)

The ICC CoJE was adopted by the ICC judges in 2005, as a first of its kind at ICTs. It stands out as demonstrative of an emerging practice, in the context of a new generation of international institutions – the ICTY and the ICTR having by then been established for over 10 years already, without the adoption of any regulatory documents for their judges.[38]

---

[36] See, for example, ICTY Statute, Article 15, see above note 10; STL Statute, Article 28, see above note 10; IRMCT Statute, Article 13, see above note 10.

[37] See, for example, ICTY RPE, Rule 19(B), see above note 13; STL RPE, Rule 32(E), see above note 13; IRMCT RPE, Rule 23(B), see above note 13.

[38] In a similar fashion, an ICC Code of Conduct for the Office of the Prosecutor was drafted as an institutional priority at an early stage, as an important means of cultivating coherence between the *being* of prosecutors and doing of investigations. See Salim A. Nakhjavani, "The Origins and Development of the Code of Conduct", in Morten Bergsmo, Klaus Rackwitz

The preamble of the ICC CoJE is brief and notably refers to the solemn undertaking, as provided for in Article 45 of the ICC Statute and fleshed out in Rule 5(1)(a) of the ICC RPE.[39] The judges further recall principles of judicial independence, impartiality and proper conduct, as well as the "need for guidelines of general application to contribute to judicial independence and impartiality and with a view to ensuring the legitimacy and effectiveness of the international judicial process". Regard is notably had to the UN Basic Principles on the Independence of the Judiciary (1985).[40]

According to Article 1 of the ICC CoJE, the Code is adopted by the judges pursuant to Regulation 126 of the Regulations of the Court. Indeed, the latter provision incorporates an explicit legal basis for the adoption of the CoJE, which is to be drawn up by the ICC President upon consultation with the judges – and to be adopted by the majority of the judges. The Regulations of the Court being adopted by the judges themselves,[41] it does appear somewhat circular to note that a legal basis for the adoption of the CoJE was adopted by the same actors who eventually adopted the CoJE itself. However, as will be seen below, this was not the case with other CoJEs, and may also be seen as demonstrative of the ICC judges' awareness of the necessity for such a Code, and consequently, for a clear legal basis for that purpose – it may, of course, be asked whether this was so because the judges were conscious of the general importance of such a Code for the purpose of ensuring the integrity of the judicial process, or whether the CoJE was adopted in order to provide a more detailed framework to flank the disciplinary procedure the judges are subjected to by virtue of Articles 46-47 of the ICC Statute and Rules 23-32 of the ICC RPE, both imposed upon them by the States Parties. Article 11(1) of the ICC CoJE would point to the latter interpretation, as it is stipulated that its principles shall "serve as *guidelines* on the essential ethical standards required of judges in the per-

---

and SONG Tianying (eds.), *Historical Origins of International Criminal Law: Volume 5*, 2017, p. 954 (https://www.toaep.org/ps-pdf/24-bergsmo-rackwitz-song).

[39] The solemn undertaking of Prosecutors also served as source for one of the central concepts of the draft ICC Code of Conduct for the Office of the Prosecutor. See *ibid.*, p. 959.

[40] Basic Principles on the Independence of the Judiciary, adopted by the Seventh United Nations Congress on the Prevention of Crime and the Treatment of Offenders held at Milan from 26 August to 6 September 1985 and endorsed by General Assembly resolutions 40/32 of 29 November 1985 and 40/146 of 13 December 1985 (https://www.legal-tools.org/doc/rnabsy/).

[41] ICC Statute, Article 52(1), see above note 10.

formance of their duties. They are *advisory* in nature and have the object of *assisting* judges with respect to ethical and professional issues with which they are confronted".[42] Academic commentators point to the same interpretation, as it has been noted that the ICC CoJE

> was adopted in response to the need for general guidelines to contribute to judicial independence and impartiality and with the aim of ensuring the legitimacy and effectiveness of the international judicial process. [...] The [ICC CoJE] provides the guidelines on the essential ethical standards required of judges according to the principles of independence, impartiality, integrity, confidentiality and diligence. As such, it will assist in assessing any complaint of misconduct alleged against a judge of the [ICC].[43]

18.3.1.2. ECCC (2008)

The preamble of the ECCC CoJE is demonstrative of its nature as a hybrid or internationalised tribunal. Indeed, reference is made to the Cambodian Code of Ethics of 2007, as well as to its foundational documents. Regard is also had, as in other CoJEs, to the UN Basic Principles on the Independence of the Judiciary (1985). Importantly, the preamble is instructive in that it appears to contain the only reference to a ratio for its adoption – the judges considered "the hybrid character of the [ECCC] and the need to adopt a code of ethics applying to both Cambodian and international judges, and incorporating both national and international norms".

An actual legal basis for its adoption is found neither in the preamble nor in the CoJE itself. Adopted by the judges in Plenary, it would appear that a potential legal basis for its adoption could be seen in Rule 18(6)(d) of the ECCC Internal Rules and Regulations, but this is nowhere specified.

18.3.1.3. ICTY (2016)

The preamble of the ICTY CoJE refers to Article 13 of the ICTY Statute, which provides for the relevant qualifications of judges – notably high moral character, impartiality and integrity. In addition, explicit reference is made to the solemn declaration required of each judge, in accordance with

---

42 Emphasis added.

43 "Article 46", in Otto Triffterer and Kai Ambos (eds.), *Commentary on the Rome Statute of the International Criminal Court*, third edition, C.H. Beck, Hart, Nomos, 2016, para. 5.

Rule 14 of the ICTY RPE. Further, the judges recall the UN Basic Principles on the Independence of the Judiciary (1985).

According to its Article 1, the ICTY CoJE is adopted by the judges pursuant to Rule 24 of the ICTY RPE. The latter provision is entitled "Plenary Meetings of the Tribunal" and incorporates in its sub-rules a range of competences of judges. Article 1 of the ICTY CoJE, however, does not specify which sub-rule is being applied in this respect – thought may have been had to Rule 24(iv) or (vi)[44] of the ICTY RPE. However, neither of these sub-rules are a perfect fit: a "decision upon matters relating to the internal function of the Chambers and the Tribunals" would have to be interpreted very broadly to cover the adoption of a legislative document. The same consideration applies to the "exercise of other functions provided for in the Statute or in the Rules" – given that, aside from the RPE, the adoption of legislative instruments by the judges (as opposed to the President) is not provided for in the ICTY Statute or its RPE.

This is symptomatic of a regulatory void, which could be explained by the fact that a CoJE was simply not envisaged for an ICT established in 1993. Having nevertheless adopted this CoJE, the judges demonstrated creativity as far as a legal basis is concerned. It is questionable whether this would have withstood a serious challenge – however, this remains a strictly hypothetical question, given that the CoJE did not contain any disciplinary mechanism, thus providing no forum for such a challenge; and, most importantly, given that such a challenge never took place, whilst the ICTY shut its doors in 2017.

18.3.1.4. STL (2016)

The preamble of the STL CoJE – in a similar fashion as the ICTY CoJE – refers back to Article 9(1) of the STL Statute, which provides for the qualifications of judges, as well as for the solemn declaration to be undertaken by each judge under Rule 24 of the STL RPE. In a unique fashion, the STL judges take note of the "process for excusal or disqualification of judges provided in Rule 25 of the [STL] Rules". Whilst the relationship between the latter proceedings and the CoJE is not further fleshed out, its mentioning does point to an obvious connection between processes of excusal and

---

[44] ICTY RPE, Rule 24(iv) and (vi), see above note 13: "Judges shall meet in plenary to [...] (iv) decide upon matters relating to the internal functioning of the Chambers and the Tribunal; [...] (vi) exercise any other functions provided for in the Statute or in the Rules".

disqualification (related to questions of impartiality) and the CoJE (which regulates the principle of impartiality).

Most interestingly, in a manner identical to the ICTY CoJE, Article 1 of the STL CoJE stipulates that it has been adopted by the judges pursuant to Rule 40 of the STL RPE, a provision entitled "Plenary Meetings of the Tribunal". The wording of the relevant provision is identical to that of the ICTY RPE mentioned above. The same conclusions thus apply: no clear legal basis is being pointed to, and neither of the potentially relevant sub-rules of Rule 40 of the STL RPE[45] is a perfect fit. In addition, as with the ICTY, the adoption of legislative instruments by the judges themselves, as opposed to the President, is not foreseen in STL Statute or RPE – safe for the adoption of the RPE itself. Here as well, the judges have demonstrated creativity in the interpretation of their competences – however, they are equally unlikely to face a legal challenge in this respect, since the STL Co-JE does not provide for any disciplinary proceedings attached to alleged violations of the CoJE.

18.3.1.5. KSC (2017)

The preamble of the KSC CoJE stands out as a more fleshed-out version of the preambles of other CoJEs. The KSC judges recall Articles 26, 27 and 31 of the Law on Specialist Chambers and Specialist Prosecutor's Office ('KSC Law'),[46] which provide respectively for their solemn declaration, for their own qualifications (high moral character, impartiality and integrity), as well as for the principles of judicial independence, impartiality and proper conduct. The KSC judges further recall – a matter of relevance to the legal basis for the adoption of the KSC CoJE – that Article 31(4) of the KSC Law provides that a judge may be dismissed if the judges, by absolute majority, find that he or she has ceased to fulfil the requirements of Articles 27 and 31 of the KSC Law. The additional references to domestic and international standards reflect the KSC's position as separate judicial chambers within the Kosovo judiciary.[47] Regard is, therefore, had to the

---

[45] STL RPE, Rule 40(ii) and (iv), see above note 13: "Judges shall meet in plenary to [...] (iv) decide upon matters relating to the internal functioning of the Chambers and the Tribunal; [...] (vi) exercise any other functions provided for in the Statute or in the Rules".

[46] The Republic of Kosovo, Law on Specialist Chambers and Specialist Prosecutor's Office, adopted on 3 August 2015 ('KSC Law') (https://www.legal-tools.org/doc/8b71c3/).

[47] See Exchange of Letters between the Kosovo President and the EU High Representative, pp. 8–9.

regulations of the principles of the judicial system as found in the Kosovo Constitution, as well as to international standards found in the UN Basic Principles on the Independence of the Judiciary (1985), the Bangalore Principles of Judicial Conduct (2002),[48] and Recommendations adopted by the Committee of Ministers of the Council of Europe entitled "Judges: Independence, Efficiency and Responsibilities" (2010).[49]

According to its Article 1, the KSC CoJE is adopted by the judges pursuant to Article 19(6) and in accordance with the above-mentioned Article 31(4) of the KSC Law. The former provision provides for a legal basis for the Specialist Chambers to "adopt internal rules, policies and practice directions that are necessary for its proper functioning, the security or fairness of proceedings or to give effect to the provisions of [the KSC] Law". Whilst it is arguable that the legal basis is also to a certain extent constructed, since there is no explicit basis for the adoption of an actual CoJE in the KSC Law, it remains the case that, in light of Article 31(4), a CoJE is necessary in order to regulate the proper functioning of the Specialist Chambers, as well as to give effect to this provision of the KSC Law, hence keeping in line with the requirements of Article 19(6) of the KSC Law. To that extent, it may be stated that the KSC CoJE provides for the most solid legal basis when compared to other CoJEs, as it draws upon provisions of its foundational documents – as opposed to documents adopted by the judges themselves. This may well be the case because of the recent adoption of its foundational document in 2015, whereby awareness of matters of judicial ethics was already engrained into the legal culture of ICTs.

18.3.1.6. IRMCT (2015, revised 2018)

The preamble of the IRMCT CoJE strikes as very similar to that of the ICTY and STL CoJEs – in particular on references to the qualification of judges and to their solemn declaration. One consideration markedly stands out, added as a result of a revision to the IRMCT adopted in April 2018: on that occasion, the IRMCT judges adopted a disciplinary procedure and, in doing so, also amended the preamble of the IRMCT CoJE, which now emphasises that the "adoption of an appropriate mechanism by which violations of this Code may be addressed reflects respect for the principle of accountability and for the principles set forth in this Code and shall further

---

[48] The Bangalore Principles of Judicial Conduct, 26 November 2002 ('Bangalore Principles') (https://www.legal-tools.org/doc/xwake8/).

[49] Recommendation of Committee of Ministers, see above note 1.

enhance the public confidence in the [IRMCT]". The adoption of this amendment, as will be fleshed out further below[50] is not only a significant step forward in terms of ensuring the accountability of judges – the ratio for it, as demonstrated in this preamble, is a fundamental shift in perspective on the part of the judges and an awareness that ensuring their own accountability is essential to increase the public confidence in the entire judicial institution.

As far as the adoption is concerned, the same considerations apply as those for the ICTY and STL CoJEs. Article 1(1) of the IRMCT CoJE broadly refers to Rule 26 of the IRMCT RPE ('Plenaries') as a legal basis for its adoption. Again, it is not further explained which sub-rule of this provision is referred to in terms of a legal basis, whilst neither of the potentially relevant ones appears to be directly applicable to the adoption of the IRMCT CoJE.[51]

18.3.1.7. Conclusion

In light of the above considerations, it is most notable that – even though the Statutes of most ICTs allow for the judges to adopt their own RPE, and would thus have given them the possibility of providing themselves with a legal basis for the adoption of CoJEs, none of them did so. Instead, in most cases, the legal basis provided remains unclear at best. In effect, progress has been made, of course, in light of the fact that CoJEs have been adopted in recent years. What this does demonstrate, however, is that the actual evolution in the awareness of the importance of CoJEs is not as deeply rooted as it may seem – it is one thing to note that there was no explicit legal basis provided in the ICTY Statute, the adoption of which dates back to 1993. However, the fact that neither the STL nor the IRMCT Statutes, adopted in 2009 respectively 2012, contain an explicit legal basis for a CoJE demonstrates that there has been no such awareness with the States adopting such Statutes. As stated above, it is the judges who triggered the progress brought about by the adoption of CoJEs – and even the judges did not go as far as amending the respective RPE of their institutions to create a clear legal basis, seemingly preferring to remain vague in this respect. As

---

[50] See Sections 18.4.1.3. and 18.4.2. below.

[51] IRMCT RPE, Rule 26(A)(iii) and (v), see above note 13: "Judges may decide in Plenary to: [...] (iii) decide upon matters relating to the internal functioning of the Chambers and the Tribunal; [...] (v) exercise any other functions provided for in the Statute or in the Rules".

always when it comes to the adoption and content of RPE of ICTs, given the lack of *travaux préparatoires*, the ratio for this remains unclear.

The most encouraging example of a legal basis may be found in the ICC Regulations of the Court, providing for an explicit legal basis – even though arguably out of necessity in light of the disciplinary system imposed by States Parties. It is further encouraging that the States Parties chose to impose a system of disciplinary proceedings – a measure not taken in respect of neither the ECCC, the ICTY, the IRMCT or the STL.

The KSC regulations are further encouraging, as they demonstrate that the foundational documents of such institutions may also incorporate the indication of a necessity to put into place disciplinary mechanisms, as demonstrated in Article 31(4) of the KSC Law.

18.3.2. Applicable Standards

The CoJEs analysed in this chapter set out a number of principles, the respective wording of which has evolved over the years. In this section, each of these principles and their evolution will be briefly presented – starting from the first adopted CoJE, the ICC CoJE, and analysing how the wording of each provision developed.

18.3.2.1. Judicial Independence

A cornerstone of judicial ethics, judicial independence is incorporated as the first article of every CoJE. The initial wording of the ICC CoJE, incorporated *verbatim* by the ECCC CoJE, read as follows:

> 1. Judges shall uphold the independence of their office and the authority of the [Court/ECCC] and shall conduct themselves accordingly in carrying out their judicial functions.
>
> 2. Judges shall not engage in any activity which is likely to interfere with their judicial functions or to affect confidence in their independence.[52]

Subsequent CoJEs of the ICTY, the STL and the IRMCT replaced Paragraph 1 of this Article with the following wording:

> 1. In the exercise of their judicial functions, Judges shall be independent of all external authority or influence.[53]

---

[52] ICC CoJE, Article 3, see above note 4; ECCC CoJE, Article 1, see above note 5.

[53] ICTY CoJE, Article 2, see above note 3; STL CoJE, Article 2, see above note 6; IRMCT CoJE, Article 2, see above note 8.

The KSC CoJE provides the most comprehensive version of this Article, having kept all three paragraphs mentioned above. Importantly, the KSC CoJE replaced the reference to the independence of "all *external* authority and influence" by independence of "*any* authority and influence".[54] This reflects a broad understanding of the concept of judicial independence, incorporating both internal and external independence, as reflected in other similar instruments.[55]

In addition, in respect of the last paragraph, the KSC CoJE adds that judges shall not engage in any activity which is likely to affect "respect for their judicial office".

In respect of the ICC, it is noteworthy that the principle of judicial independence is also incorporated at Article 40 of ICC Statute itself. Whilst Article 40(1) and (2) largely reflect the above provisions of the CoJE, Article 40(3) provides that "Judges required to serve on a full-time basis at the seat of the Court shall not engage in any other occupation of a professional nature". Article 40(4) goes further in providing for a procedure in case of disagreement on the interpretation of Article 40(2) and (3): Any question regarding their application shall be decided by a majority of judges, whereby the judge concerned shall not take part in such a decision.

A question recently arose in respect of the interpretation of Article 40(2) of the ICC Statute. The Judge in question had initially asked to resign as a full-time judge, whilst indicating her readiness to continue sitting on a non-full-time judge on a case to which she had been assigned since the beginning of the trial and which was in the deliberation stage at the relevant time. Her request was granted accordingly.[56] Shortly thereafter, the Judge put forward a second request, notifying the ICC Presidency that she had been appointed as ambassador for her country to a third country and seeking the approval of her continued participation in the relevant ICC case, whilst having taken up her position as ambassador. Regarding Article 40(2) of the ICC Statute, the Judge submitted that her new responsibility would "not in any way interfere with [her] judicial function […] [n]or would it affect confidence in her independence". In particular, she noted that her new responsibilities would be confined to the bilateral relationship

---

[54] KSC CoJE, Article 3(1), see above note 9.

[55] See, for example, Recommendation of Committee of Ministers, Recommendations 11-21 and 22-25, see above note 1.

[56] ICC, Internal Memorandum, 19 March 2019, 2019/PRES/00003-21, paras. 3–4 (https://www.legal-tools.org/doc/5a27d1/).

between her country and the third country and that she would refrain from exercising her responsibilities in this respect if and when it may have any implications for the relevant ICC case. Finally, the Judge stated that – should her request not be granted – she would submit her resignation as an ICC judge.[57]

In accordance with the procedure provided in Article 40(4) of the ICC Statute, the ICC Judges deliberated and, by absolute majority, came to the conclusion that the Judge's request was "not incompatible with the requirements of judicial independence established in [Article 40]".[58] In doing so, the Judges applied Article 40 in a concrete – rather than abstract – manner, noting that the language of the provision suggested that it is concerned with "the concrete question of whether functions actually being performed by a specific judge could affect judicial independence".[59] The majority further noted the language of Article 40(2), namely reference to any activity "likely to" affect confidence in a judge's independence, and concluded that "likelihood denotes a level of certainty beyond more speculation or possibility".[60] Having established the latter, the majority focussed on the second limb of Article 40(2) and, in this respect, took into account that the Judge's professional activities as ambassador would be entirely confined to the bilateral relationship between the Judge's country and the third country, neither of which are connected to any case before the ICC. It further noted the Judge's commitment to refraining from exercising her responsibilities where this may impact on the relevant ICC case. The majority thus concluded that it was "not likely that performing her functions as Ambassador to [the third country] would affect confidence in [the Judge's] independence as Judge of the Court".[61]

The minority took a different position. Equally concerned with the second limb of Article 40(2) of the ICC Statute, it noted that the question of the "likelihood of affecting confidence in judicial independence" is "inevitably concerned with the *appearance* of judicial independence, in the eyes of reasonable outsider observers".[62] It is noteworthy that this standard is

---

57 *Ibid.*, para. 5.
58 *Ibid.*, para. 8.
59 *Ibid.*, para. 10.
60 *Ibid.*, para. 11.
61 *Ibid.*, para. 13.
62 *Ibid.*, para. 15.

somewhat reminiscent of the test applied in respect of the appearance of impartiality in cases of disqualification of judges.[63] Applying the standard to the case at hand, the minority opined that it was "evident that the performance of an executive or political function for a State Party by an individual who remained a Judge of the Court was entirely likely to affect public confidence in judicial independence".[64] In particular, the minority contrasted the situation with a case before the ICTY, whereby a judge sought and received approval of all judges prior to seeking nomination for a political function in her country of origin, and undertook not to assume any political functions or duties prior to the completion of her tenure – the minority stressed that no such guarantees had been expressed in the present case.[65]

Much criticism has been voiced regarding the approach of the Judge in question – from alleging that she failed to disclose to the Presidency her new position as ambassador when she resigned as a full-time judge, knowing that she was thus circumventing Article 40(3) of the ICC Statute, to the pressure she allegedly put her fellow judges under in respect of the present decision, in offering the alternative to resign should her request not be granted, thus effectively threatening the entire trial she was assigned to.[66] One point raised in this respect is of particular importance to the present chapter: in their decision on this matter, the ICC Judges did not once mention the ICC CoJE, which – whilst not legally binding *per se*, nevertheless pursuant to Article 11(1) serves as "guidelines on the essential ethical standards required of judges in the performance of their duties" – and which regulates expressly, at Article 10(2) that judges "shall not exercise any political function". It is indeed questionable why this reference was not made, particularly as it would have significantly supported the minority position. Whether this was by oversight, or whether the Judges consciously chose to ignore their own CoJE for that purpose, remains unclear. Either way, it is demonstrative of the fact that the ICC judges' awareness for their very own CoJE may not be as engrained as it may seem.

---

[63] See Section 18.2. above.

[64] *Ibid.*, para. 15.

[65] *Ibid.*, para. 15, referring to ICTY, *Prosecutor v. Delalić et al.*, Decision of the Bureau on Motion on Judicial Independence, 4 September 1998, IT-96-21-T (https://www.legal-tools.org/doc/c2f2bf/).

[66] See, for example, Kevin John Heller, "Judge Ozaki Must Resign — Or Be Removed", *Opinio Juris*, 29 March 2019 (available on its web site).

18.3.2.2. Impartiality

The initial wording of the principle of impartiality adopted by the ICC Co-JE is reflected *verbatim* in the ECCC CoJE:

1. Judges shall be impartial and ensure the appearance of impartiality in the discharge of their judicial functions.

2. Judges shall avoid any conflict of interest, or being placed in a situation which might reasonably be perceived as giving rise to a conflict of interest.[67]

This largely reflects the jurisprudence discussed above in respect of the disqualification of judges.[68]

In respect of paragraph (1), the KSC CoJE implemented a slight amendment, reflecting that judges "shall exercise their functions impartially" rather than simply "be impartial".[69] This may be interpreted as the attempt to narrow the concept of impartiality further and tie it to the actual exercise of their judicial functions.

Regarding paragraph (2), one minor, yet noteworthy, amendment to the above wording was implemented into the ICTY, STL, KSC and IRMCT CoJEs: Instead of avoiding "being placed" in situations which might reasonably be perceived as giving rise to a conflict of interest, judges shall simply avoid such situations altogether:

1. Judges shall avoid any conflict of interest, *as well as situations* which might reasonably be perceived as giving rise to a conflict of interest.[70]

This may be read as reflecting the understanding that judges may not only be passively placed in such situations but that there may be situations where they actively contributed thereto – which shall be avoided altogether.

---

[67] ICC CoJE, Article 4, see above note 4; ECCC CoJE, Article 2, see above note 5; ICTY CoJE, Article 3, see above note 3; STL CoJE, Article 3, see above note 6; KSC CoJE, Article 4, see above note 9; IRMCT CoJE, Article 3, see above note 8.

[68] See Section 18.2. above.

[69] KSC CoJE, Article 4(1), see above note 9.

[70] ICTY CoJE, Article 3, see above note 3; STL CoJE, Article 3, see above note 6; KSC CoJE, Article 4, see above note 9; IRMCT CoJE, Article 3, see above note 8. Note that KSC CoJE, Article 4 further specifies "any situation".

18.3.2.3. Integrity

The principle of integrity, as reflected in the wording of the various CoJEs, has undergone significant changes since the adoption of the initial version of the ICC CoJE:

> 1. Judges shall conduct themselves with probity and integrity in accordance with their office, thereby enhancing public confidence in the judiciary.
>
> 2. Judges shall not directly or indirectly accept any gift, advantage, privilege or reward that can reasonably be perceived as being intended to influence the performance of their judicial functions.[71]

Aside from minor amendment to paragraphs (1)[72] and (2),[73] the most important change came with the addition of a new paragraph (3) in the ICTY, STL and IRMCT CoJEs:

> 3. Judges shall treat other judges and staff members with dignity and respect, and shall not engage in any form of discrimination, harassment, including sexual harassment, and abuse of authority.[74]

The addition of this paragraph marks a major step forward, even for CoJEs not attaching disciplinary measures – the inclusion of this prohibition is emblematic of an awareness that judges may commit such offences and that they should thus be subject to the same prohibitions in this respect as any staff member of international organisations.[75] This stands in stark contrast with the fact that similar prohibitions are missing from seminal documents on the principles attaching to the judiciary, a number of which

---

[71] ICC CoJE, Article 5, see above note 4.

[72] "[...] in accordance with their judicial office [...]": ICTY CoJE, Article 3(1), see above note 3; STL CoJE, Article 4(1), see above note 6; IRMCT CoJE, Article 4(1), see above note 8.

[73] "[...] the performance of their judicial functions or the independence of their office". ECCC CoJE, Article 3(2), see above note 5; ICTY CoJE, Article 4(2), see above note 3; STL CoJE, Article 4(2), see above note 6; IRMCT CoJE, Article 4(2), see above note 8.

[74] ICTY CoJE, Article 4(3), see above note 3; STL CoJE, Article 4(3), see above note 6; IRMCT CoJE, Article 4(3), see above note 8.

[75] For example, Prohibition of discrimination, harassment, including sexual harassment, and abuse of authority, 11 February 2008, ST/SGB/2008/5 (https://www.legal-tools.org/doc/ibc9oq/).

feature prominently in the preambles of the CoJEs discussed in the present paper.[76]

Stressing the significance of the concept of integrity even further, and fleshing it out in a most detailed manner, Article 5 of the KSC CoJE marks a further evolution in this respect, and it is worth repeating its relevant provision in full, highlighting relevant amendments and additions:

1. Judges shall conduct themselves with probity and integrity, *consistent with the high moral character required for their judicial office.*

2. Judges shall not directly or indirectly accept, offer or provide any gift, advantage, privilege or reward that may reasonably be perceived as being intended to influence the performance of their judicial functions.

3. Judges shall treat other Judges, *Parties, participants in the proceedings*, staff members *and others* with dignity and respect, and shall not engage in any form of discrimination, harassment, including sexual harassment, and abuse of authority.

4. *Judges shall act at all times towards one another in a spirit of collegiality and professionalism.*

5. *Judges shall be mindful at all times of their duty to uphold the standing and reputation of the Specialist Chambers.*

6. *Any Judge who is the subject of any disciplinary or workplace investigation, procedure or sanction relating to possible misconduct before any jurisdiction shall immediately provide full disclosure thereof to the President. If such a case is still at the investigatory stage, the Judge shall inform the President of any development in a timely fashion.*[77]

Article 5(1) of the KSC CoJE ties the probity and integrity of judges directly to the 'high moral character' required for their office. This is a significant step forward from the above jurisprudence on disqualification, in which these requirements for judicial office were taken into consideration to qualify the 'reasonable observer test' and thus effectively increased the

---

76. See United Nations Basic Principles on the Independence of the Judiciary, 1985, see above note 40; Bangalore Principles, see above note 48; Recommendation of Committee of Ministers, see above note 1.

77. Emphasis added.

level of a finding of bias or appearance of bias, precisely because of the relevant statutory requirements and qualifications of judges.[78] This aspect appears to be turned around in Article 5(1) of the KSC CoJE, whereby the high moral character required for the judges' office will, to the contrary, lead to an increased scrutiny when it comes to probity and integrity.

Article 5(3) of the KSC CoJE is equally significant, in that it – correctly – broadens the scope of those which judges shall treat with dignity and respect and in respect of whom they shall not engage in any form of abuse, to include Parties and participants in proceedings as well as others. Here, one may think in particular of any non-staff members of judicial institutions, such as consultants or interns, which there is no readily apparent reason to exclude from this protection. To the contrary, it appears rather concerning that it took until 2017 for a CoJE to include the latter in the protection against abuse and discrimination.

Article 5(4) of the KSC CoJE reflects a – seemingly self-evident, yet fundamental – duty in the context of the exercise of judges' profession, found in most preambles to CoJEs which recognise that "Judges are members of a collegial body". The importance of fostering this aspect of professional relation has gained momentum during the past years.[79] This is demonstrated, for example, by events dedicated to that very subject-matter.[80] Its explicit inclusion in the KSC CoJE is, therefore, a reflection of the importance that the aspect of collegiality amongst judges is gaining.

Article 5(5) and (6) of the KSC CoJE are equally important, as they reflect that judges are neither above the law nor above the suspicion of breaching the latter. In this respect, the obligations imposed upon them by these sub-provisions are of particular interest as they mirror similar provisions generally imposed upon defence counsel.[81]

---

[78] See Section 18.2. above.

[79] In a similar fashion, the ICC Code of Conduct for the Office of the Prosecutor was drafted in order to serve as a "catalyst to unify the vision and harmonise the activities of the inherently diverse membership of a unitary and permanent Office [of the Prosecutor] – one charged with unique responsibilities to uphold international justice in a world shaped by increasingly complex political, economic, social and moral crises and evolving collective patterns of response". See Nakhjavani, 2017, pp. 955–60, see above note 38.

[80] See, for example, 'ICC Judges hold retreat focusing on collegiality and various aspects of judicial proceedings', 28 September 2018, ICC-CPI-20180928-PR1412 (https://www.legal-tools.org/doc/6ba117/).

[81] See, for example, IRMCT, Code of Professional Conduct for Defence Counsel Appearing Before the Mechanism, 14 November 2012, Article 3(v) (https://www.legal-tools.org/doc/

Overall, it is to be noted that the CoJEs have contributed, over time, to strengthening the concept of the integrity of judges through the adoption of further details in respect of this provision.

18.3.2.4. Confidentiality

The initial provision as contained in the ICC CoJE underwent minor changes over the course of the adoption of subsequent CoJEs. The former read as follows:

> Judges shall respect the confidentiality of consultations which relate to their judicial functions and the secrecy of deliberations.[82]

Subsequent versions have been amended with the addition of the following section:

> Judges shall respect the confidentiality of consultations which relate to their judicial functions, the secrecy of deliberations *and the confidentiality of information acquired in the course of their duties, other than in public proceedings.*[83]

As such, the most recent versions clarify the concept initially put forward by the ICC CoJE, in that the latter did arguably not cover confidential information acquired outside of consultation and deliberations relating to judges' judicial function. In that sense, a contribution has thus been made to further detailing the obligation of confidentiality of judges.

Finally, it is noteworthy that the KSC CoJE, as the only CoJE, has incorporated a general obligation that judge "exercise the utmost discretion", which may also be read as further fleshing out the obligation of integrity of judges.

18.3.2.5. Diligence

The early CoJE of the ICC and ECCC regarding the principles of diligence read as follows:

---

eeb133/); ICC Code of Professional Conduct for counsel, Article 24(1), ICC-ASP/4/Res.1 (https://www.legal-tools.org/doc/f9ed33/); ICC Regulations of the Court, 26 May 2004, Regulation 69(3) (https://www.legal-tools.org/doc/2988d1/).

82 ICC CoJE, Article 6, see above note 4.

83 ICTY CoJE, Article 5, see above note 3; STL CoJE, Article 5, see above note 6; KSC CoJE, Article 6, see above note 9; IRMCT CoJE, Article 5, see above note 8; ECCC CoJE, Article 4, see above note 5.

1. Judges shall act diligently in the exercise of their duties and shall devote their professional activities to those duties.

2. Judges shall take reasonable steps to maintain and enhance the knowledge, skills and personal qualities necessary for judicial office.

3. Judges shall perform all judicial duties properly and expeditiously.

4. Judges shall deliver their decisions [and any other rulings][84] without undue delay.[85]

The ICTY, STL and IRMCT CoJEs subsequently chose to make paragraph (1) of this provision more concrete and to tie it to the judges' judicial duties. It was thus reformulated as follows:

1. Judges shall give precedence to their judicial duties over all other activities.[86]

The KSC CoJE combines both of the above alternatives and specifies that this provision is only applicable insofar as a judge is assigned to a Panel.[87] This is a reflection of the KSC system, which provides for a roster of judges, which – unless specifically assigned to do so – do not perform any judicial activities.[88]

Paragraph (2) above remains unchanged in subsequent CoJEs, whilst paragraphs (3) and (4) have been combined in the ICTY, STL and IRMCT CoJEs to read as follows:

3. Judges shall perform their judicial duties efficiently. These duties extend to the delivery of decisions fairly and with reasonable promptness.[89]

Finally, the KSC CoJE significantly expanded upon paragraphs (3) and (4) above and adopted the following paragraphs instead:

3. Judges shall perform all judicial duties properly, *efficiently* and expeditiously *and shall not engage in conduct incompatible with the diligent exercise of their duties.*

---

[84] This was not part of ECCC CoJE, Article 5(4), see above note 5.

[85] ICC CoJE, Article 7, see above note 4; ECCC CoJE, Article 5, see above note 5.

[86] ICTY CoJE, Article 6(1), see above note 3; STL CoJE, Article 6(1), see above note 6; IRMCT CoJE, Article 6(1), see above note 8.

[87] KSC CoJE, Article 7(1), see above note 9.

[88] KSC Law, Article 26(2) see above note 46.

[89] ICTY CoJE, Article 6(3), see above note 3; STL CoJE, Article 6(3), see above note 6; IRMCT CoJE, see above note 8.

    4. Judges shall deliver their decisions and any other rulings *fairly, with reasonable promptness and* without undue delay.

    5. *Judges shall act at all times with the view of ensuring the effectiveness of the Specialist Chambers.*[90]

The above emphasis on the efficient conduct of proceedings may be seen as a reflection of the mandate of the KSC, which includes the delivery of, *inter alia*, "fair and efficient criminal proceedings" in relation to relevant allegations, in accordance with Article 1(2) of the KSC Law.

18.3.2.6. Conduct during Proceedings

Regarding the Conduct during Proceedings, the ICC and ECCC CoJEs adopted the following provision:

    1. In conducting judicial proceedings, judges shall maintain order, act in accordance with commonly accepted decorum, remain patient and courteous towards all participants and members of the public present and require them to act likewise.

    2. Judges shall exercise vigilance in controlling the manner of questioning of witnesses or victims in accordance with the Rules and give special attention to the right of participants to the proceedings to equal protection and benefit of the law.

    3. Judges shall avoid conduct or comments which are racist, sexist or otherwise degrading and, to the extent possible, ensure that any person participating in the proceedings refrains from such comments or conduct.[91]

The ICTY CoJE contains no such provision.

Regarding Paragraph (1), the STL and IRMCT CoJEs merely supplemented the above wording with the requirements that judges also remain "attentive"[92] and "dignified" in conducting judicial proceedings,[93]

---

[90] KSC CoJE, Article 7(3)-(5), see above note 9.

[91] ICC CoJE, Article 8, see above note 4; ECCC CoJE, Article 6, see above note 5.

[92] The issue of a judge's lack of attentiveness during proceeding was indeed subject of appellate proceedings before the ICTY, Delalić *et al.* Appeal Judgment, paras. 628–629, see above note 18.

[93] STL CoJE, Article 7(1), see above note 6; IRMCT CoJE, Article 7(1), see above note 8.

whilst the KSC CoJE added to that the requirement that judges be "respect-ful".[94]

In addition, both the STL and IRMCT CoJEs specified at Para-graph (2) that judges shall exercise vigilance in controlling the manner of questioning of witnesses, "particularly when they are victims". [95] In this respect, the KSC CoJE went even further and, stressing that special atten-tion should be given to the right "and interest" of participants in the pro-ceedings. In addition, a second sentence was added to Paragraph (2): "Judges shall exercise particular vigilance in respect of vulnerable witness-es, including victims of sexual and gender based violence and children".[96] Overall, this may be seen as reflecting the evolution of the role and posi-tion of victims within international criminal justice – from mere witnesses, at the *ad hoc* tribunals to actual participants in proceedings, at the ICC, the STL and the KSC. In addition, it stresses the awareness amongst judges of the particularly vulnerable nature of certain victims – there are indications that in the past, this may not always have been the case.[97]

Finally, the KSC CoJE adopted a shortened version of Paragraph (3) above, removing the first part of the sentence and reformulating it as fol-lows: "Judges shall, to the extent possible, ensure that any person partici-pating in the proceedings refrains from comments or conduct which are degrading".[98] This shortening may simply reflect the fact that the first part of Paragraph (3) may be seen as covered by Paragraph (1) in any case – and that it would be duplicative to keep both provisions in this respect.

18.3.2.7. Public Expression and Association

The following provision is included in the ICC and ECCC CoJEs as far as Public Expression and Association is concerned:

> 1. Judges shall exercise their freedom of expression and as-sociation in a manner that is compatible with their office and that does not affect or appear to affect judicial inde-pendence or impartiality.

---

[94] KSC CoJE, Article 8(1), see above note 9.

[95] STL CoJE, Article 7(2), see above note 6; IRMCT CoJE, see above note 8.

[96] KSC CoJE, Article 8(2), see above note 9.

[97] See Binaifer Nowrojee, "'Your Justice is Too Slow' – Will the ICTR Fail Rwanda's Rape Victims?", in *United Nations Research Institute for Social Development*, Occasional Paper 10, November 2005, pp. 23–24.

[98] KSC CoJE, Article 8(3), see above note 9.

---

2. While judges are free to participate in public debate on matters pertaining to legal subjects, the judiciary or the administration of justice, they shall not comment on pending cases and shall avoid expressing views which may undermine the standing and integrity of the Court.[99]

The ICTY CoJE did not have an equivalent provision.

Regarding Paragraph (2), the STL, KSC and IRMCT CoJEs all added the obligation that judges "shall ensure that nothing in their conduct evidences disrespect for the views of another judge or staff member".[100] In addition, the KSC CoJE specifies that the judges' freedom to participate in public debate on legal matters includes academic publications.[101]

Finally, it is noteworthy that the KSC CoJE added the following two Paragraphs to this provision, which, *inter alia*, provides for the necessity to seek the approval of the President for the purpose of any media communication on matters related to the KSC and may thus be seen as a tool to streamline communication by that institution:

3. When exercising their freedom of expression, Judges shall avoid public statements or comments that may undermine the authority of the Specialist Chambers or give rise to reasonable doubt about their impartiality.

4. Judges shall seek prior approval of the President for any communication with press or media on any matters related to the Specialist Chambers.[102]

18.3.2.8. Other/Extra-Judicial Activities

On the matter of Other/Extra-Judicial Activities, the ICC and ECCC CoJEs include the following provision:

1. Judges shall not engage in any extra-judicial activity that is incompatible with their judicial function or the efficient and timely functioning of the Court, or that may affect or may reasonably appear to affect their independence or impartiality.

2. Judges shall not exercise any political function.[103]

---

[99] ICC CoJE, Article 9, see above note 4; ECCC CoJE, Article 7, see above note 5.

[100] STL CoJE, Article 8(2), see above note 6; KSC CoJE, Article 9(2), see above note 9; IRMCT CoJE, Article 8(2), see above note 8.

[101] KSC CoJE, Article 9(2), see above note 9.

[102] *Ibid.*, Article 9(3)-(4).

The ICTY CoJE did not include an equivalent provision, whilst the STL, KSC and IRMCT CoJEs did not include Paragraph (2) above in their equivalent provision.[104] It may be questioned whether this was because the judges determined that it was covering a scenario obviously falling under Paragraph (1) and that thus did not need to be further specified, or because they considered that a political function was not *per se* incompatible with a judicial function.

The case discussed above[105] demonstrates that this is not an abstract question, but that it has concrete implications for ICTs, whereby judges may be called upon to take up a position within a country's executive. It is suggested that it would perhaps have been wise to retain this provision in order to provide clarity in this respect. On the other hand, it is recalled that European Court of Human Rights jurisprudence does not regard judicial and executive functions as *per se* mutually exclusive, where matters to be decided upon in their judicial functions fall outside of the ambit of powers exercised as part of their executive functions.[106] It is perhaps in light of such jurisprudence that the categorical exclusion clause contained in Paragraph (2) above was removed by the STL, KSC and IRMCT CoJEs.

Finally, it is noted that the KSC CoJE, in fact, adopted its very own version of this provision, reflecting once more its structure as tribunal functioning with a roster of judges, who will exercise judicial functions only if and when assigned to do so by the President:

> In accordance with Article 26(4) of the Law, any activity undertaken by Judges other than that before the Specialist Chambers shall be compatible with their judicial functions and the efficient and timely functioning of the Specialist Chambers.[107]

Indeed, judges of the KSC must be able to continue their regular professional activities pending any assignment to exercise judicial functions with the KSC – as long as it is compatible with these judicial functions, and with the efficient and timely function of the institution.

---

[103] ICC CoJE, Article 10, see above note 4; ECCC CoJE, Article 8, see above note 5.

[104] STL CoJE, Article 9, see above note 6; IRMCT CoJE, Article 9, see above note 8.

[105] See Section 18.3.2.1. above.

[106] European Court of Human Rights ('ECHR'), *Sramek v. Austria*, Judgment, 22 October 1984, App. No. 8790/79, para. 40 (https://www.legal-tools.org/doc/de30a4/).

[107] KSC CoJE, Article 10, see above note 9.

18.3.2.9. Decorations and Honours

Finally, it is noted that the KSC CoJE is the only one which regulates the awarding of decorations and honours to judges:

> Judges may accept decorations and honours only where such acceptance does not give rise to a reasonable doubt as to their independence or impartiality. The President shall be informed before any such acceptance.[108]

This may, in fact, be read as simply further specifying the principles of independence and impartiality for the particular case of receiving decorations or honours.

18.3.2.10. Conclusion

The above demonstrates that – over time – judges have not only significantly expanded the level of details which describe the principles applicable to the exercise of their judicial functions, but they have also added a new range of principles, fitting the particularities of the structure of each ICT. This is a significant positive development.[109] *Vis-à-vis* States – as creators of such ICTs – it demonstrates the seriousness with which judges approach the principles applicable to their profession and their awareness of the development of these principles and of the necessity to adopt and adapt CoJEs accordingly. States should readily acknowledge this message and create a clear framework for judicial ethics in future ICTs – either by themselves adopting CoJEs, or through the creation of sound legal bases for that purpose.[110] *Vis-à-vis* parties and participants in the proceedings, it sends the unequivocal message that judges are aware that they are not 'above the law' and that, as any lawyers, they are subject to clear ethical principles. CoJEs are, therefore, a crucial tool in order to foster a culture of mutual respect amongst parties and participants in the courtroom, thus significantly strengthening the overall integrity of proceedings.

18.4. Codes of Judicial Ethics – Disciplinary Procedures

The ECCC, ICTY and STL CoJEs do not include any disciplinary procedures for the purpose of enforcing the various principles contained in those

---

[108] *Ibid.*, Article 11.
[109] See Bergsmo, 2018, p. 3, see above note 2.
[110] *Ibid.*

CoJEs. The following section will thus focus on the procedures in place at the ICC, the KSC and the IRMCT.

The disciplinary procedure at the ICC is not included in the CoJE itself – rather, the latter is found scattered throughout various regulatory documents: Articles 46 and 47 of the ICC Statute; Rules 23-32 of the ICC RPE; Regulations 119-125 of the Regulations of the Court. Both the KSC and IRMCT CoJEs include a disciplinary procedure.

These procedures will be analysed in the following, focusing on the definition of disciplinary offences, the procedure to be followed and the sanctions to be imposed.

18.4.1. Disciplinary Offences

18.4.1.1. ICC

The ICC regime differentiates between "serious misconduct and serious breach of duty", defined in Rule 24 of the ICC RPE, and "misconduct of a less serious nature", defined in Rule 25 of the ICC RPE. The former is linked to Article 46(1)(a) of the ICC Statute and may lead to removal from office, whilst the latter is tied to Article 47 of the ICC Statute and may trigger the imposition of disciplinary measures.

Rule 24(1) of the ICC RPE further differentiates between serious misconduct in, and outside the course of official duties. Pursuant to Rule 24(1)(a), the former constitutes conduct which is "incompatible with official functions, and causes or is likely to cause serious harm to the proper administration of justice before the Court or the proper internal functioning of the Court". A non-exhaustive list of three examples is included. Pursuant to Rule 24(1)(b), serious misconduct outside the course of official duties takes place where it is of grave nature that causes or is likely to cause serious harm to the standing of the Court. "Serious misconduct" has thus been interpreted to cover "not only professional conduct in relation to the duties of the office but also personal behaviour in general and is therefore broader than 'breach of duty' which relates only to the duties of the office".[111]

Pursuant to Rule 24(2), a "serious breach of duty" takes place where a judge has been "grossly negligent in the performance of his or her duties or has knowingly acted in contravention of those duties". Here also, a non-

---

[111] Triffterer and Ambos, 2016, para. 8, see above note 43.

exhaustive list of two examples is provided. It has been suggested that a "serious breach of duty" provides for a "more limited ground for removal that will specifically be assessed in relation to, *inter alia*, the duties of independence, impartiality and conscientiousness, as referred to in Articles 40 and 45" of the ICC Statute.[112] Indeed, it is noted that Article 46(1)(a) of the ICC Statute ties a removal from office to a finding that a judge committed a "serious breach of his or her duties *under this Statute*".[113] This has been interpreted as potentially covering

> all duties and responsibilities of the official concerned which flow from the Statute and not only such duties which are explicitly specified in the Statute. [...] Such an interpretation would also allow for the [ICC CoJE] to be taken into account when considering whether a Judge has acted in contravention of Articles 46 or 47 of the Statute.[114]

As far as "misconduct of a less serious nature" is concerned, Rule 25 of the ICC RPE reflects the separation between conduct in the course of (Rule 25(1)(a)) and outside the course of (Rule 25(1)(b)) judicial duties. Qualified by a lesser threshold, it has been interpreted as covering all misconduct not envisaged by Article 46.[115]

18.4.1.2. KSC

Articles 13 and 14 of the KSC CoJE respectively provide for definitions of "serious misconduct" and "misconduct of a less serious nature". In a similar fashion as for the ICC, "serious misconduct" may lead to a removal from the roster of KSC judges pursuant to Articles 21 of the KSC CoJE and 31(4) of the KSC Law – whilst "misconduct of a less serious nature" may trigger the imposition of disciplinary measures in accordance with Article 22 of the KSC CoJE.

In respect of "serious misconduct", the KSC CoJE does not provide for the clear differentiation between such conduct in the course and outside of official duties, as found in the ICC RPE. It does, however, include two alternatives at Article 13(1)(a)[116] and (b), which are almost identical to the

---

[112]   *Ibid.*, para. 8.

[113]   Emphasis added.

[114]   *Ibid.*, para. 9.

[115]   *Ibid.*, Article 47, para. 3.

[116]   Very limited variations in language are found in Article 13(1)(a)(i) ("[...] where such disclosure ~~seriously~~-prejudicial to [...]"), 13(1)(a)(ii) ("concealing *or withholding* information or

wording of Rule 24(1)(a) and (b) of the ICC RPE. In addition, Article 13(1)(b) of the KSC CoJE provides two examples, reflecting situations which could readily fall outside the course of official duties, namely:

(i) the commission of a criminal act which reflects adversely on the Judge's honesty and trustworthiness as a Judge; and

(ii) the engagement in conduct involving harassment, abuse of authority, dishonesty, fraud, deceit or misrepresentation.

In the light of the above, Article 13(1)(a) could be interpreted as reflecting conduct occurring in the course of official duties, whilst Article 13(1)(b) reflects conduct occurring outside such duties.

Article 14 of the CoJE provides a definition of "misconduct of a less serious nature". Here again, two alternatives are provided. Under Article 14(1)(a), "misconduct of a less serious nature" is conduct that "causes or is likely to cause harm to the proper administration of justice before the Specialist Chambers or the proper internal functioning of the Specialist Chambers". A non-exhaustive list of examples is provided in this respect. Pursuant to Article 14(1)(b), "misconduct of a less serious nature" is conduct that "causes or is likely to cause harm to the standing of the Specialist Chambers". No examples are provided in this respect. As in respect of Article 13 KSC CoJE, in light of the above examples, it may be suggested that Article 14(1)(a) is concerned with misconduct committed in the course of judicial duties, whilst Article 14(1)(b) captures a more broader category of misconduct which may also include instances occurring outside such duties, but which may nevertheless have an impact on the standing of the Specialist Chambers.

18.4.1.3. IRMCT

Whilst the ICC and KSC have implemented very similar definitions of misconduct, the IRMCT chose a different path. Indeed, pursuant to Article 11(2)(a) of the IRMCT CoJE, "misconduct refers to conduct that constitutes a violation of the standards set forth in this Code". The brevity of this provision is striking, and appears to have been inspired by Article 35(i) of

---

circumstances [...]") and 13(1)(a)(iii) ("[...] in order to obtain ~~unwarranted~~ favourable treatment [...]") (emphasis and strikethrough supplied by the author).

the IRMCT Code of Professional Conduct for Defence Counsel Appearing Before the Mechanism:[117]

> It shall be professional misconduct for Counsel, *inter alia*, to:
>
> (i)   violate or attempt to violate the Statute, the Rules, this Code or any other applicable law, […].

However, Article 11(2)(a) of the IRMCT CoJE, when compared to both the ICC and KSC regimes, as well as with the IRMCT regime in place for counsel is striking more in terms of what is missing than what is actually said. In particular, it is questionable whether a judge would be held responsible for an attempt to violate the IRMCT CoJE. In addition, violations are limited to the provisions of "this Code". They do not include the IRMCT Statute, RPE or any other applicable law, as it is the case for defence counsel before the IRMCT. In this respect, one may question whether the judges are applying a higher standard to counsel that to themselves.

On the other hand, the broad wording of this provision could allow for a particularly wide interpretation of "misconduct" for the purpose of the IRMCT CoJE – which, in turn, could lead to significant insecurity for the judges to whom the CoJE applies. Indeed, it is unclear what would amount to an actual 'violation' of a provision of the CoJE, particularly in light of the broad range of obligations incumbent upon judges pursuant to the CoJE. Taking Article 6(2) of the IRMCT CoJE as an example, would a judge who does not attend any lectures over the course of a few years be in violation of the obligation to "take reasonable steps to maintain and enhance their knowledge, skills and personal qualities necessary for judicial office"?

18.4.2.   Procedure before the KSC and the IRMCT

18.4.2.1. Submission of Complaint

Articles 15 of the KSC CoJE and 11(1) of the IRMCT CoJE provide that a complaint shall be transmitted directly to the President, whilst he or she may also *proprio motu* initiate proceedings.[118] Article 15(3) of the KSC CoJE specifies that, where a complaint is brought against the President, the

---

[117] IRMCT Code of Professional Conduct for Defence Counsel Appearing Before the Mechanism, see above note 81.

[118] Where the President *proprio motu* initiates proceedings, the IRMCT CoJE, see above note 8, specifies that the complaint would be addressed to the Judge who assumes the President's functions in accordance with Rule 24 of the IRMCT RPE, see above note 13. For the purpose of the present description, references to the 'President of the IRMCT' shall be read as including references to the Judge who assumes the President's functions.

Vice-President assumes his or her function for the purpose of disposing of the complaint.

Articles 15(5) of the KSC CoJE and 11(6) of the IRMCT CoJE set out the details to be contained in a complaint, which notably includes the identity of the complainant.

Article 15(1) of the KSC CoJE helpfully defines the scope of "Complainant", thus preventing anyone from claiming standing for the purpose of the disciplinary procedure under the CoJE. Indeed, complaints may be submitted by "a Judge, a staff member, a Party or a participant in the proceedings before the Specialist Chambers, the Registrar or any other person alleging that their rights or interests have been substantially affected by an alleged misconduct". By contrast, the IRMCT CoJE does not provide a definition of complainant, and it may, therefore, be assumed that anyone could file a complaint, with no limitation in respect of standing.

As for the timing of a complaint, Article 15(4) of the KSC CoJE provides for some flexibility in this respect, in specifying that a complaint must be submitted within six months after the complainant should have reasonably known about the existence or occurrence of the alleged misconduct. In addition, a matter may be pursued after this time limit if it is of general importance to the Specialist Chambers. By contrast, pursuant to Article 11(4) of the IRMCT CoJE, a complaint must be filed within 60 days of the date on which the alleged misconduct took place, or good cause must be shown for any delay. It is noted that the KSC CoJE allows for more flexibility than Article 11(4) of the IRMCT CoJE, as the time limit does not start running with the occurrence of the event in question, but with the moment in time when the complainant should have reasonably known about this occurrence.

18.4.2.2. Preliminary Verification

Article 17 of the KSC CoJE provides for the possibility of a two-layered verification and potential summary dismissal of a complaint by the KSC President. First, the KSC President shall dismiss a complaint if it is anonymous or if it is considered vexatious, misconceived, frivolous or lacking in substance or out of time. Second, where the President does not consider the complaint *prima facie* vexatious, misconceived, frivolous or lacking in substance – or where the President has initiated disciplinary proceedings *proprio motu*, the complaint is transmitted to the responding judge pursuant to Article 17(2) of the KSC CoJE. On the basis of his or her views, the

President renders a decision, determining whether the complaint should be summarily dismissed as manifestly ill-founded or not substantiated.

Similarly, pursuant to Article 12(1) of the IRMCT CoJE, a complaint is subjected to a preliminary examination in the course of which the President will examine the complaint to determine what action, if any, is warranted. Complaints which are "manifestly unsubstantiated or otherwise unreceivable" shall be summarily dismissed – the broad wording of "otherwise unreceivable" is symptomatic of the wide margin of discretion which the IRMCT President enjoys in this preliminary examination. Notably, at his or her discretion, a complaint related to a pending case may be deferred until such time as the case is disposed of. Again, at his or her discretion, the IRMCT President may also consult other judges in reaching a decision regarding a complaint. Where the IRMCT President has not summarily dismissed a complaint, it is provided to the judge concerned pursuant to Article 12(2) of the IRMCT CoJE for the purpose of providing comments thereon. Having received these comments, the President is – once again – provided with substantial discretion on how to proceed pursuant to Article 12(3) and (4) of the IRMCT CoJE: if he or she decides that "no further action in relation to the Complaint is appropriate", the complainant and judge concerned will be informed accordingly. If, on the other hand, the President decides that there is "a reasonable and sufficient basis to proceed with further action", the complainant and the judge concerned will be so advised. Again, the lack of details and hence the wide discretion enjoyed by the President is to be noted, allowing for substantial flexibility in the handling of complaints. Along these lines, Article 12(7) of the IRMCT CoJE also provides that a complaint may be closed, in case it is "informally resolved to the satisfaction of the Complainant and the Judge Concerned at any time during its pendency" – unless, exceptionally, the President decides to pursue the complaint *proprio motu.*

18.4.2.3. Investigation of Complaint

Where the KSC President does not summarily dismiss the complaint, he or she must designate a disciplinary board pursuant to Article 18(2) of the KSC CoJE, composed of three members "two of whom at least shall be from the judiciary, [...] either from judges of international or internationalised courts or judges of domestic courts with extensive experience in ethics or in the investigation of professional misconduct. The third member may be a senior appointee of the European Union". Article 18(4) of the KSC

CoJE provides for details on the investigatory powers of the disciplinary board. *Inter alia*, the disciplinary board may order the responding judge to produce documents related to the subject-matter of the complaint and to otherwise assist in and co-operate with the inquiry into the complaint in a specified manner. It may also order the Registrar to provide access to electronic data of the KSC related to the disciplinary allegations. This provides for significant clarity as to the investigatory powers and foreseeability of the procedure for the responding judge. The disciplinary board transmits preliminary conclusions to the responding judge, and invites him or her to respond accordingly. Pursuant to Article 18(6), the disciplinary board submits to the President a detailed report on the results of the inquiry, including recommendations in respect of each allegation and specific disciplinary measures to be imposed. The report is provided to the complainant and to the responding judge.

At the IRMCT, where the IRMCT President has decided that there is a "reasonable and sufficient basis to proceed with further action", he or she must establish a "panel of outside experts" pursuant to Article 13(1) of the IRMCT CoJE to investigate the allegations and report its conclusions and recommendations. This panel shall be composed of three members, who shall be "judges, former judges or other eminent jurists", taking into account geographical distribution and gender balance. Pursuant to Article 13(3) of the IRMCT CoJE, it is the IRMCT President who establishes the terms of references for the panel, which "shall contain provisions ensuring respect for the procedural rights of the complainant and the judge concerned". What investigatory powers the panel thus has is not further specified – and appears to be left to the discretion of the IRMCT President, to be determined for any given panel on a case-by-case basis. Finally, pursuant to Article 13(4), the panel shall complete its investigation and report to the President within three months of referral of the complaint.

18.4.2.4. Procedure before the Plenary

At the KSC, pursuant to Article 20(1) of the KSC CoJE, the report of the disciplinary board is only transmitted to the other judges where there has been a conclusion that the responding judge has committed one or more of the allegations in the complaint. Having deliberated upon the allegations, the judges vote thereon. It is noteworthy that, pursuant to Article 20(3) of the KSC CoJE, both the complainant, if a judge, and the responding judge, may participate in the Plenary, but do not participate in the deliberations and voting. In particular, the responding judge may be heard, answer any questions put to him or her, and provide further clarifications.

As far as the imposition of sanctions is concerned, and where the judges conclude that an allegation of *serious misconduct* has been established, they must decide by an absolute majority on the dismissal of the responding judge from the roster, pursuant to Article 21(1) of the KSC CoJE. In this respect, Article 21 of the KSC CoJE is reflective of Article 31(4) of the KSC Law. Where an absolute majority of judges favours a dismissal, Article 21(2) of the KSC CoJE provides that it shall have "immediate effect" and that the responding judge "cease[s] to be part of the Specialist Chambers". Pursuant to this provision, there is no necessity for a recommendation to the Appointing Authority to dismiss the judge and it is the Plenary which takes the actual decision of dismissal. Considering that, pursuant to Article 28(4) of the KSC Law, it is the Appointing Authority which appoints the KSC judges and places them on the roster for the duration of the existence of the KSC, it is debatable whether the KSC judges themselves have the authority to dismiss one of their peers from the roster. Article 31(4) of the KSC Law merely provides that no KSC judge may be dismissed – without specifying by whom – unless the absolute majority of judges finds that "he or she has ceased to fulfil the requirements of Articles 27 and 31". This would merely appear to provide the authority to the Plenary to determine whether a judge has ceased to fulfil these requirements. Whether, in addition thereto, this amounts to a delegation of authority to the Plenary for the actual dismissal of a judge may readily be questioned. Article 31(4) of the KSC Law is less than clear in this respect and the basic principle in cases of *actus contrarius*, applicable in European Union ('EU') administrative law,[119] would dictate that a decision such as the appointment of a judge to a roster may only be reversed by the authority who made the initial appointment, that is, the Appointing Authority. However, as there is no jurisprudence as of yet in this respect, this question must remain open for the time being.

Further, in case any allegations of *misconduct of a less serious nature* are established, Article 22(2) of the KSC CoJE provides for a catalogue of

---

[119] "[I]n accordance with a general principle of law that, in principle, a body which has power to adopt a particular legal measure also has power to abrogate or amend it by adopting an *actus contarius*, unless such power is expressly conferred upon another body." The Court of First Instance of European Communities, *Lagardière and Canal+ v. Commission*, Judgment, 20 November 2002, T-251/00, para. 130 (https://www.legal-tools.org/doc/510mj2/).

disciplinary measures which may be imposed. These include a formal and written admonishment by the Plenary, reporting to the State who nominated the responding judge, suspension from assignment to cases for a period not exceeding one year, reporting to the professional bodies to which the responding judge may belong and a pecuniary sanction not exceeding 2,000 Euro.

At the IRMCT, pursuant to Article 14(1) of the IRMCT CoJE, the President transmits the report of the panel of outside experts to all judges, with the exception of the judge concerned. The former review the report and indicate whether "(a) the complaint is well-founded; and, if so, (b) whether the matter is of sufficient severity to suggest that the removal of the judge concerned is warranted". This two-pronged procedure provides for an additional layer of safeguards for the judge concerned– three scenarios are envisaged pursuant to Article 14(3) of the IRMCT CoJE:

(iii) Where a majority of judges take the position that the complaint is not well-founded, it is closed;[120]

(iv) Where a majority of judges deem the complaint well-founded, but less than a two-third majority deem the matter of sufficient gravity to remove the judge concerned, the President shall take "such corrective action as he or she deems appropriate".[121] Again, broad discretion is provided to the President in his handling of the matter. What 'corrective action' entails is further specified at Article 14(5) of the IRMCT CoJE and "may include an oral or written reprimand, written censure, temporary suspension, or other appropriate sanction";

(v) Finally, where a two-thirds majority of the judges deem the complaint well-founded and the matter of sufficient gravity to suggest the removal of the judge concerned, the President "shall report the matter to the Secretary-General to request the removal of the judge concerned".[122] At this point, no discretion is left to the President – he or she must request the removal of the judge concerned. Whether the Secretary-General is bound by this request is a different question and may – for lack of jurisprudence in this respect – not be answered.

At this juncture, however, it is of particular interest to note that the IRMCT CoJE gives neither the IRMCT judges nor its President the actual

---

[120] IRMCT CoJE, Article 14(3)(a), see above note 8.
[121] *Ibid.*, Article 14(3)(b).
[122] *Ibid.*, Article 14(3)(c).

authority to remove an IRMCT judge from the roster. The only authority provided by the IRMCT CoJE is that of reporting the matter to the authority who (re-)appoints IRMCT judges in accordance with Article 10(2), (3) and (4) of the IRMCT Statute, that is, the UN Secretary-General, and to request the removal of the judge concerned. It is interesting to note that the authority which elects IRMCT judges, that is, the UN General Assembly in accordance with Article 10(1) of the IRMCT Statute, is not involved in the process. However, this would indicate at least to a certain extent that the administrative act of appointment may only be reversed by the authority who made an appointment –if and when the question arises at the KSC, the IRMCT CoJE will thus be an interesting source to look into in order to further interpret Articles 21 of the KSC CoJE and 31(4) of the KSC Law.

18.4.3. Procedure before the ICC

As spelled out above, the procedure before the ICC is set out in various regulatory documents, namely the ICC Statute, its RPE and the Regulations of the Court.[123] It is worth having a detailed look in this respect, particularly because the initial regulatory framework was recently amended in the ICC RPE. The following section will therefore outline the initial procedure, followed by an analysis of the amendment thereto.

18.4.3.1. Initial Procedure[124]

In its initial version, Rule 26(2) provided for any complaint to be transmitted to the Presidency, which also had the competence to *proprio motu* initiate proceedings. In accordance with this provision as well as with Regulation 119(1), the Presidency then set aside anonymous or manifestly unfounded complaints, with the assistance of three judges assigned on the basis of automatic rotation. With the possibility of seeking submissions from the persons being complained against or from the complainant, in ac-

---

[123] For the purpose of the following section, any reference to 'Article' shall be a reference to the ICC Statute; to 'Rule' shall be a reference to the ICC RPE; to 'Regulation' shall be a reference to the ICC Regulations of the Court.

[124] See ICC Rules of Procedure and Evidence, 9 September 2002, Rule 26(2) ('ICC RPE') (https://www.legal-tools.org/doc/8bcf6f/). It is noted that the initial version of Rule 26 of the ICC RPE gave the Presidency the competence to receive complaints not only against Judges, but also against the Prosecutor, the Registrar and the Deputy Registrar, as reflected not only in the initial version of Rule 26(1) of the ICC RPE but also in Regulation 119(1) of the Regulations of the Court. For the purpose of the present paper, the focus will be on complaints against Judges. As per the amended version of Rule 26(2), as set out below, the overall competence of the Presidency has now been moved to the IOM.

cordance with Regulation 119(2), these three judges made a recommendation to the Presidency on whether or not to set aside the complaint, and whether or not the complaint related to conduct which fell manifestly outside Rule 24. Pursuant to Regulation 119(3), the Presidency was free to accept or reject the recommendations of the three judges. Pursuant to Regulation 121(1), where the Presidency decided not to set aside a complaint against a judge, a question of removal from office was transmitted to a Plenary session for a vote – unless the complaint fell manifestly outside the scope of Rule 24, in which case it was considered by the Presidency directly, pursuant to Article 47, Rule 30(1) and Regulation 122.

The remainder of the procedure regarding a question of removal from office remains the same: Pursuant to Rule 29(1), the Presidency advises the Bureau of the Assembly of States Parties ('ASP') of any recommendation adopted by the Plenary in this respect. In accordance with Article 46(2), the actual decision in this respect is subsequently taken by a two-thirds majority of the States Parties upon a recommendation by a two-thirds majority of the judges. Removal from office, once pronounced, takes effect immediately in accordance with Rule 31.

When and after the Presidency determined that the conduct falls manifestly outside the scope of Rule 24, the following procedure also remains the same: In accordance with Rule 30(1), any decision to impose a disciplinary measure is taken by the Presidency. The latter include, pursuant to Rule 32, a reprimand or a pecuniary sanction which may not exceed six months of the salary of the judge. A decision of the Presidency to impose disciplinary measures may be appealed to the Plenary by the judge concerned pursuant to Regulation 122(2).

18.4.3.2. Amended Procedure

On 11 December 2018, the ASP amended Rule 26 of the ICC RPE,[125] which now provides as follows:

> 1. For the purposes of article 46, paragraph 1, and article 47 of the Statute, any complaint concerning any conduct defined under rules 24 and 25 shall include the grounds on which it is based and, if available, any relevant evidence, *and may also include the identity of the complainant.* The complaint shall remain confidential.

---

[125] Resolution on amendments to rule 26 of the Rules of Procedure and Evidence, 11 December 2018, ICC-ASP/17/Res.2 (https://www.legal-tools.org/doc/mhkgg7/).

2. All complaints shall be transmitted to the *Independent Oversight Mechanism* which may also initiate investigations on its own motion. *Any person submitting such complaints may also elect to submit a copy to the Presidency of the Court for information purposes only.*

3. *The Independent Oversight Mechanism shall assess complaints and set aside those complaints which are manifestly unfounded. Where a complaint is set aside as manifestly unfounded, the Independent Oversight Mechanism shall provide its reasons in a report which shall be transmitted to the Assembly of States Parties and the Presidency.*

4. *All other complaints shall be investigated by the Independent Oversight Mechanism. The Independent Oversight Mechanism shall transmit the results of any investigation, together with its recommendations, to the Assembly of States Parties and any other competent organ(s) as set out in articles 46 and 47 of the Statute, and rules 29 and 30.*[126]

Two crucial matters stand out.

Firstly, the competence to receive and investigate complaints against judges has been moved squarely from the Presidency to the Independent Oversight Mechanism ('IOM'), thus removing a significant competence of the ICC Presidency. New Rules 26(3) and (4) accordingly provide for the procedure to be applied in this respect. It is striking to note that the Regulations of the Court (adopted by the judges in accordance with Article 52) have not been adapted to this new version of Rule 26 of the ICC RPE (adopted and amended by the ASP in accordance with Article 51).[127] During the process leading to the adoption of the amendment, a representative of the ICC Presidency noted that the relevant Regulations of the Court "would need to be amended or deleted, but this would follow on from the amendment of the higher norm, the RPE".[128] Whether the delay in the amendment of the Regulations of the Court is merely due to the fact that

---

[126] "Draft resolution on amendments to rule 26 of the Rules of Procedure and Evidence", annexed to Report of the Working Group on Amendments, 29 November 2018, ICC-ASP/17/35 (emphasis added).

[127] See ICC Regulations of the Court, Regulations 119-122, see above note 81.

[128] "Report of the Study Group on Governance Cluster I in relation to the amendment to rule 26 of the Rules of Procedure and Evidence", annexed to Report of the Bureau on the Study Group on Governance, 27 November 2018, ICC-ASP/17/30, para. 22 ('Report ICC-ASP/17/30') (https://www.legal-tools.org/doc/faoyip/).

the amendment to Rule 26 (December 2018) was adopted after the most recent amendment to the Regulations of the Court (November 2018), is thus open for speculation.

Relevant resolutions indicate that this fundamental amendment of Rule 26 derives from the necessity to make it compatible with the operational mandate of the IOM,[129] created in 2009[130] with its operational mandate defined in 2013.[131] The ASP requested that such an amendment be considered,[132] and the amendment itself was then recommended by the Study Group on Governance[133] and the Working Group on Amendments.[134]

During consultations in respect of this amendment, the ICC Presidency noted that – since the establishment of the IOM – a practice had developed whereby the Presidency would send any complaints received to the IOM, which reported the result of its investigation to the Presidency, which – in turn – would send the report to the panel of three judges. A former head of the IOM had accordingly suggested that an amendment be adopted to reflect this practice.[135] However, during consultations, a range of States Parties noted the need to avoid "any potential conflict of interest between the role of those who judge and those who are to be judged and the necessity for an independent and impartial investigation".[136] A drafting option retaining a role for the Presidency and the judges in the investigation whilst reflecting the IOM's mandate was eventually rejected in favour of the current version, which clearly removes any role of the Presidency and judges in the investigation and thus provides for the IOM alone to conduct the investigation and make recommendations to the ASP and the Pres-

---

[129] *Ibid.*, para. 3.

[130] ICC, Establishment of an independent oversight mechanism, adopted on 26 November 2009, Resolution ICC-ASP/8/Res. 1 (https://www.legal-tools.org/doc/bf0e8c/).

[131] ICC, Independent Oversight Mechanism Resolution, adopted on 27 November 2013, ICC-ASP/12/Res.6 (https://www.legal-tools.org/doc/64ebeb/).

[132] ICC, "Mandate of the Assembly of State Parties for the intersessional period", annexed to Strengthening the International Criminal Court and the Assembly of States Parties, adopted on 14 December 2017, Resolution ICC-ASP/16/Res.6, para. 9(c) (https://www.legal-tools.org/doc/36d60d/).

[133] Report ICC-ASP/17/30, paras. 26–27, see above note 128.

[134] ICC, Report of the Working Group on Amendments, 29 November 2018, Report ICC-ASP/17/35, paras. 17–20, 28 (https://www.legal-tools.org/doc/ceidsz/).

[135] Report ICC-ASP/17/30, para. 11, see above note 128.

[136] *Ibid.*, para. 12.

idency accordingly. In favouring this option, the necessity for clarity on the leadership of investigation was stressed by a range of States Parties.[137]

In so doing, the ICC aligned its procedure with that applied at the KSC and the IRMCT, namely allowing for an investigation to be conducted by an independent body. Although the IOM is established as subsidiary body of the ASP in accordance with Article 112(4) and thus would not strictly qualify as 'external', this amendment remains a significant step forward from the initial procedure, which provided for three ICC judges respectively the Presidency to investigate and make recommendations on allegations in respect of their own colleagues. As noted by a range of States Parties, it thus constitutes a momentous step forward *vis-à-vis* the initial version of the procedure and towards guaranteeing its fairness and transparency.[138]

Ultimately, the decision on whether or not to remove a judge still remains subject to a vote by the Plenary, in accordance with Rule 29(1), and to a decision by the ASP, pursuant to Article 46(2)(a). This is similar to the procedure applied at the IRMCT and is a further confirmation of the practice of *actus contrarius* – namely that a decision of removal of a judge may ultimately only be taken by the ASP, as the body which elected the judge in the first place pursuant to Article 36(6). Further, a decision to impose disciplinary measures remains within the competence of the Presidency, in accordance with Rule 30(1). Again, this follows the procedure applied at the IRMCT, and – to a certain extent – at the KSC, where the latter decision is left with the Plenary rather than the President.

The second crucial matter regulated in the recent amendment to Rule 26 is the possibility of submitting anonymous complaints: indeed, the first sentence of the new Rule 26(1) *in fine* provides that a complaint "may" include the identity of the complainant. This is a fundamental amendment *vis-à-vis* the initial version, which provided for the Presidency to set aside anonymous complaints. In so doing, the ICC disciplinary procedure moves away from the procedure applied at the IRMCT and the KSC, where the identity of the complainant has to be included, and anonymous complaints must accordingly be summarily dismissed.[139]

---

[137] *Ibid.*, paras. 13–14.

[138] *Ibid.*, para. 12.

[139] See KSC CoJE, Articles 15(5)(a) and 17(1), see above note 9 and IRMCT CoJE, Article 11(6)(a), see above note 8; It is noted that, unlike the KSC CoJE, the IRMCT CoJE does not

During the process of adoption of this amendment, States Parties noted their concern that anonymous complaints should not automatically be set aside and stressed that "although [they] should not be the norm, there were occasions where complainants may justifiably not wish to provide their identity, for example, in cases of whistle-blowing".[140] The current wording of Rule 26(1) reflects the agreement that whilst, as a general rule, the identity of the complainant should be included, anonymous complaints should not automatically be dismissed and could exceptionally be investigated by the IOM.[141] How such complaints will be handled in practice remains to be seen. The necessity for adjustments to the IOM mandate and operational manual in order to provide for the practical application of amended Rule 26, and in particular for the "handling of anonymous complaints" was duly noted during the adoption process.[142] In general, the inclusion of anonymous complaints remains consistent with the ICC Whistle-blowing and Whistle-blower Protection Policy.[143]

18.4.4. Conclusion

Having noted the significant positive developments in respect of the definition of principles of judicial ethics, a review of the disciplinary procedures adopted at ICTs provides an ambivalent result.

Firstly, it is striking that there are only three such procedures, for a total of six CoJEs actually adopted. The ECCC, the ICTY and the STL thus remain(ed) without any proceedings attached to breaches of principles of judicial ethics professed in their respective CoJEs – and a procedure was only subsequently added in respect of the IRMCT.

Second, as far as the definition of disciplinary offences is concerned, the level of details provided in the KSC and ICC procedures is to be commended. In respect of the latter, the clear distinction between offences committed in, and outside the course of official duties is a further positive

---

provide for the obligation to dismiss an anonymous complaint. However, given the obligation to include the identity of the complainant provided in Article 11(6)(a) IRMCT CoJE, it is submitted that an anonymous complaint would have to be dismissed as unreceivable in accordance with Article 12(1), Sentence 4 IRMCT CoJE, see above note 8.

[140] Report ICC-ASP/17/30, para. 15, see above note 128.

[141] *Ibid.*

[142] *Ibid.*, para. 24(c).

[143] See ICC Whistle-blowing and Whistle-blower Protection Policy, 8 October 2014, ICC/PRESD/G/2014/003 (https://www.legal-tools.org/doc/0c36ff/); Bergsmo, 2018, pp. 3–4, see above note 2.

development, clearly demonstrating that the judicial office of a judge does not stop at the doorstep of the courtroom but that some offences – even where unrelated to actual judicial activities – are such that they would call into question the overall capacity of an individual as a judge. This is a significant positive development. As far as the IRMCT is concerned, one must bear in mind the principle of *nullum crimen sine lege* – even though arguably not directly applicable in situations of mere disciplinary offences. Because disciplinary procedures may lead to the significant sanction of removal from office, it is critical that disciplinary offences be clearly defined and, as noted above, it is certainly questionable whether the IRMCT CoJE is sufficient in this respect.

Regarding the respective procedures, a number of positive developments are notable. At the IRMCT, the KSC and, since the most recent amendment to its RPE, also at the ICC, the actual investigation into complaints is made by judicial bodies not linked in any way to the judges of each institution – whether they are actually external or entirely independent from the judges. This is a significant step forward in guaranteeing the fairness and transparency of the procedure. Allowing for anonymous complaints in exceptional circumstances at the ICC is a further step towards guaranteeing the accountability of the ICC in general and the judges in particular.

On the downside, as noted above, the disciplinary procedure at the IRMCT is striking in terms of the broad discretion afforded to the IRMCT President. Unfortunately, this discretion applied to such a wide range of procedural steps does very little in ensuring the predictability and transparency of a procedure. By way of comparison, it is positive to note that the discretion afforded to the KSC President and the ICC Presidency is significantly more limited.

In addition, as a quite fundamental matter, it is perhaps unfortunate that the actual body deciding upon the removal of a peer is – whether directly or indirectly – the Plenary, that is, the judges themselves. Whether this will guarantee a fair and transparent procedure and decision-making, or whether political considerations or personal preferences will have the upper hand in such a vote, remains to be seen. The procedure in place in all three instances certainly opens the door for the latter. On the other hand, the argument may readily be made that such an 'internal' procedure serves to guarantee the independence of the judiciary.

Also, on the downside, one central issue when reviewing the disciplinary proceedings is the lack of accessible jurisprudence to analyse whether and how the latter function in practice. It is noted that both the KSC and IRMCT CoJEs include regulations to keep any proceedings in relation thereto confidential as a matter of principle. Whilst public redacted versions of some records are envisaged,[144] it is unclear which records are concerned, how this will be handled in practice and it can thus far only be noted that there are no such records available. As far as the ICC regime is concerned, it does not provide for clear provisions regarding confidentiality. Amended Rule 26(1) of the ICC RPE merely regulates that any complaint shall remain confidential. How any other record will be handled is not further specified – and here also, the lack of any accessible jurisprudence is striking.[145]

18.5. Final Remarks

The above analysis paints a mixed picture – whereby some clear conclusions may be drawn, particularly on whether or not a culture of accountability is emerging for the judiciary in ICTs.

A review of the regulations and jurisprudence applied to motions for disqualification determined that it is less than satisfactory in holding accountable central participants in proceedings, namely the judges themselves. There was therefore a real necessity in putting systems of accountability into place– the first step of which was to further define the principles applicable to judges, and to eventually attach disciplinary procedures and sanctions to any violation thereof.

An analysis of the preambles and legal bases of various CoJEs revealed that, in doing so, judges were notably mindful of their own solemn undertakings as well as of UN or EU principles of judicial ethics. In a unique manner, the STL CoJE expressly made the link with the process of excusal and disqualification of judges, which demonstrates the close link between this process and the principles of judicial ethics adopted in the CoJEs. It is striking that the ICC is the only institution which provides an explicit legal basis for the adoption of the CoJE. For all other ICTs, the actual legal basis thereof remains unclear at best and would perhaps not withstand

---

[144] IRMCT CoJE, Articles 14(6) and 15, see above note 8 and KSC CoJE, Article 23, see above note 9.

[145] Triffterer and Ambos, 2016, para. 10, see above note 43.

a – strictly hypothetical – legal challenge. As noted above, and with the exception of the ICC, this also demonstrates that the push to adopt CoJEs ultimately came from the judges themselves, rather than from those adopting their foundational documents – that is, the States creating these ICTs. And this is perhaps where the most fundamental change of mind must occur: during the creation of such ICTs, mindful of the importance of judicial ethics and, linked thereto, of a fair and transparent system of accountability, States must put into place a solid legal basis for the adoption of such principles and disciplinary procedures attached thereto.

A detailed review of the principles contained in the various CoJEs showed an encouraging development: indeed, over time, various principles experienced significant developments, both regarding the addition of new principles as well as regarding the amount of details provided in respect of established principles. The expansion of the principle of integrity is a flagship in this respect. This significant progress is demonstrative of the fact that judges, as those adopting the CoJEs, give significant thought to the principles applied to them and to the manner in which they develop over time. It further demonstrates an awareness amongst judges that the more detailed these principles are set out, the more likely they are to foster respect by parties and participants for the judges themselves and the work performed by them. As noted above, this is a truly positive development.

The three procedures adopted in respect of CoJEs have been analysed in detail above. Significant progress has been made in this respect – not least through the actual inclusion of such procedures, but also through some clear definitions of disciplinary offences and the introduction of independent investigatory mechanisms. However, the significant discretion afforded to the President in some cases, as well as the fact that it is ultimately the judges who vote upon a removal from office is unfortunate as it calls into question the fairness and transparency of such a procedure. Ultimately, however, the lack of accessible jurisprudence remains a significant obstacle in the analysis of the efficiency of disciplinary proceedings in furthering the integrity of judicial proceedings.

Overall, however, the adoption of CoJEs as well as the disciplinary proceedings in place represent a significant step forward in creating a culture of accountability for judges in ICTs. The various issues highlighted above still require some resolution – however, it is undoubtable that such CoJEs *per se* constitute effective institutional measures to give proper effect to the 'integrity standard'. As with any novel feature of ICTs, there is a clear need for improvement in respect of a range of matters. What remains to be noted, however, is that a culture is emerging whereby judges of ICTs are becoming increasingly aware of the necessity of being subjected to ethical rules and regulations – as any staff member in ICTs, and as any judge in domestic jurisdictions, for that matter.

Recent declarations by judges themselves are demonstrative of this awareness. Most notably, Article 27 of the Paris Declaration on the Effectiveness of International Criminal Justice, adopted in October 2017 by representatives of various ICTs (the ICC, the STL, the IRMCT, the KSC) includes the following recommendation:

> Establish suitable disciplinary mechanisms in order to ensure that adopted codes of conduct are respected and to guarantee impartiality, the appearance of impartiality and the dignity of the disciplinary process. As far as possible use investigative bodies which are external to the relevant court or tribunal and entrust decision making to a separate panel of the Assembly of the Judges of the court or tribunal. Consideration could be given to establishing an investigative and decision-making body common to all international criminal courts and tribunals.[146]

In a similar vein, the recent *Oslo Recommendations for Enhancing the Legitimacy of International Courts*, finalised in July 2018 by representatives of various ICTs (the ECCC, the STL, the Special Criminal Court in the Central African Republic, the IRMCT, the ICC, the KSC) and international courts (*inter alia*, the International Court of Justice, the World Trade Organization Appellate Body, the International Tribunal for the Law of the Sea, the European Court of Human Rights, the African Court on Human and Peoples' Rights), included the following recommendations regarding "Ethics and Judicial Integrity":

- Each international court should have a code of judicial ethics whose provisions are well known to judges.

- Judges should behave in a manner that does not cast doubt upon their independence, integrity, and impartiality.

- In situations where serious ethics violations by a judge are alleged and require an investigation, consideration should be given to the appoint-

---

[146] Paris Declaration on the Effectiveness of International Criminal Justice, 16 October 2017, p. 4 (https://www.legal-tools.org/doc/ow1amx/).

ment of an external committee, provided the institution allows such a procedure, composed of individuals with relevant knowledge and experience, to conduct the investigation and make recommendations.[147]

Each of the above demonstrate a further evolution in the reflection of judges, and ultimately further progress *vis-à-vis* the current CoJEs. Most notably, this concerns the appointment of external committees to conduct investigations and make recommendations on potential ethics violations, as recommended in the *Oslo Recommendations*. The *Paris Declaration* is perhaps even more progressive, in that it recommends that consideration be given to establishing an investigative and a decision-making body common to all criminal courts and tribunals, thus guaranteeing further independence of such a body, not only at the investigative but also the decision-making stage. Whether any of these recommendations will be adopted in practice remains to be seen. In any case, it is a distinct – and encouraging – sign to the States adopting ICT Statutes that judges are aware of the necessity for strong ethical frameworks for their judicial activities.

---

[147] Oslo Recommendations for Enhancing the Legitimacy of International Courts, 26 July 2018, p. 2 (https://www.legal-tools.org/doc/4g0kcc/).

19

Reflections on Integrity in International Criminal Justice and Regional Human Rights Courts

Erik Møse[*]

19.1. Introduction

For this volume I would like to provide some reflections on integrity challenges facing international criminal courts and regional human rights courts. This may seem surprising at first sight, as the two groups of courts seemingly perform different tasks: criminal courts decide whether to convict or acquit individuals after trials, whereas human rights institutions establish State responsibility based on complaint procedures and examination of reports from States. Moreover, each group includes courts with different characteristics. In the criminal sphere, the two *ad hoc* tribunals set up in the 1990s to address the atrocities in the former Yugoslavia and Rwanda ('IC-TY' and 'ICTR', respectively) in many ways differed from the hybrid courts set up from 2002 with respect to Sierra Leone, Cambodia and Lebanon ('SCSL', 'ECCC' and 'STL', respectively). The International Criminal Court ('ICC'), established by the Rome Statute in 1998,[1] is unique, as it is the only permanent international criminal court. Turning to the three regional courts in the human rights field – the European Court of Human Rights, the Inter-American Court of Human Rights, and the African Court of Human and Peoples' Rights – they have different structures and their powers are not identical.

This said, these courts certainly have common features. They are international; they intervene because of alleged deficiencies at the national level; their aim is to reduce the occurrence of human rights abuses; and they frequently find themselves in the public spotlight, facing more or less

---

[*] **Erik Møse** is Judge of the Supreme Court of Norway. He was previously Judge of the European Court of Human Rights, and President of the International Criminal Tribunal for Rwanda.

[1] Rome Statute of the International Criminal Court, 17 July 1998 (http://www.legal-tools.org/doc/7b9af9/).

well-founded criticism. Consequently, it is not without interest to reflect on common integrity challenges facing international criminal courts and human rights courts. The main focus of this chapter is on the two institutions where I have personal experience – the ICTR in Arusha and the European Court of Human Rights in Strasbourg.

19.2. General Remarks

Human rights courts and international criminal courts were set up to address human rights violations and even large-scale abuses at the national level. It is therefore difficult to argue against their *existence*. They represent values above discussion. Very few would openly object to the principles underpinning the European Convention on Human Rights ('ECHR') – human rights, the rule of law, and democracy.[2] Similarly, it is difficult not to be in favour of justice and the fight against impunity for serious international crimes, which were the main reasons behind the creation of international criminal courts.[3]

Criticism therefore usually concentrates on the *functioning* of these institutions. For instance, it is argued that human rights and criminal courts are costly, inefficient or unfair. When the focus is on the courts' work, rather than on their existence, they become more vulnerable. There are several reasons for this.

First, these international institutions are relatively *new institutions*. The first criminal courts – the ICTY and the ICTR – were established in 1993[4] and 1994 respectively, and the ICC commenced its work in 2002, after the entry into force of the Rome Statute. The human rights court in Strasbourg in principle started its activities from 1959, but received few cases in the 1960s and the 1970s. By comparison, many national courts have existed for much longer, some of them for centuries. Few observers

---

[2] These principles are reflected in the Preamble of the ECHR, 4 November 1950 (https://www.legal-tools.org/doc/8267cb) and in Articles 1–3 of the Statute of the Council of Europe, 5 May 1949, and have frequently been confirmed in the case-law of the European Court of Human Rights.

[3] See, for instance, the preamble of Security Council Resolution 955 (1994) on the Establishment of an International Tribunal and adoption of the Statute of the Tribunal, UN Doc. S/RES/955 (1994), 8 November 1994 (http://www.legal-tools.org/doc/f5ef47/).

[4] Security Council Resolution 827 (1993) on Establishment of the International Tribunal for Prosecution of Persons Responsible for Serious Violations of International Humanitarian Law Committed in the Territory of the Former Yugoslavia since 1991, UN Doc. S/RES/827 (1993), 25 May 1993 (https://www.legal-tools.org/doc/b4f63b).

question their institutional legitimacy, even if opinions may differ on individual judgments.

Second, the *composition* of international courts reflects different legal traditions and national cultures, concerning both judges and staff. Even though their work takes place within the framework of statutory provisions, rules of procedure and case-law, there will be room for discretion. Some national observers may not trust that these courts will conclude with the 'right' result in sensitive cases where perceptions may vary according to geographical origin. The situation is different with respect to a national court where the judges have been educated and have gained experience within a society based on one legal tradition.

A third common feature, linked to the previous one, is *distance*. With the exception of the hybrid courts in Sierra Leone and Cambodia, most international courts work outside the country where the atrocities or other human rights violations took place. For instance, the ICTR's headquarters were placed in Arusha, Tanzania due to shortage of suitable premises in Kigali, the capital of Rwanda, because of appearances of justice and fairness, and as a consequence of security risks in bringing the leaders of the former regime into Rwanda if they were to be prosecuted there.[5] The ICC in The Hague, with cases potentially coming from the entire world and more than 120 States Parties, obviously needed one permanent seat. The European Court of Human Rights, with currently 47 States Parties, was placed in Strasbourg, a town with historical links to France and Germany. When an international court considers cases relating to States where it is not located, this may create a feeling of remoteness within the population of the country concerned. It also leads to difficulties of communication for the court, as it becomes more challenging to convince the inhabitants of that State that the proceedings are relevant to them. Outreach programmes and other information measures are essential but may not eliminate their feeling of distance.

In addition to these three aspects of reticence, there is a fourth factor: *unrealistic expectations*. After large-scale atrocities, there will be a cry for justice from victims and public opinion. However, as the number of perpe-

---

[5] Security Council Resolution 977 (1995) on the Decision to Designate Arusha as the Seat of the ICTR, UN Doc. S/RES/977 (1995), 22 February 1995 (https://www.legal-tools.org/doc/396c27). See also: Report of the Secretary-General Pursuant to Paragraph 5 of Security Council Resolution 955 (1994), UN doc. S/1995/134, 13 February 1994 (https://www.legal-tools.org/doc/b38d44d).

trators will normally be high, the international criminal courts cannot possibly deal with all of them, but have to focus on the leaders. This may lead some observers to believe that the process is selective. In addition, the volume and complexity of cases dealing with international crimes slow down the trials, again creating disappointment. Similarly, the Strasbourg Court is considered by many applicants in Europe their only beacon of hope; they have – rightly or wrongly – no confidence that their national authorities, including the judiciaries, will redress human rights violations. Nonetheless, because of the Court's large workload, the process usually takes years, which may lead to impatience and disappointment.

These four general characteristics are among the reasons why international courts are under scrutiny by several groups. In addition, States Parties contributing to the institutions' big budgets want value for their money. Meanwhile, the slow progress of international criminal courts leads to what has often been referred to as 'tribunal fatigue'.[6] Some countries may have a specific interest in the outcome, for instance, Rwanda with respect to the ICTR, and the respondent State in Strasbourg. In the courtroom, not only will the parties in criminal cases (the prosecution and the defence) and in human rights proceedings (the applicant and the respondent State) follow the bench closely, but witnesses or victims will also notice mistakes or weaknesses. More generally, the media, non-governmental organizations, academic observers, and the world community at large attach importance to the international courts' performance.

It is therefore essential that there be no doubt about the legitimacy of an international court. Its credibility depends on the performance of the many individuals working inside each institution – judges as well as staff. Institutional legitimacy requires individual integrity.

19.3. Inefficiency

In conformity with the overall focus of this anthology, this contribution focuses on personal integrity. This said, there is no watertight division between the institutional legitimacy of an institution and the performance of its employees. Their daily activities should be in conformity with the aims

---

[6] This term has even found its way into the literature: see, for instance, Roger P. Alford, "The Proliferation of International Courts and Tribunals: International Adjudication in Ascendance", in *Proceedings of the Annual Meeting (American Society of International Law)*, 2000, vol. 94, pp. 160–165.

of a well-functioning institution. For this reason, there is a need for a common 'insider culture'. A good illustration is efficiency.

Starting with the international criminal courts, it is a recurring criticism that they are slow or even inefficient. The criticism against the ICTR in the first years of its existence is a good illustration. First, it took some time before the trials could start. Only after the arrest of the first accused person in May 1996, a considerable period after the Security Council Resolution of November 1994, was it possible to start the trials, leading to the first judgment in September 1998.[7] Second, the overall strategy changed. Originally, the Prosecutor's plan was to conduct one single trial with 29 accused persons.[8] However, the Tribunal then decided to have many single-defendant and some multi-defendant trials. This was the right decision, but required adjustments and caused delays.

More generally, reforms were necessary to improve the Tribunal's overall efficiency. Many lessons were learned on how to handle complex international trials and acquire sufficient institutional knowledge. The tripartite structure – the Prosecution, the Registry and the Chambers – complicated the situation. Gradually, the leadership in the three branches joined forces to solve problems in a concrete and practical way through increased co-ordination, consultation and co-operation.

Structural reforms were also necessary. Given the Tribunal's huge workload, the number of judges was first increased from six to nine in 1999; then gradually to 18 from 2003, through the possibility of appointing up to nine *ad litem* judges for specific cases.[9] The number of courtrooms increased from two to four, facilitating the hearing of several trials in parallel.

As a result of the need to adopt such measures, it took time to demonstrate visible results of efficiency reforms and thereby *increase* out-

---

[7] ICTR, *The Prosecutor v. Jean-Paul Akayesu*, Trial Chamber I, Judgement, 2 September 1998, ICTR-96-4-T (https://www.legal-tools.org/doc/b8d7bd).

[8] See ICTR, *The Prosecutor v. Théoneste Bagasora and 28 others*, ICTR-98-37. On 31 March 1998, the indictment was dismissed by Judge Khan; on 8 June 1998 (ICTR-98-37-I), the Prosecutor's appeal was dismissed by the Appeals Chamber (ICTR-98-37-A).

[9] Security Council Resolution 1165 (1998) on the Establishment of a 3rd Trial Chamber of the International Tribunal for Rwanda, UN Doc. S/RES/1165 (1998), 30 April 1998 (https://www.legal-tools.org/doc/08eb7a); Security Council Resolution 1512 (2003) on the Amendment of articles 11 and 12 quarter of the Statute of the International Criminal Tribunal for Rwanda, UN Doc. S/RES/1512 (2003), 27 October 2003 (https://www.legal-tools.org/doc/47fcbe).

---

side observers' confidence in the newly established ICTR. The experience from other criminal courts reveals a similar pattern. There is considerable wisdom in the German expression 'Aller Anfang ist schwer' ('All beginnings are difficult') – also for international courts.

For the Court in Strasbourg, which gradually started its work in the 1960s, the main challenge after the 1990s has rather been to *maintain* the confidence of observers. Following the fall of the Berlin Wall and the enlargement of the Council of Europe to include the previous communist countries, the number of States Parties to the ECHR rose to 47. Consequently, the number of new applications increased steadily and in 2011 reached around 160,000 pending cases. Many of them were 'repetitive applications' against the same States, demonstrating systemic domestic problems that had not been adequately addressed by those States, in spite of the Court's previous judgments establishing violations. Even if the Court was not to blame for this backlog, there were recurring discussions about its efficiency and future, leading to expressions that it was 'drowning' or 'a victim of its own success'. This represented a serious challenge to the Court's legitimacy and led to far-reaching proposals for an overall reform of the supervisory system established by the ECHR.[10]

Following in-depth studies and ministerial conferences, the Council of Europe introduced several reforms, the most important one being the adoption of Protocol 14 to the ECHR.[11] In particular, this protocol allowed a single judge to declare an application inadmissible when it had no prospect of success. This rapidly led to a significant reduction of the backlog. The protocol also increased the Court's efficiency by giving a committee of three judges – not only a chamber of seven – the power to render unanimous judgments based on well-established case-law. During the last few years, the number of pending applications has varied between 50,000 and 60,000.[12] This reduction of the backlog, amounting to almost 100,000 cases, visibly demonstrated that there was no basis for any criticism to the effect that the Court as an institution and its employees were inefficient. Conse-

---

[10] European Court of Human Rights, "Interlaken Declaration", 19 February 2010; European Court of Human Rights, "Izmir Declaration", 27 April 2011; as well as several follow-up proposals within the Council of Europe.

[11] Council of Europe, Protocol No. 14 to the European Convention on Human Rights, 13 May 2004 (https://www.legal-tools.org/doc/dd5017).

[12] For an overview over up-to-date statistics regarding current pending cases by the European Court of Human Rights, see "Statistics" (available on its web site).

quently, the plans for an overall reform of the ECHR's supervisory system were not followed up. Recent ministerial conferences have instead focused on the need to strengthen the existing court system and on the principle of subsidiarity.[13] Last but not least, the Court has constantly tried to streamline its internal working methods in order to increase its judicial output.

19.4. Personal Integrity – Some Illustrations

Criticism relating to the personal integrity of individuals working in international courts may cover quite different situations. It is my impression that allegations of *mismanagement*, or even corruption or other illegal acts, are rare. Should such criticism occur, it is important that the institution carry out thorough investigations, even if the person accused of such behaviour has left, in order to clarify whether the allegation has any factual basis and, if so, to take necessary measures and demonstrate a rupture with the past.

I cannot recall any relevant illustrations from Strasbourg. In Arusha, there was, in the early years, serious operational deficiencies, in particular in the Registry. This resulted in administrative improvements from 1997. Subsequently, there were occasionally other allegations, for instance, about unsatisfactory witness protection if a witness had been assaulted after returning to Rwanda subsequent to his testimony. Such assertions were always subject to thorough investigations, leading to the finding that there was no basis for criticism against the Tribunal.

A more common form of criticism relates to what could generally be called *questionable behaviour* in connection with the judicial proceedings. This may take different forms. Below follow a few examples.

Starting with the behaviour *in the courtroom*, criticism against the Strasbourg proceedings are extremely rare. The hearings normally last only two to three hours and consist of oral pleadings (about 45 minutes from each party), brief questions from the judges, and responses.

The situation is more complicated in international criminal courts with trials lasting for up to hundreds of days, covering a variety of situations. For instance, the cross-examination of witnesses who are also victims of grave crimes presents challenges to lawyers testing their credibility

---

[13]   See, to some extent, European Court of Human Rights, "Brighton Declaration", 20 April 2020, and more clearly "Brussels Declaration", 27 March 2015, and "Copenhagen Declaration", 13 April 2018.

even if they will normally take into account that such witnesses are vulnerable.

In all court settings, it is essential that judges' *questions* not be perceived as biased, as this may easily lead to doubts about the legitimacy of the institution. Needless to say, this does not in any way limit a judge's independence or freedom of expression. There are many ways to formulate a question.

A point of particular relevance to international criminal trials is that the judges must avoid unnecessary *use of time* in the courtroom; otherwise their court will be perceived as inefficient (see Section 19.2 above). It is necessary to find the right balance between efficient and fair proceedings, for instance, when the parties ask for more time. There are examples of what some observers would characterize as an unnecessary consumption of time, both with respect to the taking of evidence and during discussions of procedural issues.

Another illustration, which is relevant to both groups of international courts, relates to the use of *separate opinions* (concurring or dissenting). While national systems differ on the acceptance of such opinions, most international courts allow them, either explicitly or by implication. There is no doubt that such opinions may be necessary and useful, and it goes without saying that their use does not in itself raise any risk to the legitimacy of a court. However, if some judges resort to this possibility too frequently, or if a separate opinion is quite lengthy (perhaps even longer than the majority judgment), there is a risk that the message of the court's judgments become less clear and leave observers with the impression that the court is more divided than it really is. Lengthy opinions also require considerable resources (for example, translation and checking of footnotes) and may even slow down the delivery of the judgment. Finally, it may be worth recalling that separate opinions should be drafted in a way that is respectful to the view of the majority.[14]

Integrity issues may also arise in connection with the *daily management* outside the context of the judicial proceedings. A recurring theme has been to what extent a judge may be absent from the court in order to carry out *extra-judicial activities*. Over the years, the general policy has generally become stricter. The question now arises with respect to teaching or attending conferences. As will be seen below (fourth and fifth remarks under

---

[14] See also Section 19.5. below, text accompanying notes 21 *et seq.*

Section 19.5.), current internal codes and international guidelines provide that such tasks must not reduce the efficiency of the court. One example is the guidelines for judges' teaching activities, adopted by the Strasbourg Court's bureau in 2011.[15] In principle, teaching shall take place during periods of 'light schedule' (periods when there are no hearings). Otherwise, it is only acceptable outside normal working hours, which in practice means in the evenings, during weekends and vacations.

This said, conferences provide an opportunity for judges to offer balanced information about their court's functioning and thereby respond to unfounded criticism which may affect the institution's legitimacy. It is therefore necessary to find the right balance between this task and their daily workload, which is heavy.

In the same vein, it is important for a court, through its leadership or its information office, to *provide correct information*. For instance, some observers of the ICTR argued that those accused of genocide lived in privileged conditions during pre-trial detention in Arusha, referring to the Tribunal's local prison as 'Arusha Hilton'. In fact, it was quite spartan, far from luxurious, but better than many African prisons because it complied with international standards and was inspected regularly by an independent non-governmental organization. The Tribunal decided to invite a group of journalists into the prison to observe the conditions, and the criticism ended.

Another example relates to the legal officers that assist judges in criminal and human rights courts with legal research and drafting. Occasionally, there may be rumours that they also decide the outcome of the cases. Such stories are baseless; the judges are in total control and do not hesitate to change drafts. Similarly, during my time in the Strasbourg Court, I heard national speculations that judgments based on a 'dynamic' or 'evolutive' interpretation were the result of Registry lawyers with an agenda. I never experienced anything of that sort. For integrity reasons, it is important to refute this kind of rumours and explain how the institution functions.

19.5. The Way Forward

The aim of this anthology is to revisit a wealth of issues relating to integrity in international justice, as the six parts address the topic from different

---

[15] Guidelines for "Judges' teaching activities", adopted by the European Court of Human Rights' Bureau on 5 October 2011.

perspectives. Below follow six general remarks regarding integrity in international justice, starting with the *statutory texts* of international courts.

The word 'integrity' does not appear in all statutes as rightly recalled by the policy brief from which this project originated.[16] For instance, Article 21(1) and (3) of the ECHR, on the criteria for office, simply provides that the judges shall be of "high moral character" and that they "shall not engage in any activity which is incompatible with their independence, impartiality or with the demands of a full-time office". On the other hand, Article 12 of the ICTR Statute about qualifications and election of judges states that the judges shall be persons of "high moral character, impartiality and integrity". According to its Article 15(1) about the Prosecutor, he or she shall be of "high moral character" and possess "the highest level of competence and experience" with the investigations and prosecutions of criminal cases.

Of these texts, only one refers to integrity. Both statutes focus on the judges, whereas the ICTR Statute includes the Prosecutor. They do not mention any other professional groups. Other court statutes provide a similar picture.

In my view, it is difficult to see a need to revise the statutory texts, for instance, by inserting the word 'integrity' or by providing that this requirement applies to all professional groups working in the institution. A revision process would be lengthy and require negotiations and agreement by all States Parties. It could create the incorrect impression that integrity issues are a general problem in international courts. Furthermore, it is open to doubt whether such amendments would make a significant difference in the daily life of the courts.

Second, the *rules of procedure* of human rights and criminal courts contain very few provisions of relevance to integrity. This is not surprising, as they focus on the procedural aspects of the judicial proceedings. In most courts, the rules are adopted by the plenary of the judges and hence easier to amend than statutory texts. However, whether there is a need for reform will ultimately depend on the situation of each court. Given the technical character of the rules of procedure, supplementing them with provisions on integrity may not be the best way forward.

---

[16] Morten Bergsmo, "Revisiting Integrity in International Justice", FICHL Policy Brief Series No. 93 (2018), Torkel Opsahl Academic EPublisher, Brussels, 2018 (https://www.legal-tools.org/doc/e550f7/).

Third, of greater interest are the *internal codes of conduct*. In the criminal field, it is worth noting that, already in 2005, the judges of the ICC adopted a Code of Judicial Ethics for judges, which contains provisions on judicial independence, impartiality, integrity, confidentiality, diligence, conduct during proceedings, public expression and association, and extrajudicial activities.[17] There is also an extensive Code of Conduct for the Office of the Prosecutor from 2013.[18]

In 2018, the judges of the International Residual Mechanism for International Criminal Tribunals, which succeeded the ICTY and the ICTR, adopted a code of professional conduct.[19] Its governing principles include similar provisions as the ICC code for judges and provides for a complaint procedure. Its Article 3 about integrity provides that judges "shall conduct themselves with probity and integrity, thereby enhancing public confidence in the judiciary". They shall not accept or offer gifts, shall treat others with respect and not engage in discrimination, harassment or abuse of authority.

Turning to the human rights field, the Strasbourg Court adopted a resolution on judicial ethics in 2008.[20] It contains provisions on many issues, for instance, independence, impartiality, integrity, diligence and competence, discretion, freedom of expression, and additional activities. Principle III on integrity states that judges' conduct must be consistent with the high moral character that is a criterion for judicial office, and that they should be mindful at all times of their duty to uphold the standing and reputation of the Court.

These internal codes of conduct all use the word 'integrity', define the concept and regulate important situations. It is true that some provisions are formulated in a general way, but in their totality, they provide im-

---

[17] ICC, *Code of Judicial Ethics*, 2 January 2005, ICC-BD/02-01-05 (https://www.legal-tools.org/doc/383f8f).

[18] ICC, *Code of Conduct for the Office of the Prosecutor*, entry into force 5 September 2013 (https://www.legal-tools.org/doc/3e11eb). It includes, *inter alia*, provisions on general standards, independence, honourable conduct, faithful conduct, conscientious conduct, impartiality, confidentiality, public expression and association, conflict of interest, and non-acceptance of gifts.

[19] International Residual Mechanism for Criminal Tribunals, *Code of Professional Conduct of the Judges of the Mechanism*, MICT/14/Rev.1, 9 April 2018, (https://www.legal-tools.org/doc/23cc92 (MICT/14)).

[20] European Court of Human Rights, *Resolution on Judicial Ethics*, adopted by the Plenary Court on 23 June 2008.

portant guidance. The question remains whether there should be similar guidelines also for other members of international courts than the judges.

Fourth, discussions of integrity should also take into account *international guidelines*. In 2004, the International Law Association adopted the *Burgh House Principles* on the independence of the judiciary.[21] The 17 principles focus on independence and impartiality, are generally formulated, and take into account that each international court has its own characteristics and functions. In the present context, it is worth noting that Principle 2 makes specific reference to the need to choose judges "of high moral character, integrity and conscientiousness". The other provisions regulate a wide variety of issues linked to the legitimacy and effectiveness of the international judicial process.[22]

Of interest is also the resolution adopted in 2011 by the Institut de Droit international, which deals with the position of international judges.[23] One of its aims was to promote the authority and effectiveness of international justice. Article 2 highlights the importance of "the intellectual and moral character" of the judges in international courts. The resolution contains seven articles.[24]

In 2018, during a conference with the participation of judges from international courts, the *Oslo Recommendations* for enhancing the legitimacy of international courts was adopted by the participants of the Brandeis Institute for International Judges.[25] While emphasizing that the primary work

---

[21] The Study Group of the International Law Association on the Practice and Procedure of International Courts and Tribunals in association with the Project on International Courts and Tribunals, "The Burgh House Principles on the Independence of the International Judiciary", 2004 (available on International Law Association's web site).

[22] The 17 principles deal with independence and freedom from interference; nomination, election and appointment; security of tenure; service and remuneration; privileges and immunities; budget; freedom of expression and association; extra-judicial activity; past links to a case or to a party; interest in the outcome of a case; contacts with a party; post-service limitation; disclosure; waiver, withdrawal or disqualification; and misconduct.

[23] Institut de Droit international, Sixth Commission, "The Position of the International Judge", adopted on 9 September 2011.

[24] The seven articles give guidance concerning selection of judges; term of judicial functions; status of judges; remuneration and conditions of service; organization of international courts and tribunals (with emphasis on independence); immunities and privileges; and international part-time judges.

[25] The "Oslo Recommendation for Enhancing the Legitimacy of International Courts", 26 September 2018 (https://www.legal-tools.org/doc/4g0kcc/), was drafted collectively on 2 June and finalised on 26 July 2018 by the participants of the Brandeis Institute for Interna-

of judges is to produce well-reasoned and timely judgments, the recommendation also recognizes that ensuring the legitimacy of international courts may still require more from both judges and their institutions.

The recommendation contains five parts.[26] Section B deals specifically with ethics and judicial integrity. It recommends that each international court should have a code of judicial ethics; that judges should behave in a manner that does not cast doubt upon their "independence, integrity, and impartiality"; and that dissenting or separate opinions should be delivered "with restraint and formulated in respectful language so as not to undermine the authority of the court".

Section E states that, in view of the complex and shifting global context, courts must increasingly pay attention to communicating their decisions, tasks and responsibility. It further recommends that judges should endeavour to promote the tasks and functioning of their courts by explaining their work to the public, although the primary responsibility rests with the courts' presidents and communication departments.

Fifth, it follows from this overview that several texts regulate integrity issues of relevance to international judges, whereas there is less material concerning prosecutors and members of the courts' registries. It would appear that the best way forward is not to elaborate new general texts for judges, but rather to adopt a *specific approach*. Each court should, in light of its particular situation, reflect on whether there is a need to improve in certain areas and try to foster a common culture within the institution.

Sixth, international courts need senior officials with a highly professional approach, based on the fulfilment of duty, as has been rightly highlighted.[27] It is therefore important that the process of *election* of judges and other key officials ensure that the best candidates be selected.

At the national level, candidates for the highest posts in the judiciary have previously worked in other positions and are known in legal circles.

---

tional Judges. The conference (30 May to 2 June 2018) was organized by the International Center for Ethics, Justice and Public Life (Brandeis University) and the PluriCourts Centre for the Study of the Legitimate Roles of the Judiciary in the Global Order (Faculty of Law, University of Oslo).

[26] The five sections (A to E) cover the following topics: nomination and selection of international judges; ethics and judicial integrity; efficiency of proceedings; transparency of proceedings and access to judicial output; and role of judges in outreach and interactions with the public.

[27] Bergsmo, 2018, see above note 16.

This facilitates the appointment procedure and reduces the risk of surprises. In international elections, however, the candidates are usually unknown to those electing them. It is therefore advisable to ensure transparency of elections of international judges and other high officials.

One interesting example is the European Court of Human Rights' election process. Each State Party nominates three candidates, and the Parliamentary Assembly of the Council of Europe elects one of them in respect of the State concerned. The Assembly has adopted several recommendations to improve the election process, the underlying approach being that the national selection should be "rigorous, fair and transparent in order to enhance the quality, efficacy and authority of the Court".[28] In particular, the national application procedure, both the announcement and the final recommendation, should be as transparent as possible. Moreover, the Assembly's election process, which includes interviews with the candidates, has been improved in many ways.

The Committee of Ministers also established a committee with the task to scrutinize the *curricula vitae* of the nominated candidates and give advice before the three names are transmitted to the Assembly.[29] The committee has seven members with judicial experience. It has influenced the nomination process in some countries.

19.6. Final Remarks

Criticism against institutions is common both at the national and international levels. It concerns various entities: legislative, judicial and administrative. This is not surprising but rather reflects that the institutions are relevant, exercise power, and hence should be scrutinized. Criticism is a sign of interest in their work and may lead to improvements. An institution that adopts a defensive attitude and does not react to well-founded criticism risks losing its legitimacy.

Gradually, the international judiciary has become subject to debate. Even though criminal courts and human rights courts differ in many ways,

---

[28] For the many resolutions by the Parliamentary Assembly about the election of the judges to the Strasbourg Court, see generally: Parliamentary Assembly of the Council of Europe, *Procedure for the election of judges to the European Court of Human rights as of 15th of April 2019*, SG-AS (2020) 03 rev 3, 30 September 2020.

[29] Council of Europe, CM/Res/(2010)26 on the establishment of an Advisory Panel of Experts on Candidates for Election as Judge to the European Court of Human Rights, 10 November 2010.

both groups have been subject to criticism relating to institutional legitimacy and personal integrity. There is a need to respond to such challenges, either by refuting unfounded allegations or through the adoption of measures, for instance by carrying out investigations and reform. Over the years, internal codes and international guidelines have identified integrity issues and have recommended best practices. International courts have to respond to criticism as a matter of priority and in a transparent way, thereby dispelling any doubts about their legitimacy. More generally, there should be a common culture of integrity within the institution.

20

Integrity and Independence in
the Delivery of Accountability:
Harnessing International and Domestic
Frameworks in Pursuit of Justice for ISIL Crimes

Karim A.A. Khan and Jonathan Agar[*]

> [...] a prince's court
> is like a common fountain, whence should flow
> Pure silver drops in general, but if 't chance
> Some curs'd example poison't near the head,
> Death and diseases through the whole land spread.[1]

20.1. Introduction

'Integrity' is perhaps as often cited as it is too seldom considered in legal discourse. It is for this reason that this anthology edited by Morten Bergsmo and Viviane Dittrich is so welcome – and so sorely needed. The word 'integrity', the concept and values that are embraced by it, are neither throw-away lines, or redundant surplusage. Rather, without the integrity of a criminal investigation, a legal process, or a lawyer, an investigator or other official engaged within it, due process is rendered a remote possibility.

---

[*]   **Karim A.A. Khan** QC, Assistant Secretary-General, is Special Adviser and Head of the UN Investigative Team to promote Accountability for crimes committed by Da'esh/ISIL ('UNITAD'). As a barrister, he has been engaged as counsel for prosecution, victims or the defence in cases before the ICC, the International Criminal Tribunal for the former Yugoslavia ('ICTY'), International Criminal Tribunal for Rwanda ('ICTR'), Special Court for Sierra Leone ('SCSL'), Extraordinary Chambers in the Courts of Cambodia ('ECCC'), the Special Tribunal for Lebanon ('STL'), and the European Union Rule of Law Mission in Kosovo ('EULEX') court in Kosovo and the Special Panel for Serious Crimes in East Timor. He has also worked as a legal adviser in the Office of the Prosecutor ('OTP') of both the ICTY & ICTR and in the Crown Prosecution Service and the Law Commission of England and Wales. **Jonathan Agar** is a Legal Officer in the Office of the Special Adviser, UNITAD. Previously, he has held positions with the United Nations Office of Legal Affairs, the United Nations Office on Drugs and Crime, and the United Kingdom Government Legal Service. This article is written by the authors in their personal capacity and does not represent the views of the United Nations.

[1]   John Webster, *The Duchess of Malfi*, Act 1, Scene 1.

Without integrity in all its various forms, the law and its processes are liable to be brought into disrepute. The consequence will be an erosion of trust in the vital pillar of justice and her various institutions.

The quote from John Webster's play that frames this chapter articulates a reality that integrity and leadership must commence from those 'at the top' and percolate down. It warns of the danger and consequences that will arise when the leadership is tainted or seen as polluted. But, as this chapter will also seek to demonstrate, it is also the case that integrity in the investigation of crimes, in accountability mechanisms and in the adjudication of crimes, requires a self-sustaining ecosystem in which – simultaneously – all parts are imbued with the quality of 'integrity' and in which all parts scrutinize and, thereby, reinforce or help ensure the integrity of each other.

As the work and activities of international courts, mechanisms and investigative teams come under increasing scrutiny, our adherence to these principles is rendered even more essential. As the voices of those States and other actors questioning the value and legitimacy of international action with respect to criminal accountability grow louder, advocates of global action must not be impeded by concerns and criticisms regarding the transparency and effectiveness of the existing international criminal justice architecture.

The responsibility for placing these principles of independence, impartiality and integrity at the centre of the cause of international criminal justice ultimately resides with those charged with leading relevant entities. As intimated, a culture of integrity must start with the heads of mechanisms both leading by example and empowering senior and mid-level management to implement an effective normative and institutional integrity framework. A culture of integrity should be developed that cascades down from mission leadership in a manner that ensures coherence of delivery and a common and sincere commitment by all team members, international and national, to its adherence.

While the central importance of the principles of integrity and impartiality to the delivery of justice remains constant, the mechanisms and policies introduced to implement these concepts must respond to the context in which they seek to operate. The application of integrity frameworks within international criminal justice mechanisms established in recent times will necessarily address challenges sometimes similar and at other times different to those encountered 20 years ago at the time of the adoption of the

Rome Statute. The mandates and consequent integrity challenges faced by such entities reflect the evolving political and diplomatic context.

Indeed, recent developments in the social and political environments in many States have not only increased scrutiny of existing institutions,[2] but have also had a significant impact on the context in which new international criminal justice entities are born. Increased emphasis has been placed, in particular, on how the international community can promote and support accountability in a manner that emphasizes co-operation and collaboration with national authorities and full respect for national sovereignty and the jurisdiction of States over crimes committed in their territories.

Such innovation of approach with respect to the promotion of criminal accountability is not just necessary but must be welcomed. It is essential that the international community is able to demonstrate an ability to reflect changing political contexts in new additions to the international criminal justice architecture. However, such changes also pose fundamental questions concerning the issue of integrity. For example, how do we continue to effectively uphold the principles of integrity and independence of international criminal justice mechanisms while ensuring that States are able to strengthen their role as stakeholders in the process of justice, and allow them to embrace and support the mandates of such entities? How can we address the perceived tension between the principles of independence and collaboration in a manner that maintains a viable – yet principled – political consensus for international action?

This chapter will reflect on some of the initial lessons to be drawn from the work undertaken by the United Nations ('UN') Investigative Team to Promote Accountability for Crimes Committed by Da'esh/ISIL ('UNITAD') in constructing a normative, institutional and cultural system of integrity within the framework of its mandate pursuant to the UN Security Council resolution 2379 (2017).[3] Considering the engagement and co-operation with national authorities, as well as the integration of a significant national staffing component, the implementation of integrity measures by UNITAD might provide an indicator as to how international criminal

---

[2] See Morten Bergsmo, "Revisiting Integrity in International Justice", FICHL Policy Brief Series No. 93 (2018), Torkel Opsahl Academic EPublisher, Brussels, 2018 (https://www. legal-tools.org/doc/e550f7/).

[3] United Nations Security Council ('UNSC'), Resolution 2379 (2017), Threats to International Peace and Security, UN Doc. S/RES/2379, 21 September 2017 ('S/RES/2379') (https://www.legal-tools.org/doc/1510b4/).

justice entities can continue to adapt their integrity systems to their evolving mandates and operational imperatives.

With respect to the core normative framework, we will consider in particular the interconnection and interaction between the broader framework provided by the UN Charter,[4] the UN Staff Rules and Regulations,[5] and other system-level instruments, and the increasingly specialized integrity architecture specific to the mandate and operational particularities of UNITAD. Attention will be paid in this regard to how the concept of integrity is addressed in the provisions of Security Council resolution 2379 (2017), the Terms of Reference regarding the activities of UNITAD in Iraq, as approved by the Security Council on 13 February 2018,[6] as well as the tailored integrity policies and practices implemented since the establishment of the Team. Some of these are bespoke to UNITAD and some are simply functions of established good practice that is essential to ensuring the integrity of evidence. Chain of custody, a preference for the best evidence, where available, proper interview protocols and interaction with witnesses, and a degree of circumspection regarding hearsay without supporting evidence, are all factors that are tried and tested – and recognizable elements, in one form or another, in most legal systems.

Drawing on the experience gained since the commencement of the activities of UNITAD in Baghdad in October 2018, consideration will be given to three key aspects of its work which have engaged the concepts of integrity, impartiality and independence. First, we will consider the individual and personal level of integrity. We will reflect on how common concepts of impartiality and independence can be instilled in all staff members within an organization that draws not only on the talents of over 150 staff

---

[4] Charter of the United Nations, 1 UNTS XVI, 24 October 1945, Articles 100 and 101 in particular ('UN Charter') (https://www.legal-tools.org/doc/6b3cd5/).

[5] Most recently, see amendments introduced through UN General Assembly resolution, Human Resources Management, UN Doc. A/RES/72/254, 24 December 2017 ('A/RES/72/254') (https://www.legal-tools.org/doc/cc7il5/), as promulgated by the Secretary-General through Secretary-General's Bulletin, UN Doc. ST/SGB/2018/1, effective from 1 January 2018 (https://www.legal-tools.org/doc/zn5lba/).

[6] Terms of reference of the Investigative Team to support domestic efforts to hold Islamic State in Iraq and the Levant (Da'esh) accountable for acts that may amount to war crimes, crimes against humanity and genocide committed in Iraq, established pursuant to Security Council resolution 2379 (2017), attached as Annex to Letter dated 9 February 2018 from the Secretary-General addressed to the President of the Security Council, UN Doc. S/2018/118, 14 February 2018 ('Terms of reference') (https://www.legal-tools.org/doc/niw4cw/).

members from over 40 countries world-wide, but also seeks to integrate
and harness the talents of a significant number of national criminal law experts.

Second, the concept of integrity is assessed from the perspective of
those individuals with whom UNITAD has engaged as a core part of its
investigative activities, in particular witnesses, survivors and members of
impacted communities. Integrity measures are of particular importance
here in ensuring that the most vulnerable individuals, including victims of
sexual and gender-based violence, do not suffer double-victimization, either through societal stigmatization connected through their suffering or
through reliving their experiences in a manner that is not aligned with best
practice.

Finally, we will consider integrity in relation to institutional independence. This issue is of particular relevance in light of the specific emphasis within the mandate of UNITAD with respect to co-operation and
collaboration with national authorities, as well as its ultimate objective of
supporting the implementation of effective judicial proceedings at the national level.

As reflected below, we consider that the success of any international
criminal accountability mechanism, and in particular those established in
the current political and diplomatic context, will largely depend on the
recognition that the principles of integrity and co-operation, and of independence and respect for sovereignty, do not represent competing interests
to be balanced but, may be viewed – perhaps more often than expected – as
mutually reinforcing pillars on which effective action is built. Our experience also underlines the often mutually reinforcing and complementary
nature of deontological and consequential approaches[7] to integrity. This
includes adherence to international standards and best practice in the fields
of, *inter alia*, information management and security, witness protection and
support, and evidence-collection as a precondition for effective investigative action capable of producing case-files on which national prosecutions
may be built.

---

[7] See Alexander Heinze and Shannon Fyfe, "Prosecutorial Ethics and Preliminary Examinations at the ICC", in Morten Bergsmo and Carsten Stahn (eds.), *Quality Control in Preliminary Examination: Volume 2*, Torkel Opsahl Academic EPublisher, Brussels, 2018 (https://
www.legal-tools.org/doc/dff594/).

20.2. The Normative Integrity Framework for the Establishment of a United Nations Criminal Accountability Mechanism

20.2.1. The Crimes of ISIL and a Response by the International Community

In the current climate of increased scepticism regarding the value and legitimacy of collective action in the field of criminal justice, the international community was confronted with some of the most severe, co-ordinated and egregious atrocities in recent times. Between June 2014 and December 2017, ISIL captured, controlled and operated with impunity over large swathes of territory in Iraq, committing grave abuses of international human rights law, international criminal law, and international humanitarian law. The subsequent liberation of large areas from its control served to expose the magnitude of the crimes inflicted on the inhabitants of these territories. Witness testimony revealed a plethora of abuses including executions, torture, amputations, ethno-sectarian attacks, destruction and looting of cultural heritage, and rape and sexual slavery imposed on women and girls. Thousands of children became victims, witnesses and forced perpetrators of these atrocities.[8]

As ISIL was driven from its strongholds in Iraq, and as territories were wrestled from their control, the focus of victims and impacted communities turned to the imperative of ensuring that senior ISIL members were held accountable for the crimes they have committed, on the basis of objective, evidence-based investigation and analysis. It was further recognized, both by entities representing those groups most impacted by ISIL crimes and by national governments and non-governmental agencies, that the detailed and factual presentation of ISIL atrocities in fair and transparent criminal proceedings could serve to vindicate the requirements of justice and strengthen efforts to establish a basis for broader reconciliation in Iraq. By exposing the extent and gravity of crimes committed, accountability processes could also serve to undermine the ideological underpinnings

---

[8] See Report of the Office of the United Nations High Commission for Human Rights on the human rights situation in Iraq in the light of abuses committed by the so-called Islamic State in Iraq and the Levant and associated groups, UN Doc. A/HRC/28/18, 13 March 2015 (https://www.legal-tools.org/doc/8a4f0d/), and "They came to destroy": ISIL Crimes Against the Yazidis, Report of the Independent International Commission of Inquiry on the Syrian Arab Republic, UN Doc. A/HRC/32/CRP.2, 15 June 2016 (https://www.legal-tools.org/doc/24962f/).

of their movement, thereby reducing the ability of its form of violent extremism to spread further.

In the initial conceptual discussions amongst States on the establishment of a potential international mechanism addressing ISIL crimes, emphasis was placed on the need for any international action to be based on the principle of respect for national jurisdiction, as well as effective co-operation and co-ordination with relevant national authorities. At the same time, many States and other actors emphasized the need for the future mechanism to be able to act independently and impartially so as to ensure the integrity of its work as well as strengthen the admissibility of evidentiary material collected before national courts, both in Iraq and other States. From the outset, the Team's work has been bound to these dual imperatives of respect for national sovereignty and the principle of independence, which were viewed as central to its ability to conduct its work effectively and in a manner ensuring that evidence collected could serve as an effective basis for domestic prosecutions.

It is in this context that the Government of Iraq, on 9 August 2017, formally requested the assistance of the international community in making sure that members of ISIL are held accountable for their crimes in Iraq, including where those may amount to crimes against humanity, war crimes, or genocide. Following extensive negotiations led by the United Kingdom as penholder, the Security Council responded with one voice, unanimously adopting resolution 2379 (2017).[9] It requested the Secretary-General to establish an Investigative Team, headed by a Special Adviser, "to support domestic efforts to hold ISIL accountable by collecting, preserving, and storing evidence in Iraq of acts that may amount to war crimes, crimes against humanity, and genocide committed by the terrorist group ISIL in Iraq".[10] In addition to this core investigative mandate, paragraph 3 of this resolution provides that the Special Adviser, while avoiding duplication of effort with other relevant UN bodies, will also promote throughout the world, accountability for acts that may amount to war crimes, crimes against humanity, or genocide committed by ISIL, and work with survivors, in a manner consistent with relevant national laws, to ensure their interests in achieving accountability for ISIL are fully recognized.

---

[9] S/RES/2379, see above note 3. The mandate was unanimously extended through UN Security Council resolution 2490 (2019), Threats to international peace and security, UN Doc. S/RES/2490, on 20 September 2019 (https://www.legal-tools.org/doc/l2hnjy/).

[10] S/RES/2379, para. 3, see above note 3.

Following extensive engagement between the UN and the Government of Iraq, the Terms of Reference regarding the activities of the Investigative Team in Iraq were agreed and approved by the Security Council on 13 February 2018. The document presented an enhanced framework for cooperation and collaboration between the Government of Iraq and the Investigative Team in the implementation of this mandate, while providing the more detailed legal basis underpinning the impartial and independent nature of its work.

20.2.2. The Normative Integrity Framework of the United Nations Investigative Team to Promote Accountability for the Crimes Committed by Da'esh/ISIL

Throughout both resolution 2379 (2017) and the Terms of Reference, we see how the core normative integrity framework of the Investigative Team intertwines and adapts to these fundamental operational principles of independence and respect for national sovereignty. The interconnected nature of these imperatives is crystallized on two levels, individual and institutional, personal and organizational. Through the legal framework established by the Council to govern the Team's work, and as reflected in its investigative activities in the first year of its operation in Iraq, we see the interconnected nature of measures aimed at securing the integrity of actions undertaken by Team members and the independence, impartiality and ultimate value of its work to the communities it was established to serve.

20.2.2.1. United Nations Security Council Resolution 2379 (2017)

Within the core substantive mandate of the Investigative Team, reflected in paragraph 2 of Resolution 2379 (2017), the Security Council included a both deontological and consequentialist framework for the integrity of the Team's investigative work. Specifically, its work in collecting, preserving and storing evidence in Iraq of acts that may amount to war crimes, crimes against humanity, and genocide committed by ISIL must be carried out "to the highest possible standards",[11] with detail of such standards to be included in the Terms of Reference. The purpose in the application of such standards is to "ensure the broadest possible use before national courts, and complementing investigations being carried by the Iraqi authorities, or investigations carried out by authorities in third countries at their request".[12]

---

[11] *Ibid.*, para. 2.
[12] *Ibid.*

In addition to this broad deontological principle of "highest possible standards", the Council emphasizes in paragraph 6 of resolution 2379 (2017) that the Team should be "impartial, independent and credible"[13] and that it must operate in a manner consistent with "the Terms of Reference, the Charter of the United Nations and United Nations best practice, and relevant international law including international human rights law".[14]

It is this reference to "the highest possible standards" that provides much of the immediate basis for the integrity framework developed since the establishment of the Investigative Team, serving as a guiding principle in the introduction and development of policies, procedures and practices with respect to evidence and information management, witness protection and support, testimonial evidence collection, chain of custody processes, and recruitment practices. In the implementation of this principle, Security Council resolution 2379 (2017) is clear that the Terms of Reference are the primary source to be referenced.[15] In addition, best practices and procedures from existing international accountability mechanisms, including the International Criminal Tribunals for the former Yugoslavia and Rwanda ('ICTY' and 'ICTR' respectively) and the International Criminal Court, have also been an important source of guidance, as well as recognized international standards and UN and other policy guidelines such as the UN Guidelines on the Role of Prosecutors,[16] and the International Protocol on the Documentation of Investigation of Sexual Violence in Conflict.[17]

One aspect of integrity is retaining a focus on core competencies. The requirement of doing the basics properly includes: simply following the evidence and interviewing witnesses in a structured way; collecting physical and documentary evidence in a manner that best ensures its admissibility; conducting gap analysis reviews to ensure awareness of the historical, religious, cultural and political environment; and being alive to the reality that different narratives may be given by witnesses not only

---

[13] *Ibid.*, para. 6.

[14] *Ibid.*

[15] *Ibid.*, para. 2.

[16] UN Guidelines on the Role of Prosecutors, Adopted by the Eighth United Nations Congress on the Prevention of Crime and the Treatment of Offenders, Havana, Cuba, 27 August to 7 September 1990 (https://www.legal-tools.org/doc/15b063/).

[17] Sara Ferro Ribeiro and Danae van der Straten Ponthiz, *International Protocol on the Documentation and Investigation of Sexual Violence in Conflict*, on behalf of the Foreign and Commonwealth Office, second edition, London, 2017.

from the vagaries of witness recollection and perspective, but sometimes may also be influenced by societal and community context. Awareness of all these factors – and a determination to 'get to the truth' based upon solid evidence and a constant reassessment of what is collected – is a prerequisite to the integrity of any investigation.

Beyond the establishment of a broad normative basis for the integrity framework of the Team, resolution 2379 (2017) also puts in place a transparency measure with respect to the work of the Team by requesting the Special Adviser to complete reports on the activities of the Team 90 days after commencing work, and thereafter every 180 days, and to present these reports to the Security Council. While such a reporting mechanism is well aligned with the standard practice of the Council concerning entities established pursuant to its legislative powers, these reports and associated briefings provide an important opportunity to explain the broad strategic approach to be adopted by the Team in the conduct of its work, and the basis for decisions relative to the allocation of investigative focus and resources. To date, these reports have, *inter alia*, served to outline the core strategic principles governing its work,[18] the three initial investigative priorities of its Field Investigation Units,[19] the addition of further dedicated investigative capacity in order to address crimes committed by ISIL against Christian, Kaka'i, Shabak, Sunni and Turkmen communities;[20] and the adaptation of its strategic approach in the third reporting period to allow the Team

---

[18] First report of the Special Adviser and Head of the United Nations Investigative Team to Promote Accountability for Crimes Committed by Da'esh/Islamic State in Iraq and the Levant, UN Doc. S/2018/1031, 15 November 2018, paras. 19–27 (https://www.legal-tools.org/doc/7bq4w0/).

[19] Second report of the Special Adviser and Head of the United Nations Investigative Team to Promote Accountability for Crimes Committed by Da'esh/Islamic State in Iraq and the Levant, UN Doc. S/2019/407, 17 May 2019, para. 13 ('Second report of the Special Adviser') (https://www.legal-tools.org/doc/siofyo/). These three initial investigative priorities are: (a) Attacks committed by ISIL against the Yazidi community in the Sinjar district in August 2014; (b) Crimes committed by ISIL in Mosul between 2014 and 2016, including the execution of religious minorities, crimes involving sexual and gender-based violence, and crimes against children; (c) The mass killing of unarmed Iraqi air force cadets from Tikrit Air Academy in June 2014.

[20] Third report of the Special Adviser and Head of the United Nations Investigative Team to Promote Accountability for Crimes Committed by Da'esh/Islamic State in Iraq and the Levant, UN Doc. S/2019/878, 13 November 2019, para. 10 (https://www.legal-tools.org/doc/b5y1rx/).

to respond rapidly to opportunities to support ongoing domestic proceedings through targeted shorter-term investigative and analytical work.[21]

Through these reports, the Team has sought to be as open and transparent as possible about its strategic approach, priorities and use of resources, while maintaining appropriate levels of confidentiality and protecting the ongoing integrity of the investigative process. This approach to reporting is not merely a mechanism for informing Member States and the public as to the Team's progress, but also provides an accountability tool, through which the effectiveness of its work can be assessed, albeit in broad terms, by the Security Council, relevant stakeholders (including impacted communities, non-governmental organizations and the public). Moreover, the preparation and finalization of such reports represent a relevant opportunity for self-reflection and critical evaluation of the effectiveness of the working methods and have, in the case of all reports produced to date, led to adaptations to our strategic approach.

In taking such an approach to its reporting requirement, the Team considers itself as fulfilling a broader duty, in line with 'the highest possible standards' not only to investigate, record and analyse, but also to inform and to demonstrate transparency in its activities, thereby enhancing the legitimacy and integrity of its work. Indeed, in light of limitations including United Nations documentation word limits, the existing reporting requirement does not provide a sufficiently broad platform from which this duty of transparency can be discharged. Looking forward, the Team is seeking to develop additional mechanisms through which a more comprehensive, and detailed approach can be taken with respect to the communication of its strategic approach and overarching progress in the delivery of its mandate. The recent establishment of the Team's web site[22] is a further resource in this regard, while social media platforms such as Facebook[23] and Twitter,[24] widely used in Iraq and the diaspora, are already being leveraged by the Team as a means of keeping stakeholders apprised of its activities. As a further step in support of the principle of transparency, the Team is also presently assessing its full range of standard operating procedures with a view to making them publicly available. In doing so the Team also hopes to

---

[21] *Ibid.*, para. 6.

[22] See https://www.unitad.un.org/

[23] See "UNITAD IRAQ", Facebook (available on its web site).

[24] See "UNITAD", Twitter (available on its web site).

support other national and international accountability actors in improving policies and practice in areas including witness protection, evidence-collection and psycho-social support. These endeavours are carried out while retaining appropriate levels of confidentiality given the often highly sensitive nature of the criminal investigations being undertaken by the Team.

20.2.2.2. Integrity as Addressed in the Terms of Reference Regarding the Operation of UNITAD in Iraq

The Terms of Reference, the key source of guidance regarding the implementation of the 'highest possible standards' to be followed by the Team, include more detailed provisions addressing considerations of integrity, which have, in turn, been expanded upon during the operationalization of its work as more tailored integrity policies.

As reflected above, the Terms of Reference address the issue of integrity directly within the context of sections addressing the structure and composition of the Team. Commencing with leadership, paragraph 11 of the Terms of Reference provides that the Special Adviser and Head of the Team "shall be a person of high moral character and integrity" and "shall have a proven record of independence and impartiality and be committed to upholding justice, accountability and human rights and ensuring gender equality".[25] As addressed further in Section 20.3.1. below, a detailed set of provisions are provided with respect to the staffing of the Team, emphasizing the need for its members to be "impartial and experienced professionals" and to benefit from expertise in a range of areas including international criminal law, human rights law, Iraqi criminal law and procedure, sexual and gender-based crimes, and the rights of women and children.

Building on existing obligations of all United Nations staff members, as reflected upon further below, paragraph 18 of the Terms of Reference underlines that the Special Adviser and all members of the Team shall "exercise their mandate and discharge their functions in full independence and with the utmost impartiality and shall not seek or accept instructions in regard to the performance of their functions from any government or any external source".[26] Furthermore, all staff members "shall maintain the highest

---

[25] See Terms of reference, para. 11, see above note 6.

[26] *Ibid.*, para. 18.

standards of efficiency, competence and integrity in the discharge of their functions".[27]

Addressing the core evidence-collection activities of the Team, the Terms of Reference provide a more detailed framework with respect to the standards and key principles to be applied, while mirroring its simultaneously deontological and consequentialist approach. The Team shall assess the evidence and materials in its possession, based on their "reliability and probative value"[28] and will ensure its preservation and storage "in accordance with international criminal law standards and taking into account Iraqi criminal and procedure laws, in order to ensure their broadest possible usability and admissibility in fair and independent criminal proceedings, consistent with applicable international law".[29]

Addressing the issue of integrity in the context of the Team's work with victims, paragraph 21 of the Terms of Reference requires that appropriate measures be taken to respect and ensure respect for the "privacy, interests and personal circumstances of victims, in the light of their age, sex, sexual orientation, gender and health, and taking into account the nature of the crime, in particular where it involves sexual violence, gender violence or violence against children".[30] Furthermore, the Team is required to adopt procedures and methods of work for the protection of victims and witnesses to ensure that they "and any other persons who cooperate with the Investigative Team can do so in safety and security".[31] In line with this approach, the Team is required to seek to obtain the informed consent of all witnesses and other sources prior to sharing evidence with domestic authorities.[32]

The imperative of engaging with victims and witnesses in line with the principles of integrity and dignity is further reflected in the section of the Terms of Reference addressing co-operation between the Team and the Government of Iraq. \It provides in paragraph 44(f) that the Government will ensure effective co-ordination with respect to the protection of "all those who come into contact with the Investigative Team, and an undertaking that no such person shall, as a result of such contact, suffer harassment,

---

[27] *Ibid.*

[28] *Ibid.*, para. 6.

[29] *Ibid.*, paras. 7, 19.

[30] *Ibid.*, para. 21.

[31] *Ibid.*, para. 22.

[32] *Ibid.*, para. 20.

threats, acts of intimidation, ill-treatment or reprisals". As reflected further in Section 20.3.2 below, the implementation of integrity measures concerning victims and witnesses has been an early priority in the establishment of the integrity framework of the Team.

20.2.2.3. The Broader UN Integrity Framework

As a United Nations Secretariat entity, the Team is also embedded in the established governance framework of the Organization, including relevant integrity policies, procedures and practices applicable to its over 43,000 staff members. As noted above, this point is emphasized in both Security Council resolution 2379 (2017) and the Terms of Reference of the Team which provide, collectively, that its procedures of work must be consistent with, *inter alia*, the Charter of the UN and UN policies and best practice.

As with all Secretariat entities, the ultimate starting point for the integrity framework of the Team is the Charter itself and in particular Chapter XV regarding the functioning of the Secretariat. Article 100 of the Charter emphasizes the exclusively international and independent functions exercised by staff members, prohibiting them from seeking or receiving instructions "from any government or from any other authority external to the Organization".[33] Staff members must also "refrain from any action which might reflect on their position as international officials responsible only to the Organization".[34] Furthermore, upon joining the Organization, Member States undertake, pursuant to paragraph 2 of Article 100, to respect the "exclusively international character of the responsibilities of United Nations staff and not to seek to influence them in the discharge of their responsibilities".[35] It is underlined that all staff shall be appointed by the Secretary-General and that in making such appointments paramount consideration will be given to the necessity of securing the "highest standards of efficiency, competence, and integrity".[36]

The United Nations Staff Regulations and Rules, as approved by the General Assembly pursuant to Article 101 of the Charter,[37] as well as the

---

[33] UN Charter, see above note 4.
[34] *Ibid.*
[35] *Ibid.*
[36] *Ibid.*
[37] A/RES/72/254, see above note 5.

United Nations Financial Regulations and Rules,[38] provide further detailed elements of the Organizational integrity matrix, applicable to all Secretariat staff members including those of UNITAD.[39]

Staff Regulation 1.1(d) reiterates the requirement of Article 100 of the Charter by providing that the Secretary-General shall seek to ensure that the paramount consideration in the determination of the conditions of service shall be the necessity of securing staff of the highest standards of efficiency, competence and integrity, with due regard paid to the importance of recruiting staff on as wide a geographical basis as possible. The Staff Regulations further set out several "core values" and "general rights and obligations" of staff members and addresses in further detail what the concept of integrity means within the Organizations normative framework. Staff Regulation 1.2 (b) in particular provides that the concept of integrity "includes, but is not limited to, probity, impartiality, fairness, honesty and truthfulness in all matters affecting their work and status".

Building on these conceptual underpinnings, Staff Regulations 1.2(c) and (g) elaborate some of the basic obligations placed on staff members, as well as the protections afforded to them, in the implementation of this concept of integrity, providing that:

> (b) Staff members have the duty to report any breach of the Organization's regulations and rules to the officials whose responsibility it is to take appropriate action and to cooperate with duly authorized audits and investigations. Staff members shall not be retaliated against for complying with these duties;

> (g) Staff members shall not use their office or knowledge gained from their official functions for private gain, financial or otherwise, or for the private gain of any third party, including family, friends and those they favor. Nor shall staff members use their office for personal reasons to prejudice the positions of those they do not favor.

---

[38] See UN General Assembly, Resolution adopted by the General Assembly on 24 December 2012, UN Doc. A/RES/67/246, 24 December 2012 (https://www.legal-tools.org/doc/l0arge/) and Secretary General's bulletin 2013/4, Financial Rules and Regulations of the United Nations, UN Doc. ST/SGB/2013/4, 1 July 2013 (https://www.legal-tools.org/doc/zos34u/).

[39] See also the Secretary-General's Bulletin, Status, basic rights and duties of United Nations Staff Members, UN Doc. ST/SGB/2016/9, 21 July 2016 (https://www.legal-tools.org/doc/mjxin2/). This contains a commentary by the Secretary-General to assist staff members in better understanding the obligations applicable to staff conduct.

Further developing these obligations and protections regarding the reporting of acts of corruption and other integrity breaches, the Secretary-General's Bulletin on Protection against Retaliation[40] provides detailed guidance for the implementation of the requirement on all staff members to report observed misconduct including suspected fraud, waste, abuse and corruption, as well as the procedural protections available to those that do come forward. The introduction of strengthened measures in this area represented a key focus of the reform agenda of Secretary-General António Guterres. It includes introducing the ability for the UN Ethics Office and Office of Internal Oversight Services to take preventive action where a risk of retaliation has been identified, the extension of protection from retaliation beyond staff members to contractors, and greater transparency as to measures taken against members found to have retaliated against them.

In addition to benefiting from the overarching United Nations ethics and integrity policy framework, UNITAD and other criminal justice entities within the UN Secretariat are also embedded into the organizational and institutional architecture in this field. Broadly, these can be divided into two strands: (i) efforts to promote an organizational culture informed by ethics and integrity, with a focus on prevention measures such as conflicts of interest detection and remediation, financial disclosure systems, and protection from retaliation policies led primarily by the United Nations Ethics Office; and (ii) measures related to the detection and investigation of alleged acts of misconduct, inclusive of integrity breaches, led by the Office of Internal Oversight Services. The work of the Ethics Office is of particular relevance and support during the start-up stages of an entity within the Organization, with the Office able to provide valuable advice with respect to the establishment of ethics functions and the application of preventive policies within the specific context of a new entity. A confidential one-to-one ethics briefing for all incoming Assistant-Secretary-Generals is a particularly welcome initiative, ensuring that the vision of the Secretary-General with respect to ethics and integrity framework can be clearly articulated by mission leadership and cascaded down to incoming staff members of the new entity. The voluntary publication of financial disclosures made by senior UN officials is a further important measure in instilling confidence with respect to the integrity of senior management. This initia-

---

[40] Secretary General's Bulletin, Protection against retaliation for reporting misconduct and for co-operating with duly authorized audits or investigations, UN Doc. ST/SGB/2017/2, 20 January 2017 (https://www.legal-tools.org/doc/bhpac4/).

tive, in which the first author participates, is particularly effective in demonstrating the absence of conflicts of interest amongst mandate-holders.

The cross-organization training and awareness-raising activities led by the Ethics Office, such as the Leadership Dialogue undertaken in 2020 on the issue of conflicts of interest, have allowed members of the Team to develop a better understanding of how to engage with the broader ethical infrastructure of the United Nations. These initiatives, in which all staff members of the Team must participate, also provide a further example of how the effective implementation of an ethics framework begins with the actions and 'tone from the top' from senior management.[41]

The presence of a pre-existing policy and institutional integrity framework into which a new entity such as UNITAD can be embedded is essential in providing a mature and clear architecture for ethical conduct by all staff members from the outset of its work. The policies, practices and institutional structures highlighted above have served as an important basis for action regarding integrity matters in areas including conflicts of interest, information-management and protection from retaliation.

However, given the breadth of activities undertaken by United Nations entities, cross-organization policies cannot comprehensively address the specific integrity challenges faced by staff members in the exercise of their particular functions. This is particularly the case for members of accountability mechanisms such as UNITAD,[42] in which ethical and integrity challenges associated with the exercise of investigative functions require tailored solutions based on best practices developed in prior judicial and investigative mechanisms.

In recognition of this, emphasis has been placed in the early stages of operation of UNITAD on the development and implementation of specialized measures addressing some of the specific integrity challenges faced in the conduct of its investigative work.

---

[41] "United Nations Leadership Dialogue", *UN Ethics Office* web site (available on UN's web site).

[42] Similar considerations will apply for recently-established entities such as the International, Impartial and Independent Mechanism ('IIIM') to assist in the Investigation and Prosecution of Persons for the Most Serious Crimes Under International Law committed in the Syrian Arab Republic since March 2011 and the Independent Investigative Mechanism for Myanmar ('IIMM').

20.3. The Development and Implementation of Integrity Policies in the Operationalization of an International Criminal Justice Mechanism

> Courage is the most important attribute of a lawyer. It is more important than competence and vision. It can never be delimited, dated or outworn and it should pervade the heart, the halls of justice and the Chambers of the mind.[43]

Robert F. Kennedy's famous quote sears itself on the memory in a way that great oratory so often does. Whilst the quote unfairly diminishes or relegates the importance of competence (and all that entails) as a bedrock attribute for all lawyers, it elegantly casts light upon a truth. Be that as it may, courage is certainly the bedfellow of integrity. It contains within that concept a determination to ensure that right is done, regardless of external considerations or pressures on the investigator, counsel or institution concerned. It calls to mind the dictum *fiat justitia ruat caelum*: "let justice be done though the heavens fall".

This is important in any accountability mechanism which will inexorably traverse the myriad fault lines between national, regional and international politics, different interests, competing histories and dearly held and oft-repeated narratives. Through all that, cases must be built not on the popularity of a submission or the acclaim with which a position is advocated, but on solid evidence. As reflected further in this section, there can be no hierarchy of victims in the work conducted by such mechanisms.

This objective process of investigation certainly requires courage. More specifically, the courage to follow evidence and principle with unwavering commitment. An appreciation of the various aspects of integrity and how these are incorporated into tailored effective procedures and methodologies specific to the operational imperatives and investigative priorities of the relevant entity is essential to such an approach. Furthermore, an approach based on courage, requires that individuals are supported in the implementation of these specialized frameworks to ensure that there is no integrity gap across the Team. If integrity is lacking in one area, the consequences may be monumental. This is brought into the starkest of relief when evidence collected is presented in criminal trials requiring proof be-

---

[43] Robert F. Kennedy, University of San Francisco School of Law, 29 September 1962.

yond reasonable doubt, and when the duties and responsibilities of various actors are so frequently challenged.[44]

In constructing its own specialized integrity framework, the Investigative Team has sought to accommodate the legitimate demands of States, non-governmental organizations, but most importantly those of survivors and impacted communities, by placing emphasis on operationalizing its mandate while also dedicating resources to ensuring an adequate integrity framework is developed to guide initial activities. UNITAD, as all recently-established international criminal justice entities, has been required to demonstrate its ability to deliver on its mandate and satisfy the needs of stakeholders from the outset of its work. The commencement of investigative activities and the establishment of core integrity policy frameworks are, therefore, processes that must be carried out in parallel.

It should be recognized that this simultaneous demand for the establishment of specialized deontological structures and the delivery of core functions is not a challenge particular to UNITAD or even specific to the current political climate.[45] These simultaneous challenges have been faced by other international mechanisms including the ICTY, the ICTR, and indeed the ICC where the Office of the Prosecutor was required to develop the regulations and code of conduct governing its work while at the same time taking forward its first investigations and prosecutions. The degree to which this was achieved is a matter that may be debated. There have certainly been challenges. This is starkly reflected by the fact that whilst the Rome Statute came into force in 2002, no such regulations or code were in place by the time the Prosecutor submitted the *Lubanga* Case to the Trial Chamber in June 2008. With respect to the code of conduct, this remained the case for a further five years until the *Defence* sought an order in *Muthaura* that the ICC Code of Conduct apply to the Prosecution given the absence of a dedicated code being promulgated by the Prosecutor in the preceding 11 years.[46]

---

[44] For example, evidence may be excluded if obtained in a manner contrary to that provided for international human rights law, and cases may be unnecessarily 'politicised' because of the use of intermediaries or witnesses from only one side of the political divide.

[45] Although it is perhaps worth recalling that unlike IIIM and IIMM, UNITAD was not preceded with a commission of Experts or Inquiry, the materials of which would be turned over to the mechanism when established.

[46] See ICC, *The Prosecutor v. Francis Kirimi Muthaura and Uhuru Muigai Kenyatta*, Trial Chamber, Joint Defence Application for an Order to the Prosecutor for the provision of a list containing the bar memberships and good standing status of Prosecution trial lawyers ex-

We explore below three aspects of the specific integrity challenges and solutions that the Investigative Team has addressed during this initial period of our work, specifically that of personal integrity, integrity in engagement with survivors and impacted communities, and institutional integrity and independence.

20.3.1. Building a Team Aligned with Principles of Integrity and Independence

The interconnected and complementary nature of the two core pillars of the Investigative Team's mandate, and the central importance of ensuring the integrity of the Team's work in the delivery of its mandate, is of particular prominence in the framework addressing the composition and activities of its staff members.

Pursuant to both paragraph 5 of resolution 2379 (2017) and paragraph 14 of the Terms of Reference, Iraqi investigative judges, and other criminal experts, including experienced members of the prosecution services, must be appointed to the Team, working "on an equal footing alongside international experts". Building on this principle of equality and balance between the national and international components within the Team, the Terms of Reference further provide that the appointment of national criminal experts, while ultimately made by the Special Adviser, must be carried out in consultation with the Government of Iraq. This represents an attempt by the Council to balance the need to integrate the principle of adaptation to national contexts and respect for the sovereignty of Iraq into the traditional framework of international accountability mechanisms.

In this context, implementing a common integrity culture and normative framework in which all members of the Team consider themselves personally invested is central to our ability to function effectively as a cohesive unit. As referenced above, this integration of collective principles of integrity and impartiality starts with leadership of the Team, with paragraph 11 of the Terms of Reference providing that the Team shall be headed by a

---

pected to make submissions at trial and Request that the Trial Chamber promulgate a protocol of professional ethics applicable to Prosecution lawyers, 17 January 2013, ICC-01/09-02/11 (https://www.legal-tools.org/doc/c9e14f/); and Decision on the Defence application concerning professional ethics applicable to prosecution lawyers, which confirmed the code would apply to the OTP in the interim prior to the promulgation of a code by the OTP, 31 May 2013, ICC-01/09-02/11 (https://www.legal-tools.org/doc/d27ea0/).

Special Adviser of high moral character and integrity and possessing the highest level of professional competence.

Since the first author's appointment in August 2018, he has sought to ensure that these principles and qualities are reflected in his leadership but, most importantly, also transmitted down through all teams and units. In developing our staffing structure, which now totals around 150 staff members based in Iraq, our objective has been to create a symbiotic relationship of mutual learning between national and international elements, thereby establishing a common identity and commitment to delivery of accountability with respect to ISIL crimes. By forging a common sense of purpose across all components of the Team, we provide a stable basis upon which the principles of integrity, impartiality and independence can be integrated into all aspects of our work.

20.3.1.1. Empowering National Expertise Ensuring Gender Balance Within the Team

This commitment to the development of a cohesive and balanced approach to our work is reflected in the staffing structure adopted at the outset of the development of the Team in 2018, with national experts integrated into all key substantive sections, including the Field Investigation Units and Analysis and Evidence Unit, as well as specialist entities, such as the Sexual and Gender-Based Violence and Children's Unit, Forensic Sciences Unit and Witness Protection and Support Unit. This priority given to ensuring an effective national component across all key parts of the Team has further been reflected in our development of specialized, supplementary projects funded through extrabudgetary funds provided by Member States. Specifically, through these supplementary operational projects, additional specialized units are being established in areas including digitization of evidentiary material, financial crimes and protection of cultural heritage, all of which incorporate at least one-third of national expert staffing.

In addition to ensuring the national component of the Team is sufficiently prioritized and resourced, attention has been paid to providing a specialized function within the Team allowing national experts to effectively guide and support the engagement of the Team with national authorities. To this end, a dedicated National Engagement and Support Unit has been established, headed by the most senior Iraqi national expert within the Team. The creation of a dedicated entity to ensure appropriate and informed strategic advice is provided to the Special Adviser, and to facilitate effective co-operation and collaboration with the Government of Iraq, is integral to the satisfaction of a key pillar of the mandate of the Team, while also reflecting the unique and crucial value provided by its national component in the delivery of operational priorities.

Beyond the important balance sought between national and international staff members, a broader geographic and gender balance within the Team has also served as an important element in developing an environment conducive to both the effective delivery of the mandate of the Team and the development of a culture of integrity and respect. To this end, priority was given in our recruitment strategy to ensuring qualified female candidates, as well as those from underrepresented regions, were actively identified and encouraged as part of our work in building the initial Team. This has been a successful approach, with women currently accounting for 48 per cent of substantive and support staff, and with all regional groups of the United Nations currently represented in our staffing structure. More than half of the senior management positions are held by female staff members.[47] The principal legal systems of the world are also represented within the team.

20.3.1.2. Forging a Common Identity and Integrity Framework Across International and National Components

Effective adherence to the principles of integrity and impartiality first requires the construction of a common identity and strategic vision, ensuring that both national and international components view themselves as delivering as one in pursuit of a clearly identified common objective. The establishment and communication of clear strategic investigative priorities early on in the Team's work, based on engagement with national authorities, survivors, local communities and other national entities, has been key in this regard, with dedicated Field Investigation Units tasked with pursuing individual priorities. In addition, the establishment of structured and regular fora in which Team members are able to share progress in the work of individual units ensures that action remains co-ordinated and strategic objectives can be adjusted based on experience gained through our field-based investigative activities.

Building on the establishment of this initial collective strategic vision, the Team has constructed its integrity framework by harnessing relevant

---

[47] Second report of the Special Adviser, para. 16, see above note 19

United Nations policies, practices and procedures while also developing specialized measures addressing the specific integrity challenges faced by the Team in the implementation of its mandate. Priority has been placed on ensuring a common understanding of the standards of conduct applicable to all Team members.

As referenced above, our starting point is the UN Charter,[48] which, through its Articles 100 and 101, addresses the issue of integrity and confidentiality in broad terms. These principles are further reflected in the oath of office signed by all Secretariat staff members upon joining the Organization under which staff members declare and promise to exercise in all loyalty, discretion and conscience, the functions entrusted to them as international civil servants.

In light of the often-sensitive nature of the evidentiary material collected by the Team, as well as the requirements under the Terms of Reference that our work be conducted to the highest possible standards to ensure the broadest possible use before national courts, the issue of confidentiality and information-management represents a particularly important issue to be addressed as part of our integrity framework. Reflecting this imperative, the Team has sought to develop specialized solutions that build on the existing United Nations framework. Specifically, in line with section 5.3 of the Secretary-General's Bulletin entitled "Information sensitivity, classification and handling",[49] stricter controls beyond those required at an organizational level have been developed by UNITAD.

As part of the efforts of the Team to tailor confidentiality and information-handling policy to the specific demands of its mandate and composition, a Statement of Principles on Confidentiality and Information-Management was developed at an early stage in our work, which must be signed by all staff members as part of their onboarding process. Designed as an initial step in the adaption of existing Secretariat-wide requirements to the specific information-security challenges of UNITAD, the Statement of Principles emphasizes that, as part of the Investigative Team, staff members must ensure, *inter alia*, that: (i) the discharge of their functions with the Team are exercised with the utmost discretion; (ii) no information is communicated to external entities except as authorized by the Head of the

---

[48]   UN Charter, see above note 4.

[49]   Secretary-General's Bulletin, Information sensitivity, classification and handling, UN Doc. ST/SGB/2007/6, 12 February 2007 (https://www.legal-tools.org/doc/3bfra2/).

Investigative Team; (iii) all information collected by the Team is registered in the UNITAD information-management system and classified in line with organizational information-handling policies; and, (iv) any electronic transfer of information within the Team is conducted only through the use of protected and secure means of communication.

Through the establishment of a common and tailored confidentiality policy, the Investigative Team has sought to ensure a collective understanding of staff members obligations and engender a joint commitment to a culture of implementation of the highest standards of integrity in our work. This approach, harnessing organizational frameworks while also developing tailored guidance and policies applicable to the specific demands and integrity challenges faced by the Team, has been applied to a variety of areas of our work.

20.3.2. Integrity in Engagement with Survivors, Witnesses and Impacted Communities

The relevance and fundamental importance of the concept of integrity in the working modalities of international investigative and judicial mechanisms is clearly shown when considering their engagement with witnesses and survivors of the crimes in relation to which accountability is sought. In asking those that have suffered from violence, displacement and sexual and gender-based crimes to reengage with their memories of such events, it is essential that effective and tailored mechanisms are put in place to ensure that the integrity of investigative practices and procedures are upheld and the dignity of such witnesses and survivors is prioritized above all else.

The need to integrate integrity measures into witness and survivor engagement has been particularly pronounced in the work of UNITAD, as part of which investigators, legal officers and other team members are required to work with some of the most vulnerable victims of ISIL crimes, including those who have survived mass killings, sexual slavery and, in some cases, complete destruction of their communities. In response to this imperative, we have sought to develop both an institutional and policy-based response that prioritizes the delivery of specialized, targeted support to those with which we engage, as well as clear guidance for staff members to ensure a consistent and principled approach aligned with international criminal law standards.

20.3.2.1. Integrity in Investigative Prioritization with Respect to Impacted Communities: No Hierarchy of Victims

The victims of ISIL come from diverse communities across Iraq. No community, religion, gender or ethnic group was spared the cruelty and venality of the Un-Islamic vision propagated by this terrorist organization. While international attention has at times been focused on horrendous crimes against some particular communities – other heinous acts against other religious or ethnic groups have received less attention. Even though there were various reasons for this, the imperative to ensure the actual and perceived integrity of its investigations, and the implementation of its mandate more broadly, required that UNITAD emphasized from the very outset of its work that there was "no hierarchy of victim" with respect to the focus of investigative activities.

Whilst resources would be deployed by UNITAD in light of the scale or extent of crimes committed by ISIL in specific locations, and in relation to the most serious crimes committed against particular communities, a concerted attempt was made to ensure that all victim groups felt engaged and valued from the beginning of the work of the Team in Iraq. This involved an assurance that crimes committed by ISIL against all groups would be documented and recorded and cases built based upon credible evidence. This approach is critical in any context. We have repeatedly seen that the view that 'some lives matter more than others' is one that all too easily takes root and festers in a manner that not only is inimical to justice but which – too often – contains the seeds to future conflict and misery.

By 2020, UNITAD was able to fulfil its pledge that investigations were ongoing in relation to the principal groups that had been targets of ISIL crimes. Linked to this was a requirement not to label crimes prematurely. Certain reports had labelled crimes under a particular category under international criminal law; however, UNITAD explained to survivor groups and affected communities that any such labelling and categorization would only be based upon its own independent investigations. The candour in explaining this was well understood by the affected communities. Indeed, it may have been one of the measures that helped build their trust and confidence in the work of UNITAD during the early months of its activities.

As a general point, there can be no integrity in engaging with impacted communities without honesty. It is imperative that a team is cognizant of what international criminal justice *can* do and, at the same time, be willing to explain to these communities frankly what it *cannot* do. It must be borne in mind that these impacted communities have very often survived devastating events. Indeed, they may still be reliving these experiences due to psychological or physical injuries, or the reality of the predicament in refugee camps or as displaced communities. Very often, some actors, either NGOs, national authorities or agencies, may present justice to them as transformational. Whilst it can be in some ways, it is trite that it does not bring the dead back to life or restore a family that has endured horrors that should never have been imagined, never mind carried out. In these circumstances, a candid discussion about the limitations of 'justice', and the difficulties in achieving it, can be kinder and more credible. In fact, when this is combined with an explanation of the importance of preserving a record, collecting evidence, and endeavouring to hold criminals to account in fair trials, impacted communities can be galvanized in a way that is indispensable to an investigation. Even if momentarily disappointed, or sobered by certain realities, they will see the investigative team as honest and sincere. This form of personal and collective integrity may have a significant impact on how a team is perceived and received by an affected community given the importance of managing expectations.

20.3.2.2. Institutional Responses to the Implementation of Witness Protection Policies Aligned with Principles of Integrity

In developing an integrity-based framework concerning the engagement with survivors and witnesses, it may be assumed that the core policies and practices of the relevant mechanism or entity would represent the starting-point. However, in no other area of our work are the human resources, the institutional expertise of an entity more important. Priority must, therefore, above all, be given to securing and effectively structuring the institutional architecture of the Team focused on ensuring the effective delivery of an approach prioritizing the dignity of survivors and witnesses and the provision of support and protection to reduce to an absolute minimum the risk of re-traumatization.

In developing this institutional framework, UNITAD has prioritized the establishment of two key pillars: (i) a dedicated Witness Protection and Support Unit ('WPSU'), with responsibility for ensuring that the Team engages with all survivors and victims in a manner aligned with international standards; and (ii) a specialized Gender Crimes and Crimes against Children Unit ('GCCU') charged with ensuring that the work of the Investigative Team with respect to such crimes is conducted in a manner that deliv-

ers a coherent approach to investigative activities and addresses the specific
cultural, psychological and medical considerations inherent in the engagement of the Team with the most vulnerable of survivors.

In developing the WPSU, priority has been given in particular to ensuring the Team is able to address the psychological needs of victims and
witnesses. Clinical psychologists have formed an integral part of the initial
staffing of this Unit and have been deployed to both assist in the development of the initial policy and normative integrity framework of the Team as
well as support and guide the early operational investigative activities of
the Field Investigation Units.

Specifically, these specialists have worked to develop a dedicated reception facility within UNITAD premises that provides an emotionally safe
and secure environment in which witnesses and survivors can be received
by members of the Team. This has included the incorporation of elements
within the physical infrastructure of UNITAD facilities addressing cultural
sensitivities, gender considerations and the specific needs of children. Both
the WPSU and the GCCU also play a central role in the conduct of investi-
gation-specific threat and risk assessments to identify the level of vulnerability of witnesses and survivors, and identify any specific protection
measures or approaches that are required to be implemented prior to the
witnesses being interviewed or further engaged with by investigators.

With respect to the operational work of the Team, the clinical psychologists play a crucial role in providing initial briefings and sensitization
sessions with witnesses to ensure they fully understand the focus and objectives of the Team's work and how their testimony contributes to its efforts in supporting national accountability processes. Where deemed necessary, psychologists may assist in the conduct of the investigative interview
to ensure the wellbeing of the witness is kept in constant view. Following
the conclusion of interviews, these experts conduct a debrief with the witness to ensure that they feel comfortable about the interview procedure and
also carry out an assessment to identify whether a referral of the individual
to a psychosocial or mental/medical health service-provider would be necessary for the provision of further services. Efforts are presently being
made to establish a psycho-social and mental health service provider network for this purpose, with two such referral organisations having been
secured at the time of writing.

This specialized expertise within the UNITAD staffing structure has
also been supplemented through co-operation and partnerships with exter-

nal entities such as with the Human Rights in Trauma Mental Health Program at Stanford University who have provided support with respect to the development of standard operating procedures and practices for engagement with vulnerable witnesses and a forthcoming field guide on trauma-informed approaches to investigative activities. Such collaboration reflects a broader commitment by the Team to leverage the work and expertise of entities both within the UN system and externally, so as to develop the strongest possible standards of investigative practices.

Drawing on the expertise of their specialized staffing structure, as well as its external partnerships, the leadership of the WPSU and the GCCU have, in turn, led the development of the tailored integrity framework of the Team as relevant to the interaction of its members with witnesses, victims and survivors. The rapid development and operationalization of this framework have been crucial in engendering the trust of impacted communities in Iraq which has also allowed those most vulnerable individuals to come forward with their accounts and enhance their effective participation in the accountability process.

20.3.2.3. Specialized Integrity Policies and Practices with Respect to Survivors and Witnesses

Drawing on the specialized institutional and staffing architecture of the Team regarding witness and survivor engagement, the Team has put in place a tailored policy framework that seeks to ensure all investigative work is adapted to address the specific needs of ISIL victims and witnesses. The central policy in this regard is the Witness Protection Strategy, developed by the WPSU and the GCCU at the outset of the Team's work, which builds upon previous models adopted at the ICTY, the ICTR, Special Court for Sierra Leone, the ICC and the Special Tribunal for Lebanon, in particular concerning the conduct of threat assessments and the consequent implementation of specialized protection procedures with respect to individual witnesses.

The guiding operating principle of the Team under this strategic approach is to limit the potential exposure of witnesses to identified threats, by ensuring that interviews are conducted according to a systematic and deliberate planning process and on the basis of an identified investigative need. However, the strategy does not aim to ensure only physical safety and confidentiality but takes into account the needs of witnesses in a holistic manner including psychological wellbeing, dignity, privacy, respect, appropriate assistance, sensitivity to special needs, consent and right to information. Staff members are further guided as to how key international standards and relevant parts of the domestic legal framework are to be incorporated into their operational investigative activities, in particular, the collection of testimonial evidence through the conduct of interviews.

The strategy details four levels of protection to be provided to potential witnesses to ensure the confidentiality of witnesses' interaction with the Investigative Team, protection of their security, physical and psychological well-being, privacy and dignity, and which are proportionate to the assessed risks. First, good practice guidelines are developed by the Unit, with expert input from its clinical psychologists, in relation to contact and interaction with witnesses. Emphasis is placed here on creating an operational awareness and a systematic approach, which aims to enhance the confidentiality of witnesses' interaction with the Investigative Team and sensitivity to their needs. As a second tier, and based on the initial investigation specific threat and risk assessment conducted by the WPSU, local operational measures have been developed in close co-ordination with competent national authorities. Here in particular, the National Operations Centre under the Office of the Prime Minister has provided invaluable support in the establishment of all operational procedures relevant to the investigative activities of the Team. At this level, specific attention has been paid to agreeing on a response mechanism to witness security emergencies, as well as the introduction of increased local protective measures at locations where witnesses reside, including internal displacement camps.

As a third element of our strategic approach, the Investigative Team has put in place an initial set of procedural protection measures aimed at limiting the disclosure of information which could lead to the identification of a protected witness, and support measures aimed at creating such conditions which will best facilitate the testimony of vulnerable witnesses to the fullest possible extent. Reflecting the need to develop this policy framework in parallel with the commencement of investigative activities, a provisional set of procedures has been put in place in this regard, which is being refined based on experience gained from the initial engagement with witnesses and is now presently being finalized into a set of formal standard operating procedures.

Finally, in co-operation with Iraqi authorities, steps are being taken to develop a specialized witness protection programme. The programme is aimed at limiting the disclosure of information which could lead to the identification of a protected witness, and support measures aimed at creating such conditions which will best facilitate the testimony of vulnerable witnesses to the fullest possible extent.

Based on this overarching strategic approach, a more detailed set of standard operating procedures and guidelines implementing this integrity framework is being put in place through the joint efforts of the WPSU and the GCCU. It includes the development of a good-practices guideline for investigators on the contact and interaction with witnesses, operational awareness, and a systematic approach in ensuring the confidentiality of witnesses' interaction with the Investigative Team and sensitivity to the specific needs of individual witnesses.

20.3.3. Institutional Integrity and Independence as an Operational Tool

The initial field-based activities of the Team, and in particular the early assistance we have provided with respect to the excavation of mass grave sites in northern Iraq, have shown how the ability to demonstrate our institutional independence, impartiality and integrity is crucial in providing a basis for effective co-operation with Iraqi authorities and other partners in Iraq. We have seen that the independent nature of our role and the imperative to work closely with Iraqi authorities in the implementation of our mandate, do not represent countervailing weights to be balanced but are in fact mutually supportive pillars at the foundation of our work.

Our ability to demonstrate the independent and impartial nature of the Team has been of particular importance in our initial engagement with ethnic minority communities following our arrival in Baghdad, in particular with respect to the excavation of mass grave sites in northern Iraq. Through dialogue with Yazidi community representatives and victims organizations in late 2018, a clear need was identified for the Team to assist in providing reassurance to the victims' families that the process of identification of bodies in mass grave sites and the analysis of forensic material collected through this process would be conducted both in line with international standards and with sensitivity to religious and cultural norms of that community. These communities emphasized the involvement of the Investigative Team as an impartial, independent actor as central to their confidence and support for the excavation process.

Our ability to serve as a neutral and impartial entity has also been crucial in allowing the Team to facilitate co-operation with both national authorities and the Kurdistan Regional Government in this field. In advance of excavation activities, the Investigative Team worked with the Mass Graves Directorate of the Martyrs Foundation of the Government of Iraq, the Medico-Legal Directorate of the Iraqi Ministry of Health and the Ministry of Martyrs and Anfal Affairs of the Kurdistan Regional Government to ensure relevant practices and procedures conformed to international standards. Similarly, UNITAD facilitated the signing of an agreement that allowed DNA samples held by the Kurdistan Regional Government to be included in a national database maintained by the Medico-Legal Directorate in Baghdad, allowing for a significantly increased chance of achieving DNA matches. Recognizing this, work has adopted a 'lead from behind' modality in which the substantive expertise and impartial role of the Investigative Team have been leveraged to increase standards or work and thereby strengthen the confidence of impacted communities in the excavation process.

Conceptually, a shift in approach was encouraged in order to align working methods with those used in criminal investigations, ensuring that mass grave sites were treated as formal crime scenes. Following the conduct of initial capacity assessments by the Team, targeted training sessions and in-depth technical consultations were conducted to enhance processes and practices for, *inter alia*, the gathering of ante-mortem and post-mortem information, evidence collection mechanisms, security arrangements for excavation sites and facilities for the storage of biological material. During the excavation process, guidance and assistance to national authorities were provided to ensure that key steps were carried out in line with international standards, including site coding, surface surveys, excavation activities, preservation of the crime scene, adherence to appropriate field protocols, the completion of evidence collection forms and the classification and packing of evidentiary material. To date, this has led to the completion of the excavation of 17 mass grave sites in Kojo village, sites of some of the most serious crimes committed by ISIL during the period of 2014 – 2015, as well as the commencement of work on a mass grave sites on the outskirts of Mosul of largely Sunni victims executed by ISIL and the "grave of the mothers" at Solagh Institute in Sinjar, with excavations commencing in 2020.

20.4. Conclusion: The Central Role of Integrity in the Delivery of Justice

> Integrity without knowledge is weak and useless, and knowledge without integrity is dangerous and dreadful.[50]

The development and implementation of integrity measures can often be viewed as an afterthought, an unwelcome distraction or, at worst, an impediment to the real, meaningful work of international criminal justice institutions or indeed any professional organization. However, upon commencement of activities of a newly-establishment entity such as UNITAD, as preparations for investigative work begin and a vision for the practical implementation of a mandate is put in place, the fallacy and short-sightedness of this view are exposed.

Far from representing an extraneous element to be managed, the principle of integrity represents the central pillar around which all action must be built. As has been shown in this chapter, the implementation of a comprehensive integrity framework is crucial in protecting the credibility and perceived utility of our work. Our approach to this issue cannot be piecemeal. A holistic, indivisible framework, addressing both individual and institutional integrity, and prioritizing the dignity of the most vulnerable victims with which we engage, must be prioritized. The implementation of such an approach requires concerted action and a serious, and visible commitment from entity leadership to its implementation from the very outset of our work.

For UNITAD, placing the implementation of integrity measures at the heart of our initial work has also served as a tool, a key to be used in unlocking one of the central dynamics within our mandate. By maintaining a focus on the core principle of integrity, we have been able to demonstrate that the dual-core imperatives, that of ensuring independence and seeking co-operation with domestic authorities, and that of demonstrating impartiality and pursuing national engagement, do not present a dichotomy. In fact, the opposite is true: when assessed through the prism of integrity, the mutually reinforcing nature of those imperatives becomes clear. This approach has now been demonstrated in concrete and tangible terms through the collection of accounts from victims, the excavation of gravesites and the production of initial analytical products that will ultimately allow

---

[50] Samuel Johnson, "Rasselas", 1759, Ch. 41.

Member States to hold those responsible for the crimes of ISIL to account, in line with the rule of law and due process.

As the Investigative Team has moved into the fully operational phase of its work, and as it begins to provide direct support for domestic accountability processes, its ability to address new challenges will depend on its capacity to continue to simultaneously leverage its unique position as an impartial and independent entity, and maintain the continued support of the people of Iraq. Our experience shows that adherence to the principles of integrity and impartiality will be central to our ability to effectively support the Government of Iraq in addition to effectively delivering on the promises made to victims and survivors that those responsible for inflicting crimes on their communities will be held accountable for their crimes.

The lessons learned from the initial stages of the work of UNITAD can be extrapolated and applied to the activities and approach of international criminal justice mechanisms more broadly. If we are to ensure the continued trust of Member States, impacted communities and the broader public in international criminal justice institutions as effective mechanisms for the delivery of criminal accountability, we must renew our commitment to placing the principle of integrity at the centre of our work and ensure a comprehensive approach is adopted with respect to its implementation. As confidence in the administration of justice wanes, and as the utility of the international rules-based system comes under pressure, a concerted focus on upholding the highest possible standards of integrity, efficiency and impartiality has never been more needed.

At a time when common standards and the idea of justice itself can often seem in peril, in an environment where it is sometimes fallaciously alleged that there is no truth – only competing facts – justice must be guarded like never before. Integrity must remain the sentry on guard.

21

––––––––

The Wider Policy Framework of Ethical Behaviour: Outspoken Observations from a True Friend of the International Criminal Court

Cyril Laucci[*]

21.1. Introduction

In this chapter, I will offer several observations on the relationship between the legal and policy frameworks of international institutions and integrity. Before that, however, I would like to compliment the International Nuremberg Principles Academy and the Centre for International Law Research and Policy ('CILRAP') for organizing the international conference 'Integrity in International Justice' in the Peace Palace in The Hague in December 2018, and for initiating the Integrity Project which has resulted in this comprehensive anthology. It actually takes courage to address such issues, which are usually taken for 'granted without saying'. It requires looking at integrity in international justice without fear or bias, comparing the way things are with the way they should be. This is indeed the actual support international justice needs: the frankness of true friends, instead of the flattery of courtesans. It requires going beyond the complacent fascination and deference for international justice institutions and their officials, remembering that these institutions are ultimately made up of women and men, with their own limits, needs and dilemmas, whatever the qualities of such individuals. It also requires looking deeper into the governance and policy framework of these organisations to find what, if anything, is going wrong, instead of entering superfluous judgments as to the alleged poor quality of their personnel and officials as the sole explanation for their failure to fulfil their mandate. The best civil servants and officials can do barely better than the worst ones if a proper policy framework governing their action is miss-

––––––––

[*] Dr. **Cyril Laucci** was Legal Advisor in the Registry of the International Criminal Court from 2009 to 2015. He is currently Lead Counsel for Mr. Ali Muhammad Ali Abd-Al-Rahman before the ICC, Director at The Legal Carpentry, and Project Manager on Strengthening Internal Justice Systems at European Molecular Biology Laboratory.

ing. The main difference is that the first priority for good civil servants and officials in such a case is addressing policy gaps, and promulgating a proper legal framework for their sound action.

Rules alone cannot guarantee integrity. Norms are useful in setting a standard framework of reference on which individuals can rely to assess the integrity of a given behaviour. In most cases, rules and policies – when they exist – provide ready-made answers and guidance for international civil servants to learn about the integrity that is expected from them. By itself, compliance with policies will not always be sufficient to lead one towards integrity and ethical behaviour. Nevertheless, clear guidelines will, at least, provide a framework within which individual dilemmas can find ready-made solutions for ethical action. In case of policy gaps, individual civil servants are left with no such guidance. Hence, the identification of ethical behaviour essentially relies on individual value judgments. In such a scenario, those who care about integrity, and are sufficiently enlightened to identify the right behaviour succeed, while those who lack integrity, or the capacity to uphold it consistently, fail.

Furthermore, for those who fail, disciplinary action is made more difficult – if at all possible – in the absence of clearly defined disciplinary breaches. *Nullum crimen sine lege* does apply to disciplinary action.[1] Policy gaps and failures to prevent unethical behaviour are thus impediments to disciplinary liability and a cause of impunity. In turn, the consequential perception of impunity plays as a strong deterrent to integrity. Where integrity breaches are protected from disciplinary action, they may facilitate the career development and promotion of offenders; at the same time, those who restrain their actions and try to advise adherence to ethical behaviour in all circumstances are perceived as trouble-makers. Unethical behaviour generates its own dynamics of solidarity between offenders, and retaliation against those who refuse to depart from integrity. Naming and shaming those who err is made difficult by the absence of rule that define and repress the phenomenon. It also exposes non-like-minded staff members and whistle-blowers who care for integrity to retaliation, as easy scapegoats immolated on the ground of the alleged lack of efficiency resulting from their willingness to play by rules which, to all effects, do not exist.

---

[1] International Labour Organization Administrative Tribunal ('ILOAT'), *In re Berte and Beslier*, Judgment, 20 December 1983, No. 566, p. 5 (http://www.legal-tools.org/doc/395956/).

It is generally agreed that a strong policy and legal framework alone is not an absolute guarantee of integrity in the management of an international institution; yet, policy gaps are pitfalls on the road of civil servants towards integrity and ethical behaviour. Some can avoid these, and maintain the clarity of mind to find their way to integrity in all circumstances. Still, others may fall, and their institution would then have failed to provide them with the necessary guidance.

21.1.1. Five Examples

Having regard to the Integrity Project, useful reflections may come from considering an international organization working in the field of international justice which recruits and employs hundreds of staff members, often for years, without a legally promulgated recruitment and selection procedure, discussed in Section 21.3.1. below. Section 21.3.2. describes an organization which deploys hundreds of staff members and other contractors on field missions in sensitive, post-conflict environments without any binding policy on mandatory security requirements or diplomatic clearance. In Section 21.3.3., this chapter elaborates on an organization without properly promulgated rules and procedures governing staff appeals and disciplinary proceedings, and where, by way of consequence, staff appeals and disciplinary actions fare quashed, faced by properly grounded appeals by those who are aware of such normative gaps. I will then consider an organization which enters a statement of principles combatting fraud and protecting whistle-blowers, but which fails to promulgate the necessary procedures to implement these in Section 21.3.4. Finally, Section 21.3.5. looks at an organization which does not comply, on a daily basis, with its own Information Protection Policy and thus fails to protect classified information regarding its judicial proceedings, the protection of its witnesses, victims and staff members in accordance with its own legal standards.

Without entering any conclusion with regards to the adherence of such organizations to the applicable integrity standards, I believe that we can reasonably conclude that each one of the organizations mentioned above has not set up the basic policy and legal framework and, as a consequence, fails to provide its staff and officials with the minimal guidance they should receive in order to uphold integrity standards in each organization's areas of activity.

This reasonable conclusion becomes a matter of serious concern when the five examples mentioned above are all related to the same organization, perhaps even more so when such organization is the central body in international criminal justice: the International Criminal Court ('ICC') (see Section 21.2. below). I am expressing this concern as a true friend of the ICC, with the genuine wish that the management of the Court may eventually heed my advice and take the necessary measures to correct the course. I am sharing this advice with the intent of making sure that, should the management persist in refusing to react, the concerned individuals risk facing the criticism arising from not addressing the policy gaps that undermine the daily action of this important institution, preventing the satisfactory fulfilment of its mandate of prosecuting the most serious crimes of international concern. Two years after making this advice public at the Peace Palace Conference of December 2018, I can see, with sadness, that it has remained unsuccessful so far: the final report of the Independent Expert Review ('IER') delivered on 30 September 2020 still flags "potentially outdated administrative issuances or those that are contradictory to principles set out in decisions of the International Labour Organisation – Administrative Tribunal (ILOAT) against the Court", and suggests, in its Recommendation R12, that "a systemic process should further be put in place to enable the Court's internal legal framework's compliance with ILOAT decisions, as soon as practicable after such a decision involving the Court is delivered, to identify and implement any necessary amendments".[2] This chapter is written with the genuine hope of saving the ICC from a future where it may decline by itself, by failing to uphold the highest standards of integrity, without need for a decisive action of its usual, numerous and powerful foes.

21.2. Overview of the Structure of the Internal Legal and Policy Framework of the International Criminal Court

The legal framework of relevance for the topic at hand is not composed by the usual sources of ICC law: although some articles of the Rome Statute referred to below are relevant, the other provisions governing the mandate and judicial proceedings of the Court in the Statute, the Rules of Procedure and Evidence, and other regulations have no direct relevance.

The combined provisions of Articles 38(3)(a), 42(2) and 43(2) of the Rome Statute entrust the Registrar, as "principal administrative officer of

---

[2] *Independent Expert Review of the International Criminal Court and the Rome Statute System: Final Report*, 30 September 2020, para. 59 and Recommendation R12, pp. 22–23 ('IER Report') (https://www.legal-tools.org/doc/cv19d5).

the Court" exercising his or her functions under the authority of the President of the Court and the Presidency, in charge of its "proper administration, with the exception of the Office of the Prosecutor", with the main responsibility of establishing the machinery governing the daily administration of the Court.

On the basis of these combined provisions, the ICC Presidency issued, on 9 December 2003, the first ever Presidential Directive of the Court setting up the "Procedures for the Promulgation of Administrative Issuances".[3] Section 1.1 of this Presidential Directive defines the various types of administrative issuances that can be issued by the Court: (a) Presidential Directives; (b) Administrative Instructions; and (c) Information Circulars. The list is limitative. Sections 2–4 define the scope of each type of issuances, their hierarchy, and the authority entrusted with their promulgation. Sections 5 and 6 set up the procedure for the consultation, promulgation, publication and review of administrative issuances. Section 7 provides general guidelines for their interpretation. The Presidential Directive of 9 December 2003 thus plays a preeminent, quasi-constitutional role of organic law (in French, *loi organique*), immediately under the Rome Statute, next to the Staff Regulations adopted under Article 44(3) of the Statute, and at the very top of the administrative and policy framework of the Court. All subsequent administrative issuances, more than one hundred,[4] were promulgated in accordance with this Presidential Directive.

21.2.1. Instances of Non-Observance of the Terms of the Presidential Directive of 2003

A quick review of the corpus of ICC administrative issuances reveals that, though promulgated pursuant to Presidential Directive of 9 December 2003, they were not necessarily compliant with its provisions. Since the delivery of the author's speech at the Peace Palace Conference of December 2018, the Court has fortunately taken action and redressed some of these issues, as mentioned in the relevant footnotes below.

---

[3]   International Criminal Court ('ICC'), Procedures for the Promulgation of Administrative Issuances, 9 December 2003, ICC/PRESD/G/2003/001 (http://www.legal-tools.org/doc/6a92e0/).

[4]   ICC, "Administrative Issuances" (available on its web site). The full list – unfortunately not up to date – of ICC administrative issuances.

21.2.1.1. Administrative Issuances Outside the Exhaustive List

First, many administrative issuances have been promulgated by instruments which do not form part of the exhaustive list of administrative issuances under Section 1.1 of the Presidential Directive of 9 December 2003. For example, the "ICC Recruitment Guidelines for Established Posts" of 2 November 2009, which govern the selection and recruitment of staff members[5] (see Section 21.3.1. below); the "Guidelines on Special Post Allowances" of 1 August 2007;[6] and the document published under the reference ICC/HRS/2007/7229 governing Official Working Hours of the Court and Official Holidays of 1 June 2007.[7] Although the latter document bears the label 'Information Circular' on its first page, it was not promulgated and is not published as such.

21.2.1.2. Administrative Issuances Adopted Outside of Their Given Scope

There have been several instances of administrative issuances adopted exceeding the scope of the specific instruments used for their promulgation, as defined under Sections 2 to 4 of the Presidential Directive of 9 December 2003. Such issuances include general procedures promulgated by way of Information Circulars, whereas a Presidential Directive or an Administrative Instruction would have been required under Sections 2 or 3 of the Presidential Directive of 9 December 2003. For instance, the "Rules of Procedure of the Appeals Board" promulgated by Information Circular ICC/INF/2006/003 of 21 March 2006[8] (see Section 21.3.3. below); the "Guidelines on Staff Training and Development" promulgated by Information Circular ICC/INF/2006/009 of 27 March 2006;[9] the "Rules of Pro-

---

[5]   ICC, Recruitment guidelines for Established Posts, Professional and higher General Service categories, 2 November 2009 (http://www.legal-tools.org/doc/50ed6b/) (not fixed).

[6]   ICC, Guidelines on Special Post Allowances (SPA), 1 August 2007, ICC/HRS/2007/7385 (http://www.legal-tools.org/doc/018904/) (not fixed).

[7]   ICC, Official Working Hours of the Court and Official Holidays, 1 June 2007, ICC/HRS/2007/7229 (http://www.legal-tools.org/doc/471713/) (partially fixed by ICC/AI/2019/004, 28 October 2019 (https://www.legal-tools.org/doc/asnyvr/)).

[8]   ICC, Rules of Procedure of the Appeals Board, 21 March 2006, ICC/INF/2006/003 (http://www.legal-tools.org/doc/fb03b5/) (fixed by ICC/AI/2019/005, 28 October 2019 (https://www.legal-tools.org/doc/2ekgxu/)).

[9]   ICC, Staff Training and Development – Guidelines, 27 March 2006, ICC/INF/2006/009 ('Staff Training and Development – Guidelines') (http://www.legal-tools.org/doc/317ad3/) (not fixed).

---

cedure of the Disciplinary Advisory Board" promulgated by Information Circular ICC/INF/2007/003 of 7 May 2007[10] (see Section 21.3.3. below); the setting up of the ICC Security and Safety Section, and various inter-organ fora created for the purpose of ensuring security at the Court and responding to crisis, promulgated by Information Circular ICC/INF/2008/003 of 22 January 2008[11] (see Section 21.3.2. below); "Mandatory Security Arrangements" for ICC field missions promulgated by Information Circular ICC/INF/2011/006 of 23 August 2011[12] (see Section 21.3.2. below); the procedure governing the delivery of "UN Laissez-Passer" for ICC missions promulgated by Information Circular ICC/INF/2015/008 of 19 March 2015[13] (see Section 21.3.2. below); and the "Guidelines on Language Proficiency and Language Incentives" promulgated by Information Circular ICC/INF/2016/011 of 30 December 2016.[14]

21.2.1.3. Other Instances of Flawed Administrative Issuances

The practice of the Court has brought other kinds of problematic administrative instances, such as those that are manifestly obsolete which were not reviewed, as required under Section 5.2 of the Presidential Directive of 9 December 2003: for example, the "ICC Information Protection Policy" promulgated by Administrative Instruction ICC/AI/2007/001 of 19 June 2007[15] (see Section 21.3.5. below).

Other administrative issuances refer to subsequent, subordinate instruments for the implementation of the general principles they provide,

---

[10] ICC, Rules of Procedure of the Disciplinary Advisory Board, 7 May 2007, ICC/INF/2007/003 ('Rules of Procedure of the Disciplinary Advisory Board') (http://www.legal-tools.org/doc/c7e8f0/) (fixed by ICC/AI/2019/006, 28 October 2019 (https://www.legal-tools.org/doc/43ztuk/)).

[11] ICC, An executive statement by the Registrar on the ICC Security and Safety Section (SSS), Joint Threat and Assessment Group (JTAG), Joint Crisis Management Team (JCMT) and Information Security Management Forum (ISMF), 22 January 2008, ICC/INF/2008/003 ('Executive Statement') (http://www.legal-tools.org/doc/278a95/) (not fixed).

[12] ICC, Mandatory Security Arrangements, 23 August 2011, ICC/INF/2011/006 ('Mandatory Security Arrangements') (http://www.legal-tools.org/doc/676299/) (not fixed).

[13] ICC, United Nations Laissez-Passer, 19 March 2015, ICC/INF/2015/008 ('United Nations Laissez-Passer') (http://www.legal-tools.org/doc/9a62af/) (not fixed).

[14] ICC, Guidelines on Language Proficiency and Language Incentives, 30 December 2016, ICC/INF/2016/011 (http://www.legal-tools.org/doc/ee42ad/) (fixed by ICC/AI/2019/007, 28 October 2019 (https://www.legal-tools.org/doc/sxt7ql/)).

[15] ICC, ICC Informational Protection Policy, 19 June 2007, ICC/AI/2007/001 (http://www.legal-tools.org/doc/04b126/) (not fixed).

which were not followed by the announced implementing issuances: for instance, the "ICC Anti-Fraud Policy" promulgated by Presidential Directive ICC/PRESD/G/2014/002 of 13 May 2014 (see Section 21.3.4. below);[16] and the "ICC Whistleblowing and Whistle-blower Protection Policy" promulgated by Presidential Directive ICC/PRESD/G/2014/003 of 8 October 2014 (see Section 21.3.4. below).[17]

21.2.2. The Rank of the Presidential Directive of 2003

Until recently, the frequent non-observance of the Presidential Directive of 9 December 2003 had led to a perception, widely shared within the Court, that the Directive may not necessarily be binding. Indeed, in this light, the Presidential Directive may be seen to represent an early and long-time gone era of the ICC development when all important decisions could be achieved in agreement between the various organs of the Court, and should be considered as guidelines rather than as a compulsory instrument. Though legally questionable, this perception was rarely challenged and had not led to a judicial determination until 24 January 2018.

On 24 January 2018, the Administrative Tribunal of the International Labour Organization ('ILOAT'), which is the ultimate body of appeal in ICC staff appeal and disciplinary cases pursuant to Regulation 11.2 of the ICC Staff Regulations[18] and Section 6.4 of Administrative Instruction ICC/AI/2008/001 of 5 February 2008,[19] issued its Judgment No. 3907.[20] In this Judgment, the ILOAT quashes an administrative decision and heavily sanctions the ICC as a result of its non-observance of the Presidential Directive of 9 December 2003 in the promulgation of another administrative issuance. Importantly, the ILOAT rules:

> In conclusion, pursuant to the Presidential Directive [of 9 December 2003], the Principles and Procedures should have been

---

[16]   ICC, ICC Anti-Fraud Policy, 13 May 2014, ICC/PRESD/G/2014/002 ('ICC Anti-Fraud Policy') (http://www.legal-tools.org/doc/a5168a/) (not fixed).

[17]   ICC, ICC Whistleblowing and Whistleblower Protection Policy, 8 October 2014, ICC/PRESD/G/2014/003 ('ICC Whistleblowing and Whistleblower Protection Policy') (http://www.legal-tools.org/doc/0c36ff/) (not fixed).

[18]   ICC, Staff Regulations, 30 September 2016, ICC/PRESD/G/2016/002 ('ICC Staff Regulations') (http://www.legal-tools.org/doc/bc0ddb/).

[19]   ICC, Disciplinary Procedure, 5 February 2008, ICC/AI/2008/001 ('Disciplinary Procedure') (http://www.legal-tools.org/doc/094a22/).

[20]   ILOAT, F v. ICC, Judgment, 24 January 2018, No. 3907 (http://www.legal-tools.org/doc/c1fdba/).

---

promulgated by an Administrative Instruction or, arguably, by a Presidential Directive. As the promulgation of the Principles and Procedures by Information Circular was in violation of the Presidential Directive, they were without legal foundation and are, therefore, unlawful as are the decisions taken pursuant to the Principles and Procedures.[21]

The ILOAT ruling should have dissipated any doubt as to the compulsory nature of the Presidential Directive of 9 December 2003. The ILOAT confirms that not only this Presidential Directive is preeminent in the policy framework of the ICC and compulsory, but its non-observance in the promulgation of other administrative issuances is a cause of unlawfulness of the ill-promulgated provisions, and of all administrative decisions taken on their basis. The organ promulgating an administrative issuance in violation of the Presidential Directive of 9 December 2003 – be it the President, the Prosecutor or the Registrar – is found to have no authority to overcome this primary illegality by way of exercising its own policy attributions.

In light of the abovementioned long, yet non-exhaustive, list of instances of non-observance of the Presidential Directive of 9 December 2003 in the promulgation of administrative issuances, ILOAT Judgment No. 3907 had very significant consequences on the internal legal framework of the ICC. Potentially, each and every administrative issuance not in compliance with the terms of the Presidential Directive – such as, for instance, the ICC Recruitment Guidelines for Established Posts – may be challenged; furthermore, each and every decision taken on the basis of such issuances, like the appointment of staff members, may be quashed. This is a cause of high insecurity for the Court, which cannot safely rely on substantial aspects of its own internal legal framework in support of its day-to-day administrative decisions. As a consequence of the ILOAT ruling, there is now a potential for litigation every time an administrative decision perceived as adverse is taken on the basis of one of the administrative issuances listed above. To some extent, this is also a cause of legal insecurity for ICC staff

---

[21] *Ibid.*, p. 26; ILOAT, *A v. ICC*, Judgment, 24 January 2018, No. 3903, p. 20 (http://www.legal-tools.org/doc/b3ed30/); ILOAT, *G v. ICC*, Judgment, 24 January 2018, No. 3904, p. 20 (http://www.legal-tools.org/doc/06301a/); ILOAT, *L. (No. 3) v. ICC*, Judgment, 24 January 2018, No. 3908, p. 9 (http://www.legal-tools.org/doc/619e5a/); ILOAT, *B. v. ICC*, Judgment, 26 June 2018, No. 4004, p. 6 (http://www.legal-tools.org/doc/dca542/); ILOAT, *T.P. and M. v. ICC*, Judgment, 26 June 2018, No. 4007, p. 5 (http://www.legal-tools.org/doc/bcf9cb/).

members, even though they can nonetheless rely on unlawfully promulgated administrative issuances in support of their claimed acquired rights on the basis of the *tu patere legem quam ipse fecisti* principle: the organization is bound to comply with the rules it has itself defined in favour of its staff, even if these are found unlawful. Strikingly, ICC staff members are in a much more favourable position than the Court itself, since they can, in support of their rights, rely on provisions which the Court cannot rely upon any longer in support of its decisions.

ILOAT Judgment No. 3907 clarifies that the Court cannot anymore consider its Presidential Directive of 9 December 2003 as mere guidance and disregard its provisions in the preparation, promulgation and implementation of administrative issuances. It should have led the Court to conduct, on an urgent basis, a comprehensive review of its policy framework in order to abide by the provisions of its Presidential Directive of 9 December 2003, and particularly its Section 5.2 which requires that

> officials responsible for promulgating administrative issuances shall see to it that issuances in effect within their respective spheres of competence are reviewed periodically so as to ensure that the rules, instructions and procedures that they prescribe are up to date, that obsolete administrative issuances are abolished with the minimum delay and that new issuances or amendments to existing issuances are promulgated as required.

Almost three years after the issuance of ILOAT Judgment No. 3907, no such review has taken place, despite all efforts made to raise the attention of the high management of the Court on the urgency of the review. Let us hope that the above-mentioned IER Recommendation R12 will have the power to trigger it.

21.3. Main Areas of Policy Gaps and Their Potential Impact on the Perception of Integrity at the ICC

As stated in the introduction to the present chapter, policy gaps, when they are not addressed, leave the organization's staff members and officials with no guidance as to the way of upholding the highest standards of integrity, and have the potential impact of feeding a perception of impunity for unethical behaviour, which in turn deters strict adherence to integrity standards.

21.3.1. Selection of Staff Members

There is no legally promulgated administrative issuance governing the selection and recruitment of staff members at the ICC. On 2 November 2009, the Registrar of the ICC informally promulgated "Recruitment Guidelines for Established Posts – Professional and higher and General Service categories".[22] Under Section 1, these Guidelines govern the procedures for the recruitment of staff members on established posts and positions funded by general temporary assistance. They provide rules and procedures regarding the advertisement of vacancy announcements, the classification of posts, the submission of applications, the composition of interview panels, the short-listing, assessment and final selection of candidates and the use of rosters. Unfortunately, the Court failed to resort to one or the other kind of administrative issuances listed in Section 1.1 of the Presidential Directive of 9 December 2003. As a consequence, and in light of ILOAT Judgment No. 3907, these Recruitment Guidelines were promulgated in violation of the Presidential Directive of 9 December 2003, they are without legal foundation and are, therefore, unlawful, as are all the administrative decisions taken on the basis of these guidelines, that is, each and every recruitment procedure which applied the Recruitment Guidelines.

This does not mean that each and every staff member working at the Court was unlawfully hired and shall see his or her appointment cancelled. Though unlawful, the individual administrative decisions appointing staff members created acquired rights for the incumbents, and most of them were not appealed. These acquired rights cannot be challenged on the basis of the unlawfulness of the individual administrative decisions originating them. Except in the few cases where recruitment decisions are appealed, such decisions cannot be quashed or cancelled. In the rare appeals, for example, by other unsuccessful applicants, reliance on the unlawfulness of the Recruitment Guidelines on the basis of ILOAT Judgment No. 3907 provides a solid ground for the quashing of the impugned decisions and the cancellation of the challenged recruitment processes. This situation is obviously a factor of high vulnerability for the Court, whose recruitment processes – virtually all of them – can be successfully challenged.

---

[22] ICC, ICC Recruitment guidelines for Established Posts, Professional and higher General Service categories, 2 November 2009, ICC/INF/2012/020 (https://legal-tools.org/doc/50ed6b).

However, this risk is limited by the fact that the right to challenge recruitment decisions, like any other administrative decisions, is limited to staff members who are already working for the Court under Article II.1 of the ILOAT Statute and is not open to external applicants. Only internal applicants can challenge a recruitment process and, except in rare situations, internal applicants will refrain from challenging such a decision by fear of retaliation or other adverse consequences for their career within the Court. The non-implementation of the principles governing the protection of whistle-blowers (see Section 21.3.4. below) thus plays as a powerful deterrent against the lodging of appeals against appointment decisions. Finally, the absence of reaction from the management of the Court and of review of the Recruitment Guidelines after the issuance of Judgment No. 3907 feeds the perception that, notwithstanding the clear and unambiguous ruling of the ILOAT, the Recruitment Guidelines may nonetheless be valid, for whatever reason, in the mind of the majority of staff members, who are not sufficiently acquainted with administrative subtleties. All these mitigating factors concur in limiting the risk of challenges against recruitment decisions and containing it, below the advantages of keeping things as they are. As long as a binding and properly promulgated selection and recruitment procedure is not in force, the hiring manager has the possibility of disregarding the existing Recruitment Guidelines every time they do not serve his or her purposes or those of the Human Resources Section.

Paradoxically, the procedure governing the selection and recruitment of the most precarious category of staff members, employed under short-term appointments, was properly promulgated by way of Administrative Instruction ICC/AI/2016/001 of 28 January 2016.[23] Section 4 of that Administrative Instruction governs the advertisement of vacancy announcements and provides relaxed selection and appointment processes, ensuring full discretion to the hiring manager in the selection of staff on short-term appointments. This Administrative Instruction shows *a contrario* that the ICC management is aware of the proper way of promulgating recruitment procedures, and that nonetheless, when it does so, it only promulgates loose provisions, ultimately preserving the capacity of hiring managers to select and appoint the persons of their choosing.

---

[23] ICC, Short-Term Appointments, 28 January 2016, ICC/AI/2016/001 (http://www.legal-tools.org/doc/286b48/).

The legal possibility of disregarding the Recruitment Guidelines opens the door to all possible allegations of discrimination, favouritism, nepotism, blacklisting, or other unethical behaviour in relation to recruitments for established posts in the ICC. It provides an explanation as to why subsequent internal staff surveys show that ICC staff members have a low level of confidence in the fairness of recruitment processes, and questions the very capacity of the Court to select, appoint and keep at its service the most qualified staff members, as required under Article 44 of the Rome Statute. In its final report, the IER notes the symptoms, but fails to identify the cause: none of its essentially cosmetic Recommendations R91 to R96 on recruitment addresses the lack of properly promulgated and enforceable selection and recruitment procedure.[24] The failure to address this key issue by the IER is a missed opportunity to create a sound policy basis for the hiring of ICC staff fulfilling basic standards of integrity.

21.3.2. Field Operations

Among the more than one hundred administrative issuances of the ICC, a very few are related to field operations and missions.

Appendix 1 to Information Circular ICC/INF/2008/003 of 22 January 2008[25] provides in Section 3 – 'Field Security' that the Registry Security and Safety Section ('SSS') is in charge of completing Security Risk Assessments and planning co-ordination for the deployment of all security staff – only! – in the field, assessing risks and planning security missions, acting as a focal point to obtain security clearance for ICC staff travelling on mission to ensure compliance with the Court's obligations arising from membership of the UN security management system, liaising with other organizations – like the UN Department of Safety and Security ('UNDSS') and Department of Peace Keeping Operations – monitoring all mission-related security reports and incidents, identifying security shortfalls and highlighting required remedial actions, and leading and managing the SSS personnel in the field. The Information Circular of 22 January 2008 further establishes various internal bodies in charge of coordinating on security issues: the 'ICC Joint Threat Assessment Group', the 'ICC Joint Crisis Management Team' and the 'ICC Information Security Management Forum'. The composition, functioning and responsibilities for each body are

---

[24] IER Report, paras. 218–227 and Recommendations R91 to R96, pp. 70–74, see above note 2.
[25] Executive Statement, see above note 11.

detailed in Appendices II, III and IV of the Information Circular of 22 January 2008, respectively.

Information Circular ICC/INF/2011/006 of 23 August 2011,[26] on the other hand, provides some 'Mandatory Security Arrangements'. These include attendance of security briefings delivered by SSS or UNDSS personnel, the completion of basic and advanced security training prior to deployment on field missions, the delivery of security clearance from UNDSS, the timely submission of a mission plan "at least 30 days prior to travel" and of a "detailed mission plan" (not defined) "at least 14 days prior to travel". The Information Circular of 23 August 2011 specifies that "the compliance with the mandatory security arrangements is also taken into consideration in case of investigation of an incident and may impact insurance coverage and other related compensation".

Information Circular ICC/INF/2015/008 of 19 March 2015[27] provides the procedure for the delivery of a UN Laissez-Passer (UNLP). An earlier version of the same issuance was promulgated by Information Circular ICC/INF/2005/005 of 22 August 2005[28] and superseded by the Information Circular of 19 March 2015.

However, these three key issuances governing field operations are unenforceable because they were, once again, illegally promulgated and are largely obsolete: most of the time, they are not complied with.

The three Information Circulars of 22 January 2008, 23 August 2011 and 19 March 2015 promulgate general procedures of a permanent nature. As such, these shall have been promulgated by way of a Presidential Directive or an Administrative Instruction pursuant to Sections 2 and 3 of the Presidential Directive of 9 December 2003. Since the issuance of ILOAT Judgment No. 3907 of 24 January 2018, the unlawfulness of these administrative issuances and all administrative decisions taken pursuant to these is *res judicata*. Yet, the management of the Court is not taking steps to address this issue.

From 6 June to 2 July 2012, four ICC staff members were illegally arrested and detained in Zintan, Libya, while on a mission for the Court. In response to the arrest of its four staff members, the ICC Joint Crisis Man-

---

[26] Mandatory Security Arrangements, see above note 12.

[27] United Nations Laissez-Passer, see above note 13.

[28] ICC, Guidelines for the use of the United Nations Laissez Passer, 22 August 2005, ICC/INF/2005/005 (http://www.legal-tools.org/doc/5ac2df/).

agement Committee, established by the Information Circular of 22 January 2008 to respond to this specific type of crisis, was not even activated. The release of the four ICC staff members was followed by two post-incident reports, and a Judgment issued by the ILOAT on 26 June 2018 upon a claim from one of the four arrested ICC staff members. The first post-incident report, issued by the ICC Independent Oversight Mechanism ('IOM') in October 2012, finds that there were significant gaps in the ICC's mission planning framework: no agreement had been entered with the Libyan authorities concerning the privileges and immunities of the ICC staff members; the activities that the ICC staff members intended to pursue during their mission had not been defined in advance by means of an exchange of *Notes Verbales*; the security recommendations made by the ICC Field Security Unit during the preparation of the mission had not been implemented.[29] A revised version of this first post-incident report dated 21 February 2013 further concludes that

> both in preparing the mission and attempting to resolve the crisis, the Court was greatly hindered by a poor guidance framework and absence of advanced planning. By taking action, in both areas, to strengthen the Court's system, the Court can hopefully avoid future similar crises and, when crisis is unavoidable, be able to react more robustly.[30]

The second post-incident report, issued on 3 June 2013 by an external expert tasked by the ICC, also found that there had been a lack of adequate preparation for the mission to Libya.[31] In its Judgment No. 4003 of 24 June 2018, the ILOAT finds that

> the Complainant's ordeal in Libya was a direct result of the ICC's failure to properly prepare for the mission, specifically its failure to: (a) establish a diplomatic basis by ensuring that a Memorandum of Understanding was established and/or *Notes Verbales* were exchanged with the Libyan authorities prior to the mission's initiation; (b) establish a mission plan which identified the objectives of the mission, the locations to visit and persons to be met, as well as naming the Head of Mission and clarifying the specific responsibilities of the team members; and (c) ensure that all security protocols were followed

---

[29] ILOAT, *A v. ICC*, Judgment, 26 June 2018, No. 4003, pp. 2–3 ('Judgment 4003') (http://www.legal-tools.org/doc/81bbe3/).

[30] *Ibid.*, para. 4.

[31] *Ibid.*, para. 5.

and advice was implemented to guarantee the safety and security of the staff members on mission.[32]

After the occurrence of such a serious event as the Zintan crisis of 2012, no step was taken to strengthen the policy regarding field missions and activities, privileges and immunities and compliance with field security rules. The findings and recommendations made in the two post-incident reports were not implemented. The rulings of the ILOAT in Judgment No. 4003 did not lead to significant change in the mission preparation, mission planning, privileges and immunities and field security policies of the Court.

The most significant actions taken by the ICC management in relation to field operations and security since the Zintan crisis of 2012 and the issuance of the post-incident reports consist in a restructuring of the ICC Security and Safety Section, done as part of a wider restructuring of the ICC Registry services in 2014-2015, and the promulgation of the Information Circular of 19 March 2015 on UN Laissez-Passer, replacing the earlier Information Circular of 22 August 2005.

The restructuring of the ICC Security and Safety Section essentially consisted in separating the field security, security analysis, crisis management and mission planning functions from the SSS, and entrusting them to a new Division of External Operations,[33] distributed between a new External Operations Support Section[34] and each individual Field Office. This change was implemented without amending or updating the Information Circular of 22 January 2008 entrusting the Security and Safety Section with these important functions to adapt it to the new structure and redistribution of functions. The Information Circular of 22 January 2008, already not complied with at the time of the Zintan crisis, has now become totally obsolete as a result of the restructuration of the Registry security and field management services. The failure to review or abolish the Information Circular of 22 January 2008 is in further breach of Section 5.2 of the Presidential Directive of 9 December 2003. One may also legitimately question how a restructuring that dilutes security and mission planning functions and responsibilities between, at least, three different working units instead of one without amending the applicable legal and policy framework may

---

[32] *Ibid.*, para. 16.

[33] ICC, Comprehensive Report on the Reorganisation of the Registry of the International Criminal Court, August 2016, para. 325 (http://www.legal-tools.org/doc/cbc6cc/).

[34] *Ibid.*, paras. 428, 447-448, 552.

have contributed to address and fix the policy concerns raised in the two subsequent post-incidents reports on the Zintan crisis.

As already mentioned, the Information Circular of 19 March 2015 on UN Laissez-Passer is unlawful and unenforceable as a result of its promulgation, in breach of the Presidential Directive of 9 December 2003. In addition, it provides that UN Laissez-Passer delivered to ICC staff and officials shall contain an insert affirming that its bearer "is entitled to be accorded the privileges and immunities provided for in the Agreement on the Privileges and Immunities of the International Criminal Court of 9 September 2002 or in other agreements or arrangements defining the privileges and immunities of the Court". The Information Circular of 19 March 2015 fails to inform potential bearers of the Laissez-Passer on the implications and limits of these privileges and immunities, in particular the need for an exchange of *Notes Verbales* with the local authorities and the fact that the ICC privileges and immunities only apply in States Parties to the Agreement on the Privileges and Immunities of the Court. Many current Situation countries are not Parties to the Agreement, like Côte d'Ivoire, Kenya, Sudan, Libya and Burundi, and ICC bearers of Laissez-Passer may also travel to other non-situation countries which also are not Parties to the Agreement on the Privileges and Immunities of the Court, such as the following countries under preliminary examination: Afghanistan, Bangladesh, Myanmar, Guinea (which signed the Agreement on 1 April 2004 but did not ratify it), Iraq, Nigeria, Palestine, Philippines or Venezuela (which signed on 16 July 2003 but did not ratify). By providing an insert that affirms that ICC bearers of Laissez-Passer enjoy privileges and immunities without the necessary information and caveats, the Information Circular of 19 March 2015 fails to discharge the Court's duty of care[35] *vis-à-vis* its staff and officials who may believe, on the face of the insert in their UN Laissez-Passer, that they enjoy privileges and immunities when they do not. The failure to secure the privileges and immunities of the four ICC staff members played a central role in the materialization of the Zintan crisis of 2012, and resulted in the adverse Judgment No. 4003 issued by the ILOAT; nevertheless, it has not led the Court to learn from its past mistakes and address this issue properly. The fact that the Information Circular of 19 March 2015 was issued after the Zintan crisis and the issuance of the two post-incident reports highlighting this policy gap certainly plays as a factor

---

[35] Judgment 4003, p. 12, see above note 29.

aggravating the liability of the ICC management for its failure to discharge the duty of care.

The ICC policy on mission preparation, diplomatic clearance, privileges and immunities and mandatory security arrangements remains loose, largely obsolete and noncompliant with the structure of the internal legal framework of the Court. At any moment in time, an event similar to the Zintan crisis of 2012 can re-occur, perhaps leading to a much worse result. The management of the Court is taking a huge responsibility *vis-à-vis* the life and security of its own staff and all other persons sent on ICC field missions, such as counsel, by persisting in not addressing this problem in spite of the *res judicata* rulings of the ILOAT in its Judgments Nos. 3907 and 4003. The IER report does not suggest otherwise in its above-mentioned Recommendation R12, but it strangely addresses the specific issue of field activities with respect to the Office of the Prosecutor only and succinctly,[36] without considering the wider picture of the ICC-wide policy framework governing field presence and the preparation of field missions. Like for recruitment, the IER report thus missed the main problem here.

In light of the huge risk that follows the failure to review the ICC field operations policies, one can legitimately wonder the reasons of the ICC management for not addressing this serious issue, whereas its attention was repeatedly drawn thereon. Their inaction feeds a perception that the field operations policy framework is deliberately left as it is in order to keep the greater flexibility in the conduct of field operations that a loose legal environment provides. As long as a more stringent policy framework is not in place, ICC staff members can be sent on missions without the need for ensuring in advance that they are covered by privileges and immunities, or to disclose in advance a detailed mission plan defining the exact purpose of the mission, the foreseen activities and the locations to be visited. This gives room to maximum flexibility in the conduct of missions, with last-minute changes always possible. It echoes the concerns voiced in a recent CILRAP conference on 22-23 February 2019 by a Senior Legal Officer of the ICC Chambers about the serious challenges encountered by the Office of the Prosecutor in planning investigations in advance.[37] It also opens the

---

[36] IER Report, paras. 779–784 and Recommendations R293 to R298, pp. 251–253, see above note 2.

[37] Gilbert Bitti, "Quality control in Case Preparation and the Role of the Judiciary of the International Criminal Court", CILRAP Film, New Delhi, 23 February 2019 (https://www.cilrap.org/cilrap-film/190223-bitti/).

door to all possible allegations of unethical behaviour, such as the under-taking of unofficial, parallel, non-transparent business while on a mission.

Flexibility on field missions may arguably be in the interests of the Court, but it can no longer be considered as such once, as with the Zintan crisis of 2012, it has proved to be at the cost of the security of ICC staff members and other persons at risk on account of the activities of the Court.

21.3.3. Staff Appeal and Disciplinary Procedures, Including the Independent Oversight Mechanism

The provisions governing staff appeal and disciplinary procedures before the ICC include general principles enshrined in Articles X and XI of the ICC Staff Regulations,[38] and Chapters X and XI of the ICC Staff Rules,[39] a description of the internal disciplinary procedure in Administrative Instruc-tion ICC/AI/2008/001 of 5 February 2008,[40] rules of procedures applicable before the internal Appeals Board and Disciplinary Advisory Board prom-ulgated by Information Circulars ICC/INF/2006/003 of 27 March 2006[41] and ICC/INF/2007/003 of 7 May 2007,[42] and specific grievance complaint procedures for cases of harassment and unequal treatment, including dis-crimination provided under Sections 6-7 of Administrative Instruction ICC/AI/2005/005 of 14 July 2005[43] and Sections 5-6 of Administrative Instruc-tion ICC/AI/2005/006 of 14 July 2005.[44] On 27 November 2013, the As-sembly of States Parties ('ASP') also adopted its resolution ICC-ASP/12/Res. 6 with the Operational Mandate of the IOM established under Article 112(4) of the Rome Statute in an annex.[45] The Operational Mandate of the

---

[38] ICC Staff Regulations, see above note 18.

[39] ICC, Staff Rules of the International Criminal Court, 27 July 2015, ICC/AI/2015/004/Corr.1 Anx (http://www.legal-tools.org/doc/2a5274/).

[40] Disciplinary Procedure, see above note 19.

[41] Rules of Procedure of the Appeals Board, see above note 9; replaced by ICC/AI/2019/005, 28 October 2019.

[42] Rules of Procedure of the Disciplinary Advisory Board, see above note 10; replaced by ICC/AI/2019/006, 28 October 2019.

[43] ICC, Sexual and Other Forms of Harassment, 14 July 2005, ICC/AI/2005/005 (http://www.legal-tools.org/doc/619941/).

[44] ICC, Equal Employment Opportunity and Treatment, 14 July 2005, ICC/AI/2005/006 (http://www.legal-tools.org/doc/9c4023/).

[45] ICC Assembly of State Parties ('ICC ASP'), "Independent Oversight Mechanism", 27 No-vember 2013, ICC-ASP/12/Res.6 (http://www.legal-tools.org/doc/64ebeb/).

IOM provides, *inter alia*, that it plays a role in the investigation of disciplinary cases against staff members and elected officials.

Though apparently complete, the procedural framework applicable to staff appeals and disciplinary cases actually maintains significant gaps, which are likely to impact on the integrity of internal proceedings, should litigants elect to rely on them in support of their claims, thus making the Court highly vulnerable in case of appeal before the ILOAT.

Chapter XI of the ICC Staff Rules makes the submission of appeal cases to the internal Appeals Board a mandatory step in the internal phase of the proceedings on any staff appeal against an administrative decision. Rule 111.3 provides general principles governing the procedure before the Appeals Board. However, the Rules of Procedure of the Appeals Board govern the more detailed aspects of the procedure before the Appeals Board, such as the composition of Appeals Board panels, the recusal of its members, the filing, format and content of submissions, the disclosure of relevant documents, the drafting and content of the Panel's recommendation and other aspects. Yet, the Rules of Procedure were initially promulgated as an annex to Information Circular ICC/INF/2006/003 of 27 March 2006, whereas Sections 2 and 3 of the Presidential Directive of 9 December 2003 required the promulgation of general procedures by way of Presidential Directive or Administrative Instruction. This was fixed by the promulgation of Administrative Issuance ICC/AI/2019/005 on 28 October 2019. Until that date, pursuant to the ruling of the ILOAT at paragraph 25 of its Judgment No. 3907, the Rules of Procedure of the Appeals Board were unlawful, as were all decisions taken pursuant to them, that is, all final decisions on staff appeal cases. The invalid promulgation of the Rules of Procedure of the Appeals Board thus formed a solid basis for the quashing of any final decision on a staff appeal case before the ILOAT. This made the ICC highly vulnerable to any challenge made by its staff members against its administrative decisions, whatever their merits. In the case of the majority of staff members who were not aware of this gap, or who did not feel confident enough to challenge the validity of the Rules of Procedure of the Appeals Board, this risk remained limited. On the contrary, those staff members who had this knowledge, and had enough confidence in their legal skills to measure the consequences of the unlawfulness of the Rules of the Appeals Board, could be confident that they would succeed in their appeal against any decision they may have elected to challenge.

Chapter X of the ICC Staff Rules and Section 3 of the Administrative Instruction of 5 February 2008 provide that the referral of disciplinary cases to the Disciplinary Advisory Board is a mandatory step in the internal phase of disciplinary proceedings against ICC staff members. The same requirement applies to grievance procedures for harassment and unequal treatment, including discrimination, pursuant to Section 7.3 of Administrative Instruction ICC/AI/2005/005 of 14 July 2005 and Section 6.3 of Administrative Instruction ICC/AI/2005/006 of 14 July 2005. Yet, the Rules of Procedure of the Disciplinary Advisory Board were initially promulgated as an annex to Information Circular ICC/INF/2007/003 of 7 May 2007, whereas Sections 2 and 3 of the Presidential Directive of 9 December 2003 required the promulgation of general procedures by way of Presidential Directive or Administrative Instruction. This was fixed by the promulgation of Administrative Issuance ICC/AI/2019/006 on 28 October 2019. Until that date, like the Rules of Procedure of the Appeals Board, pursuant to the ruling of the ILOAT at paragraph 25 of its Judgment No. 3907, the Rules of Procedure of the Disciplinary Advisory Board were unlawful, as were all decisions that rely on them, that is, all final decisions on disciplinary and grievance cases. The invalid promulgation of the Rules of Procedure of the Disciplinary Advisory Board formed a solid basis for chalenging the lawfulness of every final decision on disciplinary action before the ILOAT. This implied that no disciplinary action could succeed before the Court against a staff member who was aware of this gap, and feeled sufficiently confident to challenge the validity of the Rules of Procedure of the Disciplinary Advisory Board. For this minority of staff members – the few who are most aware of procedural subtleties, or who are well-advised – this created a situation of total impunity for unsatisfactory conduct, as no disciplinary action could succeed against them. For those who adhered to the highest standards of integrity, and wished to report unsatisfactory conduct by way of grievance complaint – where applicable – or other reporting under the ICC Whistleblowing Policy (see Section 21.3.4. below), this created a situation of deep sorrow, as they were aware that offenders could carry on their misconducts in full impunity, as long as they knew about this gap.

The operational mandate of the IOM was adopted by Resolution ICC-ASP/12/Res. 6 of the ASP in 2013 (the 'Operational Mandate'). Section 2.1 of the Presidential Directive of 9 December 2003 provides:

> A Presidential Directive shall be required for the promulgation
> of procedures for the implementation of regulations, resolu-

tions and decisions adopted by the ASP, including: [...] (c) Promulgation of regulations and rules governing [...] the monitoring of implementation and methods of evaluation.

As briefly alluded to by Karim A.A. Khan in his chapter and previous presentation,[46] and flagged by the International Criminal Court Bar Association in a legal analysis of February 2018,[47] since the promulgation of Resolution ICC-ASP/12/Res. 6, no Presidential Directive was issued to implement its provisions within the internal legal framework of the Court. Furthermore, the specific administrative issuances governing activities of relevance to the IOM Operational Mandate, such as disciplinary proceedings, have not been amended, nor abolished, nor replaced, whereas paragraph 3 of Resolution ICC-ASP/12/Res. 6 of the ASP had invited the Court in 2013 to complete the review of its policies "necessary for the full operationalization of all functions of the IOM" within one year. This has not been done. In his 2017 Annual Report to the ASP, the former Head of the IOM rightfully flagged that the procedural provisions of the IOM Operational Mandate "contradict or appear at odds" with "pre-existing investigation-related authorities and procedures".[48] Worse, Administrative Instruction ICC/AI/2019/006, which repromulgated the old Rules of Procedure of the Disciplinary Advisory Board on 28 October 2019, did not amend these to insert a provision on the role of the IOM in disciplinary proceedings, this leaving it outside of the ICC disciplinary scheme. The non-adaptation of the relevant administrative issuances governing disciplinary procedures within the Court in breach of paragraph 3 of Resolution ICC-ASP/12/Res. 6 of the ASP has several consequences on the integrity of disciplinary proceedings. It would not be an overstatement to submit that, since the adoption of the IOM Operational Mandate, not a single disciplinary procedure within the Court is protected from being successfully challenged on the ground of procedural flaws, irrespective of whether the IOM was involved in it. The non-compliance of the Court with paragraph 3 of Resolution ICC-ASP/12/Res. 6 of the ASP and its consequences were overlooked by the IER. Its report limits itself to noting that "the IOM does not yet enjoy

---

[46] Karim A.A. Khan, "Integrity and the Limits of Internal Oversight Mechanisms", CILRAP Film, The Hague, 2 December 2018 (https://www.cilrap.org/cilrap-film/181202-khan/).

[47] ICCBA Legal Advisory Committee, "Legal Analysis: ICC Internal Accountability Mechanisms and Policies", February 2018 ('Legal Analysis of ICC Internal Accountability Mechanisms and Policies') (http://www.legal-tools.org/doc/929bc0/).

[48] ICC ASP, Annual Report of the Head of the Independent Oversight Mechanism, 17 October 2017, ICC/ASP/16/8, para. 15 (http://www.legal-tools.org/doc/aab4bb/).

the full confidence and trust of all staff",[49] which is, by far, an understatement of the symptom, without identifying the cause.

In disciplinary cases where the IOM fulfils its investigative function under Sections 27 to 41 of its Operational Mandate, the parties – the person whose conduct is alleged to be unsatisfactory and, where applicable, the complainant – can challenge its intervention on the basis of the absence of a Presidential Directive implementing the Operational Mandate within the internal policy framework of the Court in accordance with Section 2.1 of the Presidential Directive of 9 December 2003. The ILOAT Judgment No. 3907 would support such a claim. This can be used to demonstrate a breach of procedure, and claim the quashing of the disciplinary decision: disciplinary measures may be cancelled, with financial compensation for prejudice or, in case of acquittals, complainants may get financial compensation for the Court's failure to protect their rights. Either party may also claim that the transmission of confidential information about the disciplinary charges and, where applicable, grievance complaints to the IOM amounts, in the absence of a proper legal basis for its intervention, to unauthorized disclosure, a compromise of classified information and unsatisfactory conduct pursuant to Sections 1.7, 16.1(b) and 40.3 of the ICC Information Protection Policy (see Section 21.3.5. below). This could be the basis for further disciplinary action against the officials who transmitted the classified information to the IOM and against the IOM staff members themselves, if they disclosed it to further recipient(s) in the course of the performance of their functions.

On the other hand, in disciplinary cases that do not involve the IOM, the parties can both claim, in case of an adverse decision, that the IOM should have been involved pursuant to Section 33 of the IOM Operational Mandate, which provides: "All reports of misconduct or serious misconduct, including possible unlawful acts, made against an elected official, staff member or contractor shall, if received by the Court, be submitted to the IOM".[50] The Court could claim that, in the absence of proper implementation pursuant to Section 2.1 of the Presidential Directive of 9 December 2003, the requirement of referral to the IOM under Section 33 of its Operational Mandate did not apply, but the challenging party could rely on the fact that the ASP is the legitimate authority of the Court, in charge of

---

[49] IER Report, para. 285, p. 93, see above note 2.
[50] See above note 45.

establishing the IOM pursuant to Article 112(4) of the Rome Statute and on the *tu patere legem quam ipse fecisti* principle in support of her or his challenge. Additionally, the ICC failure to comply with its Presidential Directive of 9 December 2003 with respect to the implementation of the Operational Mandate of the IOM cannot be used by the Court against a litigant pursuant to the *nemo auditur suam propriam turpitudinem allegans* principle.[51]

The abovementioned policy gaps impacting on staff appeal and disciplinary cases are highly prejudicial to the overall perception of the Court's adherence to the highest integrity standards. It is also a factor of the major vulnerability of the Court in staff litigation cases. Most disturbingly, it also feeds a perception of a double standard between those staff members who are well acquainted with the policy gaps impacting on the integrity of internal proceedings – or well-advised – and the others. The members of the first category, which necessarily includes the vast majority of the high management of the Court, can, if they like, enjoy quasi-total impunity for any misconduct, as they know that they can rely on the existing irregularities to quash any adverse decision, and can negotiate amicable settlements in a position of force. For the second category, which necessarily includes the vast majority of the lower level, non-managerial staff of the Court, it feeds a perception of helplessness against the potential abuses they may endure from the higher management, falling in the first category, in full impunity. All in all, the impossibility of safeguarding the integrity of staff appeal and disciplinary cases questions the very existence of the rule of law in the institution mandated to be the central body of international criminal justice. This is a situation that no responsible manager of the Court should normally leave unaddressed, once aware of it.

21.3.4. Anti-Fraud and Whistleblowing Policies

In 2014, the ICC promulgated the general principles of its anti-fraud and whistleblowing policies by way of Presidential Directive ICC/PRESD/G/2014/002 of 13 May 2014[52] and Presidential Directive ICC/PRESD/G/2014/003 of 8 October 2014[53] respectively. Both Directives provide, at Sections 6.1 and 5.1 respectively, that they shall be translated into relevant

---

[51] ILOAT, Judgment, 4 February 2004, No. 2318, p. 6 (http://www.legal-tools.org/doc/35b9a6/).
[52] ICC Anti-Fraud Policy, see above note 16.
[53] ICC Whistleblowing and Whistleblower Protection Policy, see above note 17.

administrative issuances to ensure a comprehensive system to combat fraud and to protect whistle-blowers. As already flagged by the International Criminal Court Bar Association in February 2018,[54] with the exception of an Administrative Instruction of 6 October 2015 on Financial Disclosure,[55] no such procedure was promulgated. The principles of the ICC Anti-Fraud and Whistleblowing Policies are yet to be implemented by appropriate procedures. The failure to promulgate procedures for the implementation of the Anti-Fraud and Whistleblowing Policies is in breach of Section 5.2 of the Presidential Directive of 9 December 2003, which affirms the responsibility of the ICC management for ensuring that "new issuances or amendments to existing issuances are promulgated as required".

In addition to the formal breach that is the failure to promulgate the procedures required to implement the Anti-Fraud and Whistleblowing policies, whistle-blowers in the Court are left with no procedure to seek and obtain protection against retaliation. In the absence of procedures, *bona fide* whistle-blowers reporting perceived fraud or unsatisfactory conduct in compliance with their duty as staff members under Section 4.1 of the Anti-Fraud Policy and/or Section 1.3(a) of the Whistleblowing Policy have no procedural venue to obtain the protection against retaliation theoretically offered to them under Section 4.4 of the Anti-Fraud Policy and/or Sections 2.2 and 4.5 of the Whistleblowing Policy. Like for the IOM, the IER report takes note of the symptom when it reads that "there is a perception from staff that individuals who officially complain may still bear a personal risk and the repercussions, including possible reprisals for a staff member, if publicly known, stand very high",[56] but it does not identify the cause. The non-implementation of appropriate procedures to protect whistle-blowers and/or those reporting fraud constitutes, in itself, a violation of the aforesaid policies, providing a valid ground for seeking compensation before the ILOAT for the Court's failure to comply with its duty to protect. More generally, this failure questions the genuineness of the Court's stated commitment to combat fraud and protect whistle-blowers, and the adherence of its management to the corresponding high standard of integrity. Read in light of the policy gaps affecting the integrity of internal disciplinary proceed-

---

[54] Legal Analysis of ICC Internal Accountability Mechanisms and Policies, see above note 47.

[55] ICC, Disclosure Requirements – Financial Disclosure Programme of the Court ('ICC-FDP') and IPSAS related party disclosures, 6 October 2015, ICC/AI/2015/005 (http://www.legal-tools.org/doc/bbdb4c/).

[56] IER Report, para. 287, p. 94, see above note 2.

ings before the ICC (see Section 21.3.3. above), this lack of compliance provides more substance to the perception of impunity for misconduct, it plays as a further deterrent to the fulfilment of staff members' reporting obligations, and further questions the existence of the rule of law within the Court.

21.3.5. Protection of Information

The framework principles governing the protection of information within the ICC are provided in a three-page Presidential Directive of 8 March 2005 entitled "Information Security Policy".[57] This Presidential Directive basically requires that all 'users' of information produced, transmitted and stored for and by the Court "must comply with the security provisions and restrictions placed on them by the Court" and further underlines that the policy is binding both on the Court and "all those who seek access to its information". The ICC Information Protection Policy promulgated by Administrative Instruction ICC/AI/2007/001 of 19 June 2007[58] governs most aspects of the classification of ICC records, in any medium or form, judicial and non-judicial alike. It defines the protection levels applicable to information within the ICC, the criteria applicable to the classification of information. It also provides rules governing its classification and handling, dissemination on a 'need-to-know' basis and disclosure of classified information, and the actions to be taken in cases of suspected compromise of information security, including potential disciplinary action.

On 4 December 2013, the ICC amended Regulation 14 of the Regulations of the Registry ('RoR') and redefined the levels of confidentiality applicable to its judicial records. The four levels of classification under Regulation 14 of the RoR are now: (a) 'Public', which is similar to 'UNCLASSIFIED' under Section 5.4 of the ICC Information Protection Policy; (b) 'Confidential', which is similar to '[ICC] CONFIDENTIAL' under Section 5.10 of the ICC Information Protection Policy; (c) 'Under Seal', which is similar to '[ICC] SECRET' under Section 5.13 of the ICC Information Protection Policy; and (d) 'Secret', which has no equivalent under the ICC Information Protection Policy. The classification '[ICC] RESTRICTED' provided under Sections 3.3(b) and 5.5-5.7 of the ICC Information Protec-

---

[57] ICC, Information Security Policy, 8 March 2005, ICC/PRESD/G/2005/001 (http://www.legal-tools.org/doc/3ae5ed/).

[58] ICC, ICC Information Protection Policy, 19 June 2007, ICC/AI/2007/001 (https://www.legal-tools.org/doc/04b126/).

tion Policy also has no equivalent under Regulation 14 of the RoR; in contrast, it is defined as the default classification for unmarked documents under Section 5.14 of the ICC Information Protection Policy.

As a result of the amendment of Regulation 14 of the RoR, the ICC Information Protection Policy of 2007 has become largely obsolete. The numerous inconsistencies between this policy and the other instruments of the Court is a factor of high insecurity for the daily operations of the Court, in particular its judicial activities. Some of these risks were flagged in February 2018 by the International Criminal Court Bar Association.[59] As a consequence of the largely perceived obsolescence of the ICC Information Protection Policy, there is now a wide consensus within the Court as to its inapplicability, which has led to a Court-wide tacit agreement to disregard it, instead of amending it. As a matter of general practice, the Office of the Prosecutor does not mark judicial documents – in particular witness statements – which are not (yet) filed in the records of a case or situation proceedings as to their level of classification, or marks them as [ICC] RESTRICTED only. Accordingly, these witness statements shall be deemed [ICC] RESTRICTED only under the ICC Information Protection Policy and are not confidential – and thus public – under Regulation 14 of the RoR. This situation creates a high risk of incidental or malevolent dissemination of highly sensitive information compromising the protection of victims, witnesses and other persons at risk on account of such information. *Bona fide* recipients of such sensitive information may not know that this information is classified, because it is not marked so, and may disseminate it further, thus increasing the risk. The sensitivity of this information should normally require, by nature, its classification as Confidential. This issue was raised before the Court in the *Gbagbo and Blé Goudé* case.[60] Trial Chamber I confirmed that witness statements – though not marked – were

---

[59] Legal Analysis of ICC Internal Accountability Mechanisms and Policies, see above note 47.

[60] In French only: ICC, *Le Procureur c. Laurent Gbagbo et Charles Blé Goudé*, Version Publique Expurgée du Rapport du Conseiller Juridique désigné en vertu de la règle 74 du Règlement de procédure et de preuve pour assister le témoin P-0046, 21 Février 2017, ICC-02/11-01/15-810-Red, paras. 18–19 (https://www.legal-tools.org/doc/e61f0c/); ICC, *Le Procureur c. Laurent Gbagbo et Charles Blé Goudé*, Observations Additionnelles relatives à l'immunité du témoin P-0046 et à la confidentialité de sa déposition auprès des enquêteurs du Bureau du Procureur, 20 Février 2017, ICC-02/11-01/15-815, paras. 7–14 (https://www.legal-tools.org/doc/621750/).

classified confidential[61] and instructed the Office of the Prosecutor to reassess the degree of compliance of its practice with the relevant administrative instructions of the Court.[62] Nothing has been done after this ruling to address this issue. One cannot exclude that the Office of the Prosecutor's persistent failure to mark and protect its witnesses' statements properly had an impact on its capacity to present a case that may support a conviction at trial, and on the acquittal of the two accused persons on 15 January 2019: how could the Prosecutor secure witness evidence without protecting the confidentiality of their statements properly? Not marking these documents and information, if confidential, amounts to a compromise under Section 1.7 of the ICC Information Protection Policy, and to unsatisfactory conduct incurring potential disciplinary action under its Section 40.3. As long as the Office of the Prosecutor will persist in not protecting its witnesses' statements properly, one can see this as a reason – not a justification – for not addressing the issues impacting on the integrity of disciplinary proceedings already mentioned (see Section 21.3.3. above).

The consequences of the failure to ensure the confidentiality of witnesses' statements on the fairness of the ICC proceedings is a matter for judicial determination by judges. However, at the same time, the absence of appropriate marking is placing victims, witnesses and other persons at risk on account of unmarked information.

In any case, the obsolescence of the 2007 ICC Information Protection Policy cannot serve as a justification for disregarding it, but rather triggers a duty to review it pursuant to Section 5.2 of the Presidential Directive of 9 December 2003. As for the previous aspects, the ICC management is in breach of this Presidential Directive for not having reviewed and adapted the ICC Information Protection Policy to the new version of Regulation 14 of the Regulations of the Registry since, at least, December 2013. This is a serious responsibility that the ICC management is once again accepting, endangering the Court's witnesses, victims, staff members, and other persons at risk on account of the activities of the Court, whereas their protection is considered a shared responsibility of "all the organs of the Court and

---

[61] ICC, *Le Procureur c. Laurent Gbagbo et Charles Blé Goudé*, Transcript of 15 February 2017, ICC-02/11-01/15, p. 3, lines 6-11 (https://www.legal-tools.org/doc/9f8359/).

[62] ICC, *Le Procureur c. Laurent Gbagbo et Charles Blé Goudé*, ICC-02/11-01/15, Transcript of 22 February 2017, p. 48 lines 23-25 to p. 49 lines 1-5 (https://www.legal-tools.org/doc/4dc909/).

those involved with the trial".[63] As is the case for field operations, the discrepancy of the current practices of the Office of the Prosecutor with the existing information protection policies provides the only rational explanation – still, not a justification – for the Court's failure to address the widely known and acknowledged issues impacting the security of classified information within the Court.

Once again, one can only hope that the IER Recommendation R12 mentioned above with respect to the undertaking of a full review of the ICC policy framework will have, despite its lack of specificity, the power to lead the Court to amend and update its Information Protection Policy, inasmuch as there is internal willingness to do so. An offer made, on 30 January 2020, by the author of the present chapter to provide a ready-made amended version of the ICC Information Protection Policy addressing its current flaws was declined the same day, on the sole ground that it came from the author (thus seemingly giving higher priority to the responding staff member's personal bias against the author, than the superior interest of the Court to protect its information, displaying what integrity normally advises against). Recommendation R12 has thus been ready for implementation with respect to the ICC Information Protection Policy even before it was made, but it is still fiercely resisted.

21.4. Conclusion

This chapter highlighted five examples of gaps in the ICC legal and policy framework. These gaps are serious, and lead to the conclusion that the minimum basic requirements are not met in terms of policy and legal framework, and that the ICC is failing, so far, to provide its staff and officials with the minimal guidance they should receive in order to uphold the highest integrity standards.

In the absence of such guidance, the onus of upholding the highest standard of integrity bears on ICC staff members and officials only. We shall trust in their capacity to do so. The requirements of Articles 36(3)(a), 42(3), 43(3) and 44(2) of the Rome Statute that the ICC Judges, Prosecutor and Registrar shall be persons of high moral character and that the staff members be selected according to the highest standards of efficiency, com-

---

[63] ICC, *The Prosecutor v. Thomas Lubanga Dyilo*, Decision on various issues related to witnesses' testimony during trial, 29 January 2008, ICC-01/04-01/06-1140, para. 36 (https://www.legal-tools.org/doc/8367f1/).

petency and integrity are there to give trust in their capacity to lead their way towards integrity without the need for such guidance.

The worst, however, is always possible. Like in Victor Hugo's *Ruy Blas*, even allegedly honest ministers and virtuous advisors do sometimes loot their organization.[64] At paragraphs 15 and 17 of its Judgment No. 4003 issued on 26 June 2018, the ILOAT rules that the behaviour of the former Registrar of the Court, Mr. Herman von Hebel – who was deemed a person of high moral character pursuant to Article 43(3) of the Rome Statute – amounted to "abuse of power, bad faith and retaliation" against one of the four ICC staff members arrested and illegally detained in Zintan in 2012. Though isolated, this instance reminds us that the guarantees provided in the Rome Statute alone, though important, are not all, and fall short from guaranteeing integrity and ethical behaviour in all circumstances.

By persisting in its failure to address the important policy and legal issues detailed in the present contribution and provide the ICC with the robust policy framework called for in the IOM's post-incident report on the Zintan crisis of 21 February 2013, and many times since, up until the more recent IER report of 30 September 2020, the management of the Court and of the ASP as a whole accepted a great risk. Having tried several times to persuade those concerned to take necessary measures, I hope that the present contribution may strengthen the awareness of the importance of the applicable standards of integrity at the ICC.

---

[64] Victor Hugo, Ruy Blas, III:2 : "Bon appétit, Messieurs ! Ô Ministres intègres ! Conseillers vertueux ! Voilà votre façon de servir, serviteurs qui pillez la maison !".

22

Does the International Criminal Court
Really Need an Ethics Charter?

Suhail Mohammed and Salim A. Nakhjavani[*]

22.1. Introduction

In December 2018, the Assembly of States Parties ('ASP') received the report of its external auditor on Human Resources Management.[1] The report – which draws on 25 interviews with officials and staff, and the results of a staff questionnaire – includes the following puzzling observations:

> The Court does not have an ethics charter. This situation may be surprising given its mission. However, the first chapter of the Staff Regulations, in article 1.2 on "fundamental values", addresses various points that may be covered by such a charter: general rights and obligations, confidentiality, honorary distinctions, gifts or remuneration, conflicts of interest, employment and activities outside the Court, and the use of the Court's property. Although it has *real legal significance*, it *does not have the moral impact of an ethics charter binding on staff*.[2]

Having made these observations, the external auditor reaches his finding:

> In its regulations, the International Criminal Court has a series of legal rules regarding ethics but without requiring its staff to adhere to a more complete "ethics charter", which would add

---

[*] **Suhail Mohammed** is a Candidate Legal Practitioner at Bowmans, South Africa. He has completed B. Pharm., LL.B. with distinction from the University of the Witwatersrand, Johannesburg, South Africa. **Salim A. Nakhjavani** is an Adjunct Professor of Law, University of the Witwatersrand, South Africa, an Advocate of the High Court, South Africa and a Member of the Johannesburg Bar. He was awarded the B.C.L., LL.B. with a *magna cum laude* from McGill University, and an LL.M. first class from the University of Cambridge, United Kingdom.

[1] ICC, Final audit report on Human Resources management, 24 July 2018, ICC-ASP/17/7 ('Audit report') (https://www.legal-tools.org/doc/5qtwby/).

[2] *Ibid.*, para. 238 (emphasis added).

to the *statutory aspect a moral message adapted to a jurisdiction.*[3]

A straightforward recommendation follows: "The External auditor recommends that the ICC develop and publish an ethics charter".[4]

One year later, the requisite report on Human Resources Management was tabled for the consideration of the ASP.[5] There was no direct mention of an ethics charter, which, it seemed, had been politely shelved, in the best traditions of the international civil service.[6] Rather, "[a]ctivities are also planned to reinforce the Court's ethical framework, including training on harassment prevention and strengthening informal conflict resolution mechanisms".[7]

The situation may indeed be "surprising", but for reasons other than the one identified by the external auditor. The Court has made two of these other reasons explicit. First, the current focus on harassment prevention is prompted by painful realities about the apparent prevalence of harassment, sexual harassment, and abuse of authority at the ICC[8] that may not have been disclosed to the external auditor or were omitted from the external auditor's report. Second, the (mis)management of misconduct has become a serious institutional risk to the mandate of the ICC, and a costly one.[9]

---

[3] *Ibid.*, p. 38, "Finding", under paras. 238–240 (emphasis added).

[4] *Ibid.*, "Recommendation 9".

[5] ICC, Report of the Court on Human Resources Management, 25 July 2019, ICC-ASP/18/4 ('Report of the Court on Human Resources Management') (https://www.legal-tools.org/doc/pys2zp/).

[6] See, for instance, Philip Allott's satirical critique, *Curing the Madness of the Intergovernmental World*, 8 July 2014, p. 4 (originally given as "The Idea of International Society", Alec Roche Lecture, 2006, Oxford, available on the web site of the Squire Law Library, University of Cambridge).

[7] Report of the Court on Human Resources Management, para. 13, p. 2, see above note 5.

[8] See ICC, Annual Report of the head of the Independent Oversight Mechanism ('IOM'), 11 November 2019, ICC-ASP/18/22, para. 14, p. 4 (https://www.legal-tools.org/doc/2u1ipr/), noting that complaints of harassment, sexual harassment and abuse of authority made up just over 40 per cent of the 32 complaints to the IOM between 1 October 2018 and 30 October 2019.

[9] See, for example, ICC, Report of the Committee on Budget and Finance on the work of its thirty-second session, 3 June 2019, paras. 140–152 (https://www.legal-tools.org/doc/q91xoa/); noting specifically "with concern the increased number of litigation cases and their significant financial impact" (para. 149), and provision of almost EUR 1 million for some 27 cases pending before the International Labour Organization Administrative Tribunal.

One further reason remains obscure, at least in public documents issued by the ICC so far: its "moral message" to its staff is *not missing*.

This observation finds clear expression in the Final Report of the Independent Expert Review of the International Criminal Court and the Rome Statute System, dated 30 September 2020. The Independent Expert Review, which was authorised by ICC-ASP/18/Res.7, takes up the recommendation of the external auditor for the adoption of a single Court-wide Ethics Charter laying down the minimum professional standards expected of all individuals working with the Court.

The rationale behind the recommendation of the Independent Expert Review was that the existing ethical framework is "fragmented, and does not provide for clear common principles and minimum standards applicable to all individuals affiliated with the Court".[10] A unified, Court-wide Ethics Charter would, according to the Expert Review, "unite all individuals affiliated with the Court under the same principles, under the One Court Principle".[11]

The Independent Expert Review, then, makes one thing clear: it is not the case that the ICC is missing a "moral message", but rather that this message is clouded, as a consequence of the fragmented presentation of the ICC's multiple ethical codes and instruments.

The ICC normative framework is clothed with not less than six codes of ethical and professional conduct, aside from the content of the Statute itself, Article 1.2 of the Staff Regulations, and the moral authority of the solemn undertakings of officials and staff. These are, in order of entry into force: the Code of Judicial Ethics, adopted by the judges of the Court (2005);[12] the Code of Professional Conduct for counsel, adopted by the ASP (2005);[13] the Code of Conduct for Investigators, promulgated by the Registrar (2008);[14] the Code of Conduct for Staff Members, promulgated

---

[10] ICC, Independent Expert Review of the International Criminal Court and Rome Statute System, Final Report, 30 September 2020 (https://www.legal-tools.org/doc/cv19d5/).

[11] *Ibid.*

[12] ICC, Code of Judicial Ethics, 2 January 2005, ICC-BD/02-01/05 (https://www.legal-tools.org/doc/383f8f/).

[13] ICC, Code of Professional Conduct for counsel, 2 December 2005, ICC-ASP/4/Res.1 (https://www.legal-tools.org/doc/f9ed33).

[14] ICC, Code of conduct for investigators, 10 September 2008, ICC/AI/2008/005 ('ICC Code of conduct for investigators') (https://legal-tools.org/doc/c86582).

by the Registrar (2011);[15] the Code of Conduct for the Office of the Prosecutor, promulgated by the Prosecutor (2013);[16] and the Code of Conduct for Intermediaries (2014).[17] A notable exclusion from this panoply of profession-specific standards appears to be the interpreters' and translators' profession, which was subject to specific ethical standards at the International Criminal Tribunal for the former Yugoslavia[18] and the Special Court for Sierra Leone.[19]

So, the ICC's "moral message" to its staff is not missing. Far from it – at least on paper. But transmission does not imply reception. The real question is how the message is translated into action, both individually and collectively. And the real challenge is that there may be little appetite for the promulgation of yet more ethical standards in a social space already inundated by expressions of moral righteousness, and in a world weary of empty speech.

Moreover, any proposal for additional normative standards must be assessed against the compliance burden of near-inevitable *double deontology*. We use this term to refer to a situation of being "subject simultaneously to two [or more] professional codes of conduct".[20] Indeed, it may be more accurate, in the context of the ICC, to refer to *multiple deontology*, and to distinguish two forms: *horizontal* and *vertical*. They encompass situations where a lawyer is bound by multiple codes of ethical conduct within the ICC normative framework (*horizontal multiple deontology*); and also between the ICC framework and their home State(s) of registration, admission or enrolment for purposes of legal practice (*vertical multiple deontology*).

---

[15] ICC, Code of Conduct for Staff Members, 4 April 2011, ICC/AI/2011/002 (https://legal-tools.org/doc/75f9db).

[16] ICC, Code of Conduct for the Office of the Prosecutor, 5 September 2013 ('OTP Code') (https://legal-tools.org/doc/3e11eb).

[17] ICC, Code of Conduct for Intermediaries, 1 March 2014 (https://legal-tools.org/doc/eac2f0).

[18] International Criminal Tribunal for the former Yugoslavia, the Code of Ethics for Interpreters and Translators Employed by the International Criminal Tribunal for the former Yugoslavia, 8 March 1999, IT/144 (https://www.legal-tools.org/doc/xix9r7/).

[19] Special Court for Sierra Leone, Code of Ethics for Interpreters and Translators Employed by the Special Court for Sierra Leone, 25 May 2004 (https://legal-tools.org/doc/c56846).

[20] Council of Bars and Law Societies of Europe, *Guidelines for Bars and Law Societies on Free Movement of Lawyers within the European Union*, p. 9. The English term comes from the original French ("double déontologie").

We attempt to proceed scientifically in our ethical analysis. As Ibn Sina proposed in his treatise, *al-Burhân*,[21] one appropriate method to acquire first principles is *tajriba*, or experimentation.[22] Ibn Sina's account of *tajriba* follows a two-step process,[23] which we have adapted to assist us in answering the question with which this chapter opens: "Does the International Criminal Court really need an ethics charter?".

Our first step in this 'thought experiment' is to assess whether the current existing framework is capable of communicating and entrenching the ICC's "moral message". The second step will use this premise in a syllogism to show that this existing capability militates against the need for an additional ethics charter, as recommended by the external auditor on Human Resources Management.

In the first step, we analyse, in particular, whether the proper implementation of the existing ethical codes can entrench the culture of ethics contained in this "moral message" to its staff. We then consider whether the publication of an additional ethics charter may actually retard the achievement of the external auditor's specified objectives, because of the added 'compliance burden' flowing, in part, from problems of *double deontology*.

In the second step, we will consider the specific objectives that are implied – and appear to underpin – the external auditor's recommendation for an additional ethics charter. We will then examine whether the conclusions from the first step of our analysis would satisfy the external auditor's objectives.

Our experimentation may not be double-blind, but it is blind in at least one respect – problematically, but inevitably: we do not know, and can never know, the reality of the lived ethics of staff in the offices and corridors of the ICC. Our analysis does not rest on qualitative or quantitative methodology, on surveys of staff. To quote Maurice Mendelson in a new context, we must "beware of the 'weaving of nets to sieve the mist'".[24]

---

[21] Ash-shifâ, al-Burhân, A. Badawi (eds.), *Cairo: Association of Authorship*, Translation and Publication Press, 1966.

[22] Jon McGinnis, "Scientific Methodologies in Medieval Islam", in *Journal of the History of Philosophy*, July 2003, vol. 41, no. 3, p. 307.

[23] *Ibid.*, p. 317.

[24] Maurice H. Mendelson, "The Formation of Customary International Law", in *Recueil des cours*, 1998, vol. 272, p. 174, citing D.J. Enright, *The Alluring Problem: An Essay on Irony*, 1986, p. 5.

22.2. Does the Existing Ethical Framework Communicate a "Moral Message"?

The external auditor's report suggests that an "ethics charter" be developed, which would "add to the statutory aspect a moral message adapted to a jurisdiction".[25] The report suggests that the envisioned charter canvass the following points, which echo the "fundamental values" contemplated in Article 1.2 of the Staff Regulations: "general rights and obligations, confidentiality, honorary distinctions, gifts or remuneration, conflicts of interest, employment and activities outside the Court, and use of the Court's property".[26] It appears that the "moral message", which the external auditor finds apposite can be adequately delivered in the form of codified guidelines in respect of the above-mentioned points. The question, then, is whether or not the existing framework addresses these points in sufficient detail to convey the "moral message" envisioned by the external auditor. To frame this question in another way, how might the external auditor have responded to question: Does the ICC's existing ethical framework *already* contain the "moral message" that the proposed ethics charter seeks to communicate?

In a nutshell, our answer is yes. The substantiation lies in the constellation of ICC codes of conduct that have already entered into force. In proving this, we will analyse these codes (with a specific focus on the OTP's Code of Conduct, given its relative breadth and depth, and its infancy) through the prism of "fundamental values" which the external auditor recommended that the ICC codify through the proposed ethics charter. Additionally, the robustness of these existing codes will be tested against what information is publicly available on past ethical lapses and failures involving ICC staff and officials.

The OTP's Code of Conduct begins by laying out five fundamental rules.[27] These rules enshrine the values of independence, impartiality, non-discrimination, respect for the rule of law, a dedication to upholding fundamental human rights, and maintaining the integrity of the Court.[28] These five fundamental rules are reiterated in Section 4 of the OTP's Code of Conduct, titled "General Principles". The foundation and principles of this Code echo the "fundamental values" that are contemplated in Article 1.2 of

---

[25] Audit report, p. 38, "Finding", under paras. 238–240, see above note 1.

[26] *Ibid.*, para. 239.

[27] ICC Code of conduct for investigators, see above note 14.

[28] *Ibid.*

the Staff Regulations which forms the basis for the external auditor's recommendation. This is the first demonstration of the congruency between the OTP's Code of Conduct and the proposed ethics charter.

The next point of analysis is Section 3 of the OTP's Code of Conduct, the "Purpose of the Code". This section explains that the Code seeks to "establish a set of minimum standards of conduct […] as a supplement to the general standards of conduct as promulgated in the Code of Conduct for Staff Members, the Staff Regulations, the Staff Rules, the Code of Conduct for Investigators and any other document that may be relevant to the performance of their duties". In addition to this, the General Principles of the OTP's Code of Conduct (found in Section 4) explicitly indicates that the OTP is to be primarily guided by, *inter alia*, the principle of "professional ethics and integrity". The external auditor's report explains that the existing standards contained in Article 1.2 of the Staff Regulations "has a series of legal rules regarding ethics but without requiring its staff to adhere to a more complete ethics charter".[29] The OTP's Code of Conduct, it seems, has the potential to function as the "complete ethics charter" that has been contemplated by the external auditor, in respect of a subset of staff – those serving in the OTP. This is premised on the fact that the OTP's Code of Conduct not only expands upon the "legal rules regarding ethics" (which are located in Article 1.2 of the Staff Regulations), but also requires the staff of the OTP to adhere to these clearly defined standards of conduct. Both of these points, at least on their face, seem to achieve the objectives laid out by the external auditor. Additionally, the manner in which the OTP's Code of Conduct functions seems to align with the objectives of the external auditor in that it supplements the "fundamental values" in Article 1.2 of the Staff Regulations, instead of subsuming that Article.

The external auditor's recommendation, however, was not solely aimed at the OTP. Indeed, it was envisioned that the proposed ethics charter would be applicable to all ICC staff. This, presumably, intended to not only include the ICC's four constituent organs, but also the counsel who practise before the Court. It is worth noting, then, that the same commitment to the "fundamental values" contained in Article 1.2 of the Staff Regulations has been made binding on members of each of these offices (including counsel who practise before the Court) through their own separately applicable codes of conduct. These codes of conduct rightly vary in rela-

---

[29] Audit report, p. 38, "Finding", under paras. 238–240, see above note 1.

tion to the specific duties that flow from fundamental values, and differ accordingly in terms of the management of conflicts of interests, confidentiality, general obligations, remuneration and employment outside of the Court. However, the essence of these codes remains the same: that they are a set of ethical and professional guidelines which regulate standards of conduct in relation to the fundamental values in Article 1.2 of the Staff Regulations. This fact is mostly uncontroversial, and is easily ascertainable from the explicit language of each of these individual codes. The content of each of these codes, which have entered into force over a period between 2005 and 2011, would seem to satisfy the external auditor's objectives in the same manner as we described in relation to the OTP's Code of Conduct.

However, an ethics charter that broadly commits itself to upholding the "fundamental values" contained in Article 1.2 of the Staff Regulations but fails to provide more definitive guidelines on *how* that can be achieved will only ring hollow.

The next point that must be addressed, then, is whether the existing of codes are – at least formally – capable of practicably fulfilling that commitment. It is helpful to address this point through the lens of the actual language of the existing guidelines, but perhaps more effective to do so through an analysis of how these guidelines would (and could have been) applied in publicly disclosed ethical lapses or failures which have affected the Court in the past. We turn to consider three specific incidents arising during the *Lubanga* trial; in respect of the Prosecutor's editorial in the Darfur situation;[30] and during the *Ruto and Sang* and *Gbagbo* trials.

22.2.1. The *Lubanga* Trial

The ethical turbulence associated with the *Lubanga* trial has been well documented.[31] The issue was the disclosure of confidential documents by the OTP during the course of the trial. During the trial, the Prosecutor had failed to disclose a cache of documents which contained potentially exculpatory evidence, citing "confidentiality" as the rationale for such conduct.[32] This failure was characterised as a "wholesale and serious abuse" by the Trial Chamber.[33] The question that must be answered here is, firstly,

---

[30] See Section 22.2.2. and note 36 below. See also Milan Markovic, "The ICC Prosecutor's Missing Code of Conduct", in *Texas International Law Journal*, 2011, vol. 47, no. 1.

[31] For a deeper discussion surrounding this particular case, see *ibid*.

[32] ICC, *The Prosecutor v. Thomas Lubanga Dyilo*, Trial Chamber, ICC-01/04-01/06, para. 17.

[33] *Ibid*., para. 76.

whether the existing OTP Code of Conduct – which would have been directly applicable, had it been in force at the material time – would have been capable of providing adequate guidance in relation to this issue; and secondly, if that is not the case, whether the proposed ethics charter would be capable of providing suitable guidance in this same instance.

The OTP's Code of Conduct appears to address the issue of disclosure of documents in Section 3. This section, however, is broadly stated, and simply places an emphasis on the OTP's obligation to

> comply with the applicable rules on disclosure of evidence and inspection of material in the possession or control of the Office in a manner that facilitates the fair and expeditious conduct of the proceedings and fully respects the rights of the person under investigation or the accused, with due regard for the protection of victims and witnesses.

The breadth of this rule has been critiqued by commentators,[34] as it does not provide "any useful clarity or guidance to members of the OTP to aid their interpretation of the Statute".[35] It certainly does not go as far as the draft rule on disclosure that has been proposed by Markovic,[36] which would provide strict guidelines as to the legal steps that the OTP ought to follow in respect of the disclosure of confidential documents during the trial process.

In our view, the broad terms of the duty of confidentiality in the OTP's Code do not limit the effectiveness of its ethical standards concerning the issue of confidentiality. This is because, in our view, the Code of Conduct ought not to constitute a crystallised guideline on trial procedure or strategy. Its primary function is to provide an ethical and professional underpinning which must be borne in mind when devising strategies which, really, are a matter of procedural and evidentiary law, not ethics, and should always be guided by the ICC Statute, the Rules of Procedure and Evidence, and previous decisions made by the Court (where appropriate).[37] In this regard, the current Code of Conduct fulfils its purpose. That is because it places an imperative on the OTP to interpret these sources of law

---

[34] Lawrence Pacewicz, "International Criminal Court Code of Conduct for the Office of the Prosecutor", in *International Legal Materials*, 2014, vol. 53, no. 2, p. 398.

[35] *Ibid.*

[36] Markovic, 2011, pp. 221–222, see above note 30.

[37] Rome Statute of the International Criminal Court, 17 July 1998, Article 21 ('ICC Statute') (http://www.legal-tools.org/doc/7b9af9/).

in such a manner that fulfils its obligation in terms of Section 3, while also affording the OTP the flexibility required to properly pursue prosecutions, as required by the mandate of that Office. What staff are guided to weigh is this interface between the Code of Conduct and the law governing trials at the ICC.

For the sake of argument, let us assume that the OTP's current Code of Conduct fails to provide adequate guidance with respect to the issue of disclosure. The question that then arises is whether the external auditor's proposed ethics charter would be capable of filling the gap. We do not think it would, for straightforward reasons: the external auditor's proposal is not specifically aimed at the OTP. Instead, it is aimed at ICC staff in general. Such a charter could only be couched as generally – if not more so – as the OTP's existing Code of Conduct, which is tailored to idiosyncratic issues such as prosecutorial obligations of disclosure. To the extent the OTP's Code of Conduct were deficient in the depth of guidance on disclosure, the more effective solution would likely be to amend or supplement the existing Code of Conduct, not to promulgate an ethics charter.

22.2.2. The Darfur Situation and the Prosecutor's Editorial

In 2010, the Appeals Chamber reversed the Pre-Trial Chamber's decision to grant an arrest warrant for Omar Al-Bashir for crimes committed in Darfur during the period of March 2003 to July 2008.[38] The ratio that underpinned this decision was that the Pre-Trial Chamber applied the incorrect standard of proof in determining whether an arrest warrant ought to have been granted.[39] Almost immediately thereafter, the Prosecutor, Luis Moreno-Ocampo, authored a piece which was published in *The Guardian*, titled "Now end this Darfur denial".[40]

In the piece, the Prosecutor claimed that the original decision by the Pre-Trial Chamber had found that "Bashir's forces have raped on a mass scale in Darfur" and had "deliberately inflict[ed] on the Fur, Masalit and Zaghawa ethnic groups living conditions calculated to bring about their

---

[38] ICC, The *Prosecutor v. Omar Hassan Ahmad Al Bashir*, Appeals Chamber, Judgment on Appeal Against the "Decision on the Prosecution's Application for a Warrant of Arrest against Omar Hassan Ahmad Al Bashir", 3 February 2010, ICC-02/05-01/09-73, para. 2 (https://www.legal-tools.org/doc/9ada8e/).

[39] *Ibid.*, paras. 41–42.

[40] Luis Moreno-Ocampo, "Now end this Darfur denial", *The Guardian*, 15 July 2010.

physical destruction".[41] The Pre-Trial Chamber, however, had made no such findings; instead, it had only made a determination in relation to the granting of a warrant of arrest under Article 58(1) of the Rome Statute.[42] The misleading nature of this editorial was widely criticised, with some going so far as suggesting that its publication constituted sufficient grounds to consider removing the Prosecutor from office.[43]

The same reflective question that we applied to the *Lubanga* issue must be applied in this instance, too. Would the OTP's Code of Conduct – were it in force at the material time – have provided adequate clarity on this issue of extrajudicial speech; and if not, would the external auditor's proposed ethics charter be capable of providing such clarity?

Section 8 of the OTP's Code of Conduct, titled "Public Expression and Association", is dedicated to addressing the issue of prosecutorial speech. Article 39 under that section specifically addresses the issue of extrajudicial speech, stating that

> Members of the Office shall refrain from making any public pronouncements, outside the context of the proceedings before the Court, that they know, or reasonably ought to know, may be disseminated by means of public communication, and may have a substantial likelihood of prejudicing the judicial proceedings or the rights of any person in the proceedings before the Court.

This standard of conduct seems to be capable of directly addressing the issue that had arisen in respect of the Al-Bashir editorial, insofar as it provides an almost explicit prohibition on speech that would "prejudic[e] […] the rights of any person in proceedings before the Court". In the Al-Bashir case, such prejudice takes the form of the derogation of Al-Bashir's right to be presumed innocent until proven guilty before the Court.[44]

The standard does not, however, follow the more detailed iteration advanced by Markovic,[45] which would prohibit "speaking to the media about the merits of particular cases or the guilt or innocence of certain accused before judgment by the Court, and making any public statements re-

---

[41] *Ibid*; see also, Markovic, 2011, p. 230, see above note 30.

[42] *Ibid*.

[43] Kevin Jon Heller, "The Remarkable Arrogance of the ICC Prosecutor", *Opinio Juris*, 20 July 2010 (available on its web site).

[44] Markovic, 2011, p. 231, see above note 30.

[45] *Ibid.*, p. 235.

garding the character, credibility, reputation, or record of an accused or any witness".[46] This version is more comprehensive than what is contained in the existing OTP Code of Conduct, but ultimately seeks to protect against the same harm as contemplated by Section 8 of that Code: prejudicing the rights of persons in proceedings before the Court. The existing Code is effective in preventing this harm, as has been acknowledged by academic commentators.[47] This is despite the existing rule being cast in broader terms than those Markovic envisioned. The rationale for this is that his catalogue of protected targets of extrajudicial speech – "the character, credibility, reputation, or record of an accused" person – are generally accepted as ingredients of a fair trial. The existing Code, then, takes each of these considerations into account, while simply framing them in the context of fair trial rights. In this regard, the guidance of the OTP's Code appears sufficient, in the sense that it would have curbed the publication of comment in the nature of the Prosecutor's editorial.

Limits on extrajudicial speech also apply to counsel practising before the Court, as well as comments made by judges before whom the proceedings are unfolding. In this respect, the Code of Professional Conduct for Counsel and the Code of Judicial Ethics find application.

The Code of Professional Conduct for Counsel implicitly addresses this issue in Article 24(1), where it is stated that "Counsel shall take all necessary steps to ensure that his or her actions or those of counsel's assistants or staff are not prejudicial to the ongoing proceedings and do not bring the Court into disrepute". This Article, cast broadly, seems to encompass extrajudicial speech to the extent that it is capable of prejudicing the rights of persons in proceedings before the Court (and thus the proceedings themselves). The guidelines in this respect are less specific than those which apply to the OTP. This distinction, however, is not inappropriate when one considers the higher duty of care that is applicable to the OTP.[48] Notwithstanding that difference, the Code of Professional Conduct for Counsel provides the necessary framework to address the issue of extrajudicial speech of the kind that is reflected in the Prosecutor's editorial.

Similarly, the Code of Judicial Ethics – in Article 9 – clearly and unequivocally prohibits judges from commenting on pending cases. This pro-

---

[46] *Ibid.*

[47] Pacewicz, 2014, p. 398, see above note 34.

[48] *Ibid.*, fn. 259.

hibition is reflective of the stringent level of impartiality that is expected of ICC judges. This prohibition ensures that no person appearing in proceedings before the Court – and thus before the judges of the Court – will be thought to be denied the presumption of innocence that the Rome Statute affords to them.

Let us assume, once again for the sake of argument, that these existing codes do not go far enough with regard to the regulation of extrajudicial speech for the purpose of protecting the rights of persons in proceedings before the Court. The question, once again, is whether the proposed ethics charter would be sufficient in achieving that goal, when overlaid on the existing codes.

Any ethics charter applicable across the ICC to all staff would not be capable of providing staff serving in each organ, or counsel who practise before the Court, with anything more comprehensive than what their currently existing codes already provide for. A general ethics charter can only address issues, well, generally. It is likely to be incapable of addressing the differing 'standards of expression' that are appropriate for each individual office. The guidelines would be sparser than what already exists, and would not overcome the same shortcomings that might have already been identified in respect of the existing ethical framework. It is for this reason, we suggest, that the external auditor's proposed ethics charter would do nothing more than what has already been done.

22.2.3. The *Ruto and Sang* and *Gbagbo* Trials

The *Ruto and Sang* trial,[49] like the *Lubanga* trial, is "one of ICC legend".[50] The *Ruto* and *Sang* trial saw Kenyan defendants appear before the Court, having been charged with crimes against humanity.[51] In this case, the Trial Chamber noted its concern regarding the Prosecutor's various disclosure failures, and needed to make an order ensuring that the Prosecution would act in full conformity with its disclosure obligations.[52] The ethical breach

---

[49] ICC, *The Prosecutor v. William Samoei Ruto and Joshua Arap Sang*, Trial Chamber, ICC-01/09-01/11.

[50] Constance Rachel Turnbull, "Understanding and Improving the 2013 Code of Conduct for the Office of the Prosecutor for the International Criminal Court", in *Georgetown Journal of Legal Ethics*, 2018, vol. 31, p. 891.

[51] *Ibid.*

[52] *The Prosecutor v. William Samoei Ruto and Joshua Arap Sang*, Trial Chamber, ICC-01/09-01/11, para 59.

---

that tainted the *Gbagbo* trial[53] was of a similar nature. In that case, the issue in question revolved around the (dis)use of evidence which "might have cut against the investigative angle".[54]

As stated previously, the heart of our enquiry is whether the existing ethical framework provides (or would have provided) adequate guidelines that, if applied in these cases, would have provided greater clarity in respect of the intersection between disclosure of evidence, confidentiality and objective truth-seeking. The second step of the enquiry also reflects our previous undertakings and, therefore, addresses whether the external auditor's proposed ethics charter would provide better guidance in respect of this same intersection.

Sections 1 and 3 of the OTP's Code of Conduct are particularly helpful in this respect. Section 1 provides clear guidance as to how a Prosecutor ought to deal with the objective truth-seeking component of this enquiry. In addressing this issue, Rule 49 explains that:

> In compliance with the duty to establish the truth under article 54(1)(a) of the Statute, the Office shall investigate incriminating and exonerating circumstances equally in all steps involved in the planning and conduct of investigative and prosecutorial activities. In particular, Members of the Office shall: [...] b) consider all relevant circumstances when assessing evidence, irrespective of whether they are to the advantage or the disadvantage of the prosecution.

This is particularly helpful as it frames the ethical duties of the OTP through a statutory lens, namely Article 54(1)(a) of the Rome Statute, as well as a professional and ethical responsibility to not discriminate between incriminating and exonerating evidence. This is particularly helpful in cases such as *Ruto and Sang* and *Gbagbo*, as it crystallises a specific instance when the Prosecutor must actively consider Article 54(1)(a), which places an obligation on him or her to "investigate incriminating and exonerating circumstances equally" – namely when assessing evidence during the case-preparative phase. The helpfulness of Rule 49 is buttressed by the language of Rule 49(b), which is far more comprehensive than the statutory duty contained in Article 54(1)(a) in that it places particular emphasis on the manner in which the OTP should assess evidence which may disadvantage

---

[53]   ICC, *The Prosecutor v. Laurent Gbagbo*, Trial Chamber, ICC-02/11-01/11-49.

[54]   Turnbull, 2018, p. 892, see above note 50.

the Prosecutor's case. The existence of this rule, according to Turnbull, "means that it is unlikely that such abuses will be repeated without prosecutorial sanctions".[55]

Section 3 of the OTP Code would have found expression, too. Rule 53(a) obliges the OTP to disclose any evidence (within the boundaries of the applicable rules on disclosure) "that shows or tends to show the innocence of the accused, or to mitigate the guilt of the accused, or which may affect the credibility of prosecution evidence". This rule, like Rule 49(a), provides the OTP with clear guidance as to how it should conduct itself in respect of the disclosure of evidence which may exonerate a person in proceedings before the Court. The existence of this rule, much like Rule 49(a), would ostensibly reduce the probability of instances of the *Ruto and Sang* or *Gbagbo* kind unfolding in the future.

As with the issue of extrajudicial expression, the issue of failing to disclose evidence which is determined to be prejudicial to one's own case, but which appears to be objectively true, is one that poses an ethical challenge to counsel who appear before the Court, and not only the OTP. In this respect, the Code of Professional Conduct for Counsel is instructive. Article 24(3) of that document is particularly applicable in such instances. It states that "Counsel shall not deceive or knowingly mislead the Court. He or she shall take all steps necessary to correct an erroneous statement made by him or her or by assistants or staff as soon as possible after becoming aware that the statement was erroneous". This obligation embedded in Article 24(3) mirrors that which is made binding upon the OTP in Rules 49 and 53, insofar as it can be reasonably understood that actively withholding of evidence on the basis that it is prejudicial to one's own case constitutes deception of the Court. This understanding can hardly be seen as controversial, and the applicability of Article 24(3) is therefore a natural corollary of such conduct. In this regard, it is clear that counsel, when dealing with situations such as those which arose in the cases of *Ruto and Sang* and *Gbagbo*, would be properly guided as to how they should (and should not) conduct themselves during the course of proceedings.

At this juncture we ask once again whether an additional set of guidelines – the proposed ethics charter – would supplement the effectiveness of the existing codes. Once again, any Court-wide ethics charter would necessarily be cast in general terms. Such a charter could only reit-

---

[55] *Ibid.*

erate the general legal obligation to assess evidence impartially. This obligation, then, would likely resemble the normative content of Article 54(1)(a), but be made applicable to a broader range of ICC staff than that article, which concerns only the OTP. This general proposition, then, will provide a certain degree of guidance in the sense that it places an ethical duty on members of the Court, which will function in tandem with the statutory duty that exists in the Rome Statute. This guidance, however, will not be any more comprehensive – nor any more helpful – than the existing codes of conduct, which not only confer the same 'dual duty' onto the Court's staff, but also goes on to further explain the specific importance of assessing and disclosing evidence which would be prejudicial to one's own case. The external auditor's proposed ethics charter, then, will provide no further guidance than what is contained within the existing ethical framework.

22.2.4. Reflection

Each of the above-mentioned incidents falls into various constituents of the "fundamental value" composite that the external auditor's proposal seeks to construct. As has been demonstrated, the existing statutory framework at the ICC is sufficiently robust to achieve such construction on its own. Put otherwise, the "moral message" which the external auditor wishes to communicate through the publication of an ethics charter is capable of being delivered by the existing constellation of ethical codes in force at the ICC.

22.3. Entrenching the ICC's "Moral Message" in Practice

Having established that the necessary "moral message" has, at least formally, been promulgated to the staff serving at every constituent office of the ICC, we must now consider how this "moral message" might permeate at the level of culture.[56] We will then consider whether an additional ethics charter would be helpful in further entrenching the "moral message".

The literature in management science makes plain that the mere existence of ethics charters and codes of conduct, does not in itself guarantee

---

[56] The distinction that we have drawn between "formal" and "informal" communication refers to the difference between having an ethical framework in place and ensuring the implementation of that ethical framework in a manner that results in the adoption of the ethical values contained within that framework.

ethical conduct by staff within an organisation.[57] This is especially true in instances when enforcement is lacking.[58] There is no reason why this logic would not apply to the ICC, whose robust ethical framework, it would appear, has not spontaneously generated virtue in all individuals under all circumstances.

We first explore some of the reasons which may render the ICC's existing ethical framework susceptible to serious ethical breaches, and secondly, consider approaches that might mitigate this risk of breaches of this kind.

A great many large organisations have fallen into ethical default, despite having ethical guidelines in place.[59] This fact prefaces the first leg of our analysis, that being some of the reasons which render organisations susceptible to ethical breach, even when those organisations are governed by robust ethical frameworks. Webley and Werner[60] suggest that the chasm between "policy and practice" is rooted in two interlinked considerations: a) ineffective ethics programmes (which we understand as referring to 'formal' implementation, such as an ethics code) and b) deficiencies in corporate culture – in other words, a lack of embedding.[61]

In respect of the first factor, Webley and Werner suggest that an ineffective ethics code might "only encompass a narrow set of issues without addressing wider obligations or commitments".[62] Additionally, it is suggested that an ineffective ethics code may constitute nothing more than "a set of rules that the employees are expected to follow, rather than values-based and providing guidance on how to handle ethical dilemmas".[63] Lastly, Webley and Webber suggest that another hallmark of an ineffective ethics

---

[57] Simon Webley and Andrea Werner, "Corporate Codes of Ethics: Necessary But Not Sufficient", in *Business Ethics: A European Review*, 2008, vol. 17, no. 4, p. 405; Pablo Ruiz, Ricardo Martinez, Cristina Diaz and Job Rodrigo, "Level of Coherence Among Ethics Program Components and Its Impact on Ethical Intent", in *Journal of Business Ethics*, 2015, vol. 128, no. 4, pp. 725–742.

[58] Jennifer J. Kish-Gephart, David A. Harrison and Linda Klebe Treviño, "Bad Apples, Bad Cases, and Bad Barrels: Meta-Analytic Evidence About Sources of Unethical Decisions at Work", in *Journal of Applied Psychology*, 2010, vol. 95, no. 1, pp. 1–31.

[59] Webley and Werner, 2008, p. 406, see above note 57.

[60] *Ibid.*

[61] *Ibid.*

[62] *Ibid.*

[63] *Ibid.*

code addresses employee behaviour, but excludes important decision-makers within the organisation.[64]

As explained above, the ICC's existing framework goes a long way in addressing specific concerns which may arise during the course of a staff member's responsibilities, as well as providing clarity in respect of the broader ethical commitments that the ICC comes to expect from its associates. Additionally, the existing framework is non-discriminatory, in the sense that Article 1.2 of the Staff Regulations is made equally applicable to each and every one of the ICC's staff, irrespective of their role within the organisation.

The next consideration, then, is what Webley and Werner call a "lack of embedding".[65] The authors explain that a gap between practice and policy emerges when an ethical code is not effectively embedded or communicated to the organisation. Simply put, they say, "it is not sufficient to send a booklet to all staff and expect them to adhere to its contents".[66] The importance of ensuring that an ethical code is embedded within an organisation cannot be understated.

In 1994, the US-based Ethics Resource Centre published its first National Business Survey.[67] This survey relied on feedback from approximately 4,000 employees in that country. It found that companies with ethics policies clearly expressed through ethics programmes showed positive upturns in ethical compliance. A negative response was attached to companies which had communicated ethics policies but omitted the expression thereof through proper ethical programmes.[68] The clearest conclusion to be drawn from this report, then, was that the existence of a code without a supporting ethics programme only increases organisational awareness of ethical issues, but does not go far enough in reducing the incidence of ethical breaches.[69]

---

[64] *Ibid*, citing Brian J. Farrell and Deirdre M. Cobbin, "A Content Analysis of Codes of Ethics in Australian Enterprises", in *Journal of Managerial Psychology*, 1996, vol. 11, no. 1, pp. 37–55.

[65] *Ibid.*

[66] *Ibid.*

[67] Rebecca Goodell, *Ethics in American Business: Policies, Programs and Perceptions Report of a Landmark Survey of U.S. Employees*, Ethics Resource Center, Washington, DC, 1994.

[68] *Ibid.*

[69] *Ibid.*, p. 37.

This finding was repeated in a 2004 Canadian study.[70] This study revolved around 57 interviews of employees and managers of four Canadian companies in respect of the effectiveness of codes of ethics within their organisations. On the back of this conclusion, the author of this study went on to suggest that "the mere existence of a code will be unlikely to influence employee behaviour" and that companies which "merely possess a code might legitimately be subject to allegations of window dressing".[71] The outcomes of these studies suggest that to bolster the probability of ethical compliance within an organisation, that organisation must supplement its ethical code – or in the case of the ICC, the existing constellation of codes of conduct – with an immersive, formal programme that ingrains its ethical commitments into the consciousness of the Court's staff. On this point, structure and function are clearly interlinked. As suggested elsewhere, an expressly virtues- or values-based code may hold more promise than duty-based rules as 'conversation-starters', and not 'conversation-enders' at the ICC, where staff are drawn from different 'home' legal systems and legal cultures.[72]

Another issue that does seem to arise, however, is in relation to what may be limited disciplinary action associated with breaches of the ICC's existing codes of conduct. This is particularly true in relation to the OTP's Code of Conduct.[73]

On 21 July 1998, the late Chief Justice of South Africa – the first of the democratic era – Ismail Mahomed, gave a speech to the International Commission of Jurists in Cape Town. He explained how, absent the exercise of the apparatus of the State in enforcing the orders of courts, they "could easily be reduced to paper tigers with the ferocious capacity to snarl and to roar but no teeth to bite and no sinews to execute their judgments which may then be mockingly reduced to pieces of sterile scholarship, toothless wisdom or pious poetry".[74]

---

[70] Mark S. Schwartz, "Effective Corporate Codes of Ethics: Perception of Code Users", in *Journal of Business Ethics*, 2004, vol. 55, no. 4, pp. 323–343.

[71] *Ibid.*

[72] See Salim A. Nakhjavani, "ICC Statute Article 45", Lexsitus Lecture, CILRAP Film, 28 September 2017, Johannesburg (www.cilrap.org/cilrap-film/45-nakhjavani/).

[73] Turnbull, 2018, p. 900, see above note 50.

[74] Ismail Mahomed, "The Independence of the Judiciary", in *South African Law Journal*, 1998, vol. 115, no. 4, pp. 658-667.

In this same vein, an ethics charter that lacks a disciplinary element, which imposes corrective. sanctions upon those who breach its provisions will be nothing more than "toothless wisdom" (or "pious poetry", depending on one's cynicism). The need for such measures for the proper implementation of an ethics code within an organisation is widely recognised.[75]

Whilst some of the existing codes of conduct (such as the Code of Professional Conduct for Counsel) go into significant depth as to how breaches of that code ought to be dealt with, others (such as the OTP's Code of Conduct) only go so far as extending a right to the Prosecutor to impose appropriate disciplinary measures against members of that office who are found to have breached its provisions.[76] This is problematic when one considers how this regime would function in the instance that the misconduct flows from either a direct instruction from the Prosecutor, or worse still, is conducted by the Prosecutor her- or himself.[77] This lacuna in the OTP's Code should be promptly addressed, as it provides an unwelcome 'impunity-gap' on the ethical plane.

We now turn to impediments to the implementation of an organisation's "moral message" at the level of corporate culture.[78]

In 2005, a second US National Business Ethics Survey found that although the enactment of formal ethical policies did impact ethical outcomes within participating organisations, the outcomes of those policies were also determined by the culture which prevailed within those same organisations.[79] In light of this, Webley and Werner[80] sought to distil the factors which hinder the proliferation of ethical culture within organisations. Their research found that the following points were particularly significant: a) a lack of commitment of top management; b) pressure to meet targets; and c) a fear of retaliation.[81]

---

[75] Timothy L. Fort, "Steps for Building Ethics Programs", in *Hastings Business Law Journal*, 2005, vol. 1, no. 1, p. 201.

[76] OTP Code, para. 75, see above note 16.

[77] Turnbull, 2018, p. 900, see above note 50.

[78] Webley and Werner, 2008, p. 408, see above note 57.

[79] Ethics Resource Center, *National Business Ethics Survey – How Employees View Ethics in Their Organizations 1994–2005*, 2005, Washington, DC.

[80] Webley and Werner, 2008, p. 408, see above note 57.

[81] *Ibid.*

The first point is derived from a study conducted in 1999,[82] wherein 10,000 employees from across six different American corporations were interviewed about their experiences with the ethical codes and programmes put in place by their employers. The outcome of this study suggested that "top management commitment was important to the scope and control orientation of corporate ethics programmes", and that "such commitment was the only factor that was strongly associated with having a programme that is orientated towards shared values".[83] These findings, according to Webley and Werner, suggest that a top-down approach to ethics is an important component of developing a culture of ethics within an organisation.[84]

As suggested elsewhere, the OTP's Code provides a useful example of embedding this top-down approach, because of the express and heightened duty on the Prosecutor and Deputy Prosecutors to provide "an impeccable example" to the staff of that Office, and to provide "appropriate guidance, direction and support in the promotion and cultivation of the standards expected of the Office".[85]

The second point was borne out of an ethics survey conducted by the American Management Association in 2005.[86] All 1,000 respondents in this survey were asked "what they considered to be the factors that are most likely to cause people to compromise an organisation's ethical standards".[87] In response, approximately 70 per cent of them referred to the "pressure to meet unrealistic business objectives/deadlines" as being a major factor in this regard.[88]

---

[82] Linda Klebe Trevino, Gary R. Weaver, David G. Gibson and Barbara Ley Toffler, "Managing Ethics and Legal Compliance: What Works And What Hurts", in *California Management Review*, 1999, vol. 41, no. 2, pp. 131–151.

[83] *Ibid.*

[84] Webley and Werner, 2008, p. 408, see above note 57.

[85] See OTP Code, para. 15, see above note 16; see also Salim A. Nakhjavani, "The Origins and Development of the Code of Conduct" in Bergsmo, Klaus Rackwitz and SONG Tianying (eds.), *Historical Origins of International Criminal Law: Volume 5*, Torkel Opsahl Academic EPublisher, Brussels, 2017, p. 961 (https://www.toaep.org/ps-pdf/24-bergsmo-rackwitz-song).

[86] *The Ethical Enterprise – Doing the Right Things in the Right Ways, Today and Tomorrow (A Global Study of Business Ethics 2005-2015)*, American Management Association, New York, 2006; Raymond Baumhart, *An Honest Profit – What Businessmen Say About Ethics in Business*, Holt, Rinehart and Winston, New York, 1968.

[87] Webley and Werner, 2008, p. 408, see above note 57.

[88] *Ibid.*

This pressure is presumably even more pronounced at an organisation such as the ICC, which has been tasked with the onerous mandate of prosecuting "the most serious of crimes of concern to the international community as a whole".[89] ICC staff, then, are burdened with achieving an objective that transcends that which has been cited by the respondents in the American Management Association's study. This is because their objectives go beyond the realm of commercial enrichment, and, instead, require them to seek justice for victims of gross violations of rights, and for the international community as a whole. In this sense, they carry the weight of the world's expectations on their shoulders. The weight of this expectation will no doubt be an important factor in determining whether or not the ICC's organisational culture is capable of being set up in a manner that upholds the stringent duties contained within the existing ethical framework, while allowing the Court's staff to execute their mandate effectively towards the international community. The three examples of ethical lapses we considered earlier in this chapter are, to our minds, clear indication that the ICC – or the OTP, at the very least – has previously found itself in a position whereby it was able to justify an ethical breach in order to achieve a specific objective: the successful prosecution of persons accused of having committed crimes that "deeply shock the conscience of humanity".[90]

The question that arises here is how to ameliorate the risks that are associated with the pursuit of these weighty objectives. One suggestion is to characterise ethical conduct as an objective in itself. This approach mirrors Webley and Werner's recommendation, which puts ethical considerations at the centre of corporate strategy as a means of promoting an ethical culture within an organisation.[91] This approach holds promise particularly for those organs and actors within the ICC directly responsible for criminal proceedings that preserve the rights of the charged person or the accused, both substantively and procedurally.

An ethical breach by an actor at the core of criminal proceedings may itself vitiate the fairness of those proceedings. Placing emphasis on ethical considerations as an objective in themselves, – as ends, not means – has the potential of not only ensuring that ICC staff are dissuaded from 'cutting corners' to achieve their broader goal of pursuing international jus-

---

[89] ICC Statute, Article 5, see above note 37.
[90] ICC Statute, Preamble, 2nd recital, see above note 37.
[91] Webley and Werner, 2008, p. 412, see above note 57.

tice, but also ensuring that their progress towards that goal is unimpeachable.

This last suggestion aligns closely with the findings of the 2004 Ethics at Work survey of the UK-based Institute of Business Ethics.[92] About a third of respondents who admitted to witnessing unethical conduct at their workplaces revealed they had chosen not to disclose their observations. This was predicated on the fact that they felt that "speaking up" would jeopardise their job security or place them at odds with their colleagues.[93] Indeed, having to work under a climate of fear or retaliation naturally serves a chilling factor against the disclosure of ethical breaches by persons operating within that workspace. The ICC, like all workplaces, is likely to have cultivated a culture whereby its staff are somewhat hesitant to make such disclosures, whether it be out of fear of castigation or otherwise.

One potential solution that had been advanced during the drafting process of the OTP Code of Conduct, but now finds no expression in the final version of that Code,[94] or of the Code of Professional Conduct for counsel – nor, indeed, in other codes – is the explicit recognition of a feature of a legal culture familiar in all major legal systems. In the practice of law as a liberal profession, or as an independent practitioner (such as barristers, advocates and the like), a great deal of ethical decision-making is premised on seeking informal – but well-informed – advice from more experienced practitioners, on a collegial basis of confidentiality. The informal conversation and advice, once rendered, are consigned to the *oubliette*. Among independent legal practitioners, this culture only 'works' where the more senior practitioner is committed to the independence and integrity of the profession above personal interest.

There is no substantial reason, in our view, why such a channel cannot be brought 'in-house' at the ICC, and for it to exist outside a staff member's management line. It is an advisory role that demands a certain calibre of person, to be sure; but the same check on possible abuse that has embedded this aspect of ethical practice among independent bars and law societies across legal cultures – that is, a longstanding, unwavering commitment to the institution and to the rule of law – must be expected of the

---

[92] S. Webley and P. Dryden, *Ethics at Work: A National Survey*, London: Institute of Business Ethics, 2005.

[93] *Ibid.*

[94] Nakhjavani, 2017, p. 957, see above note 85.

international civil service. It bears noting that the calibre of person with the demonstrated capacity to consistently subordinate individual to institutional interest – the likes of Noblemaire and Flemming – is not some kind of inaccessible hero of virtue. That person should be nothing other than an ordinary staff member of the Court.

Moreover, there is a profound, but often unarticulated ethical dimension to the first principles set out in the ICC Staff Rules: First, "[s]taff taff members of the Court are international civil servants. Their responsibilities as staff members of the Court are not national, but exclusively international";[95] and second, "[t]he interest of the Court and the obligations that staff members have towards it shall always take precedence over their other interests or ties".[96]

22.4. Double Deontology: Desperately Seeking Coherence

The problem of *vertical* double deontology, as between ethical standards binding on legal practitioners at the ICC and in their home States, is not particularly vexing, at first glance. The Code of Professional Conduct for Counsel sidesteps the problem by framing it only in terms of enforcement – the proverbial 'pain point'. That is, the disciplinary regime applicable under the Code operates "without prejudice" to the "disciplinary powers" of any other "disciplinary authority".[97] There is a rule of complementarity *sui generis* that suspends proceedings before the ICC's disciplinary authority in cases where a national authority is acting with respect to the same misconduct, unless the national authority is "unwilling or unable to conclude the disciplinary procedure".[98]

The unstated assumption is that a breach of standards matters less than when one has not yet been caught, and absent the prospect of conflicting disciplinary measures. The approach has a practical basis, nevertheless, because the rule of thumb, across various national jurisdictions, is that counsel appearing in a foreign or international court must uphold all the ethical rules by which they are bound. It is only when their conduct is formally called into question that the Code applicable at the ICC needs to provide a deadlock-breaking mechanism.

---

[95] ICC, *Staff Rules of the International Criminal Court*, 27 July 2015, Rule 101.1 ('Staff Rules') (https://www.legal-tools.org/doc/2a5274/).

[96] *Ibid.*, Rule 101.3.

[97] *Ibid.*, Rule 101.3.

[98] *Ibid.*, Article 38(4).

What this Code conspicuously fails to do is to guide counsel on their conduct when the substantive ethical standards of their home jurisdiction and that of the Court conflict. A simple but real example is where counsel are subject to a referral rule in their home jurisdiction, but then accept a contractual appointment as counsel at the ICC without formally suspending their legal practice in their home jurisdiction, where they continue to represent clients and take instructions. Are counsel entitled to insist on a brief from the ICC to be channelled through a solicitor or attorney in their home jurisdiction? Such a brief is unlikely at best. Would counsel then be breaching the referral rule to act for a client facing trial at the ICC?

Horizontal double deontology – as between multiple, overlapping ethical standards applicable at the ICC – is a significantly harder problem. Axiomatically, when overlaid as a general set of standard on the existing, more specific codes, an ethics charter creates an overlap by design. The question is what to do about it.

The OTP provides the most useful example here, because it is guaranteed functional independence by the Rome Statute. Should an OTP staff member disclose actual or imminent misconduct to a person outside the OTP because of their overarching duty to the "interest of the Court" and their "obligations towards it" under Staff Rule 101.3? The OTP's Code itself is clear, in Article 12: "When given reason to believe that a departure from these standards has occurred or is about to occur, Staff members shall report the matter to their supervisors or the Prosecutor".

Resorting to the language of rights and duties starts from an assumption of competition: the duty to act in the interest in the Court is weighed against the duty to report within the OTP reporting line. This is singularly unhelpful, because there is no clear basis on which to 'balance' these duties and reach a concrete ethical decision and course of action. A more useful approach may well be to seek coherence and to inculcate a culture of ethical behaviour centred on the requirements of a coherent life.

Despite the sustained attention of legal theorists, the concept of coherence (especially in legal argument) has proven elusive. In a useful survey of arguments on coherence in legal theory, Bertea observes that:

> While there is wide agreement among contemporary legal theorists on the characterization of coherence in the negative as lack of inconsistencies, it is still a question how coherence might be defined in positive terms. Coherence is generally held to be something more than logical consistency of propo-

sitions. But it is not entirely clear what this 'something more' amounts to. Thus, coherence is often described in figurative language as the equivalent of 'hanging together', 'making sense as a whole', 'cohesion', 'consonance' and 'speaking with one voice'. A coherent set might then be described as a 'tightly-knit unit'. Which makes coherence a 'kind of internal interconnectedness', a 'plausible connection' that is not lineal and asymmetrical but circular and symmetrical: the elements of a coherent structure are mutually supporting and reinforc-ing.[99]

We understand coherence this way: rights and duties may conflict. But values and qualities of character do not, if one accepts that each expresses a universal human potentiality of a single human being. How, then, might staff members' duty to act in the interests of the Court and their duty to report misconduct within the OTP reporting line begin to *cohere?*

What emerges immediately is that their ethical reasoning will not rest on abstract conceptions of their duties. They will interrogate the values underlying Staff Rule 101.3 and Article 12 of the OTP Code, in respect of the very specific, finely-grained facts of the misconduct of which they are aware. They will take the OTP Code not as a series of rules, but as a cohesive whole, including its standards on faithful conduct, which include the following four illustrative examples of what it means to fulfil "the trust reposed in the Office of the Prosecutor":

(a) loyalty to the aims, principles and purposes of the Court;

(b) acting within the boundaries of inherent or delegated powers and functions;

(c) due deference to the authority of the Prosecutor [...];

(d) respect for the principles of this Code, and a concerted effort to prevent, oppose and address any departure therefrom.

At that point, they will take their decision, whatever it might be – one which any reasonably objective disciplinary authority would characterise as a considered, responsible, mature choice.

---

[99] Stefano Bertea, "The Arguments from Coherence: Analysis and Evaluation", in *Oxford Journal of Legal Studies*, 2005, vol. 25, no. 3, pp. 371–72 (footnotes omitted).

22.5. What Might the External Auditor Have Hoped to Achieve?

The objective of the external auditor has been outlined in significant detail above, but for the sake of structure, it is probably worth summarising. Simply, the external auditor seeks to supplement the existing statutory framework with a "moral message". This "moral message" should echo the "fundamental values" contained in Article 1.2 of the Staff Regulations. According to the external auditor, the essence of these values is captured by the listed points, those being "general rights and obligations, confidentiality, honorary distinctions, gifts or remuneration, conflicts of interest, employment and activities outside the Court, and use of the Court's property".[100] The external auditor believes that the proposed ethics charter ought to address staff conduct with respect to said points. The existence of guidelines, which address these points is the barometer by which the need for an additional ethics charter ought to be judged.

We have tried to show how the existing ethical framework – both its general statements (as in the Staff Rules) and its details in specific codes – covers and surpasses what could be achieved practically by a single ethics charter covering all staff of the ICC. The real question is implementation, and the problem is complex. It calls for an honest reading of reality at the level of culture – beyond the totting up of complaints filed and complaints resolved. This is important to interrogate the ways that ethical standards are modelled by officials and senior staff; how these standards are embedded in staff orientation and ongoing training; the formal and informal approaches that staff might and actually do take to reach ethical decisions; and the nature, depth and persistence of conversations on ethics among the staff of the Court, both within and between its organs.

---

[100] Audit report, para. 239, see above note 1.

PART V:
INTEGRITY AND THE LENS OF CASES

23

Reflections on Integrity in
the Prosecution of International Cases

Teresa McHenry and Ann Marie Ursini[*]

23.1. Introduction

Integrity in international justice – what is it, and how do we get it? And why is the issue so vexing, particularly if everyone agrees that it is important? People would likely agree on the key means to achieve integrity: leadership; culture; training; resources; and accountability. But integrity in international justice is impossible to define and ultimately achieve without a clear sense of what these ideals should look like in practice, especially when practitioners and judges from different domestic legal systems must operate together, often in newly-created international and hybrid legal systems.

As a prosecutor with over 30 years of experience with international crimes, I[1] bring a pragmatic, rather than an academic or theoretical, approach to the subject of integrity in international criminal cases. For most of my career, I have dealt with international crime and justice, mostly at the United States ('US') Department of Justice ('DOJ') but also for five years

---

[*] **Teresa McHenry** is the head of the Human Rights and Special Prosecutions Section ('HRSP') within the Criminal Division of the US Department of Justice. She previously served as the head of the Domestic Security Section, the head of the Alien Smuggling Task Force, a trial attorney in the Organized Crime and Racketeering Section, and an Assistant US Attorney for the District of Columbia, all within the US Department of Justice. From 1994 until 1998, she served with the Office of the Prosecutor, International Criminal Tribunal for the former Yugoslavia. She serves as a member of the Commission for the Control of Interpol's Files, filling the position of a lawyer with human rights expertise. She has a B.A. *magna cum laude*, from Rice University and a J.D., *magna cum laude*, from Harvard Law School. **Ann Marie Ursini** is a Senior Trial Attorney at HRSP, where she has worked since 2013. She previously practiced in the US Attorney's Office for the Northern District of California and in the Office of the Prosecutor at the International Criminal Court. She earned a B.A., *magna cum laude*, from California State University, Stanislaus, a J.D. from Santa Clara University School of Law, where she served as Editor-in-Chief of the *Santa Clara Journal of International Law*, and an LL.M. with distinction in National Security Law from Georgetown University School of Law.

[1] First person pronouns hereinafter reference Teresa McHenry.

at the Office of the Prosecutor ('OTP') of the International Criminal Tribunal for the former Yugoslavia ('ICTY'), starting in 1994, when the Tribunal was just beginning. For the last eight years, I have led the Human Rights and Special Prosecutions Section at the US DOJ, where I supervise trial attorneys prosecuting cases in the US justice system involving international crimes.

In my career, and particularly at the outset of the ICTY, colleagues and I have grappled with questions of what integrity means in the context of international justice. Most obviously, prosecutors must make difficult choices on who to prosecute and what charges to bring, and those big decisions frequently garner intense attention from outside observers. But prosecutors, judges, and defence counsel must also navigate myriad challenges involving personnel, politics, investigative practices, witness issues, disclosure obligations, and more. These challenges can be difficult enough on the domestic stage; internationally, their complexity is compounded.

My goal is to address some of the questions posed in the policy brief on which this project is based[2] from the perspective of a prosecutor, and to provide examples and pose questions related to real-world ethical issues that arise in the prosecutions of international crimes, including how international efforts can involve challenges which are unique and different from most domestic cases. Hopefully, illustrating these challenges will encourage future efforts to enhance integrity to similarly focus on practical questions and areas for improvement.

23.2. International Justice: Inside and Outside Perspectives

The nascent years of the ICTY were exciting and fascinating, but also incredibly challenging. It would be hard to overstate how little we knew and had to work with in terms of structure at the time.

The ICTY generated great interest from non-governmental organizations ('NGOs'), scholars, academics and others, many of whom wanted to do work that would assist persons working at the Tribunal. I remember, for example, a period in which dozens of published articles were written with the intent of making the legal case for charging rape as a war crime. But from my vantage point, the articles were unhelpful, because everyone I

---

2   Morten Bergsmo, "Revisiting Integrity in International Justice", FICHL Policy Brief Series No. 93 (2018), Torkel Opsahl Academic EPublisher, Brussels, 2016 (http://www.toaep.org/pbs-pdf/93-bergsmo/).

knew at the Tribunal already agreed with their premise. I am not aware of any prosecutor at the Tribunal who disagreed that rape could be a war crime, a crime against humanity, or a method of genocide; in fact, we charged rape as a war crime early in the Tribunal's work.[3]

My fellow prosecutors and I at the ICTY were not struggling with whether rape could be a war crime. But we were struggling with numerous practical, procedural and legal issues that arose in the course of prosecuting this and other international crimes. We could have used help from academics and others as we struggled to go beyond what we knew from our domestic legal systems. For instance, an overview of how different countries balance a defendant's right to information about a rape victim's medical history with a victim's right to privacy about intimate medical issues would have been useful. I worked on the first multi-defendant case at the ICTY, in which the defendants sought separate trials, and it would have been valuable to have an analysis of how different domestic systems, particularly non-jury systems, determined when severance of co-defendants' trials did or did not contribute to the integrity of a case and fairness to the defence.

Since my time at the ICTY, there have been significant efforts to address these and other challenges faced by the courts. I hope to further this effort by sharing, from a practitioner's perspective, some of the practical challenges we face in bringing integrity to the work of international justice.

23.3. Investigations and Resources

In international justice, even the initial questions of who and what to investigate are tremendously complicated. At the ICTY, there was much discussion and internal debate about who should be investigated and charged, and, crucially, how resources should be allocated to various investigations. Everyone wanted to be fair and lead a process with integrity. But the facts were not fully known, the conflict was ongoing, and the Tribunal was working to survive such that it needed to demonstrate tangible results in the short term. There were hard questions to grapple with: what does fairness mean in the context of international investigations and charging? How do we stay true to the ICTY's mission of providing accountability for high-level perpetrators? How could we deter and prevent future crimes? Further, how did our goals interact with political realities?

---

[3] International Criminal Tribunal for the former Yugoslavia ('ICTY'), *Prosecutor v. Delalić et al.* ('Čelebići case'), Indictment, 19 March 1996, IT-96-21-T (https://www.legal-tools.org/doc/a40836/).

The mission of the ICTY, and of international justice mechanisms generally, is to provide accountability for the highest-level perpetrators of atrocity crimes – those who otherwise would likely benefit from impunity. As has been much-discussed since, the OTP decided to pursue relatively lower-level targets at the outset. On its face, this decision did not meet the purpose of the Tribunal, namely to hold accountable those persons at the highest levels of responsibility. But the hope was that this choice would allow prosecutors to demonstrate the Tribunal was active and develop the evidence and expertise needed to work up the chain of command and charge persons at higher levels. Ultimately, the ICTY was able to do just that, even though at the beginning of the Tribunal, critics of the approach wondered if focusing on these lower-level defendants was a wise use of the Tribunal's resources.[4]

Resource limitations necessitate hard decisions about where to focus investigations, in both domestic and international systems. In my current position at the US DOJ, my office and investigators with whom we work are constantly evaluating how to allocate limited resources, with one tension being how many resources we devote to situations in which there is a significant crime base but where it may be difficult to get jurisdiction over a subject, versus situations where we have fewer or less serious crimes, but where there is a subject known to be in the US and who could be arrested.

Resource limitations are even more complex on the international stage, where investigations often require evidence or access to information only available through the co-operation of a State Party, which may have strong disincentives to be helpful. In international justice, there is an expectation that prosecutors will fully and fairly review and consider evidence of crimes committed by all parties to a conflict, but it is rare that prosecutors of large-scale international crimes have the same level of access to evidence with respect to different parties to the conflict.

---

[4] The question of how senior the perpetrator must be to merit attention and resources from an international court is a recurring one. Interesting, the International Criminal Court OTP Strategic Plan issued after the CILRAP project conference in The Hague in December 2018, contains language embracing, in some circumstances, "a strategy of building upwards by focusing on mid-level or notorious perpetrators first, with the aim of reaching the level of the most responsible persons at a later stage". International Criminal Court, Office of the Prosecutor, Strategic Plan 2019-2021, 17 July 2019, pp. 19–25 ('ICC-OTP Strategic Plan 2019-2021') (https://www.legal-tools.org/doc/7ncqt3).

Initially, for example, the Bosnian Serbs were not co-operating with the ICTY, even for investigations involving Bosnian Serb victims. Later, when the OTP sought evidence from the Bosnian government – a party ostensibly co-operating with the OTP – regarding responsibility for certain crimes committed on the Bosnian side, we found the co-operation less than robust. (Ultimately, much later, we got the information from the Bosnian government and determined it would have been very helpful to the prosecution's case, but we were already well into trial and the judges found it untimely and refused to allow it into evidence.)

Co-operation by States is still a major challenge in international justice. These dynamics raise hard questions – how strongly, and using what means, should prosecutors push for assistance? How long do you wait for a State's co-operation before deciding to bring charges based on what evidence you have in hand? Is it 'fair' that persons who are nationals of a co-operative State will be punished, but those from an uncooperative State may not be because the State will not provide important evidence?

23.4. Witnesses

During investigations at the ICTY, the OTP faced a number of challenges regarding witnesses during the investigation.

23.4.1. Witness Preparation

One of the most obvious and frustrating examples of how definitions of integrity varied and conflicted among attorneys from different legal systems was in the preparation of witnesses prior to testimony. I remember numerous discussions about this with ICTY colleagues from different countries. Prosecutors from the United States offered that, in our domestic cases, we would be derelict if we failed to meet with witnesses before they testified to tell them what kinds of questions to expect, answer questions they had about the proceeding, and, depending on the anticipated nature and length of the witness testimony, conduct mock examinations.[5] One of

---

[5] Some practitioners from systems where witness preparation is not routine mistakenly believe this preparation is akin to coaching or scripting a witness. I would never instruct a witness what to say (other than to listen to the questions closely and tell the truth) or provide a script of how they should respond to my questions. The goals of preparing a witness before their testimony are to ensure the witness had an opportunity to hear and understand the types of questions I planned to ask in a low-pressure environment, where we could work out differences in understanding or, in some cases, language barriers, before the witness was faced with the intimidating challenge of speaking in court. Additionally, in an adversarial jury sys-

my Australian colleagues said that if they did the same thing in their domestic system, their actions would be frowned upon; another colleague, from Europe, said preparing a witness in this way, which in the US would be considered standard practice, would be a criminal offence!

Like so many things at the ICTY, we had to figure out workable solutions that met our respective definitions of integrity in the proceedings along the way. For instance, I remember the first evidentiary hearing held at the ICTY for judges to hear witnesses and confirm an indictment, in the *Nikolić* case.[6] The judges informed the prosecutors that we should not 'prepare' the witnesses by talking to them about their testimony in any way. For this type of hearing, there is no defendant or defence counsel present, and there is no cross-examination, so we decided not to object to the judges' instructions, and we called witnesses to testify without preparing them beforehand. The first day of witness testimony was a total mess. Witnesses did not understand what was being asked, they wanted to talk about things other than what we asked, and the judges were extremely frustrated by the amount of irrelevant testimony and wasted time. After one day of testimony, we got word that the judges had changed their minds and now wanted us to prepare our witnesses before they testified. This was only one hearing in one case, and I am certain that other judges and other courts have and will handle these issues differently; I wonder to what extent international courts have tried to standardize expectations in terms of witness preparation or offered guidance to attorneys, and whether they have been able to achieve a practical, workable balance.

23.4.2. Witness Statements

Another complexity that frequently arises in international cases is the issue of multiple witness interviews and statements, taken by NGOs, journalists, activists, domestic and international investigators, intermediaries and others. An NGO active in Liberia recently told me that they are aware that some witnesses have been interviewed by persons from as many as eight

---

tem, preparation helps prosecutors ensure they do not inadvertently ask questions that would elicit testimony precluded by our rules of evidence and allows prosecutors to assess the strength of their case. There is a saying among American attorneys: never ask a question in court to which you do not know the answer. Working with witnesses ahead of a court appearance is, in our system, an essential part of an attorney's preparation, and we do a disservice to our client and the witness if we do not adequately prepare.

6   ICTY, *Prosecutor v. Nikolić*, IT-94-2.

different countries. The existence of multiple prior statements taken from different investigating entities presents a host of issues, including challenges in evaluating the credibility of a particular witness if their statements do not perfectly overlap. The quality of the statements may vary dramatically, depending on the training and background of the interviewer, the quality of the translation, the timing of the interview, who is present for the interview, and other factors. The existence of multiple prior witness statements creates problems for prosecutors, who must carefully consider their disclosure obligations when determining whether to obtain copies of statements taken by others, particularly when the prosecutors do not know the circumstances under which other statements were taken and how reliable or accurate they are, and understanding that we may have disclosure obligations for any statements.

23.4.3. Witness Security and Privacy

Witness security is among the biggest challenges prosecutors face, and we spend tremendous time trying to ensure that witnesses or their families are not unsafe because of us, or at the very least that witnesses understand the risks and resources we can and cannot provide. There is a natural tension between our obligation to disclose information to the defence and the need to conceal, even if temporarily, information that can put witnesses at risk. In my domestic system, prosecutors, defence counsel and judges are familiar and comfortable with these precautions, such as protective orders, which limit how the defence can use or distribute sensitive information the government has disclosed or which authorize redactions of personally identifying information contained in the disclosure. Defence counsel take these orders very seriously, as they understand their professional reputations will be harmed and they may be subject to court-imposed sanctions if they do not comply with protective orders.

In most systems, there is also the option of filing a document under seal, so that the parties and the judge can see it but it is not open to the public, usually based on some showing from the filing party that it is too sensitive to be public. Courts and their staff have routine procedures for dealing with sealed filings, so the parties can generally rely on the fact the contents of sealed filings will not become public. Internationally, though, mechanisms for protecting information has not been a smooth process. At the ICTY, in the *Čelebići* trial, we had sensitive lists of protected witness names publicly disclosed in a Bosnian newspaper, and we saw sensitive medical information disclosed in open court. I know that later ICTY cases and other tribunals have struggled with and continue to struggle with these issues, particularly given the limitations of sanctions for attorneys who do not comply with court rules and orders in the international context.

23.5. Discovery and Disclosure

In my experience, prosecutors take their disclosure obligations very seriously and, next to witness security issues, this is one of the biggest challenges for prosecutors. Disclosure is particularly difficult in large fact- and document-intensive cases like those prosecuted at the international level. On large cases, prosecutors need strong case management support personnel and appropriate technology up to the task of organizing and redacting an incredible volume of documents. In some cases, a prosecutor may not even be able to review every piece of paper (or PDF page) in their case, but must rely on processing information by type and source.

One consequence of the substantial resources needed to handle disclosure obligations is that prosecutors must exercise discretion in limiting the information they themselves obtain. Prosecutors used to seek more medical records than we do now, but because of disclosure obligations and privacy concerns of victims, we now are more discerning. In the case of electronic evidence, the prevalence of technology has exponentially increased the volume of information available. For instance, in my office, a recent search warrant for one social media account for a period of only a few months returned over 10,000 pages of content, most of which required costly and time-consuming translation. The volume of available information combined with resource constraints force prosecutors and investigators to narrowly tailor their requests in order to return a manageable amount of information, particularly if the records must be translated or redacted to remove sensitive information, such as witness addresses. As we work to be discerning, however, we have to be careful to make sure that we are not failing to obtain or failing to disclose information important to the case.

23.6. Institutional Ethics Advice and Support

In order to perform a difficult job with integrity, lawyers, staff and others working in international criminal justice must have resources available to help them ensure they understand and maintain high standards of ethical conduct, and that there are mechanisms to report or deal with unethical behaviour. As the concept paper of the project indicates, it is important for international institutions to create institutional measures to build "cultures of integrity" within the courts.[7] But what do and should such measures look like and how can we "give maximum effect to existing 'integrity mechanisms', including oversight mechanisms"?[8]

In my current position at the US DOJ, I am lucky to have access to several officers and advisors within the Department whose job it is to help maintain the integrity of our prosecutions. One resource is a designated ethics officer within my Division. For certain matters, the ethics officer has a formal role, such as approving my ability to present at conferences and reviewing the public financial disclosure forms I have to fill out every year detailing the financial assets my husband and I have and our financial transactions over last year. She helps me and other attorneys in the Criminal Division avoid actual or perceived conflicts of interest. She also advises our attorneys of the legal restrictions applicable for certain political activity prosecutors must avoid so as not to appear politically motivated or impartial in their work. Just as important as her official role is her role as informal advisor. I can easily just call her to talk through a range of topics; she has a store of practical knowledge about how persons have handled similar issues in the past, and what the legal and ethical guardrails may be.

Additionally, DOJ attorneys have access to the Department's Professional Responsibility Advisory Office ('PRAO'), which advises attorneys on professional responsibilities related to attorney's authority to investigate, litigate or provide legal advice according to Department guidelines and the particular State ethics rules governing each attorney. Our office has frequently consulted PRAO regarding planned investigative steps to ensure we are complying with the patchwork of applicable ethical guidelines for prosecutors, which depend on the State in which a particular attorney is licensed and where he or she is practicing.

There are also persons to whom attorneys and staff can report internal problems, such as sexual harassment by colleagues. Additionally, various ethics professionals provide required annual training for DOJ personnel on topics including sexual harassment, ethical obligations in investigations, discovery and disclosure requirements, and other topics vital to conducting the work of the Department with appropriate standards of integrity. Further,

---

[7] Bergsmo, 2018, see above note 2.

[8] *Ibid.*

written guidance gives prosecutors parameters on when to charge or decline cases, navigate and disclose conflicts of interest, and handle other matters.

I do not know to what extent these models of having ethical expertise within an institution can be or have been replicated in other systems, including international systems, but I suspect we could all benefit from shared best practices on an international scale.

23.7. Courtroom Conduct and Personnel

Another hard issue relating to trials and integrity is conduct in the courtroom. As the concept paper indicates, States Parties are generally responsible for the election of judges and prosecutors.[9] The responsibility is "important" and requires "vigilance", since the "high officials of international courts define the culture of integrity within their institutions".[10] All would agree that staffing – particularly for high-level and high-visibility roles, including judges – is vital, but in practice, goals regarding personnel with integrity and the necessary skills may not always be met. Further examination of best practices or new practical steps, be they additional disclosure forms to identify possible conflicts of interests or mandated training, may be helpful.

When I was at the Tribunal, we struggled with the conduct of one of the judges who fell asleep during portions of the trial. During the trial, prosecutors, defence counsel and, I believe, other judges were aware of the situation. The defence did not raise it formally during trial but did raise it on appeal. Ultimately, the Appeals Chamber acknowledged that video evidence established that the judge was regularly asleep (one time for 30 minutes!) and that the judge's conduct was inappropriate, but found that appellants had failed to establish that the judge's inattention caused them actual prejudice, and so rejected the defence motion to dismiss.[11]

On another occasion, several prosecutors were complaining among themselves about a particular judge at the Tribunal, wondering how he got appointed – it seemed obvious from his performance during proceedings that he was not qualified to be a judge. One of my intrepid colleagues de-

---

[9] *Ibid.*

[10] *Ibid.*

[11] Čelebići case, Appeals Chamber, Judgement, 20 February 2001, IT-96-21-A, paras. 625–49 (https://www.legal-tools.org/doc/051554).

cided we should look up his background online. As it turns out, his credentials were incredibly impressive. We all looked at his resume, stunned into silence, until one prosecutor spoke up: "I want fingerprints, because there is no way that the judge here at the Tribunal is the same judge whose resume we are reading". Choosing appropriate judges, then, involves more than finding a sterling resume.

Judges are not the only problem. International systems struggle to consistently hire qualified, competent personnel at all levels. In my career at the US DOJ, I have been on several hiring committees, and I know a person's resume is not always an indicator of how strong an employee they will be, which is why we use in-depth reference checks, writing samples, interviews and other means to evaluate candidates. Like so much else, hiring is more complicated internationally. At some point during my time at the ICTY, maybe because I had been vocal about the need to improve hiring practices, I was drafted to serve on a few hiring committees. I learned how incredibly hard it is, maybe even impossible, to conduct meaningful reference checks for practitioners from other countries where you do not know anyone, you do not know the system, and you do not know the culture. It is possible that some people are great at working in their own domestic system, but that does not necessarily mean they will be a great fit for an international justice system.

Because of how difficult it is to evaluate the strength of a candidate from a different legal system, I have observed that it can be hard to get hired by international bodies if you do not know someone already in the system. I think this hurts the practice of international law and may lead to a host of issues, including the lack of diversity and fundamental fairness. I suspect this is not necessarily because people in hiring positions only want to hire their friends, but that, in the absence of a hiring system that reliably identifies good candidates, some believe the safest way to hire someone you have some confidence in is to hire someone you already know, or at least someone who knows someone you know.

I wonder whether a useful exercise would be to conduct further examination of practical steps to improve the hiring or appointments in all parts of international justice. For example, should there be some sort of international bar association group that could conduct more in-depth, educated and impartial vetting of candidates?

A final challenge that I think is worth mentioning, both because I saw it at the Tribunal and I have seen it in my own system, has to do with how institutions deal with problematic behaviour of staff members. Alcoholism, drug abuse, sexual harassment and other problematic behaviour by and among personnel happens, and it is important that we all continue to improve on the ways we identify and respond to these issues.

In order for integrity to exist in an institution, there must be a culture of ethical behaviour, and there must be resources for personnel in need. At the US DOJ, we have a unit dedicated to assisting employees dealing with substance abuse, caring for elderly relatives, arranging child-care, and a host of other means of support and assistance. Additionally, we have personnel, both in and outside of an employee's chain of authority, to whom employees can report harassment, misuse of government resources, and other problems. Nonetheless, we continue to struggle with these issues. We need discussion and further thought on how we can create office cultures and systems where employees can seek help and where problematic behaviour is appropriately reported and dealt with.

23.8. Conclusion

Achieving integrity in international justice raises complex, evolving questions, and I greatly appreciate the Centre for International Law Research and Policy (CILRAP) and the International Nuremberg Principles Academy for creating a forum for discussion. In my presentation at the Integrity in International Justice conference in The Hague and in this chapter, I have tried to highlight some of the practical concerns prosecutors and others face while trying to maintain high standards of integrity in international justice, and I have suggested persons outside of those justice mechanisms could assist by focusing their formidable research and analysis on considerations practical to those in the courts.

Attorneys and staff working in international entities face particular challenges because they are trying to be effective outside of the judicial system for which they were trained and outside their domestic culture and norms. Having access to resources on comparative criminal law practices and issues that are particularly complicated by virtue of being international cases would be extremely helpful, as would efforts to create cultures of ethics.

Integrity in international justice must mean integrity among and between its participants – prosecutors, defence counsel and judges – but also in the functioning of the courts and systems themselves. New challenges arise all the time, and those working inside these institutions can benefit from the practical, topical analysis of outside observers. Several of the issues I have addressed have already been the subject of much thought and attention by those inside and outside the courts.[12] But with each new case, each new judge, and each new practitioner, these issues arise in new and different forms. The quest for integrity is perennial. I welcome the opportunity to share my thoughts and experience, and hopefully to encourage practical efforts to improve things in the future.

---

[12] For example, the recent ICC-OTP Strategic Plan identifies staff well-being as a key component of the strategy. "Staff well-being" under the strategy includes, among other topics, gender equality in recruitment, development, and leadership; ethics and standards of conduct, including with regard to harassment; and reducing stress among the workforce, who may be subject to secondary trauma. The prominent placement of staff well-being in the Strategic Plan appears to indicate an acknowledgement that, for an institution to function with integrity, its personnel must be treated with – and expected to demonstrate – integrity as well. ICC-OTP Strategic Plan 2019-2021, pp. 27–28, see above note 4.

24

Individual Integrity and Independence of Judges: The Akay Saga

Antonio Angotti, Basil Saen and Shan Patel*

24.1. Introduction

Judge Aydin Sefa Akay, the (former) Turkish judge on the *Ngirabatware* bench at the International Residual Mechanism for Criminal Tribunals ('MICT' or 'Mechanism'), was arrested in the aftermath of the attempted *coup d'état* against the Erdoğan Government. Accused of terrorism-related offences, Akay was convicted by a criminal court of first instance on the charge of being a member of the Fetullahist Terrorist Organization. He was sentenced to seven years and six months of imprisonment and, consequently, lost his seat on the MICT roster. This chapter will present reflections on the integrity of some individuals in one way or another involved in the non-reappointment of Judge Akay. The Akay saga will, in other words, serve as a practical case-in-point, providing a concrete integrity test.

The chapter will start by outlining the facts of the Akay situation, collating relevant information disclosed to the public. Then, the behaviour of selected individuals will be reflected upon on the basis of applicable codes of conduct and other integrity-grounded considerations. These individuals include the United Nations ('UN') Secretary-General ('UNSG'), UN Legal Counsel, MICT Counsel for the Office of the Prosecutor along with the Prosecutor himself ('OTP' or 'Prosecution'), Defence Counsel for Ngirabatware, Peter Robinson, at the relevant point in time, and MICT President and Pre-Review Judge Theodor Meron. By applying the integrity

* **Antonio Angotti** is a licensed attorney in Florence, Italy and a Fellow at the Centre for International Law Research and Policy (CILRAP). He holds a law degree from the University of Florence and an LL.M. from the Pennsylvania State University. **Basil Saen** is an attorney at the Brussels Bar, where he focuses on white-collar crime, criminal procedure and investigations and a teaching assistant at the Institute for International Law of the University of Leuven (KU Leuven). He holds a Master of Law from the University of Leuven (KU Leuven). **Shan Patel** is Research Assistant at the Department of International Law and Dispute Resolution, Max Planck Institute Luxembourg for Procedural Law and read, *inter alia*, international criminal law and human rights at the London School of Economics and Political Science.

standard to a specific factual narrative, we aim to identify and concretize how integrity affects international criminal justice in practice.

The concept of integrity considered in the framework of the Integrity Project,[1] and therefore in this chapter, draws predominantly from Dag Hammarskjöld's description as comprising "respect for *law* and […] for *truth*".[2] Both elements are important, but protecting and upholding them simultaneously may prove difficult. Actors of international justice must display increasingly exemplary behaviour, particularly in light of States' reinvigorated efforts furthering national sovereignty and their attempts to curb supranational influence.[3] Hence, in advocating this respect for law and truth, the international judiciary and supranational organizations are to safeguard against national pressures prejudicial to integrity.[4] Transparency should be held in high regard, especially in such situations. When international criminal tribunals are involved, States Parties will, in many cases, be responsible for the election of the international judiciary. Whenever national politics or policies risk interfering with States' responsibilities regarding international justice, it is necessary for individuals within international organizations to take a stance and sometimes showcase "freedom from corrupting influences".[5] Throughout this chapter, this balancing exercise will stand at the forefront of the analysis.

The United Nations International Civil Service Advisory Board reported that integrity must be judged on the basis of the *total* behaviour of a person.[6] Indeed, as Bergsmo points out, the word integrity comes from the Latin *integer*, meaning whole or complete.[7] In that respect, our reflections upon integrity are unavoidably a fractional analysis. Such limitations not-

---

[1] See Morten Bergsmo, "Revisiting Integrity in International Justice", FICHL Policy Brief Series No. 93 (2018), Torkel Opsahl Academic EPublisher, Brussels, 2018 (http://www.toaep.org/pbs-pdf/93-bergsmo).

[2] Dag Hammarskjöld, "The International Civil Servant in Law and in Fact", in Wilder Foote (ed.), *Servant of Peace: A Selection of Speeches and Statements of Dag Hammarskjöld, Secretary-General of the United Nations 1953-1961*, Harper & Row, New York, 1962, p. 348 (emphasis added) (http://www.legal-tools.org/doc/64bcae/).

[3] Bergsmo, 2018, see above note 1.

[4] *Ibid.* See also Morten Bergsmo, "Integrity as Safeguard Against the Vicissitudes of Common Justice Institutions", CILRAP Film, The Hague, 1 December 2018 (www.cilrap.org/cilrap-film/181201-bergsmo/).

[5] *Ibid.*, p. 2.

[6] See International Civil Service Advisory Board, "Report on Standards of Conduct in the International Civil Service", 8 October 1954 (http://www.legal-tools.org/doc/d94c61/).

[7] Bergsmo, 2018, p. 2, see above note 1.

withstanding, aside from freedom from corruptibility, the Policy Brief sets forth a variety of interesting traits included in a broad understanding of integrity equally valuable to recall, including truthfulness and fidelity.[8] These traits resonate strongly with both the facts presented below and our reflections on integrity in relation thereto.

Lastly, the ethics of international civil servants are indeed fundamental to understand how desirable conduct can be inspired and obtained. Institutional integrity must be matched by the integrity of the individuals involved, who can act as a buffer against external influences. Given the plurality of actors and motives surrounding international justice, the Akay saga reveals how examples of individual integrity may provide the bricks for a wider reflection on its role and the risks of its absence.

24.2. Reflections on Questions of Integrity of the Concerned Individuals

Before expanding on the integrity of a number of concerned individuals, a brief overview will be presented of the circumstances surrounding Aydin Sefa Akay's criminal conviction in the Republic of Turkey and his subsequent non-reappointment as a judge of the Mechanism.

24.2.1. The Akay Saga

On or around 21 September 2016, Akay, who served as a judge on the Mechanism's *Ngirabatware* bench, was arrested in Turkey, his country of origin.[9] His arrest was linked to "the events of July 2016 directed against the constitutional order of Turkey".[10] Elements of the Turkish military attempted a *coup d'état* against the Government of Turkey on 15 July 2016. In response, a state of emergency was declared and routinely extended, leading to human rights concerns.[11] According to Human Rights Watch, the Government "embarked on a wholesale purge of public officials, police,

---

[8] *Ibid.*

[9] International Residual Mechanism for Criminal Tribunals, *Prosecutor v. Augustin Ngirabatware*, Appeals Chamber, Transcript of Hearing, 17 January 2017, MICT-12-29, p. 2 ('MICT, *Ngirabatware*') (http://www.legal-tools.org/doc/d35912/).

[10] *Ibid.*

[11] Kareem Shaheen, "Suffocating Climate of Fear in Turkey Despite End of State of Emergency", in *The Guardian*, 19 July 2018. Shaheen notes that the state of emergency ended in July 2018, but that a "suffocating climate of fear" continued to engulf the country.

teachers, judges and prosecutors".[12] Critics aver that the state of emergency has been used to detain, intimidate, and prosecute Government opponents for lengthy periods and without trial.[13] Specifically, with regard to government interference with the independence of the judiciary, the Office of the United Nations High Commissioner for Human Rights documented "increased executive control over, and interference with the judiciary and prosecution service; the arrest, dismissal and arbitrary transfer of judges and prosecutors to other courts; and recurring instances of threats against lawyers".[14] These internal politics and circumstances surrounding the arrest and criminal conviction of Akay, though worrisome by rule of law standards, will not be further discussed in this chapter. Notwithstanding, such context is important to understand and assess the actions taken *vis-à-vis* Akay.

After his arrest, Akay sought release by domestic petition and filed an application before the European Court of Human Rights.[15] Nevertheless, he remained in detention, affecting the Mechanism's ability to function and ultimately leading to a standstill in the *Ngirabatware* proceedings,[16] with corresponding implications to the accused's right to a fair trial. Several motions were filed by the parties to the *Ngirabatware* case, followed by decisions issued by Judge Meron, explicitly dealing with the Akay matter. At the same time, correspondence was exchanged between the MICT, through its President, the Defence Counsel for Ngirabatware, other UN officials and institutions and the Government of Turkey.

On 5 October 2016, President Meron issued a letter to the UN Security Council ('UNSC'), describing the Akay situation, alerting the UNSC of the matter, and asking to have his letter circulated as an official UNSC

---

[12] Human Rights Watch, "World Report 2017: Turkey", para. 1 (available on the Human Rights Watch's web site).

[13] Shaheen, 2018, see above note 11.

[14] Office of the UN High Commissioner for Human Rights ('OHCHR'), "Report on the Impact of the State of Emergency on Human Rights in Turkey, Including an Update on the South-East", March 2018, para. 48 (available on the OHCHR's web site).

[15] MICT, *Ngirabatware*, Order to the Government of the Republic of Turkey for the Release of Judge Aydin Sefa Akay, 31 January 2017, para. 13, see above note 9('Order for Release') (http://www.legal-tools.org/doc/a4975e/) (citing European Court of Human Rights, *Akay v. Turkey*, Referral No. 59/17).

[16] Letter from the President of the International Residual Mechanism for Criminal Tribunals, T. Meron, Regarding the Detention of Turkish Judge Aydin Sefa Akay to the UN Security Council, UN Doc. S/2016/841, 5 October 2016.

document.[17] From that moment on, Meron continued to bring the issue up in his communications with the UNSC, up to and including his last address to the UNSC as President of the Mechanism.[18]

Meron met with then-UNSG Ban Ki-moon on 8 November 2016. The MICT President drew the UNSG's attention to the situation and expressed his grave concern. He stated that absent a speedy release of Akay, "a dangerous precedent for the rule of law, for the principle of judicial independence, and for international justice" would be established.[19]

The following day, he brought the issue to the attention of the UN General Assembly ('UNGA'). In his address to the UNGA, Meron stressed the importance of diplomatic immunity granted to MICT judges, which allows them to "work remotely as much as possible and away from the seats of the Mechanism".[20] Akay himself was working from his country of origin, Turkey, at the moment of his arrest. Meron informed the UNGA that the UN Office of Legal Affairs ('UNOLA') had formally asserted Akay's immunity on behalf of the UNSG.[21] Meron expressed his regret that Turkey did not issue any formal communication on the matter to the Mechanism or the UN, and explicitly called upon Turkey to comply with its international obligations under Chapter VII of the UN Charter and immediately release Akay from detention.[22]

Notably, Ngirabatware's Counsel, Robinson, filed a motion the next day asking, *inter alia,* to order Turkey to cease prosecution of Akay so that the latter could continue his judicial functions on the MICT bench.[23] On 28 November 2016, Meron, as Pre-Review Judge, invited Turkey to file a response to the motion.[24] No such response was however issued.[25] During the

---

[17] *Ibid.*

[18] MICT, President Theodor Meron, "Address to the UN Security Council", 11 December 2018 (available on the MICT's web site).

[19] MICT, "President Meron Meets with UN Secretary-General Ban Ki-moon", 9 November 2016, para. 4 (available on the MICT's web site).

[20] MICT, President Theodor Meron, "Address to the UN Security Council", 9 November 2016, p. 3 (available on the MICT's web site).

[21] *Ibid.*

[22] *Ibid.*

[23] MICT, *Ngirabatware*, Motion for Order to Government of Turkey or for Temporary Provisional Release, 10 November 2016, see above note 9 (http://www.legal-tools.org/doc/a2f168/).

[24] MICT, *Ngirabatware*, Invitation to the Government of the Republic of Turkey, 28 November 2016, see above note 9 (http://www.legal-tools.org/doc/069a4c/).

[25] MICT, *Ngirabatware*, Order for Release, para. 7, see above note 15.

hearing of 17 January 2017, the primary purpose of which was to provide Turkey with the opportunity to be heard on the motion issued by Ngirabatware on 10 November 2016, ample consideration was accorded to Akay's situation.[26] However, no representative of Turkey attended.[27] Moreover, the Government apparently refused to receive the invitation to the hearing, turning away the diplomatic couriers who sought to deliver them at its embassies both in Tanzania and in the Netherlands.[28] Robinson described how he himself even cycled to the Turkish embassy in The Hague in an attempt to deliver news about the hearing, without success.[29]

Hence that, on 31 January 2017, Pre-Review Judge Meron issued an 'Order to the Government of the Republic of Turkey for the Release of Judge Aydin Sefa Akay', noting that such an order was "entirely appropriate and necessary to ensure that the review proceedings can conclude".[30] Turkey was to cease all legal proceedings against Akay and to release him from detention before 14 February 2017.[31] By 6 March 2017, in the absence of action, Turkey was found to have failed to comply with its obligations under Article 28 of the MICT Statute[32] to cooperate with the Mechanism and comply without undue delay to the order issued on 31 January 2017.[33] As a result, the matter was to be reported to the UNSC.[34] On 9 March 2017, President Meron notified the UNSC of Turkey's failure to cooperate.[35] Within 24 hours, Turkey provided an official response through a letter of its Permanent Representative to the UN, addressed to the President of the UNSC.[36] The Turkish Government stressed that Akay was arrested on the charge of being a member of the Fetullahist Terrorist Organization,

[26] MICT, *Ngirabatware*, Transcript of Hearing, p. 2, see above note 9.
[27] *Ibid.*, p. 3; MICT, *Ngirabatware*, Order for Release, para. 8, see above note 15.
[28] MICT, *Ngirabatware*, Transcript of Hearing, p. 6, see above note 9.
[29] *Ibid.*
[30] MICT, *Ngirabatware*, Order for Release, para. 16, see above note 15.
[31] *Ibid.*, para. 18.
[32] Resolution 1966 (2010), UN Doc. S/RES/1966, 22 December 2010, para. 16 ('MICT Statute') (http://www.legal-tools.org/doc/e79460/).
[33] MICT, *Ngirabatware*, Decision on Republic of Turkey's Non-Compliance with Its Obligations to Cooperate with the Mechanism, 6 March 2017 (http://www.legal-tools.org/doc/47e335/).
[34] *Ibid.*, p. 2.
[35] MICT, "Mechanism Notifies United Nations Security Council of Turkey's Non-Compliance", 16 March 2017 (available on the MICT's web site).
[36] Letter dated 10 March 2017 from the Permanent Representative of Turkey to the United Nations addressed to the President of the Security Council, UN Doc. S/2017/210, 10 March 2017.

an offence punishable under the Turkish Penal Code. The Permanent Representative further claimed that the Mechanism was not entitled to issue the 31 January 2017 order, that it clearly overstepped its mandate, and that the order was a "flagrant and worrying attempt to interfere with the independent judicial process" of Turkey.[37] As a result, Turkey consistently considered the order to be null and void.[38]

In June 2017, Akay was convicted by a Turkish criminal court of first instance in Ankara for being a member of the Fetullahist Terrorist Organization. He was sentenced to seven years and six months of imprisonment. Following his provisional release pending appeal, Akay resumed his judicial functions for the Mechanism. President Meron expressed his regret for Turkey's actions and called on the Government to "take urgent steps to respect the protected status of Judge Akay and to resolve the situation consistent with international law".[39]

Consequently, in his 22 June 2018 letter to the President of the UNSC, the UNSG noted that, under Article 9 of the MICT Statute, judges are to be "persons of high moral character, impartiality and integrity who possess the qualifications required in their respective countries for appointment to the highest judicial offices".[40] The UNSG stated that the Turkish Government had informed the Secretariat that Akay's eligibility was tarnished and that he "does not possess the qualifications for appointment to the highest judicial office in Turkey under the applicable law".[41] The UNSG concluded that, in light of the information which the Government of Turkey apparently had furnished, Judge Akay "does not currently meet the qualification requirements for judges of the Mechanism under Article 9, paragraph 1, of the Statute and, consequently, cannot be considered for reappointment".[42]

That being the case, on 29 June 2018, the UNSG did not reappoint Judge Akay as a judge of the MICT.[43] In reaction, President Meron again

---

[37] *Ibid.*, p. 2.

[38] *Ibid.*

[39] MICT, "Statement of the Mechanism on Conviction of Judge Aydin Sefa Akay by Turkish Criminal Court of First Instance", 15 June 2017, para. 3 (available on the MICT's web site).

[40] Letter dated 22 June 2018 from the Secretary-General addressed to the President of the Security Council, UN Doc. S/2018/626, 26 June 2018, p. 1.

[41] *Ibid.*

[42] *Ibid.*, p. 2.

[43] MICT, "Statement of the President on the Non-Reappointment of Judge Akay", 3 July 2018 (available on the MICT's web site).

expressed his regret and disagreement.[44] Meron furthered that "the decision not to reappoint Judge Akay is profoundly troubling on multiple levels".[45] With regard to the fact that the decision not to reappoint Akay was based on information provided by the Turkish Government, Meron averred that

> the acquiescence to the position advanced by the Government of Turkey represents a de facto acceptance of a State's actions undertaken in contravention of the diplomatic immunity asserted by the United Nations, a dangerous precedent to set.[46]

He concluded by stressing the importance of judicial independence, which he deems "a cornerstone principle of the rule of law", and the danger this precedent holds for the integrity of the Mechanism, as well as for the overall project of international criminal justice.[47]

On 23 July 2018, President Meron assigned Judge Lee G. Muthoga to replace Judge Akay on the *Ngirabatware* bench.[48] Several months later, in December 2018, the Turkish Judge Yusuf Aksar was elected to the judicial roster of the Mechanism.[49]

Most notably, in early 2019, Judge Christoph Flügge resigned from the MICT citing, among other concerns, political interference by Turkey and the United States. He claimed Turkey's allegations against Akay to be "baseless" and stated that Akay's non-reappointment had been enabled by the connivance of the UN.[50] According to Flügge, other judges of the Mechanism protested to the course of events, but without success. Finally, Flügge, much like Meron, underlined the importance of judicial independence, stating that:

> [e]very incident in which judicial independence is breached is one too many. Now there is this case, and everyone can invoke it in the future. Everyone can say: 'But you let Turkey get its way.' This is an original sin. It can't be fixed.[51]

---

[44] *Ibid.*

[45] *Ibid.*, para. 1.

[46] *Ibid.*, para. 5.

[47] *Ibid.*, para. 6.

[48] MICT, *Ngirabatware*, Order Replacing a Judge in a Case before the Appeals Chamber, 23 July 2018, see above note 9 (http://www.legal-tools.org/doc/96d930/).

[49] MICT, "General Assembly Elects Judge Yusuf Aksar of Turkey to Serve as Mechanism Judge", 7 January 2019 (available on the MICT's web site).

[50] Daniel Boffey, "UN Court Judge Quits The Hague Citing Political Interference", in *The Guardian*, 28 January 2019. See also Stefan Willeke, "Ich bin zutiefst beunruhigt", in *Die Zeit*, 25 January 2019.

[51] *Ibid.*

In his last address as President of the Mechanism, Meron availed of the opportunity to bring the Akay issue to the attention of the UNSC once again. He expressed his profound regret that a different and better resolution was not found, and indicated how, going forward, it would be important that "fair and transparent processes be developed to determine whether any proposed non-reappointment of a Judge accords with the fundamental principles of the rule of law".[52]

24.2.2. Questions of Integrity for Selected Individuals

With the factual narrative described above as context, the behaviour of a number of selected individuals will be reflected upon in terms of integrity. These individuals are the UNSG, the UN Legal Counsel, the Prosecution, Defence Counsel for Ngirabatware, Robinson, and MICT President and Pre-Review Judge Meron. The actions of Judge Akay himself will not be assessed due to the lack of relevant information disclosed to the public.

24.2.2.1. The United Nations Secretary-General[53]

24.2.2.1.1. Normative Framework

The UN Charter principally governs the prerogatives ascribed to and conduct expected of the UNSG.[54] The UNSG is the chief administrative officer of the Secretariat, which is one of the principal organs of the organization and is, as such, accorded legal status on par with the UNSC, UNGA, the Economic and Social Council, the International Court of Justice and the Trusteeship Council.[55] Though it is the Secretariat as a whole that is mentioned in Article 7 of the UN Charter, practice dictates the reference to mean the UNSG specifically.[56] After all, Chapter XV of the Charter only concretely spells out specific duties for the UNSG and leaves those for the remainder of the Secretariat staff to the UNSG's discretion.[57]

---

[52] MICT, "Address to the UN Security Council", p. 2, see *supra* note 17.
[53] Ban Ki-moon and António Guterres have both been confronted with the Akay saga during their respective terms as UNSG. Whenever temporal references are made in relation to conduct, the SG to which this pertains has been specified.
[54] Charter of the United Nations, 24 October 1945, ch. XV ('UN Charter') (outlining the object and purpose of the Secretariat and, in particular, its leadership).
[55] *Ibid.*, Article 7.
[56] Kjell Skjelsbæk and Gunnar Fermann, "The UN Secretary-General and the Mediation of International Disputes", in Jacob Bercovitch (ed.), *Resolving International Conflicts*, Lynne Rienner Publishers, London, 1996, p. 78.
[57] UN Charter, Articles 98, 100, 101, see above note 54.

Despite the legal equivalence as a principal organ, the wording of Article 98 of the UN Charter indicates that the UNSG will perform functions "as entrusted to him", revealing some level of dependency. More so, the fact that appointment to the position happens at the behest of the UNSC and UNGA compounds this point.[58] However, this did not withhold Hammarskjöld from claiming "authority to act in his capacity as Secretary-General, rather than as a representative or spokesperson of the General Assembly".[59]

Aside from the UN Charter, the International Civil Service Commission ('ICSC') Standards of Conduct, to which all international civil servants must abide, including the UNSG, clarify that there is an incumbent "duty [...] to maintain the best possible relations with Governments and avoid any action that might impair this".[60] Whereas this seems to imply that the UNSG is expected to acquiesce, at least to some degree, to the political decision-making of Member States, the contrary holds true. Article 100(1) of the UN Charter clarifies that neither the UNSG nor its staff are to solicit or accept directions from "any government or from any other authority external to the Organization". That said, the very nature of the UNSG position equally renders some level of political engagement crucial.[61] While that may be so, as the ethical guidelines also straightforwardly posit, interference by international civil servants with domestic affairs is wholly unacceptable.[62] Meanwhile, the ICSC Standards of Conduct go on to enu-

---

[58] *Ibid.*, Article 97.

[59] Carsten Stahn and Henning Melber, "Human Security and Ethics in the Spirit of Dag Hammarskjöld: An Introduction", in Carsten Stahn and Henning Melber (eds.), *Peace Diplomacy, Global Justice and International Agency*, Cambridge University Press, 2014, pp. 20–21.

[60] See International Civil Service Commission ('ICSC'), *Standards of Conduct for the International Civil Service*, 2013, para. 29 ('ICSC Standards of Conduct'), approved by United Nations Common System: Report of the International Civil Service Commission, UN Doc. A/RES/67/257, 3 June 2013. The 2013 ICSC Standards of Conduct replaced the 2001 revision of the ethical standards adopted in 1954.

[61] Indeed, Haack and Kille point to the duality in the UNSG mandate, encompassing both the political and administrative dimension. See Kirsten Haack and Kent J Kille, "The UN Secretary-General and Self-Directed Leadership: Development of the Democracy Agenda", in Joel E Oestreich (ed.), *International Organizations as Self-Directed Actors: A Framework for Analysis*, Routledge, Oxford, 2012, pp. 29–59. See also Skjelsbæk and Fermann, 1996, p. 79, see above note 56; Simon Chesterman (ed.), *Secretary or General? The UN Secretary-General in World Politics*, Cambridge University Press, 2007.

[62] Staff Rules and Regulations of the United Nations, UN Doc. ST/SGB/2017/1, 1 January 2017, Regulation 1.2 (d)-(e) (these references can likewise be found in the 2014 version); ICSC Standards of Conduct, 2013, para. 29, see above note 60.

---

merate how public support is crucial for any UN organization – and, indeed, the UN system in general. Civil servants, in that regard, have an ongoing "responsibility to promote a better understanding of the [system]".[63] The independence codified in the UN Charter, thus, must continuously be balanced with the duty to furnish the most optimal relations with States while acting to the benefit of the organization.

Although the UN Charter indeed makes a direct mention of integrity and does so in the context of the Secretariat, the reference pertains to sought after traits that underpin employment considerations.[64] Notwithstanding the fact that the concept accrued prominence over time, it is not mentioned in the preamble neither is it found *verbatim* elsewhere nor conceptually delineated in the UN Charter. However, Article 101 of the UN Charter allows inferring that holding the requisite integrity is pertinent to UN employees which, in turn, implies that all staff must act with integrity when discharging official functions. In that sense, when read in conjunction with the UN Staff Regulations and ICSC Standards of Conduct, it becomes clear that integrity is considered one of the "great traditions of public administration" entrenched in all aspects of civil service.[65]

24.2.2.1.2. Actions

Intent on steering clear of an in-depth discussion on the immunities of international judges, this aspect cannot be ignored in assessing the manner in which the UNSG, as the representative of the international community, handled the Akay situation.[66] It must be acknowledged that, in November 2016, the UNOLA did, in fact, call upon the Turkish government to halt legal proceedings against Judge Akay on behalf of then-UNSG Ban Ki-moon, drawing attention to the diplomatic immunity granted to members of, *inter alia*, the MICT bench.[67] Prior to that, on 25 October 2016, the UNO-

---

[63] ICSC Standards of Conduct, 2013, para. 35, see above note 60.

[64] UN Charter, Article 101(3), see above note 54.

[65] ICSC Standards of Conduct, 2013, paras. 2, 5, 22, see above note 60; Staff Rules and Regulations of the United Nations, 2017, Regulation 1.2 (b), see above note 62.

[66] For a discussion of both the functional and personal immunity of judges in relation to the situation of Akay, see Ady Niv, "The Immunity of Judge Akay in Turkey: A Test Case for International Judges' Immunity and Independence", in *ASIL Insights*, 2018, vol. 22, no. 14.

[67] See United Nations, "Briefing by Spokesperson for Secretary-General, Stéphane Dujarric", 10 November 2016 (available on the UN Audiovisual Library's web site). For a factual overview of the Akay situation, see above Section 24.2.1.

LA had likewise pointed to the immunity bestowed upon Akay.[68] Noting the dangers of disregarding UN officials' immunities, this reaction is to be readily expected and falls well within the confines of stewardship conferred upon the UNOLA and UNSG, respectively.

Further, correspondence between Robinson and Stephen Mathias, Assistant Secretary-General for Legal Affairs, allows us to infer that UNSG António Guterres met with President Erdoğan on 11 February 2017.[69] Whether the situation concerning Judge Akay had been discussed was, rather unsurprisingly, neither confirmed nor denied seeing the confidential nature of diplomatic conversations. Mathias did note, however, that "the position of the Organization remain[ed] unchanged" from its October 2016 assertion.[70] It remains unknown whether the UNSG undertook any additional action toward Turkey in relation to the matter. As such, it is vital to note that the reflections expressed below remain limited to the information available to the public at large. Recalling the inherent importance of public support and transparency outlined in the Standards of Conduct, however, this seems symbolically – if not symptomatically – apt.

The next time the UNSG engaged publically with the situation surrounding Judge Akay was when he, on 22 June 2018, addressed the President of the UNSC to advise non-reappointment.[71] According to the correspondence, "[t]he Government [of Turkey] has provided supporting material in this regard" which upon review satisfied the UNSG that Akay does not fulfil the Article 9 MICT Statute requirements for a seat on the bench.[72] What the so-called 'information furnished' by the Turkish Government entails, remains unclear.

24.2.2.1.3. Reflections on Integrity

At the heart of institutional behaviour, and embodied in the UN Charter, one finds deep-rooted ideals resonating with independence and integrity.[73]

---

[68] MICT, *Ngirabatware*, Motion to Initiate Contempt Proceedings, 3 April 2017, annex E, see above note 9 (http://www.legal-tools.org/doc/a1a511/).

[69] *Ibid.*, paras. 1–2.

[70] *Ibid.*, para. 3.

[71] Letter dated 22 June 2018 from the Secretary-General addressed to the President of the Security Council, 2018, see above note 40.

[72] *Ibid.*, para. 7.

[73] See, for example, Kent J. Kille (ed.), *The UN Secretary-General and Moral Authority: Ethics and Religion in International Leadership*, Georgetown University Press, Washington, D.C., 2007.

In this context, a commonality between UNSG officeholders is raised; namely, how "[t]hey often engaged the charter with an almost religious reverence as a sacred text and perceived themselves as the embodiment of the charter and its ethical code".[74] If this indeed holds true, it can be argued that seemingly dubious Member State conduct should warrant the most transparent approach. The mere indication of political manoeuvring on the part of the Turkish Government would thus invoke the UNSG's moral authority and necessitate action to prevent dubiety in his office – thereby also protecting the organization and safeguarding the reverence for the Charter. Although arguably, that might be the case in terms of the ethical expectations of civil service, the UNSG is under no legal obligation to do so.

As the UN Staff Regulations and ICSC Standards of Conduct reveal, civil servants must conduct themselves with the promotion of the UN system in mind.[75] This, too, supports the idea that any challenges to independence and integrity should be dealt with in a perspicuous manner, visible to the public. Transparency, after all, promotes understanding. More so, procedural transparency becomes even more crucial when concerns have been raised by those operating within the system itself, for example, Judges Theodor Meron and Christoph Flügge, rather than by external spectators. Furthermore, the leading position of the UNSG allows "for [the] raising [of] ethical concerns in international affairs".[76] Even the semblance of interference with the international judiciary or contempt for diplomatic immunities should qualify as such an ethical concern, as it is flagrantly dismissive of the ideals of independence and integrity enshrined in the UN Charter. The UNSG, as the spokesperson for the global interest, occupies a prime position to remove any and all such manifestations of ethical opaqueness.[77] After all, perception matters.[78]

---

[74] Kent J. Kille, "The Secular Pope: Insights on the UN Secretary-General and Moral Authority", in Kille (ed.), 2007, p. 352, see *ibid.*

[75] See above notes 63 and 65.

[76] Kille, 2007, pp. 352–353, see above note 74.

[77] Simon Chesterman, "The Secretary-General We Deserve?", in *Global Governance*, 2015, vol. 21, no. 4, pp. 505–506. See also Jodok Troy, "Two "Popes" to Speak for the World: The Pope and the United Nations Secretary General in World Politics", in *The Review of Faith & International Affairs*, 2017, vol. 15, no. 4, p. 71.

[78] See, for example, Dina F. Haynes, "Ethics of International Civil Service: A Reflection on How the Care of United Nations Staff Impacts the Ability to Fulfill Their Role in Harmonizing the World", in *Hamline Journal of Public Law & Policy*, 2008, vol. 30, no. 1, pp. 208–209. See also David M. Malone, "Eyes on the Prize: The Quest for Nonpermanent Seats on the UN Security Council", in *Global Governance*, 2000, vol. 6, no. 1, pp. 3–23; Elia Arm-

Arguably, to the benefit of the 'best possible' relationship with the Turkish Government, it seems that the UNSG should refrain from being readily critical of affairs that clearly fall within the national sphere of competence, such as domestic security and prosecutorial policy.[79] However, such restraint should not be equated to complete abstinence whenever UN core values are at stake. The UNSG "is supposed to expound these ideas in his public statements and be an embodiment of them in his diplomatic actions".[80] This would certainly resonate with Hammarskjöld. Albeit so, with limited tools at his disposal to himself rectify Member States' actions – let alone those deemed 'solely' morally egregious – the practicability of additional UNSG intervention could be questioned.[81] Moreover, the measure by which to assess whether the assertion of Akay's immunity to Turkey was indeed an appropriate manner in which to discharge moral duties is entirely arbitrary. Notwithstanding the potential consequences for the rule of law or the independence of the international judiciary, there was no legal obligation, whether Charter-based or otherwise, incumbent on the UNSG to take any additional action out of his own initiative. He followed the letter of the law.

1.1.1.1. The United Nations Legal Counsel

24.2.2.1.4. Normative Framework

As head of the Office of Legal Affairs, the Under-Secretary-General and UN Legal Counsel ('UN Legal Counsel'), Miguel de Serpa Soares, is a second actor whose integrity of conduct is of interest. Before evaluating the actions of the UNOLA and, in particular, the UN Legal Counsel individually, one must recall the organizational hierarchy at play. The UNSG bulletin on the structure of the Secretariat shows how the 1UNOLA is one of its

---

strong, "Integrity, Transparency and Accountability in Public Administration: Recent Trends, Regional and International Developments and Emerging Issues", United Nations, New York, 2005, pp. 1–10.

[79] Simultaneously, with the outcry relating to the Akay situation originating predominantly in academia and legal practice, insofar is public knowledge, there is no second government directly involved with whom the UNSG is to equally furnish this so-called best possible rapport.

[80] Skjelsbæk and Fermann, 1996, p. 84, see above note 56. See also Hammarskjöld, 1962, see above note 2. In his address at Oxford University, Hammarskjöld enunciated how one ought to be "politically celibate" but not a "political virgin", further strengthening the supposition that civil service is a continuous balancing act.

[81] Ian Johnstone, "The Role of the UN Secretary-General: The Power of Persuasion Based on Law", in *Global Governance*, 2003, vol. 9, no. 4, pp. 441–442.

---

organizational units, "the head of which is accountable to the Secretary-General".[82] Next to providing a clear chain of accountability, this denotes that the Standards of Conduct and Staff Regulations guiding international civil servants are likewise the applicable normative confines in this framework.[83]

A second UNSG bulletin clarifies the mandate of the UNOLA further.[84] From a managerial perspective, it indicates that the UN Legal Counsel is "responsible for ensuring efficiency, transparency and accountability" of the work conducted under UNOLA purview.[85] More concretely, this includes operational duties in support of the international criminal tribunals and the global criminal justice project as a whole.[86] When examining the UNOLA's aims more closely, another relevant point is that the Office of the Legal Counsel, one of its departments, is tasked with, *inter alia*, "[p]reparing legal opinions, studies and advice on [...] the Convention on the Privileges and Immunities of the United Nations".[87] In all, noting the points of contention at the heart of the Akay situation, the UN Legal Counsel and UNOLA indeed seem the appropriate source of advice within the Secretariat.

24.2.2.1.5. Actions

On 6 July 2017, while addressing the International Law Commission ('ILC'), the UN Legal Counsel referred to the challenges the UN faced related to privileges and immunities.[88] In doing so, he made direct mention of the situation regarding Judge Akay.[89] As the meeting records show, de Serpa Soares gave the ILC a general overview of the facts related to the Akay situation. From his synopsis, one can extrapolate that, as has been noted earlier in this chapter, the UNOLA had reminded Turkey of the dip-

---

[82] UN Secretary-General, *Organization of the Secretariat of the United Nations*, UN Doc. ST/SGB/2015/3, 22 July 2015, sec. 3. See also UN Secretary-General, *Organization of the Office of Legal Affairs*, UN Doc. ST/SGB/2008/13, 1 August 2008, sec. 3.1.

[83] See above Section 24.2.2.1.1. On the accountability chain, see also *Organization of the Office of Legal Affairs*, 2008, sec. 3, 4, see above note 82.

[84] *Ibid.*

[85] *Ibid.*, sec. 3.2.

[86] *Ibid.*, sec. 3.5.

[87] See, for example, the core functions outlined on its website: UN Office of Legal Affairs, "Office of the Legal Counsel" (available on the UNOLA's web site).

[88] International Law Commission, *Provisional Summary Record of the 3371st Meeting*, UN Doc. A/CN.4/SR.3371, 6 July 2017, pp. 4–5.

[89] *Ibid.*

lomatic immunity conferred on members of the MICT in November 2016 and pointed to its keystone importance for international civil service. Moreover, it is apparent that the UNOLA, in its assertion, availed itself of the opportunity to highlight the explicit decision of the UNSC to accord MICT judges those immunities and, in addition, recalled that international civil servants serve the organization indiscriminately of nationality.[90] Mr. de Serpa Soares went on to emphasize how UNOLA "was considering how to react to the conviction [in first instance] given its inconsistency with the judge's diplomatic immunity".[91] Since then, according to publicly available information, the Akay situation was not again mentioned to the ILC.

It is clear that shortly after Judge Akay's arrest, at the direction of then-UNSG Ban Ki-moon, the UNOLA asserted immunity.[92] Correspondence between Robinson and the UNOLA demonstrates how the former had requested the UN Legal Counsel to urge UNSG Guterres to reach out to President Erdoğan. In response, Robinson was informed that "[t]he Secretariat has been monitoring this question since last year and will continue to do so".[93] When asked for evidence related to the meeting of 11 February 2017 between UNSG Guterres and President Erdoğan, the UNOLA did not deny that the meeting took place, nor could it seeing the widespread media attention it had received, but fell back on the confidentiality of diplomatic conversations to avoid disclosing its content.[94]

24.2.2.1.6. Reflections on Integrity

Whether or not the UN Legal Counsel acted with the requisite independence and integrity in discharging his duties is difficult to ascertain. With the vast majority of the exchanges between the UNSG and UNOLA, as well as

---

[90] *Ibid.*, p. 5. Remarkably, when the MICT Statute was approved by the Security Council, Turkey held one of its rotating seats and voted in favour of its adoption, see 6463rd Meeting Records, UN Doc. S/PV.6463, 22 December 2010, p. 3.

[91] Provisional Summary Record of the 3371st Meeting, 2017, see above note 88.

[92] MICT, *Ngirabatware*, Motion to Initiate Contempt Proceedings, annexes C, E, see above note 68. See also above note 67.

[93] MICT, *Ngirabatware*, Motion to Initiate Contempt Proceedings, annex C, see above note 68. For our reflections on the integrity of Defence Counsel, see below Section 1.1.1.3.

[94] *Ibid.*, annex E. Confirming the meeting between the UNSG and President Erdoğan, see also "In Turkey, UN Chief Guterres Discusses Syria, Iraq, Cyprus with President", in *UN News*, 11 February 2017 (available on the UN News' web site); Shebab Khan, "UN Secretary-General Says Fight Against Extremists in Syria Needs Political Solution", in *The Independent*, 11 February 2017; "Erdoğan, BM Genel Sekreteri Guterres ile bir araya geldi", in *SputnikNews Türkiye*, 11 February 2017.

those between UNOLA and Member States, inaccessible due to their confidential nature, any opinion will necessarily carry qualified weight. The UNSC meeting records nevertheless provide some valuable insight insofar that the efforts of the UN Legal Counsel and his office have been lauded by some Member State Representatives. For example, Senegal "commend[ed] the work being carried out by the Office of Legal Affairs of the Secretariat" surrounding the Judge Akay and "welcome[d] the efforts [...] to seek a happy conclusion to this matter".[95] Although final conclusions cannot be drawn from this praise, it seems that the behaviour of the relevant UNOLA officials fell in line with expectations. Such conduct is to be expected, taking into account the fact that independence and integrity are core values at the organization, essential for civil servants such as the UN Legal Counsel, as a member of the Secretariat. On top of that, the UNSG bulletin specifically notes that the Secretariat must "promote the principles of the Charter" in its functioning, adding validity to such a supposition.[96]

The duties of the UN Legal Counsel include, in addition, ensuring the transparency of his office.[97] Despite the absence of any indication in the UNSG bulletin as to whom this transparency of conduct is owed, read together with the Standards of Conduct and Staff Regulations, one can assume that the Office services the general public and should allow the latter to scrutinize UNOLA conduct. Unsurprisingly, the transparency-related duties link to the requirement obliging the international civil servant to promote the public's understanding of the UN system.[98] Notwithstanding any responsibilities that indeed might be owed to the public at large by virtue of his status as a civil servant, as counsel to the UNSG and the UN bodies, de Serpa Soares has a foremost – and overriding – duty to his client. This could explain the relative lack of information furnished by the UN Legal Counsel, as well as the UNOLA, and would categorize the conduct portrayed as evidencing sufficient levels of integrity, within the confines of the available professional latitude. In addition, the fact that President Meron, a central voice in the Akay saga, consistently expressed his gratitude to "Mr. Miguel de Serpa Soares [...] for [...] ongoing and critically important

---

95 7829th Meeting Records, UN Doc. S/PV.7829, 8 December 2016, p. 13; 7960th Meeting Records, UN Doc. S/PV.7960, 7 June 2017, p. 15.
96 Organization of the Secretariat of the United Nations, 2015, sec. 2, see above note 82.
97 Organization of the Office of Legal Affairs, 2008, sec. 3.2, see above note 82.
98 ICSC Standards of Conduct, 2013, para. 35, see above note 60.

assistance", one can assume that requisite levels of integrity were displayed.[99]

1.1.1.2. The Office of the Prosecutor of the International Residual Mechanism for Criminal Tribunals[100]

24.2.2.1.7. Normative Framework

The MICT Prosecution is bound by the Standards of Professional Conduct of Prosecution Counsel ('Standards').[101] Adopted by the then-Prosecutor, Hassan Bubacar Jallow, these Standards are guided by a number of considerations listed in the first article. One of these considerations affirms that "Prosecutors, who in the MICT represent the international community, play a crucial role in the administration of justice".[102] The Prosecution is expected "to assist the Tribunal to arrive at the truth and to do justice for the international community, victims and accused",[103] and to respect the rights of the accused, including the right to a fair trial by an impartial and independent judiciary.[104] The MICT Standards likewise outline a cooperative approach to the fulfilment of a part of the duties of the OTP: the Prosecution must see that the legitimate interests of the international community are duly reflected in the administration of justice, and must do so in cooperation with the Mechanism.

In addition, the Guidelines on the Roles of Prosecutors ('Guidelines'), adopted by the Eighth UN Congress on the Prevention of Crime and the Treatment of Offenders,[105] hold particular value due to the Mechanism having received its mandate from the UNSC. Article 12 of the Guidelines is,

---

[99] 7829th Meeting Records, 2016, p. 5, see above note 95; 7960th Meeting Records, 2017, p. 6, see above note 958278th Meeting Records, UN Doc. S/PV.8278, 6 June 2018, p. 2. It should be acknowledged that Meron never explicitly linked his expression of gratitude to assistance in the Akay matter.

[100] At the time of writing, Mr. Serge Brammertz is the MICT Chief Prosecutor.

[101] MICT, Prosecutor's Regulation No. 1 (2013) on Standards of Professional Conduct of Prosecution Counsel, MICT/12, 29 November 2013 ('MICT Standards for Prosecution') (http://www.legal-tools.org/doc/d71ab0/).

[102] *Ibid.*, Article 1.

[103] *Ibid.*, Article 2(h).

[104] *Ibid.*, Article 2(a).

[105] Guidelines on the Roles of Prosecutors, Eight UN Congress on the Prevention of Crime and the Treatment of Offenders, UN Doc. A/CONF.144/28/Rev.1, 27 August 1990, p. 188 ('UN Guidelines on the Roles of Prosecutors') (http://www.legal-tools.org/doc/658aba/), welcomed by Resolution 45/166 (18 December 1990), UN Doc. A/RES/45/166, 18 December 1990.

however, careful in its reference to the duty to cooperate with the court in protecting the accused person's right to a fair trial. Indeed, it states that "Prosecutors shall [...] perform their duties fairly [...] contributing to ensuring due process".[106]

The Standards of Professional Responsibility and Statement of Essential Duties and Rights of Prosecutors of the International Association of Prosecutors[107] ('IAP Standards') should be considered a document with significant persuasive power: more so, as it is mentioned in Article 1 of the MICT Standards.[108] Article 4.3 of the IAP Standards explicitly demands that "Prosecutors [...] safeguard the rights of the accused in co-operation with the court",[109] which should be read alongside the duty enshrined in Article 1 of the IAP Standards to "always protect an accused person's right to a fair trial".[110]

The obligation to cooperate with the court to ensure the accused's right to a fair trial by an independent judiciary is crucial for the case at hand. This specific duty defines the role of the MICT Prosecution beyond the successful prosecution of cases. When fair trial rights are in peril, the OTP must work with the MICT adjudicatory arm to avert such threats. In the *Ngirabatware* case, complying with the aforementioned obligation would have meant acting in defence of Judge Akay's independence in order to preserve Ngirabatware's right to a fair trial.

24.2.2.1.8. Actions

There were two potential avenues for the Prosecution through which to protect the independence of the *Ngirabatware* bench. First, pursuant to UNSC Resolution 1966 (2010),[111] the Prosecutor of the Mechanism, along with the President, submit biannual progress reports to the UNSC. In the reports of November 2016[112] and May 2017,[113] as described below, the

---

[106] *Ibid.*, Article 12, p. 192.
[107] International Association of Prosecutors, Standards of Professional Responsibility and Statement of Essential Duties and Rights of Prosecutors, 23 April 1999 ('IAP Standards') (available on the IAP's web site).
[108] MICT Standards for Prosecution, Article 1, see above note 101.
[109] IAP Standards, Article 4.3, see above note 107.
[110] *Ibid.*, Article 1.
[111] MICT Statute, see above note 32.
[112] Assessment and Progress Report of the President of the International Residual Mechanism for Criminal Tribunals, Judge Theodor Meron, for the Period from 16 May to 15 November 2016, UN Doc. S/2016/975, 17 November 2016, Annex I, paras. 13, 38, 90.

President brought to the attention of the UNSC the issue of Judge Akay's independence. The Prosecutor, on the contrary, did not mention Akay or the *Ngirabatware* proceedings at all.

A second avenue to protect the independence of the MICT judge became available during the proceedings of the *Ngirabatware* case itself when significant discussion on judicial independence took place. In the hearing of 17 January 2017,[114] the Prosecution[115] emphasized how "a way forward has to be found so that the fair trial issues that have arisen in this case can be resolved without any further delay", holding that "an order to Turkey is not a guaranteed solution" while expressing "concern about the prospect of [Turkey's] timely compliance with any order issued".[116] The Prosecution suggested to replace Judge Akay on the bench and, to that end, provided legal grounds for the different possibilities granted by the Statute as well as the MICT Rules of Procedure and Evidence.[117] While it is fair to note that the 'remedies' suggested during the course of the hearing would have, for the most part, preserved Akay's immunity, the Prosecution seemingly did not weigh the far-reaching consequences in terms of judicial independence. The OTP has been shown to pursue one main interest: moving the case forward, arguably willing to waive judicial independence in order to minimize delays. This aim has been clearly articulated during the hearing when the Prosecution affirmed that "ensuring an immediately available review bench that can move forwards with deliberations in this case is the priority".[118]

Other case documents contribute to outline the overall attitude of the OTP. In its Response to Ngirabatware's Motion for Order to Government of Turkey or for Temporary Provisional Release, the Prosecution contended that "a period of two months does not, in the particular circumstances of this case, amount to undue delay given the complexity of the matter before the Appeals Chamber" and requested the dismissal of both the motion and

---

[113] Assessment and Progress Report of the President of the International Residual Mechanism for Criminal Tribunals, Judge Theodor Meron, for the Period from 6 November 2016 to 15 May 2017, UN Doc. S/2017/434, 17 May 2017, Annex I, paras. 12–14, 38, 89.

[114] MICT, *Ngirabatware*, Transcript of Hearing, see above note 9.

[115] Ms. Michelle Jarvis appeared for the Prosecution, with Mr. Mathias Marcussen as Co-Counsel and Mr. Iain Reid as Case Manager.

[116] MICT, *Ngirabatware*, Transcript of Hearing, p. 14, see above note 9.

[117] *Ibid.*

[118] *Ibid.*

the request for an oral hearing.[119] The Prosecution did not mention the detention of Judge Akay. Regardless, the implications of the matter were not lost on the OTP. During the proceedings, the Prosecution acknowledged in several instances how, ultimately, fair trial rights were severely impacted.[120]

24.2.2.1.9. Reflections on Integrity

The normative framework for the OTP outlines an obligation to protect the accused person's right to a fair trial in cooperation with the court in order to properly contribute to the administration of justice. The *Ngirabatware* proceedings show how the Prosecution prioritized the swift ending of the case while disregarding, to some extent, Ngirabatware's right to be judged by an independent judiciary. The OTP also refrained from condemning or pressuring the Government of Turkey, both in the proceedings itself and in its reporting to the UNSC, even though the MICT Prosecutor is bound to represent the international community.[121] As the international community holds a legitimate interest in the independence of international judges and in the preservation of diplomatic immunity, it can be argued that the Prosecution did not properly fulfil its mandate in this regard. The actions of the OTP narrowly focused on furthering the case, perhaps in order to remain non-aligned on the matter of Judge Akay's conviction and imprisonment. However, we conclude that even if the observed actions may not be directly construed as a violation of the relevant norms, the MICT Prosecutor was certainly not neutral in terms of integrity. Acting with integrity would have demanded to fully embrace the duty to protect the right of the accused to an impartial judge, contributing to the efforts of the Mechanism, and to safeguard judicial independence in the name and for the sake of the international community.

---

[119] MICT, *Ngirabatware,* Prosecution Response to Motion for Order to Government of Turkey or for Temporary Provisional Release, 18 November 2016, (http://www.legal-tools.org/doc/762b6c/).
[120] See MICT, *Ngirabatware*, Transcript of Hearing, p. 14, see above note 9.
[121] MICT Standards for Prosecution, Article 1, see above note 101.

1.1.1.3. Defence Counsel[122]

24.2.2.1.10. Normative Framework

Article 14 of the Code of Professional Conduct for Defence Counsel Appearing Before the Mechanism demands loyalty towards a client.[123] In the same article, however, counsel is imposed a "duty to the Mechanism to act with independence in the interests of justice".[124] Those interests must be put before the counsel's own interests, and before the interests of any other person, organization, or State. Read together with Article 20, which demands that counsel "at all times have due regard to the fair conduct of the proceedings",[125] the obligation to pursue the interests of justice is hierarchically at the highest level, particularly when due process rights are at stake.

24.2.2.1.11. Actions

As becomes apparent from the hearing of 17 January 2017, Robinson gave precedence to the defence of judicial independence and its significance for the juridical process over the provisional release of his client. In the transcript of the hearing, between 20 to 25 lines are dedicated to the release of Ngirabatware, whereas approximately 200 lines are dedicated to the implications of Judge Akay's detention.[126] Robinson reacted to the suggestion of the OTP to replace Judge Akay on the bench contending that the detention of the Judge was "a broader issue than what the Prosecution is talking about when it comes to judicial independence".[127] Robinson admitted that, from the perspective of Ngirabatware, replacing Akay would have been the easiest solution in order to move forward. However, Robinson explicitly stated that he was not willing to allow the replacement "at the expense of a lack of integrity and independence of the system itself".[128] Throughout the hearing, Robinson put the protection of judicial independence at the centre of his arguments.

---

[122] Mr. Ngirabatware was, at the time of the events we refer to, assisted by Mr. Peter Robinson.
[123] MICT, Code of Professional Conduct for Defence Counsel Appearing Before the Mechanism, 14 November 2012, MICT/6, Article 14 (http://www.legal-tools.org/doc/eeb133/).
[124] *Ibid.*
[125] *Ibid.*, Article 20.
[126] MICT, *Ngirabatware*, Transcript of Hearing, see above note 9.
[127] *Ibid.*, pp. 28–29.
[128] *Ibid.*, p. 29.

The motions filed by Robinson on behalf of Ngirabatware eventually led to the hearing, which was primarily convened to provide Turkey with the opportunity to be heard.[129] Counsel took individual initiatives to invite the Government of Turkey to appear at the hearing, going so far as, on the morning of the hearing, attempting to contact the Turkish authorities in person.[130] Furthermore, as the attachments to the Motion to Initiate Contempt Proceedings show,[131] Robinson continued to solicit responses and information relevant to the matter of Judge Akay with letters directed to the Turkish government, the UN Legal Counsel and the UN Assistant Secretary-General of Legal Affairs.[132]

24.2.2.1.12. Reflections on Integrity

The Defence Counsel is not an organ of the Mechanism. Notwithstanding, he or she has a duty to protect the interests of justice. In the issue discussed here, the interests of justice had been jeopardized by undue interference with the independence of the *Ngirabatware* bench. Robinson had an obligation to put the interests of justice before those of any other person, including his client. Accordingly, he gave precedence to the defence of Akay's independence. Nevertheless, Robinson managed to uphold his duty of loyalty to Ngirabatware appropriately, insofar that it did not prejudice judicial independence, by motioning for his client's provisional release.

As Defence Counsel appearing before the Mechanism, Robinson discharged his obligations, as defined in the aforementioned provisions, dutifully, demonstrating a firm understanding and adherence to the letter and the spirit of the applicable code of conduct.

1.1.1.4. President and Judge of the International Residual Mechanism for Criminal Tribunals

Judge Meron has been the President of the Mechanism from 1 March 2012 to 18 January 2019. During his lengthy judicial career, questions concerning his integrity have been raised, which should be mentioned due to their relevance to the topic at hand. In 2013, former ICTY Judge Frederik Harhoff expressed concerns – in a letter leaked to a Danish tabloid newspaper – over the pressure President Meron was perceived to have exercised

---

[129] *Ibid.*, p. 2.
[130] *Ibid.*, p. 6.
[131] MICT, *Ngirabatware,* Motion to Initiate Contempt Proceedings, para. 5, see above note 68.
[132] *Ibid.*, pp. 12–13, 15-16, 18, 20-21, 25-26. See also Section 1.1.1.1.

on other ICTY judges to promote a legal opinion which Harhoff deemed desirable for certain States.[133] Subsequent United States diplomatic cables leaked by WikiLeaks exacerbated this concern.[134] More recently, controversy has arisen over certain early release rulings adopted by Judge Meron; particularly in the case of Rwandan genocide advocate Ferdinand Nahimana.[135] In his last presidential speech at the UNSC, Judge Meron himself acknowledged with regret the "pain or concern" that some of his early release decisions might have caused to victims and their communities.[136] On the issue of the independence of Judge Akay, however, Judge Meron used every possible avenue to defend judicial independence, which he has consistently deemed critical for the rule of law.

24.2.2.1.13. Normative Framework

The hierarchy of the principle of judicial independence is made clear by the Code of Professional Conduct for the Judges of the Mechanism ('Code').[137] Article 10(2) provides that "nothing in this Code is intended in any way to limit or restrict the judicial independence of the judges",[138] which constitutes, therefore, a fundamental principle. Accordingly, the UN Basic Principles on the Independence of the Judiciary[139] ('Principles') unconditionally prohibit "inappropriate or unwarranted interference with the judicial process",[140] underlining that respecting judicial independence "entitles and requires the judiciary to ensure that judicial proceedings are conducted fair-

---

[133] Frederik Harhoff, "Mystery Lane: A Note on Independence and Impartiality in International Criminal Trials", FICHL Policy Brief Series No. 47 (2016), Torkel Opsahl Academic EPublisher, Brussels, 2016 (http://www.toaep.org/pbs-pdf/47-harhoff/).

[134] See Gunnar M. Ekeløve-Slydal, "ICTY Shifts Have Made Its Credibility Quake", FICHL Policy Brief Series No. 49 (2016), Torkel Opsahl Academic EPublisher, Brussels, 2016 (http://www.toaep.org/pbs-pdf/49-slydal); Julija Bogoeva, "International Judges and Government Interests: The Case of President Meron", FICHL Policy Brief Series No. 48 (2016), Torkel Opsahl Academic EPublisher, Brussels, 2016 (http://www.toaep.org/pbs-pdf/48-bogoeva).

[135] Gregory S. Gordon, "Measuring Integrity in Post-Conviction Proceedings" CILRAP Film, The Hague, 2 December 2018 (https://www.cilrap.org/cilrap-film/181202-gordon/).

[136] MICT, "Address to the UN Security Council", p. 3, see above note 18.

[137] MICT, Code of Professional Conduct for the Judges of the Mechanism, 9 April 2018, MICT/14/Rev. 1 (http://www.legal-tools.org/doc/23cc92/).

[138] *Ibid.*, Article 10(2).

[139] Basic Principles on the Independence of the Judiciary, Seventh UN Congress on the Prevention of Crime and the Treatment of Offenders, UN Doc. A/CONF.121/22/Rev.1, 26 August 1985.

[140] *Ibid.*, Article 4.

ly and that the rights of the parties are respected".[141] The use of the term 'ensure' arguably construes an active duty to remove impediments to the fair conduct of judicial proceedings. The MICT Statute, in addition, affirms the aforementioned principle in its Article 18.[142]

Considering how judicial independence is paramount for the respect of the accused's right to a fair trial, judges have the duty to ensure its respect at all times. It could be argued that no value should surpass the protection of judicial independence, as the fair trial rights of the accused lie at the very core of the rule of law. The explicit mention of the obligation to ensure an expeditious trial should not be construed as being hierarchically superior to the rights of the accused, as the Statute equally mandates "full respect" for the latter too.

In the case at hand, complying with Article 18 of the MICT Statute in a manner consistent with the Principles would have meant according priority to the right of the accused to be judged by an independent judiciary. The provision of Article 10(2) of the Code should be construed as according priority to the protection of judicial independence over any other obligation the Code confers upon MICT judges.

24.2.2.1.14. Actions

The actions of Judge Meron in defence of Judge Akay's independence have shown consistency with his views on judicial independence and its unconditionality. In a 2005 article,[143] Meron made two statements that are relevant to the topic at hand. First, he affirmed that a President of an international criminal tribunal has a duty to "protect the Tribunal as a whole from inappropriate encroachment", even if said encroachment originates from the Security Council itself.[144] Second, he wrote that "the President's role as spokesperson for the Tribunal involves him in diplomatic and political

---

[141] *Ibid.*, Article 6.
[142] MICT Statute, p. 13, see above note 32. Article 18 reads: "[t]he Single Judge or Trial Chambers conducting a trial shall ensure that the trial is fair and expeditious and that proceedings are conducted in accordance with the Rules of Procedure and Evidence, with full respect for the rights of the accused and due regard for the protection of victims and witnesses".
[143] Theodor Meron, "Judicial Independence and Impartiality in International Criminal Tribunals", in *The American Journal of International Law*, 2005, vol. 99, no. 2, pp. 359–369.
[144] *Ibid.*, p. 365.

functions".[145] Judicial proceedings are not, therefore, the only avenue that a President should use in order to fulfil his duties towards the Tribunal.

Judge Meron, consistent with the views he expressed in the past, began his defence of Judge Akay with a letter to the President of the UNSC, exercising his political functions as the MICT President.[146] The letter, dated 5 October 2016, is the first of a series of initiatives taken by Judge Meron to draw attention to the ongoing detention of Judge Akay, and its far-reaching consequences on judicial independence, the rule of law and the effective functioning of the Mechanism. Indeed, Meron conveyed to the UNSC that he did not

> consider it possible, under the circumstances, to reconcile full respect for the fundamental principle of judicial independence, on the one hand, with, on the other hand, the removal of Judge Akay from the bench to which he has been assigned.[147]

In his official capacity as President of the Mechanism, Judge Meron filed two progress reports to the UNSC, on 17 November 2016 and 17 May 2017, in which he raised the issue of Akay's detention, noting the broader implications on the ability of the Mechanism to fulfil its mandate.[148] The President's annual report of August 2017 likewise mentioned the assertion of diplomatic independence of Judge Akay, and the Government of Turkey's non-compliance with the Mechanism's order to cease all legal proceedings against Akay and to release him from detention.[149] In his personal capacity, Meron has stressed the impact of Akay's detention on the principle of the rule of law, affirming that "all of us who care about justice and

---

[145] *Ibid.*

[146] Letter from the President of the International Residual Mechanism for Criminal Tribunals, T. Meron, Regarding the Detention of Turkish Judge Aydin Sefa Akay to the UN Security Council, 2016, see above note 16.

[147] MICT, "Address to the UN Security Council", 8 December 2016 (available on the MICT's web site).

[148] Assessment and Progress Report of the President of the International Residual Mechanism for Criminal Tribunals, Judge Theodor Meron, for the Period from 16 May to 15 November 2016, 2016, see above note 112; Assessment and Progress Report of the President of the International Residual Mechanism for Criminal Tribunals, Judge Theodor Meron, for the Period from 6 November 2016 to 15 May 2017, 2017, see above note 113.

[149] UN General Assembly, UN Security Council, Fifth Annual Report of the International Residual Mechanism for Criminal Tribunals, UN Doc. A/72/621, UN Doc. S/2017/661, 1 August 2017, para. 26.

are committed to the rule of law must do our utmost to defend this fundamental principle [judicial independence]".[150]

During the course of the 17 January 2017 *Ngirabatware* hearing, as already mentioned above, the solutions suggested by the Prosecution centred around replacing Judge Akay on the bench while preserving his assignment as a judge of the Mechanism in order to maintain his diplomatic immunity. Judge Meron, however, intervened to keep the focus on the implications on due process and judicial independence. He pointed out that a judge of the Mechanism should always be consulted before assigning him to a panel, and that the consent of a judge must be sought when the President makes such administrative deliberations. Ultimately, Judge Meron conveyed that the replacement of Judge Akay would have weighed heavily on judicial independence, and recalled that he had deemed such replacement inappropriate in his communications to the UNSC and the UNGA.[151]

Following the hearing, Meron ordered the Government of Turkey to release Judge Akay.[152] The Order was adopted after the President's invitations to Turkey to spontaneously release Akay were ignored. At the same time, Judge Meron denied the Motion to initiate contempt proceedings on the grounds that it fell outside of the mandate and the powers of the Mechanism, which had already taken appropriate steps reporting the issue to the UNSC.[153]

It has already been mentioned that, notwithstanding the efforts of Judge Meron, Judge Akay was not reappointed to the Mechanism. In his final appearance before the UNSC as the MICT President, Meron expressed "profound regret that a different and better resolution for the situation of my former colleague, Judge Aydin Sefa Akay, was not found".[154] In his last speech as President of the Mechanism, he furthermore argued that

> at a time when the world is facing deeply troubling trends related to the undermining of independent judiciaries and the weakening of the rule of law, we at the United Nations simply cannot afford to be anything less than exemplary when it

---

[150] Theodor Meron, "The Future of International Criminal Justice", Remarks at the Embassy of the Republic of Poland in The Hague on the Occasion of the Awarding of the Officer's Cross of the Order of Merit, 16 May 2017, p. 4 (available on the MICT's web site).

[151] MICT, *Ngirabatware*, Transcript of Hearing, p. 29, see above note 9.

[152] MICT, *Ngirabatware*, Order for Release, see above note 15.

[153] MICT, *Ngirabatware*, Decision on a Motion to Initiate Contempt Proceedings, 26 April 2017, see above note 9 (http://www.legal-tools.org/doc/838408/).

[154] MICT, "Statement, Address to the UN Security Council", p. 3, see above note 18.

comes to our own handling of interference with judicial independence and actions undertaken in contravention of UN immunities.[155]

24.2.2.1.15. Reflections on Integrity

The two roles that President and Judge Meron held throughout the Akay saga have led to concurring obligations. As President of the Mechanism, he had a duty to protect the independence of the MICT judges in order to ensure the proper functioning of the institution. As Meron himself expressed, his role as President demanded diplomatic and political engagement;[156] an obligation he discharged through his reports and addresses to, and communications with, the relevant UN organs.

As a judge in the *Ngirabatware* case, Meron's duty was to ensure the fairness of the trial and the "full respect for the rights of the accused", as demanded by Article 18 of the MICT Statute.[157] The obligation to ensure the expeditiousness of the proceedings could not be entirely performed without affecting the fairness of the trial. Judge Meron's refusal of compromises that would have impacted on the right of Ngirabatware to an independent judiciary, such as Akay's replacement, was consistent with the Statute and the UN Basic Principles on the Judiciary.

Accordingly, Meron did everything in his power "to ensure that judicial proceedings are conducted fairly"[158] and to shield the judicial process from "inappropriate or unwarranted interference".[159] In doing so, he respected the boundaries of his role, displaying due constraint and limiting his actions to the means granted to him as a Judge and as President of the MICT. Arguably, the matter would have been less complicated for Meron, had he accepted to replace Judge Akay on the *Ngirabatware* bench, following the avenue proposed by the OTP during the hearing of 17 January 2017.[160] In this hypothetical situation, Judge Akay would have preserved diplomatic immunity due to his continuous assignment to MICT cases. Nevertheless, disregarding the consolidated practice of seeking the consent of a judge before altering his or her assignments would have resulted in an unreasonable compromise with respect to judicial independence. Hence, it

---

[155] *Ibid.*
[156] Meron, 2005, p. 365, see above note 143.
[157] MICT Statute, Article 18, see above note 32.
[158] Basic Principles on the Independence of the Judiciary, Article 6, see above note 139.
[159] *Ibid.*, Article 4.
[160] MICT, *Ngirabatware*, Transcript of Hearing, see above note 9.

was Meron's duty to refuse any such replacement; had he replaced Judge Akay, the resulting bench would have been indirectly determined by the illegitimate influence of the Government of Turkey on the MICT's inner workings. Consequently, Ngirabatware's right to a fair trial by an independent judiciary would have been compressed for the sake of convenience and, perhaps, expeditiousness. Conflictingly, *Judge* Meron's duties mandated him to care most about the rights of the accused, while *President* Meron had a duty to act in a manner which would ensure the proper functioning of the Mechanism.

As described above, the initiatives of Judge Meron were met by silence on the part of the UN institutions. Meron was joined in his effort by the Defence Counsel, while the MICT Prosecutor elected to prioritize the expeditiousness of the *Ngirabatware* proceedings over judicial independence. Notwithstanding the adversities, Meron consistently upheld the obligations pertinent to his roles as President and Judge, without letting other considerations – such as political convenience – influence his actions. His behaviour is exemplary of individual integrity; displaying adherence to the values protected by the applicable norms of conduct while remaining within the boundaries set by his roles.

24.3. Institutional, Professional and Personal Integrity: One and the Same?

Provisions such as Article 9 MICT Statute, titled "Qualification of Judges",[161] can be found in several instruments establishing internationalized criminal courts or tribunals.[162] Article 9 MICT Statute requires judges, among others, to be of "high moral character" and to "possess the qualifications required in their respective countries for appointment to the highest judicial offices". As noted by Bergsmo, the term integrity is – in international criminal law – a *legal* requirement laid down in provisions such as Article 9 MICT Statute.[163]

---

[161] MICT Statute, Article 9, see above note 32.
[162] See, for example, Statute of the International Criminal Tribunal for the former Yugoslavia, 25 May 1993, Article 13 (http://www.legal-tools.org/doc/b4f63b/); Statute of the International Criminal Tribunal for Rwanda, 8 November 1994, Article 12 (http://www.legal-tools.org/doc/8732d6/); Rome Statute of the International Criminal Court, 17 July 1998, Article 36 (http://www.legal-tools.org/doc/7b9af9/).
[163] Bergsmo, 2018, p. 3, see above note 1.

Dag Hammarskjöld equates integrity with "respect for law and respect for *truth*" and with "conscience".[164] Jacques Lemoine brings "the moral qualities of *dedication, fairness and impartiality*" under the concept of integrity.[165] These notions subsume something wider than what is demanded by a narrow interpretation of Article 9 MICT Statute. Some of the actors in the Akay saga, such as the UNSG and the UN Legal Counsel, clearly operated within the borders of the law. They followed Article 9 MICT Statute to the letter: Akay indeed forewent the "qualifications required in [his] respective countr[y] for appointment to the highest judicial offices"; indeed, he was charged with and convicted for a grave crime.

Logically, following the Statute, he could not be reappointed as a judge on the roster of the Mechanism. It appears, however, that Akay's conviction amounted to undue influence on judicial independence. It also seems that the response of certain individuals to this issue did not adequately defend this fundamental principle of international justice, resulting in the non-reappointment of the judge, which can be deemed problematic from a rule of law perspective.

Those who followed only the letter of Article 9 MICT Statute perhaps lost sight of other, underlying yet fundamental values of the integrity standard. They showed neither loyalty nor dedication to a principal actor of international justice or to the fundamental virtues of truth and transparency. Others, namely Defence Counsel Peter Robinson and Judge Theodor Meron, can serve as examples acting in line with the integrity standard. It has to be noted that they were allowed to do so in the roles they were accorded. Meron, as President of the Mechanism, had to ensure that his chamber functioned, which is not possible when one of its judges is detained. Robinson had his own interests, as counsel, in fighting for Akay, in whose absence the procedure pertaining to his client could not proceed.

Nevertheless, both Robinson and Meron seem to have gone beyond their professional obligations. Robinson explored all possible avenues to bring the Akay matter to the surface and to the attention of those who could have made a difference. Similarly to Meron, he attempted to affect Akay's situation, or at least make it known to the public. In the end, it is rather disappointing that both were blocked by institutionalism, confidentiality and an extensive reach of State sovereignty. Nevertheless, although of not much

---

[164] Hammarskjöld, 1962, p. 348, see above note 2 (emphasis added).
[165] Jacques Lemoine, *The International Civil Servant: An Endangered Species*, Martinus Nijhoff Publishers, The Hague, 1995, p. 257 (emphasis added).

use to Akay, who remains behind bars, their conduct shows that it is possible to intertwine integrity – understood broadly – and professional obligations resulting from their specific roles.

The Akay saga has put the integrity of concerned individuals to the test. While the Government of Turkey was pursuing its national interests, the UN institutions and international civil servants involved did not pose the needed resistance. The efforts of the parties which upheld the integrity standard could not steer the outcome: nevertheless, they represent a meaningful expression of the behaviour to be expected from individuals in such roles and, as the authors of this chapter hope, provide a lasting example for the future.

Finally, it must be noted that achieving or acting with integrity is not a one-time test, and it demands much more than meeting the normative requirements at the moment of appointment to a judicial institution. It is an ongoing struggle for all international civil servants and high officials in international justice. This is eloquently described by the concept of self-oblivion, as expressed by Dag Hammarskjöld – the constant exercise of force of will, and the careful balancing of one's personal interests and values, on the one hand, with the values one has chosen to embrace, professionally, on the other hand: with a readiness to 'surrender' to the latter. The resulting actions would likely protect the spirit of the law and its founding principles, in addition to its letter and the obligations that are spelt out: "[y]ou will find that the freedom of the continual farewell, the hourly self-surrender, gives to your experience of reality the purity and clarity which signify–self-realization".[166]

---

[166] Dag Hammarskjöld, *Markings*, Faber and Faber, London, 1964, p. 77.

25

The Disqualification of Judge Frederik Harhoff:
Implications for Integrity

Mohamed Badar and Polona Florijančič[*]

In 2013, a leaked e-mail message by Judge Frederik Harhoff (the 'Letter') put into question the integrity of the International Criminal Tribunal for the former Yugoslavia ('ICTY'). As a result of what he perceived to be a change in the ICTY jurisprudence concerning aiding, abetting, and joint criminal enterprise liability after the acquittals in the *Gotovina and Markač* Appeals Judgement, the *Perišić* Appeals Judgement, and the *Stanišić and Simatović* Trial Judgement, Judge Harhoff made the following statements in his Letter:

> Right up until autumn 2012, it has been a more or less set practice at the court that military commanders were held responsible for war crimes that their subordinates committed during the war in the former Yugoslavia. […] However, this is no longer the case. Now apparently the commanders must have had a *direct intention* to commit crimes – and not just knowledge or suspicion that the crimes were or would be committed. […] The result is now that not only has the court taken a significant step back from the lesson that commanding military leaders have to take responsibility for their subordinates' crimes (unless it can be proven that they knew nothing about it) – but also that the theory of responsibility under the specific "joint criminal enterprise" has now been reduced

---

[*] Professor **Mohamed Badar** holds the Chair in Comparative and International Criminal Law at Northumbria Law School, Northumbria University, Newcastle. He has published extensively on issues related to comparative and international criminal law, and his work has been cited by international and national criminal courts. He previously served as Senior Prosecutor and Judge in Egypt (1997-2006). Dr. **Polona Florijančič** is an independent researcher who has taught and published in the fields of international criminal law and human rights law among other fields. She has also conducted field research for the EUROMED justice project on criminal co-operation and counter-terrorism in the MENA region (2017-2019). She obtained her Ph.D. in International Trade Law and Development and an LL.M. in International Human Rights from Brunel University (London), and an LL.B. from the European Faculty of Law, Slovenia.

from contribution to crimes (in some way or another) to demanding a *direct intention* to commit crime (and so not just acceptance of the crimes being committed). Most of the cases will lead to commanding officers walking free from here on.[1]

As a result, Judge Harhoff was declared biased and removed from the *Šešelj* case. Some years later, it is argued here that two things are clear: Judge Harhoff's disqualification was, in our considered opinion, unjust – there was no bias on his part that could justify his removal from the *Šešelj* case. Furthermore, his concerns about a dangerous change in the jurisprudence were legitimate, and his views have been vindicated in subsequent rulings.

However, there was another element to the Letter, namely speculations about possible external and internal pressures put on fellow judges by the President of the Tribunal, Theodor Meron, as the reason behind the change in jurisprudence. Judge Harhoff posed the rhetorical question: "how [does] this military logic pressure the international criminal justice system? Have any American or Israeli officials ever exerted pressure on the American presiding judge [...] to ensure a change of direction? We will probably never know".[2]

While the disqualification decision omits any reference to said speculations, they seem to be the *de facto* reason behind the removal of Judge Harhoff from the *Šešelj* case and effectively the ICTY. If this is indeed the case, such a response sends a very negative signal about the Tribunal that, apparently, preferred to sweep serious concerns under the rug rather than allow investigations or open discussions about them, perpetuating the culture of silence, and discouraging whistleblowing and honest criticism from within.

25.1. Disqualification without Bias

The Statute of the ICTY guarantees an accused a 'fair and expeditious trial' with full respect for the rights of the accused.[3] Article 13 of the Statute en-

---

[1] The International Criminal Tribunal for the former Yugoslavia ('ICTY') Judge Frederik Harhoff's email, 6 June 2013 annexed to ICTY, *Prosecutor v. Stanišić and Župljanin*, Appeals Chamber, Prosecution Response to Rule 115 Motion on behalf of Mićo Stanišić seeking admission of additional evidence, 9 July 2013, IT-08-91-A (https://www.legal-tools.org/doc/956cc2/).

[2] *Ibid.*

[3] Statute of the ICTY, 25 May 1993, Article 20 (https://www.legal-tools.org/doc/b4f63b).

shrines an additional element of the right to fair trial as it requires judges of the Tribunal to be "persons of high moral character, impartiality and integrity". This principle is embodied in Rule 15 of the Rules of Procedure and Evidence, which precludes a judge from sitting in a trial or appeal in any case in which he or she has a personal interest or concerning which the judge has or has had any association which might affect his or her impartiality.[4] The Appeals Chamber has observed further that:

    A. A Judge is not impartial if it is shown that actual bias exists.

    B. There is an unacceptable appearance of bias if:

        i) a Judge is a party to the case, or has a financial or proprietary interest in the outcome of a case, or if the Judge's decision will lead to the promotion of a cause in which he or she is involved, together with one of the parties. Under these circumstances, a Judge's disqualification from the case is automatic; or

        ii) the circumstances would lead a reasonable observer, properly informed, to reasonably apprehend bias.[5]

On 9 July 2013, Vojislav Šešelj filed a motion seeking the disqualification of Judge Frederik Harhoff based on the Letter.[6] On 28 August 2013, the panel of appointed Judges[7] ('Special Chamber') issued a decision (the 'Disqualification Decision' or simply, the 'Decision') granting this motion by majority (the 'Majority').[8] After deliberating for 18 months, Judge Harhoff was removed from the case just six weeks away from pronouncing a verdict, despite the fact that "the Rules of Procedure and Evidence do not

---

[4]   ICTY, Rules of Procedure and Evidence, UN Doc. IT/32/Rev.50, 8 July 2015, adopted pursuant to Article 15 of the Statute of the Tribunal, incorporates amendments from 1994 to November 2015, Rule 15(A) (https://www.legal-tools.org/doc/30df50/).

[5]   ICTY, *Prosecutor v. Furundžija*, Appeals Chamber, Judgement, 21 July 2000, IT-95-17/1-A, paras. 189–190 ('Furundžija Appeal Judgment') (https://www.legal-tools.org/doc/660d3f/).

[6]   ICTY, *Prosecutor v. Šešelj*, Trial Chamber, Professor Vojislav Šešelj's Motion for Disqualification of Judge Frederik Harhoff, 9 July 2013, IT-03-67-T (https://www.legal-tools.org/doc/a7ccdc).

[7]   It should be mentioned that Judges Moloto and Hall had sat on other cases with Judge Harhoff.

[8]   ICTY, *Prosecutor v. Šešelj*, Chamber Convened by Order of the Vice-President, Decision on Defence Motion for Disqualification of Judge Frederik Harhoff and Report to the Vice-President, 28 August 2013, IT-03-67-T ('Disqualification Decision') (https://www.legal-tools.org/doc/5b4aa1).

provide for a case where a motion for disqualification can be made during deliberations".[9]

With regards to the Letter, in paragraph 13 of the Decision, the Majority stated:

> By referring to a 'set practice' of convicting accused persons without reference to an evaluation of the evidence in each individual case [...] there are grounds for concluding that a reasonable observer, properly informed, would reasonably apprehend bias on the part of Judge Harhoff in favour of conviction [...]. This appearance of bias is further compounded by Judge Harhoff's statement that he is confronted by a professional and moral dilemma which [...] is a clear reference to his difficulty in applying the current jurisprudence of the Tribunal.

In this statement, as well as in the whole Decision, the Majority's reasoning disregarded entirely a memorandum sent by Judge Harhoff to Judge Antonetti, the Presiding Judge in the *Šešelj* case, as well as the latter's report.[10] In the memorandum, Judge Harhoff explicitly clarified the context and meaning of various parts of the Letter. He explained that it should have been read in conjunction with the two news articles that he had previously shared with the same recipients and which gave the necessary background for understanding the concerns expressed in the Letter.[11] For example, an article in *The Economist* noted that the judgments in *Perišić*

---

[9] ICTY, *Prosecutor v. Šešelj*, President of the Chamber, Decision to Unseal the Report of the Presiding Judge to the President of the Tribunal or Alternatively the Judge Designated by him Regarding the Motion for Disqualification of Judge Harhoff, 4 September 2013, IT-03-67-T, p. 3 ('Decision to Unseal the Report') (https://www.legal-tools.org/doc/e91251).

[10] According to Rule 15(B), the Presiding Judge of the Chamber has to confer with the judge against whom bias is alleged before sending a report to the President of the Tribunal. After the panel issued the decision to disqualify Judge Harhoff, Judges Antonetti and Lattanzi sent a joint request for clarification to the panel and the Vice-President drawing their attention to the fact that neither the report of the Presiding Judge nor the written comments of the Judge in question had been mentioned in the decision. On the same day, Judge Harhoff also sent a request that the panel of judges consider the two documents. The ICTY Prosecutor, Serge Brammertz, sent a motion for review of the decision. *Ibid.*, p. 1.

[11] ICTY, Internal Memorandum from Judge Frederik Harhoff to Judge Jean-Claude Antonetti, Motion for Disqualification of Judge Frederik Harhoff filed by the Accused Vojislav Šešelj/Report, 8 July 2013, annexed to *Prosecutor v. Šešelj*, President of the Chamber, Decision to unseal the report of the Presiding Judge to the President of the Tribunal or alternatively the Judge designated by him regarding the motion for disqualification of Judge Harhoff, 4 September 2013, IT-03-67-T ('Harhoff, Memorandum') (https://www.legal-tools.org/doc/e91251/).

---

and *Stanišić and Simatović* meant it was now more difficult to convict senior officials,[12] while an article in the *New York Times* noted that *Stanišić and Simatović* had raised the standard of proof for joint criminal enterprise ('JCE') convictions, and that this was part of a trend in recent jurisprudence at the Tribunal that could be viewed as protecting the interests of more powerful countries.[13] It was these sentiments that Judge Harhoff sought to echo in his Letter, by noting that this change of practice would henceforth probably make it very hard to convict any of the superior military commanders; he considered the new requirements introduced would be very difficult to prove, for example, the specific direction requirement for aiding and abetting (see Section 25.2.1.).[14]

Furthermore, Judge Harhoff asserted that the Letter was never intended as a legal intervention,[15] but rather as an informal private communication and was for that reason "not very clear on the distinction between JCE, aiding and abetting and command responsibility".[16] He considered that it went "without saying that no one can be convicted of a crime unless the evidence convincingly supports a finding of guilt", but he did not highlight this because it was not the gist of the Letter.[17] Rather his concern was with the Appeals Chamber's acquittals, which, in his understanding, presented a departure from the Tribunal's practice and made it impossible to convict generals in the future.[18]

In his own words, in terms of JCE, he considered the new practice to require "more than just the degree of intent associated with knowledge, *i.e.* that the supreme commanders could only be convicted in the future if *a stronger degree of intent* could be proven at trial".[19]

Finally, Judge Harhoff also clarified that the 'moral and professional dilemma' he referred to at the end of the Letter was directed at the potential

---

[12] "Two puzzling judgments in the Hague: The International Criminal Tribunal for the Former Yugoslavia Lost Credibility", *The Economist*, 1 June 2013 (available on its web site).

[13] Eric Gordy, "What Happened to the Hague Tribunal?", *The New York Times*, 2 June 2013 (available on its web site).

[14] See, for example, the specific direction by the accomplice, Harhoff, Memorandum, p. 3, see above note 11.

[15] *Ibid.*, p. 2.

[16] *Ibid.*

[17] *Ibid.*, pp. 2–3.

[18] *Ibid.*, p. 1.

[19] *Ibid.*, p. 3.

situation in which he might "discover that [the] Tribunal had somehow submitted to pressure or influence from military stakeholders outside the Tribunal".[20] By his own accord, this may not have been an accurate depiction of the impact of the change of the Tribunal's practice, but it did "not in any way suggest a belief or indeed a desire" on his part to have generals convicted irrespectively of the evidence of their *mens rea* and *actus reus*.[21]

Perhaps most important for the question of bias *vis-à-vis* Šešelj is the fact that the Letter does not mention either him or the trial against him at all.[22] The main point about criminal responsibility only relates to 'senior military officers', which does not apply to Šešelj, because he was not a senior military officer and was not charged with having wielded command authority over military forces. On the other hand, there is no prejudice expressed in the Letter against Serbs or Muslims or Croats, or indeed against generals as such.[23] Furthermore, the Presiding Judge in the trial vouched for Judge Harhoff by stating that he had shown great professionalism and proved himself completely impartial towards the accused.[24]

Despite this, the Decision on Judge Harhoff's disqualification states: "With regard to Judge Harhoff's reference to military commanders, the Chamber notes that the accused is charged with participating in a JCE by *inter alia* directing paramilitary forces including a group known as 'Šešelj's men'".[25] This statement is rather disingenuous since it was precisely because of the fact that Šešelj did not hold any official rank, title or authority in the military and did not exercise conventional command responsibility over those committing crimes, that the Prosecution could only claim an 'ideological and moral' authority in the context of JCE charges.[26] What is more, the Trial Chamber in *Šešelj* had already in its Rule 98*bis* de-

---

20 *Ibid.*

21 *Ibid.*

22 *Ibid.*, p. 1.

23 *Ibid.*

24 "Antonetti: Don't let Harhoff be 'doubly victimized'", *Sense Agency*, 4 September 2013 (available on its web site).

25 Disqualification Decision, para. 12, see above note 8, referring to ICTY, *Prosecutor v. Šešelj*, Third Amended Indictment, 7 December 2007, IT-03-67-T, paras. 8, 10 (https://www.legal-tools.org/doc/f427f1/).

26 ICTY, *Prosecutor v. Šešelj*, Transcript, 19 February 2009, IT-03-67-T, T. 3815 (Testimony of prosecution expert witness Theunens); ICTY, *Prosecutor v. Šešelj*, Trial Chamber, Prosecution's Closing Brief, 5 February 2012, IT-03-67-T, para. 593 (https://www.legal-tools.org/doc/61hng5/).

cision (both in the majority and dissenting opinions) expressed a preference for instigation as the mode of liability most appropriate to describe the actions of the accused.[27]

In his report on the Letter, Judge Antonetti reminded that other judges had made public statements on the jurisprudence of the Tribunal, but they had not been disqualified.[28] Similarly, the Prosecution stated that "in criticising recent jurisprudence, [the Letter] was no different from many other public statements disagreeing with the jurisprudence of the Tribunal".[29] Despite this, the Majority claimed that the Letter did differ from other such public statements made by judges in that Judge Harhoff referred to what he perceived as a 'set practice' of convicting military commanders for the war crimes committed by their subordinates and made clear his dissatisfaction with his perceived change in the Tribunal's direction in this regard.[30] The Majority bizarrely implies that the 'set practice' here meant a practice of convictions *without evaluating the evidence in each individual case*.[31] Such a strange implication could only be made by an 'informed person' had the person a) not considered the Letter in its entirety or b) not known anything about Judge Harhoff's professionalism or indeed his previous adjudications at the Tribunal. It is thus not surprising that the Majority conveniently declared the consideration of those adjudications to be irrelevant.[32]

In this context, it is important to note that Judge Harhoff "was not just any judge at the tribunal".[33] He participated from the very beginning in the efforts to establish liability for international crimes. He worked as a Senior Legal Officer at the International Criminal Tribunal for Rwanda ('ICTR') in its first three years of existence, was a member of the Danish delegation at the Rome Conference, and served three years as a Senior Le-

---

[27] ICTY, *Prosecutor v. Šešelj*, Transcript, 4 May 2011, IT-03-67-T, T. 16827 (Rule 98*bis* proceedings).

[28] Decision to Unseal the Report, p. 2, see above note 9.

[29] Disqualification Decision, para. 3, see above note 8; ICTY, *Prosecutor v. Šešelj*, Prosecution's Response to Motion for Disqualification of Judge Frederick Harhoff, 17 July 2013, IT-03-67-T, para. 5 (https://www.legal-tools.org/doc/afc254/).

[30] Disqualification Decision, para. 12, see above note 8.

[31] *Ibid.*, para. 13.

[32] *Ibid.*, para. 9.

[33] Martin Burcharth, "The email that went around the world", *Information*, 7 December 2013 (available on its web site).

gal Officer at the ICTY where he was later appointed judge. Furthermore, he has worked as an Associate Professor at the University of Copenhagen and Professor of International Law at the University of Southern Denmark.[34] He sat as a judge in four Trial Chambers at the ICTY, and an evaluation of this work by the Special Chamber would have further been important in terms of countering Šešelj's submission that there was a specific anti-Serb bias present on the part of Judge Harhoff. He, in fact, took part in convicting the Bosnian Serb general Dragomir Milošević and the Bosnian Serb interior minister and the security chief in Banja Luka, but he also took part in convicting the Bosnian Muslim general Rasim Delić for war crimes committed by *mujahideen* warriors. Furthermore, the two Appeals Chamber judgments which Judge Harhoff criticized in the Letter concern both Croats and Serbs.[35] He does refer as an example only to the "ethnic cleansing of non-Serbs as part of the common purpose" of the JCE as alleged in many indictments, but as he explains in his memorandum, this does not imply that he holds JCE-expulsions of other ethnicities only as a matter for the Serbs.[36]

Writing his dissenting opinion to the Decision on the disqualification, Judge LIU, expressed his concern with what he called "the cursory approach taken by the Majority" and its failure to properly contextualize the statements or take into account the highly informal nature of the Letter.[37] Most importantly, LIU stated that he was not convinced that Judge Harhoff's failure to refer to "an evaluation of the evidence in each individual case"[38] creates the appearance that he is reluctant to apply the Tribunal's law and rules of procedure and evidence or that he is in favour of conviction of accused before the Tribunal.[39] He also disagreed with the Majority's conclusion that the reference to 'a professional and moral dilemma' reflected a difficulty on Judge Harhoff's part to apply the current jurisprudence of the Tribunal.[40]

The defence of the former Bosnia and Herzegovina ('BiH') Army Main Staff commander, Rasim Delić, also called for a review of his judge-

---

[34] *Ibid.*

[35] Harhoff, Memorandum, p. 1, see above note 11.

[36] *Ibid.*

[37] Disqualification Decision, Dissenting Opinion of Judge Liu, paras. 6–7, see above note 8.

[38] *Ibid.*, para. 13.

[39] *Ibid.*, para. 7.

[40] *Ibid.*

ment on the basis of Judge Harhoff's alleged 'bias'. However, the Appeals Chamber dismissed the motion for review since Delić had already passed away at the time and neither his next-of-kin nor Counsel had *locus standi in judicio*.[41] The saga, nonetheless, received a more interesting update in 2016 with the appeal in the *Stanišić and Župljanin* case.[42] Perhaps unsurprisingly, the appellants seized the opportunity and claimed that the disqualification of Judge Harhoff from the *Šešelj* proceedings, although not legally binding, must lead to the same result in the proceedings against them.[43] They submitted that they were specifically included in the category of persons likely to be convicted as a result of Judge Harhoff's predisposition,[44] and repeated the finding of the Majority in the Special Chamber that his views demonstrated a belief in convicting accused persons under JCE liability without proving the requisite legal elements.[45]

One could hardly argue with their logic that if there had been a bias in terms of sitting as a judge on the *Šešelj* trial, it would equally have exist-

---

[41] ICTY, *Prosecutor v. Delić*, Appeals Chamber, Decision on Defence Motion for Review, 17 December 2013, IT-04-83-R.1, p. 2 (https://www.legal-tools.org/doc/d61bd1/).

[42] ICTY, *Prosecutor v. Stanišić and Župljanin*, Appeals Chamber, Judgement, 30 June 2016, IT-08-91-A ('Stanišić and Župljanin Appeal Judgement') (https://www.legal-tools.org/doc/e414f6/).

[43] ICTY, *Prosecutor v. Stanišić and Župljanin*, Appeals Chamber, Additional Appellant's brief on behalf of Mićo Stanišić, 26 June 2014, IT-08-91-A, paras. 33–52 ('Stanišić Additional Appeal Brief') (https://www.legal-tools.org/doc/509154/); ICTY, *Prosecutor v. Stanišić and Župljanin*, Stojan Župljanin Supplement to Appeal Brief (Ground Six), 26 June 2014, IT-08-91-A, paras. 4–13, 28-29 ('Župljanin Additional Appeal Brief') (https://www.legal-tools.org/doc/e6a556/); ICTY, *Prosecutor v. Stanišić and Župljanin*, Additional brief in reply on behalf of Mićo Stanišić, 25 July 2014, IT-08-91-A, paras. 28–30 ('Stanišić Additional Reply Brief') (https://www.legal-tools.org/doc/48470a/). The Prosecution argued, amongst other things, that the unanimous Trial Judgment in *Stanišić and Župljanin* shows that the Special Chamber's majority interpretation of the Letter was incorrect and that Harhoff's Memorandum was erroneously considered to be immaterial. See ICTY, *Prosecutor v. Stanišić and Župljanin*, Appeal Hearing, 16 December 2015, AT. 133-134 ('Appeal Hearing'); The Prosecution also argued that a conclusion contrary to the Disqualification Decision in *Prosecutor v. Šešelj* would be consistent with prior instances where different chambers reached different conclusions based on different arguments and evidence. ICTY, *Prosecutor v. Stanišić and Župljanin*, Prosecution Consolidated Supplemental Response Brief, 18 July 2014, IT-08-91-A, para. 31 (https://www.legal-tools.org/doc/6301a0/).

[44] Appeal Hearing, AT. 79, 84, 152, see above note 43.

[45] Stanišić Additional Appeal Brief, paras. 65–71, 73, 78-9 (referring to Letter pp. 3–4), see above note 43; Župljanin Additional Appeal Brief, paras. 4, 10-13, see above note 43. See Appeal Hearing, 16 December 2015, AT. 149-154, see above note 43; Stanišić Additional Reply Brief, paras. 12, 34-35, see above note 43.

ed in their case, yet the Appeals Chamber found the opposite. Regarding both the 'deep professional and moral dilemma' expressed in the Letter as well as the 'set practice'[46] described therein, the Appeals Chamber accepted the explanations from Judge Harhoff's memorandum[47] and, taking into account the whole Letter, it was not convinced that it would lead a reasonable observer properly informed to conclude that Judge Harhoff was predisposed to convicting the accused persons.[48] Thus, the Appeals Chamber reached drastically different conclusions from the Special Chamber, yet it seems that the only difference between the *Šešelj* and the *Stanišić and Župljanin* cases was that the former was still ongoing at the time, while the Trial Judgment in the latter had already been issued at the date of the publication of the Letter.[49] A rather superficial difference and hardly one which could explain why the same judge, holding the same convictions, would be biased in one and not the other, particularly since bias was alleged on the basis of a predisposition against the faithful application of the law.[50]

While strongly criticizing Judge Harhoff's views on the law as expressed in the Letter and stating that they do not align with the jurisprudence of the Tribunal,[51] the Appeals Chamber recalled that personal convictions and opinions of ICC Judges are not in themselves a basis for inferring a lack of impartiality.[52] Furthermore, it stated that the Trial Chamber had applied the correct legal standard for JCE liability[53] to the circumstances of the case in question and not the views expressed in the Letter.[54]

---

[46] Letter, p. 1, see above note 1.

[47] Stanišić and Župljanin Appeal Judgement, para. 56, see above note 42; Harhoff, Memorandum, p. 3, see above note 11.

[48] *Ibid.*, para. 56.

[49] *Ibid.*, para. 54.

[50] *Ibid.*, para. 37, fns. 148, 149.

[51] *Ibid.*, para. 52.

[52] ICTY, *Prosecutor v. Delalić et al.*, Appeals Chamber, Judgement, 20 February 2001, IT-96-21-A, para. 699 ('Čelebići Appeal Judgement') (https://www.legal-tools.org/doc/051554/), referring to *Prosecutor v. Anto Furundžija*, Appeals Chamber, Judgement, para. 203 ('Furundžija Appeal Judgement') (https://www.legal-tools.org/doc/660d3f/). See also Scottish High Court of Justiciary, *Hoekstra v. HM Advocate*, Judgment, 2000; New South Wales Court of Appeal, *Newcastle City Council v. Lindsay*, Judgment, 2004, paras. 35–36.

[53] ICTY, *Prosecutor v. Stanišić and Župljanin*, Trial Chamber, Judgement, vol. 1, 27 March 2013, IT-08-91-T, paras. 99–106 ('*Stanišić and Župljanin*, Trial Judgement') (https://www.legal-tools.org/doc/2ed57f/).

[54] The following paragraphs from Stanišić and Župljanin Appeal Judgement are significant in this regard, paras. 51–53, see above note 42:

While the Appeals Chamber's reasoning reflects slight confusion about what exactly it considered Judge Harhoff's views on the applicable law to have been at the time, it seemed to rectify the matter by considering that, regardless, "Judge Harhoff as a Judge of the Tribunal could disabuse his mind of any irrelevant personal beliefs or predispositions".[55]

The Appeals Chamber particularly notes that a reasonable observer properly informed would be aware that: (i) Judge Harhoff's comments only generally concern the mode of liability of joint criminal enterprise; (ii) none of the cases referred to by Judge Harhoff altered the scope of joint criminal enterprise liability, contrary to his assertions; and (iii) it has never been the law or practice, contrary to Judge Harhoff's statement, to "convict leaders for the crimes committed with their knowledge within a framework of a common goal". Further, it is the Appeals Chamber's view that a reasonable observer properly informed of all relevant circumstances would be aware of the relevant jurisprudence of the Tribunal. A reasonable observer would therefore be aware that knowledge on the part of an accused that crimes were committed is insufficient to find an accused responsible under either the first or the third category of joint criminal enterprise.

The Appeals Chamber notes that a reasonable observer would also consider the fact that Judge Harhoff neither distinguished the facts nor the respective modes of liability relevant to the *Gotovina and Markač* Appeal Judgement, the *Perišić* Appeal Judgement, and the *Stanišić and Simatović* Trial Judgement. Based on his views on the law and practice, which do not align with the Tribunal's jurisprudence, coupled with his sweeping generalisations of the judgements in question, Judge Harhoff expressed deep dissatisfaction with what he considered a change in "set practice" at the Tribunal. However, the Appeals Chamber recalls that personal convictions and opinions of Judges are not in themselves a basis for inferring a lack of impartiality. Additionally, a reasonable observer, properly informed, would take into account that at no time did Judge Harhoff direct his comments to Stanišić and Župljanin. Thus, the Appeals Chamber is not convinced by Stanišić's submission that Judge Harhoff was predisposed to convicting Stanišić and Župljanin.

Regarding Župljanin's argument that sections of the Trial Judgement indicate that the wrong *mens rea* standard was applied, the Appeals Chamber is not convinced that a reasonable observer would consider that these cited sections reflect, or were influenced, by the same opinions that Judge Harhoff expressed in the Letter. In this regard, the Appeals Chamber notes that the Trial Chamber applied the correct legal standard for JCE liability to the circumstances of the case and not the views expressed in the Letter. Further, a reasonable observer would also take into account Judge Harhoff's statement that he did not set out in the Letter all of the applicable principles necessary to assess criminal liability, including proof beyond a reasonable doubt.

[55] *Ibid.*, para. 55, referring to ICTY, *Prosecutor v. Šainović et al.*, Appeals Chamber, Judgement, 23 January 2014, IT-05-87-A, para. 181 ('Šainović *et al.*, Appeal Judgement') (https://www.legal-tools.org/doc/81ac8c/); Furundžija Appeal Judgement, paras. 196–197, see above note 52.

25.2. Was Judge Harhoff Really Wrong about a Change in Jurisprudence?

While the Letter is not written in legal language and thus seems to compound JCE with aiding and abetting, Judge Harhoff has explained in his memorandum that his main concern was with the use of the 'specific direction' requirement for aiding and abetting, which for him presented a parting from set practice. While the compounding of JCE and aiding and abetting may seem unprofessional, it is hardly surprising in the context of the ICTY where the 'catch-all' practice has seen many accused charged and even convicted under several modes of liability for the same conduct. Although efforts have been made to avoid this, it is an indisputable characteristic of the Tribunal. Judge Harhoff's use of a sort of layman explanation of the situation is, in fact, not far off in describing the practice of catching those responsible for war crimes 'one way or another'.

Even before Judge Harhoff's Letter was made public, the series of acquittals had provoked a storm of complaints from international lawyers, human rights groups and other judges at the court, who claimed in private that the rulings had abruptly rewritten legal standards that had been applied in earlier cases.[56] So, was there an actual departure from set jurisprudence?

25.2.1. Specific Direction

The specific direction standard was applied at the appeal in *Perišić*. The case concerned a Serbian general, who was convicted at trial for having aided and abetted the crimes committed by the Army of Republika Srpska ('VRS') in Sarajevo and Srebrenica, through the provision of weapons and personnel. At the appeal, however, the Judgment stated that when the accused is remote from the crime, they have to 'specifically direct' their assistance towards the perpetration of specific crimes and not only generally towards the realization of activities which could be either lawful or unlawful.[57] While it established that the assistance policy was set at a higher political level, its implementation would have automatically satisfied the specific direction requirement had it been criminal as such.[58] However, since the policy was aimed at supporting and assisting the VRS – an army wag-

---

[56] Marlise Simons, "Judge at War Crimes Tribunal Faults Acquittals of Serb and Croat Commanders", *The New York Times*, 14 June 2013 (available on its web site).

[57] ICTY, *Prosecutor v. Perišić*, Appeals Chamber, Judgement, 28 February 2013, IT-04-81-A ('Perišić, Appeal Judgement') (https://www.legal-tools.org/doc/f006ba/).

[58] *Ibid.*, paras. 51, 53.

ing war, not a criminal organization – and its general war effort, not specific crimes, the specific direction requirement was not considered to have been met.[59]

Similarly, the *Stanišić and Simatović* Trial Judgment affirmed that crimes had been committed and detailed the connections between the accused parties and the physical perpetrators. It further affirmed the existence of a JCE to create ethnically homogeneous populations and concrete contributions to the realization of this enterprise. Despite this, it held that in order to establish guilt, evidence would have to prove that the support provided to the physical perpetrators was 'specifically directed towards the commission of the crimes' that is "specifically directed to assist, encourage, or lend moral support to the perpetration of [the] crime".[60]

Judge Harhoff saw the specific direction requirement as a dangerous departure from previous jurisprudence, whereas both panels considering his bias claimed that there was no such departure. Other commentators at the time also considered the specific direction as established jurisprudence based on the fact that in *Vasiljević*, as well as in *Jokić*, the Tribunal determined liability for aiding and abetting on a finding that there was a specific direction to assist the perpetration of the crimes. Thus, it has been argued that the Tribunal in *Perišić*, as well as in *Stanišić and Simatović*, did not depart from previous standards but that, instead, the peculiar circumstances of these cases directed a different outcome (that is, the fact that the accused were officials in one country while the armed conflict was unfolding and crimes were committed in another). However, to say this is to mask the fact that the jurisprudence on specific direction was far from 'established' up until that point and, if anything, there were more reasons to find, as Judge Harhoff did, a departure from previous jurisprudence than its application.

The 'specific direction' requirement in aiding and abetting was, in fact, part of the jurisprudence at the Tribunal since *Tadić*, that is, since the introduction of the concept of JCE.[61] However, *Tadić* did not cite any prior

---

[59] *Ibid.*, para. 53.

[60] ICTY, *Prosecutor v. Stanišić and Simatović*, Trial Chamber, Judgement, vol. 2, 30 May 2013, IT-03-69-T, para. 1264 (https://www.legal-tools.org/doc/698c43/).

[61] ICTY, *Prosecutor v Tadić*, Appeals Chamber, Judgement, 15 July 1999, IT-94-1-A, para. 229(iii) (https://www.legal-tools.org/doc/8efc3a/):

> (iii) The aider and abettor carries out acts specifically directed to assist encourage or lend moral support to the perpetration of a certain specific crime (murder, extermination, rape, torture, wanton destruction of civilian property, etc.) and this support has a sub-

source on 'specific direction', and it used it merely to justify a lack of any such standards in determining liability under JCE. As such, the 'specific direction' was an *obiter dictum* and one which arguably served judicial creativity in the way of widening the interpretation of the scope of criminal liability, but then ironically, in *Perišić*, it ended up being used to overly restrict this scope. Even Judge Ramaroson, one of the judges in the *Perišić* Appeals majority, pointed out in his separate opinion that in *Tadić*, the Appeals Chamber merely tried to differentiate between JCE and aiding and abetting liability and did not envisage specific direction as an essential component of the *actus reus* of the latter.[62]

What is more, there was generally no agreement among the majority in *Perišić* as to the precise meaning of 'specific direction', and only one opinion actually viewed it as it was described in the majority judgment, that is, as an essential component of the *actus reus*. For their part, Judges Agius and Meron explained that it should fall within the mental element as a purposive *mens rea*, fulfilled when an individual "specifically aimed to assist relevant crimes".[63] Ramaroson considered the requirement to be part of the *mens rea*, if anything, but that it could not be dependent on geographical or temporal distance from the final crime, as the majority implied by requiring explicit consideration of specific direction only in such cir-

---

stantial effect upon the perpetration of the crime. By contrast, in the case of acting in pursuance of a common purpose or design, it is sufficient for the participant to perform acts that in some way are directed to the furthering of the common plan or purpose.

[62] Perišić, Appeal Judgement, Opinion Séparée du Juge Ramaroson sur la Question de la Visée Spécifique dans la Complicité par Aide et Encouragement, paras. 2–4, see above note 57. In the same vein, the *Šainović et al.*, Appeal Judgement ultimately concluded that the *Tadić* discussion was not aimed at systematically defining aiding and abetting liability (as was done in *Furundžija*), but was instead included in order to better defining joint criminal enterprise, see para. 1623, see above note 55. See also ICTY, *Prosecutor v. Aleksovski*, Appeals Chamber, Judgement, 24 March 2000, IT-95-14/1-A, para. 163 (https://www.legal-tools.org/doc/176f05/), see also ICTY, *Prosecutor v. Blagojević and Jokić*, Appeals Chamber, Judgement, 9 May 2007, IT-02-60-A ('Blagojević and Jokić, Appeal Judgement') (https://www.legal-tools.org/doc/c32768/), which similarly noted that *Tadić* Appeal only sought to contrast JCE with aiding and abetting and was not a complete statement on the law of aiding and abetting.

[63] Perišić, Appeal Judgement, Joint Separate Opinion of Judges Theodor Meron and Carmel Agius, para. 3, see above note 57; Norman Farrell, "Attributing Criminal Liability to Corporate Actors: Some Lessons from the International Tribunals", in *Journal of International Criminal Justice*, 2010, vol. 8, no. 3, p. 890: "such a requirement is not part of either the *actus reus* or *mens rea* of aiding and abetting".

---

cumstances.[64] The mere disagreements on the essential questions about the nature of the 'specific direction' element put into question the assertion that it was established jurisprudence prior to *Perišić*. Furthermore, Judge LIU rejected the very existence of the specific direction condition, claiming the majority was introducing an additional requirement, never analysed in previous cases, which would make it more difficult to convict those "responsible for knowingly facilitating the most grievous crimes".[65]

Judge LIU's opinion, and thereby Judge Harhoff's opinion as well, has since been vindicated by the Special Court of Sierra Leone ('SCSL') in the *Charles Taylor* Judgment and by the ICTY Judgments in *Šainović*, *Popović* and *Stanišić and Simatović*. It has further been noted that the Statute of the International Criminal Court ('ICC') holds no such requirement for aiding and abetting.[66]

To understand the confusion, one has to look at the relevant case law. In *Furundžija*, which presented an actual detailed study of the elements of aiding and abetting, no specific direction requirement was identified.[67] *Furundžija* and the subsequent jurisprudence specified the *actus reus* as providing assistance to a crime by making a *substantial contribution* or having a *substantial effect* on its perpetration.[68] This was described as as-

---

[64] Perišić, Appeal Judgement, Opinion Séparée du Juge Ramaroson, paras. 7–8, see above note 57; Perišić, Appeal Judgement, para. 39:

> not all cases of aiding and abetting will involve proximity of an accused individual's relevant acts to crimes committed by principal perpetrators. Where an accused aider and abettor is remote from relevant crimes, evidence proving other elements of aiding and abetting may not be sufficient to prove specific direction. In such circumstances, the Appeals Chamber, Judge Liu dissenting, holds that explicit consideration of specific direction is required.

[65] *Ibid.*, Partially Dissenting Opinion of Judge Liu, para. 3.

[66] Dhruv Sharma, "Specific Direction: An Unspecific Threshold", in *Groningen Journal of International Law*, 2019, vol. 6, no. 2, p. 320; Antonio Coco and Tom Gal, "Losing Direction: The ICTY Appeals Chamber's Controversial Approach to Aiding and Abetting in *Perišić*", in *Journal of International Criminal Justice* 12, 2014, vol. 12, no. 2, p. 358.

[67] ICTY, *Prosecutor v. Furundžija*, Trial Chamber, Judgement, 10 December 1998, IT-95-17/1-T, paras.193-226 (*actus reus*) and 236-241 (*mens rea*) ('Furundžija Trial Judgement') (https://www.legal-tools.org/doc/e6081b/) endorsed, *inter alia*, by ICTY, *Prosecutor v. Blaškić*, Appeals Chamber, Judgement, 29 July 2004, IT-95-14-A, para. 46 (https://www.legal-tools.org/doc/88d8e6/).

[68] Furundžija Trial Judgement, para. 235, see above note 67; see also Special Court for Sierra Leone, *Prosecutor v Taylor*, Appeals Chamber, Judgment, 26 September 2013, SCSL-03-01-A, para. 368 ('Taylor Appeal Judgement') (https://www.legal-tools.org/doc/3e7be5/). For an

sistance which increased the likelihood that the crime would be perpetrated or that it could be perpetrated in a certain manner.[69] As for the *mens rea*, the aider and abettor must have knowledge that the assistance will substantially contribute to the commission of the crime.[70] This standard does not imply certainty but rather the knowing acceptance of a risk that, in the ordinary course of events, the behaviour will substantially contribute to the crime.[71] Unlike a member of a JCE, an aider and abettor does not need to share the principal perpetrator's criminal intent.

Blagojević and Jokić Appeal Judgment was the first appellate judgment to deal directly with this matter. It noted that the *Blaškić* Appeals Judgment's confusing approach cited both the *Vasiljević* Appeal Judgment as well as the *Furundžija* Trial Judgment, which had conflicting positions on the matter.[72] The Judgment held that, while the *Tadić* Appeal Judgment had never been explicitly departed from, other appeals judgments had not included a specific direction requirement. This could be explained by "the fact that such a finding will often be implicit in the finding that the accused has provided practical assistance to the principal perpetrator which had a substantial effect on the commission of the crime".[73] The Chamber thus considered it as part of the *actus reus*. In so finding, the *Blagojević and*

---

overview, see Antonio Cassese, Paola Gaeta *et al.*, *Cassese's International Criminal Law*, 3rd edn., Oxford University Press, 2013, at pp. 193 *et seq.*

[69] ICTY, *Prosecutor v. Tadić*, Trial Chamber, Opinion and Judgement, 7 May 1997, IT-94-1-T, para. 688 (https://www.legal-tools.org/doc/0a90ae/). This standard is usually deemed to be higher than the 'significant' contribution demanded for a JCE. See Judgment, ICTY, *Prosecutor v. Kvočka et al.*, Appeals Chamber, Judgement 28 February 2005, IT-98-30/1, para. 97 (https://www.legal-tools.org/doc/006011/), and ICTY, *Prosecutor v. Gotovina et al.*, Appeals Chamber, Judgement, 16 November 2012, IT-06-90, para. 149 ('Gotovina Appeal Judgement') (https://www.legal-tools.org/doc/03b685/).

[70] ICTY, *Prosecutor v. Mrkšić et al.*, Appeals Chamber, Judgement, 5 May 2009, IT-95-13-1-A, para. 49 (https://www.legal-tools.org/doc/40bc41/). See also ICTY, *Prosecutor v. Orić*, Appeals Chamber, Judgement, 3 July 2008, IT-03-68-A, para. 43 (https://www.legal-tools.org/doc/e053a4/).

[71] SCSL, *Prosecutor against Brima*, Trial Chamber, Judgement, 20 June 2007, SCSL-04-16-T, para. 776 (https://www.legal-tools.org/doc/87ef08/); Furundžija Trial Judgment, para. 246, see above note 67; ICTY, *Prosecutor v Blaškić*, Trial Chamber, Judgement, 3 March 2000, IT-95-14-T, para. 287 (https://www.legal-tools.org/doc/e1ae55/); ICTY, *Prosecutor v. Orić*, Trial Chamber, Judgement, 30 June 2006, OT-03-68-T, para. 288 (https://www.legal-tools.org/doc/37564c/). See also The Hague Court of Appeal, Judgment, *Prosecutor v. van Anraat*, 9 May 2007, 2200050906-2, para. 11.16 (https://www.legal-tools.org/doc/1e1b4b/).

[72] Blagojević and Jokić, Appeal Judgement, paras. 185–188, see above note 62.

[73] *Ibid.*, para. 189.

Jokić Appeal Judgment failed to articulate a definite and unequivocal position on whether 'specific direction' was required or not under the law of aiding and abetting, and could be read to support or reject 'specific direction'. The Appeals Chamber in *Mrkšić* and *Šljivančanin* interpreted *Blagojević* as "confirm[ing] that 'specific direction' is not an essential ingredient of the *actus reus* of aiding and abetting".[74] Later, in *Lukić* and *Lukić*, the Appeals Chamber again confirmed this interpretation and held that "there [was] no "cogent reason" to depart from this jurisprudence".[75] However, on this point, the ICTY Appeals Chamber was not unanimous. Judge Güney was unconvinced by the majority's reasoning for not departing from the *Mrkšić and Šljivančanin* Appeals Judgment. He found that the facts of the *Lukić and Lukić* case did not warrant consideration of the specific direction question, but that, in any event, the *Mrkšić and Šljivančanin* Appeals Judgment's consideration of the issue should be seen as an *obiter dictum*, and that specific direction was likely already implicit in the *actus reus* definition.[76] Judge Agius also rejected the majority's analysis of the issue, finding that the *Mrkšić and Šljivančanin* Appeal Judgment had departed from past jurisprudence and was not supported by the *Blagojević and Jokić* Appeal Judgment. However, Judge Agius found that the 'specific direction' requirement was implicitly satisfied by the facts of the *Lukić and Lukić* case.[77]

The Appeals Chamber in *Perišić*, in one way or another, dismissed previous jurisprudence which did not take specific direction into account. It claimed that *Mrkšić* neither intended to depart from well-established jurisprudence nor provided adequate reasons to do so.[78] From *Blagojević et al.*, it drew the conclusion that while 'specific direction' may be implied in some cases, in others, it needed to be analysed and proven separately.[79] Still, it dismissed other jurisprudence on the basis that it was not dealing with defendants who were not proximate to the crimes and were thus irrele-

---

[74] ICTY, *Prosecutor v. Mrkšić and Šljivančanin*, Appeals Chamber, Judgement, 5 May 2009, IT-95-13-1-A, para. 159 (https://www.legal-tools.org/doc/40bc41/).

[75] ICTY, *Prosecutor v. Lukić and Lukić*, Appeals Chamber, Judgement, 4 December 2912, IT-98-32/1-A, paras. 159, 424 (https://www.legal-tools.org/doc/da785e/).

[76] *Ibid.*, Separate and Partially Dissenting Opinion of Judge Güney, paras. 10–11.

[77] *Ibid.*, Separate Opinion of Judge Agius, paras. 1–6.

[78] Perišić, Appeal Judgement, paras. 32–36, see above note 57.

[79] *Ibid.*, para. 15.

vant.[80] However, neither Brđanin nor Krstić, for example, were present at the place where crimes were being committed, for which they were found responsible as aiders and abettors.[81] Coco and Gal thus find Brđanin's conduct in many ways similar to Perišić's.[82]

In the context of the ICC, one commentator called the 'specific direction' requirement "counter-intuitive to the objectives of the ICC as it unreasonably increases evidentiary requirements at the Court and consequently makes the fight against impunity, an already challenging task, even more difficult".[83] The ICTY Office of the Prosecutor claimed that it had no foundation in customary international law, was contrary to prior Appeals Chamber jurisprudence, lacked coherence as a legal doctrine and most importantly, undermined respect for international humanitarian law.[84]

Finally, in the *Šainović* Appeal Judgement, delivered on 23 January 2014, the *Perišić* Appeal Judgement's reasoning was unequivocally overturned and the 'specific direction' requirement was found to be in "direct and material conflict with the prevailing jurisprudence […] and with customary international law".[85] The same conclusion was reached by the Appeals Chamber of the SCSL in the *Taylor* Appeal Judgement.[86]

The majority in the *Šainović* Appeal Judgment (Judge Tuzmukhamedov dissenting[87]) found the *Perišić* Appeals Chamber's interpretation of *Mrkšić and Šljivančanin* Appeal Judgement and the *Lukić and Lukić* Appeal Judgement to be in effect at odds with the plain reading of the judgments and to have disregarded positions expressly taken and clearly set out

---

[80] *Ibid.*, para. 38 and fn. 100.

[81] Coco and Gal, 2014, pp. 356–357, see above note 66.

[82] *Ibid.*, p. 356.

[83] Sharma, 2019, p. 320, see above note 66 .

[84] ICTY, Office of the Prosecutor Statement of the ICTY Prosecutor, "Statement of the ICTY Prosecutor Serge Brammertz", 24 June 2013 ('Statement of Serge Brammertz').

[85] Šainović *et al.*, Appeal Judgement, para. 1650, see above note 55.

[86] Taylor Appeal Judgement, paras. 471–486, see above note 68.

[87] Šainović *et al.*, Appeal Judgement, Dissenting opinion of Judge Tuzmukhamedov, paras. 40–47, see above note 55, Judge Tuzmukhamedov declined to take a position on specific direction, arguing instead that it was not necessary to determine the issue on the facts of the case because Lazarević, commander of the VJ's Priština corps stationed in Kosovo, was not geographically remote from the crime scene. The Majority, in footnote 5320, explained that the issue of specific direction was explicitly raised by the Parties and that it was a legal issue of "general significance to the Tribunal's jurisprudence".

therein.[88] It further emphasized that in prior jurisprudence "no independent specific direction requirement was applied by the Appeals Chamber to the facts of any case before it", but only "substantial contribution as an element of the *actus reus* has consistently been required".[89] After having reviewed post-World-War II judgments, relevant national legislation and other international law sources (such as the International Law Commission's Draft Code of 1996), the Appeals Chamber further reached the conclusion that 'specific direction' was not an essential element of the *actus reus* of aiding and abetting in customary international law.[90]

In 2015, the Appeals Chamber also quashed the acquittal of *Stanišić and Simatović*, the former head and deputy head of the Serbian secret police, for crimes committed in Bosnia and Croatia. According to the Judgment, the Trial Chamber failed to properly reason its decision regarding the participation of the accused in a JCE, because it could not analyse their *mens rea* without determining the *actus reus* of JCE, whereas it erred in law regarding aiding and abetting, that is by considering that specific direction was an element of its *actus reus*.[91]

Based on the correction of the jurisprudence, the Office of the Prosecutor even filed a motion before the Appeals Chamber requesting that it reconsider its acquittal of *Perišić*, stating that "the erroneous reversal of Mr. Perišić's lawful convictions and 27 year sentence must be corrected to redress *the grave injustice* caused to the tens of thousands of men, women and children killed or injured in Sarajevo and Srebrenica and to their families".[92] The motion was, however, denied by an Appeals Chamber panel presided by Judge Meron.

While Judge Harhoff may have been vindicated in terms of criticizing specific direction in his Letter, it is rather ironic that he himself seemed to have endorsed the requirement in the past. Judge Harhoff was part of the majority in *Stanišić and Župljanin*, which stated in the Trial judgment that

---

[88] *Šainović et al.*, Appeal Judgement, paras. 1621–1622, see above note 55.

[89] *Ibid.*, para. 1625.

[90] *Ibid.*, paras. 1627, 1648 (analysis of the cases) and paras. 1649–1650 (conclusion).

[91] This is unsurprising, since the three votes in the majority were all judges who formed the *Šainović* Appeals Chamber majority (Pocar, LIU, Ramaroson), while one of the judges was in the *Perišić* Appeals Chamber majority (Agius).

[92] ICTY, Statement of Prosecutor Serge Brammertz in relation to the motion for reconsideration submitted by the Prosecution in the Perišić case, 3 February 2014 ('Statement of Prosecutor 2014') (https://www.legal-tools.org/doc/195e1f/).

> despite the involvement of the police in the commission of extermination in some instances, there is no evidence that Stanišić's acts or omissions were specifically directed to assist, encourage, or lend moral support to the perpetration of extermination nor was he aware of the perpetrators intent to commit the crime. Therefore, the Trial Chamber finds that Stanišić is not criminally responsible for aiding and abetting the crime of extermination.[93]

Meron had previously rejected applying the 'specific direction' standard to a couple of indicted generals in two appeals cases in 2007 and 2009.[94]

25.2.2. The Case of *Gotovina* and Joint Criminal Enterprise

A further target of criticism in Judge Harhoff's Letter was the acquittal of General Ante Gotovina, which is unsurprising since the Appeal Judgment raises many concerns with its complete overturn of the findings of the Trial Judgment. The Trial Chamber in *Gotovina* unanimously held that the highest ranks of the Croatian leadership formed a JCE aimed at the permanent removal of the Serb civilian population from the Krajina region of Croatia by force or threat of force, which amounted to and involved persecution (deportation, forcible transfer, unlawful attacks against civilians and civilian objects, and discriminatory and restrictive measures), deportation, and forcible transfer.[95] The Trial Chamber relied on a series of events to reach the conclusion on this aim, including transcripts of a meeting of Croatian leaders at Brioni and the preparation of 'Operation Storm'; crimes committed by the Croatian military and police against the remaining Serb civilian population and property in the aftermath of 'Operation Storm'; the Croatian leadership's policies on the return of Croatian displaced persons and refugees; and discriminatory property laws targeting the Serb minority.[96]

The Appeals Chamber, however, overturned the Judgment's findings by a three to two majority by zooming in on one of the bases of the Trial Chamber's findings, the controversial so-called 200-meters standard. The Trial Chamber considered any shells falling further away from a legitimate

---

[93] Stanišić and Župljanin, Trial Judgement, para. 786, see above note 53.

[94] Burcharth, 2013, see above note 33.

[95] ICTY, *Prosecutor v Gotovina et al.*, Trial Chamber, Judgement, 15 April 2011, IT-06-90-T, paras. 2314–15 (https://www.legal-tools.org/doc/d0d665/).

[96] *Ibid.*, paras. 1756–58, 1843-46, 1970-2098, 2304-12.

military target as evidence of an unlawful and indiscriminate attack on the population of the shelled towns. The Appeals Chamber took advantage of the unreasoned nature of this standard to counter the finding of the unlawfulness of the artillery attacks and, in turn, considered that without the context of unlawful shelling all other evidence indicating the existence of a JCE was lacking.[97]

For example, the majority there contended that:

> discussions of pretexts for artillery attacks, of potential civilian departures, and of provision of exit corridors could be reasonably interpreted as referring to lawful combat operations and public relations efforts. Other parts of the Brioni Transcript, such as Gotovina's claim that his troops could destroy the towns of Knin, could be reasonably construed as using shorthand to describe the military forces stationed in an area, or intending to demonstrate potential military power in the context of planning a military operation.[98]

In his dissent, Judge Pocar stated that "[i]n light of the Trial Chamber's careful and detailed review of the minutes of the Brioni Transcript, these suggestions are simply grotesque".[99] Considering the limited powers of review that are set for appeals procedures at the ICTY, by overturning crucial factual findings the Appeals Chamber essentially declared that 'no reasonable trier of fact' could have found that JCE to exist on the evidence presented to the Trial Chamber.

Judge Pocar fundamentally dissented from the entire Appeal Judgement, which he claimed "contradicts any sense of justice".[100] Similar to Judge Harhoff, he also expressed his suspicions about hidden motives behind the Decision. In his words, "one might wonder what the Majority wanted to achieve by quashing the mere existence of the JCE rather than concentrating on Gotovina's and Markač's significant contributions to the JCE. I leave it as an open question".[101] It would thus appear that here also Judge Harhoff's criticism concerned an objectively speaking problematic judgment, albeit one which cannot be re-examined to prove the legitimacy of his concerns.

---

[97] Gotovina Appeal Judgment, paras. 91–96, see above note 69.

[98] *Ibid.*, para. 93, footnotes omitted.

[99] *Ibid.*, Dissenting Opinion of Judge Pocar, para. 26.

[100] *Ibid.*, para. 39.

[101] *Ibid.*, para. 30.

25.3. Punishment for Questioning the Court's Independence?

The impartiality of a court is intrinsically linked to its independence. Both external and internal independence are necessary for each judge to operate completely impartially.[102] In other words, there needs to be judicial independence both from any political interference by any government, intergovernmental organization, or other external stakeholder, as well as from internal influences of actors within the Court, such as other judges, the Registrar, Prosecutor, or Defence.[103] Both aspects of judicial independence were put into question by Judge Harhoff's Letter. In fact, the implication was that external pressure might have been behind the internal pressure put on fellow judges by the President of the Tribunal.[104] Commenting on the Letter, the Chatham House Milestones in International Criminal Justice noted that it raised many questions, including whether the allegations were true.[105] It, however, continued that

> an issue that was more immediately problematic was the allegation of judicial misconduct. For a judge to publicly defame his fellow judges in this manner and bring the ICTY into disrepute, has been said to raise doubts over his fitness for judicial office and his position as an ICTY judge.[106]

This hierarchy of priorities is rather odd and may reflect the real reasons behind the dismissal of Judge Harhoff under the guise of 'bias'. We mention in this connection a statement by Kevin Jon Heller, who called the court's Decision to remove Judge Harhoff "absolutely the right decision", since accusing the president of a tribunal of being a puppet of the Israeli and the US governments without offering any kind of evidence was, according to him, fundamentally unethical, appalling, widely speculative, and implausible.[107]

---

[102] Steven Freeland, "Judicial Decision-Making in International Criminal Courts: "Effective" Justice?", in *Griffith Journal of Law and Human Dignity*, 2015, vol. 3, no. 1, p. 71.

[103] *Ibid.*

[104] *Ibid.*

[105] John R.W.D. Jones *et al.*, *Milestones in International Criminal Justice: Recent Legal Controversies at the UN Yugoslav Tribunal*, Chatham House, London, 2013.

[106] *Ibid.*

[107] Marie Dhumieres, "Judge Thrown off Yugoslavia War Crimes Tribunal for Criticising Change of Direction in Verdicts", *The Independent*, 24 September 2013 (available on its web site).

Regardless of how ethical or unethical one may find Judge Harhoff's speculations, they could hardly provide a legal basis for a finding of bias against any particular accused. It is no surprise that in its Decision, the Special Chamber did not refer to these speculations at all. Even Judge Harhoff's 'professional and moral dilemma' was interpreted as having nothing to do with a fear of outside influence, despite his memorandum specifically explaining it to be just that.[108] Our personal impression is therefore that the Decision may have been nothing more than a masked 'punishment' for an action for which no sanction is actually proscribed, namely the violation of an informal 'code of silence' that prohibits criticizing other judges in public.

Since it was not actually prohibited behaviour, Judge Harhoff's Letter has prompted calls for a code of conduct – interestingly, coming from defence counsel – which would prohibit such statements in the future.[109] Judge Harhoff himself expressed the view that judges should refrain from criticizing colleagues and their rulings in public.[110] Yet he added a caveat: "Unless you talk to them first, that is. But all previous attempts to raise debate within the Tribunal about the change in our jurisprudence had been soundly rejected by President Meron".[111] He claimed that several other judges[112] had called for an internal debate of the 'specific direction' standard, but the idea was "categorically rejected by President Meron". Thus, Judge Harhoff felt it would be futile for him to raise the question within the court.[113]

While such a stance is understandable, it still remains a mystery why he did not voice his concerns also in the form of a separate opinion, which would have been far less controversial, in the case of *Mićo Stanišić and Stojan Župljanin*, where he was part of the majority in the Trial Chamber endorsing the specific direction standard.[114]

---

[108] Harhoff, Memorandum, see above note 11.

[109] Colleen Rohan and Gregor Guy-Smith, "Comment on Judge Harhoff's Letter", 19 June 2013, International Criminal Law Bureau.

[110] Burcharth, 2013, see above note 33.

[111] *Ibid.*

[112] It has also been claimed elsewhere that several fellow judges endorsed Harhoff's objections, but preferred to remain anonymous, see Martin Burcharth, "Fellow Judges support ousted colleague's criticism of Hague Tribunal", *Information*, 6 December 2013 (available on its web site).

[113] *Ibid.*

[114] Stanišić and Župljanin, Trial Judgement, para. 786, see above note 53.

25.3.1. Claims of Pressure Exerted on Fellow Judges

Judge Harhoff's claims of internal pressure being exerted were confirmed by a number of senior officials at the Court, albeit anonymously in an article published by the *New York Times*.[115] They claimed judges had been perturbed by pressures from Meron to deliver judgments before they were ready and that he was furthermore shutting down debate in the panels on the decisions to be taken.[116] If these allegations were true, Meron was disregarding an element of deliberations that ensures impartiality, which he himself invokes in an article on judicial independence at the ICTY, where he describes how judges "discuss the case among themselves prior to agreeing on a decision, and this discussion helps to correct any latent biases, because a judge is confronted with, and has to respond to, logical arguments of his colleagues".[117]

It has been argued that Meron did not pressure colleagues to achieve particular rulings, but rather to implement the ICTY Completion Strategy. In 2003, Wikileaks documents revealed that Meron was considered by the US ambassador as the tribunal's pre-eminent supporter of the US government's efforts in terms of the Completion Strategy.[118] While internal pressure seems to have actually taken place, for one reason or another, such pressure may be nothing more than a natural occurrence of courts and tribunals.

The more controversial issue was the question of potential external pressure. Judge Harhoff's speculations regarding this issue were just *that*, and in the specific context in which they were raised may or may not have been warranted. However, it would be "incredibly naïve to think that judg-

---

[115] Simons, 2013, see above note 56.

[116] *Ibid.*:

> After the only session to deliberate the acquittal that Judge Meron had drafted in the case of the two Croatian generals, one official said, the judge abruptly declined a request by two dissenting judges for further debate [...] In his letter, Judge Harhoff also said Judge Michele Picard of France was recently given only four days to write her dissent against the majority decision to acquit two Serbian police chiefs, Jovica Stanišić and Franko Simatović. 'She was very taken aback by the acquittal and deeply upset about the fast way it had to be handled,' said an official close to the case.

[117] Theodor Meron, "Judicial Independence and Impartiality in International Criminal Tribunals", in *The American Journal of International Law*, 2005, vol. 99, no. 2, p. 361.

[118] WikiLeaks, "ICTY: Ambassador Prosper's Meetings with ICTY President and Registrar", 7 November 2003.

es are not influenced by considerations of policy or even pure politics".[119] Milanović reminds us that "the specific direction business in *Perišić* was clearly motivated by the desire to delineate between culpable and non-culpable remote complicity in international crimes", no doubt considering the implications for current and future conflicts and the potentially associated trials.[120]

In their briefs, Perišić's lawyers openly took as a parallel to the situation which was at hand, the so-called 'humanitarian intervention' in Libya, and claimed that, without applying the 'specific direction' standard, "assistance given to a party of a conflict in the knowledge that crimes are likely to be committed by that party will result in a finding of guilt irrespective of the humanitarian intent or impact of that assistance".[121] They characterized the intervention in Libya by the UK, France, US and Canada, among others, as support given to a 'rights-based' uprising against the 'regime' of Muammar Gaddafi under the Responsibility to Protect doctrine in response to widespread reports of serious violations of international humanitarian and human rights law committed by 'Gaddafi's forces'.[122] Yet, at the same time, Perišić's lawyers implied that the 'bigger picture' should have been enough reason for those providing assistance to the irregular non-state armed groups *with knowledge of the potential for that assistance to aid in some way in the commission of crimes and such crimes being subsequently committed*, to not be subject to criminal sanction for aiding and abetting.[123]

To consider the commission of crimes as acceptable in the pursuit of the presumed greater good is a dangerous slippery slope. As Stewart posits: "Should we suddenly redefine torture to accommodate practices that are now ubiquitous in the war on terror?".[124] Moreover, such regime change interventions have not aged well, not in Libya, nor elsewhere, and their humanitarianism is far from clear and should not be presumed.

---

[119] Marko Milanović, "Danish Judge Blasts ICTY President", *EJIL: Talk!*, 13 June 2013, comments section (available on its web site).

[120] *Ibid.*

[121] ICTY, *Prosecutor v. Perišić*, Public Redacted Version of the Appeal Brief of Momčilo Perišić, 10 April 2012, IT-04-81-A, paras. 20–21 ('Perišić Appeal Brief') (https://www.legal-tools.org/doc/b20df0/).

[122] *Ibid.*, para. 25.

[123] *Ibid.*, paras. 27–28.

[124] James G. Stewart, "The ICTY Loses its Way on Complicity – Part 2", *Opinio Juris*, 3 April 2013 (available on its web site).

The defence brief in *Perišić* further stated: "The facts surrounding the Libyan conflict are far from unique. It is foreseeable that the international community will be called upon to make similar decisions in the future in non-international armed conflicts such as Syria".[125] In fact, the international community was not *called upon*, not in Syria, not in the case of other regime change interventions, yet several States nevertheless provided support to so-called 'moderate rebels' at great expense to the Syrian population when aid landed in the hands of terrorists.

At the hearing in *Šainović*, the Prosecution noted that a 'remote' aider and abettor might even be able to provide more effective assistance than a 'proximate' aider and abettor, and have more extensive knowledge of the circumstances of the crimes, especially if he/she is a high-ranking official of an army involved in a conflict.[126] Considering the vast intelligence possessed by Western countries which involve themselves in regime-change interventions, at least the knowledge that the assistance will substantially contribute to the commission of crimes will usually be present, if not outright intent to provide such substantial contribution. To assume that such support could never be beyond the pale, and that it does not deserve to be scrutinized against the same rigorous standards at international criminal tribunals as the support given from 'up-close', is a position that reflects the dogmatic belief in the good of the West and its infallibility in foreign policy. Where judges hold such naïve beliefs, no further external pressure is necessary.

However, here again, we enter the world of speculation since the examples of Syria or Libya were not actually mentioned in the *Perišić* Appeal Judgment and we do not know how the judges took them into account, if at all. There was, nonetheless, undoubtedly a shift in the Tribunal towards protecting the interests of the military. As William Schabas stated at the time: "A decade ago, there was a very strong humanitarian message coming out of the tribunal, very concerned with the protection of civilians. It was not concerned with the prerogatives of the military and the police. This message has now been weakened; there is less protection for civilians and human rights".[127]

---

[125] Perišić Appeal Brief, para. 30, see above note 121.

[126] *Prosecutor v. Šainović et al.*, Appeals Chamber, Transcript, 13 March 2013, para. 454. For the whole rejection of the specific direction requirement by the Office of the Prosecutor, see paras. 440–461.

[127] Simons, 2013, see above note 56.

In the words of Dag Hammarskjöld, whose name has become synonymous with the integrity of an international civil servant, a person in such a role must remain wholly uninfluenced not merely by national but also group interests or ideologies.[128] Thus, regardless of whether Judge Harhoff's speculations about direct outside pressure were a reflection of the reality or not, the concern for military interests and the protection of an interventionist ideology over justice puts into question the legitimacy of the decisions criticized by Judge Harhoff and those pushing for them. Against this background, the fact that he voiced his concerns about what he saw as a grave issue in terms of the court's impartiality can be understood as speaking in favour of his moral character and integrity and not *vice versa*.

Richard Dicker, the Human Rights Watch International Justice Program Director, commented that Judge Harhoff's e-mail raised a legitimate question, especially concerning the acquittals of *Perišić* and *Stanišić and Simatović*, which created a very dangerous and undermining precedent of immunizing senior officials when they are not present at the scene of the crimes, while reminding that they are usually 'smart enough' not to put their criminal instructions into writing.[129] In the words of Hammarskjöld,

> if integrity in the sense of respect for law and respect for truth were to drive [an international civil servant] into positions of conflict with this or that interest, then that conflict is a sign of his neutrality and not of his failure to observe neutrality – [in other words] it is in line, not in conflict with his duties as an international civil servant.[130]

The judgments considered in Judge Harhoff's Letter had important implications not only for the immediate victims of the crimes under consideration, but also the narratives of 'guilt' and 'innocence' of the main nations involved in the conflict – no small matter in terms of achieving justice or reconciliation in the affected communities. For example, with regard to *Gotovina*, Milanović noted that the acquittal of the individuals on trial may have been the correct decision, but the dismissal of the views of the Trial Chamber on so many issues and particularly the existence of any JCE (with or without the two accused) served to harden the conflicting nationalist nar-

---

[128] Jacques Lemoine, *The International Civil Servant: An Endangered Species*, Kluwer Law International, 1995, p. 45, citing Dag Hammarskjöld, *The International Civil Servant in Law and in Fact*, Oxford University Press, 1961.

[129] Dhumieres, 2013, see above note 107.

[130] Lemoine, 1995, p. 46, see above note 128.

ratives in Croatia and Serbia, of which the 'victorious' brand is even more poisonous and harder to cure.[131] Similarly, Nakarada observed that with this judgment, the Croatian government was proclaimed innocent, and the victims were humiliated.[132] This and the subsequent dropping of the charges against the Albanian leader of the Kosovo Liberation Army, Ramush Haradinaj, made even those Serbs who were previously supportive of the ICTY as an institution of justice now believe that it was highly biased, that is treating victims unequally depending on their ethnic origin.[133] In terms of Perišić, who was the top figure within the Yugoslav Army, his conviction in 2011 was immensely significant for Bosniaks,[134] while Stanišić was the first intelligence chief of a country to be judged by an international criminal tribunal. As Orentlicher noted, even if Judge Harhoff's speculations about external influence were just that – speculations – in the eyes of many Bosnians "it was the proverbial smoking gun".[135]

Keil and Perry describe how the expectations from the Tribunal have been exceptionally high in terms of fighting impunity:

> However after the acquittals in the cases of *Gotovina et al.*, *Haradinaj et al.* and *Perišić* as well as the *Stanišić and Simatović* first instance verdicts, the standing of the Tribunal among victims in BiH is likely to be less favourable, judging by the reactions of victim associations and discussions in the media.[136]

Fifteen victims' associations from BiH called for the resignation of Meron, yet their call was simply ignored. According to media reports, after five weeks of silence, the President of the Association of Mothers of the

---

[131] Marko Milanović, "The Gotovina Omnishambles", *EJIL: Talk!*, 18 November 2012 (available on its web site).

[132] Radmila Nakarada, "Acquittal of Gotovina and Markač: A Blow to the Serbian and Croatian Reconciliation Process", in *Utrecht Journal of International and European Law*, 2013, vol. 29, no. 76, pp. 102–105.

[133] *Ibid.*

[134] Anton Vukpalaj, "Acquittals at the International Criminal Tribunal for the former Yugoslavia (ICTY) in 2012-2013: the domestic implications", in *Studies of Transition States and Societies*, vol. 10, no. 1, 2018, p. 8, citing D. Karabegović and O. Zorić, "Bosnian Consternation at Serbian Security Officers IWPR", in *Institute for War and Peace Reporting*, 2013.

[135] Diane Orentlicher, *Some Kind of Justice: The ICTY's Impact in Bosnia and Serbia*, Oxford University Press, 2018, p. 186.

[136] Soeren Keil and Valery Perry (eds.), *State-Building and Democratization in Bosnia and Herzegovina*, Southeast European Studies, 2015, p. 153.

Srebrenica and Žepa Enclaves, Munira Subašić, and Murat Tahirović, President of the Organization of Victims and Witnesses of Genocide, came to The Hague "to talk to the Tribunal's officials and get some answers".[137] Although they were received by Meron himself,[138] he refused to allow them a further meeting with other judges. Instead, he suggested that they write a letter to him specifying what they wanted to ask them, and then he would talk to them – a proposal Subašić found useless considering how he ignored their first letter. Generally, Subašić had little positive to say about Meron on this particular occasion, characterizing him as "a very cunning man – cunning as a man; cunning as a politician", and claiming he was holding monopoly power over the court, filling bottomless barrels, and telling tales for kids to the victims.[139] On the other hand, Tahirović stated that the victims' representatives would leave The Hague with a strong impression that there "is a clear conflict and disagreement" among the judges.[140]

The victims' associations had also written to the UN Secretary-General Ban Ki Moon asking him to establish an independent commission to investigate the allegations made in the Letter sent by Judge Harhoff, and to see if the Tribunal had really 'changed its course' under the pressure of 'military establishments' of some influential countries, yet they never received a response. It is important to note, that the acquittals, also driven by Meron, which have granted the release of several genocide convicts at the ICTR, have similarly caused shock in the affected communities and raised calls for reviews, which were likewise ignored. IBUKA, the genocide survivors' umbrella organization in Rwanda, has repeatedly called for an urgent investigation of all the controversial decisions, which it said have only served to benefit genocide perpetrators. In one of its protest letters to the UN, it stated:

> The international community failed Rwandans during the Genocide against the Tutsi yet it had its mission present in the country, today there's an attempt, through international justice,

---

[137] "Instead of Resignation, Meron Offers Victims 'New Chapter'", *Sense Agency*, 26 July 2013 (available on its web site) ('Sense Agency').

[138] As well as the Tribunal's Registrar John Hocking and Chief Prosecutor Serge Brammertz.

[139] *Govori priče za djecu, puni sode bez dna*, TV Tribunal 596, video, 27 July 2013 (on file with the authors).

[140] Sense Agency, see above note 137.

to minimize the gravity of the genocide by releasing its top architects.[141]

25.4. Conclusion

As Lemoine noted, "[t]here can be no impartiality without independence from outside influence and notably from governments, including, and perhaps primarily, from one's own".[142] Speaking from his own experience, Meron himself acknowledged the existence of governmental influence on international judges by arguing for life-long appointments in order to offset it.[143] Whether justified or not, imagined or real, suspicions of outside influence should be taken seriously when raised in an honest manner at such high levels within an international tribunal.

The fact that both at the ICTY and the ICTR, calls for investigations fell on deaf ears is a failure of the system to ensure impartiality. Furthermore, if there was, in fact, no direct outside influence that dictated the numerous acquittals, raising open-ended questions such as the ones posed by Judge Harhoff or Judge Pocar should not be considered something to fear, prohibit or punish, but rather an opportunity to elaborate clearly on why such perceptions are erroneous. Certainly, their suspicions were not merely felt by them, but rather by numerous people affected by or having knowledge of the relevant conflicts; thus, an open discussion would have been invaluable.

The Appeals Chamber in *Čelebići* stated that "justice should not only be done, but should manifestly and undoubtedly be seen to be done"[144] and is founded on the need to ensure public confidence in the judiciary.[145] As the Office of the Prosecutor rightly noted: "To preserve its positive reputa-

---

[141] "Judge Who Freed 10 Genocide Convicts Seeks New UN Contract", *KT Press*, 29 January 2018 (available on its web site).

[142] Lemoine, 1995, p. 43, see above note 128.

[143] Meron, 2005, see above note 117.

[144] Furundžija Appeal Judgement, para. 195, see above note 52. See International Criminal Tribunal for Rwanda ('ICTR'), *Prosecutor v. Seromba*, The Bureau, Decision on Motion for Disqualification of Judges, 25 April 2006, ICTR-2001-66-T, para. 9 (with references cited therein) (https://www.legal-tools.org/doc/9d6128/).

[145] Čelebići Appeal Judgement, para. 707, see above note 52; ICTR, *Prosecutor v. Karemera et al.*, Trial Chamber, Decision on Joseph Nzirorera's Motion for Disqualification of Judge Byron and Stay of the Proceedings, 20 February 2009, ICTR-98-44-T, para. 6 (https://www.legal-tools.org/doc/f27eb3/); Stanišić and Župljanin Appeal Judgement, para. 43, see above note 42.

tion moving forward, the Tribunal must make allowance for valid criticism. It must use the constructive aspects of the debate generated as a springboard for strengthening its processes".[146] Instead, the Tribunal chose to simply get rid of Judge Harhoff, "to wash away the stain that [his] email had put on the court".[147] One could argue that this reaction was the stain itself, sending a signal to the public as well as other judges and insiders that any criticism, whistleblowing or questioning would be severely punished instead of being met with a response of self-reflection by the institution.

On a positive note, as the Office of the Prosecutor has noted, the Court and its Appeals Chamber "demonstrated its independence, impartiality and capacity for critical reflection, strengthening the international justice system and the rule-of-law" in overturning the *Perišić* Appeal Judgement's flawed holding.[148]

---

[146] Statement of Serge Brammertz, see above note 84.

[147] Burcharth, see above note 33.

[148] Statement of Prosecutor 2014, see above note 92.

26

Integrity in
International Criminal Law:
Post-Conviction Proceedings

Gregory S. Gordon[*]

> By establishing the Mechanism, the Council has helped to
> guarantee that the closure of the two pioneering ad hoc tribu-
> nals does not open the way for impunity to reign once more.
>
> MICT President Theodor Meron[1]

26.1. Introduction

On 14 December 2016, based on a decision by the President of the United
Nations International Residual Mechanism for Criminal Tribunals
('MICT'), convicted Rwandan genocidaire Ferdinand Nahimana was
granted early release.[2] Nahimana, referred to by some as the 'Rwandan
Goebbels', is considered the propaganda master of the Rwandan Geno-

---

[*] **Gregory S. Gordon** is Professor and formerly served as Associate Dean (Develop-
ment/External Affairs) and Director of the Ph.D.–M.Phil. Programme at the Faculty of Law,
The Chinese University of Hong Kong. Before joining the legal academy, he served as a
prosecutor with the United States Department of Justice and the International Criminal Tribunal for Rwanda. Professor Gordon is also a Research Fellow at the Centre for International Law Research and Policy (CILRAP). In 2017, his book *Atrocity Speech Law: Foundation,
Fragmentation, Fruition* (Oxford University Press), which coined a new term for the law related to hate speech in international criminal law, proposed a paradigm shift in the field with
introduction of the "Unified Liability Theory for Atrocity Speech Law". The author would
like to thank Jan Stone for her outstanding research assistance on this project.

[1] Theodor Meron, Speech before the UN Security Council, 7 June 2012, in United Nations
International Residual Mechanism for Criminal Tribunals ('MICT'), "About" (available on
its web site).

[2] MICT, *The Prosecutor v. Nahimana*, Public Redacted Version of the 22 September 2016
Decision of the President on the Early Release of Ferdinand Nahimana, 5 December 2016,
MICT-13-37-ES.I, para. 35 ('Nahimana Early Release Decision') (https://legal-tools.org/
doc/1l5p1y); Firouzeh Mitchell, "Early Release for Two ICTR Convicts, Possible War
Crimes in Aleppo, and Amnesty Law in Colombia", *ICL Media Review*, 15 December 2016
(available on its web site).

cide.[3] His December 2003 conviction and 30-year sentence by the International Criminal Tribunal for Rwanda ('ICTR') on various hate speech-related genocide and crimes against humanity charges was grounded in his founding/guiding the operations of Radio Télévision Libre des Milles Collines ('RTLM').[4] Also referred to as 'Radio Machete', RTLM urged Rwandan Hutus to slaughter Tutsis over the airwaves, helping fuel a genocide against the country's ethnic minority in 1994, during which close to 800,000 victims perished in approximately three months.[5]

From a superficial perspective, without studying the defendant's background too closely, the release decision raises no red flags. Nahimana had hit the two-thirds mark of his 30-year sentence and a MICT practice had developed allowing ad hoc tribunal convicts with good behaviour to be set free after serving two-thirds of their sentences.[6]

Yet, closer scrutiny raises troubling issues of integrity. The early release decision was made by Judge Theodor Meron, who had sat in judgement of Nahimana during the merits phase of the proceedings against the RTLM founder.[7] At that juncture, Meron took issue with the basis of Nahimana's liability and dissented on the grounds that the sentence was too harsh.[8] Meron had disagreed with the other judges on his panel, finding that Nahimana's liability connected to hate speech was illegitimate in light of freedom of expression concerns explicitly grounded in the zealous free speech bent of US First Amendment jurisprudence.[9] Further, that appellate

---

3   Vincent Gasana, "When a Judge Undermines the Legacy of International Justice", *The New Times*, 4 June 2018 (available on its web site).

4   "Journalists Jailed for Inciting Rwandan Genocide", *The Guardian*, 4 December 2003 (available on its web site).

5   Sharon Lafraniere, "Court Finds Rwanda Media Executives Guilty of Genocide", *The New York Times*, 3 December 2003 (available on its web site).

6   Barbara Hola, "Early Release of ICTR Convicts: The Practice Beyond the Outrage", *JusticeInfo.Net*, 5 July 2019 (available on its web site).

7   James Karuhanga, "Government, Survivors Raise Concern over UN's Early Release of Genocide Convicts", *The New Times*, 16 December 2016 (available on its web site).

8   International Criminal Tribunal for Rwanda ('ICTR'), *Prosecutor v. Ferdinand Nahimana et al.*, Appeals Chamber, Judgement, 28 November 2007, ICTR-99-52-A ('Nahimana Case Appeals Judgement'), Partially Dissenting Opinion of Judge Theodor Meron, para. 22 (http://www.legal-tools.org/doc/4ad5eb/); Gregory S. Gordon, *Atrocity Speech Law: Foundation, Fragmentation, Fruition*, Oxford University Press, Oxford, 2017, pp. 235–236.

9   *Ibid.*, pp. 235–236. (A previous chapter by the author on this case focused on the national power politics underlying and surrounding the Nahimana Early Release Decision: "On the Early Release of the "Rwandan Goebbels": American Free Speech Exceptionalism and the

panel had reduced Nahimana's sentence from life to 30 years.[10] As a member of that panel who had advocated for a lighter penalty, Meron logically played a role in Nahimana's even being in a position to request release at such an early juncture.

Thus, Meron subsequently sitting as the lone decision-maker on Nahimana's application for early release taints the procedure with the stain of bias and/or lack of impartiality. Not surprisingly, as we will see below, other jurisdictions, with both common and civil law moorings, frown upon such adjudicatory double-dipping and prohibit it.

In light of Meron's compromised position, one would have expected, at the very least, that the decision be made pursuant to a full and fair briefing and hearing procedure respecting due process protections. However, that was not the case. As already indicated, it was a unilateral decision.[11] There was no hearing. And, with no hearing, there was no input in open court from victims, prosecutors, UN or government officials or non-governmental organizations.[12] Furthermore, Meron's written decision was heavily redacted. This raises other serious integrity issues regarding transparency and procedural coherency, which this chapter will also explore.

The chapter proceeds in five parts. After this introduction, Section 26.2. examines the case of *The Prosecutor v. Ferdinand Nahimana et al.* and the involvement of Judge Theodor Meron during the merits phase of that proceeding. It then reviews Meron's presiding over Nahimana's early release application before the MICT. Next, Section 26.3. considers the rules on early release and Judge Meron's decision in respect of Nahimana's application. In light of the troubling ethical and due process issues raised by this decision, Section 26.4. examines the relevant law on judicial bias and disqualification at the MICT, at international criminal judicial institutions in general and in domestic jurisdictions. Based on this, Section 26.5. makes

---

Ghost of the Nuremberg–Tokyo Commutations", in Morten Bergsmo, Mark Klamberg, Kjersti Lohne and Christopher B. Mahony (eds.), *Power in International Criminal Justice*, Torkel Opsahl Academic EPublisher, Brussels, 2020. While there is some overlap, the current chapter views the case strictly from a deontological and/or professional responsibility perspective consistent with this volume's focus on the theme of "Integrity in International Justice".)

[10] *Ibid.*, p. 410. Nahimana Case Appeals Judgement, para. 1052, see above note 8.

[11] Linda Melvern, "Early Release of Genocide Criminals One More Betrayal", *The New Times*, 21 April 2017 (available on its web site).

[12] *Ibid.*

recommendations for the MICT in terms of reforming early-release application procedures as well as adding or strengthening judicial integrity provisions that will ensure greater fairness, transparency and due process in future post-conviction proceedings.

26.2. Proceedings at the ICTR

26.2.1. *The Prosecutor v. Nahimana*: Background

Formerly a Belgian colony, Rwanda's first steps toward independence in 1959 were accompanied by majority Hutus committing widespread and horrific atrocities against minority Tutsis.[13] The mass killings and violence were motivated by Hutu resentment of Tutsis, who had been placed in power and favoured during Belgian rule, which finally ended in 1962. The violence created a Central and East African Tutsi diaspora from which a Ugandan group, the Rwandan Patriotic Front ('RPF') launched a 1990 military invasion into the mother country.[14] Owing to an enfeebled economy and international pressure, Rwandan President Juvénal Habyarimana participated in UN-sponsored negotiations that culminated in the so-called Arusha Peace Accords. The latter stipulated the formation of a transitional government that included RPF participation.[15]

Habyarimana's governing clique included hard-line Hutus who bristled at the idea of power-sharing and began to use the media to attack the accords, the international community, and, most vituperatively, the Tutsis themselves.[16] And they began to draw up a plan for Tutsi genocide. The intellectual darling of this extremist cadre, known as the 'Akazu', was Rwandan history professor Ferdinand Nahimana.[17] After a successful career as an academic, Nahimana was appointed by Habyarimana as the director of ORINFOR, the Rwandan government's public communications apparatus. Part of ORINFOR's portfolio included the official national radio station, known as Radio Rwanda.

---

[13] "Rwanda: How the Genocide Happened", *BBC News*, 17 May 2011 (available on its web site).

[14] *Ibid.*

[15] *Ibid.*

[16] Chris McGreal, "Rwanda's Himmler: The Man Behind the Genocide", *The Guardian*, 18 December 2008 (available on its web site).

[17] Godfrey Mwakikagile, *Civil Wars in Rwanda and Burundi: Conflict Resolution in Africa*, New Africa Press, Pretoria, 2013, p. 269.

During his tenure there, in what some have referred to as a 'dress rehearsal' for the Rwandan Genocide,[18] Nahimana had Radio Rwanda broadcast a knowingly fabricated 'news bulletin' informing listeners that the Tutsis had compiled a list of Hutu targets to be murdered in Bugesera (a Tutsi district in Eastern Province, Rwanda).[19] Radio Rwanda aired this fudged 'news' to extremist Hutu *Interahamwe* militias and members of the Presidential Guard, who were synchronously being transported to that locale.[20] Nahimana's voice soon came on the same airwaves and implored listeners to "*[a]nnihilate* these Machiavellian plans of the enemy Inyenzi-Inkotanyi".[21] He then referred to the Tutsis as 'cockroaches' (*inyenzi*) and warned that they were "preparing to overthrow the country".[22] Enraged by the broadcast and then deposited at the doorstep of an exclusive Tutsi enclave, these heavily armed militia, arriving in Bugesera by the truckload, slaughtered scores of innocent civilians.[23]

Most of Rwanda, and the international community at large, were in an uproar over this orchestrated butchery. Bowing to the attendant pressure, President Habyarimana fired Nahimana from his ORINFOR post.[24] Having been sacked from his government position as head of communications, Nahimana turned to the private sector to find a comparable position.

And this coincided with the extremist Hutus drawing up the burgeoning template for a Tutsi genocide. In particular, as part of the mounting hate speech campaign against the Tutsis, in July 1993, Nahimana spearheaded the establishment of RTLM.[25] In the hate language it disseminated over the airwaves, Nahimana's station attempted to dehumanize the Tutsis by, among other things, referring to them as '*inyenzi*' (cockroaches) and using other dehumanizing metaphors.[26] Additionally, it called for violence against

---

[18] Gordon, 2017, pp. 51–52, see above note 8.

[19] Aimable Twagilimana, *Historical Dictionary of Rwanda*, Rowman & Littlefield, London, 2007, p. 123.

[20] Linda Melvern, *Conspiracy to Murder: The Rwandan Genocide*, Verso, London, 2006, pp. 26–28.

[21] Dina Temple-Raston, *Justice on the Grass: Three Rwandan Journalists, Their Trial for War Crimes, and a Nation's Quest for Redemption*, Free Press, New York, 2005, pp. 27–28.

[22] *Ibid.*, p. 28.

[23] *Ibid.*, p. 27.

[24] *Ibid.*, p. 29.

[25] Jolyon Mitchell, "Remembering the Rwandan Genocide: Reconsidering the Role of Local and Global Media", in *Global Media Journal*, 2007, vol. 6, no. 11, p. 3.

[26] *Ibid.*, p. 4.

certain Tutsi individuals.[27] Pre-genocide, Nahimana had responsibility for hiring broadcasters and shaping RTLM's content. Monitoring the violence being spurred by RTLM's broadcasts, the Rwandan government convened meetings with Nahimana and other RTLM managers and warned them that the anti-Tutsi inflammatory broadcasts needed to end.[28] Nonetheless, they did not.

Once the genocide began on 6 April 1994, RLM's content became even more inflammatory and played a significant role in fuelling the bloodshed that claimed the lives of approximately 800,000 innocent civilian Tutsis and non-conforming Hutus in less than three months.[29] Nahimana claimed to have had no control over RTLM after 6 April 1994, testifying at his trial that he had taken refuge at the French embassy and was then evacuated by French troops to Bujumbura, Burundi.[30] Yet, the record established by other evidence at the trial was to the contrary. This included Nahimana's visiting the RTLM station during the genocide, media interviews where he indicated a management role in the radio station, suggesting to witnesses that he approved of the RTLM broadcasts, and being spotted in the company of another RTLM manager at the Ministry of Defence.[31] And, most damning of all, trial evidence established that, during the genocide, at the request of a French official, Nahimana ordered RTLM announcers to halt the broadcast of certain incendiary content, after which such broadcasts ceased.[32]

26.2.2. The Trial Chamber Proceedings

After Cameroon arrested Nahimana in March 1997 and surrendered him to the ICTR, the latter charged him with: (1) conspiracy to commit genocide; (2) instigation to genocide (advocacy for genocide when the crime is committed and the advocacy made a substantial contribution); (3) direct and

---

[27] Gordon, 2017, p. 53, see above note 8.

[28] ICTR, *Prosecutor v. Ferdinand Nahimana et al.*, Trial Chamber, Judgment and Sentence, 3 December 2003, ICTR-99-52-T, paras. 571–607 ('Nahimana Case Trial Judgement') (http://www.legal-tools.org/doc/45b8b6/).

[29] Frank Chalk, "Hate Radio in Rwanda", in Howard Adelman and Astri Suhrke (eds.), *The Path of a Genocide: The Rwanda Crisis from Uganda to Zaire*, Routledge, London, 2017, p. 97 (noting that RTLM played an important role as an inciter and co-ordinator of the Rwandan Genocide).

[30] Gordon, 2017, p. 151, see above note 8.

[31] *Ibid.*, pp. 151–152.

[32] *Ibid.*, p. 152. Nahimana Case Trial Judgement, para. 563, see above note 28

public incitement to commit genocide (advocacy not necessarily leading to commission, that is, an inchoate crime); (4) complicity in genocide; and (5) crimes against humanity (persecution and extermination).[33] Within Article 6 of the Statute (Individual Criminal Responsibility), these charges against Nahimana were pursuant to subsection (1), that is, direct commission, but also pursuant to subsection (3), superior responsibility, in respect of direct and public incitement to commit genocide and crimes against humanity (persecution). In other words, superior responsibility was not charged as a mode of liability for the other crimes.[34]

In December 2003, after 230 trial days, and pursuant to Article 6(1), the ICTR found Nahimana guilty of genocide, direct and public incitement to commit genocide, conspiracy to commit genocide, and crimes against humanity (extermination and persecution). It also found him guilty of incitement and persecution pursuant to Article 6(3) (superior responsibility). In sentencing him to life in prison, Judge Navanethem Pillay observed:

> As the mastermind of RTLM, Nahimana set in motion the communications weaponry that fought the "war of media, words, newspapers and radio stations" he described in his Radio Rwanda broadcast of 25 April as a complement to bullets. Nahimana also expressed his intent through RTLM, where the words broadcast were intended to kill on the basis of ethnicity, and that is what they did.[35]

26.2.3. The Appeals Chamber Proceedings

In April 2004, Nahimana (along with his co-defendants) filed a notice of appeal and was assigned the following Appeals Chamber panel: (1) Judge Fausto Pocar, presiding (Italy); (2) Judge Mohamed Shahabuddeen (Guyana) ; (3) Judge Mehmet Güney (Turkey); (4) Judge Andrésia Vaz (Senegal); and (5) Judge Theodor Meron (United States).[36]

---

[33] *Ibid.*, para. 8.

[34] *Ibid.* Jean-Bosco Barayagwiza, another RTLM founder/director, was arrested in the same raid and charged with the same crimes although supplemented in reference to his leadership of a Hutu extremist political party (*Coalition pour la Défense de la République* or CDR) – thus, CAH-murder was included in his indictment. *Ibid.*, para. 14. Another Hutu extremist journalist, Hassan Ngeze, editor-in-chief of the radically anti-Tutsi newspaper *Kangura*, was arrested in Kenya in 1997, charged with similar crimes and tried with Nahimana and Barayagwiza. *Ibid.*, para. 19.

[35] *Ibid.*, para. 966.

[36] Nahimana Case Appeals Judgement, see above note 8.

Subsequently, Nahimana's appellate brief challenged three key aspects of the Trial Chamber's decision: (1) it contested all of the interlocutory decisions rendered on issues relating to the validity of the proceedings; (2) it claimed errors of law and fact related to fair trial protections; and (3) it pointed to errors of law and fact in connection with the merits decision.[37] As a threshold matter, the panel rejected Nahimana's arguments regarding the validity and fair trial violations.

Further, the main grounds for conviction against Nahimana on the merits were affirmed. More specifically, the Appeals Chamber upheld those portions of the decision below dealing with the elements of direct and public incitement to commit genocide.[38] Significantly, in respect of incitement, the judges ruled:

> The Appeals Chamber considers that the Trial Chamber did not alter the constituent elements of the crime of direct and public incitement to commit genocide in the media context (which would have constituted an error) [...] Furthermore, the Appeals Chamber notes that several extracts from the [Trial Chamber] Judgment demonstrate that the Trial Chamber did a good job of distinguishing between hate speech and direct and public incitement to commit genocide [...]. The Appeals Chamber will now turn to the Appellants' submissions that the Trial Chamber erred (1) in considering that a speech in ambiguous terms, open to a variety of interpretations, can constitute direct incitement to commit genocide, and (2) in relying on the presumed intent of the author of the speech, on its potential dangers, and on the author's political and community affiliation, in order to determine whether it was of a criminal nature. The Appellants' position is in effect that incitement to commit genocide is direct only when it is explicit and that under no circumstances can the Chamber consider contextual elements in determining whether a speech constitutes direct in-

---

[37] See, for example, *ibid.*, para. 224 (rejecting argument that late filing of broadcast translations caused prejudice); para. 226 (rejecting argument regarding admission of evidence); para. 229 (amending the prosecution list found not to be prejudicial); para. 235 (argument regarding obstruction to defense investigation found not to have merit); para. 257 (no proof that right to have defense witnesses appear under the same condition as prosecution witnesses was violated).

[38] *Ibid.*, para. 695.

citement to commit genocide. For the reasons given below, the Appeals Chamber considers this approach overly restrictive.[39]

Similarly, the Appeals Chamber upheld the convictions based on hate speech as crimes against humanity (persecution). The Trial Chamber had found that "hate speech targeting a population on the basis of ethnicity, or other discriminatory grounds, reaches a sufficient level of gravity [as required by the case law] and constitutes persecution under Article 3(h) of its Statute" and unlike the crime of indictment, it does not require a call to action because it is not a provocation to cause harm but, as an affront to human dignity, "is the harm itself".[40]

Pushing back against this analysis, Nahimana claimed on appeal that hate speech could not serve as the *actus reus* for the persecution offense because it was not criminalized under customary international law. The majority of the panel, with only Meron dissenting, did not agree. It focused on the question of whether hate speech violated fundamental rights and whether the gravity threshold was met.[41] In accord with the Trial Chamber, it found that hate speech *per se* violates the right to human dignity, and hate speech "inciting to violence" violates the right to security (the chamber also noted that hate speech on its own could not violate the rights to life or physical integrity as it would require intermediate actors to facilitate the requisite injuries to constitute a breach of these rights).[42]

Regarding the gravity criterion, four of the judges (minus Meron) specified that they did not feel compelled to decide whether "mere hate speeches not inciting violence" were sufficient as a cumulative approach was needed in respect of all pertinent media offerings. In the case at bar, per the judges, hate speech was

> accompanied by calls for genocide against the Tutsi group and [took] place in the context of a massive campaign of persecution directed at the Tutsi population of Rwanda, this campaign

---

[39] *Ibid.*, paras. 696, 697.

[40] *Ibid.*

[41] *Ibid.*, paras. 986, 987.

[42] *Ibid.*, para. 986. I have been critical of this portion of the Appeals Chamber judgment as the panel squandered a golden opportunity to clarify whether hate speech on its own, as part of a widespread or systematic directed against a civilian population, can constitute the *actus reus* for CAH-persecution. Gordon, 2017, pp. 233, 234, 335, 336, see above note 8.

> being also characterized by acts of violence (killings, torture and ill-treatment, rapes …) and of destruction of property.[43]

Notwithstanding these setbacks, the appeal was successful in reversing liability based on pre-6 April (that is, the start of the genocide) transmissions. Similarly, the Appeals Chamber invalidated the convictions for instigation to genocide, incitement to genocide, and crimes against humanity (extermination and persecution) premised on Article 6(1) liability – that is, Nahimana's direct 'commission' of the crimes (namely, the illicit broadcasts). Since parts of the convictions were reversed, the Appeals Chamber reduced Nahimana's life sentence to thirty years (with credit being given, under Rule 101(D) of the ICTR Rules of Procedure and Evidence, for the period already spent in detention).[44]

26.2.4. Meron's Dissent

Even though Nahimana's sentence of incarceration was drastically reduced, in spite of upheld convictions for incitement to genocide and crimes against humanity (based on superior responsibility), Judge Meron thought the considerably watered-down punishment was still too harsh. His dissent focused on the majority opinion's being too permissive regarding speech as the basis for liability. To begin, Meron observed that, "[t]he sheer number of errors in the Trial Judgement indicates that remanding the case, rather than undertaking piecemeal remedies, would have been the best course".[45]

He then turned to his objections regarding speech-focused liability. Under any circumstances, he opined, "mere hate speech may not be the basis of a criminal conviction".[46] Solely when it rises "to the level of inciting violence or other imminent lawless action" may it be criminalized, he concluded.[47] To back this pronouncement, he cited, among other things, the US Constitution and US Supreme Court jurisprudence, noting that:

---

[43] Nahimana Case Appeals Judgment, para. 988, see above note 8 (ellipsis in the original).

[44] *Ibid.*, para. 1052. With reference to the other two Media Trial defendants, Ngeze's sentence was reduced to 35 years. Barayagwiza had been technically sentenced to life in prison but had it reduced to 35 years, with credit for time served (bringing it to twenty-seven), due to certain procedural irregularities. *Ibid.*, para. 1039. Based on the portions of the convictions that were overturned, he was granted a further sentence reduction of three years by the Appeals Chamber. *Ibid.*, para. 1097.

[45] Nahimana Case Appeals Judgment, Partially Dissenting Opinion of Judge Theodor Meron, para. 1, see above note 8.

[46] *Ibid.*, para. 13.

[47] *Ibid.*, para. 12.

[T]he government may not prohibit the expression of an idea simply because society finds the idea itself offensive or disagreeable [...]. [U]nder the rubric of persecution, to criminalize unsavory speech that does not constitute actual imminent incitement might have grave and unforeseen consequences.[48]

Then Judge Meron criticized the persecution charge on a separate ground. He pointed to the prosecution's not demonstrating a link between any RTLM broadcasts for which Nahimana was responsible and the widespread or systematic attack against the civilian population that was the underlying basis for the crimes against humanity charge. The conviction should be overturned, he asserted, on that independent ground as well.[49]

Given his view that Nahimana's guilt based on persecution was invalid, and that only portions of the incitement liability survived appeal, he believed that Nahimana's 30-year sentence was too severe. In the words of Judge Meron:

> Because I would reverse the conviction of Appellant Nahimana for persecution, I believe that the only conviction against him that can stand is for direct and public incitement to commit genocide under Article 6(3) and based on certain post-6 April broadcasts. *Despite the severity of this crime, Nahimana did not personally kill anyone and did not personally make statements that constituted incitement. In light of these facts, I believe that the sentence imposed is too harsh*, both in relation to Nahimana's own culpability and to the sentences meted out by the Appeals Chamber to Barayagwiza and Ngeze, who committed graver crimes. Therefore, I dissent from Nahimana's sentence.[50]

---

[48] *Ibid.* paras. 11–12, citing United States Supreme Court ('US SC'), *Texas v. Johnson*, 21 June 1989, 491 U.S. 397, p. 414; US SC, *Brandenburg v. Ohio*, 9 June 1969, 395 U.S. 444, p. 447; US SC, *Watts v. United States*, 21 April 1969, 394 U.S. 705, p. 708.

[49] Judge Meron merely stated this with no authority supporting him – in point of fact, per existing law, no causal nexus need be shown – rather, the prosecutor must only prove that the broadcasts were part of the attack, with the RTLM announcers being conscious that they were part of the attack. See Gordon, 2017, p. 10, see above note 8, noting that the crime against humanity of hate speech as persecution is committed as "part of a widespread or systematic attack directed against any civilian population, with knowledge of the attack". This does not mean that there must be a "causal nexus" between the hate speech and the attack. Judge Meron merely asserted this without support.

[50] Nahimana Case Appeals Judgment, Partially Dissenting Opinion of Judge Theodor Meron, para. 1, see above note 8 (emphasis added).

26.3. Developments Post-ICTR Proceedings

26.3.1. Judge Meron's Nomination to the MICT

On 22 December 2010, via UN Security Council Resolution 1066, the Council created the MICT.[51] It was established to maintain the "jurisdiction, rights and obligations and essential functions" of the ICTR and ICTY.[52] The portion representing the ICTR assumed that tribunal's functions on 1 July 2012 and is based in Arusha, Tanzania (the ICTY branch, based in The Hague, followed suit on 1 July 2013).[53] The MICT has three separate organs – a judiciary, a prosecutor and a registrar.[54] Each is directed by an appointee given a renewable four-year term.[55]

The MICT has a roster of 25 judges (only employed when necessary) and they are nominated by their countries of origin.[56] Additionally, the Mechanism designates one permanent judge to function as its President.[57] For its part, the United States nominated Theodor Meron, who in March 2012 was then chosen as the MICT's first president by the UN Secretary-General.[58] The UN renewed his term in 2016.[59] In January 2019, Judge Carmel Agius was elected as President of the MICT, replacing Theodor Meron.[60]

26.3.2. Nahimana's Incarceration and Application for Early Release

After his conviction, on 3 December 2008, ICTR prisoner Ferdinand Nahimana was transferred across the African continent, from Arusha to Bamako Central Prison, Mali, where he was meant to serve the remainder of his

---

[51] United Nations Security Council, resolution 1066, 22 December 2010, UN Doc. S/RES/1966 (2010) ('SC Resolution 1066') (https://www.legal-tools.org/doc/e79460). The MICT's Statute ('MICT Statute') is attached thereto.

[52] *Ibid.*

[53] MICT, "Mechanism for International Criminal Tribunals (MICT) Begins Work in The Hague", press release, 1 July 2013 (https://www.irmct.org/en/news/mechanism-international-criminal-tribunals-mict-begins-work-hague); Chandra Lekha Sriram, Olga Martin-Ortega and Johanna Herman, *War, Conflict and Human Rights: Theory and Practice*, second edition, Routledge, London, 2014, p. 178.

[54] UNSC Resolution 1066, Articles 8–15, see above note 51.

[55] *Ibid.*, Articles 10, 14, 15.

[56] MICT, "Judges" (available on its web site).

[57] *Ibid.*

[58] MICT, "Judge Theodor Meron" (available on its web site).

[59] *Ibid.*

[60] MICT, "Judge Carmel Agius" (available on its web site).

---

sentence.[61] On 15 February 2016, Nahimana filed an application for early release under Article 26 of the MICT Statute.[62] This statutory provision contains one of the MICT's core duties – supervising enforcement of sentences handed down by the ICTR or the ICTY. Article 26 vests the MICT President with the power to supervise and enforce ICTR and ICTY sentences and decide on requests for pardon or commutation of sentences.[63] In particular, it declares that "[t]here shall only be pardon or commutation of sentence if the President of the Mechanism so decides on the basis of the interests of justice and the general principles of law".[64] Thus, President Meron was given sole discretion to rule on Nahimana's application.

Approximately six months after the application was filed, on 29 August 2016, in accordance with paragraphs 3, 4, and 5 of the MICT Practice Direction on the Procedure for the Determination of Applications for Pardon, Commutation of Sentence, and Early Release of Persons Convicted by the ICTR, ICTY or the Mechanism ('Practice Direction'),[65] the following information was gathered and transmitted via a memorandum from the Registry to Judge Meron: (1) a 13 July 2016 letter from the Mali Ministry of Justice and Human Rights; (2) an 11 April 2016 letter from the former Warden of Koulikoro Prison (where Nahimana was incarcerated) [transmitting (a) an 11 April 2016 report on the status of incarceration; (b) an 11 April 2016 psycho-social report; (c) a 28 December 2015 psychiatric examination report from Policlinique Pasteur]; (3) a 3 August 2016 letter from Koulikoro Prison Warden Abdoulaye Fofana; and (4) a 25 August 2015 memorandum from the MICT Office of the Prosecutor.[66]

Then, on 8 September 2016, the MICT sent the aforementioned items to Nahimana, who filed a responsive pleading on 22 September.[67] These, then, were the sole materials upon which Judge Meron considered the mer-

---

[61] Paul R. Bartrop, "Nahimana, Ferdinand", in Paul R. Bartrop and Steven L. Jacobs (eds.), *Modern Genocide: The Definitive Resource and Document Collection, Volume 4*, ABC-CLIO, Santa Barbara, 2015, p. 1774.

[62] Nahimana Early Release Decision, para. 1, see above note 2.

[63] MICT Statute, Article 26, see above note 51.

[64] *Ibid.*

[65] Mechanism for International Criminal Tribunals, Practice Direction on the Procedure for the Determination of Applications for Pardon, Commutation of Sentence, and Early Release of Persons Convicted by the ICTR, the ICTY or the Mechanism, 5 July 2012, MICT/3, paras. 3, 4 and 5 ('MICT Practice Direction') (http://www.legal-tools.org/doc/244989/).

[66] *Ibid.*, para. 5.

[67] *Ibid.*, para. 6.

its of Nahimana's early release application. It bears emphasizing that the MICT governing instruments grant sole jurisdiction for release decisions to the MICT President without calling for a hearing or input from other stakeholders, including the MICT prosecutor or any relevant victims.[68] It should also be noted that, in this case, Meron's written decision, which will be the object of the analysis that follows, is heavily redacted. So, notwithstanding the narrow scope of due process just described, from this perspective alone, there are apparent transparency deficits.

Even apart from all this, however, the unredacted portion of the decision is problematic in its own right and raises issues regarding integrity in the post-conviction proceedings for defendants convicted by the *ad hoc* tribunals and now before the MICT seeking early release. Those issues will now be considered.

26.3.3. Examination of the Early Release Decision

26.3.3.1. An Overview of the Relevant Rules

The unredacted portion of the decision began with a consideration of the MICT Rules of Procedure and Evidence ('RPE'). Rule 150 of the RPE provides: "The President shall, upon such notice, determine, *in consultation with any Judges of the sentencing Chamber* who are Judges of the Mechanism, whether pardon, commutation of sentence, or early release is appropriate".[69] This is reinforced by MICT Practice Direction 7, which requires the President to consult with other judges by forwarding information, including the President's comments about the case, to "Judges of the sentencing Chamber who are Judges of the Mechanism".[70]

Rule 151 then states:

> In determining whether pardon, commutation of sentence, or early release is appropriate, the President shall take into account, *inter alia*, the gravity of the crime or crimes for which the prisoner was convicted, the treatment of similarly-situated prisoners, the prisoner's demonstration of rehabilitation, as

---

[68] For example, MICT Statute, Article 26, see above note 51; MICT Practice Direction, para. 9, see above note 65.

[69] MICT, Rules of Procedure and Evidence, 26 September 2016, MICT/1/Rev.2, Rule 150 ('MICT RPE') (emphasis added).

[70] MICT Practice Direction, para. 7, see above note 65.

well as any substantial cooperation of the prisoner with the Prosecutor.[71]

26.3.3.2. MICT RPE Rule 151 Analysis

26.3.3.2.1. Gravity

26.3.3.2.1.1. The Offences

The bulk of Meron's ruling centred on Rule 151. He started by recognizing that the offenses for which Nahimana had been found guilty were of great gravity.[72] In doing so, he cited the Media Case Trial Chamber's insight that the "power of the media to create and destroy fundamental human values comes with great responsibility" and that those "who control such media are accountable for its consequences".[73] Similarly, Meron alluded to the Trial Judgment finding that RTLM fostered contempt for Rwanda's Tutsi citizens and unequivocally called for their liquidation, which, in fact, led to their mass slaughter.[74] He also recognized the Trial Chamber's conclusion that if the downing of President Habyarimana's plane on 6 April 1994 was the 'trigger' for the killings that followed, that RTLM was 'the bullet in the gun' and that the killings resulted in part from its effectively disseminated

---

[71] *Ibid.*, Rule 151. In addition, Meron referred to Article 3(2) of the 13 May 2016 Agreement between the United Nations and the Government of the Republic of Mali on the Enforcement of Sentences Pronounced by the International Criminal Tribunal for Rwanda or the International Residual Mechanism for Criminal Tribunals (https://legal-tools.org/doc/ulm6wv) provides that the conditions of imprisonment shall be governed by the law of Mali Subject to the Supervision of the Mechanism. Nahimana Early Release Decision, para. 10, see above note 2. Article 8 of the Enforcement Agreement provides. *inter alia.* that, following notification of eligibility for early release under Malian law, the President shall determine whether early release is appropriate on the basis of the interests of justice and the general principles of law, and the Registrar shall transmit the decision of the President to Mali, which shall execute the terms of the decision promptly. *Ibid.* In this case, Meron observed, according to the provisions of Article 35 of Mali's Law No. 01-003 of 27 February 2001 on the prison system and supervised education, "detainees who have provided sufficient proof of their improvement could be eligible for parole or semi-custodial treatment". *Ibid.*, para. 11. Meron noted in his decision that the Malian authorities state that Nahimana "meets the conditions set out in Malian legislation for parole or semi-custodial treatment", *ibid.* Meron noted, however, that that even if Nahimana were eligible for early release under Mali's domestic law, "early release of persons convicted by the ICTR falls exclusively with in the discretion of the President pursuant to Article 26 of the Statute and Rules 150 and 151 of the Rules". *Ibid.*, para. 12.

[72] *Ibid.*, para. 14.

[73] *Ibid.*, quoting Nahimana Case Trial Judgment, para. 945, see above note 28.

[74] *Ibid.*, quoting Nahimana Case Trial Judgment, para. 949, see above note 28

---

messages.[75] This, in turn, furnished 'conclusive evidence' of genocidal intent.[76]

26.3.3.2.1.2. Nahimana's Role

Meron then examined the crucial part Nahimana played in conceiving, launching, moulding and operating RTLM. He described Nahimana as the "mastermind" of RTLM, who, during the Rwandan Genocide, voiced his gratification that the radio station he founded had been "instrumental in awakening" the Hutu population and "halting" the "Tutsi ethnic group" when large-scale slaughter had been taking place for almost a month.[77] Nahimana's writings alluded to the "Tutsi league" – a "veiled reference to the Tutsi population as a whole", which he denigrated as Rwanda's enemy.[78] In this way, then, he operationalized the communications weaponry that fought what he referred to as the war of "media, words, newspapers and radio stations", which he described during the genocide as a complement to bullets.[79]

26.3.3.2.1.3. Nahimana's Awareness

Meron also emphasized Nahimana's knowledge of his criminal activity during the genocide. He made reference to the Trial Chamber's conclusion that "Nahimana was 'fully aware of the power of words' and used 'the radio – the medium of communication with the widest reach – to disseminate hatred and violence'".[80] As a result, the Trial Chamber found, and Meron conceded, "without a firearm, machete or any physical weapon", Nahimana "caused the deaths of thousands of innocent civilians".[81] For this, he bore superior responsibility since he did not use his *de facto* power and authority to avert the "genocidal harm" the RTLM transmissions catalysed.[82]

---

[75] *Ibid.*, quoting Nahimana Case Trial Judgment, para. 953, see above note 28

[76] *Ibid.*, quoting Nahimana Case Trial Judgment, para. 965, see above note 28

[77] *Ibid.*, para. 15, quoting Nahimana Case Trial Judgment, para. 966, see above note 28.

[78] *Ibid.*

[79] *Ibid.*

[80] *Ibid.*, para. 16, quoting Nahimana Case Trial Judgment, para. 1099, see above note 28.

[81] *Ibid.*, quoting Nahimana Case Trial Judgment, para. 1102, see above note 28

[82] *Ibid.*, quoting Nahimana Case Trial Judgment, para. 972, see above note 28.

26.3.3.2.2. Treatment of Similarly Situated Prisoners

Meron then turned to the next Rule 151 criterion – the requirement of equal treatment for "similarly-situated" prisoners in connection with early release applications. The ratio provided here was clipped and shallow:

> In this respect, I recall that ICTR convicts like Nahimana, are considered 'similarly situated' to all other prisoners under the Mechanism's supervision and that all convicts supervised by the Mechanism are to be considered eligible for early release upon the completion of two-thirds of their sentences, irrespective of the tribunal that convicted them.[83]

This was supported by a lone footnote, number 30, in which Meron referred to two other early release decisions – one each from the ICTY and ICTR, respectively. In each case – *Prosecutor v. Borovčanin* (August 2016 decision) and *Prosecutor v. Bisengimana* (December 2012 decision) – the defendant had been released after serving two-thirds of his sentence.

26.3.3.2.2.1. *The Prosecutor v. Borovčanin*

In the first case, defendant Ljubomir Borovčanin's guilt stemmed from a fairly limited hierarchical role tied to two incidents in Bosnia in July 1995, during which he was a police brigade deputy commander. He was found guilty of war crimes and crimes against humanity in reference to: (1) aiding and abetting in the forcible transfer of civilians out of Potočari; and (2) failing to punish his subordinates who took part in killing prisoners in front of a warehouse in Kravica.[84] Borovčanin was sentenced to 17 years and did not appeal.[85] Significantly, he was originally on trial with Vujadin Popović, Ljubiša Beara and Drago Nikolić, who all exercised overall leadership positions in reference to the charged crimes.[86] The Trial Chamber's sentenc-

---

[83] *Ibid.*, para. 19, see above note 2.

[84] International Criminal Tribunal for the former Yugoslavia, "Ljubomir Borovčanin Transferred to Denmark to Serve Sentence", press release, 11 November 2011 (https://legal-tools.org/doc/qw7qxb); MICT, *The Prosecutor v. Borovčanin*, Public Redacted Version of the 14 July 2016 Decision of the President on the Early Release of Ljubomir Borovčanin, 2 August 2016, MICT-13-37-ES.I, para. 3 ('Borovčanin Early Release Decision') (http://www.legal-tools.org/doc/2e491d/).

[85] Borovčanin Early Release Decision, para. 3, see above note 84.

[86] "Bosnian Serb Srebrenica Convict Ljubomir Borovčanin Freed", in *Balkan Transitional Justice*, 2 August 2016 (available on its web site).

ing Popović and Beara to life in prison, and Nikolić to 35 years,[87] helps place Borovčanin's subordinate role into its proper perspective.

26.3.3.2.2.2. *The Prosecutor v. Bisengimana*

The other case cited by Judge Meron in this portion of the early release decision was the ICTR matter of *Prosecutor v. Bisengimana*. There, the defendant was the mayor of a town called Gikoro in the Kigali-Rural Prefecture of Rwanda.[88] In December 2005, he pled guilty to aiding and abetting crimes against humanity (murder, extermination) committed against Tutsis in his town between 13 and 15 April 1994. As with *Borovčanin*, this was a rather low-level official. Even more striking, though, when contrasted with Nahimana, was the fact that Bisengimana had actually co-operated with prosecutors by pleading guilty.

26.3.3.2.2.3. The Absence of Legal Authority in Footnote 30

Quite conspicuously, Meron's footnote 30 did not cite legal authority for the proposition that "all convicts supervised by the Mechanism are to be considered eligible for early release upon the completion of two-thirds of their sentences, irrespective of the tribunal that convicted them". He merely referenced the two cases of *Borovčanin* and *Bisengimana*, suggesting this had been the MICT's practice (even though, as suggested above, the two convicts in those cases do not seem to be similarly situated to the high-ranking Ferdinand Nahimana). Meron did observe that a "convicted person having served two-thirds of his or her sentence shall be merely eligible to apply for early release and not entitled to such release, which may only be granted by the President as a matter of discretion, after considering the totality of the circumstances in each case".[89] With this in mind, after first confirming that, by Meron's calculations, Nahimana served two-thirds of his sentence by 27 March 2016, Meron went on to consider: (1) demonstration of rehabilitation; (2) substantial co-operation; and (3) "humanitarian concerns".

---

[87] *Ibid.*

[88] MICT, *Prosecutor v. Bisengimana*, Decision of the President on Early Release of Paul Bisengimana and on Motion to File a Public Redacted Application, 11 December 2012, MICT-12-07, para. 3 ('Bisengimana Early Release Decision') (http://www.legal-tools.org/doc/a7d60f/; https://legal-tools.org/doc/urptdm).

[89] Nahimana Early Release Decision, para. 19, see above note 2.

26.3.3.2.3. Demonstration of Rehabilitation

Turning to the demonstration of rehabilitation, Meron relied on the reports from the Malian prison officials. The "Psycho-Social Report", for instance, noted that "Nahimana is consistently ready to assist his fellow inmates complete tasks required by the prison authorities. and he lives "in perfect harmony" with both the prison inmates and the prison administration".[90] Paragraph 24 is the most substantial in this portion of the decision and it is characterized by similar statements. Somewhat comical among these is the suggestion that the bookish Nahimana would physically help to "restrain" his compatriots *vis-à-vis* prison officials – which is noted as "quite an achievement among a group of intellectuals".[91]

26.3.3.2.4. Substantial Co-operation

That a former history scholar and university administrator would be polite behind bars is no great revelation. What is enlightening, however, comes in the paragraph that follows. Moreover, it is an omission. The topic is Nahimana's acceptance of responsibility. Significantly, the paragraph demonstrated the RTLM mastermind has absolutely no contrition for his central role in the Rwandan Genocide. Meron could only offer that Nahimana "has never 'questioned or minimised the genocide' or the 'criminal nature of numerous broadcasts of the RTLM' during that time".[92] Nevertheless, Meron had to aver, because Nahimana put it in his own Application for Release (para. 4), that "he has disputed his own responsibility for these crimes".[93] This is in stark contrast to the other two early decision releases cited by Meron – *Borovčanin* and *Bisengimana*. In the former, the Bosnian Serb deputy police commander did not appeal his conviction or sentence and expressed that he had "no doubt whatsoever" that what he did "during the war was wrong".[94] In the latter, the former mayor pled guilty, which the decision noted "constitutes cooperation with the Prosecution".[95]

Consequently, Meron had to admit that Nahimana "has at no time cooperated with [the Prosecution] in the course of his trial, appeal, or at

---

[90] *Ibid.*, para. 22.

[91] *Ibid.*, para. 24. It must be noted that a nerd helping physically "restrain" other nerds from armed prison guards does not seem like much of a feat!

[92] *Ibid.*, para. 25.

[93] *Ibid.*

[94] Borovčanin Early Release Decision, paras. 22–23, see above note 84.

[95] Bisengimana Early Release Decision, para. 30, see above note 88.

any point while serving his sentence". So, despite no evidence or remorse or co-operation, Meron was able only to wanly intone that "Nahimana's lack of cooperation with the Prosecution […] is a neutral factor in determining whether or not to grant him early release".[96]

26.3.3.2.5. Humanitarian Concerns

As for the final Rule 151 factor, "humanitarian concerns", Meron alluded to Nahimana's Application submission that "his age and ill health are grounds for early release".[97] No substantiation or details regarding the "ill health" were provided (it should be pointed out, though, once again, that the Decision is heavily redacted). It is noted that, at the time the application was submitted, Nahimana was in his mid-60s – not the sort of extremely advanced age, where grave health problems could easily be supposed. Not surprisingly then, Meron rejected the ill health assertion and was dubious of Nahimana's claim that his age was a factor.[98]

26.3.3.2.6. Conclusion of the Rule 151 Analysis

This was followed by a concluding paragraph. Having checked off few of the boxes he seemed to indicate were important, and acknowledging the gravity of Nahimana's crimes, Meron perfunctorily granted Nahimana's Application in one skeletal sentence: "While the crimes of which Nahimana was convicted are very grave, the fact that Nahimana already completed two-thirds of his sentence as of 27 March 2016, and the fact that he has demonstrated some signs of rehabilitation weigh in favour of his early release".[99]

26.3.3.3. MICT RPE Rule 150 Analysis

Up to now, we have examined Meron's consideration of Nahimana's Application for Early Release pursuant to Rule 151 of the MICT RPE. Yet, the RPE demands more – the President must also take into account Rule 150, which requires him to consult with other judges (and, as we have seen, Practice Direction 7 mandates this as well). But Meron gave only short shrift to this provision, noting quite cursorily by way of footnote: "Other

---

[96] Nahimana Early Release Decision, para. 30, see above note 2.

[97] *Ibid.*, paras. 32–33.

[98] *Ibid.*, para. 34. The then-86-year-old Meron could presumably speak from personal experience in that regard.

[99] *Ibid.*, paras. 35–37.

than myself, none of the Judges of the sentencing Chamber are judges of the Mechanism. On that basis, no consultations with other Judges of the Mechanism pursuant to Rule 150 of the Rules are required in determining his Application".[100]

26.4. Overall Analysis of the Early Release Decision

26.4.1. Failure to Comply with MICT RPE Rules 151 and 150

The first aspect of the decision to consider is the coherence and probity of the document itself. This, in turn, hinges on Meron's analysis pursuant to RPE Rules 151 and 150 – the heart of the early release merits decision. Furthermore, here it is clear that Judge Meron failed to comply with the spirit, if not the letter, of the explicit instructions provided in those rules.

26.4.1.1. The Rule 150 Analysis

In this respect, his treatment of Rule 150 stands out. As will be recalled, that provision requires the President to consult "with any Judges of the sentencing Chamber who are Judges of the Mechanism, whether pardon, commutation of sentence, or early release is appropriate".[101]

In this regard, Judge Meron hung his hat on a technicality – it is true that no member of the sentencing bench was on the MICT roster at that time (again, it is not a group of full-time paid judges but persons on call who are paid only for work performed when assigned to them). However, Judge Fausto Pocar, a member of the sentencing panel who disagreed with Meron, was still a judge at the ICTY – as was Meron himself.[102] It would have been quite feasible to solicit Judge Pocar's views given the close structural and personnel link between the ICTY and the MICT. Regardless, Judge Meron failed to do even that.

It is worth noting that the MICT seems to have taken cognizance of the technical loophole Judge Meron exploited in the *Nahimana* Early Release Decision. The Mechanism recently amended Rule 150 to mandate that "[i]f none of the Judges who imposed the sentence are Judges of the Mechanism, the President shall consult with at least two other Judges".[103]

---

[100] *Ibid.*, para. 8, footnote 15.

[101] MICT RPE Rule 150, see above note 69.

[102] United Nations International Criminal Tribunal for the former Yugoslavia, "The Judges" (available on ICTY's web site) indicating that Judge Fausto Pocar and Judge Theodor Meron were still on the ICTY bench.

[103] MICT RPE, 4 March 2019, MICT/1/Rev.5, Rule 150, cf. above note 69.

Going even further, and consistent with the practice of the Residual Mechanism for the Special Court for Sierra Leone, Rule 150 could be revised to require the early release application decision-maker to consult with at least one judge from the panel that issued the final version of the sentence imposed on the defendant.[104] In the age of the Internet, this is eminently feasible.

26.4.1.2. The Rule 151 Analysis

26.4.1.2.1. Extreme Gravity and Non-Similarly-Situated Prisoners

Examining the Rule 151 analysis also reveals serious issues. The evaluation begins auspiciously with consideration of the gravity of Nahimana's crimes. The gist of this section is that the RTLM founder was a principal architect of the Rwandan Genocide and desired the impact 'Radio Machete' had on fomenting and fuelling the massacres. Yet, what follows can only be described as cognitive dissonance. In particular, the "equal treatment of similarly-situated prisoners" exposition is a non-sequitur and internally incoherent. How could Meron assert that a Bosnian Serb police brigade deputy commander and a Kigali-suburb mayor were "similarly situated" vis-à-vis the Rwandan Genocide's propaganda master? The imbalance in criminal responsibility alone renders the comparison absurd.

26.4.1.2.2. Absence of Rehabilitation or Co-operation

But that disparity is exacerbated when one considers that these lower-level players co-operated (through a guilty plea and non-appeal) and expressed contrition. Nahimana fought every step of the way and continued to deflect blame for his actions until the day of his release. What is worse, a bit of research by the MICT would have revealed that Nahimana's lack of repentance only intensified after he began serving his sentence.

In a document he published on the Internet titled "Debate on the Book of Jean Baptiste Nkuliyingoma", Nahimana passionately denied any sort of responsibility whatsoever in reference to his hate media activities both before and during the Rwandan Genocide.[105] In the document, he

---

[104] Residual Special Court for Sierra Leone, Rules of Procedure and Evidence, 30 November 2018, Rule 124 ('RSCSCL RPE') (http://www.legal-tools.org/doc/2b02c6/) (requiring the early release decision-maker to consult "with the Judges who imposed the sentence").

[105] Ferdinand Nahimana, "Débat Sur le Livre de Jean Baptiste Nkuliyingoma: Inkundura. Amateka y'intambara ya ruhekura yakuyeho igitugu ikimika ikindi", 9 February 2012 (translated by the author).

blanketly assigned all blame to the RPF and its alleged dissemination of propaganda in the previous 20-plus years (alluding to, for instance, the "propaganda, the rumor, and the false presentation of actual facts between 1990 and 1994 meant to demonize the opponents of the RPF and hide the true nature of this movement").[106] Among other core points of denial Nahimana asserted here:

1. He alleged that the text of the communiqué read on Radio Rwanda, when he was in charge of that radio station before the founding of RTLM, as reported in various histories of Rwanda, was a fabrication of Jean-Pierre Chrétien (Nahimana's thesis supervisor) in his 1995 book *Les Médias du Génocide* and that the communiqué was selectively redacted and read out of context without his knowledge and contrary to his wishes. In any event, he insisted, the overall message of the communiqué was an appeal for nonviolence.[107] (This assertion is contrary to trial testimony as well as the histories of experts beyond reproach, such as Alison Des Forges in her book *Leave None to Tell the Story*: "In March 1992 [when Nahimana was its director], Radio Rwanda warned that Hutu leaders in Bugesera were going to be murdered by Tutsi, false information meant to spur the Hutu massacres of Tutsi".[108])

2. Similarly, Nahimana claimed that he was not responsible for the reading of the communiqué and was sacked from ORINFOR [the agency he directed that ran Radio Rwanda] by backchannel manoeuvrings of the RPF – not because of indignation throughout Rwandan society and the international community, which, as we have seen, pressured the government to remove Nahimana from the ORINFOR post [as was widely reported].[109] He also asserted that he was offered a consular post in Germany but turned it down to return to the University.[110] (But according to Allison Des Forges: "He gave up teach-

---

[106] *Ibid.*, p. 6.

[107] *Ibid.*, pp. 13–14.

[108] Alison Des Forges, *"Leave None to Tell the Story": Genocide in Rwanda*, Human Rights Watch, New York, 1999, p. 79.

[109] Nahimana, 2012, pp. 14–18, see above note 105. See also Temple-Raston, 2005, p. 29, see above note 21 (reporting that many in Rwanda and the international community at large were appalled by the orchestrated slaughter in Bugesera and that, as a result of this, then-Rwandan President Juvenal Habyarimana fired Nahimana from his ORINFOR post).

[110] *Ibid.*, pp. 15–16.

ing to take charge of government propaganda at ORINFOR. After being forced from this position, Nahimana was supposed to become the Rwandan ambassador in Bonn, but the German government refused to accept him. He tried to go back to the university, but his colleagues there also protested against his return".)[111]

3. It is false, he alleged, that the virulently anti-Tutsi newspaper *Kangura* and its editor-in-chief, Hassan Ngeze (Nahimana's co-defendant in the Media Trial], were the mouthpiece of Hutu extremism – in fact, they were a front for the RPF to spread anti-Tutsi hate speech so extreme that it would discredit the Habyarimana regime and Hutus in general.[112] Nahimana also claimed that Ngeze had been financed by the American government, which funded his journalistic coverage of the genocide (and distribution of images of the massacres to American news outlets).[113] (These allegations are so clearly spurious and against the great weight of evidence adduced at trial, that there is no need to even muster a detailed response.)

4. Nahimana acknowledged taking part in RTLM's pre-6 April management but claimed that the media outlet did not broadcast a radical Hutu hard-line anti-Tutsi message – it was only after 6 April that RTLM's content became genocidal. He averred, however, that he had no control at that point.[114] (Nonetheless, he overlooked the specific instances of RTLM's pre-6 April incitement – explicitly brought to his attention through communications with the Ministry of Information (whose existence he acknowledged) and entirely ignored his important position in the genocidal rump government, his damning quotes during the genocide, and his successfully instructing RTLM to refrain from attacking UN peacekeepers, given at the behest of the French ambassador.)

Moreover, Nahimana made incredible assertions of acquittal – suggesting that the Appeals Chamber Judgment fully exonerated him:

> When he [Nkuliyingoma] speaks about RTLM, he clearly opines that he and its shareholders had the intention and had

---

[111] Des Forges, 1999, p. 85, see above note 108.

[112] Nahimana, 2012, pp. 11–12, see above note 105.

[113] *Ibid.*, p. 12. Nahimana notes that Ngeze testified to this effect before the ICTR and has maintained this claim ever since. *Ibid.*

[114] *Ibid.*, pp. 21–25.

made the decision to use RTLM as a tool of incitement to commit crimes of extermination and genocide. This accusation does not stand up to scrutiny and cannot go unchallenged. If certain debates and analyses disseminated on RTLM's air waves before 6 April 1994 did not correspond to the views or beliefs or certain persons or groups of persons, especially due to their tone or orientation, which was sometimes provocative, indeed denigrating, I do not deny that. But that cannot constitute grounds for accusing the RTLM shareholders to have been motivated by the desire to commit genocide at the time RLTM was founded. The judges of the ICTR Appeals Chamber were of this opinion. After examining the legal documents, the list of the RTLM corporation's shareholders, my role within this corporation and the broadcasts of this radio station, they overturned the Trial Chamber's guilty verdicts against me as a principle for the "*crimes of genocide, direct and public incitement to commit genocide, conspiracy to commit genocide, and extermination and persecution as crimes against humanity*".[115]

Two sentences after this, he alluded to his "acquittal" in no uncertain terms. What Nahimana failed to include, however, was that he was convicted of incitement to genocide and crimes against humanity (persecution) on grounds of superior responsibility. Nor did he mention that he likely would have been convicted of the other crimes if those had been charged under a theory of superior responsibility (and not merely pursuant to direct personal responsibility under Article 6(1) of the ICTR Statute).

Nonetheless, this text is replete with denials and blame shifting. In it, as well, Nahimana declared that those who think RTLM was part of the extremist Hutu blueprint for Tutsi genocide merely spew "unfounded accusations" and have "manifestly twisted the truth".[116] He even went so far as to assert that his atrocity convictions were owing to a frame-up by Reporters without Borders media expert Hervé Deguine, who brought RTLM's genocidal broadcasts to international attention during the 1994 Tutsi massacres. According to Nahimana:

> In fact, the names "*Radio Hate*" and "*Radio Télé La Mort [Tele-Death] (RTLM)*" are the invention of the association

---

[115] *Ibid.*, pp. 18–19, emphasis in the original and author's translation from French.

[116] *Ibid.*, p. 19, referring to "accusations si infondées" and saying that anyone who believes this have "manifestement tordu la verité" (author's translation from French).

> Reporters Sans Frontières (RSF) (Reporters without Borders). It coined these names after July 1994, publicized them and found support for them from certain Rwandan journalists who were looking for work, money and name-recognition as well as through Jean Baptiste Nkuliyingoma, the Minister of Information of the RPF's first government during this month of July 1994. Hervé Deguine of RSF coordinated this propaganda campaign. He received money from RSF to put together a collection of commissioned fabrications and publish them under the title *Rwanda : les médias du genocide* [*Rwanda: The Media of Genocide*]. He personally organized the witch-hunt and verbal and written attacks against me; he caused me to be arrested; he caused me to be convicted.[117]

Nahimana's bald-faced rejection of his own guilt in this tract has been featured elsewhere. Also easy to find on the Internet is Jean-Baptiste Nkuliyingoma's commentary, which observes that Nahimana's online invective adopts "a clearly visible strategy to exculpate himself of all the crimes for which he was found guilty by the ICTR, both at the Trial Chamber and Appeals Chamber levels".[118] Despite being easily accessible via a very simple Google search, Judge Meron's Early Release Decision made no reference to Nahimana's egregious demonstration of denial.

26.4.1.2.3. Acknowledging Unfounded Claims of Ill Health and Offering Insufficient Grounds for Granting the Application

Even worse, Meron implicitly acknowledged the falsity of Nahimana's bad health claims. As a result, having already pointed out the Hutu propagandist's tremendous responsibility as a key architect of the Rwandan Genocide, and acknowledged that early release is an eligibility *privilege*, not a guarantee, Meron merely parroted the words of Malian prison officials regarding Nahimana's docile prison demeanour. In effect, he ignored a memorandum submitted by the Prosecutor, which referenced Nahimana's lack of co-operation and equated the RTLM founder with low-level convicts who co-operated and/or admitted their guilt. Thus, early release was to be granted, even though Nahimana had demonstrated not a shred of remorse and arguably fabricated claims of ill-health. Meron merely alluded to Na-

---

[117] *Ibid.*, p. 23 (author's translation from French).

[118] Jean-Baptiste Nkuliyingoma, "The Book *Inkundura*: Can Ferdinand Nahimana Be Both Judge and Jury?", in *La Tribune Franco-Rwandaise*, 19 February 2012 (available on its web site) (author's translation from French).

himana's having arrived at the two-thirds mark of his sentence and having shown "some signs of rehabilitation" (although Meron never indicated specifically what they were).

26.4.1.2.4. A Lack of Legal Support for the Two-Thirds Rule

Moreover, what is the legal support for eligibility for early release at the two-thirds mark in the first place? As it turns out, there is no statutory support for it.[119] It was simply a practice adopted by the judges at the *ad hoc* tribunal for the former Yugoslavia. However, the ICTR had a different practice from the ICTY. In contrast to the ICTY, the ICTR used a three-quarters standard.[120] The greater severity of the crimes before the ICTR, which arose within the context of a widespread and systematic genocidal campaign where approximately 800,000 were murdered in approximately three months, accounted for the policy divergence between the two tribunals.[121]

Further, as noted by Jonathan Choi, this early release practice runs against the policy aims of the ad hoc tribunal framers as it confuses parole with commutation:

> The ICTY seems to have implemented early release policies that are significantly more generous than its framers intended. It has adopted something like a *presumption* that prisoners need only serve two thirds of their sentences, apparently out of confusion between commutation and parole [...] However, it is important to note at this point that the Statute only contemplates the convicted person's eligibility for pardon or commutation of sentence, *not* for parole. This is a crucial distinction because, as we will see, domestic actors grant commutation much less often than they do parole. The plain language of the Statutes suggests that their framers intended early release to be similarly rare.[122]

So, if the early release policy is problematic in the first place, it is exacerbated at the ICTY, where a two-thirds standard was applied. How is it, then, that the two-thirds standard was transposed to ICTR convicts at the

---

[119] Jonathan H. Choi, "Early Release in International Criminal Law", in *The Yale Law Journal*, vol. 123, no. 6, 2014, pp. 1792–1793.

[120] *Ibid.*, p. 1793.

[121] *Ibid.*

[122] *Ibid.*, pp. 1793–1794, emphasis added.

MICT? The answer is simple: Judge Theodor Meron. In the 2012 *Besingimana* early release decision, as President of the MICT, he simply made a unilateral decision to apply the two-thirds rule to Rwandan genocidaires.[123] In his words:

> While I acknowledge that adoption of the two-thirds eligibility threshold might constitute a benefit not previously recognised for persons convicted by the ICTR, I do not consider that this can justify discriminating between the different groups of convicted persons falling under the jurisdiction of the Mechanism.[124]

26.4.2. Failure to Comply with Principles of Integrity

26.4.2.1. On a Judicial Level – the Appearance of Lack of Impartiality and/or Bias

The shortcomings of the early release ruling are put into a clearer perspective when one considers the deontological normative framework surrounding it. Does the relevant law on judicial ethics support placing Judge Meron in the position of being the sole decision-maker? A review of the law reveals a negative answer to this question.

Although the Charter of the International Military Tribunal at Nuremberg did not address the qualifications of judges and prohibited any challenges to the composition of the bench, the statutes and rules of modern international criminal tribunals subject judges to principles of ethical conduct.[125] Among these, to safeguard defendants' rights and uphold institutional credibility, all such modern tribunals mandate that judges be independent and impartial.[126]

The MICT is no exception. Per MICT RPE Rule 18(A): "A Judge may not sit in any case in which the Judge has a personal interest or concerning which the Judge has or has had any association which might affect his impartiality. The Judge shall in any such circumstance withdraw, and

---

[123] Bisengimana Early Release Decision, paras. 20–21, see above note 88.

[124] *Ibid.*, para. 21.

[125] Milan Markovic, "International Criminal Trials and the Disqualification of Judges on the Basis of Nationality", in *Washington University Global Studies Law Review*, 2014, vol. 13, no. 1, p. 2.

[126] *Ibid.* See, for example, International Criminal Court, Code of Judicial Ethics, 9 March 2005, Res. ICC-BD/02-01-05, Articles 3, 4 (http://www.legal-tools.org/doc/383f8f/).

the President shall assign another Judge to the case".[127] Here, as Meron was President at the time of the *Nahimana* Early Release Decision, Rule 18 also provides the most senior judge would appoint a new judge to the case.[128]

In the *Nahimana* matter, Rule 18(A) clearly suggests excluding Meron as the decision-maker in reference to the early release application. Meron had a "previous association with the case" as an appellate judge on Nahimana's merits adjudication, and he had an "association that might affect his impartiality" given that he dissented as to one of the key bases of conviction that was upheld and he explicitly called for a reduction of the defendant's sentence.

Complementing Rule 18(A), the related Rule 18(D) provides that "[n]o Judge shall sit on any appeal in a case in which that Judge sat in first instance".[129] Although this rule is not exactly on point here (as the early release application was not technically an "appeal"), in conjunction with Rule 18(A), Meron's service on the merits appeal panel and then in the follow-up early release application capacity also militates in favour of exclusion for the latter.

These points are underscored by the MICT's "Code of Professional Conduct for the Judges of the Mechanism" (MICT Judicial Conduct Code), which had been adopted in 2015 and was in place when Judge Meron ruled on Nahimana's early release application. The Preamble of the Code explicitly recognizes that the "impartiality of judges is fundamental to ensuring public confidence in a fair and transparent international judicial process".[130] In addition, Article 3(1) of the Code mandates that "Judges shall be impartial and ensure the appearance of impartiality in the discharge of their judicial functions".[131]

This is in line with national judicial ethics rules. For example, on lack of impartiality grounds, the American Bar Association Model Code of 1Judicial Conduct, Rule 2.11(A)(6)(d) requires disqualification of a judge who has "previously presided as a judge over the matter in another

---

[127] MICT RPE, Rule 18(A), see above note 69.

[128] *Ibid.*

[129] *Ibid.*

[130] Mechanism for International Criminal Tribunals, Code of Professional Conduct for the Judges of the Mechanism, 11 May 2015, MICT/14/Art. 3 ('MICT Judicial Conduct Code') (http://www.legal-tools.org/doc/23cc92/) (current code date is 9 April 2018; language on this article has not changed).

[131] *Ibid.*, Article 3.

court".[132] Similarly, pursuant to Canon 3(C)(1)(e) of the Code of Conduct for United States Judges,

> A judge shall disqualify himself or herself in a proceeding in which the judge's impartiality might reasonably be questioned, including but not limited to instances in which [...] (e) the judge has [...] participated as a judge (in a previous judicial position) concerning the proceeding or has expressed an opinion concerning the merits of the particular case in controversy.[133]

Civil law jurisdictions adopt a comparable deontological stance. Mali, for instance, whose legal system is rooted in French law,[134] deals with a lack of judicial impartiality in Articles 15 and 16 of its Code of Ethics for Magistrates. Article 15 "is comparable to that of [ABA] Model Rule 2.11",[135] which, as we have just seen, mandates disqualification of a magistrate who has previously served as a judicial officer over the same matter in another tribunal.

Even if the rules were not so specific, the spirit of general judicial ethical standards would strongly suggest excluding Judge Meron from being the sole adjudicator in reference to Nahimana's early release application. The portions of the MICT Judicial Conduct Code referred to above demonstrate this. And *ad hoc* tribunal jurisprudence is consistent. Thus, in

---

[132] American Bar Association, Model Code of Judicial Conduct, Rule 2.11(A)(6)(d).

[133] Code of Conduct for United States Judges, 12 March 2019, Canon 3(C)(1)(e) ('Code of Conduct'). Although the Code of Conduct was created to govern the lower courts, for the US Supreme Court, "the Code remains the starting point and key source of guidance for the Justices", John G. Roberts Jr., 2011 Year-End Report on the Federal Judiciary, THIRD BRANCH (Admin. Office of the US Courts), December 2011, pp. 3–5. Similarly, Congress's enactment of 28 U.S.C. § 455 directing recusal circumstances for federal judges has been used as a standard by the Justices, *ibid.* at 7-9, as noted in recent recusals by Associate Justice Neil Gorsuch in US SC, *Royal v. Murphy*, 2018 (a case denied an *en banc* hearing during Gorsuch's tenure on the appeals court); and Associate Justice Brett Kavanaugh, who has recused himself from three cases for the 2018-2019 term: *Jam v. International Finance Corporation*, *Lorenzo v. Securities and Exchange Commission*, and *Azar v. Allina Health Services* (Kavanaugh served on the DC Circuit three-judge panel in two of these cases and participated in an *en banc* order for the third).

[134] Nicolas Boring, "Malian Rules of Judicial Ethics: A Comparative Study", in *United States Library of Congress*, September 2014 ("The Malian judicial system, like that of other former French colonies such as Côte d'Ivoire, Senegal, Burkina Faso, and Benin, is strongly based on France's legal traditions").

[135] *Ibid.* Mali, Loi No. 02-054 du 16 décembre 2002 portant statut de la magistrature (Law No. 02-054 of December 16, 2002 on the Status of Judges), 31 December 2002, Articles 15, 16.

Prosecutor v. Furundžija, an ICTY Appeals Chamber held that "a Judge should not only be subjectively free from bias, but also that there should be nothing in the surrounding circumstances which objectively gives rise to an appearance of bias".[136] Once again, notwithstanding Meron's stated disagreement regarding the disposition of Nahimana's Media Case merits conviction and sentence, which clearly shows subjective bias, his service on the merits appeals panel, apart from the dissent, arguably gives rise to an appearance of bias from an objective perspective.

26.4.2.2. On a Systemic Level – the Appearance of Lack of Due Process and Fairness

As we have seen, Judge Meron's handling of the *Nahimana* early release application raised questions of integrity in reference to his personal approach in ruling on the matter. But the way the application was treated also raises integrity concerns from a systemic perspective. In other words, it is generally considered that a judge's ethical duty encompasses the fair administration of justice, implicitly assuring that due process to all parties is afforded. As noted by Alfred and Bruce Gitelson, "[p]rocedural due process is not merely for the parties but, additionally, for the court itself".[137] As a result, judges have an affirmative duty "to do justice by rendering to every [person her] due under the same law, equally, fairly".[138]

The MICT RPE hints at this ethical obligation in Rule 17, which requires judges, upon investiture, to make a solemn declaration promising to perform their duties "honourably, faithfully, impartially and conscientiously".[139] The MICT Judicial Conduct Code, which again, was in place at the time of Meron's ruling on the *Nahimana* early release application, is even more specific. Rule 4.1 of the code declares that "Judges shall conduct themselves with probity and integrity in accordance with their judicial office, thereby enhancing public confidence in the judiciary".[140]

---

[136] International Criminal Tribunal for the former Yugoslavia , Prosecutor v. Furundžija, Appeals Chamber, Judgement, 21 July 2000, IT-95-17/1-A, para. 189 (http://www.legal-tools.org/doc/660d3f/).

[137] Alfred and Bruce Gitelson, "A Trial Judge's Credo Must Include His Affirmative Duty to be an Instrumentality of Justice", in *Santa Clara Lawyer*, 1966, vol. 7, no. 1, p. 24.

[138] *Ibid.*, p. 7.

[139] MICT RPE, Rule 17, see above note 69.

[140] MICT Judicial Conduct Code, Article 4, see above note 130.

National deontological codes are even more specific. For example, per Canon 3(A)(4) of the Code of Conduct for United States Judges, "[a] judge should accord to every person who has a legal interest in a proceeding [...] the full right to be heard according to law".[141] In the case of the *Nahimana* early release application, this might have included the prosecution and victims, among others.

Similar ethical mandates are enshrined internationally, as seen in the 2002 UN-sponsored "Bangalore Principles of Judicial Conduct", which were the product of a conference held in the presence of a UN special rapporteur and the Consultative Committee of European Judges.[142] That model code combines the overlapping ethical principles of both common law and civil law judicial cultures. Notably, Principle 5 declares that "[e]nsuring equality of treatment to all before the courts is essential to the due performance of the judicial office".[143] Principle 5.3 then specifies that "[a] judge shall carry out judicial duties with appropriate consideration for *all persons*, such as the parties, witnesses, lawyers".[144] Besides, according to Principle 6.5, "[a] judge shall perform all judicial duties [...] fairly".[145]

26.4.3. The Integrity Deficits Placed in Perspective: The Residual Special Court for Sierra Leone

The problems highlighted above in connection with Judge Meron's treatment of the *Nahimana* early release application stand in stark relief when compared to the deontological and normative protocols of a sister mechanism – the Residual Special Court for Sierra Leone ('RSCSL'). In particular, the RSCSL RPE contain a dedicated section covering "Pardon, Commutation of Sentence and Early Release" that includes carefully crafted rules requiring consultation with the Prosecution (representing the interests of victims and witnesses) and also with judges who imposed the sentence.[146] In particular, RSCSL RPE Rule 124 provides:

---

[141] Code of Conduct, Canon 3(A)(4), see above note 133.

[142] Eric J. Maitrepierre, "Ethics, Deontology, Discipline of Judges and Prosecutors in France", Resource Materials Series No. 80, p. 266.

[143] Judicial Group on Strengthening Judicial Integrity, *The Bangalore Principles of Judicial Conduct*, 2002, Principle 5.

[144] *Ibid.*, Principle 5.3 (emphasis added).

[145] *Ibid.*, Principle 6.5.

[146] Residual Special Court for Sierra Leone, Rules of Procedure and Evidence, 2 December 2017, Part IX, Rules 123, 124 ('RSCSL RPE') (http://www.legal-tools.org/doc/76a01e/).

There shall only be pardon, commutation of sentence or early release if the President of the Residual Special Court, in accordance with Article 24 of the RSCSL Statute and in consultation with the Judges who imposed the sentence where possible, and after considering the position of the Prosecutor, which shall incorporate the interests of Prosecution witnesses and victims, as well as the convicted person individually or through counsel, so decides on the basis of the interests of justice and the general principles of law.[147]

These protocols are bolstered by the Practice Directions on the Conditional Early Release of Persons Convicted by the Special Court for Sierra Leone assigning to the Registrar, in connection with handling convicted prisoners, specific and extensive information-gathering and reporting tasks (Directions 4-7), decision-making procedures (Direction 8), prisoner agreement requirements (Direction 10), monitoring mechanisms (Direction 11), and consequences for violations of the prisoner agreements (Direction 12).[148] Direction 9(C) deals with the imposition of conditions for early release. Annex C of the Practice Directions contains a long list of general conditions found in an Early Release Agreement template appended to the back of the Practice Directions. Those conditions include, among others, not committing new offenses, not possessing firearms, not inciting crimes, and not engaging in violent behaviour.[149]

The early release decision in the case of *Prosecutor v. Moinina Fofana*, whose defendant was a senior leader of the Kamajors militia and Civil Defence Forces in the Sierra Leone Civil War, demonstrates strict compliance with these protocols. Fofana, who had been convicted for crimes against humanity and sentenced to 15 years, was granted early conditional release with certain restrictive stipulations spelled out quite clearly. Those included: (1) completion of a behavioural training rehabilitation program; (2) not approaching and/or intimidating relevant witnesses; (3) not engaging in secret meetings intended to plan civil unrest or join local politics; (4) strictly observing reporting schedules set by a designated local Monitoring Authority and the Registrar; (5) personally reporting to special-

---

[147] *Ibid.*, Rule 124.

[148] Residual Special Court for Sierra Leone, Practice Directions on the Conditional Early Release of Persons Convicted by the Special Court for Sierra Leone, 1 October 2013 ("SCSL Practice Directions') (http://www.legal-tools.org/doc/0260c4/).

[149] *Ibid.*

ly-designated reporting centres, at least twice every month; and (6) accepting regular visits made by the office of the Registrar to provide assurance of security to such vulnerable former witnesses as may desire it.[150]

26.4.4. Summary of Integrity Deficits in the *Nahimana* Early Release Decision

A review of the record and decision in the *Nahimana* application for early release raises serious questions about whether the relevant proceedings adhered to either the letter or spirit of the well-established principles just considered. The reasons for this are legion: (1) a unilateral, lone-judge decision-making process; (2) the judge ruling on the early release application after having been a member of the merits appeals panel; (3) that judge, at the merits stage, having dissented for policy reasons on the legal grounds for the conviction and the appropriateness of the punishment; (4) an arbitrarily-imposed two-thirds-mark release eligibility policy imposed previously by that same judge with no chance to have it vetted or litigated; (5) no independent office or agency, such as a 'Prisoner Release Analysis Unit', capable of thoroughly reviewing the record and all other relevant materials, conducting appropriate research and providing insights to the decision-maker in advance of a decision on the merits; (6) the absence of a hearing where prosecutors, victims and/or other witnesses could be heard; (7) failure to impose conditions for early release premised on meeting certain key benchmarks, such as expression of remorse, assurances of refraining from speaking in public to defend past criminal conduct or to justify new ethnic animosity; (8) the absence of any monitoring authority in the release jurisdiction to ensure compliance with the conditions; (9) a heavily redacted written decision on early release; and (10) the lack of a mechanism to allow for review of the early release decision.

26.5. Recommended Reforms

So, in light of all the issues highlighted in this chapter, how can we reform the system to avoid the problematic process and outcome seen in the *Nahimana* case, as well as ensure adherence to principles of integrity in future post-conviction proceedings? Here, the recommendations are related to

---

[150] Residual Special Court for Sierra Leone, *Prosecutor v. Moinina Fofana*, Public Decision of the President on Application for Conditional Early Release, 11 August 2014, SCSL-2004-14 (http://www.legal-tools.org/doc/1027ef/).

both deontology and system coherence or fairness (which also has deontological implications).

26.5.1. Providing for Broader Deontological Coverage Within the Existing MICT Governing Documents

Although, as we have seen, the MICT RPE and Code of Judicial Conduct contain some guidance regarding the deontological duties of its magistrates, this is not sufficiently systemic or rigorous. For instance, while the Code of Judicial Conduct deals with impartiality, it is only in very general terms. The MICT RPE is more specific and bars judges from presiding over matters when having any association that might affect impartiality or sitting on an appeal where having previously sat in first instance. Nevertheless, that document does not address the precise situation of the judge who previously presided over the same matter in another court.

Moreover, the current RPE does not generally ensure that important instances of adjudication, such as ruling on early release applications, generate sufficient judicial consensus via, at a minimum, three-judge panels (as opposed to a single judge sitting alone). Nor does the RPE provide for the bare due process guarantee of participation of all relevant stakeholders in such proceedings or the opportunity for appeal (which, we have seen, has adjudicator-ethics implications). These issues need to be fixed in both the RPE and perhaps in the MICT Statute and the Code of Judicial Conduct itself.

26.5.2. Fixing Early Release Decision Protocols and Procedure

The problems outlined above in respect of the Nahimana early release decision suggest the fixes necessary to make the system work properly. Those will be considered in turn below.

26.5.2.1. Return to the Three-Quarters Early Release Eligibility Standard

As we have seen, as a threshold matter, it is not clear whether there is bona fide legal support for eligibility for early release in the first place.

Switching back to a three-quarters standard for ICTR convicts would be an important first step. However, given that we are also dealing with mass atrocity crimes in respect of ICTY convicts too, perhaps the three-quarters standard should be applied to them as well.

26.5.2.2. Establishment of a Prisoner Release Analysis Unit

At the domestic level, penal systems contemplating early release of convicts routinely employ agencies to analyse the propriety and/or advisability
of the release. For example, in many United States jurisdictions, it is typical for a 'Parole Board' (established to analyse suitability for 'parole', a
type of early release on conditions of rehabilitation and community safety)
to employ experts who create a 'Parole Eligibility Report'. That document
informs the decision-maker of whether there is "a reasonable assurance,
after consideration of all of the facts and circumstances, including the prisoner's mental and social attitude, that the prisoner will not become a men-
ace to society or to the public safety".[151]

Similarly, in France, early release may be effectuated via "*la libération conditionnelle*" (conditional liberation.[152] In order to decide whether a
prisoner is eligible for conditional liberation, a *Comité Consultatif de
Libération Conditionnelle* (Consultative Committee for Conditional Liberation) prepares a report as to the suitability for conditional liberation of
eligible prisoners, and this report guides the judge in making decisions.[153]

Instituting a 'Prisoner Release Analysis Unit' at the MICT would be
another key recommendation for reforming the early release decision procedural regime. The unit would be staffed by persons with expertise in various aspects of law enforcement, especially those related to corrections,
including psychology, social work and criminal justice.[154] As in domestic
jurisdictions, they would prepare a report for the relevant members of the
MICT judiciary to make informed and sound decisions regarding the early
release of ICTR and ICTY convicts.

---

[151] Michigan Department of Corrections, "The Parole Process" (available on its web site).

[152] France, Code de procédure pénale (Code of Criminal Procedure), 2 March 1959, Articles
729–733 ('French Code of Criminal Procedure') (https://legal-tools.org/doc/388101). See
also Christopher L. Blakesley, "Conditional Liberation (Parole) in France", in *Louisiana
Law Review*, 1978, vol. 30, no. 1, pp. 2–3.

[153] French Code of Criminal Procedure, Article 730, see above note 152; Blakesley, pp. 39–40,
see above note 152.

[154] Radek Gadek, "Federal Probation Officer Career, Job Description & Salary Info", *Criminal
Justice Online Blog*, 31 January 2019 (available on its web site) (describing qualifications of
personnel in comparable positions, in particular, US Probation Officers).

26.5.2.3. Hearing for All Relevant Stakeholders

As highlighted previously, the *Nahimana* early release decision was made without an opportunity for all relevant stakeholders to be heard. For purposes of ensuring due process and fairness to all concerned parties, such a hearing is routine in domestic jurisdictions. In the United States, for instance, pursuant to Section 2967.19(F) of the Ohio Revised Code: "The court shall not grant [a Petition for Early Release] to an offender without holding a hearing".[155] Further, under subsection (H) of that provision:

> If the court schedules a hearing under this section, at the hearing, the court shall afford the offender and the offender's attorney an opportunity to present written information and, if present, oral information relevant to the offender's early release. *The court shall afford a similar opportunity to the prosecuting attorney, victim or victim's representative*, as defined in section 2930.01 of the Revised Code, *and any other person the court determines is likely to present additional relevant information.*[156]

Similarly, in France, there is a hearing on applications for conditional liberation where, in addition to the prisoner, the prosecution and victims can be heard.[157] For convicts sentenced to more than ten years, that hearing is held before the *Tribunal d'Application des Peines* (for lesser sentences, before the *Juge d'Application des Peines*).[158]

It is submitted that a comparable hearing in connection with applications for early release before the MICT would go a long way toward compensating for the current regime's due process deficits. In particular, it would crucially invest the procedure with greater institutional integrity (with corresponding deontological benefits).

26.5.2.4. Imposing Conditions if Early Release Is Granted

Penal regimes that incorporate the early release option always do so premised on sufficient evidence of the prisoner's satisfying certain basic conditions both prior to and after release (for the latter, based on the probabilities in light of the evidence). In his article "The Innocent Prisoner's Dilemma:

---

[155] Ohio Revised Code, 22 March 2019, Title 29, Section 2967.19(F).

[156] *Ibid.*, Section 2967.19(H) (emphasis added).

[157] British Embassy Paris, *Information Pack for British Prisoners in France*, British Embassy Paris, 30 June 2014.

[158] *Ibid.*

Consequences of Failing to Admit Guilt at Parole Hearings", Daniel Medwed provides a helpful list of these, which includes expressions of remorse, the likelihood of recidivism by the inmate, public safety, behaviour during incarceration, institutional record, the nature of the crime and criminal history, and evidence of rehabilitation.[159]

One could easily imagine similar conditions being imposed in respect of granting early release to ICTR or ICTY convicts at the MICT. In addition to the criteria enumerated by Daniel Medwed, MICT conditions could also take into account securing promises from the prisoner that have relevance in the mass atrocity context, such as refraining from speaking in public to defend past criminal conduct or spur a fresh outbreak of ethnic animosity. These could be incorporated explicitly into the MICT Practice Directions.

Indeed, only recently, the MICT has begun to impose such conditions. In January 2019, Rwandan genocidaire Aloys Simba was the first ICTR or ICTY convict to be released early under certain defined conditions.[160] Among others, he was asked to pledge not to "interfere in any way with the proceedings of MICT, or administration of justice"; to "conduct himself honorably and peacefully [...] and not to engage in secret meetings intended to plan civil unrest or any political activities"; and not to "discuss [his] case, including any aspect of the 1994 genocide against the Tutsi in Rwanda with anyone [...] nor make any statements denying the 1994 genocide".[161] What is more, as demonstrated above, releasing convicts early under quite restrictive conditions has also been a feature of the Special Court for Sierra Leone.[162]

---

[159] Daniel Medwed, "The Innocent Prisoner's Dilemma: Consequences of Failing to Admit Guilt at Parole Hearings", in *Iowa Law Review*, 2008, vol. 93, pp. 493, 510, 511.

[160] Hola, 5 July 2019, see *supra* note 6. Simba, a retired lieutenant colonel and former member of parliament who had directed militias in the massacre of Tutsis in Gikongoro, had been convicted by the ICTR of genocide and crimes against humanity (persecution) and sentenced to twenty-five years imprisonment. See ICTR, *The Prosecutor v. Aloys Simba*, Trial Chamber I, Judgement and Sentence, 13 December 2005, ICTR-01-76, (http://www.legal-tools.org/doc/373ff0/).

[161] Hola, 5 July 2019, see above note 6.

[162] *Ibid.*

26.5.2.5. Establishing a Monitoring Authority to Ensure Compliance with Release Conditions

Imposing conditions for early release is meaningless if a prisoner's post-release compliance with those conditions cannot be monitored. Thus, it follows that a local monitoring authority must be put in place. The Residual Special Court for Sierra Leone has such a mechanism. It would appear to consist of an agreement with local authorities in the community where the prisoner is released to supervise compliance with the release conditions.[163] At the MICT, as at the RSCSL, this would operate under the supervision of the Registrar.[164]

26.5.2.6. Unredacted Decisions and Appellate Review

Finally, as suggested above, for purposes of increasing transparency and fairness, written decisions in respect of early release applications at the MICT should be unredacted so that all of the judicial reasoning can be considered by the parties and the public. Related to this, to the extent that the reasoning is found wanting, the parties before the MICT in such matters should have the right to appeal. Clearly, the soundness of Meron's decision can be called into question here but it is difficult to know all of his points of consideration given the prominent portions of the decision that are blacked out. What is worse, quite unfortunately in light of its very poor quality, that decision cannot be appealed.

Unredacted written decisions and the right of review are common features in early release procedural regimes. Incorporating them into the MICT framework would, therefore, be consistent with best practices and in furtherance of promoting integrity in international criminal law post-conviction proceedings.[165]

26.6. Conclusion

'Integrity', the subject of this volume, has two distinct meanings. On the one hand, according to the Cambridge Dictionary, it refers to "the quality

---

[163] Residual Special Court for Sierra Leone, Practice Direction on the Early Release of Persons Convicted by the Special Court for Sierra Leone, 1 October 2013, Annex C (http://www.legal-tools.org/doc/0260c4/).

[164] *Ibid.*

[165] See, for example, California Department of Corrections and Rehabilitation, "Life Parole Process" (available on its web site).

of being honest and having strong moral principles [and standards]".[166] At the same time, it encompasses the notion of "wholeness and unity". Our examination here of integrity in post-conviction proceedings in international criminal law has implicated both of these definitions.

Certainly, much of the analysis in this chapter has focused on the deontological deficits in the *Nahimana* Early Release Decision. The anaemic nature of the MICT's governing documents insofar as judicial ethics are concerned, the fact that a judge who had sat on the merits appeals panel, and explicitly expressed dissatisfaction with the grounds for conviction and the extent of punishment, then served as the lone decision-maker for an application for early release, and the subsequent poorly reasoned and internally incoherent decision itself – all these factors raise serious questions about the judge's compliance with standard canons of professional responsibility, particularly lack of impartiality and/or existence of bias. Thus, the first aspect of 'integrity' has featured prominently in these pages.

Nevertheless, that other dimension of 'integrity', to wit, wholeness, cohesion, coherence (which as explained by Alfred and Bruce Gitelson, has deontological implications)[167] has also come into play. One must surely call into question whether the early release decision-making regime at the MICT reflects a holistic vision of the overall procedural scheme. In the first place, only a rather myopic view of the *ad hoc* tribunal or MICT procedural landscape would ignore the distinct possibility that a judge from the ICTY or the ICTR might sit as a decision-maker in respect of an early release application at the MICT. After all, the MICT judicial roster is nothing short of an honour roll of emeritus *ad hoc* tribunal magistrates. 'Integrity', in this context, would undoubtedly include a provision in the MICT Statute excluding the decision-maker from presiding over the early release decision if he or she participated in making the *ad hoc* merits decision. This is doubly true if he or she took issue with the grounds for conviction and/or the extent of punishment.

As well, 'integrity' in terms of wholeness or coherence comes into play when the gravity of prisoners' crimes vis-à-vis one another is ignored and the voices of important stakeholders, most prominently victims, are entirely excluded. Similarly, the absence of an unredacted written opinion supporting the early release decision, as well as the right of appeal for

---

[166] Cambridge Dictionary, "Integrity" (available on its web site).

[167] Gitelson and Gitelson, 1966, p. 24, see above note 137.

those parties, including the prosecution, whose interests are affected by that decision, betrays a substantial lack of inclusive perspective.

This chapter has explained how these deontological and tunnel-vision problems can be remedied. Beefing up the imperatives in the existing MICT Code of Judicial Conduct, the RPE and the Statute regarding impartiality, bias, and prior service in the same matter would go a long way toward ensuring that the *Nahimana* early release decision problems do not replicate themselves going forward. At the same time, returning to the three-quarters early release policy for ICTR convicts, expanding the scope of process to include a prisoner release analysis unit, requiring submission of a report featuring that unit's analysis, identifying a local monitoring mechanism to ensure compliance with conditions, and mandating a balanced or participatory briefing regime or court hearing, transparent written decisions and a right of appeal could remedy the structural integrity issues.

Unfortunately, in many ways, it is too late for meaningful change in respect of ICTR defendants. As reported by Barbara Hola:

> Between 1998 and 2015, the ICTR convicted 59 former governmental and public officials, military, militiamen, journalists, clergy and businessmen for their involvement in the genocide of Rwanda's Tutsis. By now […] twenty-one have been set free from prisons in West Africa and Europe. Only five served their whole sentences.[168]

That said, important ICTR defendants are still incarcerated and reforming the early release regime may yet have a significant impact. Most prominently, using the two-thirds rule, Théoneste Bagosora, the chief architect of the Rwandan Genocide, often referred to as 'Rwanda's Himmler', is now eligible for early release.[169] It is a given that he will file an early re-

---

[168] Hola, 5 July 2019, see above note 6. As Hola notes, "[t]he proportion of those who were granted early release before serving their full sentence is even higher at the ICTY. Out of 59 individuals who are by now out of prison, 55 (93%) have been released early by the Yugoslav Tribunal". *Ibid.*

[169] McGreal, 18 December 2008, see above note 16. As McGreal notes:

> You might call him the Heinrich Himmler of Rwanda. Theoneste Bagosora was less grand than the Nazi SS leader, eschewing pitch-black uniforms and grand military parades, but he espoused an ideology as hateful and ultimately as deadly as the man who oversaw the Holocaust. And he was just as organised […] Bagosora was at the centre of what the prosecution called 'preparing the apocalypse'.

> Bagosora was originally sentenced to life in prison but the sentence was reduced on appeal to 35 years. See "Rwanda Genocide: Bagosora's Life Sentence Reduced", *BBC News*,

lease application, and so the clock is ticking. A lack of ethical and procedural integrity has already resulted in the unjust early release of the
'Rwandan Goebbels'; it is hoped that an integrity course correction will
mean a different result for the 'Rwandan Himmler'.

---

14 December 2011 (available on its web site). Using the two-thirds formula, he is eligible
for early release beginning in July 2019. Hola, 5 July 2019, see above note 6.

PART VI:
INDEPENDENCE AND INTEGRITY

Judicial Independence and Accountability at International Criminal Courts and Tribunals

Ivana Hrdličková and Adrian M. Plevin[*]

27.1. Introduction

The legal profession has existed for over two thousand years. From the Greek city-states and the Roman Empire to the present day, lawyers have actively executed a vital role in the formulation and application of the law.[1] Because of this role and the nature of their duties and obligations to their clients, lawyers are subjected to a higher standard of conduct than most citizens in terms of personal integrity, professional conduct and ethics. Yet the role of the judge is separate and apart from that of others in the legal profession. Judges occupy the most prestigious role in the profession, holding positions of authority which presuppose respect for the highest standards of personal and moral responsibility. As a result, judges are expected

---

[*] Judge **Ivana Hrdličková** holds a Ph.D. from Charles University. She is the President of the Special Tribunal for Lebanon ('STL'). She began her career as a Judge in the Czech Republic in 1990 and has presided over both civil and criminal cases. Since 2008, Judge Hrdličková also acts as a legal expert of the Council of Europe. She participated in a number of international legal and judicial projects, such as the Euro-Mediterranean efforts to increase judicial co-operation between the Mediterranean-European Development Agreement countries. **Adrian Plevin** obtained his LL.M degree from Leiden University. He is a Legal Officer in the Office of the President and Appeals Chamber of the STL. He began his career in domestic civil and criminal litigation practice, serving as a member of the Human Rights Committee of the Law Society of South Australia. He has since held positions in the Appeals Chamber and Office of the President of the United Nations International Criminal Tribunal for the former Yugoslavia ('ICTY'). The authors are indebted to Nicolas Guillou, Cécile Ouba and Helen Brown for their comments and contributions to earlier iterations of this chapter. Any errors or inaccuracies remain the authors' alone. The opinions, views, conclusions and recommendations contained in this chapter are expressed by the authors in their private capacity and do not necessarily reflect those of any respective national judiciary, the STL or ICTY, nor can be attributed to those entities and institutions, nor the United Nations in general.

[1] See, for example, Anton Hermann Chroust, "Legal Profession in Ancient Athens", in *Notre Dame Law Review*, 1954, vol. 29, no. 4, pp. 339–389; Anton Hermann Chroust, "Legal Profession in Ancient Imperial Rome", in *Notre Dame Law Review*, 1955, vol. 30, no. 4, pp. 521–616; Edward M. Harris and Lene Rubinstein (eds.), *Law and the Courts in Ancient Greece*, Duckworth, London, 2004.

to adhere to even stricter standards than other lawyers. These factors are equally true of the international judge.[2]

Being an international judge entails occupying an office that society views with prestige and vests with substantial power afforded only to a select few. At the same time, it presumes that the office-holder will embody the highest standards of personal and professional moral conduct. For many, being an international judge is more than a job; it is a calling and the culmination of many years of experience in the profession. In this context, it bears recalling the words of the American philanthropist J.D. Rockefeller Jr., that "every right implies a responsibility; every opportunity, an obligation; every possession, a duty". It is precisely because of the powers given to international judges that it is crucial to ensure their responsibility and accountability.

The accountability of judges entails, *stricto sensu*, an expectation of transparent and well-reasoned decisions and judgments delivered in accordance with the law. In most jurisdictions, this is ensured through the principle of open justice and by subjecting the vast majority of judicial decisions to the possibility of appeal.[3] But judicial accountability is not limited to procedural remedies for litigants. It also entails accountability of the judicial milieu: the responsibility of individual judges and judicial institutions to perform their functions for the ultimate benefit of the communities they serve, and the specific responsibility to account for the use of public resources and expenditure of public finances. To adopt the words of Chief Justice Tom Bathurst of the New South Wales Supreme Court:

> The courts receive funds from the public purse. To my mind that carries with it an obligation of accountability, not only to deliver quality judgments, but to be able to demonstrate that money is being spent efficiently. Accountability promotes good decision-making and ensures that the power of courts to spend money is not uncontrolled.[4]

Bathurst distinguishes (legitimate) transparency and accountability from (illegitimate) executive interference in the judicial branch. In this chapter, we explore how the regulation of duties, obligations and responsi-

---

[2] See Daniel Terris *et al.*, *The International Judge: An Introduction to the Men and Women Who Decide the World's Cases*, Brandies University Press, Waltham, 2007.

[3] See Tom Bathurst, "Separation of Powers: Reality or Desirable Fiction?", Judicial Conference of Australia Colloquium, Sydney, 11 October 2013, para. 21.

[4] *Ibid.*, para. 22.

bilities of judges is achieved legitimately without compromising the cornerstone of any successful criminal justice system: the independence of the judiciary. The chapter proceeds on the premise that guaranteeing judicial independence is an essential means for ensuring fair, independent and impartial trials in any successful justice system, international courts and criminal tribunals being no exception.[5] More specifically, we examine the concept of judicial accountability and explore possible future means of ensuring that the balance between independence and accountability at international criminal tribunals continues to promote universal values that underpin international justice and the rule of law. In so doing, we affirm the view that judicial accountability should not be considered a threat to legitimate judicial independence, but rather promoted as a means of strengthening and protecting it.

Amidst current concerns that multilateralism is under growing pressure, which may increase the scrutiny of international courts,[6] this anthology and the joint research project by the Centre for International Law and Research Policy ('CILRAP') and the International Nuremberg Principles Academy (the 'Integrity Project') presents a welcome forum for exploring the relationship between the integrity of international courts and the independence and accountability of international judges. Thus, the focus of this chapter is an exploration of the relationship between judicial independence and accountability, and the importance of its institutionalization for international criminal courts and tribunals. As one of the core aims of the Integrity Project is to explore 'integrity' in the context of international justice, we deal with the former component first, examining the relationship between integrity and accountability, before addressing the correlation between judicial accountability and judicial independence.

We then turn to the latter, and explore the progressive development of both international standards and the regulation of judicial accountability

---

[5] See, for example, Theodor Meron, "Judicial Independence and Impartiality in International Criminal Tribunals", in *American Journal of International Law*, 2005, vol. 99, no. 2, p. 359. Throughout this chapter, the term 'international judges' is used in a general sense to denote judges holding office at international courts and tribunals, irrespective of their status as national judges or international judges in the case of hybrid criminal tribunals such as the Special Tribunal for Lebanon ('STL') or Extraordinary Chambers in the Courts of Cambodia ('ECCC').

[6] Morten Bergsmo, "Revisiting Integrity in International Justice", FICHL Policy Brief Series No. 93 (2018), Torkel Opsahl Academic EPublisher, Brussels, 2018, p. 1 (https://www.toaep.org/pbs-pdf/93-bergsmo/).

at international courts and tribunals. In response to some of the core questions arising from the Integrity Project, relating to measures available to States and institutions moving forward, we examine the recommendation arising from the Paris Declaration on the Effectiveness of International Criminal Justice, regarding the establishment of a common disciplinary mechanism for all international criminal tribunals.[7]

27.2. The Integrity-Accountability Paradigm

The integrity of a society's judiciary is essential to ensuring public confidence in judicial proceedings and key to ensuring the legitimacy and functionality of a given judicial system. Integrity is essential for ensuring societies can trust in their judges and judicial institutions, and indeed, is essential to the rule of law itself. So critical is the concept of confidence in the judiciary that it pressed French novelist and playwright, Honoré de Balzac, to implore that "to distrust the judiciary marks the beginning of the end of society. Smash the present patterns of the institution, rebuild it on a different basis [...] but don't stop believing in it".[8]

The word 'integrity' itself is derived from the French term '*intégrité*', meaning innocence, blamelessness and purity; and evolved from the Latin, '*integer*', meaning whole or complete.[9] It is the quality of being honest and having strong moral principles, and refers to a personal choice to hold oneself to consistent and noble standards (that is, ethics).[10] This definition suffices when conceptualizing integrity as applied to the individual judge.

---

[7] Representatives of International Courts and Tribunals, *Paris Declaration on the Effectiveness of International Criminal Justice*, 16 October 2017 ('Paris Declaration') (https://www.legal-tools.org/doc/ow1amx/).

[8] Honoré de Balzac, quoted in Otto Kirchheimer, *Political Justice: The Use of Legal Procedure for Political Ends*, Princeton University Press, Princeton, 1961, p. 175. See Arthur Selwyn Miller, "Public Confidence in the Judiciary: Some Notes and Reflections", in *Law and Contemporary Problems*, 1970, vol. 35, no. 1, p. 69.

[9] Bergsmo, 2018, p. 2, see above note 6.

[10] On the interplay between law, morality, and ethics, see, for example, Peter Michael Stephen Hacker and Joseph Raz, *Law, Morality, and Society: Essays in Honour of H.L.A. Hart*, Clarendon Press, Oxford 1977; H.L.A. Hart, *Law, Liberty, and Morality*, Stanford University Press, Stanford, 1963; Jocelyn M. Pollock-Byrne and Jocelyn M. Pollock, *Ethics in Crime and Justice: Dilemmas and Decisions*, Brooks/Cole, Pacific Grove, 1989; Roscoe Pound, "Law and Morals–Jurisprudence and Ethics", in *North Carolina Law Review*, 1945, vol. 23, no. 4, pp. 185–222; Joseph Raz, *Ethics in the Public Domain*, Clarendon Press, Oxford, 1994.

But what about when we speak of the intrinsically related yet separate notion of integrity of judicial institutions? Here, integrity often demands the adherence of individuals within a judicial system to a firm moral
code. But it also requires the application of rules or principles, by which
judicial institutions are governed, rather than the application of some common denominator of conduct of judicial office-holders. In this sense, the
strongest judicial institutions are those which are comprised of members
who uphold high standards of personal integrity and who are governed
equally by defined principles that permit institutional integrity to also
flourish. This notion was recognized in the preamble of the Bologna and
Milan Global Code of Judicial Ethics 2015, adopted at the International
Conference of Judicial Independence, which proclaims that:

> Public confidence in the judicial system and in the moral au-
> thority and integrity of the judiciary is of the utmost im-
> portance in a modern democratic society and it is essential that
> judges, individually and collectively, respect and honour judi-
> cial office as a public trust and strive to enhance and maintain
> confidence in the judicial system.[11]

Maintaining public confidence in the integrity of the judiciary thus
requires not only the identification of applicable ethical and professional
standards, but the application and enforcement of them. Accountability,
therefore, serves as both a means of ensuring personal integrity of individual judges and as a method of assuring institutional integrity.

In the context of international criminal courts and tribunals, this institutional integrity is crucial to ensuring that international criminal justice
remains credible. Credibility does not demand that these courts and tribunals strive for judicial outcomes that satisfy the interests of their myriad
stakeholders – such as prosecutors and defence counsel, victims of crimes,
accused persons, the legal community, civil society, or the States that provide the funding and diplomatic support necessary for these institutions to
function. Rather, credibility requires that stakeholders can be confident that
the exercise of judicial powers at these international bodies is professional,
ethical and motivated only by the fair interpretation and application of the
law, irrespective of the outcome of individual decisions.

---

[11] Bologna and Milan Global Code of Judicial Ethics, June 2015, Preamble ('Global Code of
Judicial Ethics') (https://www.legal-tools.org/doc/cq44mw/). See Bangalore Principles of
Judicial Conduct ('Bangalore Principles'), 25–26 November 2002, Preamble
(https://www.legal-tools.org/doc/xwake8/).

Stated alternatively, in order to ensure their integrity, international criminal courts and tribunals must strive to achieve two aims. The first is related to the composition of the judiciaries of these institutions. They must be comprised of professional, capable judges, possessing the highest possible moral standards. This is commensurate with the practice of appointing judges to international criminal courts and tribunals that have been carefully selected to be persons of high moral character, impartiality and integrity,[12] and who possess, depending on the jurisdiction, "the qualifications required in their respective states for appointment to the highest judicial offices",[13] "experience",[14] "extensive judicial experience",[15] or experience

---

[12] The Republic of Kosovo, Law on Specialist Chambers and Specialist Prosecutor's Office ('KSCSPO'), 3 August 2015, 05/L-053, Article 27(1) ('Law on KSCSPO') (https://www.legal-tools.org/doc/8b71c3/); International Residual Mechanism for Criminal Tribunals ('IRMCT'), Statute of the International Residual Mechanism for Criminal Tribunals, 22 December 2010, Article 9(1) ('IRMCT Statute') (http://www.legal-tools.org/doc/30782d/); International Criminal Tribunal for Rwanda ('ICTR'), Statute of the International Criminal Tribunal for Rwanda [as amended], 8 November 1994, Article 12 ('ICTR Statute') (http://www.legal-tools.org/doc/8732d6/); ICTY, Updated Statute of the International Criminal Tribunal for the former Yugoslavia, 25 May 1993, Article 13 ('ICTY Statute') (http://www.legal-tools.org/doc/b4f63b/); Agreement between the United Nations and the Lebanese Republic on the establishment of a Special Tribunal for Lebanon ('STL Agreement') (https://www.legal-tools.org/doc/e1635d/), Attachment: Statute of the Special Tribunal for Lebanon, 30 May 2007, Article 9(1) ('STL Statute') (http://www.legal-tools.org/doc/da0bbb/); Cambodia, Law on the Establishment of Extraordinary Chambers in the Courts of Cambodia for the Prosecution of Crimes Committed during the period of Democratic Kampuchea (as amended), 27 October 2004, Article 10 new ('Law on ECCC') (http://www.legal-tools.org/doc/9b12f0/); Agreement between the United Nations and the Government of Sierra Leone on the Establishment of a Special Court for Sierra Leone, 12 April 2002 ('SCSL Agreement') (http://www.legal-tools.org/doc/797850/), Attachment 1: Statute of the Special Court for Sierra Leone, Article 13(1) ('SCSL Statute') (http://www.legal-tools.org/doc/aa0e20/); Agreement between the United Nations and the Government of Sierra Leone on the Establishment of a Residual Special Court for Sierra Leone('RSCSL'), 11 August 2010 ('RSCSL Agreement'), Attachment: Statute of the Residual Special Court for Sierra Leone, Article 11(2) ('RSCSL Statute') (http://www.legal-tools.org/doc/4768bc/); Rome Statute of the International Criminal Court ('ICC'), 17 July 1998, Article 36.3(a) ('ICC Statute') (http://www.legal-tools.org/doc/7b9af9/).

[13] ICC Statute, Article 36.3(a), see above note 12; see *ibid.*, Article 36.3(b); Law on KSCSPO, Article 27(1), see above note 12.

[14] Cf. IRMCT Statute, Article 9(1), see above note 12; ICTR Statute, Article 12, see above note 12; ICTY Statute, Article 9, see above note 12; SCSL Statute, Article 13(2), see above note 12.

[15] STL Statute, Article 9(1), see above note 12.

in criminal law, including international law and human rights.[16] Naturally
then, there is a legitimate expectation[17] – albeit an unwritten one – that
such highly-qualified judges will comply with equally high standards of
professionalism and conduct, in order to give effect to the very principles
of judicial independence that underpin universal values relating to fair and
independent trials.[18] As will be seen below, the relationship between integrity and accountability is reflected in various international instruments,[19]
such as the United Nations ('UN') Basic Principles on the Independence of
the Judiciary,[20] which have been endorsed by the UN General Assembly as
setting out the core principles related to the functionality of judiciaries ca-

---

[16] Law on ECCC, Article 10 new, see above note 12; ICC Statute, Article 36.3(b), see above
note 12.

[17] This expectation is given credence through the strong presumption in favour of judges satisfying these requirements (of impartiality) recognized in the jurisprudence of international
criminal tribunals. See, for example, ICTR, *Nahimana v. The Prosecutor*, Bureau, Decision
on Request for Disqualification of Judge Pocar, 6 June 2012, ICTR-99-52B-R, para. 9
(http://www.legal-tools.org/doc/c4c5ef/); ICTY, *Prosecutor v. Furundžija*, Appeals Chamber,
Judgement, 21 July 2000, IT-95-17/1-A, para. 197 (http://www.legal-tools.org/doc/660d3f/);
ICTY, *Prosecutor v. Stanišić and Župljanin*, Appeals Chamber, Judgement, 30 June 2016,
IT-08-01-A, para. 44 (http://www.legal-tools.org/doc/e414f6/); STL, *In the matter of El
Sayed*, The President of the Tribunal, Decision on Mr. El Sayed's Motion for the Disqualification of Judge Chamseddine from the Appeals Chamber Pursuant to Rule 25, 5 November
2010, CH/PRES/2010/09, para. 17 (http://www.legal-tools.org/doc/fda41c/); and decisions
of the plenary of judges of the international criminal court see, for example, ICC, *Prosecutor
v. Nourain, Presidency*, Annex to the Notification of the Decision on the Defence Request
for the Disqualification of a Judge, 5 June 2012, ICC-02/05-03/09-344-Anx (http://www.
legal-tools.org/doc/a15116/).

[18] Expounding upon this view in the domestic context, Devlin and Dodek consider the accountability of judges as one of the essential components of ensuring effective judicial independence, together with selection criteria, the irremovability of judges, and the provision of
appropriate resources to the judiciary. Richard Devlin and Adam Dodek, "Regulating Judges:
Challenges, Controversies and Choices", in Richard Devlin and Adem Dodek (eds.), *Regulating Judges: Beyond Independence and Accountability*, Edward Elgar, Cheltenham, 2016,
pp. 5–11. But see Jeffrey L. Dunoff and Mark A. Pollack, "The Judicial Trilemma", in
American Journal of International Law, vol. 111, no. 2, April 2017, pp. 225–276, who view
independence and accountability, along with transparency, as the three core values giving
rise to an interlocking series of trade-offs. *Ibid.*, p. 225.

[19] Throughout this chapter, the terms 'international instruments' and 'international standards'
are used in a broad sense to denote instruments and standards adopted by States through the
UN General Assembly ('UNGA'), by international organizations, such as the UN Economic
and Social Council ('ECOSOC'), and through civil society organizations and initiatives. See
section 27.4. below.

[20] UN, Basic Principles on the Independence of the Judiciary, 13 December ('UN Basic Principles') (https://www.legal-tools.org/doc/rnabsy/).

---

pable of implementation across all the world's diverse legal systems and cultures.[21] The Bangalore Principles, for example, describe 'integrity' as an essential principle to the proper discharge of the judicial office, and emphasize that a judge shall "ensure that his or her conduct is above reproach in the view of a reasonable observer".[22] They also state that "[t]he behavior and conduct of a judge must reaffirm the people's faith in the integrity of the judiciary".[23] The international standards examined in this chapter show that this expectation is typically envisaged through the regulation of judges through the prescription of standards of professional conduct, on the one hand, and the existence of disciplinary mechanisms, on the other.[24]

This leads us to conclude that the second aim for international courts and tribunals, in order to ensure their integrity, is to strive for transparent regulatory frameworks capable of ensuring professional and ethical conduct standards are consistently observed, applied and enforced. It is not surprising, then, that the exploration of "individual awareness and integrity as professionalism" and "institutional integrity measures available to international courts" are two of the key foci of the Integrity Project.[25] Cumulatively, these aims form a vital part of efforts to ensure a robust and transparent system of international criminal justice, comprised of effective and efficient bodies, capable of optimizing the resources provided to them in pursuing justice for international(ized) crimes and protecting the fundamental rights of accused persons and the interests of victims.

27.3. Judicial Independence and Accountability

American statesman, and one of the founding fathers of the United States, Alexander Hamilton, famously defended the role of the independent judiciary in his essay, *Federalist No. 78*, declaring:

> Whoever attentively considers the different departments of power must perceive, that, in a government in which they are separated from each other, the Judiciary, from the nature of its

---

[21] UNGA, Seventh United Nations Congress on the Prevention of Crime and the Treatment of Offenders, UN Doc. A/RES/40/32, 29 November 1985 (https://www.legal-tools.org/doc/qwiloh/); UN General Assembly, Human Rights in the Administration of Justice, UN Doc. A/RES/40/146, 13 December 1985 (https://www.legal-tools.org/doc/qwiloh/).

[22] Bangalore Principles, Article 3, see above note 11.

[23] *Ibid.*, Article 3.2.

[24] See sections 27.4. and 27.5. below.

[25] Bergsmo, 2018, pp. 2–3, see above note 6.

---

functions, will always be the least dangerous to the political
rights of the Constitution, because it will be least in a capacity
to annoy and injure them. The Executive not only dispenses
the honors, but holds the sword of the community. The legislature not only commands the purse, but prescribes the rules by
which the duties and rights of every citizen are to be regulated.
The Judiciary, on the contrary, has no influence over either the
sword or the purse, no direction either of the strength or of the
wealth of the society, and can take no active resolution whatever. It may truly be said to have neither force nor will, but
merely judgment, and must ultimately depend upon the aid of
the executive arm even for the efficacy of its judgments.[26]

The pursuit and defence of an independent judiciary in line with this
theory of separation of powers has long since been replicated across the
globe. The principle of judicial independence – entailing respect towards
the judiciary and its fundamental functions, and its freedom from encroachment from the legislative and executive arms of government – is
now deeply rooted in many contemporary legal systems and cultures.
While the concept of executive and legislative 'arms of government' does
not transpose so neatly to the international arena,[27] we can still view the
separation of the judicial powers from the influence of political pressures
as a cornerstone of independent, impartial and fair international criminal
trials.

At the domestic level, this separation of power serves both the citizens of the State, and the judges. Externally, it promotes the interests and
legitimacy of the State on the international plane. Internally, and if it works
effectively, it promotes a functional judicial system. While the concept of
judicial independence has spread almost universally, including to international courts and tribunals, it is frequently prone to misinterpretation, misunderstanding and confusion, including amongst members of the judiciary.
Indeed, the principle of judicial independence is prone to frequent over-

---

[26] Alexander Hamilton, *The Federalist Papers No. 78: The Judiciary Department* (available on
the web site of the Congress of the United States of America).

[27] Ernst-Ulrich Petersmann, "How to Constitutionalize International Law and Foreign Policy
for the Benefit of Civil Society", in *Michigan Journal of International Law*, 1998, vol. 20,
no. 1, p. 13; cf. Dapo Akande, "The International Court of Justice and the Security Council:
Is There Room for Judicial Control of Decisions of the Political Organs of the United Nations", in *International and Comparative Law Quarterly*, 1997, vol. 46, no. 2, p. 309–343;
Stefan Talmon, "The Security Council as World Legislature", in *The American Journal of
International Law*, 2005, vol. 99, no. 1, pp. 175–193.

statement, especially in the context of conditions of judicial service or funding of the court system.[28] In reality, judicial independence is intended to protect the justice system as a whole, the rule of law and public trust in the judiciary. As former Australian Chief Justice Gerard Brennan declared, "independence does not exist to serve the judiciary; nor to serve the interests of the other two branches of government. It exists to serve and protect not the governors but the governed".[29] Indeed, Hamilton himself emphasized that judges should only hold office "during good behaviour".[30]

In this manner, the defence of judicial independence at international criminal courts and tribunals serves to protect the *judicial functions* of the judge from external influence. In order to perform their duties, judges must be free from external influence – not only from the executive and legislative 'arms of government', but also from other portions of society: the corporate sector, businesses, individuals and the media. Fairness and impartiality demand not that judges be shielded from criticism or accountability, but that they are free from fear of any retaliation when performing judicial functions. Judges must be free to decide cases solely on the basis of the evidence before them and in accordance with the law, and protected from the threat of reprisals for the decisions they make. The appearance of this judicial independence is just as important as the existence of it – as stated in the well-quoted maxim of former Lord Chief Justice of England, Gordon Hewart, that "[i]t is of fundamental importance that justice should not only be done, but should manifestly and undoubtedly be seen to be done".[31]

Judges decide cases between individuals and, not only in the criminal domain, between individuals and the State. In the international sphere, their role can extend to adjudicating disputes between States themselves and, in international criminal law, between individuals and prosecutors of institutions created as, or by, multilateral organizations representing the societal interests of numerous States or the international community as a whole. Thus, in order to ensure public confidence that cases are decided impartial-

---

[28] Murray Gleeson, "The Role of the Judge and Becoming a Judge", National Judicial Orientation Programme, Sydney, 16 August 1998.

[29] Gerard Brennan, "Judicial Independence", Australian Judicial Conference, Australian National University, Canberra, 2 November 1996.

[30] Hamilton, 1999, pp. 463–471, see above note 26.

[31] England and Wales High Court (King's Bench Division), *R v. Sussex Justices, ex parte McCarthy*, Decision, 9 November 1923, [1924] 1 KB 256, p. 259. See Bangalore Principles, Article 32, see above note 11.

ly and fairly, the independence of international judges must be protected. In practice, this protection is granted by ensuring and promoting their independence; not to serve judges' own personal benefit, but to serve the interest of the international public and the various stakeholders of which it is comprised.[32] The discussion of promoting and protecting the independence of international criminal law judges in this chapter should be understood in this context.

Notwithstanding the universality of the underlying principles of judicial independence that exist, when it comes to promoting and protecting judicial independence of international judges, the systems at different international courts and tribunals are far from uniform.[33] Moreover, despite the inexorable correlation between independence and accountability of judges having been explored in-depth in relation to national judiciaries,[34]

---

[32] Cf. Brennan, 1996, see above note 29.

[33] See section 27.4 below.

[34] See, for example, Amy B. Atchison, *et al.*, "Judicial Independence and Judicial Accountability: A Selected Bibliography", in *Southern California Law Review*, 1998, vol. 72, no. 2–3, pp. 723–810; Paul D. Carrington, "Judicial Independence and Democratic Accountability in Highest State Courts", in *Law and Contemporary Problems*, 1998, vol. 61, no. 3, pp. 79–126; Francseco Contini and Richard Mohr, "Reconciling Independence and Accountability in Judicial Systems", in *Utrecht Law Review*, 2007, vol. 3, no. 2, pp. 26–43; Consultative Council of European Judges ('CCJE'), Opinion No. 1 on Standards concerning the Independence of the Judiciary and the Iremmovability of Judges, 23 November 2001 (http://www.legal-tools.org/doc/ca5224/); CCJE, Opinion No. 3 on the principles and rules governing judges' professional conduct, in particular ethics, incompatible behaviour and impartiality, 19 November 2002 (http://www.legal-tools.org/doc/81c8b5/); Devlin and Dodek, 2016, pp. 1–33, see above note 18; Nuno Garoupa and Tom Ginsburg, "Guarding the Guardians: Judicial Councils and Judicial Independence", in *The American Journal of Comparative Law*, 2009, vol. 57, no. 1, pp. 103–134; Charles H. Geyh, "Judicial Independence, Judicial Accountability, and the Role of Constitutional Norms in Congressional Regulation of the Courts", in *Indiana Law Journal*, 2003, vol. 78, no. 1, pp. 153–221; Hoong Phuon Lee (ed.), *Judiciaries in Comparative Perspective*, Cambridge University Press, 2011; Andrew Le Sueur, "Developing Mechanisms for Judicial Accountability in the UK", in *Legal Studies*, 2004, vol. 24, no. 1–2, pp. 73–98; Carlos Santiso, "Economic Reform and Judicial Governance in Brazil: Balancing Independence with Accountability", in *VII Congresso Internacional de CLAD sobre la Reforma del Estado y de la Administración Pública*, Panama, 28–31 October 2003, pp. 1–16; Shimon Shetreet, "Judicial Independence and Accountability in Israel", in *International and Criminal Law Quarterly*, 1984, vol. 33, no. 4, pp. 979–1012; Frances Kahn Zemans, "The Accountable Judge: Guardian of Judicial Independence", in *Southern California Law Review*, 1999, vol. 72, pp. 625–655. The authorities cited in this footnote, and footnotes 35 and 36 below, are not intended to represent exhaustive lists.

there is very little written on the issue as it relates to international judges.[35] There is less still in the context of international criminal courts and tribunals.[36] Mackenzie and Sands attribute this to the fact that independence is culture-specific and "it is less apparent what the meaning of independence and impartiality in the context of the international courts should be".[37] While that may be true in practice, in principle, the universality of the various international instruments regarding judicial independence belies this assessment or, at the very least, suggests that the reality is more nuanced.[38]

The Preamble to the UN Basic Principles, for example, recognizes that the independence of the judiciary is essential to fully realizing the right of every person to equality before the law, to the presumption of innocence and to a fair and public hearing by a competent, independent and impartial tribunal established by law. These rights are enshrined variously under the Universal Declaration of Human Rights,[39] the International Covenant on Civil and Political Rights[40] and, to a lesser extent, the International Covenant on Economic, Social and Cultural Rights.[41] But the UN Basic Principles also decree that it is a fundamental aspect of judicial accountability that judges may be subject to suspension or removal for misconduct or reasons of incapacity that render them unfit to discharge their duties.[42]

---

[35] See Dunoff and Polack, 2017, see above note 18; Kenneth J. Keith, "Challenges to the Independence of the International Judiciary", International Law Programme Speech Transcript, Chatham House, 26 November 2014; Kenneth J. Keith, "Challenges to the Independence of the International Judiciary: reflections on the International Court of Justice", in *Leiden Journal of International Law*, 2017, vol. 30, no. 1, pp. 153–154.

[36] See, for example, Michael G. Karnavas, "Judicial Ethics in the International Tribunals", drawn from Michael G. Karnavas's lecture at the ADC-ICTY Twelfth Defence Symposium, 24 January 2014, Paul Mahoney, "The International Judiciary – Independence and Accountability", in *The Law and Practice of International Courts and Tribunals*, 2008, vol. 7, pp. 313–349.

[37] R. Mackenzie and P. Sands, "International Courts and Tribunals and the Independence of the International Judge", in *Harvard International Law Journal*, 2003, vol. 44, pp. 271, 275.

[38] On the academic debate in this context, see Lorne Neudorf, *The Dynamics of Judicial Independence*, Springer, Cham, 2017, pp. 1–9.

[39] UN, Universal Declaration of Human Rights, UN Doc. A/RES/217(III) A, 10 December 1948, Article 10 (https://www.legal-tools.org/doc/085437/).

[40] UN, International Covenant on Civil and Political Rights, 23 March 1976, Articles 14, 26 (https://www.legal-tools.org/doc/2838f3/).

[41] International Covenant on Economic, Social and Cultural Rights, 3 January 1976, Preamble (https://www.legal-tools.org/doc/06b87e/).

[42] UN Basic Principles, Article 18, see above note 20. See also *ibid.*, Preamble.

Indeed, many of the international instruments on judicial independence enshrine similar principles. The Bangalore Principles, for example, recognizing that judicial independence is a "pre-requisite to the rule of law and a fundamental guarantee of a fair trial",[43] espouse the principle that judges must be "accountable for their conduct to appropriate institutions established to maintain judicial standards".[44] Likewise, the Commonwealth (Latimer House) Principles on the Three Branches of Government state unequivocally that the principles of judicial accountability and independence "underpin public confidence in the judicial system and the importance of the judiciary as one of the […] pillars upon which a responsible government relies".[45] These principles are considered in further detail in Section 27.4. below. The analysis therein suggests that the existence of disciplinary mechanisms, consistent with established standards of judicial conduct, are recognized internationally – if not universally – as fundamental to the independence of the judiciary and to the establishment of conditions under which justice can be pursued.

Accountability is all the more important in the international context, considering the effect of immunities which, both conceptually and in practice, afford wide latitude to protect international judges from criminal and civil suits. Contrary to some judicial systems at the national level, *all* international criminal tribunal judges are afforded immunities protecting them from criminal prosecutions and civil lawsuits.[46] Although this immunity can always be waived – usually by the authority responsible for judicial

---

[43] Bangalore Principles, Article 1, see above note 11.

[44] *Ibid.*, Preamble.

[45] Commonwealth Heads of Government, Commonwealth (Latimer House) Principles on the Three Branches of Government, November 2003, Article VII(b) ('Latimer House Principles') (https://www.legal-tools.org/doc/c502bd/).

[46] See, for example, Law on ECCC, Articles 41, 42 new, see above note 12; ICTY Statute, Article 30(2), see above note 12; ICTR Statute, Article 29(2), see above note 12; STL Agreement, Article 11, see above note 12; SCSL Agreement, Article 12(2), see above note 12. In the case of the KSCSPO, see Law on KSCSPO, Article 56.1, see above note 12 and Netherlands-Kosovo, Agreement between the Kingdom of the Netherlands and the Republic of Kosovo concerning the Hosting of the Kosovo Relocated Specialist Judicial Institution in the Netherlands, 15 February 2016, Article 19 ('KSCSPO Agreement') (https://www.legal-tools.org/doc/muyojl/). In respect of the RSCSL, see RSCSL Agreement, Article 10(1), see above note 12 and UNGA, Convention on the Privileges and Immunities of the United Nations, 13 February 1946, Section 20 ('Privileges and Immunities Convention') (http://www.legal-tools.org/doc/f68109/).

appointments[47] – it serves as a robust safeguard against attempts to destabilize judges when performing legitimate judicial functions. But the existence of such immunities and the infrequency of their wavier signals the need for efficient internal oversight mechanisms aimed at enforcing the ethical principles and conduct standards recognized in the various international declarations on the judiciary, judicial ethics, and judicial independence.

At the national level, the legitimacy and authority of the courts is tied to their independence.[48] In order to give effect to these fundamental principles on the international plane, the foundational texts of many international and regional judicial institutions recognize that judges may only be removed from office in the event of misconduct or incapacity, or when a judge ceases to fulfil the required conditions for their ongoing membership of a court or tribunal.[49] But in order to promote and protect judicial independence, mechanisms by which accountability can be ensured must be established. The function of these mechanisms is to ensure that complaints

---

[47] For most international criminal tribunals, this power lies with the UN Secretary-General. See STL Agreement, Article 11(2), see above note 12; Vienna Convention on Diplomatic Relations, 18 April 1961, Article 32 (http://www.legal-tools.org/doc/fda998/). In the case of the KSCSPO, the power appears to be vested with the President. See KSCSPO Agreement, Article 30, see above note 46, referring to Kosovo, Law No. 04/L-274, On the Ratification of the International Agreement between the Republic of Kosovo and the European Union on the European Rule of Law Mission in Kosovo, 23 April 2014, Article 1.2.3, in turn, referring to Kosovo, On the Status, Immunities and Privileges of Diplomatic and Consular Missions and Personnel in Republic of Kosovo and of the International Military Presence and Its Personnel, 20 February 2008, Article 7. In respect of the RSCSL, see RSCSL Agreement, Article 10(1), see above note 12, and Privileges and Immunities Convention, Section 20, see above note 46.

[48] Mackenzie and Sands, 2003, p. 275, see above note 37.

[49] See, for example, Council of Europe ('CoE'), European Convention on Human Rights, 4 November 1950, Article 23(4) (http://www.legal-tools.org/doc/8267cb/); Organization of American States (OAS) General Assembly, Statute of the Inter-American Court of Human Rights, 1 October 1979, Article 20(1) (https://www.legal-tools.org/doc/3eb97d/); ICC Statute, Article 46.1, see above note 12; UN, Statute of the United Nations Administrative Tribunal, 24 November 1949, Article 3(3) (https://www.legal-tools.org/doc/fwa4o9/); UN, Statute of the International Court of Justice, 18 April 1946, Article 18 (https://www.legal-tools.org/doc/fdd2d2/); UNGA, Administration of Justice at the United Nations, UN Doc. A/RES/63/253, 24 December 2008, Annex I, Article 4(10) and Annex II, Article 3(10) (https://www.legal-tools.org/doc/56xnx6/); International Tribunal on the Law of the Sea, Statute of the International Tribunal for the Law of the Sea (Annex VI of the United Nations Convention on the Law of the Sea), 10 December 1982, Article 9 (https://www.legal-tools.org/doc/zlbrua/).

can be raised against judges and that judges are answerable for their actions to an appropriate authority, in order to ensure that they comply with core ethical principles and standards of conduct. Indeed, we can say that there is a positive correlation between judicial accountability, on the one hand, and effective judicial independence, on the other. In this sense, judicial accountability is one among a number of key concepts central to promoting and protecting judicial independence. Other such concepts include the character requirements individuals must meet in order to be appointed to judicial office in the first place,[50] the requirement that the judiciary be supplied with appropriate resources to enable it to carry out its functions free from external interference, and the general irremovability of judges.[51]

Accountability serves as an agent of strengthening effective, independent judiciaries for at least two principal reasons:

1. First, effective regulation is essential to ensure that all users of the judicial system – including judges themselves – know what is expected of them, what they can do, and what they cannot do in the performance of their duties. While this may seem self-evident, the reality of hybridized international criminal justice is that what may be considered totally acceptable under the domestic legal tradition of one actor may be considered unethical or improper in another. Insofar as international criminal courts and tribunals are *sui generis*, the point must be made that the creation of these institutions did not in and of itself instil them with clear judicial ethical standards or professional conduct rules. All the while, the judges appointed to these tribunals come from disparate legal traditions, and no *sui generis* system of judicial ethics was likely to emerge in a regulatory vacuum organically. Regulation then serves, first and foremost, as a means of identifying – in a more concrete manner than the references in foundational texts to 'highest moral standards', 'impartiality' and 'integrity' – the professional and ethical conduct standards that judges are expected to uphold.

2. Second, any judiciary is ultimately an arm of government,[52] and judges ultimately perform a civil *service*, even if their independence makes

---

[50] See Silvia Fernández de Gurmendi, "Judges: Selection, Competence, Collegiality", in *American Journal of International Law Unbound*, 2018, vol. 112, pp. 163–167.

[51] See Devlin and Dodek, 2016, pp. 5–11, see above note 18.

[52] Bathurst, 1996, para. 3, see above note 3.

plain they are not civil *servants*.[53] It is a legitimate expectation of any society – including the international community – to know of the existence of rules defining acceptable conduct of judges and to be confident that systems are in place to provide effective remedies, in the event that standards of judicial conduct are not upheld, beyond esoteric processes designed *ad hoc* or occurring behind closed doors. When a judge fails to uphold the high standards expected of them, it should be clear to those outside of the judiciary that the judge will be held to account. Indeed, at the domestic level, the traditionally anti-reformist view that public confidence may be "undermined if every bit of dirty judicial laundry were aired in public",[54] have effectively been rebuked.

In concrete terms, then how can society know what to expect from judges and to what extent judges are really accountable? The codification of professional conduct and ethical standards represents the most obvious solution to inform the public, as well as other actors within the judiciary – including judges themselves – of what is expected, what is tolerated, and what is not. In the international judicial system, as in domestic systems, it has long been debated by judges whether the codification of professional and ethical standards is a necessity. Those against formal regulation argue that it is never possible – and potentially unwise to attempt – to determine all of ethical rules and behavioural standards applicable to judges in the abstract. As a consequence, it is argued that written codes can only ever be very generic. In truth, however, such limitations need not undermine the utility of codification. Understanding the boundaries of ethical and professional conduct of judges necessarily demands that consideration be given to a host of factors that influence the conduct of judges at the national level, including international norms, societal values, legal traditions, or even the extent to which religious morals permeate societal understandings of appropriate judicial conduct. Each of these factors contributes to the formulation of moral and ethical standards that affect the practice of law and the interactions of courts and society. Because of these disparate influences, even generic codes of conduct serve to provide beneficial guidance as to acceptable standards for judges within a specific legal system, to the judiciary and external actors alike. This utility is amplified in the international

---

[53] *Ibid.*, para. 16.

[54] Tim Dare, "Discipline and Modernize: Regulating New Zealand Judges", in Devlin and Dodek (eds.), *Regulating Judges: Beyond Independence and Accountability*, Edward Elgar, Cheltenham, 2016, pp. 293–312, 295.

field. Nonetheless, it is not remarkable to expect that, while still respecting international norms, it may be legitimate that the application of standards is tailored according to the culture and legal traditions reflected in each judicial system.

If it is accepted that the codification of ethical standards, despite the limitations described above, is a beneficial practice, another question arises: is it possible, or even necessary, to regulate the enforcement of these ethical rules? Many discussions have been conducted on how to enforce rules on judges' behaviour while at the same time guaranteeing that such mechanisms will not be used as tools of political will against judges whose rulings contradict the interests of the executive.[55] Almost thirty-five years after the adoption of the UN Basic Principles – and going on two-hundred more since Hamilton's essay – the balance between the courts and other branches of government continues to generate tension.[56] It is this continuing tension – an anticipated side-effect of the separation of judicial power from other arms of government – that is perhaps the strongest argument in favour of judiciaries taking the lead to ensure public confidence through transparent accountability mechanisms.[57] Procedures for investigating and, if necessary, disciplining judges, according to law, thus serve to protect the interests of the judiciary, executive and legislative authorities, and, most importantly, society at large.

27.4. International Standards Regulating the Accountability of Judges

27.4.1. Early Efforts to Regulate Judicial Accountability and Independence

In 1980, UN ECOSOC authorized the Sub-Commission on Prevention of Discrimination and Protection of Minorities ('ECOSOC Sub-Commission'), to appoint Laxmi Mall Singhvi as Special Rapporteur on the independence and impartiality of the judiciary, jurors and assessors, and the independence of lawyers.[58] In August of the following year, the Special Rapporteur submitted to the ECOSOC Sub-Commission draft principles on judicial independence that had been formulated by a Committee of Experts hosted by

---

[55] See, generally, Devlin and Dodek, 2016, see above note 18.

[56] See Bathurst, 1996, see above note 3.

[57] *Ibid.*

[58] ECOSOC, Draft Universal Declaration on the Independence of Justice, E/CN.4/Sub.2/1985/18/Add.5/Rev.1, 24 August 1987, p. 1 ('Singhvi Declaration') (https://www.legal-tools.org/doc/9pxw6x/).

the International Institute of Higher Studies in Criminal Sciences ('IIHSCS'),[59] in Syracuse, Italy ('Syracuse Principles').[60] The seven substantive chapters of the Syracuse Principles cover issues from the definition of independence of the judiciary; the qualification, selection and training of judges; posting, transfer and promotion of judges; retirement, discipline, removal and immunity; working conditions, administrative and financial arrangements; the role of the judiciary in a changing society; and the interrelation between judicial independence and the protection of human rights. Relevantly, the Syracuse Principles also provide for disciplinary proceedings to be conducted "before a court or board composed of and selected by members of the judiciary",[61] removal from office for criminal acts or "gross or repeated neglect or physical or mental incapacity",[62] disciplinary action based upon established standards of judicial conduct,[63] and the disqualification of judges in certain circumstances.[64]

The New Delhi Code of Minimum Standards of Judicial Independence, adopted by the International Bar Association in 1982 (also known as the 'IBA Minimum Standards'),[65] is largely analogous to the Syracuse Principles. In relation to the discipline and removal of judges, it deviates in providing that, unless a judge requests otherwise, disciplinary procedures should be held *in camera*,[66] that disciplinary tribunals under the authority of the legislature should be "predominantly" composed of members of the judiciary,[67] and in no uncertain terms, that "[t]he head of the court may legitimately have supervisory powers to control judges on administrative

---

[59] The Committee of Experts was organized jointly by the International Association of Penal Law, the International Commission of Jurists, and the Centre for the Independence of Judges and Lawyers.

[60] See International Institute of Higher Studies in Criminal Sciences ('IIHSCS'), "Draft Principles on the Independence of the Judiciary", in Reed Brody (ed.), *Centre for Independence of Judges and Lawyers*, No. 25–26, p. 59 (https://www.legal-tools.org/doc/p5qixp/).

[61] *Ibid.*, Article 13, see *ibid.*, Articles 14–15.

[62] *Ibid.*, Article 16.

[63] *Ibid.*, Article 14.

[64] *Ibid.*, Article 23.

[65] International Bar Association ('IBA'), "Minimum Standards of Judicial Independence", in Reed Brody (ed.), *Centre for Independence of Judges and Lawyers Bulletin*, No. 25–26, p. 105 ('New Delhi Code') (https://www.legal-tools.org/doc/p5qixp/).

[66] *Ibid.*, Article 28.

[67] *Ibid.*, Article 31.

---

matters".[68] The New Delhi Code also specified that, whether or not proceedings were *in camera* or public, judgments may be published.[69]

The following year saw the adoption of the Universal Declaration on the Independence of Justice at the First World Conference on the Independence of Justice in Montreal ('Montreal Declaration').[70] Uniquely, the Montreal Declaration was the first instrument to recognize the distinction between principles applicable to *national* and *international* judges, respectively. In respect of removal and discipline of judges, while the provisions relating to national judges develop upon the Syracuse Principles and New Delhi Code,[71] those relating to international judges are relatively barren, providing that judges can only be removed from office by other members of their court and in accordance with their Statutes.[72] Nominally rejecting the universality of the principles applicable to domestic judges to international judges, the Montreal Declaration also calls for the context-specific application of conduct rules to *ad hoc* judges and arbitrators.[73]

Although the Syracuse Principles, New Delhi Code and Montreal Declaration represent international civil society initiatives (albeit with the heavy involvement of judges from various legal systems), the ideas they espouse largely inspired other instruments that were created in a multilateral context in the years and decades that followed. Despite their nuances and the key differences described above, these early texts otherwise remain remarkably similar in scope and content. While in practical terms, this similarity might be attributable to the involvement of key individuals in their creation,[74] the very fact that the principles were adopted in a range of international fora speaks to their universal appeal.

---

[68] *Ibid.*, Article 32.

[69] *Ibid.*, Article 28.

[70] Universal Declaration on the Independence of Justice, 10 June 1983 ('Montreal Declaration') (https://www.legal-tools.org/doc/p6ek6z/).

[71] For example, by providing for the presumption of confidentiality of complaints at the initial stage, providing for the right of appeal, and providing protections for judges serving in courts that are abolished. Montreal Declaration, Articles 2.32, 2.37, 2.39, see above note 70.

[72] *Ibid.*, Articles 1.18–1.19.

[73] *Ibid.*, Article 1.20.

[74] See Neudorf, 2017, p. 4, see above note 38.

27.4.2. UN System: Towards Possible Universality

The early initiatives described above ultimately contributed to the adoption of the UN Basic Principles at the Seventh Congress on the Prevention of Crime and the Treatment of Offenders in Milan in 1985.[75] The latter represented the first inter-State effort related to the regulation of judges. The UN Basic Principles were soon endorsed by resolution of the UN General Assembly, which also encouraged their implementation.[76] Formulated to assist Member States to secure and promote the independence of their judiciaries,[77] according to the UN Basic Principles, the independence of the judiciary is an essential element of a functional judicial system which should "be guaranteed by the State and enshrined in the Constitution or law of the country".[78] But if the drafters intended to focus on shielding the judiciary from the interference of other arms of government,[79] they did not shy away from establishing internationally recognized standards related to the discipline, suspension and removal of judges from office, in a manner not dissimilar to the Syracuse Principles of four years prior.[80] Accordingly, the UN Basic Principles promote equitable adjudication of complaints against judges, for example: requiring that a complaint made against a judge in their judicial and professional capacity shall be processed expeditiously and fairly.[81] Clearly, however, the focus of the provisions relating to the discipline, suspension and removal of judges is on the protections afforded to judges against the risk of abuse of process through complaint procedures. Thus, the UN Basic Principles afford judges the right to a fair hearing,[82] and prescribe that they shall be subject to suspension or removal on one of two grounds only: "reasons of incapacity or behavior that renders them unfit to discharge their duties".[83] In addition, they provide that "[d]ecisions in disciplinary, suspension or removal proceedings should be subject to an

---

[75] UN Basic Principles, see above note 20; see Neudorf, 2017, p. 4, see above note 38.

[76] See above Section 27.2.

[77] UN Basic Principles, Preamble, see above note 20.

[78] *Ibid.*, Article 1.

[79] See, for example, *ibid.*, Articles 1–7 (Independence of the judiciary), 8–9 (Freedom of expression and association), 11–14, (Conditions of service and tenure), 15–16 (Professional secrecy and immunity).

[80] See *ibid.*, Articles 17–20.

[81] *Ibid.*, Article 17.

[82] *Ibid.*

[83] *Ibid.*, Article 18.

independent review",[84] though the commitment is watered down in the case of "decisions of the highest court and those of the legislature in impeachment or similar proceedings".[85] In this manner, the Principles unambiguously provide for the role of judicial complaints mechanisms but are cautious not to endorse procedures that might endanger the legitimate protections of the judiciary. This implicit recognition of the limits of the judicial functions and the balance between judicial freedoms and judicial accountability would go on to underpin the various international standards that were adopted subsequently.

Similar considerations are evident, for example, in the 1989 Singhvi Declaration, adopted by the ECOSOC Sub-Commission to assist States in the implementation of the UN Basic Principles.[86] As to the discipline and removal of judges, a number of principles in the Declaration are aimed at protecting judges from political interference. For example, the Declaration provides that even though the power to remove a judge may be vested in the legislature by impeachment or joint address, "proceedings for judicial removal or discipline when such are initiated shall be held before a Court or a Board predominantly composed of members of the judiciary",[87] though this is somewhat weaker than the protection envisaged in this regard by the Syracuse Principles. The Singhvi Declaration also affirms the rule that the removal of judges should be exceptional: "judges shall not be subject to removal except on proved grounds of incapacity or misbehavior rendering them unfit to continue in office".[88] As to the applicable procedure, the Declaration envisages that disciplinary or removal proceedings must be based upon established standards,[89] guarantee the judge fairness and the opportunity of a full hearing,[90] and, in going further than the New Delhi Standards, that judgements rendered in disciplinary proceedings against judges, whether *in camera* or public, *should* be published.[91]

---

[84] *Ibid.*, Article 20.
[85] *Ibid.*
[86] Singhvi Declaration, p. 1, see above note 58.
[87] *Ibid.*, Article 26(b).
[88] *Ibid.*, Article 30.
[89] *Ibid.*, Article 27.
[90] *Ibid.*, Article 28.
[91] *Ibid.*, Article 29.

27.4.3. Regional Initiatives

During the 1990s, a number of regional efforts also demonstrated the global reach of initiatives related to identifying judicial independence and accountability standards. In Europe, the Council of Europe ('CoE') adopted a recommendation on the independence, efficiency and role of judges.[92] The Recommendation called, *inter alia*, for States to consider establishing special competent bodies under the control of the judiciary for hearing disciplinary complaints, including for failures to carry out duties in an efficient manner, with full respect for the rights enshrined in the European Charter of Human Rights.[93] Later, in 1998, the CoE adopted the European Charter on the Statute of the Judge,[94] which, together with its explanatory memorandum, proclaims that "[j]udges have no monopoly over miscarriages of justice" and advocates the role of an independent body to refer complaints to an appropriate disciplinary body.[95]

The initiatives of LAWASIA, an advocacy group for the legal profession in the Asia-Pacific region, culminated in 1995, with the adoption of the LAWASIA Beijing Statement.[96] That document recognizes that, traditionally, some societies had functioned with disciplinary procedures under the ambit of the legislature, but that in others, this was not appropriate, and disciplinary procedures under the control of the judiciary should be favoured.[97] It also provides for many of the procedural protections espoused in earlier initiatives.[98]

Commonwealth nations, too, developed principles directed at the accountability of judges. The Latimer House Guidelines, adopted in 1998, were agreed by representatives of twenty Commonwealth nations.[99] The

---

[92] CoE Committee of Ministers, Recommendation No. R (94) 12 of the Committee of Ministers to Member States on the Independence, Efficiency and Role of Judges, 13 October 1994 (https://www.legal-tools.org/doc/d67e7z/).

[93] *Ibid.*, Principle VI(1)–(3).

[94] CoE, European Charter on the Statute for Judges and Explanatory Memorandum, 8–10 July 1998, DAJ/DOC (98) 23 (https://www.legal-tools.org/doc/gbx10x/).

[95] *Ibid.*, Explanatory Memorandum, para. 5.3.

[96] LAWASIA, Beijing Statement of Principles of the Independence of the Judiciary in the LAWASIA Region, 28 August 1997 (https://www.legal-tools.org/doc/y6gatr/).

[97] *Ibid.*, Articles 23–24.

[98] See, for example, *ibid.*, Articles 26–29.

[99] Commonwealth Heads of Government, Parliamentary Supremacy, Judicial Independence, Latimer House Guidelines for the Commonwealth, 19 June 1998 ('Latimer House Guidelines') (https://www.legal-tools.org/doc/c502bd/).

Guidelines concern the separation of powers and '*trias politica*' at the domestic level and, in relation to the judiciary, echoed the core recommendations of earlier documents, limiting the grounds for removal of judges,[100] recognizing the legitimate role of independent disciplinary tribunals and of the chief judge of the courts in disciplinary proceedings,[101] and also providing for the legitimate public criticism of judicial performance as a means of ensuring accountability.[102] Importantly, they also called for the adoption of codes of ethics to be developed and adopted by each judiciary as a means of ensuring accountability.[103] The Latimer House Guidelines were supplemented by the Latimer House Principles, adopted by the Commonwealth Heads of Government in 2003. The Latimer House Principles recognized that:

> Judges are accountable to the Constitution and to the law which they must apply honestly, independently and with integrity. The principles of judicial accountability and independence underpin public confidence in the judicial system and the importance of the judiciary as one of the three pillars upon which a responsible government relies.[104]

The Principles called for any disciplinary procedure to be "fairly and objectively administered", and prescribed that "proceedings which might lead to the removal of a judicial officer should include appropriate safeguards to ensure fairness".[105]

27.4.4. Judicial Regulation in the Twenty-First Century

Perhaps the most important international instrument regarding judicial accountability is the Bangalore Principles of Judicial Conduct.[106] Two reasons are noteworthy: the duration and breadth of consultations leading to its adoption – which involved judges from common law and civil law jurisdictions, as well as judges of the International Court of Justice and the UN Special Rapporteur on the Independence of Judges and Lawyers, Dato' Param Cumaraswamy – as well as the prescriptiveness and detail of the

---

[100] *Ibid.*, Articles VI(1)(a)(i).
[101] *Ibid.*, Articles VI(1)(a)(i)–(ii).
[102] *Ibid.*, Articles VI(1)(a)(iii).
[103] *Ibid.*, Articles V(1)(a).
[104] Latimer House Principles, Article VII(b), see above note 45.
[105] *Ibid.*
[106] Bangalore Principles, see above note 11.

provisions it contains defining acceptable judicial conduct. The Bangalore Principles establish standards structured around six core values: independence, impartiality, integrity, propriety, equality and finally, competence and diligence. Premised on the supposition that judges are accountable for their conduct to appropriate institutions established to maintain judicial standards,[107] the Bangalore Principles do not provide for common values regarding either the operation of accountability frameworks or disciplinary mechanisms. Not only did the Bangalore Principles break with the practice of prescribing requirements for an independent judiciary, but their close focus on the permissible conduct of judges represented the first internationalized attempt to define professional and ethical conduct standards for judges. The universality of these principles should not be understated. They are "seen more and more as a document which *all* judiciaries and legal systems can accept unreservedly".[108] Indeed, the UN Commission on Human Rights and ECOSOC each endorsed the Bangalore Principles in 2003 and 2006, respectively.[109]

The Bangalore Principles were followed, in 2010, by the Measures for the Effective Implementation of the Bangalore Principles of Judicial Conduct ('Implementation Measures'), designed "as guidelines or benchmarks for the effective implementation of the Bangalore Principles".[110] Divided into two parts, the Implementations Measures set out the responsibilities of both the judiciary and the State. With respect to the latter, the

---

[107] *Ibid.*, Preamble.

[108] UN Office on Drugs and Crime, *Commentary on the Bangalore Principles of Judicial Conduct*, 2007, p. 5 (emphasis added). Elsewhere, Appleby, Le Mire, Devlin, Dodek, Dare, and Cravens note the reluctance of common law jurisdictions (Australia, Canada, New Zealand, and the United States) to embrace judicial regulation. See Gabrielle Appleby and Suzanne Le Mire, "The Australian Judiciary: Resistant to Reform", in Devlin and Dodek, 2016, pp. 35–54, see above note 18; Sarah M.R. Cravens, "Regulating Judges in the United States: Concerns for Public Confidence", in Devlin and Dodek, 2016, pp. 390–407, see above note 18; Dare, 2016, pp. 295–296, see above note 54; Richard Devlin and Adam Dodek, "'Fighting Words': Regulating Judges in Canada", in Devlin and Dodek, 2016, pp. 76–104, see above note 18.

[109] UN Commission on Human Rights, Independence and Impartiality of the Judiciary, Jurors and Assessors and the Independence of Lawyers, 23 April 2003, p. 1 (https://www.legal-tools.org/doc/17afdm/); ECOSOC, Strengthening Basic Principles of Judicial Conduct, UN Doc. E/2006/INF/2/Add.1, 27 July 2006, para. 2 (https://www.legal-tools.org/doc/yiyqyy/).

[110] Measures for the Effective Implementation of the Bangalore Principles of Judicial Conduct (The Implementation Measures), 22 January 2010, p. 3.

Implementation Measures envisage disciplinary proceedings against judges
"only for serious misconduct",[111] and contend that:

> Conduct that gives rise to disciplinary sanctions must be dis-
> tinguished from a failure to observe professional standards.
> Professional standards represent best practice, which judges
> should aim to develop and towards which all judges should
> aspire. They should not be equated with conduct justifying
> disciplinary proceedings. However, the breach of professional
> standards may be of considerable relevance, where such
> breach is alleged to constitute conduct sufficient to justify and
> require disciplinary sanction.[112]

Additionally, the Implementation Measures propose the establishment of a body for receiving complaints and determining whether they
should then be referred to a specific body vested with the power to discipline judges that is "independent of the legislature and executive, composed of serving or retired judges but which may include in its membership
persons other than judges".[113] The latter body would conduct proceedings
in accordance with procedures guaranteeing the full rights of defence, including appeal.[114] It also recommends publication of the outcome of any
such disciplinary process involving the sanction against a judge.[115]

Directed exclusively at international judges, the 2010 Burgh House
Principles on the Independence of the International Judiciary recognize the
particular challenges facing the international judiciary in view of the non-
national context in which they operate,[116] that is, where the *trias politica*
lens – through which judicial independence is traditionally viewed – is not
directly applicable.[117] The Burgh House Principles attempt to set up a general framework for judicial misconduct, compelling each court to establish
rules of procedure to address specific complaints of misconduct or breach
of duty on the part of a judge that may affect independence or impartiali-

---

[111] *Ibid.*, Article 15.1.

[112] *Ibid.*, fn. 9.

[113] *Ibid.*, Articles 15.2–15.4.

[114] *Ibid.*, Articles 15.5–15.6.

[115] *Ibid.*, Article 15.7.

[116] Burgh House Principles on the Independence of the International Judiciary, August 2004
('Burgh House Principles') (https://www.legal-tools.org/doc/2cncgo/). See P. Sands *et al.*,
"The Burgh House Principles on the Independence of the International Judiciary", in Law
and Practice of International Courts and Tribunals, 2005, vol. 4, no. 2, pp. 247–260.

[117] See above note 27.

ty.[118] It also recommends that the governing instruments of the court shall provide for appropriate measures, including the removal from office of a judge,[119] and provides not for publication of disciplinary decisions, but communication of the outcome of any complaint to the complainant.[120] These principles also appear in the Mount Scopus International Standards of Judicial Independence, first adopted in 2008 and revised subsequently in 2011 and 2012.[121]

When compared to the earlier European instruments, the CCJE's Magna Carta of Judges, adopted in 2010, is more detailed with respect to judicial ethics and responsibilities, but less prescriptive in terms of the requirements of disciplinary mechanisms.[122] Perhaps its key contribution to regulation in this area is advocating for the creation of a Council for the Judiciary or like body, "itself independent from the legislative and executive powers, endowed with broad competences" for all matters relating to the status and organization of judges, that is, including disciplinary measures.[123] Notably, the Magna Carta of Judges is intended to "apply *mutatis mutandis* to judges of all European and international courts".[124]

In 2015, the Global Code of Judicial Ethics was adopted in an effort to clarify standards of ethical conduct for judges and "to afford the judiciary a framework for regulating judicial conduct".[125] Although its provisions with respect to national judges and concerning ethical standards for international judges are far more prescriptive than those in the instruments that preceded it, its provisions related to accountability mechanisms do not further build upon the Burgh House Principles and Mt Scopus Standards.[126]

---

[118] Burgh House Principles, Article 17.1, see above note 116.

[119] *Ibid.*, Article 17.3.

[120] *Ibid.*, Article 17.4.

[121] Mount Scopus Standards on the Independence of Judges, 19 March 2008, Articles 26.1–26.4 ('Mt. Scopus Standards') (https://www.legal-tools.org/doc/gciwle/).

[122] See CCJE, Magna Carta of Judges (Fundamental Principles), 19 November 2010, Articles 18–22 ('Magna Carta of Judges') (https://www.legal-tools.org/doc/r7r1c2/). These fundamental principles built upon earlier studies of the CCJE in relation to the independence of the judiciary. See CCJE, 2001, see above note 34; CCJE, 2002, see above note 34.

[123] Magna Carta of Judges, Article 13, see above note 122.

[124] *Ibid.*, Article 23.

[125] Global Code of Judicial Ethics, Preamble, see above note 11.

[126] *Ibid.*, p. 14.

Though the need for judicial disciplinary mechanisms is now stressed in the vast majority of international instruments related to judicial independence, there is not yet consensus in practice as to how disciplinary proceedings should be organized. While several of these instruments provide for safeguards to protect judges against the improper use of disciplinary procedures to remove judges from office, and substantial effort has been made to detail ethical and unethical professional conduct for international judges, it is far more difficult to discern universally applicable disciplinary procedures. This is true for key aspects, including who has the authority to trigger an investigation, the body responsible for conducting investigations in disciplinary proceedings, and the final arbiter tasked with determining if a breach of standard has occurred and, if so, the disciplinary sanction to be applied. Moreover, there is also no clear consensus on the type of sanctions that should be available. If removal is presented as the sanction of last resort in several international instruments, several other types of sanctions can be contemplated, such as reprimand, change of functions, or regression.

27.5. Regulating Judicial Conduct at International Criminal Courts and Tribunals

27.5.1. Litigation as a Means of Ensuring Accountability

The contemporary system of international criminal justice was born with the establishment of the International Criminal Tribunal for the former Yugoslavia ('ICTY') in 1993, which was followed soon after by the establishment of the International Criminal Tribunal for Rwanda ('ICTR') in 1994. Hybrids of civil and common law traditions though they were,[127] these *ad hoc* tribunals, and the later hybrid courts – the Extraordinary Chambers in the Courts of Cambodia ('ECCC'), the Special Court for Sierra Leone ('SCSL') and the Special Tribunal for Lebanon ('STL') – lacked any regulatory framework relating to standards of judicial conduct or oversight of the conduct of judges reminiscent of those that exist in national systems.

This did not mean, however, that there was *no* recourse when questions arose as to the professional standards to which the judges of these tribunals were to be held to account. Two such mechanisms existed:

---

[127] See, for example, Alphons A.A. Orie, "Accusatorial v. Inquisitorial Approach in International Criminal Proceedings Prior to the Establishment of the ICC and in Proceedings Before the ICC", in Antonio Cassese *et al.* (eds.), *The Rome Statute of the International Criminal Court: A Commentary*, vol. 2, Oxford University Press, 2002, pp. 1439–1495 (http://www.legal-tools.org/doc/01addc/).

1. The first was that available under Rule 15 of the ICTY Rules of Procedure and Evidence ('RPE'), which enabled a party to seek the disqualification of a judge where the judge has "a personal interest or concerning [...] or any association which might affect his or her impartiality".[128] Analogous provisions were incorporated into the rules of procedure and evidence of the ECCC,[129] the ICTR,[130] the SCSL,[131] and the STL,[132] as well as those of the International Criminal Court ('ICC'),[133] the Kosovo Specialist Chambers and Specialist Prosecutor's Office ('KSCSPO'),[134] the International Residual Mechanism for Criminal Tribunals ('IRMCT'),[135] and the Residual Special Court for Sierra Leone ('RSCSL').[136]

2. The second was by raising the issue through the course of litigation, as was done, for example, by appellant Esad Lanžo, who complained in arguments on appeal before the ICTY, that Judge Karibi-Whyte, the Presiding Judge at trial, "was asleep during substantial portions of the trial".[137]

The effectiveness of such mechanisms as a means for adjudicating judicial conduct or capacity, however, is questionable.[138] This is true *in ab-*

---

[128] ICTY, Rules of Procedure and Evidence, 8 July 2015, Rule 15 ('ICTY RPE') (http://www.legal-tools.org/doc/30df50/).

[129] ECCC, Internal Rules (Rev. 9), 16 January 2015, Rule 34 ('ECCC Internal Rules') (http://www.legal-tools.org/doc/b8838e/).

[130] ICTR, Rules of Procedure and Evidence, 13 May 2015, Rule 15 (http://www.legal-tools.org/doc/c6a7c6/).

[131] SCSL, Rules of Procedure and Evidence, 31 May 2012, Rule 15 (http://www.legal-tools.org/doc/4c2a6b/).

[132] STL, Rules of Procedure and Evidence, 10 April 2019, Rule 25 (https://www.legal-tools.org/doc/qop639/).

[133] ICC, Rules of Procedure and Evidence, 9 September 2002, Rule 43 ('ICC RPE') (http://www.legal-tools.org/doc/8bcf6f).

[134] KSCSPO, Rules of Procedure and Evidence before the Kosovo Specialist Chambers including Rules of Procedure for the Specialist Chamber of the Constitutional Court, 25 August 2017, Rule 20 (https://www.legal-tools.org/doc/opmwoy/).

[135] IRMCT, Rules of Procedure and Evidence, 18 December 2019, MICT/1/Rev.6, Rule 18 (https://www.legal-tools.org/doc/n7lau1/).

[136] RSCSL, Rules of Procedure and Evidence of the Residual Special Court for Sierra Leone (as revised), 6 November 2018, Rule 15 (http://www.legal-tools.org/doc/76a01e/).

[137] ICTY, *Prosecutor v. Delalić et al.*, Appeals Chamber, Judgement, 20 February 2001, IT-96-21-A, para. 620. ('Čelebići Case') (http://www.legal-tools.org/doc/051554/).

[138] See Sands *et al.*, 2005, p. 247, see above note 116.

stracto, as these procedures are only available to the litigating parties, and thus exclude any prospect of other persons raising complaints regarding judicial misconduct or incapacity.[139] It is also true *in concreto*. For example, while the ICTY Appeals Chamber found that Judge Karibi-Whyte's conduct "cannot be accepted as appropriate conduct for a judge",[140] there is no indication of whether any disciplinary action was taken against Karibi-Whyte. To the contrary, Landžo's Counsel was chastised for raising this "opportunistic" ground of appeal rather than addressing the issue during trial.[141] Indeed, according to the Appeals Chamber, the complaint of Karibi-Whyte's sleeping was only ever secondary to Counsel's primary motivation, namely complaining about Karibi-Whyte's "lack of judicial temperament, self-restraint and common decency",[142] which itself was neither raised before nor addressed by, the ICTY Appeals Chamber.

---

[139] But, as is inherently recognized in codes of conduct subsequently adopted by international courts and tribunals, it is not only in-court behaviour or judicial decision-making that ought to fall under the purview of regulated judicial conduct. See in this section below.

[140] Čelebići Case, Judgement, para. 629, see above note 137.

[141] *Ibid.*, para. 650. For criticisms, see, for example, Michael Bohlander, "The International Criminal Judiciary – Problems of Judicial Selection, Independence and Ethics", in Michael Bohlander (ed.), *International Criminal Justice: A Critical* Analysis of Institutions and Procedures, Cameron May, London, 2007, pp. 375–383 (http://www.legal-tools.org/doc/774cfc/); Mark S. Ellis, *Sovereignty and Justice: Balancing the Principle of Complementarity between International and Domestic War Crimes Tribunals*, Cambridge Scholars Publishing, Cambridge, 2014, pp. 259–261. While it is true that Judge Karibi-Whyte's mandate as an ICTY Judge was not renewed, in the words of Grunstein and Banerjee "it is unclear whether this was related to his somnolence during the trial", see Ronald R. Grunstein and Dev Banerjee, "The Case of 'Judge Nodd' and Other Sleeping Judges—Media, Society, and Judicial Sleepiness", in *Sleep*, 2007, vol. 30, no. 5, p. 627. Moreover, the Appeals Chamber did not find that Karibi-Whyte's conduct amounted to "serious misconduct or incapacity", which if it was considered as a basis for his non-renewal, is equally concerning. Cf. the situation of Judge Frederik Harhoff, an *ad litem* judge of the ICTY, whose removal from office ultimately followed his disqualification, as he was not seized of any other judicial proceedings. Harhoff was disqualified following the decision of a Panel of three judges assigned under Rule 15 of the ICTY RPE, on the basis of their finding of apprehended bias following the publication of a letter written by Harhoff, which it considered indicated 'reasonably apprehended bias in favour of conviction […] further compounded by [his] clear difficulty in applying the current jurisprudence of the Tribunal'. See ICTY, *Prosecutor v. Šešelj*, Rule 15 Panel, Decision on Defence Motion for Disqualification of Judge Frederik Harhoff and Report to the Vice-President, 28 August 2013, IT-03-67-T (http://www.legal-tools.org/doc/5b4aa1/). Whether or not Harhoff's actions amounted to serious misconduct was not addressed by the Panel.

[142] Čelebići case, para. 658, see above note 137.

Similarly, the ECCC's equivalent to ICTY Rule 15 came under scrutiny when the ECCC Trial Chamber, seized of allegations of Judge Nil Nonn's past accepting of bribes,[143] "conceded that '[a] pattern of improper conduct [...] may call into question a person's qualifications to act as a judge of the ECCC, [but] [n]o relevant mechanisms are provided in the ECCC Law and Agreement'".[144] In that case, the ECCC Trial Chamber itself noted the limitations of the mechanism enshrined within the ECCC Internal Rules, finding that "the ECCC cannot confront general questions of judicial independence and integrity directly, it can [only] ensure that *Accused in proceedings before it* benefit from proceedings that are fair and conducted in accordance with international standards".[145]

While the ICTY Rule 15 and its analogues might be appropriate for assessing the statutorily required impartiality of judges, it is less appropriate as a mechanism for assessing questions that may arise in relation to the 'high moral character' and 'integrity' that are a prerequisite to their appointment.[146]

In the case of the ICC, the drafters of the ICC Statute took a broader approach to addressing questions of judicial conduct and capacity than the precedent set by the *ad hoc* tribunals and followed by the hybrid tribunals. As a result, the ICC Statue provides for a mechanism separate to the disqualification procedure. Under that process, judges – as well as the Prosecutor, the Registrar and their respective Deputies – can be removed from office on one of three grounds: serious misconduct,[147] a serious breach of statutory duties,[148] or the inability to exercise functions required by the ICC

---

[143] ECCC, *Co-Prosecutors v. Chea et al.*, Ieng Sary's Application to Disqualify Judge Nil Nonn Due to his Personal Admission that he has Accepted Bribes and Request for a Public Hearing or in the Alternative Leave to Reply to any Submissions Presented by Judge Nil Nonn in his Response to this Application, 14 January 2011, 002/19-09-2007-ECCC/TC (https://www.legal-tools.org/doc/a48970/).

[144] Ellis, 2014, p. 261, see above note 141. See ECCC, *Co-Prosecutors v. Chea et al.*, Trial Chamber, Decision on Ieng Sary's Application to Disqualify Judge Nil Nonn and Related Requests, 28 January 2011, 002/19-09-2007-ECCC/TC, para. 9 ('Nil Nonn case') (http://www.legal-tools.org/doc/e3e419/).

[145] Nil Nonn case, para. 15 (emphasis added), see above note 144.

[146] See above section 27.2.

[147] ICC Statute, Article 46.1(a) see above note 12.

[148] *Ibid.*

Statute.[149] Separate provisions in the ICC Statute provide for complaints relating to, and the imposition of disciplinary measures for, "misconduct of a less serious nature",[150] a concept which is defined in the ICC RPE.[151]

27.5.2. Codes of Conduct and Accountability Mechanisms

In addition to its regulatory framework, the judges of the ICC were first among their counterparts at other contemporary international criminal courts and tribunals to adopt a Code of Judicial Ethics.[152] They did so in March 2005, some three months prior to the issuance of the first indictments against Joseph Kony and others.[153] By that point, the ICTY and ICTR had adopted Codes of Professional Conduct for Counsel,[154] but had not yet taken the step of introducing instruments concerning the professional conduct of judges. At the ECCC, inspiration appears to have flowed from the ICC Judicial Code. The Plenary of Judges at the ECCC adopted its Code of Judicial Ethics in September 2008,[155] some six months prior to the commencement of the Extraordinary Chambers' inaugural trial proceedings the following February.[156]

Judicial conduct standards appear to have gained greater attention towards the end of the decade that followed, as the original *ad hoc* tribunals prepared to close, and the IRMCT assumed their residual jurisdictions. In May 2015, the IRMCT adopted its first Code of Professional Conduct for the Judges of the Mechanism.[157] While the ICTR had closed its doors by the end of 2014, the trend of codifying judicial ethics was followed by

---

[149] *Ibid.*, Article 46.1(b). With respect to the operation of this complaints mechanism, see, for example, ICC RPE, Rules 23–32, see above note 133.

[150] ICC Statute, Article 47, see above note 12.

[151] ICC RPE, Rule 25(1), see above note 133.

[152] See ICC, Code of Judicial Ethics, 9 March 2005 ('ICC Judicial Code') (https://www.legal-tools.org/doc/383f8f/).

[153] ICC, "Kony et al. Case" (available on the ICC's web site).

[154] See ICTY, Code of Professional Conduct for Counsel Appearing Before the International Tribunal, 22 July 2009, IT/125 REV. 3 (https://www.legal-tools.org/doc/rtgkbb/); ICTR, Code of Professional Conduct for Defence Counsel, 14 March 2008 (https://www.legal-tools.org/doc/51efe3/); ICTR, Standards of Professional Conduct Prosecution Counsel, 14 September 1999 (https://www.legal-tools.org/doc/nz7gv4/).

[155] ECCC, Code of Judicial Ethics, 5 September 2008 ('ECCC Judicial Code') (https://www.legal-tools.org/doc/5dys4p/).

[156] ECCC, "Initial hearing in Case 001" (available on the ECCC's web site).

[157] IRMCT, Code of Professional Conduct for the Judges of the Mechanism, 11 May 2015, MICT/14 ('IRMCT Judicial Code') (http://www.legal-tools.org/doc/23cc92/).

the ICTY in July 2016,[158] and the latter's code remained in effect until the institution's closure at the end of 2017. The STL also followed suit in 2016, adopting its own Code of Professional Conduct for Judges in September of that year.[159] As well as defining concepts of independence, impartiality, integrity, confidentiality and diligence,[160] these 'ethical codes' and 'codes of conduct' typically govern conduct during proceedings, public expression and association, and extra-judicial activity.[161] In this way, they cover the conduct of judges both inside and outside of the courtroom and their particular institution. When compared to the Global Judicial Code of Ethics, however, it is clear that that the instruments adopted at the international courts and tribunals are the far less prescriptive of the two.

Up to this point, the ICC was the only international criminal court or tribunal with a formal process for hearing complaints against the judiciary outside of the litigation context, and the only to provide the possibility of their removal from office as a disciplinary sanction or in response to proven incapacity. That changed following the first plenary of the Roster of Judges of the Kosovo Specialist Chambers in March 2018.[162] The KSCSPO judges adopted a Code of Judicial Ethics for Judges, mirroring the ICC's model that, in addition to defining "serious misconduct" and "misconduct of a less serious nature",[163] provided for a disciplinary procedure for receiving, handling and adjudicating complaints against judges.[164] In doing so, the KSCSPO seems to have spurred a small flurry of activity at other tribunals. The judges of the IRMCT adopted a revised Code of Professional

---

[158] ICTY, Code of Professional Conduct for the Judges of the Tribunal, 6 July 2016 ('ICTY Judicial Code') (https://www.legal-tools.org/doc/55lsey/).

[159] STL, Code of Professional Conduct for the Judges of the Special Tribunal for Lebanon, 27 September 2016, STL-CC-2016-04 ('STL Judicial Code') (https://www.legal-tools.org/doc/oird6k/).

[160] ECCC Judicial Code, Articles 1–5, see above note 155; ICC Judicial Code, Articles 3–7, see above note 152; IRMCT Judicial Code, Articles 2–6, see above note 157; ICTY Judicial Code, Articles 2–6, see above note 158; STL Judicial Code, Articles 2–6, see above note 159.

[161] ECCC Judicial Code, Articles 6–8, see above note 155; ICC Judicial Code, Articles 8–10, see above note 152; IRMCT Judicial Code, Articles 7–9, see above note 157; STL Judicial Code, Articles 7–9, see above note 159. The ICTY Judicial Code notably contained no such clause.

[162] KSCSPO, *First Report*, 2016–2018, March 2018, p. 9.

[163] KSCSPO, Code of Judicial Ethics for Judges Appointed to the Roster of International Judges of the Kosovo Specialist Chambers, 14 March 2017, KSC-BD-01/COR2, Articles 13–14 (https://www.legal-tools.org/doc/wl7m65/).

[164] *Ibid.*, Articles 15–23.

Conduct for the Judges of the Mechanism in April 2018, this time incorporating a disciplinary procedure.[165] For its part, on 1 March 2018, the STL adopted a Judicial Accountability Mechanism, annexed to its Conditions of Compensation and Service of Judges, upon the extension of its renewable mandate.[166]

As will be seen in the following section, this trend towards formalizing regulation of judicial ethics and professional conduct standards[167] has not been limited to the above internal regulatory documents. To the contrary, the issue of judicial accountability has been recognized on the world stage, as a core consideration for the future viability of international criminal justice.

27.5.3.   The Paris Declaration: A Vision of the Future?[168]

In the autumn of 2017, the National School for the Judiciary (*École nationale de la magistrature* or 'ENM') of France hosted an expert conference on the topic of the effectiveness of international criminal justice, chaired by former ICC Judge, Bruno Cotte ('Paris Conference'). Delegates included the Presidents of four international criminal courts and tribunals,[169] the Head of the International, Impartial and Independent Mechanism for Syria, and the President of the Extraordinary African Chambers.

The Conference resulted in the adoption of the Paris Declaration on the Effectiveness of International Criminal Justice, consisting of 31 separate, though interrelated recommendations focused around the central themes of predictability (and transparency), expediency, and judicial gov-

---

[165] IRMCT, Code of Professional Conduct for the Judges of the Mechanism, 9 April 2018, MICT/14/Rev. 1 (https://www.legal-tools.org/doc/5deknw/).

[166] STL, Conditions of Service and Compensation of Judges of the Special Tribunal for Lebanon, 9 February 2018, Annex 2: Procedure Establishing a Judicial Accountability Mechanism.

[167] Although a conceptual distinction could be made between judicial ethics (that is, factors guiding judicial decision-making) on the one hand, and professional conduct standards (that is, rules of conduct governing the behaviour of judges) on the other, no clear distinction exists in the various instruments adopted by the ECCC, ICC, ICTY IRMCT, KSCSPO or STL. Indeed, the ethical codes and professional conduct standards are largely similar, despite the different lexicon used. For present purposes, this chapter does not seek to distinguish 'professional conduct standards,' of judges from 'judicial ethics' and the terms are used variably, as complementary or interchangeable.

[168] The authors were delegates at the Paris Conference on the Effectiveness of International Criminal Justice, Paris, 16 October 2017.

[169] Namely, ICC, ICTY, KSCSPO and STL.

ernance. The Declaration openly acknowledges that "while international courts and tribunals must be provided with the necessary resources to fulfil their mandate, they must also be accountable".[170] To this end, a number of recommendations focus on the accountability of international criminal courts and tribunals and their judges broadly, dealing with issues from the adoption of codes of conduct,[171] the collection of data about the functioning of courts and tribunals,[172] the development of transparent performance indicators,[173] and the effective auditing of international criminal courts and tribunals.[174] Of these, a number envisage cross-institutional cooperation. For instance, Article 28 encourages the collection (and sharing) of statistical data across international criminal courts and tribunals to identify possible common challenges and foster the dissemination of best practices, while Article 29 calls for reflection upon the identification of performance indicators aimed at making the work of international criminal courts and tribunals as a whole more transparent, in order to benefit from qualitative information capable of enhancing procedures and practices.

For present purposes, the most significant suggestion is the call for the establishment of suitable disciplinary mechanisms. In particular, in emphasizing the importance of the impartiality and the dignity of the disciplinary process, the Paris Declaration calls for international courts and tribunals to give consideration to establishing an investigative and decision-making body common to all international criminal courts and tribunals for the purposes of ensuring standards of judicial conduct are adopted and respected.[175] The Paris Declaration hints at the form this joint disciplinary mechanism might take, recommending that, as far as possible, international courts and tribunals utilize external investigative bodies and entrust disciplinary decisions to a panel separate to the plenary of judges of that court or tribunal.[176]

But what motivates this new call to action? The context of the Paris Conference itself, devoted to increasing the effectiveness of international criminal justice as whole, lends some indication. Judicial accountability

---

[170] Paris Declaration, Preamble, see above note 7.
[171] *Ibid.*, Article 26.
[172] *Ibid.*, Article 28.
[173] *Ibid.*, Article 29.
[174] *Ibid.*, Article 30.
[175] *Ibid.*, Article 27.
[176] *Ibid.*

mechanisms are but one tool in an array of potential methods by which to strengthen the governance of judiciaries of international courts and tribunals and to improve their functionality. They serve to consolidate public and stakeholder confidence in the belief that the high standards of integrity expected of international judges are upheld in practice, which in turn, serves to strengthen confidence in international criminal justice as a whole. The need for such mechanisms is palpable. As once observed by the former UN Assistant Secretary-General for Legal Affairs, Ralph Zacklin, speaking of the *ad hoc* tribunals, "[t]he decentralization of power and accountability, coupled with the need to respect judicial and prosecutorial independence, have been chronic problems".[177] An independent, joint judicial disciplinary mechanism presents a meaningful way of strengthening confidence in the integrity of both individual courts and tribunals and the system of international criminal justice as a whole. Symbolically, it would also serve to demonstrate to the public and stakeholders the authenticity of efforts to ensure the highest standards of ethical and professional conduct amongst the international judiciary, despite international courts and tribunals having previously lagged behind the development of international standards.

Another motivating factor is the climate of wavering confidence in international criminal courts and tribunals to deliver what was envisaged of them, which shows no signs of abating. For instance, in commemorating the twentieth anniversary of the Rome Conference on the establishment of the ICC, (former ICTY and IRMCT President) Theodor Meron and academic Maggie Gardener observed that:

> it is [...] undeniable that Rome project still falls short of the expectations of the participants at the groundbreaking conference in Rome, with their visions of creating [an] international criminal court [...] that is efficient, economic, and fair, and one that applies a full panoply of human and due rights processes.[178]

That sentiment was echoed by the United Kingdom's Legal Adviser to the ICC Assembly of States Parties ('ASP'),[179] who went on to argue, in

---

[177] Ralph Zacklin, "The Failings of Ad Hoc International Tribunals", in *Journal of International Criminal Justice*, 2004, vol. 2, no. 2, p. 543.

[178] Theodor Meron and Maggie Gardener, "Introduction to the Symposium on the Rome Statute at Twenty", in *American Journal of International Law Unbound*, 2018, vol. 112, p. 155.

[179] Andrew Murdoch, "UK Statement to the ICC Assembly of States Parties 17th Session, ICC ASP, 17th Session", *Gov.uk*, 5 December 2018 (available on its web site).

the context of strengthening the credibility of the ICC, that it "surely goes without saying that the Court must act in accordance with the highest possible standards of good governance and professionalism".[180] While negative perceptions of the credibility of international criminal justice and proposals for reform are neither unique to the judiciary nor particularly new,[181] the prevalence of the phenomenon should not lead to a false assurance that the problem is benign. One need only recall the forewarning of the Permanent Representative of New Zealand, that "[w]hen a Court loses credibility in the eyes of a large sector of community opinion, then those with political and legislative responsibility have a right, and a duty, to act to restore that credibility and effectiveness".[182] If the independence of international criminal courts and tribunals is truly valued, it is incumbent upon their judiciaries to welcome changes that ensure that such a threshold of credibility loss is never crossed.

Merits aside, the Paris proposal raises a number of questions that would have to be answered before a viable joint disciplinary mechanism could be established. These range from questions about sustainable funding models, to issues of competence (for example, how it might be possible that such a body could investigate and determine allegations of judicial misconduct across various international courts and tribunals) and even whether a new joint mechanism could complement, for example, the statutory procedures provided for at the ICC.

Each of these questions are worthy of further discussion and merit considered debate. The protection of legitimate judicial independence should feature heavily in future discussions in this regard. One can envis-

---

[180] Meron and Gardener, 2018, see above note 178.

[181] See, for example, Antonio Cassese, Report on the Special Court for Sierra Leone Submitted by the Independent Expert, 12 December 2006 (https://www.legal-tools.org/doc/6tr996/); Silvia Fernández de Gurmendi, "Enhancing the Court's Efficiency: From the Drafting of the Procedural Provisions by States to their Revision by Judges", in *Journal of International Criminal Justice*, 2018, vol. 16, no. 2, pp. 341–361; Open Society Justice Initiative and Coalition for International Justice, "Unfulfilled Promises: Achieving Justice for Crimes Against Humanity in East Timor", 2004, pp. 34–45 (http://www.legal-tools.org/doc/06eaf7/); Carsten Stahn, "The Future of International Criminal Justice", in *Hague Justice Journal*, 2009, vol. 4, no. 3, pp. 257–266; Hans-Peter Kaul, "Construction Site for More Justice: The International Criminal Court after Two Years", in *American Journal of International Law*, 2005, vol. 99, no. 2, pp. 370–384; Zacklin, see above note 177.

[182] Jim McLay, "Report of the International Criminal Court: Statement delivered by H.E. Mr. Jim McLay, Permanent Representative of New Zealand", *New Zealand Foreign Affairs and Trade*, 31 October 2013 (available on its web site).

---

age, however, an entity legally separate from any individual court or tribunal bound by procedures consistent with internationally recognized minimum standards. Inspiration might be taken from the procedures applied by bodies such as the UN Office of Internal Oversight, as a means of ensuring fair, transparent, investigations of judicial complaints. Disciplinary proceedings could be determined by disciplinary boards composed of members with extensive judicial experience who are shortlisted, selected, or nominated by the judiciary. All protections of a fair hearing could be guaranteed to judges, and fair, consistent and transparent complaints, investigation and disciplinary processes could contribute to improved public confidence and a greater understanding of the almost unexplored field of international judicial legal ethics in practice.

There is also impetus for the initiatives on the international stage to continue. It must be observed that the uniform international standards of ethics and professional conduct for international judges are comparatively scarce in detail when compared with standards for national judges. At the same time, the progressive development of the international standards demonstrates that there is room and opportunity for international criminal courts and tribunals themselves to contribute to the establishment of norms. Representative, round-table conferences, like the Paris Conference, could take a central role, for example, in formulating a uniform code of conduct for judges of international criminal courts and tribunals. This would not only supplement the judicial ethics and conduct codes already in force at existing international criminal courts and tribunals but could be an essential step in paving the way for cross-institutional initiatives such as a joint accountability mechanism.

27.6. Conclusion

If effective international criminal courts and tribunals are intended as a key feature of international criminal justice, it is essential to ensure their proper functioning and credibility. The legitimacy – if not the very survival – of these institutions and the contemporary system of international criminal justice as a whole, depends upon it. Ensuring the accountability of judicial institutions and the integrity and impartiality of individual judges who hold office is an essential component of continuing to guarantee fair, free, independent trials in accordance with the highest international standards.

International criminal courts and tribunals have recognized this. Although standards relating to international judges have developed slower than those relating to national judges, the ICC, the IRMCT, the KSCSPO and the STL have each adopted disciplinary mechanisms designed to ensure that complaints of misconduct can be raised, heard and adjudicated to promote accountability without compromising legitimate judicial independence. In doing so, these courts and tribunals have recognized the accountability of judicial institutions and personnel as an absolutely essential component of judicial independence. International justice has both the capacity and impetus, however, to consolidate efforts to improve effectiveness, including in the oversight of judicial accountability. If the Global Code of Judicial Ethics presents model ethical standards applicable to judicial office-holders at international courts and tribunals, the Paris Declaration's proposal for a joint accountability mechanism could represent the current gold-standard in ensuring the highest quality of regulation of judicial accountability. As a potential next step, consistent with the development of international standards on the independence of the judge, judiciaries in international criminal courts and tribunals should move towards the development of a more detailed code of conduct, applicable to all of their judges.

In attempting to secure the long-term credibility and legitimacy of international criminal justice, there is impulse for common ethical and professional conduct minimum standards applicable to all judges serving in this field, and for a joint accountability mechanism to ensure they are respected. The Paris Declaration could prove to be the first step in this direction, yet the proposal for a joint accountability mechanism should not be considered in isolation. Rather, it should be viewed alongside other proposals for reform and improvement of judicial governance generally.[183] Moreover, calls for reform on the international stage should be considered in context. Since the beginning of the contemporary era of international standards of judicial regulation, efforts to strengthen judicial independence and accountability have developed side-by-side. The development of ethical and professional standards and minimum guarantees of accountability rightfully go hand-in-hand with efforts to bolster the independence of the judiciary, stave off unwarranted encroachment on the exercise of judicial powers, and improve the quality of justice and the rule of law.

---

[183] See, for example, Fernández de Gurmendi, above note 50, identifying potential improvements in the procedures used to appoint international judges.

28

Prosecutorial Language, Integrity and Independence

Richard J. Goldstone[*]

28.1. Introduction

Politics plays a crucial role in international criminal justice. It shapes international criminal law and establishes the institutions of criminal justice. Indeed, without the politics, there would be no international criminal justice. The politics is at play both externally and internally with regard to every such judicial institution. External politics includes the inevitability that State officials will seek, whether directly or indirectly, to influence decisions made by international criminal courts. Internally, there is the reality that some judges will attempt, directly or indirectly, to influence the policy and decisions of the office of the prosecutor. Those forms of political pressures are the reality and the background against which one should consider the language used by international prosecutors and their integrity and independence. In what follows, I will rely primarily on my own experiences as the first chief Prosecutor of the United Nations International Tribunals for the former Yugoslavia ('ICTY')[1] and Rwanda ('ICTR').[2]

I would add that the actual and perceived integrity and independence of international prosecutors are essential not only to the office of the prosecutor, but to the court as a whole. Without it, the court will lose critical support from governments and the prosecutor will lose crucial respect, confidence and trust from the judges.[3]

---

[*] **Richard J. Goldstone** is a retired Justice of the Constitutional Court of South Africa. He served as the first Chief Prosecutor of the International Criminal Tribunals for the former Yugoslavia and Rwanda.

[1] Established by Security Council Resolution 827, UN Doc. S/RES/827 (1993), 25 May 1993 (http://www.legal-tools.org/doc/dc079b/).

[2] Established by Security Council Resolution 955, UN Doc. S/RES/955 (1994), 8 November 1994 (http://www.legal-tools.org/doc/f5ef47/).

[3] Morten Bergsmo, "Revisiting Integrity in International Justice", FICHL Policy Brief Series No. 93 (2018), Torkel Opsahl Academic EPublisher, Brussels, 2018, p. 1 (https://www.toaep.org/pbs-pdf/93-bergsmo/).

28.2. The Political Pressure on Prosecutors from Outside the Institution and Contact with Governmental Officials

The circumstances in which I came to be appointed as chief Prosecutor for the ICTY provides a good illustration of the external politics of international criminal justice.[4] The United Nations Security Council decided that it would make the appointment of the chief Prosecutor and that, unusually, its appointment of the Prosecutor of the ICTY would require consensus between its members. The practical effect of that decision was to grant an effective veto power to each of the 15 members of the Security Council, and not only the Permanent Five. The appointment was to be made on the nomination of the Secretary-General.[5]

The first eight nominations made by Secretary-General Boutros Boutros-Ghali were opposed by one or more members of the Security Council. They were found unacceptable, according to reports at the time, because of the nationality or religion of the nominees. These politics of the Security Council delayed the appointment of the Prosecutor for more than six months. It ended with my appointment in consequence of newly elected President Nelson Mandela acceding to a request from the Secretary-General to support the nomination of a South African as chief Prosecutor. Boutros-Ghali realised that in the middle of 1994, a nomination supported by Mandela was not likely to be opposed by any member of the Security Council. It was that support that led to my rapid appointment by the Security Council in July of 1994.[6]

The absence of a chief Prosecutor for some eight months after their appointment caused the judges to feel angry and frustrated at having no judicial work to do. In the result, when I arrived in The Hague, the judges were demanding rapid indictments and trials. To this end, they summoned me to report regularly to plenary sessions held by the judges. Whilst I felt obliged to respond positively to these summonses, I was acutely aware that I was required to protect both the integrity and independence of my Office. There was also the integrity of the judges themselves. They had to be protected from acquiring information that might result in a conflict of interests and consequential calls for their recusal. At that early stage, no indictments

---

[4] Compare, in this regard, *ibid.*, p. 2, sect. 3.

[5] Statute of the International Criminal Tribunal for the former Yugoslavia ('ICTY'), 25 May 1993, Article 16(4) (http://www.legal-tools.org/doc/b4f63b/).

[6] UN Security Council, Resolution 936 (1994), UN Doc. S/RES/936 (1994), 8 July 1994.

had been issued and there was thus no reason for the judges and Prosecutor not to confer. That situation changed immediately when the first indictments were issued. The relationship between the judges and the Prosecutor became more formal. In all of those interactions with the judges, the use of careful language was essential. The relationship was fraught with the danger of compromising the independence of the judges and the Prosecutor as well as the institution as a whole.

Equally important was the use of careful language in relation to briefings of the media. There was intense public interest in the first truly international criminal court, and favourable press was highly relevant to receiving adequate funding from the then cash-strapped United Nations. I had to present an optimistic face to the public without disclosing sensitive information relating to the detail or direction of investigations. I had learnt from my South African experiences that the only safe policy was to say nothing to journalists 'off the record' that might be embarrassing if it came to be made public. I found that an open and transparent relationship with journalists was appreciated and received by them with understanding. Subject to those restraints, I regularly provided the media with background briefings and, in particular, explained what was to come in the following days. Only on one occasion did that policy lead to a journalist ignoring an embargo by using the information prior to a public announcement. In that exceptional case, the information reported was accurate, but it was hardly fair to those journalists who had respected the embargo.

No international prosecutor can or should avoid contact with outside agencies, whether governmental or private. On my appointment as chief Prosecutor of both the ICTY and the ICTR, I took the view that it was not appropriate for an international prosecutor's office to send investigators or other officers to work in any country without consulting the government of such country. That applied, in my opinion, notwithstanding that my appointment had been made by the United Nations Security Council acting under its peremptory Chapter VII powers. It was the politics of the situation that dictated a diplomatic approach. To that end, I visited the capitals of the relevant European countries in the case of the ICTY and African countries in the case of the ICTR. I met with the respective ministers of justice and foreign affairs. The response, with one exception, was that my investigators would be welcome to work in their countries. In most cases, it was suggested that their names and the details of their visits should be conveyed to the relevant Ambassador in The Hague so that the government concerned could be helpful to my investigators in case of need.

The one exception was the French government. They initially insisted that any interview on French soil, even with a willing witness, was to be conducted before an investigating magistrate. I explained that this was quite impractical and would compel me to bring such a witness to The Hague or to arrange to meet the witness in Brussels. After a number of meetings with the legal advisor at the Quai D'Orsay, we reached a compromise. If the person to be interviewed was a French official, the interview would indeed have to be conducted before an investigating magistrate. In the case of a non-official, there was no longer a problem.

The approach to the governments was a useful and often a fruitful opportunity to meet the relevant ministers face to face and open direct lines of communication that became helpful in the months that followed. I could furnish many illustrations of those benefits. To refer to one of them: an important Bosniak witness felt under serious physical threat where he lived in Bosnia and Herzegovina, and I requested the government of Denmark to grant protection to the witness and his family. The fact that I had met the Danish Minister of Foreign Affairs facilitated the speedy consent to my request. I doubt that I would have been able to achieve that result if the contacts with the Minister had been solely in exchanges of e-mail messages.

I did not, on any occasion during these many contacts and meetings, feel that the independence of my Office was directly or indirectly compromised. The ground rules for a new institution in the international community had to be laid down from the very outset. I had made it clear more than once, at press conferences, that any inappropriate approach from any government would forthwith be made public.

The other important government contacts I found necessary related to the receipt of confidential intelligence information from relevant governments and especially the United States. I was fortunate to find that the General Counsel at the Central Intelligence Agency, Elizabeth Rindskopf Parker, was fully supportive of the work of the ICTY. After many detailed discussions, we were able to forge a formal relationship between the Office of the Prosecutor and the government of the United States, providing for intelligence information to be shared with the Prosecutor. In order to implement that agreement, the Rules of Procedure and Evidence of the ICTY required amendment to enable the Prosecutor to receive confidential information, but only as lead information that could not be used against the interests of any defendant. The information could only be made public with the express consent of the provider of the information.[7] That rule has been replicated with regard to the ICTR and the International Criminal Court.

Fortunately, as a United National official, I was co-opted to the diplomatic circuit in The Hague. I found it extremely useful to attend national day celebrations at the various embassies. I found that these were more working occasions than solely social. At one point, because of the serious state of the United Nations finances, all travel by United Nations officials had been put on hold. This was disastrous for the work of the ICTY, where travel was crucial to our investigators' work. I inquired from the finance office at United Nations headquarters in New York whether we could use unallocated funds from the ICTY Trust Fund for travel. The curt and unspecific response was that the funds were not available. That was strange indeed. At a national day reception, the following day, I found myself speaking with the Ambassador of Pakistan. I informed him of my problem. I reminded him that Pakistan had donated USD 1 million to the ICTY Trust Fund. I informed him that what I had told him was on the record and that I would appreciate it if he were to request his colleague in New York to inquire from the United Nations Secretariat why the Trust Fund could not be used for travel by ICTY investigators. Whether that request was the cause, I do not know, but within 24 hours the consent to use those funds was granted. I would stress, in the context of this book, that the language in which my request was formulated was important. I was not giving the Ambassador information that might in any way compromise the independence of my Office or of the ICTY.

28.3. Relationship with the United Nations Secretary-General

My earliest discussions at the United Nations were with the then newly appointed Deputy Secretary-General for Legal Affairs, former Ambassador Hans Corell of Sweden. I should mention that Hans Corell soon became a good friend and that friendship continues to the present day. During my time as a United Nations international prosecutor, Corell, sometimes to my frustration, refused ever to give me advice. He considered that my independence was so central to my mission as chief Prosecutor, that it was not consistent with that independence for a senior United Nations official to

---

[7]   ICTY, Rules of Procedure and Evidence, Rule 70(B) (adopted 11 February 1994, amended 4 October 1994, 30 January 1995 and 12 November 1997) (https://legal-tools.org/doc/30df50/).

give me advice. Of course, I respected and appreciated his highly principled approach.

It soon turned out that the idea of independence held by Secretary-General Boutros-Ghali was a very different and unusual one. Some months into my term of office, I was requested to visit the Secretary-General in his office in New York. He quickly came to the point: he had obtained details of my travel schedules from the ICTY Registrar's office and he was of the strong view, he said, that I had been neglecting my duties in The Hague by traveling too frequently. He added that some United Nations ambassadors had complained to him that I was too frequently in Washington, D.C. I explained the need for my travels and added politely but firmly that I would have to continue with a busy travel schedule. It was not a pleasant meeting. Apart from his complaint, I objected to his deviously requesting information about my travel from the Tribunal Registry in The Hague.

Our difficult relationship came to a head with regard to the indictment of Radovan Karadžić in July 1995. Before announcing that we were proceeding against the 'president' of *Republika Srpska* and his army chief, Ratko Mladić, I decided it was necessary to give a few days' confidential notice to institutions whose security might be compromised by the announcement: The United Nations, which had troops in the former Yugoslavia serving with the United National Protection Force (UNPROFOR); the United Nations High Commissioner for Refugees, which had investigators in the field; and the Dutch government, which hosted the ICTY. Their personnel could have been placed at risk by a United Nations prosecutor taking action against leading actors in the armed conflicts in the former Yugoslavia who were regarded as heroes by the Serb nationalist communities. Some of the right-wing supporters of Karadžić and Mladić were not astute in making a distinction between different organs of the United Nations or indeed of the international community.

The civil head of the United Nations forces in the former Yugoslavia at the time was Akashi Yasushi. I found Akashi to be a supporter of the ICTY who never failed to give me his warm co-operation. It was not a good time for me to be seen in Zagreb, where Akashi had his office. I explained that I had important information to convey to him in confidence, and he generously agreed to meet me in Geneva a few days later. I informed him that I was sharing the information with him on a 'need to know' basis. I expected that he would share it with the United Nations battalion commanders who might wish to take extra safety precautions on the day of the announcement. He asked if he could share the information with the Secretary-General. I responded that the decision was for him to make. He informed me that he felt obliged to do so.

Some days after the announcement, which received huge media attention, I was again summoned to meet with the Secretary-General. He informed me of his extreme displeasure at the decision to proceed against Karadžić and Mladić. He was of the view that the peace negotiations then under way were more important than prosecuting the Bosnian Serb leaders. His priority was to bring an end to the war that was still raging in the former Yugoslavia. My actions were calculated, he said, to jeopardise and possibly put an end to those negotiations. I fully understood his position and I told him so. However, I stated that my duty and obligation under the Security Council Statute establishing the ICTY was to bring indictments for war crimes when the evidence justified so doing. He then informed me that he considered that it had been my duty to consult him before taking so important a step. I referred him to the Statute that guaranteed my independence. I added that, in any event, he had been informed ahead of my announcement of the then coming indictment. He acknowledged that Akashi had so informed him. He informed me that he respected my independence and that is why he had not approached me – I should have approached him! I responded that it had never occurred to me to consult him. I said that I assumed he would have advised me to postpone the indictments. He agreed. I quietly added that I was happy not to have consulted him. Our discussion ended with him informing me that he had great difficulty in dealing with a senior United Nations official who was not subject to his orders.

I might add that, unbeknown to either the Secretary-General or me, it was the indictment of Karadžić that made possible the Dayton meeting and agreement in November 1995, which indeed brought an end to the war. Had Karadžić been free to travel to Dayton, the meeting would not have taken place. Karadžić knew that if he set foot in the United States, he would be arrested and sent for trial to The Hague. It would not have been politically possible, some four months after the Srebrenica massacre, for the leaders of Bosnia and Herzegovina to have met in the same room with Karadžić.

Then there was a bizarre discussion with the Secretary-General towards the end of 1995. I had been invited to deliver one of the opening addresses at a ceremony in Nuremberg to mark the fiftieth anniversary of the Nuremberg Trial of the major Nazi leaders. The proceedings were to take place in the same courtroom. My host was the Lord Mayor of the City of Nuremberg. The invitation was extended to my wife as well as a colleague and his wife. It was arranged that we would fly from Amsterdam to Nuremberg on a Saturday morning. On the Wednesday prior to our visit, I received a call from the *Chef de cabinet* of the Secretary-General, Jean-Claude Aimee. He informed me that the Secretary-General understood that I was traveling to Nuremberg on the weekend. When I confirmed that information, he informed me that he had to convey an instruction from the Secretary-General to the effect that I was not to travel to Nuremberg. Somewhat shocked, I inquired as to the reason for the instruction. He informed me that he had no idea. I told Mr. Aimee that unless there was a very good reason for my not going to Nuremberg, I was not prepared to embarrass either my Office or the Mayor of Nuremberg. I asked to speak to the Secretary-General. He was in the air, said Aimee, and would be in his office at about 21:30 CET that evening. I requested Mr. Aimee to inform the Secretary-General that I wished to discuss his instruction with him. I gave him the telephone number of our dinner host that evening, the then President of the International Court of Justice. That evening, the Secretary-General did indeed call. He confirmed the instruction and explained that because of the serious state of the United Nations finances, he had had to cancel travel by all United Nations staff. I informed the Secretary-General that we were going to Nuremberg as the guests of the City of Nuremberg and that it would not involve any funding at all from the ICTY or the United Nations. "Oh", said the Secretary-General, "that is very different. Enjoy your trip!". I had shared my problem with the small dinner group assembled. They were as puzzled as I had been and amazed at the response I had received from the Secretary-General. We agreed that the incident exemplified the manner in which Boutros-Ghali micromanaged the huge United Nations bureaucracy, and that it was important that my independence allowed me to question instructions from the Secretary-General.

In short, it is necessary for any international prosecutor to have frequent interactions with governments and, in the case of a United Nations tribunal, with the Secretary-General and other high United Nations officials. It is crucial in those contacts to be transparent and to use language that is calculated to make apparent the independence and integrity of the office of the prosecutor.

28.4. The International Criminal Tribunal for Rwanda

The politics surrounding the establishment of the ICTR were almost as fraught as those of the ICTY. At the end of the genocide in Rwanda, in the middle of 1994, Rwanda held a non-permanent seat on the Security Council. It requested an international criminal tribunal, along the general lines of the ICTY, to bring the perpetrators to justice. However, it soon became apparent that the government of Rwanda had in mind a domestic tribunal sitting in Kigali, its capital, rather than a remote institution like the ICTY sitting in The Hague, a substantial distance from the former Yugoslavia. Its own justice system had been destroyed by the genocide – almost all of its judges and prosecutors had been slaughtered. The government of Rwanda wanted an international judicial body as a substitute for its own justice system.

However, the Security Council, for understandable reasons, could not contemplate sending international judges and staff to hold trials in Rwanda. The ability of the government, let alone the Tribunal, to protect the lives of its staff would present an insurmountable hurdle. Imagine the position of judges who might acquit an alleged genocidaire and have thousands of victims calling for revenge. The Security Council decided to set up the Tribunal in Arusha, in neighbouring Tanzania with the Office of the Prosecutor in Kigali. The great majority of the witnesses were located in Rwanda and that is where investigators would have to interview them. This approach of the Security Council was unacceptable to Rwanda and it withdrew its request for the establishment of an international tribunal. Notwithstanding this decision by the government of Rwanda, the Security Council, for its part, insisted on setting up such an institution. As with the ICTY, it would use its peremptory powers under Chapter VII of the Charter of the United Nations. When the resolution was put to the vote, 13 members of the Security Council voted in favour, China abstained, and Rwanda cast the single negative vote.[8]

The Security Council also decided that, in order to introduce unity of practice and procedure, the chief Prosecutor of the ICTY would also be the chief Prosecutor of the ICTR. So, virtually overnight, I was obliged to set up an Office of the Prosecutor in Kigali. The politics clearly dictated that I should meet as soon as possible with the government of Rwanda. I required their co-operation in setting up my Office in their capital. However, in No-

---

[8]   UN Security Council, Resolution 955, 1994, see above note 2.

vember 1994, there were no United Nations funds available for the ICTR. It was a donation to the United Nations Trust Fund for Rwanda from Switzerland that made it possible for me to visit Kigali in the first week of December 1994. President Bizimungu and Deputy President Kagame were welcoming and agreed to assist me in setting up an office. I doubt that they would have been so accommodating if I had delayed a visit to Kigali.

In all of my dealings with regard to the ICTR, language played a crucial role. The United States was insisting that the word 'genocide' should not be used as that might place on it burdens under the Genocide Convention.[9] The Rwandan survivors and the government that had put an end to the killing and violence had no doubt that genocide had been committed. Until the evidence to establish the commission of genocide became overwhelming, diplomacy and the prospect of garnering funding for the ICTR compelled me to speak with great circumspection. I referred to slaughter, massive war crimes and so forth. I could not afford to antagonise either side.

On the government side, apart from the physical establishment of an office with staff including experienced investigators, I required the assistance of the Rwandan police to accompany and guarantee the safety of investigators and their staff when they travelled around the country. This was forthcoming, but at a price. The police were tipped off as to the identity of the witnesses, and frequently they would question the witnesses in the days after our interviews with them. Fortunately, we were on the same side.

It was difficult to recruit staff prepared to work in the very difficult circumstances that prevailed in the months after the genocide had come to an end. Accommodation was at a premium and not very pleasant. For security reasons, the United Nations was not prepared to allow families to accompany any member of the ICTR staff. We required experts with the ability to converse in both English and French. The Rwandan government was not prepared to have French nationals in Rwanda as they regarded France as having been complicit in the commission of the genocide. So, too, Algerians. Fortunately, we were successful in recruiting top-rate French-Canadians to work for us in Kigali, including the first head of investigations.

---

9   The Convention on the Prevention and Punishment of the Crime of Genocide was adopted by the United Nations General Assembly on 9 December 1948 as General Assembly Resolution 260, UN Doc. A/RES/260 (III) (http://www.legal-tools.org/doc/cee5ed/).

Particularly in the early days of the ICTR, the use of careful language was crucial if the independence and integrity of the Tribunal and the Office of the Prosecutor were to be recognised and respected. That recognition had to come from the government of Rwanda, the United Nations and the global community. The difficulty of my task was substantially eased by the advice and friendship of the head of the United Nations Mission in Rwanda, Shaharyar Khan of Pakistan. Ambassador Khan, a former Pakistan Ambassador to France and High Commissioner to the United Kingdom, was a consummate diplomat who efficiently and helpfully steered me through the political jungle that then obtained in Rwanda.

Perhaps the most difficult negotiation with Rwanda related to the transfer to the ICTR of the real architect of the genocide, Théoneste Bagosora. He had been arrested in Cameroon and requests for extradition had been made by both Rwanda and Belgium. The Security Council resolution and the Statute for the ICTR gave the Tribunal primacy, and I insisted that the main perpetrator of the genocide should be brought to trial before the ICTR. When I met with the whole Rwandan cabinet, I made it clear that, rather than agree to Bagosora being transferred to Rwanda, I would suggest to the Security Council that the mission of the ICTR be brought to an end. After a tense and rather unpleasant meeting, the government of Rwanda conceded. There were no courts then sitting in Rwanda and Bagosora would likely have been murdered if he had been transferred to the custody of the Rwandan forces. He was subsequently convicted by the ICTR on charges including genocide and ultimately sentenced to 35 years in prison.[10] Yet again, appropriate language was crucial both in my dealings with the Rwandan government and in the public statements and press conferences that followed. It was essential to uphold the independence of the ICTR and at the same time to avoid, to the extent possible, embarrassing or alienating the government of Rwanda.

28.5. Civil Society

Non-governmental organisations have played an important role with regard to international criminal justice. It was their pressure that galvanised Western States during 1993 to support the establishment of the ICTY and later the ICTR. They publicised the reports of journalists emanating from the war zones in the former Yugoslavia.

---

[10] ICTY, *Prosecutor v. Bagosora and Nsengiyumva*, Appeals Chamber, Judgement, 14 December 2011, ICTR-98-41-A (https://legal-tools.org/doc/52d501).

It was civil society that began the successful campaign to have recognised what, for centuries, had been ignored: the role played by gender-
related crimes in warfare and, in particular, systematic mass rape. Reports
emerged early of gender crimes having been committed in both the former
Yugoslavia and Rwanda. Soon after I arrived in The Hague in August 1994,
I began to receive what became a deluge of letters, many hand-written,
pleading for me to give appropriate attention to the investigation of mass
rape as a method of warfare practised by the Serb forces in Bosnia and
Herzegovina. What impressed me was that the letters were not stereotyped.
They came from women and men in many countries. I was more impressed
than I would have been by a petition signed by many thousands of people. I
decided that all the letter-writers were entitled to a personalised response. I
appointed Patricia V. Sellers, one of the lawyers in my Office, to take care
of gender-related issues, both internal and external. One of her first tasks
was to draft appropriate responses to the many letters. It was important to
acknowledge the importance of the issue that had been raised and to make
it clear that their calls would receive a positive response from the Office of
the Prosecutor.

I also tasked Patricia V. Sellers with ensuring that any gender issues
in our Office were promptly and efficiently investigated and resolved. This
was important in an Office in which the largest department was the almost
all-male Investigations Section. It was difficult in the middle of the 1990s
to find experienced female police investigators who were willing to move
to The Hague to work for an *ad hoc* Tribunal. Fortunately, there were no
serious issues, and those that did emerge were efficiently and successful
handled by Sellers. It was important that at each monthly meeting of the
whole staff of the Office, I would stress the importance for the gender issue
and make it clear that Sellers was acting on my behalf and with my full authority. On one occasion, it was necessary to reprimand members of the
Investigations Section for telling sexist jokes. I made it clear that how they
behaved in their own homes was their business, but how they behaved in
our Office was my business.

When one of the female judges on the ICTY, Elizabeth Odio Benito
of Costa Rica, raised the absence of a charge of rape in one of the very first
indictments, it was made clear to her that at that time the only reference to
rape in the Statute was to be found in the definition of crimes against humanity. Such crimes required the commission of widespread or systematic
attacks, and that was not a case that we were able to make. Judge Odio Be-

nito suggested that rape be included in grave breaches of the Geneva Conventions. Whatever the demerits of that suggestion, the combined effects of the push from civil society and from the judges left little doubt that we were being called upon to give priority to gender crimes. Similar pressure came from the only female judge of the ICTR, Navi Pillay.

Very quickly, gender-related crimes were included in indictments, and in the ICTR, Judge Pillay wrote the judgment in which, for the first time, mass rape was recognised as an act of genocide.[11] The campaign continued into the debate on the Rome Statute for the International Criminal Court. The holistic definition of gender crimes to be found in that Statute is the result.[12]

So again, language became all-important in the relationship between the members of staff of the Offices of the Prosecutor of the ICTY and the ICTR, and in the relationship between those Offices, the media, civil society organisations and the general public.

28.6. Conclusion

I hope that I have been able to demonstrate the importance of language and its relationship to the integrity and independence of an international prosecutor. The politics relating to international criminal justice lies at the heart of the issues that arise on an almost daily basis. The obligations make it essential to meet and negotiate with governments, the United Nations, and non-governmental institutions, including the media.

There are always people who, for good reason or bad, are opposed to the very concept of international justice. As Morten Bergsmo points out, they are waiting to expose any inappropriate conduct and to magnify it in the public domain.[13] The attack by John Bolton, former National Security Adviser of the Trump Administration, is a case in point.[14] More recently, similar attacks have been made by the present Secretary of State Pompeo.[15]

---

[11] ICTR, *Prosecutor v. Akayesu*, Trial Chamber, Judgement, 2 September 1998, ICTR-96-4-T (http://www.legal-tools.org/doc/b8d7bd/).

[12] Rome Statute of the International Criminal Court, 17 July 1998, Articles 7(1)(g), 8(2)(b)(xxii), and 8(2)(e)(vi) (http://www.legal-tools.org/doc/7b9af9/).

[13] Bergsmo, 2018, p. 1, see above note 3.

[14] See Olivia Gazis, "In first major address, John Bolton attacks old foe", *CBS News*, 10 September 2018.

[15] See Marlise Simons and Megan Specia, "U.S. Revokes Visa of I.C.C. Prosecutor Pursuing Afghan War Crimes", *New York Times*, 5 April 2019.

It is important not to provide ammunition to opponents of international criminal justice in general, and the ICC in particular.

Transparency in the conduct of an international prosecutor is essential. Not only transparency with regard to what might be shared with the public, but also transparency with regard to those many issues that have to remain confidential. No less essential is the quality and integrity of the staff of any international prosecutor's office, and the mutual trust that must exist between them and the prosecutor. The success of the institution depends upon it.

29

Integrity and the Preservation of Independence in International Criminal Justice

David Donat Cattin and Melissa Verpile[*]

29.1. Introductory Notes: An NGO's Perspective

This chapter does not intend to address the topic of integrity and independence of International Criminal Court ('ICC') organs from the perspective of a non-governmental organisation ('NGO'). However, the democratic governance's features of the NGO that these authors are affiliated with will address the often-untold criticism concerning the purported lack of accountability, legitimacy and, at times, even integrity of certain civil society organisations.[1]

Parliamentarians for Global Action ('PGA') is a political organisation composed of Members of Parliaments, and it is an NGO with general consultative status to the United Nations ('UN') Economic and Social Council. As of the time of writing, approximately 1,300 individual lawmakers from

---

[*]   **David Donat Cattin** is the Secretary-General of Parliamentarians for Global Action ('PGA'). Over the last 20 years, he has worked to promote the universality and effectiveness of the Rome Statute of the International Criminal Court in approximately 100 countries. He holds a post-doctorate diploma from the Centre for Studies and Research of The Hague Academy of International Law (2002), a Ph.D. in Public International Law (2000) from the Faculty of Law of the University of Teramo (Italy). His writings on international criminal law appeared on well-known scholarly works, such as Triffterer's *Commentary on the Rome Statute of the ICC*, Nomos; Flavia Lattanzi and William Schabas, *Essays on the Rome Statute of the ICC*, il Sirente, vol. I, 1999, vol. II, 2004; and Larissa van den Herik and Carsten Stahn, *The Diversification and Fragmentation of International Criminal Law*, Brill, 2012. He co-edited and contributed to the book in honour of Professor (Judge) Flavia Lattanzi entitled *International Law and the Protection of Humanity*, Brill, 2016. Since May 2012, he has been Adjunct Professor of International Law at New York University Center for Global Affairs. **Melissa M. Verpile** is a senior legal officer of the International Law and Human Rights Programme at PGA, specifically incorporating international legal standards to domestic legislation to strengthen the rule of law and the protection of human rights. She holds a Master of Laws (LL.M.) in US and Comparative Law from Fordham University School of Law and a Master of Public Policy and Development from University Paris Descartes (Paris V). She is fluent in French, English, Spanish, Italian, Haitian Creole and Portuguese.
[1]   Jens Steffek and Kristina Hahn (eds.), *Evaluating Transnational NGOs: Legitimacy, Accountability, Representation*, Palgrave Macmillan UK, Springer, 2010.

---

137 national and regional legislative bodies are members of PGA. The Secretary-General of PGA heads the Secretariat, based in New York and The Hague, and is appointed by the Board of the organisation. The Board is comprised of 15 parliamentarians elected every two years by the PGA International Council, the representative body of the global membership composed of National Groups. The Secretary-General (or the Secretariat) has a duty to carry out the result-oriented implementation of the organisation's strategic plan and vision with integrity and efficiency.

Regarding these elected positions, Board members may not be re-elected for more than two consecutive terms of two years, while the Secretary-General may not be appointed for more than three terms of three years. This shows how the leadership of an NGO can be the democratic emanation of its constituency, which demands that service to the organisation be carried out in line with principles of transparency, effectiveness and accountability. These principles do not substantially differ from those discussed in the context of public entities, including inter-governmental organisations. The perspective of an NGO whose leadership is chosen through a democratic process is not substantially different from the perspective of other stakeholders from democratic institutions.

Given that States historically failed to prevent and punish international crimes, the global membership of PGA determined that it was necessary to create and support an international legal order in which the exercise of international criminal jurisdiction would address the impunity gap while obligating States to exercise their duty to prosecute domestically. This was discussed in a several debates held during PGA's Annual Fora and at meetings of its Board and International Council. Such a strong policy framing the work of PGA has been undertaken under the assumption that the 'international rule of law' is *not yet* a reality, but a goal to be attained through the progressive development and codification of international law.

In the framework of the 'Integrity Project' of the Centre for International Law Research and Policy (CILRAP) and the International Nuremberg Principles Academy, contributors have been invited to reflect on different aspects of the role of the individual in international judicial institutions. In view of the first seventeen years of ICC praxis, this chapter will try to shed light on the interplay between the notion of integrity and the maintenance of a core pillar of the judicial mandate, that is, the independence of judges and prosecutors.

It is essential to reflect on this topic in the current international context. Multilateralism is in crisis, there is a growing lack of confidence of constituents in their institutions, certain powerful countries lay outside the international accountability system for the most serious crimes of concern to the international community as a whole, and justice has been elusive to victims of mass atrocity crimes. Consequently, in this climate of mistrust, scrutiny is heightened for institutions like the International Criminal Court ('ICC'), the first permanent, independent, international court with jurisdiction to investigate and prosecute individuals accused of committing international crimes.

29.2. Towards the Inception of *an* International Rule of Law: The Creation of the Rome Statute of the ICC

In his 2004 Report on the Rule of Law and Transitional Justice in Conflict and Post-Conflict Societies, the UN Secretary-General defined the rule of law as

> a principle of governance in which all persons, institutions and entities, public and private, including the State itself, are accountable to laws that are publicly promulgated, equally enforced and independently adjudicated, and which are consistent with international human rights norms and standards. It requires, as well, measures to ensure adherence to the principles of supremacy of law, equality before the law, accountability to the law, fairness in the application of the law, separation of powers, participation in decision-making, legal certainty, avoidance of arbitrariness and procedural and legal transparency.[2]

This comprehensive definition has been promoted by the parliamentary membership of PGA before 1998, the year the Rome Statute of the ICC was adopted. Indeed, the vision of the organisation is to contribute to the creation of a rules-based international order. The construction of an international rule of law is an ongoing process, whereby there is an established system of public international law characterized by a decentralized and hor-

---

[2] The rule of law and transitional justice in conflict and post-conflict societies: Report of the Secretary-General, UN Doc. S/2004/616, 23 August 2004 (https://www.legal-tools.org/doc/77bebf). On 30 April 2004, PGA organized a roundtable with States' representatives and UN officials to provide input to the drafting of this definition. See PGA, *Annual Report 2004*, p. 19.

izontal system of law enforcement.[3] The international law system is based on the concept of equality of States and characterized by the lack of separation of powers, insofar as States concentrate powers and functions that are institutionally attributed to the legislative and executive governmental branches at the domestic level. The Rome Statute 'sub-system' is a self-contained system that reproduces the features of the judiciary in the domestic rule of law, as it is based on the principle of equality of all individuals before the law, which lies at the heart of the exercise of State power within effective and functioning legal systems.[4] In this sense, the Rome Statute constitutes a major innovation in global affairs and is an active step towards the idea of an international rule of law.

In order to fully achieve the establishment of an international rule of law, key institutions, including the ICC, face enormous external challenges. Twenty-two years after the adoption of the Rome Statute, there are not only external obstacles but serious internal challenges that undermine the institution and its legacy. One of the fundamental challenges is the perceived lack of integrity of the institution and its proceedings, which is a self-inflicted wound.

29.3. The Statutory Requirement of Integrity: The Mere Application of the Rome Statute?

The notion of the individual is central to international criminal law. The Rome Statute includes in its general principles of law that of individual criminal responsibility,[5] and its preamble affirms that the object and purpose of the treaty is to put an end to impunity for "the most serious crimes of concern to the international community as a whole" in respect of the in-

---

[3] Fragmentation of international law: Difficulties arising from the diversification and expansion of international law, UN Doc. A/CN.4/L.682, 13 April 2006, p. 246, para. 486 (https://www.legal-tools.org/doc/dda184): "A key point made in this study is that normative conflict is endemic to international law. Because of the spontaneous, decentralized and unhierarchical nature of international law-making - law-making by custom and by treaty - lawyers have always had to deal with heterogeneous materials at different levels of generality and with different normative force."

[4] For a description of the Rome Statute as a self-contained system, see David Donat Cattin, "Decision-making in the International Criminal Court: Functions of the Assembly of States Parties and Independence of the Judicial Organs", in Flavia Lattanzi and William Schabas (eds.), *Essays on the Rome Statute of the International Criminal Court-volume II*, il Sirente, 2004, pp. 69–84.

[5] See Rome Statute of the International Criminal Court, 17 July 1998, Article 25, Part 3 ('ICC Statute') (https://www.legal-tools.org/doc/e5faa8/).

---

dividual. Moreover, the Statute creates a system of norms that essentially applies to individuals (accused persons and victims) and is substantially implemented by individuals as organs (namely the Judges and the Prosecutor,[6] albeit nominated and elected by States). It does not seem unusual that the ICC constitutive charter would indicate professional requirements and those pertaining to the character of officials of an international judicial body, given this prominent responsibility to humankind.

Integrity may refer to the behaviour of an individual who adheres to moral and ethical principles, which are reflected in legal norms (for example, fair and impartial trial). In the context at hand, this adherence to a set of moral or ethical principles is to be understood as the application of the highest standards and best practices both in the conduct of professional duties and in the behaviour of court officials wielding the powers of a criminal court, which can, *inter alia*, deprive an accused and/or convicted person of personal liberty during the exercise of their duties. In this sense, and for the purposes of this chapter, the authors retain the definition of 'integrity' presented by Morten Bergsmo in his policy brief as a concept often used in connection with "high moral character".[7]

Both concepts are found in Articles 36 and 42 of the Rome Statute respectively, regarding the qualifications, nomination and election of judges as well as the principles attached to the Office of the Prosecutor ('OTP') and *a fortiori* the qualities expected of its officials. 'Integrity' and 'high moral character' are legal concepts closely linked to those of probity and independence, which is a pre-condition for impartiality. As in any domestic or international judicial institution, independence is quintessential to justice. The ICC Judges are bound by the Rome Statute provisions to appropriately apply the Statute and other sources of law listed in Article 21, with full independence, regardless of any political preference or external influence. The organs of the ICC have significant jurisdictional power, which implies great responsibility. Hence the importance of having judges at the Court who are adequately competent and display qualities intrinsic to a high moral character. To answer the question posed in the title of this section, the correct application of the Rome Statute provisions by judges during the Court's proceedings safeguards the integrity of the ICC. Court officials

---

[6] All the organs of the ICC as defined in *ibid.* Article 34 consist of individuals.

[7] Morten Bergsmo, "Revisiting Integrity in International Justice", FICHL Policy Brief Series No. 93 (2018), Torkel Opsahl Academic EPublisher, Brussels, 2018 (https://www.legal-tools.org/doc/e550f7).

who correctly apply the Rome Statute display a level of competence that protects the institution from external attacks on the soundness of its decisions. In the Rome Statute, integrity seems to refer to competence linked to the professional responsibility of the judges and Prosecutor as well as to the fact that these individual organs shall be – and perceived to be – incorruptible and impartial in all situations and cases before them.

29.4. The Preservation of Independence and Integrity at the ICC *Despite* its Assembly of States Parties (ASP)

The Rome Statute established a system which, notwithstanding its weaknesses, deserves to be protected, effectively implemented, and, when useful and appropriate, reviewed, reformed and improved. To do so, all stakeholders, including civil society organisations, should strive to reduce the influence of politics in the conduct of prosecutorial and judicial affairs, as much as the reality allows for. Actors, including PGA, have a propensity to call for criticism of the ICC on issues that have now become apparent to international law practitioners. However, caution is essential: safeguarding the Rome Statute system has become a pressing matter, and criticism should be delivered in a constructive manner.

Integrity is a central component of *complementarity* in the sense that the ICC is a 'court of last resort' where States are unable or unwilling to act to genuinely investigate and prosecute individuals allegedly responsible of committing international crimes, which may be a question of national integrity. When situations of inability or unwillingness arise, it means that there is a disintegration of the State or bad faith on the part of its authorities, which may result in 'sham justice' or inertia. In the face of these situations, which are not uncommon in the twenty-first century, we can no longer let impunity reign at the international and domestic levels.

To achieve the goal of effectively fighting impunity, ICC organs must be credible, effective and independent. Integrity is, therefore, a precondition of the Court's effective operations. The effective realization of the object and purpose of the Rome Statute is to be understood as integral to that exercise of integrity and independence.

The Rome Statute explicitly set a requirement to preserve the independence of the judges from the influence of the executive branch of government, as "[j]udges shall not engage in any activity which is likely to interfere with their judicial functions or to affect confidence in their independence".[8] Preserving the independence of ICC judges also means respecting the separation of powers to avoid conflicts of interest. On 18 February 2019, when Judge OZAKI Kuniko of Japan, a member of the Chamber trying Bosco Ntaganda, conveyed to her peers that she may have to resign as a "full-time judge"[9] because she had been appointed as the Japanese Ambassador to Estonia, this constituted a serious breach of her fiduciary duties to the ICC. This also fuelled Court detractors who argued that the institution is not impartial (following a similar rationale to the legal metaphor of the *fruit from the poisonous tree* to argue that the decisions of the Court would also be tainted by the lack of impartiality). On 4 March 2019, a plenary session of the ICC Judges on the matter concluded "that it was clear that the prohibitions in Article 40(2) of the Statute did not apply in the concrete circumstances, […] that Judge Ozaki's independence would not be undermined by assuming the role of Ambassador of Japan to Estonia".[10] Such finding by the majority is inherently problematic and could undermine the independence of the ICC unless remedied. Such a remedy rescued the Court as a result of the public scrutiny that followed the above-cited decision. In April 2019, Judge Ozaki resigned from her diplomatic post in Estonia, and, in June 2019, the plenary of the Judges and the Appeals Chamber dismissed the defence's motion for the disqualification of the judge.[11]

This controversy is emblematic of the approach to integrity and independence within the Rome Statute system, given that the entire issue would not have even emerged if the State Party of the nationality of the judge in question had not appointed a sitting judge to an executive position of government. An ambassadorial appointment of this nature would not have been even imaginable within a domestic jurisdiction, and it reveals the 'original sin' committed by States that nominate career diplomats for judicial positions at the ICC, supported by the practice of other States that voted for this type of candidates.

---

[8] ICC Statute, Article 40, to be read in the framework of Part 4, see above note 5.

[9] International Criminal Court ('ICC'), *The Prosecutor v. Bosco Ntaganda*, Decision on your request of 18 February 2019, Internal Memorandum, 19 March 2019, ICC-01/04-02/06 (https://www.legal-tools.org/doc/5a27d1).

[10] *Ibid.*, p. 6, para. 14.

[11] ICC, *Prosecutor v. Bosco Ntaganda*, The Presidency, Notification of the Decision of the Plenary of Judges on the Defence Request for the Disqualification of Judge Kuniko Ozaki from the case of *The Prosecutor v. Bosco Ntaganda*, 20 June 2019, ICC-01/04-02/06-2355 (https://www.legal-tools.org/doc/d7252b).

States Parties should be fully aware of the object and purpose of the Rome Statute, which is – as the Romans used to say, *'repetita iuvant'* – "to put an end to impunity for the most serious crimes of concern to the international community as a whole", in accordance with the Preamble to the Statute. Yet, some stakeholders of the Court, including States Parties to the Rome Statute, may forget this object and purpose and focus on the national interests of their country in their relations with the Court. Another scenario, albeit less common, is that diplomatic personnel interfacing with the ICC as an international organisation may give precedence to their personal agendas over a common agenda to protect the integrity of the Rome Statute system. Such personal considerations are legitimate; however, they do not justify any departure from the standards outlined in the Rome Statute. The level of commitment required to exercise a judicial function at the ICC is higher than the one we may be witnessing in some instances today. It is imperative to recall that 123 States Parties have joined this accountability system, and one of the roles and responsibilities of the ASP is to adopt measures that ensure the protection of the integrity and independence of the Court.

29.5. Reconciling Ideals and Reality: A Functional Approach

Public international law practitioners recall vividly the process and the principled ideals underlying the creation of the ICC, echoed in the Preamble to the Rome Statute. Twenty-two years later, this project to prevent and punish the perpetrators of genocide, crimes against humanity, war crimes and the crime of aggression is under attack, by States Parties and non-States Parties alike. In the framework of a politically intricate global context, the international community needs to adjust its course.

If the ICC issues an arrest warrant against former President Omar Al Bashir, accused of five counts of crimes against humanity, two counts of war crimes, and three counts of genocide,[12] and the warrant fully satisfies the legal requirements, all actors of the international community and, in particular, representatives of ICC States Parties should be aware that they are under the obligation to refrain from 'shaking hands' with Al Bashir, a fugitive from justice. Yet, the 2018 proceedings on this prominent case before the Appeals Chamber revolved around issues (primarily raised by Jor-

---

[12] See ICC, *Prosecutor v. Omar Hassan Ahmad Al Bashir*, The Appeals Chamber, Judgment in the Jordan Referral re Al-Bashir Appeal, 6 May 2019, ICC-02/05-01/09 OA2 (https://www.legal-tools.org/doc/0c5307).

dan and the rather non-ritual and unusual *amici curiae*, the League of Arab States and the African Union[13]) that are part of the body of international law since the Allied powers issued the 1943 declaration in Moscow. According to the declaration, the leaders of Axis powers did not have immunity from prosecution if an international jurisdiction concluded that the evidence against them proved their individual responsibility for international crimes, as enshrined in the 1945 London Charter, ratified by all members of the international community at the time. Therefore, the debates before the ICC Appeals Chamber should not have revolved around Jordan's obligation to arrest Al Bashir. On 6 May 2019, the ICC Appeals Chamber confirmed the ICC Pre-Trial Chamber II's decision regarding the fact that Jordan failed to comply with its obligations under the Rome Statute by not arresting Al-Bashir and surrendering him to the ICC while he was on Jordanian territory attending the League of Arab States' Summit on 29 March 2017. Despite the determination of lack of co-operation, there was no consequence for Jordan at the ASP level or at the level of the UN Security Council, which referred the Darfur situation to the ICC pursuant to resolution 1593 on 31 March 2005, given that Jordan was deemed to be constructively engaging with the ICC.

Dissent is a key tool to make advancements in any institutional framework, including the Rome Statute system, and uncritical support may be analogous to a 'kiss of death' and be as detrimental to the system as the above-criticized failure of some States Parties to enforce the arrest warrants against Omar Al Bashir when he was the President of Sudan. NGOs who supported and continue to support the implementation of the Rome Statute's mandate have often made critical assessments of the ICC organs' performance at various stages of its institutional development.

For example, when the first ICC Prosecutor presented to States Parties, NGOs and other stakeholders the OTP's strategy for 'focused investi-

---

[13] An *amicus curiae* is 'a friend' of the Court, providing legal advice to the Judges in a gratuitous, free and independent manner in order to help the jurisdictional organ to fulfil its complex mandate. While individual academics or practitioners advising the Court '*pro bono causa*' can fulfil adequately the role of *amici curiae*, it is questionable whether their input may be equated to the one provided by academics or practitioners hired by an international organization, which is paying these jurists in order to pursue and advance the official policies of the organization. It is hereby submitted that the role and *locus standi* of *amici curiae* before the ICC should be reserved only to individual friends of the Court, who are not motivated by the interest of a client, but only by their personal interest to assist the judges in their interpretation of the Rome Statute and other sources of applicable law under Article 21.

gations' during the early years of his mandate, PGA expressed serious concerns. The rationale for 'focused investigations' hinged on the determination that 'Milošević-like trials' were not desirable for the ICC. It is the view of the authors that the complexity of the Milošević 'mega-trial' did not represent a negative model, regardless of its procedural outcome, due to the extreme gravity and complexity of the crimes for which a head of State or government should be brought to justice. In fact, the concept of 'focused investigations' may not be desirable in most situations and cases falling under the ICC's jurisdiction, given the need to investigate atrocity-type crimes in a satisfactory manner, which entails the need to investigate their contextual elements (for instance, the widespread or systematic attack against any civilian population characterizing the notion of crimes against humanity). It must be stressed that the PGA representative expressed concerns regarding the idea of 'focused investigation' since the first consultations between NGOs and the OTP, and before the commencement of the early ICC proceedings.

A few years later, the pre-occupation stemming from the policy of the first Prosecutor of the Court was in some regards assuaged by the policy adopted by the second Prosecutor. The inclination to try to conduct relatively fast and representative (focused) investigations, to be followed by focused prosecutions and adjudications, did not bring about fast and focused criminal proceedings, as illustrated by the cases *The Prosecutor v. Thomas Lubanga Dyilo* and *The Prosecutor v. Germain Katanga*. As such proceedings developed, NGOs expressed other concerns to the OTP regarding evidence-related matters, including methods of evidence collection and digital and technologically derived evidence, as well as the excessive reliance on witness evidence. These concerns have been partially addressed by the second Prosecutor in her OTP policies.

But the most serious problem of integrity of the judicial process is associated with the issue of competence of the prosecutorial and judicial organs of the Court. As identified by one of the authors of this chapter, this concerns, for example, the unsound decision of the pre-trial and trial chambers in the cases of the Kenyan situation to continue issuing summons to appear voluntarily in the courtroom against all accused, including the then Deputy Prime Minister Kenyatta and Member of Parliament Ruto. In meetings with NGOs and consultations with the OTP and representatives of the Court's chambers, one of the present authors highlighted the Rome Statute's provisions requiring the issuance of an arrest warrant. Indeed, this relates to when the accused is either threatening to reiterate crimes or commit new crimes or is at risk of escaping or is posing threats to the integrity of evidence (including threats to the safety, security, wellbeing and privacy of victims and witnesses). Even in the face of an agreement between the Prosecutor and the defence on the voluntary appearance of the accused, the relevant chamber could have *proprio motu* transformed the summons to appear into a warrant of arrest, including an order to remain in detention in a safehouse in the ICC's host State. Former UN Under-Secretary General for Legal Affairs, Hans Corell, expressed similar concerns.[14]

Kenyatta and Ruto forged an unexpected alliance when they were travelling between The Hague and Nairobi. They called it "Jubilee Coalition" and, after every appearance at the Court, they went back home as candidates for the presidency and vice-presidency, presenting themselves at times as the victims of a neo-colonial Court against African leaders, and, other times, chanting the role of the law-abiding citizens who respect court orders and defend themselves against allegations while accepting to be treated as every other individual 'equal' before the law. Their propaganda efforts proved successful as, in March 2013, they resulted in presidential election victory while they were accused persons of crimes against humanity before the ICC. When they assumed power, they launched an unprecedented State-driven campaign to destroy the ICC's credibility, making use of the State apparatus. Assisted by extremely effective defence counsel teams, the two accused succeeded in obtaining a decision to halt proceedings against them. In the OTP's view, this outcome was the consequence of their actions to threaten and attack witnesses and victims, and tamper with the evidence that the Prosecutor had disclosed during the proceedings.

If the Prosecutor's allegations are genuine, how could the relevant Court organs have prevented this failure? The answer might be found in the recommendations made by NGOs, including PGA, well before Kenyatta and Ruto won the presidential elections, namely, to apply the Rome Statute provisions and transform the summons to appear voluntarily into valid arrest warrants. When there is a risk for the integrity of evidence, including the testimony of witnesses who may disappear, the ICC Pre-Trial Chamber has the ability to "provide for the protection and privacy of victims and

---

[14] See Hans Corell, "Challenges for the International Criminal Court", in *International Judicial Monitor*, Winter 2014.

witnesses, the preservation of evidence, the protection of persons who have been arrested or appeared in response to a summons, and the protection of national security information".[15] These are grounds for transforming a summons to appear into an arrest warrant. In the *Situation in the Republic of Kenya*, neither the Prosecutor nor the judges carried out their judicial duties effectively under the Rome Statute to protect witnesses under Article 68 – which is applicable to all stages of the proceedings[16] – and prevent offences against the administration of justice. The unintended and indirect result of this situation was that the National Alliance candidate Uhuru Kenyatta backed by the Jubilee Alliance won the Kenyan presidential elections with 50.05 per cent on 4 March 2013. This case revealed many of the shortfalls of the Rome Statute system.

As illustrated above, NGOs play a critical role in safeguarding the Rome statute system by pointing to deficiencies and lack of confidence in ICC proceedings stemming from a lack of competence, integrity or independence of its organs, as well as from deficiencies of the ASP and its Member States.

As in 2002–06, in 2018–19 the ICC was confronted with the vision of John Bolton, former US Under-Secretary of State for Arms Control and International Security Affairs from 2001 to 2004 and Ambassador to the UN from August 2005 to December 2006 under President George W. Bush, and President Trump's National Security Advisor from April 2018 to September 2019. Bolton supported the Iraq War in 2003 and, closer to our time and topic, Bolton stated:

> on the eve of September 11th, I want to deliver a clear and unambiguous message on behalf of the president of the United States. The United States will use any means necessary to protect our citizens and those of our allies from unjust prosecution by this illegitimate court. We will not cooperate with the ICC. We will provide no assistance to the ICC. We will not join the ICC. We will let the ICC die on its own. After all, for all intents and purposes, the ICC is already dead to us. […].

---

[15]   ICC Statute, Article 57, Part 5, see above note 5.

[16]   See David Donat Cattin, "Article 68: Protection of Victims and Witnesses and their Participation in the Proceedings", in Otto Triffterer and Kai Ambos (eds.), *Commentary on the Rome Statute of the ICC*, third edition, Beck/Hart Publishers/Nomos, 2015, pp. 1686–1687.

> [T]he International Criminal Court unacceptably threatens American sovereignty and US national security interests.[17]

Bolton considered the ICC to be illegitimate because he defined it as 'a supranational court' that 'threatens US sovereignty'. Fake news! All of us have the duty to protect the integrity of the Rome Statute and explain to Bolton that there is no supranational institution here with overarching powers of any kind. The ICC is an international, not supranational, court, which depends on the monopoly of the use of force by States, which are required to carry out its orders, requests and decisions.

29.6. Ailments Stemming from the Functioning of the ICC Are Not a Fatality

Antonio Cassese, a giant of international law and jurisprudence, opened the doors of The Hague to international justice at a time when nobody believed that the International Criminal Tribunal for the former Yugoslavia would have had an impact. Judge Cassese was the first president of the *ad hoc* Tribunal, while Judge Richard J. Goldstone was its first prosecutor. When the ICC became a *permanent* fixture of international law and was saluted as "a gift of hope to the future generations",[18] several individuals, who were more interested in their individual careers than the principles and norms of international criminal law and justice that the Rome Statute embodies, managed to join the Court. Whereas the Tribunal started as a rather utopian project, the ICC commenced its operations on solid foundations, which inevitably attracted personnel and elected officials seeking solid employment.

Some detractors of the Court, including Bolton, accused the ICC of not being accountable. But how can this court be unaccountable if the ASP has the possibility, unknown in most national systems, to "remove from office" its highest officials? The ASP is a political body with many prerogatives of different natures. The ASP is a legislator because it can amend the Statute; it is an administrator with executive powers, as it approves the

---

[17] John Bolton, *Protecting American Constitutionalism and Sovereignty from International Threats*, 10 September 2018, Address to the Federalist Society in Washington, D.C. (https://www.legal-tools.org/doc/84c2b4/).

[18] See Kofi Annan's statement at the 18 July 1998 ceremony held at the Campidoglio, City Hall of Rome, reproduced in UN Press Release. Secretary-General says Establishment of International Criminal Court is Gift of Hope to Future Generations, UN Doc. SG/SM/6643-L/2891, 21 July 1998 (https://www.legal-tools.org/doc/e7c55e).

budget; and, it has oversight prerogatives. With a vote by two-thirds, the ASP can 'fire' a judge, on the basis of a recommendation issued by at least two-thirds of the judges. More significantly, the ASP can remove the Prosecutor from office simply with a vote of 51 per cent, provided that such decisions are motivated on legal grounds under the Rome Statute (for example, the Prosecutor is liable of miscarriage of justice).

The main difficulty making accountability work lies in the fact that the ASP is not performing some of its functions. It never set-up a committee to determine disciplinary measures, nor did it set-up a standing committee with hired experts in the field to tackle issues. Although there is a functioning Internal Oversight Mechanism, this spear is not enough to deal with major issues. The ICC is accountable to a system, but actors of the system have not performed at the level indicated in the Rome Statute. The final report of the Independent Expert Review is an important step forward, but it is up to the Assembly to take relevant action within the framework of its pivotal statutory mandate.[19]

29.7. Moving Forward to Protect the Integrity of the Rome Statute

PGA commemorated the twentieth anniversary of the Rome Statute by organizing a forward-looking conference in the Sala della Protomoteca, in Campidoglio (Rome).[20] This event took place at the initiative of the Vice-President of the European Parliament with portfolio-responsibility for human rights and democracy (Fabio Massimo Castaldo, MEP), and was hosted by the Mayor of Rome. The conference gathered distinguished representatives of the three branches of power of the Italian State, PGA members from the European and Dominican Republic Parliaments, ICC judges, legal experts, NGO representatives, members of the press, academics and students. All stakeholders agreed that one of the main problems of the Court relates to the lack of competence of its officials, which often translates into lack of efficiency and effectiveness.

One of the proposed solutions advocated by PGA to improve the Court's overall performance is a reform of the system of nomination and election of the judges and the Prosecutor. Articles 36 to 44 of the Statute

---

[19] See Independent Expert Review, Independent Expert Review of the International Criminal Court and the Rome Statute System: Final Report, 30 September 2020 (https://www.legal-tools.org/doc/cv19d5/).

[20] PGA, "Conference on the Commemoration of the 20th Anniversary of the Statute of the International Criminal Court", 23 July 2018.

have not been fully implemented and, notwithstanding all the efforts to differentiate the elections for the highest ICC officials from those of other international organisations, States Parties have not yet ensured that only the best candidates apply to judicial positions at the ICC. Within the framework of nomination processes for international judicial institutions, a seconded judge of the European Court of Human Rights ('ECtHR') presented a study on the correlation between the ECtHR's impressive increase in productivity derived from the reforms of the system of judicial nomination and election. Reforms in the same vein as those of the ECtHR are needed to professionalize and depoliticize the nomination process and, albeit to a lesser extent, the election process of the ICC Judges. During the conference, Judge Marc Perrin de Brichambaut rightly noted that ICC judges are elected by States and that one could not eliminate that element of legitimacy from the system. As much as jurists like the idea of an independent body, the Rome Statute system makes 'full' independence difficult to achieve. However, States can take measures to increase the transparency of the process, which will increase the faith and the integrity of the ICC.

In this respect, PGA has advocated for States to propose at the ASP a resolution on enhanced procedures for the nomination of judicial candidates. The resolution should include several concrete measures: (1) The publicity of the calls for applications to become a candidate in each country as a precondition for valid nominations; and (2) the binding nature of opinions issued by the Advisory Committee on Nominations of Judges.

These two measures appear to be simple and they may not require an amendment to Article 36 of the Rome Statute, which can be interpreted as containing a minimum standard of qualifications and characteristics of a valid judicial nomination, whereby nothing is provided in respect of the domestic procedure to achieve nominations. One of the PGA proposals, reflected in a non-paper submitted by Liechtenstein to a relevant Working Group of the ASP set up in New York during 2019, regarded the possibility for States to have confidential consultations with the Advisory Committee on Nominations. As such, States would receive appropriate input in case the Committee would make a determination that a candidate proposed by a State would not comply with the requirements of competence, integrity and 'high moral character' under the Rome Statute. Even if the stand-alone resolution adopted by the 2019 ASP reinforces the role of this Advisory Committee, the proposal was not accepted by some States, which used and abused the argument that the process of nomination is a 'State-driven' process in order to avoid to self-impose a public procedure to attract the best possible judicial candidates for the ICC. In a similar vein, a few States rejected the Liechtenstein proposal for merit-based, pre-established criteria for the selection of national nominees through open and public calls for proposals, and the Working Group did not decide through a majority vote.

Hence, the lack of unanimity and the search for 'consensus' drove the ASP to the lowest common denominator, now reflected in the resolution on the review of the procedure for the nomination and election of judges.[21] Therefore, this ASP resolution falls short of the PGA recommendations to ensure that States impose on themselves a merit-based, pre-established and transparent procedure at the national level (Open Call for Nominations, aforementioned) to be carried out by each State to produce a ranking-list headed by the best possible candidate. The list would have been transmitted to the Advisory Committee on Nominations for its independent assessment. Several elements of the PGA proposal were reflected in proposals tabled by Liechtenstein and the UK that received significant support from States in the ASP Working Group. However, a few determined States managed to impede consensus on the text. The matter was not open to a vote within the Working Group and the ASP itself, and an agreement on the text was found on few improvements concerning the functioning of the Advisory Committee on Nominations. This decision-making process suggests that the 'diplomatic method' is one of the main 'enemies' or impediments of the international justice system, which should be supported by an ASP that should decide on the basis of the democratic method.

Preserving the Rome Statute system means protecting the advancements we have made since World War II to protect the rule of law and the human rights of vulnerable populations. The supremacy of the law should not be a controversial principle before domestic or international jurisdictions. The Rome Statute created the ICC as a court of last resort in a rather complex system. We have an enormous challenge to do all that is in our power to uphold the wise and immortal words of the Chief Prosecutor for the United States Army at the Einsatzgruppen Trial, Mr. Benjamin B. Ferencz: "Never give up hope, never stop trying to make this a more humane world [...]. The time is now, and the place is here".

---

[21] ICC, Assembly of State Parties, Resolution on the review of the procedure for the nomination and election of judges, 6 December 2019, ICC-ASP/18/Res.4 (https://www.legal-tools.org/doc/bswpis).

30

Integrity and Independence:
Common Standards and
Uneven Cost of Implementation

Adedeji Adekunle[*]

30.1. Introduction

Integrity and independence are key qualities required of persons appointed as the Prosecutor and Judges of the International Criminal Court ('ICC'). Both Articles 36 and 42 of the Statute of the ICC[1] refer to persons of "high moral character" and emphasize independence and impartiality. These qualifications are reinforced by the undertaking in Article 45 of the Statute, to enter into their respective duties impartially and conscientiously as well as the elaboration of separate codes of ethical conduct for judges of the Court,[2] the Office of the Prosecutor ('OTP')[3] and the staff of the Court.[4]

These codes – for example, the Code of Conduct for the OTP – underscore the importance of impartiality and independence as fundamental attributes of the office. This chapter examines whether, and if so, to what extent account should be taken of the diverse background of staff in evalu-

---

[*] Professor **Adedeji Adekunle** is a Senior Advocate of Nigeria and Visiting Fellow of the National Human Rights Institute of the Nigerian Human Rights Commission. He was Director General of the Nigerian Institute of Advanced Legal Studies ('NIALS') until May 2019. A former Special Adviser to Nigeria's Attorney General and Minister of Justice on various aspects of criminal justice administration. He was Secretary of the 2004 Law Revision Committee. He has authored a Guide to Judicial officers on Nigeria's Administration of Criminal Justice Act 2015 and several other monographs. The author acknowledges with gratitude the assistance of Joke Adediran and Bola Omojola, both promising researchers in the International Law Department of NIALS.

[1] Rome Statute of the International Criminal Court, 17 July 1998, Articles 36 and 42 ('ICC Statute') (http://www.legal-tools.org/doc/7b9af9/).

[2] ICC, Code of Judicial Ethics, 2 January 2005 ('ICC Code of Judicial Ethics') (https://www.legal-tools.org/doc/383f8f/).

[3] ICC, Code of Conduct for the Office of the Prosecutor, 5 September 2013 ('ICC Code of Conduct for the OTP') (https://www.legal-tools.org/doc/3e11eb/).

[4] ICC, Code of Conduct for Staff Members, 4 April 2011 (https://www.legal-tools.org/doc/75f9db/).

---

ating a case of non-compliance.[5] First, it matters that concepts like "integrity" and "impartiality" are not just seen as necessary components of a justice framework, but also that there is sufficient understanding of what they connote in the context of an institutional framework and what consequences follow a breach.[6] Evenness and objectivity in enforcement are just as important as adopting an ethics code. Therefore, to avoid unfairness, international civil servants and high officials in international courts must have a sufficient understanding of what the concepts mean by contextualizing them within the framework of their beliefs and norms.

Secondly, while it is no doubt important to have a universal understanding of ethical concepts, the reality is that this is hardly the case as individual understandings of what these concepts mean may vary. During the international conference on 'Integrity in International Justice', Ambassador Paschke observed, "the UN staff represents, on the whole, a peculiar mix of diverse attitudes and underlying ethics".[7]

In that case, it becomes necessary to set institutional pathways to clearly illustrate what will not be tolerated and provide mechanisms to prevent such conduct.

This is not to encourage a dilution of objective standards even if pressures or the cost of compliance differ. It, however, requires a deeper assessment of the different backgrounds and cultures of international officials and the fashioning of mechanisms to highlight objective standards and ensure widespread awareness and counselling of how to identify and deal with pressures to depart from these standards.

Such pressure can be brought to bear on the integrity and independence of international officials directly (where the official or the interest exerting the pressure is the direct beneficiary) or indirectly (official acting for

---

[5] It has been suggested that the ambiguity produced by this confluence of legal traditions and culture in international courts may be significant, and it cannot be dispelled by an assumed "judicial instinct". See Brandeis Institute for International Judges, "Toward the Development of Ethics Guidelines for International Courts", in Brandeis Institute for International Judges, *Authority and Autonomy: Defining the Role of International and Regional Courts*, Brandeis University, Waltham, MA, 2003.

[6] Morten Bergsmo, "Revisiting Integrity in International Justice", FICHL Policy Brief Series No. 93 (2018), Torkel Opsahl Academic EPublisher, Brussels, 2018 (http://www.toaep.org/pbs-pdf/93-bergsmo/).

[7] Karl Theodor Paschke, "On the Efforts to Uphold Standards of Integrity Through the Work of the United Nations Internal Oversight Services", CILRAP Film, 2 December 2018 (https://www.cilrap.org/cilrap-film/181202-paschke).

other interests (States)). The pressure may also be political, economic, cultural or even historical. While all international justice personnel subscribe to a uniform code and are expected to suppress their subjective prejudices in the discharge of their duties, this is easier said than done when external challenges to their independence are presented.

30.2. Ethical Gaps in the Prosecutorial Function of the Court

Recent revelations about the conduct of Luis Moreno-Ocampo, the first ICC Prosecutor, in office and also thereafter, have provoked discussions on the effectiveness of the integrity requirements and safeguards, particularly for the OTP.[8] It is no secret that whereas a draft code of conduct had been elaborated for the OTP, it was only after the election of Fatou Bensouda as the second ICC Prosecutor in 2012 that an ethics code for the Office was adopted.[9]

It may well be that the lateness in coming of the Code had a profound effect on the conduct of Ocampo and some of his staff, as demonstrated by a series of judicial disapprovals over some decisions of the OTP in relation to charges brought against Thomas Lubanga. The latter was charged for war crimes under Articles 8(2)(b)(xxvi) and 8(2)(e)(vii) of the ICC Statute, namely the enlistment and conscription of children into the Union des Patriotes Congolais and the Forces Patriotiques pour la Libération du Congo in connection with the internal conflict in the DRC.

These unfortunate incidents[10] betrayed profound integrity gaps on the part of the OTP and a preoccupation with a 'winning at all costs' mentality even if this amounted to an abuse of the process of court.

In the first case, the Prosecutor had improperly sought to shield exculpatory material from the defendant by invoking a limited power to enter into confidentiality agreements with information-providers, under Article

---

[8]   Morten Bergsmo, Wolfgang Kaleck, Sam Muller and William H. Wiley, "A Prosecutor Falls, Time for the Court to Rise", FICHL Policy Brief Series No. 86 (2017), Torkel Opsahl Academic EPublisher, Brussels, 2017 (http://www.legal-tools.org/doc/41b41a/). It has also been observed that a fallout of the first 15 years when the ICC was more mission oriented than values driven is its weak culture of institutional integrity. See Brigid Inder, "Conformity, Leadership and the Culture of Integrity", CILRAP Film, 1 December 2018 (https://www.cilrap.org/cilrap-film/181201-inder).

[9]   See above note 3.

[10]   For an extensive discussion of these incidents as well as others See Milan Markovic, "The ICC Prosecutor's Missing Code of Conduct", in *Texas International Law Journal*, 2011, vol. 47, p. 201.

54(3) of the Statute. The Court criticized the prosecutor's routine recourse to Article 54(3)(e) for obtaining a wide range of materials under the cloak of confidentiality, in order to identify from those materials evidence to be used at trial. In the words of the Court:

> This is the exact opposite of the proper use of the provision, which is, exceptionally, to allow the prosecution to receive information or documents which are not for use at trial but which are instead intended to "lead" to new evidence. The prosecution's approach constitutes a wholesale and serious abuse, and a violation of an important provision which was intended to allow the prosecution to receive evidence confidentially, in very restrictive circumstances. The logic of the prosecution's position is that all of the evidence that it obtains from information-providers can be the subject of Article 54(3)(e) agreements.[11]

In the Court's view, the Prosecution had incorrectly used Article 54(3)(e) when entering into agreements with information-providers, with the consequence that a significant body of exculpatory evidence which would otherwise have been disclosed to the accused is to be withheld from him, thereby improperly inhibiting the opportunities for the accused to prepare his defence.

In the second case, the Prosecutor had declined to comply with the Trial Chamber's order to disclose the identity of an intermediary to the defence, citing grave security and safety concerns. The Court took a dim view of this and observed that:

> The Prosecutor has chosen to prosecute this accused. In the Chamber's judgment, he cannot be allowed to continue with this prosecution if he seeks to reserve to himself the right to avoid the Court's orders whenever he decides that they are inconsistent with his interpretation of his other obligations. In order for the Chamber to ensure that the accused receives a fair trial, it is necessary that its orders, decisions and rulings

---

[11] ICC, Situation in Democratic Republic of the Congo, *The Prosecutor v Thomas Lubanga Dyilo*, Trial Chamber, Decision on the consequences of non-disclosure of exculpatory materials covered by Article 54(3)(e) agreements and the application to stay the prosecution of the accused, together with certain other issues raised at the Status Conference on 10 June 2008, 13 June 2008, ICC-01/04-01/06-1401 (http://www.legal-tools.org/doc/e6a054/).

are respected, unless and until they are overturned on appeal,
or suspended by order of the Court.[12]

On yet another occasion, the Court had to warn the prosecutor when
he resorted to the media and misrepresented proceedings in the *Lubanga*
case, by predicting a long jail term for Lubanga based on the testimonies of
"courageous and credible witnesses" of the prosecution.[13] Subsequently,
the Prosecutor himself authored an editorial where he misrepresented the
decision of the Trial Chambers, which had authorized the issue of arrest
warrants against Al Bashir, the Sudanese leader charged for war crimes, in
a way portraying that Al Bashir had actually been convicted.[14] While these
events seem to have drawn more attention to the OTP, the overall dampen-
ing effect on confidence is evident. To what extent can these unhappy incidents be attributed to the absence of a code for the OTP? Put another way,
could the existence of a code have prevented these cases of indiscretion?
What role or influence is wielded by a code of ethics in such an office? In
Markovic's view, the lack of an ethics code by the ICC imposed "conflicting obligations" on the ICC Prosecutor, as seen in the above instances. He
concludes that the conflicting obligations were resolved in ways that have
undermined the ICC's credibility and diminished confidence in the Court.[15]

30.3. Uniform Standards of Integrity and Ethics Code

It should be noted that the diversity of cultures and legal traditions, which
is a feature of many international organizations, including the ICC, and
which invariably instructs the need for a standard uniform code is not neu-
tralized by the mere existence of a code. In fact, it is this diversity and the
conflicts inherent in the duties of the OTP and Judges that give life to the
ethical standards. Markovic, for example, had observed that because of the
differences in legal and social backgrounds among OTP attorneys, different

---

[12] ICC, Situation in Democratic Republic of the Congo, *The Prosecutor v. Thomas Lubanga
Dyilo*, Trial Chamber, Redacted Decision on the Prosecution's Urgent Request for Variation
of the Time-Limit to Disclose the Identity of Intermediary 143 or Alternatively to Stay Proceedings Pending Further Consultations with the VWU, 8 July 2010, ICC-01/04-01/06-
2517-Red (http://www.legal-tools.org/doc/cd4f10/).

[13] ICC, Situation in Democratic Republic of the Congo, *The Prosecutor v. Thomas Lubanga
Dyilo*, Trial Chamber, Decision on the press interview with Ms Le Fraper du Hellen, 12 May
2010, ICC-01/04-01/06-2433 ('ICC Lubanga du Hellen interview Decision') (http://
www.legal-tools.org/doc/3b613a/).

[14] Discussed in Markovic, 2011, p. 230, see above note 10.

[15] *Ibid.*, pp. 201 and 211.

attorneys might have different perspectives of their work and interpretations of the provisions of a code of conduct.[16] He further emphasized the uniqueness of the OTP when compared with adversarial prosecutorial systems when he observed that the role of the ICC Prosecutor is more in accordance with the civil law tradition, which, thus, sets the establishment of truth as a Prosecutor's ultimate goal.[17]

While the prescription of codes serves to provide a general ethics guide, understanding and forestalling the diverse challenges to integrity and impartiality that can confront officials of the Court is required in order to take proactive measures to prevent unethical behaviour. Judges of the Court and high officials of the OTP are required to exhibit impartiality and high moral character in the performance of their duties. Article 40 of the ICC Statute, in particular, provides that Judges shall be independent in the performance of their functions and shall not engage in any activity that is likely to interfere with their judicial functions or to affect confidence in their independence. Similar obligations on the staff of the OTP exist under Article 40, which provides that staff of the Office shall not seek or act on instructions from any external source and also specifically obliging the Prosecutor not to engage in any activity, which is likely to interfere with his or her prosecutorial functions or to affect confidence in his or her independence.

Integrity can be described as the moral worth of an individual. Its presence evokes a sense of confidence and justice, while the absence of it promotes suspicion and distrust. Impartiality, as well as honesty, are therefore, crucial indices of integrity. This is the sense in which the Statute uses the phrase "high moral character"[18]: the inquiry focuses on what kinds of perceptions are evoked by the conduct in question?

Although these attributes are required for all the staff of the Court – indeed any 'international civil servant' – the conduct of the Prosecutor, members of the OTP, and the Judges command more attention, given the complex political environment in which the ICC operates. Unlike judges, however, whose official duties are deliberative and joint, the actions and decisions of the OTP are attributed singly to the Prosecutor.[19] The Prosecu-

---

[16] *Ibid.*, pp. 207–209.

[17] *Ibid.*, p. 211.

[18] See ICC Statute, Article 42.3, see above note 1.

[19] The OTP is regarded in this sense by its first Senior Legal Adviser, Morten Bergsmo, as the "weakest link". See Morten Bergsmo, "Institutional History, Behaviour and Development",

tor cannot refrain from taking politically sensitive steps simply on the ground that this would provoke controversy. However, "he is requested to be fully aware of these human reactions and meticulously check himself so that they are not permitted to influence his actions".[20]

Apart from the personal integrity of officials, there is also institutional integrity. This approximates to the values and norms that an institution champions or through which it measures integrity and punishes infractions and can often be located in the corporate ethics code or collectively in the ethics codes for members of the Institution.

If prosecutorial discretion and choices are complicated in domestic legal systems, the need for guidance in the ICC, which thrusts upon the Prosecutor the unique responsibilities for seeking the truth (by according equal weight to the investigation of incriminating and exculpatory material)[21] cannot be over-emphasized. A code of conduct provides a uniform, objective and ethical rationale for the application of the provisions of the Statute and Rules. Without it, uneven and subjective application of the hard law to situations will be unavoidable. Such codes are characterized by Nakhjavani as a set of fundamental beliefs, attitudes, habits of thought and action, learnt and practised over time and in diverse contexts, which are inseparable from the act of legal characterization itself and its occasionally world-shaping effects.[22]

30.3.1. Judges

Articles 3, 4 and 5 of the Code of Judicial Ethics require Judges of the ICC to be independent, impartial and to demonstrate integrity in the course of their duties. These provisions also emphasize the need for judges to avoid putting themselves in situations that conflict with or interfere with their integrity or duties.

---

in Morten Bergsmo, Klaus Rackwitz and SONG, Tianying (eds.), *Historical Origins of International Criminal Law: Volume 5*, FICHL Publication Series No. 24, Torkel Opsahl Academic EPublisher, Brussels, 2017, p. 7 (https://www.legal-tools.org/doc/09c8b8).

20 Dan Hammarskjöld, "The International Civil Servant in Law and in Fact", in Wilder Foote (ed.), *The Servant of Peace: A Selection of the Speeches and Statements of Dag Hammarskjöld, Secretary-General of the United Nations, 1953–1961*, The Bodley Head, 1962, p. 348 (https://www.legal-tools.org/doc/64bcae/).

21 ICC Statute, Article 54(1)(a), see above note 1.

22 See Salim A. Nakhjavani, "The Origins and Development of the Code of Conduct", in Bergsmo, Rackwitz and SONG (eds.), 2017, p. 954, see above note 18.

30.3.2. Office of the Prosecutor

Although the OTP is required under the Statute to act independently as a separate organ of the Court, a substantive Code of Conduct for the OTP was not adopted until 2013. Prior to this, the general terms of Articles 44 of the Statute applied to the Prosecutor and the Deputy Prosecutor, while Staff Rules and the Code of Conduct for Staff Members applied to the staff.[23]

Unlike the Staff Rules and the Code of Conduct for Staff Members, the Code of Conduct for the OTP applies to the Prosecutor, the Deputy and all members of the Office as well as interns, visiting professionals, *gratis* personnel, and staff members of other organizations on short term assignment to the Court. Also, unlike the Code of Judicial Ethics, the ethics framework for the OTP is more elaborate, going as far as illustrating situations that come under the general normative framework of the Statute. It outlines, in Section 2, some examples of how the duty to act independently under Article 42 of the Statute can be breached or observed. For instance, it forbids members of the OTP from acting or seeking to act on instructions from any external source, or from activities that may negatively affect the confidence of others in the independence or integrity of the OTP; or from activities which may interfere with their duties; or from which it can reasonably be inferred that their independence has been compromised.[24]

30.4. Pressures

The power wielded by the Prosecutor and Judges of the ICC is not inconsequential. Insulating discretion from personal or proprietary interests can be Herculean in the midst of the pressure and the dynamics of the international criminal justice system. The illustrations and instances cited in the Code of Conduct for the OTP provide different scenarios by which pressure can be brought to bear on the integrity and independence of Judges as well as the staff of the OTP – for instance, where there is a personal interest in a case, or a personal or professional relationship with any of the parties or victims.[25]

---

[23] Under Article 44 of the ICC Statute, these are personnel appointed by the Prosecutor and the Registrar. Markovic rightly doubts the application of these Rules to the Prosecutor or Deputy Prosecutor. Markovic, 2011, p. 206, see above note 10.

[24] ICC Code of Conduct for the OTP, Section 2, para. 23(a), see above note 3.

[25] *Ibid.*, Section 9, para. 42.

Although the Code of Judicial Ethics did not contain similar illustrations, they are of equal significance to Judges of the Court. Such pressures
can be characterized as political, economic, cultural or even historical. Furthermore, they can vary in intensity and type depending on the socio-legal
background or even status of the official. Naturally, the higher the status of
the official, the more intense the pressure will be. The Prosecutor, Judges,
and other high officials necessarily find themselves in the eye of the public,
whether willingly or unwillingly. They must rise beyond showmanship and
focus on the essentials of their job. The internal conflicts are considerable.
Together with the inherently political nature of most international crimes
like war crimes and genocide, no one should doubt that States will exert
pressure on these officials directly or otherwise. While a code of ethics and
integrity will not prevent these pressures, it will greatly assist the Prosecutor and the staff of the OTP in dealing with them. However, much more
needs to be done in order to secure widespread understanding and compliance. In the next section, diverse scenarios of the pressure dynamics and
the impact of socio-cultural factors are examined with a view to demonstrating the need for an institutional compliance mechanism.

30.4.1. Political Pressure

Political pressure is often brought to bear in the course of the appointment
or tenure of the official. In a seminal article on the international civil servant, Dag Hammarskjöld highlighted two complementary factors: first, that
international bodies must perforce work with persons from different nationalities and second, that these persons more often than not have the political support of their country of origin or a bloc of States.[26] The motives
for support vary, but as Morten Bergsmo puts it, whatever the motive, there
is no lack of efforts by States to promote candidates that can be "influenced" or subsequently shown up as ineffectual or ridiculed.[27] The ICC
operates in a complex political environment and depends greatly on governments for wide-ranging matters such as the smooth conduct of preliminary examination or the exercise of investigation powers, witness protection or, indeed, its budget. In such circumstances, some measure of 'political protection' from an influential State or bloc of interests is inevitable.
Where decisions or actions of the Court coincide with the interests of such
a 'protector', perceptions of bias cannot be avoided even if this is purely

---

[26] Hammarskjöld, 1962, p. 339, see above note 20.
[27] See Bergsmo, 2017 pp. 7, 8, 30 and 31, see above note 19.

accidental. Judge Goldstone has characterized the impact of politics on justice and integrity as a fact of life that should not be ignored.[28]

Despite the fairly straightforward process outlined in Articles 36 and 42 of the ICC Statute for the nomination and election, respectively of Judges and the Prosecutor of the Court, the process is laced with intricate political and diplomatic undertones.[29] The provisions envisage an election by an absolute majority of members of the Assembly of States Parties, however, so far, this has been the case only with Judges. The first and current Prosecutor of the Court were elected to date by consensus, which, in my opinion, mutes dissenting voices and accentuates the political influence. While consensus may give rise to negotiations and horse-trading, it has certain political connotations, which usually prevent States, developing ones in particular, from blocking consensus during international negotiations. Since the process of decision-making through consensus is conducted openly, many developing countries are concerned about the consequences of their objections and thus prefer to remain silent in order not to be seen as stumbling blocks to the consensus.[30]

30.4.2. Economic Pressure

It has been observed that by instituting nine-year non-renewable terms for the Prosecutor and similarly for Judges, the Statute has reduced threats to independence as well as other drawbacks of re-election.[31] On the other hand, an official, may on account of a single term, become more susceptible to economic or cultural pressures arising from concern about a career after service to the Court. Another source of pressure, therefore, is attributable to future career prospects at the end of service in the ICC. Hence, will a Prosecutor or a Judge nearing the end of their terms make decisions or issue judgments more favourable to some States, as insurance for a future position at home or elsewhere?

---

[28] Richard J. Goldstone, "Prosecutorial Language, Integrity and Independence", CILRAP Film, 2 December 2018 (https://www.cilrap.org/cilrap-film/181202-goldstone).

[29] *Ibid.*

[30] This is a common feature of the dynamics of the UN political system and is alluded to also by Paschke, 2018, see above note 7.

[31] Brandeis Institute for International Judges, "Challenges to Judicial Independence" in Brandeis Institute for International Judges, *Toward an International Rule of Law*, Brandeis University, Waltham, MA, 2010. See also ICC Statute, Article 36(9) (Judges) and Article 42(4) (Prosecutor), see above note 1.

The nature of the work of the ICC Prosecutor and Judges involves making decisions that many powerful States find unpleasant. This "stepping on toes" often places a judge in an adverse position for seeking future job opportunities in such States. In reaction to the preliminary examinations conducted by the Prosecutor on alleged war crimes in Afghanistan, the United States issued a "warning" to the ICC to desist from conducting the investigations and had threatened to "use any means necessary to protect its citizens from unjust prosecution by [the] illegitimate court".[32] Part of the threat was a "policy of U.S. visa restrictions on those individuals directly responsible for any ICC investigation of U.S. personnel" as well as economic sanctions.[33] The US eventually revoked the visa of the Chief Prosecutor in April 2019,[34] and subsequently imposed sanctions on her and her staff member Mr. Phakiso Mochochoko. It is not surprising that, eventually, the ICC Pre-Trial Chamber II rejected the request of the Chief Prosecutor to open an investigation probe into US involvement in Afghanistan, albeit on the ground that "an investigation into the situation in Afghanistan at this stage would not serve the interests of justice".[35] The Chamber elaborated further that although all the relevant requirements were met as regards both jurisdiction and admissibility, the current circumstances of the situation in Afghanistan were such as to make the prospects for a successful investigation and prosecution extremely limited.[36] While the basis for the decision is practical, it also demonstrates the delicate interplay between international justice and international politics. The action of the US in this situation is a form of economic pressure as judges of the Court may be pressurized to consider the likelihood of losing career prospects in the US after their tenure, if the threat by the latter is eventually carried out.

It is obvious also that some of the challenges or threats to independence outlive the position and do not necessarily disappear by foreclosing

---

[32] See *Al Jazeera*, "Full text of John Bolton's speech to the Federalist Society", 10 September 2018.

[33] See Michael R. Pompeo, "Remarks to the Press", US Department of State, 15 March 2019, available on Department of State's web site.

[34] *BBC News*, "US revokes visa of International Criminal Court prosecutor", 5 April 2019, available on its web site.

[35] ICC, Situation in the Islamic Republic of Afghanistan, Pre-Trial Chamber, Decision Pursuant to Article 15 of the Rome Statute on the Authorisation of an Investigation into the Situation in the Islamic Republic of Afghanistan, 12 April 2019, ICC-02/17-33 (https://www.legal-tools.org/doc/2fb1f4).

[36] *Ibid.*, para. 96.

re-election or term renewals. Ethics compliance officers must, for example, consider situations where the international justice official exhibits conduct calculated to catch attention of the 'market place' and position themselves for a post-retirement career as for example where an official slants his or her actions or pronouncements (including dissenting judgments) so as to demonstrate ideological or conceptual persuasions that can influence a chair in a university or form the basis of a commissioned authorship or consultancy after his tenure.[37] It must, however, be said that this kind of pressure is probably not of major concern for accomplished jurists or experts – they already have some competitive edge. However, it will be a major challenge for officials of lesser experience and for whom service at the ICC is a unique 'door opening' activity.

30.4.3. Historical Pressure

It is also important to appreciate that some pressures can be applied by a State that is peculiarly situated in relation to the international justice official. Consider the potential influence wielded by a former colonial power in terms of educational, professional and social opportunities and how such influence can challenge the independence of the international justice official who is a national of a former colony. The factors at play are diverse and are a combination of the educational and cultural background of the justice official. The situation becomes complicated where another State leverages such relational dynamics to exert pressure. Global alliances can give rise to a regional power leveraging on the historical tie of another nation to seek to compromise the integrity of an official. This pressure can work in several ways – taking a course of action or refraining from it in order to receive favour or avoid the disapproval of a State or a bloc of States.

Historical pressure can also be discussed along the lines of the dependence on foreign aids by developing countries. It has been noted that foreign aids can be used in the promotion of neo-colonial agenda,[38] and events have indeed shown that donor States would withdraw aids from developing countries due to defiance or unyieldingness of the latter to certain

---

[37] Brandeis Institute for International Judges, 2003, p. 6, see above note 5.

[38] Stephanie Itimi, "Is Foreign Aid a facilitator of Neo-Colonialism in Africa?", in *Journal of African Cultural Studies*, 2018 (on file with the author).

standards.[39] An instance was the foreign aid cut to Uganda when it enacted its anti-gay law.[40] This supports the view that foreign aid is a tool that can be used by donor States to advance a specific agenda. In the light of historical pressure in this discourse, a justice official from a State that is dependent on aids by some particular States may be pressurized by his or her home State as regards the interests of the donor States.

30.4.4. Socio-Cultural Pressure

There are some other forms of pressure that are socio-cultural and which may or may not be concerned with career prospects or job security. What, for example, constitutes independence in terms of the OTP or a Judge? Individual or cultural perspectives of the concept of independence vary. Whereas in some countries, the duty of independence of a Prosecutor does not prevent notification of an intended course of action to a supervisor or superior official discussion of the case with the prosecutor's colleagues, expressing pre-determined views can be problematic in an international court.[41] Considering the dynamics of the ICC, there are no clear answers. Context, as usual, plays a role. We should not also forget that the duty of independence is yoked with that of confidentiality, and even if the official stoically rebuffs external pressure in such discussions, the mere fact of participating in such discussions and disclosure of some material could amount to a breach of the code.

Another area of difficulty is interaction and communication. Judges in many countries are perhaps familiar with the need to be circumspect in conversations concerning their work. The same cannot, however, be said about prosecutors and investigators. In some national jurisdictions, for example, in Nigeria, press releases and interviews concerning arrested suspects or ongoing trials are routine – sometimes with damning conclusions made on the guilt of the suspects. However, this should not be the case, given the sensitive and inquisitorial nature of ICC investigations and prosecutions. This was clearly the position of the Trial Chambers in the *Lubanga* case while criticizing the OTP when, in a press interview, an OTP staff misrepresented proceedings in the *Lubanga* case and predicted a long jail

---

[39]   *BBC News*, "Cameron threat to dock some UK aid to anti-gay nations", 30 October 2011, available on its web site.

[40]   *Al Jazeera*, "Uganda hit with foreign aid cuts over anti-gay law", 27 February 2014, available on its web site.

[41]   See Goldstone, 2018, see above note 28.

term for Lubanga based on the "courageous and credible witnesses" of the prosecution.[42]

There are less subtle pressures such as monetary gifts or in-kind assistance rendered to the official, relatives or associates. Some so-called 'social obligations' – customary gifts in societies where social events are intricately connected with class or status are problematic. Events that provide the challenge in Nigeria or for a Nigerian will probably not matter to officials of other nationalities. In some countries, for example, monetary gifts during social events or welcome/farewell gifts are customary. For international officials working in these environments, for example, examination or investigation teams of the OTP, what is required is not simply an ethics code but also guidance on these socio-cultural issues so as to conform to the constitutional tone without offending host States.

It is instructive that the Code of Conduct for the OTP addresses this kind of unethical conduct. It must always be remembered that officials must guard against the appearance of bias as well as actual bias. The Code, therefore, provides in Section 6.30 that:

> impartial conduct includes
>
> 1. respect for the presumption of innocence. In particular, Members of the Office shall not publicly express an opinion on the guilt or innocence of a person under investigation or the accused outside the context of the proceedings before the Court;
>
> 2. refraining from expressing an opinion that could, objectively, adversely affect the required impartiality, whether through communications media, in writing or public addresses, or through any other actions outside the context of the proceedings before the Court […].

In the absence of a generally applicable international standard to determine the acceptable norms, judicial officers will be left to adhere to the customary ethical norms in their States. The challenge this poses is that a judicial officer whose socio-cultural background allows certain social interactions and relationships may do so innocently meanwhile, it may later give room for pressure. However, no one should be in doubt that judicial officers cannot plead the customary gift excuse where this is offered by a litigant or counsel to a litigant.

---

[42] ICC Lubanga du Hellen interview Decision, see above note 13.

30.4.5. Post-Employment Pressures

Cases or matters in which an official has been or is likely to have been professionally involved do not, of course, terminate with the departure of the official or expiration of the official's tenure. Conflicting interests can arise even after the employment is terminated, particularly where knowledge and goodwill gained in the course of duty – as Judge or Prosecutor is exploited in a private consultancy. This question is of major importance considering the fact that unrestricted engagements of this nature can exert as much pressure on the official or other officials while in office (by compromising his independence in order to gain an advantage of employment) or after leaving office (by disclosing or accessing sensitive information on an ongoing case). Shortly after he left office, the first Prosecutor of the Court, Moreno-Ocampo, was engaged as a consultant to Hassan Tatanaki, a prominent figure in Libya and business partner to Seif al-Islam Gaddafi, son of the former Libyan leader Muammar Gaddafi. The fact that in 2009 he opened an investigation into Muammar and Seif Gaddafi on suspicion of crimes against humanity and that Tatanaki was closely connected with the Gaddafi regime did not seem to matter to Moreno-Ocampo, who reportedly said that the purpose of the consultancy was to help end the civil war.[43] Among several other reported infractions after his disengagement, Moreno-Ocampo allegedly made money from assisting persons suspected of having aided violations in Libya with help from some staff in the OTP.[44]

Some existing rules and regulations relating to Staff of the Court[45] provide limited bases for post-employment obligations. For instance, the Staff Regulations of the ICC in Regulation 1.2(i) specifies the obligations of the staff, and this includes utmost discretion with regard to all matters of official business.[46] Regulation 1.2 (i) goes on to state: "Those obligations do not cease upon separation from service". Also, the Staff Rules of the

---

[43] See Barney Thomson, "Former ICC prosecutor in Row over Lucrative Consultancy Work", *Financial Times*, 6 October 2017, available on its web site.

[44] See Bergsmo, 2018, p. 2, see above note 6.

[45] The applicability of these Rules to elected officials – for example, Judges, the Registrar and the Prosecutor or Deputy Prosecutor – is in doubt. See Markovic, 2011, p. 206, see above note 10.

[46] ICC, Staff Regulations, 12 September 2003 ('ICC Staff Regulations') (https://www.legal-tools.org/doc/3542d3).

ICC in Rule 101.4 provide: "The obligations of staff members regarding confidentiality shall not cease upon separation from service".[47]

However, to avoid possible conflict of interest obligations, there is a need for stronger provisions. To what extent, therefore, can some reasonable restraint be imposed on international justice officials with regard to the nature of their post-employment engagements?

Such clauses are features of employment contracts under the domestic law of States where their validity is hinged on whether the clause is unfairly restrictive, that is, in terms of geographical or temporal scope; or essential to protect the business or corporate interests of the former employer; or against the public interest. Similarly, a Secretary-General's Bulletin on post-employment restrictions[48] in the context of procurements states that:

> former staff members who have participated in the UN procurement process may not seek or accept employment with any UN contractor or vendor for a period of one year following separation from service. Restrictions on UN lobbying for a period of two years also exist for former staff members who participated in the procurement process.[49]

In-service staff members involved in the procurement process are required to refrain from soliciting or accepting offers of future employment from any UN contractor or vendor; where an offer is received from a vendor, the staff member is required to report the incident and recuse themselves from any further dealings with that contractor or vendor. Without a doubt, there is a strong public interest element in preventing a former staff of the Court from exploiting confidential information to his or her advantage. However, the precise scope of such a restriction may have to be limited to ICC matters and only for a reasonable period (one year perhaps).

Two additional points should be made. First, there is the possibility that such clauses will discourage many professionals from making their services available to an international court. It is also in the public interest to avoid this situation. In my view, however, this should not be of major concern. Many professionals are already familiar with confidentiality and fidelity obligations to clients, some of which are lifelong. Therefore, intro-

---

[47] ICC, Staff Rules of the ICC, 25 August 2005 ('ICC Staff Rules') (https://www.legal-tools.org/doc/10f5c7).

[48] Secretary General's Bulletin – Post-employment restrictions, UN Doc ST/SGB/2006/15, 26 December 2006.

[49] *Ibid.*, Sections 2.1 and 2.2.

ducing restraint clauses in the contract for engaging such professionals cannot be strange.

Second, while the clause is contractual, we note that it flows from the Court's corporate ethics on integrity and independence.[50] In particular, Section 9.42 of the Code of Conduct for the OTP provides: "Members of the Office shall abstain from any conduct which may, directly or indirectly, be in conflict with the discharge of their official duties during terms of service or may compromise the independence and trust reposed in the Office, following separation of service".

Similarly, Section 9.44 restrains a former staff member from accepting engagement or appointment as defense counsel or member of a defense team in any of the proceedings before the Court for a period of 12 months from the day of separation, unless specifically authorized by the Prosecutor. Although the operation of this provision is conditional on a declaration by the concerned staff, it is suggested that such declaration should not be optional and that a similar obligation should apply to Judges of the Court.

30.5. An Ethics Compliance Mechanism

What flows from the above is that integrity challenges for officials in the field of international justice in these rapacious and dangerous times are increasingly complex and dynamic. Despite the diverse cultures represented in an organization like the ICC, codes of conduct, or ethics can only prescribe objective standards of conduct. Compliance or enforcement must also be done evenly and objectively. This does not, however, ignore the need to resolve or lessen the impact of vulnerabilities arising from diversity. The key to this is taking proactive, supportive measures that aid voluntary compliance.

This is the weak link in the ICC's ethics compliance mechanism. The extant codes provide that apart from immediate supervisors, requests for guidance or reports of actual or potential breaches should be directed at the elected officials, namely, the Prosecutor or the Deputy Prosecutor in the case of the OTP's Code or the President or the Vice President in the case of the Judicial Ethics. In fact, these officials may have limited knowledge, time, or experience to guide on ethics issues, or there may be some other limiting factor as to where the official's conduct is related to the concern.

---

[50] ICC Staff Regulations, Section 1.2(i), see above note 46; ICC Staff Rules, Section 101.4(d), see above note 47.

Such questions relate, *inter alia*, to what kinds of social or professional engagements should be attended? What kinds of gifts are acceptable? Which social media is safe are few examples of dilemmas that can arise in ways that even the elected official is unable to provide guidance despite the obligation under Section 2.1.15 of the Code for the OTP to set an impeccable example of conduct for the staff members and provide, inter alia, appropriate direction, guidance and support in the promotion and cultivation of the standards expected of the Office.[51]

With over 1,400 staff members, the ICC does not have an adequate institutional framework to support staff compliance on ethics issues. This is surprising, given that concern for an advisory and supportive unit on compliance featured prominently at the early stages of developing a code of conduct.[52] Although the Code of Conduct for the OTP prescribes a proactive mechanism by requiring that the Legal Advisory Section shall assist the Prosecutor in promoting awareness of and compliance with the Code, this responsibility should be formalized.

The lack of an ethics and compliance office in the ICC is chiefly responsible for the critical policy gaps and errors of judgment discussed earlier. Indeed, if officials operate in an institution with a weak culture of integrity and a high level of impunity, there is not much one can expect in terms of individual integrity.[53]

The Independent Oversight Mechanism (IOM) established per Article 112(4) of the Rome Statute and which became operational only in 2017, at first sight, seems to meet the need for an institutional ethics compliance mechanism. However, closer scrutiny yields severe limitations.[54] The purpose of the IOM is to provide *meaningful oversight* of the Court through its mandate to conduct internal court inspections, evaluations, and investigations. Inspections and evaluations are aimed mainly at ensuring efficient operations and are activated at the request of the Bureau or the Assembly of States Parties. The IOM mandate also allows it to undertake, subject to available resources, evaluations, and inspections at the direct request of a

---

[51] See also ICC Code of Conduct for the OTP, Sections 2.2.24 (independence) and 3.9.43 (conflict of interest), see above note 3.

[52] Nakhjavani, 2017, p. 957, see above note 22.

[53] Inder, 2018, see above note 8; See also Paschke, 2018 see above note 7.

[54] Bergsmo *et al.*, 2017, see above note 8; see also Karim A.A. Khan, "Integrity and the Limits of Internal Oversight Mechanisms", CILRAP Film, 2 December 2018 (https://www.cilrap.org/cilrap-film/181202-khan/).

Head of Organ. However, it cannot initiate either an evaluation or inspection without having received an authorized request to do so. An investigation, on the other hand, can be undertaken by the IOM at its own discretion into any report of misconduct or retaliation that it receives concerning an elected official or member of Court personnel. Misconduct in the context of ICC staff members and other personnel is non-compliance with a relevant ICC rule, regulation, or other administrative instruction, including relevant standards of conduct. Misconduct in the context of elected officials and their specific functions is separately detailed in the Court's Rules of Procedure and Evidence. It seems clear, therefore, that the mandate of the IOM as far as misconduct or unethical conduct is concerned essentially consists in investigating a report relating to conduct of an official of the Court – and even so, it must consult with the Head of an organ before such an investigation so as not to prejudice an ongoing investigation. The IOM cannot investigate alleged misconduct of a former staff or official and quite clearly is not concerned with counselling staff on ethics compliance.[55] It may, however, through its work, provide credible, useful and evidence-based information to the decision-makers and other relevant stakeholders.[56]

However, given the diverse challenges to independence and integrity that may arise, and bearing in mind that disclosure or requests for guidance may require confidentiality, a proactive and independent mechanism is required.[57] Such a mechanism, such as the UN Ethics Office, if established, will prevent or mitigate damage to institutional reputation by providing guidance to staff in perceived or actual situations of doubt.[58] There is no need to have an elaborate structure for such an office as the functions can, in my view, be effectively combined with the office of the legal adviser of the ICC. The fears that haunted an earlier draft about entrusting such a mandate in a person, for example, whether such person would be trusted or

---

[55] *Ibid.*

[56] ICC, "The Independent Oversight Mechanism (IOM) Mandate", available on its web site.

[57] See Women's Initiatives for Gender Justice, "A Critical Time for the ICC's Integrity", 12 October 2017 (http://www.legal-tools.org/doc/e2fbc7/), which called for two new compliance mechanisms – an Integrity Advisory Board and an Ethics/Compliance Office in the Court.

[58] The UN Ethics Office was established in 2005 offers confidential ethics advice, ethics awareness and education, protection against retaliation for reporting misconduct, financial disclosure programme and promotion of coherence and common ethics standards across the UN. See UN Ethics Office, "What is the UN Ethics Office", available on its web site ('UN Ethics Office web site').

would not become overbearing[59] are now significantly doused successful by the models provided to us by the Ombudsman of the EU and the UN Ethics Office.

The justification to be proactive in institutions such as the ICC is self-evident. Whenever a case of alleged impropriety is attributed to an official of the ICC, the resulting damage to the institution and loss of public confidence are unquantifiable.[60] When serious 'integrity' problems within international courts become manifest, they tend to affect the external reputation of and support for the institution and erode morale among the staff. Quite apart from such crisis management after the damage is done, focusing on the standard and practice of 'integrity' is an open-ended necessity for international justice institutions. The structure and practice of such an office are already well demonstrated in the practice and institutional procedures of the UN Ethics office. Established in 2005 for the purpose of securing the highest standards of integrity among the UN staff, the main functions of the UN Ethics Office[61] are to:

1. administer the UN financial disclosure programme;
2. protect staff against retaliation for reporting misconduct and for co-operating with duly authorized audits or investigations;
3. provide confidential advice and guidance to staff on ethical issues, for example, conflict of interest, including administering an ethics helpline; and
4. develop standards, training and education on ethics issues, in co-ordination with the Office of Human Resources Management and other offices as appropriate, including ensuring annual ethics training for all staff.

According to the web site of the Office, the justification for its existence is first, the changing and dynamic nature of the work of the UN, second, the complexities of a rapidly-evolving environment in which decisions are taken, and third, the challenge of objective and uniform standards, given the multi-cultural staff of the UN in duty stations in every region of

---

[59] See Nakhjavani, 2017, pp. 957–958, see above note 22.

[60] See Bergsmo *et al.*, 2017, see above note 8.

[61] See Secretary General's Bulletin – Ethics Office – Establishment and Terms of reference, UN Doc ST/SGB/2005/22, 30 December 2005.

the world.[62] In its advisory mandate, the Office treats all requests and advisories with confidentiality.

Through this service, the staff members are better able to describe their problems or concerns, identify the rules and regulations that may apply, examine their options, and understand the consequences. Through the advisory process, the staff is better able to make ethical decisions that serve the interest of the UN. Ethics advice is confidential to the person requesting assistance. The Office has also published several guides on conflicts of interest, financial disclosures, and an Ethics Roadmap for the guidance of staff. It is also instructive that a similar mechanism exists under the European Union where a Complaints and Inquiry Unit clarifies on request, in concrete terms, the meaning of ethical principles on integrity and conflict of interest to staff members of the European Union – another multi-cultural organization.[63]

30.6. Conclusion

Although the standards of independence and integrity are required for all staff (including elected officials of the Court), the conduct of the Prosecutor, members of the OTP, and the Judges command more attention, given that international criminal trials are more complex, more expensive, and more difficult to accomplish than domestic prosecutions. If proceedings are prejudiced on account of misconduct by the Prosecutor, it has a significantly negative effect on the resources and time of the Court.[64]

While Codes on ethical standards are important, the conflicts and pressures inherent in the duties of the persons of diverse cultures and background that work as officials of the OTP, as Judges and indeed other staff confront these officials in equally diverse ways. The establishment of a proactive independent mechanism similar to the UN Ethics Office will address these concerns by supporting staff compliance on ethics through counselling and issuing guidelines.

---

[62] UN Ethics Office web site, see above note 57.

[63] Marta Hirsch-Ziembinska, "Integrity and the Work of the European Ombudsman", CILRAP Film, 2 December 2018 (https://www.cilrap.org/cilrap-film/181202-ziembinska).

[64] Jenia Turner, "Policing International Prosecutors", in *NYU Journal of International Law and Politics*, 2012, vol. 45, no. 1, pp. 210–211.

31

Integrity and the Inevitable Political Exposure of International Criminal Justice

Christopher Staker[*]

A large amount of subject matter that could be said to fit under this title has already been addressed by others. This contribution is, in fact, concerned with one specific manifestation of the problem of political exposure, arising from the fact that certain aspects of the international criminal justice system fall within the responsibility of political rather than independent judicial or prosecutorial decision-makers.

If asked to what extent it is appropriate for aspects of the criminal justice system to be entrusted to or influenced by political decision making, the instinctive first reaction of many would be to respond that even the tiniest amount of political influence would taint and corrupt the integrity of the entire process. That view may, of course, be a fundamental truth in relation to some parts of the system. When judges retire at the end of a case to consider their verdict, they should obviously conduct their deliberations in complete independence and with complete impartiality, without outside influence of any kind, political or otherwise, and should base their decision solely on the evidence before them and the law.

However, when the entire criminal justice system is considered as a whole, it can be seen on reflection that it is simplistic to suggest that political decision-making should never play any part anywhere in the system at all. In a domestic legal system, where political decision-makers are the legislature, the executive, or even the electorate as a whole, it will for instance typically be a political decision-maker (the legislature) that creates and defines substantive crimes and the maximum penalties for those crimes. It

---

[*] Dr. **Christopher Staker** is a Barrister at 39 Essex Chambers in London. He has been counsel in cases before the International Court of Justice, International Tribunal for the Law of the Sea, International Criminal Tribunal for the Former Yugoslavia ('ICTY'), Special Court for Sierra Leone, and European Court of Human Rights. Previously, he has been Principal Legal Secretary at the International Court of Justice; Deputy Prosecutor of the Special Court for Sierra Leone; Senior Appeals Counsel at the ICTY; and Counsel Assisting the Solicitor-General of Australia. He originally trained as a diplomat with the Australian Department of Foreign Affairs. He holds a doctorate degree from Oxford.

will be political decision-makers who determine the annual budgets of the various organs of the criminal justice system. In some systems, political decision-makers (the executive or the legislature) will appoint, or have a role in the appointment of, judges and chief prosecutors[1] (and indeed, in some systems, judges and even chief prosecutors may be directly elected by the population).[2] In some systems, political decision-makers may issue certain instructions[3] or guidance[4] to prosecution authorities. There may also be other ways in which political decision-makers play a role in the criminal justice system more directly.[5]

---

[1] See, for instance, J. van Zyl Smit, *The Appointment, Tenure and Removal of Judges under Commonwealth Principles: A Compendium and Analysis of Best Practice (Report of Research Undertaken by Bingham Centre for the Rule of Law*, British Institute of International and Comparative Law, London, 2015, p. xvi:

> Only 19% of Commonwealth jurisdictions have executive-only appointment systems in this sense (appointments to the highest court are reserved for the executive in another 8% of jurisdictions, and the appointment of the Chief Justice in a further 23% of jurisdictions). […] In 21% of Commonwealth jurisdictions there is some legislative involvement in the appointment of judges, usually by way of confirmation of candidates selected by a judicial appointments commission.

[2] Jed Handelsman Shugerman, *The People's Courts*, 2012, Harvard University Press, p. 3 ("Almost 90 percent of state judges [in the United States] face some kind of popular election"); Michael J. Ellis, "The Origins of the Elected Prosecutor", in *The Yale Law Journal*, 2012, vol. 121, no. 6, pp. 1528, 1530 ("The United States is the only country in the world where citizens elect prosecutors").

[3] See, for instance, United Nations General Assembly, Human Rights Council, Report of the Special Rapporteur on the independence of judges and lawyers, Gabriela Knaul, UN Doc. A/HRC/20/19, 7 June 2012, para. 73 (https://www.legal-tools.org/doc/dqtiml/) ("In order to ensure a fair and consistent approach in criminal justice policy, general guidelines can be issued by the prosecution service itself (internally) and by nonprosecutorial authorities (externally)"), para. 74 ("the issue of instructions by nonprosecutorial authorities should be: transparent, consistent with lawful authority and subject to established guidelines to safeguard the actuality and the perception of prosecutorial independence"), para. 116 ("Case-specific instructions to prosecutors from external organs should be avoided. However, in extraordinary cases, when such instructions are deemed necessary, they should be in writing and formally recorded and carefully circumscribed to avoid undue interference or pressure. Prosecutors should have the right to challenge the instructions received, especially when they are deemed unlawful or contrary to professional standards or ethics").

[4] For example, South Australia, Director of Public Prosecutions Act 1991, 6 July 1992, section 9(2) (https://www.legal-tools.org/doc/zg1tc7/) ("The Attorney-General may, after consultation with the Director [of Public Prosecutions], give directions and furnish guidelines to the Director in relation to the carrying out of his or her functions").

[5] For instance, in certain jurisdictions, the Attorney-General, a government minister, has the power to issue *ex officio* indictments or to terminate a prosecution by issuing a *nolle prosequi*.

Depending on the system, the judiciary may deliberately exercise restraint in certain respects in order not to encroach on areas that the judiciary acknowledges properly to fall within the domain of political organs of the State. For instance, courts in a common law country may take the view that they have no power through the development of case law to create new common law offences or to widen the scope of existing common law offences, now seen as a function of the legislature.[6] On the other hand, a judgment of a court that significantly changes what had previously been understood to be the scope of a provision of the criminal law may be welcomed in certain circumstances as an expansion and strengthening of the rule of law.[7] However, certain judicial development of the law has at the same time been criticised by some as undermining the rule of law as a result of the entry by the judiciary into an essentially political sphere.[8]

---

[6]   United Kingdom, House of Lords ('UKHL'), *R. v. Withers*, Judgment, 20 November 1974, [1975] AC 842, pp. 854, 860, 863, 867, 877; England and Wales, Court of Appeal, *R. v. Misra and Srivastava*, Judgment, 8 October 2004, [2004] EWCA Crim 2375, [2005] 1 Cr App R 328, paras. 29–34; UKHL, *R. v. Rimmington*, Judgment, 27 October 2005, [2005] UKHL 63, [2006] 1 Cr App Rep 17, paras. 33–35. See also UKHL, *R. v. Jones*, Judgment, 29 March 2006, [2006] 1 AC 136 dealing with the question whether crimes under international law are automatically assimilated into UK domestic law, in which Lord Hoffmann referred at para. 60 to "the democratic principle that it is nowadays for Parliament and Parliament alone to decide whether conduct not previously regarded as criminal should be made an offence".

[7]   See, for instance, the extrajudicial observations of a then justice of the High Court of Australia in Michael Kirby, *Judicial Activism: Authority, Principle and Policy in the Judicial Method*, Sweet & Maxwell, London, 2004, pp. 82–83:

> the judicial abolition of spousal immunity for rape, without waiting for legislative change, was informed by strong contemporary advances in the recognition of the rights of women; [...] In such a changed world, it was intolerable to expect contemporary judges to give effect to the old rule, made by predecessors centuries earlier. [...] [I]n doing so, they gave voice to what would have been the overwhelming opinion of contemporary society. [...] Who will say that the judges were wrong to redefine the common law in that way? Be sure that some would denounce such action as egregious 'judicial activism'. If so, it is an epithet that the judges will gladly bear.

[8]   See, for instance, the extrajudicial observations of a then justice of the High Court of Australia in Dyson Heydon, "Judicial Activism and the Death of the Rule of Law", in *Otago Law Review*, 2004, vol. 10, no. 4, p. 493:

> The expression 'judicial activism' is here used to mean using judicial power for a purpose other than that for which it was granted, namely doing justice according to law in the particular case. It means serving some function other than what is necessary for the decision of the particular dispute between the parties. Often the illegitimate function is the furthering of some political, moral or social programme: the law is seen not as the touchstone by which the case in hand is to be decided, but as a possible starting point or catalyst for developing a new system to solve a range of other cases. Even more com-

Thus, in any domestic legal system, there may be an ongoing debate as to the boundaries of those areas that should be the exclusive preserve of political and judicial decision-making respectively, and of areas in which each may legitimately play a role.[9]

Similar issues inevitably arise also in the sphere of international law, including international criminal law, where political decision-makers are primarily States, acting either individually, or collectively as members of political bodies such as the UN Security Council or the Assembly of States Parties of the International Criminal Court. A decision by a State to act in a certain way, or to vote in a certain way as a member of an organ of an international organisation, being a decision taken by a political branch of that State's government, is inherently political, whether that State is thereby seeking to give effect to its own self-interest or is seeking to act altruistically in the long term interests of the international community as a whole.

Some political decision making in the international criminal justice system may be more or less analogous with that which exists in domestic legal systems. Examples in the case of the International Criminal Court include the functions of the Assembly of States Parties in adopting the Elements of Crimes and the Rules of Procedure and Evidence (analogous in a way to the adoption of substantive and procedural criminal law by domestic legislatures), and its adoption of the annual budget and the election of the Judges and the Prosecutor.

However, in the case of the International Criminal Court, some of the political decision making that is hard-wired into the system has no ready analogy with domestic legal systems. Provisions dealing with the way that the Court's jurisdiction is triggered are an obvious example. For the Court to exercise its jurisdiction, one way or another, a prior political decision is required. For jurisdiction to be exercised under Article 13(a) or (c) of the Statute of the Court, the requisite precedent political decision is that of a State referred to in Article 12(2) either to become a party to the Statute of

---

monly the function is a discursive and indecisive meander through various fields of learning for its own sake.

[9] See, for instance, the extrajudicial observations of a judge of the United Kingdom Supreme Court: Lord Hodge, "The scope of judicial law-making in the common law tradition", Max Planck Institute of Comparative and International Private Law Hamburg, Germany, 28 October 2019, para. 24 ("What have judges said about those boundaries? The answer is that judges recognise that there is a boundary to judicial law-making but there is no consensus as to where it is") (available on the Supreme Court's web site).

the Court or to make a declaration under Article 12(3) of the Statute. For jurisdiction to be exercised under Article 13(b), the requisite precedent political decision is that of the Security Council to refer a situation to the Prosecutor. For jurisdiction to be exercised under Article 13(a), a further requisite precedent political decision is that of the relevant State to refer the situation to the Prosecutor under Article 14(1) of its Statute. The exercise of jurisdiction by the Court over the crime of aggression is subject to further political decision-making, including the decision of the relevant State whether or not to make or withdraw a declaration under Article 15*bis*(4), and the decision of the Security Council to make (or not) a determination under Article 15*bis*(6)-(8). Furthermore, the processes of the Court may be interrupted by a political decision of the Security Council under Article 16 to request a deferral of an investigation or prosecution.

Thus, the question whether the International Criminal Court can or cannot exercise jurisdiction in relation to a specific situation will depend not just on political decisions taken at the time that the Court was initially established, but by real-time political decisions taken by States contemporaneously with decision-making by the Prosecutor and Chambers of the Court.

A further feature of the International Criminal Court that has no obvious analogy with domestic legal systems is Article 127 of its Statute, which confers on each State Party the right to withdraw from the Statute. References to general principles established in domestic legal systems thus provide no guidance on how the Prosecutor or Chambers of the Court should react, for instance, to a situation where a group of States threatens to withdraw from the Statute on the basis that those States are dissatisfied with the direction that prosecutorial decisions are taking.

On one view, it might be said that such a situation would amount to an unjustifiable attempt by the States concerned to exert political influence over the Prosecutor,[10] and that maintenance of the integrity of the system would require the Prosecutor to not be influenced or to be seen to be influenced by such political pressures. This view might lead to the conclusion that a Prosecutor of integrity should refuse to change course in response to such threats to withdraw from the Statute, even in the hypothetical extreme

---

[10] Compare the statement of Canada at the seventeenth session of the Assembly of States Parties, December 2018, p. 5: "We remain concerned about efforts to undermine the Court's work, be it threats directed at the Court and its personnel, politically motivated withdrawals or unexecuted arrest warrants".

case where the result would lead to the withdrawal from the Statute of every State Party, such that the Court itself would cease to exist.

However, a contrary view can also be put. A State which is not a party to the Statute might well decide against becoming a party – at least for the time being – on the ground that it is not impressed by the current direction of prosecutorial decision-making. Nothing in the Statute could prevent a non-State Party from so deciding or from publicly stating its reasons for that decision, and it is unlikely that many would characterise such statements by a non-State Party as an assault on the integrity of the Court. It is difficult to see why the position is any different in the case of a State Party contemplating withdrawal from the Statute, given that Article 127 of the Statute gives States Parties an unequivocal right to withdraw. Any decision by a State Party to do so will inevitably be a political decision. The Statute in no way limits the reasons upon which a decision of the State Party to withdraw may be based.[11] Indeed, some might argue that Article 127 is an essential safety valve, enabling States Parties to decide to be no longer bound by the Statute if they feel that the political compromises reflected in the Statute are not being respected, or that the Court is not properly performing the functions that it was set up to serve. Without that safety valve, some States Parties might not have willingly become parties to the Statute in the first place. While the Prosecutor and the Chambers clearly are not bound to take any particular action in response to threats by a State to withdraw from the Statute, it may be argued that it would be contrary to the intentions of the Statute for the organs of the Court to remain totally oblivious to any expressions of dissatisfaction by States Parties.[12]

Of course, it would be inherently contrary to the integrity of the system for any organ of the Court to be influenced by threats of a State Party to withdraw from the Statute if a particular verdict is not reached in a particular case. However, that does not necessarily mean that it would be contrary to the integrity of the system for organs of the Court to take into account the views of States Parties (or indeed, even non-States Parties) in relation to more general matters of prosecutorial policy. It is noteworthy, for instance, that a statement of Canada at the Assembly of States Parties in December 2018, while criticising "politically motivated withdrawals",

---

[11] Roger S. Clark, "Article 127", in Otto Triffterer and Kai Ambos (eds.), *The Rome Statute of the ICC*, third edition, Nomos, 2016, mn. 1.

[12] *Ibid.*, pp. 5–6.

went on to call for "an exit strategy for ongoing preliminary investigations where the evidence available does not support the timely or successful prosecution", adding that "[k]eeping these cases active is not an efficient use of Court resources regardless of the political price of their withdrawal".[13]

This leads to consideration of a further difference between domestic legal systems and international criminal courts and tribunals, which is that international criminal courts are very selective in the prosecutions that they bring. In domestic legal systems, the general position tends to be that all cases are prosecuted where there is sufficient evidence to justify it, unless there is some specific reason why it is not in the interests of justice to do so. On the other hand, in the case of an international criminal court, there is inevitably evidence of more crimes by more apparent perpetrators than could ever be practicably prosecuted, thus requiring decisions to be made as to which persons should be prosecuted for which particular crimes. Again, it might well be contrary to the integrity of the system if political decision-makers sought to influence which specific persons should be prosecuted on which specific charges. However, it does not necessarily follow that it would be inconsistent with the integrity of the institution for political actors to seek to persuade organs of the Court, for instance, that there is good empirical evidence that a focus on certain types of crimes would have the greatest effect of promoting peace and reconciliation in a particular post-conflict State, or would have the greatest effect in deterring the commission of future crimes under international law.

Questions of fundamental importance thereby arise as to the appropriate limits of the matters within the international criminal justice system that may or should appropriately be regulated or influenced by political actors – and the line beyond which political influences cease to be proper and become a threat to the integrity of the institution. A related issue is the question of who has responsibility for recognising that this boundary has been crossed, and for doing something about it. That in turn leads to the further question of exactly what should be done about it. The answers to these questions will not necessarily be uncontroversial.

---

[13] See *ibid.*: "In the case of the Specialized Agencies, a custom has perhaps developed that that States explain why it is that they are withdrawing, in order to give the entity an opportunity to alter any course of action that the withdrawing State finds unacceptable".

Although the theme of the conference and this book has been individual integrity rather than institutional integrity, in any discussion of political influences on the criminal justice process, the two inevitably overlap. A political body seeking to influence the judicial or prosecutorial activities of an international criminal court will likely focus its efforts on a judge or the judges collectively, or on the prosecutor. It is the actions of those individuals in responding to such forces that will shape the integrity of the institutions themselves. Institutional integrity therefore requires those individuals to have an appreciation of what responses to such influences would be appropriate or inappropriate, as well as a willingness and ability to act accordingly.

An essential step in preserving the integrity of the international criminal justice system in the face of political exposure is thus to achieve a common understanding of the appropriate role of political decision-makers and its limitations. In the absence of such a common understanding, it is hard for individual prosecutors or judges to know if they are appropriately maintaining their own independence and integrity or not.

A worthwhile project for the future would be to try to establish some kind of guidelines on these issues. Such guidelines, if formulated in calm deliberation following full consultation and debate, would no doubt be of great assistance to the prosecutors and judges of international criminal courts. As well as being a point of reference for prosecutors and judges to explain and justify their responses in particular cases, such guidelines may assist in deterring inappropriate political pressures from being exerted in the first place.

It is beyond the scope of this contribution to consider the detailed process by which such guidelines might be adopted, let alone what the content of such guidelines might be. Addressing the issues above may well prove to be a complex and difficult task. That, if so, would underscore the need for a major initiative in this area. Preservation of the integrity of the international criminal justice system is fundamental. If there are any uncertainties about precisely what this requires, energetic and committed efforts should be made to resolve them.

32

Some Reflections on
Integrity in International Justice

David Re[*]

In 2013, I wrote a short article with the bright and cheery title of "The Glass is Half-full for International Criminal Law".[1] Revisiting the topic seven years later, however, my then more youthful sanguinity is now a far more cautious optimism. This results from intervening personal experiences and some institutional and political developments. My purpose here is to briefly explore some of these issues.

Consequently, in sharing some of these personal experiences as I do below, and my reflections on integrity in international justice generally, my hope is that these concrete examples may inform where normative but nonetheless more abstract notions may struggle.[2] The combination of experience and observation may help to illuminate some institutional obstacles and challenges. The more important aim here, though, is to pose the slightly more pessimistic question of whether too many structural impediments exist to achieve a level of integrity that can ever match the high internal and external expectations for international justice.

32.1. No International Justice System Exists

Comparing the national and international, and using the national as a possible model is useful, although the differences between the two are quite

---

[*] **David Re** is the Presiding Judge of the Trial Chamber of the Special Tribunal for Lebanon. (since 2013). Before that he was an international judge of the Court of Bosnia and Herzegovina in Sarajevo and a prosecuting trial attorney and senior prosecuting trial attorney at the International Criminal Tribunal for the former Yugoslavia ('ICTY') in The Hague. He has worked in international justice institutions since 2002. In Australia, between 1986 and 2001, he worked as a barrister, a prosecutor and a solicitor in private practice, and as a research officer for the New South Wales Attorney-General's Department. He was an NGO observer at the negotiations for the Rome Statute of the International Criminal Court in 1998. He has also legally consulted for the OSCE, and the UNDP in South Sudan.

[1] David Re, "The Glass is Half-full for International Criminal Law", in Global Policy, 2013, vol. 4, no. 3, p. 317.

[2] Some of these are eloquently expressed in chapters in this book such as Hans Corell's Chapter 5 ("The Dag Hammarskjöld Legacy and Integrity in International Civil Service").

pronounced. Essential to understanding the dimension of the issue is that, unlike in national justice systems, no international justice *system* as such exists.

The various permanent and temporary institutions do not operate within the framework of a coherent functioning justice system. Each institution stands alone.[3] The international criminal courts and tribunals, for example – hybrid, *ad hoc* or permanent – are simply trial courts with a single level of appeal that operate as self-functioning institutions outside of a wider justice system. This dislocation from a true justice system, in my view, lies at the heart of the challenges in developing and maintaining institutional integrity, which includes that of its personnel. And central to this is that no outside appellate oversight mechanisms exist.

32.2. Some Personal National Experiences

To compare the national and international, and looking first to the national, my personal starting point was in Australia where I began my legal career. While working as a lawyer and prosecutor in the 1980s and 1990s, and then as a self-employed barrister, I rarely encountered ethical challenges or matters involving personal or institutional integrity. Most involved dealings with the police and the differing professional ethics between the legal profession and those of a disciplined paramilitary force. Lawyers are bound by their professional codes and subject to disciplinary action upon complaint, and unlike police have independent duties of honesty and candour to the courts.

In Australia, as opposed to in the international criminal courts and tribunals, prosecuting lawyers (generally) are not investigators and rely upon the police to gather evidence. While working as a prosecutor I encountered some corrupt police officers; some were exposed in a lengthy public commission of inquiry, and subsequently tried and imprisoned. The commission laid bare police corruption that in some cases had become institutional, but generally was confined to specific units. In its aftermath, much, but by no means all, was cleaned up.

The prosecutor's office where I worked, by contrast, almost never experienced what could be considered as corrupt conduct, although like

---

[3] The international human rights courts, though, are in a slightly different category at the peak of a treaty-based system applying international human rights law, by making declarations of rights when domestic remedies are exhausted.

any other comparable institution naturally it experienced individual ethical lapses. Generally, though, ethical standards were tacitly enforced by virtue of the professional codes, the internal office systems, and the wider institutional framework, in which the office was an integral component of the justice system. Many factors contributed to this tight internal and external institutional integrity. On a personal professional level, lawyers are admitted to practice and must complete ethics courses. Personal professional reputation in a national system is critical. Like in any field of professional specialisation, prosecutors and defence lawyers are reasonably known to each other. Their professional universe is quite small and people talk. They are on public display in their court work. They are reasonably well remunerated. Moreover, judges enforce ethical standards.

Maintaining personal professional reputation in the national 'pond' is fundamental. Institutional integrity can become self-regulating as a result of internal peer pressure to act professionally and with integrity. Nationally, unlike in the international sphere, an integrity check for a job applicant is a mere telephone call away. Someone always knows something good, bad or indifferent about the candidate.

On a wider institutional level, the prosecutor's office is part of a structure in which other institutions function together to provide integrity to the wider system. A critical media can scrutinise judicial and other decisions and conduct. Parliamentary committees have oversight over some aspects of the justice system. Independent complaints and disciplinary mechanisms exist – for lawyers, police, judicial officers and civil servants. Judicial review is available for many administrative decisions. Courts can enforce rights – including those of staff and officials – with orders, injunctions and declarations. Statutory auditors examine the accounts of public institutions and publish full reports. Justice institutions must publish annual reports that include detailed and audited financial information. An independent ombudsman's office may inquire into alleged misconduct. Standing anti-corruption bodies have powers of investigation and compulsion against self-incrimination, and may hold public hearings. Some of these institutions also have educative functions.

Taken together, they represent a sophisticated, interwoven body of norms that operate to provide legitimacy to the justice system as a whole. This builds a degree of transparency into the system and, unlike in international justice, a properly functioning national justice system is not politicised.

32.3. The Institutions of International Justice

The institutions of international justice in which I have worked, however, do not resemble anything that I experienced in my formative legal years. On a personal level, this was evident when I entered the international system in 2002, first as a prosecuting trial attorney in the Office of the Prosecutor of the International Criminal Tribunal for the Former Yugoslavia ('ICTY').

An obvious difference with the national level was that the ICTY's institutional framework had neither the internal nor external safeguards guaranteeing integrity that are built in to any properly functioning national justice system. At that stage, the ICTY and the International Criminal Tribunal for Rwanda ('ICTR') were the only functioning international criminal courts or tribunals. Both were temporary and within the umbrella of the United Nations ('UN'), which, although having its own 'principal judicial organ' in the International Court of Justice, did not have the dedicated justice bureaucracy of national systems. Neither *ad hoc* institution was part of a justice *system*. Most of the other accompanying national institutional features mentioned above, including the independent external oversight present in those systems, were also absent.

On another level I was also immediately struck by several stark differences with legal practice in Australia. These included the dramatic dissimilarity in the quality of the investigations (which was generally much lower at the ICTY), and the more casual attitude towards professional obligations, including codes of conduct. Such was the Office's disjointed and fragmented nature that its self-regulating behavioural code was weak. Some examples are provided below.

The reasons for this are complex, but my sense generally was that this politicised *ad hoc* institution lacked the internal motivation that could foster a culture of rule- and ethics-based integrity. This is aside from the deficit of external integrity safeguards in the UN system. Inevitably, this external shortfall must negatively influence internal conduct, and hence institutional integrity.

The transient and political nature of such an institution, and indeed most other international justice institutions – the International Criminal Court ('ICC'), which is permanent but nonetheless operates in very political waters, is an obvious exception – must contribute to this. Working, for example, as a lawyer, investigator or analyst in an international justice institution is not generally viewed as a long-term career move. It certainly is not for judges, all of whom have limited terms of office. By contrast, a national civil servant can have a career path with a natural progression involving internal promotion and moving between different agencies, with career breaks and work exchanges.

Most who work in the various international institutions are passing through in a manner different to comparable national workplaces, especially at the hybrid and *ad hoc* institutions. This creates a phenomenon in which personal and professional reputation – which is so significant in one's own national system – regrettably, becomes less important so far from home. The consequences of breaching ethical standards may be close to non-existent.

Internationally, codes of professional conduct are rarely invoked. As a judge, I have seen lawyers comporting themselves in a manner that I do not believe they would dare replicate before the courts of their own countries. And in my experience, international judges seem to have a somewhat touching shyness towards enforcing the codes against transgressing lawyers, even in issuing the routine warning that would be expected in a domestic court. The price of this timidity in 'keeping the peace' with advocates can degrade professional standards and thus institutional integrity.

The same can be said of the institutional practice of employing people who are not admitted to national legal practice, and hence whose professional conduct essentially cannot be regulated through professional codes. Similarly, assigning a lawyer as defence co-counsel to defend an accused charged with committing international crimes, but one who has never appeared in court or had a client, must diminish confidence in an institution, and hence its overall structural integrity. But these three examples could be easily rectified by appropriate institutional action.

32.4. As an International Prosecutor: Some Institutional Integrity Issues

Giving some specific examples of 'lapses' in institutional integrity that I have personally encountered may assist, as it could provide an insight into the dimension of the issue.

In the first instance, as an international prosecutor at the ICTY, in a case to which I was assigned, I was charged with examining the totality of the evidence against the two accused. It became apparent that the prosecution had at most a *prima facie* case against the two accused on two of the seven indicted counts (one count for each accused). The evidence was otherwise insufficient to proceed to trial. Further investigation with an adjournment, or alternatively abandoning five counts, was required. A memorandum to this effect was prepared, bearing the signatures of the four prosecuting lawyers. A very senior official, however, instructed the case to proceed, notwithstanding this assessment, and then, additionally, neglected to inform the Prosecutor of the existence of the memo. The case commenced. I moved to another one. As I believed that the Prosecutor should be made aware of this evidentiary deficiency, I informed the Prosecutor of the true state of the evidence. The case still proceeded, and eventually on appeal, only two counts survived – namely, those for which there had been some evidence at the trial's commencement. The case should not have gone to trial on the other counts: but it did at enormous cost to the institution and the two accused. That this occurred reveals a major lapse in institutional integrity. Was it avoidable? Absolutely. But why this course was taken was never explained.

In raising this example, I recognise a counter-argument: namely, that as a judge had confirmed the indictment it should be left to a trial chamber at that point to determine the sufficiency of the evidence. However, against this is that if the prosecutors in the case have formed the view that, based on an *insufficiency* of evidence, 'no reasonable prospect of conviction' exists, the case should not proceed. I subscribe to this latter view: as a matter of prosecutorial integrity, and hence that of the system itself, in these circumstances it is unconscionable to advance to trial.

In another case in which I was involved at a late stage, I became aware that prosecution officials had deliberately failed to disclose to the accused crucial exculpatory evidence during the phase of the case related to that evidence. The suppressed evidence was disclosed only at a later point.

In a third case, the prosecution misled the Trial Chamber and the defence by failing to disclose something that was highly relevant to an application to amend an indictment. When I belatedly discovered this, I was instructed not to bring it to the attention of either the chamber or the defence. Ultimately, however, no prejudice occurred as the prosecution failed in its application, and, moreover, the accused was acquitted. Both factors, however, are beside the point regarding standing ethical obligations, especially in something as fundamental as amending the charging instrument.

In a fourth case, in which I was the lead counsel, it became apparent that certain investigators were being less than candid about the circumstances of interviewing witnesses, during which they had allegedly identified an accused person. The investigators were attempting to conceal what had occurred. My solution was to put everything relevant to this before the chamber and to disclose it to the defence.

In these examples, unlike in a properly functioning national system, there was essentially nowhere to go to rectify these systemic failures. This represents a major structural obstacle to fostering internal integrity.

32.5. As an International Judge: Some Institutional Integrity Issues

Regarding judges: almost all who I have worked with have integrity and competence. However, and regrettably, as an international judge I have also encountered breaches of integrity which, had they occurred domestically, would have resulted in swift and possibly severe consequences. Some conduct I have witnessed could be considered as corrupt.

Shockingly, I have been on the receiving end of judges attempting to interfere in witness testimony in a trial, and I have seen attempts to make judicial decisions for political reasons. I have also encountered judges routinely submitting false leave returns, in effect defrauding the institution by claiming benefits they were not entitled to receive, and subsequent high-level attempts to manipulate the records to cover-up this institutionalised wrong-doing. I have also seen a judge continue to sit in a case in which the judge had an obvious conflict that should have disqualified them from further involvement.

This reaches the point when 'integrity lapses' move beyond the opportunism of some individuals and become entrenched. At that point, the internal processes have failed, and there is no one to report it to. I have also encountered indifference, and worse, by the United Nations Office of Legal Affairs – as the judicial appointing authority, and presumably for political reasons – to these transgressions.

Judicial officers behaving in this manner in a properly functioning national justice system would be the subject of complaint, discipline and removal from office, and also possible prosecution with the attendant criminal penalty. Such 'lapses' would be rightly viewed as attacking the integrity of the justice system and dealt with accordingly. Internationally, however, political considerations can intervene, resulting in the concealment of matters going to the heart of judicial integrity and, consequently, public credibility.[4]

Turning a blind eye to, or attempting to cover up, such transgressions facilitates the degradation of standards and makes a mockery of the statutory requirements that judges serving in international institutions have high moral character and integrity. As Judge Erik Møse points out,

> it is important that the institution carries out thorough investigations, even if the person accused of such behaviour has left, in order to clarify whether the allegation has any factual basis and, if so, to take necessary measures and demonstrate a rupture with the past.[5]

In this respect, sunlight is the best disinfectant.

Another institutional barrier to institutional integrity is the inadequate manner of dealing with applications to disqualify a judge from hearing a matter. Lacking structural recourse to external judicial mechanisms, international courts and tribunals must resort to using their own internal means to decide these issues. Some use a panel of three judges (without any appeal from the decision) while others sit in plenary to determine such applications.

The drawbacks in having a full plenary of judges deciding applications to disqualify one or more of their own are obvious. The judges are effectively deciding whether their judicial colleagues are actually biased or could be perceived to be so. Further, potential future conflicts of interest will inevitably arise, for example, an application to disqualify an entire trial chamber may involve some potential appellate judges deciding in plenary an issue that could reappear in an appeal. The non-appealable three-judge panel model suffers exactly the same defects.

By contrast, in some national systems the judge first decides whether they should continue in the case, and the applicant may appeal an adverse decision to another court. This model, in my view, provides greater institutional integrity and hence credibility. Again, the fact that the institutions stand alone, unlike in national systems, with no appeal possible beyond the

---

4   Politicising the disciplining and removal of judges must be avoided. See for example, Report of the Special Rapporteur on the independence of judges and lawyers, Diego García-Sayán, A/75/172, 17 July 2020.

5   See Erik Møse, "Reflections on Integrity in International Criminal Justice and Regional Human Rights Courts", Chapter 19, Section 4 ("Personal Integrity – Some Illustrations").

court itself, provides a structural impediment to achieving institutional integrity and wider credibility.

Also connected with this is that conflicts of interest in international settings, in my personal experience, also seem to assume less importance than in national systems, no matter how blindingly obvious they may be to an outside observer.

To give another minor illustrative example of a lapse in institutional integrity – and one potentially explicable by cultural institutional factors – in the Court of Bosnia and Herzegovina I once had a national prosecutor casually drop by into my office, interpreter in tow, to ask me if I had any helpful hints on what he should say in his closing submissions in the case. I firmly but politely explained that 'no' this was not how things were done.

I emphasise that these are only *some* of the things that I have *personally* experienced, and, moreover, that this is only what I have experienced (as opposed to having heard about). Logic dictates that more must be out there. But I also highlight that the overwhelming majority of my colleagues in international justice are ethical, competent and professional. The thread running through these negative examples speaks more to the institutional failures that permit them.

Finally, the reports of corruption at the Extraordinary Chambers in the Courts of Cambodia are legion. By contrast, in the cases of the Kosovo Specialist Chambers, the ICTY and ICTR, political decisions were made not to include judges of the countries from the conflict. This model, which can go a long way to preserving institutional integrity, is one worth emulating in future hybrid institutions.

32.6. The Political Dimension

Coming to an important structural obstacle in the political dimension, it is emphasised that all international justice institutions – including UN fact-finding missions and accountability mechanisms – have political roots. The appointment and election of senior officials, including prosecutors and judges, is an intensely political process, and the winners are not necessarily appointed on merit, although of course many excellent candidates manage to get through the process.

An example of a major political and legal institutional integrity failure in a fact-finding mission occurred in the United Nations International Independent Investigating Commission ('UNIIIC') from 2005 onwards. Successive UNIIIC Commissioners remained publicly silent while four high-level prisoners, who had been detained on the Commission's request, were imprisoned in Lebanon without charge for almost four years. This continued despite the collapse of the evidence founding their arrests, and the UN Human Rights Council's Working Group on Arbitrary Detention finding that the continued detentions were arbitrary and thus breached Lebanon's obligations under the International Covenant on Civil and Political Rights.[6]

This episode produced a mixed result for international justice. On one hand the UNIIIC as a UN international justice institution failed a basic integrity test, while another UN institution – acting as a watchdog and inquirer – passed it with flying colours. The political dimension, however, triumphed until the formal establishment of the Special Tribunal for Lebanon, and its Pre-Trial Judge ordering Lebanon to immediately release the four. This example demonstrates how political considerations can outplay those of international human rights law and institutional integrity.

Directly connected with the political nature of international justice, and international criminal justice in particular, is that some personnel – including lawyers – have a dual but unrevealed role in working for their government in one form or another while simultaneously being employed by the institution. Loyalties are thus divided in a manner that will be rare in a domestic criminal justice system. This of course infringes the formal contractual rules and statutory obligations of neutrality of international civil servants, and on its face at least, would appear to undermine institutional integrity.

This goes hand in hand with the political nature of the institutions and their work,[7] and in particular in international criminal justice in investigating targets and situations or cases. Irrespective of what countries publicly say about supporting the aims of international criminal justice, for example ('ending impunity', 'bringing justice to the victims', 'ensuring that this never happens again', and so on) – and while of course there are very vocal exceptions, such as the Trump administration's opposition to specific ICC investigations – numerous state and non-state actors have motives to

---

[6] Promotion and Protection of all Human Rights, Civil, Political, Economic, Social and Cultural Rights, Including the Right to Development. Opinions adopted by the Working Group on Arbitrary Detention, A/HRC/10/21/Add.1, 4 February 2009, Opinion No. 37/2007.

[7] I am excluding the work of the permanent international human rights courts here, although all applications have a state as a respondent, and states naturally desire a favourable outcome in each case against them.

further, neutralise or even to end investigations or prosecutions. This can include influencing the evidence and the choice of defendant.

A perusal of a trove of leaked government cables – assuming their authenticity, of course – revealed extensive contact between court and tribunal employees and appointed and elected officials, and government officials. The government officials are merely going about their normal business in assisting the institutions, while obtaining information and attempting to influence what the courts and tribunals do. Much in the cables is of the mundane – meetings, briefings, issues of co-operation and so on, all of which is properly within a court's stated mandate. The courts rely on these contacts for their survival. Some contacts, however, greatly exceed this and reveal a level of 'outreach' going well beyond the contractual, in certain instances appearing to breach the normative principles against taking instructions from outside sources.

This is an obvious but unresolvable issue of institutional integrity, but one coming to light only by the fact of publication. The usual employment 'solution' here would be to terminate the services of such an official. But as they will not be found out, this will not happen. Nothing – codes, contracts, exhortations, pleas to 'do the right thing' – can prevent officials with divided loyalties from so acting. It may be why they are there. Only the gullible could believe that there is a solution to this, short of an enforceable international agreement to refrain from doing this. But that, like trying to agree on an international definition of 'terrorism', will surely never happen.

A classic example of the interplay between international politics and those of international court officials was uncovered in 2017 when ostensible communications between the first ICC Prosecutor and French officials revealed that he had sought the detention of the former president of Côte d'Ivoire, Laurent Gbagbo, many months before seeking to open a preliminary investigation into any situation. Assuming that the content of the hacks or leaks are correct – and it appears that none of those named in the documents have either confirmed or denied their accuracy – it goes without saying that, irrespective of the allegations, a prosecutor cannot seek a person's detention without a lawful basis to do so, such as a court-authorised arrest warrant. This lack of due process strikes at the heart of institutional integrity. Maybe these were the (alleged) actions of a rogue top official, but while institutional safeguards theoretically exist to prevent these types of misdeeds, refraining from acting in such a manner is very much a matter of personal and professional integrity. Policing such personal misconduct is virtually impossible.

Because of the political nature of judicial elections and appointments, the international system is also ill-equipped to deal with the examples of judicial wrong-doing described above. (Ironically though, the public judicial election process is usually more transparent than the national selection of candidates for nomination for election.) An element of protecting national interest may also intrude – at the very least in avoiding national embarrassment – as most judges are state-nominated. While some formal mechanisms exist, they need be properly used in order to remedy some of the things described. This requires institutional will and perseverance.

There is no easy solution to this political dimension, one that lies at the core of the integrity of international justice. States have political objectives that may either coincide or conflict with those expressed in the statutes of the courts and tribunals and as put into practice. This will never go away. Beyond recognising that it goes with the territory of international justice, little can be done internally other than maintaining vigilance, and attempting to erect internal barriers that may help to resist irregular and improper outside pressures. However, structural changes including introducing truly independent external oversight – and additional independent judicial protections – would make a huge difference. But this requires political will and consensus.

32.7. Are There Too Many Structural Impediments to Achieve Institutional Integrity? Some Suggestions

This leads to my initial question of 'whether too many structural impediments exist to achieve a level of integrity that can ever match the high internal and external expectations for international justice'?

Fundamental to the debate about integrity in international justice is recognising that some international institutions are structured in a way that makes it difficult to attain the normal levels of institutional integrity that are so vital for the credibility of national systems. It is naive to think that states will forego forms of attempted influence over the international institutions they have created and in which they have so much invested. A pessimist will accordingly conclude that that this is beyond change, and that reforming internal mechanisms could provide the most realistic prospects for success.

Prevention, though, is clearly preferable to a cure. In the 1980s, a centrist Australian political party had a very popular catch cry, inelegantly expressed as 'Keep the bastards honest'. This slogan's noble aim, I believe, can be achieved both internally and externally in international justice, but this will not be easy.

Internally, encouraging a thriving culture of transparency and questioning and reflection is an obvious step towards this aim. Flatter and less authoritarian hierarchies can promote this.

Good behaviour must be encouraged, but without overbearing vigilance. Officials and staff must be able to get on with their jobs without fear of over-surveillance or interference in their work. By analogy, partners in law firms owe fiduciary duties towards each other, and this and the notion of a partnership provides the motivation for self-regulating professional and personal conduct: each partner is essentially watching the others.

Independent complaint and disciplinary mechanisms are also part of the solution. But even there, caution must be exercised. I have seen staff being 'weaponised' to bring complaints disproportionate to the alleged transgression, in circumstances where mediation or counselling would have been the more appropriate course. Truly independent ethics offices in which officials and staff could confide and seek advice could assist.

Externally, standing independent oversight mechanisms are essential, like the examples noted above of auditors, ombudsman, and the availability of judicial administrative review. 'Independent' is the key term here. External consultancy review can be helpful, especially in identifying matters that may otherwise not come to light. However, external 'experts' briefly parachuting themselves into a complex international institution such as the ICC, for example, with broad terms of reference requiring rapid reporting, while of some use, can probably achieve no more than window-dressing and recommendations that merely, in many cases, state the obvious.

The lack of external legal mechanisms to enforce legal rights is a key impediment to achieving institutional integrity. The institutions have immunity from civil suit under international conventions and host state agreements. International justice officials and staff, for example, thus have no court before which they can seek redress in respect of legal rights that do not involve an adverse administrative decision. For this reason, I advocate either providing the existing courts and tribunals with these ancillary powers – but through establishing separate court divisions with dedicated judges – or, preferably, by creating legally enforceable judicial mechanisms that are independent of the institutions. This should include applications to disqualify judges. These steps could help neutralise some of the political factors described above. As a suggested solution, just in The Hague, for example, there are more than enough judges in the various international justice institutions to jointly perform these functions for other courts and tribunals. Allowing this would require amending the statutory instruments of these institutions. This must be achievable. It would also create a form of connected international justice.

International judges also lack statutory whistle-blower protections. This is a structural issue. The UK Supreme Court has unanimously ruled that judges are entitled to the same whistle-blower protection as employees.[8] This precedent should be embraced. Court and tribunal statutes and internal regulatory documents should guarantee such protections to judges and mandate formal enforceable assurances against retaliation. For staff, whistle-blower protections are often 'toothless tigers'. Those of the United Nations are a classic case in point. Whistle-blowers are typically viewed with suspicion and as trouble-makers (which some of course are) rather than ethically-minded individuals attempting to report wrong-doing. It is much easier to turn a blind eye, look the other way, or simply decamp if the stench overwhelms, rather than offering oneself as a martyr at the altar of moral and legal rectitude. Remedying this, however, should be relatively easy. The solution is both cultural and regulatory. There are numerous national models for both that are worth emulating.

32.8. Conclusion: Cautious Optimism Tempered by Realism

No system can attain institutional perfection, but the experiences described above demonstrate avoidable wrongdoing that systemic failures either permit, or allow to flourish. Some should be quite preventable by the use of internal regulatory mechanisms and promoting a culture of integrity and honesty. But this requires leadership and vigilance. If the leadership lies at the root of the problem (like in the Gbagbo example above) – and especially if a leader has a long term ahead of them – we then go straight back to the structural and normative, and the need for strong internal and external regulatory mechanisms that can address these short-comings. This would include, as suggested, creating independent legal mechanisms to enforce

---

[8]   United Kingdom, Supreme Court, *Gilham v. Ministry of Justice*, Judgment, 16 October 2019, UKSC 44 (2019).

legal rights. And like many others, I add that much greater care must be taken in nominating suitable officials to serve in international justice institutions. Many reforms in this respect have been proposed, but short of somehow magically removing the political dimension from the appointment, nomination and election process – or injecting into it a novel level of transparency – probably little will change.

To conclude, attaining and maintaining adequate levels of integrity is difficult. It requires recognition of the structural obstacles, and some adjustment of expectations to make achieving these goals even a semi-realistic aim. External structural change is crucial. I remain an optimist but now with a glass swishing between half-full and half-empty, depending on the viewing angle.

INDEX

A

Adab Al-Qāḍī, 121
  integrity, 118
Adorno, Theodor
  Aesthetic Theory, 500
Aeschines, 62
  democratic virtues, 64
Agramunt, Pedro, 176
AI Wei Wei, 507
AidToo (#) movement, 536
Aimee, Jean-Claude, 1072
Akay, Aydin Sefa, 919
  arrest, 921
  conviction, 925
  High Commissioner for Human Rights (UN),
    922
  immunity (UN), 923, 932
  non-reappointment, 930
Aksar, Yusuf, 926
Ala Al-Deen Al-Taraabulsi, 111
Alexander, Jeffrey, 505
al-Fairūzābādī, 102
Alī Ibn Abī Ṭālib, 99, 112, 116
  Mālik Al-Ashtar, letter to, 135
  Message to the Judiciary, 150
Al-Mughnī
  integrity, 118
Al-Shahīd Al-Sadr
  Adab Al-Qāḍī, 112
Ambos, Kai, 648
American Bar Association
  documentation (international crimes), 623
  Model Code of Judicial Conduct, 1011
Annan, Kofi, 4, 528
Aquinas, Thomas, 493
  virtue, 87, *See* also Cardinal Virtues
Arbour, Louise, vii, 412
  integrity, 475
  International Criminal Tribunal for Rwanda,
    418
  International Criminal Tribunal for the
    former Yugoslavia, 475
  leadership, 418
Aristophanes, 59, 60

Aristotle
  aesthetics, 90
  Cardinal Virtues, 88
  On the Parts of Animals, 59
  Politics, 58
  Republic, 59
  virtue, 87
armed conflict
  displacement, 312
  low-intensity, 312
Ashworth, Andrew, 647
Assange, Julian
  torture, 481
Australia
  Community Protection Act, 293
  justice system, 1126
  Kable case (High Court), 293
Azerbaijan
  Council of Europe, 158

B

Bagosora, Théoneste, 1023
Ban Ki-moon, 923, 934
Bangalore Principles of Judicial Conduct, 93,
    103, 231, 242, 256, 265, 1049
  accountability, 1049
  Commentary (UNODC), 232, 257
  effective implementation, 1050
  Judicial Integrity Group, 231
Barr, William, 8
Basic Principles on the Independence of the
    Judiciary, 231, 242, 753, 754, 942, 1033
  adoption, 1046
  Article 2, 131
  Preamble, 1038
Bathurst, Tom, 1028
Bensouda, Fatou, 7
  code of conduct (ICC-OTP), 1097
  Statement on the *Bemba* Appeals Chamber's
    decision, 302
Bergsmo, Morten, iv, vii, xv, 279, 309, 399,
    404, 421, 628, 634, 920, 947
  Faustian curtain (integrity), 42
Bleasdale, Marcus, 508
Blewitt, Graham, 419

R

Rackwitz, Klaus, iv, v, x
Rankin, Melinda, 640
Rapp, Stephen, 631
realpolitik, 484
Residual Special Court for Sierra Leone
  commutation and early release, 1014
Responsibility to Protect (doctrine)
  Libya, 975
revolving doors, phenomenon, 598
  Ombudsman (EU), 598
Rhode, Deborah L., 10
Rhodes, Kingston, 541
Rindskopf Parker, Elizabeth, 1068
Roberts, Paul, 645, 685, 705, 725
Robinson, Peter, 923
  correspondence (UN), 934
  Motion for Order to Government of Turkey
    (MICT), 938
  Ngirabatware case, 940, 941
Rockefeller, John D., Jr., 1028
Rogall, Klaus, 689, 700
Rules of Procedure and Evidence (ICC)
  Rule 24, 774, 784
  Rule 25, 775
  Rule 26, 783, 784, 785, 790
  Rule 29(1), 784
  Rule 30, 784
  Rule 32, 784
  Rule 49, 888
  Rule 5(1), 753
  Rule 77, 729
  Rule 9, 284
Rules of Procedure and Evidence (ICTY)
  Rule 15, 455, 953, 1054
  Rule 24, 755
  Rule 46, 446, 462
  Rule 65 *ter*, 439, 440
  Rule 66, 439
  Rule 67, 439, 443, 451
  Rule 68, 446, 450
  Rule 95, 708
Rules of Procedure and Evidence (MICT)
  Rule 150, 996, 1003
  Rule 151, 996, 1002
  Rule 18, 1010
Rwanda
  colonisation, 986
  ethnicities, 986
  Interahamwe, 987

Radio Télévision Libre des Milles Collines
  ('Radio Machete'), 984

S

Sallust
  Conspiracy of Catiline, 77
  virtue, 80
Saudi Arabia
  Khashoggi, Jamal, 606
self-evaluation, 217
self-oblivion, v, 949, *See also* Hammarskjöld,
  Dag
self-restraint, 217
Sellers, Patricia V., 1076
Shahabuddeen, Mohamed, 989
Sharí'ah
  Adab Al-Qāḍī, 101
  Al-qāḍī, 113
  Arabic language, 98, 102
  competence, diligence, 133
  corruption, 141
  disciplinary action, 142
  equality, 129
  ethics, judicial, 99
  ijmā, 98
  ijtihád, 98, 111, 114
  impartiality, 131
  independence, 132
  integrity, 96, 139, 145
  integrity (emotional), 134, 137
  jurisprudence (*fiqh*), 98
  objectives, 111
  Qur'án, 96, 100
  requirements (judiciary), 121, 123
  resoning (independent-individual). *See infra*
    ijtihád
  sources, 95, 104, 146
  Sunnah, 96, 100, 105, 113
Sherwin, Richard
  digital baroque, 496
Sibidé, Michel, 541
Socrates. *See* Plato
Söderman, Jacob, 595
SONG Tianying, v
Special Court for Sierra Leone
  convictions, 397
  integrity, 617
  Taylor case, 965
Special Tribunal for Lebanon
  establishment, 1134
  judicial ethics (code), 755, 1058

T

U

V

W

TOAEP TEAM

Editors

Antonio Angotti, Editor
Olympia Bekou, Editor
Mats Benestad, Editor
Morten Bergsmo, Editor-in-Chief
Alf Butenschøn Skre, Senior Executive Editor
Eleni Chaitidou, Editor
CHAN Icarus, Editor
CHEAH Wui Ling, Editor
FAN Yuwen, Editor
Manek Minhas, Editor
Gareth Richards, Senior Editor
Nikolaus Scheffel, Editor
SIN Ngok Shek, Editor
SONG Tianying, Editor
Moritz Thörner, Editor
ZHANG Yueyao, Editor

Editorial Assistants

Pauline Brosch
Marquise Lee Houle
Genevieve Zingg

Law of the Future Series Co-Editors

Dr. Alexander (Sam) Muller
Professor Larry Cata Backer
Professor Stavros Zouridis

Nuremberg Academy Series Editor

Dr. Viviane E. Dittrich, Deputy Director, International Nuremberg Principles Academy

Scientific Advisers

Professor Danesh Sarooshi, Principal Scientific Adviser for International Law
Professor Andreas Zimmermann, Principal Scientific Adviser for Public International Law
Professor Kai Ambos, Principal Scientific Adviser for International Criminal Law
Dr.h.c. Asbjørn Eide, Principal Scientific Adviser for International Human Rights Law

Editorial Board

Dr. Xabier Agirre, International Criminal Court
Dr. Claudia Angermaier, Austrian judiciary
Ms. Neela Badami, Narasappa, Doraswamy and Raja

OTHER VOLUMES IN
THE *NUREMBERG ACADEMY SERIES*

Linda Carter and Jennifer Schense (editors):
Two Steps Forward, One Step Back: The Deterrent Effect of International Criminal Tribunals
Torkel Opsahl Academic EPublisher
Brussels, 2017
Nuremberg Academy Series No. 1 (2017)
ISBN: 978-82-8348-186-0

Tallyn Gray (editor):
Islam and International Criminal Law and Justice
Torkel Opsahl Academic EPublisher
Brussels, 2018
Nuremberg Academy Series No. 2 (2018)
ISBNs: 978-82-8348-188-4 (print) and 978-82-8348-189-1 (e-book)

Viviane E. Dittrich, Kerstin von Lingen, Philipp Osten and Jolana Makraiová (editors):
The Tokyo Tribunal: Perspectives on Law, History and Memory
Torkel Opsahl Academic EPublisher
Brussels, 2020
Nuremberg Academy Series No. 3 (2020)
ISBNs: 978-82-8348-137-2 (print) and 978-82-8348-138-9 (e-book)

All volumes are freely available online at http://www.toaep.org/nas/. For printed copies, see http://www.toaep.org/about/distribution/. For reviews of earlier books in this Series in academic journals and yearbooks, see http://www.toaep.org/reviews/.

The International Nuremberg Principles Academy (Nuremberg Academy) is a non-profit foundation dedicated to the advancement of international criminal law and human rights. It was established by the Federal Republic of Germany, the Free State of Bavaria, and the City of Nuremberg in 2014. The activities and projects of the Academy are supported through contributions from the three founding entities and financially supported by the Federal Foreign Office of Germany.

Lightning Source UK Ltd.
Milton Keynes UK
UKHW051258261120
374038UK00011BA/457/J